Peter Carr Gedenkschrift

Research Advances in Mathematical Finance

Peter Carr Gedenkschrift

Research Advances in Mathematical Finance

Edited by

Robert A Jarrow
Cornell University, USA

Dilip B Madan
University of Maryland, USA

World Scientific

NEW JERSEY • LONDON • SINGAPORE • BEIJING • SHANGHAI • HONG KONG • TAIPEI • CHENNAI • TOKYO

Published by

World Scientific Publishing Co. Pte. Ltd.
5 Toh Tuck Link, Singapore 596224
USA office: 27 Warren Street, Suite 401-402, Hackensack, NJ 07601
UK office: 57 Shelton Street, Covent Garden, London WC2H 9HE

Library of Congress Cataloging-in-Publication Data
Names: Jarrow, Robert A, editor. | Madan, Dilip B, editor.
Title: Peter Carr Gedenkschrift : research advances in mathematical finance / edited by
Robert A Jarrow, Cornell University, USA, Dilip B Madan, University of Maryland, USA.
Description: Hackensack, NJ : World scientific, [2024] | Includes bibliographical references.
Identifiers: LCCN 2023030467 | ISBN 9789811280290 (hardcover) |
ISBN 9789811280306 (ebook for institutions) | ISBN 9789811280313 (ebook for individuals)
Subjects: LCSH: Finance--Mathematical models. | Gedenkschrift, Peter Carr.
Classification: LCC HG106 .P47 2024 | DDC 332.01/51--dc23/eng/20230714
LC record available at https://lccn.loc.gov/2023030467

British Library Cataloguing-in-Publication Data
A catalogue record for this book is available from the British Library.

Cover photo courtesy of NYU Tandon Finance and Risk Engineering.

For any available supplementary material, please visit
https://www.worldscientific.com/worldscibooks/10.1142/13491#t=suppl

Desk Editors: Aanand Jayaraman/Lai Ann

Typeset by Stallion Press
Email: enquiries@stallionpress.com

https://doi.org/10.1142/9789811280306_fmatter

Preface

The first of March of 2022 was when we learned that our dear friend, colleague and fellow researcher into the mathematical aspects of finance suddenly passed away at the young age of 63. His departure was deeply felt by all who knew him. His enthusiasm for life and learning was contagious. We immediately decided to publish a Gedenkschrift in his honor. This book is the result. It contains 21 papers presented at a conference held for Peter at the Robert H. Smith School of Business on November 11 and 12, 2022. The topics covered are quite diverse and reflect the wide range of Peter's interests. The book starts with tributes to Peter presented at his Memorial Service held at the First Unitarian Congregational Society in Brooklyn Heights on March 19, 2022. The tributes detail the many aspects of a life filled with joy in all dimensions. We also include a collection of pictures taken over Peter's professional life.

https://doi.org/10.1142/9789811280306_fmatter

About the Editors

Robert A. Jarrow is the Ronald P. and Susan E. Lynch Professor of Investment Management at Cornell's SC Johnson College of Business. He is a co-creator of the Heath—Jarrow—Morton (HJM) model, the reduced form credit risk model and the forward price martingale measure. He was the first to distinguish forward/futures prices and to study market manipulation using arbitrage-pricing theory. He has written 7 textbooks and has over 200 academic journal publications.

His research has won many awards, including the Graham and Dodd Scrolls Award 2001, the CBOE Pomerance Prize 1982, the Ross Best Paper Award 2008 and the Bernstein Fabozzi/Jacobs Levy Award 2009. In 1997, he was named IAFE Financial Engineer of the Year. He is in the Fixed Income Analysts Society Hall of Fame, *Risk* magazine's 50-member Hall of Fame, and listed in the Who's Who of Economics. He received *Risk* magazine's Lifetime Achievement Award in 2009. He also serves on various academic journal and industry advisory boards.

Dilip B. Madan is the Professor Emeritus of Mathematical Finance at the Robert H. Smith School of Business. Currently, he serves as a consultant to Morgan Stanley and Norges Bank Investment Management. He is a founding member and Past President of the Bachelier Finance Society. He received the 2006 von Humboldt award in applied mathematics, was the 2007 *Risk* magazine Quant of the Year, received the 2008 Medal for Science from the University of Bologna, held the 2010 Eurandom Chair, was inducted into the Circle of Discovery of the College of Computer, Mathematical and Natural Sciences in 2014 and is the IAQF Financial Engineer of the Year 2021. He has published over 200 papers and serves on the Advisory Board of Frontiers of Mathematical Finance and as a Director of the Scientific Association of Mathematical Finance.

https://doi.org/10.1142/9789811280306_fmatter

Contents

https://doi.org/10.1142/9789811280306_fmatter

Introduction

Peter Carr was an avid researcher in many areas of mathematical finance. This breadth of interests is well documented in this book by the writings of his co-researchers who, in memory of the wonderful times spent together, contributed to his Gedenkschrift. Given the diversity of the topics presented, for ease of reference, we list in alphabetical order of the submitting or presenting author the titles and abstracts for the numerous contributions.

Backtestability and the Ridge Backtest, Carlo Acerbi and Balasz Szekeley

We propose a formal definition of backtestability for a statistical functional of a distribution: a functional is backtestable if there exists a backtest function depending only on the forecast of the functional and the related random variable, which is strictly monotonic in the former and has zero expected value for an exact forecast. We discuss the relationship between elicitability and identifiability which turn out to be necessary conditions for backtestability. The variance and the expected shortfall are not backtestable for this reason. We compare (absolute) model validation in the context of hypothesis tests, via backtest functions, versus (relative) model selection between competing forecasting models, via scoring functions. We define a backtest to be sharp when it is strictly monotonic with respect to the real value of the functional and not only to its forecast. This decides whether the expected value of the backtest determines also the prediction discrepancy and not only its significance. We show that the quantile backtest is not sharp and in fact it provides no information whatsoever on its true value. The expectile is also not sharp; we provide bounds for its true value, which are looser for outer confidence levels. We then introduce the notion of ridge backtests, applicable to particular non-backtestable functionals, such as the variance and the expected shortfall, which coincide with the attained minimum of the scoring function of another elicitable auxiliary functional (the mean and the value at risk, respectively). This permits approximated sharp backtests up to a small and one-sided sensitivity to the prediction of the auxiliary variable. The ridge mechanism explains why the variance has always been *de facto* backtestable and allows for similar efficient ways to backtest the expected shortfall. We discuss the relevance of this result in the current debate of financial regulation (banking and insurance), where value at risk and expected shortfall are adopted as regulatory risk measures.

A Deep Learning Scheme for Solving Nonlinear Partial Differential Equations, Maxim Bichuch and Ke Chen

We study the convergence of a deep learning algorithm applied to a general class of fully nonlinear second-order partial differential equations. By using a suitable finite difference approximation to the loss function of the deep learning scheme, we are able to apply existing numerical solutions to convergence theorems. We apply our results and illustrate this convergence to the finite horizon optimal investment problem with a proportional transaction cost in single- and multi-asset settings.

Data-Driven Non-parametric Robust Control under Dependence Uncertainty, Erhan Bayraktar and Tao Chen

We consider a multi-period stochastic control problem where the multivariate driving stochastic factor of the system has known marginal distributions but uncertain dependence structures. To solve the problem, we propose to implement the non-parametric adaptive robust control framework. We aim to find the optimal control against the worst-case copulae in a sequence of shrinking uncertainty sets which are generated from continuously observing the data. Then, we use a stochastic gradient descent ascent algorithm to numerically handle the corresponding high-dimensional dynamic inf-sup optimization problem. We present the numerical results in the context of utility maximization and show that the controller benefits from knowing more information about the uncertain model.

Option Pricing Generators, Umberto Cherubini

We characterize a class of option pricing models by their algebraic structure. Option prices are monoids, that is, operators endowed with the commutativity and associativity property and an identity element. If the price on the underlying asset is bounded, the operator corresponds to the concept of t-conorm, while if it is defined on the positive real line, the operator is a pseudo-addition. These operators have the same no-arbitrage properties as the classical option pricing models but are also associative. Each model in this class is characterized by a univariate increasing function that is defined as the generator of the model. The generator encodes a synthetic representation of the probability structure of the underlying asset. We provide no-arbitrage conditions for the generators and practical guidelines to construct them.

Representation for Martingales Living After a Random Time with Applications, Tahir Choulli and Ferdoos Alharbi

Our financial setting consists of a market model with two flows of information. The smallest flow $\mathbb{F}$ is the "public" flow of information which is available to all agents, while the larger flow $\mathbb{G}$ has additional information about the occurrence of a random time τ. This random time can model the default time in credit risk or death time in life insurance. Hence, the filtration $\mathbb{G}$ is the progressive enlargement of $\mathbb{F}$ with τ. In this framework, under some mild assumptions on the pair $(\mathbb{F};\tau)$, we describe explicitly how $\mathbb{G}$-local martingales can be represented in terms of $\mathcal{F}$-local martingale and parameters of τ. This representation complements Choulli, Daveloose and Vanmaele [10] to the case when martingales live "after τ." The application of these results to the explicit parametrization of all deflators under $\mathbb{G}$ is fully elaborated. The results are illustrated in the case of the jump-diffusion model and the discrete-time market model.

Derivatives Risks as Costs in a One-Period Network Model, Dorinel Bastide, Stéphane Crépey, Samuel Drapeau and Mekonnen Tadese

We present a one-period XVA model encompassing bilateral and centrally cleared trading in a unified framework with explicit formulas for most quantities at hand. We illustrate possible uses of this framework for running stress test exercises on a financial network from a clearing member's perspective or for optimizing the porting of the portfolio of a defaulted clearing member.

Approximation with Independent Variables, Freddy Delbaen and Chitro Majumdar

Given a square-integrable m-dimensional random variable X on a probability space $(\Omega, \mathcal{F}, P)$ and a subsigma algebra $\mathcal{A}$, we show that there exists another m-dimensional random variable Y, independent of $\mathcal{A}$ and minimizing the L^2 distance to X. Such results have importance to fairness and bias reduction in artificial intelligence, machine learning and network theory.

Pricing Autocallables under Local-Stochastic Volatility, Walter Farkas, Francesco Ferrari and Urban Ulrych

This chapter investigates the pricing of single-asset autocallable barrier reverse convertibles in the Heston local-stochastic volatility (LSV) model. Despite their complexity, autocallable structured notes are the most traded equity-linked exotic derivatives. The autocallable payoff embeds an early-redemption feature generating strong path- and model-dependency. Consequently, the commonly used local volatility (LV) model is overly simplified for pricing and risk management. Given its ability to match the implied volatility smile and reproduce its realistic dynamics, the LSV model is, in contrast, better suited for exotic derivatives, such as autocallables. We use quasi-Monte Carlo methods to study the pricing given the Heston LSV model and compare it with the LV model. In particular, we establish the sensitivity of the valuation differences of autocallables between the two models with respect to payoff features, model parameters, underlying characteristics and volatility regimes. We find that the improved spot volatility dynamics captured by the Heston LSV model typically result in higher prices, demonstrating the dependence of autocallables on the forward skew. Moreover, we show that the parameters of the stochastic component of LSV models enable controlling for the autocallables' price while leaving the fit to European options unaffected.

Not All Oil Storage Shocks Are Alike: The Case of WTI during Times of COVID, Helyette Geman and Yuanye Ma

The goal of this chapter is two-fold: (a) revisit and adjust the theory of storage of Kaldor (1936) and Working (1939) for the WTI crude oil during the period 2017 to November 2020. We show that the inventory was a much more explanatory factor than production during the period surrounding the moment when the pandemic news broke in the Western world, a feature that can be explained by the remarkable lack of storage that existed in the United States at that time and took, for the first time in the history of oil markets, WTI prices to negative territories; (b) employ neural network methods to forecast WTI oil prices between January 2017 and December 2020. Our results are excellent before April 20, 2020, but unsurprisingly exhibit a larger RMSE during the period surrounding the crash which contained prices of mixed signs.

Total Positivity and Relative Convexity of Option Prices, Paul Glasserman and Dan Pirjol

This chapter studies total positivity and relative convexity properties in option pricing models. We introduce these properties in the Black–Scholes setting by showing the following: out-of-the-money calls are totally positive in strike and volatility, out-of-the-money puts have a reverse sign rule property, calls and puts are convex with respect to at-the-money prices, and relative convexity of option prices implies a convexity-in-time property of the underlying. We then extend these properties to other models, including scalar diffusions, mixture models and certain Lévy processes. We show that relative convexity typically holds in time-homogeneous local volatility models through the Dupire equation. We develop implications of these ideas for empirical option prices, including constraints on the at-the-money skew. We illustrate connections with models studied by Peter Carr, including the variance-gamma, CGMY, Dagum and logistic density models.

Supervised Deep Neural Networks (DNNs) for Pricing/Calibration of Vanilla/Exotic Options Under Various Different Processes, Tugce Karatas, Amir Oskoui and Ali Hirsa

We apply supervised deep neural networks (DNNs) for pricing and calibration of both vanilla and exotic options under both diffusion and pure jump processes with and without stochastic volatility. We train our neural network models under different numbers of layers, neurons per layer and various different activation functions in order to find which combinations work better empirically. For training, we consider various different loss functions and optimization routines. We demonstrate that deep neural networks exponentially expedite option pricing compared to commonly used option pricing methods which consequently make calibration and parameter estimation super fast.

Asset Price Bubbles, Wealth Preserving, Dominating and Replicating Trading Strategies, Robert Jarrow and Yuxuan Liu

This chapter studies an arbitrage-free, competitive and frictionless market with trading in a single risky asset and money market account, where the risky asset exhibits a price bubble. We analyze two sets of self-financing and admissible trading strategies in this market. The first is simple trading strategies, and the second is trading strategies that replicate or super-replicate the risky asset's payoffs at the model's horizon. We show that, in both sets, there exist wealth-preserving trading strategies, i.e., trading strategies whose initial value equals the present value of their future cash flows. And, in the second set, we show that there are wealth-preserving replicating trading strategies that dominate buying and holding the risky asset. The practical applications of these insights are discussed.

EMA-type Trading Strategies Maximize Utility under Partial Information, Xiaodong Chen and Roger Lee

Consider a partially informed trader who does not observe the true drift of a financial asset. Under Gaussian price dynamics with stochastic unobserved drift, including cases of mean-reversion and momentum dynamics, we take a filtering approach to solve explicitly for trading strategies which maximize expected logarithmic, exponential and power utility. We prove that the optimal strategies depend on the current price and an exponentially weighted moving average (EMA) price and, in some cases, current wealth, not on any other stochastic variables. We establish optimality over all price-history-dependent strategies satisfying integrability criteria, not just EMA-type strategies. Thus, the condition that the optimal trading strategy depends purely on EMA and current price is not an assumption but rather a consequence of our theorems. We solve explicitly for the optimal parameters of the EMA-type strategies and verify optimality rigorously, relative to a universe of admissible strategies defined by a broad, natural and simple sup-integrability condition on the utility of wealth.

Option Returns, Dilip Madan, Wim Schoutens and King Wang

Nonlinear martingale theory is used to form lower and upper price processes straddling a martingale. The martingale return is then modeled in terms of risk charges associated with the returns on the straddling lower and upper processes. The move to physically expected returns is made via the usual covariation risk factors. There are however two covariation terms: one for the lower and the other for the upper return. The expected returns are then seen to incorporate in addition to covariation considerations that address the martingale, the risk charges that assess out-of-martingale issues. The theory is tested on prices of options for 10 underliers over 170 days covering 4 maturities and 21 strikes. It is observed that the risk charges have positive significant coefficients while the upper covariation has a positive price with the lower covariation receiving a negative price.

Supermartingale Breiner's Theorem with Full Marginals Constraints, Erhan Bayraktar, Shuoqing Deng and Dominykas Norgilas

We explicitly construct the supermartingale version of the Fréchet–Hoeffding coupling in the setting with infinitely many marginals constraints. This extends the results of Henri–Labordère, Tan and Touzi [12] obtained in the martingale setting. Our construction is based on the Markovian iteration of one-period optimal supermartingale couplings. In the limit, as the number of iterations goes to infinity, we obtain a pure jump process that belongs to a family of local Lévy models introduced by [6]. Finally, we show that the constructed process solves the continuous time supermartingale optimal transport problem for a particular family of (path-dependent) cost functions. The explicit computations are provided in the following three cases: the uniform case, the Bachelier model and the geometric Brownian motion case.

Forward-Backward Stochastic Neural Networks: Deep Learning of High-dimensional Partial Differential Equations, Maziar Raissi

Classical numerical methods for solving partial differential equations suffer from the curse of dimensionality mainly due to their reliance on meticulously generated spatio-temporal grids. Inspired by modern deep learning-based techniques for solving forward and inverse problems associated with partial differential equations, we circumvent the tyranny of numerical discretization by devising an algorithm that is scalable to high dimensions. In particular, we approximate the unknown solution by a deep neural network which essentially enables us to benefit from the merits of automatic differentiation. To train the aforementioned neural network, we leverage the well-known connection between high-dimensional partial differential equations and forward-backward stochastic differential equations. In fact, independent realizations of a standard Brownian motion will act as training data. We test the effectiveness of our approach for a couple of benchmark problems spanning a number of scientific domains including Black–Scholes–Barenblatt and Hamilton–Jacobi–Bellman equations, both in 100 dimensions.

How to Design a Derivatives Market? Bastien Baldacci, Paul Jusselin and Mathieu Rosenbaum

We consider the problem of designing a derivatives exchange aiming at addressing clients' needs in terms of listed options and providing suitable liquidity. We proceed into two steps. First, we use a quantization method to select the options that should be displayed by the exchange. Then, using a principal–agent approach, we design a make-take fees contract between the exchange and the market maker. The role of this contract is to provide incentives to the market maker so that he offers small spreads for the whole range of listed options, hence attracting transactions and meeting the commercial requirements of the exchange.

A Moment Matching Calibration under the Bilateral Gamma Model and Its Applications, Jinqyan Zhang and Wim Schoutens

This paper provides a closed-form solution for a moment matching calibration under the Bilateral Gamma (BG) model. The BG model is an exponential Lévy model with a bilateral gamma distribution as the underlying distribution. The famous Variance Gamma (VG) model is a special case of this BG model. Compared with the variance gamma distributions, bilateral gamma distributions allow more flexible tail behaviors. Model calibration is a vital and classical problem of option pricing. The standard calibration process applies a search algorithm to find an optimal parameter set by minimizing an objective function representing the error between the model and market quotes. However, numerical optimization often suffers from local minima, an ill-posed problem, and the optimal result is sensitive to the initial value of the search algorithm. Moment matching calibration follows an alternative approach. It estimates the model parameters by matching a series of moments of the model with the corresponding market-implied moments. Hence, instead of applying a search algorithm, it obtains the optimal parameters by solving the moment matching equations, and thus, it avoids the mentioned issues. Previous studies have developed the moment matching calibration for the mentioned VG model. This paper provides an analytical solution to the moment matching equations for the BG model. Next, we evaluate its performance in a numerical study and compare a few variations of the methodology. As theoretically expected, the moment matching calibration under the BG model outperforms the moment matching calibration under the VG model. In terms of minimizing root-mean-squared errors, also as expected, it is suboptimal by construction compared with the search algorithm under the BG model. We quantify the gap and note that the straightforward moment matching calibration is obtained almost instantaneously in contrast to the search algorithm, which is rather time-consuming. Accordingly, we combine the moment matching calibration and standard calibration by using the moment matching solution as a plausible initial value for the search algorithm and improve model performance as such.

Exploiting Arbitrage Requires Short Selling, Eckhard Platen and Stephan Tappe

We show that in a financial market given by semimartingales, an arbitrage opportunity, provided it exists, can only be exploited through short selling. This finding provides a theoretical basis for differences in regulation for financial service providers that are allowed to go short and those without short sales. The privilege to be allowed to short sell gives access to potential arbitrage opportunities, which creates by design a bankruptcy risk.

Power Laws in Market Microstructure, Umut Çetin and Henri Waelbroeck

We develop an equilibrium model for market impact of trades when investors with private signals execute via a trading desk. Fat tails in the signal distribution lead to a power law for price impact, while the impact is logarithmic for lighter tails. Moreover, the tail distribution of the equilibrium trade volume obeys a power law. The spread decreases with the degree of noise trading and increases with the number of insiders. In case of a monopolistic insider, the last slice traded against the limit order book is priced at the fundamental value of the asset reminiscent of Ref. [17]. However, competition among insiders leads to aggressive trading, hence vanishing profit in the limit. The model also predicts that the order book flattens as the amount of noise trading increases converging to a model with proportional transaction costs with non-vanishing spread.

An Extension with Illustrations of the Azéma–Yor Algorithm for Solving Skorohod Embedding Problem, Yuri Imamura and Ju Yi Yen

We recall and illustrate four methods: Azéma–Yor algorithm, Vallois algorithm, excursion method and Azéma exponential result, each one allowing us to solve the Skorokhod embedding problem. In doing so, we consider more general stopping times than in the original Azéma–Yor algorithm.

Part I

Tributes and Pictures

https://doi.org/10.1142/9789811280306_0001

Chapter 1

Tributes

Tributes to Peter Carr are presented here in alphabetical order after the tributes of family members, the editors of this work and the conference dinner keynote speaker.

1. Carol Marquardt

Thank you all for being here today.

Peter was born on December 22, 1958, in Toronto, Canada. He was the oldest of the three sons of Larry and Livia Caruana, who had immigrated from Malta. His childhood was filled with family get-togethers with his many cousins, Sunday dinners at Swiss Chalet and countless games of road hockey with friends and neighbors. In high school, he was senior class treasurer and he competed on the quiz bowl team. He studied business at the University of Toronto, where he found his true calling in a finance class taught by Professor Dan Thornton. I later met Professor Thornton after Peter and I were married, and he told me that Peter was the smartest undergrad he'd ever met with a completely intuitive understanding of finance. I'm sure that assessment would surprise none of Peter's colleagues who are here today.

Peter then got a doctorate in finance. He only applied to four programs, all of them in California, wanting to escape the cold of Canada. He chose UCLA and arrived a few months early in June of 1983, eager to get started. He was overwhelmed by the beauty of the campus. The jacaranda trees were in full bloom and he told me he felt unbelievably lucky to be there. His luck continued when he immediately fell into a fantastic living arrangement, chauffeuring a blind psychotherapist to the Braille Institute three days a week in exchange for free rent in her Bel Air guest cottage with maid service included. It was at UCLA that he also developed his love for ultimate frisbee, which later became a Father's Day tradition for us.

While he enjoyed California living, Peter also worked very hard at UCLA. His dissertation chairman, Michael Brennan, emailed me last week and wrote: "Peter was my first PhD student at UCLA and I have been very proud of him though in truth I can take little credit for his accomplishments, for we taught him none of the mathematics that he needed to contribute to the field in which he made such significant contributions. *He had to learn the math himself.*" Peter was self-taught, which explains his enormous library of math books, which at one point were spread across five different locations in Manhattan.

Peter then began his career as a finance academic at Cornell, teaching option pricing to MBA students and working on his research. And during his first semester at Cornell, he also taught himself to ice skate. Back in the 1980s, the business school had an annual tradition in which the faculty played ice hockey against the female students, and apparently, the faculty had been consistently losing these matches. So, when Peter, a young Canadian, was hired, expectations were very high — finally, the faculty might have a chance to win this thing. The only problem was that Peter, though a very experienced road hockey player, had never really learned to ice skate all that well. But he was determined to help out the team, so he devoted his lunch hours to practicing every day at Lynah Rink, which was across the street from the business school. By the time the game rolled around that winter, he was an amazing skater. I was able to attend a few of these games and you could just see how much joy he got from being out on the ice. Still, the faculty team never won a match — when Peter played, he made sure that every game magically ended in a draw.

I met Peter at a picnic at a state park just outside of Ithaca, New York. It was Saturday, September 7, 1991. He was just coming off the volleyball court, and I was walking toward it, drinking a Canadian beer, which he took as a promising sign. I was instantly charmed by his friendliness and sense of humor and frankly, I was a little surprised to learn that he was a faculty member because he seemed way too down-to-earth and in way too good a mood to be a tenure-track professor. On our first date, he amused me with his parlor trick of naming the day of the week for any date in history, and he related his love of the Beatles and of classic TV from the 1960s and 1970s. I thought he was adorable. And he was smart. On our second date, he quizzed me with a series of brainteasers, which he collected and shared with his students to help them prepare for job interviews. I thought it was kind of fun, so it was only later that I wondered — was that a test? Fortunately for us, I guess I passed and we happily spent the next 30 years together.

Eventually, Peter left academia and we moved to New York, a city we both adored. Peter spent 20 years working in the financial industry, where he enjoyed the fast pace, the challenge of working on difficult problems and collaborating with talented colleagues. However, he remained an academic at heart, interested in the world of ideas and the beauty of mathematics. An insomniac, he awoke early every morning to work on research before heading to the office, and he continued to publish in the top journals in finance while pursuing a career on Wall Street. Ironically, he published far more articles while working in the industry than he did while he was an actual academic! Things came full circle though when he returned to academia full-time in 2016 as chair of the finance and risk engineering department at NYU Tandon. I think this really was the perfect job for him — combining what he loved best about the two worlds. He also felt particularly blessed with his staff at FRE — he never stopped raving about them — and as a result, he was one of the few people I've known that actually liked being a department chair! To make things even better, we moved to Brooklyn in 2017, and Peter had a five-minute commute on a Citi Bike. The more relaxed vibe in Brooklyn perfectly suited him. He loved exploring new neighborhoods and new restaurants, and he ran in Prospect Park several times a week. On so many levels, Peter was the happiest he'd ever been during his time at Tandon.

But the happiest day of Peter's life — by far — was August 9, 2001, the day our daughter Olivia was born. He called his mother to share the good news, and she later told me she had never heard him so overjoyed. Peter took particular glee in parading Olivia around on his shoulders, though it always made me nervous, and he only reluctantly stopped when she got too tall. He was an active dad, taking Olivia on bike rides through the city, first in a baby seat and later on a tandem bike. They spent countless hours together at the local playgrounds, where Olivia always wanted to be pushed higher and higher on the swings. He walked her to elementary school every morning, which I know was a very special time for them both. The three of us traveled as a family whenever we could, and we have many happy memories of trips to London, Paris, Stockholm, Istanbul, Budapest, Prague, Vienna, Hong Kong, Cancun, the Bahamas, Hawaii, Machu Picchu and the Galapagos Islands and of course many trips to Disney and the Wizarding World. Peter always overpacked for these trips, bringing so many books, files and electronic devices that we'd sometimes need to buy clothes for him when we arrived. And even at Disney World, he would work on proofs in a Mickey Mouse notebook while waiting in line with Olivia for the rides. The pandemic ended most of those adventures, but it also gave us more time together at home, time that I will now especially treasure.

Much has already been written about Peter's kindness and generosity, his almost compulsively helpful nature — he loved nothing better than doing a favor for a friend. And Peter had lots of friends — I'm happy to see so many of you here today. He saw the best in everyone. The only people who truly annoyed him were drivers who blocked the box and French waiters who refused to bring the check.

Peter was also known for his enthusiasm for the latest technology. Of course, those close to Peter knew how much he loved his car, a Tesla Model S, but Peter had fun trying out Google glasses, virtual reality headsets, voice-activated appliances and any device with the word "smart" in front of it. His last tech purchase was a smart soap dispenser, and I cannot figure out how it works.

Peter's last day at home was January 29th. He wasn't feeling well, so he spent the day in bed, which I don't remember ever happening before. I take some small comfort in knowing that he spent that last day doing the things he loved — he worked on a proof and he enjoyed his favorite food. Olivia and I were nearby. At 7 p.m., he watched his beloved Toronto Maple Leafs play the Detroit Red Wings. The Leafs won, 7 to 4. Soon after that, we realized something was terribly wrong, and we called an ambulance. And for the next month, we prayed for a miracle.

Many people have since sent kind messages of support and sympathy. Someone wrote to say that the miracle we had been praying for had in fact already occurred — the miracle was that Peter and I had ever met at all, that we were able to have our beautiful daughter Olivia and build a good life together in this wonderful city. And I know that they're right. And I also know that I should be grateful for getting to spend 30 years with the nicest guy in the world. But I wanted more — and Olivia wanted more — and I think everyone here today wanted more time with Peter, too.

2. Jim Carr

Good morning everyone, to all of you in this beautiful room and to everyone who is watching on Zoom. I'm Jim Carr, one of Peter's two brothers, and I wanted to start by saying how grateful I am for the outpouring of support our family has received over the past month, whether through phone calls, social media posts or the many tributes from academia and industry. Peter was an inspiration to so many people, in so many ways. As a friend, a colleague or a mentor. And while many of you know him as Professor Peter Carr, the distinguished author of many ground-breaking papers in quantitative finance, I had the privilege of growing up with Peter and sharing in many of his early life experiences that would shape his character going forward.

So, as I was reflecting on what I would say today, I realized that others were far more qualified to speak to Peter's many professional accomplishments and that I'd like to journey back to his formative years, where his contagious smile, his innate curiosity and generous spirit were evident even then. Those same qualities which bring us together today to celebrate his life and the influence he has had on so many people.

So let's rewind the clock and in honor of Peter's love of the Beatles, I'd like to embark on what I'll call the Magical Mystery tour of Peter's early days.

Our journey begins in the late sixties. A time when anything seemed possible. The Beatles sang "All you need is love," the Apollo space mission was closing in on landing a man on the moon and even Peter's beloved Toronto Maple Leafs hockey team defied tradition and had actually won the Stanley Cup. A miracle not since repeated, I may add.

Our family lived on the outskirts of Toronto, Canada. My mother and father had emigrated from the Mediterranean island of Malta where their childhood had been upended by the air raid sirens and severe rations of World War II. The war prevented them from completing their education, so when they moved to Canada, they worked hard to ensure that we grow up in a stable environment and could get a solid education. We had a fun childhood as we'd play street hockey with the local kids like Mike Klimeck and Rob Wilson, catch turtles in a nearby Humber River or get together with our many relatives.

It was pretty evident early on that Peter had a way with numbers. He loved math and would have us test him on how quickly he could do calculations in his head. This came in handy when we'd get together and play his favorite board game at the time, which, of course, was Monopoly. Peter would always be the banker and would enjoy figuring out how much change was owed for a particular transaction and explaining how mortgages worked to his younger siblings. This may have been the first inkling that Peter was destined for the world of Wall Street finance.

So, after mastering Monopoly, Peter wanted to try his hand at making money in the real world. But how? In those days, opportunities were limited for a 13-year-old. Then, one day, while Peter was watching our neighborhood paperboy deliver the paper to our house and an idea hit him. Paperboys were paid for each paper they delivered, so Peter reasoned he could deliver far more papers with a paper route in an apartment building, rather than trudge door to door through rain and snow in the neighborhood. So next thing you know, Peter got a paper route in the largest building in the area. He then worked out a system where he would load all the papers into the elevator, press the button for the top floor and when the door opened he would run into the hallway, throw the papers to each apartment and then run back before the doors closed. Timing is everything. He'd then push the elevator button for the next floor and do it all over again. Rinse and repeat. In an hour, he could deliver hundreds of newspapers that would have taken days of delivering in the neighborhood. He then decided to expand the operation further by taking on two additional buildings and even hiring me to help him. He continued expanding until he had built a paper delivery empire that became the largest paper route in the country. Not bad for a kid who wasn't old enough to get a drivers license. And it beat mowing lawns. Eventually, Peter sold his route for a profit but gave one of the routes to me for free, which allowed me to earn a little money as well. So, even as a little kid, Peter had developed a keen mind for business, for developing innovative approaches and for helping others to succeed. He had proven he could win at Monopoly *and* in the real world.

Peter also developed a passion for teaching and academia. This, too, had its roots in his childhood. My father, who flew in from LA to be with us today, likes to tell this story of how Peter used to love watching the TV show, Gilligan's Island. For those of you who haven't heard of it, Gilligan's Island was a fun show about the antics of seven castaways shipwrecked on a deserted island off the coast of Hawaii. If you know the show, there's a character known as "The professor" who had a profound influence on young Peter. Peter would be inspired by the Professor's encyclopedic knowledge, his ability to write long equations on a blackboard and invent all sorts of gadgets to help get off the island. Peter was so enthralled by the Professor that when my father would ask Peter what he wanted to be when he grew up, he would enthusiastically exclaim "A Professor." He was too young to properly pronounce the word, but even at a young age, Peter had a clear vision of his future career path. It's no wonder that years later Peter would cultivate his own encyclopedic knowledge and be found writing complex equations on blackboards or playing with some new-fangled gadget. So, thank you Gilligan's Island for providing an incredible role model for Peter and starting him on the road to academia.

Fast forward a few years and the next stop on our Magical Mystery tour was Peter's formal education. In high school, he made friends easily and quickly became one of the top students. He especially loved math and finance, and as Carol mentioned, he eventually did a bachelor's in commerce degree and MBA at the University of Toronto.

Peter had a strong influence on the careers of many people. Myself included. He was an important factor in my own decision to complete the commerce degree at the University of Toronto and eventually an MBA. Peter's enthusiasm and passion were contagious to many.

Carol also mentioned that once Peter finished his MBA, he packed up and moved to LA to pursue his PhD. There's a story behind that as well. So, Peter eventually left our home in Toronto and headed to

LA in his beat-up 1970s VW rabbit packed with all his belongings. Unfortunately, he ran into a problem when his car was broken into in Las Vegas. The thieves took all of Peter's worldly possessions, his clothes, books, everything. Peter was devastated but was determined not to let some thief get in the way of pursuing his dreams. So, he continued to UCLA in what was now an empty beat-up VW rabbit. Fortunately, his luck turned around when he arrived in LA and saw a notice for a place to rent in the exclusive Bel Air neighborhood at an incredibly low price. He immediately called the number and an elderly lady told him the rent was low because she needed someone to drive her around from time to time. Peter seized the opportunity and arranged to meet the lady at her house later that afternoon. The only problem was that Peter didn't have any nice clothes to wear to his first meeting with her. All of his clothes had been taken when his car was broken into. So Peter, being ever resourceful, went on a mission to buy a new shirt, pants and shoes. He found someone to tailor his clothes and even went and got a haircut to look his absolute best. By the time Peter had finished running his errands, the sun had started to set. He drove up the woman's driveway and was a little surprised that there were no lights on in the home. He knocked on the door and waited. Nothing. He knocked again. Still nothing. He was starting to think that maybe all the trouble and expense he had gone through to get the clothes, shoes and haircut had been for nothing. He tried knocking one final time and the door slowly opened to reveal a little old lady with thick dark glasses and a white cane. Peter stood there dumbfounded realizing she was completely blind. He had spent all day buying clothes to make a good first impression and she couldn't even see him. Realizing the irony of the situation, Peter relayed his predicament to the old woman and they both broke out laughing. They bonded instantly and so began a relationship between Peter and that old lady that lasted several years while he completed his PhD at UCLA. He would drive her around from time to time and in return, he lived in a beautiful home in the hills of Bel Air while paying student rates. It was a great example of Peter's adaptability, resourcefulness and warm sense of humor that drew people toward him.

Fast forward again and over the ensuing years we would keep in touch and get together for holidays and vacations. Of course, Peter would go on to do great things in industry and academia. His contributions to quantitative finance are many. But the seeds had been sown all those years earlier in his experiences growing up as a kid: playing board games and building a paper route. In our 30s and 40s, when my brothers and I would get together, we'd inevitably pull out the Monopoly game and Peter would once again be the banker. We'd watch old reruns of Gilligan's Island or watch a hockey game. Regrettably, the Leafs never did win the Stanley cup again, but Peter never lost hope.

So now we arrive at this final stop on our Magical Mystery tour. It's been a wonderful journey, but all journeys end eventually, and unfortunately, this one ended far too soon. The last month has been very difficult as we process the loss of Peter. I will miss his passion, brilliance and infectious smile. His love of life and his generosity.

I came across a quote recently that spoke to me about Peter and the influence he has had on all of us. It reads:

"A life well lived leaves others better off."

And so, Peter, on behalf of the many people in this room today, those watching on Zoom and those who have been touched by you on your journey, I want to say "thank you, for leaving us all a little better off."

And thank you all for being here today to honor my brother.

3. Laurence Caruana

All three of us brothers — Peter, Jim and Laurence — went to the same high school in Toronto, and its Latin motto — *Semper ad Excellentiam* — quickly became engraved in our memories. Peter embodied that noble maxim in a very natural way: *"Always Strive towards Excellence."* And yet, he always had his own unique way of doing things, and I'm sure he would have amended that maxim to say: *"Strive towards Excellence — but with a touch of humor as well."*

Many of the people in this room know Professor Carr for his many accomplishments in the field of Finance. But, as his brother, I remember him in a more personal way — for the many times that he, as a young man, showed excellence in all that he did. It was just a natural part of his character, like a gift from birth, and there were many times in which he distinguished himself from the time he was a child. He always did so with natural grace and not a little laughter.

Whenever my Dad speaks of Peter as a pre-schooler, even today, my 88-year-old father recalls how Peter learned to speak quite early, and that he could name every one of the scale model cars that were in his collection. As a four year child, Peter was already showing a remarkable talent for memory.

In 1967, when Peter was nine years old, we moved to a new neighborhood in the west of Toronto called Edenbridge. It was a large new house, built by my father and uncles, with a long backyard leading down to the park with its river and forests. This is where Peter would join the neighborhood kids for a variety of exploits: catching snakes and frogs in summer, skating along the frozen river in winter and, every Saturday afternoon, playing street hockey just around the corner on Clay Court.

Peter shared with his best friend, Mike Klimek, a real passion for sports. As Mike later recalled in his tribute to Peter, "I'll always remember the day that we played all the local jocks and athletes of the school. We were both rather nervous. As it turned out, we ended up beating them. I had the game of my life in net and Peter razzle-dazzled them with his footwork and stick-handling."

Yes, Hockey has always been a huge part of life for Canadians, and without fail, Peter's gang of friends would gather every Wednesday and Saturday evening in our living room — to watch the Maple Leafs game on TV, usually with a pizza from Bellini's restaurant around the corner, and a case of Labatt's Blue beer or Red Cap ale. And — usually — the Leafs would lose, but that was all part of the tradition. Peter remained a faithful Leaf fan all of his life.

My brother was a typical teenager of the late sixties and early seventies. In his room you could find piles of *Mad* magazine, sci-fi books by Ray Bradbury or Isaac Asimov, and a whole collection of *Ripley's Believe It or Not.* But he also had a curious fondness for almanacs and atlases — any thick book crammed with facts. Most of all, he loved books that taught you how to sharpen your thinking skills, or increase your reading speed and expand your memory recall. He never treated his mental acuity simply as a gift but also worked very hard to cultivate his mind's capacity through constant learning and diligent practice. So within our family, Peter became notorious for his unique ability to remember dates of global events or calculate, for example, the weekday of any given date in history.

Those prodigious mental skills allowed him to distinguish himself in high school, not only through his excellent grades but also in two unique ways. In his final year, he was elected to the four-member Executive of the Student Council, serving as School Treasurer. And, along with three of the other brightest kids in school, he appeared on *Reach For the Top*. This was a nationwide TV quiz show, where high school teams competed for the top prize. His broad knowledge in so many subjects made him a formidable addition to the team.

In his more solitary moments, Peter would relax by playing snooker on the billiard table in the basement. The family house had a billiard table because the original Caruana house in Malta was situated next door to a Sports Club, where his father and uncles often played pool before they emigrated. Peter kept up this family tradition by becoming a very proficient player in the game. I think it appealed to his mathematical side since he would view the table from a variety of angles, and plan his shots many moves ahead — always lining up the white ball for the next perfect shot. An uncle who was highly skilled in the game, Uncle Mike, often came by to challenge him. And in this way, Peter learned the Maltese style of playing International Snooker, with all its hooks and angles. Eventually, they both participated in the Maltese-Canadian Club Competition, and Peter came away with First Prize, accompanied by a large golden trophy surmounted by a pool player.

3.1. *Semper ad Excellentiam*

Peter's mental acuity served him well during his academic studies, and he completed a Bachelor of Commerce Degree with very high standing. This garnered him a position at Coopers & Lybrand, and it was his intention, at the time, to become a Chartered Accountant. This was Peter's first big step into the World of Business, and we marveled at his transformation, since he now dressed in a pin-stripe suit, came home with a big briefcase filled with ledgers, and even changed his name from Caruana to Carr.

I'd moved out of the family home by then, and I remember having dinner with him one evening at the Café May in Toronto. He explained to me, with great excitement, all his new duties as an auditor but — I came away from the dinner wondering if he was really on the right career path. Well, to give Peter his due, he soon realized that as well. Within a year, he'd give up on accounting and was pursuing graduate studies at the University of Toronto.

This is an important quality about my brother which we should not overlook. Throughout his life, he had an unusual willingness to change his career path from Industry to Academia, and then back again. After he left Toronto in 1984 to begin his PhD in L.A., I saw Peter much less often. And I myself moved to Europe around the same time. So when our family came together in 1993 to celebrate Christmas at Peter and Carol's beautiful little home in Ithaca, Peter was now an Associate Professor at Cornell. But, by the time he visited me in Paris, in 2005, he was working on Wall Street.

Over the years I watched at a distance as his life became more complete: marrying the love of his life, having a beautifully-gifted child, and growing together into a happy family in Manhattan and Brooklyn.

Somehow, each time we met up, he was either advancing in his career on Wall Street or publishing new papers and teaching part-time at places like NYU. He always managed to keep a foot in both camps: Industry and Academia. I believe he was genuinely *intrigued by both*, rising to *the challenges of each*, and *seeking excellence in both*. As many of you know, Peter gave up some very lucrative opportunities on Wall Street to return to Academia full-time as chair of Tandon's Department of Finance and Risk Engineering.

This last change in his career path is, I believe, one of the most beautiful and noteworthy aspects of his legacy. He'd certainly left his mark in the field of Finance, as we can see from the many honors and prizes awarded to him, and by the different pricing models and formulas bearing his name. But, in the last decade of his life, he chose to dedicate himself to Mathematics and Finance in a different way: by dedicating himself to others.

He had a profound impact on the lives of his colleagues and students — those people who would, in turn, form the next generation of Finance and Risk Engineering. Even before he left us, he was looking into the future, and into the hearts of those people he knew and trusted to be the true bearers of his legacy — those who, like him, were in pursuit of excellence in all that they did, but also with a little smile, a twinkle of the eye, and a touch of humor in their hearts.

Thank you for remembering my brother, Peter Carr.

4. Dilip B. Madan

Peter Carr left us, saddened and shocked, on the morning of March 1, 2022, after an earlier devastating internal hemorrhage. I spoke with Peter on January 29 asking about his response to my remarks on a discussion that took place at a virtual seminar on January 25, the second day of the Spring semester of 2022. He replied that he had not been feeling well and would get back to me when he was better. This was the first time and now also the last time that Peter responded in such a manner. I have never known him to be in such a state. Something was clearly amiss.

Undoubtedly, Peter leaves us with many wonderful memories of our interactions with him and here I try and relate some of them. I first met Peter in the summer of 1991 at a Cornell conference that initiated the journal *Mathematical Finance*. At the time, I had just arrived back in the United States after twelve years in Australia and was an unknown personality in the U.S. community of mathematicians with an interest in Finance. The meeting was brief but we got to appreciate each other. We got to know each other much better in the fall of 1995 when I spent the Fall semester on sabbatical at Cornell. Many discussions followed on the theory of no-arbitrage pricing.

By the summer of 1996, Peter had moved from Cornell to essentially head the quant group at Morgan Stanley. He may not have been the head but was recognized for his brilliance, intellect and energy as such by those around him. His natural inclination was to question, debate and challenge what is being discussed from multiple directions in the friendliest way possible. Recognizing this, the rest of the team just fell into place.

Peter arranged to have me hired as a consultant at Morgan Stanley in the summer of 1996 and I have since spent two to three days a week there. The spring of 1995 saw the birth of the variance gamma model with skewness added to it. Trader overrides were posing a strain on capital requirements supporting the option trading business. Marking to the variance gamma model was proposed, tried out on a small set of underliers and then adopted firm wide. The marking activity needed fast computation of variance gamma prices for thousands of underliers at market close. It must have been Thanksgiving of 1996, when my family and I were making our annual visit to my brother-in-law in Connecticut, where instead of joining the families to go shopping, the following Friday, I met Peter at Morgan Stanley and worked on developing the fast Fourier transform method for pricing options. This is what made the marking possible. Neither Peter nor I were interested in shopping. For many years, the Friday after Thanksgiving was spent this way. These two papers are among our most cited papers. Many asked Peter to take charge of the model and its implementation. But Peter's active mind had to move on to other pastures. It cannot stand in the light of any past glories.

Since then, we have worked in many ways and places. When it comes to financial mathematics, Peter did not take breaks. We worked in Sydney, Budapest, Paris and London on numerous occasions. Once on the barrier reef in Australia when most of the conference party was taking dives or snorkeling, Peter could be seen on deck, laptop in hand, interviewing colleagues on matters of mathematical detail. He embraced early on the idea of proof in mathematics and loved it all the way. Directing donations to the math museum is most appropriate.

Peter moved on to revising the VIX computation and developing hedges for the variance and volatility swaps. I interacted with him on hedging insurance risks. We worked on the implications of the absence of static arbitrage. This led us to the study of additive processes of which the Sato process was another contribution. My conversation with Peter between January 25 and 29 of this year was on additive processes and has led to a new paper, now without him, that we could have coauthored. Peter, prolific with both ideas and the personalities he engaged with, has published with many other coauthors on numerous aspects of the subject and we may note in this regard the extensive work with Liuren Wu, Roger Lee, Gurdip Bakshi, Andrey Itkin, Johannes Ruf, Travis Fisher, Matthew Lorig, Lorrenzo Torricelli, Sergey Nadtochiy to mention a few.

Apart from the papers and investigations, Peter gave freely of his time in delivering courses at conferences during the years he was with the financial industry. I participated in a few of these. One of these was a week-long course, in January 2012 at the Tata Institute of Fundamental Research in Bombay, my hometown. Peter could not take financial remunerations for these and diverted the funds to be received to various causes. One of which was funding my FestSchrift conference in 2006. In 2016 Peter, Philip Protter, Rene Carmona and I worked in bringing the World Congress of the Bachelier Finance Society to New York.

Let me close by noting that there is much to fondly remember Peter by. I remember a night in Paris when we went to dinner at a restaurant with no menu but you got what the house had prepared that day. The line to enter was too long and at Peter's suggestion, we returned the next night to be first in line. Another time in the financial district of London, we went to a pub and on some rare occasions Peter would take an alcoholic beverage, standard fare for me, but to my surprise, he took to a cherry-flavored beer. A bit courageous for my taste, but Peter delved into the new easily. Bought an electric vehicle easily and really enjoyed driving it. Would go out of the way to extend the ride. In Sydney, we enjoyed the early morning swim at Manly beach followed by Tasmanian scallops, one of my favorites there. He bought me a gigantic wine glass that holds a bottle of wine so I could say I just had one glass of wine at night! On another occasion, Peter stayed at my house overnight for a joint presentation in Baltimore the next morning. Peter was using the shower in my daughter's bedroom when there were just the two of us in the house. Neither of us, with three PhDs between us, could figure out how to turn the shower on. We gave up and he finally showered in my bedroom shower.

His spirit will definitely live on in our memories and our lives. Many thanks Peter for uplifting all the lives you touched so deeply.

5. Robert Jarrow

Peter was a special and unique scholar because of his inquisitiveness and eagerness to understand finance. He loved solving problems and learning the math that enabled him to do so. This story demonstrates these qualities. It is about the first time I met him when he was interviewing for an academic position at Cornell.

I was head of Cornell's recruiting committee, and we invited Peter for a campus visit. At a Saturday night dinner, he asked me an insightful question about the Black–Scholes formula and the stop-loss trading strategy with respect to options. To my chagrin, I didn't know the answer. I promised Peter that I would think about the problem.

He was leaving Ithaca to go back to UCLA on a Sunday evening. I wanted to fulfill my promise to Peter before he left, so I worked on the problem the Sunday morning. I called him at his hotel and told him that I thought I'd found the answer to the problem. We talked about the proof and decided together that the answer was correct. The solution involved the notion of a local time for a Brownian motion. Later, after he came to Cornell, we worked on generalizing this and published the result in the *Review of Financial Studies,* 1990, entitled "The stop-loss start-gain paradox and option valuation: a new decomposition into intrinsic and time value."

Peter used to say that my working on that question so quickly was the reason he came to Cornell. I doubt that this was the whole story. But I was glad that I worked on the problem that Sunday morning, pleased that we hired Peter and delighted that he came to Cornell. We became great friends.

Over the years, whenever Peter and I met, we chatted about finance-related research and never tired of the conversations. I admired his sharp mind and creative insights. The negative of our discussions was that this often made us boring dinner party guests. The positive is that because of those talks, we coauthored many other papers together and I am a better scholar. For that and Peter's friendship, I will be forever grateful.

6. Philip Protter

I celebrate Peter Carr, and sing to him,
And what I assume you shall assume,
For every atom belonging to Peter as good belongs to you.

Peter Carr had many attributes and probably most people here know and/or have experienced many if not most of them. What people may be less aware of is the symbolic role he provided to the profession. Before I explain that remark, let me give a quick summary of his career.

Peter began as an academic at the Cornell Business School. This was an important time for him if for no other reason than he met his wife Carol there. While at Cornell, he was mentored by Bob Jarrow, but (in an internecine fight having nothing to do with Peter) Cornell made one of his biggest mistakes — and Cornell has some doozies to its credit — when he denied Peter tenure, back in 1996.

I didn't know Peter back then, but I imagine he became disgusted with academia and its pettiness and decided to try his luck in the rough and tumble world of investment banking. To say he excelled with brilliance at Morgan Stanley, then Bloomberg and then Morgan Stanley a second time is not only self-evident but perhaps even an understatement. He became a managing director with around 70 people reporting to him.

I don't know what it's like to manage so many people in an investment bank, but I remember asking a friend who was chair of an 80-person department at Purdue what it was like, and he said it was like running a very large kindergarten class. Peter seemed to do it effortlessly. I very much doubt it was effortless, however; it's just that he made it seem that way.

Let's return to the symbolic function Peter fulfilled. While in the industry, Peter did original research. This is not like a dog playing the piano, no: Peter did first-rate research. There is a measurement in academia that measures the impact of one's work within the research community, known as the H-index. My own H-index is 50, which is considered to be quite good. Dilip Madan, for comparison, is 54. Peter has an H-index of 60. That's amazing.

These days, academics working in the generalized area of investment finance, such as myself, have PhD students who debate whether to continue in academia or to continue on "Wall Street." It's a difficult decision because it's almost impossible, once the die is cast, to change one's mind. Academia is not for everyone, by a long shot. Salaries are lower, and the beginning of one's career, unless you're lucky, involves picking up and moving a couple or even a few times, from this school to that school, with the schools often located far apart. It can wreak havoc on family life.

Many a time, students have told me that they're going into the banking world, but they will be keeping up a busy agenda of research while they work. I explain, in as kind a manner as possible, that unless they are Peter Carr, it's more or less a pipe dream. They will have neither the time nor the energy to conduct such a scenario. A job in the industry means, unless one is Peter, forgetting about research. I even think companies like Morgan Stanley should have written above their doors, "Abandon all hope of doing research, ye who work here."

"But what about Peter Carr?" They ask. I'm usually too kind to reply, "I served with Peter Carr. I knew Peter Carr. Peter Carr is a friend of mine. Trust me: You're no Peter Carr."

My mother taught High School English, and at the risk of her turning over in her grave to hear me say this, Peter is almost unique. I only add the caveat "almost" because I'm a probabilist/statistician and we always allow for the possibility of there being more than one outlier. Well, let me tell you: If you have to be an outlier, then being Peter Carr is the way to go.

Peter Carr is the most wonderful outlier I can imagine. His memory lives on within us all.

7. Barry Blecherman

At Peter's memorial service, Carol mentioned that Peter liked to do research thinking first thing in the morning, before leaving for work. Working with Peter these past six years, I was often the beneficiary of this AM passion. Even if he hadn't been thinking about research, Peter was almost always excited about something when he arrived at Tandon. It often happened that the first faculty member Peter would see when he arrived in our suite of offices would be me. Each time this happened, it was special — I had the chance for what would typically be the better part of an hour to be Peter's audience, to try to be his sounding board.

This was a wonderful way for me to begin my workday. Instead of diving straight into administrative work, my day might begin with a discussion of differential equations or tropical geometry. Or hockey. Or world events and their impact on markets. Or hockey. Or electric cars — comparing and contrasting his Tesla and my Mustang was a frequent topic. Or hockey. With Peter being a Toronto Maple Leafs fanatic (last Stanley Cup win in 1967) and me being a hardcore Philadelphia Flyers fan (most recent Stanley Cup in 1975), we talked about and moaned about hockey a lot.

Peter was always excited to share with others what was exciting his mind — what a gift I had to be his colleague. I miss him every day, especially in the morning.

8. Sébastian Bossu

In 2005, I gave a talk about variance and correlation swaps at Emanuel Derman's practitioner seminar, based on my early industry papers. Peter came to the talk and that's how I met him. At dinner, I enjoyed being in the company of several famous quants. Listening to Peter, I was immediately dazzled by his active mind and passion for research, by how much he knew and how willingly he shared his knowledge, and by just how stimulating our conversations were. I recall that he told me about Matytsin's formula, a very clever result that was not well known at the time, and that I utilized about ten years later when I investigated the delta of variance swaps.

Peter loved ideas so much that you could always trust him to judge your work entirely on its merit yet with a benevolent and altruistic nature. In a field and an industry so fiercely competitive, Peter was refreshingly friendly, open-minded and synergetic. He would always give you credit for engaging in the world of ideas and encourage you to go further.

I often ran into Peter at conferences, enjoying his wonderful talks and happy quant banter during breaks. We only corresponded from time to time until about 2017 when we began to collaborate on joint academic articles. I like to think we instinctively had mutual esteem for each other, due to a number of *self-similarities*: we both studied business and mathematics, in that order; we both came from countries where French is an official language; we both were "hybrids" — a career concept he coined — with one foot in academia and the other in the industry; we both liked nerd jokes: at a Morgan Stanley seminar, I remember how Peter's face instantly lit up, bursting into laughter after I quipped that correlation swaps really should be called "eigenswaps".

In virtually every dimension I can think of, Peter simply seemed ahead of us all. More intense. More genuine. More supportive. More knowledgeable. More enthusiastic. More people-oriented. More generous. A brilliant mind who loved models, Peter himself was an incredibly inspirational *quant model* just about impossible to *replicate*. Indeed, I would argue that the question of Peter Carr's replicability may yet be the hardest open problem posed to the quantitative finance community after his untimely disappearance.

Still, as Peter liked to say, nothing is truly impossible as long as we are willing to *make an assumption*. In his spirit, allow me to observe that, while it does seem impossible for *one* mortal to be another Peter Carr, things begin to look much better once we extend the solution space to multiple dimensions. In fact, I would like to submit to the quantitative finance community the following conjecture that, in the limit as d goes to infinity, where d is the number of quants following in Peter's footsteps, Peter's greatness is replicable with probability 1. Now let us prove it!

9. Agostino Capponi

I will never forget when I first met Peter. It was in 2008 at a conference in Los Angeles, and Peter was a very well-established academic who I had only known through this influential research. I was a PhD student, who had just begun working in financial mathematics. Peter spent half an hour chatting and listening to me on my counterparty risk research. He gave me plenty of useful advice, which played a fundamental role in my career. I was positively surprised and very pleased to see Peter following up with me regularly after our first meeting to discuss research and provide feedback.

Peter was also an active sportsman. I still preserve good memories of when we went joking in Pittsburgh during Steve Shreve's birthday conference. While running, Peter and I discussed his current research on machine learning to predict variance. Peter was able to keep up with running and discuss his research insights deeply at the same time. If it were possible to write while running, Peter would have written the entire paper. Absolutely, amazing.

Peter was a continuous source of ideas, thoughts and inspiration. He was able to animate conferences with sharp and thought-provoking questions, and with his participation, he was able to transform each session into a very engaging and entertaining event.

Beyond his incredible intelligence, enthusiasm and energy, what struck me about Peter has always been his open-mindedness, generosity and humbleness. He has been always open to discuss research and ideas with anybody, regardless of their level of seniority or education.

We have lost a pillar of our community, a person with a continuous flow of ideas and a strong supporter of young researchers. We will miss not only the outstanding researcher but also the amazing person behind the influential research.

10. Pasquale Cirillo

I first met Peter in 2015 at a conference. I was immediately captured by the passion and the love he showed for finance and probability. His enthusiasm was contagious. As a student, I studied some of his fundamental papers, and it was a great honor to meet him in person.

A couple of years later we met again at NYU, where he had become the Department Chair of FRE. I was visiting Nassim Taleb for some joint work. Peter remembered me (I was positively shocked!) and invited me to give a talk in the seminar series of the department.

After my talk, Peter, Nassim and I had a lovely dinner, and Peter asked me whether I wanted to be involved in teaching at FRE, for the new boot camp he had in mind to welcome students.

That was when we also started working together on some joint research involving pseudo-analysis, size distributions and inequality indices. I enjoyed working with Peter, he taught me a lot of things. He was a never-ending source of knowledge.

For more than three years we have been collecting notes, sketches and working papers. I have tons of materials, including many of his hand-written comments. They are a little treasure to me.

We have spent hours together sitting in his office at FRE every time I was in New York for the boot camp. And we have spent hours online over the years, working remotely.

Last January 28, we were scheduled for another Zoom meeting, but Peter was not there. I did not worry, I knew Peter was very busy.

The next day he wrote me he was sorry for not showing up, that he was feeling weak, but that we would meet again in a few days. It never happened.

Peter was a great scholar, but most of all a terrific person. He was always friendly, curious and supportive. We both loved good food and we shared a lot of tips about places to try. Last summer I discovered a new Persian restaurant in Brooklyn, and Peter fell in love with it. He kept thanking me for the suggestion. This was Peter: a number one yet humble and thankful.

I feel blessed for meeting him, and I will miss him.

My thoughts are with his family, whom he was tremendously proud of and which he always used to talk with that blink of love in his eyes.

11. J.P. Delavin

Peter was the smartest, funniest and most supportive mentor a student could ever ask for. He showed me kindness even before I set foot in New York when I was having problems with my scholarship for my master's, and he remained a constant source of wisdom and inspiration throughout my stay there.

During my time at Tandon, Peter was my professor for two classes and the research advisor for my capstone project. One of my favorite things that he did during our weekly meetings for my project was just sitting in complete silence whenever he encountered a difficult problem. I always relished those moments and would always think to myself: I am seeing a genius at work. He usually came out of those silences with great insight on how to answer the problem at hand, but he also sometimes ended up unable to find a solution during our session. The next day, however, I would find an email from him very early in the morning on how to answer the question.

Even after I graduated and returned to the Philippines, Peter offered to continue to meet with me weekly to prepare for my PhD applications. He set aside hundreds of hours of his time for someone who was not even his student anymore. Even though we did spend most of our time talking about research, what I will miss the most from our Zoom calls are stories about his time in academia, working on Wall Street, interesting YouTube videos and stack exchange entries, and the latest app or gadget that he had discovered that week. I will also miss his almost encyclopedic knowledge of mathematicians. (During one of our meetings last December, he even joked that he would also like a mathematical equation in his tombstone, like Ludwig Boltzmann. I did not know that this conversation would be relevant so soon.)

Thank you so much, Peter, for helping me pursue my dreams. It is heartbreaking to think that I am starting my PhD journey without getting one final piece of advice from you. I hope you are in a much better place now and that I and all your former students can make you proud. We will miss you so much.

12. Sara Tomeo DeLusant

On paper, Peter was my boss, but in life, he was so much more than that to me. He was a friend, a mentor and my truly biggest supporter. We worked together for about a decade: first at Morgan Stanley, and later at NYU. To find the right words or stories to do justice to a soul like Peter's feels like almost an impossible task.

I have so many fond memories of Peter. When we were at MS, we would go on recruiting trips together using Peter's math fame to help lure students into the program! No matter how much money he made or recognition he got, nothing was beneath him. I distinctly remember him stacking pizzas on his arms to help me bring them into a recruiting session at UCLA. He had no shame and was always there to lend a helping hand to that needed it, both figuratively and literally.

During our time together at NYU over the last five years, I felt a level of support I never had before. Working for Peter meant someone always had my back; he believed so fiercely in me and in our mission for the program. His enthusiasm for the positive changes our team was making to the program was contagious, and it energized and motivated me.

There are so many things that I'll remember about Peter: His love for math, of course. The Toronto Maple Leaves. His love for runs and bike rides around Prospect park, his recent love for the show "Ted Lasso", his fascination with tech gadgets and so many other little things.

Peter truly was a light in my life and almost everyone's life that knew him. Peter saw the best in every single person and gave everyone the benefit of the doubt.

It really didn't matter whether you were a managing director at a global bank or a student who just finished their BS degree and wanted to come to NYU, Peter treated you exactly the same as anyone else. That is a rare quality. I'll miss him so much.

I loved Peter's "matter-of-fact" way of delivering a message. He did not sugarcoat anything but still was always so kind. He didn't have a bad bone in his body.

It's hard to find the light in unexpected and unfair losses like the loss of Peter. Since the loss of Peter, though, I have found both peace and joy in reading about all of the lives that Peter touched; there were too many to count. Not just lives touched but actually changed. To leave behind a legacy like this is something really, really special. I hope that we can all carry a little bit of Peter's positive legacy with us and pass it along. In that way, Peter will always live on.

They really, really don't make them better than Peter. If you were lucky enough to know Peter, you were, truly, lucky enough.

13. Carmen Montes De Oca

I worked closely with Peter on a daily basis since he joined Tandon 6 years ago. Peter's absence is deeply felt in the office and in our lives. Not only was he the best boss but he was also kind and caring to all.

I will always be grateful to have had the honor of working for an amazing and brilliant person, as he was. He made my life better and I know he did too for so many others lucky enough to have counted him as a mentor, student, colleague or friend. My favorite memories of Peter are far too many to recount. He will be greatly missed but never forgotten. His legacy will live on in our hearts and minds.

May he Rest In Peace and may we all find comfort in our treasured memories of our time with Peter.

14. Paul Glasserman

A city bus turns out to be a good place for a tour of the early history of option pricing theory, if you're sitting next to Peter and attending a conference called *45 Years After the Publication of Black–Scholes–Merton*. It helps if the bus is rolling through an ancient city, in this case, Jerusalem.

With his usual enthusiasm and good cheer, Peter shared his fascinating investigation into the earliest papers in the field. He was driven to understand how the foundational ideas of pricing PDEs, continuous-time hedging and arbitrage pricing had taken shape. He pointed out subtle but important differences between the published papers we know and earlier working papers that are almost lost to history. He shared email exchanges with the field's founders on their recollections of their discoveries. I think Peter had plans to write something on the early history of option pricing, and it's hard to imagine almost anyone else up to that challenge.

The conversation was pure Peter: his boundless enthusiasm for ideas, his eagerness to share, his admiration for foundational work and his commitment to scholarship. I had many interactions with Peter over the past 27 years, but this one will always stand out.

Peter was the glue for the quant community. I feel gratitude for his past support, appreciation for his many contributions and a terrible sense of loss at his passing.

15. Julien Guyon

Peter was so many people at a time, a remarkable researcher with very successful careers in both the financial industry and academia, a prolific writer, a great colleague who loved collaborating and sharing ideas, and a profoundly kind human being ready to help anyone, whatever their rank or statute, and discuss finance and mathematics at any time of the day or night. But to me, he will remain this ever-smiling young man.

An anecdote will stay in my mind forever. I was leading a full-day workshop on nonlinear option pricing with my friend and former colleague Pierre Henry-Labordère at the Global Derivatives conference (now QuantMinds). I think it was in 2017. As usual, the attendees were young professionals in their late 20s and early 30s, sent by their employers to catch up with some recent research in quantitative finance. As we welcome the participants as they enter the classroom and take a seat, Peter shows up, fresh and smiling as always, sits among them, just a humble student among the students, eager to always learn more, despite the fact that he was one of the most recognized figures in the field. Peter actually spent the whole day with us, happy to learn new stuff, taking notes, and asking (obviously very good) questions. Peter was actually showing us the secret of eternal youth: learn something every day, stay curious, stay humble. This is why he knew so many things in both mathematics and finance. This is also why I still cannot believe that Peter is no longer with us in person, this ever-smiling young man.

Peter, you are dearly missed, I cherish the memory of our many inspiring discussions about volatility modeling and derivatives pricing and your kind invitations to talk at Morgan Stanley and NYU Tandon. Be sure that you live, and live well, in the minds of a whole community that thanks you for all your contributions, for inspiring so many young aspiring quants and for being a role model for so many of them and so many of us.

16. Ali Hirsa

I had known Peter since 1996 and was introduced to him by my PhD advisor, Professor Madan. I had the pleasure of working in his group, writing papers and articles with him and attending more than 30 conferences in 14 cities, 9 countries and 3 continents.

At the start of each conference, the first thing Peter would ask was "shall we go running early morning or before dinner?" He loved running. I was his running mate!

He was not necessarily a good dancer, I recall that from my wedding, but you should have seen him on the ice. My son and I ran into Peter and Olivia about 10 years ago at the Lasker Rink (north of Central Park). Peter could really dance on the ice; I asked, "Peter, I did not know you can skate so beautifully" and he replied, "what did you expect I am Canadian!"

I would never forget the excitement on his face anytime he would learn a new mathematical trick or see an interesting problem, resembling the face of a kid seeing ice cream or chocolate.

Those who knew Peter, know about his love for books. Massive collection of them, the so-called Peter's Library! You can find almost any topic you were looking for in his library!

One last thing before I forget, Peter's love for spicy food! To Peter, food would not be spicy enough unless he would sweat and he LOVED it.

When we were coming up with a title for one of our papers, Peter said let's name it "Why be backward?" and he looked at me, smiled and said: "I am a forward-looking guy!" And he was.

Aside from being brilliant, aside from his significant contributions to the field of financial mathematics and quantitative finance, he was a generous, gentle, genuine and very kind person. Peter was always willing to help, a true mentor and a great teacher. You did not need to know him for long to know these traits about him. He touched so many hearts and had a big impact on lots of people's career paths including mine.

A poem from the famous Persian poet Saadi: "A good man will never die, dead in the one who is not remembered in a positive way". Peter lives forever in our hearts and our memories!

17. Bruno G. Kamdem

I met Professor Carr for the first time through Professor Geman at the Eastern Conference in Mathematical Finance (ECFM) in 2017 at NYU. I met Professor Carr again at the ECMF at BU in 2019. Although highly regarded and respected in the academic and finance communities, he was approachable and amicable. He believed in people's potential, regardless of their race or color. He has made such an indelible impact on my emerging academic career.

Professor Carr was the perfect balance between high intelligence, deep wisdom and sincere humility. The loss of Professor Carr is terribly sad and is leaving a big hole almost impossible to fill. I pray that God brings comfort to his wife and children (Psalm 68:19, 20). I pray that God remembers Professor Peter Carr for what he has done for better humankind (Nehemiah 5:19).

18. Ajay Khanna

Hello everybody. It's a privilege to be here and speak a few words about Peter, an extremely nice yet exceptional human being who has brought us all together today.

I first met Peter at Cornell in the late 1980s where he was just starting out as an assistant professor in finance, and I was completing my PhD in OR. Given his friendly nature and being a somewhat youthful professor, he was very approachable and we became friends. We went on to work closely together again when I was managing an equity derivatives book as a trader at Morgan Stanley. This was in the late 1990s when Peter was the in-house option expert in the research group. He introduced me to Dilip, and the three of us enjoyed each other's company at work and beyond. We kept up our relationship over the decades, even after Peter's departure from Morgan, and would periodically meet up for meals or drinks.

I'd like to recount a story Peter shared with me, about something he often told incoming Morgan Stanley summer interns during their option training classes with him.

When I first met Peter as a student at Cornell, I would always address him very respectfully as Professor Carr, even though we weren't very far apart in age, he was a professor to me. It was always stuff like:

Hi Professor Carr.

Professor Carr want to join us for a drink?

Professor Carr what's the difference between a put and call option?

Prof Carr can I borrow Skorokhod's book on Stochastic processes?

And so on.

After finishing my PhD, I accidentally became an assistant professor at NYU, with a growing interest in finance which was quite hot at that time. Our communication took on a slightly different tone, mostly phone calls, as this was before email:

Hey Peter, what's the financial intuition behind the smooth pasting requirement?

Peter please could you comment on my paper with Kaushik on American options?

etc.

The respectful Professor Carr language was dropped for the more collegial Peter.

Fast forward through more years and we are both at Morgan Stanley.

I had started a few years earlier and was working a relatively junior position on the derivatives trading desk and Peter had just joined as a senior derivatives quant in research.

Apparently, as the story goes, on Peter's very first stroll across the trading floor, he heard a voice loudly shout out from across the vast room:

"Carr! Can you come here please? Need your help with pricing this new payoff."

As you can guess, the shouter was me.

So, he would say that is how one goes from the respectful Professor Carr to collegial Peter and finally, to the super casual

Carr!

Peter was probably just entertaining the interns with war stories during breaks from learning about option theory. He was probably also poking fun at the absurd importance that even average traders enjoyed in those days in relation to super knowledgeable and expert quants. This was before full on electronic trading was the norm.

But I am sure the story was told with a smile and I know we laughed when he recounted it to me. For Peter nearly always had an unruffled openness and humility about his success that kept him smiling, happy and totally relatable, even through many a vigorous debate.

To me, this was a very unique quality in that world — this humility and openness was in stark contrast to how self-importantly others regarded their own intelligence and success on Wall Street and in the larger community of math and finance.

But beyond how our relationship evolved with age, there is a common thread that strikes me about this story, how, at each stage, I was always looking for his help and advice. Since the news of his passing, I have connected with several mutual ex-colleagues and they too have invariably brought up an incident or two about how Peter aided them in some critical and unforgettable way during their interactions with him.

Here's a story from George George, another former colleague of Peter's from Morgan Stanley:

GG was looking to switch over from the IT department where he was a young quant to the better-paid and more fast-moving front office research team. GG had a PhD in engineering but limited finance knowledge.

In the interview process, George Courtadon gave him a day to come up with a solution for a difficult payoff to value.

GG found some guidance in one of Wilmot's books, but there was a key step which involved an absence of arbitrage argument that GG couldn't quite follow, so he decided to wing it by writing that the step obviously follows by no-arbitrage. The next day when Courtadon looked at his derivation, he asked GG to explain the no-arbitrage step, and GG said he had it last night but was having a hard time recalling it. Turns out, Courtadon himself couldn't crack it either, so resident options guru Peter was called in.

As luck would have it, Courtadon had to step away to take an urgent phone call and Peter quickly figured out the difficult step, explained it to George, told him he could claim it as his own solution and left the room. Well, not surprisingly George impressed Courtadon on his return and got the job.

This particular story is just one of many I have heard about Peter — similar stories which exemplify his skills, collaborative nature and super generosity, once again attributes rare in Wall Street where taking credit for a solution often leads to multiple gains in income and success.

This GG story trends in another direction too and what I think was one of Peter's lasting contributions to the math finance community.

He was a bridge for so many engineers, physicists, computer science and math types, who had great quant skills and experience but were struggling either with finance concepts or simply just breaking into the world of finance because of lack of contacts and experience.

Many got started in the field with a selfless assist from Peter. Peter must have mentored tons of such young professionals (including this accidental professor who also did not have a financial background). In my various jobs at Wall Street, I had the opportunity to interact with plenty of young quants, who without exception all looked up to Peter. Moreover, many told of having received some form of assistance from him. Informing these young quants about my long association with Peter always enhanced my reputation with them.

Peter was brilliant and had a passion for people and ideas. His generosity with his encyclopedic knowledge and connections made him Google before Google and LinkedIn before LinkedIn. Most importantly to me, his humility, openness and generosity kept him 100% human and relatable. He was the best kind of teacher, leading by example. And because of the connections he created and fostered on this human level, he left an indelible mark in the field where there is now a Peter-shaped hole we will now have to fill with memories.

Hey Carr, you will be missed!

19. Roger Lee

Peter's exuberant energy, amazing generosity, boundless creativity and transcendent enduring insights will continue to warm my heart, elevate our spirits and illuminate our paths in the profession, for all the years to come.

Thank you to Peter's family and Carol and Olivia, for sharing him with us.

We know how much music meant to him. I don't know whether he liked a band called The Bravery, but their lyrics express my thoughts to Peter:

All that I can think to say
is I'll be with you every day.
Not even Earth can hold us.
Not even life controls us.
Not even the ground can keep us down.
The memories in my head
Are just as real as the time we spent.
You'll always be close to me, my friend.
This is not the end.

20. Supavitch Nakburee

It took me a bit of time to gather my countless memories with my beloved professor, Peter Carr. He is one of the most significant people in my life. He is like a father who provided the first light in my quantitative journey. He is a teacher, a mentor, a supporter, a neighbor and a real-life role model. Could you imagine you would ever have a legendary financial figure who is down-to-earth, friendly and willing to teach and support you? I am very fortunate that I once met a person like him. It is hard to picture my graduation ceremony without him standing alongside me.

I first met Professor Carr during the Fall semester of 2020. I was fortunate enough to join a student club connected to the MSFE program at NYU Tandon that usually had a bi-weekly meeting with him.

It is common to feel yourself being nervous before introducing yourself to him, especially when you know that he is a famous person. This happened to literally everyone. The opposite happened when you started introducing yourself to him, as he never stopped initiating a conversation with you. He was very friendly and open-minded. He was always smiling and made people laugh at his jokes. His sense of humor relaxed everyone who had a conversation with him.

Because of his motivation and inspiration, I got involved in a research paper with him, even though he knew that my research experience was limited back then. He dedicated himself to teaching me in a research class for more than a year. He gave that opportunity to me, to his other students and to everyone surrounding him. His good hopes drove me and others forward. He built people up. He trained thousands of quants for the industry. His passion inspired people, and he always wanted to see you getting better. By all definitions, he was a true leader and the one that I want to grow up to be. I could not and will never stop thinking about him during every accomplishment I make in the future.

I am very emotional about the loss, and I am sorry for everyone who shared similar experiences with me. My heart is with his family. MSFE at Tandon will never be the same, but it will keep growing. His legacy will continue, and we will make him proud.

He left on a jet plane that is never coming back again. However, I will always keep a picture of him laughing and cheering me from somewhere in a good place.

Rest In Peace Professor Peter Carr.

I am very grateful and very lucky to have met you.

You'll always be my role model.

21. Conall O'Sullivan

I met Peter for the first time in 2018. I was slightly nervous given Peter's achievements in the field of quantitative finance/financial engineering. I needn't have been. Within a few minutes, we were discussing our shared admiration of Irish mathematician William Rowan Hamilton, how one of his favorite films was the Irish movie The Commitments (about a dysfunctional soul band set in recession hit

1980s Dublin probably best watched with subtitles given the strong Dublin accents) and, of course, all things quant and financial engineering related.

Peter once wrote "If you want to be a quant, my advice is to see it as a calling, not a job. The money is incidental. It comes and goes. A good idea never goes away and if you are lucky, you'll have a few before we all fade away into obscurity." Peter was a fountain of many brilliant ideas. Combine that with generosity, humbleness, good cheer and massive work ethic (the list goes on) and you have a very rare but winning combination. I'll miss our chats, Peter, but fading away into obscurity is not for you, my friend!

22. Zahra Patterson

In memory of Peter Carr,

My name is Zahra Patterson, program manager in the Department of Finance and Risk Engineering at NYU Tandon.

I was fortunate enough to work in Peter Carr's dream team in FRE. He and I worked together on the BQE Lecture Series, the departmental newsletter and special events.

Peter cared deeply about the department, his entire staff, every faculty member, student, alumni and our rankings.

Under Peter's strong leadership, FRE thrived. Peter was never in a bad mood. In fact, he always had a smile on his face, a funny story to tell or would give an update about Brooklyn's ever-changing landscape.

He became my personal cheerleader when I graduated from NYU Steinhardt. He made us all feel special and a part of something truly special. No matter how busy Peter was, he always took time to say "thank you!" In one of our last email exchanges, I asked what he needed from me for an upcoming Grad. Admissions event and Peter said, "Just your incredible EQ, Z!" That's what made Peter special to me.

Peter stood up for his staff members whenever we encountered problems on campus. He was always ready to send an email, make that phone call or schedule a meeting on our behalf.

Not only did he stand up for me on occasions, but when Peter learned that my son was a victim of a gang assault that left him blind in his right eye, Peter wanted to help in ways that I'll never forget. I am eternally grateful to Peter who showed compassion to my son, whom he'd never met but wanted to see justice finally prevail. Peter will be missed beyond measure.

I would like to recite a few lines from one of Peter's favorite bands: The Beatles

There are places I'll remember
All my life though some have changed
Some forever, not for better
Some have gone and some remain

Peter, you will remain in our hearts forever and your legacy will live on in FRE.

Our lives are forever changed for the better because of your vision, trust and kind spirit. Thank you for always making me feel seen, heard and valued.

Rest in eternal peace.

ZP

My condolences to the entire Carr family.

23. Thomas Philips

I first met Peter 10 years ago when a mutual friend suggested that I talk to him about an option pricing problem I was having some difficulty with. We talked over dinner, and he promptly pulled out his pen, took hold of a napkin and drew a picture which immediately clarified my thinking. So typical of Peter!

But Peter was much, much more than a quick study: he was a deep, polymathic and open-minded thinker, a great listener, a ferociously quick absorber (and re-explainer) of new and unfamiliar ideas, a warm, pleasant and engaging personality, and most importantly, an extraordinarily generous person, both with his time and with his thoughts. He had the rare ability to bring out the best in everyone he interacted with, and was very supportive of curricular experiments that departed from the mainstream, so long as our students learned something of value. It didn't take long to convince him that our students would benefit from an exploration of econometric models to value Bordeaux wines, big data techniques to value real estate, and the Edwards–Bell–Ohlson equation to value firms, alongside their study of traditional cash flow-based valuation methods and corporate finance. Small wonder, then, that our department's ratings soared during his tenure!

The last time we talked was on a cold day in January 2022. We shared our concerns about the health of our elderly relatives, as well as our excitement about all the new things we were going to try in our classrooms in the Spring semester: the new topics we would cover, the guest speakers we would invite and the students from other Tandon departments who would try their hands at an FRE course. After our meeting ended, we laughed, shook hands, promised to meet to talk about what had worked and what had not, and then waved goodbye to each other. The thought never crossed my mind that this would be our last laugh together. His broad smile and his outstretched hand will remain etched in my memory forever.

Thank you, Peter, for everything you did, both for the department and for the world. You will be sorely missed and will forever live in our hearts.

24. David C. Shimko

I met Peter Carr in 1987. I had just started my first full-time academic job, teaching finance at the University of Southern California. Peter was in his last year of graduate school at UCLA. He had been a professional accountant for a few years before going for his PhD, so he was a few years older than me. While at USC, I frequented the weekly UCLA seminar series across town, at a time when so many great financial minds were there, such as Richard Roll, Michael Brennan, Eduardo Schwartz and Francis Longstaff, to drop a few names. Berkeley was not that far away, with Hayne Leland and Mark Rubinstein in residence. Peter and I became friends quickly, and we had common interests in derivatives pricing at the time. I had recently published a paper valuing insurance contracts by integrating the Black–Scholes option pricing model. I remember one day Peter told me he thought my formula was wrong, but a month later told me I was right after all. We had a healthy and fun academic relationship.

I tried to get Peter to interview for an Assistant Professor position at USC in 1988, but he had other ideas. He joined Cornell upon his graduation, and I went to Wall Street a few years later. I never left derivatives, building my career in commodity finance, financial risk management, security design, credit and corporate finance. Peter specialized in derivatives theory and trading. He had a brilliant academic beginning, publishing an eye-popping work with Robert Jarrow on local time, which was a novel way to price the extrinsic value of an option based on how much "time" the stock price spent at the exercise price of the option in a continuous-time stochastic process. This was a brilliant mathematical insight, but I would have to say the practical value was more pedagogical. Peter continued to write prolifically, contributing to not only the theory of mathematical finance but also to the practice. Demand for his insight was increasing in financial circles. Peter started to become known in both academic and professional venues on the East Coast. We saw each other at conferences and industry dinners regularly, covering the globe.

Peter left Cornell for Wall Street but never lost the academic bug completely. He worked for hedge funds and trading companies like Susquehanna but also held important roles managing groups of quants, at places as venerable as Morgan Stanley. He had a rare combination of academic curiosity, technical capability, personal humility and a sincere desire to help others that made him an effective leader, an able contributor, a true collaborator and an inspiration to many young quants. Through Peter's work, mathematicians and physicists were able to see immediately how they could apply their seemingly unrelated skills to financial problems. At NYU, Peter's ongoing work has become broader, some very applied and some very abstract. He has cultivated thankful PhD students, coauthors, postdocs and visiting faculty with a seemingly unending supply of academic energy.

Over the years, I saw Peter at conferences and we kept in close touch with each other's work. When one of my consulting ventures failed, he was my first phone call. He had just joined NYU FRE as the chair. He needed someone to teach corporate finance, and I fit the bill.

At funerals, I have often heard people say, "I would not be where I am were it not for the dearly beloved Mr. X." In my case, there is no truer statement I could make. Without Peter's encouragement and support, I would not be teaching at NYU Tandon. Without his excitement in converting an MBA finance course into a valuation course suitable for master's students in financial engineering, I would not have been able to create a brand new curriculum and write a book for the course. Without Peter Carr, I would not have been inspired to continue to publish new research in my 60s, a time when most academics are on to other things.

While working on my class and the book last summer, I discovered it was very difficult to teach option pricing to master's students who had never seen stochastic calculus before and developed a new derivation that requires only college-level calculus. In disbelief, Peter asked me to prove it to him. I stood at the whiteboard outside his office and explained it. When I finished, he asked me to stop and held up his hand. After about a half-minute, he broke out in laughter, with a tear in his eye. How can it have been so easy? Why didn't we see this before? The proof remained unerased from his whiteboard for several weeks. He offered guidance and urged me to publish it immediately. The paper will likely appear this summer.

Anyway, I have proven my statement. *Quod Erat Demonstrandum.* Without Peter Carr, I would not be where I am today. I wish I could have thanked him more before he left us. I hope we can sustain and build on his unique and profound legacy. Now, I am the one with the tear in my eye. May his memory be a continuous blessing for all of us.

Peter Carr (left) and David C. Shimko in Los Angeles, 1987. Maggie Copeland, foreground.

25. Ron Slivka

You Are Still With Us Peter.

While I will miss our professional conversations and your ever-insightful comments, I know your presence will endure in the reflections of all those whose lives you have touched, and that is comforting to so many of us who have valued your friendship and advice. Rest well good colleague.

26. Peter Dan Stefanica

While thinking about how to honor Peter's memory today, I realized that what Peter would have really wanted us to do was to think of some problems we can model and then take out a napkin and start working them out. Well, we cannot do that, but that's what Peter would have loved us to do.

Peter was unique. I always thought of Peter as simultaneously being the best academic in industry and the best practitioner in academia. His moving seamlessly from industry to academia only made this more obvious: he became the best practitioner in academia and the best academic in industry, at the same time.

Peter was always hugely successful in his work, be it industry or academia, and success came so naturally to him that it became a given. However, behind the scenes, Peter worked tirelessly and with laser focus to ensure that was going to be the case.

When he joined Morgan Stanley as Head of Global Modelling, Peter asked me to set up head quant and former head quant at two NY banks. We all met at a Swedish restaurant close to Baruch. While initially surprised, I realized during the meeting Peter's wisdom in making sure that he had all the information needed to be the best at his new role.

When Peter joined NYU from Morgan Stanley, we met in my office and I was peppered with Peter's questions. (I was wearing this same shirt I wear today. I remember Peter jokingly complimenting me on how it fits the persona of an MFE program director in academia.) As you would expect, I learned a lot just from Peter's questions and from the insights they revealed. Peter was an amazing person and a truly transformational one.

Peter and I met more than 20 years ago at a seminar that he gave at Baruch. After the seminar, we ended up working with Liuren on the board on an alternative solution to one of the results he presented.

That was just a constant when meeting with Peter — every time we met, we ended up doing math. I did mention napkins in the beginning — they were the primary medium for doing math in our meetings since boards are scarcely available at restaurants. That happened constantly.

Peter and I met once over lunch when he was at Bloomberg, and for the first time, Peter was not smiling at the beginning. He just sat down and looked at me for about ten seconds and then he said "Dan, you have no idea how lucky you are not to have a boss." Clearly, that was a difficult day at work. Well, by the end of lunch, we were doing math on napkins and Peter was happy again! Talking math and working on problems with others always made Peter happy!

I just realized that the first blurb on the back page of my first book is from Peter. I was very flattered when he volunteered to do that, and now it will be there forever.

And speaking of forever, Olivia, this is a grievous loss, but please keep in mind that everyone in here (and a lot more people out there) are friends and nothing would make us happier than to help you. So please, please keep in mind that for anything that you would need help and support with, there is a friend of Peter who will gladly provide it. For you and in Peter's honor.

Carol, the same goes for you as well, and, in particular, please make sure that Olivia knows that for anything that she needs, there is someone who wants to help her.

Peter, may you rest in peace. We will honor your memory and we will take care of everything in your absence.

27. Leon Tatevossian

Peter and I met in the mid-1990s during the first period that he worked at Morgan Stanley. I worked there from 1989 to 1992. A colleague of his, whom I knew from my MS years, introduced us. (I think this was at an NYU math-finance event.) Soon after that, the first of the many seminar and conference presentations given by my friend Peter that I attended took place.

During Peter's illness, I spoke with many professional colleagues about Peter's unique and unforgettable qualities. As Bruno remarked, Peter's love of his subject was "radiant." All of us noted his wonderful talent for and dedication to clear exposition. His PowerPoint slides were works of art. How did Peter reach that perfect balance? Each page had the right amount of content. The theme of the talk was visible throughout and you saw how it all fit together. The drill-down into each detail came at just the right point. How did Peter pull that off each time?

As you got to know Peter you learned that this skill at explanation was a singular part of his personality. He was devoted to his field and devoted equally to sharing his ideas: how some of the concepts are intuitive and some not so intuitive. And he did this with the most amazing modesty and with those just learning the subject, infinite patience.

My brother Armand, who knew Peter longer than I did, having met him in 1990, told me about sharing a meal with Peter, Carol, and Olivia in a Montauk restaurant in 2019. There was another patron in the restaurant and Armand found out that this person was a finance student. Armand mentioned this to Peter and Carol. After a while Armand left the table for a bit, and when he returned he saw Peter explaining an idea or formula to this person, using a paper napkin as paper. The quant-finance-on-a-paper-napkin trick was on display in every meal I enjoyed with Peter.

Peter was fond of classifying finance quants as either "P-quants" or "Q-quants." The "P-quants" work with the "real world" or "physical" probabilities of market outcomes, extrapolating these probabilities from past behavior (and maybe economic models). "Q-quants" are in derivatives land: Under assumptions that ensure hedging, they invoke adjusted probabilities (called the "Q-measure") to price derivatives and impute prices of exotic derivatives from prices of standard ones.

I can clearly picture this scenario: Peter explaining this P-versus-Q characterization, with his usual limitless enthusiasm, to a group of students. Me, off to the side, absorbing it and thinking: How clever. I'm going to use that formulation myself. And when I think about it, that scenario represents one of many situations where Peter's brilliance made an impact, and continues to make an impact, on me.

For so many parts of mathematical finance, Peter was my go-to person for questions. I would send an email, and he would write back (often very quickly) with a reformulation. He loved to engage you. It was sometimes a bit intimidating because Peter would explain (gently) that focusing on my original question was leaving out a much more interesting, and consequential, story. It would remind me that there was a lot that I didn't know. That's one of my fondest memories.

Farewell Peter. It was a profound honor to be your friend and colleague.

28. Claudio Tebaldi

A journey with Peter Carr across quantum fields, for fun.

It is well recognized that game changers turn the hardest challenge into the best opportunity. So did Peter in the early days of our collaboration.

Although we met many years ago, we started working on a joint project only in the early days of 2020 when I was invited by Peter to present a paper for an NYU Tandon BQE Lecture. Peter proposed to work on an operator extension of the famous Ross (1978) arbitrage pricing argument. Many of the arguments he was proposing are close in spirit to the operator algebras approach to quantum mechanics. This was for me, not for him, a great surprise and brought me back to the years of my PhD, so I reviewed and enthusiastically shared with him some notes, written many years ago at the International Center for Theoretical Physics in Trieste, that appeared now useful in a completely different context.

During my stay in NYC, while I was enjoying Peter's friendship and the nice atmosphere at Tandon, the COVID pandemic started spreading and killing in Italy. I cannot forget the frustration when our collaboration was suddenly interrupted by the flight ban imposed on European airlines. Together with my wife, we had to decline a kind invitation for dinner by Peter and his wife and rush to the airport to take one of the last available flights back home. A sense of missed opportunity was mixed with uncertainty about the future, with lockdown policy appearing for the first time in Western countries.

Winston Churchill once said that the pessimist sees the difficulty in every opportunity while the optimist sees the opportunity in every difficulty. No question that Peter belonged to this second category.

Soon after my return back to Italy, Peter proposed to continue our discussion online in a weekly meeting to be held, to my great surprise, on Sunday. I must admit that, at first, I was puzzled by that unconventional choice. *Ex post*, I realize it was brilliant, already endogenizing the stay-at-home policy and the necessity to find the right balance between "smart working" and "smart fun." In fact, also

Peter was a quantum mechanics enthusiast, and the Sunday meeting was intended to be "smart fun," a good substitute for a bike ride on a sunny day, for both of us.

During these two years, these meetings have been a unique opportunity to share ideas and reorganize our diverse understanding of those topics. As usual, Peter's approach was unconventional, innovative and close to applications. His proposal was to hardwire basic financial principles of no-arbitrage valuation in the (stochastic) geometry underlying quantum mechanics. Do not consider this project exotic or a purely intellectual exercise. In fact, it is the first step in paving the way toward a rigorous formulation of quantum computation for financial applications.

Brilliant connections between option pricing and mechanics are disseminated through his contributions dating back to the early days of option pricing. For example, in an appendix of a paper on semi-static hedging of barrier options in the presence of jumps, he shows that the no-arbitrage condition can be expressed as the exactness condition for a differential form. It is not difficult to recognize here the Poincaré–Cartan form of classical mechanics. In a private communication, Peter pointed out that the conservation of energy is replaced here by the conservation of the P&L.

After long discussions and a lot of fun, finally, in January 2022, Peter was quite satisfied with our understanding of the so-called quantization procedure. In a first draft discussed and dated January 23rd, he states: *The main idea of this paper is to treat the market price of risk and the amount of risk as linear operators rather than as numbers... this conceptual leap is identical to Heisenberg's reformulation of mechanics using matrices, as recognized by Born.* Quantization of no-arbitrage is connected to Feller's (1957) scale and speed factorization of a one-dimensional infinitesimal generator.

The bad news about Peter came too fast, less than one week later. In his last email, Peter wrote me that he could not make the January 30th meeting. I thank Peter for sharing this intellectual journey.

His intellectual leadership and generosity reverberate now in the acute sense of loneliness we feel for his early departure. The huge body of knowledge that Peter leaves also in this new research field, now looks like "a heap of broken images," hard to reconstruct absent his guidance. However, when there is a will, there is a way.

May Peter Paul Carr rest in peace.

29. Lorenzo Torricelli

Good morning everyone,

My name is Lorenzo, I come from Italy, and I am a colleague and friend of Peter. I met him in 2019 during a conference in Perugia, when I asked him a question during his talk. He apparently liked it, so he got back in touch, and we have been talking online every Tuesday ever since. I never met him in person again, and I regret it. Mostly, our conversations were about work, but there was a lot of space for casual chat and general intellectual debate, which was enlightening just the same. I will cherish those moments for the rest of my life. The atmosphere was always relaxed and informal, and despite the great insight on a large number of topics I have always gained by talking to him, our conversations always had more the feeling of a friendly weekly catch-up than that of research meetings. This was, to me, his greatness. The way I knew him was that of a light-spirited, enthusiastic person who loved his job to the bone without ever being overwhelmed by it. And he was to me such an incredibly kind and generous person. I feel I owe him much and that wasn't able to repay him somehow, but then again I deep down know that this is a wrong thought, because what he did for me really was just for the sake of giving.

If any proof is needed of how charismatic Peter was, just look at me. I really only met him once and yet here I am celebrating his memory. All I really need to say, all I came here to say today, is thank you. Thank you Peter for sharing with me your exceptional ideas: your brilliance and genius have motivated my working life like nothing did before. Thank you for putting in me a degree of trust and belief I never imagined someone could have. Thank you Peter for giving me the self-confidence for pushing forward with my plans and projects, even when I was doubting myself. Thank you for having unquestionably been during these two years the colleague who most supported me, and believed in my potential. Thank you Peter for being an exemplary professional, scholar and colleague. Thank you Peter for being such an inspiration to me and to many others. You might not have fulfilled your lifetime ambition of a perfect American option formula. But you have given us so, so much more.

Thank you Peter.

30. Jeff Wang

Thank you for everything, Peter. Thank you for encouraging my PhD research, for advising my career choice, for the amazing opportunity to be a part of the FRE community and, most importantly, for always being supportive of me.

I feel tremendously fortunate to have met you, you've had a huge impact on my life, and your passing is extremely hard for everyone. I will forever remember your smile, your kindness and your encouragement. Rest in peace, my mentor and friend.

31. Ju Yi Yen

It was in 2005, when Peter and I both attended a conference held in Charlottesville, Virginia, I told him that we (Michael Fu and I) would like to organize a conference in celebration of the 60th birthday of Dilip Madan. A few days later, Peter wrote me an email, "Regarding funding for Dilip's 60th, my present plan is to use some money owed to me as a speaker for a Risk course I co-taught last July. I represented Bloomberg, so Bloomberg would be the official sponsor of the event, not me. I don't know the exact amount of money, it's on the order of $25K but it has a positive standard deviation of about $4K. If there is money left over, it should go to you as the organizer, or to a charity, but not to me." (I passed the leftover donation to the University of Maryland College Park Foundation.)

Peter and I then worked closely together during 2006 to prepare for this conference. I left the east coast in the summer of the same year to start a postdoc position in the south. Knowing that I would appreciate any opportunities to take a break from the south, Peter invited me to visit New York (both NYU and Bloomberg) during the summer of 2007. I was honored, on a few occasions, he introduced me to his colleagues as someone he trusted. During my three-month visit, we met frequently and discussed a wide range of topics. I remember he particularly enjoyed practicing the Doomsday algorithm and could easily figure out the day of the week for any given date in a minute or two. I also remember fondly that he always made sure that he arrived home before his daughter fell asleep so that he could spend quality time with her every evening. Peter was truly kind and generous to me. I asked him what I could do for him in return; he replied, "Come to attend my 60th birthday conference!"

This year marks the 20th anniversary since the publication of the article "The Fine Structure of Asset Returns: An Empirical Investigation" by Peter Carr, Hélyette Geman, Dilip Madan and Marc Yor. This article introduced the renowned CGMY model, named after the authors. As its name implies, the model has four parameters C, G, M, Y. "These parameters play an important role in capturing various aspects of the stochastic process under study. The parameter C may be viewed as a measure of the overall level of activity. [$\cdots$] The parameters G and M, respectively, control the rate of exponential decay on the right and left of the Lévy density, leading to skewed distributions when they are unequal. [...] The parameter Y is particularly useful in characterizing the fine structure of the stochastic process" (quoted from the article).

Peter once told me that the selection of the name of each C, G, M, Y parameter was not random; the name of each parameter was carefully matched with the characteristics of one of the corresponding authors. "Keeping the other parameters constant [...], we see that the aggregate activity level may be calibrated through movements in C" (quoted again from the article). Words fail to describe how Carr's movements shaped the aggregate activity level of the field of quantitative finance.

32. Jiming Yu

I worked for Peter at Morgan Stanley. My deepest condolences to Carol and Peter's entire family, and may Peter Rest In Peace. The news was so sudden to me that I couldn't believe it in the first 2 days or so.

Peter was the greatest mentor to me. He was my manager's manager at MS (he was Global Head of Market Modeling), but he directly worked with me on a regular basis like equals, and I have learned a tremendous amount from him. Our work culminated in a paper published in 2012 on a topic of intense interest in both industry and academia, under his guidance and his drive to produce something out of our work. He subsequently helped me further develop and expand my career by introducing me to crucial people and giving me the precious opportunity to work for another team to expand my horizons in mathematical finance.

After a few years at MS, I wished to transition to a different type of job (another business in MS), and he was very understanding and gave me all the help and green lights; he helped me again in 2018 when I was looking for a job after MS. All above are not what usual managers of managers do; Peter has gone above and beyond to help me in any way he can. I owe him a great deal, most of my professional career so far — this is not with exaggeration at all.

There are numerous other ways that Peter helped me, by trying to propel me to higher achievements. He took me to the Princeton conferences on quantitative finance a few times, and during our work, meals and seminars, he provided me with the opportunities to meet quite a few important researchers in the field, either in academia or industry. He is the role model as an advisor and a mentor to me.

After MS, it was great news to hear that he became the Chair of the Department of Finance and Risk Engineering at NYU. We have kept in touch, and I have watched some of his videos on LinkedIn and browsed through his new papers since then (I cannot really say I understand them well given the depth of his papers). I distinctly remember that I briefly chatted with him over the email just last Christmas, and he mentioned a few papers related to the mathematical finance professor whose work appeared in a TV series in recent years. That was like yesterday.

When I was interviewing with MS in 2010, I was thrilled to learn that Peter was the Global Head of the group I was interviewing with — Peter has been a legend in both the financial industry and academia and has been one of my idols I have long admired since I was in graduate school. In the interviews, Peter was very nice and talked to me like an equal — I was a little nervous and have always looked up to him (including now and forever). It was my great honor to have the opportunity to work for him and have had him as my mentor.

Peter will forever be remembered!

https://doi.org/10.1142/9789811280306_0002

Chapter 2

Pictures and Statements

1. Kevin Atteson 1 and 2

Early in my time working with Peter, he and I were in a meeting with HR about compensation. An HR person was explaining how they grade people's performance across multiple factors.

Suddenly realizing how HR's approach worked, Peter replied with his usual enthusiasm to the HR person, who had had little mathematical training, "It's just tensor analysis!"

2. J.P. Fouque

A great time in Santa Barbara: Center for Financial Mathematics and Actuarial Research (CFMAR). 10th Anniversary Conference. May 19, 2017 to May 21, 2017, Peter was an enthusiastic supporter of the center. He spoke on the inaugural day on October 16, 2006.

3. Robert Jarrow

A meeting at Cornell when the *Journal of Mathematical Finance* was created.

4. Dilip Madan

A rooftop bar in Bombay across the street from where I (Dilip Madan) grew up when Peter and I were teaching courses at the Tata Institute of Fundamental Research on Financial Mathematics in a program designed by Freddy Delbaen in January 2012.

5. Leon Tatevossian 1 and 2

Peter at a quant panel discussion with Emmanuel Derman, Douglas Breeden and Cliff Asness.

6. PC and MB

Peter Carr with Michael Bloomberg.

7. Ju Yi Yen

The CGMY picture taken in 2006 at the 60th Birthday Conference for Dilip Madan that Peter funded.

8. Conference Pictures

1. Group Photo on last day of Conference, November 12, 2022
2. Lunch Table at Conference
3. Picture of people who interacted with Peter at Morgan Stanley and were at the conference

MARYLAND
ROBERT H. SMITH

Part II

Papers Presented at the Peter Carr Gedenkschrift Conference

https://doi.org/10.1142/9789811280306_0003

Chapter 3

Backtestability and the Ridge Backtest*

Carlo Acerbi[†,§] **and Balazs Szekely**[‡,¶]

[†]*LARIX risk consulting, Genève, Switzerland*
Ecole Polytechnique Fédérale de Lausanne, Switzerland
[‡]*Morgan Stanley, Budapest, Hungary*
[§]*carlo.acerbi@larixriskconsulting.com*
[¶]*szbalazs@math.bme.hu*

Abstract
We propose a formal definition of backtestability for a statistical functional of a distribution: a functional is backtestable if there exists a backtest function depending only on the forecast of the functional and the related random variable, which is strictly monotonic in the former and has zero expected value for an exact forecast. We discuss the relationship with elicitability and identifiability which turn out to be necessary conditions for backtestability. The variance and the expected shortfall are not backtestable for this reason. We compare (absolute) model validation in the context of hypothesis tests, via backtest functions, versus (relative) model selection between competing forecasting models, via scoring functions. We define a backtest to be sharp when it is strictly monotonic with respect to the real value of the functional and not only to its forecast.

*A preliminary version in this chapter appeared on SSRN in 2017 [2]. The authors are grateful to prof. Carol Alexander and four anonymous referees for their valuable comments that led to major improvements in this chapter. This paper is the private opinion of the authors and does not necessarily reflect the policy and views of Morgan Stanley.

This decides whether the expected value of the backtest determines also the prediction discrepancy and not only its significance. We show that the quantile backtest is not sharp and in fact it provides no information whatsoever on its true value. The expectile is also not sharp; we provide bounds for its true value, which are looser for outer confidence levels. We then introduce the notion of ridge backtests, applicable to particular non-backtestable functionals, such as the variance and the expected shortfall, which coincide with the attained minimum of the scoring function of another elicitable auxiliary functional (the mean and the value at risk, respectively). This permits approximated sharp backtests up to a small and one-sided sensitivity to the prediction of the auxiliary variable. The ridge mechanism explains why the variance has always been *de facto* backtestable and allows for similar efficient ways to backtest the expected shortfall. We discuss the relevance of this result in the current debate of financial regulation (banking and insurance), where value at risk and expected shortfall are adopted as regulatory risk measures.

Keywords: Elicitability, Backtestability, Quantile, Expectile, Expected shortfall, Model validation, Ridge backtest

1. Motivation and Objectives

Backtest procedures for testing forecasts of a risk measure are common in the statistical and probabilistic disciplines, notably in the field of financial risk management. Backtesting in general, however, remains to date a collection of disparate practices in the wait for a clear definition. Whether a statistical functional is backtestable and whether a methodology is a backtest have long been vague questions prone to controversy.

1.1. *Understanding Backtestability*

In this chapter, we address the problem of formalizing the concept of backtestable functional[1] and backtesting procedure. We will try to distill the key features that make it possible to perform the common backtests of functionals, such as the mean, the quantile and the variance. Inferring these features, however, is not so

[1]In this chapter, we'll use the term *functional* to mean a statistical functional of a distribution. We will alternatively use also the term *risk measure*, although restrictive.

straightforward because even finding what these simple cases have in common requires some care. For instance, we will see that the quantile is completely atypical in that it does not require the issuance of a predictive distribution, and the variance is not even backtestable, strictly speaking. It's probably because of subtleties like these that the concept of backtestability still awaits formalization after decades of industry practices.

Backtesting a functional (a risk measure, for instance) is not so straightforward as it may seem; indeed, not any functional can be backtested, which may come as a surprise even to experienced risk managers. When you make a sequence of bets, say, through a season of horse races, you can easily check if your predictions were correct simply because the winning horse is publicly declared at the end of any race. But if you make a prediction y on a statistical functional $\mathbf{y}$ (say the variance, $\boldsymbol{\sigma}^2$) of a distribution F of future events (say portfolio profit/losses X), neither the distribution F nor the true value of the risk measure $\mathbf{y}(F)$ is publicly announced at the end of the day. What is revealed is just a single random draw $X = x$ from an unknowable real-world distribution F. The difficult point here is as follows: How to compare a prediction of a functional $\mathbf{y}$ against a single outcome of its random variable X? This is possible only when there exists a test function $Z(y, x)$ depending only on these observable quantities — *ex ante* prediction y of the functional and *ex post* realization x of the random variable — whose expected value somehow reveals if predictions are over/underestimated. For a given functional $\mathbf{y}$, however, the existence of such a test function is not granted *a priori*; as a matter of fact, many functionals are not backtestable.

1.1.1. *Quantile: The Prototype of all Backtests. Or maybe not*

A common example of a backtesting procedure is provided by the quantile. Suppose that a prediction y_t is issued for a quantile $\mathbf{q}_\alpha$ with confidence level $\alpha \in (0, 1)$. If the prediction were correct, the realization x_t should be lower than y_t with probability[2] equal to α (Figure 1). Over multiple predictions at different times t, the expected number of quantile "shootouts" $x_t < y_t$ should be a fraction

[2]Let's assume for the moment that F be continuous.

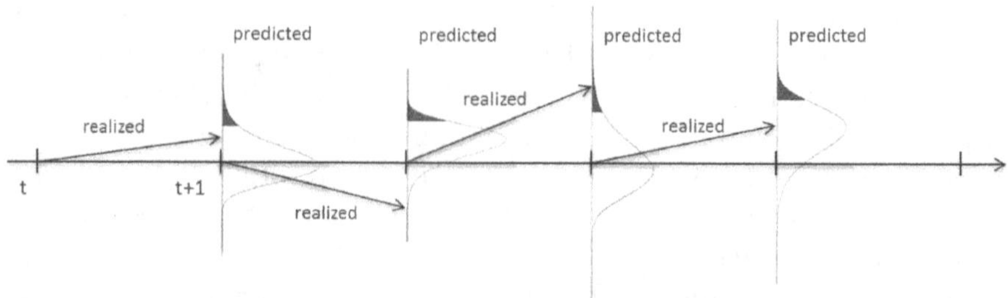

Figure 1. Testing risk predictions is difficult because the true risk is not observable *a posteriori*. What is revealed is just one random draw.

α of all predictions. A lower (bigger) number of shootouts would signal that the model tends to underestimate (overestimate) the quantile. The procedure has been adopted within Basel regulation for capital adequacy, for backtesting a bank's value at risk ($\mathbf{VaR} = -\mathbf{q}$) model, for over two decades [5, 6].

At the heart of this procedure lies the fact that for quantiles there exists a test function

$$Z_{\mathbf{q}_\alpha}(y, x) = \mathbf{1}_{\{x \leq y\}} - \alpha$$

such that

$$\mathbb{E}_F[Z_{\mathbf{q}_\alpha}(y, X)] \gtreqless 0 \quad \text{if } y \gtreqless \mathbf{q}_\alpha(F).$$

The sign of the realized test function $\bar{z}_{\mathbf{q}} = (1/T)\sum_{t=1}^{T} Z_{\mathbf{q}_\alpha}(y_t, x_t)$ over successive predictions y_t is used to detect the tendency to under- or over-estimations. We will take the existence of such a function as the definition of backtestability for a given functional with some additional requirements and distinctions.

Remark 1.1. The case of quantile backtest, although prototypical in some sense, is very special in some others. In the case of an exact prediction, the test variable $Z_{\mathbf{q}_\alpha}$ is distributed along a Bernoulli distribution of parameter α and zero mean and therefore $\bar{z}_{\mathbf{q}}$ follows a binomial distribution $B(T, \alpha)$, with zero mean, independently of the predictive model P. For this reason, computing the p-value for a realization of $\bar{z}_{\mathbf{q}}$ in the null hypothesis that the predictions are correct requires only generation and storage of the point predictions y_t but not of the predictive distributions P_t. The quantile backtest can be performed also if the forecaster issues outright point predictions

y_t not derived from any predictive distribution. We will see that in the case of all other backtestable functionals, the distribution of $\bar{z}_{\mathbf{q}}$ under the predictive model is model-dependent requiring the generation and storage of the predictive distributions P_t for computing p-values. See also Remark 3.12.

Another peculiar feature of the quantile backtest is the discontinuity of the test function which requires smoothness and strict monotonicity conditions on the distribution functions involved. See Proposition 3.2.

1.2. *Backtesting in the Financial Regulation Debate*

Although the scope of this chapter is more general, the initial motivation for the present publication comes from financial risk management.

The question of whether the Expected Shortfall (**ES**) [4, 29] can be backtested or not has been the subject of a lively debate over the past years since it was found that this risk measure doesn't possess a property called elicitability [17]. Part of the controversy stems from the fact that in the absence of a formal definition of backtestability, its precise connection with elicitability remains unclear.

The subject is paramount in the current regulatory debate. In 2013, the Basel Committee of Banking Supervision (BCBS), after a proposal exposed to public consultation, took the decision [12] of replacing Value at Risk (**VaR**) with **ES** for capital adequacy internal models. The decision is now part of the final rules of the new Basel Accord [6] that banks are currently implementing.

A similar debate was the subject of a public consultation [18] from the International Association of Insurance Supervisors on Insurance Capital Standards in December 2014; the result of the consultation was in this case exactly the opposite with IAIS finally opting for the adoption of **VaR** in the Capital Standard [19]. Among the motivations for this choice was the absence of a backtest for **ES** (see Table 3 in [18]).

ES has a number of advantages over **VaR**, among which is its ability to detect tail risks, respecting basic rules of risk diversification and convexity. But when it comes to financial regulation, backtestability — whatever it exactly means — is not a negotiable property. The term backtesting, as commonly intended in the risk industry, refers to the practice of validating *ex ante* model predictions of some risk measure against observed *ex post* realizations of the random variable it refers to. It's the only way for verifying if a risk model makes acceptable predictions or not. Banks have been following backtesting practices for decades because **VaR** — despite all its deficiencies — lends itself to straightforward backtesting. If it were ascertained that **ES** cannot be backtested in any possible way, related risk models could not be validated, and for instance the BCBS should seriously reconsider its decision.

Currently, Basel regulation [6] imposes banks to compute the capital charge for their internal models based on **ES**, but in the absence of an accepted backtest for this measure, it requires an unconvincing patchwork of model validations, based on **VaR** backtests at two different quantiles plus two so-called P&L attribution tests (Kolmogorov–Smirnov and Spearman correlation between the realized P&L as repriced by the front office and by the risk management pricing libraries). Whether and how **ES** can be backtested have become urgent questions.

1.3. *Structure of the Chapter and Main Findings*

In Section 2, we define the notation and the experiment setup and we review the established concepts of elicitation and identification, which will take us very close to a proper definition of backtestability. In Section 2.2.2, we discuss how elicitability serves the purpose of conducting relative non-directional tests of goodness between competing models issuing point predictions on a distribution functional.

In Section 3, we pose the central definition of backtestability, corresponding to strictly y-increasing identification and y-convex elicitation. Non-elicitable functionals, such as the variance and the expected shortfall, are not backtestable. We show that convexity forces the scoring and backtest functions of the mean, the quantile and the expectile to be essentially unique (Corollaries 3.8 and 3.9). Section 3.1.3 describes the proper hypothesis backtesting procedure that allows for absolute validation of a model issuing entire predictive distributions.

In Section 3.2, we note that only some backtests (such as the mean backtest) are monotonic also with respect to the true value of the functional under the real-world distribution. We call them sharp because their expected value uniquely determines the true value of the functional, providing information not only on the significance but also on the magnitude of a prediction discrepancy. Non-sharp backtests provide limited information on the true value in the form of an attainable range. We show (Proposition 3.17) that the quantile backtest tells basically nothing about the true value of the functional. Expectiles are not sharp either unless $\alpha = 1/2$ and we provide bounds for the location of the true value (Proposition 3.19).

In Section 4, we show that some special non-backtestable functionals admit what we call a ridge backtest. This is an approximated backtest, affected by the predictions of a second, elicitable, auxiliary functional, with respect to which the test displays only limited and one-sided sensitivity. Such mechanism allows for effective backtests when the bias side happens to be prudential for the purpose of the ridge backtest (Proposition 4.2). The variance and the expected shortfall are shown to admit a ridge backtest. The result opens the way for effective backtests of the expected shortfall.

2. Preliminary Concepts

In this section, we describe the setup, set the notation and briefly review a number of concepts and results in the related literature.

2.1. *Backtest Experiment Setup*

Let $X \in \mathbb{R}$ be a random variable distributed along an unknowable real-world distribution function F. Let $\mathbf{y}$ be a functional of X, which we will alternatively denote as $\mathbf{y}(F)$, $\mathbf{y}(X)$ or simply $\mathbf{y}$ depending on the context. $\mathbf{y}$ may be real-valued or interval-valued as in the case of quantiles (see Section A.1).

We will consider a discrete sequence of times $t = 0, 1, \ldots, T$ and random variables X_t observed at every $t > 0$. Let F_t denote the distribution of X_t. We will assume that at any time $t-1$, a forecast y_t for the functional $\mathbf{y}$ is issued by some model based on the information available up to time $t-1$. Most of the time, as this is the standard practice in financial risk management, we will assume that an entire forecast distribution P_t for the random variable X_t is issued by the model and used to generate the prediction $y_t = \mathbf{y}(P_t)$. We will abstract completely from the nature of the model, which can be any sort of algorithm, procedure, divination or guesswork.

To pave the ground for a definition of backtestability, we first review some useful concepts.

2.2. *Elicitability*

A central concept as well as an established tool for the evaluation of point forecasts is the notion of *elicitability* [17].

Definition 2.1. A functional $\mathbf{y}$ is called $\mathcal{F}$–*elicitable*[3] if there exists a *scoring function* $S_{\mathbf{y}}(y, x)$ such that the functional can be expressed as the minimizer of the expectation

$$\mathbf{y}(F) = \arg\min_{y} \mathbb{E}_F \left[S_{\mathbf{y}}(y, X) \right], \qquad \forall F \in \mathcal{F},\ X \sim F. \tag{1}$$

An interpretation of this definition is that the expected scoring function plays the role of a penalty function for possible forecasts y of the functional because it is minimized in expectation by a perfect forecast $y = \mathbf{y}(F)$.

We are primarily interested in the case when the class of distribution functions $\mathcal{F}$ is *maximal*, in the sense that it contains all distributions F for which both the functional $\mathbf{y}(F)$ and the expected scoring function $\mathbb{E}_F[S_{\mathbf{y}}]$ are integrable. In this case, we will omit to denote $\mathcal{F}$ and simply speak of elicitable functionals.

Common examples of elicitable functionals include the following (Table 1):

Table 1. Common examples of elicitable functionals and their canonical scoring functions.

$\mathbf{y}$	$S_{\mathbf{y}}(y, x)$	$\mathcal{F}_S$
$\boldsymbol{\mu}$	$(y - x)^2$	Maximal
$\mathbf{q}_{1/2}$	$\lvert y - x \rvert$	Maximal
$\mathbf{q}_\alpha$	$\alpha(x - y)_+ + (1 - \alpha)(x - y)_-$	Maximal
$\mathbf{e}_\alpha$	$\alpha(x - y)_+^2 + (1 - \alpha)(x - y)_-^2$	Maximal

[3] Our definition of elicitability corresponds to strict elicitability in Ref. [17]. We are not interested in the non-strict case.

- The mean $\boldsymbol{\mu}(F) = \mathbb{E}_F[X]$ is the minimizer of the expected squared error and therefore has scoring function

$$S_{\boldsymbol{\mu}}(y,x) = (y-x)^2\,.$$

- The median — the 1/2-quantile $\mathbf{q}_{1/2}(F)$ — is the minimizer of the expected absolute error and therefore has scoring function

$$S_{\mathbf{q}_{1/2}}(y,x) = |y-x|\,.$$

- More generally, any α-quantile, for $\alpha \in (0,1)$ (see A.1), is elicited by a scoring function

$$S_{\mathbf{q}_\alpha}(y,x) = \alpha(x-y)_+ + (1-\alpha)(x-y)_-\,,$$

  a well known fact in quantile regression.
- Expectiles $\mathbf{e}_\alpha(F)$ [13, 26] (see A.3) are elicitable with scoring function

$$S_{\mathbf{e}_\alpha}(y,x) = \alpha(x-y)_+^2 + (1-\alpha)(x-y)_-^2\,.$$

  Expectiles represent a remarkable example because for $\alpha \leq 1/2$, the associated risk measure (of opposite sign) was proven to be in Ref. [30] the only elicitable functional which is also a coherent measure in the sense of Ref. [7].

Examples of non-elicitable functionals include the expected shortfall (see A.2) [17] and also the popular variance $\boldsymbol{\sigma}^2$ of a distribution [22].

2.2.1. *Characterization of Scoring Functions: Osband's Principle*

When the scoring function of a functional exists, it is not unique. For example, it is immediate to check that a scoring function $S_{\mathbf{y}}(y,x)$ is defined up to *inessential transformations*

$$S_{\mathbf{y}}(y,x) \to aS_{\mathbf{y}}(y,x) + b(x), \tag{2}$$

where $a > 0$ and b is any function.

More general non-trivial scoring functions for the same functional can be obtained by the following group of transformations:

$$S_{\mathbf{y}}(y,x) \to \int^{y} a(t)\partial_t S_{\mathbf{y}}(t,x)\,dt + b(x) \tag{3}$$

for any function $a(t) > 0$. The so-called *Osband's principle* [16,17,28] states not only that these transformations are sufficient for generating a different scoring function but also that they are necessary: if two scoring functions for the same functional exist, they must be connected by a transformation of this type.

Applications of Osband's principle therefore permit to characterize all scoring functions of a functional. For instance, Ref. [17] reports the most general expression for the scoring function of the quantile

$$S_{\mathbf{q}_\alpha}(y,x) = (\mathbf{1}_{\{x \le y\}} - \alpha)(g(y) - g(x)), \quad g \text{ non-decreasing}, \tag{4}$$

and for the mean,

$$S_{\boldsymbol{\mu}}(y,x) = \phi(x) - \phi(y) - \phi'(y)(x-y), \quad \phi \text{ convex}. \tag{5}$$

A natural notion of the simplest possible, *canonical* scoring function, however, seems to emerge, defined only up to inessential transformations. Importantly, canonical scoring functions respect scale invariance[4], namely basic dimensional analysis rules, when x and y are thought of as not dimensionless (say $[x] = \$$). This is a crucial property for applications in finance, which is clearly violated by the introduction of non-constant choices for the function $a(t)$ in the group of transformations (3). Non-scale-invariant scoring functions require the introduction of some scale parameter in the form of a dimensionful constant.

Interestingly, we will see (Corollary 3.8) that for the quantile, the mean and the expectile, only canonical scoring functions are convex in the prediction variable y, a fact that will turn out to be crucial for backtestability: backtestability functions will essentially be unique (see Section 3.1.1).

We conclude this section by recalling Ref. [17] that elicitability is invariant with respect to strictly monotonic transformations

[4]See Ref. [17] for a discussion on scale invariance.

$g : \mathbb{R} \to \mathbb{R}$, in the sense that if $\mathbf{y}$ is elicitable, then also $\mathbf{y}_g = g(\mathbf{y})$ is elicitable with $S_{\mathbf{y}_g}(y, x) = S_{\mathbf{y}}(g^{-1}(y), x)$. In particular, a functional is elicitable if and only if its opposite is elicitable so that we can equivalently speak of the elicitability of the quantile $\mathbf{q}$ or of $\mathbf{VaR} = -\mathbf{q}$, for instance. Similarly, we can equivalently speak of the non-elicitability of the variance $\boldsymbol{\sigma}^2$ and the standard deviation $\boldsymbol{\sigma}$.

2.2.2. *Model Selection via Scoring Functions*

The importance of elicitability stems from the fact that it allows one to say something about predictions of a functional based only on realizations of the random variable, which is exactly the problem we posed ourselves in Section 1. If a functional is elicitable, the *realized mean score*,

$$\bar{s}_{\mathbf{y}} = \frac{1}{T} \sum_{t=1}^{T} S_{\mathbf{y}}(y_t, x_t), \tag{6}$$

measured over a sequence of forecasts y_t for the functional $\mathbf{y}(X)$ and realizations x_t of the random variable X can be used to set up a contest of *relative* quality between different models labeled by k issuing sequences of forecasts $y_t^{(k)}$. The idea is that, for a fixed sequence of realizations x_t, the smaller the mean score $\bar{s}_{\mathbf{y}}^{(k)}$, the better the model k.

The big advantage of this type of test is that it doesn't require an entire predictive probability distribution P_t for issuing the predictions y_t; the numbers y_t are all that is needed, and the forecast model can be of whatever type, including bullet predictions y_t at any t.

Note however that a test of this type is inherent of *relative* type between competing models: if there is a single model, the mean score will tell nothing on the quality of its predictions in *absolute* terms. For this reason, as we pointed out in Ref. [1], this type of procedure allows for *model selection* among multiple models running in parallel, rather than *model validation* which needs an absolute scale for testing models, and is the goal of a proper backtesting procedure (see Section 3.1.3).

We also note that a realized mean score test is not directional in the sense that it will not reveal whether a model under- or overestimates the functional. So, you may end up preferring a small risk underestimation to a large overestimation, which may not be what you want if your goal is of prudential type. In the context of model validation for prudential financial regulation, it is clearly important to look for directional validation methods, which is what a backtesting procedure should provide. A step in this direction is provided by identifiability.

2.3. *Identifiability*

A close concept to elicitability is *identifiability.*

Definition 2.2. A functional $\mathbf{y}$ is called $\mathcal{F}$-*identifiable*[5] if there exists an *identification function* $I_{\mathbf{y}}(y,x)$ such that

$$\mathbb{E}_F\left[I_{\mathbf{y}}(y,X)\right]=0, \text{ iff } y\in\mathbf{y}(F), \quad \forall F\in\mathcal{F},\, X\sim F. \tag{7}$$

In most common cases, identifiability and elicitability occur jointly, when equation (7) represents the first-order stationarity condition of a scoring function global minimum

$$S(y,x)=\int^{y} I(t,x)dt, \tag{8}$$

whose expected value $\mathbb{E}_F[S(y,X)]$ has a global minimum in $y\in\mathbf{y}(F)$. Tables 1 and 2 summarize some (canonical) scoring and identification functions for the analyzed examples, all of which are related by Eq. (8).

We conventionally set the sign of identification functions in accordance to (8), namely such that the function be increasing around $y=\mathbf{y}(F)$. Canonical identification functions (and backtest functions in the following) are therefore defined up to an overall inessential positive multiplicative constant; more general identification functions are generated by Osband's principle (3) for any function $a(y)>0$

$$I_{\mathbf{y}}(y,x)\to a(y)I_{\mathbf{y}}(y,x). \tag{9}$$

Similar to elicitability, we will simply speak of identifiability, without specifying $\mathcal{F}$, when the class is maximal, namely when it contains all

[5]Strictly identifiable in most literature.

Table 2. Common examples of canonical identification functions. $c \in [-\alpha, 1-\alpha]$, see Remark 2.4.

$\mathbf{y}$	$I_{\mathbf{y}}(y,x)$	$\mathcal{F}_I$
$\boldsymbol{\mu}$	$y-x$	Maximal
$\mathbf{q}_{1/2}$	$\mathbf{1}_{\{y>x\}} - \mathbf{1}_{\{y<x\}} + 2c\mathbf{1}_{\{y=x\}}$	$F(x)$ cont. in $\mathbf{q}_{1/2}$
$\mathbf{q}_\alpha$	$(1-\alpha)\mathbf{1}_{\{y>x\}} - \alpha\mathbf{1}_{\{y<x\}} + c\mathbf{1}_{\{y=x\}}$	$F(x)$ cont. in $\mathbf{q}_\alpha$
$\mathbf{e}_\alpha$	$(1-\alpha)(x-y)_- - \alpha(x-y)_+$	Maximal

distribution functions for which $\mathbf{y}(F)$ and $\mathbb{E}_F[I_{\mathbf{y}}]$ are finite. Equation (8) implies that the maximal class for identifiability includes the maximal class for elicitability.

Also identifiability (and later backtestability) is invariant with respect to strictly monotonic transformations $g : \mathbb{R} \to \mathbb{R}$, in the sense that if $\mathbf{y}$ is identifiable, then also $\mathbf{y}_g = g(\mathbf{y})$ is identifiable with $I_{\mathbf{y}_g}(y,x) = I_{\mathbf{y}}(g^{-1}(y), x)$.

Remark 2.3. As opposed to all other examples in Table 2, the quantile (and the median as a special case) is not identifiable under a maximal class $\mathcal{F}$ of distributions via the proposed (canonical) function but requires further continuity conditions on $F(x)$ at least in $x = \mathbf{q}_\alpha$. To illustrate the point let $F(x)$ be discontinuous in $x = \mathbf{q}_\alpha$. We will have $F(\mathbf{q}_\alpha^-) = F(\mathbf{q}_\alpha^+) - \Pr[X = \mathbf{q}_\alpha] < F(\mathbf{q}_\alpha^+)$ and $F(\mathbf{q}_\alpha^-) \le \alpha \le F(\mathbf{q}_\alpha^+) = F(\mathbf{q}_\alpha)$. We can immediately check that the expected value of the identification function for a correct prediction $y = \mathbf{q}_\alpha$

$$\mathbb{E}_F[I_{\mathbf{q}_\alpha}(\mathbf{q}_\alpha, X)] = -\alpha(1 - F(\mathbf{q}_\alpha)) + (1-\alpha)F(\mathbf{q}_\alpha^-) + c\Pr[X = \mathbf{q}_\alpha]$$

is in general different from zero. The problem is intrinsic to the discontinuity of the map $y \mapsto I_{\mathbf{q}}(y,x)$ and is common to any other identification function of the quantile derived from the most general scoring function (4).

Remark 2.4. The identification function of the quantile in Table 2 (and the backtest function in Table 3) is defined up to a term concentrated in $x = y$. The most general form is

$$I^c_{\mathbf{q}_\alpha}(y,x) = (1-\alpha)\mathbf{1}_{\{y>x\}} - \alpha\mathbf{1}_{\{y<x\}} + c\mathbf{1}_{\{y=x\}}, \tag{10}$$

for any choice of $c \in [-\alpha, 1-\alpha]$. For instance, the popular choices $I^{1-\alpha}_{\mathbf{q}_\alpha}(y,x) = \mathbf{1}_{\{y \ge x\}} - \alpha$ and $I^{-\alpha}_{\mathbf{q}_\alpha}(y,x) = \mathbf{1}_{\{y>x\}} - \alpha$ are obtained by setting $c = 1-\alpha$ and $c = -\alpha$, respectively.

Table 3. Common examples of backtest functions. These are unique up to a positive constant (see Corollary 3.9).

$\mathbf{y}$	$Z_{\mathbf{y}}(y,x)$	$\mathcal{F}_Z$
$\boldsymbol{\mu}$	$y-x$	Maximal
$\mathbf{q}_{1/2}$	$\mathbf{1}_{\{y>x\}} - \mathbf{1}_{\{y<x\}} + 2c\mathbf{1}_{\{y=x\}}$	$F(x)$ str. incr., cont. in $\mathbf{q}_{1/2}$
$\mathbf{q}_\alpha$	$(1-\alpha)\mathbf{1}_{\{y>x\}} - \alpha\mathbf{1}_{\{y<x\}} + c\mathbf{1}_{\{y=x\}}$	$F(x)$ str. incr., cont. in $\mathbf{q}_\alpha$
$\mathbf{e}_\alpha$	$(1-\alpha)(x-y)_- - \alpha(x-y)_+$	Maximal

The range for c comes from the fact that

$$\mathbb{E}_F[I^c_{\mathbf{q}_\alpha}(y,X)] = F(y) - d\Pr[X=y] - \alpha \equiv F_d(y) - \alpha, \tag{11}$$

with $d = 1-\alpha-c$. We need to require that $F_d(y) \equiv F(y) - d\Pr[X = y] \in [F(y^-), F(y^+) = F(y)]$, otherwise there can be solutions to $\mathbb{E}_F[I^c_{\mathbf{q}_\alpha}(y,X)] = 0$ different from $y = \mathbf{q}_\alpha$. This forces $d \in [0,1]$ and therefore $c \in [-\alpha, 1-\alpha]$.

Note that we would have obtained the same restriction simply by imposing (10) to be non-decreasing in y.

3. Backtesting: Definitions, Methods and Properties

We now have the elements for attempting a definition of backtestability. For a reason that will be clear from Remark 3.3, we consider in this section functionals $\mathbf{y}$ that are single-valued and we adopt the correspondingly simpler notation.

3.1. *Backtestability*

We define backtestability in such a way to be able to rank forecasts on a scale where positive (negative) values denote over-(under-) estimation and larger mispredictions rank further away from zero. This will also allow us to set up a meaningful hypothesis-testing framework in probabilistic terms.

Definition 3.1. We define a functional $\mathbf{y}$ to be $\mathcal{F}$-*backtestable* if there exists a *backtest function* $Z_{\mathbf{y}}(y,x)$ such that

$$\mathbb{E}_F\left[Z_{\mathbf{y}}(y,X)\right] = 0, \text{ iff } y = \mathbf{y}(F), \quad \forall F \in \mathcal{F}, \tag{12}$$

which is strictly increasing in the prediction y, $\forall F \in \mathcal{F}$.

$$\mathbb{E}_F\left[Z_{\mathbf{y}}(y_1, X)\right] < \mathbb{E}_F\left[Z_{\mathbf{y}}(y_2, X)\right] \quad \text{if } y_1 < y_2. \tag{13}$$

The requirement is very natural: posing this definition, the sign of $\mathbb{E}_F\left[Z_{\mathbf{y}}(y, X)\right]$ will coincide with the sign of the prediction discrepancy $y - \mathbf{y}(F)$

$$\begin{cases} \mathbb{E}_F\left[Z_{\mathbf{y}}(y, X)\right] < 0 & \text{if } \ y < \mathbf{y}(F) \\ \mathbb{E}_F\left[Z_{\mathbf{y}}(y, X)\right] > 0 & \text{if } \ y > \mathbf{y}(F) \end{cases}, \tag{14}$$

and given two predictions that both overestimate (or underestimate) the functional, the worse prediction will generate a strictly worse (i.e., farther from zero) expected backtest function

$$\begin{cases} \mathbb{E}_F\left[Z_{\mathbf{y}}(y_1, X)\right] < \mathbb{E}_F\left[Z_{\mathbf{y}}(y_2, X)\right] < 0 & \text{if } \ y_1 < y_2 < \mathbf{y}(F) \\ \mathbb{E}_F\left[Z_{\mathbf{y}}(y_1, X)\right] > \mathbb{E}_F\left[Z_{\mathbf{y}}(y_2, X)\right] > 0 & \text{if } \ y_1 > y_2 > \mathbf{y}(F) \end{cases}. \tag{15}$$

Backtestability is slightly more restrictive than identifiability in that it requires the expected value of the identification function to be strictly increasing in the prediction variable y. For this, it is necessary that the identification function be non-decreasing in y for all x and it is sufficient that it is strictly increasing.

The canonical identification functions of $\boldsymbol{\mu}$ and $\mathbf{e}_\alpha$ are strictly increasing in y and therefore constitute valid backtest functions on the same distribution class $\mathcal{F}$ of identifiability, which is maximal.

The identification function (10) of the quantile $\mathbf{q}_\alpha$ is non-decreasing in y for any c but not strictly increasing. We therefore need to check under what distribution functions we obtain strict monotonicity with respect to y of the expected identification function. From (11), remembering that $F(y^-) \leq F_d(y) \leq F(y^+)$, we can immediately conclude that for the expectation to be strictly increasing in y, it is necessary and sufficient to restrict to distribution functions that are overall strictly increasing.[6] We can conclude the following:

Proposition 3.2. *The quantile* $\mathbf{q}_\alpha$ *is backtestable only on the class*

$$\mathcal{F} = \{F |\ \textit{overall strictly monotonic; continuous in } \mathbf{q}_\alpha\}. \tag{16}$$

---

[6]We call strictly increasing a distribution function when it is strictly increasing in the interior of its domain, namely except where it takes the value 0 or 1.

In most practical applications, the scope of a quantile backtest will typically be the smaller class of distributions which are overall both continuous and strictly monotonic.

Remark 3.3. Given that the quantile is backtestable only on strictly increasing distributions on which the quantile is single-valued, we restrict throughout this section to functionals $\mathbf{y}$ which are single-valued. We don't have other interesting examples of interval-valued backtestable functionals.

In all the examples shown in Table 2, the identification functions are non-decreasing in y and, as we have shown, they represent also valid backtest functions although in the case of the quantile, this is true only on a smaller class of distributions. We summarize the results in Table 3.

It is possible to construct examples of identifiable functionals that are not backtestable, but they are somewhat *ad hoc*.

Example 3.4. The functional $\mathbf{y}$ defined via (1) by a non-y-concave scoring function like

$$S_{\mathbf{y}}(y, x) = 1 - \frac{1}{\cosh(x - y)} \tag{17}$$

is identifiable over its maximal $\mathcal{F}$, but the identification function

$$I_{\mathbf{y}}(y, x) = \partial_y S_{\mathbf{y}}(y, x) = -\frac{\sinh(x - y)}{\cosh^2(x - y)} \tag{18}$$

is not non-decreasing with respect to y as is any further transformation of type (9). The functional $\mathbf{y}$ is therefore not backtestable.

3.1.1. *Essential Uniqueness of Backtest Functions*

While identification functions of a given functional are defined up to a non-trivial group of transformations (9), backtest functions seem to be unique up to a positive multiplicative constant. We don't have a general proof of this statement. We show this in the cases of the mean, the quantile and the expectile.

Proposition 3.5. *In the family of identification functions of the mean*

$$I_{\boldsymbol{\mu}}(y,x) = \phi''(y)(y-x) \qquad \phi \textit{ convex} \tag{19}$$

derived from the most general scoring function (5), *the only one which is non-decreasing in* y *for all* x *is the canonical one where* ϕ'' *is a constant.*

Proof. We need to impose that

$$\partial_y[\phi''(y)(y-x)] = \phi'''(y)(y-x) + \phi''(y) \geq 0. \tag{20}$$

We know that $\phi'' \geq 0$. But if $\phi'''(y) \neq 0$ at some y, there exists some x for which the above expression goes negative. Therefore, $\phi'''(y) = 0$ which implies that $\phi'' = const.$ □

Proposition 3.6. *In the family of identification functions of the quantile*[7]

$$I_{\mathbf{q}_\alpha}(y,x) = g'(y)(\mathbf{1}_{\{y\geq x\}} - \alpha) \quad g \textit{ increasing} \tag{21}$$

derived from the most general scoring function (4), *the only one which is non-decreasing in* y *for all* x *is the canonical one obtained with* $g(t) = t$ *up to a positive constant.*

Proof. We need to impose that

$$\partial_y[g'(y)(\mathbf{1}_{\{y\geq x\}} - \alpha)] = g''(y)(\mathbf{1}_{\{y\geq x\}} - \alpha) + g'(y)\delta(x-y) \geq 0, \tag{22}$$

for all y and x. But whatever the sign of $g''(y)$, we know that the term $(\mathbf{1}_{\{y\geq x\}} - \alpha)$ is both positive and negative depending on x and y. The only possibility is therefore that $g''(y) = 0$, which imposes $g(t) = t$. □

Proposition 3.7. *The only identification function of the expectile which is non-decreasing in* y *for all* x *is the canonical one in Table* 2 *up to a constant.*

[7]For simplicity, we fix $c = 1 - \alpha$ in the general expression (10). The choice is irrelevant for the result.

Proof. The proof is similar to Proposition 3.5. From Osband's principle, Eq. (3), we know that all the identification functions of the expectile can be written as

$$I^a_{\mathbf{e}_\alpha}(y,x) = a(y) I_{\mathbf{e}_\alpha}(y,x), \tag{23}$$

where $a(y) > 0$, and

$$I_{\mathbf{e}_\alpha}(y,x) = (1-\alpha)(x-y)_- - \alpha(x-y)_+ \tag{24}$$

is the canonical one. If we impose $\partial_y I^a_{\mathbf{e}_\alpha}(y,x) \geq 0$, we get that for all x and y

$$a'(y) I_{\mathbf{e}_\alpha}(y,x) + a(y)\left[(1-\alpha)\mathbf{1}_{\{y>x\}} + \alpha\mathbf{1}_{\{y<x\}}\right] \geq 0. \tag{25}$$

The second term is positive. If there existed some y for which $a'(y) \neq 0$, then it would be possible to find some x for which this expression is negative. Therefore, $a = const.$ □

We summarize with stating the following:

Corollary 3.8. *Up to inessential transformations, the only scoring functions for the mean, the quantile and the expectile that are y-convex are the canonical ones listed in Table* 1.

Corollary 3.9. *Up to a positive constant, the only backtest functions of the mean, the quantile and the expectile are the canonical identification functions listed in Table* 3.

3.1.2. *Backtestability and Elicitability*

It is immediate to show that backtestability implies elicitability.

Proposition 3.10. *If* $\mathbf{y}$ *is* $\mathcal{F}$*-backtestable with backtest function* $Z_{\mathbf{y}}(y,x)$, *then it is also* $\mathcal{F}'$*-elicitable with y-convex scoring function*

$$S_{\mathbf{y}}(y,x) = \int^y Z_{\mathbf{y}}(t,x)\,dt, \tag{26}$$

on the class $\mathcal{F}'$ *of distributions F for which* $S_{\mathbf{y}}(y,X)$ *is integrable.*

Proof. $y \mapsto \mathbb{E}_F[Z_{\mathbf{y}}(y, X)]$ strictly increasing ensures that $y \mapsto \mathbb{E}_F[S_{\mathbf{y}}(y, X)]$ is convex and has a global minimum in $y = \mathbf{y}(F)$. □

The above proposition tells us that convexity of the scoring function is a necessary condition for backtestability and that the backtest function is the y-subdifferential of the scoring function.[8]

Elicitability with a strictly y-convex and smooth scoring function implies backtestability. If the smoothness condition is not met, like in the case of the quantile, restrictions on $\mathcal{F}$ may be necessary to ensure backtestablity.

Proposition 3.11. *If* $\mathbf{y}$ *is* $\mathcal{F}$*-elicitable with scoring function* $S_{\mathbf{y}}(y, x)$ *which is strictly convex and continuously differentiable in* y*, then it is also* $\mathcal{F}'$*-backtestable with* $\mathcal{F}' \supseteq \mathcal{F}$ *and backtest function*

$$Z_{\mathbf{y}}(y, x) = \partial_y S_{\mathbf{y}}(y, x). \tag{27}$$

Proof. straightforward. □

3.1.3. *Model Validation via Backtest Functions*

For a proper model validation of absolute type, we require[9] that the forecast $y_t = \mathbf{y}(P_t)$ be formulated via an entire predictive distribution function P_t. We can then exploit (14) which becomes

$$\mathbb{E}_F\left[Z_{\mathbf{y}}(\mathbf{y}(P), X)\right] \lesseqgtr \mathbb{E}_P\left[Z_{\mathbf{y}}(\mathbf{y}(P), X)\right] = 0 \quad \text{if}\ \mathbf{y}(P) \lesseqgtr \mathbf{y}(F) \tag{28}$$

to test whether the prediction $\mathbf{y}(P)$ over-/under-estimates the real value $\mathbf{y}(F)$.

A standard hypothesis testing framework can be set up using as a test statistic the average realization $\bar{z}_{\mathbf{y}}$ of the backtest function over

[8]It is interesting to note that the condition on c in Remark 2.4, although derived from different requirements, corresponds exactly to the subdifferential range in the non-differentiable point of the scoring function of the quantile.

[9]Quantile will represent an exception, as it does not require resampling of the predictive backtest distribution.

the period $t = 1, \ldots, T$ with functional predictions y_t and observations $X_t = x_t$ of the random variable.

$$\bar{z}_{\mathbf{y}} = \frac{1}{T}\sum_{t=1}^{T} Z_{\mathbf{y}}(y_t, x_t). \tag{29}$$

The sampling distribution of the test is represented by the model distribution $P_{\bar{Z}}$ of the average backtest function

$$\bar{Z}_{\mathbf{y}} = \frac{1}{T}\sum_{t=1}^{T} Z_{\mathbf{y}}(y_t, X_t), \quad X_t \sim P_t. \tag{30}$$

For any chosen significance level $\eta \lesssim 1$ (such as $\eta = 95\%$), we can determine a rejection region of P-measure $1-\eta$ for $\bar{z}_{\mathbf{y}}$. This will span one or both tails of the $P_{\bar{Z}}$ distribution, depending on whether the test is one- or two-sided.

Let's consider for instance the typical example in banking regulation of a one-sided test intended to check if the forecasts $\mathbf{y}_t$ of a risk model are prudential enough. The null hypothesis is that the model issues predictions that do not underestimate the risk measure:

$$H_0 : \mathbf{y}(P_t) \geq \mathbf{y}(F_t) \quad \forall t = 1, \ldots, T.$$

The rejection region will span the left tail of the distribution: $\bar{z}_{\mathbf{y}} \in (-\infty, c_\eta]$, where $c_\eta = P_{\bar{Z}}^{-1}(1-\eta)$.

The distribution $P_{\bar{Z}}$ in many cases can be obtained analytically or via central limit asymptotics. In the absence of analytical or asymptotic results, one can always simulate the model distribution $P_{\bar{Z}}$ of the random variable $\bar{Z}_{\mathbf{y}}$, generating a suitably large number M of scenarios:

$$\begin{aligned} &\text{simulate independent} \quad X_t^i \sim P_t \qquad \forall t = 1, \ldots, T, \quad \forall i = 1, \ldots, M, \\ &\text{compute test scenarios } \bar{z}_{\mathbf{y}}^i = \tfrac{1}{T}\sum_{t=1}^{T} Z_{\mathbf{y}}(\mathbf{y}(P_t), X_t^i) \qquad \forall i = 1, \ldots, M. \end{aligned}$$

The critical threshold will be estimated by $c_\eta = \bar{z}_{\mathbf{y}}^{M(1-\eta):M}$, where $\bar{z}_{\mathbf{y}}^{i:M}$ denotes the sample's order statistics. Finally, the null hypothesis will be rejected if $\bar{z}_{\mathbf{y}} \leq c_\eta$.

Remark 3.12. The case of quantile backtesting (like the standard **VaR** backtest in Basel regulation) is exceptional in the sense that the distribution $P_{\bar{Z}}$ is binomial, independent of the model P. Implementation of the backtest is therefore much more straightforward, in particular for what concerns data storage. To backtest a quantile, it is sufficient to record, for every t, the numerical prediction y_t and the realization x_t, while for other functionals, it is necessary to record also the entire probability distribution P_t for resampling purposes.

However, from a conceptual point of view, the standard quantile backtest based on the counting of "exceedances" (i.e., on $Z_{\mathbf{q}_\alpha}(y,x) = \mathbf{1}_{\{y \geq x\}} - \alpha$) follows exactly the same logic as the above hypothesis test.

3.2. *Sharp backtests*

Backtestability requires the expectation of the backtest function to be strictly monotonic with respect to the prediction variable: worse predictions rank worse, given a real distribution. We can however reverse the logic and ask ourselves the following questions: Is the converse true? Is a given prediction ranking better in a backtest if the real value of the functional is closer to it than if it is farther? The question is legitimate: we would like our validation system to send louder warnings for larger discrepancies. If that weren't the case, for instance, a traffic light indicator for ongoing risk model validation could turn from yellow to red over time when in fact the prediction precision is actually improving or vice versa, from red to yellow when it is worsening.

And yet, natural as it sounds, the requirement,

$$\mathbb{E}_{F_1}[Z_{\mathbf{y}}(y,X)] > \mathbb{E}_{F_2}[Z_{\mathbf{y}}(y,X)] \quad \text{iff } \mathbf{y}(F_1) < \mathbf{y}(F_2),\ \forall y, \tag{31}$$

namely that the expected backtest function be strictly decreasing with respect to the true value of the functional, is not implied by the definition of backtest function and in fact fails to hold in the notable cases of quantiles and expectiles as we will see. We therefore add to backtestability the above requirement and pose the following more restrictive:

Definition 3.13. We define the backtest $Z_{\mathbf{y}}(y,x)$ of a $\mathcal{F}$-backtestable functional $\mathbf{y}$ to be *sharp* if it is strictly decreasing in the value $\mathbf{y}(F)$, in the sense that

$$\mathbb{E}_{F_1}\left[Z_{\mathbf{y}}(y,X)\right] > \mathbb{E}_{F_2}\left[Z_{\mathbf{y}}(y,X)\right] \quad \text{iff } \mathbf{y}(F_1) < \mathbf{y}(F_2);\ \forall F_1, F_2 \in \mathcal{F}, \forall y. \tag{32}$$

Condition (32) implies in particular[10] that $\mathbb{E}_{F_1}(Z_y(y,X)) = \mathbb{E}_{F_2}(Z_y(y,X))$ if $\mathbf{y}(F_1) = \mathbf{y}(F_2)$ which means that $\mathbb{E}_F(Z_y(y,X))$ is a function of $\mathbf{y}(F)$ only and not of all F. An equivalent definition is therefore the following:

Definition 3.14. We define the backtest $Z_{\mathbf{y}}(y,x)$ of $\mathcal{F}$-backtestable functional $\mathbf{y}$ to be *sharp*, if for all $F \in \mathcal{F}$, the expectation

$$\mathbb{E}_F\left[Z_{\mathbf{y}}(y,X)\right] = \psi_{\mathbf{y}}(y,\mathbf{y}(F)) \tag{33}$$

is a function $\psi_{\mathbf{y}} : \mathbb{R}^2 \to \mathbb{R}$ of the prediction y and of the true value $\mathbf{y}(F)$, which is strictly increasing in the former and strictly decreasing in the latter.

The importance of sharp backtests (and the reason why we call them sharp) is understood by noting that for any value z of the expected value (33), there's one and only one compatible value

$$\mathbf{y}(F) = \psi_{\mathbf{y}}^{-1}(y,z) \tag{34}$$

of the real value $\mathbf{y}(F)$, where by $\psi_{\mathbf{y}}^{-1}$ we denote the inverse function of the second argument of $\psi_{\mathbf{y}}$. This is a fundamental point: a sharp backtest will quantify also the discrepancy of a prediction and not only the model acceptance probability as generic backtests do.

Remark 3.15. The point has been overlooked for a long time in the case of **VaR** backtesting for banking regulation. A bank may lose the regulator's model approval if it repeatedly ranks red in a traffic light system even if, as we will see, this could be caused by very small discrepancies between prediction and real values. And more worryingly, the traffic light could be yellow or even green even when the underestimation is large. As a matter of fact, the color of the traffic light, in

[10]Note the iff in (32).

the case of **VaR**, tells absolutely nothing about the distance between predicted and real **VaR** values, as Proposition 3.17 will show. Sharp backtests, on the contrary, measure both the significance and the discrepancy extent of a prediction.

It is immediate to check that the backtest of the mean μ is sharp. As a matter of fact, all functionals that are explicitly defined as an expectation or strictly increasing functions thereof have a sharp backtest.

Proposition 3.16. *Let $g, h : \mathbb{R} \to \mathbb{R}$, g strictly monotonic and let*

$$\mathbf{y}(F) \equiv g(\mathbb{E}_F[h(X)]),$$

then $\mathbf{y}$ is $\mathcal{F}$-backtestable on maximal $\mathcal{F}$ with sharp backtest function

$$Z_{\mathbf{y}}(y, x) = \nu\, g^{-1}(y) - \nu\, h(x), \tag{35}$$

where $\nu \in \{\pm 1\}$ is the sign of g'.

Proof. By direct calculation of $\nu g(\mathbb{E}_F[Z_{\mathbf{y}}(y, X)])$. □

3.2.1. *Information Content of the Quantile and Expectile Backtests*

We will show that both the backtests of the quantile and the expectile are not sharp. It is therefore interesting to study how informative a backtest of these functionals is in localizing the real value.

Let's begin by analyzing the quantile, recalling that its backtest function is unique, up to a positive multiplicative constant and the choice of c in (10).

Proposition 3.17. *The backtest of the quantile $\mathbf{q}_\alpha$ is not sharp on its $\mathcal{F}$-backtestability class* (16).

For any prediction y and expected value $z = \mathbb{E}_F[Z_{\mathbf{q}_\alpha}(y, X)]$ of the backtest function, the attainable range of $\mathbf{q}_\alpha(F)$ is given by

$$\begin{cases} \mathbf{q}_\alpha(F) \in (-\infty, y) & \text{if } z > 0 \\ \mathbf{q}_\alpha(F) \in (y, +\infty) & \text{if } z < 0 \end{cases}. \tag{36}$$

Proof. For the proof, we fix $c = 1 - \alpha$ in (10) so that $Z_{\mathbf{q}_\alpha}(x, y) = \mathbf{1}_{\{y \geq x\}} - \alpha$. It is easy to see that the choice is completely inessential.

If $F \in \mathcal{F}$, then $z = F(y) - \alpha$. If $z > 0$, $\exists F_1, F_2 \in \mathcal{F}$ such that $F_1^{-1}(\alpha) = y - \epsilon$ as well as $F_2^{-1}(\alpha) = -M$, for arbitrarily small $\epsilon > 0$ and large $M > 0$. If $z < 0$, $\exists F_1, F_2 \in \mathcal{F}$ such that $F_1^{-1}(\alpha) = y + \epsilon$ as well as $F_2^{-1}(\alpha) = +M$. This proves the range conditions on $\mathbf{q}_\alpha = F^{-1}(\alpha)$.

Then, $Z_{\mathbf{q}_\alpha}$ is not sharp because the values of y and z do not determine $\mathbf{q}_\alpha(F)$. □

The result of the above proposition is quite dramatic. In plain English, it means that the backtest gives you no clue whatsoever on the location of the real quantile, even if you knew the exact value of expected backtest function. It can be anywhere. Also note that to enforce the missing property (32), we should restrict to a class $\mathcal{F}'$ such that

$$\mathbb{E}_{F_1}\left[Z_{\mathbf{q}_\alpha}(y, X)\right] - \mathbb{E}_{F_2}\left[Z_{\mathbf{q}_\alpha}(y, X)\right] = F_1(y) - F_2(y) > 0,$$

when $\mathbf{q}_\alpha(F_1) < \mathbf{q}_\alpha(F_2)$, for all $F_1, F_2 \in \mathcal{F}'$ and for all y. But this means $F_1 <_{1^{st}} F_2$ in the sense of first stochastic dominance. Therefore, the only classes on which the backtest of the quantile can be made sharp are totally ordered by first stochastic dominance. No class of this type makes any sense for practical application purposes so that in practical terms we can affirm that the quantile backtest is not sharp at all.

The only information on the location of the true quantile provided by its backtest is restricted to whether the real value is above or below the prediction.

Remark 3.18. One may confuse the result of Proposition 3.17 with the elementary fact that a quantile is blind to the magnitude of the risks in the tail, in the sense that the position of the quantile doesn't tell you anything on how severe the further tail events are. The above result has nothing to do with this. The backtest of the quantile tells nothing on the position of the true quantile which in turn tells nothing on the position of the risks of the tail. We are speaking in other words of a (long-overlooked) problem on top of another (well-known) one.

We now consider the expectile.

Proposition 3.19. *The backtest of the expectile* $\mathbf{e}_\alpha$ *is not sharp on its maximal* $\mathcal{F}$*-backtestability class unless* $\alpha = 1/2$*, where it trivially coincides with the mean of the distribution.*

For any prediction y *and expected value* $z = \mathbb{E}_F[Z_{\mathbf{e}_\alpha}(y, X)]$ *of the backtest function, the attainable range of* $\mathbf{e}_\alpha(F)$ *is given by*

$$\begin{cases} \mathbf{e}_\alpha(F) \in (y - z/\alpha, y - z/(1-\alpha)] & \textit{if } z > 0 \quad \textit{and} \quad \alpha < 1/2 \\ \mathbf{e}_\alpha(F) \in (y - z/(1-\alpha), y - z/\alpha] & \textit{if } z < 0 \quad \textit{and} \quad \alpha < 1/2 \\ \mathbf{e}_\alpha(F) \in [y - z/(1-\alpha), y - z/\alpha) & \textit{if } z > 0 \quad \textit{and} \quad \alpha > 1/2 \\ \mathbf{e}_\alpha(F) \in [y - z/\alpha, y - z/(1-\alpha)) & \textit{if } z < 0 \quad \textit{and} \quad \alpha > 1/2 \\ \mathbf{e}_\alpha(F) = y - 2z & \qquad\qquad \textit{if} \quad \alpha = 1/2 \end{cases}. \tag{37}$$

Proof. If $F \in \mathcal{F}$, then the map $u \mapsto h(u) = \mathbb{E}_F[Z_{e_\alpha}(u, X)]$ can be shown to be strictly increasing and convex (concave) for $\alpha < 1/2$ (resp., $\alpha > 1/2$) with first derivative $h'(u) = \alpha + (1-2\alpha)F(u)$ and asymptotes

$$\begin{aligned} h(u) &\sim \alpha(u - \mathbb{E}_F[X]) && \text{if } u \to -\infty, \\ h(u) &\sim (1-\alpha)(u - \mathbb{E}_F[X]) && \text{if } u \to +\infty. \end{aligned}$$

Let us prove (37) for $z > 0$ and $\alpha < 1/2$. It is convenient to plot the function on the plane $(u, h(u))$. The expectile is the value $u^\star$ that solves $h(u) = 0$. From $h(y) = z > 0$ and the fact that the minimum and maximum slopes of the function h are α and $1 - \alpha$, we conclude that $\mathbf{e}_\alpha \in [y - z/\alpha, y - z/(1-\alpha)]$. But given that $z > 0$, the point $(u, h(u)) = (\mathbf{e}_\alpha, 0)$ can be on the right asymptote but not on the left. Therefore, the right extreme of the interval can be attained, but the left one cannot.

A distribution family for $\chi \in (0, 1]$ that spans the entire range is given by

$$F_\chi(x) = \chi\left(x \geq y - \frac{z}{\chi(1-\alpha)}\right) + (1-\chi)(x \geq y) \qquad \chi \in (0, 1].$$

One can easily prove that $\mathbb{E}_{F_\chi}[Z_{\mathbf{e}_\alpha}(y, X)] = z$ and

$$\mathbf{e}_\alpha(F) = y - \frac{z}{\chi + \alpha - 2\chi\alpha} \in (y - z/\alpha, y - z/(1-\alpha)].$$

The three other cases in (37) can be proven in an analogous way.

Then, $Z_{\mathbf{e}_\alpha}$ is not sharp for $\alpha \neq 1/2$ because the above would contradict (34). □

The result is clear. The expectile has a sharp backtest on $\mathcal{F}$ if and only if $\alpha = 1/2$, where it coincides with the mean of the distribution. For $\alpha \neq 1/2$, the real expectile is bounded in a range which is smaller and smaller as α approaches 1/2. The information content of the backtest in other words decreases when the expectile is used as an extreme tail measure. In the limits $\alpha \to 0, 1$, the range size diverges.

Interestingly, from the proof, we learn that $h'(u) = \alpha + (1 - 2\alpha)F(u)$, and therefore, $h(u) = C + \alpha u + (1 - 2\alpha)\int^u F$. So, similar to the quantile case, in order to impose the expectile backtest to be sharp, we should restrict to distributions F_1, F_2 such that $\forall y$

$$\mathbb{E}_{F_1}\left[Z_{\mathbf{e}_\alpha}(y, X)\right] - \mathbb{E}_{F_2}\left[Z_{\mathbf{e}_\alpha}(y, X)\right] \propto \int^y (F_1 - F_2) > 0,$$

whenever $e_\alpha(F_1) < e_\alpha(F_2)$, which means that we should restrict to classes of distributions which are totally ordered by second-order stochastic dominance $F_1 <_{2nd} F_2$; as in the case of the quantile, this is again too restrictive a condition for any practical application. The expectile in practice admits no sharp backtest, but in the trivial case, $\alpha = 1/2$.

We conclude this section by noting that the backtest of the expectile is in some sense "sharper" than the one of the quantile but less and less so for the values of α which are most interesting for risk management purposes, namely down in the tails. Both the quantile and the expectile backtests have very poor resolution properties in terms of localizing the true value of the risk measure for small confidence levels.

4. Ridge Backtests

An intuitive way for checking the backtestability of a functional $\mathbf{y}$ is looking for an expression of the type $\mathbb{E}[I_{\mathbf{y}}(\mathbf{y}(X), X)] = 0$, depending only on the functional itself and the random variable X. If the functional doesn't lend itself to expressions of this type, the functional is probably not elicitable to begin with, although a formal conclusive proof may be non-trivial.

Functionals like the variance $\boldsymbol{\sigma}^2$ and the expected shortfall **ES** (see Appendix A.2) have been proven to be not elicitable [17, 22] and are therefore not backtestable. This should not sound surprising. A zero expectation involving the variance, for instance, exists, following directly from its definition

$$\mathbb{E}_F[\boldsymbol{\sigma}^2(F) - (X - \boldsymbol{\mu}(F))^2] = 0, \tag{38}$$

but it irreducibly depends also on another functional, the mean $\boldsymbol{\mu}$. This is in a nutshell the reason why the variance is not elicitable.

Similarly, from (57), it is immediate to obtain a null expectation for the **ES**,

$$\mathbb{E}_F\left[\mathbf{ES}_\alpha(F) - \mathbf{VaR}_\alpha(F) - \frac{1}{\alpha}(X + \mathbf{VaR}_\alpha(F))_-\right] = 0. \tag{39}$$

Also, this expression, however, involves another functional, the Value at Risk, **VaR**.

In general, starting from a relation of the type

$$\mathbb{E}[I(\mathbf{y}_2(X), \mathbf{y}_1(X), X)] = 0, \tag{40}$$

involving two functionals $\mathbf{y}_1$ and $\mathbf{y}_2$, a single backtest procedure may tell very little on the prediction quality of either one because deviations from zero expectation may be ascribed to discrepancies in either of the predictions y_1 and y_2. If the goal is, say, to backtest $\mathbf{y}_2$, then the dependency on $\mathbf{y}_1$ will represent a spurious sensitivity that pollutes the backtest.

In this situation, one may try to perform a preliminary backtest on say $\mathbf{y}_1$, if it is separately backtestable, and then use the joint relationship (40) to backtest $\mathbf{y}_2$, "conditionally to $\mathbf{y}_1$ being correct". This is essentially the strategy we adopted in [1], with the backtests Z_1 and Z_2 for $\mathbf{y}_2 = \mathbf{ES}$, in the assumption that the prediction for $\mathbf{y}_1 = \mathbf{VaR}$ had previously been tested. This strategy, however, poses two serious problems. First of all, what if the prediction of $\mathbf{y}_1$ turns out to be not correct? What is the sensitivity of the backtest for $\mathbf{y}_2$ to this discrepancy? But second, and more importantly, how can one ascertain at all that the prediction for $\mathbf{y}_1$ is spot on, given that via hypothesis testing we can at most rule out large discrepancies and only up to some significance level?

It is clear from these arguments that a useful backtest methodology for $\mathbf{y}_2$ based on a condition of type (40) can be obtained only if some model-independent mechanism ensures small sensitivity on predictions to $\mathbf{y}_1$. Incidentally, this is exactly what happens for the variance and the expected shortfall. These two measures are very special in that they are the attained minimum of the scoring function of a partner variable, $\boldsymbol{\mu}$ and **VaR**, respectively.

We pose the following:

Definition 4.1. We say that a functional $\mathbf{y}_2$ admits a *ridge $\mathcal{F}$-backtest*

$$Z_{\mathbf{y}_2}(y_2, y_1, x) = y_2 - S_{\mathbf{y}_1}(y_1, x) \tag{41}$$

if the functional (or a strictly monotonic transformation thereof) can be expressed as the minimum of the expected $\mathcal{F}$-scoring function $S_{\mathbf{y}_1}$ of an elicitable *auxiliary functional* $\mathbf{y}_1$

$$\begin{cases} \mathbf{y}_2(F) = \min_y E_F[S_{\mathbf{y}_1}(y, X)] \\ \mathbf{y}_1(F) = \arg\min_y E_F[S_{\mathbf{y}_1}(y, X)] \end{cases}, \quad F \in \mathcal{F}. \tag{42}$$

The utility of this definition is explained in the following:

Proposition 4.2. *Let $Z_{\mathbf{y}_2}$ be a ridge $\mathcal{F}$-backtest for $\mathbf{y}_2$ with auxiliary functional $\mathbf{y}_1$ as in Definition 4.1. Then, we have the following:*

- *The expected backtest is zero in the correct predictions for $\mathbf{y}_2$ and $\mathbf{y}_1$*

$$\mathbb{E}_F[Z_{\mathbf{y}_2}(\mathbf{y}_2(F), \mathbf{y}_1(F), X)] = 0 \quad \forall F \in \mathcal{F}. \tag{43}$$

- *$Z_{\mathbf{y}_2}$ acts as a backtest for $\mathbf{y}_2$ up to a one-sided bias depending only on y_1*

$$B(y_1) = \mathbb{E}_F[S_{\mathbf{y}_1}(y_1, X) - S_{\mathbf{y}_1}(\mathbf{y}_1(F), X)] \geq 0, \tag{44}$$

in the sense that

$$\begin{aligned} \mathbb{E}_F[Z_{\mathbf{y}_2}(y_2, y_1, X)] &= y_2 - \mathbf{y}_2(F) - \mathbb{E}_F[S_{\mathbf{y}_1}(y_1, X) - S_{\mathbf{y}_1}(\mathbf{y}_1(F), X)] \\ &= y_2 - \mathbf{y}_2(F) - B(y_1) \\ &\leq y_2 - \mathbf{y}_2(F) \quad \forall y_1. \end{aligned} \tag{45}$$

- *If* $\mathbb{E}_F[S_{\mathbf{y}_1}(y_1, X)]$ *is continuously differentiable in* $y_1 = \mathbf{y}_1(F)$ *for* $F \in \mathcal{F}' \subseteq \mathcal{F}$, *then*

$$\mathbb{E}_F[Z_{\mathbf{y}_2}(y_2, y_1, X)] = y_2 - \mathbf{y}_2(F) - \mathcal{O}(y_1 - \mathbf{y}_1(F))^2. \tag{46}$$

- $Z_{\mathbf{y}_2}$ *is a sharp backtest for* $\mathbf{y}_2$ *up to the bias term* (44).

Proof. Equation (43) follows from the definition (41) and from (45). The inequality in (44) follows from the second equality in (42). Equation (45) follows from (41) and (44), noting that (42) implies $\mathbf{y}_2(F) = \mathbb{E}_F[S_{\mathbf{y}_1}(\mathbf{y}_1(F), X)]$.

If $\mathbb{E}_F[S_{\mathbf{y}_1}(y_1, X)]$ is continuously differentiable in the minimum $y_1 = \mathbf{y}_1(F)$, it is at least quadratic which shows (46). The last assertion follows directly from the inspection of (45). □

The above proposition tells us some important facts. When you climb a mountain walking on a ridge, if you lose your way on either side, you can at least be sure that you find yourself below where you should be. Similarly, a ridge backtest for a functional $\mathbf{y}_2$ has a one-sided dependence on the prediction y_1 of the auxiliary functional $\mathbf{y}_1$. This allows one to draw bounded conclusions on the forecast y_2.

Suppose for instance that $\mathbf{y}_2$ is a risk measure and we want to test against underestimations. These will produce a negative expected backtest

$$\mathbb{E}_F[Z_{\mathbf{y}_2}(y_2, y_1, X)] < 0 \quad \text{if } y_2 < \mathbf{y}_2(F), \tag{47}$$

irrespective of the prediction y_1. An imperfect prediction y_1 will only make the result more negative, or in other words, the sensitivity to $\mathbf{y}_1$ makes the test only more prudential. Importantly, the magnitude of this bias will be small around a correct prediction $y_1 = \mathbf{y}_1(F)$ where it vanishes. Under smooth conditions, the sensitivity to y_1 will be zero at first order.

As a consequence, a (non-backtestable) functional admitting a ridge backtest can be approximately backtested for prudential purposes when the sign of the bias is in line with the objective of the test. The implementation of the ridge backtest follows the same steps described in Section 3.1.3.

Any scoring function $S_{\mathbf{y}_1}$ (even non-convex) of any elicitable functional $\mathbf{y}_1$ generates an example of ridge backtest by just taking (42) as the definition of $\mathbf{y}_2$.

4.1. *Variance*

The variance admits a ridge backtest. It is well known that

$$\boldsymbol{\sigma}^2(F) = \min_m \mathbb{E}_F[(X-m)^2] = \min_m \mathbb{E}_F[S_{\boldsymbol{\mu}}(X,m)], \tag{48}$$

where $S_{\boldsymbol{\mu}}$ is the canonical scoring function of the mean in Table 1. The variance therefore admits a ridge $\mathcal{F}$-backtest on the maximal class where it is integrable. Its backtest function is given by

$$Z_{\boldsymbol{\sigma}^2}(v,m,x) = v - (x-m)^2, \tag{49}$$

where v and m represent the predictions of the variance and the mean, respectively. The sensitivity to predictions m of the mean is quadratic around $m = \boldsymbol{\mu}(F)$ because $S_{\boldsymbol{\mu}}(y,x)$ is continuously differentiable in y.

The existence of a ridge backtest explains the apparent paradox that despite the fact that the variance is not elicitable (hence not backtestable), it has never been difficult to perform effective backtests, under even rudimental predictions for the mean, such as $m = 0$. Estimation errors in the mean affect the backtest very mildly and only in the prudential direction of penalizing possible underestimations of the variance.

Trivially, being a strictly monotonic transformation of the variance, the standard deviation $\boldsymbol{\sigma} = \sqrt{\boldsymbol{\sigma}^2}$ also admits a ridge backtest

$$Z_{\boldsymbol{\sigma}}(s,m,x) = s^2 - (x-m)^2, \tag{50}$$

for predictions s, as per Definition 4.1.

4.2. *Expected Shortfall*

Let's consider the case of the expected shortfall $\mathbf{ES}_\alpha = -\mathbf{TM}_\alpha$ and $\mathbf{VaR}_\alpha = -\mathbf{q}_\alpha$; see Appendices A.1 and A.2 for definitions. To show that **ES** admits a ridge backtest, we recall from (59) that[11]

$$\mathbf{ES}_\alpha = \min_v \left\{ v + \frac{1}{\alpha}\mathbb{E}[(X+v)_-] \right\},$$

$$\mathbf{VaR}_\alpha = \arg\min_v \left\{ v + \frac{1}{\alpha}\mathbb{E}[(X+v)_-] \right\}. \tag{51}$$

The corresponding backtest function (which is defined up to a positive constant) for predictions e of $\mathbf{ES}_\alpha$ can be written as

$$\begin{aligned} Z_{\mathbf{ES}_\alpha}(e,v,x) &= e - v - (1/\alpha)(x+v)_- \\ &= e - v + (1/\alpha)(x+v)\mathbf{1}_{\{x+v<0\}}, \end{aligned} \tag{52}$$

which is a ridge $\mathcal{F}$-backtest for **ES** on all distributions $F \in \mathcal{F}$ where it exists.

The scoring function of $\mathbf{VaR}_\alpha$ is however not continuously differentiable. The sensitivity to v of the backtest is zero at first order only requiring the same conditions under which the quantile is identifiable, namely that the distribution F be continuous in $\mathbf{q}_\alpha(F) = -\mathbf{VaR}(F)$.

We observe that the ridge backtest (52) is very similar to test Z_2 proposed in Ref. [1], which can be written as

$$Z_2(e,v,x) = e + (1/\alpha)x\mathbf{1}_{\{x+v<0\}}. \tag{53}$$

This expression was derived from (58) in the "simplifying" but unfortunate assumption of continuous distributions under which it satisfies $\mathbb{E}[Z_2(\mathbf{ES},\mathbf{VaR},X)] = 0$. In reality, this test suffers from significant linear sensitivity on the **VaR** prediction v, as it fails to reflect the mechanism of the ridge backtest for **ES**. The sensitivity is present even for continuous distributions, which may appear surprising. Backtest (52) has to be preferred in any circumstance over test (53).

Example 4.3. To illustrate this point, we consider the following experiment: let $F = N(0,1)$ be a real distribution and let

[11]To check that $\hat{S}_{\mathbf{q}_\alpha}(q,x) = -q + (1/\alpha)(x-q)_- = v + (1/\alpha)(x+v)_-$ is a scoring function for $\mathbf{q}_\alpha$ and therefore for $\mathbf{VaR}_\alpha$, note that it coincides with the scoring function $S_{\mathbf{q}_\alpha}$ in Table 1 up to the inessential transformation:

$$\hat{S}_{\mathbf{q}_\alpha}(q,x) = S_{\mathbf{q}_\alpha}(q,x)/\alpha - q.$$

$P_v = N(\mu_v, \sigma_v^2)$ be a family of predictive distributions which forecast $\mathbf{ES}_\alpha = 5\%$ exactly ($e = \mathbf{ES}_\alpha(P_v) = \mathbf{ES}_\alpha(F)$) but yield varying predictions $v = \mathbf{VaR}_\alpha(P_v)$ around $\mathbf{VaR}_\alpha(F)$. Figure 2 plots the behavior of the mean over $T = 250$ days of the two tests in a backtesting procedure (as in Section 3.1.3) meant to exclude underestimations up to significance level $\eta = 95\%$.

From the plot, we see that Z_2 displays significant linear sensitivity to v, possibly leading to model rejection (a type I error) also for relatively small underestimations $v < \mathbf{VaR}_\alpha(F)$. Test $Z_{\mathbf{ES}}$ on the other end displays much lower sensitivity in v, in fact zero at first order, and is affected only in the prudential direction. Rejection can still occur but only for huge estimation errors of $\mathbf{VaR}_\alpha$.

Let's now instead consider predictions chosen in such a way that they all underestimate the expected shortfall $\mathbf{ES}_\alpha(P_v) = 0.8\mathbf{ES}_\alpha(F)$. Figure 3 shows that the linear sensitivity of Z_2 this time can be responsible for the failure to reject a wrong model (type II error), something that will never happen with $Z_{\mathbf{ES}}$ given that its bias sign is prudential.

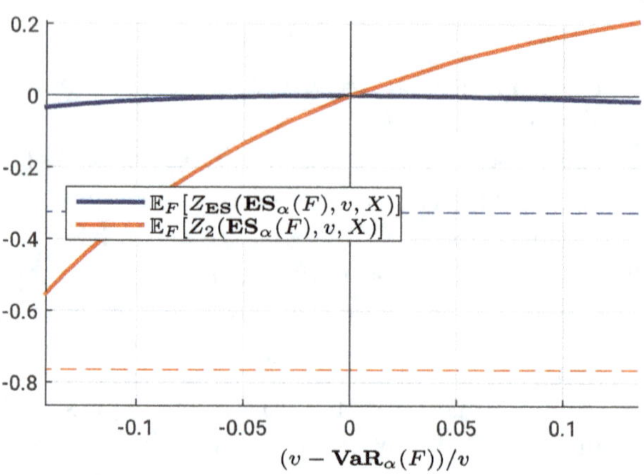

Figure 2. Dependence on v of tests $Z_{\mathbf{ES}}$ and Z_2 in the case of correct predictions for $\mathbf{ES}$. Dashed lines represent critical values at 5% for the two tests. Note the linear sensitivity of the latter and the muted, quadratic sensitivity of the former. We can see that Z_2 can easily generate a type I error.

Source: Ref. [3].

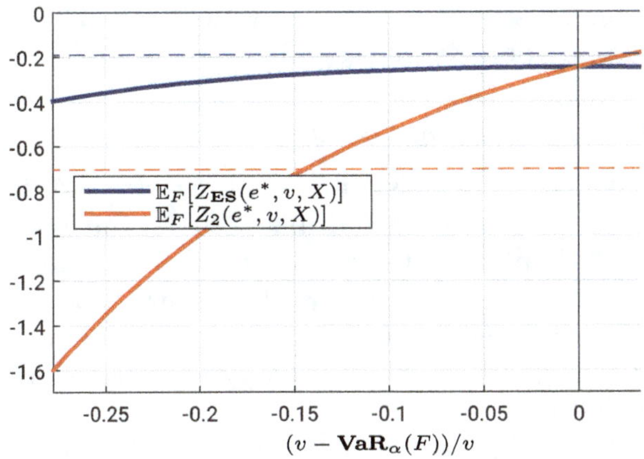

Figure 3. Similar example in the case of an underestimation $e = 0.8\mathbf{ES}$. Z_2 can generate a type II error, while $Z_{\mathbf{ES}}$ cannot.

Source: Ref. [3].

Remark 4.4 (Ridge backtest and banking regulation). The fact that the **ES** admits a ridge backtest is relevant for model validation purposes in the financial industry, notably the banking regulation debate discussed in Section 1.2. The **ES** has long been considered non-backtestable, and strictly speaking, this is true, as our definition of backtestability confirms. We now know, nonetheless, that it admits a backtest which is prudential and negligibly biased, unless **VaR** is grossly misspecified. And up to this bias, the backtest is sharp, namely it provides information also on the magnitude and not only the significance of a prediction discrepancy, as opposed to a traditional **VaR** backtest. Note that if **VaR** were indeed to be completely misspecified, a significant prudential bias would result with the sole effect of rejecting models which issue accidentally correct predictions of **ES** despite a completely wrong model distribution. This may even be a desirable property from a banking regulation point of view.

It is worth observing that in a ridge backtest, the direction of the bias is inherent to the functional and cannot be chosen at will. In the case of **ES** imagined as a risk measure, it is a fortunate coincidence that the bias turns out to be prudential. If for whatever reason someone wanted to test against overestimations of **ES** there would be no ridge backtest that does a prudential job.

For a broader discussion on the relevance of the **ES** ridge backtest for banking regulation, we refer to Ref. [3].

4.2.1. *An Overview of the Literature on* **ES** *Backtesting*

Over the past years, a long list of different *backtests* for **ES** have been proposed in the literature by multiple authors: this may be puzzling because in this chapter, on the contrary, we prove that the **ES** is not backtestable, once we adopt a sensible definition of backtestability, 3.1. Indeed, none of the proposed methods qualifies as a backtest in the sense of our definition, nor it could, given the lack of elicitability of **ES**. It would be naive however to blame the definition as overly restrictive because the common problem to all these proposals is concrete: as we learned from Section 4, any attempt to test predictions of $\mathbf{ES}_\alpha$ will inevitably be affected also by some sensitivity to predictions of other distributional features, for instance, $\mathbf{VaR}_\alpha$. For this reason, all of the proposed **ES** backtests cannot ensure to reward better predictors of **ES**, which is exactly what we would expect for them to be called **ES** backtests.

For instance, the tests proposed in Refs. [1] and [24] (tests 1 and 2) are correct backtests of $\mathbf{ES}_\alpha$ only conditionally to the $\mathbf{VaR}_\alpha$ prediction being exact, and they bear significant linear sensitivity to $\mathbf{VaR}_\alpha$ mispredictions, a fact that is not remarked in those papers. Note that the ridge backtest for **ES** is in the same league, but at least it stands out in that the sensitivity to **VaR** is small and prudential under any distributional assumptions.

In some other cases [9–11, 23, 25], what is actually being tested is not **ES** but some other quantity introduced by pure analogy. Instructive is the case of [9–11, 23] where the test variable is chosen to be the *generalized breach indicator*

$$X_{\mathbf{ES}} \equiv \frac{1}{\alpha}\int_0^\alpha \mathbf{1}_{\{X<-\mathbf{VaR}_p\}}dp$$

chosen in analogy with formula (56). Natural as this choice may sound, it is a fact that the p-average of $\mathbf{VaR}_p$ breach rates is not the breach rate of the p-average of $\mathbf{VaR}_p$ (i.e., the **ES**). Under this test, a perfect predictor of **ES** can rank as anything in between a bad overestimator and a bad underestimator, depending on other features of the predictive distribution.

In other cases, the decision to approximate **ES** is declared, such as in Ref. [14], where the authors adopt the average of four $\mathbf{VaR}_p$ as a proxy. The authors of Ref. [21] elaborate on this idea and propose a multinomial test over the breach frequencies of those **VaR** levels. The authors also introduce the useful distinction between explicit and implicit backtests for **ES**, admitting that the latter are tests of the entire tail distribution, only indirectly related to **ES**. Among these implicit tests, they mention their own paper [21], the seminal work [20] and the above-mentioned [9–11]; we also add test 3 in Ref. [1].

Finally, an interesting body of literature [8, 15, 27] is represented by proposals based on the joint elicitability of **ES** and **VaR** introduced in Refs. [1, 16]. This is however yet another way of admitting that a pure evaluation of **ES** predictions is not possible and some joint evaluation of **ES** and **VaR** predictions is necessary. Moreover, as the authors in Ref. [27] state, there is no natural classical choice for the functional form of the joint scoring function, and any legitimate choice will change the importance of **VaR** in the backtest, something that in our opinion deserves further study.

5. Conclusions

Despite the existence of widespread and consolidated practices, a clear definition of backtestability of a functional has long struggled to emerge. We believe that if there's a property that deserves this name, it is the existence of a backtest function, namely a function only of the prediction and the random variable (the only two quantities that are observable in an experiment), which is strictly monotonic in the prediction and has zero expected value when the prediction is correct. This is what allows to set up a proper hypothesis backtesting.

Not all backtests, however, are also strictly monotonic in the real value of the functional, for a fixed prediction. We call this property sharpness because the expected value of such a backtest determines exactly the real value of the functional, providing information also on the extent of the discrepancy of a wrong prediction. Sharpness is a natural requirement for a backtest if we want louder warnings for worse discrepancies. Non-sharp backtests (quantile and expectile) provide limited if any information at all on the possible real values of the functional.

Some functionals (variance and expected shortfall), despite being not backtestable, admit a backtest function that depends also on another auxiliary variable (resp., the mean and value at risk) but on an extremal point. The corresponding backtest (ridge backtest) has muted sensitivity with respect to the prediction of the auxiliary variable and known bias sign. This is the mechanism that has always allowed for effective tests of variance predictions without caring much if the predictions of the mean were accurate.

We show that the same ridge backtest mechanism allows for effective ways to backtest the expected shortfall. For a fortunate circumstance, the muted bias due to value at risk predictions falls on the right side of prudence when it comes to detecting underestimations of the expected shortfall, which represents the natural use case for a risk measure. This backtest is also sharp, as opposed to the backtest of value at risk which is completely blind to the magnitude of prediction errors. This result is relevant for banking regulatory standards, which are now adopting expected shortfall as a risk measure for capital adequacy but are still based on backtests of value at risk.

Appendix

A. Definitions of Relevant Functionals

We collect the definitions adopted for the concepts of quantile, tail mean and expectile. When changed sign, these functionals are used to define tail risk measures on a profit–loss distribution, respectively, known as value at risk, expected shortfall and expectile risk.

In this section, X denotes a random variable with distribution function F and integrability properties specified case by case. We will denote by $\alpha \in (0, 1)$ a confidence level, typically small.

A.1. *Quantile and Value at Risk*

Definition A.1 (Quantile and value at risk). Given a r.v. $X \in L_0$, we define the *α-quantile* as the interval-valued quantity

$$\mathbf{q}_\alpha(F) = [x_\alpha, x^\alpha], \tag{54}$$

where the lower and upper quantiles are respectively defined by

$$\begin{cases} x_\alpha = \inf\{x|F(x) \geq \alpha\} \\ x^\alpha = \sup\{x|F(x) \leq \alpha\} \end{cases}. \tag{55}$$

We define *value at risk* as the opposite of the quantile, $\mathbf{VaR}_\alpha = -\mathbf{q}_\alpha$.

$\mathbf{q}_\alpha$ is a single-valued functional if and only if the inverse image $F^{-1}(\alpha)$ is single-valued or empty for all $\alpha \in (0,1)$.

A.2. *Tail Mean and Expected Shortfall*

Definition A.2 (Tail Mean and Expected Shortfall). Given a random variable[12] $X \in L_1$, we define the *tail mean* as [4]

$$\mathbf{TM}_\alpha(F) = \frac{1}{\alpha}\int_0^\alpha \mathbf{q}_t(F)\,dt. \tag{56}$$

We define the *expected shortfall* as the opposite of the tail mean, $\mathbf{ES}_\alpha = -\mathbf{TM}_\alpha$.

An equivalent useful formulation [4] is given by[13]

$$\begin{aligned} \mathbf{TM}_\alpha(F) &= \frac{1}{\alpha}\mathbb{E}_F\{X\mathbf{1}_{\{X-\mathbf{q}_\alpha(F)<0\}} + \mathbf{q}_\alpha(F)[\alpha - \mathbf{1}_{\{X-\mathbf{q}_\alpha(F)<0\}}]\} \\ &= \mathbf{q}_\alpha(F) - \frac{1}{\alpha}\mathbb{E}_F[(X-\mathbf{q}_\alpha(F))_-]. \end{aligned} \tag{57}$$

Note that when $\mathbf{TM}_\alpha$ exists, it is always single-valued, even when $\mathbf{q}_p$ is interval-valued for some $p \in [0,\alpha]$. Formulae (56) and (57) do not depend on the choice of a single value $\mathbf{q}_p \in [x_\alpha, x^\alpha]$ when needed. Also, (57) remains valid if strict inequalities $<$ are replaced with $\leq$. See Ref. [4].

---

[12] It is sufficient to require that only the left tail be L_1.

[13] We use the standard notation for the positive part $(x)_+ = \max(x,0) = x\mathbf{1}_{\{x>0\}}$ and negative part $(x)_- = -\min(x,0) = -x\mathbf{1}_{\{x<0\}}$ of a number x.

We report here also two widely used alternative expressions that hold for continuous distributions.

$$\mathbf{TM}_\alpha(F) \overset{F\,\text{cont.}}{=} \frac{1}{\alpha}\mathbb{E}_F\{X\mathbf{1}_{\{X-\mathbf{q}_\alpha(F)<0\}}\} \overset{F\,\text{cont.}}{=} \mathbb{E}_F\{X|X<\mathbf{q}_\alpha(F)\}. \tag{58}$$

More generally, the equalities hold for all distributions for which $Prob\{X < \mathbf{q}_\alpha(F)\} = \alpha$. For non-continuous distributions, on the contrary, these three expressions may all be different.

Finally, we recall the classical result of Uryasev and Rockafellar [4, 29] that shows that Eq. (57) can be expressed as an optimization, in which $\mathbf{ES}_\alpha$ plays the role of the attained minimum and $\mathbf{VaR}_\alpha$ of the minimizer of the same expression (a scoring function for $\mathbf{VaR}_\alpha$).

$$\mathbf{ES}_\alpha(F) = \min_v \left\{ v + \frac{1}{\alpha}\mathbb{E}_F[(X+v)_-] \right\},$$

$$\mathbf{VaR}_\alpha(F) = \arg\min_v \left\{ v + \frac{1}{\alpha}\mathbb{E}_F[(X+v)_-] \right\}. \tag{59}$$

A.3. *Expectile*

Definition A.3 (Expectile). For $X \in L_1$, the *expectile* $\mathbf{e}_\alpha(F)$ is defined as the solution of [13, 26]

$$\alpha\mathbb{E}_F[(X-\mathbf{e}_\alpha(F))_+] = (1-\alpha)\mathbb{E}_F[(X-\mathbf{e}_\alpha(F))_-]. \tag{60}$$

In the special case $\alpha = 1/2$, the expectile coincides with the mean of the distribution.

The corresponding tail risk measure, differing by an overall sign, is sometimes called *expectile risk* or more often simply expectile without risk of ambiguity.

References

[1] C. Acerbi and B. Szekely. Back-testing expected shortfall. *Risk*, 27(11):76–81, 2014.

[2] C. Acerbi and B. Szekely. General properties of backtestable statistics. SSRN preprint, 2017. https://ssrn.com/abstract=2905109.

[3] C. Acerbi and B. Szekely. The minimally biased backtest for ES. *Risk Magazine*, September 2019.

[4] C. Acerbi and D. Tasche. On the coherence of expected shortfall. *Journal of Banking & Finance*, 26:1487–1503, 2002.

[5] Basel Committee on Banking Supervision. Amendment to the capital accord to incorporate market risks, 1996. http://www.bis.org/publ/bcbs24.pdf.

[6] Basel Committee on Banking Supervision. Minimum capital requirements for market risk, 2019. http://www.bis.org/bcbs/publ/d457.pdf.

[7] P. Artzner, F. Delbaen, J. M. Eber, and D. Heath. Coherent measures of risk. *Mathematical Finance*, 9(3):203–208, 1999.

[8] S. Bayer and T. Dimitriadis. Regression based expected shortfall backtesting. *Journal of Financial Econometrics*, 20(3):437–471, 2022.

[9] N. Costanzino and M. Curran. Backtesting General spectral risk measures with application to expected shortfall, SSRN preprint, 2015 https://ssrn.com/abstract=2514403

[10] N. Costanzino and M. Curran. A simple traffic light approach to backtesting expected shortfall. *Risks*, 6(1):1–7, 2018.

[11] Z. Du and J. C. Escanciano. Backtesting expected shortfall: Accounting for tail risk. *Management Science*, 63(4):901–1269, 2017.

[12] Basel Committee on Banking Supervision. Fundamental review of the trading book: A revised market risk framework, Consultative Paper, 2013.

[13] F. Bellini, B. Klar, A. Müller, and Rosazza E. Gianin. Generalized quantiles as risk measures. *Insurance: Mathematics and Economics*, 54(C):41–48, 2014.

[14] S. Emmer, M. Kratz, and D. Tasche. What is the best risk measure in practice? A comparison of standard measures. *The Journal of Risk*, 18(2):31–60, 2015.

[15] T. Fissler, T. Gneiting, and J. F. Ziegel. (2015) Expected shortfall is jointly elicitable with value–at–risk: Implications for backtesting, *Risk*, December 2015.

[16] T. Fissler and J. F. Ziegel. Higher order elicitability and Osband's principle. *The Annals of Statistics*, 44(4):1680–1707, 2016.

[17] T. Gneiting. Making and evaluating point forecasts. *Journal of the American Statistical Association*, 106(494):746–762, 2011.

[18] International Association of Insurance Supervisors. Risk-based global insurance capital standard, public consultation document, 2014.

[19] International Association of Insurance Supervisors. Risk-based global insurance capital standard, Version 1.0, public consultation document, 2016.

[20] J. Kerkhof and B. Melenberg. Backtesting for risk-based regulatory capital. *Journal of Banking & Finance*, 28(8):1845–1865, 2004.

[21] M. Kratz, Y. H. Lok, and A. J. McNeil. Multinomial VaR backtests: A simple implicit approach to backtesting expected shortfall. *The Journal of Banking & Finance*, 88(C):393–407, 2018.

[22] N. Lambert, D. M. Pennock, and Y. Shoham. Eliciting properties of probability distributions. *Proceedings of the 9th ACM Conference on Electronic Commerce, EC 08*, 2008.

[23] R. Loser, D. Wied, and D. Ziggel. New backtests for unconditional coverage of expected shortfall. *Journal of Risk*, 21:4, 2018.

[24] A. J. McNeil and R. Frey. Estimation of tail-related risk measures for heteroscedastic financial time series: An extreme value approach. *Journal of Empirical Finance*, 7(3-4), 2000.

[25] F. Moldenhauer and M. Pitera. Backtesting expected shortfall: A simple recipe. *The Journal of Risk*, 22(1):17–42, 2019.

[26] W. K. Newey and J. L. Powell. Asymmetric least squares estimation and testing. *Econometrica*, 55(4):819–847, 1987.

[27] N. Nolde and J. F. Ziegel. Elicitability and backtesting: Perspectives for banking regulation. *The Annals of Applied Statistics*, 11(4):1833–1874, 2017.

[28] K. H. Osband. Providing incentives for better cost forecasting. Ph.D. thesis, University of California, Berkeley, 1985.

[29] R. T. Rockafellar and S. Uryasev. Conditional value–at–risk for general loss distributions. *Journal of Banking & Finance*, 26(7):1443–1471, 2002.

[30] J. F. Ziegel. Coherence and elicitability. *Mathematical Finance*, 26(4):901–918, 2016.

https://doi.org/10.1142/9789811280306_0004

Chapter 4

A Deep Learning Scheme for Solving Fully Nonlinear Partial Differential Equation

Maxim Bichuch[*,‡] **and Ke Chen**[†,§]

[*]*Department of Mathematics, SUNY at Buffalo, 317 Mathematics Building Buffalo, NY 14260, USA*

[†]*Department of Applied Mathematics and Statistics, Whiting School of Engineering, Johns Hopkins University, 3400 North Charles St., Baltimore, MD 21218, USA*

[‡]*mbichuch@buffalo.edu*

[§]*kchen78@jhu.edu*

Abstract

We study the convergence of a deep learning algorithm applied to a general class of fully nonlinear second-order partial differential equations. By using a suitable finite difference approximation to the loss function of the deep learning scheme, we show the convergence of the numerical solution to the unique viscosity solution. We apply our results and illustrate this convergence to the finite horizon optimal investment problem with proportional transaction costs in single and multi-asset settings.

Keywords: Deep learning, Machine learning, Partial differential equation, Convergence, Optimal investment, Transaction costs

1. Introduction

Convergence of the numerical solution to the true solution is a classical question in numerical analysis. When the true solution is known, this question can be easily answered once the numerical solution is obtained, but when the true solution is unknown, the question becomes significantly more difficult. In recent years, numerical solutions using neural networks applied to financial problems have gained significant attention. In this chapter, our goal is to prove convergence of a numerical solution from a neural network to viscosity solution of a fully nonlinear Partial Differential Equation (PDE). We then illustrate it by numerically solving the finite horizon optimal investment problem with transaction costs, a problem whose analytical solution is not known in multi-asset setting.

Ref. [23] summarized that a two-layer perception is not able to approximate functions unless the functions belong to a very special class but left the approximation capability of multilayer problem open. The celebrated result of Ref. [19] rigorously presented that the standard multilayer feedforward networks (even single hidden layer network) can approximate any Borel measurable function with sufficiently many neurons on the hidden layer. This result was later improved in Ref. [20] who proved further that with an appropriately smooth activation function, the multilayer feedforward networks are able to approximate not only the function itself but also its derivatives even in a generalized sense. These results are now usually referred to as the universal approximation theorems. They show that the approximators from the multilayer neural networks estimate a large class of functions in different norms, such as L_∞ or $\mathbf{W}^{k,p}$ norms. Ref. [15] also presented similar result and illustrate these results with the inverse problem of chaotic dynamics.

These results in turn were used to study the possibility of solving ordinary differential equations and PDEs using artificial neural network. Ref. [22] proposed a numerical method to solve linear and nonlinear PDEs. They used a linear Poisson equation and thermal conduction with nonlinear heat generation as examples to show how straightforward the method is and compared the numerical solution with the analytic solutions to show that the method can provide good-quality solutions. Ref. [21] proposed a method to solve initial boundary value problem using feedforward deep neural networks which can fit the boundary conditions. Their idea is to split the solution of the PDE into two parts: a smooth part without any optimization parameters that can exactly fit the initial/boundary condition and the other part with adjustable parameters which will vanish on the boundary. They verify the efficiency of their method by comparing the numerical solutions with the solutions from the Galerkin finite element method. Ref. [1] introduced a method to incorporate the structure of the PDE and its boundary and/or initial conditions into the structure of the networks. They obtained promising results when applying their algorithm to a damped free vibration problem and a one-dimensional non-steady groundwater flow problem. In addition to the fixed boundary problems, deep learning scheme can also be used to solve free boundary problems. Ref. [31] introduced a new algorithm based on an analogy between the Backward Stochastic Differential Equation (BSDE) and reinforcement learning. By using the error between the solution of the BSDE and the terminal condition as the loss function, they solved a number of high-dimensional nonlinear PDEs from physics and finance such as the Hamilton–Jacobi–Bellman (HJB) equation numerically. Solving optimal control problems with neural networks is also discussed in Ref. [7]. Deep learning of optimal control through PDE solutions is discussed in Ref. [14,16] and in many references therein. Free boundary problems appear also in optimal stopping problem, and their solution by deep learning is done, e.g., by Refs. [4,5]. Additional deep learning techniques are discussed in Refs. [6,9,12,26–28]. Ref. [17] applied this simulation-based deep learning approach to solve the risk-sharing equilibrium problem with general convex costs on the agents' trading rate. Ref. [30] solved another type of free boundary problem, the Stefan problem, with deep neural network. Their numerical result showed that it is possible to learn the solution and the boundary together by using two or more neural networks, one is to learn the solution and the others are used to learn the free boundaries, and adding the characterization of the free boundary into the loss function.

Although there has been enough empirical evidence for the solvability of deep neural network for partial differential equation, to the best of our knowledge, there are few results that also prove convergence of their deep learning scheme from theoretical perspective. Ref. [29] presented a deep learning algorithm with both numerical results and an accompanied theorem that showed the existence of numerical approximator together with a proof of convergence. They presented a Deep Galerkin Method (DGM): a deep learning algorithm for solving PDEs. In addition to the elegant numerical results for solving different kinds of PDEs, they proved that the loss function converges to zero, and the approximated function f_n will converge to the unique solution in the $\mathbf{L}^q$, $q > 1$ sense. However, a crucial assumption to use these results is the *a priori* knowledge that the true solution is smooth is required.

In financial mathematics, a common example of a nonlinear PDE is an HJB equation. While the existence and uniqueness of a viscosity solution are usually not difficult to prove, it can be very hard to show that this solution is in fact a classical solution of the PDE. Ref. [3] showed that the solution to a monotone, stable and consistent numerical scheme converges to the viscosity solution locally uniformly. Ref. [25] showed that a degenerate elliptic property of a finite difference scheme is stronger than monotone and stable but much easier to verify. In this chapter, we propose a deep learning scheme which suitably approximates the loss function via a finite difference with which the existence of numerical approximator and convergence result is then proved.

The rest of this chapter is structured as follows: In Section 2, we present the background, the motivation, the construction of our deep learning scheme and our main theoretical results. In Section 3, we use the finite difference equation of the finite horizon optimal investment problem with proportional transaction cost as an example to show how to construct the loss function. In Section 4, we solve the one- and two-dimensional finite horizon optimal investment problems with transaction costs numerically with the deep learning scheme. We conclude with a brief summary in Section 5.

2. Deep Learning Method for Solving Fully Nonlinear Second-Order Degenerate Elliptic Problem

In this section, we propose a deep learning scheme for solving a general class of fully nonlinear second-order degenerate elliptic PDE, especially an HJB equation. Our scheme is a combination of finite difference scheme and deep learning. We are then able to prove the convergence of this scheme to the true (viscosity) solution of the PDE. The loss function is constructed using finite difference and using the fact that the minimizer of the loss function is the (unique) solution to the finite difference scheme. In Section 2.1, we go over the related definitions and results. We explain the idea of why a finite difference approximation is used to construct the loss function, and, in Section 2.2, we provide a set of sufficient conditions for the existence of numerical approximator and the convergence result for a general class of second-order fully nonlinear equations.

2.1. *Motivation and Theoretical Preparation*

Consider a second-order fully nonlinear degenerate elliptic PDE

$$\begin{cases} F(x, u, Du, D^2u) = 0, & x \in \Omega, \\ u(x) = g(x), & x \in \partial\Omega, \end{cases} \tag{1}$$

with a unique viscosity solution u and where $\Omega \subset \mathbb{R}^n$ is open and bounded, $n \geq 1$. Suppose that F is proper, that is,

Assumption 2.1. 1. For $x \in \mathbb{R}^n,\ s \in \mathbb{R},\ p \in \mathbb{R}^n,\ M, \tilde{M} \in \mathbb{S}(n)$,

$$F(x, s, p, M) \geq F(x, s, p, \tilde{M}), \quad \text{if } M \leq \tilde{M}, \tag{2}$$

where $\mathbb{S}(n)$ is the set of square, symmetric matrices of size n, and where $M \leq \tilde{M}$ means $\tilde{M} - M$ is positive semi-definite.

2. For $x \in \mathbb{R}^n,\ t, s \in \mathbb{R},\ p \in \mathbb{R}^n,\ M \in \mathbb{S}(n)$,

$$F(x, t, p, M) \geq F(x, s, p, M), \quad s \leq t. \tag{3}$$

Property (2) is referred to as the degenerate elliptic property, and together with (3), F is said to be proper. While these two properties of F are fundamental properties, they cannot guarantee the existence of a classical solution. On the other hand, if u is a viscosity solution of problem (1), $F(x, u, Du, D^2u)$ may not be (pointwise) well defined. Hence, it is not suitable to use $\mathbf{L}^2$ loss function for solving this PDE.

Throughout this chapter, we will assume that the operator F satisfies Assumption 2.1 and write $F[u](x) \equiv F(x, u(x), Du(x), D^2u(x)), \forall x \in \Omega$.

The idea is to construct a suitable loss function to make sure that our deep learning scheme converges to a finite difference scheme. In turn, according to Ref. [3], a finite difference scheme that is monotone, stable and consistent will converge to the viscosity solution of (1) locally uniformly. However, it is usually hard to check the monotonicity and stability of a finite difference scheme. Thanks to Ref. [25], a degenerate elliptic scheme enjoys monotonicity and stability, a property we will use to construct our loss function in this chapter. Next, we briefly introduce the consistency and degenerate elliptic properties of a finite difference scheme.

For a real-valued function u, let $F_{\Delta x}[u]$ be the finite difference scheme of F for u. In general, the scheme can be defined locally, that is, at any fixed point x, let $D_{\Delta x}u(x), D^2_{\Delta x}u(x)$ be the finite difference approximation of the first- and second-order derivatives evaluated at x. For example, $(D_{\Delta x})_i u(x) = \frac{u(x+\Delta x e_i)-u(x-\Delta x e_i)}{2\Delta x}$, $(D^2_{\Delta x})_i u(x) = \frac{u(x+\Delta x e_i)-2u(x)+u(x-\Delta x e_i)}{\Delta x^2}$, where $\{e_i\}_{i=1,\dots,n}$ is the standard basis. Then, $F_{\Delta x}[u](x) = F(x, u(x), D_{\Delta x}u(x), D^2_{\Delta x}u(x))$. As the finite difference approximation of the derivatives depends on the difference between $u(x)$ and the function evaluated at other points in $\mathcal{M}_{\Delta x}(x)$ inside $\mathcal{N}_{\Delta x}(x)$, a neighborhood of x, therefore $F_{\Delta x}[u](x)$ can be expressed as a function of $x, \Delta x, u(x), u(x_j) - u(x)$, for some $x_j \in \mathcal{M}_{\Delta x}(x)$. Then, there exist a function $H(\Delta x, x, u(x), u(x_j) - u(x)|_{x_j \in \mathcal{M}_{\Delta x}(x)})$ such that

$$F_{\Delta x}[u](x) = H\left(\Delta x, x, u(x), u(x) - u(x_j)|_{x_j \in \mathcal{M}_{\Delta x}(x)}\right). \tag{4}$$

We can now introduce the definitions of consistency, stability and monotonicity:

Definition 2.2 (Consistent Scheme). A finite difference scheme $F_{\Delta x}$ is consistent if for any $u \in C^\infty(\bar{\Omega})$, $x \in \Omega$:

$$F_{\Delta x}[u](x) \to F(x, u(x), Du(x), D^2u(x)), \qquad \text{as } \Delta x \to 0. \tag{5}$$

Definition 2.3 (Degenerate Elliptic Scheme). A scheme $F_{\Delta x}$ for PDE (1) is degenerate elliptic, if for any fixed $x \in \Omega$ and $\Delta x \in \mathbb{R}^+$ small enough, the function $G(\cdot,\cdot)$ is non-decreasing in each variables, where $G(y, \mathbf{z}) = H(\Delta x, x, y, \mathbf{z})$, $(y, \mathbf{z}) \in \mathbb{R}^{|\mathcal{M}_{\Delta x}(x)|+1}$ and H as in (4).

To ensure the existence of a numerical solution, we need two more properties of the numerical scheme: proper and Lipschitz continuity.

Definition 2.4 (Proper Scheme). A finite difference scheme $F_{\Delta x}$ is proper if there is a constant $\delta > 0$ such that for any $x \in \Omega$, $\mathbf{z} \in \mathbb{R}^{|\mathcal{M}_{\Delta x}|}$, $y_1, y_2 \in \mathbb{R}$, $y_1 \leq y_2$, we have that

$$H(\Delta x, x, y_1, \mathbf{z}) - H(\Delta x, x, y_2, \mathbf{z}) \geq \delta(y_2 - y_1). \tag{6}$$

Definition 2.5 (Lipschitz Continuous Scheme). A finite difference scheme $F_{\Delta x}$ is Lipschitz continuous if there is a constant $L > 0$ such that for all $x \in \Omega$, $\mathbf{z}_1, \mathbf{z}_2 \in \mathbb{R}^{|\mathcal{M}(x)|+1}$,

$$|H(\Delta x, x, \mathbf{z}_1) - H(\Delta x, x, \mathbf{z}_2)| \leq L||\mathbf{z}_1 - \mathbf{z}_2||_{l^\infty}. \tag{7}$$

Assumption 2.6. The finite difference scheme $F_{\Delta x}$ is proper, Lipschitz continuous and degenerate elliptic.

Let $\mathcal{N}$ be a grid of $\bar{\Omega}$ and $I = \{1, \ldots, |\mathcal{N}|\}$ be the index of the points in $\mathcal{N}$. Denote $u^{\Delta x}$ as a continuous function defined on the closure of the domain Ω which is the solution to the finite difference scheme $F_{\Delta x}$, i.e., satisfying $F_{\Delta x}[u](x_i) = 0, i \in I$. Additionally, let $\hat{u}^{\Delta x}$ be the deep learning approximator. For convenience, let $u_i^{\Delta x} = u^{\Delta x}(x_i), \hat{u}_i^{\Delta x} = \hat{u}^{\Delta x}(x_i),\ x_i \in \mathcal{N}, i \in I$.

Remark 2.7. 1. The uniqueness of the solution to the finite difference scheme $F_{\Delta x}$ can only be on the points of the grid. That is, for a fixed grid $\mathcal{N}$, the solution of $F_{\Delta x}[u] = 0$ is unique if $F_{\Delta x}[u](x_i) = 0, F_{\Delta x}[v](x_i) = 0,\ x_i \in \mathcal{N}$ then $u|_{\mathcal{N}} \neq v|_{\mathcal{N}}$.

2. According to Ref. [25][Theorem 8], a proper and Lipschitz continuous degenerate elliptic scheme has a unique numerical solution.

The idea is to first approximate the viscosity solution u by finite difference solution $u^{\Delta x}$ and in turn approximate it with the deep neural network solution $\hat{u}^{\Delta x}$. Then, we can conclude the convergence result of $\hat{u}^{\Delta x}$ to $u^{\Delta x}$ which in turn converges to u.

We construct the loss function for the deep learning algorithm as

$$\mathcal{R}(v) = \sum_{i=1}^{|\mathcal{N}|} (F_{\Delta x}[v](x_i))^2. \tag{8}$$

Therefore, the solution $u^{\Delta x}$ exists and is unique by Remark 2.7 and is the (unique up the grid values) global minimizer of (8).

Before we present the theoretical results, let's define some notation related to the neural network. The function space defined by a shallow network with N neurons on the hidden layer and $h\colon \mathbb{R}^n \to \mathbb{R}$ as the activation function on the hidden layer is the set

$$\mathcal{G}^N(h) = \{\hat{u}(\cdot;\Theta) : \mathbb{R}^n \to \mathbb{R} : \ \hat{u}(x) = \sum_{i=1}^{N} \beta_i h(\sum_{j=1}^{n} w_{j,i} x_j + b_j)\}, \quad (9)$$

where $\Theta = (\beta_1, \dots \beta_n, w_{1,1}, \dots w_{n,N}, b_1, \dots, b_n)$ is the set of training parameters of the deep learning scheme.$\beta_i, w_{j,i} \in \mathbb{R}, \ b_i \in \mathbb{R}^n, \ i = 1, \dots, n, \ j = 1, \dots, N$. Also, set

$$\mathcal{G}(h) = \cup_{N=1}^{\infty} \mathcal{G}^N(h). \quad (10)$$

2.2. *Existence of Numerical Solution and Convergence Result*

Theorem 2.8. *Fix a grid $\mathcal{N}$. Suppose that Assumption 2.6 holds and $h \in \mathbf{C}(\mathbb{R}^n)$ is non-constant and bounded. Then, for every $\epsilon > 0$, there exists a function $v \in \mathcal{G}(h)$ such that*

$$\mathcal{R}(v) \le \epsilon.$$

Proof. According to Assumption 2.6 and by Remark 2.7, there exist a unique solution $u^{\Delta x}$ to the finite difference scheme on the grid $\mathcal{N}$. By linear interpolation, assume that $u^{\Delta x}$ is a continuous function on the entire domain $\bar{\Omega}$. By the universal approximation theorem of Ref. [18][Theorem 3], for fixed $\epsilon > 0$, there exists a function $v \in \mathcal{G}(h)$ such that

$$\sup_{x \in \bar{\Omega}} |v(x) - u^{\Delta x}(x)| \le \frac{\sqrt{\epsilon}}{L\sqrt{N}}, \quad (11)$$

where L is the Lipschitz constant of the finite difference scheme $F_{\Delta x}$. Hence, for every $i \in I$, $|F_{\Delta x}[v](x_i)| \le L\frac{\sqrt{\epsilon}}{L\sqrt{N}} = \sqrt{\frac{\epsilon}{N}}$ which implies that $\mathcal{R}(v) \le \epsilon$. □

Next, we estimate the error bound for the deep learning algorithm.

Theorem 2.9. *Fix a grid $\mathcal{N}$ and an $\epsilon > 0$. Suppose $F_{\Delta x}$ is a finite difference scheme satisfying Assumption* 2.6. *Let $u^{\Delta x}$ be the unique solution to this finite difference scheme. Let $\hat{u}^{\Delta x}$ be an output of the neural network satisfying $\mathcal{R}(\hat{u}^{\Delta x}) < \epsilon$, then*

$$\max_{1\leq i\leq|\mathcal{N}|} |\hat{u}^{\Delta x}(x_i) - u^{\Delta x}(x_i)| \leq C\sqrt{\epsilon}, \tag{12}$$

where C is a constant that may only depend on δ, the constant in the definition of a proper scheme 2.4.

Proof. From the assumption that $\mathcal{R}(\hat{u}^{\Delta x}) = \sum_{i=1}^{|\mathcal{N}|}(F_{\Delta x}[\hat{u}](x_i))^2 < \epsilon$, it follows that for every $i \in I$, we have that $(F_{\Delta x}[\hat{u}](x_i))^2 < \epsilon$, and thus $|F_{\Delta x}[\hat{u}^{\Delta x}](x_i)| \leq \sqrt{\epsilon}$.

Define $\hat{v}^{\Delta x} = \hat{u}^{\Delta x} + \frac{\sqrt{\epsilon}}{\delta}$, then $F_{\Delta x}[\hat{v}^{\Delta x}](x_i) - F_{\Delta x}[\hat{u}^{\Delta x}](x_i) \geq \delta(\hat{v}^{\Delta x}(x_i) - \hat{u}^{\Delta x}(x_i)) = \sqrt{\epsilon}$, and hence, $F_{\Delta x}[\hat{v}_{\Delta x}](x_i) \geq 0$. According to Ref. [25][Theorem 5], we have that $u^{\Delta x} \leq \hat{v}^{\Delta x}$, and hence, $u^{\Delta x} - \hat{u}^{\Delta x} \leq \frac{\sqrt{\epsilon}}{\delta}$.

Now, let $v^{\Delta x} = u^{\Delta x} + \frac{\sqrt{\epsilon}}{\delta}$, then similarly, $F_{\Delta}[v^{\Delta}](x_i) \geq \sqrt{\epsilon}$ and in turn, $\sqrt{\epsilon} \geq F_{\Delta x}[\hat{u}^{\Delta x}](x_i)$. Then again, by Ref. [25][Theorem 5], we have that $\hat{u}^{\Delta x} \leq v^{\Delta x}$, and we conclude that $\hat{u}^{\Delta x} - u^{\Delta x} \leq \frac{\sqrt{\epsilon}}{\delta}$.

Altogether, it follows that we have $\max_{1\leq i\leq|\mathcal{N}|} |\hat{u}^{\Delta x}(x_i) - u^{\Delta x}(x_i)| \leq \frac{\sqrt{\epsilon}}{\delta}$. □

Finally, combining this with the fundamental result for the convergence of numerical schemes for fully nonlinear, degenerate elliptic equation of Ref. [3] summarized in Theorem 2.10, we have our convergence locally uniformly convergence result.

Theorem 2.10. *Suppose $F_{\Delta x}$ is a consistent, stable and monotone numerical scheme for problem* (1), *then the solution to the numerical scheme converges locally uniformly to the unique viscosity solution of* (1).

Corollary 2.11. *Suppose $F_{\Delta x}$ is a consistent and degenerate elliptic numerical scheme for problem* (1), *then the solution to the numerical scheme converges locally uniformly to the unique viscosity solution of* (1).

Proof. According to Ref. [25][Theorem 3], a degenerate elliptic scheme enjoys both monotonicity and strong form of stability. Hence, by Theorem 2.10, the solution to the numerical scheme converges locally uniformly to the unique viscosity solution. □

2.3. *Construction of Degenerate Elliptic Finite Difference Scheme*

The goal now is to construct a degenerate elliptic finite difference scheme with a good accuracy. Once we achieve that, we can create a loss function and by appealing to the universal approximation theorem of Ref. [18][Theorem 3] and Theorem 2.9 to provide theoretical guarantee for the existence of numerical solution and convergence result for deep learning algorithm. In general, even for a second-order linear PDE, it is not easy to construct a monotone scheme with quadratic order accuracy. However, this does not mean it is impossible to build a degenerate elliptic scheme, if we accept lower accuracy. The main issue comes from the second-order cross-derivative term. In this section, we introduce a way to construct degenerate elliptic finite difference scheme with $O(\sqrt{\Delta x})$ stencil.

2.3.1. *Remove the Second-order Cross-derivatives*

To construct a degenerate elliptic scheme, the main issue comes from the second-order cross-derivative terms. Hence, the first step is removing the cross-derivatives by using local coordinate transformation. In this section, we focus on how to remove the second-order cross-derivatives so that we use second-order linear equation with only second-order terms as an example. Note that the method also works for general second-order degenerate elliptic partial differential equations.

Consider

$$\begin{cases} -\operatorname{trace}\big(A(x)D^2u(x)\big) = 0, & x \in \Omega, \\ u(x) = g(x), & x \in \partial\Omega, \end{cases} \tag{13}$$

where $A(x) \in \mathbb{S}^n \subset \mathbb{S}(n)$, and $\mathbb{S}^n$ is the set of symmetric, positive semi-definite matrices, for any $x \in \Omega$. Therefore, for any $x \in \Omega$, there exists a diagonal matrix $L(x)$ whose diagonal elements are the eigenvalues of $A(x)$ and an orthonormal matrix $V(x)$ whose columns are eigenvectors of $A(x)$ such that $V^T(x)A(x)V(x) = L(x)$.

Then,

$$\begin{aligned} A(x)D^2u(x) &= V(x)L(x)V^T(x)D^2u(x) \\ &= V(x)L(x)V^T(x)D^2u(x)V(x)V^T(x). \end{aligned} \quad (14)$$

Denote $V(x) = (v_1(x), \dots, v_n(x))$, where $\{v_i(x)\}_{i=1,\dots,n}$ is a set of orthonormal basis in $\mathbb{R}^n$, $L(x) = diag(l_1(x), l_2(x), \dots, l_n(x))$ and $H(x) = V^T(x)D^2u(x)V(x) = \{h_{ij}(x)\}_{i,j=1,\dots,n}$.

Then, $A(x)D^2u(x)$ is similar to $L(x)H(x)$ which implies that

$$\mathrm{trace}(A(x)D^2u(x)) = \mathrm{trace}(L(x)H(x)) = \sum_{i=1}^{n} l_i(x)h_{ii}(x). \quad (15)$$

Because $h_{ii}(x) = v_i^T(x)D^2u(x)v_i(x)$ which is exactly $\frac{\partial^2 u}{\partial v_i^2}(x)$. Finally, the second-order cross-derivatives have been eliminated:

$$-\mathrm{trace}\big(A(x)D^2u(x)\big) = -\sum_{i=1}^{n} l_i(x)\frac{\partial^2 u}{\partial v_i^2}(x), x \in \Omega. \quad (16)$$

Remark 2.12. Indeed, the step of diagonalization at every reference point is slow and takes a considerable amount of memory for high-dimensional problems. However, when we use deep learning to solve it, we don't need to do this on every reference point but on the mini-batch points. For example, if we use stochastic gradient descent method, we only need to do the diagonalization on one batch point at each step.

Remark 2.13. To implement this step, the algorithm to find eigenvalues and eigenvectors is needed. When the dimension is low, we suggest using analytic solution instead of approximation; see Appendix A.1 for more details about this.

2.3.2. *Multilinear Interpolation and $O(\sqrt{\Delta x})$ Wide Stencil*

To construct a degenerate elliptic scheme for a high-dimensional problem, the main difficulty comes from constructing a monotone scheme specially when there is second-order cross-derivatives especially for the variable coefficient case. In general, it may not be easy to build monotone approximation schemes even for linear second-order equations. Ref. [11] provide a counter-example explicitly to show that for a given fixed stencil (a geometric arrangement of a nodal group that relate to the point of interest by using a numerical approximation routine), it is possible to find a linear elliptic equation for which no second-order accurate monotone scheme can be built. However, if we reduce the order of accuracy, it is possible to construct monotone or even degenerate elliptic scheme. Let's briefly discuss the motivation and procedure in this section.

After the cross-derivatives are replaced by directional derivatives, we can use finite difference to approximate the directional derivatives. The only issue left is that the two end points along the eigenvector direction may not coincide with the mesh point. Hence, when constructing finite difference scheme, we have to use the mesh points around it to approximate the function value there. This approximation introduces another error, therefore a wide stencil has to be used to construct a consistent finite difference scheme. In this section, we use a two-dimensional case as an example to explain and illustrate this method, which in turn can be generalized for higher dimensions.

For a fixed point $x \in \Omega$, to construct a degenerate elliptic scheme for problem (13), we use finite difference to approximate directional derivatives instead of the second-order cross-derivatives locally at x. That is,

$$\begin{aligned} \frac{\partial^2 u}{\partial \mathbf{v}^2}(x) &\approx \frac{u(x+\mathbf{v}\sqrt{\Delta x}) + u(x-\mathbf{v}\sqrt{\Delta x}) - 2u(x)}{\Delta x}, \\ \frac{\partial^2 u}{\partial \mathbf{w}^2}(x) &\approx \frac{u(x+\mathbf{w}\sqrt{\Delta x}) + u(x-\mathbf{w}\sqrt{\Delta x}) - 2u(x)}{\Delta x}, \end{aligned} \tag{17}$$

where $\mathbf{v}, \mathbf{w}$ are the two orthogonal unit eigenvectors of $A(x)$.

There are two issues in (17) that need to be explained and then solved:

1. Even if x is a grid point, $x + \mathbf{v}\sqrt{\Delta x}, x - \mathbf{v}\sqrt{\Delta x}, x + \mathbf{w}\sqrt{\Delta x}, x - \mathbf{w}\sqrt{\Delta x}$ may not be on the grid.
2. Why is $O(\sqrt{\Delta x})$ stencil being used instead of $O(\Delta x)$?

To deal with the first point, we use bilinear interpolation which is widely used in computer vision and image processing. In the following discussion of this section, let's focus on the mesh point, though the procedure is the same for constructing a finite difference scheme at any point in the domain. Suppose x_i is an interior grid point.

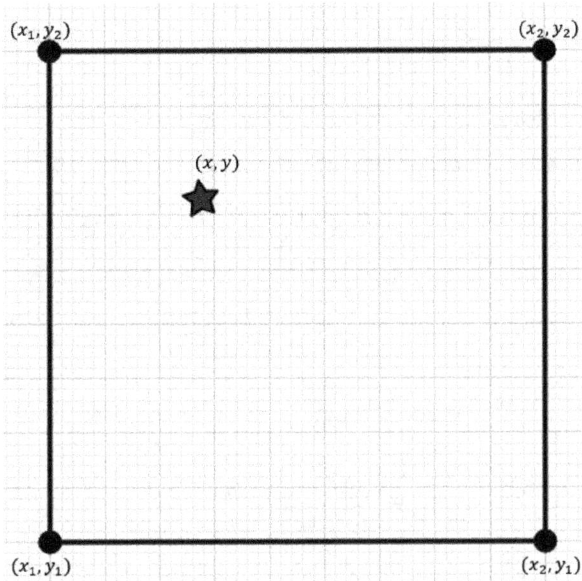

Figure 1. The bilinear interpolation of (x, y) will use a convex combination of vertices $(x_1, y_1), (x_1, y_2), (x_2, y_1), (x_2, y_2)$ of a square.

Even if $x_i + \mathbf{v}\sqrt{\Delta x}$ is not a mesh point on the grid, it must be on the closure of a mesh square. We use a convex combination of the function values at the four vertices to approximate the function value at the desired point. Suppose $(x, y) \in \mathbb{R}^2$ is in the closure of a square with vertices $(x_1, y_1), (x_1, y_2), (x_2, y_1), (x_2, y_2)$ illustrated in Figure 1. Then, (x, y) can be expressed as a convex combination of the four vertices. However, the convex combination is not unique.

The idea is that the function value $f(x, y)$ is going to be approximated by the convex combination of $f(x_1, y_1), f(x_1, y_2), f(x_2, y_1), f(x_2, y_2)$ as follows:

$$f(x, y) \approx w_1 f(x_1, y_1) + w_2 f(x_1, y_2) + w_3 f(x_2, y_1) + w_4 f(x_2, y_2). \quad (18)$$

To ensure that the approximate is accurate, the bilinear interpolation requires that there is no error when $f(x, y)$ is either x or y or xy, i.e., one of the coordinates, or the product of the two. With this additional condition, the weights of the four edges $w_1, \ldots, w_4$ need to satisfy

$$\begin{aligned}
&w_1 + w_2 + w_3 + w_4 = 1, \\
&w_1x_1 + w_2x_1 + w_3x_2 + w_4x_2 = x, \\
&w_1y_1 + w_2y_2 + w_3y_1 + w_4y_2 = y, \\
&w_1x_1y_1 + w_2x_1y_2 + w_3x_2y_1 + w_4x_2y_2 = xy. \qquad (19)
\end{aligned}$$

This linear system has a unique solution given by

$$\begin{aligned}
w_1 &= \frac{(x_2 - x)(y_2 - y)}{(x_2 - x_1)(y_2 - y_1)}, \\
w_2 &= \frac{(x_2 - x)(y - y_1)}{(x_2 - x_1)(y_2 - y_1)}, \\
w_3 &= \frac{(x - x_1)(y_2 - y)}{(x_2 - x_1)(y_2 - y_1)}, \\
w_4 &= \frac{(x - x_1)(y - y_1)}{(x_2 - x_1)(y_2 - y_1)}. \qquad (20)
\end{aligned}$$

Next, let's discuss the reason for why the $O(\sqrt{\Delta x})$ stencil is used. Let (x, y) be a point on the closure of mesh grid with vertices $(x_i, y_i), (x_i, y_i + \Delta x), (x_i + \Delta x, y_i), (x_i + \Delta x, y_i + \Delta x)$. Then, for a function u defined on the closure of Ω, the bilinear interpolation $I_{\Delta x}u(x, y)$ of u at (x, y) with weights w_1, w_2, w_3, w_4 corresponding to $(x_i, y_i), (x_i, y_i + \Delta x), (x_i + \Delta x, y_i), (x_i + \Delta x, y_i + \Delta x)$ is given by

$$\begin{aligned}
I_{\Delta x}u(x, y) = {}& w_1u(x_i, y_i) + w_2u(x_i, y_i + \Delta x) + w_3u(x_i + \Delta x, y_i) \\
&+ w_4u(x_i + \Delta x, y_i + \Delta x). \qquad (21)
\end{aligned}$$

Lemma 2.14. *Let $u \in \mathbf{C}^\infty(\mathbb{R}^2)$ and (x, y) be a point on the closure of mesh grid with vertices $(x_i, y_i), (x_i, y_i + \Delta x), (x_i + \Delta x, y_i), (x_i + \Delta x, y_i + \Delta x)$. Then, $I_{\Delta x}u(x, y) - u(x, y) = O((\Delta x)^2)$.*

Proof. By Talyor expansion,

$$u(x_i, y_i) = u(x, y) + \frac{\partial u}{\partial x}(x, y)(x_i - x) + \frac{\partial u}{\partial y}(x, y)(y_i - y) + O((\Delta x)^2),$$

$$u(x_i, y_i + \Delta x) = u(x, y) + \frac{\partial u}{\partial x}(x, y)(x_i - x) + \frac{\partial u}{\partial y}(x, y)(y_i + \Delta x - y) + O((\Delta x)^2),$$

$$u(x_i+\Delta x, y_i) = u(x,y) + \frac{\partial u}{\partial x}(x,y)(x_i+\Delta x - x) + \frac{\partial u}{\partial y}(x,y)(y_i - y) + O((\Delta x)^2),$$

$$u(x_i+\Delta x, y_i+\Delta x) = u(x,y) + \frac{\partial u}{\partial x}(x,y)(x_i+\Delta x - x) + \frac{\partial u}{\partial y}(x,y)(y_i+\Delta x - y) + O((\Delta x)^2). \tag{22}$$

Then,

$$\begin{aligned} &I_{\Delta x}u(x,y) - u(x,y) \\ &= \frac{\partial u}{\partial x}(x,y)\left(w_1(x_i - x) + w_2(x_1 - x) + w_3(x_1+\Delta x - x) + w_4(x_1+\Delta x - x)\right) \\ &\quad + \frac{\partial u}{\partial y}(x,y)\left(w_1(y_i - y) + w_2(y_i+\Delta x - y) + w_3(y_i - y)\right. \\ &\quad \left.+ w_4(y_i+\Delta x - y)\right) + O((\Delta x)^2) \\ &= \frac{\partial u}{\partial x}(x,y)\left(w_1 x_i + w_2 x_1 + w_3(x_1+\Delta x) + w_4(x_1+\Delta x) - x\right) \\ &\quad + \frac{\partial u}{\partial y}(x,y)\left(w_1 y_i + w_2(y_i+\Delta x) + w_3 y_i + w_4(y_i+\Delta x) - y\right) + O((\Delta x)^2) \\ &= O((\Delta x)^2). \end{aligned} \tag{23}$$

The last equality in (23) holds because the weights (w_1, w_2, w_3, w_4) satisfy the linear system (18). □

This theorem implies that when the bilinear interpolation is used, another error of order $O((\Delta x)^2)$ would be introduced in the numerator of (17). If a narrow stencil ($O(\Delta x)$ stencil) is used, the order of the local truncation error of the second-order central finite difference scheme becomes $O(1)$ which makes the numerical scheme non-consistent. While by using the wide stencil, we can at least have a consistent finite difference scheme with order $O(\sqrt{\Delta x})$.

Finally, we write down the numerical scheme in the following. There are three cases when using a wide stencil to approximate $\frac{\partial^2 u}{\partial \mathbf{v}^2}(\mathbf{x}_i)$ (similar cases for $\frac{\partial^2 u}{\partial \mathbf{w}^2}(\mathbf{x}_i)$).

Case 1: Both $\mathbf{x}_i + \mathbf{v}\sqrt{\Delta x}, \mathbf{x}_i - \mathbf{v}\sqrt{\Delta x}$ are interior points of domain Ω, as illustrated in Figure 2.

In this case,

$$\frac{\partial^2 u}{\partial \mathbf{v}^2}(\mathbf{x}_i) \approx \frac{I_{\Delta x}u(\mathbf{x}_i + \mathbf{v}\sqrt{\Delta x}) + I_{\Delta x}u(\mathbf{x}_i - \mathbf{v}\sqrt{\Delta x}) - 2u(\mathbf{x}_i)}{\Delta x}. \tag{24}$$

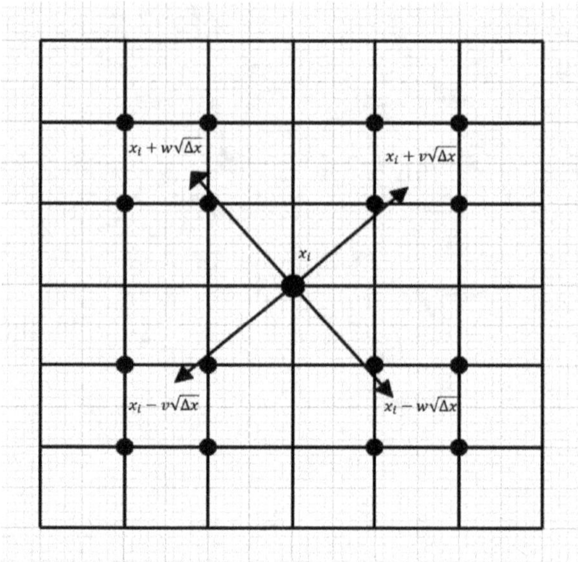

Figure 2. Wide Stencil Case 1: All end points along eigenvector direction are interior points.

Case 2: One of $\mathbf{x}_i + \mathbf{v}\sqrt{\Delta x}, \mathbf{x}_i - \mathbf{v}\sqrt{\Delta x}$ lies outside of the domain Ω, as illustrated in Figure 3. In this case,

$$\frac{\partial^2 u}{\partial \mathbf{v}^2}(\mathbf{x}_i) \approx \frac{\frac{u(\mathbf{x}_i+\mathbf{v}\eta)-u(\mathbf{x}_i)}{\eta} + \frac{I_{\Delta x}u(\mathbf{x}_i-\mathbf{v}\sqrt{\Delta x})-u(\mathbf{x}_i)}{\sqrt{\Delta x}}}{\frac{\eta+\sqrt{\Delta x}}{2}}, \tag{25}$$

where $\mathbf{x}_i + \mathbf{v}\eta$ is on $\partial\Omega$.

Case 3: Both $\mathbf{x}_i + \mathbf{v}\sqrt{\Delta x}, \mathbf{x}_i - \mathbf{v}\sqrt{\Delta x}$ lie outside the domain Ω, as illustrated in Figure 4.

In this case,

$$\frac{\partial^2 u}{\partial \mathbf{v}^2}(\mathbf{x}_i) \approx \frac{\frac{u(\mathbf{x}_i+\mathbf{v}\eta_1)-u(\mathbf{x}_i)}{\eta_1} + \frac{u(\mathbf{x}_i-\mathbf{v}\eta_2)-u(\mathbf{x}_i)}{\eta_2}}{\frac{\eta_1+\eta_2}{2}}, \tag{26}$$

where $\mathbf{x}_i + \mathbf{v}\eta_1, \mathbf{x}_i - \mathbf{v}\eta_2$ are on $\partial\Omega$.

Theorem 2.15. *Let* $\{\mathbf{x}_i\}_{i=1}^{|\mathcal{N}|}$ *be the grid points with mesh size* Δx, *and let the numerical scheme* $F_{\Delta x}[u](\mathbf{x}_i) = 0, i = 1, \ldots, |N|$, *for*

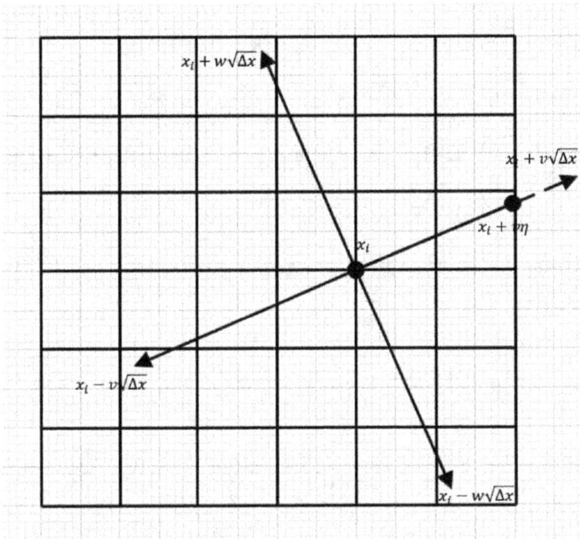

Figure 3. Wide Stencil Case 2: One of the end points along eigenvector direction is outside the domain.

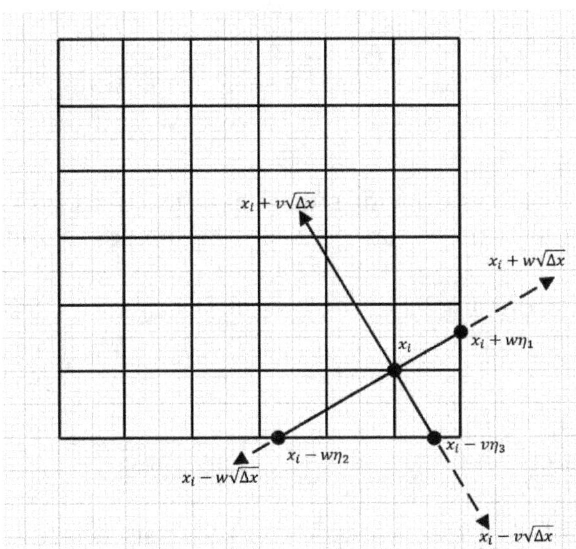

Figure 4. Wide Stencil Case 3: Both end points along eigenvector direction are outside the domain.

problem (13) *be given by* (17)–(26). *Further, assume that every entry of* $A(x)$ *is in* $\mathbf{C}(\bar{\Omega})$. *Then, for any* $\phi \in \mathbf{C}^\infty(\Omega)$,

$$-\text{trace}(A(\mathbf{x}_i)D^2\phi(\mathbf{x}_i)) - F_{\Delta x}[\phi](\mathbf{x}_i)$$
$$= \begin{cases} O(\Delta x) & \textit{all 4 wide stencil points in } \Omega, \\ O(\sqrt{\Delta x}) & \textit{otherwise.} \end{cases} \tag{27}$$

Proof. **Case 1:** Both wide stencil points $\mathbf{x}_i + \mathbf{v}\sqrt{\Delta x}, \mathbf{x}_i - \mathbf{v}\sqrt{\Delta x}$ are inside Ω.

$$\begin{aligned}
&\frac{\partial^2\phi}{\partial \mathbf{v}^2}(\mathbf{x}_i) - \frac{I_{\Delta x}\phi(\mathbf{x}_i + \mathbf{v}\sqrt{\Delta x}) + I_{\Delta x}\phi(\mathbf{x}_i - \mathbf{v}\sqrt{\Delta x}) - 2\phi(\mathbf{x}_i)}{\Delta x} \\
&= \frac{\partial^2\phi}{\partial \mathbf{v}^2}(\mathbf{x}_i) - \frac{\phi(\mathbf{x}_i + \mathbf{v}\sqrt{\Delta x}) + \phi(\mathbf{x}_i - \mathbf{v}\sqrt{\Delta x}) - 2\phi(\mathbf{x}_i)}{\Delta x} \\
&\quad + \frac{\phi(\mathbf{x}_i + \mathbf{v}\sqrt{\Delta x}) + \phi(\mathbf{x}_i - \mathbf{v}\sqrt{\Delta x}) - 2\phi(\mathbf{x}_i)}{\Delta x} \\
&\quad - \frac{I_{\Delta x}\phi(\mathbf{x}_i + \mathbf{v}\sqrt{\Delta x}) + I_{\Delta x}\phi(\mathbf{x}_i - \mathbf{v}\sqrt{\Delta x}) - 2\phi(\mathbf{x}_i)}{\Delta x} \\
&= O(\Delta x) + O(\Delta x).
\end{aligned} \tag{28}$$

The first $O(\Delta x)$ comes from the local truncation error of central discretization of the second-order derivative and the second $O(\Delta x)$ from Lemma 2.14.

Case 2: One of the two wide stencil points is inside Ω. Without loss of generality, suppose $\mathbf{x}_i + \mathbf{v}\sqrt{\eta}$ is on the boundary and $\mathbf{x}_i - \mathbf{v}\sqrt{\Delta x}$ is inside Ω.

$$\begin{aligned}
\frac{\partial^2\phi}{\partial \mathbf{v}^2}(\mathbf{x}_i) &= \frac{\frac{\phi(\mathbf{x}_i+\mathbf{v}\eta)-\phi(\mathbf{x}_i)}{\eta} + \frac{\phi(\mathbf{x}_i-\mathbf{v}\sqrt{\Delta x})-\phi(\mathbf{x}_i)}{\sqrt{\Delta x}}}{\frac{\eta+\sqrt{\Delta x}}{2}} + O\left(\frac{(\Delta x)^2}{\sqrt{\Delta x}\frac{\eta+\sqrt{\Delta x}}{2}}\right) \\
&= O\left(\sqrt{\Delta x} - \eta\right) + O\left(\frac{(\Delta x)^2}{\sqrt{\Delta x}\frac{\eta+\sqrt{\Delta x}}{2}}\right) = O(\sqrt{\Delta x}).
\end{aligned} \tag{29}$$

Case 3: Neither of the two wide stencil points is inside Ω.

$$\frac{\partial^2\phi}{\partial \mathbf{v}^2}(\mathbf{x}_i) - \frac{\frac{u(\mathbf{x}_i+\mathbf{v}\eta_1)-u(\mathbf{x}_i)}{\eta_1} + \frac{u(\mathbf{x}_i-\mathbf{v}\eta_2)-u(\mathbf{x}_i)}{\eta_2}}{\frac{\eta_1+\eta_2}{2}} = O(\eta_1 - \eta_2) = O(\sqrt{\Delta x}). \tag{30}$$

By exactly the same argument, the local truncation error for $\frac{\partial^2 \phi}{\partial \mathbf{w}^2}(\mathbf{x}_i)$ can be proved. Finally, because the every entry of $A(x)$ is in $\mathbf{C}(\bar{\Omega})$, according to Gershgorin circle theorem, the eigenvalues of $A(x)$ are uniformly bounded which implies the result (27). □

Theorem 2.16. *In the same setting as Theorem* 2.15, *the numerical scheme $F_{\Delta x}[u]$ is degenerate elliptic and Lipschitz continuous with respect to its arguments.*

Proof. The proof follows from (23)–(26), as the coefficient of $u(\mathbf{x}_i), u(\mathbf{x}_i) - u(\mathbf{x}_j)$ in $F_{\Delta x}[u](x_i)$ are all non-negative and bounded, the numerical scheme is degenerate elliptic and bounded. □

Remark 2.17. For a class of general second-order degenerate elliptic fully nonlinear partial differential equation,

$$F\left(\text{trace}\big(A(x)D^2u(x)\big)\right) = 0, \tag{31}$$

the above method constructing a finite difference scheme still works as well. See Appendix A.2 for more details.

3. A Deep Learning Solver for Finite Horizon Optimal Investment with a Proportional Transaction Cost

Optimal investment with a proportional transaction cost is a well-known topic in financial mathematics. There are many different settings of the problem. In this chapter, we focus on finite horizon optimal investment with a proportional transaction cost, and we use this problem to illustrate the convergence of the numerical solution from the neural network.

Consider a financial market in consisting of one risk-free asset (money market account) and n stocks. The corresponding asset prices, denoted as $S_0(t), S_1(t), \ldots, S_n(t)$, are modeled by stochastic differential equations in equation (32).

$$\begin{aligned} dS_0(t) &= rS_0(t)dt, \\ dS_i(t) &= \mu_i S_i(t)dt + \sigma_i S_i(t)dW_i(t), \quad i = 1, 2, \ldots, n, \end{aligned} \tag{32}$$

where the $W_i(t), i = 1, 2, \ldots, n$ are standard Brownian motions defined on filtered probability space $(\Omega, \mathcal{F}, \{\mathcal{F}_t\}_{0 \le t \le T}, \mathbb{P})$ with constant instantaneous correlation $\rho \in (-1, 1)$, $r > 0$ is the constant risk-free rate, and μ_i, σ_i are the expected return and standard deviation of the stock i, $i = 1, 2, \ldots, n$, and $T > 0$ is the terminal time.

Let $X(t)$ and $Y_i(t), i = 1, 2, \ldots, n$, be the amount of wealth invested in the risk-free asset and the ith stock, respectively. In the presence of the proportional transaction cost $\lambda_i \in (0, 1)$, the corresponding dynamics for the value of risk-free account and the value of stock account i are describe as

$$
\begin{aligned}
dX(t) &= rX(t)dt - \sum_{i=1}^{n}(1+\lambda_i)dL_i(t) + \sum_{i=1}^{n}(1-\lambda_i)dM_i(t),\\
dY_i(t) &= \mu_i Y_i(t)dt + \sigma_i Y_i(t)dW_i(t) + dL_i(t) - dM_i(t), i = 1, 2, \ldots, n,\\
(X(0-), &Y_1(0-), \ldots, Y_n(0-)) = (x, y_1, \ldots, y_n),
\end{aligned}
\tag{33}
$$

where $L_i(t)$ and $M_i(t)$ are right-continuous with left-limit, non-negative and non-decreasing $\{\mathcal{F}_t\}_{t\leq 0}$-adapted processes with $L_i(0-) = 0, M_i(0-) = 0, i = 1, \ldots, n$. The processes $L_i(t)$ and $M_i(t)$ stand for the cumulative amount of dollar value transferred from the stock account i to the money market account and the cumulative amount of dollar value transferred from money market account to the stock account i up to time t, respectively. For simplicity, for each stock i, suppose the proportional transaction costs on both sides, purchasing and selling, are the same, denoted as λ_i. Define $\mathbf{y} = (y_1, \ldots, y_n)$ and the solvency region $\mathbb{K}$.

$$
\mathbb{K} = \left\{(x, \mathbf{y}) \in \mathbb{R}^{n+1} : x + \sum_{i=1}^{n} y_i - \sum_{i=1}^{n} \lambda_i |y_i| > 0\right\} \tag{34}
$$

and $\mathbf{y} = (y_1, \ldots, y_n)$. Any position in solvency region means that the net wealth (after liquidation) is positive. Assume that the initial wealth allocation of an investor $(x, \mathbf{y}) \in \mathbb{K}$ is inside the solvency region. A investment policy $(L_1, \ldots, L_n, M_1, \ldots, M_n)$ is admissible for a position $(x, \mathbf{y}) \in \mathbb{K}$ starting from $s \in [0, T)$ if $(X(t), Y_1(t), \ldots, Y_n(t))$ given by (33) with $(X(s-), Y_1(s-), \ldots, Y_n(s-)) = (x, \mathbf{y})$ never leaves the closure of the solvency region $\mathbb{K}$ for all times $t \in [s, T]$. Denote the collection of the admissible investment policy as $\mathcal{A}(s, x, \mathbf{y})$. Using the power utility function with risk-aversion parameter $p \in (0,1)$ defined in (35),

$$U(c) = \frac{c^p}{p}, \; c \in [0, +\infty). \tag{35}$$

The goal is to maximize the expected utility of the terminal wealth. Hence, for $(t, x, \mathbf{y}) \in [0,T] \times \bar{\mathbb{K}}$, the value function $V(t, x, \mathbf{y})$ is defined as

$$V(t,x,\mathbf{y}) = \sup_{\mathcal{P} \in \mathcal{A}(t,x,\mathbf{y})} \mathbb{E}_t^{x,\mathbf{y}} \left[U \left(X(T) + \sum_{i=1}^{n} Y_i(T) - \sum_{i=1}^{n} \lambda_i |Y_i(T)| \right) \right], \tag{36}$$

where $\mathbb{E}_t^{x,\mathbf{y}}[.]$ denotes the conditional expectation, conditioned on $X(t-) = x, Y_1(t-) = y_i, \ldots, Y_n(t-) = y_n$.

Assumption 3.1. Throughout this chapter, fix any $\beta > 0$ satisfying $\beta > rp + \frac{p\mathbf{r}_e \Sigma^{-1} \mathbf{r}_e}{2(1-p)}$, where Σ is the covariance matrix of the stock returns and $\mathbf{r}_e = (\mu_1 - r, \mu_2 - r, \ldots, \mu_n - r)^T$ is the vector of excess returns for the stocks.

Then, using the change of variables (see Ref. [8] for more details, motivation and derivation),

$$\begin{aligned} V(t,x,y) &= e^{\beta(T-t)}(x+y)^p \, u\left(t, \frac{y}{x+y}\right) v_\beta(t,x,y), \\ &\beta \geq 0, (t,x,y) \in [0,T] \times \bar{\mathbb{K}}. \end{aligned} \tag{37}$$

Then, u satisfies the following HJB equation (also see Ref. [8]):

$$\begin{cases} \min\{\mathcal{L}u(t,\mathbf{z}), \min_{1 \leq i \leq n} \mathcal{B}_i u(t,\mathbf{z}), \min_{1 \leq i \leq n} \mathcal{S}_i u(t,\mathbf{z})\} = 0, (t,\mathbf{z}) \in [0,T) \times \mathbb{K}_u, \\ u(T,\mathbf{z}) = U(1 - \sum_{i=1}^{n} \lambda_i |z_i|), \mathbf{z} \in \partial \mathbb{K}_u, \end{cases} \tag{38}$$

where $\mathbb{K}_u = \{\mathbf{z} \in \mathbb{R}^n : 1 - \sum_{i=1}^n \lambda_i |z_i| > 0\}$ and

$$\begin{aligned}
\mathcal{L}u &= -u_t(t,\mathbf{z}) - p(\tilde{A}(p) - d^{(1)}(\mathbf{z}))u(t,\mathbf{z}) \\
&\quad - \sum_{i=1}^n d^{(2)}(\mathbf{z}) \frac{\partial u}{\partial z_i}(t,\mathbf{z}) - \sum_{i,j=1}^n d^{(3)}(\mathbf{z}) \frac{\partial^2 u}{\partial z_i \partial z_j}(t,\mathbf{z}), \\
\mathcal{B}_i u &= \lambda_i p u(t,\mathbf{z}) - \sum_{j=1}^n (\delta_{ij} + \lambda_i z_j) \frac{\partial u}{\partial z_j}(t,\mathbf{z}), \\
\mathcal{S}_i u &= \lambda_i p u(t,\mathbf{z}) + \sum_{j=1}^n (\delta_{ij} - \lambda_i z_j) \frac{\partial u}{\partial z_j}(t,\mathbf{z}),
\end{aligned}$$

and

$$\begin{aligned}
\tilde{A}(p) &= A(p) - \frac{\beta}{p} = -\frac{\beta}{p} + r + \frac{\mathbf{r}_e \Sigma^{-1} \mathbf{r}_e}{2(1-p)}, \\
d^{(1)}(\mathbf{z}) &= \frac{1}{2}(1-p)(\mathbf{z}-\theta)^T \Sigma (\mathbf{z}-\theta), \\
d_i^{(2)}(\mathbf{z}) &= z_i \sum_{j=1}^n (\delta_{ij} - z_j) \left((\mu_j - r) + \sum_{k=1}^n (p-1)\rho_{jk}\sigma_j\sigma_k z_k \right), \\
d_{ij}^{(3)}(\mathbf{z}) &= z_i z_j \sum_{k,l=1}^n \frac{1}{2} \rho_{kl}\sigma_k\sigma_l (\delta_{ki} - z_k)(\delta_{lj} - z_l), \\
\delta_{ij} &= \begin{cases} 1, & i = j, \\ 0, & i \neq j. \end{cases}
\end{aligned}$$

We will now illustrate how to find a suitable loss function to solve the optimal investment problem with transaction costs numerically in one and two dimensions.

3.1. *One-dimensional Optimal Investment in Finite Time Horizon*

In case of only one stock, in order to find the solution to the finite time optimal investment with a proportional transaction cost, we need to solve the auxiliary problem (38) with $n = 1$. In this section, we only explicitly write down the formula at mesh points. The procedure to define a finite difference scheme is exactly the same for all other points.

Let $(t_i, z_j), i = 0, \dots, M; j = 0, \dots, N$ be the uniform grids of $[0, T] \times [-\frac{1}{\lambda}, \frac{1}{\lambda}]$ and $\Delta t = t_i - t_{i-1}, \Delta z = z_j - z_{j-1}$. After constructing a finite difference scheme for problem (38) that satisfies Assumption 2.6, it is straightforward to build a deep learning solver with guarantee for the existence of numerical approximator and the convergence. For any function v defined on $[0, T] \times \bar{\mathbb{K}}_u$, define $v^{i,j} = v(t_i, z_j)$ at reference point $(t_i, z_j), i = 0, \dots, N, j = 0, \dots M$, and at reference point $(t_i, z_j), i = 0, \dots, N-1, j = 1, \dots M-1$; the finite difference schemes for the three linear operators are

$$\mathcal{L}_{\Delta t,\Delta z}[v](t_i, z_j) \tag{39}$$

$$= \begin{cases} \frac{v^{i,j}-v^{i+1,j}}{\Delta t} - p(\tilde{A}(p) - d^{(1)}(z_j))v^{i,j} - d^{(2)}(z_j)\frac{v^{i,j+1}-v^{i,j}}{\Delta z} \\ \quad -d^{(3)}(z_j)\frac{v^{i,j+1}+v^{i,j-1}-2v^{i,j}}{(\Delta z)^2}, \\ \qquad\qquad\qquad\qquad\qquad\qquad : \ d^{(2)}(z_j) \geq 0, \\ \frac{v^{i,j}-v^{i+1,j}}{\Delta t} - p(\tilde{A}(p) - d^{(1)}(z_j))v^{i,j} - d^{(2)}(z_j)\frac{v^{i,j}-v^{i,j-1}}{\Delta z} \\ \quad -d^{(3)}(z_j)\frac{v^{i,j+1}+v^{i,j-1}-2v^{i,j}}{(\Delta z)^2} \\ \qquad\qquad\qquad\qquad\qquad\qquad : \ \text{otherwise,} \end{cases}$$

$$\mathcal{B}_{\Delta t,\Delta z}[v](t_i, z_j) = \lambda p v^{i,j} - (1 + \lambda z_j)\frac{v^{i,j+1} - v^{i,j}}{\Delta z}, \tag{40}$$

$$\mathcal{S}_{\Delta t,\Delta z}[v](t_i, z_j) = \lambda p v^{i,j} + (1 - \lambda z_j)\frac{v^{i,j} - v^{i,j-1}}{\Delta z}. \tag{41}$$

Hence, the finite difference scheme corresponding to (38) is

$$\begin{aligned} F_{\Delta t,\Delta z}[v](t_i, z_j) = \min\{&\mathcal{L}_{\Delta t,\Delta z}[v](t_i, z_j), \\ &\mathcal{B}_{\Delta t,\Delta z}[v](t_i, z_j), \mathcal{S}_{\Delta t,\Delta z}[v](t_i, z_j)\}. \end{aligned} \tag{42}$$

At the boundary points $(t_i, z_0), i = 0, \dots, M-1$ or $(t_i, z_N), i = 0, \dots, M-1$,

$$F_{\Delta t,\Delta z}[v](t_i, z_0) = v^{i,0}, F^{i,N}_{\Delta t,\Delta z}[\mathbf{v}] = v^{i,N}. \tag{43}$$

While at the terminal time points $(t_M, z_j), j = 0, \ldots, M$,

$$F_{\Delta t,\Delta z}[v](t_M, z_j) = v^{M,j} - U(1 - \lambda|z_j|). \tag{44}$$

Before we transform the finite difference scheme to the loss function, we verify the properties needed for $F_{\Delta t,\Delta z}$ in Assumption 2.6. Thanks to Ref. [25], we only need to verify degenerate elliptic and proper properties of the three finite difference schemes inside the minimum function one by one.

Theorem 3.2. *Assume that β is large enough so that Assumption* 3.1 *holds. Then, the finite difference scheme defined in* (42), (43) *and* (44) *is degenerate elliptic.*

Proof. For the reference point $(t_i, z_j), i = 0, 1, \ldots, M, j = 0, 1, \ldots, N$, the finite difference scheme $F^{i,j}_{\Delta t,\Delta z}(\mathbf{v})$ is a function of $v^{i,j}$ and $v^{i,j} - v^{0,0}, v^{i,j} - v^{i,j-1}, v^{i,j} - v^{i,j+1}, \ldots, v^{i,j} - v^{M,N}$. Because of Assumption 3.1, the term $-p(\tilde{A}(p) - d^{(1)}(z)$ is strictly positive for $z \in \mathbb{K}_u$, and the terms $d^{(3)}(z), \lambda p, 1 + \lambda z, 1 - \lambda z$ are non-negative there as well. Therefore, from the constructions 39, it follows that $F^{i,j}_{\Delta t,\Delta z}(\mathbf{v})$ is a non-decreasing function of each variable. We conclude that the finite difference scheme defined in (42), (43) and (44) is a degenerate elliptic scheme. □

Theorem 3.3. *Assume that β is large enough so that Assumption* 3.1 *holds. Then, the finite difference scheme defined in* (42), (43) *and* (44) *is proper.*

Proof. According to Assumption 3.1, the coefficient $-p\Big(\tilde{A}(p) - d_1(z)\Big)$ of the the first argument of $\mathcal{L}^{i,j}_{\Delta t,\Delta z}v$ is a strictly positive and bounded below by $-p\tilde{A}(p)$ which is independent of z. For $\mathcal{B}^{i,j}_{\Delta t,\Delta z}v$ and $\mathcal{S}^{i,j}_{\Delta t,\Delta z}v$, the coefficient λp of the first arguments is strictly positive as well. Together, these imply that the finite difference scheme defined in (42), (43) and (44) is proper. □

Next, we verify the Lipschitz continuous property of the finite difference scheme. We start with the following observation:

Lemma 3.4. *Let I be a finite index set, and $f^i : \mathbb{R}^d \mapsto \mathbb{R},\ i \in I$ is a Lipschitz continuous function with Lipschitz constant L_i, then* $\min_{i\in I}\{f^i(x)\}$ *is a Lipschitz continuous function.*

Proof. By assumptions, for any $x, y \in \mathbb{R}^d$ and $i \in I$, $|f^i(x) - f^i(y)| \leq L_i|x-y| \leq L|x-y|$, where $L = \max_{i\in I}\{L_i\}$. Consider, for example, the case when $\min_{i\in I}\{f^i(x)\} = f^1(x), \min_{i\in I}\{f^i(y)\} = f^2(y)$. Then,

$$\begin{aligned}
&\min_{i\in I}\{f^i(x)\} - \min_{i\in I}\{f^i(y)\} \leq f^2(x) - f^2(y) \leq L|x-y|,\\
&\min_{i\in I}\{f^i(y)\} - \min_{i\in I}\{f^i(x)\} \leq f^1(y) - f^1(x) \leq L|x-y|.
\end{aligned} \tag{45}$$

Hence, $|\min_{i\in I}\{f^i(x)\} - \min_{i\in I}\{f^i(y)\}| \leq |f^2(x) - f^2(y)| \leq L|x-y|$. □

Theorem 3.5. *The finite difference scheme defined in* (42),(43) *and* (44) *is a Lipschitz continuous scheme.*

Proof. Because of the linear structure of $\mathcal{L}_{\Delta t,\Delta z}, \mathcal{B}_{\Delta t,\Delta z}, \mathcal{S}_{\Delta t,\Delta z}$ with respect to their argument, and having uniformly bounded coefficients, it follows that each of them is Lipschitz continuous. Then, by Lemma 3.4, this is a Lipschitz continuous scheme. □

Theorem 3.6. *The finite difference scheme defined in* (42), (43) *and* (44) *is a consistent scheme.*

Proof. For any $\phi \in C^\infty([0,T] \times [-\frac{1}{\lambda}, \frac{1}{\lambda}])$, by Taylor expansion, we know

$$\begin{aligned}
&\frac{\phi(t+\Delta t, z) - \phi(t,z)}{\Delta t} = \phi_t(t,z) + O(\Delta t),\\
&\frac{\phi(t,, z+\Delta z) - \phi(t,z)}{\Delta z} = \phi_z(t,z) + O(\Delta z),\\
&\frac{\phi(t,, z) - \phi(t,z-\Delta z)}{\Delta z} = \phi_z(t,z) + O(\Delta z),\\
&\frac{\phi(t,, z+\Delta z) + \phi(t, z-\Delta z) - 2\phi(t,z)}{(\Delta z)^2} = \phi_{zz}(t,z) + O((\Delta z)^2).
\end{aligned} \tag{46}$$

Hence, by the linear structure of the operators with uniformly bounded coefficient in $[0,T] \times [-\frac{1}{\lambda}, \frac{1}{\lambda}]$,

$$\begin{aligned}
\mathcal{L}_{\Delta t,\Delta z}\phi &= \mathcal{L}\phi + O(\Delta z + \Delta t),\\
\mathcal{B}_{\Delta t,\Delta z}\phi &= \mathcal{B}\phi + O(\Delta z),\\
\mathcal{S}_{\Delta t,\Delta z}\phi &= \mathcal{S}\phi + O(\Delta z).
\end{aligned} \tag{47}$$

Then, arguing similar to the way it is done in Lemma 3.4, we have that

$$F_{\Delta t,\Delta z}[\phi] = \min\{\mathcal{L}\phi, \mathcal{B}\phi, \mathcal{S}\phi\} + O(\Delta z + \Delta t). \tag{48}$$

Therefore, $F_{\Delta t,\Delta z}[\phi] \to \min\{\mathcal{L}\phi, \mathcal{B}\phi, \mathcal{S}\phi\}$ as $\Delta t + \Delta z \to 0$. □

Then, we directly get a deep learning solver for the one-dimensional finite time optimal investment with a proportional transaction cost problem by setting the loss function as

$$\mathcal{R}(v) = \sum_{i=0}^{N}\sum_{j=0}^{M}(F^{i,j}_{\Delta t,\Delta z}[v])^2. \tag{49}$$

3.2. *Two-dimensional Optimal Investment in Finite Time Horizon*

When there are two risky assets, we again perform a reduction of variables similar to (37). Then, let $(t^i, z_1^j, z_2^k), i = 0,\ldots,N; j = 0,\ldots,M; k = 0,\ldots,M$ be the mesh points of $[0,T]\times\bar{\mathbb{K}}_u$ with mesh size $\Delta t, \Delta z$ and denote the collection of grid points as $\mathcal{N}$. For convenience, for any function u defined on the closure of the domain, define $u^{i,j,k} = u(t^i, z_1^j, z_2^k)$.

Note that all the five operators inside the min operator are linear operators, and according to the building blocks introduced in Ref. [25], we only need to construct a degenerate elliptic finite difference scheme for each of the operators. The constructions of $\mathcal{B}_1 u, \mathcal{B}_2 u, \mathcal{S}_1 u, \mathcal{B}_2 u$ are straightforward. For any $(t^i, z_1^j, z_2^k) \in \mathcal{N}$ which is a interior point, we define

$$\begin{aligned} &\mathcal{B}_1^{\Delta t,\Delta z}[u](t^i, z_1^j, z_2^k)\\ &= \begin{cases} \lambda u^{i,j,k} - (1+\lambda z_1^j)\frac{u^{i,j+1,k}-u^{i,j,k}}{\Delta z} - \lambda z_2^k\frac{u^{i,j,k+1}-u^{i,j,k}}{\Delta z}, & z_2^k \le 0,\\ \lambda u^{i,j,k} - (1+\lambda z_1^j)\frac{u^{i,j+1,k}-u^{i,j,k}}{\Delta z} - \lambda z_2^k\frac{u^{i,j,k}-u^{i,j,k-1}}{\Delta z}, & z_2^k < 0. \end{cases} \end{aligned} \tag{50}$$

$$\begin{aligned} &\mathcal{B}_2^{\Delta t,\Delta z}[u](t^i, z_1^j, z_2^k)\\ &= \begin{cases} \lambda u^{i,j,k} - (1+\lambda z_2^k)\frac{u^{i,j,k+1}-u^{i,j,k}}{\Delta z} - \lambda z_1^j\frac{u^{i,j+1,k}-u^{i,j,k}}{\Delta z}, & z_1^j \le 0,\\ \lambda u^{i,j,k} - (1+\lambda z_2^k)\frac{u^{i,j,k+1}-u^{i,j,k}}{\Delta z} - \lambda z_1^j\frac{u^{i,j,k}-u^{i,j-1,k}}{\Delta z}, & z_1^j < 0. \end{cases} \end{aligned} \tag{51}$$

$$\mathcal{S}_1^{\Delta t,\Delta z}[u](t^i, z_1^j, z_2^k)$$
$$= \begin{cases} \lambda u^{i,j,k} + (1-\lambda z_1^j)\frac{u^{i,j,k}-u^{i,j-1,k}}{\Delta z} - \lambda z_2^k \frac{u^{i,j,k+1}-u^{i,j,k}}{\Delta z}, z_2^k \le 0, \\ \lambda u^{i,j,k} + (1+\lambda z_1^j)\frac{u^{i,j,k}-u^{i,j-1,k}}{\Delta z} - \lambda z_2^k \frac{u^{i,j,k}-u^{i,j,k-1}}{\Delta z}, z_2^k < 0. \end{cases} \tag{52}$$

$$\mathcal{S}_2^{\Delta t,\Delta z}[u](t^i, z_1^j, z_2^k)$$
$$= \begin{cases} \lambda u^{i,j,k} + (1-\lambda z_2^k)\frac{u^{i,j,k}-u^{i,j,k-1}}{\Delta z} - \lambda z_1^j \frac{u^{i,j+1,k}-u^{i,j,k}}{\Delta z}, z_1^j \le 0, \\ \lambda u^{i,j,k} + (1-\lambda z_2^k)\frac{u^{i,j,k}-u^{i,j,k-1}}{\Delta z} - \lambda z_1^j \frac{u^{i,j,k}-u^{i,j-1,k}}{\Delta z}, z_1^j < 0. \end{cases} \tag{53}$$

It is easy to verify that all the finite difference schemes above are degenerate elliptic, proper and Lipschitz schemes.

To construct the finite difference scheme for the second-order operator $\mathcal{L}u$, we split $\mathcal{L}u$ into two pieces: the pure second-order part and other terms whose orders are strictly smaller than two, denoted respectively as $-\operatorname{trace}(A(z_1,z_2)D^2u(t,z_1,z_2))$ and $-u_t(t,z_1,z_2) + d_0(z_1,z_2)u + \mathbf{d}_1^T(z_1,z_2)Du(t,z_1,z_2)$, where

$$A(z_1,z_2) = \begin{pmatrix} a_{11}(z_1,z_2) & a_{12}(z_1,z_2) \\ a_{12}(z_1,z_2) & a_{22}(z_1,z_2) \end{pmatrix},$$
$$a_{11}(z_1,z_2) = \frac{1}{2}\left(\sigma_1^2 z_1^2(1-z_1)^2 - 2\rho\sigma_1\sigma_2 z_1^2(1-z_1)z_2 + \sigma_2^2 z_1^2 z_2^2\right),$$
$$a_{12}(z_1,z_2) = \frac{1}{2}\Big(\sigma_1^2 z_1(1-z_1)z_2^2 + \sigma_2^2 z_2(1-z_2)z_1^2$$
$$- \rho\sigma_1\sigma_2 z_1 z_2(1-z_1)(1-z_2) - \rho\sigma_1\sigma_2 z_1^2 z_2^2\Big),$$
$$a_{22}(z_1,z_2) = \frac{1}{2}\left(\sigma_2^2 z_2^2(1-z_2)^2 - 2\rho\sigma_1\sigma_2 z_2^2(1-z_2)z_1 + \sigma_1^2 z_1^2 z_2^2\right),$$
$$\mathbf{d}_1^T(z_1,z_2)Du(t,z_1,z_2) = \begin{pmatrix} d_{11}(z_1,z_2) \\ d_{12}(z_1,z_2) \end{pmatrix},$$

$$d_{11}(z_1,z_2) = z_1(1-z_1)\left(\mu_1 - r + (p-1)(\sigma_1^2 z_1 + \rho\sigma_1\sigma_2 z_2)\right)$$
$$- z_1 z_2\left(\mu_2 - r + (p-1)(\rho\sigma_1\sigma_2 z_1 + \sigma_2^2 z_2)\right),$$
$$d_{12}(z_1,z_2) = z_2(1-z_2)\left(\mu_2 - r + (p-1)(\sigma_2^2 z_2 + \rho\sigma_1\sigma_2 z_1)\right)$$
$$- z_1 z_2\left(\mu_1 - r + (p-1)(\rho\sigma_1\sigma_2 z_2 + \sigma_1^2 z_1)\right).$$

Consider $-u_t(t, z_1, z_2) + d_0(z_1, z_2)u + \mathbf{d}_1^T(z_1, z_2)Du(t, z_1, z_2)$. We can find a suitable finite difference scheme with a narrow stencil. Specifically, for any interior point $(t^i, z_1^j, z_2^k) \in \mathcal{N}$, we construct the finite difference as

$$
\begin{aligned}
&-u_t(t^i, z_1^j, z_2^k) + d_0(z_1, z_2)u(t^i, z_1^j, z_2^k) + \mathbf{d}_1^T(z_1, z_2)Du(t^i, z_1^j, z_2^k)\\
&\approx \begin{cases}
\frac{u^{i,j,k}-u^{i+1,j,k}}{\Delta t} + d_0(z_1^j, z_2^k)u^{i,j,k} + d_{11}(z_1^j, z_2^k)\frac{u^{i,j,k}-u^{i,j-1,k}}{\Delta z} \\
\quad + d_{12}(z_1^j, z_2^k)\frac{u^{i,j,k}-u^{i,j,k-1}}{\Delta z} \\
\qquad\qquad : d_{11}(z_1^j, z_2^k) \geq 0, \text{`}d_{12}(z_1^j, z_2^k) \geq 0, \\
\frac{u^{i,j,k}-u^{i+1,j,k}}{\Delta t} + d_0(z_1^j, z_2^k)u^{i,j,k} + d_{11}(z_1^j, z_2^k)\frac{u^{i,j+1,k}-u^{i,j,k}}{\Delta z} \\
\quad + d_{12}(z_1^j, z_2^k)\frac{u^{i,j,k}-u^{i,j,k-1}}{\Delta z} \\
\qquad\qquad : d_{11}(z_1^j, z_2^k) < 0,\ d_{12}(z_1^j, z_2^k) \geq 0, \\
\frac{u^{i,j,k}-u^{i+1,j,k}}{\Delta t} + d_0(z_1^j, z_2^k)u^{i,j,k} + d_{11}(z_1^j, z_2^k)\frac{u^{i,j,k}-u^{i,j-1,k}}{\Delta z} \\
\quad + d_{12}(z_1^j, z_2^k)\frac{u^{i,j,k+1}-u^{i,j,k}}{\Delta z} \\
\qquad\qquad : d_{11}(z_1^j, z_2^k) \geq 0,\ d_{12}(z_1^j, z_2^k) < 0, \\
\frac{u^{i,j,k}-u^{i+1,j,k}}{\Delta t} + d_0(z_1^j, z_2^k)u^{i,j,k} + d_{11}(z_1^j, z_2^k)\frac{u^{i,j+1,k}-u^{i,j,k}}{\Delta z} \\
\quad + d_{12}(z_1^j, z_2^k)\frac{u^{i,j,k}-u^{i,j,k-1}}{\Delta z} \\
\qquad\qquad : d_{11}(z_1^j, z_2^k) < 0,\ d_{12}(z_1^j, z_2^k) < 0.
\end{cases}
\end{aligned}
\tag{54}
$$

Finally, consider the second-order term $-\operatorname{trace}(A(z_1, z_2)$ $D^2u(t, z_1, z_2))$. Since it has second-order cross-derivatives, it is impossible to construct a monotone scheme with a narrow stencil in general, and hence, the mixed derivatives term needs to be removed. As $A(x)$ is positive semi-definite, it is diagonalizable. Diagonalize A as $A(z_1, z_2) = V(z_1, z_2)L(z_1, z_2)V^T(z_1, z_2)$, where $L(z_1, z_2)$ is a diagonal matrix. Denote the eigenvalues as $l_i(z_1, z_2), i = 1, \ldots, d$, and denote the orthonormal eigenvectors and the columns of $V(z_1, z_2)$ as $\{\mathbf{v}_1(z_1, z_2), \ldots, \mathbf{v}_d(z_1, z_2)\}$. We then have

$$
-\operatorname{trace}(A(z_1, z_2)D^2u(z_1, z_2)) = -\sum_{i=1}^{d} l_i(z_1, z_2)\frac{\partial^2 u}{\partial \mathbf{v}_i^2}(z_1, z_2). \tag{55}
$$

Although the cross-derivatives have been removed, if the eigenvectors do not line up with the grids, it is impossible to find the second-order accurate monotone scheme. That is, at a grid point, (t^i, z_1^l, z_2^k), $(t^i, z_1^l + \mathbf{v}_m \Delta z, z_2^k), (t^i, z_1^l - \mathbf{v}_m \Delta z, z_2^k)$ are not grid points, which means we cannot use $\frac{u(t^i, z_1^l + \mathbf{v}_m \Delta z, z_2^k) + u(t^i, z_1^l - \mathbf{v}_m \Delta z, z_2^k) - 2u(t^i, z_1^l + \mathbf{v}_m \Delta z, z_2^k)}{(\Delta z)^2}$. Here, we follow the idea of Ref. [10] in two dimension and use a stencil of length $\sqrt{\Delta z}$ and bilinear interpolation weights to get a $\frac{1}{2}$-order accurate monotone scheme which is also degenerate elliptic. We refer to Appendix A for the details of the wide stencil scheme and bilinear interpolation.

Combining with 54, and denoting the finite difference scheme of $\mathcal{L}u$ as $\mathcal{L}^{\Delta t, \Delta z}u$, we define the finite difference scheme for F as

$$F_{\Delta t, \Delta z}[u] = \min\{\mathcal{L}^{\Delta t, \Delta z}u, \mathcal{B}_1^{\Delta t, \Delta z}u, \mathcal{B}_2^{\Delta t, \Delta z}u, \mathcal{S}_1^{\Delta t, \Delta z}u, \mathcal{S}_2^{\Delta t, \Delta z}u\}. \tag{56}$$

This scheme will then have the following properties.

Theorem 3.7. *The finite difference scheme* 56 *is a proper, degenerate elliptic, Lipschitz continuous and consistent scheme.*

Proof. The proper, degenerate elliptic and Lipschitz continuous properties are satisfied by the construction of the scheme. For any $\phi \in \mathbf{C}^\infty([0, T] \times \bar{\mathbb{K}}_u)$, according to 2.15 and the linear structure of the $\mathcal{L}\phi$, we have for any $(t^i, z_1^j, z_2^k) \in ([0, T) \times \mathbb{K}_u) \cap \mathcal{N}$,

$$\mathcal{L}^{\Delta t, \Delta z}[\phi](t^i, z_1^j, z_2^k) = \mathcal{L}\phi(t^i, z_1^j, z_2^k) + O(\Delta t + \sqrt{\Delta z}), \tag{57}$$

and also

$$\begin{aligned}
\mathcal{B}_1^{\Delta t, \Delta z}[\phi](t^i, z_1^j, z_2^k) &= \mathcal{B}_1\phi(t^i, z_1^j, z_2^k) + O(\Delta z),\\
\mathcal{B}_2^{\Delta t, \Delta z}[\phi](t^i, z_1^j, z_2^k) &= \mathcal{B}_2\phi(t^i, z_1^j, z_2^k) + O(\Delta z),\\
\mathcal{S}_1^{\Delta t, \Delta z}[\phi](t^i, z_1^j, z_2^k) &= \mathcal{S}_1\phi(t^i, z_1^j, z_2^k) + O(\Delta z),\\
\mathcal{S}_2^{\Delta t, \Delta z}[\phi](t^i, z_1^j, z_2^k) &= \mathcal{S}_2\phi(t^i, z_1^j, z_2^k) + O(\Delta z).
\end{aligned} \tag{58}$$

Finally, similar to Lemma 3.4,

$$F^{i,j,k}_{\Delta t,\Delta z}[\phi] = \min\{\mathcal{L}\phi, \mathcal{B}_1\phi, \mathcal{B}_2\phi, \mathcal{S}_1\phi, \mathcal{S}_2\phi\}(t^i, z_1^j, z_2^k) + O(\Delta t + \sqrt{\Delta z}), \tag{59}$$

which implies consistency. □

Therefore, a deep learning solver with the loss function

$$\mathcal{R}(u) = \sum_{i=0}^{N}\sum_{j=0}^{M}\sum_{k=0}^{M}(F^{i,j,k}[u])^2$$

provides a with theoretical guarantee for the two-dimensional finite time optimal investment with a proportional transaction cost problem.

4. Numerical Experiment

In this section, we present some numerical results by using the deep learning solver to solve the optimal investment with a proportional transaction cost when there is one stock or two stocks. The deep neural network is the fully connected feedforward neural network with sigmoid function as the activation function. In the following subsections, we provide some numerical results of the optimal investment problem with the deep learning solver.

4.1. *Numerical Results in One Stock Case*

In this section, we present the numerical results for the finite horizon optimal investment with a proportional transaction cost and maturity $T = 10$. The model parameters used in this section are listed in Table 1. With these choices, the Merton point is $\theta = \frac{\mu - r}{(1-p)\sigma^2} \approx 0.444$ which ensures that when the proportional two-side transaction cost λ is small, all the assumptions of Theorems 3.3, 3.5 and 3.6 are satisfied.

4.1.1. *No-trade Interval at $t = 0$ with Different Levels of Proportional Transaction Cost*

In this section, we show that our algorithm provides good estimation of no-trade region by comparing with the asymptotic solutions when the proportion transaction cost λ is small at the initial time $t = 0$.

Table 1. Table of parameters for one stock case.

Parameters	Symbol	Value
Expected return of the stock	μ	10%
Volatility of the stock	σ	0.3
Risk-free rate	r	8%
Risk aversion coefficient	p	0.5
Objective discounting rate	β	0.1
Terminal time	T	10

Table 2. Table of approximated no-trade intervals and asymptotic no-trade intervals with different levels of proportional transaction costs at time 0.

λ	$(\hat{l}, \hat{r})$	$d(\theta, \hat{l})$	$d(\hat{r}, \theta)$	Asymptotic interval
0.1	$(-0.0132, 0.7358)$	0.4576	0.2914	(0.1810,0.7079)
0.07	$(0.0721, 0.6838)$	0.3724	0.2394	(0.2105,0.6784)
0.05	$(0.1622, 0.6544)$	0.2822	0.2100	(0.2353,0.6536)
0.03	$(0.2244, 0.6330)$	0.2203	0.1886	(0.2681,0.6208)
0.01	$(0.3046, 0.5685)$	0.1398	0.1240	(0.3222,0.5667)
0.005	$(0.3431, 0.5382)$	0.1013	0.0937	(0.3474,0.5415)

Ref. [8] provided the asymptotic analysis for the value function. The problem setting there is exactly the same as the model setting in this section. We then compare our results against those asymptotic results. Using the parameters from Table 1, we report these results at time $t = 0$ as a function of the transaction costs λ in Table 2.

From Table 2, it is clear that the no-trade interval shrinks with the decreasing level of proportional transaction cost and the buy stock boundary (left end point) is much more sensitive than the right boundary (right end point). By comparing with the asymptotic intervals especially when the level of the proportional transaction cost is small (1% and 0.5%), the deep learning algorithm provides an accurate estimation of no-trade intervals.

4.1.2. *Change of No-trade Interval as Time Change*

At the maturity, investors must liquidate their risky positions when calculating their total wealth. Hence, it is not optimal to buy risky

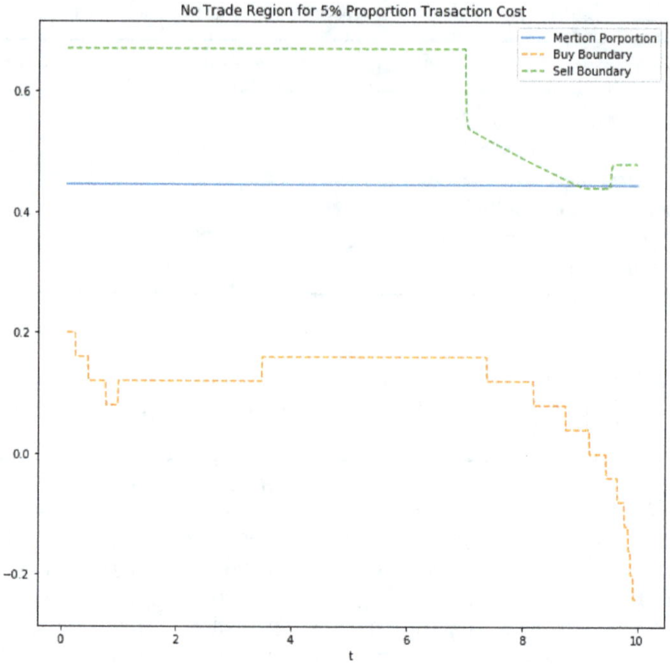

Figure 5. Evolution of no-trade region.

assets close to maturity if the wealth invested into the risky assets is non-negative. By Ref. [13], the buy boundary vanishes and the sell boundary converges when approaching $\frac{T-t}{\lambda}$. Figure 5 shows the approximation boundary of changing of no-trade intervals which is consistent with the analysis of Ref. [13].

4.1.3. *Approximated Value Function*

Finally, in this section, we provide the approximate value function at time 0. From Figure 6, it is clear that the approximated value function at time 0 is a concave function and is in fact smooth (including the peak when scaled appropriately).

4.2. ***Numerical Results in Two Stock Case***

When there are two stocks, we study the behavior of the no-trade region with respect to different levels of the transaction cost and different correlations between the stock returns.

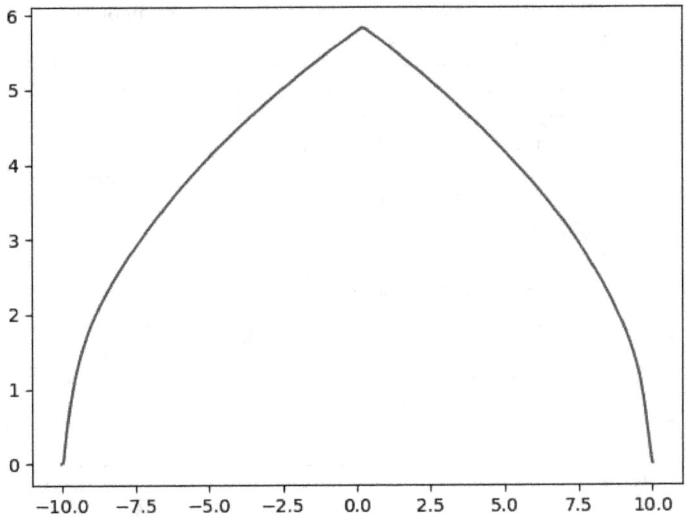

Figure 6. Value function at time 0.

4.2.1. *Effects of Difference Levels of the Proportional Transaction Cost*

In this section, we show the numerical approximation of no-trade regions with different levels of the proportional transaction cost. We use the parameters used from Table 3. Figure 7 is the numerically computed no-trade region with different levels of transaction cost. Similar to the one stock case, the size of no-trade region decreases as the transaction cost becomes smaller. For the two uncorrelated identical stocks case, the no-trade regions are almost perfect squares. However, the centers of the squares are not the Merton proportion, which also implies the buy-stock boundaries (left and bottom boundaries) are much more sensitive to the changing levels of transaction cost.

4.3. *Effects of Correlations between the Stocks*

In this section, we present the numerical results of the no-trade regions with different correlations between the two identical stock returns with parameters from Table 4. The covariance matrix is defined through the variances σ_1^2, σ_2^2 and the correlation between the

Table 3. Table of parameters for two uncorrelated stock case.

Parameters	Symbol	Value
Expected return of the stock 1	μ_1	10%
Expected return of the stock 2	μ_1	10%
Volatility of the stock 1	σ_1	0.3
Volatility of the stock 2	σ_2	0.3
Risk-free rate	r	8%
Risk aversion coefficient	p	0.5
Objective discounting rate	β	0.1
Terminal time	T	10

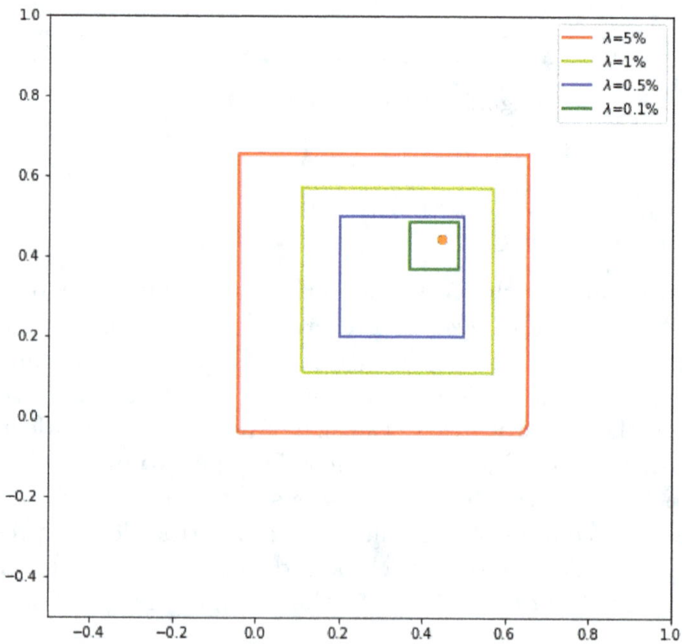

Figure 7. No-trade region with different levels of transaction cost.

two stock returns ρ by

$$\Sigma = \sigma\sigma^T = \begin{pmatrix} \sigma_1^2 & \rho\sigma_1\sigma_2 \\ \rho\sigma_1\sigma_2 & \sigma_2^2 \end{pmatrix}. \tag{60}$$

Table 4. Table of parameters for two uncorrelated stock case.

Parameters	Symbol	Value
Expected return of the stock 1	μ_1	8%
Expected return of the stock 2	μ_1	8%
Risk-free rate	r	3%
Risk aversion coefficient	p	0.5
Objective discounting rate	β	1
Terminal time	T	10
Proportional transaction cost	λ	2%

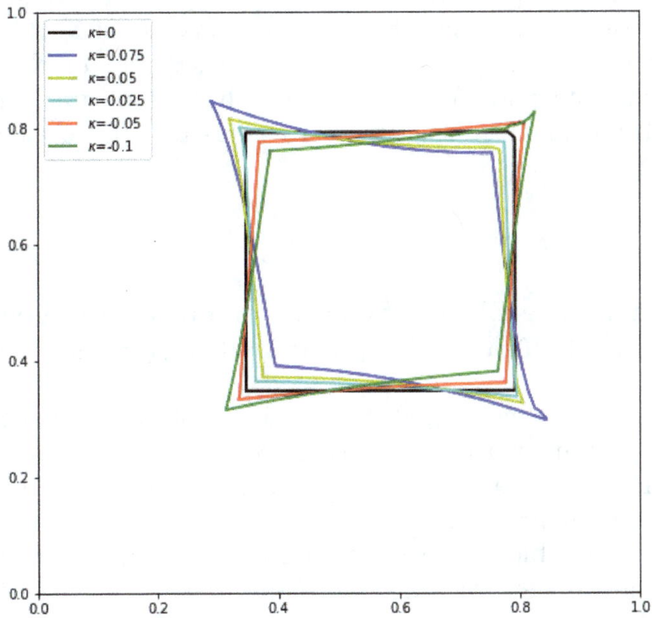

Figure 8. Effect of correlation.

In this chapter, we define the covariance matrix through σ with one hyperparameter κ

$$\sigma = \begin{pmatrix} 0.4 - \kappa & \kappa \\ \kappa & 0.4 - \kappa \end{pmatrix}. \tag{61}$$

In Figure 8, we plot the no-trade region at time 0 with κ equal to one of the following: $-0.1, -0.05, 0, 0.025, 0.05$ and 0.075. The results are consistent with the expectation and the existence result presented in Ref. [24] and Ref. [2]. As expected, there is higher tolerance for deviation along the $(1, -1)$ direction from the Merton proportion as the correlation between the two stock returns increases. The financial sense behind the phenomenon is that the excess proportion will hedge each other because of the positive correlation.

5. Conclusion

In this chapter, we present the numerical solvability of a deep leaning scheme for a general class of fully nonlinear partial differential equation, for which we prove the existence of numerical approximator and convergence results. The solver is a combination of finite difference and deep learning. It is a scheme with no restriction on the structure of the neural network. We use the finite horizon optimal investment with a proportional transaction cost to illustrate the efficiency of our scheme.

Appendix

A. Degenerate Elliptic Scheme for Fully Nonlinear Partial Differential Equation with Wide Stencil

In Section 3.2, we mentioned that it might not be easy to construct a monotone scheme with second-order accuracy for every second-order linear PDE. However, this does not mean it is impossible to build a degenerate elliptic scheme. In fact, if we accept a lower accuracy, it's usually possible to construct a degenerate elliptic scheme. There are several ways to use wide stencil to construct degenerate elliptic scheme. In this appendix, we introduce the $O(\sqrt{\Delta x})$ method which is used in this manuscript.

A.1. *Analytic Equation to Remove the Second-order Cross-derivatives for Two-dimensional Problem*

Consider

$$\begin{cases} -\operatorname{trace}\big(A(x)D^2u(x)\big) = 0, & x \in \Omega, \\ u(x) = g(x), & x \in \partial\Omega, \end{cases} \tag{62}$$

where $A(x) \in \mathbb{S}^2$ is positive semi-definite for any $x \in \Omega \subset \mathbb{R}^2$.

Let

$$A(x) = \begin{pmatrix} a_{11}(x) & a_{12}(x) \\ a_{12}(x) & a_{22}(x) \end{pmatrix}. \tag{63}$$

Then, the eigenvalues of $A(x)$ are

$$\begin{aligned} l_1(x) &= \frac{(a_{11}(x) + a_{22}(x)) + \sqrt{((a_{11}(x) - a_{22}(x))^2 + 4a_{12}^2(x)}}{2}, \\ l_2(x) &= \frac{(a_{11}(x) + a_{22}(x)) - \sqrt{((a_{11}(x) - a_{22}(x))^2 + 4a_{12}^2(x)}}{2}, \end{aligned} \tag{64}$$

and corresponding eigenvectors $\mathbf{v}(x), \mathbf{w}(x)$ are

$$\mathbf{v} = \begin{pmatrix} \frac{a_{12}(x)}{\sqrt{(a_1^2 2(x) + (a_{11}(x) - l_1(x))^2}} \\ \frac{l_1(x) - a_{11}(x)}{\sqrt{(a_1^2 2(x) + (a_{11}(x) - l_1(x))^2}} \end{pmatrix}, \mathbf{w} = \begin{pmatrix} \frac{a_{12}(x)}{\sqrt{(a_1^2 2(x) + (a_{11}(x) - l_2(x))^2}} \\ \frac{l_2(x) - a_{11}(x)}{\sqrt{(a_1^2 2(x) + (a_{11}(x) - l_2(x))^2}} \end{pmatrix}. \tag{65}$$

Finally, we have

$$-\text{trace}(A(x)D^2u(x)) = -l_1(x)\frac{\partial^2 u}{\partial \mathbf{v}^2}(x) - l_2(x)\frac{\partial^2 u}{\partial \mathbf{w}^2}(x). \tag{66}$$

A.2. *Removing the Cross-derivatives for Fully Nonlinear Degenerate Elliptic Equation*

Consider

$$\begin{cases} F\left(\text{trace}\big(A(x)D^2u(x)\big)\right) = 0, & x \in \Omega, \\ u(x) = g(x), & x \in \partial\Omega, \end{cases} \tag{67}$$

where $A(x) \in \mathbb{S}^n$ is positive semi-definite for any $x \in \Omega$.

Theorem A.1. *Consider problem* (67); *suppose* F *is degenerate elliptic, then at each point* $x \in \Omega$, *define* $p_i(x) = \frac{\partial u}{\partial v_i}(x)$, *for any* $\epsilon \geq 0, i = 1, 2, \ldots, n$,

$$F\left(\sum_{j=1}^{n} l_j(x)p_j(x)\right) \leq F\left(\sum_{j=1, j\neq i}^{n} l_j(x)p_j(x) + l_i(x)(p_i(x) + \epsilon)\right). \tag{68}$$

Proof. According to equations (15) and (16),

$$
\begin{aligned}
&F\left(\sum_{j=1}^{n} l_j(x)p_j(x) + l_i(x)(p_i(x)+\epsilon)\right)\\
&= F\left(\sum_{j=1, j\neq i}^{n} l_j(x)v_j^T(x)D^2u(x)v_j(x) + l_i(x)(v_i^T(x)D^2u(x)v_i(x) + \epsilon v_i^T(x)v_i(x))\right)\\
&= F\left(\text{trace}(L(x)V^T(x)(D^2u(x)+\epsilon Z(x)))V(x)\right)\\
&= F\left(\text{trace}(V(x)L(x)V^T(x)(D^2u(x)+\epsilon Z))V(x)V^T(x)\right)\\
&= F\left(\text{trace}(A(x)(D^2u(x)+M)\right) \leq F\left(\text{trace}(A(x)D^2u(x))\right) = F\left(\sum_{j=1}^{n} l_j(x)p_j(x)\right),
\end{aligned}
\tag{69}
$$

where $z_{ii}=1, z_{ij}=0, j\neq i$ and $M(x)=\epsilon Z$ and the inequality comes from the elliptic degenerate property of equation (67). □

References

[1] L. P. Aarts and P. Van Der Veer. Neural network method for solving partial differential equations. *Neural Processing Letters*, 14(3):261–271, 2001.

[2] A. Altarovici, M. Reppen, and H. Mete Soner. Optimal consumption and investment with fixed and proportional transaction costs. *SIAM Journal on Control and Optimization*, 55(3):1673–1710, 2017.

[3] G. Barles and P. E Souganidis. Convergence of approximation schemes for fully nonlinear second order equations. *Asymptotic Analysis*, 4(3):271–283, 1991.

[4] S. Becker, P. Cheridito, and A. Jentzen. Deep optimal stopping. *Journal of Machine Learning Research*, 20:74, 2019.

[5] S. Becker, P. Cheridito, A. Jentzen, and T. Welti. Solving high-dimensional optimal stopping problems using deep learning. *European Journal of Applied Mathematics*, 32(3):470–514, 2021.

[6] J. Berg and K. Nyström. A unified deep artificial neural network approach to partial differential equations in complex geometries. *Neurocomputing*, 317:28–41, 2018.

[7] D. Bertsekas and J. N. Tsitsiklis. *Neuro-Dynamic Programming.* Athena Scientific, Nashua, New Hampshire, 1996.

[8] M. Bichuch. Asymptotic analysis for optimal investment in finite time with transaction costs. *SIAM Journal on Financial Mathematics*, 3 (1):433–458, 2012.

[9] J. Blechschmidt and O. G. Ernst. Three ways to solve partial differential equations with neural networks? A review. *GAMM-Mitteilungen*, 44(2):e202100006, 2021.

[10] Y. Chen, J. Wan and J. Lin. Monotone mixed finite difference scheme for Monge-Ampéere equation. *Journal of Scientific Computing*, 76:1839–1867, 2018.

[11] M. G. Crandall and P.-L. Lions. Convergent difference schemes for nonlinear parabolic equations and mean curvature motion. *Numerische Mathematik*, 75(1):17–41, 1996.

[12] S. Cuomo, V. Schiano D. Cola, F. Giampaolo, G. Rozza, M. Raissi, and F. Piccialli. Scientific machine learning through physics-informed neural networks: Where we are and what's next. *Journal of Scientific Computing*, 92:1–62, 2022. *arXiv preprint arXiv:2201.05624*.

[13] M. Dai and F. Yi. Finite-horizon optimal investment with transaction costs: A parabolic double obstacle problem. *Journal of Differential Equations*, 246(4):1445–1469, 2009.

[14] S. Fecamp, J. Mikael, and X. Warin. Deep learning for discrete-time hedging in incomplete markets. *Journal of computational Finance*, 25(2):51–85, 2021.

[15] A. R. Gallant and H. White. On learning the derivatives of an unknown mapping with multilayer feedforward networks. *Neural Networks*, 5(1):129–138, 1992.

[16] M. Germain, H. Pham, and X. Warin. Deep backward multistep schemes for nonlinear pdes and approximation error analysis. *SIAM Journal of Scientific Computing*, 44(1): A28–A56, 2022. *arXiv preprint arXiv:2006.01496*.

[17] L. Gonon, J. Muhle-Karbe, and X. Shi. Asset pricing with general transaction costs: Theory and numerics. *Mathematical Finance*, 31 (2):595–648, 2021.

[18] K. Hornik. Approximation capabilities of multilayer feedforward networks. *Neural Networks*, 4(2):251–257, 1991.

[19] K. Hornik, M. Stinchcombe, and H. White. Multilayer feedforward networks are universal approximators. *Neural Networks*, 2(5):359–366, 1989.

[20] K. Hornik, M. Stinchcombe, and H. White. Universal approximation of an unknown mapping and its derivatives using multilayer feedforward networks. *Neural Networks*, 3(5):551–560, 1990.

[21] I. E. Lagaris, A. Likas, and D. I. Fotiadis. Artificial neural networks for solving ordinary and partial differential equations. *IEEE Transactions on Neural Networks*, 9(5):987–1000, 1998.

[22] H. Lee and I. S. Kang. Neural algorithm for solving differential equations. *Journal of Computational Physics*, 91(1):110–131, 1990.

[23] M. Minsky and S. Papert. *Perceptrons: An Introduction to Computational Geometry.* MIT Press, Cambridge, MA, 1969.

[24] K. Muthuraman. A computational scheme for optimal investment–consumption with proportional transaction costs. *Journal of Economic Dynamics and Control*, 31(4):1132–1159, 2007.

[25] A. M. Oberman. Convergent difference schemes for degenerate elliptic and parabolic equations: Hamilton–Jacobi equations and free boundary problems. *SIAM Journal on Numerical Analysis*, 44(2):879–895, 2006.

[26] H. Owhadi. Bayesian numerical homogenization. *Multiscale Modeling & Simulation*, 13(3):812–828, 2015.

[27] M. Raissi, P. Perdikaris, and G. E. Karniadakis. Machine learning of linear differential equations using gaussian processes. *Journal of Computational Physics*, 348:683–693, 2017a.

[28] M. Raissi, P. Perdikaris, and G. E. Karniadakis. Physics informed deep learning (Part i): Data-driven solutions of nonlinear partial differential equations. *Journal of Computational Physics*, 378:686–707, 2019. *arXiv preprint arXiv:1711.10561.*

[29] J. Sirignano and K. Spiliopoulos. DGM: A deep learning algorithm for solving partial differential equations. *Journal of Computational Physics*, 375:1339–1364, 2018.

[30] S. Wang and P. Perdikaris. Deep learning of free boundary and Stefan problems. *Journal of Computational Physics*, 428:109914, 2021.

[31] E. Weinan, J. Han, and A. Jentzen. Deep learning-based numerical methods for high-dimensional parabolic partial differential equations and backward stochastic differential equations. *Communications in Mathematics and Statistics*, 5(4):349–380, 2017.

https://doi.org/10.1142/9789811280306_0005

Chapter 5

Data-Driven Non-Parametric Robust Control under Dependence Uncertainty

Erhan Bayraktar* **and Tao Chen**†

Department of Mathematics, University of Michigan, Ann Arbor
530 Church Street, Ann Arbor, MI 48109, USA
**erhan@umich.edu*
†*chenta@umich.edu*

Abstract

We consider a multi-period stochastic control problem where the multivariate driving stochastic factor of the system has known marginal distributions but uncertain dependence structure. To solve the problem, we propose to implement the non-parametric adaptive robust control framework. We aim to find the optimal control against the worst-case copulae in a sequence of shrinking uncertainty sets which are generated from continuously observing the data. Then, we use a stochastic gradient descent ascent algorithm to numerically handle the corresponding high-dimensional dynamic inf-sup optimization problem. We present the numerical results in the context of utility maximization and show that the controller benefits from knowing more information about the uncertain model.

Keywords: Non-parametric adaptive robust control, Model uncertainty, Stochastic control, Adaptive robust dynamic programming, Wasserstein distance, Markovian control problem, Utility maximization, Copula, Machine learning, Stochastic gradient descent ascent

1. Introduction

In this chapter, we propose a non-parametric approach for solving a stochastic Markovian control problem in discrete time under a special type of uncertainty. We assume that the multivariate driving random factor of the underlying stochastic process has known marginals and unknown dependence. Naturally, to deal with such kind of uncertainty, one can choose a parametric family of copula functions and learn the unknown parameter from the observed data. In this work, we avoid making such postulations to prevent model misspecification. When it comes to handling model uncertainty, there are different approaches, parametric and non-parametric, developed in the past decades to incorporate learning into solving control problems with unknown system models (cf. Refs. [14], [6], [15], [8]). However, earlier studies show that a pure learning approach without awareness of the model risk is prone to risk caused by estimation error and often leads to overly aggressive controls and system outcomes with high variances. On the other hand, the central idea of robust control goes back to Ref. [13]. A large body of research has been devoted to this area since then and produced fruitful results. Robust techniques are extremely successful in dealing with model risk, but if the learning phase is lacking in the framework, corresponding controls can be overly conservative and even trivial. Our work aims to address all the issues mentioned above when handling dependence uncertainty by applying the non-parametric adaptive robust methodology proposed in Ref. [2] and developing an efficient numerical scheme for implementing such a method. The main idea of adaptive robust control is to consider a specific type of sequential game: the controller first constructs a sequence of uncertainty sets by continuously observing the system data; then, at each time step, the nature chooses one model from the time-t uncertainty set that is the worst for the controller; finally, the controller will apply an optimal control in response, and both players (the controller and the nature) repeat the same process at latter time steps. Note that such a framework is data-driven and the learning phase is integrated into the optimization phase. Regarding constructing the desired uncertainty sets, we refer to Refs. [3] and [1] for the parametric case in discrete time and continuous time, respectively. Discussion of constructing time-dependent uncertainty sets in discrete time in the non-parametric case can be found in our earlier work [2]. In summary, to deal with the dependence uncertainty, we use the method described in the aforementioned papers to build uncertainty sets in terms of the Wasserstein ball centered at the non-parametric estimators of the copula by utilizing the concentration results for the empirical distribution and the Wasserstein distance (cf. Refs. [9], [11]) and formulate the corresponding robust control problem. Practically, numerical search of the worst-case copula in a Wasserstein ball is extremely difficult. One can utilize the results presented in Ref. [12] to obtain a duality result for solving the relevant inf-sup optimization problem. However, as we will see in the sequel, the Bellman equation derived in this framework has unavoidable high dimension. Thus, solving such an optimization problem using brute force is virtually impossible. Toward this end, we design a stochastic gradient descent ascent algorithm to mitigate the computational burden. On top of that, we use the Gaussian process regression model to approximate the corresponding value function. The gradient of such an approximation can be explicitly computed, and this fact increases the numerical efficiency in the dynamic programming backward recursion.

The rest of this chapter is organized as follows. We begin Section 2 with setting up the model and then discuss the stochastic process that represents the learning of the unknown dependence, and the construction of the uncertainty sets which contain all the considered copulae at different time steps. Section 3 is dedicated to the formulation of the non-parametric adaptive robust control framework. We investigate the solution of the non-parametric adaptive robust control problem in Section 4. In this section, we prove the Bellman principle of optimality for the problem and show the existence of measurable worst-case model selector as well as the existence of measurable optimal control. We also discuss the comparison among several different methods that can be used to handle the stochastic control problem under dependence uncertainty. Finally, in Section 5, we consider an illustrative example, namely the uncertain utility maximization problem where the investor needs to allocate the wealth among the money market account and several risky assets without knowing the true dependence of return processes of the risky assets. We apply the non-parametric adaptive robust control approach to such a problem and provide a numerical solver by using machine learning techniques, such as stochastic gradient descent ascent and the Gaussian process. Numerical results presented in this section show that knowing more about the distribution of the underlying stochastic process leads to an optimal trading strategy that is more balanced between profit seeking and risk aversion.

2. Non-Parametric Adaptive Robust Control Problem Subject to Dependence Uncertainty

Let $(\Omega, \mathscr{F})$ be a measurable space and $T \in \mathbb{N}$ be a fixed time horizon. Let $\mathcal{T} = \{0, 1, 2, \ldots, T\}$, $\mathcal{T}' = \{0, 1, 2, \ldots, T-1\}$ and $\mathcal{T}'' = \{1, 2, \ldots, T\}$. On the space $(\Omega, \mathscr{F})$, we consider a controlled stochastic process $X = \{X_t,\ t \in \mathcal{T}\}$ taking values in $\mathbb{R}^d$ with dynamics

$$X_{t+1} = S(t, X_t, \varphi_t, Z_{t+1}), \quad t \in \mathcal{T}'. \tag{1}$$

The above $Z_t = (Z_t^{(1)}, \ldots, Z_t^{(n)})$, $t \in \mathcal{T}''$, is an n-dimensional i.i.d. sequence adapted to the natural filtration of the process X which is denoted by $\mathbb{F} = \{\mathcal{F}_t, t \in \mathcal{T}\}$. The process $\varphi = \{\varphi_t, t \in \mathcal{T}'\}$ is also $\mathbb{F}$-adapted and takes values in a measurable subset $A \subset \mathbb{R}^m$. For every $t \in \mathcal{T}'$, the function $S(t, \cdot, \cdot, \cdot) : \mathbb{R}^d \times A \times \mathbb{R}^n \to \mathbb{R}^d$ is deterministic and continuous. In addition, we denote by $\mathcal{A}_t$ the set of all processes that take values in A and are adapted to the filtration $\mathbb{F}_t := \{\mathcal{F}_s, t \le s \le T-1\}$. Each element in $\mathcal{A}_t$ is called an admissible control starting at time t, and we use the convention $\mathcal{A} = \mathcal{A}_0$. In this work, we assume that the process Z is observable, and for every fixed $t \in \mathcal{T}''$, the marginal distributions of Z_t are known to the controller, but the dependence structure among marginals is unknown and needs to be learned. We write $\mathcal{P}(\mathbb{R}^n)$ as the set of all distributions on $\mathbb{R}^n$. Finally, let $\ell : \mathbb{R}^d \to \mathbb{R}$ be continuous, bounded from above, and play the role of the loss function. In this work, denote by F_* the true distribution of Z_t, $t \in \mathcal{T}''$; we will formulate and solve a robust optimization problem aiming to minimize the expected loss with the restriction that the worst-case distribution of Z_t, $t \in \mathcal{T}''$, matches the marginals of F_*. To proceed, we specify the following notations which will be used throughout:

- For any $z \in \mathbb{R}^n$, $z^{(i)}$, $i \in \mathcal{N} := \{1, \ldots, n\}$, is the ith component of z.
- For any CDF F of an n-dimensional random variable, $F^{(i)}$, $i \in \mathcal{N}$, is the ith marginal CDF.
- For any CDF F of an n-dimensional random variable, $F^{-1} = (F^{(1),-1}, \ldots, F^{(n),-1})$.
- For any CDF F of an n-dimensional random variable and $z \in \mathbb{R}^n$,

$$\begin{aligned} F \circ z &= (F^{(1)}(z^{(1)}), \ldots, F^{(n)}(z^{(n)})), \\ F^{-1} \circ z &= (F^{(1),-1}(z^{(1)}), \ldots, F^{(n),-1}(z^{(n)})). \end{aligned}$$

- For any function f on $\mathbb{R}^n$, and CDF F of an n-dimensional random variable,

$$\begin{aligned} f \circ F &= f(F^{(1)}, \ldots, F^{(n)}), \\ f \circ F^{-1} &= f(F^{(1),-1}, \ldots, F^{(n),-1}). \end{aligned}$$

In order to deal with the dependence uncertainty, we will take the copula perspective and note that

$$F_*(z) = C_* \left(F_*^{(1)} \left(z^{(1)} \right), \ldots, F_*^{(n)} \left(z^{(n)} \right) \right), \tag{2}$$

where C_* is the unknown true copula function of Z_t. Here, we make a standing assumption that $F_*^{(i)}$, $i \in \mathcal{N}$, is continuous and strictly increasing. Consequently, the copula function C_* is unique. In the sequel, we will write $\mathbb{P}_F$ and $\mathbb{E}_F$ as the probability measure and expectation, respectively, associated with the distribution function F.

In the first step, having in mind the possibility that the parametric family which C_* belongs to could be unknown, we need to define an estimator for C_* based on the observed data of Z in a non-parametric manner. There are essentially two different ways to achieve this. One is to use the up-to-time t information of Z to construct a multidimensional empirical distribution $\widehat{F}_t$ for F_* and define an estimator of C_* via (2). The other is to consider a kernel-based estimator of

F_* which is a smoothed version of $\widehat{F}_t$ instead. One example in such a family of methods is the so-called perturbed empirical distribution. Both approaches have their advantages: using the empirical distribution will simplify the numerical computation, while the kernel-based method offers a better estimator that is more in line with the assumption that $F_*^{(i)}$, $i \in \mathcal{N}$, are continuous. To this end, we consider the following estimator of F_* (in a recursive format):

$$\widehat{F}_{t+1}(z) = \frac{(t_0 + t)\widehat{F}_t(z) + H_{t+1}(z - Z_{t+1})}{t_0 + t + 1}, \quad z \in \mathbb{R}^n, \tag{3}$$

where H_t is a sequence of continuous distribution function such that $\lim_{t\to\infty} H_t = \mathbb{1}_{[0,\infty)^n}$ if t is allowed to go to infinity, or $H_t \equiv \mathbb{1}_{[0,\infty)^n}$ for any considered t. The former choice corresponds to constructing $\widehat{F}$ as the perturbed empirical distribution and the latter is the case of choosing $\widehat{F}$ to be the usual empirical distribution.

Next, we define

$$\widehat{C}_t(u) = \widehat{F}_t(F_*^{-1} \circ u), \quad u \in [0,1]^n, \tag{4}$$

and $\widehat{C}_t$ is an estimator of the copula C_*. Moreover, we have

$$\widehat{C}_{t+1}(u) = \frac{(t_0 + t)\widehat{C}_t(u) + H_{t+1}(F_*^{-1} \circ u - Z_{t+1})}{t_0 + t + 1} =: R(t, \widehat{C}_t, Z_{t+1}),$$
$$u \in [0,1]^n. \tag{5}$$

Remark 2.1. We want to stress that even though F_* is uncertain, we assume that the marginals $F_*^{(i)}$, $i \in \mathcal{N}$, are known, and therefore due to our definition F_*^{-1} is also known to the controller.

In many works, regardless of knowing $F_*^{(i)}$, $i \in \mathcal{N}$, or not, the empirical copula is defined as $\widehat{C}_t(u) = \widehat{F}_t(\widehat{F}_t^{-1} \circ u)$ which means using the empirical marginals instead of the true ones to construct the estimator for the copula. Note that in such a construction, due to the discontinuity of $\widehat{F}_t$, the resulting $\widehat{C}_t$ is not necessarily a copula. On the other hand, for $H_t \equiv \mathbb{1}_{[0,\infty)^n}$, the estimator of C_* defined in (4) is not a copula either. Hence, any application or computation purely based on either of these two estimators could be problematic. We argue that, for this reason, one should consider a robust framework to mitigate the inherent risk that comes from the statistical estimation procedure.

To proceed, we fix the notations $\widehat{F}$ and $\widehat{C}$ for estimators defined as in (3) and (4) and assume that, for any $0 \leq \alpha \leq 1$, there exists a deterministic function $r(\alpha, t_0, t)$ decreasing in $t \in \mathcal{T}'$ such that

$$\mathbb{P}(d_{W,p}(\widehat{C}_t, C_*) \leq r(\alpha, t_0, t)) \geq 1 - \alpha, \tag{6}$$

where $d_{W,p}$ is the Wasserstein distance between distributions in $\mathcal{P}([0,1]^n)$ of order $p \geq 1$. In application, regarding the construction of $r(\alpha, t_0, t)$ and for $H_t \equiv \mathbb{1}_{[0,\infty)^n}$, we will use the concentration results for the empirical distribution in Ref. [11, Theorem 2] by imposing necessary integrability assumptions on C_*. The takeaway is that there exists some function $r(\alpha, t_0, t)$ satisfying (6).

The uncertainty of C_* is then modeled, by using (6), in terms of the confidence region as

$$\mathcal{C}_t^\alpha(\widehat{C}_t) = \left\{ C \in \mathcal{P}([0,1]^n) : d_{W,p}(\widehat{C}_t, C) \leq r(\alpha, t_0, t) \right\}, \tag{7}$$

and the set $\mathcal{C}_t^\alpha$ is called the uncertainty set of C_*. Since $[0,1]^n$ is a compact subset of $\mathbb{R}^n$, then $d_{W,p}$ is a metric on $\mathcal{P}([0,1]^n)$. Throughout, we consider the metric space $(\mathcal{P}([0,1]^n), d_{W,p})$. As mentioned earlier, we will adopt the adaptive robust control framework to our setup in this project. Hence, we are going to find the worst-case copula function in $\mathcal{C}_t^\alpha$ and search for the optimal control in reaction to such a worst-case copula. One needs to realize that $\mathcal{C}_t^\alpha$ includes all types of distributions on $[0,1]^n$ and in general these distributions do not necessarily have uniform marginals. In other words, not all $C \in \mathcal{C}_t^\alpha$ are copulae, and this issue will be addressed in the sequel.

Before we discuss and formulate the non-parametric adaptive robust control problem under dependence uncertainty, we first provide the following technical results for preparation:

Lemma 2.2. *For fixed $t \in \mathcal{T}'$, the mapping $R(t, \cdot, \cdot) : \mathcal{P}([0,1]^n) \times \mathbb{R} \to \mathcal{P}([0,1]^n)$ is continuous.*

Proof. We will prove the result for H_t, $t \in \mathcal{T}'$, being continuous distribution functions. Regarding the case of $H_t \equiv \mathbb{1}_{[0,\infty)}$, we refer the readers to [8] or Lemma 3.1.

Assume that $(C_i, z_i) \to (C, z)$, where $C_i, C \in \mathcal{P}([0,1]^n)$, $z_i, z \in \mathbb{R}$, $i = 1, 2, \ldots$. Then, $d_{W,p}(C_i, C) \to 0$ and $z_i \to z$. Denote $\mu_{C_i,z_i} = R(t, C_i, z_i)$ and $\mu_{C,z} = R(t, C, z)$, and $\mathcal{M} := \{f : |f(z) - f(z')| \leq \|z - z'\|,\ z, z' \in [0,1]^n\}$. Note that $[0,1]^n$ is compact, so for any $p \geq 1$, there exists a constant b_p such that $d_{W,p}(F, G) \leq b_p d_{W,1}(F, G)$ for any $F, G \in \mathcal{P}([0,1]^n)$. Hence, we have that

$$\begin{aligned} d_{W,p}(\mu_{C_i,z_i}, \mu_{C,z}) &\leq b_p d_{W,1}(\mu_{C_i,z_i}, \mu_{C,z}) \\ &= b_p \sup\left\{\int_{[0,1]^n} f d\mu_{C_i,z_i} - \int_{[0,1]^n} f d\mu_{C,z} : f \in \mathcal{M}\right\}. \end{aligned}$$

By the construction of the function R, we obtain

$$\begin{aligned} \sup\left\{\int_{[0,1]^n} f d(\mu_{C_i,z_i} - \mu_{C,z}) : f \in \mathcal{M}.\right\} &= \sup\left\{\frac{t_0 + t}{t_0 + t + 1}\int_{[0,1]^n} f d(C_i - C)\right. \\ &\quad \left. + \frac{\int_{[0,1]^n} f d(H_{t+1}(F_*^{-1} \circ u - z_i) - H_{t+1}(F_*^{-1} \circ u - z))}{t + t_0 + 1}\ :\ f \in \mathcal{M}\right\}. \end{aligned}$$

Note that

$$\begin{aligned} H_{t+1}(F_*^{-1} \circ u - z_i) &= \mathbb{P}(\widetilde{H} \leq F_*^{-1} \circ u - z_i) \\ &= \mathbb{P}\left(\left(F_*^{(1)}(\widetilde{H}^{(1)} + z_i^{(1)}), \ldots, F_*^{(n)}(\widetilde{H}^{(n)} + z_i^{(n)}\right) \leq u\right), \end{aligned}$$

where $\widetilde{H}$ is a multidimensional random variable with distribution H_{t+1}. Then, we get that

$$\begin{aligned} &\sup\left\{\int_{[0,1]^n} f d(H_{t+1}(F_*^{-1} \circ u - z_i) - H_{t+1}(F_*^{-1} \circ u - z)) :\ f \in \mathcal{M}\right\} \\ &\quad = \sup\left\{\mathbb{E}\left[f\left(F_*^{(1)}(\widetilde{H}^{(1)} + z_i^{(1)}), \ldots, F_*^{(n)}(\widetilde{H}^{(n)} + z_i^{(n)}\right)\right]\right. \\ &\qquad \left. - \mathbb{E}\left[f\left(F_*^{(1)}(\widetilde{H}^{(1)} + z^{(1)}), \ldots, F_*^{(n)}(\widetilde{H}^{(n)} + z^{(n)}\right)\right] : f \in \mathcal{M}\right\} \\ &\quad \leq \mathbb{E}\left[\left\|\left(F_*^{(1)}(\widetilde{H}^{(1)} + z_i^{(1)}), \ldots, F_*^{(n)}(\widetilde{H}^{(n)} + z_i^{(n)})\right)\right.\right. \\ &\qquad \left.\left. - \left(F_*^{(1)}(\widetilde{H}^{(1)} + z^{(1)}), \ldots, F_*^{(n)}(\widetilde{H}^{(n)} + z^{(n)})\right)\right\|\right]. \end{aligned}$$

Since F_*^j, $j \in \mathcal{N}$, are all bounded continuous functions, thus by dominated convergence theorem,

$$\sup\left\{\frac{\int_{[0,1]^n} fd(H_{t+1}(F_*^{-1}\circ u - z_i) - H_{t+1}(F_*^{-1}\circ u - z))}{t+t_0+1} : f \in \mathcal{M}\right\} \to 0$$

as $z_i \to z$. On the other hand,

$$\sup\left\{\frac{t_0+t}{t_0+t+1}\int_{[0,1]^n} fd(C_i - C) : f \in \mathcal{M}\right\} = \frac{t_0+t}{t_0+t+1} d_{W,1}(C_i, C).$$

In view that $d_{W,1}(C_i, C) \leq d_{W,p}(C_i, C)$ for $p \geq 1$, we have that $d_{W,p}(C_i, C) \to 0$ implies that the above term converges to 0 as well. Therefore, $d_{W,p}(\mu_{C_i,z_i}, \mu_{C,z}) \to 0$ and the mapping $R(t, \cdot, \cdot)$ is continuous. □

Another important property that $\mathcal{C}_t^\alpha$ satisfies as a set-valued function is upper hemi-continuity (u.h.c.) and it is stated in the following:

Lemma 2.3. *For every $t \in \mathcal{T}'$, the set-valued function $\mathcal{C}_t^\alpha$ is upper hemi-continuous.*

Proof. We need to show that for any $C \in \mathcal{P}([0,1]^n)$ and any open set E such that $\mathcal{C}_t^\alpha(C) \subset E \subset \mathcal{P}([0,1]^n)$, there exists a neighborhood D of C such that for all $C' \in D$, $\mathcal{C}_t^\alpha(C') \subset E$.

To this end, let $\varepsilon = \mathrm{dist}(C, \partial E) - r(\alpha, t_0, t)$ where $\mathrm{dist}(C, \partial E)$ is the shortest Wasserstein-p distance from C to the boundary of E. Since E is an open set, then $\varepsilon > 0$. Hence, we take D as the Wasserstein-p ball centered at C with radius ε. It is clear that for any $C' \in D$, we have $\mathcal{C}_t^\alpha(C') \subset E$. Therefore, for fixed $t \in \mathcal{T}'$, $\mathcal{C}_t^\alpha$ is u.h.c. □

3. Non-parametric Adaptive Robust Control Problem

Now we proceed to formulate the non-parametric adaptive robust control problem assuming the true copula function C_* is unknown. Recall that we consider $\mathcal{P}([0,1]^n)$ with the metric $d_{W,p}$. Obviously, $(\mathcal{P}([0,1]^n, d_{W,p})$ is separable and complete. Hence, it is a Polish space and thus a Borel space. We define the augmented state process

$Y = \{Y_t = (X_t, \widehat{C}_t), t \in \mathcal{T}\}$, and such a process has the following dynamics:

$$Y_{t+1} = \mathbf{G}(t, X_t, \varphi_t, Z_{t+1}) := (S(t, X_t, \varphi_t, Z_{t+1}), R(t, \widehat{C}_t, Z_{t+1})), \quad t \in \mathcal{T}'. \tag{8}$$

According to the assumption that S is continuous and Lemma 2.2, we get that $\mathbf{G}$ is continuous and therefore Borel measurable.

3.1. *Transition Kernel of the State Process*

Through the rest of this chapter, we will write $\mathcal{C}_t^{\alpha}(Y_t) := \mathcal{C}_t^{\alpha}(\widehat{C}_t)$ for $Y_t = (X_t, \widehat{C}_t)$. For $C \in \mathcal{P}([0,1]^n)$, one would like to define the transition kernel of Y as

$$Q_t(dy'|y, a, F) = \mathbb{P}_{C \circ F^*}(\mathbf{G}(t, y, a, Z_{t+1}) \in dy').$$

However, $C \circ F^*$ is a well-defined distribution on $\mathbb{R}^n$ only when $C^{(i)}$, $i \in \mathcal{N}$, is left continuous at 1 and

$$\lim_{u \to 0} C^{(i)}(u) = 0.$$

Distribution $C \in \mathcal{P}([0,1]^n)$ does not satisfy the above conditions and will result in a distribution $C \circ F^*$ putting mass on infinity. To overcome this problem, we consider $\overline{\mathbb{R}} = \mathbb{R} \bigcup \{-\infty, \infty\}$ with order topology and hence Borel σ-algebra $\mathcal{B}(\overline{\mathbb{R}}) = \sigma\left(\mathcal{B}(\mathbb{R}) \bigcup \{[-\infty, x), (x, \infty], x \in \mathbb{R}\}\right)$. Note that we take the convention $\infty - \infty = 0$. We also consider a metric on $\overline{\mathbb{R}}$ consistent with $\mathcal{B}(\overline{\mathbb{R}})$. Consequently, we have $\overline{\mathbb{R}}^n$ equipped with the product topology and it is a Polish space as well as a Borel space. In addition, we consider $\mathcal{P}(\overline{\mathbb{R}}^n)$ the set of all probability distributions on $\overline{\mathbb{R}}^n$ with topology consistent with weak convergence. For any $F \in \mathcal{P}(\mathbb{R}^n)$, we denote by $\overline{F}$ its extension in $\mathcal{P}(\overline{\mathbb{R}}^n)$ as $\overline{F}(x) = F(x)$ for $x \in \mathbb{R}^n$, and $\overline{F}$ being the limit of F for x that has component equals to infinity. Naturally, we change the state space of X to $\overline{\mathbb{R}}^d$ and define the augmented state space $E_Y = \overline{\mathbb{R}}^d \times \mathcal{P}([0,1]^n)$ with product topology. It is then a Borel space, and the Borel σ-algebra $\mathcal{E}_Y$ coincides with the product σ-algebra. In addition, for any relevant real-valued function f, we write

$$f(\infty) = \lim_{x\to\infty} f(x),$$
$$f(-\infty) = \lim_{x\to-\infty} f(x).$$

To proceed, for any $t \in \mathcal{T}'$, $(y,a) \in E_Y \times A$, and distribution $C \in \mathcal{P}([0,1]^n)$, Q_t is a probability measure on $\mathcal{E}_Y$ such that

$$Q_t(D|y,a,C) = \mathbb{P}_{C\circ F_*}(\mathbf{G}(t,y,a,Z_{t+1}) \in D), \quad D \in \mathcal{E}_Y.$$

In particular, when C is a copula, $C\circ F_*$ is an n-dimensional probability distribution on $\mathbb{R}^n$ with marginals $F_*^{(1)},\ldots,F_*^{(n)}$. One important property of Q_t is that it is Borel measurable for fixed $t \in \mathcal{T}'$. Such a property is crucial for showing the existence of measurable optimal control and worst-case copula. To this end, we extend Lemma 2.2 to the general case and provide the following technical results:

Lemma 3.1. *For every fixed $t \in \mathcal{T}'$, the mapping*

$$\overline{R}(t,F,z') = \frac{(t_0+t)F(z) + \overline{H}_{t+1}(z-z')}{t_0+t+1}, \quad F \in \mathcal{P}(\overline{\mathbb{R}}^n),\ z,z' \in \overline{\mathbb{R}}^n, \tag{9}$$

is continuous on $\mathcal{P}(\overline{\mathbb{R}}^n) \times \overline{\mathbb{R}}^n$.

Proof. Assume that $(F_i, z_i') \to (F, z_0')$ and it implies that $F_i \to F$ in distribution and $z_i' \to z_0'$. Take any continuity set B of $\overline{R}(t,F_0,z_0')$. That is, for the boundary ∂B of B, the probability $\mathbb{P}_{\overline{R}(t,F_0,z_0')}(\partial B)$ is equal to 0. Therefore, we get that B is also a continuity set of F and $\overline{H}_{t+1}(z-z_0')$.

Now, since $F_i \to F_0$ in distribution, then by the Portmanteau lemma, we know

$$\lim_{i\to\infty} \mathbb{P}_{F_i}(B) \to \mathbb{P}_{F_0}(B).$$

On the other hand, for any $z' \in \overline{\mathbb{R}}^n$, $\overline{H}_{t+1}(z-z') = \mathbb{P}(\widetilde{H} \le z-z') = \mathbb{P}(\widetilde{H} + z' \le z)$, where $\widetilde{H}$ is the random variable with distribution

$\overline{H}_{t+1}$. Since z'_i converges to the constant z'_0, then $\widetilde{H} + z'_i \to \widetilde{H} + z'_0$ in distribution. In turn, we get

$$\lim_{i\to\infty} \mathbb{P}_{\overline{H}_{t+1}(z-z'_i)}(B) \to \mathbb{P}_{\overline{H}_{t+1}(z-z'_0)}(B).$$

To summarize, we have that

$$\lim_{i\to\infty} \mathbb{P}_{\overline{R}(t,F_i,z'_i)}(B) = \mathbb{P}_{\overline{R}(t,F_0,z'_0)}(B),$$

and $\overline{R}(t,F,z')$ is continuous on $\mathcal{P}(\overline{\mathbb{R}}^n) \times \overline{\mathbb{R}}^n$. □

With this result in hand, we define the transition kernel on the product space $\overline{\mathbb{R}}^n \times \mathcal{P}(\overline{\mathbb{R}}^n)$ with product topology. That is, fix $t \in \mathcal{T}'$, for any $(x, F, a, G) \in \overline{\mathbb{R}}^n \times \mathcal{P}(\overline{\mathbb{R}}^n) \times A \times \mathcal{P}(\overline{\mathbb{R}}^n)$, and any set D belongs to the Borel σ-algebra of $\overline{\mathbb{R}}^n \times \mathcal{P}(\overline{\mathbb{R}}^n)$, we write

$$\overline{Q}_t(D|x, F, a, G) = \mathbb{P}_G((S(t, x, a, Z_{t+1}), \overline{R}(t, F, Z_{t+1})) \in D).$$

Then, we show the measurability of $\overline{Q}_t$, $t \in \mathcal{T}'$.

Lemma 3.2. *For every fixed $t \in \mathcal{T}'$, $\overline{Q}_t$ is a continuous stochastic kernel on $\overline{\mathbb{R}}^n \times \mathcal{P}(\overline{\mathbb{R}}^n)$ given $\overline{\mathbb{R}}^n \times \mathcal{P}(\overline{\mathbb{R}}^n) \times A \times \mathcal{P}(\overline{\mathbb{R}}^n)$.*

Proof. It is enough to prove that for any bounded continuous function f on $\overline{\mathbb{R}}^n \times \mathcal{P}(\overline{\mathbb{R}}^n)$, we have

$$\int_{\overline{\mathbb{R}}^n \times \mathcal{P}(\overline{\mathbb{R}}^n)} f(y)\overline{Q}_t(dy|x, F, a, G) \tag{10}$$

is continuous w.r.t. (x, F, a, G). To this end, we view that

$$\int_{\overline{\mathbb{R}}^n \times \mathcal{P}(\overline{\mathbb{R}}^n)} f(y)\overline{Q}_t(dy|x, F, a, G) = \int_{\overline{\mathbb{R}}^n} f((S(t, x, a, z), \overline{R}(t, F, z))dG(z).$$

By assumption on S and Lemma 3.1, for fixed $t \in \mathcal{T}'$, S and $\overline{R}$ are continuous w.r.t. other variables. Since f is also continuous, then $f((S(t, x, a, z), \overline{R}(t, F, z))$ is continuous w.r.t. (x, F, a, z). In addition, $G(z)$ can be seen as a continuous stochastic kernel on $\overline{\mathbb{R}}^n$ given (x, F, a, G) because it does not depend on (x, F, a). Hence, by [5,

Proposition 7.30], we get that

$$\int_{\overline{\mathbb{R}}^n} f((S(t,x,a,z),\overline{R}(t,F,z))dG(z)$$

is continuous w.r.t. (x,F,a,G). We immediately conclude that (10) is continuous w.r.t. (x,F,a,G). □

Next, we define the following mappings between $\mathcal{P}([0,1]^n)$ and $\mathcal{P}(\overline{\mathbb{R}}^n)$ similar to (4): for any $F \in \mathcal{P}(\overline{\mathbb{R}}^n)$,

$$C(u) := F(F_*^{-1} \circ u), \quad u \in [0,1]^n, \tag{11}$$

and for any $C \in \mathcal{P}([0,1]^n)$,

$$F(x) := C(F_* \circ x), \quad x \in \overline{\mathbb{R}}^n. \tag{12}$$

We realize that due to our assumptions on the marginals $F_*^{(i)}$, $i \in \mathcal{N}$, the mapping

$$u \to F_* \circ u, \quad u \in [0,1]^n,$$

defines a homeomorphism between $[0,1]^n$ and $\overline{\mathbb{R}}^n$. By using such an observation, we show the main result of this section as follows:

Proposition 3.3. *For each $t \in \mathcal{T}'$, the probability $Q_t(\,\cdot\,|y,a,C)$ is a continuous stochastic kernel on E_Y given $E_Y \times A \times \mathcal{P}([0,1]^n)$. Moreover, it is a Borel measurable stochastic kernel on E_Y given by $E_Y \times A \times \mathcal{P}([0,1]^n)$.*

Proof. Through the proof, all the convergence for probability distributions is understood in the weak sense. We will prove the statements in several steps:

1. Establish a mapping M_1 from $E_Y \times A \times \mathcal{P}([0,1]^n)$ to $\overline{\mathbb{R}}^n \times \mathcal{P}(\overline{\mathbb{R}}^n) \times A \times \mathcal{P}(\overline{\mathbb{R}}^n)$ that is continuous.
2. Use Lemma 3.2 to obtain the continuous mapping $\overline{Q}_t$ from $\overline{\mathbb{R}}^n \times \mathcal{P}(\overline{\mathbb{R}}^n) \times A \times \mathcal{P}(\overline{\mathbb{R}}^n)$ to $\mathcal{P}(\overline{\mathbb{R}}^n \times \mathcal{P}(\overline{\mathbb{R}}^n))$.
3. Construct a mapping M_2 from $\mathcal{P}(\overline{\mathbb{R}}^n \times \mathcal{P}(\overline{\mathbb{R}}^n))$ to $\mathcal{P}(E_Y)$, which is restricted to the family of $\overline{Q}_t(\,\cdot\,|x,F,a,G)$ and satisfies some proper form of continuity.

We also need M_1 and M_2 to satisfy $Q_t = M_2 \circ \overline{Q}_t \circ M_1$. To this end, for the first step, we take $M_1 : (x, \widetilde{C}, a, C) \mapsto (x, \widetilde{C} \circ F_*, a, C \circ F_*)$, $F, G \in \mathcal{P}([0,1]^n)$. Assume that the sequences $\{\widetilde{C}_i \in \mathcal{P}([0,1]^n), i = 1, 2, \ldots\}$ and $\{C_i \in \mathcal{P}([0,1]^n), i = 1, 2, \ldots\}$ converge to $\widetilde{C}_0 \in \mathcal{P}([0,1]^n)$ and $C_0 \in \mathcal{P}([0,1]^n)$ in distribution, respectively. It implies that for any continuity point u of $\widetilde{C}_0$, we have $\widetilde{C}_i(u) \to \widetilde{C}_0(u)$ as $i \to \infty$. In view of the homeomorphism

$$u \to F_*^{-1} \circ u, \quad u \in [0,1]^n,$$

if z is a continuity point of $\widetilde{C}_0 \circ F_*$, then $\left(F_*^{(1)}(z^{(1)}), \ldots, F_*^{(n)}(z^{(n)})\right)$ is a continuity point of $\widetilde{C}_0$. Recall that $\widetilde{C}_i$ converges to $\widetilde{C}_0$ in distribution, we get

$$\begin{aligned}\lim_{i\to\infty} \widetilde{C}_i \circ F_*(z) &= \lim_{i\to\infty} \widetilde{C}_i(F_* \circ z) = \lim_{i\to\infty} \widetilde{C}_i \left(F_*^{(1)}(z^{(1)}), \ldots, F_*^{(n)}(z^{(n)})\right) \\ &= \widetilde{C}_0 \left(F_*^{(1)}(z^{(1)}), \ldots, F_*^{(n)}(z^{(n)})\right) = \widetilde{C}_0 \circ F_*(z),\end{aligned}$$

which implies that $\widetilde{C}_i \circ F_*$ converges to $\widetilde{C}_0 \circ F_*$ in distribution. Similarly, $C_i \circ F_*$ converges to $C_0 \circ F_*$ in distribution, and Step 1 is done. Also note that Step 2 is fulfilled according to Lemma 3.2.

Next, define $M_2 : \overline{Q}_t(\,\cdot\,|x, F, a, G) \mapsto Q_t(\,\cdot\,|x, F \circ F_*^{-1}, a, G \circ F_*^{-1})$, $F, G \in \mathcal{P}(\overline{\mathbb{R}}^n)$. We will show that Q_t is continuous w.r.t. (x, F, a, G). In turn, the mapping M_2 will be continuous according to the definition of continuous parametric mapping. Let $D \in \mathcal{E}_Y$ be a closed set, and let (F_i, G_i) converge to (F_0, G_0). Similar to the discussion in Step 1, we have $F_i \circ F_*^{-1}$ and $G_i \circ F_*^{-1}$ converge to $F_0 \circ F_*^{-1}$ and $G_0 \circ F_*^{-1}$, respectively. Thus, by Lemma 2.2 and the fact that continuity in distribution and continuity in the Wasserstein sense are equivalent on $\mathcal{P}([0,1]^n)$, the function $\mathbf{G}(t, x, F \circ F_*^{-1}, a, z)$ is continuous w.r.t. (x, F, a, z). Consider any bounded continuous function f on E_Y, we get that

$$\begin{aligned}&\int_{E_Y} f(y) Q_t(dy|x, F \circ F_*^{-1}, a, G \circ F_*^{-1}) \\ &\quad = \int_{\overline{\mathbb{R}}^n} f(\mathbf{G}(t, x, F \circ F_*^{-1}, a, z)) dG(F_*^{-1} \circ z). \qquad (13)\end{aligned}$$

The integrand $f(\mathbf{G}(t, x, F \circ F_*^{-1}, a, z))$ is continuous w.r.t. (x, F, a, z). Also, we view the $G \circ F_*^{-1}$ as a continuous stochastic kernel w.r.t. (x, F, a, G). By Ref. [5, Proposition 7.30] again, the integral

$$\int_{\mathbb{R}^n} f(\mathbf{G}(t, x, F \circ F_*^{-1}, a, z)) dG(F_*^{-1} \circ z)$$

is continuous in (x, F, a, G) and so is

$$\int_{E_Y} f(y) Q_t(dy|x, F \circ F_*^{-1}, a, G \circ F_*^{-1})$$

due to (13). As a result, Q_t is continuous in (x, F, a, G), and Step 3 is complete.

Finally, we note that $Q_t = M_2 \circ \overline{Q}_t \circ M_1$. According to the above discussion and equivalence between continuity in distribution and in the Wasserstein sense on $\mathcal{P}([0,1]^n)$, Q_t is a continuous stochastic kernel. Hence, it is also a Borel measurable stochastic kernel. □

3.2. *Formulation of Adaptive Robust Control Problem*

In this work, we will formulate and solve a closed-loop feedback control problem. To this end, with slight abuse of notations, we say that a control process φ is Markovian if for every $t \in \mathcal{T}'$

$$\varphi_t = \varphi_t(Y(t)),$$

such that $\varphi_t(\cdot) : E_Y \to A$ is a measurable mapping. Similarly, a process ψ is called a Markovian model selector if

$$\psi_t = \psi_t(Y(t)),$$

where $\psi_t(\cdot) : E_Y \to \mathcal{P}([0,1]^n)$ is measurable. In the adaptive robust framework, we consider the Markovian control processes and Markovian model selectors such that $\psi_t(y) \in \mathcal{C}_t^\alpha(y)$ and $\psi_t(y)$ is restricted to be a copula for any $y \in E_Y$. For every $t \in \mathcal{T}'$, any time-t state $y_t \in E_Y$, and control process $\varphi \in \mathcal{A}_t$, we define

$$\mathbf{\Psi}_t^{y_t} = \{\psi : \psi_s(y_s) \in \mathcal{C}_s^\alpha(y_s), \quad t \leq s \leq T-1\}.$$

In addition, let $\varphi \in \mathcal{A}_t$ and δ_y be the Dirac probability measure that assigns the mass at $y \in E_Y$. Then, at time t, for the current state $Y_t = y$, define the probability measure $\mathbb{Q}^{\varphi,\psi}_{y,t}$ on the concatenated canonical space $\mathsf{X}_{s=t}^T E_Y$ as

$$\mathbb{Q}^{\varphi,\psi}_{y,t}(B_t \times \cdots \times B_T)$$
$$= \int_{B_t}\int_{B_{t+1}} \cdots \int_{B_T} \prod_{s=t}^{T-1} Q_s(dy_{s+1}|y_s, \varphi(s,y_s), \psi(s,y_s))\delta_y(dy_t).$$

Accordingly, we consider the family of probability measures $\mathcal{Q}^{\varphi}_{y,t} = \left\{\mathbb{Q}^{\varphi,\psi}_{y,t},\ \psi \in \mathbf{\Psi}^y_t\right\}$, and we write, for simplicity, $\mathcal{Q}^{\varphi}_y = \mathcal{Q}^{\varphi}_{y,0}$. Finally, for $Y_0 = y \in E_Y$, the non-parametric adaptive robust control problem in this work is formulated as

$$\inf_{\varphi \in \mathcal{A}} \sup_{\mathbb{Q}^{\psi} \in \mathcal{Q}^{\varphi}_y} \mathbb{E}_{\mathbb{Q}^{\psi}}[\ell(X_T)],$$
$$\text{s.t.} \quad \psi_t \text{ is a copula}, \qquad t \in \mathcal{T}'. \tag{14}$$

Note that for every $t \in \mathcal{T}'$, any $y \in E_Y$, search for the worst-case copula in $\mathcal{C}^{\alpha}_t(y)$ is practically impossible. To overcome such a difficulty, we adopt the method of penalty functions and use it to reformulate (14). Ultimately, for every fixed $t \in \mathcal{T}'$ and any fixed $(y,a) \in E_Y \times A$, we want to find the optimizer $\psi_t(y,a)$ such that $\psi_t(y,a) \circ F_*$ has marginals $F^{(i)}_*$, $i \in \mathcal{N}$. Hence, we denote by $C_b(\overline{\mathbb{R}})$ the set of all continuous, bounded, real-valued functions and consider the penalty function

$$\rho(\psi) = \sum_{t \in \mathcal{T}'} \rho_t(\psi_t) := \sum_{t \in \mathcal{T}'} \sum_{i \in \mathcal{N}} \sup_{f_i \in C_b(\overline{\mathbb{R}})} \left(\mathbb{E}_{(\psi_t \circ F_*)^{(i)}}[f_i] - \mathbb{E}_{F^{(i)}_*}[f_i]\right).$$

The choice of the penalty function is inspired by the criterion that characterizes the weak convergence of probability distributions, and it is similar to the penalty function used in Ref. [12]. Note that for such penalty, we have the following:

Lemma 3.4. *For any fixed $t \in \mathcal{T}'$, ψ_t is a copula if and only if $\rho_t(\psi_t) = 0$.*

Proof. If ψ_t is a copula, then it is obvious that $\rho_t(\psi_t) = 0$. On the other hand, note that for any $i \in \mathcal{N}$,

$$\sup_{f\in C_b(\overline{\mathbb{R}})} \left(\mathbb{E}_{(\psi_t\circ F_*)^{(i)}}[f] - \mathbb{E}_{F_*^{(i)}}[f]\right) \geq \mathbb{E}_{(\psi_t\circ F_*)^{(i)}}[0] - \mathbb{E}_{F_*^{(i)}}[0] = 0.$$

Hence, if $\rho_t(\psi_t) = 0$, we obtain that for any $i \in \mathcal{N}$,

$$\sup_{f\in C_b(\overline{\mathbb{R}})} \left(\mathbb{E}_{(\psi_t\circ F_*)^{(i)}}[f] - \mathbb{E}_{F_*^{(i)}}[f]\right) = 0.$$

Moreover, we get that for any $i \in \mathcal{N}$, and any $f \in C_b(\overline{\mathbb{R}})$,

$$\mathbb{E}_{(\psi_t\circ F_*)^{(i)}}[f] - \mathbb{E}_{F_*^{(i)}}[f] = 0. \tag{15}$$

Otherwise, there exists some $i \in \mathcal{N}$ and $f_0 \in C_b(\overline{\mathbb{R}})$ such that

$$\mathbb{E}_{(\psi_t\circ F_*)^{(i)}}[f_0] - \mathbb{E}_{F_*^{(i)}}[f_0] < 0.$$

In turn, for such i, we have

$$\begin{aligned}\sup_{f\in C_b(\overline{\mathbb{R}})} \left(\mathbb{E}_{(\psi_t\circ F_*)^{(i)}}[f] - \mathbb{E}_{F_*^{(i)}}[f]\right) &\geq \mathbb{E}_{(\psi_t\circ F_*)^{(i)}}[-f_0] - \mathbb{E}_{F_*^{(i)}}[-f_0] \\ &= -\left(\mathbb{E}_{(\psi_t\circ F_*)^{(i)}}[f_0] - \mathbb{E}_{F_*^{(i)}}[f_0]\right) > 0,\end{aligned}$$

and $\rho_t(\psi_t) > 0$ as a result which is a contradiction. Therefore, equality (15) holds true. Consequently, by the criterion of weak convergence, we get that ψ_t is a copula. □

The above result justifies the choice of ρ. Another advantage of using the proposed penalty function is that for any fixed $f \in C_b(\overline{\mathbb{R}})$, the linearity in $\psi_t \circ F_*$ allows us to obtain a tractable numerical computation scheme (cf. Section 5.1) for the value functions to be defined later. To proceed, we provide the following technical result on the regularity property of ρ_t, $t \in \mathcal{T}'$, which plays an important role in proving the existence of optimal control.

Lemma 3.5. *For every $t \in \mathcal{T}'$, the penalty term ρ_t is lower semi-continuous (l.s.c.).*

Proof. We will show that $\liminf_{C\to C_0}\rho_t(C)\geq\rho_t(C_0)$ for any $C_0\in\mathcal{P}([0,1]^n)$. To this end, let C_j be any sequence that converges to C_0. If $\rho_t(C_0)=+\infty$, then, for any $b\in\mathbb{R}$, there exists a family $\{f_i,i\in\mathcal{N}\}\subset C_b(\overline{\mathbb{R}})$ such that

$$\sum_{i\in\mathcal{N}}\left(\mathbb{E}_{(C_0\circ F_*)^{(i)}}[f_i]-\mathbb{E}_{F_*^{(i)}}[f_i]\right)>b.$$

Since $C_j\to C_0$, then there exists a $n_0>0$ such that for any $j\geq n_0$, we get

$$\sum_{i\in\mathcal{N}}\left(\mathbb{E}_{(C_j\circ F_*)^{(i)}}[f_i]-\mathbb{E}_{F_*^{(i)}}[f_i]\right)>\frac{b}{2},$$

where the continuity of $\mathbb{E}_{(C\circ F_*)^{(i)}}[f_i]$ in C is obtained according to the proof of Proposition 3.3. Thus, we have that

$$\rho_t(C_j)>\frac{b}{2},\quad j\geq n_0,$$

and moreover

$$\lim_{j\to\infty}\rho_t(C_j)=+\infty.$$

If $\rho_t(C_0)<+\infty$, then for any $\varepsilon>0$, there exists a family $\{f_i,i\in\mathcal{N}\}\subset C_b(\overline{\mathbb{R}})$ such that

$$\sum_{i\in\mathcal{N}}\left(\mathbb{E}_{(C_0\circ F_*)^{(i)}}[f_i]-\mathbb{E}_{F_*^{(i)}}[f_i]\right)>\rho_t(C_0)-\varepsilon.$$

Hence, from the convergence of C_j to C_0, there exists $n_0>0$, and for any $j\geq n_0$, the following inequality holds true:

$$\sum_{i\in\mathcal{N}}\left(\mathbb{E}_{(C_j\circ F_*)^{(i)}}[f_i]-\mathbb{E}_{F_*^{(i)}}[f_i]\right)>\rho_t(C_0)-2\varepsilon.$$

Thus, $\rho_t(C_j)\geq\rho_t(C_0)-2\varepsilon$ for any $j\geq n_0$, and $\lim_{j\to\infty}\rho_t(C_j)\geq\rho_t(C_0)-2\varepsilon$. Because ε is arbitrary, we get that $\lim_{j\to\infty}\rho_t(C_j)\geq\rho_t(C_0)$. In summary, we conclude that $\liminf_{C\to C_0}\rho_t(C)\geq\rho_t(C_0)$ and ρ_t is l.s.c. $\square$

In the sequel, we will consider a reformulation of (14) as follows:

$$\inf_{\varphi \in \mathcal{A}} \sup_{\mathbb{Q}^{\psi} \in \mathcal{Q}_y^{\varphi}} \left(\mathbb{E}_{\mathbb{Q}^{\psi}}[\ell(X_T)] - \rho(\psi)\right). \tag{16}$$

Before discussing the solution of (16), we want to remark that, in this work, the uncertainty set is some set of measures on $\mathcal{P}([0,1]^n)$ centered at the empirical copula. Another approach is to consider the worst-case model of Z_t, $t \in \mathcal{T}''$, chosen from some uncertainty set centered around the empirical distribution of Z_t. By imposing a penalty function similar to ρ, we can ensure that the worst-case model matches F_* in terms of the marginals. Thus, we are able to set up a problem that is similar to (16) without considering the copula. Regarding the comparison between such an approach and our method, we refer to Section 4.3. In case the marginals are also uncertain, one can extend the framework in Ref. [2] to the multidimensional case via the multivariate empirical distribution.

4. Solution of the Non-Parametric Adaptive Robust Control Problem

In this section, we show that the solution of the non-parametric adaptive robust control problem (16) is given by solving the following adaptive robust Bellman equations:

$$\begin{aligned}
V_T(y) &= \ell(x), \quad y \in E_Y, \\
V_t(y) &= \inf_{a \in A} \sup_{C \in \mathcal{C}_t^{\alpha}(y)} \Big(\mathbb{E}_{C \circ F_*}[V_{t+1}(\mathbf{G}(t,y,a,Z_{t+1}))] - \rho_t(C)\Big), \\
&\quad y \in E_Y, \ t \in \mathcal{T}'.
\end{aligned} \tag{17}$$

4.1. *Existence of Measurable Optimal Control*

To show the existence of measurable optimal control to problem (17), we denote

$$v_t(y,a,C) = \mathbb{E}_{C \circ F_*}[V_{t+1}(\mathbf{G}(t,y,a,Z_{t+1}))] - \rho_t(C), \quad t \in \mathcal{T}',$$

and provide the following preliminary results:

Proposition 4.1. *For every $t \in \mathcal{T}$, the functions v_t and V_t are upper semi-continuous (u.s.c.). Moreover, there exists a Borel measurable function ψ_t^* that takes values in the set of copulae such that for any fixed (y, a)*

$$\sup_{C \in \mathcal{C}_t^\alpha(y)} v_t(y, a, C) = v_t(y, a, \psi_t^*(y, a)). \tag{18}$$

Proof. By our assumption, the function $V_T(y) = \ell(x)$ is continuous and hence u.s.c. For any $C \in \mathcal{P}([0,1]^n)$, we write

$$\mathbb{E}_{C \circ F_*}[V_T(\mathbf{G}(T-1, y, a, Z_T))] = \int_{E_Y} V_T(y_T) dQ_{T-1}(y_T | y, a, C).$$

According to Proposition 3.3, Q_{T-1} is a continuous stochastic kernel. Then, in view of the assumption that ℓ is bounded from above and [5, Proposition 7.31], we get that

$$\mathbb{E}_{C \circ F_*}[V_T(\mathbf{G}(T-1, y, a, Z_T))]$$

is u.s.c. On the other hand, by Lemma 3.5, $-\rho_{T-1}(C)$ is u.s.c., and in turn, v_{T-1} are u.s.c.

Next, since $[0,1]^n$ is compact, then $\mathcal{P}([0,1]^n)$ (equipped with metric $d_{W,p}$) is compact. Let $\mathrm{D} = \bigcup_{(y,a) \in E_Y \times A} (\{(y,a)\} \times \mathcal{C}_t^\alpha(y))$ which can be viewed as the graph of the set-valued function $\mathcal{C}_t^\alpha(y)$. Note that $\mathcal{C}_t^\alpha(y)$ is closed and, by Lemma 2.3, is u.h.c. Hence, the set D is closed. According to Ref. [5, Proposition 7.33], the function $\check{V}_{T-1}(y, a) = \sup_{C \in \mathcal{C}_t^\alpha(y)} v_{T-1}(y, a, C)$ is u.s.c. As a result, $V_{T-1}(y) = \inf_{a \in A} \check{V}_{T-1}(y, a)$ is u.s.c. as well. Moreover, for any fixed (y, a), there exists a Borel measurable function ψ^* such that (18) holds true.

Last but not the least, for any $C \in \mathcal{C}_{T-1}^\alpha(y)$ that is not a copula, it is not hard to see that $\rho_{T-1}(C) = +\infty$. Consequently, for such C, $v_{T-1}(y, a, C) = -\infty$. For any C that is a copula, we have

$$v_{T-1}(y, a, C) = \mathbb{E}_{C \circ F_*}[V_T(\mathbf{G}(t, y, a, Z_T))] \geq -\infty.$$

This indicates that for any (y, a), $\psi_{T-1}^*(y, a)$ is a copula. The rest of the proof follows analogously. □

The above proposition proves the existence of measurable worst-case copula selector. Regarding the optimal control, we use the semi-analyticity property of the value function V_t as follows:

Proposition 4.2. *For every $t \in \mathcal{T}$, the function V_t is lower semi-analytic (l.s.a.). Moreover, for any $\varepsilon > 0$, there exists an analytically measurable function $\varphi_t^{*,\varepsilon}$ such that*

$$\sup_{C \in \mathcal{C}_t^{\alpha}(y)} v_t(y, \varphi_t^{*,\varepsilon}(y), C) = \begin{cases} V_t(y) + \varepsilon & \text{if } V_t(y) > -\infty, \\ -1/\varepsilon & \text{if } V_t(y) = -\infty. \end{cases} \tag{19}$$

In other words, $\varphi_t^{*,\varepsilon}$ is the ε-optimal control.

Proof. Since $V_T(y) = \ell(x)$ is continuous by assumption, then V_T is l.s.a. Recall

$$v_{T-1}(y, a, C, \lambda_{T-1}) = \int_{E_Y} V_T(y_T) Q_{T-1}(dy_T | y, a, C) - \rho_{T-1}(C).$$

The first term on the RHS is l.s.a. as Q_{T-1} is a Borel measurable stochastic kernel by Proposition 3.3, and the second term $-\rho_{T-1}(C)$ is l.s.a. because it is u.s.c. Therefore, the function $v_{T-1}(y, a, C)$ is l.s.a.

In view of (18) in Proposition 4.1 where ψ_{T-1}^* is Borel measurable, we deduce that

$$\widehat{V}_t(y, a) = \sup_{C \in \mathcal{C}_{T-1}^{\alpha}(y)} v_{T-1}(y, a, C)$$

is l.s.a. according to part (3) of Ref. [5, Lemma 7.30].

Next, the set A is also Borel measurable and in turn analytic. Hence, by Ref. [5, Proposition 7.50], $V_{T-1}(y)$ is l.s.a., and (19) holds true for $t = T - 1$. The rest of the proof follows analogously. $\square$

Remark 4.3. We want to stress that in general the result in Lemma 4.2 cannot be improved in the sense that one is unable to obtain the measurable optimal control instead of ε-optimal control. Following Ref. [5, Proposition 7.50], on the set

$$I = \left\{ y \in E_Y : \exists a_y \in A \text{ such that } \widehat{V}_t(y, a_y) = V_t(y) \right\}$$

one will get a universally measurable optimal control. In our setup, all the continuous points of V_t belong to I. However, due to the presence of the penalty term, it is impossible to show the lower semi-continuity of V_t to the best of our knowledge.

Now, we proceed to show that problem (16) satisfies the Bellman principle and is solved by (17).

4.2. *Dynamic Programming*

Here we will use Proposition 4.1 and Proposition 4.2 to show that problem (16) is solved by the Bellman equation (17). Denote

$$\rho_{t:T-1}(\psi) = \sum_{s=t}^{T-1} \rho_s(\psi_s),$$

then we have the main result of this section as follows:

Theorem 4.4. *For every $t \in \mathcal{T}'$, and any $y \in E_Y$, we have*

$$V_t(y) = \inf_{\varphi \in \mathcal{A}_t} \sup_{\mathbb{Q} \in \mathcal{Q}^{\varphi}_{y,t}} \left(\mathbb{E}_{\mathbb{Q}}[\ell(X_T)] - \rho_{t:T-1}(\psi)\right).$$

Proof. We will prove the statement via backward induction in $t = T-1, \ldots, 1, 0$.

When $t = T-1$ and $y \in E_Y$, we have

$$\inf_{\varphi \in \mathcal{A}_{T-1}} \sup_{\mathbb{Q}^{\psi} \in \mathcal{Q}^{\varphi}_{y,T-1}} \left(\mathbb{E}_{\mathbb{Q}^{\psi}}[\ell(X_T)] - \rho_{T-1}(\psi)\right)$$

$$= \inf_{a \in A} \sup_{C \in \mathcal{C}^{\alpha}_{T-1}(y)} \left(\int_{E_Y} V_T(y') Q_{T-1}(y'|y, a, C) - \rho_{T-1}(C)\right) = V_{T-1}(y).$$

Next, for $t = T-2, \ldots, 0$ and $y \in E_Y$, denote $\varphi^t = \{\varphi_s, s = t, \ldots, T-1\}$ and $\psi^t = \{\psi_s, s = t, \ldots, T-1\}$, then

$$\inf_{\varphi \in \mathcal{A}_t} \sup_{\mathbb{Q}^{\psi} \in \mathcal{Q}^{\varphi}_{y,t}} \left(\mathbb{E}_{\mathbb{Q}^{\psi}}[\ell(X_T)] - \rho_{t:T-1}(\psi)\right)$$

$$= \inf_{(a, \varphi^{t+1}) \in \mathcal{A}_t} \sup_{C \in \mathcal{C}^{\alpha}_t(y)} \int_{E_Y} \sup_{\mathbb{Q}^{\psi^{t+1}} \in \mathcal{Q}^{\varphi^{t+1}}_{y', t+1}}$$

$$\times \left(\mathbb{E}_{\mathbb{Q}^{\psi^{t+1}}}[\ell(X_T)] - \rho_{t:T-1}((C, \psi^{t+1}))\right) Q_t(dy'|y, a, C),$$

where by induction

$$
\begin{aligned}
&\sup_{\mathbb{Q}^{\psi^{t+1}}\in\mathcal{Q}^{\varphi^{t+1}}_{y',t+1}} \left(\mathbb{E}_{\mathbb{Q}^{\psi^{t+1}}}[\ell(X_T)] - \rho_{t:T-1}((C,\psi^{t+1}))\right)\\
&\quad = \sup_{\mathbb{Q}^{\psi^{t+1}}\in\mathcal{Q}^{\varphi^{t+1}}_{y',t+1}} \left(\mathbb{E}_{\mathbb{Q}^{\psi^{t+1}}}[\ell(X_T)] - \rho_{t+1:T-1}(\psi^{t+1}) - \lambda_t\rho_t(C)\right)\\
&\quad \geq V_{t+1}(y') - \rho_t(C).
\end{aligned}
$$

Hence, we get

$$
\begin{aligned}
&\inf_{\varphi\in\mathcal{A}_t}\sup_{\mathbb{Q}^{\psi}\in\mathcal{Q}^{\varphi}_{y,t}} \left(\mathbb{E}_{\mathbb{Q}^{\psi}}[\ell(X_T)] - \rho_{t:T-1}(\psi)\right)\\
&\quad \geq \inf_{(a,\varphi^{t+1})\in\mathcal{A}_t}\sup_{C\in\mathcal{C}^{\alpha}_t(y)}\int_{E_Y}\left(V_{t+1}(y') - \rho_t(C)\right)Q_t(dy'|y,a,C)\\
&\quad = \inf_{a\in A}\sup_{C\in\mathcal{C}^{\alpha}_t(y)}\left(\int_{E_Y}V_{t+1}(y')Q_t(dy'|y,a,C) - \rho_t(C)\right) = V_t(y).
\end{aligned}
\tag{20}
$$

On the other hand, for any $\varepsilon > 0$, let $\varphi^{t+1,\varepsilon} \in \mathcal{A}_{t+1}$ be an ε-optimal control starting at time $t+1$. We obtain that

$$
\begin{aligned}
&\sup_{\mathbb{Q}^{\psi^{t+1}}\in\mathcal{Q}^{\varphi^{t+1,\varepsilon}}_{y',t+1}} \left(\mathbb{E}_{\mathbb{Q}^{\psi^{t+1}}}[\ell(X_T)] - \rho_{t:T-1}((C,\psi^{t+1}))\right)\\
&\quad \leq \inf_{\varphi^{t+1}\in\mathcal{A}_{t+1}}\sup_{\mathbb{Q}^{\psi^{t+1}}\in\mathcal{Q}^{\varphi^{t+1}}_{y',t+1}} \left(\mathbb{E}_{\mathbb{Q}^{\psi^{t+1}}}[\ell(X_T)] - \rho_{t:T-1}((C,\psi^{t+1}))\right) + \varepsilon\\
&\quad = \left(V_{t+1}(y') - \lambda_t\rho_t(C)\right) + \varepsilon.
\end{aligned}
$$

In what follows, we have

$$
\begin{aligned}
&\inf_{\varphi\in\mathcal{A}_t}\sup_{\mathbb{Q}^{\psi}\in\mathcal{Q}^{\varphi}_{y,t}} \left(\mathbb{E}_{\mathbb{Q}^{\psi}}[\ell(X_T)] - \rho_{t:T-1}(\psi)\right)\\
&\quad \leq \inf_{a\in A}\sup_{\mathbb{Q}^{\psi}\in\mathcal{Q}^{(a,\varphi^{t+1,\varepsilon})}_{y',t+1}} \left(\mathbb{E}_{\mathbb{Q}^{\psi}}[\ell(X_T)] - \rho_{t:T-1}((C,\psi^{t+1}))\right)
\end{aligned}
$$

$$= \inf_{a\in A} \sup_{C\in\mathcal{C}_t^\alpha(y)} \int_{E_Y} \sup_{\mathbb{Q}^{\psi^{t+1}}\in\mathcal{Q}^{\varphi^{t+1,\varepsilon}}_{y',t+1}} \Big(\mathbb{E}_{\mathbb{Q}^{\psi^{t+1}}}[\ell(X_T)] - \rho_{t:T-1}((C,\psi^{t+1}))\Big)$$

$$\times\, Q_t(dy'|y,a,C)$$

$$\leq \inf_{a\in A} \sup_{C\in\mathcal{C}_t^\alpha(y)} \int_{E_Y} \left(V_{t+1}(y') - \rho_t(C)\right) Q_t(dy'|y,a,C) + \varepsilon$$

$$= \inf_{a\in A} \sup_{C\in\mathcal{C}_t^\alpha(y)} \left(\int_{E_Y} V_{t+1}(y') Q_t(dy'|y,a,C) - \rho_t(C)\right) + \varepsilon$$

$$= V_t(y) + \varepsilon.$$

Since ε is arbitrary, as a consequence,

$$\inf_{\varphi\in\mathcal{A}_t} \sup_{\mathbb{Q}^\psi\in\mathcal{Q}^\varphi_{y,t}} \left(\mathbb{E}_{\mathbb{Q}^\psi}[\ell(X_T)] - \rho_{t:T-1}(\psi)\right) \leq V_t(y). \tag{21}$$

Combining (20) and (21), we conclude that

$$\inf_{\varphi\in\mathcal{A}_t} \sup_{\mathbb{Q}^\psi\in\mathcal{Q}^\varphi_{y,t}} \left(\mathbb{E}_{\mathbb{Q}^\psi}[\ell(X_T)] - \rho_{t:T-1}(\psi)\right) = V_t(y).$$

□

The above theorem shows that problem (16) is solved via the Bellman equation (17). In the following section, we will compare the approach (16) to some different methods that can be used to handle the optimization problem under dependence uncertainty.

4.3. *Comparison to Robust Control Problem via Empirical Distribution*

In this section, we will compare three different setups that can be used for solving the proposed problem. One of the other approaches that is viable in this setup is, as we mentioned earlier, the multidimensional version of the methodology discussed in Ref. [2]. Briefly speaking, one can build confidence regions in terms of Wasserstein balls centered at the empirical distribution $\widehat{F}_t$, say, denoted as $\mathcal{C}_t^{\alpha,e}(\widehat{F}_t)$. Then, formulate the adaptive robust problem that optimizes the expected loss/utility against the worst-case model in $\mathcal{C}_t^{\alpha,e}(\widehat{F}_t)$. Obviously, doing so will ignore the available information of the marginals $F_*^{(i)}$, $i\in\mathcal{N}$. However, for a large value of T, such a method will have a decent performance as the corresponding value function will get quite close to the true one when t approaches T (cf. Ref. [2]). The associated Bellman equation is given as follows:

$$V_t^e(y') = \inf_{a \in A} \sup_{F \in \mathcal{C}_t^{\alpha,e}(y')} \mathbb{E}_F[V_{t+1}^e(\mathbf{G}(t, y', a, Z_{t+1}))], \quad t \in \mathcal{T}', \tag{22}$$

where y' is the state of the process $Y_t' = (X_t, \widehat{F}_t)$, $t \in \mathcal{T}'$. The third method is somewhat similar to the one we just described but utilizes the information of the known marginals. One can impose essentially the same penalty function as in this work and force the worst-case distribution to have correct marginals. To this end, we define the following one-step penalty function:

$$\rho_t^m(F) = \sum_{i \in \mathcal{N}} \sup_{f_i \in C_b(\mathbb{S}^{(i)})} \left(\mathbb{E}_{F^{(i)}}[f_i] - \mathbb{E}_{F_*^{(i)}}[f_i] \right),$$

for any $F \in \mathcal{C}_t^{\alpha,m}(\widehat{F}_t)$, which is the Wasserstein ball centered at $\widehat{F}_t$ that might have a different radius compared to $\mathcal{C}_t^{\alpha,e}(\widehat{F}_t)$. Also, the above $\mathbb{S}^{(i)}$ is the support of $Z_{t+1}^{(i)}$, $i \in \mathcal{N}$. The corresponding Bellman equation is

$$V_t^m(y') = \inf_{a \in A} \sup_{F \in \mathcal{C}_t^{\alpha,m}(y')} \left(\mathbb{E}_F[V_{t+1}^m(\mathbf{G}(t, y', a, Z_{t+1}))] - \rho_t(F) \right), \quad t \in \mathcal{T}', \tag{23}$$

where y' is defined the same way as in (22).

Now the question is as follows: Which framework is the best in what situation, and can the methods with imposed penalty functions take advantage of the available information of the marginals and outperform the approach that ignores it? First off, note that one can always take $\mathcal{C}_t^{\alpha,m} = \mathcal{C}_t^{\alpha,e}$ backed by the concentration result. Then, due to the presence of the penalty function $\rho_t(F)$, framework (23) is essentially searching for the worst-case distribution in a smaller set compared to (22). Therefore, we have

$$V_t^m(y') \leq V_t^e(y').$$

In other words, (23) yields smaller loss which is meant to be minimized. In this sense, the solution corresponding to (23) is better than the one corresponding to (22).

The comparison between (16) and (23) is much more complicated, and it turns out that the preference depends on additional properties of F^*. To this end, we first discuss the relationship between the uncertainty sets $\mathcal{C}_t^{\alpha}(y)$ and $\mathcal{C}_t^{\alpha,e}(y')$ where $y = (x, \widehat{C})$ and $y' = (x, \widehat{F})$ such that $\widehat{C} = \widehat{F} \circ F_*^{-1}$. This means that both methods use the exact same information at every time step $t \in \mathcal{T}'$. In the first case, when there exists a constant $B > 1$ such that

$$\|F_* \circ z_1 - F_* \circ z_2\| \le B\|z_1 - z_2\|, \tag{24}$$

where

$$F_* \circ z = \left(F_*^{(1)}(z^{(1)}), \ldots, F_*^{(n)}(z^{(n)})\right).$$

Hence, for any f_1, f_2 on $[0,1]^n$, such that

$$|f_1(u_1) - f_2(u_2)| \le \|u_1 - u_2\|^p, \quad u_1, u_2 \in [0,1]^n,$$

we get

$$|f_1(F_* \circ z_1) - f_2(F_* \circ z_2)| \le \|F_* \circ z_1 - F_* \circ z_2\|^p \le B^p\|z_1 - z_2\|^p,$$
$$z_1, z_2 \in \mathbb{R}^n.$$

Following such an observation, we have for any C

$$\begin{aligned} d_{W,p}^p(\widehat{C}, C) &= \sup_{f_1, f_2} \left(\int_{[0,1]^n} f_1(u) d\widehat{C}(u) - \int_{[0,1]^n} f_2(u) dC(u)\right) \\ &= \sup_{f_1, f_2} \left(\int_{\mathbb{R}^n} f_1(F_* \circ z) d\widehat{C}(F_* \circ z) - \int_{\mathbb{R}^n} f_2(F_* \circ z) dC(F_* \circ z)\right) \\ &\le B^p \sup_{g_1, g_2} \left(\int_{\mathbb{R}^n} g_1(z) d\widehat{C}(F_* \circ z) - \int_{\mathbb{R}^n} g_2(z) dC(F_* \circ z)\right) \\ &= B^p d_{W,p}^p(\widehat{F}, C \circ F_*), \end{aligned} \tag{25}$$

where $|g_1(z_1) - g_2(z_2)| \le \|z_1 - z_2\|^p$ for any $z_1, z_2 \in \mathbb{R}^n$. Thus, for the radius $r^m(\alpha, t_0, t)$ of $\mathcal{C}_t^{\alpha,m}(y')$, it suffices to take $r^m(\alpha, t_0, t) = r(\alpha, t_0, t)/B$. Note that, in theory one should choose $r^e(\alpha, t_0, t)$, which is the radius of $\mathcal{C}_t^{\alpha,e}$, as $r^e(\alpha, t_0, t) = r(\alpha, t_0, t)$. Hence, in this case, (23) will perform better than (22) because it has a smaller associated Wasserstein ball.

On the other hand, between (16) and (23), in view of (25), we obtain that for any $F \in \mathcal{C}_t^{\alpha,m}(y')$, there exists a corresponding $C \in \mathcal{C}_t^{\alpha}(y)$. Consequently, we can view $\mathcal{C}_t^{\alpha,m}$ as a "smaller" set than $\mathcal{C}_t^{\alpha}$. Moreover, we immediately get that

$$V_t^m(y') \leq V_t(y),$$

and (23) outperforms (16). One should note that, in this case, it is unclear which one is better between (16) and (23).

The other case is that each $\mathbb{S}^{(i)}$, $i \in \mathcal{N}$, is a compact subset of $\mathbb{R}$, and we suppose that there exists a constant $B' > 0$ such that

$$\|F_* \circ z_1' - F_* \circ z_2'\| \geq B'\|z_1' - z_2'\|, \tag{26}$$

for any $z_1', z_2' \in \prod_{i\in\mathcal{N}} \mathbb{S}^{(i)}$. Under these assumptions, for any g_1, g_2 on $\mathbb{R}^n$, such that

$$|g_1(z_1') - g_2(z_2')| \leq \|z_1' - z_2'\|^p, \quad z_1', z_2' \in \prod_{i\in\mathcal{N}} \mathbb{S}^{(i)},$$

we obtain

$$|g_1(F_*^{-1} \circ u_1) - g_2(F_*^{-1} \circ u_2)| \leq \|F_*^{-1} \circ u_1 - F_*^{-1} \circ u_2\|^p \leq \frac{1}{B'}\|u_1 - u_2\|,$$
$$u_1, u_2 \in [0,1]^n.$$

Then, for any F whose associated random variable has support $\prod_{i\in\mathcal{N}} \mathbb{S}^{(i)}$, and $F = C \circ F_*$ for some copula C, we have

$$\begin{aligned}
d_{W,p}^p(\widehat{F}, F) &= \sup_{g_1,g_2} \left(\int_{\mathbb{R}^n} g_1(z)d\widehat{F}(z) - \int_{\mathbb{R}^n} g_2(z)dF(z) \right) \\
&= \sup_{g_1,g_2} \left(\int_{\prod_{i\in\mathcal{N}} \mathbb{S}^{(i)}} g_1(z)d\widehat{F}(z) - \int_{\prod_{i\in\mathcal{N}} \mathbb{S}^{(i)}} g_2(z)dF(z) \right) \\
&= \sup_{g_1,g_2} \left(\int_{\prod_{i\in\mathcal{N}} \mathbb{S}^{(i)}} g_1(z)d\widehat{C}(F_* \circ z) - \int_{\prod_{i\in\mathcal{N}} \mathbb{S}^{(i)}} g_2(z)dC(F_* \circ z) \right) \\
&= \sup_{g_1,g_2} \left(\int_{[0,1]^n} g_1(F_*^{-1}(u)d\widehat{C}(u) - \int_{[0,1]^n} g_2(F_*^{-1}(u)dC(u) \right) \\
&\leq \frac{1}{B'} \sup_{f_1,f_2} \left(\int_{[0,1]^n} f_1(u)d\widehat{C}(u) - \int_{[0,1]^n} f_2(u)dC(u) \right) \\
&= \frac{1}{B'} d_{W,p}^p(\widehat{C}, C),
\end{aligned}$$

where $|f_1(u_1) - f_2(u_2)| \leq \|u_1 - u_2\|$ for any $u_1, u_2 \in [0,1]^n$. As a result, similar to the above discussion, we view $\mathcal{C}_t^\alpha$ as a "smaller" set than $\mathcal{C}_t^{\alpha,m}$, and we conclude

$$V_t(y) \leq V_t^m(y') \leq V_t^e(y').$$

In other words, the framework proposed in this work will perform the best among all three mentioned approaches.

Finally, we remark that when $\mathbb{S}^{(i)}$, $i \in \mathcal{N}$, are compact, and both (24) and (26) hold true, the two frameworks (16) and (23) are equivalent. If neither (24) or (26) is satisfied, it is unclear which one between (16) and (23) is more preferable.

5. Uncertain Utility Maximization with Known Marginal Distributions

In this section, we will apply the adaptive robust control methodology to the uncertain utility maximization problem where the marginal distributions of the underlying random noise are known. Note that even though our theory applies to both empirical distribution and perturbed empirical distribution, we will focus only on the case of empirical distribution in this section. The advantage of using the perturbed empirical distribution is that the resulting $\widehat{C}$ is a copula. This could be a more sounding approach in some applications, however in this work, it will increase the computation burden which is already heavy. Hence, we leave the corresponding investigation for potential future studies.

Toward this end, we first discuss the algorithm that we will implement.

5.1. *Numerical Algorithm*

From the practical point of view, one major difficulty in solving a robust control problem with Wasserstein uncertainty set such as $\mathcal{C}_t^\alpha$ is that direct searching through $\mathcal{C}_t^\alpha(y)$ to find the optimizer $\psi_t^*(y)$ is impossible. Typically, one uses a duality argument to rewrite such a problem as a scalar optimization problem. In Ref. [10], the authors provide a rather comprehensive discussion on the tractable reformulations of an optimization problem over the Wasserstein ball. With some postulation on the loss function, the authors achieve a convex reduction of the worst-case expectation problems. However, results in Ref. [10] only apply to the case of optimizing the expected loss, while in this work, we deal with a different problem as in (17)

$$\sup_{C\in\mathcal{C}_t^\alpha(y)} \left(\mathbb{E}_{C\circ F_*}[V_{t+1}(\mathbf{G}(t,y,a,Z_{t+1}))] - \rho_t(C)\right). \tag{27}$$

Due to the nonlinearity of the penalty function ρ_t, one cannot directly adopt the idea in Ref. [10] to reformulate problem (17) for the numerical purpose.

To this end, we recall the paper [12] which considers the numerical solution of a 1-period robust optimization problem with Wasserstein uncertainty set centered at the estimated copula which is similar to our worst-case copula optimization problem. Let $\{z_{-t_0+1},\ldots,z_t\}$ be the historical data of Z up to time $t\in\mathcal{T}'$, the strong duality result in Ref. [12] implies that problem (27) can be solved as

$$\inf_{\gamma\in\mathbb{R}_+, f_i\in C_b(\mathbb{R})}\left\{\gamma r(\alpha,t_0,t)^p + \sum_{i=1}^n \int_{\mathbb{R}} f_i(z)dF_*^{(i)}(z) + \frac{1}{t_0+t}\sum_{j=-t_0+1}^{t} V_{t+1}^\gamma(\mathbf{G}(t,y,a,z_j)\right\}, \tag{28}$$

where

$$V_{t+1}^\gamma(\mathbf{G}(t,y,a,z_j) = \sup_{z\in\mathbb{R}^n}\left(V_{t+1}(\mathbf{G}(t,y,a,z)) - \sum_{i=1}^n f_i(z^{(i)}) - \gamma d_{F_*}^p(z,z_j)\right), \tag{29}$$

and

$$d_{F_*}(\xi,\zeta) = d\left(\left(F_*^{(1)}(\xi^{(1)}),\ldots,F_*^{(n)}(\xi^{(n)})\right), \left(F_*^{(1)}(\zeta^{(1)}),\ldots,F_*^{(n)}(\zeta^{(n)})\right)\right). \tag{30}$$

Remark 5.1. In general, the premetric d_{F_*} is defined as

$$d_{F_*}(\xi,\zeta) = \liminf_{d(\xi_i,\xi),d(\zeta_i,\zeta)\to 0} d\left(\left(F_*^{(1)}(\xi_i^{(1)}),\ldots,F_*^{(n)}(\xi_i^{(n)})\right),\right.$$
$$\left.\left(F_*^{(1)}(\zeta_i^{(1)}),\ldots,F_*^{(n)}(\zeta_i^{(n)})\right)\right).$$

Due to our assumption that $F_*^{(i)}$, $i\in\mathcal{N}$, are continuous, so d_{F_*} becomes (30).

In Ref. [12], to use the strong duality result in practice, the authors essentially assume that the range of the random variable Z_t, $t \in \mathcal{T}$, is a finite set. Such an assumption is obviously not true in this work, and hence we will use the following treatment to overcome such an obstacle. Toward this end, denote by $C([0,1])$ the set of all continuous functions on $[0,1]$, we first apply the change of variable to (28)–(29) as follows:

$$\inf_{\gamma\in\mathbb{R}_+, f_i\in C([0,1])} \left\{ \gamma r(\alpha, t_0, t)^p + \sum_{i=1}^{n} \int_0^1 f_i\left(F_*^{(i),-1}(u)\right) du \right.$$
$$\left. + \frac{1}{t_0+t} \sum_{j=-t_0+1}^{t} V_{t+1}^{\gamma}\left(\mathbf{G}\left(t, y, a, F_*^{-1}(u_j)\right)\right) \right\},$$

where

$$V_{t+1}^{\gamma}\left(\mathbf{G}\left(t, y, a, F_*^{-1}(u_j)\right)\right)$$
$$= \sup_{u\in[0,1]^n} \left(V_{t+1}\left(\mathbf{G}\left(t, y, a, F_*^{-1}(u)\right)\right) - \sum_{i=1}^{n} f_i\left(F_*^{(i),-1}(u^{(i)})\right) - \gamma d^p(u, u_j) \right).$$

Next, we recall the Weierstrass approximation theorem which indicates that any $f_i \circ F_*^{(i),-1} \in C([0,1])$ can be approximated by polynomials. In addition, the Bernstein polynomials

$$\beta_{k,K}(u) = \binom{K}{k} u^k (1-u)^{K-k}, \quad u \in [0,1], \quad k = 0, \ldots, K,$$

form a basis for the space of polynomials of degree K. Also, note that for fixed K and any $k = 0, \ldots, K$,

$$\int_{[0,1]} \beta_{k,K}(u) du = \frac{1}{K+1}.$$

Hence, the above optimization problem is approximated as

$$\inf_{\gamma\in\mathbb{R}_+, g_{i,k}\in\mathbb{R}} \left\{ \gamma r(\alpha, t_0, t)^p + \sum_{i=1}^{n} \sum_{k=0}^{K} \frac{g_{i,k}}{K+1} \right.$$
$$\left. + \frac{1}{t_0+t} \sum_{j=-t_0+1}^{t} V_{t+1}^{\gamma}(\mathbf{G}(t, y, a, F_*^{-1}(u_j))) \right\},$$

where

$$V_{t+1}^{\gamma}(\mathbf{G}(t,y,a,F_*^{-1}(u_j)))$$
$$= \sup_{u\in[0,1]^n}\left(V_{t+1}(\mathbf{G}(t,y,a,F_*^{-1}(u))) - \sum_{i=1}^{n}\sum_{k=0}^{K} g_{i,k}\beta_{k,K}(u^{(i)}) - \gamma d^p(u,u_j)\right).$$

By including the optimization over feasible controls, the inf-sup problem we need to solve is

$$\inf_{a\in A,\gamma\in\mathbb{R}_+,g_{i,k}\in\mathbb{R}}\left\{\gamma r(\alpha,t_0,t)^p + \sum_{i=1}^{n}\sum_{k=0}^{K}\frac{g_{i,k}}{K+1} + \frac{1}{t_0+t}\sum_{j=-t_0+1}^{t} V_{t+1}^{\gamma}(\mathbf{G}(t,y,a,F_*^{-1}(u_j)))\right\}, \quad (31)$$

where

$$V_{t+1}^{\gamma}(\mathbf{G}(t,y,a,F_*^{-1}(u_j)))$$
$$= \sup_{u\in[0,1]^n}\left(V_{t+1}(\mathbf{G}(t,y,a,F_*^{-1}(u))) - \sum_{i=1}^{n}\sum_{k=0}^{K} g_{i,k}\beta_{k,K}(u^{(i)}) - \gamma d^p(u,u_j)\right). \quad (32)$$

With regard to designing a numerical algorithm to solve (31)–(32), we first note that the inf problem in (31) and the sup problem in (32) have dimensions $m + n*(K+1)+1$ and n, respectively. Hence, we have a non-trivial high dimensional inf-sup optimization problem for which a solver using brute force will be extremely inefficient and virtually impossible. On top of the inherent high dimension in optimization, it also requires a large amount of computation cost to evaluate $\frac{1}{t_0+t}\sum_{j=-t_0+1}^{t} V_{t+1}^{\gamma}(\mathbf{G}(t,y,a,F_*^{-1}(u_j)))$ given that t_0 is decently big. In view of these difficulties, we propose to use the stochastic gradient descent ascent (SGDA) method to overcome the obstacles.

To explain the idea of SGDA in our work, for any fixed $t\in\mathcal{T}'$, $y\in E_Y$, we denote

$$\hat{v}_t(a,\gamma,g,u;\hat{u}) = \gamma(r(\alpha,t_0,t)^p - d^p(u,\hat{u})) + \sum_{i=1}^{n}\sum_{k=0}^{K}\left(\frac{g_{i,k}}{K+1} - g_{i,k}\beta_{k,K}(u^{(i)})\right) + V_{t+1}(\mathbf{G}(t,y,a,F^{-1}(u))),$$

where $\hat{u} \in \{u_j, j = -t_0 + 1, \ldots, t\}$. Such a formulation comes from the considered loop as follows: Given some $(a(l), \gamma(l), g(l), u(l))$, $l = 0, 1, \ldots$,

1. uniformly simulate $\hat{u}(l) \in \{u_j, j = -t_0 + 1, \ldots, t\}$,
2. update $(a(l), \gamma(l), g(l), u(l))$ as

$$a(l+1) = a(l) - \eta(l)\frac{\partial}{\partial a}\hat{v}_t(a(l), \gamma(l), g(l), u(l); \hat{u}(l)),$$

$$\gamma(l+1) = \gamma(l) - \eta(l)\frac{\partial}{\partial \gamma}\hat{v}_t(a(l), \gamma(l), g(l), u(l); \hat{u}(l)),$$

$$g(l+1) = g(l) - \eta(l)\frac{\partial}{\partial g}\hat{v}_t(a(l), \gamma(l), g(l), u(l); \hat{u}(l)),$$

$$u(l+1) = u(l) + \eta(l)\frac{\partial}{\partial u}\hat{v}_t(a(l), \gamma(l), g(l), u(l); \hat{u}(l)),$$

   where $\eta(l)$ denote the step size,
3. Go to 1.

The above loop will stop when there is no improvement of $(a(l), \gamma(l), g(l), u(l))$ anymore, and we denote the corresponding number l of iterations as l^*.

To apply SGDA, one needs to have a functional representation of V_t, $t = 1, \ldots, T-1$, such that the above gradients of $\hat{v}_t$ can be quickly computed. To construct such a functional approximation, we first choose N so-called design points y_t^j, $j = 1, \ldots, N$, at which we solve for $V_t(y_t^j)$, $j = 1, \ldots, N$, and then build a regression model $\widetilde{V}_t$ based on the training data $(y_t^j, V_t(y_t^j))$, $j = 1, \ldots, N$. For the choice of the regression model, we will use the Gaussian process (GP) with kernel function $\mathbf{k}(\cdot, \cdot)$ of the Matern 3/2 type. For a detailed discussion of GP, one can refer to Ref. [16]. We also summarize the basic idea of GP in earlier works (cf. Refs. [7], [4], [8], [2]).

When it comes to regression, one needs to note that the second component $\widehat{C}$ of the state variable y is in general a distribution and hence infinitely dimensional, which cannot be regressed against numerically. To such end, we will approximate each $\widehat{C}$ with its first M moments of marginals and covariance among marginals. By doing so, the dimension of the state variable y is reduced to $Mn + \binom{n}{2} + 1$ and we denote the approximating vector by $\tilde{y}$.

The rationale behind choosing GP with the Matern 3/2 kernel is two-fold. On one hand, it is a regression model sophisticated enough to capture the complicated structure of V_t with minimal assumptions, as Matern 3/2 kernel is used for regressing the function that has first-order derivatives. On the other hand, the gradients of $\widetilde{V}_t$, and in turn of $\hat{v}_t$, can be analytically computed which is of particular importance to our implementation. To see this, recall that given y_t^j, $j = 1, \ldots, N$, the resulting regression model has the following representation:

$$\widetilde{V}_t(\tilde{y}) = (\mathbf{k}(\tilde{y}, \tilde{y}_t^1), \ldots, \mathbf{k}(\tilde{y}, \tilde{y}_t^N))[\mathbf{K} + \varepsilon^2\mathbf{I}]^{-1}(V_t(y_t^1), \ldots, V_t(y_t^N))^\top. \tag{33}$$

The above $\varepsilon^2\mathbf{I}$ with $\mathbf{I}$ being the identity matrix is the perturbation added to the matrix $\mathbf{K}$ to ensure that the latter is invertible. The matrix $\mathbf{K}$ satisfies that $\mathbf{K}_{ij} = \mathbf{k}(\tilde{y}_t^i, \tilde{y}_t^j)$ and

$$\mathbf{k}(\tilde{y}^1, \tilde{y}^2) = \left(1 + \sqrt{3}d_s(\tilde{y}^1, \tilde{y}^2)\right)\exp\left(-\sqrt{3}d_s(\tilde{y}^1, \tilde{y}^2)\right),$$

where d_s is the scaled Euclidean distance between y^1 and y^2 with parameter s:

$$d\left(\left(\frac{\tilde{y}^{1,(1)}}{s^{(1)}}, \ldots, \frac{\tilde{y}^{1,(n)}}{s^{(n)}}\right), \left(\frac{\tilde{y}^{2,(1)}}{s^{(1)}}, \ldots, \frac{\tilde{y}^{2,(n)}}{s^{(n)}}\right)\right),$$

where $d(\cdot, \cdot)$ is the usual Euclidean distance. The vector s is called the length scale and fitting a GP model means using the maximum-likelihood method to find the optimal value of s. After $\widetilde{V}_t$ is fitted, the product $[\mathbf{K} + \varepsilon^2\mathbf{I}]^{-1}(V_t(y_t^1), \ldots, V_t(y_t^N))^\top$ in (33) is a fixed constant vector $(\nu_t^1, \ldots, \nu_t^N)$. Therefore, (33) can be rewritten as $\widetilde{V}_t(\tilde{y}) = \sum_{j=1}^N \nu_t^j \mathbf{k}(\tilde{y}, \tilde{y}_t^j)$. As a result, the gradient of $\widetilde{V}_t$ is a linear combination of the gradients of $\mathbf{k}(\tilde{y}, \tilde{y}_t^j)$ and with the explicit formula of $\mathbf{k}$ being available, its gradient can therefore be computed analytically. There is no need to stress how important the capability of computing the gradient without any numerical approximation is in a gradient-based optimization algorithm. Our solver for problem (31)–(32) is summarized as follows: For $t = T - 2, \ldots, 0$, we have the following:

1. Assume that $V_{t+1}(y^i_{t+1})$ and $\varphi^{*,\varepsilon}_{t+1}(y^i_{t+1})$, $i = 1, \ldots, N$, are computed. Fit the GP models $\widetilde{V}_{t+1}$ and $\widetilde{\varphi}^{*,\varepsilon}_{t+1}$ by using the training data $(y^i_{t+1}, V_{t+1}(y^i_{t+1}))$ and $(y^i_{t+1}, \varphi^{*,\varepsilon}_{t+1}(y^i_{t+1}))$, $i = 1, \ldots, N$, respectively.
2. Choose $y^i_t \in E_Y$, $i = 1, \ldots, N$.
3. For each y^i_t, choose initial guesses $(a(0), \gamma(0), g(0), u(0))$, and use SGDA to compute $(a(l^*), \gamma(l^*), g(l^*), u(l^*))$. Set $V_t(y^i_t) = \hat{v}_t(a(l^*), \gamma(l^*), g(l^*), u(l^*); \hat{u}(l^*))$, and $\varphi^{*,\varepsilon}_t(y^i_t) = a(l^*)$.
4. Go to 1: Start the next recursion for $t - 1$.

To analyze the performance of the computed optimal control $\varphi^{*,\varepsilon}$, we use forward simulation to estimate the mean terminal loss over the out-of-sample paths. For $t = 0, \ldots, T-1$, we have the following:

1. Draw $N' > 0$ i.i.d. $Z^1_{t+}, \ldots, Z^{N'}_{t+1}$ from the true distribution corresponding to F_*.
2. All paths start from the initial y_0. The state along path i is updated according to $\mathbf{G}(t, y^i_t, \widetilde{\varphi}^{*,\varepsilon}_t(y^i_t), Z^i_{t+1})$, $i = 1, \ldots, N'$.
3. Obtain the terminal state X^i_T, $i = 1, \ldots, N'$, and compute

$$V^c := \frac{1}{N'} \sum_{i=1}^{N'} \ell(X^i_T)$$

as the estimated mean terminal loss.

In Section 4.3, we know that there is no complete theoretical result of the comparison between our adaptive robust method based on copula and the approach of using empirical distribution without marginal information. Hence, we will focus on such a comparison when presenting our numerical results.

5.2. *Numerical Results*

In this section, we apply the algorithm described above to the uncertain utility maximization problem. We take $d = 2$ and consider two different stocks where Z_{t+1} is the vector of log returns from time t to $t+1$, which follows a multidimensional normal distribution.

Correspondingly, let X_t be the wealth at time t with the dynamics

$$X_t = X_{t-1}\left((1-\varphi_t^{(1)}-\varphi_t^{(2)})(1+r)+\varphi_t^{(1)}e^{Z_t^{(1)}}+\varphi_t^{(2)}e^{Z_t^{(2)}}\right).$$

The above $\varphi_t^{(i)}$, $i=1,2$, is the proportion of wealth invested in stock i. The constants r and $Z_t^{(i)}$, $i=1,2$, are the interest rate and log return of stock i, respectively. In addition, we choose the loss function ℓ such that $-\ell=U$ which is the exponential utility function. Then, we are effectively facing a utility maximization problem involving two different stocks under model uncertainty.

We compare three different types of strategies: (1) adaptive robust control method with known marginals, (2) adaptive robust control method based on empirical distribution without using marginal information and (3) optimal control without uncertainty. We denote by $\varphi^{*,\varepsilon}$, φ^e and φ^{tr} the corresponding strategies, respectively. We also use V^c, V^e and V^{tr} to denote the corresponding estimated expected utility, respectively. In Section 4.3, we find that it is unclear which of $\varphi^{*,\varepsilon}$ and φ^e will perform better when the marginal CDFs are Lipschitz continuous. Hence, we will compare these two strategies for Lipschitz marginals by using numerical results presented in the sequel.

To proceed, we take the following values for our parameters: $t_0=400$, $T=10$, $N=N'=1000$, $\alpha=0.1$, $p=2$ and $M=2$. Regarding the true distribution F_*, it is bivariate normal with mean $\mu=(0.09, 0.13)$ and covariance matrix $\Sigma=\begin{pmatrix}0.25^2 & 0.85\cdot0.25\cdot0.4\\ 0.85\cdot0.25\cdot0.4 & 0.4^2\end{pmatrix}$ where all numbers are annualized. Finally, the annual interest rate is $r=0.02$. With $T=10$, it means that we consider 10 trading periods in a year.

Table 1 shows that, in terms of the expected utility, adaptive robust using marginals performs better than the approach without using the information of marginals but worse than the case of knowing the true model. Similar comparison results hold true if we look at the 30% quantile and the minimum values of the terminal wealth. On the contrary, φ^e produces the highest variance, 90% quantile and maximum of the terminal wealth, while φ^{tr} generates the lowest values in these aspects. These observations can be obtained by viewing the box plots in Figure 1. In addition, adaptive robust without information of marginals has the highest mean wealth while knowing the true model gives the lowest value.

Table 1. Expected utility, variance, 30% quantile, 90% quantile, maximum and minimum of the out-of-sample terminal wealth.

	AR	AR (no marginals)	TR
V	19.8726	19.8659	19.8857
$\mathrm{Var}(X_T)$	441.7334	628.7182	118.3159
$q_{0.30}(X_T)$	92.4007	90.4748	96.3813
$q_{0.90}(X_T)$	136.7146	144.7677	121.2001
$\max(X_T)$	190.4936	220.5724	144.6299
$\min(X_T)$	51.2641	48.7990	77.4599

Note: AR: adaptive robust; TR: no uncertainty.

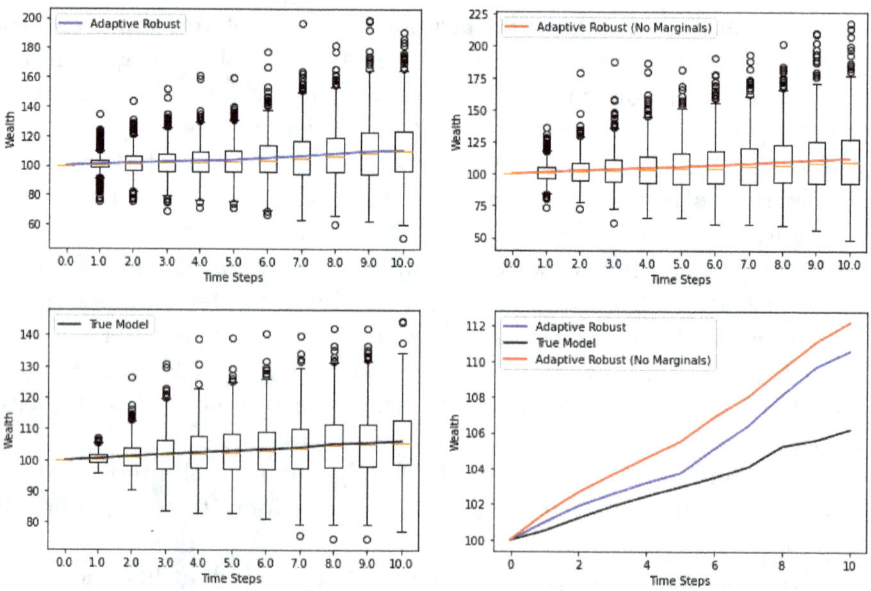

Figure 1. Evolution of the wealth along out-of-sample paths. Upper left: Box plot of the wealth generated by $\varphi^{*,\varepsilon}$; upper right: box plot of the wealth generated by φ^{e}; bottom left: box plot of the wealth generated by φ^{tr}; bottom right: comparison of mean wealth.

As we can see, when the investor knows more about the true model, the resulting terminal wealth excels in the risk management aspects, such as variance, 30% quantile and minimum value. Knowing less information about the true model will produce a higher mean, 90% quantile and maximum of the wealth which signal a strategy that is relatively more aggressive and profit seeking. By looking at the expected utility which takes into account both profit seeking and risk aversion, we note that the more information we know about the model, the higher the mean utility we obtain. With such numerical results, we conclude that, in general, knowing more about the true model leads to a more balanced and less risky optimal strategy.

References

[1] T. Bhudisaksang and A. Cartea. Online drift estimation for jump-diffusion processes. *Bernoulli — Journal of the Bernoulli Society*, 27(4):2494–2518, 2021.

[2] E. Bayraktar and T. Chen. Nonparametric adaptive robust control under model uncertainty. *SIAM Journal on Control and Optimization*. Preprint, 2022. Available at arXiv.org/abs/2202.10391.

[3] T. Bielecki, T. Chen, and I. Cialenco. Recursive construction of confidence regions. *Electronic Journal of Statistics*, 11(2):4674–4700, 2017.

[4] T. R. Bielecki, T. Chen, and I. Cialenco. Time-inconsistent markovian control problems under model uncertainty with application to the mean-variance portfolio selection. *International Journal of Theoretical and Applied Finance*, 24(1):1–28, 2021.

[5] D. P. Bertsekas and S. Shreve. *Stochastic Optimal Control: The Discrete-Time Case*. Academic Press, New York, 1978.

[6] H. F. Chen and L. Guo. *Identification and Stochastic Adaptive Control (Systems & Control: Foundations & Applications)*. Birkhäuser Inc., Boston, 1991.

[7] T. Chen and M. Ludkovski. A machine learning approach to adaptive robust utility maximization and hedging. *SIAM Journal on Financial Mathematics*, 3(12):1226–1256, 2021.

[8] T. Chen and J. Myung. Nonparametric adaptive Bayesian stochastic control under model uncertainty. Preprint, 2020. Available at arXiv.org/abs/2011.04804.

[9] E. Del Barrio, E. Giné, and C. Matrán. Central limit theorems for the wasserstein distance between the empirical and the true distributions. *The Annals of Probability*, 27(2):1009–1071, 1999.

[10] P. M. Esfahani and D. Kuhn. Data-driven distributionally robust optimization using the wasserstein metric: Performance guarantees and tractable reformulations. *Mathematical Programming*, 171:115–166, 2018.

[11] N. Fournier and A. Guillin. On the rate of convergence in wasserstein distance of the empirical measure. *Probability Theory and Related Fields*, 162:707–738, 2015.

[12] R. Gao and A. Kleywegt. Data-driven robust optimization with known marginal distributions. Technical Report. Georgia Institute of Technology, 2017.

[13] I. Gilboa and D. Schmeidler. Maxmin expected utility with nonunique prior. *Journal of Mathematical Economics*, 18(2):141–153, 1989.

[14] P. R. Kumar and P. Varaiya. *Stochastic Systems: Estimation, Identification, and Adaptive Control.* Prentice Hall, Inc., Englewood Cliffs, NJ, 2015.

[15] U. Rieder. Bayesian dynamic programming. *Advances in Applied Probability*, 7:330–348, 1975.

[16] C. E. Rasmussen and C. K. I. Williams. *Gaussian Processes for Machine Learning.* The MIT Press, Cambridge, MA, 2006.

https://doi.org/10.1142/9789811280306_0006

Chapter 6

Option Pricing Generators*

Peter Carr[†] **and Umberto Cherubini**[‡,§]

[†]*New York University, Tandon School of Engineering, Finance and Risk Engineering Department, Metrotech 1, Brooklyn, New York, 11201*

[‡]*University of Bologna, Department of Economics, Strada Maggiore 45, 40125 Bologna, Spain*

[§]*umberto.cherubini@unibo.it*

Abstract

We characterize a class of option pricing models by their algebraic structure. Option prices are monoids, that is, operators endowed with the commutativity and associativity property and an identity element. If the price of the underlying asset is bounded, the operator corresponds to the concept of t-conorm, while if it is defined on the positive real line, the operator is a pseudo-addition. These operators have the same no-arbitrage properties as the classical option pricing models but are also associative. Each model in this class is characterized by a univariate increasing function that is defined as the *generator* of the model. The generator encodes a synthetic representation of the probability structure of the underlying asset. We provide no-arbitrage conditions for the generators and practical guidelines to construct them.

Keywords: Pseudo-addition, Monoids, Implied distributions, Lamperti transforms, Copula functions

*The authors would like to thank, without implicating, Sabrina Mulinacci, Massimo Ricci, Salvatore Maglione and an anonymous referee for helpful comments.

1. Introduction

In a recent paper, Ref. [6] propose a new strategy for the evaluation of options. The focus is shifted to a product paying $\max(S_T, K)$, where S_T is the price of the underlying asset at maturity time T and K is the strike price. The product is called "a married put" because it can be attained by holding the underlying asset and a put option or, by put-call parity, holding a call option and a bond with face value equal to the strike.

The goal is to define a function

$$E_Q(\max(S_0, K)|\mathcal{F}_\tau) = m_\tau(S_\tau, K), \tag{1}$$

where $E_Q(., |\mathcal{F}_\tau)$ denotes the conditional expectation given the information available τ periods before maturity under the risk neutral measure Q. Note that our notation substitutes the standard setting $E_Q(\max(S_T, K)|\mathcal{F}_t)$. Then, by put-call parity, the function $m_\tau(S_\tau, K)$ can be used to price a call option, setting $f(S_\tau, \tau; K) = m_\tau(S_\tau, K) - B_\tau K$, where B_τ is the risk-free discount factor for term τ. The put option is obtained by computing $p(S_\tau.\tau; K) = m_\tau(S_\tau, K) - S_\tau D_\tau$, where D_τ is the discounted value of the dividend yield.

Clearly, the price of the married put must abide by specific conditions, the most important being the requirement that at maturity $\tau = 0$ it must be worth $\max(S_0, K)$. Other requirements were first introduced by Ref. [16] who gave necessary no-arbitrage conditions in his theory of rational option pricing. Necessary and sufficient conditions were analyzed in Refs. [5] and [12].

Here we take an algebraic approach to analyze the features that may be possessed by the pricing function $m_\tau(S, K)$. Starting with the standard Black and Scholes model with zero interest rates and dividend yield, one can show that the price of the married put is constrained by

$$\max(S, K) \leq m_\tau(S, K) \leq S + K.$$

In this case, the bounds are standard aggregation operators, that is, the standard sum and the $\max(S, K)$ operator. One is tempted to show under which conditions the functions $m_\tau(S, K)$ can be considered *pseudo-additions*. A pseudo-addition denotes a general aggregation operator which is increasing in both the arguments and endowed with the commutative and associative properties. Together with the definition of an identity element, this denotes a monoid. Formally, a monoid is defined as $(\mathcal{S}, \oplus)$, where $\mathcal{S}$ denotes a set and $\oplus$ an operation, with an element $e \in \mathcal{S}$ such that $x \oplus e = x, \forall x \in \mathcal{S}$.

One can easily show that $m_{\tau}(x, y)$ in the Black and Scholes formula is not a pseudo-addition because it fails to satisfy the associative property. Other models may instead qualify for a pseudo-addition representation. One is the Dagum option pricing model proposed by Ref. [6]:

$$m_{\tau}(S, K) = \left(S^{1/b_{\tau}} + K^{1/b_{\tau}}\right)^{b_{\tau}}$$

with b_{τ} strictly increasing with limits 0 and 1. It is easy to check that this option pricing formula has the same properties as the one in the Black and Scholes model but is also endowed with the associativity property.

Here we propose a general representation of associative option pricing models. The associativity property allows for a synthetic and elegant characterization of each pricing model by an increasing univariate function that is called the *generator* of the model. This generator completely encodes the probability structure of the model.

The structure of this chapter is as follows. In Section 2, we introduce the topic by analyzing the algebraic structure of the married put price in the Black and Scholes model with zero dividends and interest rates. In Section 3, we analyze the option pricing problem in a setting with bounded price of the underlying asset using t-conorm operators. In Section 4, we extend the analysis to underlying assets with prices unbounded from above. Section 5 shows how the generator characterizes the implied probability of the underlying asset. Section 6 gives guidelines and examples about how to build no-arbitrage option pricing generators. In Section 7, we report examples of smile functions obtained by several generators. Section 8 concludes.

2. Getting Started: Black and Scholes

Here we start our analysis with the most standard model. We start assuming no dividend payments and zero risk-free interest rates. In this setting, the price of the married put option in the Black and

Scholes model is

$$m_\tau(S,K) = S\Phi(d_\tau + 0.5\sigma\sqrt{\tau}) + K\Phi(-d_\tau + 0.5\sigma\sqrt{\tau}),$$

where S is the price of the underlying asset, K is the strike, τ the time to maturity, σ is volatility, and $\Phi(x)$ denotes the standard normal distribution and

$$d_\tau(S/K) = \frac{\log(S/K)}{\sigma\sqrt{\tau}}.$$

We then restrict our analysis to the algebraic properties of the function

$$\mu_\tau(x,y) = x\Phi(d_\tau(x/y) + 0.5\sigma\sqrt{\tau}) + y\Phi(-d_\tau(x/y) + 0.5\sigma\sqrt{\tau})$$

It is easy to prove the following:

Proposition 2.1. *The married put price $m_\tau(S,K)$ in the Black and Scholes model is endowed with the following properties:*

1. *commutative*: $m_\tau(x,y) = m_\tau(y,x)$,
2. *increasing in each place*: $x' > x, y' > y$ *implies* $m_\tau(x',y') \geq m_\tau(x,y)$,
3. 0 *is the identity*: $m_\tau(x,0) = x$,
4. *limit at* $\tau = 0 : \lim_{\tau\to 0} m_\tau(x,y) = \max(x,y)$,
5. *limit at* $\tau = \infty : \lim_{\tau\to\infty} m_\tau(x,y) = x + y$.

Proof. We have the following:

1. From $d_\tau(x/y) = -d_\tau(y/x)$,

$$\begin{aligned} m_\tau(x,y) &= x\Phi(d_\tau(x/y) + 0.5\sigma\sqrt{\tau}) + y\Phi(-d_\tau(x/y) + 0.5\sigma\sqrt{\tau}) \\ &= y\Phi(d_\tau(y/x) + 0.5\sigma\sqrt{\tau}) + x\Phi(-d_\tau(y/x) + 0.5\sigma\sqrt{\tau}) \\ &= m_\tau(y,x). \end{aligned} \tag{2}$$

2. Trivial.
3. From $\lim_{y\to 0} d_\tau(x/y) = \infty$, we get $\mu_\tau = x\Phi(\infty) + y\Phi(-\infty) = x$, and the rest follows from the commutativity property.
4. $\lim_{\tau\to 0} d_\tau(x/y) = \infty$ if $x > y$, implying $m_\tau(x,y) = x$, while $x < y$ leads to $\lim_{\tau\to 0} d_\tau(x/y) = -\infty$, and $m_\tau(x,y) = y$.
5. Since $\lim_{\tau\to\infty} d_\tau(x/y) = \lim_{\tau\to\infty} -d_\tau(x/y) = 0$, we have $x\Phi(\infty) + y\Phi(\infty) = x + y$.

□

Some of the properties above are recognized to be the conditions for rational option pricing pointed out in Ref. [16]. From $f(S,\tau;K) = m_\tau(S,K) - K$, condition (3) yields the following: (i) $m_\tau(S,0) = S = f(S,\tau;0)$ and (ii) $f(0,\tau;K) = m_\tau(0,K) - K = 0$. Moreover, condition (5) yields Theorem 3 in Ref. [16]: the value of a perpetual warrant is $f(S,\infty;K) = m_\infty(S,K) - K = S + K - K = S$. However, it is not difficult to find examples in which the perpetual warrant condition is not required. Instead, condition (4) is one of the no-arbitrage conditions imposed by Ref. [5]: when the time to maturity tends to zero, the price must converge to the payoff. For call options, we have $f(S,0;K) = \lim_{\tau\to 0} m_\tau(S,K) - K = \max(S,K) - K = \max(S-K,0)$. For put options, $p(S,0;K) = \lim_{\tau\to 0} m_\tau(S,K) - S = \max(S,K) - S = \max(K-S,0)$.

Refs. [5] and [12] stated sufficient conditions for no-arbitrage. Namely, a pricing formula for a call (put) option is arbitrage-free if and only if (i) it is convex and decreasing (increasing) in the strike price with derivative uniformly bounded below by -1 (above by $+1$) (no horizontal arbitrage), (ii) it is increasing with maturity (no vertical arbitrage) and (iii) the limit of the maturity tending to 0 is the payoff. We collect all the no-arbitrage requirements in Proposition 2.2.

Proposition 2.2. *In an economy with no dividends and zero interest rates, in order to avoid arbitrage opportunities, the function* $m_\tau(S,K)$ *must satisfy the following conditions*:

1. *grounded call and put prices*: $m_\tau(S,0) = S$, $m_\tau(0,K) = K$,
2. *terminal condition:* $\lim_{\tau\to 0} m_\tau(S,K) = \max(S,K)$,
3. *avoiding horizontal arbitrage*:

$$0 \leq \frac{\partial m_\tau(S,K)}{\partial K} \leq 1, \tag{3}$$

4. *avoiding vertical arbitrage*:

$$0 \leq \frac{\partial m_\tau(S,K)}{\partial \tau}. \tag{4}$$

Proof. Condition (1) makes sure that the price of put options is zero when the strike is zero: $m_\tau(S,0) - S = 0$ and call options must be zero when the underlying is worth zero: $m_\tau(0,K) - K = 0$.

Condition (2) is evident. As for the horizontal arbitrage condition, the price of put option must be increasing in the strike

$$\frac{\partial p(S,\tau;K)}{\partial K}=\frac{\partial(m_\tau(S,K)-S)}{\partial K}\geq 0$$

and the price of a call option must be decreasing in the strike

$$\frac{\partial f(S,\tau;K)}{\partial K}=\frac{\partial(m_\tau(S,K)-K)}{\partial K}=\frac{\partial m_\tau(S,K)}{\partial K}-1\leq 0.$$

The case of vertical arbitrage avoids calendar arbitrage opportunities.

□

Remember that these conditions are derived under the assumption of zero interest rates and dividend yields. While this does not change our analysis of the algebraic structure of arbitrage free option prices, in the following, we will comment on how to extend the conditions if one allows for positive interest rates and dividends.

3. Option Pricing Generators: Bounded Underlying

We now extend the analysis above to cases in which the hypothesis of the Black and Scholes model about the dynamics of the underlying asset cannot be maintained. A straightforward example is when the price of the underlying asset is bounded both from below and above. This is obviously the case when the underlying asset is a bond. However, the hypothesis that the price is bounded has been also used in general asset pricing models: it was made by Ref. [14] in the analysis of the numeraire portfolio and by Carr and Yu (2012) in their proof of the Ross recovery theorem.

If the price of the underlying asset is bounded, we can rescale it without loss of generality to the unit interval. Keeping in mind Proposition 2.1, it is natural to revisit the definition of t-conorm. The concepts of t-norm and t-conorm were first proposed by Ref. [15] and developed by Schweitzer and Sklar (1961) in their studies of statistical and probability metric spaces. In finance, this concept has been typically used in the literature on non-additive decomposable capacities (Chateauneuf, 1996, [9,11]). We report here the definition:

Definition 3.1. A function $\perp$: $[0,1] \times [0,1] \rightarrow [0,1]$ is called a *t-conorm* (or *s-norm*) if

1. $\perp(a,b) = \perp(b,a)$ for all $a, b \in [0,1]$,
2. it is non-decreasing in each argument,
3. $\perp(a,0) = a$ for all $a \in [0,1]$,
4. $\perp(\perp(a,b),c) = \perp(a, \perp(b,c))$ for all $a, b, c \in [0,1]$.

Moreover, if $\perp(a,a) > a$ for all $a \in (0,1)$, then the *t-conorm* is called *Archimedean* and if $\perp(.,.)$ is strictly increasing in $(0,1) \times (0,1)$, the t-conorm is called *strict.*

Note that the points (1) through (3) of the definition are the same as in Proposition 2.1. Condition (4) is the associative property, and it is not a property satisfied by the Black and Scholes algebra. It is then natural to merge them with Proposition 2.2 to provide an axiomatic characterization of a no-arbitrage option pricing function.

Proposition 3.2. *Assume an underlying asset price $S \in [0,1]$. Take a function $m_\tau(x,y)$ endowed with the following properties:*

1. *$m_\tau(x,y)$ is an Archimedean t-conorm,*
2. *terminal condition at $\tau = 0 : \lim_{\tau \to 0} m_\tau(x,y) = \max(x,y)$,*
3. *no horizontal arbitrage:*

$$0 \leq \frac{\partial m_\tau(x,y)}{\partial y} \leq 1,$$

4. *no vertical arbitrage:*

$$0 \leq \frac{\partial m_\tau(x,y)}{\partial \tau}.$$

Then, $m_\tau(S_\tau, K)$ is the no-arbitrage price of a married put option.

While all the conditions have been already discussed, it is important to stress the Archimedean requirement. This is a technical requirement that is quite natural to impose in an option pricing application since it amounts to assuming that at-the-money call and put option values must be positive. In fact, we have

$$f(S,\tau;S) = m_\tau(S,S) - S = p(S,\tau;S) > 0$$

for $\tau > 0$ and $S \in (0,1)$. It is clear that if the Archimedean property fails, S_τ has to be a constant.

The Archimedean property, together with the associative property that we included using the t-conorm definition, brings an important feature into the picture: the option pricing generator.

Theorem 3.3. *A function* $\perp$: $[0,1] \times [0,1] \to [0,1]$ *is a continuous Archimedean t-conorm if and only if there exists a strictly increasing function* $\psi : [0,1] \to [0,+\infty]$ *with* $\psi(0) = 0$ *such that*

$$a \perp b = \psi^{[-1]}(\psi(a) + \psi(b)),$$

where $\psi^{[-1]}$ *is the pseudo-inverse of* ψ *defined as*

$$\psi^{[-1]}(x) = \begin{cases} \psi^{-1}(x), & \text{if } x \leq \psi(1) \\ 1, & \text{if } x > \psi(1). \end{cases}$$

Moreover, ψ *is called the generator of* $\perp$ *and* $\perp$ *is* strict *if and only if* $\psi(1) = +\infty$.

This result is very well known and was proved for t-norms and t-conorms by Refs. [19] and [13]. In this model, all the information content is contained in a univariate increasing function that we call the *option pricing generator*. The generator allows then a characterization of the option pricing function.

Theorem 3.4. *The price of a married put option on a bounded underlying* $S \in [0,1]$ *satisfying Proposition* 3.2 *may be written as follows*:

$$m_\tau(S,K) = \psi_\tau^{[-1]}(\psi_\tau(S) + \psi_\tau(K)),$$

where $\psi_\tau(\cdot)$ *is called the* generator *of the option pricing model.*

4. Option Pricing Generators: Underlying Unbounded from Above

We now extend the analysis to the case in which the price of the underlying asset is unbounded from above. Monoids of increasing, commutative and associative operators defined on the positive real line are called *pseudo-additions*. The extension was first proposed by Ref. [20]. We start with the definition of pseudo-addition:

Definition 4.1. Given a set $\mathcal{S} \subseteq [0, \infty]$, a *pseudo-addition* is an operator $\oplus : \mathcal{S}\ X\ \mathcal{S} \to \mathcal{S}$ which

1. is commutative: $x \oplus y = y \oplus x$,
2. is non-decreasing in each argument: $x' \geq x, y' \geq y \to x' \oplus y' \geq x \oplus y$,
3. has 0 as identity item: $0 \oplus x = x \oplus 0 = x$,
4. is associative: $x \oplus (y \oplus z) = (x \oplus y) \oplus z$,
5. satisfies continuity: $x_n \to x, y_n \to y$ implies $x_n \oplus y_n \to x \oplus y$.

We are clearly interested in the case $\mathcal{S} = [0, \infty]$. The strategy to get there is to first partition the set $[0, \infty]$ into subsets and on these to define submonoids with respect to $([0, \infty], \oplus)$. Then, given further requirements on the operation $\oplus$, we will look for a pseudo-addition defined on the whole monoid. We start with the formal definition of these submonoids in Ref. [20].

Definition 4.2. Let $\{(\alpha_k, \beta_k) : k \in \mathcal{K}\}$ be a family of disjoint open intervals in $[0, \infty]$ indexed by a countable set $\mathcal{K}$. For each $k \in \mathcal{K}$, associate a continuous and strictly increasing function

$$g_k : [\alpha_k, \beta_k] \to [0, \infty].$$

We say that a binary operation $\oplus$ has a representation

$$\{\langle(\alpha_k, \beta_k), g_k\rangle : k \in \mathcal{K}\}$$

if and only if

$$x \oplus y = \begin{cases} g_k^{[-1]}(g_k(x) + g_k(y)), & \text{if } (x, y) \in [\alpha_k, \beta_k]^2 \\ \max(x, y), & \text{otherwise,} \end{cases}$$

where $g_k^{[-1]}$ is the pseudo-inverse of g_k defined by

$$g_k^{[-1]}(x) = g^{-1}(\min(x, g_k(\beta_k))).$$

So, a representation of pseudo-addition can be obtained for every submonoid, along the same lines followed for the bounded case.

Theorem 4.3. *A binary operation is a pseudo-addition if and only if it has a representation* $\{\langle(\alpha_k, \beta_k), g_k\rangle : k \in \mathcal{K}\}$.

This is all that can be obtained if we stick to the conditions in Definition 4.1. In the general case, then the best that can be done is to get a set of generators g_k. The representation is largely simplified if we add the Archimedean property. On this we follow Ref. [17].

Definition 4.4. A pseudo-addition on $\mathcal{S} = [0, \infty]$ satisfies the following conditions:

1. commutativity: $x \oplus y = y \oplus x$,
2. non-decreasing in each argument: $x' \geq x, y' \geq y \to x' \oplus y' \geq x \oplus y$,
3. 0 as identity item: $0 \oplus x = x \oplus 0 = x$,
4. associativity: $x \oplus (y \oplus z) = (x \oplus y) \oplus z$,
5. continuity: $x_n \to x, y_n \to y$ implies $x_n \oplus y_n \to x \oplus y$,
6. Archimedean property: $x \oplus x > x, \forall x \in (0, \infty)$,
7. finite sum of finite elements: if $x < \infty$ and $y < \infty$ then $x \oplus y < \infty$.

We can now prove the result that we are going to use.

Theorem 4.5. *A binary operation* $\oplus$ *on* $[0, \infty]$ *is a pseudo-addition if and only if there exists a continuous and strictly increasing function*

$$g : [0, \infty] \to [0, \infty]. \quad g(0) = 0 \quad g(\infty) = \infty$$

such that

$$x \oplus y = g^{-1}(g(x) + g(y)) \quad \textit{for every } x, y \in [0, \infty].$$

Proof. The proof is in Ref. [17], but we give here a sketch of it because it clarifies what is going on:

1. By Theorem 4.3, the solution must have the $\{\langle(\alpha_k, \beta_k), g_k\rangle : k \in \mathcal{K}\}$ representation. Then, we must study the set $\mathcal{K}$. If $\mathcal{K} = \emptyset$, we have $x \oplus y = \max(x, y), \forall x, y$, that violates the Archimedean property. Moreover, the Archimedean property is also violated at all points α_k, β_k except $\alpha_1 = 0$ and $\beta_1 = \infty$. Then, the set $\mathcal{K}$ is a singleton identifying a single function: $\{\langle(0, \infty), g\rangle\}$. The function is of course unique up to multiplication by a positive constant.

2. By contradiction, we prove that it cannot be $g(\infty) = M < \infty$. If this is the case, one may in fact find u such that $2g(u) > M$. Then, $u \oplus u = g^{[-1]}(2g(u)) = \infty$ violates condition (7) in Definition 4.4 which would require instead $u \oplus u < \infty$.
3. The direct part can be easily proved by verifying that the function $x \oplus y$ satisfies all the conditions for a pseudo-addition.

□

Note that the Archimedean property allows us to identify a single monoid $([0, \infty], \oplus)$ associated with a single function g, unique up to multiplication by a positive constant. Without the Archimedean property, then we would remain with an arbitrary set of submonoids. We remind that this is not at all a restriction in our application, since the Archimedean property is a requirement to ensure positive at-the-money option prices. We also note a difference with respect to the case in which the price of the underlying is bounded. The pricing function is strictly increasing and the generator is always strict.

We are now in a position to characterize the set of option prices.

Proposition 4.6. *Assume an underlying asset price $S \in [0, \infty]$. Take a function $m_\tau(x, y)$ endowed with the following properties:*

1. *$m_\tau(x, y)$ is an Archimedean pseudo-addition,*
2. *boundary condition at $\tau = 0$: $\lim_{\tau \to 0} m_\tau(x, y) = \max(x, y)$,*
3. *no horizontal arbitrage:*

$$0 \leq \frac{\partial m_\tau(x, y)}{\partial y} \leq 1,$$

4. *no vertical arbitrage:*

$$0 \leq \frac{\partial m_\tau(x, y)}{\partial \tau}.$$

Then, $m_\tau(S_\tau, K)$ is the no-arbitrage price of a married put.

Finally, we can provide a general characterization for married put prices in this set of models in terms of generators:

Theorem 4.7. *The price of a married put option on an unbounded underlying S in $\in [0, \infty]$ satisfying Proposition 4.6 is given by*

$$\mu_\tau(S, K) = g_\tau^{-1}(g_\tau(S) + g_\tau(K)),$$

where $g_\tau(\cdot)$ is called the generator *of the option pricing model.*

5. Generators and Implied Probabilities

If option prices can be uniquely represented by generators, they encode all the information about the model, that is, the probability distribution of the underlying asset. This can be easily extracted using the seminal paper by Ref. [2].

As it is well known, the probability distribution implied by a set of no-arbitrage prices of options can be recovered as the limit of call and put spreads, corresponding to the derivative of the option price with respect to the strike price. Coherently, the density is recovered as the limit of butterfly spreads, that is, the second derivative of option prices. In our setting, in which prices are completely determined by generators, the probability distribution is also completely determined by them. Moreover, writing the distribution in terms of generators would allow us to identify the requirements needed for a monoid to be a consistent arbitrage-free option price and for the corresponding generator to be eligible as an option pricing generator.

Formally, let us assume that the price of a married put could be written as

$$m_T(S_T, K) = g_T^{-1}(g_T(S_T) + g_T(K)).$$

Then, the cumulative probability distribution (CPD) of the underlying asset S at maturity can be recovered from

$$Q_T(S_0 \le K) = \frac{\partial m_T(S_T, K)}{\partial K} = \frac{g'_T(K)}{g'_T(m_T(S_T, K))},$$

where $g'_T(\cdot)$ denotes the first derivative of $g_T(\cdot)$. If we assume that the generator is twice differentiable, the density is given by the second derivative of $m_T(S_T, K)$ and we compute the following:

$$\begin{aligned}
&\frac{\partial^2 m_T(S_T, K)}{\partial K^2} \\
&= \frac{g''(K)}{g'_T(m_T(S_T, K))} - \left(g'_T(K)\right)^2 \frac{g''_T(m_T(S_T, K))}{g'_T(m_T(S_T, K))^3} \\
&= \frac{g'_T(K)}{g'_T(m_T(S_T, K))} \left(\frac{g''_T(K)}{g'_T(K)} - \frac{g'_T(K)}{g'_T(m_T(S_T, K))} \frac{g''_T(m_T(S_T, K))}{g'_T(m_T(S_T, K))} \right) \\
&= Q_T(S_0 \le K) \left(\frac{g''_T(K)}{g'_T(K)} - Q_T(S_0 \le K) \frac{g''_T(m_T(S_T, K))}{g'_T(m_T(S_T, K))} \right),
\end{aligned}$$

where $g''_T(\cdot)$ denotes the second derivatives of $g_T(\cdot)$.

Having characterized the implied probability distribution of the underlying asset, we can gather all the results to ensure that the generator used in the pricing model satisfies the no-arbitrage requirement. The conditions are reported in the following theorem:

Theorem 5.1. *A function $g_\tau(x)$ satisfies the no-arbitrage conditions in Theorem* A.1 *if the following conditions hold:*

1. *$g_\tau(x)$ is a smooth pseudo-addition generator,*
2. *for any $x < y$*

$$\lim_{\tau \to 0} \frac{g_\tau(x)}{g_\tau(y)} = 0, \tag{5}$$

3. *the function $1/g'_\tau(x)$ is convex,*
4. *for $\tau_1 > \tau_2$ we have $g_{\tau_1}(x) > g_{\tau_2}(x)$.*

The proof is reported in Appendix. It is quite intuitive that condition (2) restricts the choice of generators to make sure that the married put option converges to its payoff at maturity. Moreover, the Breeden and Litzenberger theory suggests that the smoothness requirement in condition (1) and the convexity condition (3) have to do with implied probability. Finally, condition (4) is clearly linked to the vertical no-arbitrage condition.

6. How to Build Generators

Here we give practical guidelines and examples of option pricing generators and models based on them. We have already made clear that not all increasing functions are eligible as option pricing generators. For example, $\mathcal{G}(x) = \log(x)$ is a generator of the monoid $([0, \infty], x \times y)$. Of course, this cannot work as a generator for a pseudo-sum. In fact, the range of the function is the whole real line instead of the positive part of it (see Theorem 4.5). The question is whether and how this generator of a product can be turned into the generator of a sum. A first suggestion comes from the observation that the identity element of the product is $e = 1$ and that $\log(x + 1)$ qualifies as the generator of a pseudo-sum. Moreover, it is clear that if a function qualifies as a generator of a sum, its exponentiation of a proper exponent may maintain that property.

Here we give guidelines to transform a generator into an option pricing generator. In practice, we introduce two operations on the generator to satisfy the no-arbitrage requirements:

1. shift the identity element of a generator: given a generator $\mathcal{G}(x)$ with $\mathcal{G}(e) = 0$, we define a generator $g(x)$ with $g(0) = 0$,
2. power of a generator: given a generator $\mathcal{G}(x)$, we define $g(x) = \mathcal{G}(x)^{1/\theta}$.

We start defining the identity-shifting operation:

Proposition 6.1. *Given an Archimedean monoid* $(\mathcal{S}, \oplus)$, $\mathcal{S} \subseteq [0, \infty]$ *with generator* $\mathcal{G}(x), l$ *and identity element* e, *the function* $g(x) = \mathcal{G}(x + e)$ *generates a monoid with identity element* 0 *and operation* $\oplus$ *defined as*

$$x \oplus y = \mathcal{G}^{-1}(\mathcal{G}(x + e) + \mathcal{G}(y + e)) - e. \tag{6}$$

Proof. If $y = 0$, from $\mathcal{G}(e) = 0$, we have $\mathcal{G}^{-1}(\mathcal{G}(x + e)) - e = x$. □

We now address the problem of exponentiation of the generator to make it consistent with the boundary condition $\max(S, K)$.

Proposition 6.2. *Assume an Archimedean monoid* $(\mathcal{S}, \oplus)$, $\mathcal{S} \subseteq [0, \infty]$, *with generator* $\mathcal{G}(x)$ *and identity element* e *and a function* $1/b_\tau$, $b_\tau \in (0, 1]$, *strictly increasing in* τ *and such that* $\lim_{\tau \to 0} b_\tau = 0$. *Then,*

$$m_\tau = \mathcal{G}^{-1}\left(\mathcal{G}(S + e)^{1/b_\tau} + \mathcal{G}(K + e)^{1/b_\tau}\right)^{b_\tau} - e \tag{7}$$

is the no-arbitrage price of a European married put option.

Proof. First, using proposition 6.1, it is clear that the identity element of the monoid is 0. Then, we can assume $e = 0$ without loss of generality and prove

$$\lim_{b_\tau \to 0} m_\tau(S, K) = \max(S, K).$$

From

$$\lim_{b_\tau \to 0} = \left(\mathcal{G}(S)^{1/b_\tau} + \mathcal{G}(K)^{1/b_\tau}\right)^{b_\tau} = \max(\mathcal{G}(S), \mathcal{G}(K)),$$

it follows

$$\begin{aligned}\lim_{b_\tau \to 0} m_\tau(S, K) &= \mathcal{G}^{-1}\left(\mathcal{G}(S)^{1/b_\tau} + \mathcal{G}(K)^{1/b_\tau}\right)^{b_\tau} \\ &= \mathcal{G}^{-1}(\max(\mathcal{G}(S), \mathcal{G}(K)) \\ &= \max(S, K).\end{aligned}$$

□

Note that the case $\mathcal{G}(x) = x$ gives the conjugate Dagum model used in Ref. [6].

A technical point that needs to be addressed is when the exponentiation is applied to a generator that may take values in the negative region. This is hardly the case in standard option pricing applications, when the price is defined over positive values and the generator is shifted so that it cannot produce negative values (setting $\mathcal{G}(x + e)$ in place of $\mathcal{G}(x)$). Nevertheless, the problem may emerge in option pricing applications in which the underlying can take negative values. Examples are options on interest rates, that in the European market have taken on negative values for quite a long time, or derivatives on correlation, that can take values in $[-1, 1]$. And moreover, the problem of well-defined exponentiation of a monoid generator is an interesting and challenging task in itself. If the generator $g(x)$ has a symmetric structure for positive and negative values, a natural way to perform this extension would be to make sure that the exponentiation distortion would preserve such symmetry. We would call this operation *flipping* of the generator. The operation would consist in pasting the value on the positive axis on the corresponding value of the negative part.

Of course, it is clear that in order to define the flipping operation, we should first define how to map any point of the positive range of the generator on the corresponding points in the negative region. This we do in the following definition of symmetry of a generator:

Definition 6.3. A generator $\mathcal{G}(x)$, $x \in \mathcal{S}$, is symmetric if

1. there exists $e \in \mathcal{S}$ such that $\mathcal{G}(e) = 0$,

2. there exists a function $f(x)$ such that (i) $f(e) = e$ and (ii) $\mathcal{G}(f(x)) = -\mathcal{G}(x)$.

Based on this, we can then extend the exponentiation operation over negative values as follows:

Definition 6.4. Given a generator $\mathcal{G}(x)$, $\mathcal{G}(e) = 0$, $x, e \in \mathcal{S}$, symmetric around e with function $f(x)$, we define the *Power Generator* $\mathcal{G}(x)^{[1/b]}$ as

$$\mathcal{G}(x)^{[1/b]} = \begin{cases} \mathcal{G}(x)^{1/b}, & x \geq e \\ -\left(\mathcal{G}(f(x))^{1/b_{\mathcal{T}}}\right), & x < e. \end{cases} \tag{8}$$

6.1. *Power of Lamperti Transforms*

As a first example of how to build an option pricing generator, we resort to *Lamperti transform.* We first remind that the Lamperti transform is the operator that when applied to an Ito process reduces it to a unit variance arithmetic Brownian motion.

Definition 6.5. Given an Ito process $(x_t)_t$ with diffusion term given by the function $a(x_t)$, the Lamperti transform is defined as

$$\mathcal{G}(x) = \int^x \frac{1}{a(u)} du \tag{9}$$

so that the process $\mathcal{G}(x_t)$ is an Ito process such that

$$d\mathcal{G}(x_t) = drift + dW_t,$$

where W_t is a Wiener process.

Note that the transformation changes the drift of the Ito process, but this is not the focus of our analysis. Our goal here is to use the transform $\mathcal{G}(x)$ as an option pricing generator, defining $g(x) = \mathcal{G}(x+e)^{1/b_{\mathcal{T}}}$, $b_{\mathcal{T}} \in (0, 1]$. Since Lamperti transforms yield a Wiener process under a suitable change of measure, they are clearly symmetric around a suitable function $f(x)$ as the following examples show:

Example 6.6. Assume $a(x) = x$, $x \in (0, \infty)$, so that the Ito process is a geometric Brownian motion. It is very well known that in this case the Lamperti transform is $\mathcal{G}(x) = \log(x)$. We then have $e = 1$ and $f(x)$ is given by

$$f(x) = \mathcal{G}^{-1}(-\mathcal{G}(x)) = \exp(-\log(x)) = \frac{1}{x}.$$

Example 6.7. Assume $a(x) = x(1-x)$. Then, the Lamperti transform is

$$\mathcal{G}(x) = \log\left(\frac{x}{1-x}\right)$$

and it is clear that $e = 1/2$. As for the function $f(x)$, we compute

$$\mathcal{G}^{-1}(y) = \frac{1}{1+\exp(-y)}$$

and

$$f(x) = \mathcal{G}^{-1}(-\mathcal{G}(x)) = \frac{1}{1+\exp(\log(\frac{x}{1-x}))} = 1 - x.$$

6.2. *Archimedean Copula Generators*

Generators are used in copula theory in a set of models called Archimedean copula functions (see Refs. [18] and [10] for applications in finance). The structure of this class of copulas is in fact given by

$$C(x,y) = \phi^{-1}(\phi(x) + \phi(y)) \tag{10}$$

with $x, y \in [0,1]$. It is well known that x, y represent uniform random variables and the function $C(x,y)$ is the corresponding joint distribution. The function $\phi(\cdot)$ is called the generator of the copula function. It is a decreasing convex function with $\phi(0) = 1$ and $\phi(\infty) = 0$. Clearly, from an algebraic point of view, an Archimedean copula function is a commutative and associative operation with identity element $e = 1$. We may then wonder whether these functions could be used as option pricing generators. We first observe that the identity element e should be changed from 1 to 0. The other problem is that the maximum copula function is $\min(x,y)$ while we are interested in a sequence of functions reaching $\max(x,y)$. For underlying bounded in $[0,1]$, there is a well-known result that allows us to achieve a suitable generator. This is known as generalized De Morgan law that gives a link between t-norms (of which Archimedean copula functions are a special case) and t-conorms that are option pricing generators as discussed in Section 3.

Theorem 6.8. *Given a t-norm $t(x,y), x, y \in [0,1]$, the function*

$$x \oplus y = 1 - t(1-x, 1-y) \tag{11}$$

is a t-conorm.

We remind that t-norms are defined just like t-conorms in Definition 3.1 with the difference that the identity element is 1 instead of 0. Moreover, it can be checked that $\min(x,y)$ is a t-norm, and the dual t-conorm is $\max(x,y)$. So, the generalized De Morgan law delivers all the changes needed to transform a t-norm, and a copula function, into an option pricing generator. It is also possible to establish a link between the generator of the t-norm (and the copula) and the t-conorm (and the option pricing generator). More specifically, it is easy to check that if $\phi(x)$ is the generator of the copula function, $\psi(x) = \phi(1-x)$ is the generator of the t-conorm.

Here we want to carry out a parallel analysis for the case in which the underlying is unbounded from above. A casual observation of standard Archimedean copulas reveals that the same link between copula and t-conorms can be extended to the positive real line as follows:

Proposition 6.9. *Denote $C_\theta(u,v)$ an Archimedean copula function with generator $\phi(x)$ indexed by a parameter θ such that $\lim_{\theta\to\theta^*} C_\theta(x,y) = \min(x,y)$. Assume $S, K \in [0,\infty]$. Then,*

$$\lim_{\theta\to\theta^*} S \oplus_\theta K = C_\theta\left(\frac{1}{S+1}, \frac{1}{K+1}\right)^{-1} - 1 \tag{12}$$

with generator

$$g(x) = \phi\left(\frac{1}{x+1}\right) \tag{13}$$

is a pseudo-addition.

Proof. First note that with $\lim_{\theta\to\theta^*} C_\theta(x,y) = \min(x,y)$ we have

$$\begin{aligned}
x \oplus y &= \frac{1}{\min\left(\frac{1}{x+1}, \frac{1}{y+1}\right)} - 1 \\
&= \frac{1}{\frac{1}{\max(x+1,y+1)}} - 1 \\
&= \max(x+1, y+1) - 1 = \max(x,y).
\end{aligned}$$

As for the generator,

$$g(x) = \phi\left(\frac{1}{x+1}\right)$$

we have

$$g^{-1}(s) = \frac{1}{\phi^{-1}(s)} - 1.$$

We then compute

$$\begin{aligned}
x \oplus y &= g^{-1}(g(x) + g(y)) \\
&= \frac{1}{\phi^{-1}\left(\phi\left(\frac{1}{x+1}\right) + \phi\left(\frac{1}{y+1}\right)\right)} - 1 \\
&= C_\theta\left(\frac{1}{x+1}, \frac{1}{y+1}\right)^{-1} - 1.
\end{aligned}$$

□

It may be appropriate to give a clarification on the reason why we need to include a limit with respect to the parameter θ requiring that the copula functions reach their maximum value $\min(x,y)$. The reason is that this limit is not defined for all copula functions. For cases in which the maximum copula is not reached, the pseudo-sum generator cannot reach $\max(x,y)$ and one of the no-arbitrage conditions is not satisfied.

We give here examples of these generators using the most popular Archimedean copula functions.

Example 6.10. Consider Gumbel–Hougaard copula with generator

$$\phi(x) = (-\log x)^\theta$$

with $\theta \in [1, \infty)$. Then,

$$g(x) = (\log(x+1))^\theta \quad g^{-1}(s) = \exp\left(s^{1/\theta}\right) - 1.$$

We then have

$$x \oplus y = \exp\left(\left((\log(1+x))^\theta + (\log(1+y))^\theta\right)^{1/\theta}\right) - 1.$$

Note that setting $b = 1/\theta$ gives

$$x \oplus y = \exp\left(\left((\log(1+x))^{1/b} + (\log(1+y))^{1/b}\right)^b\right) - 1$$

with $b \in (0, 1]$ that is the same generator obtained by exponentiation of the Lamperti transform of a geometric Brownian motion.

Example 6.11. The Clayton copula is characterized by the generator

$$\phi(x) = \frac{x^{-\theta} - 1}{\theta}$$

with $\theta \in [-1, \infty]$. Then,

$$g(x) = \frac{(x+1)^\theta - 1}{\theta} \quad g^{-1}(s) = (1 + \theta s)^{1/\theta} - 1.$$

Note that this generator may be also considered as the logarithm in Tsallis algebra Ref. [21]. For this reason, we call this model Clayton–Tsallis. We then have the following:

$$x \oplus y = \left((x+1)^\theta + (y+1)^\theta - 1\right)^{1/\theta} - 1.$$

6.3. *Hybrid Models: Black–Scholes–Dagum*

It is now time to compare the associative option pricing models, for which an option pricing generator exists, and the standard Black and Scholes model. Moreover, we can show that generators can be applied to other models, including the Black and Scholes one.

Associative married put option pricing models share the representation

$$m_\tau(S, K) = g_\tau^{-1}(g_\tau(S) + g_\tau(K)),$$

where $g(\cdot)$ is an increasing function (strictly increasing if the function is in $[0, \infty]$).

Note that the common feature of these models is that there exists a transformation of the married put price m_τ that yields a linear relationship to the same transformation of the variables S and K. Formally,

$$g_\tau(m_\tau(S, K)) = g_\tau(S) + g_\tau(K).$$

Let us now compare this structure with the Black and Scholes formula:

$$m_\tau(S, K) = S\Phi(d_\tau + 0.5\sigma\sqrt{\tau}) + K\Phi(-d_\tau + 0.5\sigma\sqrt{\tau})$$

with

$$d_\tau(S/K) = \frac{\log(S/K)}{\sigma\sqrt{\tau}}.$$

It is clear that this function cannot be directly reconducted to an associative function in S and K in $[0, \infty]$. However, a closer inspection of the pricing formula shows that it can be seen as associative on a set of *functions of* S and K. In fact, defining the function

$$D_\tau(x) = x\Phi\left(d_\tau(x/y) + 0.5\sigma\sqrt{\tau}\right),$$

we note that the Black and Scholes married put price can be written as follows:

$$m_\tau(S, K) = D_\tau(S) + D_\tau(K).$$

This derives from the function

$$\mu_\tau(y) = x\Phi(d_\tau(x/y) + 0.5\sigma\sqrt{\tau}) + y\Phi(-d_\tau(x/y) + 0.5\sigma\sqrt{\tau})$$

and $-d(x/y) = d(y/x)$. The financial meaning of the representation is very well known: $D_\tau(S)$ is the price of an *asset-or-nothing* (AoN) digital option and $D_\tau(K)$ is the price of a *cash-or-nothing* (CoN) digital option paying K dollars.

As for the algebraic properties of the married put function, we note that the Black and Scholes function is commutative in $D_\tau(x)$. Moreover, it is clear that it is additive in the digital prices with generator $g(x) = x$. It then makes sense to conceive that the pseudo-addition version of the Black and Scholes formula could be extended to other generators:

$$m_\tau(S, K) = g^{-1}\left(g(D_\tau(S)) + g(D_\tau(K))\right).$$

Note that this representation extends the linear no-arbitrage representation of options in terms of AoN and CoN digital options. As a representative element of this hybrid class of models, it is natural to nest the Black and Scholes model in the Dagum one.

Proposition 6.12. *The Black–Scholes–Dagum model is defined as*

$$m_\tau = \left(D_\tau(S)^{1/b(\tau)} + D_\tau(K)^{1/b(\tau)}\right)^{b(\tau)} \tag{14}$$

with

$$\begin{aligned} D_\tau(x) &= x\Phi\left(d_\tau(x/y) + 0.5\sigma\sqrt{\tau}\right) \\ d_\tau(x/y) &= \frac{\log(x/y)}{\sigma\sqrt{\tau}} \end{aligned}$$

with $b(\tau)$ increasing in $[0,1]$ and $\sigma \in (0,\infty)$. The Black and Scholes model is obtained with $b(\tau) = 1, \forall\tau$, and the Dagum model is obtained as $\sigma \to 0$ or $\sigma \to \infty$.

7. Three Examples

Here we give three examples of models characterized by generators. Please consider that this is not meant to be a full-fledged empirical analysis of these option pricing models but just a first attempt to understand the possible shapes of *smile* functions that can be generated. It is only for the sake of realism that we calibrate the models on the *at-the-money* value of traded options in a trading day. The models were calibrated on the one-year maturity option on the Italian

Table 1. Models.

Generator $g_\mathcal{T}$	Married put $m_\mathcal{T}$	Implied probability $Q_\mathcal{T}(S_0 \leq K)$
$x^{1/b_\mathcal{T}}$	$\left(S^{1/b_\mathcal{T}} + K^{1/b_\mathcal{T}}\right)^{b_\mathcal{T}}$	$\left(1 + \left(\frac{S}{K}\right)^{-1/b_\mathcal{T}}\right)^{1-b_\mathcal{T}}$
$(\log(x+1))^{1/b_\mathcal{T}}$	$\exp\left(\left((\log(1+S))^{1/b_\mathcal{T}} + (\log(1+K))^{1/b_\mathcal{T}}\right)^{b_\mathcal{T}}\right) - 1$	$\left(\frac{\log(K+1)}{\log(m_\mathcal{T}+1)}\right)^{1/b_\mathcal{T}-1} \frac{m_\mathcal{T}+1}{K+1}$
$\frac{(x+1)^{b_\mathcal{T}}-1}{b_\mathcal{T}}$	$\left((S+1)^{b_\mathcal{T}} + (K+1)^{b_\mathcal{T}} - 1)\right)^{1/b_\mathcal{T}} - 1$	$\left(\frac{K+1}{m_\mathcal{T}+1}\right)^{b_\mathcal{T}-1}$

FTSE-MIB stock index. The first model considered is the Dagum model. The other two are those proposed in the previous section: one is the logarithm exponentiated in model 6.10 and the other is the logarithm in the Tsallis algebra, model 6.11. Details of the models are reported in Table 1. The models are compared with the Black and Scholes and all of them are calibrated to have the same value for the *at-the-money* option.

The comparison of the models is reported in Figure 1 in terms of implied volatilities. The parameter $b_\mathcal{T}$ generates a smile for all the models. The Dagum and Tsallis–Clayton models produce results that are indistinguishable from the other with a smile curve that is steeper for the lower tail than for the upper tail. The power-log model is more symmetric, and the smile line lies below the Dagum model in the lower tail and above it in the upper tail. The parameters $b_\mathcal{T}$ of the models, just like the integrated variance $\sigma\sqrt{\mathcal{T}}$ in the Black and Scholes models, are increasing with maturity.

An interesting question is how the shape of the smile would evolve with maturity. Figure 2 reports the smiles for the Dagum and the power of log model for a value of the parameters three times higher, corresponding to a value of integrated variance in the Black and Scholes model equal to 0.581424. We note that while the shape of the smile for the Dagum model remains about the same as that for the shorter maturity, that one of the power of log model is substantially different. More precisely, it is shifted well below the Dagum smile for out-of-the money part of the curve and above the line for in-the-money options. In other words, the smile of power-log is rotated

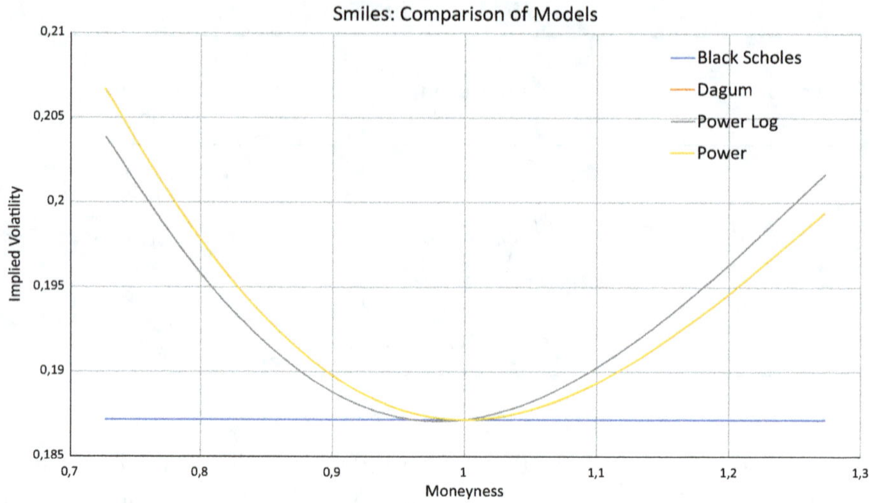

Figure 1. Smiles: Comparison of the models. Short-term low volatility.

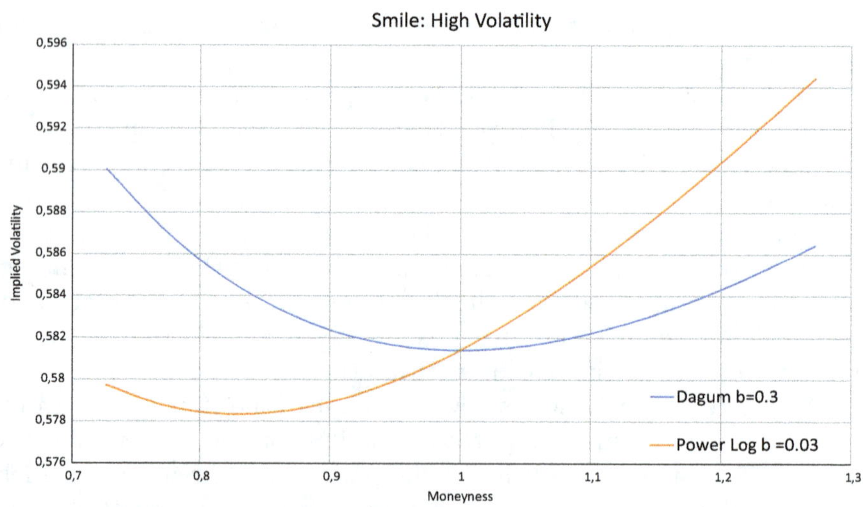

Figure 2. Smiles: Comparison of the Dagum and power of log models. Long-term high volatility.

while being shifted up, while the Dagum model is only shifted up. In this sense, the Dagum model represents a natural extension of the Black and Scholes model with the difference that the smile is not flat.

8. Conclusions

In this chapter, we have characterized a class of option pricing models that are completely described by a one-place increasing function grounded at zero called the *generator* of the option pricing model. The analysis of this generator is made possible by focusing on the pricing function of a married put option, that is, a position consisting of the underlying and a protective put. The task is then to find a set of functions that evolve toward the payoff function $\max(S, K)$ at maturity.

Existence of the generator is granted if one assumes that this pricing function is commutative, associative and Archimedean. The Archimedean assumption is particularly relevant in the option price application because it amounts to requiring that at-the-money options must have positive values. Violation of this assumption would result in a degenerate distribution. So, under the assumption that the price of the underlying is bounded, without loss of generality in $[0, 1]$, the option pricing formula is a t-conorm, while if the underlying is in $[0, \infty]$, the option pricing formula is a pseudo-addition. In both cases, the pricing functions admit the existence of an option pricing generator.

We showed how to select generators compliant with the no-arbitrage requirements. In particular, we showed that using the exponentiation of some well-known generators found in stochastic process theory (Lamperti transform), or in multivariate distribution theory (Archimedean copula functions generators), can be suitably adjusted to give possible candidates for an option price generator.

Once the option pricing generator is specified, the information concerning the risk-adjusted density of the underlying asset is completely encoded in the option pricing generator, and can be recovered using the standard Ref. [2] machinery. Cumulative distribution and probability density functions are written in terms of first and second derivatives of the option pricing generators.

We provide examples of option pricing generator comparing the power generator using the power function, leading to the Dagum distribution, a generator using exponentiation of the logarithm function and one using the Tsallis definition of the logarithm in the q-algebra. The Dagum and the power of log models instead are different, and the difference is getting larger for longer maturities. In particular, the Dagum model preserves the same smile shape for different maturities.

Appendix

Here we give proof of Theorem 5.1. The theorem is proved by the following lemmas. We give credit to Lin Yang for most of this proof that we embedded in our monoid generator analysis. We start writing the option pricing function and the no-arbitrage requirements in terms of the generator.

Theorem A.1. *Let us define a monoid* $([0,\infty],\oplus)$, *where* $\oplus$ *is an Archimedean pseudo-addition with generator* $g_\tau(x)$, *continuous and twice differentiable. Then, the function*

$$m_\tau(S_\tau, K) \equiv S_\tau \oplus K = g_\tau^{-1}(g_\tau(S) + g_\tau(K)) \tag{15}$$

denotes the arbitrage-free value of a European married put option written on the underlying S *with strike price* K *and time to maturity* τ *if an only if it satisfies the following:*

1. *Terminal condition*:

$$\lim_{\tau\to 0} g_\tau^{-1}(g_\tau(S_\tau) + g_\tau(K)) = \max(S_0, K), \tag{16}$$

2. *Horizontal arbitrage condition*:

$$\frac{\partial m_\tau(S_\tau, K)}{\partial K} = Q_\tau(S_0 \le K) = \frac{g'_\tau(K)}{g'_\tau(m_\tau(S_\tau, K))} \le 1 \tag{17}$$

$$\frac{\partial^2 m_\tau(S_\tau, K)}{\partial K^2} = Q_\tau(S_0 \le K)\left(\frac{g''_\tau(K)}{g'_\tau(K)} - Q_\tau(S_0 \le K) \times \frac{g''_\tau(m_\tau(S_\tau, K))}{g'_\tau(m_\tau(S_\tau, K))}\right) > 0, \tag{18}$$

3. *Vertical arbitrage condition:* $g_\tau(\cdot)$ *must be such that for any* $\tau_1 > \tau_2 \geq 0$,

$$m_{\tau_1}(S, K) > m_{\tau_2}(S, K). \tag{19}$$

Now we report a set of lemmas linking the requirements in Theorem A.1 with the conditions in Theorem 5.1.

Lemma A.2. *If* $g_\tau(x)$ *is a smooth generator of a pseudo-addition (condition* 1 *and condition* 2 *in Theorem* 5.1 *holds), then*

$$\lim_{\tau \to 0} m_\tau(x, y) = \max(x, y).$$

Proof. First, remind that $g(x)$ is positive and increasing, and $g_\tau^{-1}(x)$ is also increasing, being the generator of a pseudo-addition (Theorem 4.5). Now, set $\delta > 0$ and $y > x > 0$. Condition (2) gives

$$\lim_{\tau \to 0} \frac{g_\tau(y)}{g_\tau(y + \delta)} = 0$$

and

$$\lim_{\tau \to 0} \frac{g_\tau(x)}{g_\tau(y + \delta)} = 0$$

from which

$$\lim_{\tau \to 0} \frac{g_\tau(x) + g_\tau(y)}{g_\tau(y + \delta)} = 0.$$

So, for all $\delta > 0$, $y > x > 0$, and for any $\varepsilon > 0$, there exists τ_0 such that for $\tau < \tau_0$,

$$\left| \frac{g_\tau(y) + g_\tau(x)}{g_\tau(y + \delta)} \right| < \varepsilon.$$

Since $g(x)$ is positive, we get, for $\varepsilon = 1$,

$$g_\tau(x) + g_\tau(y) < g_\tau(y + \delta)$$

and

$$g_\tau(y) < g_\tau(x) + g_\tau(y) < g_\tau(y + \delta).$$

Since $g_\tau^{-1}(\cdot)$ is increasing, we obtain

$$y < g_\tau^{-1}(g_\tau(x) + g_\tau(y)) < y + \delta.$$

So, for all $\delta > 0$, there exists $\tau < \tau_0$ such that

$$\left|g_\tau^{-1}(g(x) + g(y)) - y\right| < \delta$$

and we have proved

$$\lim_{\tau \to 0} g_\tau^{-1}(g(x) + g(y)) = y > x. \qquad \square$$

Lemma A.3. *Condition* 2 *in Theorem* (5.1) *implies that* $g(x)$ *is convex.*

Proof. By contradiction, assume that, there exist $y > x$ and $t \in (0,1)$ such that for all $\tau > 0$,

$$g_\tau(tx + (1-t)y) > tg_\tau(x) + (1-t)g_\tau(y).$$

Since $g_\tau(x)$ is positive,

$$\frac{g_\tau(tx + (1-t)y)}{g_\tau(y)} > \frac{tg_\tau(x) + (1-t)g_\tau(y)}{g_\tau(y)}.$$

Applying condition (2), and reminding $y > x$, we obtain

$$\lim_{\tau \to 0} \frac{g_\tau(tx + (1-t)y)}{g_\tau(y)} = 0,$$

but the same condition yields

$$\lim_{\tau \to 0} \frac{tg_\tau(x) + (1-t)g_\tau(y)}{g_\tau(y)} = 1 - t > 0,$$

a contradiction. $\square$

Lemma A.4. *If* $m_\tau(x,y) \equiv g_\tau^{-1}(g_\tau(x) + g_\tau(y))$, *condition* (2) *in Theorem* 5.1 *implies*

$$0 \leq \frac{\partial m_\tau(x,y)}{\partial y} \leq 1. \tag{20}$$

Proof. First, we compute the derivative of inverse function

$$\frac{\partial m_T(x,y)}{\partial y} = \frac{g'_T(y)}{g'_T(m_T(x,y))},$$

and since $g'_T(\cdot)$ is positive, we have

$$\frac{\partial m_T(x,y)}{\partial y} \geq 0.$$

Next, from Lemma A.3, we have that $g(\cdot)$ is convex so that $g'(\cdot)$ is increasing. So, from $m_T(x,y) \geq y$, we obtain

$$\frac{\partial m_T(x,y)}{\partial y} = \frac{g'_T(y)}{g'_T(m_T(x,y))} \leq 1.$$

□

Lemma A.5. *$m_T(x,y)$ is convex in y if and only if $1/g'_T(\cdot)$ is convex (condition 3 in Theorem 5.1).*

Proof. From

$$\frac{\partial m_T}{\partial y} = \frac{g'_T(y)}{g'_T(m_T)},$$

we compute

$$\frac{\partial^2 m_T(x,y)}{\partial y^2} = \frac{g''_T(y)g'_T(m_T) - g'_T(y)(\partial g'_T(m_T)/\partial y)}{[g'_T(m_T)]^2}.$$

The condition for convexity then is

$$g''_T(y)g'_T(m_T) - g'_T(y)\frac{\partial g'_T(m_T)}{\partial y} \geq 0.$$

This can be written as

$$g''_T(y)g'_T(m_T) - g'_T(y)g''_T(m_T)\frac{\partial m_T}{\partial y} \geq 0$$

from which

$$g''_T(y)g'_T(m_T) - g'_T(y)g''_T(m_T)\frac{g'_T(y)}{g'_T(m_T)} \geq 0.$$

This yields the condition:

$$\frac{g''_T(y)}{[g'_T(y)]^2} \geq \frac{g''_T(m_T)}{[g'_T(m_T)]^2}.$$

Since $m_T \geq y$, this implies that the function

$$\frac{g''_T(z)}{[g'_T(z)]^2}$$

must be decreasing. But since we have

$$\frac{\partial(1/g'_T(z))}{\partial z} = -\frac{g''_T(z)}{[g'_T(z)]^2},$$

the function $1/g'_T(z)$ must be convex. The same proof can be run backward. □

Lemma A.6. *If* $\tau_1 > \tau_2$, $m_{T1} > m_{T2}$ *iff* $g_{T1}(z) > g_{T2}(z), \forall z$.

Proof. First note that $g_{T1}(\cdot) \lesseqgtr g_{T2}(\cdot)$ implies

$$g_{T1}\left(g_{T2}^{-1}(z)\right) \lesseqgtr g_{T2}\left(g_{T2}^{-1}(z)\right) = z.$$

Now if $m_{T1}(x,y) > m_{T2}(x,y)$, for $\tau_1 > \tau_1$, we have

$$\begin{aligned} g_{T1}(m_{T1}(x,y)) &= g_{T1}(x) + g_{T1}(y) \\ &> g_{T1}\left(m_{T2}(x,y)\right) \\ &= g_{T1}\left(g_{T2}^{-1}(g_{T2}(x) + g_{T2}(y))\right) \\ &> g_{T2}(x) + g_{T2}(y) \end{aligned}$$

which implies $g_{T1}(\cdot) > g_{T2}(\cdot)$. □

References

[1] J. Aczél. *Lectures on Functional Equations and Their Applications*, Academic Press, New York, 1966.

[2] D. Breeden and R. Litzenberger. Prices of state contingent claims implicit in option prices. *Journal of Business*, 51:621–651, 1978.

[3] P. Carr. Semi-static hedging and conservative fields. Mimeo, 2008.

[4] P. Carr. Lie's Canonical coordinate and Stochastic differential equations. Mimeo, 2020.

[5] P. Carr and D. Madan. A note on sufficient conditions for no arbitrage. *Finance Research Letters*, 2:125–130, 2005.

[6] P. Carr and L. Torricelli. Additive logistic processes in option pricing. *Finance and Stochastics*, 25:689–724, 2021.

[7] P. Carr and J. Yu. Risk, return and ross recovery. *The Journal of Derivatives*, 20(1):38–59, 2012.

[8] A. Chateauneuf. Decomposable capacities, distorted probabilities and concave capacities. *Mathematical Social Sciences*, 31:19–37, 1995.

[9] U. Cherubini. Fuzzy measures and asset pricing: Accounting for information ambiguity. *Applied Mathematical Finance*, 4(3):135–149, 1997.

[10] U. Cherubini, E. Luciano, and W. Vecchiato. *Copula Methods in Finance*. John Wiley Finance Series, Chichester, UK, 2004.

[11] U. Cherubini and S. Mulinacci. Extensions and distortions of λ-measures. *Fuzzy Sets and Systems*, 412:27–40, 2020.

[12] M. H. A. Davis and D. G. Hobson. The range of traded option prices. *Mathematical Finance*, 17(1):1–14, 2007.

[13] C. H. Ling. Representation of associative functions. *Publicationes Mathematicae Debrecen*, 12:189–212, 1965.

[14] J. B. Long. Numeraire portfolio. *Journal of Financial Economics*, 26(1):29–69, 1990.

[15] K. Menger. Statistical metrics. *Proceedings of the National Academy of Sciences of the United States of America*, 28(12):535–537, 1942.

[16] R. C. Merton. Theory of rational option pricing. *The Bell Journal of Economics and Management Science*, 4(1):141–183, 1973.

[17] R. Mesiar and J. Rybáric. Pseudo-arithmetical operations. *Tatra Mountains Mathematical Publications*, 2:185–192, 1993.

[18] R. B. Nelsen. *An Introduction to Copulas*, 2nd edn. Springer, New York, 2006.

[19] B. Schweizer and A. Sklar. Associative functions and statistical triangle inequalities. *Publicationes Mathematicae Debrecen*, 8:169–186, 1961.

[20] M. Sugeno and T. Murofushi. Pseudo-additive measures and integrals. *Journal of Mathematical Analysis and Applications*, 122:197–222, 1987.

[21] C. Tsallis. Possible generalization of the Boltzman-Gibbs statistics. *Journal of Statistical Physics*, 52:479–487, 1988.

https://doi.org/10.1142/9789811280306_0007

Chapter 7

Representation for Martingales Living after a Random Time with Applications

Tahir Choulli[*,‡] **and Ferdoos Alharbi**[*,†,§]

[*]*Mathematical and Statistical Sciences Department, University of Alberta, Edmonton, Canada*

[†]*College of Science and Theoretical Studies, Saudi Electronic University, Riyadh, Saudi Arabia*

[‡]*tchoulli@ualberta.ca*

[§]*ferdoos@ualberta.ca*

Abstract

Our financial setting consists of a market model with two flows of information. The smallest flow $\mathbb{F}$ is the "public" flow of information which is available to all agents, while the larger flow $\mathbb{G}$ has additional information about the occurrence of a random time τ. This random time can model the default time in credit risk or death time in life insurance. Hence the filtration $\mathbb{G}$ is the progressive enlargement of $\mathbb{F}$ with τ. In this framework, when τ is a finite honest time, we describe explicitly how $\mathbb{G}$-local martingales can be represented in terms of $\mathbb{F}$-local martingales and parameters of τ. This representation complements the recent work of Choulli, Daveloose and Vanmaele to the case when martingales live "after τ." Under some mild assumptions on the pair $(\mathbb{F}, \tau)$, we fully elaborate the application of these results to the explicit parametrization of all deflators under $\mathbb{G}$. The results are illustrated in the case of a jump-diffusion model and a discrete-time market model.

Keywords: Honest/random time, Progressively enlarged filtration, Optional martingale representation, Informational risk decomposition, Deflators

1. Introduction

This chapter considers a class of informational markets, which is defined by the pair $(\mathbb{F}, \tau)$. Herein, $\mathbb{F}$ models the "public" information that is available to all agents over time, while τ is a random time that might not be seen through the flow $\mathbb{F}$ when it occurs. This random time represents a default time of a firm in credit risk theory, a death time of an agent in life insurance where the mortality and longevity risks pose serious challenges, or the occurrence time of an event that might impact the market somehow. For detailed discussion about the relationship between our current framework with the credit risk literature, we refer the reader to Choulli *et al.* [12]. As random times can be seen before their occurrence, the flow of the agents who can see τ happening results from the progressive enlargement of $\mathbb{F}$ with τ and which will be denoted by $\mathbb{G}$ throughout the rest of this chapter.

In this setting, our first principal objective lies in quantifying the various risks induced by τ and its "correlation" with $\mathbb{F}$. Mathematically, usually a risk is represented by a random variable which can be seen as a terminal value of a martingale (the dynamic version of this risk). Thus, our objective boils down to elaborating the following representation for any $\mathbb{G}$-martingale $M^{\mathbb{G}}$:

$$M^{\mathbb{G}} = M^{(\mathrm{pf})} + M^{(\mathrm{pd},1)} + \cdots + M^{(\mathrm{pd},k)} + M^{(\mathrm{cr},1)} + \cdots + M^{(\mathrm{cr},l)}. \quad (1)$$

All terms in the right-hand side are $\mathbb{G}$-local martingales, where $M^{(\mathrm{pf})}$ represents the pure financial risk, $M^{(\mathrm{pd},i)}$ $i = 1, \ldots, k$ are the pure default/mortality risks and $M^{(\mathrm{cr},j)}$ $j = 1, \ldots, l$ are the correlation risks. The representation (1) appeared first in Azéma *et al.* [4] when $\mathbb{F}$ is a Brownian filtration and τ avoids $\mathbb{F}$-stopping times and is the end of an $\mathbb{F}$-predictable set. Then Blanchet–Scalliet and Jeanblanc (2004) focused on a restricted subset of $\mathbb{G}$-martingales stopped at τ and extends slightly the representation under a set of assumptions on the pair $(\mathbb{F}, \tau)$. Recently, the set of $\mathbb{G}$-martingales stopped at τ was fully elaborated under no assumption in Ref. [12]. The applications of this representation in credit risk can be found in [6–8] (see also Ref. [12]

for more related literature), while its application in arbitrage can be found in Ref. [15]. To the best of our knowledge, for $\mathbb{G}$-martingales living after τ and general pair $(\mathbb{F}, \tau)$, the martingales representation formula (1) remains an open question.

This chapter assumes that τ is an honest time and elaborates formula (1) for $\mathbb{G}$-martingales living after τ, and hence it complements the study considered in Ref. [12]. Then, by combining these obtained results with Ref. [12], we derive the exact form of (1) for honest times. This extends Ref. [4] to a more general setting for the pair $(\mathbb{F}, \tau)$.

Our second objective in this chapter resides in deriving direct applications of the representation (1) to the explicit description of deflators for the models $(S - S^\tau, \mathbb{G})$ in terms of the deflators of the initial model $(S, \mathbb{F})$. Here S is the discounted price processes of d-risky assets, which is mathematically an $\mathbb{F}$-semimartinagle. This complements Ref. [15], which focuses on market models stopped at τ. Therefore, again, we combined our obtained results on deflators with [15] to describe the set of all deflators for the model $(S, \mathbb{G})$ afterwards.

This chapter contains four sections including the current introduction section. The second section presents the mathematical model, its parametrization and some preliminaries that will be used throughout this chapter. The third section addresses our first goal and gives results about the representation (1). The fourth section deals with the second main objective of deflators' descriptions. This chapter has some appendices where we recall some known results for the sake of having a self-contained paper and where we relegate some technical proofs.

2. The Mathematical Framework and Preliminaries

Throughout this chapter, we consider a complete probability space $(\Omega, \mathcal{G}, P)$. For any filtration $\mathbb{H} \in \{\mathbb{F}, \mathbb{G}\}$ defined on this space, we denote $\mathcal{A}(\mathbb{H})$ (respectively, $\mathcal{M}(\mathbb{H})$) the set of $\mathbb{H}$-adapted processes with $\mathbb{H}$-integrable variation (respectively, that are $\mathbb{H}$-uniformly integrable martingale), and the total variation process of a process X — it exists — will be denoted throughout this chapter by $\text{Var}(X)$. For any process X, we denote by ${}^{o,\mathbb{H}}X$ (respectively, ${}^{p,\mathbb{H}}X$) the $\mathbb{H}$-optional (respectively, $\mathbb{H}$-predictable) projection of X. For an increasing process V, we denote $V^{o,\mathbb{H}}$ (respectively, $V^{p,\mathbb{H}}$) its dual

$\mathbb{H}$-optional (respectively, dual $\mathbb{H}$-predictable) projection. For a filtration $\mathbb{H}$, $\mathcal{O}(\mathbb{H})$, $\mathcal{P}(\mathbb{H})$ and $\mathrm{Prog}(\mathbb{H})$ represent the $\mathbb{H}$-optional, the $\mathbb{H}$-predictable and the $\mathbb{H}$-progressive σ-fields respectively on $\Omega\times[0,+\infty[$. For an $\mathbb{H}$-semimartingale X, we denote by $L(X,\mathbb{H})$ the set of all X-integrable processes in Ito's sense, and for $H\in L(X,\mathbb{H})$, the resulting integral is one-dimensional $\mathbb{H}$-semimartingale denoted by $H\bullet X := \int_0^{\cdot} H_u dX_u$. For $M\in\mathcal{M}_{loc}(\mathbb{H})$, we denote $L^1_{loc}(M,\mathbb{H})$ the subset of $L(M,\mathbb{H})$ such that the resulting integral is an $\mathbb{H}$-local martingale. Throughout this chapter, for any process X and any random time θ, we denote by X^θ the stopped process at θ given by $X^\theta_t := X_{t\wedge\theta}$, $t\geq 0$. If $\mathcal{C}(\mathbb{H})$ is a set of $\mathbb{H}$-adapted processes, then $\mathcal{C}_{\mathrm{loc}}(\mathbb{H})$ — except when it is stated otherwise — is the set of processes, X, for which there exists a sequence of $\mathbb{H}$-stopping times, $(T_n)_{n\geq 1}$, that increases to infinity and X^{T_n} belongs to $\mathcal{C}(\mathbb{H})$, for each $n\geq 1$. For any $\mathbb{H}$-semimartingale, L, the Doléans–Dade stochastic exponential denoted by $\mathcal{E}(L)$ is the unique solution to the SDE, $dX = X_- dL$, $X_0 = 1$, given by

$$\mathcal{E}_t(L) = \exp\big(L_t - L_0 - \frac{1}{2}\langle L^c\rangle_t\big)\prod_{0<s\leq t}(1+\Delta L_s)e^{-\Delta L_s}. \tag{2}$$

Our mathematical model starts with a stochastic basis $(\Omega,\mathcal{G},\mathbb{F}=(\mathcal{F}_t)_{t\geq 0},P)$, where $\mathbb{F}$ is a filtration satisfying the usual hypothesis (i.e., right continuity and completeness) and $\mathcal{F}_\infty\subset\mathcal{G}$. Financially speaking, the filtration $\mathbb{F}$ represents the flow of "public information" through time. Besides this initial model, we consider a random time τ, i.e., a $[0,+\infty]$-valued $\mathcal{G}$-measurable random variable. To this random time, we associate the process D and the filtration $\mathbb{G}$ given by

$$\begin{aligned} &D := I_{[\![\tau,+\infty[\![}, \quad \mathbb{G} := (\mathcal{G}_t)_{t\geq 0},\\ &\mathcal{G}_t = \cap_{s>0}\left(\mathcal{F}_{s+t}\vee\sigma\left(D_u,\ u\leq s+t\right)\right). \end{aligned} \tag{3}$$

The agent endowed with $\mathbb{F}$ can only get information about τ via the *survival probabilities* G and $\widetilde{G}$, known in the literature as Azéma supermartingales, and are given by

$$\begin{aligned} &G_t :=^{o,\mathbb{F}} (I_{[\![0,\tau[\![})_t = P(\tau>t|\mathcal{F}_t) \quad \text{and}\\ &\widetilde{G}_t :=^{o,\mathbb{F}} (I_{[\![0,\tau]\!]})_t = P(\tau\geq t|\mathcal{F}_t). \end{aligned} \tag{4}$$

Throughout this chapter, besides the pair $(G, \widetilde{G})$ that parametrizes τ, the following process

$$m := G + D^{o,\mathbb{F}} \tag{5}$$

plays a central role in our analysis and it is a BMO $\mathbb{F}$-martingale. For more details about this and other related results, we refer the reader to [17, paragraph 74, Chapter XX].

In this chapter, we focus on the class of honest times introduced in Ref. [5] and which we recall in the following.

Definition 2.1. A random time σ is called an $\mathbb{F}$-honest time if, for any t, there exists an $\mathcal{F}_t$-measurable random variable σ_t such that $\sigma I_{\{\sigma<t\}} = \sigma_t I_{\{\sigma<t\}}$.

The following theorem introduces two different classes of $\mathbb{G}$-martingales, which are very useful in our analysis. The first class is intimately related to an operator which transforms $\mathbb{F}$-martingales into $\mathbb{G}$-martingales, and this operator appeared naturally in the representation of $\mathbb{G}$-martingales. The second class consists of the $\mathbb{G}$-local martingale part of $M - M^\tau$, when M spans the set of $\mathbb{F}$-local martingales.

Theorem 2.2. *Suppose τ is an honest time. Then the following assertions hold:*

(a) *For any $\mathbb{F}$-local martingale M, the process*

$$\begin{aligned}\mathcal{T}^{(a)}(M) := I_{]\!]\tau,+\infty[\![} \cdot M + \frac{I_{]\!]\tau,+\infty[\![}}{1-G} \cdot [m, M] \\ + \frac{I_{]\!]\tau,+\infty[\![}}{1-G_-} \cdot \left(\sum \Delta M(1-G_-) I_{\{\widetilde{G}=1>G_-\}}\right)^{p,\mathbb{F}}\end{aligned} \tag{6}$$

is a $\mathbb{G}$-local martingale.

(b) *For any $M \in \mathcal{M}_{loc}(\mathbb{F})$, the process*

$$\widehat{M}^{(a)} := I_{]\!]\tau,+\infty[\![} \cdot M + (1-G_-)^{-1} I_{]\!]\tau,+\infty[\![} \cdot \langle m, M\rangle^{\mathbb{F}} \tag{7}$$

is a $\mathbb{G}$-local martingale.

The proof of assertion (a) can be found in Ref. [11, Proposition 4.3], while assertion (b) is given in Ref. [2, Lemma 2.6] (or see Refs. [22, Théorème 5.10] and [17, XX.79] for this assertion and related results). The superscript in the operator $\mathcal{T}^{(a)}$ refers to the case of "after τ", while that in $\mathcal{T}^{(b)}$ — which will be defined later in Theorem 3.7 — refers to the case of "before or at τ".

3. Martingale Representation Theorems

This section complements the work of Choulli *et al.* [12] and parametrizes fully and explicitly the $\mathbb{G}$-local martingales that live after τ, which we assume is an honest time. This section is divided into three sections. The first section presents our main representation results for $\mathbb{G}$-local martingales that live after τ and illustrates those results on two particular cases. The second section combines the first section with Choulli *et al.* [12] in order to derive a full and complete representation of general $\mathbb{G}$-martingales, while the last section proves the main results of the first section.

3.1. *The Case of Martingales Living After τ*

This section extends the main result of Ref. [12] to $\mathbb{G}$-local martingales which live on the stochastic interval $]\!]\tau,+\infty[\![$. It shows how to represent $\mathbb{G}$-local martingales on $]\!]\tau,+\infty[\![$ using $\mathbb{F}$-local martingales.

Theorem 3.1. *Let m be defined in* (5), *and suppose τ is an honest time. Consider an RCLL and $\mathbb{G}$-adapted process $M^{\mathbb{G}}$. Then, the following assertions hold:*

(a) $I_{]\!]\tau,+\infty[\![}\bullet M^{\mathbb{G}}$ *is a square-integrable $\mathbb{G}$-martingale (i.e., $I_{]\!]\tau,+\infty[\![}\bullet M^{\mathbb{G}}\in\mathcal{M}^2(\mathbb{G})$) if and only if there exists a unique square-integrable $\mathbb{F}$-martingale M satisfying*

$$I_{\{G_-=1\}}\bullet M=0,\quad \Delta M I_{\{\widetilde{G}=1\}}=0, \tag{8}$$

$$E\left[\int_0^\infty I_{\{\widetilde{G}_s<1\}}(1-\widetilde{G}_s)^{-1}d[M,M]_s\right]<\infty \tag{9}$$

and

$$(1-G_-)I_{]\!]\tau,+\infty[\![}\bullet M^{\mathbb{G}}=\mathcal{T}^{(a)}(M). \tag{10}$$

(b) $I_{]\!]\tau,+\infty[\![} \bullet M^{\mathbb{G}}$ *is a* $\mathbb{G}$*-local martingale with integrable variation (i.e.,* $I_{]\!]\tau,+\infty[\![} \bullet M^{\mathbb{G}} \in \mathcal{M}_{loc}(\mathbb{G}) \cap \mathcal{A}(\mathbb{G})$*) if and only if there exists a unique* $M \in \mathcal{M}_{loc}(\mathbb{F})$ *with integrable variation satisfying* (8) *and* (10).

The proof of Theorem 3.1 is relegated to Subsection 3.3 for the sake of easy exposition. Theorem 3.1 gives martingale parameterizations which are unique, explicit and complete no matter what is the model for the honest time τ. It is important to mention that, as stated in Ref. [22, Proposition (5.1), Chapter V], τ being an honest time is in general weaker than τ being the *end of an* $\mathbb{F}$*-optional random set.* In fact, these two concepts (honest time and being the end of an optional random set) coincide for *finite* random times only (i.e., when $\tau < +\infty$ P-a.s.). On the one hand, without this finiteness property of τ, the localization property might not remain valid when passing from $\mathbb{G}$ to $\mathbb{F}$. It is exactly this point that forced us to consider the two classes of square-integrable martingales and martingales with integrable variations. On the other hand, for the case of finite honest times, we can do much better and elaborate the localization version of Theorem 3.1 (i.e., we can drop the assumption of uniform integrability on $M^{\mathbb{G}}$). This is the aim of the next representation theorem. To this end, we consider the following subspace of $\mathbb{F}$-local martingales, which *naturally* appeared in our analysis and it is very intrinsic to the pair $(\mathbb{F}, \tau)$,

$$\mathbb{M}(\mathbb{F},\tau) := \left\{ M \in \mathcal{M}_{0,loc}(\mathbb{F}) : E\left[\int_0^\infty \frac{I_{\{\widetilde{G}_s<1\}}}{1-\widetilde{G}_s+|\Delta M_s|} d[M,M]_s\right] < +\infty \right\}. \tag{11}$$

Thus, in virtue of the localization defined in Section 2, we have

$$M \in \mathbb{M}_{loc}(\mathbb{F},\tau) \quad \text{if and only if}$$

$$I_{\{\widetilde{G}_s<1\}}\left(1-\widetilde{G}_s+|\Delta M_s|\right)^{-1} \bullet [M,M] \in \mathcal{A}^+_{loc}(\mathbb{F}).$$

To explain how natural this space appears in our coming results and analysis, it is worth comparing it to the space of $\mathbb{F}$-martingales of Theorem 3.1(a). To this end, we consider the case when all

$\mathbb{F}$-martingales are continuous and easily conclude that in this setting the two spaces coincide. In general, it is clear that any $\mathbb{F}$-local martingale M satisfying (9) belongs to $\mathbb{M}(\mathbb{F},\tau)$. In the following, we summarize other properties of $\mathbb{M}(\mathbb{F},\tau)$, which are interesting in themselves.

Remark 3.2. (a) If $M \in \mathcal{M}_{0,loc}(\mathbb{F})$ with integrable variation, then it belongs to $\mathbb{M}(\mathbb{F},\tau)$ or equivalently $\mathcal{M}_{0,loc}(\mathbb{F}) \cap \mathcal{A}(\mathbb{F}) \subset \mathbb{M}(\mathbb{F},\tau)$. This claim follows from combining the fact that $\mathrm{Var}(M) = \sum |\Delta M|$ (see [20, Lemma 2.61, Chapter 2]) and the following inequalities

$$\frac{I_{\{\widetilde{G}<1\}}}{1-\widetilde{G}+|\Delta M|}\bullet[M,M] = \frac{|\Delta M|}{1-\widetilde{G}+|\Delta M|}I_{\{\widetilde{G}<1\}}\bullet \mathrm{Var}(M) \leq \mathrm{Var}(M).$$

(b) Suppose M is a continuous $\mathbb{F}$-local martingale. Then $M \in \mathbb{M}(\mathbb{F},\tau)$ if and only if there exists a continuous and square-integrable $\mathbb{F}$-martingale N satisfying $M = \sqrt{1-G_-}\bullet N$. As a result, if $\mathcal{M}^c_{loc}(\mathbb{F})$ denotes the set of all $\mathbb{F}$-local martingale that are continuous, then we get

$$\Big\{\sqrt{1-G_-}\bullet N : N \text{ is a continuous and square-integrable } \mathbb{F}\text{-martingale}\Big\} = \mathbb{M}(\mathbb{F},\tau)\cap \mathcal{M}^c_{loc}(\mathbb{F}).$$

Now, we state our second representation theorem for general *finite honest times.*

Theorem 3.3. *Let m be defined in* (5), *and suppose*

$$\tau \textit{ is a finite honest time} \quad (i.e.,\ \tau < +\infty\ P\text{-}a.s.). \tag{12}$$

Consider an RCLL and $\mathbb{G}$-adapted process $M^{\mathbb{G}}$. Then the following assertions are equivalent:

(a) $cI_{]\!]\tau,+\infty[\![}\bullet M^{\mathbb{G}}$ *is a $\mathbb{G}$-local martingale (i.e.,* $I_{]\!]\tau,+\infty[\![}\bullet M^{\mathbb{G}} \in \mathcal{M}_{loc}(\mathbb{G})$).

(b) *There exists an $\mathbb{F}$-local martingale $M^{\mathbb{F}}$ satisfying*

$$M^{\mathbb{F}} I_{\{\widetilde{G}=1\}} = 0, \quad \frac{M^{\mathbb{F}}_{-} I_{\{G_{-}<1\}}}{1-G_{-}} \text{ is } \mathbb{F}\text{-locally bounded,}$$
$$I_{\{G_{-}<1\}} \bullet M^{\mathbb{F}} + \frac{M^{\mathbb{F}}_{-} I_{\{G_{-}<1\}}}{1-G_{-}} \bullet m \in \mathbb{M}_{loc}(\mathbb{F}, \tau), \tag{13}$$

and

$$(1-G_{-}) I_{]\!]\tau,+\infty[\![} \bullet M^{\mathbb{G}} = \mathcal{T}^{(a)}(M^{\mathbb{F}}) + \frac{M^{\mathbb{F}}_{-}}{1-G_{-}} I_{]\!]\tau,+\infty[\![} \bullet \mathcal{T}^{(a)}(m). \tag{14}$$

(c) *There exists a unique $M \in \mathbb{M}_{loc}(\mathbb{F}, \tau)$ such that*

$$I_{\{G_{-}=1\}} \bullet M = 0, \quad \Delta M I_{\{\widetilde{G}=1\}} = 0 \quad \text{and}$$
$$(1-G_{-}) I_{]\!]\tau,+\infty[\![} \bullet M^{\mathbb{G}} = \mathcal{T}^{(a)}(M). \tag{15}$$

The proof of this theorem is relegated to Section 3.3. It is worth mentioning that our Theorem 3.3 can be extended (without much difficulties) to the set of $\mathbb{G}$-local martingale that is locally p-integrable (for any $p \in (1, +\infty)$). Indeed, if we denote $\mathcal{M}^p_{loc}(\mathbb{G})$ such a set, and we consider

$$\mathbb{M}^{(p)}_{loc}(\mathbb{F}, \tau) := \left\{ M \in \mathcal{M}_{0,loc}(\mathbb{F}) : \left(\frac{I_{\{\widetilde{G}<1\}}}{1-\widetilde{G}+|\Delta M|} \bullet [M, M] \right)^{p} \in \mathcal{A}^{+}_{loc}(\mathbb{F}) \right\},$$

then one can state the similar theorem by substituting $\mathcal{M}^p_{loc}(\mathbb{G})$ and $\mathbb{M}^{(p)}_{loc}(\mathbb{F}, \tau)$ for $\mathcal{M}_{loc}(\mathbb{G})$ and $\mathbb{M}_{loc}(\mathbb{F}, \tau)$, respectively. This case of (locally) p-integrable local martingales is mainly motivated by the application in arbitrage theory and precisely in describing martingale densities/deflators (see Definition 4.1 for deflators) which are (locally) p-integrable. For more on these and their applications, we refer the reader to [9, 10, 16, 24] and the references therein.

Theorem 3.3 gives deep insight into the structures of the representation (see assertion (b)) and how τ affects the martingale structures through both the process m and the operator $\mathcal{T}^{(a)}$. By using this structure, we lost the uniqueness of the parametrization which holds on the set $(G_\tau < 1)$ only.

From the perspective of applications in arbitrage theory, as it is our concerns herein, it was proven in the literature that an arbitrary finite honest time τ might trigger arbitrage opportunities in the part after τ no matter how nice the initial model is. To address this issue, Ref. [2] introduced a subclass of honest times, which is rich enough and has the possibility of preserving the non-arbitrage condition after τ for a large class of initial models. Thus, the aim of the next representation theorem lies in showing that when we restrict to this subclass of honest times, the parametrization of $\mathbb{G}$-local martingales requires the full space of $\mathbb{F}$-local martingales instead.

Theorem 3.4. *Consider a process $M^{\mathbb{G}}$, and suppose that* (12) *holds and*

$$G_\tau < 1 \quad P\text{-}a.s. \tag{16}$$

Then the following assertions are equivalent:

(a) $I_{]\!]\tau,+\infty[\![} \cdot M^{\mathbb{G}} \in \mathcal{M}_{loc}(\mathbb{G})$.

(b) *There exists a unique $\widetilde{M}^{\mathbb{F}} \in \mathcal{M}_{0,loc}(\mathbb{F})$ satisfying $\widetilde{M}^{\mathbb{F}} I_{\{\widetilde{G}=1\}} = 0$ and*

$$\begin{aligned} I_{]\!]\tau,+\infty[\![} \cdot M^{\mathbb{G}} &= \frac{I_{]\!]\tau,+\infty[\![}}{1-G_-} \cdot \mathcal{T}^{(a)}(\widetilde{M}^{\mathbb{F}}) \\ &\quad + \frac{\widetilde{M}^{\mathbb{F}}_-}{(1-G_-)^2} I_{]\!]\tau,+\infty[\![} \cdot \mathcal{T}^{(a)}(m). \end{aligned} \tag{17}$$

(c) *There exists a unique $M \in \mathcal{M}_{0,loc}(\mathbb{F})$ such that*

$$I_{\{G_-=1\}} \cdot M = 0, \quad I_{\{\widetilde{G}=1\}} \Delta M = 0, \quad I_{]\!]\tau,+\infty[\![} \cdot M^{\mathbb{G}} = \mathcal{T}^{(a)}(M). \tag{18}$$

The rest of this section illustrates Theorems 3.1, 3.3 and 3.4 to the case when the initial model is a jump-diffusion model or a discrete-time market model.

Corollary 3.5. *Suppose $\mathbb{F}$ is the augmented filtration of the filtration generated by (W, N), where W is a standard Brownian motion, N is* *the Poisson process with intensity one and* $N_t^{\mathbb{F}} := N_t - t$. *Consider the pair* $(\phi^{(m)}, \psi^{(m)}) \in L^1_{loc}(W, \mathbb{F}) \times L^1_{loc}(N^{\mathbb{F}}, \mathbb{F})$ *such that*

$$m = m_0 + \phi^{(m)} \bullet W + \psi^{(m)} \bullet N^{\mathbb{F}}. \tag{19}$$

Let $M^{\mathbb{G}}$ *be an RCLL process. Then the following assertions hold:*

(a) $M^{\mathbb{G}} \in \mathcal{M}_0^2(\mathbb{G})$ *if and only if there exists a unique pair of predictable processes* (ϕ, ψ) *satisfying*

$$(\phi, \psi) I_{\{G_- = 1\}} \equiv (0, 0), \quad \psi I_{\{\psi^{(m)} = 1 - G_-\}} \equiv 0, \tag{20}$$

$$E\left[\int_0^\infty \frac{\phi_s^2 I_{\{G_s<1\}}}{1 - G_s} ds + \int_0^\infty \frac{\psi_s^2}{1 - G_s - \psi_s^{(m)}} \times I_{\{G_s + \psi_s^{(m)} < 1\}} ds\right] < \infty \tag{21}$$

and

$$M^{\mathbb{G}} - \left(M^{\mathbb{G}}\right)^{\tau} = \frac{\phi}{1 - G_-} I_{\{G_- < 1\}} \bullet \mathcal{T}^{(a)}(W) + \frac{\psi}{1 - G_-} I_{\{G_- < 1\}} \bullet \mathcal{T}^{(a)}(N^{\mathbb{F}}). \tag{22}$$

(b) *Suppose that* (12) *holds. Then for any* $M^{\mathbb{G}} \in \mathcal{M}_{0,loc}(\mathbb{G})$, *there exists a unique pair of predictable processes* (ϕ, ψ) *satisfying* (20), (22) *and*

$$V_t := \int_0^t \left(\frac{\phi_s^2 I_{\{G_s<1\}}}{1 - G_s} + \frac{\psi_s^2}{1 - G_s - \psi_s^{(m)}} I_{\{G_s + \psi_s^{(m)} < 1\}} \right) ds \in \mathcal{A}^+_{loc}(\mathbb{F}). \tag{23}$$

(c) *Suppose that both* (12) *and* (16) *hold. Then for any* $M^{\mathbb{G}} \in \mathcal{M}_{0,loc}(\mathbb{G})$, *there exists a unique pair* (ϕ_1, ψ_1) *of* $\mathbb{F}$*-predictable processes such that* $\int_0^\cdot ((\phi_1(s))^2 + (\psi_1(s))^2) ds$ *is locally integrable and*

$$M^{\mathbb{G}} - \left(M^{\mathbb{G}}\right)^{\tau} = \phi_1 \bullet \mathcal{T}^{(a)}(W) + \psi_1 \bullet \mathcal{T}^{(a)}(N^{\mathbb{F}}). \tag{24}$$

Proof. Assertion (a) is a direct consequence of Theorem 3.1(a) and the fact that for any $\mathbb{F}$-local martingale, M, there exists a unique pair (φ_1, φ_2) that is $(W, N^{\mathbb{F}})$-integrable and $M = M_0 + \varphi_1 \bullet W + \varphi_2 \bullet N^{\mathbb{F}}$.

Again by combining this fact with Theorem 3.3 (respectively, with Theorem 3.4), assertion (b) (respectively, assertion (c)) follows. This proves the corollary. □

The second popular case for $(S, \mathbb{F})$ is the discrete-time model, where we suppose that on $(\Omega, \mathcal{F}, P)$ the following assumptions hold:

$$P(\tau \in \{0, 1, \ldots, T\}) = 1, \quad \mathbb{F} := (\mathcal{F}_n)_{n=0,1,\ldots,T},$$
$$\mathcal{G}_n = \mathcal{F}_n \vee \sigma(\tau \wedge 1, \ldots, \tau \wedge n). \tag{25}$$

As a result, in this case, the pair $(G, \widetilde{G})$ that parametrizes τ in $\mathbb{F}$ takes the following forms:

$$G_n = \sum_{k=n+1}^{T} P(\tau = k|\mathcal{F}_n), \quad n = 0, \ldots, T-1, \quad \text{and}$$
$$\widetilde{G}_n = \sum_{k=n}^{T} P(\tau = k|\mathcal{F}_n), \quad n = 0, \ldots, T. \tag{26}$$

Corollary 3.6. *Consider the model given by* (25), *and suppose that τ is an honest time. Then for any $\mathbb{G}$-local martingale $M^{\mathbb{G}}$, there exists a unique $\mathbb{F}$-local martingale $M^{\mathbb{F}}$ satisfying $M_0^{\mathbb{F}} = 0$,*

$$\Delta M_n^{\mathbb{F}} I_{\{\widetilde{G}_n = 1\}} := (M_n^{\mathbb{F}} - M_{n-1}^{\mathbb{F}}) I_{\{\widetilde{G}_n = 1\}} \equiv 0,$$
$$P\text{-a.s. } n = 1, \ldots, T, \tag{27}$$

and

$$M_n^{\mathbb{G}} - M_{n\wedge\tau}^{\mathbb{G}} = \sum_{k=1}^{n} \frac{\Delta M_k^{\mathbb{F}}}{1 - \widetilde{G}_k} I_{\{\tau < k\}} = \sum_{k=1}^{n} \frac{\Delta \mathcal{T}_k^{(a)}(M^{\mathbb{F}})}{1 - G_{k-1}} I_{\{\tau < k\}},$$
$$n = 0, \ldots, T. \tag{28}$$

Proof. We start by proving the uniqueness. In fact, this boils down to proving that any $\mathbb{F}$-local martingale M satisfying (27) and

$$\frac{\Delta M_k^{\mathbb{F}}}{1 - \widetilde{G}_k} I_{\{\tau < k\}} = 0, \quad P\text{-a.s.}, \quad k = 1, \ldots, T,$$

M should be null. By taking the conditional expectation with respect to $\mathcal{F}_k$ on both sides of the above equality, we get for any $k = 1, \ldots, T$,

$$(\Delta M_k^{\mathbb{F}}) I_{\{\widetilde{G}_k < 1\}} = 0, \quad P\text{-a.s.}$$

Thus by combining this with (27) and $M_0^{\mathbb{F}} = 0$, we get

$$(\Delta M_k^{\mathbb{F}}) = (\Delta M_k^{\mathbb{F}}) I_{\{\widetilde{G}_k < 1\}} + (\Delta M_k^{\mathbb{F}}) I_{\{\widetilde{G}_k = 1\}} = 0, \quad k = 1, \ldots, T,$$

and the uniqueness is proved. For the rest of this proof, we consider the following processes:

$$\overline{M}_k^{\mathbb{G}} := M_k^{\mathbb{G}} - M_{k\wedge\tau}^{\mathbb{G}}, \quad \text{and} \quad \Delta M_k := E\left[\Delta \overline{M}_k^{\mathbb{G}} | \mathcal{F}_k\right],$$
$$k = 1, \ldots, T, \quad M_0 = E\left[\overline{M}_0^{\mathbb{G}} | \mathcal{F}_0\right].$$

Then, it is easy to check that $\overline{M}^{\mathbb{G}}$ is a $\mathbb{G}$-local martingale, M is an $\mathbb{F}$-local martingale and

$$\Delta \overline{M}_n^{\mathbb{G}} = (\Delta \overline{M}_n^{\mathbb{G}}) I_{\{\tau < n\}}, \quad P\text{-a.s.}, \quad n = 1, \ldots, T. \tag{29}$$

Furthermore, in virtue of this latter equality and the fact that $(\tau < n) \subset (\widetilde{G}_n < 1) \subset (G_{n-1} < 1)$ P-a.s., we deduce that $(\Delta \overline{M}_n^{\mathbb{G}}) I_{\{\widetilde{G}_n = 1\}} = 0$ P-a.s. and hence we get

$$(\Delta M_n) I_{\{\widetilde{G}_n = 1\}} = E\left[(\Delta \overline{M}_n^{\mathbb{G}}) I_{\{\widetilde{G}_n = 1\}} \, | \mathcal{F}_n\right] = 0, \quad P\text{-a.s.}$$

This proves the existence of an $\mathbb{F}$-local martingale M satisfying (27). Now we prove that this M satisfies (28). To this end, we combine (29) with [22, Proposition 5.3(b)] and derive

$$\begin{aligned}
\frac{\Delta M_n}{1 - \widetilde{G}_n} I_{\{\tau < n\}} &= \frac{E\left[\Delta \overline{M}_n^{\mathbb{G}} I_{\{\tau < n\}} \, | \mathcal{F}_n\right]}{1 - \widetilde{G}_n} I_{\{\tau < n\}} \\
&= E\left[\Delta \overline{M}_n^{\mathbb{G}} I_{\{\tau < n\}} \, | \mathcal{G}_n\right] = \Delta \overline{M}_n^{\mathbb{G}}.
\end{aligned}$$

Thus, the first equality in (28) follows immediately, while the second equality is a direct consequence of (27) combined with

$$\mathcal{T}_n^{(a)}(N) := \sum_{k=1}^{n} \frac{P(\tau \leq k-1|\mathcal{F}_{k-1})}{P(\tau \leq k|\mathcal{F}_k)} I_{\{\tau<k\}} \Delta N + \sum_{k=1}^{n} I_{\{\tau<k\}} E[\Delta N_k I_{\{P(\tau\geq k|\mathcal{F}_k)=1\}} | \mathcal{F}_{k-1}],$$

for any $\mathbb{F}$-local martingale N. This ends the proof of the corollary. □

3.2. *The Case of Arbitrary $\mathbb{G}$-Martingales*

This section combines Theorem 3.1, 3.3 and/or 3.4 with either Ref. [12, Theorems 2.20 and 2.21] or [15, Theorem 2.6]. These combinations give representation results which extend both Refs. [12] and [4] to the most general setting. To this end, we recall some results and notations from Refs. [1, Theorem 3] and [12, Theorems 2.3 and 2.11].

Theorem 3.7. *The following assertions hold:*

(a) *For any $M \in \mathcal{M}_{loc}(\mathbb{F})$, the process*

$$\mathcal{T}^{(b)}(M) := M^\tau - \widetilde{G}^{-1} I_{]\!]0,\tau]\!]} \bullet [M, m] + I_{]\!]0,\tau]\!]} \bullet \left(\sum \Delta M I_{\{\widetilde{G}=0<G_-\}}\right)^{p,\mathbb{F}} \tag{30}$$

is a $\mathbb{G}$-local martingale.

(b) *The process*

$$N^{\mathbb{G}} := D - \widetilde{G}^{-1} I_{]\!]0,\tau]\!]} \bullet D^{o,\mathbb{F}} \tag{31}$$

is a $\mathbb{G}$-martingale with integrable variation. Moreover, $H \bullet N^{\mathbb{G}}$ is a $\mathbb{G}$-local martingale with locally integrable variation for any H belonging to

$$\mathcal{I}^{o,\mathbb{F}}_{loc}(N^{\mathbb{G}}, \mathbb{G}) := \left\{K \in \mathcal{O}(\mathbb{F}) \,|\, |K| G \widetilde{G}^{-1} I_{\{\widetilde{G}>0\}} \bullet D \in \mathcal{A}_{loc}(\mathbb{G})\right\}. \tag{32}$$

Furthermore, for any $q \in [1, +\infty)$ and a σ-algebra $\mathcal{H}$ on $\Omega \times [0, +\infty)$, we define

$$L^q\left(\mathcal{H}, P \otimes dD\right) := \left\{X\ \mathcal{H}\text{-measurable}:\ E[|X_\tau|^q I_{\{\tau<+\infty\}}] < +\infty\right\}. \tag{33}$$

In the following, we elaborate on our representation results for $\mathbb{G}$-martingales:

Theorem 3.8. *Suppose that τ is an honest time, let $M^{\mathbb{G}}$ be a right-continuous-with-left-limits and $\mathbb{G}$-adapted process with $M_0^{\mathbb{G}} = 0$, and consider the $\mathbb{F}$-stopping time R given by*

$$R := \inf\left\{t \geq 0:\ \widetilde{G}_t = 0\right\}.$$

Then the following assertions hold:

(a) *$M^{\mathbb{G}}$ is a square-integrable $\mathbb{G}$-martingale if and only if there exists a unique quadruplet*

$$\left(M^{(\mathbb{F},b)}, M^{(\mathbb{F},a)}, \varphi^{(o)}, \varphi^{(pr)}\right) \in \mathcal{M}_0^2(\mathbb{F}) \times \mathcal{M}_0^2(\mathbb{F}) \times L^2\left(\mathcal{O}(\mathbb{F}), P \otimes G\widetilde{G}^{-1} dD\right) \times L^2\left(\text{Prog}(\mathbb{F}), P \otimes dD\right)$$

and satisfying the following properties:

$$M^{(\mathbb{F},b)} = (M^{(\mathbb{F},b)})^R, \quad \Delta M^{(\mathbb{F},b)} I_{\{\widetilde{G}=0\}} = 0,$$

$$\varphi^{(o)} = \varphi^{(o)} I_{[\![0,R[\![}, \quad E[\varphi^{(pr)}_\tau | \mathcal{F}_\tau] = 0, \tag{34}$$

$$I_{\{G_-=1\}} \bullet M^{(\mathbb{F},a)} \equiv 0, \quad \Delta M^{(\mathbb{F},a)} I_{\{\widetilde{G}=1\}} \equiv 0, \tag{35}$$

$$M^{\mathbb{G}} = \frac{I_{]\!]0,\tau]\!]}}{G_-} \bullet \mathcal{T}^{(b)}(M^{(\mathbb{F},b)}) + \varphi^{(o)} \bullet N^{\mathbb{G}} + \varphi^{(pr)} \bullet D + \frac{I_{]\!]\tau,+\infty[\![}}{1-G_-} \bullet \mathcal{T}^{(a)}(M^{(\mathbb{F},a)}), \tag{36}$$

$$E\left[\int_0^\infty \frac{I_{\{\widetilde{G}_s>0\}}}{\widetilde{G}_s} d[M^{(\mathbb{F},b)}, M^{(\mathbb{F},b)}]_s\right] < \infty \quad \textit{and}$$

$$E\left[\int_0^\infty \frac{I_{\{\widetilde{G}_s<1\}}}{1-\widetilde{G}_s} d[M^{(\mathbb{F},a)}, M^{(\mathbb{F},a)}]_s\right] < \infty. \tag{37}$$

(b) $M^{\mathbb{G}}$ *is a* $\mathbb{G}$*-local martingale with integrable variation if and only if there exist unique pairs*

$$\left(M^{(\mathbb{F},b)}, M^{(\mathbb{F},a)}\right) \in (\mathcal{M}_{0,loc}(\mathbb{F}) \cap \mathcal{A}_{loc}(\mathbb{F})) \times (\mathcal{M}_{0,loc}(\mathbb{F}) \cap \mathcal{A}(\mathbb{F}))$$

and

$$(\varphi^{(o)}, \varphi^{(pr)}) \in I^o_{loc}(N^{\mathbb{G}}, \mathbb{G}) \times L^1\left(\mathrm{Prog}(\mathbb{F}), \mathrm{P} \otimes dD\right)$$

satisfying (34), (35),

$$E\left[\int_0^\infty \frac{|G_-^{-1}\Delta M_s^{(\mathbb{F},b)} + G_s\varphi_s^{(o)}|}{\widetilde{G}_s} I_{\{\widetilde{G}_s>0,\ cG_->0\}} dD_s^{o,\mathbb{F}} + \sum_{s>0} \frac{|G_-^{-1}\Delta M_s^{(\mathbb{F},b)} - \varphi_s^{(o)}\Delta D_s^{o,\mathbb{F}}|}{\widetilde{G}_s} G_s I_{\{\widetilde{G}_s>0,\ G_->0\}}\right] < \infty \tag{38}$$

and

$$M^{\mathbb{G}} = \frac{I_{]\!]0,\tau]\!]}}{G_-^2} \bullet \mathcal{T}^{(b)}(M^{(\mathbb{F},b)}) + \varphi^{(o)} \bullet N^{\mathbb{G}} + \varphi^{(pr)} \bullet D + \frac{I_{]\!]\tau,+\infty[\![}}{1-G_-} \bullet \mathcal{T}^{(a)}(M^{(\mathbb{F},a)}). \tag{39}$$

(c) *Suppose that* $G > 0$ (*i.e.,* $R = +\infty$ P*-a.s.*) *and* (12) *holds. Then* $M^{\mathbb{G}} \in \mathcal{M}_{loc}(\mathbb{G})$ *if and only if there exists a unique quadruplet*

$$\left(M^{(\mathbb{F},b)}, M^{(\mathbb{F},a)}, \varphi^{(o)}, \varphi^{(pr)}\right) \in \mathcal{M}_{0,loc}(\mathbb{F}) \times \mathbb{M}_{loc}(\mathbb{F}, \tau) \times I^o_{loc}(N^{\mathbb{G}}, \mathbb{G}) \times L^1_{loc}\left(\mathrm{Prog}(\mathbb{F}), \mathrm{P} \otimes dD\right)$$

satisfying (34), (35) *and*

$$M^{\mathbb{G}} = \mathcal{T}^{(b)}(M^{(\mathbb{F},b)}) + \varphi^{(o)} \bullet N^{\mathbb{G}} + \varphi^{(pr)} \bullet D + \frac{I_{]\!]\tau,+\infty[\![}}{1-G_-} \bullet \mathcal{T}^{(a)}(M^{(\mathbb{F},a)}). \tag{40}$$

(d) *Suppose that* $G > 0$ (*i.e.*, $R = +\infty$ *P-a.s.*), *and both* (12) *and* (16) *hold. Then* $M^{\mathbb{G}} \in \mathcal{M}_{loc}(\mathbb{G})$ *if and only if there exists a unique quadruplet*

$$\left(M^{(\mathbb{F},b)}, \overline{M}^{(\mathbb{F},a)}, \varphi^{(o)}, \varphi^{(pr)}\right) \in \mathcal{M}_{0,loc}(\mathbb{F}) \times \mathcal{M}_{0,loc}(\mathbb{F})$$
$$\times\ I^o_{loc}(N^{\mathbb{G}}, \mathbb{G}) \times L^1_{loc}(\mathrm{Prog}(\mathbb{F}), \mathrm{P} \otimes \mathrm{dD})$$

satisfying (34), (35) *and*

$$M^{\mathbb{G}} = \mathcal{T}^{(b)}(M^{(\mathbb{F},b)}) + \varphi^{(o)} \bullet N^{\mathbb{G}} + \varphi^{(pr)} \bullet D + \mathcal{T}^{(a)}(\overline{M}^{(\mathbb{F},a)}). \tag{41}$$

Proof. On the one hand, it is clear that, due to Ref. [2, Proposition B.1-(b)], which claims that $(1 - G_-)^{-1} I_{\{G_- < 1\}}$ is $\mathbb{F}$-locally bounded when both (12) and (16) hold, we put

$$\overline{M}^{(\mathbb{F},a)} := (1 - G_-)^{-1} I_{\{G_- < 1\}} \bullet M^{(\mathbb{F},a)}$$

and conclude that assertion (d) follows immediately from assertion (c). On the other hand, it is clear that assertion (c) is the consequence of applying Theorem 3.3 to $M^{\mathbb{G}} - (M^{\mathbb{G}})^{\tau}$ and [15, Theorem 2.6] to $(M^{\mathbb{G}})^{\tau}$, and combining the obtained results afterwards using

$$M^{\mathbb{G}} = (M^{\mathbb{G}})^{\tau} + M^{\mathbb{G}} - (M^{\mathbb{G}})^{\tau} =: (M^{\mathbb{G}})^{\tau} + \overline{M}^{\mathbb{G}}. \tag{42}$$

This proves both assertions (c) and (d). Thus, the rest of this proof focuses on proving assertions (a) and (b) in parts 1 and 2, respectively.

Part 1. Herein, we prove assertion (a). To this end, we suppose $M^{\mathbb{G}}$ is a square-integrable martingale, and hence both $(M^{\mathbb{G}})^{\tau}$ and $\overline{M}^{\mathbb{G}}$ are square-integrable martingales. On the one hand, by applying Theorem 3.1(a) to $\overline{M}^{\mathbb{G}}$ yields the existence of a unique $M^{(\mathbb{F},a)} \in \mathcal{M}_{0,loc}(\mathbb{F})$ fulfilling (35), the second condition in (37) and

$$\overline{M}^{\mathbb{G}} = I_{]\!]\tau,+\infty[\![}(1 - G_-)^{-1} \bullet \mathcal{T}^{(a)}(M^{(\mathbb{F},a)}). \tag{43}$$

On the other hand, by applying [12, Theorem 2.21] to $(M^{\mathbb{G}})^{\tau}$, we get the existence of the unique $\left(M', \varphi^{(o)}, \varphi^{(pr)}\right)$ which belongs to

$\mathcal{M}_{0,loc}(\mathbb{F}) \times I^o_{loc}(N^{\mathbb{G}}, \mathbb{G}) \times L^1_{loc}(\text{Prog}(\mathbb{F}), P \otimes dD)$ satisfying (34) and

$$(M^{\mathbb{G}})^{\tau} = \frac{I_{]\!]0,\tau]\!]}}{G_-^2} \bullet \mathcal{T}^{(b)}(M') + \varphi^{(o)} \bullet N^{\mathbb{G}} + \varphi^{(pr)} \bullet D. \qquad (44)$$

By looking closely at the proof of Ref. [12, Theorem 2.20] and using Ref. [12, Theorem 2.17-(c)], we easily conclude that $(M^{\mathbb{G}})^{\tau}$ is square integrable iff $\varphi^{(pr)}) \in L^2(\text{Prog}(\mathbb{F}), P \otimes \text{dD})$, and both $\varphi^{(o)} \bullet N^{\mathbb{G}}$ and $I_{]\!]0,\tau]\!]} G_-^{-2} \bullet \mathcal{T}^{(b)}(M')$ are square integrable. Direct calculations show that $\varphi^{(o)} \bullet N^{\mathbb{G}} \in \mathcal{M}^2(\mathbb{G})$ if and only if $\varphi^{(o)} \in L^2\left(\mathcal{O}(\mathbb{F}), P \otimes G\widetilde{G}^{-1}\text{dD}\right)$, and $I_{]\!]0,\tau]\!]} G_-^{-2} \bullet \mathcal{T}^{(b)}(M') \in \mathcal{M}^2(\mathbb{G})$ is equivalent to

$$E\left[\int_0^{\infty} \frac{I_{\{G_{s-}>0\}} I_{\{\widetilde{G}_s>0\}}}{G_{s-}^2 \widetilde{G}_s} d[M', M']_s\right] = E\left[\int_0^{\tau} \frac{1}{G_{s-}^4} d[\mathcal{T}^{(b)}(M'), \mathcal{T}^{(b)}(M')]_s\right] < +\infty. \qquad (45)$$

In virtue of the first and second conditions in (34), which are fulfilled by M', and $\widetilde{G}^{-1} \geq 1$, the above inequality implies that $I_{\{G_->0\}} G_-^{-1}$ is M'-integrable, and $M^{(\mathbb{F},b)} := I_{\{G_->0\}} G_-^{-1} \bullet M' \in \mathcal{M}^2(\mathbb{F})$. Furthermore, by inserting it in (45), we deduce that $M^{(\mathbb{F},b)}$ fulfills the first condition in (37), as well as the first and second conditions in (34). This proves the existence of the quadruplet $\left(M^{(\mathbb{F},b)}, M^{(\mathbb{F},a)}, \varphi^{(o)}, \varphi^{(pr)}\right) \in \mathcal{M}_0^2(\mathbb{F}) \times \mathcal{M}_0^2(\mathbb{F}) \times L^2\left(\mathcal{O}(\mathbb{F}), P \otimes G\widetilde{G}^{-1}\text{dD}\right) \times L^2(\text{Prog}(\mathbb{F}), \text{P} \otimes \text{dD})$ and fulfilling (34), (35), (36) and (37). For the reverse sense, it is clear that for any such quadruplet satisfying these conditions, one can easily check that all the four processes $\varphi^{(pr)} \bullet D$, $\varphi^{(o)} \bullet N^{\mathbb{G}}$, $I_{]\!]0,\tau]\!]} G_-^{-1} \bullet \mathcal{T}^{(b)}(M^{(\mathbb{F},b)})$ and $I_{]\!]\tau,+\infty[\![}(1-G_-)^{-1} \bullet \mathcal{T}^{(a)}(M^{(\mathbb{F},a)})$ are square-integrable $\mathbb{G}$-martingales. This ends the proof of assertion (a).

Part 2. This part proves assertion (b). Similarly as in part 1, we suppose $M^{\mathbb{G}} \in \mathcal{A}(\mathbb{G}) \cap \mathcal{M}_{loc}(\mathbb{G})$ and note that this fact implies that both $(M^{\mathbb{G}})^{\tau}$ and $\overline{M}^{\mathbb{G}}$ belong to $\mathcal{A}(\mathbb{G}) \cap \mathcal{M}_{loc}(\mathbb{G})$. Then a direct application of Theorem 3.1(b) to $\overline{M}^{\mathbb{G}}$ implies the existence of a unique $M^{(\mathbb{F},a)} \in \mathcal{M}_{0,loc}(\mathbb{F}) \cap \mathcal{A}(\mathbb{F})$ fulfilling (35) and (43). As the assumption $M^{\mathbb{G}} \in \mathcal{A}(\mathbb{G})$ yields the uniform integrability of $(M^{\mathbb{G}})^{\tau}$, then we apply [12, Theorem 2.21] to it and deduce the existence of the unique $\left(M', \varphi^{(o)}, \varphi^{(pr)}\right)$ which belongs to $\mathcal{M}_{0,loc}(\mathbb{F}) \times I^o_{loc}(N^{\mathbb{G}}, \mathbb{G}) \times L^1_{loc}\left(\mathrm{Prog}(\mathbb{F}), P \otimes dD\right)$ satisfying (34) and (44). By looking closely at the proof of [12, Theorem 2.21], one can easily note that the assumption $M^{\mathbb{G}} \in \mathcal{A}(\mathbb{G})$ forces $\varphi^{(pr)}$ to belong to $L^1\left(\mathrm{Prog}(\mathbb{F}), P \otimes dD\right)$, and

$$\varphi^{(o)} \bullet N^{\mathbb{G}} + I_{]\!]0,\tau]\!]} G_-^{-2} \bullet \mathcal{T}^{(b)}(M') \in \mathcal{A}(\mathbb{G}). \tag{46}$$

As $\varphi^{(o)} \bullet N^{\mathbb{G}} \in \mathcal{A}_{loc}(\mathbb{G})$, we deduce that $I_{]\!]0,\tau]\!]} G_-^{-2} \bullet \mathcal{T}^{(b)}(M') \in \mathcal{A}_{loc}(\mathbb{G})$. This implies that the non-decreasing process $Y := \sum |\Delta M'| G_-^{-1} \widetilde{G}^{-1} I_{\{G_->0,\ \widetilde{G}>0\}}$ takes finite values on $]\!]0, \tau]\!]$ or equivalently $I_{]\!]0,\tau]\!]} \leq I_{\{Y<\infty\}}$. Then by taking the $\mathbb{F}$-optional projection, we get $\{\widetilde{G} > 0\} \subset \{Y < \infty\}$. Then by combing this with the second condition in (34), we conclude that the process Y has a finite variation, and as a result M' has a finite variation and $I_{\{G_-<1\}} G_-^{-1}$ is M'-integrable. Thus, we put $M^{(\mathbb{F},b)} := I_{\{G_->0\}} \bullet M'$ and it is easy to check that $M^{(\mathbb{F},b)} \in \mathcal{M}_{loc}(\mathbb{F}) \cap \mathcal{A}_{loc}(\mathbb{F})$ and satisfies the first and second conditions of (34). Then by combining Ref. [20, Lemma 2.61-(b), Chapter 2] and (46), we conclude that the pair $(\varphi^{(o)}, M^{(\mathbb{F},b)})$ satisfies (38). This proves the existence of unique pairs $\left(M^{(\mathbb{F},b)}, M^{(\mathbb{F},a)}\right) \in \left(\mathcal{M}_{0,loc}(\mathbb{F}) \cap \mathcal{A}_{loc}(\mathbb{F})\right) \times \left(\mathcal{M}_{0,loc}(\mathbb{F}) \cap \mathcal{A}(\mathbb{F})\right)$ and $(\varphi^{(o)}, \varphi^{(pr)}) \in I^o_{loc}(N^{\mathbb{G}}, \mathbb{G}) \times L^1\left(\mathrm{Prog}(\mathbb{F}), \mathrm{P} \otimes \mathrm{dD}\right)$ satisfying (34), (35), (38) and (39). For the reverse sense, it is easy to verify that, for such quadruplet fulfilling those conditions, the three processes $I_{]\!]0,\tau]\!]} G_-^{-1} \bullet \mathcal{T}^{(b)}(M^{(\mathbb{F},b)})$, $\varphi^{(pr)} \bullet D$ and $\varphi^{(o)} \bullet N^{\mathbb{G}} + I_{]\!]\tau,+\infty[\![}(1 - G_-)^{-1} \bullet \mathcal{T}^{(a)}(M^{(\mathbb{F},a)})$ belong to $\mathcal{A}(\mathbb{G}) \cap \mathcal{M}_{loc}(\mathbb{G})$. This proves assertion (b), and the proof of the theorem is complete. □

Besides giving a representation for any uniformly integrable $\mathbb{G}$-martingale, which extends Ref. [12, Theorems 2.20 or 2.21] to any $\mathbb{G}$-martingale uniformly integrable, this theorem also extends [4, Théorème 3] to the most general case, where $\mathbb{F}$ is an arbitrary filtration satisfying the usual conditions, and τ is an arbitrary honest time which might not be an end of an optional random set and/or might not avoid $\mathbb{F}$-stopping times. Both assertions (c) and (d) of Theorem 3.8 can be extended to the case of $\mathcal{M}^p_{loc}(\mathbb{G})$, for any $p \in (1, +\infty)$.

3.3. Proof of Theorems 3.1, 3.3, and 3.4

The proofs of these theorems rely essentially on connecting $\mathbb{G}$-martingales with $\mathbb{F}$-adapted processes having some structures. This fact, which is interesting in itself, is singled out in the following lemma:

Lemma 3.9. *Suppose τ is an honest time and $M^{\mathbb{G}} \in \mathcal{M}_{loc}(\mathbb{G})$. Then the following assertions hold:*

(a) *If $M^{\mathbb{G}} \in \mathcal{M}(\mathbb{G})$ and σ is an $\mathbb{F}$-stopping time, then there exists a unique $\mathbb{F}$-martingale $\overline{M}^{\mathbb{F}}$ satisfying*

$$(M^{\mathbb{G}} - (M^{\mathbb{G}})^{\tau})^{\sigma} = \overline{M}^{\mathbb{F}} \frac{(I_{]\!]\tau,+\infty[\![})^{\sigma}}{1-G^{\sigma}}, \quad \overline{M}^{\mathbb{F}} = (\overline{M}^{\mathbb{F}})^{\sigma}, \quad \textit{and}$$
$$\{\widetilde{G}^{\sigma} = 1\} \subset \{\overline{M}^{\mathbb{F}} = 0\}. \tag{47}$$

Here $(I_{]\!]\tau,+\infty[\![})^{\sigma}$ is the stopped process (i.e., $(I_{]\!]\tau,+\infty[\![})^{\sigma} = I_{\{\sigma>\tau\}}I_{]\!]\tau,\sigma]\!]} + I_{\{\sigma>\tau\}}I_{]\!]\sigma,+\infty[\![}$).

(b) *If (12) holds, then there exists a unique $\mathbb{F}$-martingale $\overline{M}^{\mathbb{F}}$ such that the $\mathbb{F}$-predictable process $\overline{M}^{\mathbb{F}}_{-}(1-G_{-})^{-1}I_{\{G_{-}<1\}}$ is $\mathbb{F}$-locally bounded, and*

$$M^{\mathbb{G}} - (M^{\mathbb{G}})^{\tau} = \overline{M}^{\mathbb{F}} \frac{I_{]\!]\tau,+\infty[\![}}{1-G} \quad \textit{and} \quad \{\widetilde{G} = 1\} \subset \{\overline{M}^{\mathbb{F}} = 0\}. \tag{48}$$

(c) *If $M \in \mathcal{M}_{loc}(\mathbb{F})$ satisfying $\{\widetilde{G} = 1\} \subset \{M = 0\}$, then*

$$\Big(\sum \Delta M \Delta m I_{\{\widetilde{G}=1>G_{-}\}}\Big)^{p,\mathbb{F}} = -M_{-}(1-G_{-})^{-1}I_{\{G_{-}<1\}} \bullet \Big(I_{\{\widetilde{G}=1\}} \bullet [m,m]\Big)^{p,\mathbb{F}}, \tag{49}$$

and $\mathcal{T}^{(a)}(M)$ defined via (6) satisfies

$$\mathcal{T}^{(a)}(M) = I_{]\!]\tau,+\infty[\![} \bullet M + \frac{I_{]\!]\tau,+\infty[\![}}{1-\widetilde{G}} \bullet [m,M] - \frac{M_{-}I_{]\!]\tau,+\infty[\![}}{(1-G_{-})^2} \bullet \Big(I_{\{\widetilde{G}=1>G_{-}\}} \bullet [m,m]\Big)^{p,\mathbb{F}}. \tag{50}$$

Proof. We start this proof by noting that (50) follows immediately from combining (49) and Theorem 2.2(a). Finally, due to $\{\widetilde{G}=1\}\subset\{M^{\mathbb{F}}=0\}$, we easily derive

$$\sum \Delta M^{\mathbb{F}}\Delta m I_{\{\widetilde{G}=1>G_-\}} = -\sum M^{\mathbb{F}}_-(1-G_-)I_{\{\widetilde{G}=1>G_-\}}$$
$$= -\frac{M^{\mathbb{F}}_-}{1-G_-}I_{\{\widetilde{G}=1>G_-\}}\bullet[m,m],$$

and hence the proof of assertion (c) is complete. Thus, the remaining part of this proof focuses on proving assertions (a) and (b) in two parts.

Part 1. Here we prove assertion (a). To this end, we remark that there is no loss of generality in assuming that $(M^{\mathbb{G}})^{\tau}\equiv 0$. Thanks to Lemma A.2(a) (see also [22] and [5]), there exists an $\mathbb{F}$-optional process X such that

$$M^{\mathbb{G}} = M^{\mathbb{G}}I_{]\!]\tau,+\infty[\![} = XI_{]\!]\tau,+\infty[\![}.$$

It is clear that X is RCLL on $]\!]\tau,+\infty[\![$, and

$$(M^{\mathbb{G}})^{\sigma} = X^{\sigma}(I_{]\!]\tau,+\infty[\![})^{\sigma}.$$

Then consider the process $\overline{M}^{\mathbb{F}} := ({}^{o,\mathbb{F}}((M^{\mathbb{G}})^{\sigma}))^{\sigma}$, which is a uniformly integrable $\mathbb{F}$-martingale satisfying

$$\overline{M}^{\mathbb{F}} = X^{\sigma}({}^{o,\mathbb{F}}((I_{]\!]\tau,+\infty[\![})^{\sigma}))^{\sigma} = X^{\sigma}(1-\widetilde{G}^{\sigma}) \quad \text{and}$$
$$\{\widetilde{G}^{\sigma}=1\}\subset\{\overline{M}^{\mathbb{F}}=0\}.$$

In the above equality, we used the fact $({}^{o,\mathbb{F}}((I_{]\!]\tau,+\infty[\![})^{\sigma}))^{\sigma} = 1-\widetilde{G}^{\sigma}$ can be proved easily. Therefore, by combining these remarks with $\widetilde{G}=G$ on $]\!]\tau,+\infty[\![$ (see Ref. [17, XX.79] for details), we get

$$(M^{\mathbb{G}})^{\sigma} = X^{\sigma}(I_{]\!]\tau,+\infty[\![})^{\sigma} = \frac{\overline{M}^{\mathbb{F}}}{1-\widetilde{G}^{\sigma}}(I_{]\!]\tau,+\infty[\![})^{\sigma} = \frac{\overline{M}^{\mathbb{F}}}{1-G^{\sigma}}(I_{]\!]\tau,+\infty[\![})^{\sigma}.$$

This proves (47), and the proof of assertion (a) is complete as soon as we prove the uniqueness of $\overline{M}^{\mathbb{F}}$. To this end, we suppose that there exist two $\mathbb{F}$-martingales M and M' satisfying (47), and put $M'' := M - M'$. Hence, we get

$$\frac{M''}{1-\widetilde{G}^\sigma}(I_{]\!]\tau,+\infty[\![})^\sigma = 0 \quad \text{or equivalently} \quad M''(I_{]\!]\tau,+\infty[\![})^\sigma = 0.$$

Then by taking the $\mathbb{F}$-optional projection in both sides of the latter equation and stopping at σ afterwards, we deduce that $(M-M')(1-\widetilde{G}^\sigma) = 0$. This implies that $\{\widetilde{G}^\sigma < 1\} \subset \{M = M'\}$ on the one hand. On the other hand, we have $\{\widetilde{G}^\sigma = 1\} \subset \{M = M' = 0\}$. Thus, we deduce that the two $\mathbb{F}$-martingales M and M' are indistinguishable. This ends the proof of assertion (a).

Part 2. Here we prove assertion (b). To this end, we suppose that condition (12) holds and without loss of generality, we assume that $(M^{\mathbb{G}})^\tau \equiv 0$. As $M^{\mathbb{G}} \in \mathcal{M}_{loc}(\mathbb{G})$, there exists a sequence of $\mathbb{G}$-stopping times $(\sigma_n^{\mathbb{G}})_n$ that increases to infinity and $(M^{\mathbb{G}})^{\sigma_n^{\mathbb{G}}}$ is a uniformly integrable martingale. On the one hand, in virtue of the assumption (12) and [2, Proposition B.1-(a)], we obtain the existence of a sequence of $\mathbb{F}$-stopping times (σ_n) that increases to infinity almost surely, and

$$\max(\tau, \sigma_n^{\mathbb{G}}) = \max(\sigma_n, \tau), \quad P\text{-a.s.} \quad n \geq 1.$$

On the other hand, by applying assertion (a) to each pair $(M^{\mathbb{G},n}, \sigma_n)$, where $M^{\mathbb{G},n} := (M^{\mathbb{G}})^{\sigma_n^{\mathbb{G}}} = (M^{\mathbb{G}})^{\sigma_n}$, we obtain a sequence of $\mathbb{F}$-martingales $(\overline{M}^{(\mathbb{F},n)})_n$ satisfying

$$M^{\mathbb{G},n} = (M^{\mathbb{G}})^{\sigma_n^{\mathbb{G}}} = \frac{\overline{M}^{(\mathbb{F},n)}}{1-G^{\sigma_n}}(I_{]\!]\tau,+\infty[\![})^{\sigma_n} \quad \text{and} \quad \overline{M}^{(\mathbb{F},n)} I_{\{\widetilde{G}^{\sigma_n}=1\}} = 0. \tag{51}$$

By combining the uniqueness of $\overline{M}^{\mathbb{F},n}$ satisfying (51) (see assertion (a)) and $M^{\mathbb{G},n} = (M^{\mathbb{G},k})^{\sigma_n}$ for any $k \geq n$, we deduce that

$$\overline{M}^{(\mathbb{F},n)} = (\overline{M}^{(\mathbb{F},k)})^{\sigma_n} \quad \text{for any } k \geq n. \tag{52}$$

Then we put

$$\sigma_0 := 0, \quad \overline{M}^{\mathbb{F},0} := 0, \quad \text{and} \quad \overline{M}^{\mathbb{F}} := \sum_{n=1}^{+\infty} I_{]\!]\sigma_{n-1},\sigma_n]\!]} \bullet \overline{M}^{\mathbb{F},n}.$$

As σ_n increases to infinity almost surely and by using $(\overline{M}^{\mathbb{F}})^{\sigma_n} = \sum_{k=1}^n I_{]\!]\sigma_{k-1},\sigma_k]\!]} \bullet M^{(\mathbb{F},k)} \in \mathcal{M}_{loc}(\mathbb{F})$ and $(\mathcal{M}_{loc}(\mathbb{F}))_{loc} = \mathcal{M}_{loc}(\mathbb{F})$, we deduce that $M^{\mathbb{F}} \in \mathcal{M}_{loc}(\mathbb{F})$. Furthermore, thanks to (52), we get

$$(\overline{M}^{\mathbb{F}})^{\sigma_n} = \sum_{k=1}^{n} I_{]\!]\sigma_{k-1},\sigma_k]\!]} \cdot \overline{M}^{(\mathbb{F},k)} = \sum_{k=1}^{n}((\overline{M}^{(\mathbb{F},k)})^{\sigma_k} - (\overline{M}^{(\mathbb{F},k)})^{\sigma_{k-1}})$$
$$= \sum_{k=1}^{n}(\overline{M}^{(\mathbb{F},k)} - \overline{M}^{(\mathbb{F},k-1)}) = \overline{M}^{(\mathbb{F},n)}.$$

By combining this with (51), we derive

$$\overline{M}^{\mathbb{F}} I_{\{\widetilde{G}=1\}} = \lim_{n\longrightarrow+\infty}(\overline{M}^{\mathbb{F}})^{\sigma_n} I_{\{\widetilde{G}^{\sigma_n}=1\}} = \lim_{n\longrightarrow+\infty}\overline{M}^{(\mathbb{F},n)} I_{\{\widetilde{G}^{\sigma_n}=1\}} \equiv 0,$$

$$M^{\mathbb{G}} = \lim_{n\longrightarrow\infty}(M^{\mathbb{G}})^{\sigma_n^{\mathbb{G}}} = \lim_{n\longrightarrow\infty}\frac{\overline{M}^{(\mathbb{F},n)}}{1-G^{\sigma_n}}(I_{]\!]\tau,+\infty[\![})^{\sigma_n}$$
$$= \lim_{n\longrightarrow\infty}\frac{(\overline{M}^{\mathbb{F}})^{\sigma_n}}{1-G^{\sigma_n}}(I_{]\!]\tau,+\infty[\![})^{\sigma_n} = \frac{\overline{M}^{\mathbb{F}}}{1-G}I_{]\!]\tau,+\infty[\![}.$$

This proves the first part of assertion (b). Now we address the second part, which states that the process $\overline{M}^{\mathbb{F}}_{-}(1-G_{-})^{-1}I_{\{G_{-}<1\}}$ is $\mathbb{F}$-locally bounded. Thus, as $M^{\mathbb{G}}$ is RCLL and adapted, we conclude that $M^{\mathbb{G}}_{-}$ is $\mathbb{G}$-locally bounded, and hence, in virtue of (48), $M^{\mathbb{G}}_{-} - (M^{\mathbb{G}}_{-})^{\tau} = \overline{M}^{\mathbb{F}}_{-}(1-G_{-})^{-1}I_{]\!]\tau,+\infty[\![}$ is also $\mathbb{G}$-locally bounded. This yields the existence of a sequence of $\mathbb{G}$-stopping times $\tau_n^{\mathbb{G}}$ that increases to infinity and for all $n \geq 0$,

$$\frac{\overline{M}^{\mathbb{F}}_{-}}{1-G_{-}}I_{]\!]\tau,+\infty[\![}I_{]\!]0,\tau_n^{\mathbb{G}}]\!]} \leq n. \tag{53}$$

On the other hand, thanks to assumption (12) and [2, Proposition B.1-(a)], we obtain the existence of a sequence of $\mathbb{F}$-stopping times $\tau_n^{\mathbb{F}}$ that increases to infinity and $\tau_n^{\mathbb{G}} \vee \tau = \tau_n^{\mathbb{F}} \vee \tau$ P-a.s. Thus, by inserting this in (53), we derive that

$$I_{]\!]\tau,+\infty[\![} \leq I_{\Sigma}, \quad \Sigma := \left\{\frac{\overline{M}^{\mathbb{F}}_{-}}{1-G_{-}}I_{\{G_{-}<1\}}I_{]\!]0,\tau_n^{\mathbb{F}}]\!]} \leq n\right\} \in \mathcal{P}(\mathbb{F}).$$

Then by taking the $\mathbb{F}$-predictable projection on both sides of the above inequality, we get $1-G_{-} \leq I_{\Sigma}$, or equivalently

$$\{G_{-}<1\} \subset \Sigma := \left\{\frac{\overline{M}^{\mathbb{F}}_{-}}{1-G_{-}}I_{\{G_{-}<1\}}I_{]\!]0,\tau_n^{\mathbb{F}}]\!]} \leq n\right\}.$$

By combining this with the fact that we always have $\{G_- = 1\} \subset \Sigma$ and the fact that $\tau_n^{\mathbb{F}}$ increases to infinity, we deduce that $\overline{M}_-^{\mathbb{F}}(1-G_-)^{-1}I_{\{G_-<1\}}$ is locally bounded. This proves assertion (c), and the proof of the lemma is complete. □

Besides Lemma 3.9, the proof of Theorem 3.3 requires the following two technical lemmas:

Lemma 3.10. *Suppose that τ is an honest time. Then the following assertions hold:*

(a) *It always holds that*

$$I_{]\!]\tau,+\infty[\![} \bullet D^{o,\mathbb{F}} \equiv 0.$$

(b) *Suppose $M \in \mathcal{M}_{0,loc}(\mathbb{F})$ satisfying $I_{\{G_-=1\}} \bullet M = I_{\{\widetilde{G}=1\}}\Delta M = \mathcal{T}(M) = 0$. Then M is a null process (i.e., $M = 0$).*

(c) *Suppose that* (12) *and* (16) *hold. If $M \in \mathcal{M}_{0,loc}(\mathbb{F})$ satisfying*

$$MI_{\{\widetilde{G}=1\}} \equiv 0, \quad \textit{and} \quad I_{]\!]\tau,+\infty[\![} \bullet M = -\frac{M_-}{1-G_-} I_{]\!]\tau,+\infty[\![} \bullet m,$$

then M is a null process (i.e., $M \equiv 0$).

The proof of this lemma is relegated to Appendix C, while in the following we state our second technical lemma.

A part of the proof of Theorem 3.3 relies on the following lemma that is interesting in itself:

Lemma 3.11. *Let $N \in \mathcal{M}_{loc}(\mathbb{F})$ satisfying* (8) *(i.e., $I_{\{\widetilde{G}=1\}}\Delta N = I_{\{G_-=1\}} \bullet N = 0$), and consider $\mathrm{M}_{loc}(\mathbb{F},\tau)$ defined via* (11). *If we put $H^{\mathbb{G}} := (1-G_-)^{-1} I_{]\!]\tau,+\infty[\![}$, then the following assertions hold:*

(a) *$H^{\mathbb{G}} \in L(\mathcal{T}^{(a)}(N), \mathbb{G})$ and $H^{\mathbb{G}} \bullet \mathcal{T}^{(a)}(N) \in \mathcal{M}^2(\mathbb{G})$ if and only if*

$$E\left[\int_0^\infty \frac{I_{\{\widetilde{G}_s<1\}}}{1-\widetilde{G}_s} d[N,N]_s\right] < \infty. \tag{54}$$

(b) *$N \in \mathcal{A}(\mathbb{F})$ if and only if $H^{\mathbb{G}}$ is $\mathcal{T}^{(a)}(N)$-integrable and $H^{\mathbb{G}} \bullet \mathcal{T}^{(a)}(N) \in \mathcal{A}(\mathbb{G})$.*

(c) *Suppose that* (12) *holds. Then* N *belongs to* $\mathbb{M}_{loc}(\mathbb{F}, \tau)$ *if and only if* $H^{\mathbb{G}}$ *is* $\mathcal{T}^{(a)}(N)$*-integrable and* $H^{\mathbb{G}} \bullet \mathcal{T}^{(a)}(N) \in \mathcal{M}_{loc}(\mathbb{G})$.

The proof of the lemma is relegated to Appendix C, the rest of this subsection focuses on proving Theorems 3.1, 3.3 and 3.4.

Proof of Theorem 3.1. On the one hand, remark that the uniqueness of an $\mathbb{F}$-local martingale M, satisfying both (8) and (10), is a direct consequence of Lemma 3.10(b). On the other hand, thanks to Lemma 3.11(a), if $M \in \mathcal{M}_{loc}(\mathbb{F})$ satisfying (8)–(9)–(10), then $(1-G_-)^{-1}I_{]\!]\tau,+\infty[\![} \in L(\mathcal{T}^{(a)}(N), \mathbb{G})$ and $M^{\mathbb{G}} = (1-G_-)^{-1}I_{]\!]\tau,+\infty[\![} \bullet \mathcal{T}^{(a)}(N) \in \mathcal{M}^2(\mathbb{G})$. This proves one implication of assertion (a), while the reverse implication will be proved in Step 2.1. Similarly, again due to Lemma 3.11(c), when $M \in \mathcal{M}_{loc}(\mathbb{F}) \cap \mathcal{A}(\mathbb{F})$ satisfying (8) and (10), we deduce that $(1-G_-)^{-1}I_{]\!]\tau,+\infty[\![}$ is $\mathcal{T}^{(a)}(N)$-integrable and $M^{\mathbb{G}} = (1-G_-)^{-1}I_{]\!]\tau,+\infty[\![} \bullet \mathcal{T}^{(a)}(N) \in \mathcal{A}(\mathbb{G})$. This proves one sense in the equivalence of assertion (b), while the reserve sense will be proved in Step 2.2. Thus, the rest of this proof is divided into two steps:

Step 1. This step proves the following fact, which holds for any pair $(M^{\mathbb{G}}, N) \in \mathcal{M}_{loc}(\mathbb{G}) \times \mathcal{M}_{loc}(\mathbb{F})$.

$$\begin{aligned}&\text{If the pair } (M^{\mathbb{G}}, N) \text{ satisfies (48), then } (1-G_-)^2 \bullet M^{\mathbb{G}}\\ &\quad = (1-G_-) \bullet \mathcal{T}^{(a)}(N) + N_- \bullet \mathcal{T}^{(a)}(m).\end{aligned} \tag{55}$$

To prove this claim, we suppose that the pair $(M^{\mathbb{G}}, N)$ fulfills (48), which we recall in the following:

$$M^{\mathbb{G}} - (M^{\mathbb{G}})^{\tau} = \frac{N}{1-G} I_{]\!]\tau,+\infty[\![} \quad \text{and} \quad N I_{\{\widetilde{G}=1\}} = 0. \tag{56}$$

As a result, by combining these properties with $[\![\tau]\!] \subset \{\widetilde{G} = 1\}$, we deduce that

$$\begin{aligned}(M^{\mathbb{G}} - (M^{\mathbb{G}})^{\tau})(1-G) &= N I_{]\!]\tau,+\infty[\![} = N I_{[\![\tau,+\infty[\![}\\ &= N \bullet D + I_{]\!]\tau,+\infty[\![} \bullet N = I_{]\!]\tau,+\infty[\![} \bullet N.\end{aligned} \tag{57}$$

Thus, we apply the integration by parts formula to the left-hand side term of (57) and use Lemma 3.10(a) afterwards to derive

$$\begin{aligned}
&(M^{\mathbb{G}} - (M^{\mathbb{G}})^{\tau})(1-G)\\
&\quad = (1-G_-)I_{]\!]\tau,+\infty[\![} \bullet M^{\mathbb{G}} - (M^{\mathbb{G}}_- - M^{\mathbb{G}}_{\tau})I_{]\!]\tau,+\infty[\![} \bullet G\\
&\qquad - I_{]\!]\tau,+\infty[\![} \bullet [M^{\mathbb{G}}, G]\\
&\quad = (1-G_-)I_{]\!]\tau,+\infty[\![} \bullet M^{\mathbb{G}} - (M^{\mathbb{G}}_- - M^{\mathbb{G}}_{\tau})I_{]\!]\tau,+\infty[\![} \bullet m\\
&\qquad - I_{]\!]\tau,+\infty[\![} \bullet [M^{\mathbb{G}}, m].
\end{aligned}$$

By combining this latter equality with (57), we derive

$$\begin{aligned}
&(1-G_-)I_{]\!]\tau,+\infty[\![} \bullet N\\
&\quad = (1-G_-)^2 I_{]\!]\tau,+\infty[\![} \bullet M^{\mathbb{G}} - (M^{\mathbb{G}}_- - M^{\mathbb{G}}_{\tau})(1-G_-)I_{]\!]\tau,+\infty[\![} \bullet m\\
&\qquad - (1-G_-)I_{]\!]\tau,+\infty[\![} \bullet [M^{\mathbb{G}}, m].
\end{aligned} \tag{58}$$

Then this equation allows us to get $[M^{\mathbb{G}}, m]$ as follows:

$$\begin{aligned}
&(1-G_-)I_{]\!]\tau,+\infty[\![} \bullet [N, m]\\
&\quad = \Big((1-G_-)^2 - (1-G_-)\Delta m\Big) I_{]\!]\tau,+\infty[\![} \bullet [M^{\mathbb{G}}, m]\\
&\qquad - (M^{\mathbb{G}}_- - M^{\mathbb{G}}_{\tau})(1-G_-)I_{]\!]\tau,+\infty[\![} \bullet [m, m]\\
&\quad = (1-G_-)(1-\widetilde{G})I_{]\!]\tau,+\infty[\![} \bullet [M^{\mathbb{G}}, m]\\
&\qquad - (M^{\mathbb{G}}_- - M^{\mathbb{G}}_{\tau})(1-G_-)I_{]\!]\tau,+\infty[\![} \bullet [m, m].
\end{aligned}$$

Thus, by inserting this in (58) and using $(M^{\mathbb{G}}_- - M^{\mathbb{G}}_{\tau})I_{]\!]\tau,+\infty[\![} = N_-(1-G_-)^{-1}I_{]\!]\tau,+\infty[\![}$, we obtain

$$\begin{aligned}
&(1-G_-)^2 I_{]\!]\tau,+\infty[\![} dM^{\mathbb{G}}\\
&\quad = (1-G_-)I_{]\!]\tau,+\infty[\![} dN + \frac{1-G_-}{1-\widetilde{G}} I_{]\!]\tau,+\infty[\![} \bullet [N, m]\\
&\qquad + N_- I_{]\!]\tau,+\infty[\![} dm + \frac{N_-}{1-\widetilde{G}} I_{]\!]\tau,+\infty[\![} \bullet [m, m].
\end{aligned} \tag{59}$$

Put

$$M' := (1 - G_-) \bullet N + N_- I_{\{G_- < 1\}} \bullet m \in \mathcal{M}_{0,loc}(\mathbb{F}), \tag{60}$$

and remark that the condition $NI_{\{\widetilde{G}=1\}} = 0$ implies that

$$\begin{aligned} \Delta M' I_{\{\widetilde{G}=1\}} &= (1 - G_-)^{-1} I_{\{\widetilde{G}=1>G_-\}} \Delta N \\ &\quad + N_-(1 - G_-)^{-2} I_{\{\widetilde{G}=1>G_-\}} \Delta m \\ &= -(1 - G_-)^{-1} N_- I_{\{\widetilde{G}=1>G_-\}} \\ &\quad + N_-(1 - G_-)^{-1} I_{\{\widetilde{G}=1>G_-\}} = 0. \end{aligned} \tag{61}$$

Hence, it is easy to check that, due to this latter equality, we have

$$\begin{aligned} I_{]\!]\tau,+\infty[\![} \bullet M' + \frac{I_{]\!]\tau,+\infty[\![}}{1 - \widetilde{G}} \bullet [M', m] &= \mathcal{T}^{(a)}(M') \\ = (1 - G_-) \bullet \mathcal{T}^{(a)}(N) + N_- \bullet \mathcal{T}^{(a)}(m). \end{aligned}$$

Therefore, by inserting this equality in (59), the claim (55) follows, and this ends Step 1.

Step 2. Herein we prove assertions (a) and (b). To this end, remark that if $M^{\mathbb{G}} \in \mathcal{M}^2(\mathbb{G})$ or $M^{\mathbb{G}} \in \mathcal{A}(\mathbb{G})$, then $M^{\mathbb{G}}$ is a uniformly integrable martingale and one can apply Lemma 3.9(a) to $M^{\mathbb{G}}$ directly. As result, there exists an $\mathbb{F}$-martingale N such that the pair $(M^{\mathbb{G}}, N)$ satisfies (48). Hence, in virtue of Step 1 and its proof, we deduce the existence of an $\mathbb{F}$-martingale N such that M' defined in (60) satisfies

$$\begin{aligned} &(1 - G_-)^2 I_{]\!]\tau,+\infty[\![} \bullet M^{\mathbb{G}} = \mathcal{T}^{(a)}(M'), \\ &I_{\{\widetilde{G}=1\}} \Delta M' \equiv 0, \quad I_{\{G_-=1\}} \bullet M' \equiv 0. \end{aligned} \tag{62}$$

Step 2.1. Here we suppose $I_{]\!]\tau,+\infty[\![} \bullet M^{\mathbb{G}}$ is square integrable and prove assertion (a). Thus, due to the first and second properties in

(62), we conclude that $I_{]\!]\tau,+\infty[\![}\bullet M^{\mathbb{G}}$ is square integrable iff M' satisfies

$$\begin{aligned}
E&\left[\int_0^\infty \frac{I_{\{G_{s-}<1\}}}{(1-G_{s-})^2}\bullet [M',M']_s\right]\\
&\le E\left[\int_0^\infty \frac{I_{\{G_{s-}<1\}}I_{\{\widetilde{G}_s<1\}}}{(1-G_{s-})^2(1-\widetilde{G}_s)}d[M',M']_s\right]\\
&= E\left[\left(I_{]\!]\tau,+\infty[\![}\bullet [M^{\mathbb{G}},M^{\mathbb{G}}]\right)_\infty\right] < \infty. \qquad (63)
\end{aligned}$$

These (in)equalities are due to the definition of $\mathcal{T}^{(a)}$, the second condition in (62) and $1/(1-\widetilde{G}) \ge 1$. On the one hand, (63) implies that $I_{\{G_{s-}<1\}}(1-G_{s-})^{-1}$ is M'-integrable (or equivalently $N_- I_{\{G_{s-}<1\}}(1-G_{s-})^{-1}$ is m-integrable) and

$$M := \frac{I_{\{G_{s-}<1\}}}{1-G_{s-}}\bullet M' = I_{\{G_-<1\}}\bullet N + \frac{N_-}{1-G_-}I_{\{G_-<1\}}\bullet m \in \mathcal{M}^2(\mathbb{F}).$$

On the other hand, by inserting the above equality in (63) and (62), we obtain

$$I_{\{G_-=1\}}\bullet M = I_{\{\widetilde{G}_s<1\}}\Delta M \equiv 0, \quad E\left[\int_0^\infty \frac{I_{\{\widetilde{G}_s<1\}}}{1-\widetilde{G}_s}d[M,M]_s\right] < \infty$$
$$\text{and} \quad (1-G_-)I_{]\!]\tau,+\infty[\![}dM^{\mathbb{G}} = \mathcal{T}^{(a)}(M).$$

This proves assertion (a) and ends Step 2.1.

Step 2.2. Here we assume that $M^{\mathbb{G}} \in \mathcal{A}(\mathbb{G})$ and prove assertion (b). Thus, thanks to Ref. [20, Lemma 2.60-(b), Chapter 2] which states that $\mathrm{Var}(K) = \sum|\Delta K|$ for any local martingale K, and in virtue of (62), $I_{]\!]\tau,+\infty[\![}\bullet M^{\mathbb{G}}$ has an integrable variation if and only if $M' \in \mathcal{A}(\mathbb{F})$ and

$$E\left[\int_0^\infty \frac{I_{\{G_{s-}<1\}}}{1-G_{s-}}d\mathrm{Var(M')}_s\right] = E\left[\left(I_{]\!]\tau,+\infty[\![}\bullet \mathrm{Var(M^{\mathbb{G}})}\right)_\infty\right] < \infty. \qquad (64)$$

This equality is due to $\Delta M' I_{\{\widetilde{G}=1\}} = 0$. Thus, we deduce that $(1-G_-)^{-1}I_{\{G_-<1\}}$ is M'-integrable and $M := (1-G_-)^{-1}I_{\{G_-<1\}}\bullet M' =$

$I_{\{G_-<1\}}\bullet M+N_-(1-G_-)^{-1}I_{\{G_-<1\}}\bullet m$ belongs to $\mathcal{M}_{loc}(\mathbb{F})$ satisfying

$$I_{\{G_-=1\}}\bullet M=I_{\{\widetilde{G}=1\}}\Delta M=0,\quad (1-G_-)I_{]\!]\tau,+\infty[\![}\bullet M^{\mathbb{G}}=\mathcal{T}^{(a)}(M)$$
$$\text{and}\quad E\left[\mathrm{Var(M)}_\infty\right]<\infty.$$

This proves assertion (b), and the proof of the theorem is complete.

Proof of Theorem 3.3. On the one hand, we remark that uniqueness in assertion (c) follows from Lemma 3.10-(c). On the other hand, the implication (b)$\Longrightarrow$(c) follows immediately from putting

$$M:=I_{\{G_-<1\}}\bullet M^{\mathbb{F}}+M^{\mathbb{F}}_-(1-G_-)^{-1}I_{\{G_-<1\}}\bullet m.$$

Furthermore, (c)$\Longrightarrow$(a) is a direct consequence of Lemma 3.11(b). Thus, the rest of the proof focuses on proving (a)$\Longrightarrow$(c). To this end, we suppose (12) holds and $I_{]\!]\tau,+\infty[\![}\bullet M^{\mathbb{G}}\in\mathcal{M}_{loc}(\mathbb{G})$. Then a direct application of Lemma 3.9(b), and then Step 1 of the proof of Theorem 3.1 (i.e., the claim (55)) afterwards, we conclude the existence of an $\mathbb{F}$-martingale $M^{\mathbb{F}}$ satisfying

$$M^{\mathbb{F}}I_{\{\widetilde{G}=1\}}=0,\quad \frac{M^{\mathbb{F}}_-}{1-G_-}I_{\{G_-<1\}}\text{ is }\mathbb{F}\text{-locally bounded}\qquad(65)$$

and

$$(1-G_-)^2I_{]\!]\tau,+\infty[\![}\bullet M^{\mathbb{G}}=(1-G_-)\bullet\mathcal{T}^{(a)}(M^{\mathbb{F}})+M^{\mathbb{F}}_-I_{]\!]\tau,+\infty[\![}\bullet\mathcal{T}^{(a)}(m).$$

As $M^{\mathbb{F}}_-(1-G_-)^{-1}I_{\{G_-<1\}}$ is locally bonded (see the second property in (65)), then this process is m-integrable and the above equality is equivalent to (14). Furthermore, by applying Lemma 3.11(b) to $M:=I_{\{G_-<1\}}\bullet M^{\mathbb{F}}+M^{\mathbb{F}}_-(1-G_-)^{-1}I_{]\!]\tau,+\infty[\![}\bullet m$, we deduce that $M\in\mathbb{M}_{loc}(\mathbb{F},\tau)$. This proves that assertion (b) holds and ends the proof of the theorem.

Proof of Theorem 3.4. On the one hand, we remark that the uniqueness in assertion (b) is a direct consequence of Lemma 3.10(c), and the fact that $\mathcal{T}^{(a)}(N)=0$ is equivalent to $I_{]\!]\tau,+\infty[\![}\bullet N\equiv 0$ for any $N\in\mathcal{M}_{loc}(\mathbb{F})$ satisfying $I_{\{\widetilde{G}=1\}}\Delta N\equiv 0$. On the other hand, the proof of (a)$\Longrightarrow$(b) follows immediately from Theorem 3.3. Thanks to Ref. [2, Proposition B.1-(b)], under both assumptions (12) and (16), the process $(1-G_-)^{-r}I_{\{G_-<1\}}$ is $\mathbb{F}$-locally bounded and $(1-G_-)^{-r}I_{]\!]\tau,+\infty[\![}$ is $\mathbb{G}$-locally bounded for any $r\in(0,\infty)$. Thus, the implication (c)$\Longrightarrow$(a) is a direct consequence of this latter fact, while (b)$\Longrightarrow$(c) follows from combing the local boundedness of $(1-G_-)^{-r}I_{\{G_-<1\}}$ and putting

$$M := (1-G_-)^{-1}I_{\{G_-<1\}}\bullet \widetilde{M}^{\mathbb{F}} + \frac{\widetilde{M}^{\mathbb{F}}_-}{(1-G_-)^2}\bullet m.$$

This ends the proof of the theorem.

4. Explicit Description of All Deflators

In this section, we parametrize explicitly all deflators for the model $(S-S^\tau,\mathbb{G},P)$ in terms of the deflators of a transformed model from $(S,\mathbb{F})$. This complements [15, Theorems 3.2 and 3.4] and allows us to describe all deflators for the whole model $(S,\mathbb{G},P)$. Thus, we start this section by recalling the mathematical definition of deflators and their local martingale deflator variant.

Definition 4.1. Consider the model $(X,\mathbb{H},Q)$, where $\mathbb{H}$ is a filtration, Q is a probability and X is a $(Q,\mathbb{H})$-semimartingale. Let Z be a process.

(a) We call Z a local martingale deflator for $(X,Q,\mathbb{H})$ if $Z_0=1$, $Z>0$ and there exists a real-valued and $\mathbb{H}$-predictable process φ such that $0<\varphi\leq 1$ and both Z and $Z(\varphi\bullet X)$ are $\mathbb{H}$-local martingales under Q. Throughout this chapter, the set of these local martingale deflators will be denoted by $\mathcal{Z}_{loc}(X,Q,\mathbb{H})$.
(b) We call Z a deflator for $(X,Q,\mathbb{H})$ if $Z_0=1$, $Z>0$ and $Z\mathcal{E}(\varphi\bullet X)$ is an $\mathbb{H}$-supermartingale under Q, for any $\varphi\in L(X,\mathbb{H})$ such that $\varphi\Delta X\geq -1$. The set of all deflators will be denoted by $\mathcal{D}(X,Q,\mathbb{H})$. When $Q=P$, for the sake of simplicity, we simply omit the probability in notations and terminology.

The rest of this section is divided into three sections. The first section states our main results on deflators for the model $(S-S^\tau,\mathbb{G})$ and discusses their importance and the key intermediate results. The second section extends the result to the full model $(S,\mathbb{G})$, while the third section gives the proof of the principal results in the first section.

4.1. *Main Results*

This section describes explicitly the set of all deflators of $(S - S^\tau, \mathbb{G})$ in terms of deflators for the initial model $(S, \mathbb{F})$. Thus, throughout this section, we assume the following assumptions:

$$\tau \text{ is a finite honest time such that } \quad G_\tau < 1 \quad P\text{-a.s.} \quad \text{and}$$
$$\left\{\widetilde{G} = 1 > G_-\right\} = \emptyset. \tag{66}$$

Theorem 4.2. *Suppose that assumptions* (66) *hold, and let* $Z^{\mathbb{G}}$ *be a process such that* $(Z^{\mathbb{G}})^\tau \equiv 1$. *Then the following assertions are equivalent:*

(a) $Z^{\mathbb{G}}$ *is a deflator for* $(S - S^\tau, \mathbb{G})$ (*i.e.,* $Z^{\mathbb{G}} \in \mathcal{D}(S - S^\tau, \mathbb{G})$).
(b) *There exists a unique pair* $\left(K^{\mathbb{F}}, V^{\mathbb{F}}\right)$ *such that* $K^{\mathbb{F}} \in \mathcal{M}_{loc}(\mathbb{F})$, $V^{\mathbb{F}}$ *is an* $\mathbb{F}$*-predictable RCLL and non-decreasing process such that* $V_0^{\mathbb{F}} = K_0^{\mathbb{F}} = 0$, $\mathcal{E}(K^{\mathbb{F}})\mathcal{E}(-V^{\mathbb{F}}) \in \mathcal{D}(I_{\{G_-<1\}} \bullet S, \mathbb{F})$ *and*

$$Z^{\mathbb{G}} = \mathcal{E}(K^{\mathbb{G}})\mathcal{E}(-I_{]\!]\tau,+\infty[\![} \bullet V^{\mathbb{F}}), \quad \textit{where}$$
$$K^{\mathbb{G}} = \mathcal{T}^{(a)}(K^{\mathbb{F}}) + (1 - G_-)^{-1} I_{]\!]\tau,+\infty[\![} \bullet \mathcal{T}^{(a)}(m). \tag{67}$$

(c) *There exists a unique* $Z^{\mathbb{F}} \in \mathcal{D}(I_{\{G_-<1\}} \bullet S, \mathbb{F})$ *such that*

$$Z^{\mathbb{G}} = \frac{Z^{\mathbb{F}}/(Z^{\mathbb{F}})^\tau}{\mathcal{E}(-I_{]\!]\tau,+\infty[\![}(1 - G_-)^{-1} \bullet m)}. \tag{68}$$

The theorem gives two different characterizations for deflators of the model $(S - S^\tau, \mathbb{G})$. Precisely, assertion (b) characterizes deflators in an additive way, while assertion (c) uses a multiplicative structure. The key idea behind the equivalence between the two characterizations is singled out in the following lemma, which is interesting in itself.

Lemma 4.3. *Suppose that* (66) *is fulfilled. Then the following assertions hold:*

(a) *For any $\mathbb{F}$-semimartingale X, we always have*

$$\frac{\mathcal{E}(I_{]\!]\tau,\infty[\![}\bullet X)}{\mathcal{E}\left(-I_{]\!]\tau,\infty[\![}(1-G_-)^{-1}\bullet m\right)} = \mathcal{E}\Big(\mathcal{T}^{(a)}(X) + (1-G_-)^{-1}I_{]\!]\tau,\infty[\![}\bullet \mathcal{T}^{(a)}(m)\Big), \tag{69}$$

where $\mathcal{T}^{(a)}(X)$ is given by

$$\mathcal{T}^{(a)}(X) := I_{]\!]\tau,\infty[\![}\bullet X + \frac{I_{]\!]\tau,\infty[\![}}{1-\widetilde{G}}\bullet [X,m]. \tag{70}$$

(b) *For any $K^{\mathbb{F}} \in \mathcal{M}_{loc}(\mathbb{F})$, then*

$$M^{\mathbb{G}} := \frac{I_{]\!]\tau,\infty[\![}\bullet K^{\mathbb{F}}}{\mathcal{E}\left(-I_{]\!]\tau,\infty[\![}(1-G_-)^{-1}\bullet m\right)} \in \mathcal{M}_{loc}(\mathbb{G}). \tag{71}$$

(c) *For any $\mathbb{F}$-semimartingales X and Y, the following holds:*

$$\left[\mathcal{T}^{(a)}(X), Y\right] = \left[X, \mathcal{T}^{(a)}(Y)\right] = \frac{1-G_-}{1-\widetilde{G}} I_{]\!]\tau,\infty[\![}\bullet [X,Y]. \tag{72}$$

The proof of this lemma is relegated to Appendix C. As a particular case of Theorem 4.2, we characterize the set of all local martingale deflators for $(S-S^\tau,\mathbb{G})$, denoted by $\mathcal{Z}_{loc}(S-S^\tau,\mathbb{G})$, as follows:

Theorem 4.4. *Suppose that assumptions (66) hold, and let $K^{\mathbb{G}}$ be a $\mathbb{G}$-semimartingale such that $(K^{\mathbb{G}})^\tau \equiv 0$. Then the following assertions are equivalent:*

(a) $Z^{\mathbb{G}} := \mathcal{E}\left(K^{\mathbb{G}}\right)$ *is a local martingale deflator for* $(S-S^\tau,\mathbb{G})$.
(b) *There exists a unique $K^{\mathbb{F}} \in \mathcal{M}_{loc}(\mathbb{F})$ such that $K^{\mathbb{F}}_0 = 0$, $\mathcal{E}\left(K^{\mathbb{F}}\right) \in \mathcal{Z}_{loc}(I_{\{G_-<1\}}\bullet S,\mathbb{F})$ and*

$$K^{\mathbb{G}} = \mathcal{T}^{(a)}(K^{\mathbb{F}}) + (1-G_-)^{-1}I_{]\!]\tau,+\infty[\![}\bullet \mathcal{T}^{(a)}(m). \tag{73}$$

(c) *There exists a unique $Z^{\mathbb{F}} \in \mathcal{Z}_{loc}(I_{\{G_-<1\}}\bullet S,\mathbb{F})$ such that*

$$Z^{\mathbb{G}} = \frac{Z^{\mathbb{F}}/(Z^{\mathbb{F}})^\tau}{\mathcal{E}(-I_{]\!]\tau,+\infty[\![}(1-G_-)^{-1}\bullet m)}. \tag{74}$$

The proof of this theorem will be detailed in Section 4.3, while in the rest of this subsection, we elaborate the description of the set of all deflators for the full model $(S, \mathbb{G}, P)$ by combining Theorems 4.2 and 4.4 with Choulli and Yansori [15, Theorems 3.2 and 3.4].

Theorem 4.5. *Suppose that* (66) *holds and* $G > 0$. *Consider* $N^{\mathbb{G}}$ *given by* (31), *and let* $K^{\mathbb{G}}$ *be an arbitrary* $\mathbb{G}$-*semimartingale. Then the following assertions hold:*

(a) $Z^{\mathbb{G}} := \mathcal{E}(K^{\mathbb{G}}) \in \mathcal{D}(S, \mathbb{G})$ *if and only if there exists a quadruplet* $(Z^{(\mathbb{F},b)}, Z^{(\mathbb{F},a)}, \varphi^{(o)}, \varphi^{(pr)})$ *that belongs to* $\mathcal{D}(S, \mathbb{F}) \times \mathcal{D}(I_{\{G_-<1\}} \bullet S, \mathbb{F}) \times \mathcal{I}^{o,\mathbb{F}}_{loc}(N^{\mathbb{G}}, \mathbb{G}) \times L^1_{loc}(\mathrm{Prog}(\mathbb{F}), P \otimes dD)$ *such that*

$$\varphi^{(pr)} > -1, \quad -\frac{\widetilde{G}}{G} < \varphi^{(o)}, \quad \varphi^{(o)}(\widetilde{G} - G) < \widetilde{G},$$
$$P \otimes dD\text{-}a.e., \quad E\left[\varphi^{(pr)}_\tau | \mathcal{F}_\tau\right] = 0, \quad P\text{-}a.s. \tag{75}$$

and

$$Z^{\mathbb{G}} = \frac{(Z^{(\mathbb{F},b)})^\tau}{\mathcal{E}(G_-^{-1} \bullet m)^\tau} \frac{Z^{(\mathbb{F},a)}/(Z^{(\mathbb{F},a)})^\tau}{\mathcal{E}(-I_{]\!]\tau,+\infty[\![}(1-G_-)^{-1} \bullet m)}$$
$$\times\, \mathcal{E}(\varphi^{(o)} \bullet N^{\mathbb{G}}) \mathcal{E}(\varphi^{(pr)} \bullet D). \tag{76}$$

(b) $Z^{\mathbb{G}} := \mathcal{E}(K^{\mathbb{G}}) \in \mathcal{Z}_{loc}(S, \mathbb{G})$ *if and only if there exists a quadruplet* $(Z^{(\mathbb{F},b)}, Z^{(\mathbb{F},a)}, \varphi^{(o)}, \varphi^{(pr)})$ *which belongs to* $\mathcal{Z}_{loc}(S, \mathbb{F}) \times \mathcal{Z}_{loc}(I_{\{G_-<1\}} \bullet S, \mathbb{F}) \times \mathcal{I}^{o,\mathbb{F}}_{loc}(N^{\mathbb{G}}, \mathbb{G}) \times L^1_{loc}(\mathrm{Prog}(\mathbb{F}), P \otimes dD)$ *and satisfies both conditions* (75) *and* (76).

Proof. Remark that $\mathcal{E}(K^{\mathbb{G}})$ is a (local martingale) deflator for $(S, \mathbb{G})$ if and only if $\mathcal{E}(I_{[\![0,\tau]\!]} \bullet K^{\mathbb{G}})$ is a (local martingale) deflator for $(S^\tau, \mathbb{G})$ and $\mathcal{E}(I_{]\!]\tau,+\infty[\![} \bullet K^{\mathbb{G}})$ is a (local martingale) deflator for $(S - S^\tau, \mathbb{G})$. Thus, to prove assertion (a) (respectively, assertion (b)), we apply Theorem 4.2 (respectively, Theorem 4.4) to $\mathcal{E}(I_{]\!]\tau,+\infty[\![} \bullet K^{\mathbb{G}})$ with the model $(S - S^\tau, \mathbb{G})$ and get $Z^{(\mathbb{F},a)}$ which belongs to $\mathcal{D}(I_{\{G_-<1\}} \bullet S, \mathbb{F})$ (respectively, belongs to $\mathcal{Z}_{loc}(I_{\{G_-<1\}} \bullet S, \mathbb{F})$) and

$$\frac{Z^{\mathbb{G}}}{(Z^{\mathbb{G}})^\tau} = \mathcal{E}(I_{]\!]\tau,+\infty[\![} \bullet K^{\mathbb{G}}) = \frac{Z^{(\mathbb{F},a)}/(Z^{(\mathbb{F},a)})^\tau}{\mathcal{E}(-I_{]\!]\tau,+\infty[\![}(1-G_-)^{-1} \bullet m)}. \tag{77}$$

Then we apply Ref. [15, Theorem 3.2] (respectively, [15, Theorem 3.4)]) to $\mathcal{E}(I_{[\![0,\tau[\![} \bullet K^{\mathbb{G}})$ with the model $(S^\tau, \mathbb{G})$ and obtain the triplet $(Z^{(\mathbb{F},b)}, \varphi^{(o)}, \varphi^{(pr)})$ which belongs to $\mathcal{D}(S,\mathbb{F}) \times \mathcal{I}^{o,\mathbb{F}}_{loc}(N^{\mathbb{G}},\mathbb{G}) \times L^1_{loc}(\mathrm{Prog}(\mathbb{F}), P\otimes dD)$ (respectively, $\mathcal{Z}_{loc}(S,\mathbb{F}) \times \mathcal{I}^{o,\mathbb{F}}_{loc}(N^{\mathbb{G}},\mathbb{G}) \times L^1_{loc}(\mathrm{Prog}(\mathbb{F}), P\otimes dD)$) and satisfies (75) and

$$(Z^{\mathbb{G}})^{\tau} = \mathcal{E}(I_{[\![0,\tau]\!]} \bullet K^{\mathbb{G}}) = \frac{(Z^{(\mathbb{F},b)})^{\tau}}{\mathcal{E}(G_-^{-1}\bullet m)^{\tau}}\mathcal{E}(\varphi^{(o)}\bullet N^{\mathbb{G}})\mathcal{E}(\varphi^{(pr)}\bullet D).$$

Therefore, the proof of (76) follows immediately from combining this latter equation with (77), and this ends the proof of theorem. □

4.2. *Two Particular Cases: The Jump-Diffusion and the Discrete-Time Models*

This section illustrates the main result of the previous section on the cases where $(S,\mathbb{F})$ follows either a jump-diffusion model or a discrete-time model. Thus, we suppose that a standard Brownian motion W and a Poisson process N with intensity $\lambda > 0$ are defined on the probability space $(\Omega, \mathcal{F}, P)$ and are independent. Let $\mathbb{F}$ be the completed and right continuous filtration generated by W and N. Stock's price process is supposed to have the following dynamics:

$$S_t = S_0\mathcal{E}(X)_t, \quad X_t = \sigma\bullet W_t + \zeta\bullet N^{\mathbb{F}}_t + \int_0^t \mu_s ds, \quad N^{\mathbb{F}}_t := N_t - \lambda t. \tag{78}$$

Here μ, σ and ζ are bounded and $\mathbb{F}$-predictable processes, and there exists $\delta \in (0,+\infty)$ such that

$$\sigma > 0, \quad \zeta > -1, \quad \sigma + |\zeta| \geq \delta, \ P\otimes dt\text{-a.e.} \tag{79}$$

Theorem 4.6. *Suppose* (66) *holds and S is given by* (78)–(79)*. Then the following holds:*

(a) *$Z^{\mathbb{G}}$ is a local martingale deflator for $(S - S^{\tau}, \mathbb{G})$ with $(Z^{\mathbb{G}})^{\tau} = 1$ if and only if there exists a unique $(\psi_1, \psi_2) \in L^1_{loc}(W,\mathbb{F}) \times$*

$L^1_{loc}(N^{\mathbb{F}}, \mathbb{F})$ *satisfying*

$$Z^{\mathbb{G}} = \frac{\mathcal{E}(\psi_1 I_{]\!]\tau,+\infty[\![} \bullet W + \psi_2 I_{]\!]\tau,+\infty[\![} \bullet N^{\mathbb{F}})}{\mathcal{E}(-(1-G_-)^{-1} I_{]\!]\tau,+\infty[\![} \bullet m)}$$

and $P \otimes dt$*-a.e. on* $(G_- < 1)$, (ψ_1, ψ_2) *satisfies*

$$\mu + \psi_1 \sigma + \psi_2 \zeta \lambda = 0 \quad \text{and} \quad \psi_2 > -1. \tag{80}$$

(b) *Suppose furthermore that* $G > 0$. *Then* $Z^{\mathbb{G}}$ *is a local martingale deflator for* $(S, \mathbb{G})$ *if and only if there exist unique* $(\psi^{(1,b)}, \psi^{(2,b)})$ *and* $(\psi^{(1,a)}, \psi^{(2,a)})$ *which belong to* $L^1_{loc}(W, \mathbb{F}) \times L^1_{loc}(N^{\mathbb{F}}, \mathbb{F})$, $(\varphi^{(o)}, \varphi^{(pr)}) \in \mathcal{I}^{o,\mathbb{F}}_{loc}(N^{\mathbb{G}}, \mathbb{G}) \times L^1_{loc}(\text{Prog}(\mathbb{F}), P \otimes dD)$ *such that*

(i) $(\psi^{(1,b)}, \psi^{(2,b)})$ *satisfies* (80) $P \otimes dt$*-a.e.,*
(ii) $(\psi^{(1,a)}, \psi^{(2,a)})$ *satisfies* (80) $P \otimes dt$*-a.e. on* $(G_- < 1)$,
(iii) $(\varphi^{(o)}, \varphi^{(pr)})$ *fulfills* (75) *and*

$$\begin{aligned} Z^{\mathbb{G}} = & \frac{\mathcal{E}\left(\psi^{(1,a)} \bullet W + \psi^{(2,a)} \bullet N^{\mathbb{F}}\right)}{\mathcal{E}(-(1-G_-)^{-1} I_{]\!]\tau,+\infty[\![} \bullet m)} \\ & \times \frac{\mathcal{E}(\psi^{(1,b)} \bullet W + \psi^{(2,b)} \bullet N^{\mathbb{F}})^{\tau}}{\mathcal{E}\left(\psi^{(1,a)} \bullet W + \psi^{(2,a)} \bullet N^{\mathbb{F}}\right)^{\tau}} \\ & \times \frac{\mathcal{E}(\varphi^{(o)} \bullet N^{\mathbb{G}})}{\mathcal{E}(G_-^{-1} \bullet m)^{\tau}} \mathcal{E}(\varphi^{(pr)} \bullet D). \end{aligned}$$

The proof follows immediately from Theorems 4.4 and 4.5 and the fact that for any $M \in \mathcal{M}_{loc}(\mathbb{F})$, there exists a unique pair of $\mathbb{F}$-predictable processes $(\psi_1, \psi_2) \in L^1_{loc}(W, \mathbb{F}) \times L^1_{loc}(N^{\mathbb{F}}, \mathbb{F})$ such that $M = M_0 + \psi_1 \bullet W + \psi_2 \bullet N^{\mathbb{F}}$.

Theorem 4.7. *Suppose that the pair* $(\tau, \mathbb{F})$ *follows the model given in* (25), *and*

$$P\left(\widetilde{G}_n = 1 > G_{n-1}\right) = 0, \quad n = 1, \ldots, T. \tag{81}$$

Consider a $\mathbb{G}$*-adapted process* $Z^{\mathbb{G}}$ *and the pair* $(\widehat{Q}, \widehat{S})$ *given by*

$$\widehat{Q} := \widehat{Z}_T \cdot P, \quad \text{where } \widehat{Z}_n := \prod_{k=1}^{n} \left(\frac{1-\widetilde{G}_k}{1-G_{k-1}} I_{\{G_{k-1}<1\}} + I_{\{G_{k-1}=1\}} \right),$$

$$\widehat{S}_n := \sum_{k=1}^{n} I_{\{G_{k-1}<1\}} \Delta S_k. \tag{82}$$

Then the following assertions are equivalent:

(a) $Z^{\mathbb{G}}$ *is a deflator for* $(S - S^{\tau}, \mathbb{G})$ *(i.e.,* $Z^{\mathbb{G}} \in \mathcal{D}(S - S^{\tau}, \mathbb{G})$*) with* $(Z^{\mathbb{G}})^{\tau} = 1$.

(b) *There exists a unique* $Z \in \mathcal{D}(\widehat{S}, \widehat{Q}, \mathbb{F})$ *such that* $Z^{\mathbb{G}} = Z/Z^{\tau}$.

Proof. Remark that the process $\widehat{Z}$ is the discrete-time version of the $\mathbb{F}$-local martingale $\mathcal{E}(-(1-G_-)^{-1} I_{\{G_-<1\}} \bullet m)$. Furthermore, it is easy to check that the process $\widehat{Z}$ is a martingale, and hence the probability $\widehat{Q}$ is well defined. Thus the proof of the theorem follows from combining these remarks with Theorem 4.2. This ends the proof of the theorem. □

4.3. *Proof of Theorems 4.2 and 4.4*

The proof of these theorems requires the following two lemmas that are interesting in themselves.

Lemma 4.8. *The following equalities hold:*

$$\begin{aligned} X^G := \frac{1-G}{1-G^{\tau}} &:= I_{[\![0,\tau]\!]} + \frac{1-G}{1-G_{\tau}} I_{]\!]\tau,\infty[\![} \\ &= \mathcal{E}\Big(-\frac{1}{1-G_-} I_{]\!]\tau,\infty[\![} \bullet m\Big) =: \mathcal{E}(m^{(a,\mathbb{G})}). \end{aligned} \tag{83}$$

Proof. Remark that $X_0^G = 1$. Furthermore, by combining $G = m - D^{o,\mathbb{F}}$ and Lemma 3.10 (i.e., $I_{]\!]\tau,+\infty[\![} \bullet D^{o,\mathbb{F}} = 0$), we derive

$$\begin{aligned} dX_t^G &= I_{]\!]\tau,\infty[\![}(t) dX_t^G + I_{[\![0,\tau]\!]}(t) dX_t^G = \frac{1}{1-G_{\tau}} I_{]\!]\tau,\infty[\![}(t) d(1-G_t) \\ &= \frac{-1}{1-G_{\tau}} I_{]\!]\tau,\infty[\![}(t) dm_t. \end{aligned}$$

As a result, we conclude that the process X^G satisfies the following SDE:

$$dX = -\frac{X_-}{1-G_-} I_{]\!]\tau,\infty[\![} dm, \quad X_0 = 1, \tag{84}$$

which has a unique solution given by the RHS term of (83). □

The second lemma of this section connects $\mathbb{G}$-predictable non-decreasing processes with $\mathbb{F}$-predictable non-decreasing processes.

Lemma 4.9.

(a) *If $V^{\mathbb{G}}$ is an RCLL, non-decreasing and $\mathbb{G}$-predictable process such that $(V^{\mathbb{G}})^\tau \equiv 0$, then there exists a unique RCLL, non-decreasing and $\mathbb{F}$-predictable process $V^{\mathbb{F}}$ such that $V_0^{\mathbb{F}} = 0$,*

$$I_{\{G_-=1\}} \bullet V^{\mathbb{F}} \equiv 0 \quad \textit{and} \quad V^{\mathbb{G}} = I_{]\!]\tau,+\infty[\![} \bullet V^{\mathbb{F}}. \tag{85}$$

Furthermore $\Delta V^{\mathbb{G}} < 1$ if and only $\Delta V^{\mathbb{F}} < 1$.

(b) *If (66) holds, then*

$$\Theta_b(S - S^\tau, \mathbb{G}) = \left\{\varphi I_{]\!]\tau,+\infty[\![} : \varphi \in \Theta_b(I_{\{G_-<1\}} \bullet S, \mathbb{F})\right\}. \tag{86}$$

Here, for any filtration $\mathbb{H}$ and any $\mathbb{H}$-semimartingale X, the set $\Theta_b(X, \mathbb{H})$ is given by

$$\Theta_b(X, \mathbb{H}) := \{\varphi \text{ is } \mathbb{H}\textit{-predictable and bounded}: \ \varphi \Delta X > -1\}. \tag{87}$$

The proof of this lemma is relegated to Appendix C. Throughout the rest of this chapter, processes will be compared to each other in the following sense:

Definition 4.10. Let X and Y be two processes such that $X_0 = Y_0$. Then we denote

$$X \succeq Y \quad \text{if } X - Y \text{ is a non-decreasing process.} \tag{88}$$

Now we are in the stage of delivering the proof of Theorem 4.2.

Proof of Theorem 4.2. The proof is divided into two parts: The first part proves (b) $\iff$ (c) and the implication (c) $\Longrightarrow$ (a), while the second part focuses on proving (a) $\Longrightarrow$ (b).

Part 1. Remark that the implication (b) $\Longrightarrow$ (c) follows directly from Lemma 4.3(a), while the reverse implication is the consequence of a combination of Lemma 4.3(a) and the following fact: For any positive $\mathbb{H}$-supermartingale Z with $Z_0 = 1$, there exists a unique $M \in \mathcal{M}_{loc}(\mathbb{H})$ and a non-decreasing, RCLL and $\mathbb{H}$-predictable process V such that $V_0 = M_0 = 0$, $\Delta V < 1$, $\Delta M > -1$ and $Z = \mathcal{E}(M)\mathcal{E}(-V)$. For more details about this fact, we refer the reader to Ref. [20, Théorème (6.19)]. This ends the proof of (b) $\Longleftrightarrow$ (c). Thus, the rest of this part proves (c) $\Longrightarrow$ (a). To this end, we assume that assertion (c) holds. Then we note that, for any $\varphi \in \Theta_b(I_{\{G_-<1\}} \bullet S, \mathbb{F})$, $Z^{\mathbb{F}}\mathcal{E}(\varphi I_{\{G_-<1\}} \bullet S)$ is a positive $\mathbb{F}$-supermartingale, and

$$Z^{\mathbb{F}}\mathcal{E}(\varphi I_{\{G_-<1\}} \bullet S) = 1 + M - V,$$

where $M \in \mathcal{M}_{loc}(\mathbb{F})$, V is non-decreasing, RCLL and $\mathbb{F}$-predictable and $M_0 = V_0 = 0$. Furthermore, direct calculations show that

$$\begin{aligned}\frac{Z^{\mathbb{F}}\mathcal{E}(\varphi I_{\{G_-<1\}} \bullet S)}{(Z^{\mathbb{F}})^{\tau}\mathcal{E}(\varphi I_{\{G_-<1\}} \bullet S)^{\tau}} &= \frac{Z^{\mathbb{F}}}{(Z^{\mathbb{F}})^{\tau}}\mathcal{E}(\varphi I_{]\!]\tau,+\infty[\![} \bullet S)\\ &= 1 + I_{]\!]\tau,+\infty[\![} \bullet M - I_{]\!]\tau,+\infty[\![} \bullet V. \qquad (89)\end{aligned}$$

Then by combining this equality with Lemma 4.3(b) and the fact that

$$\frac{I_{]\!]\tau,+\infty[\![} \bullet V}{\mathcal{E}(m^{(a,\mathbb{G})})} = (I_{]\!]\tau,+\infty[\![} \bullet V) \bullet \frac{1}{\mathcal{E}(m^{(a,\mathbb{G})})} + \frac{1}{\mathcal{E}_-(m^{(a,\mathbb{G})})} I_{]\!]\tau,+\infty[\![} \bullet V$$

is a non-negative local submartingale, where $m^{(a,\mathbb{G})}$ is defined in (83), we deduce that

$$\frac{Z^{\mathbb{F}}/(Z^{\mathbb{F}})^{\tau}}{\mathcal{E}(m^{(a,\mathbb{G})})}\mathcal{E}(\varphi I_{]\!]\tau,+\infty[\![} \bullet S) \quad \text{is a non-negative } \mathbb{G}\text{-local supermartingale,}$$

and hence, this latter process is indeed a $\mathbb{G}$-supermartingale. Thus, the implication (c) $\Longrightarrow$ (a) follows immediately from this latter fact. This ends the first part.

Part 2. Here we prove (a) $\Longrightarrow$ (b). To this end, we assume that assertion (a) holds, and hence $Z^{\mathbb{G}} \in \mathcal{D}(S - S^{\tau}, \mathbb{G})$ with $(Z^{\mathbb{G}})^{\tau} = 1$.

Remark that there always exist $M \in \mathcal{M}_{0,loc}(\mathbb{F})$ and an RCLL, $\mathbb{F}$-predictable process with finite variation A such that $M_0 = A_0 = 0$,

$$\begin{aligned} S = S_0 + M + A + \sum I_{\{|\Delta S|>1\}}\Delta S \quad \text{and} \\ \max(|\Delta A|, |\Delta M|) \leq 1. \end{aligned} \tag{90}$$

By applying Proposition B.1 to the model $(S - S^\tau, \mathbb{G})$, we obtain the existence of $M^{\mathbb{G}} \in \mathcal{M}_{loc}(\mathbb{G})$ and an RCLL non-decreasing and $\mathbb{G}$-predictable process $V^{\mathbb{G}}$ such that

$$\begin{aligned} &Z^{\mathbb{G}} = \mathcal{E}(M^{\mathbb{G}})\mathcal{E}(-V^{\mathbb{G}}), \quad M_0^{\mathbb{G}} = V_0^{\mathbb{G}} = 0, \\ &\Delta V^{\mathbb{G}} < 1 \quad \text{and} \quad \Delta M^{\mathbb{G}} > -1 \end{aligned} \tag{91}$$

and

$$\begin{aligned} &\sup_{0<s\leq \cdot} |\Delta Y^{(\varphi,\mathbb{G})}| \in \mathcal{A}_{loc}(\mathbb{G}), \quad \frac{1}{1-\Delta V^{\mathbb{G}}} \bullet V^{\mathbb{G}} \succeq A^{(\varphi,M^{\mathbb{G}},\mathbb{G})}, \\ &\forall\ \varphi \in \Theta_b(S - S^{\mathbb{G}}, \mathbb{G}), \end{aligned} \tag{92}$$

where $A^{(\varphi,M^{\mathbb{G}},\mathbb{G})}$ is $\mathbb{G}$-predictable belonging to $\mathcal{A}_{loc}(\mathbb{G})$ and

$$\begin{aligned} Y^{(\varphi,\mathbb{G})} &:= \varphi \bullet (S - S^\tau) + [\varphi \bullet (S - S^\tau), M^{\mathbb{G}}], \\ &Y^{(\varphi,\mathbb{G})} - A^{(\varphi,M^{\mathbb{G}},\mathbb{G})} \in \mathcal{M}_{loc}(\mathbb{G}). \end{aligned} \tag{93}$$

Thus, by applying Theorem 3.4 to $M^{\mathbb{G}}$ and Lemma 4.9(a) to $V^{\mathbb{G}}$, we deduce the existence of a pair $(N^{\mathbb{F}}, V^{\mathbb{F}})$ such that $N^{\mathbb{F}} \in \mathcal{M}_{loc}(\mathbb{F})$ and $V^{\mathbb{F}}$ is RCLL non-decreasing and $\mathbb{F}$-predictable such that

$$\begin{aligned} &M^{\mathbb{G}} = \mathcal{T}^{(a)}(N^{\mathbb{F}}), \quad I_{\{G_-<1\}} \bullet N^{\mathbb{F}} = 0, \\ &\Delta N^{\mathbb{F}} I_{\{\widetilde{G}=1\}} = 0, \quad \Delta M^{\mathbb{G}} = \frac{1-G_-}{1-\widetilde{G}} \Delta N^{\mathbb{F}} I_{]\!]\tau,+\infty[\![}, \end{aligned} \tag{94}$$

$$V^{\mathbb{G}} = I_{]\!]\tau,+\infty[\![} \bullet V^{\mathbb{F}}, \quad I_{\{G_-=1\}} \bullet V^{\mathbb{F}} = 0 \quad \text{and} \quad \Delta V^{\mathbb{F}} < 1. \tag{95}$$

Thanks to Lemma 4.9(b), there is no loss of generality in considering $\varphi \in \Theta_b(I_{\{G_-<1\}} \bullet S, \mathbb{F})$ only. Therefore, for $\varphi \in \Theta_b(I_{\{G_-<1\}} \bullet S, \mathbb{F})$, we calculate $[M^{\mathbb{G}}, \varphi \bullet (S - S^{\tau})]$ using (94) and (90) as follows:

$$\begin{aligned}
&[M^{\mathbb{G}}, \varphi \bullet (S - S^{\tau})] \\
&\quad = [M^{\mathbb{G}}, \varphi \bullet (A - A^{\tau})] + \varphi \bullet [M^{\mathbb{G}}, M - M^{\tau}] \\
&\qquad + \sum \Delta M^{\mathbb{G}} \varphi \Delta S I_{\{|\Delta S|>1\}} I_{]\!]\tau,+\infty[\![} \\
&\quad = \varphi \bullet [M^{\mathbb{G}}, A] + \varphi \bullet [M, \mathcal{T}^{(a)}(N^{\mathbb{F}})] \\
&\qquad + \sum \frac{1 - G_-}{1 - \widetilde{G}} \Delta N^{\mathbb{F}} \varphi \Delta S I_{\{|\Delta S|>1\}} I_{]\!]\tau,+\infty[\![} \\
&\quad = \varphi \bullet [M^{\mathbb{G}}, A] + \frac{1 - G_-}{1 - \widetilde{G}} \varphi I_{]\!]\tau,+\infty[\![} \bullet [M, N^{\mathbb{F}}] \\
&\qquad + \sum \frac{1 - G_-}{1 - \widetilde{G}} \Delta N^{\mathbb{F}} \varphi \Delta S I_{\{|\Delta S|>1\}} I_{]\!]\tau,+\infty[\![}.
\end{aligned}$$

As both processes $[M^{\mathbb{G}}, A] = \Delta A \bullet M^{\mathbb{G}}$ and $M - M^{\tau} + (1 - G_-)^{-1} I_{]\!]\tau,+\infty[\![} \bullet \langle M, m \rangle^{\mathbb{F}}$ are $\mathbb{G}$-local martingales, due to Yoeurp's lemma (see Ref. [18, Théorème 36, Chapter VII, p. 245]) and Theorem 2.2(b), respectively, we derive

$$\begin{aligned}
Y^{(\varphi,\mathbb{G})} &:= \varphi \bullet (S - S^{\tau}) + [M^{\mathbb{G}}, \varphi \bullet (S - S^{\tau})] \\
&= -\frac{\varphi I_{]\!]\tau,+\infty[\![}}{1 - G_-} \bullet \langle M, m \rangle^{\mathbb{F}} + \varphi \bullet (A - A^{\tau}) \\
&\quad + \frac{1 - G_-}{1 - \widetilde{G}} \varphi I_{]\!]\tau,+\infty[\![} \bullet [M, N^{\mathbb{F}}] \\
&\quad + \sum \left(1 + \frac{1 - G_-}{1 - \widetilde{G}} \Delta N^{\mathbb{F}}\right) \varphi \Delta S I_{\{|\Delta S|>1\}} I_{]\!]\tau,+\infty[\![} \\
&\quad + \mathbb{G}\text{-local martingale.}
\end{aligned}$$

Therefore, from this equation, we deduce that $\sup_{0<s\leq \cdot} |\Delta Y^{(\varphi,\mathbb{G})}| \in \mathcal{A}_{loc}(\mathbb{G})$ if and only if

$$W := \sum \left(1 + \frac{1 - G_-}{1 - \widetilde{G}} \Delta N^{\mathbb{F}}\right) \varphi \Delta S I_{\{|\Delta S|>1\}} I_{]\!]\tau,+\infty[\![} \in \mathcal{A}_{loc}(\mathbb{G}) \tag{96}$$

and in this case we have

$$A^{(\varphi, M^{\mathbb{G}}, \mathbb{G})} = -\frac{\varphi I_{]\!]\tau,+\infty[\![}}{1-G_-} \bullet \langle M, m\rangle^{\mathbb{F}} + \varphi I_{]\!]\tau,+\infty[\![} \bullet A$$
$$+ \varphi I_{]\!]\tau,+\infty[\![} \bullet \langle M, N^{\mathbb{F}}\rangle^{\mathbb{F}} + W^{p,\mathbb{G}}. \qquad (97)$$

Remark that, in virtue of Lemma A.1, $W \in \mathcal{A}_{loc}(\mathbb{G})$ if and only if $U \in \mathcal{A}_{loc}(\mathbb{F})$ and

$$W = \frac{I_{]\!]\tau,+\infty[\![}}{1-\widetilde{G}} \bullet U, \quad \text{where}$$
$$U := \sum \left(1 - \widetilde{G} + (1-G_-)\Delta N^{\mathbb{F}}\right) \varphi \Delta S I_{\{|\Delta S|>1\}} I_{\{G_-<1\}}. \qquad (98)$$

Put

$$K^{\mathbb{F}} := N^{\mathbb{F}} - (1-G_-)^{-1} I_{\{G_-<1\}} \bullet m \in \mathcal{M}_{loc}(\mathbb{F}), \qquad (99)$$

and on the one hand we obtain

$$K^{\mathbb{G}} = \mathcal{T}^{(a)}(N^{\mathbb{F}}) = \mathcal{T}^{(a)}(K^{\mathbb{F}}) + (1-G_-)^{-1} I_{]\!]\tau,+\infty[\![} \bullet \mathcal{T}^{(a)}(m). \quad (100)$$

This proves (67). On the other hand, we remark that $\Delta M^{\mathbb{G}} > -1$ if and only if

$$]\!]\tau, +\infty[\![\subset \left\{ \frac{1-G_-}{1-\widetilde{G}} \Delta N^{\mathbb{F}} > -1 \right\},$$

which is equivalent to

$$]\!]\tau, +\infty[\![\subset \left\{ 1 - \frac{\Delta m}{1-G_-} I_{\{G_-<1\}} + \Delta N^{\mathbb{F}} > 0 \right\} = \left\{ 1 + \Delta K^{\mathbb{F}} > 0 \right\}.$$

By passing to indicator and taking the $\mathbb{F}$-optional projection, we get

$$1 - \widetilde{G} \le I_{\{1+\Delta K^{\mathbb{F}}>0\}}, \quad \text{which implies that}$$
$$\{\widetilde{G} < 1\} \subset \{1 + \Delta K^{\mathbb{F}} > 0\}. \qquad (101)$$

Due to $\{\widetilde{G} = 1 > G_-\} = \emptyset$, we easily prove that

$$\{\widetilde{G} = 1\} \subset \{\Delta K^{\mathbb{F}} = 0\} \subset \{1 + \Delta K^{\mathbb{F}} > 0\}.$$

Thus, by combining this latter fact with (101), we deduce that we always have

$$\Delta K^{\mathbb{F}} > -1. \tag{102}$$

Direct calculations show that $U \in \mathcal{A}_{loc}(\mathbb{F})$ if and only if $\sup_{0<s\leq \cdot} |\Delta Y^{(\varphi,\mathbb{F})}| \in \mathcal{A}_{loc}(\mathbb{F})$, where

$$Y^{(\varphi,\mathbb{F})} := \varphi I_{\{G_-<1\}} \bullet S + [K^{\mathbb{F}}, I_{\{G_-<1\}} \bullet S].$$

Furthermore, we derive

$$U = (1-G_-) \bullet \sum \left(1 + \Delta K^{\mathbb{F}}\right) \varphi I_{\{G_-<1\}} \Delta S I_{\{|\Delta S|>1\}} \quad \text{and}$$

$$A^{(\varphi,M^{\mathbb{G}},\mathbb{G})} = I_{]\!]\tau,+\infty[\![} \bullet A^{(\varphi,K^{\mathbb{F}},\mathbb{F})}. \tag{103}$$

By inserting this latter equality and (95) in the second condition of (93), we get

$$\frac{1}{1-\Delta V^{\mathbb{F}}} \bullet V^{\mathbb{F}} \succeq A^{(\varphi,K^{\mathbb{F}},\mathbb{F})} \quad \text{for any } \varphi \in \Theta_b(I_{\{G_-<1\}} \bullet S, \mathbb{F}).$$

Thus, by combining this with (102), we conclude that

$$Z := \mathcal{E}(K^{\mathbb{F}})\mathcal{E}(-V^{\mathbb{F}}) \in \mathcal{D}(I_{\{G_-<1\}} \bullet S, \mathbb{F}). \tag{104}$$

Therefore, assertion (b) follows immediately from combining (95), (100) and (104). This ends the second part and the proof of the theorem is complete.

Proof of Theorem 4.4. It is clear that the proof of (b) $\Longleftrightarrow$ (c) and the implication (c) $\Longrightarrow$ (a) follow the same footsteps as in the proof of the corresponding claims in Theorem 4.2 (see part 1). Hence, the details for these will be omitted herein and the rest of this proof focuses on (a) $\Longrightarrow$ (b). To this end, we remark that due to Lemma A.2, for any $\mathbb{G}$-predictable process $\varphi^{\mathbb{G}}$ satisfying $0 < \varphi^{\mathbb{G}} \leq 1$, there exists an $\mathbb{F}$-predictable process φ such that $0 < \varphi \leq 1$ and $\varphi^{\mathbb{G}} I_{]\!]\tau,+\infty[\![} = \varphi I_{]\!]\tau,+\infty[\![}$. Suppose that assertion (a) holds. Hence there exists an $\mathbb{F}$-predictable process φ such that $0 < \varphi \leq 1$ and $\mathcal{E}(K^{\mathbb{G}})(\varphi I_{]\!]\tau,+\infty[\![} \bullet S)$ is a $\mathbb{G}$-local martingale. Then, using Itô's computation rule, and using the notation and calculations in the proof of Theorem 4.2 part 2, we deduce that $Y^{(\varphi,\mathbb{G})}$ is a $\mathbb{G}$-local martingale or equivalently $W \in \mathcal{A}_{loc}(\mathbb{G})$ and

$$\begin{aligned}
0 &= -\frac{\varphi}{1-G_-} I_{]\!]\tau,+\infty[\![} \bullet \langle M, m\rangle^{\mathbb{F}} + \varphi \bullet (A - A^\tau) \\
&\quad + \frac{\varphi}{(1-G_-)^2} I_{]\!]\tau,+\infty[\![} \bullet \langle M, N^{\mathbb{F}}\rangle^{\mathbb{F}} \\
&= \varphi \bullet (A - A^\tau) + \frac{\varphi}{(1-G_-)^2} I_{]\!]\tau,+\infty[\![} \bullet \langle M, N^{\mathbb{F}} - (1-G_-)\bullet m\rangle^{\mathbb{F}}.
\end{aligned} \tag{105}$$

Thus, we deduce that $U \in \mathcal{A}_{loc}(\mathbb{F})$ and by taking the $\mathbb{F}$-predictable projections on both sides of the above equality, we get

$$\begin{aligned}
0 &\equiv \varphi I_{\{G_-<1\}} \bullet A + \varphi \bullet \langle I_{\{G_-<1\}} \bullet M, K^{\mathbb{F}}\rangle^{\mathbb{F}}, \\
K^{\mathbb{F}} &:= \frac{I_{\{G_-<1\}}}{(1-G_-)^2} \bullet (N^{\mathbb{F}} - (1-G_-)\bullet m).
\end{aligned} \tag{106}$$

This proves that $Y^{(\varphi,\mathbb{F})}$ is an $\mathbb{F}$-local martingale. Hence, by combining this latter fact with $\Delta K^{\mathbb{F}} > -1$ (which can be proved using similar arguments as in the proof of Theorem 4.2 part 2), we deduce that $\mathcal{E}(K^{\mathbb{F}}) \in \mathcal{Z}_{loc}(I_{\{G_-<1\}} \bullet S, \mathbb{F})$, and assertion (b) follows immediately. This ends the proof of the theorem.

Appendix

A $\mathbb{G}$-Processes versus $\mathbb{F}$-Processes

The following lemma connects $\mathbb{G}$-compensators with $\mathbb{F}$-compensators and is given in Ref. [2, Lemma 3.2-(b)]:

Lemma A.1. *Suppose that τ is an honest time. Then for any $\mathbb{F}$-adapted process V with locally integrable variation, one has*

$$I_{]\!]\tau,+\infty[\![} \bullet V^{p,\mathbb{G}} = I_{]\!]\tau,+\infty[\![}(1-G_-)^{-1} \bullet \left((1-\widetilde{G})\bullet V\right)^{p,\mathbb{F}}. \tag{A.1}$$

We recall the following lemma from Ref. [22, Proposition 5.3], see also Ref. [2, Proposition A.5]:

Lemma A.2. *Suppose that τ is an honest time and let H be a process. Then the following hold:*

(a) *If H is $\mathbb{G}$-optional, then there exists an $\mathbb{F}$-optional process $H^{\mathbb{F}}$ such that*

$$HI_{]\!]\tau,\infty[\![} = H^{\mathbb{F}} I_{]\!]\tau,\infty[\![}. \tag{A.2}$$

(b) *If H is $\mathbb{G}$-predictable, then there exists two $\mathbb{F}$-predictable processes J and K such that*

$$H = JI_{[\![0,\tau]\!]} + KI_{]\!]\tau,\infty[\![}. \tag{A.3}$$

If furthermore $C_1 < H \leq C_2$ hold for two constants $C_1 < C_2$, then both processes J and K satisfy the same inequalities.

B Characterization of Deflators

Here we recall Ref. [15, Proposition 3.1], which is an important result on the characterization of deflators.

Proposition B.1. *Let X be an $\mathbb{H}$-semimartingale and Z be a process. Then the following hold:*

(a) *Z is a deflator for $(X, \mathbb{H})$ if and only if there exists a unique pair (N, V) such that $N \in \mathcal{M}_{loc}(\mathbb{H})$, V is non-decreasing RCLL and $\mathbb{H}$-predictable,*

$$\begin{aligned} &Z := Z_0\mathcal{E}(N)\mathcal{E}(-V), \quad N_0 = V_0 = 0,\\ &\Delta N > -1, \quad \Delta V < 1, \end{aligned} \tag{B.1}$$

$$\begin{aligned} &\sup_{0<s\leq\cdot} |\Delta Y^{(\varphi)}| \in \mathcal{A}_{loc}(\mathbb{H}) \quad and \quad \frac{1}{1-\Delta V}\cdot V \succeq A^{(\varphi,N,\mathbb{H})},\\ &\quad \forall \varphi \in \Theta_b(X, \mathbb{H}). \end{aligned} \tag{B.2}$$

Here $Y^{(\varphi)} := \varphi{\bullet}X + [\varphi{\bullet}X, N]$, $A^{(\varphi,N,\mathbb{H})} \in \mathcal{A}_{loc}(\mathbb{H})$ is $\mathbb{H}$-predictable such that $Y^{(\varphi)} - A^{(\varphi,N,\mathbb{H})} \in \mathcal{M}_{loc}(\mathbb{H})$, and $\Theta_b(X, \mathbb{H})$ is defined in (87).

(b) *Z is a local martingale deflator for $(X, \mathbb{H})$ (i.e., $Z \in \mathcal{Z}_{loc}(X, \mathbb{H})$) if and only if there exist a real-valued positive and bounded $\mathbb{H}$-predictable process φ and a unique $N \in \mathcal{M}_{loc}(\mathbb{H})$ such that $N_0 = 0$,*

$$Z := Z_0\mathcal{E}(N), \quad \Delta N > -1,$$

$$\sup_{0<s\leq \cdot} |\varphi_s \Delta X_s|(1 + \Delta N_s) \in \mathcal{A}_{loc}(\mathbb{H}), \tag{B.3}$$

$$\varphi \bullet X + [\varphi \bullet X, N] \in \mathcal{M}_{loc}(\mathbb{H}). \tag{B.4}$$

C Proofs of Lemmas 3.10, 3.11, 4.3, and 4.9

Proof of Lemma 3.10. This proof is achieved in three parts:

Part 1. This part proves assertion (a). Thanks to Ref. [22, Proposition 5.1], we recall that τ being an honest time is equivalent to $\widetilde{G}_\tau = 1$ P-a.s. on $\{\tau < +\infty\}$. Thus, we derive

$$E\Big[I_{]\!]\tau,+\infty[\![} \bullet D^{o,\mathbb{F}}_\infty\Big] = E\Big[(1 - \widetilde{G}) \bullet D^{o,\mathbb{F}}_\infty\Big] = E\Big[(1 - \widetilde{G}_\tau) I_{\{\tau<+\infty\}}\Big] = 0.$$

The first equality follows directly from the definition of the optional projection, while the second equality is due to the definition of $D^{o,\mathbb{F}}$, see [18, Definition 73] with optional process $A = D$.

Part 2. This part proves assertion (b). Consider $M \in \mathcal{M}_{0,loc}(\mathbb{F})$ such that

$$I_{\{G_-=1\}} \bullet M = I_{\{\widetilde{G}=1\}} \Delta M = 0, \tag{C.1}$$

and $\mathcal{T}^{(a)}(M) = 0$. Then, in virtue of the second condition in (C.1) and the definition of $\mathcal{T}^{(a)}$, we get

$$0 = \mathcal{T}^{(a)}(M) = I_{]\!]\tau,+\infty[\![} \bullet M + \frac{I_{]\!]\tau,+\infty[\![}}{1 - \widetilde{G}} \bullet [M, m].$$

Thus, this yields to

$$\frac{1 - G_-}{1 - \widetilde{G}} I_{]\!]\tau,+\infty[\![} \bullet [M, m] = [\mathcal{T}^{(a)}(M), m] = 0,$$

and hence $I_{]\!]\tau,+\infty[\![} \bullet M = 0$. Therefore, by combining this with the two conditions (C.1) and

$$E\left[(I_{\{\widetilde{G}<1\}} \bullet [M,M])_\infty\right] = E\left[\int_\tau^\infty \frac{1}{1-\widetilde{G}} d[M,M]_s\right] = 0,$$

we conclude that $M \equiv 0$. This ends the proof of assertion (b), and the proof of the lemma is complete.

Proof of Lemma 3.11. Put $H^{\mathbb{G}} := (1-G_-)^{-1} I_{]\!]\tau,+\infty[\![}$ and consider $N \in \mathcal{M}_{loc}(\mathbb{F})$ satisfying

$$I_{\{G_-=1\}} \bullet N \equiv 0 \quad \text{and} \quad I_{\{\widetilde{G}=1\}} \Delta N \equiv 0.$$

Thus, in virtue of the latter condition and the definition of $\mathcal{T}^{(a)}$, we derive

$$\begin{aligned}(H^{\mathbb{G}})^2 \bullet [\mathcal{T}^{(a)}(N), \mathcal{T}^{(a)}(N)] &= \frac{I_{]\!]\tau,+\infty[\![}}{(1-G_-)^2} \bullet [\mathcal{T}^{(a)}(N), \mathcal{T}^{(a)}(N)] \\ &= \frac{I_{]\!]\tau,+\infty[\![}}{(1-\widetilde{G})^2} \bullet [N,N]. \end{aligned} \tag{C.2}$$

Therefore, due to this equality, we get

$$E\left[\int_0^\infty (H_s^{\mathbb{G}})^2 d[\mathcal{T}^{(a)}(N), \mathcal{T}^{(a)}(N)]_s\right] = E\left[\int_0^\infty \frac{I_{\{\widetilde{G}_s<1\}}}{1-\widetilde{G}_s} d[N,N]_s\right].$$

Thus, assertion (a) follows immediately from this equality. Assertion (b) is a consequence of a combination of Ref. [20, Lemma 2.61, Chapter 2] with $\Delta\mathcal{T}^{(a)}(N) = I_{]\!]\tau,+\infty[\![}(1-G_-)\Delta N/(1-\widetilde{G})$, and

$$\begin{aligned} E&\left[\int_0^\infty H_s^{\mathbb{G}} d\mathrm{Var_s}(\mathcal{T}^{(a)}(\mathrm{N}))\right] \\ &= E\left[\sum_{s>0} H_s^{\mathbb{G}} |\Delta\mathcal{T}_s^{(a)}(N)|\right] = E\left[\sum_{s>0} \frac{|\Delta N_s|}{1-\widetilde{G}_s} I_{\{s>\tau\}}\right] \\ &= E\left[\mathrm{Var}_\infty(\mathrm{N})\right]. \end{aligned}$$

The rest of this proof focuses on proving assertion (c). It is well known that $H^{\mathbb{G}}$ is $\mathcal{T}^{(a)}(N)$-integrable and $H^{\mathbb{G}} \bullet \mathcal{T}^{(a)}(N) \in \mathcal{M}_{loc}(\mathbb{G})$ if and only if $\sqrt{(H^{\mathbb{G}})^2 \bullet [\mathcal{T}^{(a)}(N), \mathcal{T}^{(a)}(N)]} \in \mathcal{A}^+_{loc}(\mathbb{G})$, which is equivalent to

$$\sqrt{I_{]\!]\tau,+\infty[\![}(1-\widetilde{G})^{-2} \bullet [N,N]} \in \mathcal{A}^+_{loc}(\mathbb{G}), \tag{C.3}$$

due to (C.2). Then by combining $[N,N] = [N^c, N^c] + \sum(\Delta N)^2$, where N^c is the continuous local martingale part of N, and [20, Proposition 2.56 and Corollary 2.57-(a), Chapter 2], we deduce that (C.3) is equivalent to

$$\frac{I_{]\!]\tau,+\infty[\![}}{(1-G_-)^2} \bullet [N^c, N^c] + \sum \frac{(1-\widetilde{G})^{-2}(\Delta N)^2}{1+(1-\widetilde{G})^{-1}|\Delta N|} I_{]\!]\tau,+\infty[\![} \in \mathcal{A}^+_{loc}(\mathbb{G}).$$

Thanks to Ref. [2, Lemma 3.2-(c)], this latter condition is equivalent to

$$\begin{aligned}
&\frac{I_{\{G_-<1\}}}{1-G_-} \bullet [N^c, N^c] + \sum \frac{(\Delta N)^2 I_{\{\widetilde{G}<1\}}}{1-\widetilde{G}+|\Delta N|} \\
&\quad = \frac{I_{\{\widetilde{G}<1\}}}{1-\widetilde{G}+|\Delta N|} \bullet [N,N] \in \mathcal{A}^+_{loc}(\mathbb{F})
\end{aligned}$$

or equivalently $N \in \mathbb{M}_{loc}(\mathbb{F}, \tau)$. This proves assertion (c) and ends the proof of the lemma.

Proof of Lemma 4.3. (1) Here we prove assertion (c). Thanks to (66) and $]\!]\tau, \infty[\![\subset \{G = \widetilde{G}\}$ (for details about this latter fact, we refer the reader to Ref. [17, XX.79]), we derive

$$\mathcal{T}^{(a)}(X) = I_{]\!]\tau,+\infty[\![} \bullet X + \frac{1}{1-\widetilde{G}} I_{]\!]\tau,+\infty[\![} \bullet [m, X]. \tag{C.4}$$

Hence, direct calculation yields

$$\begin{aligned}
\left[\mathcal{T}^{(a)}(X), Y\right] &= \left[I_{]\!]\tau,+\infty[\![} \bullet X + \frac{1}{1-\widetilde{G}} I_{]\!]\tau,\infty[\![} \bullet [m, X], Y\right] \\
&= I_{]\!]\tau,+\infty[\![} \bullet [X,Y] + \frac{1}{1-\widetilde{G}} I_{]\!]\tau,\infty[\![} \Delta m \bullet [X,Y] \\
&= \left(1 + \frac{\widetilde{G}-G_-}{1-\widetilde{G}}\right) I_{]\!]\tau,+\infty[\![} \bullet [X,Y] \\
&= \frac{1-G_-}{1-\widetilde{G}} I_{]\!]\tau,\infty[\![} \bullet [X,Y] = \left[X, \mathcal{T}^{(a)}(Y)\right].
\end{aligned}$$

This proves assertion (c).

(2) To prove assertion (a), we recall that

$$1/\mathcal{E}(X) = \mathcal{E}\left(-X + (1+\Delta X)^{-1} \bullet [X, X]\right)$$

holds for any semimartingale X such that $1+\Delta X > 0$, and this fact is a consequence of Yor's formula. Then, by combining this equality and $\Delta m = \widetilde{G} - G_-$, we derive

$$\begin{aligned}
&\frac{1}{\mathcal{E}\left(-I_{]\!]\tau,\infty[\![}(1-G_-)^{-1} \bullet m\right)} \\
&\quad = \mathcal{E}\left(\frac{1}{1-G_-} I_{]\!]\tau,\infty[\![} \bullet m + \frac{(1-G_-)^{-2}}{1 - \frac{1\!\!1_{]\!]\tau,\infty[\![}\Delta m}{1-G_-}} I_{]\!]\tau,\infty[\![} \bullet [m, m]\right) \\
&\quad = \mathcal{E}\left(\frac{I_{]\!]\tau,\infty[\![}}{1-G_-} \bullet m + \frac{I_{]\!]\tau,\infty[\![}}{(1-G_-)(1-\widetilde{G})} \bullet [m, m]\right) \\
&\quad = \mathcal{E}\left((1-G_-)^{-1} I_{]\!]\tau,\infty[\![} \bullet \mathcal{T}^{(a)}(m)\right).
\end{aligned} \tag{C.5}$$

Therefore, by using this equality and Yor's formula afterwards, for any X we obtain

$$\begin{aligned}
&\frac{\mathcal{E}\left(I_{]\!]\tau,\infty[\![} \bullet X\right)}{\mathcal{E}\left(-I_{]\!]\tau,\infty[\![}\frac{1}{1-G_-} \bullet m\right)} \\
&\quad = \mathcal{E}\left(I_{]\!]\tau,\infty[\![} \bullet X\right) \mathcal{E}\left((1-G_-)^{-1} I_{]\!]\tau,\infty[\![} \bullet \mathcal{T}^{(a)}(m)\right) \\
&\quad = \mathcal{E}\Big(I_{]\!]\tau,\infty[\![} \bullet X + (1-G_-)^{-1} I_{]\!]\tau,\infty[\![} \bullet \mathcal{T}^{(a)}(m) \\
&\qquad + \frac{I_{]\!]\tau,\infty[\![}}{1-G_-} \bullet \left[X, \mathcal{T}^{(a)}(m)\right]\Big) \\
&\quad = \mathcal{E}\left(I_{]\!]\tau,\infty[\![} \bullet X + (1-G_-)^{-1} I_{]\!]\tau,\infty[\![} \bullet \mathcal{T}^{(a)}(m) + \frac{I_{]\!]\tau,\infty[\![}}{1-\widetilde{G}} \bullet [X, m]\right) \\
&\quad = \mathcal{E}\left(\mathcal{T}^{(a)}(X) + (1-G_-)^{-1} I_{]\!]\tau,\infty[\![} \bullet \mathcal{T}^{(a)}(m)\right).
\end{aligned}$$

The third equality above follows from assertion (c). This ends the proof of assertion (a).

(3) Here we prove assertion (b). Due to the integration by part and (C.5), we get

$$\begin{aligned}
M^{\mathbb{G}} :=& \frac{I_{]\!]\tau,\infty[\![} \bullet K^{\mathbb{F}}}{\mathcal{E}\left(-I_{]\!]\tau,\infty[\![}(1-G_-)^{-1} \bullet m\right)} \\
=& \frac{(I_{]\!]\tau,\infty[\![} \bullet K)^{\mathbb{F}}_-}{(1-G_-)\mathcal{E}_-(-I_{]\!]\tau,\infty[\![}(1-G_-)^{-1} \bullet m)} \bullet \mathcal{T}^{(a)}(m) \\
&+ \frac{I_{]\!]\tau,\infty[\![}}{\mathcal{E}_-(-I_{]\!]\tau,\infty[\![}(1-G_-)^{-1} \bullet m)} \bullet K^{\mathbb{F}} \\
&+ \frac{I_{]\!]\tau,\infty[\![}}{(1-G_-)\mathcal{E}_-(-I_{]\!]\tau,\infty[\![}(1-G_-)^{-1} \bullet m)} \bullet \left[K^{\mathbb{F}}, \mathcal{T}^{(a)}(m)\right] \\
=& \frac{(I_{]\!]\tau,\infty[\![} \bullet K)^{\mathbb{F}}_-}{(1-G_-)\mathcal{E}_-(-I_{]\!]\tau,\infty[\![}(1-G_-)^{-1} \bullet m)} \bullet \mathcal{T}^{(a)}(m) \\
&+ \frac{I_{]\!]\tau,\infty[\![}}{\mathcal{E}_-(-I_{]\!]\tau,\infty[\![}(1-G_-)^{-1} \bullet m)} \bullet K^{\mathbb{F}} \\
&+ \frac{I_{]\!]\tau,\infty[\![}}{(1-\widetilde{G})\mathcal{E}_-(-I_{]\!]\tau,\infty[\![}(1-G_-)^{-1} \bullet m)} \bullet \left[K^{\mathbb{F}}, m\right] \\
=& \frac{(I_{]\!]\tau,\infty[\![} \bullet K)^{\mathbb{F}}_-}{(1-G_-)\mathcal{E}_-(-I_{]\!]\tau,\infty[\![}(1-G_-)^{-1} \bullet m)} \bullet \mathcal{T}^{(a)}(m) \\
&+ \frac{I_{]\!]\tau,\infty[\![}}{\mathcal{E}_-(-I_{]\!]\tau,\infty[\![}(1-G_-)^{-1} \bullet m)} \bullet \mathcal{T}^{(a)}(K^{\mathbb{F}}).
\end{aligned}$$

Thus, in virtue of Theorem 2.2, this proves $M^{\mathbb{G}} \in \mathcal{M}_{loc}(\mathbb{G})$, and the proof of the lemma is complete.

Proof of Lemma 4.9. This proof has two parts where we prove assertions (a) and (b), respectively:

Part 1. We start proving the uniqueness of the process $V^{\mathbb{F}}$ satisfying (85). This follows from the fact that if V is an $\mathbb{F}$-predictable process with finite variation such that

$$V_0 = 0, \quad I_{\{G_-=1\}} \bullet V = 0 \quad \text{and} \quad I_{]\!]\tau,+\infty[\![} \bullet V = 0, \tag{C.6}$$

then $V \equiv 0$. To prove this latter fact, we take the dual predictable projection in both sides of the third condition and get $(1-G_-)\bullet V =$

0 or equivalently $I_{\{G_-<1\}} \bullet V \equiv 0$. Thus, by combining this with the second condition in (C.6), we deduce that $V = I_{\{G_-=1\}} \bullet V + I_{\{G_-<1\}} \bullet V = 0$. This proves the uniqueness of $V^{\mathbb{F}}$. To prove the last statement of assertion (a), we remark that due to the second equality in (85) we get $\Delta V^{\mathbb{G}} = I_{]\!]\tau,+\infty[\![}\Delta V^{\mathbb{F}}$. Thus, $\Delta V^{\mathbb{G}} < 1$ if and only if $I_{]\!]\tau,+\infty[\![} \leq I_{\{\Delta V^{\mathbb{F}}<1\}}$. By taking the $\mathbb{F}$-predictable projection on both sides of the latter inequality, we get

$$1 - G_- \leq I_{\{\Delta V^{\mathbb{F}}<1\}}$$

or equivalently $\{G_- < 1\} \subset \{\Delta V^{\mathbb{F}} < 1\}$. By combining this with

$$\{G_- = 1\} \subset \{\Delta V^{\mathbb{F}} = 0\} \subset \{\Delta V^{\mathbb{F}} < 1\},$$

we conclude that $\Delta V^{\mathbb{F}} < 1$ always hold. This proves that $\Delta V^{\mathbb{G}} < 1$ implies $\Delta V^{\mathbb{F}} < 1$, while the reverse inclusion is obvious from the second equality in (85). This ends the proof of the last statement of assertion (a). Thus, the rest of this part focuses on the existence of the process $V^{\mathbb{F}}$ satisfying $V_0^{\mathbb{F}} = 0$ and (85). To this end, remark that there is no loss of generality in assuming that the process $V^{\mathbb{G}}$ is bounded. Thus, in virtue of Ref. [18, Théorème 47, p.119 and Théorème 59, 268] and the non-decreasiness of $V^{\mathbb{G}}$, the process $S^{\mathbb{F}} :=^{o,\mathbb{F}} (V^{\mathbb{G}})$ is an RCLL and bounded $\mathbb{F}$-submartingale. Thus, on the one hand, we deduce the existence of $M \in \mathcal{M}_{loc}(\mathbb{F})$ and an RCLL non-decreasing and $\mathbb{F}$-predictable process U such that

$$S^{\mathbb{F}} := {}^{o,\mathbb{F}}(V^{\mathbb{G}}) = S_0^{\mathbb{F}} + M + U \quad \text{and} \quad M_0 = U_0 = 0. \tag{C.7}$$

On the other hand, as $V^{\mathbb{G}}$ is a $\mathbb{G}$-predictable process such that $(V^{\mathbb{G}})^{\tau} \equiv 0$, we apply Lemma A.2 and get the existence of an $\mathbb{F}$-predictable process V such that

$$V^{\mathbb{G}} = V^{\mathbb{G}} I_{]\!]\tau,+\infty[\![} = V I_{]\!]\tau,+\infty[\![}. \tag{C.8}$$

By taking the $\mathbb{F}$-optional projection on both sides of this equality, we obtain $S^{\mathbb{F}} = V(1 - \widetilde{G})$, which yields $\{\widetilde{G} = 1\} \subset \{S^{\mathbb{F}} = 0\}$. Thus, by combing this fact with (C.8), (C.7) and Lemma 4.8, we derive

$$\begin{aligned} V^{\mathbb{G}} &= VI_{]\!]\tau,+\infty[\![} = \frac{S^{\mathbb{F}}}{1-\widetilde{G}} I_{]\!]\tau,+\infty[\![} = \frac{S^{\mathbb{F}}}{1-G} I_{]\!]\tau,+\infty[\![} = \frac{S^{\mathbb{F}} I_{]\!]\tau,+\infty[\![}}{(1-G_\tau)X^G} \\ &= \frac{I_{]\!]\tau,+\infty[\![} \bullet S^{\mathbb{F}}}{(1-G_\tau)X^G} = \frac{I_{]\!]\tau,+\infty[\![} \bullet M}{(1-G_\tau)X^G} + \frac{I_{]\!]\tau,+\infty[\![} \bullet U}{(1-G_\tau)X^G} \\ &= \frac{(I_{]\!]\tau,+\infty[\![} \bullet M)(1-G_\tau)^{-1}}{X^G} + (I_{]\!]\tau,+\infty[\![} \bullet U) \bullet \frac{(1-G_\tau)^{-1}}{X^G} \\ &\quad + \frac{(1-G_\tau)^{-1}}{X^G_-} I_{]\!]\tau,+\infty[\![} \bullet U \\ &= \underbrace{\frac{(I_{]\!]\tau,+\infty[\![} \bullet M)(1-G_\tau)^{-1}}{X^G} + (I_{]\!]\tau,+\infty[\![} \bullet U) \bullet \frac{(1-G_\tau)^{-1}}{X^G}}_{\text{is a } \mathbb{G}\text{-local martingale}} \\ &\quad + \frac{1}{1-G_-} I_{]\!]\tau,+\infty[\![} \bullet U. \end{aligned} \tag{C.9}$$

Therefore, as both processes $V^{\mathbb{G}}$ and $(1-G_-)^{-1} I_{]\!]\tau,+\infty[\![} \bullet U$ are non-decreasing and $\mathbb{G}$-predictable, we conclude that the $\mathbb{G}$-local martingale part in (C.9) is null. Hence, we obtain

$$V^{\mathbb{G}} = \frac{I_{]\!]\tau,+\infty[\![}}{1-G_-} \bullet U.$$

Therefore, by putting $V^{\mathbb{F}} = (1-G_-)^{-1} I_{\{G_-<1\}} \bullet U$, the proof of assertion (a) is complete.

Part 2. Due to Lemma A.2, remark that $\varphi^{\mathbb{G}} \in \Theta_b(S - S^\tau, \mathbb{G})$ if and only if there exists an $\mathbb{F}$-predictable and bounded process φ such that

$$\varphi I_{]\!]\tau,+\infty[\![} = \varphi^{\mathbb{G}} I_{]\!]\tau,+\infty[\![}.$$

Thus, due to $]\!]\tau,+\infty[\![\subset \{G_- < 1\}$, the above equality implies that

$$\begin{aligned} &\varphi I_{\{G_-<1\}} \Delta S > -1 \quad \text{on} \quad]\!]\tau,+\infty[\![\quad \text{or equivalently} \\ &I_{]\!]\tau,+\infty[\![} \leq I_{\{\varphi I_{\{G_-<1\}} \Delta S > -1\}}. \end{aligned}$$

Then by taking the $\mathbb{F}$-optional projection on both sides of the latter inequality, we get

$$1 - \widetilde{G} \le I_{\{\varphi I_{\{G_- <1\}}\Delta S > -1\}} \quad \text{or equivalently}$$
$$\{\widetilde{G} < 1\} \subset \{\varphi I_{\{G_- <1\}}\Delta S > -1\}.$$

By combing this latter inclusion with the fact that $\{\widetilde{G} = 1\} \subset \{G_- < 1\} \subset \{\varphi I_{\{G_- <1\}}\Delta S > -1\}$, which follows from the condition $\{\widetilde{G} = 1 > G_-\} = \emptyset$ in (66), we deduce that φ is an $\mathbb{F}$-predictable and bounded process satisfying

$$\varphi I_{\{G_- <1\}}\Delta S > -1.$$

This proves that $\varphi \in \Theta_b(I_{\{G_- <1\}} \cdot S, \mathbb{F})$, and the proof of the lemma is complete.

Acknowledgments

This research is fully supported by the Natural Sciences and Engineering Research Council of Canada, Grant NSERC RGPIN-2019-04779. The authors would like to thank Safa' Alsheyab, Jun Deng and Michèle Vanmaele for several comments/suggestions, for fruitful discussions on the topic and/or for providing important and useful related references. The authors are very grateful to an anonymous referee for the careful reading, important suggestions and pertinent comments that helped improve this chapter.

References

[1] A. Aksamit, T. Choulli, and Jeanblanc, M. On an optional semimartingale decomposition and the existence of a deflator in an enlarged filtration. In Donati-Martin, C. and Lejay, A. and Rouault, A. (eds.), *Memoriam Marc Yor — Séminaire de Probabilités XLVII*, 187–218, Springer International Publishing AG Switzerland, 2015.

[2] A. Aksamit, T. Choulli, J. Deng, and M. Jeanblanc. No-arbitrage under a class of honest times. *Finance and Stochastics*, 22(1):127–159, 2018.

[3] F. Alharbi and T. Choulli. Log-optimal portfolio after a random time: Existence, description and sensitivity analysis. arXiv:2204.03798, 2022.

[4] J. Azéma, Th. Jeulin, F. Knight, and M. Yor. *Lecture Notes in Math.* 1557, 27:133–158, 1993.

[5] M. T. Barlow. Study of a filtration expanded to include an honest time. *Probability Theory and Related Fields*, 44(4):307–323, 1978.

[6] A. Bélanger, S. E. Shreve, and D. Wong. A general framework for pricing credit risk. *Mathematical Finance*, 14(3):317–350, 2004.

[7] T. Bielecki and M. Rutkowski. *Credit Risk: Modeling, Valuation and Hedging.* Springer Finance, Berlin, 2002.

[8] C. Blanchet-Scalliet and M. Jeanblanc. Hazard rate for credit risk and hedging defaultable contingent claims. *Finance and Stochastics*, 8(1):145–159, 2002.

[9] T. Choulli, C. Stricker, and L. Krawczyk. On Fefferman and Burkholder-Davis-Gundy inequalities for $\mathcal{E}$-martingales. *Probability Theory and Related Fields*, 113:571–597, 1999.

[10] T. Choulli, C. Stricker, and J. Li. Minimal Hellinger martingale measures of order q. *Finance and Stochastics*, 11(3):399–427, 2007.

[11] T. Choulli and J. Deng. Structure conditions under progressively added information. *Theory of Probability and its Applications*, 65(3):418–453, 2020.

[12] T. Choulli, C. Daveloose, and M. Vanmaele. A martingale representation theorem and valuation of defaultable securities. *Mathematical Finance*, 30(4):1527–1564, 2020.

[13] T. Choulli and S. Yansori. Log-optimal portfolio without NFLVR: Existence, complete characterization, and duality. *Theory of Probability and its Applications*, 67(2):229–245, 2022.

[14] T. Choulli and S. Yansori. Log-optimal and numéraire portfolios for market models stopped at a random time. *Finance and Stochastics*, 26:535–585, 2022.

[15] T. Choulli and S. Yansori. Explicit description of all deflators for market models under random horizon with applications to NFLVR. *Stochastic Processes and their Applications*, 151:230–264, 2022.

[16] F. Delbaen and W. Schachermayer. Attainable claims with pth moments. *Annales de l'I. H. P., section B*, 32(6):743–763, 1996.

[17] M. Dellacherie, B. Maisonneuve, and P.-A. Meyer. Probabilités et Potentiel, chapitres XVII–XXIV: Processus de Markov (fin), Compléments de calcul stochastique, Hermann, Paris, 1992.

[18] C. Dellacherie and P.-A. Meyer. *Probabilité et Potential, Théorie des martingales.* Chapter V–VIII, Hermann, Paris, 1980.

[19] C. Fontana, M. Jeanblanc, and S. Song. On arbitrages arising with honest times. *Finance and Stochastics*, 18:515–543, 2014.

[20] J. Jacod. *Calcul stochastique et problèmes de martingale*, vol. 714. Springer-Verlag Berlin Heidelberg, 1979.

[21] J. Jacod and A. N. Shiryaev. *Limit Theorems for Stochastic Processes.* Springer, Berlin, 2003.

[22] T. Jeulin. Semi-martingales et grossissement de filtration. In *Lecture Notes in Mathematics*, Vol. 833, Springer-Verlag, Berlin, Heidelberg, New York, 1980.

[23] Y. Jiao and S. Li. Modeling sovereign risks: From a hybrid model to the generalized density approach. *Mathematical Finance*, 28(1):240–267, 2018.

[24] Ch. Stricker. Arbitrage et lois de martingale. *Annales de l'I. H. P., Section B*, 26(3):451–460, 1990.

https://doi.org/10.1142/9789811280306_0008

Chapter 8

Derivatives' Risks as Costs in a One-Period Network Model

Dorinel Bastide[*,†,‖], **Stéphane Crépey**[‡,**], **Samuel Drapeau**[§,††], **and Mekonnen Tadese**[¶,‡‡]

[†]*Laboratoire de Mathématiques et Modélisation d'Evry (LaMME), Université d'Evry/Université Paris-Saclay CNRS UMR 8071, Evry Vald'Essonne, France*
[‡]*Laboratoire de Probabilités, Statistique et Modélisation (LPSM), Sorbonne Université and Université Paris Cité, CNRS UMR 8001, Paris, France*
[§]*Shanghai Jiao Tong University, Shanghai, China*
[¶]*Woldia University, Mathematics Department, Ethiopia*
[‖]*dorinel.2.bastide@bnpparibas.com*
[**]*stephane.crepey@lpsm.paris*
[††]*sdrapeau@saif.sjtu.edu.cn*
[‡‡]*mekonnenta@wldu.edu.et*

Abstract
We present a one-period XVA model encompassing bilateral and centrally cleared trading in a unified framework with explicit formulas for most quantities at hand. We illustrate possible uses of this framework for running stress test exercises on a financial network from a clearing member's perspective or for optimizing the porting of the portfolio of a defaulted clearing member.

[*]BNP Paribas Stress Testing Methodologies & Models. This article represents the opinions of the author, and it is not meant to represent the position or opinions of BNP Paribas or its members.

Keywords: Financial network, Counterparty credit risk, Central clearing counterparties, XVA, Risk management, Reverse stress test, Economic capital, Uncertainty quantification

1. Introduction

In the wake of the 2008–2009 global financial crisis, clearing through central counterparties (CCPs) has become mandatory for standardized derivatives, while other ones remaining under bilateral setup with higher capital requirements.

One role of the CCPs[1] is to provide their clearing members with fully collateralized hedges of their market risk with their clients. But this comes at a cost to the clearing members, who pass it to their corporate clients in the form of XVA (cross-valuation adjustment) add-ons. Bearing in mind that the risks of a hedge are, by definition, of the same magnitudes as the ones of the originating position and that standardized derivatives usable as hedging assets have to be traded through CCPs, the XVA footprint of not only bilateral but also centrally cleared trading is significant and should be analyzed in detail, which is the topic of this chapter. Ref. [18, Section 6] provides a continuous-time XVA analysis in the realistic situation of a bank dealing with an arbitrary number of clients and CCPs. For the sake of tractability, this is mimicked here in a stylized one-period setup, fine-tuned to applications including risk assessment in the context of stress test exercises[2] or optimizing the porting of the portfolio of defaulted clearing members.

The first type of application is motivated by the default in 2020 of Ronin Capital, a broker/dealer firm that had clearing exposures on both CCP services Fixed Income Clearing Corporation (FICC) GSD[3] segment (123 members) and CME Futures (56 members of which 24 common with FICC GSD). If all members are assumed to be only exposed to these CCPs and their cleared clients, we can illustrate these relationships by the network depicted in Figure 1. Any common member on those two CCPs needs to ensure conservative

[1]See Ref. [27] and Ref. [28] for general CCP and XVA references, as well as Ref. [33] for a CCP survey.

[2]As required by Ref. [36, Article 302].

[3]Government Securities Division.

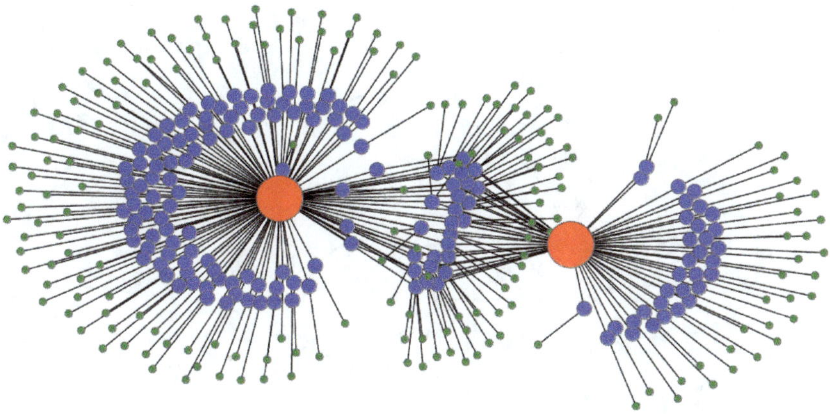

Figure 1. Network consisting of two CCPs (in red), 123 members for CCP1 seen on the left-hand side and 56 members for CCP2 on the right-hand side, with 24 common members displayed as the group of members in the middle of the two CCPs (155 members in total, in blue), and with 179 cleared clients (in green).

risk assessment that can be achieved in the proposed framework by accounting for common memberships on the two CCPs. If such common memberships are ignored, they can lead to lower loss estimates giving wrong risk view on potential losses.

The second type of application is an illustration of the results of defaulted portfolio porting as it has been the case for the trader Einer Aas on NASDAQ OMX[4] that has defaulted on 2018 with loss spillover effect on surviving members.

This chapter is outlined as follows: Section 2 sets the stage. Section 3 develops the corresponding XVA analysis. Section 4 sets up an elliptical market and credit model amenable to efficient XVA computations. Section 5 introduces the case studies. Section 6 provides numerical results of stress test exercises. Section 7 shows how to optimize the porting of defaulted members' portfolios. Section 8 concludes.

2. General Setup

We consider a finite set of market participants, also susceptible to serve as clearing members of CCPs. Derivative transactions can then

[4] Optionsmäklarna/Helsinki Stock Exchange.

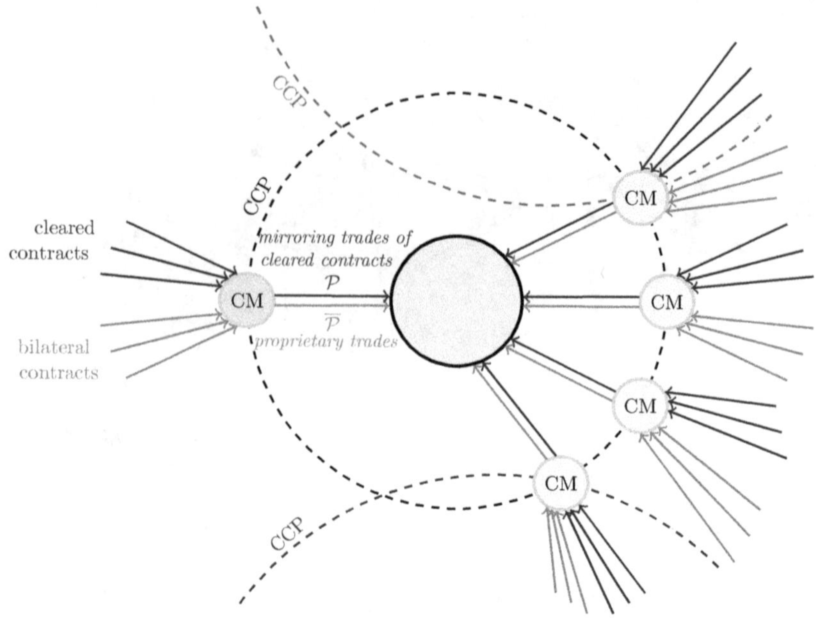

Figure 2. Promised cash flows between market participants. The reference clearing member bank is on the left.

be concluded between two individual participants or between a set of participants,[5] pooled in the form of a CCP, and a clearing member of this CCP.

The trades of a clearing member bank with a CCP are partitioned between proprietary trades, which are in effect hedges of the bilateral trading exposure of the bank, and back-to-back hedges of so-called cleared client trades, through which non-member clients gain access to the clearing services of a CCP: see Figure 2. The contractual cash flows from cleared and bilateral clients to a reference clearing member, dubbed the bank hereafter, are promised in successive turns from the bank to the CCP (cash flows denoted by $\mathcal{P}$ and $\overline{\mathcal{P}}$ on Figure 2), from the CCP to other clearing members and from the latter to their own clients. As a consequence, the CCP is flat in terms of market risk, as is also each of the clearing members. CCPs are typically siloed into different services, each devoted to a specific class of derivatives.

[5]Two or more, in practice from a few units to a few hundreds.

We first consider a setup with a single CCP service, the extension to several CCPs being done in Section 3.3.

2.1. *Defaults Settlement Rule*

As reasserted in the wake of the 2008–2009 global financial crisis by the Volcker rule, a dealer bank should be hedged as much as possible, at least in terms of market risk.[6] Jump-to-default risk, on the other hand, is hardly hedgeable in practice. Instead it is mitigated through netting and collateralization. Namely, designated netting sets of transactions between two given counterparties (two individual participants or a participant and the CCP) are jointly collateralized, i.e., guaranteed against the default of one or/and the other party. The collateral (or guarantee) comprises a variation margin, which tracks the mark-to-market (counterparty-risk-free value) of the netting set between the two parties, and non-negative amounts of initial margin posted by each party to the other, which provide a defense against the risk of slippage of the value of the netting set away from its (frozen) variation margin during its liquidation period. In the case of transactions with a CCP, there is an additional layer of collateral in the form of the (funded) default fund contributions of the clearing members, which is meant as a defense against extreme and systemic risk. For each participant, variation margin is rehypothecable and fungible across all its netting sets. Initial, margin is segregated at the netting set level. Default fund contributions are segregated at the clearing member level.

The general rule regarding the settlement of contracts of a defaulted netting set, to be instantiated in practical setups on a case-by-case basis,[7] is as follows:

Principle 2.1. If a counterparty in default is indebted toward the other beyond its posted margin, then this debt is only reimbursed at the level of this posted margin (assuming zero recovery rate of the defaulted party for simplicity in this chapter); otherwise the debt between the two parties is fully settled.

---

[6] cf. paragraph number 1851 in section 619 from Ref. [37].

[7] cf. e.g., Assumption 3.2.

Here debt is understood on a counterparty-risk-free basis.

Remark 2.2. One intuitively expects client default cash flows of the form $\mathcal{C} = (1-R)(D-M)^+$, where the "debt" D represents the pre-default value of the client derivative portfolio to the bank, M the margin posted by the client to the bank and R the recovery rate of the client. Technically, such an $(1-R)(D-M)^+$ effectively arises as

$$D - \big(M + R(D-M)^+ - (D-M)^-\big) = (1-R)(D-M)^+,$$

where $M + R(D-M)^+ - (D-M)^-$ is what the bank obtains from the client and D what the bank pays on the hedge of the portfolio. In the special case where case $R = 0$, what the bank obtains from the client simplifies to $M-(D-M)^- = D\wedge M$, in line with Principle 2.1, and the above expression to

$$D - D \wedge M = (D-M)^+.$$

We emphasize that a counterparty credit default loss $\mathcal{C} = (1-R)(D-M)^+$ (or simply $(D-M)^+$ if $R = 0$) should not be taken as an *assumption* but only arises as the result of a *computation* accounting for the cash flows of the portfolio *and its hedge*, derived in a specific market setup under the umbrella of the guiding principle 2.1 (or the corresponding extension to non-zero recovery, skipped for simplicity in this work). The exact outcome in fact depends on the refined specification of the setup at hand: see, e.g., Assumption 3.2 and the ensuing formulas (4) (in a single CCP setup) and (10) (under the multiple CCP extension) for the counterparty credit default loss $\mathcal{C}$ in the market setup of this work. Such formulas cannot be safely *guessed*, they should only be *derived* from first principles.

Remark 2.3. The above is of course a very crude description of default cash flows. Non-zero, possibly random, recoveries could be introduced at no harm from a theoretical viewpoint, as already pointed out above and done in the continuous-time setup of Ref. [18, Section 3.3]. Non-zero recoveries are of course more realistic. But, from a qualitative viewpoint that is our main objective in this work, they only soften the impacts of the defaults. Random recoveries are in line with the uncertainty about the actual level of recovery rates that are only observed *a posteriori* and can reflect the possibility of liquidating various forms of collateral, account for the output of liquidation procedures, legal resolutions, and other complex and unobservable features. For our purposes in this work, random recoveries could be used for emphasizing some extra dependencies via correlations with other random modeling features. This is all ignored hereafter for avoiding to blur the main features.

Principle 2.1 also applies to a netting set of transactions between a clearing member and a CCP. However, in our stylized setup, a CCP is nothing but the collection of its clearing members. Our CCP has no resources of its own (in particular, it cannot post any default fund contribution or "skin-in-the-game"[8]). As long as it is non-default, i.e., as long as at least one of its clearing members is non-default, our CCP can only handle the losses triggered by the defaults of some of its clearing members by redirecting these losses on the surviving ones. This participation of the surviving members to the losses triggered by the defaults of the other members corresponds in our framework to the usage by the CCP of their default fund contributions, both funded (as already introduced above) and unfunded. As will be detailed in the following equations, the funded default fund contributions are used for covering losses triggered by the defaults of clearing members over their margins. The unfunded default fund contributions correspond to additional refills that can be required by the CCP, often up to some cap in principle, without bounds in our model, in case the funded default fund contributions of the surviving members are not enough.

2.2. *XVA framework*

In a nutshell, the main XVAs are the CVA, the FVA/MVA and the KVA, where we have the following:

i. The CVA is the expected cost for the bank of the default risk of its clients.
ii. The FVA/MVA is the expected cost for the bank of its own default risk or, more precisely, of the implications of this risk

[8]such additional protection layer, though quite common in practice, is of marginal magnitude compared to the other protection layers. By omitting skin-in-the-game component, the obtained results are conservative in terms of risk management and the various formulations are simplified.

in terms of rehypothecable/segregated collateral funding spreads for the bank.

iii. The KVA is the cost for the bank of having to remunerate its shareholders at some hurdle rate for their capital at risk, capital which is required by the regulator as a provision against the residual risk left uncovered by i. and ii. (as default risk cannot be hedged by the bank).

Going into details, assume that at time 0 all the banking participants, including the reference clearing member bank,[9] with no prior endowments, enter transactions with their clients and hedge their positions, both bilaterally between them and through the CCP. As seen above, the CCP and each bank are flat in terms of market risk. However, as market participants are assumed to be defaultable with zero recovery, in order to account for counterparty credit risk and its funding and capital consequences, the reference bank (and each clearing member bank alike) requires from its corporate clients a pricing rebate (considering conventionally the bank as the "buyer") with respect to the mark-to-market (counterparty-risk-free) valuation of the deals. The corporate clients of the bank are assumed to absorb the ensuing prices via their corporate business, which is their primary motivation for these deals.

A reference probability measure $\mathbb{R}^\star$, relevant for grounding both stress test exercises and risk management analysis such as economic capital calculation, with corresponding expectation operator denoted by $\mathbb{E}^\star$, is used for the linear valuation of cash flows, using the risk-free asset as our numéraire everywhere. This choice of a numéraire simplifies equations by removing all terms related to the (assumed risk-free) remuneration of all cash and collateral accounts. The funding issue is then refocused on the risky funding side of the problem, i.e., funding costs in what follows really means excess funding costs with respect to a theoretical situation where the bank could equally borrow and lend at the risk-free rate.

More precisely, as suitable for XVA calculations Ref. [6, Remark 2.3]: given a physical probability measure defined on the

[9] cf. Figure 2.

full model σ algebra $\mathcal{A}$ and equivalent to a given risk-neutral measure on the financial sub σ algebra $\mathcal{B}$ of $\mathcal{A}$, we take $\mathbb{R}^{\star}$ equal to the risk-neutral measure on $\mathcal{B}$ and equal to the physical probability measure conditionally on $\mathcal{B}$.[10]

Following the general XVA guidelines of Ref. [18, Section 1], the XVA pricing rebate required by the reference clearing member bank from its corporate clients, dubbed funds transfer price (FTP), comes in two parts: first, the expected counterparty default losses and funding expenditures of the bank, an amount that flows into the bank liabilities and which we refer to as contra-asset valuation ($\mathrm{CA} = \mathrm{CVA} + \mathrm{FVA} + \mathrm{MVA}$ as we will see); second, a cost of capital risk premium (KVA), which instead is loss-absorbing[11] and is also used by the management of the bank as retained earnings for remunerating the shareholders of the bank for their capital at risk within the bank. All in one, the bank buys the deals from its clients at the (aggregated) price (MtM − FTP), where MtM is their counterparty-risk-free value and

$$\mathrm{FTP} = \underbrace{\mathrm{CA}}_{\text{Expected costs}} + \underbrace{\mathrm{KVA}}_{\text{Risk premium}} . \tag{1}$$

Let EC denote an economic capital of the bank corresponding to the minimum level of capital at risk that the bank should hold from a regulatory (i.e., solvency) perspective. If $\mathrm{KVA} < \mathrm{EC}$, then the bank shareholders need to provide the missing amount $(\mathrm{EC} - \mathrm{KVA})$ of capital at risk so that the actual level of capital at risk of the bank is

$$\max(\mathrm{EC}, \mathrm{KVA}),$$

while *shareholder* capital at risk reduces to

$$\max(\mathrm{EC}, \mathrm{KVA}) - \mathrm{KVA} = (\mathrm{EC} - \mathrm{KVA})^{+}. \tag{2}$$

[10] These two conditions uniquely characterize $\mathbb{R}^{\star}$ Ref. [10, Proposition 2.1].

[11] Hence, not a liability.

3. Theoretical XVA Analysis

In this section, we detail each term in the equations above, in the realistic setup of a bank involved into an arbitrary combination of bilateral and centrally cleared portfolios, in a tractable one-period setup with period length T. In the one-period XVA model of Ref. [6, Section 3], there were no CCPs and the bank was assumed to have access to a "fully collateralized back-to-back hedge of its market risk", ensuring by definition and for free to the bank a cash-flow $(\mathcal{P} - \text{MtM})$ at time 1, irrespective of the default status of the bank and its client. There, $\mathcal{P}$ denoted the contractual cash flows from the (assumed unique) client to the bank and MtM was the corresponding counterparty-risk-free value. In this chapter, we reveal the mechanism of such a "fully collateralized hedge of the market risk" of the bank, which can be achieved through central clearing but at a certain cost that we analyze.

All proofs are deferred to Section 8.

3.1. *Cash Flows*

Given disjoint sets of indices $I \ni 0$, C, and B for the clearing members (including the reference bank labeled by 0) and for the respective cleared and bilateral netting sets of the bank with its (individual) counterparties, we denote by the following:

- J_0, shortened as J, and J_i, $i \in I \setminus \{0\}$, the survival indicator random variables of the bank and of the other clearing members at time 1; $\gamma = \mathbb{R}^\star(J = 0)$, the default probability of the bank,
- $\mathcal{J} = \max_i J_i$, the survival indicator random variable of the CCP (i.e., of at least one clearing member),
- $\mathcal{P}_i$, $\text{MtM}_i = \mathbb{E}^\star \mathcal{P}_i$, and IM_i, $i \in I$, the contractual cash flows, variation margin and initial margin from the clearing member i to the CCP corresponding to the cleared clients account of the member i,
- $\overline{\mathcal{P}}_i$, $\overline{\text{MtM}}_i = \mathbb{E}^\star \overline{\mathcal{P}}_i$, and $\overline{\text{IM}}_i$, $i \in I$, the contractual cash flows, variation margin and initial margin from the clearing member i to the CCP corresponding to the proprietary (also dubbed house) account of the clearing member i,

- DF_i, $i \in I$, the funded default fund contribution posted by the clearing member i to the CCP,
- J_b, $b \in B$, the survival indicator random variable of the counterparty of the bilateral netting set b of the reference bank, $\mathcal{P}_b$, VM_b and IM_b, the associated contractual cash flows, variation margin and initial margin from the corresponding counterparty to the bank, and $\overline{\mathrm{IM}}_b$, the initial margin from the bank to this counterparty,
- J_c, $c \in C$, the survival indicator random variable of the client of the cleared trading netting set c of the bank, and $\mathcal{P}_c$, $\mathrm{MtM}_c = \mathbb{E}^{\star}\mathcal{P}_c$[12] and IM_c, the associated contractual cash flows, variation margin and initial margin from the corresponding client to the bank,[13]
- $\mathcal{L}$, the loss of the CCP, i.e., the loss triggered by the defaults of its clearing members beyond their posted collateral,[14] which is borne by the surviving members (if any),[15]
- $\mu = J\mu$, the proportion of these losses allocated to the reference clearing member bank (based on remaining survivors).

Moreover, in case $i = 0$ (so regarding the reference clearing member bank), we typically skip the index i (as in $J_0 = J$).

Assumption 3.1. $\sum_i(\mathcal{P}_i + \overline{\mathcal{P}}_i) = 0$ (the CCP is flat in terms of market risk), $\sum_c \mathcal{P}_c = \mathcal{P}_0$ (by definition of cleared trades and of their mirroring trades) and $\sum_b \mathcal{P}_b = \overline{\mathcal{P}}_0$ (the reference bank is flat in terms of market risk).

Assumption 3.1 yields the clearing conditions regarding the contractually promised cash flows, which applies to each banking participant (written there for the reference bank) and to the CCP.

Moreover, in line with Principle 2.1 that monitors the default cash flows, we have the following:

---

[12]Reflecting the fact that members of CCPs are fully collateralized.

[13]Note that a bank does not post any initial margin on its cleared client netting sets.

[14]Variation margin, initial margin and (funded) default fund contributions.

[15]See the last paragraph of Section 2.1.

Assumption 3.2. On the CCP survival event $\{\mathcal{J} = 1\}$, the CCP receives from each clearing member i

$$J_i(\mathcal{P}_i + \overline{\mathcal{P}}_i) + (1 - J_i)\Big(\mathcal{P}_i \wedge (\mathrm{MtM}_i + \mathrm{IM}_i) + \overline{\mathcal{P}}_i \wedge (\overline{\mathrm{MtM}}_i + \overline{\mathrm{IM}}_i) \\ +\big((\mathcal{P}_i - (\mathrm{MtM}_i + \mathrm{IM}_i))^+ + (\overline{\mathcal{P}}_i - (\overline{\mathrm{MtM}}_i + \overline{\mathrm{IM}}_i))^+\big) \wedge \mathrm{DF}_i\Big).$$

On the bank survival event $\{J = 1\}$ ($\subseteq \{\mathcal{J} = 1\}$), the bank receives on each cleared netting set c and bilateral netting set b

$$J_c\mathcal{P}_c + (1 - J_c)\big(\mathcal{P}_c \wedge (\mathrm{MtM}_c + \mathrm{IM}_c)\big) \quad \text{and} \\ J_b\mathcal{P}_b + (1 - J_b)\big(\mathcal{P}_b \wedge (\mathrm{VM}_b + \mathrm{IM}_b)\big),$$

whereas it pays to the CCP

$$\sum_c \mathcal{P}_c + \sum_b \mathcal{P}_b = \sum_c \big(J_c\mathcal{P}_c + (1 - J_c)\mathcal{P}_c\big) + \sum_b \big(J_b\mathcal{P}_b + (1 - J_b)\mathcal{P}_b\big).$$

We need one more condition, regarding the funding side of the problem:

Assumption 3.3. At time 0, the amounts CA and KVA sourced from the corporate clients of the bank are deposited on reserve capital and capital at risk accounts of the bank. The bank can use the amounts CA and max(EC, KVA)[16] on its reserve capital and capital at risk accounts for its variation margin borrowing purposes. Funds needed beyond CA + max(EC, KVA) for variation margin posting purposes are borrowed by the bank at its credit spread γ above OIS. Instead, the bank must borrow entirely the amounts to post as initial margin and funded default fund contributions, but this can be achieved at some blended funding spread $\widetilde{\gamma} \leq \gamma$.

The rationale for funding variation margin but not initial margin from CA + max(EC, KVA) is set out before Equation (15) in Ref. [4].

[16] Where $\max(\mathrm{EC}, \mathrm{KVA}) - \mathrm{KVA} = (\mathrm{EC} - \mathrm{KVA})^+$ is provided by the bank shareholders, cf. (2).

The motivation for the assumption $\widetilde{\gamma} \leq \gamma$ is provided in Ref. [3, Section 5], along with numerical experiments suggesting that $\widetilde{\gamma}$ can be several times lower than γ.

Lemma 3.4. *The borrowing needs of the bank for reusable and segregated collateral amount to, respectively,*

$$\left(\sum_{b}(\mathrm{MtM}_b - \mathrm{VM}_b) - \mathrm{CA} - \max(\mathrm{EC}, \mathrm{KVA})\right)^{+} \quad \textit{and}$$

$$\mathrm{IM} + \overline{\mathrm{IM}} + \mathrm{DF} + \sum_{\mathrm{b}} \overline{\mathrm{IM}}_{\mathrm{b}}. \tag{3}$$

Lemma 3.5. *On the bank survival event $\{J = 1\}$, the counterparty default losses $\mathcal{C}$ and the funding expenses $\mathcal{F}$ of the bank are given by*

$$\mathcal{C} = \sum_{b}(1 - J_b)(\mathcal{P}_b - \mathrm{VM}_b - \mathrm{IM}_{\mathrm{b}})^{+}$$
$$+ \sum_{c}(1 - J_c)(\mathcal{P}_c - \mathrm{MtM}_c - \mathrm{IM}_c)^{+} + \mu\mathcal{L}, \tag{4}$$

where

$$\mathcal{L} = \sum_{i}(1 - J_i)\big((\mathcal{P}_i - \mathrm{MtM}_i - \mathrm{IM}_i)^{+}$$
$$+ (\overline{\mathcal{P}}_i - \overline{\mathrm{MtM}}_i - \overline{\mathrm{IM}}_i)^{+} - \mathrm{DF}_i\big)^{+} \tag{5}$$

and

$$\mathcal{F} = \widetilde{\gamma}(\mathrm{IM} + \overline{\mathrm{IM}} + \mathrm{DF}) + \widetilde{\gamma}\sum_{\mathrm{b}} \overline{\mathrm{IM}}_{\mathrm{b}} + \gamma$$
$$\left(\sum_{b}(\mathrm{MtM}_b - \mathrm{VM}_b) - \mathrm{CA} - \max(\mathrm{EC}, \mathrm{KVA})\right)^{+}. \tag{6}$$

3.2. *Valuation*

Let $\mathbb{E}$ denote the expectation with respect to the bank survival measure $\mathbb{R}$ associated with $\mathbb{R}^{\star}1$, i.e., for any random variable $\mathcal{Y}$,

$$\mathbb{E}\mathcal{Y} = (1 - \gamma)^{-1}\mathbb{E}^{\star}(J\mathcal{Y}) \tag{7}$$

(expectation of $\mathcal{Y}$ conditional on the survival of the bank). As (readily) seen in Ref. [6, Section 3], we have the following:

Lemma 3.6. *For any random variable $\mathcal{Y}$ and constant Y, we have*

$$Y = \mathbb{E}^{\star}(J\mathcal{Y} + (1-J)Y) \Longleftrightarrow Y = \mathbb{E}\mathcal{Y}.$$

Under a cost-of-capital XVA approach, the bank charges its future losses to its corporate clients at a CA level making $\ell = J(\mathcal{C}+\mathcal{F}-\mathrm{CA})$, the trading loss of the shareholders of the bank, $\mathbb{R}^{\star}$ centered. In addition, given a target hurdle rate h assumed in $[0,1]$ (and typically of the order of 10%), the management of the bank ensures to the bank shareholders dividends at the height of h times their capital at risk $(\mathrm{EC}-\mathrm{KVA})^{+}$ (cf. (2)), where we model EC as $\mathbb{ES}(\ell)$, the expected shortfall of the trading loss ℓ[17] computed under the bank survival measure $\mathbb{R}$ at a quantile level[18] α (e.g., $\alpha = 99\%$ and $\alpha = 99.75\%$ in our experiments), i.e., under the dual representation of the expected shortfall[19]:

$$\mathrm{EC} = \sup\left\{\mathbb{E}[\ell\chi]\ \chi \text{ measurable}, 0 \le \chi \le (1-\alpha)^{-1}, \text{ and } \mathbb{E}[\chi] = 1\right\}, \tag{8}$$

which for atomless ℓ coincides[20] with $\mathbb{E}[\ell|\ell \ge \mathbb{V}\mathrm{a}\mathbb{R}(\ell)]$, where $\mathbb{V}\mathrm{a}\mathbb{R}$ is the $\mathbb{R}$ value-at-risk (lower quantile) at the level α. Note that, in view of (8), an expected shortfall of a centered random variable is non-negative.

The definitions of the XVA metrics corresponding to the above specifications are given in Table 1. Hence in view of (4) and (6):

$$\mathrm{CA} = \mathbb{E}^{\star}\Big(J(\mathcal{C}+\mathcal{F}) + (1-J)\mathrm{CA}\Big), \tag{9}$$

i.e., $\mathbb{E}^{\star}\Big(J(\mathcal{C}+\mathcal{F}-\mathrm{CA})\Big) = 0$, as desired.[21] The terminal cash flows of the form $(1-J)\times\cdots$ in Table 1 expressions and in (9) are thus consistent with the desired shareholder centric perspective. They can

[17] Assumed $\mathbb{R}$ integrable.

[18] Under normal distribution assumptions, such ES at percentile level 99.75% allows reaching similar loss level as with a VaR (quantile) risk metric at the level 99.9%. In practice, regulatory and economic capital indeed aims at capturing extreme losses that can occur once every 1000 years, cf. paragraph 5.1 from Ref. [12] for the detailed instructions.

[19] See, e.g., Ref. [29, Theorem 4.1].

[20] See Corollary 5.3 and representation thanks to expression (3.7) from Ref. [2].

[21] See after Lemma 3.6.

Table 1. XVA definitions, cf. Section 2.2 (with $\mathcal{C}$, $\mathcal{F}$ and $\mathcal{L}$ given by Lemma 3.5).

XVA	Expression	Full name and description
KVA	$\mathbb{E}^\star\Big(Jh(\mathrm{EC}-\mathrm{KVA})^+ + (1-J)\mathrm{KVA}\Big)$, where $\mathrm{EC} = \mathbb{ES}(J(\mathcal{C}+\mathcal{F}-\mathrm{CA}))$	Capital valuation adjustment
CA	$\mathrm{CVA}+\mathrm{MVA}+\mathrm{FVA}$	Contra-asset valuation
CVA	$\mathrm{BCVA}+\mathrm{CCVA}$	Credit valuation adjustment
BCVA	$\mathbb{E}^\star\left(J\sum_b(1-J_b)(\mathcal{P}_b-\mathrm{VM}_b-\mathrm{IM}_b)^+ + (1-J)\mathrm{BCVA}\right)$	Credit valuation adjustment for bilateral exposures
CCVA	$\mathbb{E}^\star\left(J\sum_c(1-J_c)(\mathcal{P}_c-\mathrm{MtM}_c-\mathrm{IM}_c)^+ + \mu\mathcal{L} + (1-J)\mathrm{CCVA}\right)$	Credit valuation adjustment for clearing activity exposures
MVA	$\mathrm{BMVA}+\mathrm{CMVA}$	Margin valuation adjustment
BMVA	$\mathbb{E}^\star\left(J\tilde{\gamma}\sum_b\overline{\mathrm{IM}}_b + (1-J)\mathrm{BMVA}\right)$	Margin valuation adjustment for bilateral exposures
CMVA	$\mathbb{E}^\star\Big(J\tilde{\gamma}(\mathrm{IM}+\overline{\mathrm{IM}}+\mathrm{DF}) + (1-\mathrm{J})\mathrm{CMVA}\Big)$	Margin valuation adjustment for clearing activity exposures
FVA	$\mathbb{E}^\star\left(J\gamma\big(\sum_b(\mathrm{MtM}_b-\mathrm{VM}_b)-\mathrm{CA} - \max(\mathrm{EC},\mathrm{KVA})\big)^+ + (1-J)\mathrm{FVA}\right)$	Funding valuation adjustment

also be interpreted as the amounts of reserve capital and risk margin lost by the bank shareholders, hence valued as such by CA, as their property is transferred to the liquidator of the bank if the bank defaults.

Due to these terminal cash flows, the above definition is in fact a fix-point system of equations. The split of the underlying CA equation (9) into the collection of equations in Table 1 is motivated by both interpretation and numerical considerations. From an interpretation viewpoint, it is useful to provide a more granular view of the costs of the bank provided by the split of the global CA amount between, on the one hand, bilateral and centrally cleared trading default risk components BCVA and CCVA and, on the other hand, bilateral and centrally cleared trading funding risk components BMVA and CMVA for segregated initial margin, whereas the FVA cost of funding variation margin is holistic in nature (can only be apprehended at the level of the bank balance sheet as a whole), via the feedback impact of $\mathrm{CA} + \max(\mathrm{EC}, \mathrm{KVA})$ into the FVA. From a numerical viewpoint, the collection of smaller problems in Table 1 may be easier to address than the global equation (9). Each of the smaller problems can also be handled by a dedicated desk of the bank, namely the CVA desk, for the BCVA and CCVA, and the Treasury of the bank, for the BMVA, CMVA and FVA.

Passing in the above equations to the bank survival measure $\mathbb{R}$ based on Lemma 3.6 shows that the corresponding fixed point problem is in fact well posed and yields explicit formulas for all the quantities at hand.

Theorem 3.7. *The explicit XVA formulas of Table 2 hold and we have*

$$J(\mathcal{C} - \mathrm{CVA}) = J\Big(\sum_c (1 - J_c)(\mathcal{P}_c - \mathrm{MtM}_c - \mathrm{IM}_c)^+ + \mu\mathcal{L} - \mathrm{CCVA} + \sum_b (1 - J_b)(\mathcal{P}_b - \mathrm{VM}_b - \mathrm{IM}_b)^+ - \mathrm{BCVA}\Big).$$

In particular, all the XVA (and also EC) numbers are non-negative.[22]

Remark 3.8. The reason why funding disappears from the bank trading loss, i.e., $J(\mathcal{C} + \mathcal{F} - \mathrm{CA}) = J(\mathcal{C} - \mathrm{CVA})$, is because, in a one-period setup, the collateral borrowing requirements (3) of the bank are simply constants. Hence funding triggers no risk to the bank but only a deterministic cost. In the dynamic setup of Ref. [3], funding generates both costs and risk.

[22] cf. Ref. [18, Sections 1 and 7.1].

Table 2. XVA explicit formulas (with $\mathcal{C}$, $\mathcal{F}$ and $\mathcal{L}$ given by Lemma 3.5).

XVA	Explicit formula
CCVA	$\mathbb{E}\left(\sum_c (1-J_c)(\mathcal{P}_c - \mathrm{MtM}_c - \mathrm{IM}_c)^+ + \mu\mathcal{L}\right)$
CMVA	$\widetilde{\gamma}(\mathrm{IM} + \overline{\mathrm{IM}} + \mathrm{DF})$
BCVA	$\mathbb{E}\left(\sum_b (1-J_b)(\mathcal{P}_b - \mathrm{VM}_b - \mathrm{IM}_\mathrm{b})^+\right)$
BMVA	$\widetilde{\gamma}\sum_b \overline{\mathrm{IM}}_b$
EC	$\mathbb{ES}(J(\mathcal{C} - \mathrm{CVA}))$
FVA	$\frac{\gamma}{1+\gamma}\left(\sum_b (\mathrm{MtM}_b - \mathrm{VM}_b) - (\mathrm{CCVA} + \mathrm{CMVA} + \mathrm{BCVA} + \mathrm{BMVA}) - \mathrm{EC}\right)^+$
KVA	$\frac{h}{1+h}\mathrm{EC}$

3.3. *Extension to Several CCPs or CCP Services*

In the realistic case where the reference bank is a clearing member of several services of one or several CCPs, we index all the CCP-related quantities in the above by an additional index *ccp* in a finite set disjoint from $I \cup C \cup B$. Then, with $\mathrm{CA} = \mathrm{CCVA} + \mathrm{CMVA} + \mathrm{BCVA} + \mathrm{BMVA} + \mathrm{FVA}$ as before, we have the following:

Proposition 3.9. *The counterparty default loss $\mathcal{C}$ across several counterparties and several CCPs is given by*

$$\mathcal{C} = \sum_{ccp,c}(1-J_c)(\mathcal{P}_c^{ccp} - \mathrm{MtM}_c^{ccp} - \mathrm{IM}_c^{ccp})^+ + \sum_{ccp}\mu^{ccp}\mathcal{L}^{ccp}$$
$$+ \sum_b (1-J_b)(\mathcal{P}_b - \mathrm{VM}_b - \mathrm{IM}_\mathrm{b})^+, \tag{10}$$

where

$$\mathcal{L}^{ccp} = \sum_i (1-J_i)\big((\mathcal{P}_i^{ccp} - \mathrm{MtM}_i^{ccp} - \mathrm{IM}_\mathrm{i}^{\mathrm{ccp}})^+$$
$$+(\overline{\mathcal{P}}_i^{ccp} - \overline{\mathrm{MtM}}_i^{ccp} - \overline{\mathrm{IM}}_i^{ccp})^+ - \mathrm{DF}_i^{ccp}\big)^+. \tag{11}$$

The funding expenses $\mathcal{F}$ across several CCPs and several counterparties are given by

$$\mathcal{F} = \widetilde{\gamma} \sum_{ccp} (\mathrm{IM}^{\mathrm{ccp}} + \overline{\mathrm{IM}}^{\mathrm{ccp}} + \mathrm{DF}^{\mathrm{ccp}}) + + \widetilde{\gamma} \sum_{\mathrm{b}} \overline{\mathrm{IM}}_{\mathrm{b}}$$

$$+ \gamma \left(\sum_{b} (\mathrm{MtM}_{b} - \mathrm{VM}_{b}) - \mathrm{CA} - \max(\mathrm{EC}, \mathrm{KVA}) \right)^{+} . \quad (12)$$

The only XVA definitions and explicit formulas that change with respect to Tables 1 *and* 2 *(on top of* $\mathcal{C}$ *and* $\mathcal{F}$ *generalized as above) are the ones for CCVA and CMVA, the way detailed in Tables* 3 *and* 4*. Moreover,*

$$J(\mathcal{C} - \mathrm{CVA}) = J \Bigg(\sum_{ccp,c} (1 - J_c)(\mathcal{P}_c^{ccp} - \mathrm{MtM}_c^{ccp} - \mathrm{IM}_c^{ccp})^{+} + \sum_{ccp} \mu^{ccp} \mathcal{L}^{ccp} - \mathrm{CCVA} + \sum_{b} (1 - J_b) \times (\mathcal{P}_b - \mathrm{VM}_b - \mathrm{IM}_{\mathrm{b}})^{+} - \mathrm{BCVA} \Bigg) .$$

Before passing to the case studies, we specify the calculation of economic capital under the member survival measure.

Lemma 3.10. *If* $\mathbb{R}(\ell = \mathbb{V}\mathrm{a}\mathbb{R}(\ell)) = 0$, *where* $\ell = J(\mathcal{C} - \mathrm{CVA})$, *then*

$$\mathrm{EC} = \mathbb{E}^{\star}\big(\mathcal{C} - \mathrm{CVA} \big| \mathcal{C} - \mathrm{CVA} \geq \mathbb{V}\mathrm{a}\mathbb{R}(\ell), J = 1\big). \quad (13)$$

Table 3. CCVA and CMVA definitions with several CCPs (also, $\mathcal{C}$ and $\mathcal{F}$ are now given by Proposition 3.9, as also $\mathcal{L}^{ccp}$).

XVA	Expression	Full name and description
CCVA	$\mathbb{E}^{\star}\Big(J \sum_{ccp,c} (1 - J_c)(\mathcal{P}_c^{ccp} - \mathrm{MtM}_c^{ccp} - \mathrm{IM}_c^{ccp})^{+} + \sum_{ccp} \mu^{ccp} \mathcal{L}^{ccp} + (1 - J)\mathrm{CCVA}\Big)$	Credit valuation adjustment for clearing activity exposures
CMVA	$\mathbb{E}^{\star}\Big(J \sum_{ccp} \widetilde{\gamma}(\mathrm{IM}^{\mathrm{ccp}} + \overline{\mathrm{IM}}^{\mathrm{ccp}} + \mathrm{DF}^{\mathrm{ccp}}) + (1 - \mathrm{J})\mathrm{CMVA}\Big)$	Margin valuation adjustment for clearing activity exposures

Table 4. CCVA and CMVA explicit formulas with several CCPs (also, $\mathcal{C}$ and $\mathcal{F}$ are now given by Proposition 3.9, as also $\mathcal{L}^{ccp}$).

XVA	Explicit formula
CCVA	$\mathbb{E}\left(\sum_{ccp,c}(1-J_c)(\mathcal{P}^{ccp}_c - \mathrm{MtM}^{ccp}_c - \mathrm{IM}^{ccp}_c)^+ + \sum_{ccp}\mu^{ccp}\mathcal{L}^{ccp}\right)$
CMVA	$\sum_{ccp}\widetilde{\gamma}(\mathrm{IM}^{ccp} + \overline{\mathrm{IM}}^{ccp} + \mathrm{DF}^{ccp})$

4. Market and Credit Model

We introduce a market and credit model, written under $\mathbb{R}^\star$, with parameters that can capture dependence between portfolio changes, joint defaults and possible adverse exacerbated changes of the portfolio due to their owner default known as wrong-way risk.

For any $j \in I \cup B \cup C$, denoting by F_j the marginal cdf of a financial participant j's default time τ_j, $\Delta\mathcal{P}_j := \mathcal{P}_j - \mathrm{MtM}_j$, S the Student-t cdf with 3 degrees of freedom, nom_j a (signed) nominal of the portfolio of the market participant j, σ_j its annualized relative volatility and Δ_l a positive liquidation period accounting for the time taken by the CCP to novate or liquidate[23] defaulted portfolios, we define

$$\begin{cases} \tau_j = F_j^{-1}\left(S(X_j)\right), \\ \dfrac{\Delta\mathcal{P}_j}{\mathrm{nom}_j\sigma_j\sqrt{\Delta_l}} = Y_j, \end{cases} \tag{14}$$

where

$$\begin{cases} X_j = \sqrt{\rho^{cr}}\mathcal{T} - \sqrt{\rho^{wwr}_j}\mathcal{X}_j + \sqrt{1-\rho^{cr}-\rho^{wwr}_j}\mathcal{T}_j \\ Y_j = \sqrt{\rho^{mkt}}\mathcal{E} + \sqrt{\rho^{wwr}_j}\mathcal{X}_j + \sqrt{1-\rho^{mkt}-\rho^{wwr}_j}\mathcal{E}_j. \end{cases} \tag{15}$$

Here ρ^{cr}, ρ^{mkt} and ρ^{wwr}_j are positive credit/credit, market/market and credit/market correlation coefficients, while $\mathcal{T}$, $\mathcal{T}_j$, $\mathcal{E}$, $\mathcal{E}_j$ and $\mathcal{X}_j$ are i.i.d. random variables following Student-t distributions with degree of freedom 3 such that

[23] cf. Section 7.

- $\mathcal{T}$ represents the common systemic factor for default times across members,
- $\mathcal{E}$ represents the common systemic factor for portfolio variations across members,
- $\mathcal{X}_j$ is the common factor co-driving portfolio variations and default time of market participant j,
- $\mathcal{T}_j$ is the idiosyncratic factor for market participant j's default time,
- $\mathcal{E}_j$ is the idiosyncratic factor for market participant j's portfolio variations.

Remark 4.1. In practice, margin computations rely on historical estimates based on several market-stressed periods. Our approach, instead, aims at reflecting extreme market shocks with fat-tailed Student-t distributions of degree of freedom $\nu = 3$ and volatility level within a reasonable range of $[20\%, 40\%]$. Our static formulation depicts stationary increments of the defaulted portfolios' value over the liquidation period.

In view of the above, the setup is well defined if and only if[24]

$$\rho_j^{wwr} < \min\left(1 - \rho^{cr}, 1 - \rho^{mkt}\right). \tag{16}$$

The "minus" sign in front of the common credit-market factor $-\sqrt{\rho_j^{wwr}}$ for the default time component in (15) ensures that the corresponding common factor accelerates defaults while increasing the market exposure due to the $+\sqrt{\rho_j^{wwr}}$ factor in the second part of (15).

Remark 4.2. Our model of latent variables $(\tilde{X}, \tilde{Y})$ has a (multivariate) elliptical distribution, i.e., $(\tilde{X}, \tilde{Y}) = AZ$, where, with $N = |I \cup B \cup C|$ the number of market participants in the financial network, $Z = \left(\mathcal{T}, \mathcal{E}, \mathcal{T}_1, \mathcal{X}_1, \mathcal{E}_1, \ldots, \mathcal{T}_N, \mathcal{X}_N, \mathcal{E}_N\right)^\top$ and A is the matrix

[24]Otherwise, the model for both default time and portfolio variation factors is undefined due to their idiosyncratic coefficient term $\sqrt{1 - \rho^{cr} - \rho_j^{wwr}}$ and $\sqrt{1 - \rho^{mkt} - \rho_j^{wwr}}$. Also we discard the limit cases where $\rho_j^{wwr} = 1 - \rho^{cr}$ or $\rho_j^{wwr} = 1 - \rho^{mkt}$ as they lead to a zero contribution of the idiosyncratic factors, which would be unrealistic.

implicit in (15) Ref. [31, Chapter 6]. Ref. [9] introduce a dynamic model locally elliptical in the sense of elliptical on each next time step given the information at the beginning of the time step. Under simplifying assumptions including their equation (32) and Assumption 2, they obtain (in our notation) explicit CMVA and approximate CCVA formulas. In their case, defaults are triggered by $\Delta\mathcal{P}_j$ (in our notation) falling below a Merton-like threshold. In our static setup with extra latent variables for defaults, we do not have such explicit formulas. However, Monte Carlo simulation is quite efficient and required anyway for stress test exercises that aim at identifying scenarios leading to extreme losses with adequate description such as the identification of defaulted members and their corresponding losses.

Hereafter, we describe two possible applications of our XVA framework which will be illustrated by numerical case studies in the above model. To these ends, two networks will be defined to serve the numerical illustrations: one rather educational on the use of the XVA metrics and the other one reflecting the more realistic situation depicted in Figure 1.

In the numerical applications that follow, all members play in turn the role of the reference bank in the theoretical XVA framework of Sections 2–3. The CVA and KVA computations require a Monte Carlo routine run under $\mathbb{R}^\star$ in combination with a rejection technique in order to yield simulations under the survival measures associated with different clearing members. For obtaining confidence intervals regarding the expected shortfalls that are embedded in the KVA computations, the simulations are split into several batches, from which the mean of the (partial) EC estimates yields the final EC estimate, while their standard deviation is used to define a confidence interval.

5. Case Studies Setup

In the examples that follow, market participants are identified by a number and can then be included in one of several of the considered CCPs. We restrict ourselves to cleared client trades so that the non-vanishing XVA metrics reduce to the CCVA, the CMVA and the KVA.

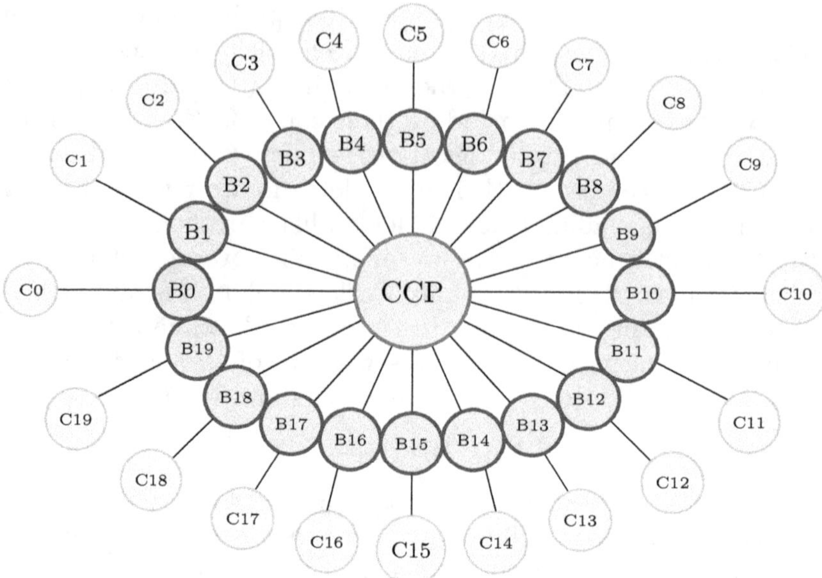

Figure 3. Financial network composed of 1 CCP, its 20 members (labeled by B) and one client per member.

5.1. *Single CCP setup and initial XVA costs*

We consider a single CCP service with 20 members labeled by $i \in 0 \cdots n = 19$, only trading for cleared clients (i.e., without bilateral or centrally cleared proprietary trading). Each member faces one client. The ensuing financial network is depicted in Figure 3.

All clients are assumed to be risk-free. For any member i, its posted IM to the CCP is calculated based on the idea of a VM call not fulfilled over a time period $\Delta_s < \Delta_l$ at a confidence level $\alpha \in (1/2, 1)$, using a VaR metric[25] applied to the non-coverage of VM call taken also to follow a scaled Student-t distribution $\mathcal{S}_\nu$ with ν degrees of freedom with cdf S_ν:

$$\mathrm{IM}_i = \mathbb{V}\mathrm{a}\mathbb{R}\big(\mathrm{nom}_i \sigma_i \sqrt{\Delta_s}\mathcal{S}_\nu\big) = |\mathrm{nom}_i|\, \sigma_i \sqrt{\Delta_s} \mathrm{S}_\nu{}^{-1}(\alpha). \tag{17}$$

The default fund is calculated at the CCP level as

$$\mathrm{Cover2} = \mathrm{SLOIM}_{(0)} + \mathrm{SLOIM}_{(1)}, \tag{18}$$

[25]Under the member survival measure.

for the two largest stressed losses over IM (SLOIM_i) among members, identified with subscripts (0) and (1), where SLOIM is calculated as the value-at-risk $\mathbb{V}\text{a}\mathbb{R}'$ at a confidence level $\alpha' > \alpha$ of the loss over IM, i.e.,

$$\begin{aligned}\text{SLOIM}_i &= \mathbb{V}\text{a}\mathbb{R}'\big(\text{nom}_i\sigma_i\sqrt{\Delta_s}\mathcal{S}_\nu - \text{IM}_i\big)\\ &= |\text{nom}_i|\,\sigma_i\sqrt{\Delta_s}\Big(S_\nu{}^{-1}(\alpha') - S_\nu{}^{-1}(\alpha)\Big).\end{aligned} \tag{19}$$

The total amount (18) is then allocated between the clearing members to define their (funded) default fund contributions as $\text{DF}_i = \dfrac{\text{SLOIM}_i}{\sum_j \text{SLOIM}_j}\text{Cover2}$.

The nom_js of other clearing members are not observable by a given one. However, following Ref. [34] and [30], $|\text{nom}|_{(i)}$ denoting the i-th largest absolute nominal amount for $i \in 0 \cdots n = 19$, a parameterization of the form

$$|\text{nom}|_{(i)} = \beta e^{-\beta'(i+1)},\ \ \beta, \beta' > 0, \tag{20}$$

can be fit to the total default fund held by the CCP[26] and the sum of its five largest default fund contributions,[27] made public each quarter for most of the CCPs. The parameters β and β' inferred from the default fund data are used to depict a similar pattern on the absolute nominal sizes.[28] The participants and portfolios' parameter inputs are detailed in Table 6, where id is the identifier of the CM, DP stands for the one-year probability of default of the member expressed in percentage points, size represents the overall portfolio size of the member detained within the CCP and vol is the annual volatility used for the portfolio variations.

The portfolios listed in Table 6 relate to the members toward the CCP (which are mirroring the ones between the members and

---

[26]Item referenced as 4.3.15 in Ref. [11], *Value of pre-funded default resources (excluding initial and retained variation margin) held for each clearing service in total, post-haircut* in the quantitative disclosure documents.

[27]Item referenced as 18.4.2 in Ref. [11]: *For each segregated default fund with 25 or more members; Percentage of participant contributions to the default fund contributed by largest five clearing members in aggregate.*; or item referenced 18.4.1 for CCP services with less than 25 members.

[28]As if the default fund amounts are proportional to the portfolio sizes.

Table 5. XVAs calculation configuration.

One-period length T	5 years
Liquidation period at default Δ_l	5 days
Portfolio variations' correlation ρ^{cr}	30%
Credit factors' correlation ρ^{mkt}	20%
Correlation between credit factors and portfolio variations ρ^{wwr}	20%
IM covering period (MPoR) Δ_s	2 days
IM quantile level	95%
Funding blending ratio $\widetilde{\gamma}/\gamma$	25%
SLOIM calculation[29] for DF Cover-2	VaR 97%
Funded DF allocation rule	$\propto$ SLOIM
$\mathcal{L}$ allocation rule ($\ni \mu$)	$\propto DF_i$
Quantile level used for clearing members EC calculation	99.75%
Hurdle rate h used for KVA computations	10.0%
Number of Monte Carlo simulations (for CCVA and KVA computations)	10M
Number of batches (for KVA computations)	100

Table 6. Member characteristics and portfolio parameters, ordered by decreasing member size.

cm id	0	1	2	3	4	5	6	7	8	9
DP (bps)	50	60	70	80	90	200	190	180	170	160
size	−242	184	139	105	−80	−61	−46	35	26	−20
vol (%)	20	21	22	23	24	25	26	27	28	29

cm id	10	11	12	13	14	15	16	17	18	19
DP (bps)	150	140	130	120	110	100	90	80	70	60
size	−15	−11	−9	−6	5	−4	−3	2	2	−1
vol (%)	30	31	32	33	34	35	36	37	38	39

their clients). The signs of the nominals are distributed so that $\sum_j \text{nom}_j = 0$, consistent with the clearing condition (first identity in Assumption 3.1, here without proprietary trades).

The parameters of the XVA costs calculations are summarized in Table 5. Note that the chosen period length of $T = 5$ years covers the bulk (if not the final maturity) of most realistic CCP portfolios.

For each member, the CCVA, CMVA and KVA costs are calculated and reported in Table 7. For KVA, two calculations have been

[29]Such confidence level at 97% for SLOIM in DF calibration allows for a ratio of default fund over initial margin of about 10% in our calculations, a ratio (of this level or less) often observed in practice.

Table 7. Initial XVA costs: estimates [value-at-risk underlying the KVA estimate] and (95% confidence level errors).

cm id	CMVA	CCVA	KVA (99%)	KVA (99.75%)
0	0.0687	0.0778 (0.3%)	0.2734 [0.1396] (0.6%)	0.5138 [0.2923] (1%)
1	0.0656	0.0805 (0.4%)	0.3407 [0.1422] (0.7%)	0.7022 [0.3806] (1.1%)
2	0.0604	0.0635 (0.4%)	0.2725 [0.1132] (0.7%)	0.5624 [0.3039] (1.1%)
3	0.0544	0.0503 (0.5%)	0.2191 [0.0903] (0.9%)	0.4549 [0.2439] (1.5%)
4	0.0485	0.0356 (0.5%)	0.1654 [0.0625] (0.9%)	0.3565 [0.185] (1.2%)
5	0.0834	0.0252 (0.5%)	0.1339 [0.0507] (0.8%)	0.2856 [0.1513] (1.2%)
6	0.0623	0.021 (0.5%)	0.1085 [0.0429] (0.8%)	0.2284 [0.1211] (1.3%)
7	0.0467	0.0187 (0.5%)	0.0883 [0.0365] (0.8%)	0.1836 [0.098] (1.1%)
8	0.0341	0.0146 (0.5%)	0.0685 [0.0282] (0.9%)	0.1432 [0.0755] (1.5%)
9	0.0256	0.0113 (0.5%)	0.0549 [0.0223] (1%)	0.1157 [0.06] (1.6%)
10	0.0187	0.009 (0.5%)	0.0429 [0.0173] (1%)	0.0908 [0.0467] (1.7%)
11	0.0132	0.007 (0.7%)	0.0328 [0.0132] (1.3%)	0.0701 [0.0354] (2.2%)
12	0.0104	0.006 (0.6%)	0.0279 [0.0111] (1.3%)	0.0598 [0.0299] (2.3%)
13	0.0066	0.0042 (0.9%)	0.0198 [0.0077] (1.9%)	0.0438 [0.0206] (3.3%)
14	0.0052	0.0037 (0.9%)	0.0174 [0.0066] (1.8%)	0.0389 [0.0177] (3.1%)
15	0.0039	0.0032 (1.3%)	0.0151 [0.0054] (2.5%)	0.0351 [0.0146] (4.3%)
16	0.0027	0.0025 (1.4%)	0.012 [0.0042] (2.7%)	0.0285 [0.0113] (4.4%)
17	0.0017	0.0018 (2%)	0.0088 [0.0029] (4%)	0.0218 [0.0078] (6.4%)
18	0.0015	0.0019 (2%)	0.0093 [0.0029] (4.1%)	0.0233 [0.008] (6.5%)
19	0.0007	0.0011 (3.7%)	0.006 [0.0015] (6.9%)	0.017 [0.0041] (9.7%)

performed: one based on ES at 99th percentile level and another one based on 99.75th percentile level. The amount in square bracket is the corresponding quantile level from which average is calculated and numbers in parentheses represent the 95% confidence interval in relative difference from calculated metric for both CCVA and KVA. All the XVA numbers decrease with the member size.

To assess the average behavior w.r.t. ρ^{cr}, ρ^{mkt} and ρ^{wwr} of the CCVA and KVA, we vary these correlations between 5% and 95%, with 5% step and display in Figures 4 and 5 the corresponding metrics, aggregated over all clearing members successively considered as the reference bank. For such tests, the default correlations ρ^{cr} and ρ^{mkt} are both set to 4% when they are not changed between 5% and 95%. This is to allow for runs with $\rho_i^{wwr} = 95\%$ satisfying condition (16).

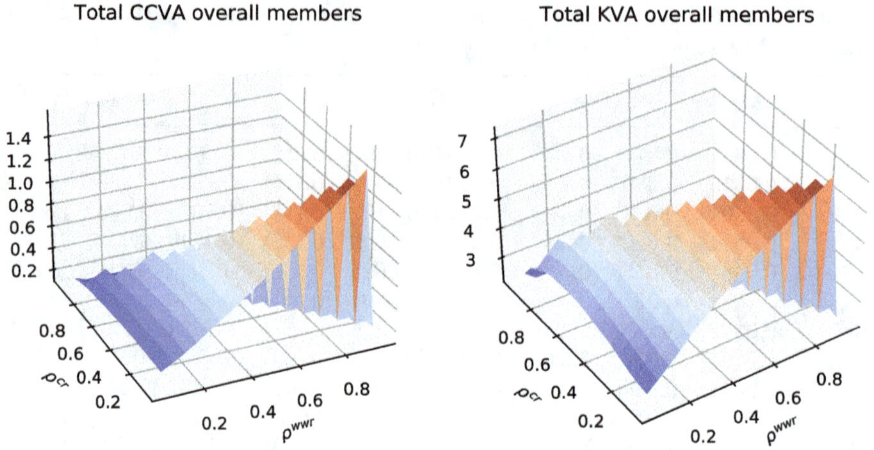

Figure 4. CCVA and KVA w.r.t. credit factors' correlation and credit and portfolio variation factors' correlation.

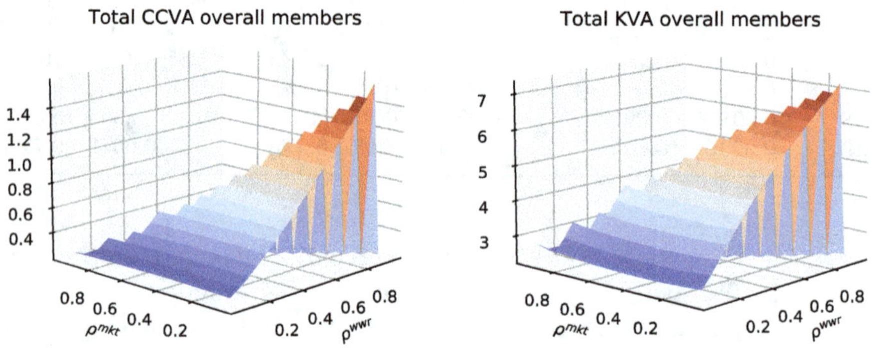

Figure 5. CCVA and KVA w.r.t. market factors' correlation and credit and portfolio variation factors' correlation.

The KVA depicts an increase w.r.t. ρ^{cr} but also w.r.t. ρ^{wwr} and very limited change w.r.t. ρ^{mkt}. The correlation ρ^{wwr} has more impact than ρ^{cr} and ρ^{mkt} (right panels in Figures 4 and 5). As seen on the left panels of Figures 4 and 5, there are very marginal changes for the aggregated CCVA w.r.t. ρ^{cr} and ρ^{mkt}, but a significant positive impact of ρ^{wwr}. This is understandable for the sensitivity to ρ^{cr} and ρ^{mkt} as, apart for modulations of the measure with respect to which each individual CCVA is assessed, the CCVA aggregated over clearing members is essentially an expectation of the CCP loss $\mathcal{L}$ (cf. the first line of Table 2). The individual CCVAs (as per the first line in Table 2) of each clearing member, however, may depend on ρ^{cr} and ρ^{mkt} (on top of ρ^{wwr}) in a strong and nontrivial manner, via the allocation coefficient μ.

5.2. *Two CCPs' network setup*

We now consider the case of Figure 1 where there are two CCPs with some common members and stress test is considered from the perspective of one of these common members. The motivation for this case is to provide a realistic example mimicking in a simplified way the trading firm Ronin Capital, which had memberships on both FICC GSD[30] segment, hereafter denominated by CCP1, and CME Futures segment, hereafter denominated by CCP2, in March 2020. It is well known that a VaR-type risk measure is not subadditive, in particular for credit portfolios as illustrated in Example 5.4 in Ref. [2] and Example 2.25 in [31] for a portfolio of defaultable bonds so that for a common member adding VaR estimates of trading losses on two CCPs separately can lead to underestimated levels with respect to the actual VaR of the global exposition of the member. As such, stress test exercises accounting for common memberships could reveal a larger value-at-risk compared to the exercise where stress tests are conducted separately on each CCP.

To perform the analysis, the following setup is considered:

- All members have only clearing client positions,[31] with 123 members on CCP1 and 56 members on CCP2, out of which 24 are common to both CCPs.
- All clients are assumed to be default-free.
- Both CCPs use configuration as per Table 5.
- The sizes of the positions are assumed exponentially distributed in the sense that from the most exposed member to the least one, absolute value of positions decrease exponentially with the form in (20) as depicted by Figures 6 and 7, respectively.

---

[30] Government Securities Division.

[31] Ronin Capital had in fact only a house account and was thus not clearing any client position.

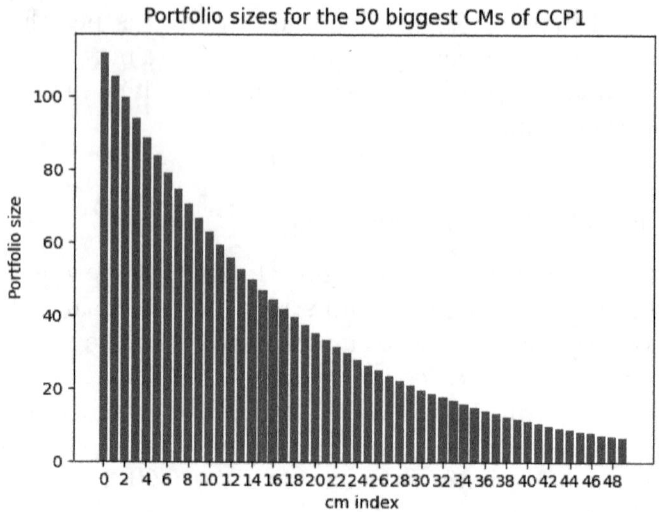

Figure 6. Decreasing absolute nom_i per member for CCP1.

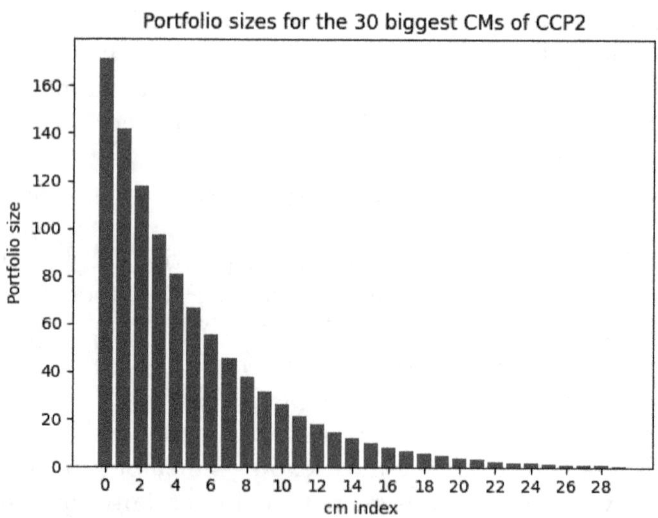

Figure 7. Decreasing absolute nom_i per member for CCP2.

- The proportion of the default fund detained by the five biggest members is 25% for CCP1 and 61% for CCP2.[32]
- The size of the default fund of CCP1 is assumed to be twice the one of the default fund of CCP2.

All data used are either public sources or have been anonymized, with default intensities ranging from 10 bps to 400 bps and portfolio volatilities ranging from 20 to 30. Similar configuration as given in Table 5 is used, apart from the number of Monte Carlo simulations reduced to 2M for memory capacity reasons.

The clearing conditions are ensured by setting the sum of the portfolio sizes nom_i to zero on each CCP. The situation of member 3, exposed to both CCPs, as the defaulting member, corresponds roughly to the situation of Ronin Capital in 2018. In particular, an annual probability of default of 0.1% corresponds roughly to a BBB rating that was assigned to Ronin Capital in 2018 for its issuances.[33]

6. Stress Test Exercises

As outlined in the capital requirements regulation detailed in Ref. [36] article 290, financial institutions must conduct regular stress test exercises of their credit and counterparty exposures. Paragraph 8 of this article also stipulates the reverse stress test[34] requirement to

> "[...] identify extreme, but plausible, scenarios that could result in significant adverse outcomes."

This is complemented by article 302 on the exposure financial institutions may have toward CCPs:

> "Institutions shall assess, through appropriate scenario analysis and stress testing, whether the level of own funds held against exposures to a CCP, including potential future credit exposures, exposures from default fund contributions and, where the

---

[32]Taken from the quantitative disclosure of both CCPs as of third quarter of 2020.

[33] https://www.spglobal.com/marketintelligence/en/news-insights/blog/banking-essentials-newsletter-july-edition-2.

[34]See dedicated definition p.12 in Ref. [16] and articles 97, 98 p. 37 in Ref. [24] for official regulatory definitions.

> institution is acting as a clearing member, exposures resulting from contractual arrangements as laid down in Article 304, adequately relates to the inherent risks of those exposures."

In practice, stress test exercises aim at assessing the capacity of financial institutions to absorb financial and economic shocks. In regular exercises, such as the ones conducted by the European Banking Authority, the shocks are usually considered under so-called *central* and *baseline* macroeconomic scenarios corresponding to a median quantile and *adverse* scenario usually taken as a 90th percentile reflecting severe yet plausible scenario that can occur once every 10 years.[35] Additionally, extreme scenarios can be considered for measuring the capital adequacy[36] for absorbing extremely severe losses around confidence level at 99.9%. From a clearing member perspective, this requires to have the capacity of scanning certain points of its trading loss distribution. In our framework, this boils down to identifying particular levels of the distribution of the trading loss $\ell = J(\mathcal{C} - \text{CCVA} - \text{BCVA})$ of the reference clearing member bank, where the different terms are detailed in Proposition 3.9.

Other types of stress test exercises, referenced as *reverse stress test*[37] Ref. [21], consist in identifying the probability of reaching a given loss level as well as describing the scenario configuration such as projected defaults and loss magnitude leading to such loss levels. The distribution must span a sufficient large spectrum of losses, including the ones targeted by the exercise, but it also has to be sufficiently rich numerically to allow identifying combinations of events leading to such losses.

Confidence intervals of corresponding extreme scenario probabilities should complement the analysis to ensure the reliability of the used model and numerical methods.

---

[35]Such confidence levels are suggested by the Federal Reserve outlining p.10 in Ref. [15] the various recession periods of the United States listed in their Table 1 p. 14. The 2021 instructions in Ref. [22] also indicate p.72 that stressed market risk factors are based on shocks specified in Ref. [25], citing Ref. [20, p. 29], with the US recessions periods as stressful economic episodes.

[36]cf. paragraph 5.1 p.11 from Ref. [12].

[37]See also dedicated definition on p.12 in Ref. [16] and articles 97, 98 p. 37 in Ref. [24] for official regulatory definitions.

Regulators have the ability to challenge financial institutions on these elements and demand for improvements.[38]

6.1. *Scenarios' identification for reverse stress test*

We now briefly explain how to identify and exploit the scenarios leading to contribute the most to economic capital, in the spirit of Ref. [7]. We denote by M the number of Monte Carlo scenario for which $J = 1$, i.e., survival of the reference bank. Its trading loss $\mathcal{C} - \mathrm{CVA}$ for a simulation m is given by $\mathcal{C}^m - \mathrm{CVA}$, where $m \in 1 \cdots M$ enumerates the simulated scenarios for which the reference member bank ends up in survival state.

To get an estimate of the economic capital based on expected shortfall, relying on Ref. [2, Definition 2.6 and Proposition 4.1], we calculate, for a high confidence level $\alpha \in (\frac{1}{2}, 1)$ and $[x]$ denoting the integer part of any real x,

$$\widehat{\mathbb{ES}}\,(\mathcal{C} - \mathrm{CVA}) := \frac{1}{M - [\alpha M]} \sum_{m=[\alpha M]+1}^{M} \left\{\mathcal{C}^{(m)} - \mathrm{CVA}\right\}, \qquad (21)$$

where the $\mathcal{C}^{(m)} - \mathrm{CVA}$s are the simulated trading losses of the reference bank ranked in increasing order.

To obtain the contribution of any simulated scenario m (with $\mathcal{C}^m \geq \mathcal{C}^{([\alpha M])}$) to the economic capital estimated by (21), we compute

$$\widehat{\mathbb{ES}}^{-m}(\mathcal{C} - \mathrm{CVA}) := \frac{1}{M - 1 - [\alpha(M-1)]} \Big\{(M - [\alpha M])\widehat{\mathbb{ES}} \times (\mathcal{C} - \mathrm{CVA}) - (\mathcal{C}^m - \mathrm{CVA})\Big\}. \qquad (22)$$

The contribution $\delta_m\widehat{\mathbb{ES}}\,(\mathcal{C} - \mathrm{CVA})$ of scenario m to $\widehat{\mathbb{ES}}\,(\mathcal{C} - \mathrm{CVA})$ is then given by

$$\delta_m\widehat{\mathbb{ES}}\,(\mathcal{C} - \mathrm{CVA}) = \widehat{\mathbb{ES}}\,(\mathcal{C} - \mathrm{CVA}) - \widehat{\mathbb{ES}}^{-m}(\mathcal{C} - \mathrm{CVA}). \qquad (23)$$

To illustrate the various flavors of stress test exercises that can be conducted by a CCP member, we report numerical results for the two

[38]This may entail re-assessment of the Pillar 2 guidance additional capital requirement set in the annual Supervisory Review and Evaluation Process reported by Banks, cf. Ref. [23] for a brief definition and use and Ref. [14] for more extensive details as well as Ref. [17] for similar requirements.

network examples introduced in Section 5. We start with a reverse stress test exercise on example covered by Table 6. For this first illustration, a specific extreme loss is targeted and the corresponding probability of loss reaching at least such target level is estimated. We then consider the example illustrated by Figure 1 where projected loss levels for specific confidence levels are indicated for the members with common memberships on the two CCPs.

6.2. *Numerical results*

In Table 8, we report, for the example summarized in Table 6, the 99.9th percentile trading loss levels, referenced as extreme quantile, with corresponding (asymmetric) confidence intervals based on the approach proposed in Ref. [32, Section G.2]. This is done for every clearing member successively playing the role of the reference bank in the setup of Sections 2–3. We also compute the probabilities of reaching a loss equal to 1.5 times the obtained extreme quantile level, referenced as RST scenario, with corresponding confidence levels.[39]

Our description of the scenarios leading to such losses includes the identified defaulted members, the generated losses and the allocated loss coefficient of the reference clearing member (CM1 in this example). Table 9 provides the description of the 20 worst scenarios, contributing the most to the EC estimation for the second biggest member, that is, CM1.[40] Most of these scenarios are driven by significant losses stemming from CM0's default, reflecting the highly concentrated position of CM0. We observe that several scenarios illustrate the cases where more than one clearing member defaults such as 2nd to 5th scenarios for which not only CM0 generates most

[39]The calculation of the latter confidence intervals of the probability of being above a quantile relies on the same numerical approach based on batches used for KVA calculations. Also, the batch approach leads to reasonably tight confidence intervals for the RST scenario probabilities.

[40]Its theoretical number of scenarios above the RST loss level should be 4,153, i.e., the number of MC simulations of 10M multiplied by CM1's survival probability over 5 years and by CM1's RST loss level probability estimated in Table 8 as 0.0428%, which is of course far too many to report. Nonetheless, a focus on the 20 worst ones already illustrates the type of information that can be exploited for such exercises.

Table 8. Stress test (ST) extreme quantile, 1.5× ST extreme quantile and RST probability to breach 1.5 times the 99.9th quantile loss level, for each member, based on 10M simulations.

cm id	99.9%	1.5 × 99.9%	RST scenario probability
0	4.9022 (−0.9%, 0.9%)	7.3534	0.0387% (5%)
1	6.7852 (−0.9%, 1%)	10.1778	0.0428% (4.4%)
2	5.4194 (−1%, 1%)	8.1291	0.0435% (4.4%)
3	4.3402 (−0.9%, 0.9%)	6.5103	0.0437% (4.3%)
4	3.3843 (−0.9%, 1%)	5.0764	0.0452% (4.5%)
5	2.7516 (−0.9%, 1%)	4.1274	0.044% (4.6%)
6	2.1804 (−1%, 0.9%)	3.2706	0.0437% (3.9%)
7	1.7481 (−1%, 1%)	2.6221	0.0434% (4.2%)
8	1.3452 (−1%, 1.2%)	2.0178	0.0435% (4.1%)
9	1.0714 (−1%, 1%)	1.6071	0.0433% (4.2%)
10	0.8362 (−1%, 1.1%)	1.2544	0.0429% (4.4%)
11	0.6325 (−0.9%, 1%)	0.9487	0.0427% (4.4%)
12	0.5330 (−1%, 0.9%)	0.7995	0.0431% (4.2%)
13	0.3688 (−0.9%, 0.9%)	0.5533	0.0428% (4.6%)
14	0.3186 (−1%, 1%)	0.4779	0.0429% (4.4%)
15	0.2626 (−0.9%, 1.1%)	0.394	0.0427% (4.3%)
16	0.2037 (−1.1%, 1.2%)	0.3055	0.0427% (4.4%)
17	0.1403 (−1.1%, 1%)	0.2105	0.0434% (4%)
18	0.1458 (−1%, 1%)	0.2187	0.0427% (4.1%)
19	0.0753 (−1%, 0.9%)	0.113	0.0431% (4%)

Note: Parentheses: Corresponding 95% confidence intervals.

of the loss but also other defaulting members generate significant losses yet of less magnitude compared to CM0.

From CM1 viewpoint (i.e., with CM1 in the role of the reference clearing member), 18 scenarios entail significant losses over the collateral posted by the defaulted CM0 (positive first entries in the last column of Table 9). CM0 bears a very large concentrated position compared to other members. Even if CM0 has more IM and DF requirements than others, this is still not enough: this example highlights that employed DF allocation rules in this example dilute the DF collateral requirements for concentrated positions. It also illustrates that scenarios with multiple defaults do not necessarily lead to extreme losses, due to the fact that members with medium or small positions have large default fund contributions stemming from others' concentrated positions.

Table 9. Economic Capital 20 worst scenarios' details for member 1 in decreasing order of total loss where column with header μ indicates allocated coefficient loss to member 1 and n is the number of defaults within the scenario.

Rank	Loss	n	μ	Defaulters	Losses triggered by defaulters
1	17.22	2	0.23	CM0, 7	842.25, 0
2	12.68	6	0.31	CM0, 2, 5, 9, 11, 14	300.22, 0, 92.28, 36.03, 20.83, 0
3	12.16	5	0.29	CM0, 2, 5, 14, 15	335.56, 0, 112.91, 0, 9.67
4	11.82	7	0.33	CM0, 3, 5, 7, 8, 9, 14	394.96, 0, 0, 0, 0, 0.65, 0
5	11.05	5	0.26	CM0, 5, 6, 10, 15	465.41, 0, 0.59, 0, 0.05
6	10.99	1	0.21	CM0	566.93
7	10.74	1	0.19	CM2	608.58
8	9.23	2	0.23	CM0, 7	451.35, 0
9	9.1	1	0.21	CM0	469.81
10	8.83	5	0.31	CM0, 2, 5, 8, 12	300.42, 14.38, 0, 0, 0
11	8.57	3	0.23	CM0, 6, 16	408.40, 1.88, 0
12	8.41	3	0.22	CM0, 16, 17	429.53, 0, 0
13	8.22	12	0.51	CM0, 3, 4, 5, 6, 7, 8, 9, 10, 11, 13, 16, 17	81.53, 0, 32.12, 22.44, 17.66, 0, 0, 9.95, 6.19, 4.84, 2.63, 1.51, 0
14	8.09	2	0.23	CM0, 7	395.87, 0
15	7.87	1	0.21	CM0	406
16	7.86	8	0.31	CM0, 4, 6, 7, 8, 9, 12, 14	275.27, 0, 0, 0, 0, 0, 0, 0
17	7.83	2	0.22	CM0, 9	391.07, 0
18	7.49	12	0.55	CM0, 2, 4, 5, 6, 7, 8, 9, 10, 11, 13, 16, 18	51.85, 0, 27.98, 25.76, 20.82, 0, 0, 8.41, 4.26, 5.33, 3.21, 1.62, 0
19	6.85	7	0.36	CM0, 2, 3, 7, 8, 12, 17	0, 84.82, 70.26, 29.05, 20.74, 0, 2.06
20	6.7	3	0.22	CM0, 10, 11	330.03, 0.39, 0.34

In Table 10, we report, for the example illustrated in Figure 1 with 2 CCPs, the trading loss levels (value-at-risks) at confidence levels 90% and 99.9%, for the 24 common members on the two CCPs. The corresponding numbers in the case where the two CCPs would be considered separately are reported in columns VII and IX.

For members with very low size on one of the two CCPs compared to the other, considering the common memberships or not does not affect the loss estimates, as expected.[41] For other members, however, at 90% confidence levels, the value-at-risks are significantly higher (compare columns VII and VIII in Table 10) when the common membership is considered compared to the stand-alone value-at-risks calculation conducted on each CCP and summed, especially for the first ten members. On the contrary, at the confidence level 99.9%, the sum of the stand-alone value-at-risks is well above the value-at-risk when common memberships are taken into consideration (columns IX and X in Table 10). These two situations illustrate that a regulator and the board (top management) of the bank could equally and rightfully criticize a simplistic stand-alone approach, too aggressive in some cases (making it unacceptable by the regulator) and over-conservative in others (making it unacceptable by the board).

7. Optimizing the Porting of Defaulted Client Portfolios

In case a clearing member defaults, the CCP tentatively novates part of the CCP portfolio of the defaulted member through auctions among the surviving clearing members Ref. [13, 19], and it liquidates the residual on the market. A natural baseline is that the CCP novates (auctions among surviving members) client trades and their mirroring client account positions, collectively dubbed client positions for brevity hereafter, whereas house account positions are liquidated.

The liquidation side of the procedure cannot be handled in our modeling setup, which does not embed the fundamentals of price formation (our MtM processes are assumed to be exogenously given). On the other hand, an XVA-based procedure can be used for

[41] As the CCP with the very low size compared to the other should have marginal impact.

Table 10. Quantile loss levels (confidence errors) for 90% and 99.9% confidence levels across members for the example with 2 CCPs and 155 members including 24 common members.

I	II	III	IV	V	VI	VII	VIII	IX	X
3	0.1	19.9	21	−97.48	23	0.0755 (−1.5%, 1.5%)	0.0794 (−1.1%, 1.1%)	4.0067 (−1.8%, 1.7%)	3.6185 (−1.8%, 1.8%)
4	0.1	80.79	24	−18.79	22	0.0687 (−1.5%, 1.4%)	0.0739 (−0.9%, 1%)	3.4324 (−2%, 2%)	3.0625 (−1.5%, 1.9%)
9	3.1	−31.58	29	17.74	23	0.0478 (−1.3%, 1.3%)	0.0624 (−0.7%, 0.7%)	1.9749 (−1.8%, 2.3%)	1.6109 (−2%, 2.1%)
12	0.1	17.97	21	−16.75	24	0.0351 (−0.9%, 0.9%)	0.0423 (−0.6%, 0.6%)	1.0592 (−1.8%, 1.9%)	0.8008 (−2%, 2.3%)
13	0.1	−14.9	22	15.81	25	0.0337 (−0.9%, 0.9%)	0.0403 (−0.6%, 0.6%)	0.9738 (−1.8%, 1.9%)	0.7319 (−2%, 2.2%)
14	0.2	12.34	23	−14.93	26	0.0323 (−0.9%, 0.9%)	0.0385 (−0.6%, 0.6%)	0.8805 (−1.7%, 1.9%)	0.6518 (−1.5%, 1.5%)
15	0.1	−10.23	24	14.09	27	0.0311 (−0.8%, 0.9%)	0.0364 (−0.6%, 0.6%)	0.8245 (−1.8%, 1.8%)	0.6175 (−2.1%, 1.8%)
17	0.3	−7.03	26	−13.3	28	0.0295 (−0.8%, 0.8%)	0.0337 (−0.5%, 0.6%)	0.6991 (−1.8%, 1.8%)	0.5259 (−2.1%, 1.7%)
19	0.2	−4.83	28	12.56	29	0.0278 (−0.7%, 0.8%)	0.0309 (−0.5%, 0.5%)	0.622 (−1.8%, 1.8%)	0.4808 (−1.8%, 2%)
22	3.9	2.75	20	−11.86	30	0.0301 (−0.7%, 0.7%)	0.0315 (−0.6%, 0.6%)	0.524 (−1.9%, 2%)	0.4439 (−1.6%, 2.2%)
26	0.1	1.3	24	11.2	20	0.0159 (−0.7%, 0.7%)	0.0164 (−0.6%, 0.6%)	0.3061 (−1.8%, 1.8%)	0.2695 (−2%, 2.1%)
27	0.1	1.07	25	−10.57	21	0.0157 (−0.7%, 0.7%)	0.016 (−0.7%, 0.6%)	0.2958 (−1.7%, 1.7%)	0.2649 (−2%, 2%)
28	1.5	0.89	26	9.98	22	0.0163 (−0.7%, 0.7%)	0.0166 (−0.7%, 0.6%)	0.2831 (−1.8%, 2.1%)	0.2533 (−2.1%, 2%)
31	0.1	−0.51	29	−9.42	23	0.0151 (−0.7%, 0.7%)	0.0151 (−0.6%, 0.7%)	0.2723 (−1.7%, 1.8%)	0.2547 (−1.9%, 1.8%)
34	0.1	0.29	21	8.89	24	0.0147 (−0.6%, 0.7%)	0.0147 (−0.6%, 0.6%)	0.2539 (−1.7%, 1.8%)	0.2469 (−2%, 1.8%)
35	0.1	−0.24	22	−8.4	25	0.0145 (−0.6%, 0.7%)	0.0144 (−0.6%, 0.6%)	0.2482 (−1.8%, 1.7%)	0.242 (−2%, 1.8%)
36	0.1	0.2	23	7.93	26	0.0142 (−0.6%, 0.6%)	0.0141 (−0.7%, 0.6%)	0.2427 (−1.8%, 1.6%)	0.2375 (−2%, 1.8%)
39	0.1	−0.11	26	−7.48	27	0.0138 (−0.6%, 0.6%)	0.0138 (−0.6%, 0.6%)	0.2361 (−1.8%, 1.7%)	0.2328 (−1.8%, 1.7%)
40	0.5	0.09	27	7.07	28	0.0138 (−0.7%, 0.6%)	0.0138 (−0.7%, 0.7%)	0.225 (−2%, 1.6%)	0.2218 (−2%, 1.4%)
44	0.1	0.04	20	−6.67	29	0.0132 (−0.6%, 0.6%)	0.0131 (−0.6%, 0.6%)	0.2224 (−1.8%, 1.7%)	0.2217 (−1.8%, 1.7%)
49	0.1	−0.02	25	6.3	30	0.0129 (−0.6%, 0.6%)	0.0129 (−0.6%, 0.7%)	0.2168 (−1.8%, 1.7%)	0.2163 (−1.8%, 1.7%)
50	0.1	0.01	26	−5.95	20	0.0081 (−0.6%, 0.6%)	0.0081 (−0.6%, 0.6%)	0.1366 (−1.7%, 1.7%)	0.1364 (−1.7%, 1.7%)
51	0.1	−0.01	27	5.61	21	0.008 (−0.6%, 0.6%)	0.008 (−0.6%, 0.6%)	0.1355 (−1.8%, 1.7%)	0.1352 (−1.8%, 1.7%)
55	0.1	−0.01	20	−5.3	22	0.008 (−0.6%, 0.6%)	0.008 (−0.6%, 0.6%)	0.134 (−1.7%, 1.7%)	0.1338 (−1.8%, 1.8%)

Notes: Legend for column headers: I. Member Id, II. DP (%), III. Size on CCP1, IV. Volatility on CCP1, V. Size on CCP2, VI. Volatility on CCP2, VII. 90th Perc. stand-alone, VIII. 90th Perc., IX. 99.9th Perc. stand-alone, X. 99.9th Perc.

rendering what would be the output of an idealized, efficient auction, assuming a large number of clearing members Ref. [35, Section 3.3]. Namely, supposing that the reference clearing member, labeled as 0 in Sections 2–3, defaults at time 0, i.e., just after that all portfolios have been settled, for each surviving member CM$*$ successively envisioned as a potential taker of the defaulted (client) positions of CM0, one computes the incremental (Δ) XVAs of porting the defaulted positions to CM$*$, for each surviving member (CM$*$ included[42]). The corresponding incremental XVA numbers are then summed over metrics and survivors, resulting in the funds transfer price (FTP$*$) of porting defaulted client positions to CM$*$. The effective taker is then the surviving member for which the ensuing FTP$*$ is the smallest.[43] See Ref. [5, Section 5.2] for more details on such "XVA Pareto optimally driven" novation procedures.

In what follows, based on the example in Table 6 (which only involves client positions), we analyze from this perspective a first scenario of a single default on the CCP.

Taking the first case with a single default, we first assume the scenario whereby CM0 defaults at time 0. Table 11 summarizes the total ΔXVA$*$ aggregated over survivors, across members $*$ from 1 to 19, in increasing order of the FTP$*$ indicated in the last column. Based on the results of Table 11, CM1 appears to be the potential taker leading to the least overall FTP costs across all surviving members. This is understandable as this member's portfolio size (184 in Table 6) nets the most the defaulted member's portfolio size (-242) with volatility and credit default probability similar to[44] the ones of the defaulted member.

As CM1 concentrates more risks due in particular to non-perfect offset[45] between its prior positions and the defaulting one, there is

[42]Note that all members are impacted by additional margin to fund due to the re-calibration of their DF by the CCP, whereas only the member taker of the portfolio sees in addition its IM adjusted.

[43]Or, indifferently in case of multiple minima, one of the minimizing FTP$*$ members.

[44]In particular, not significantly higher than.

[45]By offset we refer to risk reduction when taking over some additional position. The effect of correlation is such that an opposite sign in portfolio size does not imply an equal offset of the risk of the aggregated positions. For instance, even

Table 11. Total ΔXVA∗ aggregated over survivors corresponding to the different surviving CM∗, i.e., for ∗ other than 0, assuming an instant default of CM0 at time 0. In parentheses, the contributions to ΔXVA∗ of CM∗ itself.

Surv. member ∗	Total ΔCMVA∗	Total ΔCCVA∗	Total ΔKVA∗	Total FTP∗
1	0.0768 (0.0295)	−0.0511 (−0.0038)	−0.9182 (−0.1709)	−0.8926 (−0.1452)
2	0.0921 (0.0428)	−0.047 (0.0028)	−0.8262 (−0.0866)	−0.7811 (−0.0411)
3	0.1054 (0.0576)	−0.0394 (0.0088)	−0.7307 (−0.0185)	−0.6647 (0.0479)
19	0.1298 (0.0818)	−0.0253 (0.039)	−0.6785 (0.2818)	−0.574 (0.4026)
18	0.1417 (0.0939)	−0.0192 (0.0379)	−0.5995 (0.2693)	−0.477 (0.401)
17	0.1549 (0.107)	−0.0138 (0.0377)	−0.5547 (0.2702)	−0.4137 (0.4149)
16	0.1688 (0.1208)	−0.0088 (0.037)	−0.4435 (0.2665)	−0.2835 (0.4243)
15	0.1814 (0.1334)	−0.0032 (0.0363)	−0.3841 (0.2622)	−0.2059 (0.4319)
4	0.1525 (0.1022)	−0.0364 (0.0159)	−0.2671 (0.0427)	−0.151 (0.1608)
14	0.1903 (0.1426)	0.0035 (0.0353)	−0.3146 (0.253)	−0.1208 (0.4309)
13	0.2061 (0.1582)	0.008 (0.035)	−0.2108 (0.2583)	0.0033 (0.4515)
12	0.2171 (0.1692)	0.0101 (0.0335)	−0.1767 (0.2458)	0.0506 (0.4485)
8	0.234 (0.1881)	0.02 (0.0264)	−0.1305 (0.1778)	0.1235 (0.3924)
11	0.2285 (0.1807)	0.0147 (0.0326)	−0.101 (0.2415)	0.1422 (0.4548)
7	0.2327 (0.1876)	0.02 (0.0235)	−0.0949 (0.1501)	0.1578 (0.3612)
10	0.2385 (0.1908)	0.0188 (0.0311)	−0.0259 (0.2316)	0.2314 (0.4535)
9	0.2478 (0.2003)	0.0205 (0.029)	0.0442 (0.2158)	0.3125 (0.4451)
6	0.2687 (0.2225)	0.0215 (0.0205)	0.2937 (0.1399)	0.5839 (0.3828)
5	0.2728 (0.2274)	0.0189 (0.0163)	0.3527 (0.0922)	0.6444 (0.3359)

an increase in its IM reflected through an increase in CMVA. But the new risk of CM1 is less than the sum of the former risks of CM0 and CM1, hence the ΔCCVA aggregated across surviving members is reduced. This only happens when CM1 takes over the defaulting portfolio, other potential takers leading to an overall increase in the CCVA. As for the KVA, there is a reduction effect for CM1 when CM1 is the taker (see the term in parentheses in Table 11), and an overall decrease in the total KVA (aggregated over all surviving members), which is also the case for most members. Having CM1 as the taker allows one to obtain the most significant decrease in ΔKVA.

As expected, among the three XVA components, KVA is the main determinant of the optimal taker, see Table 12.

---

with opposite sizes and same volatilities but for $\rho^{mkt} \in (0, 1/2)$, the member ends up with more risk.

Table 12. Standard deviation across surviving members $*$ of the ΔXVA$*$ for the example with 1 CCP and 20 members, assuming an instant default of CM0 at time 0.

ΔCMVA	ΔCCVA	ΔKVA
0.0593	0.0251	0.3557

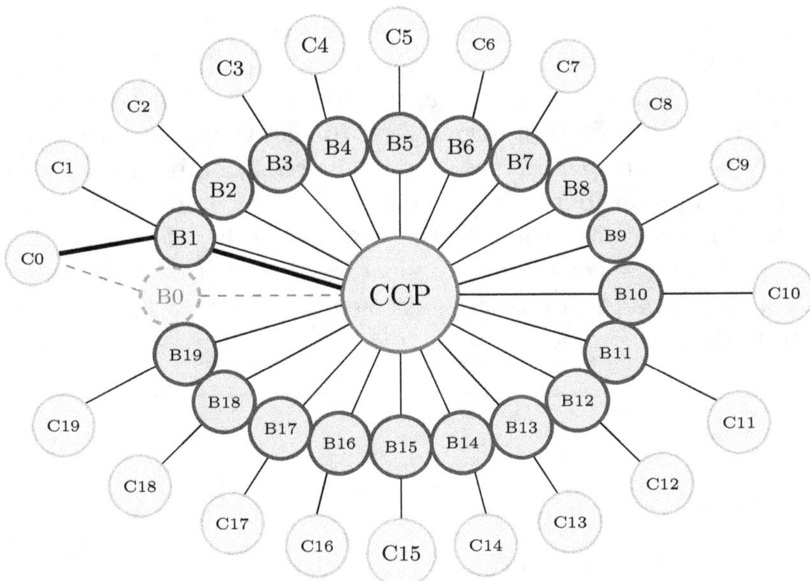

Figure 8. The 1-CCP, former 20-member financial network with 19 members post CM0 default. Defaulted CM0, labeled "B0" in the presented network, is represented as pale dashed node with pale dashed links to reflect former exposures to its client and toward the CCP. The optimal porting of CM0 portfolio with CM1, labeled "B1", is outlined with bold links to reflect the new exposures for CM1.

Once the CCP has re-allocated all defaulted client positions, the resulting financial network formerly depicted in Figure 3 becomes the network with 19 members shown in Figure 8. The thick lines represent the new portfolio exposures for CM1 and the pale dashed lines show the defaulted CM0 positions.

8. Conclusion

We have proposed a fully integrated risk management framework that can be used for stress test analysis, including reverse stress test in line with regulatory requirements, or for optimizing the porting of defaulted portfolios, in a setup encompassing all the trades (bilateral as centrally cleared and their hedges) of a reference bank. The framework includes dependence between financial participants' portfolios, joint defaults and a configurable wrong-way risk feature. This is done in a numerically tractable static setup (although already quite demanding on large financial networks).[46] A possible improvement would be to incorporate regulatory constraints, such as minimum regulatory capital requirements and liquidity leverage ratios. More fundamentally, in this chapter, we tackle the derivatives' risk problem from a pure counterparty credit risk viewpoint: if members, clients and counterparties are all default-free, then in view of Proposition 3.9, all considered XVAs are zero so that our setup becomes trivial. Another dimension to the problem is liquidity Ref. [8, 26]. Depending on the considered applications,[47] credit or liquidity is the main force at hand. A challenging research project would be to integrate both in a common setup.

Appendix

A Proofs

A.1. *Proof of Lemma 3.4*

On the bilateral trades of the bank and their hedges, the Treasury of the bank receives $\sum_b \mathrm{VM}_b$ of variation margin from its counterparties and has to post an aggregated amount $\sum_b \mathrm{MtM}_b$ of variation margin. Assumption 3.3 then leads to (3).

[46]The dynamic extension considered in Ref. [18, Section 6] is only workable at a much higher computational burden, using the simulation and learning techniques of Ref. [1].

[47]See, e.g., the beginning of Section 7.

A.2. *Proof of Lemma 3.5*

In view of Lemma 3.4 and Assumption 3.3, the (risky) funding expenses of the bank correspond to the formula (6) for $\mathcal{F}$. Regarding $\mathcal{C}$, on the CCP survival event $\{\mathcal{J}=1\}$, the CCP receives, by Assumption 3.2,

$$\sum_i \Big(J_i(\mathcal{P}_i+\overline{\mathcal{P}}_i) + (1-J_i)\Big(\mathcal{P}_i \wedge (\mathrm{MtM}_i + \mathrm{IM}_i) \\ +\overline{\mathcal{P}}_i \wedge (\overline{\mathrm{MtM}}_i + \overline{\mathrm{IM}}_i) + \big((\mathcal{P}_i - (\mathrm{MtM}_i + \mathrm{IM}_i))^+ \\ +(\overline{\mathcal{P}}_i - (\overline{\mathrm{MtM}}_i + \overline{\mathrm{IM}}_i))^+\big) \wedge \mathrm{DF}_i\Big)\Big). \tag{24}$$

By the CCP clearing condition in Assumption 3.1,

$$0 = \sum_i (\mathcal{P}_i+\overline{\mathcal{P}}_i) = \sum_i \big(J_i(\mathcal{P}_i+\overline{\mathcal{P}}_i) + (1-J_i)(\mathcal{P}_i+\overline{\mathcal{P}}_i)\big).$$

Hence (24) is equal to

$$-\sum_i (1-J_i)\big((\mathcal{P}_i - \mathrm{MtM}_i - \mathrm{IM}_i)^+ \\ +(\overline{\mathcal{P}}_i - \overline{\mathrm{MtM}}_i - \overline{\mathrm{IM}}_i)^+ - \mathrm{DF}_i\big)^+ = -\mathcal{L}$$

by definition (5) of $\mathcal{L}$.

On the bank survival event $\{J=1\}$ ($\subseteq \{\mathcal{J}=1\}$), by the respective Assumptions 3.2 and 3.1, the bank receives from its clients and counterparties

$$\sum_c \Big(J_c\mathcal{P}_c + (1-J_c)\big(\mathcal{P}_c \wedge (\mathrm{MtM}_c + \mathrm{IM}_c)\big)\Big) \\ + \sum_b \Big(J_b\mathcal{P}_b + (1-J_b)\big(\mathcal{P}_b \wedge (\mathrm{VM}_b + \mathrm{IM}_b)\big)\Big), \tag{25}$$

respectively, pays to the CCP

$$\sum_c \mathcal{P}_c + \sum_b \mathcal{P}_b = \sum_c \big(J_c\mathcal{P}_c + (1-J_c)\mathcal{P}_c\big) \\ + \sum_b \big(J_b\mathcal{P}_b + (1-J_b)\,\mathcal{P}_b\big). \tag{26}$$

Subtracting (25) from (26), we obtain

$$\sum_c (1-J_c)(\mathcal{P}_c - \mathrm{MtM}_c - \mathrm{IM}_c)^+ + \sum_b (1-J_b)(\mathcal{P}_b - \mathrm{VM}_b - \mathrm{IM}_\mathrm{b})^+.$$

On top of this comes the participation $\mu\mathcal{L}$ of the bank to the CCP default losses, which yields formula (4) for $\mathcal{C}$.

A.3. *Proof of Theorem 3.7*

By the result recalled after (8), EC is non-negative as an expected shortfall under $\mathbb{R}$ of the random variable $J(\mathcal{C}+\mathcal{F}-\mathrm{CA})$, which is centered under $\mathbb{R}^\star$ and therefore under $\mathbb{R}$, by (7). The first four formulas in Table 2 directly follow from the definitions of Table 1 and Lemma 3.6, which also implies that $\mathrm{KVA} = \mathbb{E}\big(h(\mathrm{EC}-\mathrm{KVA})^+\big) = h(\mathrm{EC}-\mathrm{KVA})^+$. As h is non-negative, this KVA semilinear equation is equivalent to

$$(\mathrm{KVA} > \mathrm{EC} \text{ and } \mathrm{KVA} = 0) \text{ or } \left(\mathrm{KVA} \le \mathrm{EC} \text{ and } \mathrm{KVA} = \frac{h}{1+h}\mathrm{EC}\right),$$

where $(\mathrm{KVA} > \mathrm{EC}$ and $\mathrm{KVA} = 0)$ contradicts the non-negativity of EC, whereas, for $h \in [0,1]$ as assumed and $\mathrm{EC} \ge 0$, $\mathrm{KVA} = \frac{h}{1+h}\mathrm{EC}$ implies $\mathrm{KVA} \le \mathrm{EC}$, i.e., $\max(\mathrm{EC},\mathrm{KVA}) = \mathrm{EC}$. This and Lemma 3.6 yield

$$\begin{aligned}\mathrm{FVA} &= \mathbb{E}\Big(\gamma\big(\sum_b(\mathrm{MtM}_b - \mathrm{VM}_b) - \mathrm{CA} - \mathrm{EC}\big)^+\Big)\\ &= \gamma\big(\sum_b(\mathrm{MtM}_b - \mathrm{VM}_b) - \mathrm{CA} - \mathrm{EC}\big)^+.\end{aligned}$$

As $\mathrm{CA} = \mathrm{CCVA} + \mathrm{CMVA} + \mathrm{BCVA} + \mathrm{BMVA} + \mathrm{FVA}$, this is an FVA semilinear equation, which, as γ is non-negative, is equivalent to the FVA formula

$$\begin{aligned}\mathrm{FVA} = \frac{\gamma}{1+\gamma}\Bigg(&\sum_b(\mathrm{MtM}_b - \mathrm{VM}_b) - (\mathrm{CCVA} + \mathrm{CMVA} + \mathrm{BCVA}\\ &+ \mathrm{BMVA}) - \mathrm{EC}\Bigg)^+.\end{aligned}$$

Last, we have $\mathrm{EC} = \mathbb{ES}(J(\mathcal{C}+\mathcal{F}-\mathrm{CA}))$, where the identity $\mathcal{C}+\mathcal{F}-\mathrm{CA} = \mathcal{C}-\mathrm{CVA}$ and the formula for $J(\mathcal{C}-\mathrm{CVA})$ in Table 2 are obtained by substituting the already derived XVA formulas in (4) and (6).

A.4. *Proof of Proposition 3.9*

In the case of several CCP services, the second line in (3) must be turned into $\sum_{ccp}\left(\mathrm{IM}^{\mathrm{ccp}}+\overline{\mathrm{IM}}^{\mathrm{ccp}}+\mathrm{DF}^{\mathrm{ccp}}\right)+\sum_{\mathrm{b}}\overline{\mathrm{IM}}_{\mathrm{b}}$; the terms in the first lines of (4) and (6) must be summed over the various CCP services in which the bank is involved as a clearing member. The rest of the analysis proceeds as before.

A.5. *Proof of Lemma 3.10*

If $\mathbb{R}(\ell=\mathbb{V}\mathrm{a}\mathbb{R}(\ell))=0$, then, by the ES formula recalled after (8), we have

$$
\begin{aligned}
\mathrm{EC}=\mathbb{ES}(\ell)&=\mathbb{E}\big(J(\mathcal{C}-\mathrm{CVA})\big|J(\mathcal{C}-\mathrm{CVA})\geq\mathbb{V}\mathrm{a}\mathbb{R}(\ell)\big)\big)\\
&=\frac{\mathbb{E}\left(J(\mathcal{C}-\mathrm{CVA})\mathbb{1}_{\left\{J(\mathcal{C}-\mathrm{CVA})\geq\mathbb{V}\mathrm{a}\mathbb{R}(\ell)\right\}}\right)}{\mathbb{R}\big(J(\mathcal{C}-\mathrm{CVA})\geq\mathbb{V}\mathrm{a}\mathbb{R}(\ell)\big)}\\
&=\frac{\mathbb{E}^{\star}\left((\mathcal{C}-\mathrm{CVA})\mathbb{1}_{\left\{(\mathcal{C}-\mathrm{CVA})\geq\mathbb{V}\mathrm{a}\mathbb{R}(\ell)\right\}}\mathbb{1}_{\{J=1\}}\right)}{\mathbb{R}^{\star}\big((\mathcal{C}-\mathrm{CVA})\geq\mathbb{V}\mathrm{a}\mathbb{R}(\ell),J=1\big)},
\end{aligned}
$$

using (7) on both numerator and denominator expressed in expectation form, which yields (13).

Acknowledgments

We thank Paul Besson, Head of Quantitative research, Euronext, and Mohamed Selmi, Head of Market Risk, LCH SA, for useful discussions. This work benefited from the support of the grant *When Credit Meets Liquidity: The Clearing Member Default Resolution Issue*, under the aegis of the Europlace Institute of Finance, France. The research of S. Crépey benefited from the support of the *Chair Stress Test, RISK Management and Financial Steering*, led by the

French École polytechnique and its Foundation and sponsored by BNP Paribas.

References

[1] L. Abbas-Turki, S. Crépey, and B. Saadeddine. Pathwise CVA regressions with oversimulated defaults. *Mathematical Finance*, 33, 274–307, 2023.

[2] C. Acerbi and D. Tasche.On the coherence of expected shortfall. *Journal of Banking & Finance*, 26:1487–1503, 2002.

[3] C. Albanese, Y. Armenti, and S. Crépey. XVA metrics for CCP optimization. *Statistics & Risk Modeling*, 37(1–2):25–53, 2020.

[4] C. Albanese, S. Caenazzo, and S. Crépey. Credit, funding, margin, and capital valuation adjustments for bilateral portfolios. *Probability, Uncertainty and Quantitative Risk*, 2(7):26, 2017.

[5] C. Albanese, M. Chataigner, and S. Crépey. Wealth transfers, indifference pricing, and XVA compression schemes. In Y. Jiao (Ed.), *From Probability to Finance—Lecture Note of BICMR Summer School on Financial Mathematics*, Mathematical Lectures from Peking University Series, Springer, 2020, pp. 219–248.

[6] C. Albanese, S. Crépey, R. Hoskinson, and B. Saadeddine. XVA analysis from the balance sheet. *Quantitative Finance*, 21(1):99–123, 2021.

[7] C. Albanese, S. Crépey, and S. Iabichino. Quantitative reverse stress testing, bottom-up. *Quantitative Finance*. Conditionally Accepted, 23(5), 2022.

[8] H. Amini, D. Filipovic, and A. Minca. Systemic risk in networks with a central node. *SIAM Journal on Financial Mathematics*, 11(1):60–98, 2020.

[9] L. Andersen and A. Dickinson. Funding and credit risk with locally elliptical portfolio processes: An application to CCPs. *Journal of Financial Market Infrastructures*, 7(4):27–70, June, 2019.

[10] P. Artzner, K.-T. Eisele and T. Schmidt, No Arbitrage in Insurance and the QP-Rule (May 22, 2020). Available at SSRN: https://ssrn.com/abstract=3607708 or http://dx.doi.org/10.2139/ssrn.3607708?.

[11] Bank of International Settlements and OICV-IOSCO. Public quantitative disclosure standards for central counterparties, 2021. Retrieved on June 14, 2021 on https://www.bis.org/cpmi/publ/d125.pdf.

[12] Basel Committee on Banking Supervision. An explanatory note on the Basel II IRB risk weight functions, 2005. Retrieved on July 19, 2021 on https://www.bis.org/bcbs/irbriskweight.htm.

[13] Basel Committee on Banking Supervision. A discussion paper on central counterparty default management auctions, 2019a. Retrieved on November 11, 2019 on https://www.bis.org/cpmi/publ/d185.pdf.

[14] Basel Committee on Banking Supervision. Overview of Pillar 2 supervisory review practices and approaches, 2019b. Retrieved on November 25, 2021 on https://www.bis.org/bcbs/publ/d465.pdf.

[15] Board of Governors of the Federal Reserve System. Rules and regulations, policy statement on the scenario design framework for stress testing. *Federal Register*, November, 2013. Retrieved on November 15, 2021 on https://www.gpo.gov/.

[16] Board of Governors of the Federal Reserve System. Guidance on stress testing for banking organizations with total consolidated assets of more than $10 billion. *SR Letter 12-7*, May 2012. Retrieved on November 19, 2021 on https://www.federalreserve.gov/supervisionreg/.

[17] Board of Governors of the Federal Reserve System. Amendments to the regulatory capital, capital plan, and stress test rules, October, 2020. Retrieved on November 15, 2021 on https://www.federalreserve.gov/newsevents/pressreleases/bcreg20200304a.htm.

[18] S. Crépey. Positive XVAs. *Frontiers of Mathematical Finance*, 1(3):425–465, 2022. doi: 10.3934/fmf.2022003.

[19] Default Risk Management Working Group. Uniform CCP terminology for default management auctions. Technical report, Commodity Futures Trading Commission (CFTC), 2016. Retrieved on November 11, 2019 on https://www.cftc.gov/sites/default/files/idc/groups/public/@aboutcftc/documents/file/mrac062716_uniformccp.pdf.

[20] Dordu, B., R. Edge, and D. Schwindt. Measuring the severity of stress-test scenarios. *FEDS Notes*, May 5, 2017. Retrieved on November 15, 2021 on https://www.federalreserve.gov/econres/notes/feds-notes/.

[21] M. Eichhorn, T. Bellini, and D. Mayenberger. *Reverse Stress Testing in Banking: A Comprehensive Guide.* De Gruyter, Berlin, Boston, 2021.

[22] European Bank Authority. 2021 eu-wide stress test - methodological note, 2021. Retrieved on July 19, 2021 on https://www.eba.europa.eu/eba-launches-2021-eu-wide-stress-test-exercise.

[23] European Central Bank. Pillar 2 guidance (P2G), 2021. Retrieved on November 25, 2021 on https://www.bankingsupervision.europa.eu/banking/srep/html/p2g.en.html.

[24] European Central Bank. ECB guide to the internal capital adequacy assessment process (ICAAP). *Banking Supervision*, November, 2018. Retrieved on November 19, 2021 on https://www.bankingsupervision.europa.eu/home/html/index.en.html.

[25] European Systemic Risk Board. Macro-financial scenario for the 2020 EU-wide banking sector stress test. *European Banking Authority*, November, 2013. Retrieved on November 15, 2021 on https://www.eba.europa.eu/eba-launches-2020-eu-wide-stress-test-exercise.
[26] U. Faruqui, W. Huang, and E. Takats. Clearing risks in OTC derivatives markets: The CCP-bank nexus. *BIS Quarterly Review*, December 2018.
[27] J. Gregory. *Central Counterparties: Mandatory Central Clearing and Initial Margin Requirements for OTC Derivatives.* Wiley, Southern Gate, United Kingdom, 2014.
[28] J. Gregory. *The xVA Challenge: Counterparty Credit Risk, Funding, Collateral and Capital.* Wiley, Southern Gate, United Kingdom, 2015.
[29] M. Kaina and L. Rüschendorf. On convex risk measures on l^p-spaces. *Mathematical Methods of Operations Research*, 69(3):475–495, 2009.
[30] A. Lipton. Systemic risks in central counterparty clearing house networks. In L. A. M. Pykhtin (Ed.), *Margin in Derivatives Trading*, 2018, pp. 367–401. Risk Books, London.
[31] A. J. McNeil, R. Frey, and P. Embrechts. *Quantitative Risk Management: Concepts, Techniques and Tools* (revised ed.). Princeton Series in Finance, Princeton, New Jersey, United States, 2015.
[32] W. Q. Meeker, G. J. Hahn, and L. A. Escobar. *Statistical Intervals, A Guide for Practitioners and Researchers.* Wiley, Hoboken, New Jersey, United States, 2017.
[33] A. J. Menkveld and G. Vuillemey. The economics of central clearing. *Annual Review of Financial Economics*, 13:153–178, 2021.
[34] D. Murphy and P. Nahai-Williamson. Dear prudence, won't you come out to play? approaches to the analysis of central counterparty default fund adequacy. *Financial Stability Paper*, 30:1–21, October, 2014.
[35] R. Oleschak *et al.* Central counterparty auctions and loss allocation. Technical report, Swiss National Bank, 2019.
[36] The European Parliament and the Council of the European Union. Regulation (EU) No 575/2013 of the European parliament and of the council of 26 June 2013 on prudential requirements for credit institutions and investment firms and amending regulation (EU) No 648/2012. *Official Journal of the European Union*, 2013. Retrieved on July 19, 2021 on https://eur-lex.europa.eu/legal-content/EN/TXT/PDF/?uri=CELEX:32013R0575&qid=1626646160733&from=EN.
[37] The United States Congress. Dodd-Frank Wall Street reform and consumer protection act, July, 2010. https://www.congress.gov/111/plaws/publ203/PLAW-111publ203.pdf.

https://doi.org/10.1142/9789811280306_0009

Chapter 9

Approximation with Independent Variables

Freddy Delbaen[*,‡] **and Chitro Majumdar**[†,§,¶]

[*] *Departement für Mathematik, ETH Zürich, Rämistrasse 101, 8092 Zürich, Switzerland, also Institut für Mathematik, Universität Zürich, Winterthurerstrasse 190, 8057 Zürich, Switzerland*

[†] *RSRL, Chitro Majumdar (Corresponding Author), Jumeirah Beach Residence (JBR), Dubai, United Arab Emirates*

[‡] *delbaen@math.ethz.ch*

[§] *chitro.majumdar@rsquarerisklab.com*

[¶] *chitromajumdar@icloud.com*

Abstract

Given a square integrable m-dimensional random variable X on a probability space $(\Omega, \mathcal{F}, \mathbb{P})$ and a sub sigma-algebra $\mathcal{A}$, we show that there exists another m-dimensional random variable Y, independent of $\mathcal{A}$ and minimizing the L^2 distance to X. Such results have an importance to fairness and bias reduction in artificial intelligence, machine learning and network theory.

Keywords: Independence, Approximation, Transport theory, Optimal transport plan, Monge-Kantorovich

1. Notation and Preliminaries

We use standard probabilistic notation, $(\Omega, \mathcal{F}, \mathbb{P})$ is a probability space and $\mathcal{A} \subset \mathcal{F}$ is a sub σ-algebra. All random variables will be square-integrable and all norms will be the L^2 norm. For random variables $X\colon \Omega \to \mathbb{R}^m$, the norm is then defined as $\|X\|^2 = \int |X|^2 \mathbb{P}[d\omega]$, where for $x \in \mathbb{R}^m$, $|x|$ denotes the Euclidean norm of x. The problem we want to solve is the following: Given a random variable $X\colon \Omega \to \mathbb{R}^m$, $X \in L^2$, can we find a random variable $Y\colon \Omega \to \mathbb{R}^m$ which is independent of the σ-algebra $\mathcal{A}$ and which minimizes $\|X-Y\|$ among all m-dimensional random variables that are independent of $\mathcal{A}$?

The motivation to study this problem found its origin in artificial intelligence and neural networks. If a random outcome X is observed that is subject to perturbations described by the information structure or sigma-algebra $\mathcal{A}$, then we would like to replace X with a random variable Y that is independent of these perturbations or biases. We use the L^2 distance as a measure for approximation, but the method of proof of the existence of Y also works for $L^p, 1 \leq p < \infty$, distances. However, in this case, the relation with correlation coefficients disappears.

The idea of the proof is to use results of transport theory and the Wasserstein metric. We do not need the deeper results of this theory, so the reader can look up the necessary tools in any book on this topic, see, for instance, [9]. To find an independent random variable that solves our problem, we will use a parametrized form of the solution of suitable Monge–Kantorovich problems. To solve the necessary measurability issues, we will state and prove some (probably known) measurability results on the dependence of optimal transport plans. In case the dimension $m = 1$, the use of transport theory can be simplified and can be replaced — as is well known from transport theory — by the use of commonotonicity. The optimization of the L^2 distance is then based on the inequalities 368 page 261 and 378 page 278 in Ref. [4].

To avoid possible complications with sets of measure zero, we will suppose that $\mathcal{A}$ contains all null sets of $\mathcal{F}$. Since we are looking for a random variable that is independent of $\mathcal{A}$, we suppose that there is a $U\colon \Omega \to [0,1]$ uniformly distributed and independent of $\mathcal{A}$. This condition is equivalent to the condition that $\mathcal{F}$ is atomless with respect to $\mathcal{A}$, see Ref. [3]. It guarantees the existence of random variables with arbitrary distribution.

We now recall some facts about conditional distributions and independence. The reader can look up the details in Ref. [7], page 126, Theorem 5, where the theorems are proved for $\mathbb{R}^m$ (the cases we will use), but they remain valid for Polish spaces, see Ref. [2].

Lemma 1.1. *Let E be a Polish space equipped with its Borel sigma-algebra $\mathcal{E}$. Let $Z\colon \Omega \to E$ be a measurable function. Furthermore, let $\mathcal{A} \subset \mathcal{F}$ be a sub sigma-algebra. There exists a kernel $\mu\colon \Omega \times \mathcal{E}$ such that*

1. *for each $F \in \mathcal{E}$, the mapping $\omega \to \mu(\omega, F)$ is $\mathcal{A}$ measurable,*
2. *for almost every $\omega \in \Omega$, the mapping $F \to \mu(\omega, F)$ defines a probability on $\mathcal{E}$,*
3. *for each bounded measurable function $h\colon E \to \mathbb{R}$, the conditional expectation is given by $\mathbb{E}[h(Z) \mid \mathcal{A}](\omega) = \int_E h(x)\mu(\omega, dx)$ almost everywhere.*

Lemma 1.2. *With the notation of the previous lemma, we have that Z is independent of $\mathcal{A}$ if and only if almost everywhere $\mu(\omega, .) = \nu$, where $\nu = \mathbb{P} \circ Z^{-1}$ is the distribution of Z.*

Lemma 1.3. *Z is independent of $\mathcal{A}$ if and only if for each $A \in \mathcal{A}$ and each bounded continuous function $h\colon \mathbb{R} \to \mathbb{R}$ we have $\mathbb{E}[h(Z)\mathbf{1}_A] = \mathbb{P}[A]\,\mathbb{E}[h(Z)]$. For sets the situation is easier, a set $B \in \mathcal{F}$ is independent of $\mathcal{A}$ if and only if $\mathbb{E}[\mathbf{1}_B \mid \mathcal{A}] = \mathbb{P}[B]$.*

2. Realization of Measures with Random Variables

It is well known that for a Polish space $(E, \mathcal{E})$ an arbitrary probability measure α on $\mathcal{E}$ can be realized with a random variable, a Borel measurable function $\psi\colon [0, 1] \to E$, meaning that the distribution of ψ equals α. We need a parametrized version of this result. The following theorem, due to Blackwell and Dubins, [1] says a lot more than we need.

Theorem 2.1. *For a Polish space $(E, \mathcal{E})$, let $\mathbf{M}$ be the set of probability measures on $\mathcal{E}$. There exists a Borel measurable function $h\colon \mathbf{M} \times [0, 1] \to E$ such that for each $\alpha \in \mathbf{M}$, the distribution of $h(\alpha, .)$ ($[0, 1]$ is equipped with the Lebesgue measure λ) is precisely α. Furthermore, if $\alpha_n \to \alpha$ is a weak* converging sequence, then $h(\alpha_n, t) \to h(\alpha, t)$ λ almost surely.*

Remark 2.2. We do not need the continuity part of the theorem. We only need the existence and the Borel measurability of h.

Remark 2.3. The Blackwell–Dubins theorem is a refinement of the Skorohod theorem which says that if $\mu_n, n \geq 1$ is a sequence of probability measures on a Polish space E, converging weak* to a probability measure μ, then there exists a sequence of Borel measurable functions $X_n, n \geq 1$, and a Borel measurable function X such that $X_n \colon [0,1] \to E$, $X_n \to X$, almost everywhere and the distribution of X_n is μ_n. Of course, the distribution of X is then μ. This allows one to replace the weak* convergence with a pointwise convergence of measurable functions. We will, without mentioning, use this trick when we use the monotone convergence theorem, Fatou's lemma and truncation arguments for weak* convergence.

3. The Wasserstein Metric and Transport Problems

For two probability measures μ, ν on $\mathbb{R}^m$, each having second moments, i.e., $\int_{\mathbb{R}^m} |x|^2 d\mu + \int_{\mathbb{R}^m} |x|^2 d\nu < \infty$, we denote by $\Pi(\mu,\nu)$ the set of probability measures γ on $\mathbb{R}^m \times \mathbb{R}^m$ such that the marginals of γ are precisely μ and ν. Obviously, this set is closed in the weak* topology of probability measures on $\mathbb{R}^m \times \mathbb{R}^m$. The set $K(\mu,\nu)$ denotes the subset of $\Pi(\mu,\nu)$ realizing the minimum of $\int_{\mathbb{R}^m \times \mathbb{R}^m} |x-y|^2 d\gamma$ on $\Pi(\mu,\nu)$. The set $K(\mu,\nu)$ was shown to exist by Kantorovitch and is the object of transport theory [9]. To make the statements easier to read, let us denote by $\mathbf{M}_2(k)$ the set of probability measures on $\mathbb{R}^k$ having finite second moment. There are two topologies on $\mathbf{M}_2(k)$ that are of interest to us. The first one is the weak* topology and the second one is the topology asking the convergence of $\int f d\gamma$, where f runs through the set of continuous functions that are quadratically bounded, i.e., there is a constant C such that for all $x \in \mathbb{R}^k$ we have $|f(x)| \leq C(1+|x|^2)$. This topology, which we denote by $\mathcal{T}_2$, turns $\mathbf{M}_2(k)$ into a Polish space. As easily seen, $\mu_n \to \mu$ for $\mathcal{T}_2$ if and only if $\mu_n \to \mu$ weak* and $\int_{\mathbb{R}^k} |x|^2 d\mu_n \to \int_{\mathbb{R}^k} |x|^2 d\mu$. The square of the Wasserstein distance $W(\mu,\nu)$ between two elements $\mu,\nu \in \mathbf{M}_2(m)$ is defined as $W^2(\mu,\nu) = \int_{\mathbb{R}^m \times \mathbb{R}^m} |x-y|^2 d\gamma$, where $\gamma \in K(\mu,\nu)$.

Theorem 3.1. *With the notation introduced in the preceding paragraph, the set*

$$\{(\mu,\nu,\gamma) \mid \mu,\nu \in \mathbf{M}_2(m), \gamma \in K(\mu,\nu)\}$$

is closed in $\mathbf{M}_2(m) \times \mathbf{M}_2(m) \times \mathbf{M}_2(2m)$, *equipped with the product topology of the corresponding* $\mathcal{T}_2$ *topologies. For each* $(\mu, \nu) \in \mathbf{M}_2(m) \times \mathbf{M}_2(m)$, *the set* $K(\mu, \nu)$ *is compact for* $\mathcal{T}_2$. *The Wasserstein distance is continuous on* $\mathbf{M}_2(m) \times \mathbf{M}_2(m)$ *for the product topology of the* $\mathcal{T}_2$ *topologies.*

Proof. These results are standard but for completeness we will give a proof, [9]. We will prove the closedness of the graph in such a way that it includes a proof of compactness. Let $\mu_n \to \mu, \nu_n \to \nu$ for the $\mathcal{T}_2$ topology. Let γ_n be a sequence with $\gamma_n \in K(\mu_n, \nu_n)$. We will show that the sequence contains a subsequence that converges to an element of $K(\mu, \nu)$. That will prove the closedness of the graph and compactness of $K(\mu, \nu)$. We have $\int |(x, y)|^2 d\gamma_n = \int |x|^2 d\mu_n + \int |y|^2 d\nu_n \to \int |x|^2 d\mu + \int |y|^2 d\nu < \infty$. It follows that the sequence $(\gamma_n)_n$ is relatively weak* compact. Without loss of generality, we may suppose that $\gamma_n \to \gamma_0$ for the weak* topology. Obviously, $\gamma_0 \in \Pi(\mu, \nu)$. Using truncation and the monotone convergence theorem, we have $\int |(x, 0)|^2 \, d\gamma_0 = \int |x|^2 \, d\mu, \int |(0, y)|^2 \, d\gamma_0 = \int |y|^2 \, d\nu$. This shows that $\gamma_n \to \gamma_0$ for the $\mathcal{T}_2$ topology. The dominated convergence theorem shows that $\int |x - y|^2 \, d\gamma_n \to \int |x - y|^2 \, d\gamma_0$. In other words, $\lim_n W^2(\mu_n, \nu_n) = \int |x - y|^2 \, d\gamma_0 \geq W^2(\mu, \nu)$. But the triangle inequality for the Wasserstein distance as well as its relation to weak* convergence shows that $W(\mu_n, \nu_n) \leq W(\mu_n, \mu) + W(\mu, \nu) + W(\nu, \nu_n)$, and by taking limits for $n \to \infty$, we get $\limsup W(\mu_n, \nu_n) \leq W(\mu, \nu)$. This in turn gives $\gamma_0 \in K(\mu, \nu)$. □

Remark 3.2. The set $\mathbf{M}_2(k)$ equipped with the weak* topology is a Lusin space (because $\mathcal{T}_2$ is a finer Polish topology). The Borel sets for $\mathcal{T}_2$ and for the weak* topology are therefore the same, see [6], and hence the set

$$\{(\mu, \nu, \gamma) \mid \mu, \nu \in \mathbf{M}_2(m), \gamma \in K(\mu, \nu)\}$$

is a Borel set when the product space is equipped with the product of the weak* topologies. An element $\gamma \in K(\mu, \nu)$ is sometimes called a transport plan.

The following theorem is a direct application of Novikov's selection theorem for Borel sets with compact sections [8]:

Theorem 3.3. *There is a Borel measurable map*

$$\kappa\colon \mathbf{M}_2(m) \times \mathbf{M}_2(m) \to \mathbf{M}_2(2m)$$

such that for every $\mu, \nu \in \mathbf{M}_2(m)$, $\kappa(\mu, \nu) \in K(\mu, \nu)$.

Remark 3.4. It is easy to find examples showing that a continuous selection does not exist.

4. Obvious Properties of the Solution

Lemma 4.1. *Let* $\mathcal{A} \subset \mathcal{F}$ *be a sub sigma-algebra and let* $X \in L^2$. *If* Y *is independent of* $\mathcal{A}$ *and satisfies*

$$\|X - Y\| = \inf\{\|X - Z\| \mid Z \textit{ independent of } \mathcal{A}\},$$

then $\mathbb{E}[X] = \mathbb{E}[Y]$.

Proof. This is rather obvious since $\mathbb{R}^m \to \mathbb{R}_+, \alpha \to \|X - Y - \alpha\|^2$ attains its minimum for $\alpha = \mathbb{E}[X - Y]$. □

Lemma 4.2. *Let* $\mathcal{A} \subset \mathcal{F}$ *be a sub sigma-algebra and let* $X \in L^2$. *If* X *is* $\mathcal{A}-$*measurable, then*

$$\|X - \mathbb{E}[X]\| = \inf\{\|X - Z\| \mid Z \textit{ independent of } \mathcal{A}\}.$$

In other words, the solution to the optimization problem (as in the previous lemma) is $Y = \mathbb{E}[X]$.

Proof. Because of the previous lemma, we can change the optimization in the following way:

$$\inf\{\|X - Z\| \mid Z \text{ independent of } \mathcal{A} \text{ and } \mathbb{E}[Z] = \mathbb{E}[X]\}.$$

We then find

$$\|X - Z\|^2 = \|X - \mathbb{E}[X]\|^2 - 2\langle X - \mathbb{E}[X], Z - \mathbb{E}[Z]\rangle + \|Z - \mathbb{E}[Z]\|^2.$$

The middle term is zero because of the independence of X and Z. The optimal choice for Z is therefore $Z = \mathbb{E}[Z] = \mathbb{E}[X]$. □

The statement in the following theorem can be void since we do not know if an optimal solution exists. However, in the following section, we will show by construction that an optimal solution exists under some additional hypotheses.

Theorem 4.3. *The optimal choice in*

$$\inf\{\|X - Z\| \mid Z \text{ independent of } \mathcal{A}\}$$

is given by $Y = V + \mathbb{E}[X]$, *where* V *is the optimal choice for the random variable* $X - \mathbb{E}[X \mid \mathcal{A}]$.

Proof. Take $V \in L^2$ and independent of $\mathcal{A}$. Let us write $Y = V + \mathbb{E}[X]$ where as we know $\mathbb{E}[X] = \mathbb{E}[Y]$ for the relevant random variables. Then we write

$$X - Y = (X - \mathbb{E}[X \mid \mathcal{A}] - V) + (\mathbb{E}[X \mid \mathcal{A}] - \mathbb{E}[X]),$$

which is a sum of two orthogonal variables. Indeed $(X - \mathbb{E}[X \mid \mathcal{A}]) \perp L^2(\mathcal{A})$ and $V \perp L_0^2(\mathcal{A})$, the space of m-dimensional $\mathcal{A}$-measurable random variables with expectation equal to zero. Hence,

$$\|X - Y\|^2 = \|X - \mathbb{E}[X \mid \mathcal{A}] - V\|^2 + \|\mathbb{E}[X \mid \mathcal{A}] - \mathbb{E}[X]\|^2.$$

Therefore, $\|X - Y\|^2$ is minimal if $\|X - \mathbb{E}[X \mid \mathcal{A}] - V\|^2$ is minimal. □

Remark 4.4. We know that being uncorrelated is different from being independent. In the preceding theorem, the random variable V is the best independent approximation of the random variable $X - \mathbb{E}[X \mid \mathcal{A}]$ which is uncorrelated to the variables in $L^2(\mathcal{A})$. So, the initial problem is in fact equivalent to the replacement of uncorrelated random variables by independent random variables.

5. The Construction of the Solution

The idea is to "decompose" X along the atoms of $\mathcal{A}$. This is done by constructing a factorization of X through a product space where the first factor is Ω equipped with the sigma-algebra $\mathcal{A}$. Then, on each atom of $\mathcal{A}$, we will find Y as the solution of a Monge–Kantorovich problem:

(1) Let $\Phi\colon \Omega \to \Omega\times\mathbb{R}^m\times[0,1]$ be defined as $\Phi(\omega) = (\omega, X(\omega), U(\omega))$. It is measurable for $\mathcal{F}$ and $\mathcal{A}\otimes\mathcal{R}^m\otimes\mathcal{R}_{[0,1]}$, where $\mathcal{R}^m$ is the Borel σ-algebra on $\mathbb{R}^m$ and $\mathcal{R}_{[0,1]}$ the Borel $\sigma-$algebra on $[0,1]$.

(2) On $\Omega\times\mathbb{R}^m\times[0,1]$, we define $\chi(\omega,x,t) = x$ and $\tau(\omega,x,t) = t$. Clearly, $\chi\circ\Phi = X$ and $\tau\circ\Phi = U$.

(3) The image probability $(\mathbb{P}\circ\Phi^{-1})$ of Φ can now be disintegrated, see [7] for the existence of the conditional distributions. There exist kernels:
$\mu_{X,U} : \Omega\times(\mathcal{R}^m\otimes\mathcal{R}_{[0,1]}) \to [0,1]$, $\mathcal{A}-$ measurable,

$\mu_X : \Omega\otimes\mathcal{R}^m \to [0,1]$, $\mathcal{A}$-measurable, such that

$\mathbb{P}\circ\Phi^{-1}(A\times B\times C) = \int_A \mathbb{P}[d\omega]\mu_{X,U}(\omega, B\times C)$, $\quad A\in\mathcal{A}, B\in \mathcal{R}^m, C\in\mathcal{R}_{[0,1]}$

$\mathbb{P}\circ\Phi^{-1}(A\times B\times[0,1]) = \int_A \mathbb{P}[d\omega]\mu_X(\omega,B), A\in\mathcal{A}, B\in\mathcal{R}^m.$

Almost surely the measure $\mu_X(\omega,.)$ is the marginal distribution of the probability measure $\mu_{X,U}(\omega,.)$. Because of independence, the conditional distribution of U (given $\mathcal{A}$) is always the Lebesgue measure λ on $[0,1]$.

Theorem 5.1. *We use the notation of the previous section. Let $Y\colon \Omega\to\mathbb{R}^m, Y\in L^2$, be independent of $\mathcal{A}$. Let ν be the distribution of Y. Then,*

$$\|X-Y\|^2 \ge \int_\Omega \mathbb{P}[d\omega]\, W^2(\mu_X(\omega),\nu).$$

Proof. Since $\|X\|^2 = \mathbb{E}[|X|^2] = \int_\Omega \mathbb{P}[d\omega]\int_{\mathbb{R}^m}|x|^2\mu_X(dx)$, we have that almost surely $\mu_X(\omega)\in\mathbf{M}_2(m)$. The disintegration of the distribution of Y given by $\mathcal{A}$ is — because of independence — trivially the constant ν, of course $\nu\in\mathbf{M}_2(m)$. The mapping $\Omega\to\mathbf{M}_2(m); \omega\to\mu_X(\omega)$ is $\mathcal{A}$-measurable when $\mathbf{M}_2(m)$ is endowed with its Borel σ-algebra. The integral in the statement of the theorem therefore makes sense since also $W(.,\nu)$ is Borel measurable, even continuous, on $\mathbf{M}_2(m)$. Let $\mu_{X,Y}$ be the disintegration of the distribution of the couple (X, Y) given by $\mathcal{A}$. Since

$$\|X - Y\|^2 = \int_\Omega \mathbb{P}[d\omega] \int_{\mathbb{R}^m \times \mathbb{R}^m} |x - y|^2 \mu_{X,Y}(\omega)(dx, dy),$$

and since

$$\int_{\mathbb{R}^m \times \mathbb{R}^m} |x - y|^2 \mu_{X,Y}(\omega)(dx, dy) \geq W^2(\mu_X(\omega), \nu) \text{ almost surely,}$$

the theorem follows. □

Theorem 5.2. *There is a probability measure ν_0 where the function*

$$\mathbf{M}_2(m) \to \mathbb{R}_+; \nu \to \int_\Omega \mathbb{P}[d\omega]\, W^2(\mu_X(\omega), \nu)$$

attains its minimum.

Proof. Let ν_n be a sequence so that the integrals converge to the infimum. The second moment of ν_n can be calculated using the Wasserstein distance to the Dirac measure δ_0, concentrated at $0 \in \mathbb{R}^m$. Then we use $W(\nu_n, \delta_0) \leq W(\mu_X, \delta_0) + W(\mu_X, \nu_n)$ and integrate. Since the sequence has uniformly bounded second moments, Prohorov's theorem implies that it is a relatively weak* compact. By selecting a subsequence, we may suppose that it converges weak* to a probability measure ν_0. Obviously, we have that $\nu_0 \in \mathbf{M}_2(m)$. The Wasserstein metric satisfies for any fixed $\alpha \in \mathbf{M}_2(m)$

$$W(\alpha, \nu_0) \leq \liminf W(\alpha, \nu_n).$$

From there it follows using Fatou's lemma that $\int_\Omega \mathbb{P}[d\omega] W^2(\mu_X(\omega), \nu_0)$ realizes the minimum. □

The only problem that remains is to find a random variable that has distribution equal to ν_0 that is independent of $\mathcal{A}$ and gives almost surely the Wasserstein distance to $\mu_X(\omega, .)$. Using the results from transport theory, we will construct Y for each $\omega \in \Omega$ or better for a set of full measure. $Y(\omega)$ will be a function of $X(\omega)$ and $U(\omega)$. This will guarantee measurability. Y will have conditional to $\mathcal{A}$ and be independent of ω, the distribution ν_0. This will guarantee independence and it will in fact conclude the construction. The details may look a little bit complicated, but the construction is in fact the obvious way to follow.

Theorem 5.3. *There is a random variable* $Y : \Omega \to \mathbb{R}^m$ *that is independent of* $\mathcal{A}$*, has* ν_0 *as its distribution and realises the infimum*

$$\|X - Y\| = \inf\{\|X - Z\| \mid Z \text{ independent of } \mathcal{A}\}.$$

Proof. We use the functions h and κ from Theorems 3.1 and 3 and make the reasoning for each ω separately. We start by looking at the measure $\mu_{X,U}$ on $\mathbb{R}^m \times [0,1]$. On this set, there are two obvious maps $\chi(x,t) = x$ having distribution $\mu_X(\omega)$ and $\tau(x,t) = t$ having distribution, the Lebesgue measure λ. We now use on $\mathbb{R}^m \times \mathbb{R}^m$ the measure $\kappa(\mu_X(\omega), \nu_0)$. We disintegrate this measure with respect to the first coordinate giving a kernel $\alpha(\omega, x, .)$ which is measurable in (ω, x). To be precise, we have

$$\kappa(\mu_X(\omega), \nu_0)(A \times B) = \int_A \mu_X(\omega)(dx)\alpha(\omega, x, B).$$

We now define $v(\omega, x, t) = h(\alpha(\omega, x), t)$. By construction and by definition of the kernel α, we have that for each ω the map

$$v(\omega) : \mathbb{R}^m \times [0,1] \to \mathbb{R}^m$$

has distribution ν_0. The definition of κ implies that

$$W^2(\mu_X(\omega), \nu_0) = \int_{\mathbb{R}^m \times [0,1]} |\chi(x,t) - v(\omega, x, t)|^2 \mu_{X,U}(dx, dt).$$

We now put $Y = v \circ \Phi$ and recall that $X = \chi \circ \pi(\Phi)$ where π maps $\Omega \times \mathbb{R}^m \times [0,1]$ onto $\mathbb{R}^m \times [0,1]$. The construction guarantees that Y has the distribution ν_0 and is independent of $\mathcal{A}$. As we saw, this means that Y is the best approximation of X by a random variable independent of $\mathcal{A}$. □

6. A Case with Few Independent Random Variables

Let us first recall the following definition:

Definition 6.1. $\mathcal{F}$ is atomless conditionally to $\mathcal{A}$ if for every $A \in \mathcal{F}$, $\mathbb{P}[A] > 0$, there is $B \subset A$ such that

$$\mathbb{P}\left[0 < \mathbb{E}[\mathbf{1}_B \mid \mathcal{A}] < \mathbb{E}[\mathbf{1}_A \mid \mathcal{A}]\right] > 0.$$

Proposition 6.2. *The existence of $U: \Omega \to \mathbb{R}$, uniformly distributed on $[0,1]$ and independent of $\mathcal{A}$, is equivalent to the condition that $\mathcal{F}$ is atomless conditionally to $\mathcal{A}$.* [3]

If no such condition exists, then the existence of a uniformly $[0,1]$ distributed independent random variable, U, is no longer guaranteed. Nevertheless, in some cases, the existence of an optimal approximating random variable Y can be shown to exist. Let us illustrate this with the following rather extreme example. Suppose $\mathcal{F}$ is generated by $\mathcal{A}$ and one set $A, 0 < \mathbb{P}[A] < 1$. We suppose that A is independent of $\mathcal{A}$ and look for other sets in $\mathcal{F}$ that are independent of $\mathcal{A}$. We first recall that

$$\mathcal{F} = \{(A \cap B) \cup (A^c \cap C) | B, C \in \mathcal{A}\}.$$

Suppose first that $\mathbb{P}[A] = \frac{1}{2}$ (from the general case, it will follow that this is indeed an isolated case) and take $B \in \mathcal{A}$, then

$$\mathbb{P}(A \cap B) \cup (A^c \cap B^c) = \mathbb{P}[A \cap B] + \mathbb{P}[A^c \cap B^c] = \frac{1}{2}\mathbb{P}[B] + \frac{1}{2}\mathbb{P}[B^c] = \frac{1}{2}.$$

Now $D = (A \cap B) \cup (A^c \cap B^c)$ is independent of $\mathcal{A}$. Indeed

$$\mathbb{E}[1_D \mid \mathcal{A}] = \mathbb{E}[1_A \mid \mathcal{A}]1_B + \mathbb{E}[1_A^c \mid \mathcal{A}]1_{B^c} = \frac{1}{2}.$$

So the conditional expectation is constant and for sets this is equivalent to independence. All sets that are independent of $\mathcal{A}$ are of this form. Indeed for $(A \cap B) \cup (A^c \cap C)$, we have

$$\mathbb{E}[1_D \mid \mathcal{A}] = \frac{1}{2}\mathbf{1}_B + \frac{1}{2}\mathbf{1}_C$$

and this is a constant only if $B = C = \Omega$ ($\mathbb{P}[D] = 1$), $B = C = \emptyset$ ($\mathbb{P}[D] = 0$) or $C = B^c$ and then $\mathbb{P}[D] = \frac{1}{2}$.

Suppose that $\mathcal{D}$ is a sigma-algebra that is independent of $\mathcal{A}$, then $\mathcal{D} = \{\emptyset, \Omega, D = (A \cap B) \cup (A^c \cap B^c), D^c\}$, where $B \in \mathcal{A}$. Indeed let $D_1 = (A \cap B_1) \cup (A^c \cap B_1^c), D_2 = (A \cap B_2) \cup (A^c \cap B_2^c)$ be two elements in $\mathcal{D}$, then unless we have trivial cases, $D_1 \cap D_2$ is not of the form $(A \cap C) \cup (A^c \cap C^c)$. It follows that random variables Y that are independent of $\mathcal{A}$ can only take at most two different values. Suppose that X is $\mathcal{F}$ measurable, then it can be written as

$X = f\mathbf{1}_A + g\mathbf{1}_{A^c}$, where f, g are $\mathcal{A}$ measurable. To avoid irrelevant complications, we suppose that $f, g \geq 0$. Let $Y = \alpha\mathbf{1}_D + \beta\mathbf{1}_{D^c}$, where $D = (A \cap B) \cup (A^c \cap B^c)$ with $B \in \mathcal{A}$. The norm of the difference $X - Y$ can now be calculated.

$$
\begin{aligned}
&\|X - Y\|^2 \\
&\quad = \|f\mathbf{1}_A + g\mathbf{1}_{A^c} - \alpha\left(\mathbf{1}_{B\cap A} + \mathbf{1}_{b^c\cap A^c}\right) - \beta\left(\mathbf{1}_{B^c\cap A} + \mathbf{1}_{B\cap A^c}\right)\|^2 \\
&\quad = \|(f-\alpha)\mathbf{1}_{B\cap A} + (g-\alpha)\mathbf{1}_{B^c\cap A^c} + (f-\beta)\mathbf{1}_{B^c\cap A} \\
&\qquad + (g-\beta)\mathbf{1}_{B\cap A^c}\|^2 \\
&\quad = \mathbb{E}\left[(f-\alpha)^2\mathbf{1}_{B\cap A}\right] + \mathbb{E}\left[(g-\alpha)^2\mathbf{1}_{B^c\cap A^c}\right] \\
&\qquad + \mathbb{E}\left[(f-\beta)^2\mathbf{1}_{B^c\cap A}\right] + \mathbb{E}\left[(g-\beta)^2\mathbf{1}_{B\cap A^c}\right] \\
&\quad = \frac{1}{2}\left(\mathbb{E}\left[(f-\alpha)^2\mathbf{1}_B\right] + \mathbb{E}\left[(g-\alpha)^2\mathbf{1}_{B^c}\right]\right) \\
&\qquad + \frac{1}{2}\left(\mathbb{E}\left[(f-\beta)^2\mathbf{1}_{B^c}\right] + \mathbb{E}\left[(g-\beta)^2\mathbf{1}_B\right]\right) \\
&\quad = \frac{1}{2}(\mathbb{E}[(f-\alpha)^2\mathbf{1}_B + (g-\alpha)^2\mathbf{1}_{B^c}] \\
&\qquad + \mathbb{E}[(f-\beta)^2\mathbf{1}_{B^c} + (g-\beta)^2\mathbf{1}_B]) \\
&\quad = \frac{1}{2}\left(\mathbb{E}\left[(f\mathbf{1}_B + g\mathbf{1}_{B^c} - \alpha)^2\right] + \mathbb{E}\left[(f\mathbf{1}_{B^c} + g\mathbf{1}_B - \beta)^2\right]\right).
\end{aligned}
$$

The optimal choices for α, β are

$$
\begin{aligned}
\alpha &= \mathbb{E}[f\mathbf{1}_B + g\mathbf{1}_{B^c}] \\
\beta &= \mathbb{E}[f\mathbf{1}_{B^c} + g\mathbf{1}_B],
\end{aligned}
$$

and then the expression becomes (after rearrangement)

$$
\frac{1}{2}\left(\mathbb{E}[f^2] + \mathbb{E}[g^2] - \left(\mathbb{E}[f\mathbf{1}_B + g\mathbf{1}_{B^c}]^2 + \mathbb{E}[f\mathbf{1}_{B^c} + g\mathbf{1}_B]^2\right)\right).
$$

We can now choose the set B so that the expression on the right becomes as big as possible. An optimal choice is $B = \{f \geq g\} \in \mathcal{A}$

(because f, g are non-negative). We then find

$$\frac{1}{2}\left(\mathbb{E}[(f \vee g)^2] - \mathbb{E}[(f \vee g)]^2 + \mathbb{E}[(f \wedge g)^2] - \mathbb{E}[(f \wedge g)]^2\right).$$

For the optimal random variable Y, we get

$$Y = \mathbb{E}[f \vee g]\mathbf{1}_A + \mathbb{E}[f \wedge g]\mathbf{1}_{A^c}.$$

Let us now quickly analyze the case $\mathbb{P}[A] \neq \frac{1}{2}$, then for

$$D = (A \cap B) \cup (A^c \cap C)$$

such that D is independent of $\mathcal{A}$, we find

$$\mathbb{P}[D] = \mathbb{P}[A]\mathbb{P}[B] + \mathbb{P}[A^c]\mathbb{P}[C] = \mathbb{P}[C] + \mathbb{P}[A](\mathbb{P}[B] - \mathbb{P}[C]).$$

The conditional expectation is given by

$$\mathbb{E}[1_D \mid \mathcal{A}] = \mathbb{P}[A]\mathbf{1}_B + \mathbb{P}[A^c]\mathbf{1}_C.$$

We first deal with the case $\mathbb{P}[D] = 0$ which is only possible if $B = C = \emptyset$. Next we suppose that $\mathbb{P}[B \cap C] > 0$. Then on $B \cap C$, the conditional expectation is equal to 1 and since it must be a constant, it is 1 on Ω. This means $\mathbb{P}[D] = 1 = \mathbb{P}[B] = \mathbb{P}[C]$. The remaining case is when $\mathbb{P}[B \cap C] = 0$. Then because $\mathbb{P}[A] \neq \mathbb{P}[A^c]$, we must have that either B or C is the empty set and that $B = C^c$. That means that either $D = A$ or $D = A^c$. There is not much choice for a set (and hence for a random variable) to be independent of $\mathcal{A}$. The calculation of the optimal choice for Y is left to the reader.

7. A One-Dimensional Example

In this final section, we analyze an easy one-dimensional example. The space $(\Omega, \mathcal{F}, \mathbb{P})$ satisfies the following:

(1) There are two sub σ−algebras $\mathcal{X}, \mathcal{N}$ that are independent and together generate $\mathcal{F}$.
(2) $\mathcal{N}$ is generated by a random variable $N\colon \Omega \to \mathbb{N} = \{1, 2, 3, \ldots\}$.
(3) $\mathcal{X}$ is generated by a sequence of independent identically distributed random variables $X_n\colon \Omega \to \mathbb{R}_+$.
(4) The random variables $(X_k)_k, N$ are in L^2.

(5) The distribution function $\mathbb{F}_X$ of X_1 is strictly increasing, continuous and defines a homeomorphism between $\mathbb{R}_+$ and $[0, 1)$.

We define $S_n = \sum_{k=1}^n X_k$ and are interested in $\xi = \sum_n S_n \mathbf{1}_{N=n}$. Such random variables arise in insurance mathematics where N describes the number of claims and the variables X_k are the claim sizes. We want to approximate ξ by a random variable η that is independent of $\mathcal{N}$. The first idea is to replace ξ by $\mathbb{E}[\xi \mid \mathcal{X}] = \sum_n S_n \mathbb{P}[N = n]$ as this yields a variable that is independent of $\mathcal{N}$ and it is the best $\mathcal{X}$ measurable approximation of ξ. As we will see, this intuition does not give the best result. From the preceding sections, it follows that the best approximation must be commonotone with S_n on each set $\{N = n\}$. The conditional expectation $\sum_k S_k \mathbb{P}[N = k]$ does not necessarily satisfy this condition. We will follow the construction as outlined in the preceding sections.

First, let us remark that the distribution functions $\mathbb{F}_{S_n}$ of the sums S_n are all homeomorphisms between $\mathbb{R}_+$ and $[0, 1)$. Furthermore, the variables $\mathbb{F}_{S_n}(S_n)$ are uniformly distributed on $[0, 1]$ and independent of $\mathcal{N}$. We first look for the optimal distribution of the solution. Let us denote by $\mathbb{G}$ this distribution function. The inverse function of $\mathbb{G}$ does not need to exist but we can take one of the generalized inverses and denote this by $\mathbb{G}^{-1}$. In fact, we will find $\mathbb{G}^{-1}$ and this will define the distribution function $\mathbb{G}$. The solution to our problem will then be $\eta = \sum_n \mathbb{G}^{-1}(\mathbb{F}_{S_n}(S_n))\mathbf{1}_{N=n}$, where, of course, we must still find the optimal $\mathbb{G}$. We remark that the random variable η is constructed using the variable N and hence set-theoretically it depends on something related to N but nevertheless it is stochastically independent of N.

We now calculate $\|\xi - \eta\|^2$.

$$
\begin{aligned}
&\|\xi - \eta\|^2 \\
&\quad = \int (\xi - \eta)^2 \mathbb{P}[d\omega] \\
&\quad = \sum_n \int_{\{N=n\}} (S_n - \mathbb{G}^{-1}(\mathbb{F}_{S_n}(S_n)))^2 \mathbf{1}_{N=n} \, \mathbb{P}[d\omega] \\
&\quad = \sum_n \mathbb{P}[N = n] \int_{\mathbb{R}_+} (x - \mathbb{G}^{-1}(\mathbb{F}_{S_n}(x)))^2 \, d\mathbb{F}_{S_n}(x)
\end{aligned}
$$

$$= \sum_n \mathbb{P}[N = n] \int_0^1 (\mathbb{F}_{S_n}^{-1}(u) - \mathbb{G}^{-1}(u))^2 \, du$$

$$= \sum_n \mathbb{P}[N = n] \int_0^1 \left(\mathbb{F}_{S_n}^{-1}(u)^2 - 2\,\mathbb{F}_{S_n}^{-1}(u)\mathbb{G}^{-1}(u) + \mathbb{G}^{-1}(u)^2\right) du$$

$$= \|\xi\|^2 + \int_0^1 \left(-2\left(\sum_n \mathbb{P}[N = n]\,\mathbb{F}_{S_n}^{-1}(u)\right)\mathbb{G}^{-1}(u) + \mathbb{G}^{-1}(u)^2\right) du.$$

This expression has a minimum when

$$\mathbb{G}^{-1}(u) = \left(\sum_n \mathbb{P}[N = n]\,\mathbb{F}_{S_n}^{-1}(u)\right).$$

We can now define η in such a way that its distribution is precisely $\mathbb{G}(u)$, where $\mathbb{G}$ is defined in the line above. One easily checks that this indeed defines a distribution function of a random variable. To achieve this, we define for each n the function ϕ_n such that

$$\phi_n(\mathbb{F}_{S_n}^{-1}(u)) = \left(\sum_k \mathbb{P}[N = k]\,\mathbb{F}_{S_k}^{-1}(u)\right) = \mathbb{G}^{-1}(u),$$

and then we define $\eta = \sum_n \phi_n(S_n)\mathbf{1}_{N=n}$. The functions ϕ_n can also be seen to satisfy $\phi_n(x) = \mathbb{G}^{-1} \circ \mathbb{F}_{S_n}(x)$.

Remark 7.1. We made the regularity assumptions on $\mathbb{F}_{X_1}$ and supposed that $N \geq 1$ to avoid some technical complications when defining the inverse functions and the functions ϕ_n. A generalization is possible but it will be messy and must use the existence of an independent function U as described in the preceding sections. Because of the regularity of $\mathbb{F}_{X_1}$, the existence of U is immediate, indeed the variables $\mathbb{F}_{S_n}(S_n)$ are uniformly $[0, 1]$ distributed and independent of $\mathcal{N}$.

Remark 7.2. We also remark that

$$\|\xi - \eta\| < \|\xi - \mathbb{E}[\xi \mid \mathcal{X}]\|.$$

The solution to the optimal transport problem was easy since we could use commonotonicity arguments, based on the already mentioned inequalities of [4]. A more advanced conclusion holds. Let us recall that a random variable ψ dominates a random variable ζ in the convex order if for every convex function $\varphi\colon \mathbb{R} \to \mathbb{R}$, we have $\mathbb{E}[\varphi(\zeta)] \le \mathbb{E}[\varphi(\psi)]$. The integrals make sense as soon as both $\psi, \zeta \in L^1$ since convex functions are bounded below by affine functions. In our setting, there is no problem since all random variables are in L^2. The notation for this ordering is $\zeta \preceq \psi$. Clearly, $\zeta \preceq \psi$ implies $\mathbb{E}[\psi] = \mathbb{E}[\zeta]$ and $\mathbb{E}[\zeta^2] \le \mathbb{E}[\psi^2]$. We will show the following:

Proposition 7.3. $\mathbb{E}[\xi \mid \mathcal{X}] \preceq \eta \preceq \xi$.

Proof. Let φ be a convex function defined on $\mathbb{R}$. From [5], we recall that

$$\mathbb{E}\left[\varphi\left(\sum_n \mathbb{P}[N=n]\, S_n\right)\right] \le \int_{[0,1]} \varphi\left(\sum_k \mathbb{P}[N=k]\, \mathbb{F}_{S_k}^{-1}(u)\right) du.$$

This shows that $\mathbb{E}[\xi \mid \mathcal{X}] \preceq \eta$. To show the other dominance we suppose without loss of generality that $\varphi(0) = 0$ and calculate $\mathbb{E}[\varphi(\xi)]$

$$\begin{aligned}
\mathbb{E}[\varphi(\xi)] &= \mathbb{E}\left[\varphi\left(\sum_n \mathbf{1}_{N=n} S_n\right)\right] \\
&= \sum_n \mathbb{E}\left[\mathbf{1}_{N=n}\varphi(S_n)\right] \\
&= \sum_n \mathbb{P}[N=n]\, \mathbb{E}[\varphi(S_n)] \\
&= \sum_n \mathbb{P}[N=n] \int_{[0,1]} \varphi(\mathbb{F}_{S_n}^{-1}(u))\, du \\
&= \int_{[0,1]} \sum_n \mathbb{P}[N=n]\, \varphi(\mathbb{F}_{S_n}^{-1}(u))\, du \\
&\ge \int_{[0,1]} \varphi\left(\sum_n \mathbb{P}[N=n]\, \mathbb{F}_{S_n}^{-1}(u))\right) du = \mathbb{E}[\varphi(\eta)].
\end{aligned}$$

This shows that $\eta \preceq \xi$. □

References

[1] D. Blackwell and L. E. Dubins. An extension of Skorohod's almost sure representation Theorem. *Proc. Amer. Math. Soc.*, 89(4):691–692, 1983.

[2] P. Billingsley. *Probability and Measure*, Anniversary Edition. Wiley, New Jersey, 2012.

[3] F. Delbaen. Conditionally atomless extensions of sigma algebras. arxiv 2003.09254, John Wiley & Sons, Inc., Hoboken, NJ, 2012.

[4] G. Hardy, J. E. Littlewood, and G. Polya. *Inequalities.* Cambridge Mathematical Library, Cambridge, 1934.

[5] R. Kaas, J. Dhaene, D. Vyncke, M. Goovaerts, and M. Denuit. A simple geometric proof that comonotonic risks have the convex-largest sum. *ASTIN Bulletin*, 32(1):71–80, 2002.

[6] K. R. Parthasarathy. *Probability Measures on Metric Spaces.* Academic Press, New York, 1967.

[7] M. M. Rao and R. J. Swift. *Probability Theory with Applications*, 2nd Edition. Springer, New York, 2006.

[8] S. M. Srivastava. *A Course on Borel Sets.* GTM 180, Springer, New York, 1998.

[9] M. Thorpe. *Introduction to Optimal Transport.* F2.08, Centre for Mathematical Sciences, University of Cambridge, Cambridge, UK, 2018.

https://doi.org/10.1142/9789811280306_0010

Chapter 10

Pricing Autocallables under Local-Stochastic Volatility

Walter Farkas[*,†,‡,¶], **Francesco Ferrari**[*,‖], **and Urban Ulrych**[*,‡,§,**]

[*]*Department of Banking and Finance, University of Zurich, Switzerland*
[†]*Department of Mathematics, ETH Zurich, Switzerland*
[‡]*Swiss Finance Institute, Switzerland*
[§]*College of Management of Technology, EPFL Lausanne, Switzerland*
[¶]*walter.farkas@bf.uzh.ch*
[‖]*francesco.ferrari@bluewin.ch*
[**]*urban.ulrych@epfl.ch*

Abstract

This chapter investigates the pricing of single-asset autocallable barrier reverse convertibles in the Heston local-stochastic volatility (LSV) model. Despite their complexity, autocallable structured notes are the most traded equity-linked exotic derivatives. The autocallable payoff embeds an early redemption feature generating strong path and model dependency. Consequently, the commonly used local volatility (LV) model is overly simplified for pricing and risk management. Given its ability to match the implied volatility smile and reproduce its realistic dynamics, the LSV model is, in contrast, better suited for exotic derivatives, such as autocallables. We use quasi-Monte Carlo methods to study the pricing given the Heston LSV model and compare it with the LV model. In particular, we establish the sensitivity of the valuation differences of autocallables between the two models with respect to payoff features, model parameters, underlying characteristics and volatility regimes. We find that the improved spot-volatility dynamics captured by the Heston LSV model typically result in higher prices, demonstrating the dependence of autocallables on the forward-skew and vol-of-vol risk. Moreover, we show that the parameters of the stochastic component of LSV models enable controlling for the autocallables, price while leaving the fit to European options unaffected.

Keywords: Exotic derivatives pricing, Local-stochastic volatility, Implied volatility smile dynamics, Barrier reverse convertibles, Quasi Monte Carlo methods

1. Introduction

Equity-linked yield enhancement structured notes offer more attractive returns compared to traditional fixed-income securities. Accordingly, such exotic derivatives experience great demand, especially in low-interest rate environments. Structured notes are unsecured debt obligations comprising a bond and typically a single payoff or multiple derivative payoffs. The barrier reverse convertible (BRC) is one such yield enhancement structured product. It consists of a zero-coupon bond, a short down-and-in (D&I) put option and a stream of coupon payments. The autocall feature complements the BRC with Bermudan up-and-out (U&O) barriers, which, if hit, trigger the early redemption of the note. As a result of the increased risk exposure, autocallables offer higher coupons compared to standard fixed maturity structured products. Therefore, they can provide a better fit to the risk-return appetite of investors who are seeking income in low-yield environments.

The issuance volume of such exotic derivatives has increased exponentially since the first autocallable was traded in 2003 [12]. According to Ref. [40], autocallable products are the most traded equity-linked exotic derivatives of the last 20 years with average yearly volumes topping 100 billion euros. Despite their high demand, the hedging of such derivatives continues to be problematic due to their significant path dependency and complex dynamics [42]. Furthermore, leading issuers have recently experienced trading losses, forcing them to rethink this business [4, 5].

The local volatility (LV) model, first proposed in Refs. [13, 15] as an extension of the Black–Scholes model [7] capable of reproducing the observed implied volatility (IV) smile, remains to date a standard model for pricing and risk managing structured derivatives at equity trading desks [11,44]. However, its limitations are widely documented in the literature. In particular, the LV model does not capture the realistic dynamics of the IV smile [14,26,38] and thus systematically misprices the forward-smile and the vol-of-vol risk [6]. Autocallables are sensitive to the IV dynamics because of their path-dependent nature. Consequently, the LV model is in general not suited for pricing and hedging autocallables [11].

Stochastic volatility (SV) models, such as the Heston model [30], tend to be more consistent with the observed market dynamics but are commonly not able to fit the short end of the implied volatility surface (IVS). The local-stochastic volatility model, introduced by Ref. [32], aims to address the limitations of LV and SV models by combining their advantages. Hence, the local-stochastic volatility (LSV) model is consistent with the market prices of European options, and the dynamics of the IV smile. As such, it oughts to be suitable for modeling exotic options, such as those embedded in autocallable derivatives.

Despite the popularity of autocallables, academic literature has dedicated limited attention to them [23]. From a qualitative viewpoint, Ref. [8] presents several autocallable payoffs and discusses the embedded risks as well as the hedging implications. The references to valuation methods include a partial differential equation (PDE) framework for autocallables with discrete and continuous U&O barriers [12], an analytical pricing formula in a Black–Scholes setting [23], an LV valuation add-on accounting for the complex spot-volatility dynamics [40] and a recursive method to obtain a static hedging portfolio replicating the payoff under a general Markov diffusion [34].

On the other hand, by employing Monte Carlo (MC) methods, Ref. [18] suggested a specific variance reduction technique for pricing autocallables, and Ref. [2] developed an algorithm that allows for stable differentiation to improve the calculation of Greeks. The autocallables literature in an LSV setting contains an analysis of the impact of SV in the case of a multi-asset autocallable referencing the worst performing underlying in a basket [11]. Moreover, a brief comparison of an FX autocallable price under LV versus LSV is given in Ref. [10] within the context of a study of the convergence of an Euler scheme for a Heston-like LSV model.

The impact of boosting LV with an SV component may be well understood by practitioners for a single-asset autocallable [11], yet, to the best of our knowledge, no academic paper provides an extensive analysis of its prices in LV versus LSV models. In light of the industry relevance, the central purpose of this chapter is to perform such analysis. In the existing LSV literature, such comparison is done, e.g., on forward-starting options in [9, 32, 43, 44] present some results for American-style binary and barrier FX options in the Heston LSV model. References [29] and [41] study the price difference of call spread cliquets. Finally, Ref. [39] exhibits a price comparison of at-the-money (ATM) straddles on the realized variance and the VIX index.

In this chapter, we compare the fair values of different single-asset autocallable BRCs referencing major US indices obtained with the LSV and the LV models. In the spirit of Ref. [32], we augment the LV model with the Heston SV model [30]. Therefore, the LSV model resulting from matching the diffusion terms of both models using Gyöngy's mimicking theorem [25] is Heston-like. We calibrate the LSV model with the non-parametric Monte Carlo (MC) approach of Ref. [44]. The LV function is obtained through its association with the IVS via Dupire's formula, whereby the extended surface stochastic volatility inspired (eSSVI) parametrization [28] is employed to obtain a smooth arbitrage-free IVS.

We aim to identify the autocallables, payoff features that embed the largest model dependency and study the sensitivity of the autocallable price with respect to the Heston parameters and the impact of underlying specific characteristics as well as the evolution of valuation differences with the volatility regime. The price estimates are obtained with quasi-MC (QMC) methods and antithetic variates for variance reduction. Generally, we find autocallable derivatives to be valued higher in the Heston LSV model compared to the LV model and hence the price differences to be positive. In particular, our analysis consists of four parts.

First, we study the impact of payoff features and identify those that imply larger price differences between the LSV and LV models. Namely, the features embedding higher model dependency as well as exposure to the vol-of-vol and the forward-smile risk. Indeed, we establish that the composition of the autocallable payoff has an impact on the valuation differences. For instance, longer U&O barrier observation tenors and higher coupon levels lead to larger price differences, whereas the effect of higher D&I barrier levels is decreasing or increasing depending on the maturity of the note.

Second, we test the effect of changing the parameters driving the stochastic component of the Heston LSV model. The observed impact is reduced to the SV parameters as the prices of European options are unchanged by construction. The valuation differences increase with the volatility-of-variance η, whereas they decrease with the speed of mean reversion κ, the correlation ρ and the long-term level of variance θ. The effect of the initial level of variance V_0 is negligible. We motivate our observation based on the respective resulting forward IV skews.

Third, we analyze underlying specific characteristics, such as the dividend yield and the implied volatility level. We find that lower forwards reduce the valuation differences. Indeed, for sufficiently low forward and long maturity, the Heston LSV price becomes even smaller than the LV price. Moreover, underlyings exhibiting higher implied volatility levels tend to produce larger valuation differences.

Finally, we study the impact of the volatility regime. We find the difference between Heston LSV and LV model valuations to be positively related to the market's implied volatility level. This is only partially explained by higher coupons that can be financed by selling a more expensive put option. Indeed, the main drivers are the higher volatility-of-variance η and lower spot-variance correlation ρ resulting from the calibration of the Heston model in stressed markets.

This chapter is organized as follows: Section 2 presents the employed dataset and the construction of an arbitrage-free IVS, which serves as the foundation of this chapter. Section 3 defines the LSV model and discusses its advantages in comparison to the LV and SV models. Section 4 studies the impact of payoff features, model parameters, underlying characteristics and market regimes on the autocallable price difference in the Heston LSV and LV models. Section 5 concludes. Additional explanations and figures are delegated to Appendices A and B.

2. Implied Volatility Surface

2.1. *Dataset*

The dataset employed in our analysis is retrieved from IvyDB US, which is a comprehensive database of historical prices for the entire US-listed index and equity options markets compiled by OptionMetrics and accessible through the Wharton Research Data Services [36]. We obtain US dollar zero-coupon interest rate curves, underlying security prices and the corresponding historical option prices.

The historical option price data contain the best bid and offer prices across all exchanges. In accordance with the standard market convention, we use mid option prices to compute implied forwards, implied dividend yields inclusive of borrow rates and implied volatilities. To ensure that we retain only informative options, we filter the dataset as follows: we drop in-the-money (ITM) options because they are notably inaccurate due to infrequent trading, and we exclude options with bid prices under twice the minimum tick size of USD 0.05, i.e., USD 0.10 [1]. Moreover, for expiries where both A.M. and P.M. settled options are listed, we drop options with P.M. settlement from the dataset.

In our experiments, we focus on US broad equity market indices, such as the S&P 500 (SPX), the Nasdaq-100 (NDX), the Dow Jones Industrial Average (DJX) and the Russell 2000 (RUT). First, excluding a few exceptions, index options are European-style in contrast to American-style stock options. Hence, we can readily use Black–Scholes (BS) formula to price these options and compute implied volatilities. Second, by focusing on equity indices, we avoid the nontrivial treatment of discrete cash dividends coupled with proportional dividends and their prediction. Third, the liquidity of index options is notably higher than their single stock equivalents, and additionally, more listed expiries are available. Therefore, greater and more reliable data points can be used as inputs in the calibration of the model and the implied volatility surface parametrization. Fourth, autocallable structured notes referencing US equity indices represent a large share of the equity exotic derivatives market. These arguments justify our choice.

2.2. *Parametrization*

When pricing exotic path-dependent derivatives in accordance with market-observed vanilla option prices, the implied volatility surface serves as the crucial input parameter of any pricing model. The absence of static arbitrage is key. In fact, any arbitrage violation can lead to mispricings occurring due to negative transition probabilities [16].

For the Black–Scholes option price $C^{BS}(\cdot)$ and the market-observed option price $C^{MKT}(\cdot)$, both referencing the same underlying, implied volatility is defined as the value $\hat{\sigma}$ such that $C^{BS}(K,T,\hat{\sigma}) = C^{MKT}(K,T)$. Namely, it is the value of the volatility parameter σ that matches the observed market price with the price obtained using the Black–Scholes formula. Implied volatilities generally form a U-shaped pattern across strikes. Consequently, the function $K \mapsto \hat{\sigma}(K,T)$, which, for any fixed maturity T, assigns to each strike K the value $\hat{\sigma}(K,T)$, is commonly referred to as the IV smile or skew. The collection of all IV smiles constitutes the implied volatility surface, i.e., the two-dimensional mapping $\hat{\sigma} : (K,T) \mapsto \hat{\sigma}(K,T)$.

Figure 1 portrays the implied volatilities calculated from mid prices of SPX options as of January 23, 2020, across all listed regular expires and in forward-moneyness $K/F(0,T)$ space, where $F(t,T)$ denotes the price specified in a contract at time t to be paid at time T for the underlying asset, i.e., the forward price. The IV smiles are clearly violating the Black–Scholes assumption of constant volatility and reflecting the stylized facts of IV [17]. In fact, the implied volatility smiles show large curvature for short expires that progressively flattens out for longer-dated options. Additionally,

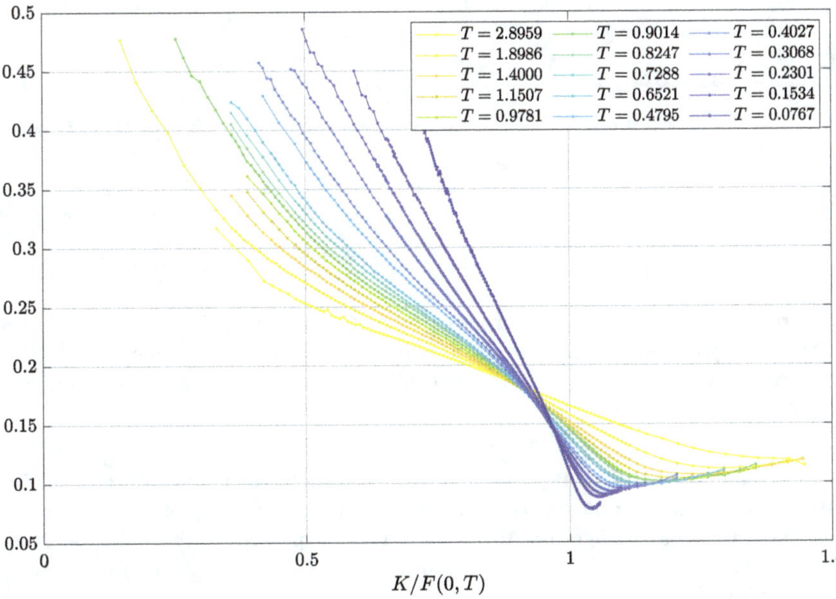

Figure 1. Implied volatilities in forward-moneyness $K/F(0,T)$ space computed from SPX mid option prices across all the listed regular expiries as of January 23, 2020.

the at-the-money-forward (ATMF) term structure of implied volatility is upward sloping.

We follow a parametric approach for the construction of implied volatility surfaces.[1] Thereby, a single non linear parametric function for the entire surface, or typically for each smile, is defined and fitted to market data [17]. An example of such an approach is the stochastic volatility inspired (SVI) parametrization of [19] based on the large-time asymptotic behavior of the IV smile generated by the Heston model [20]. In our application, we rely on the eSSVI parametrization of total implied variance proposed in Ref. [28]. This approach extends the surface SVI[2] (SSVI) model from Ref. [21], hence the acronym

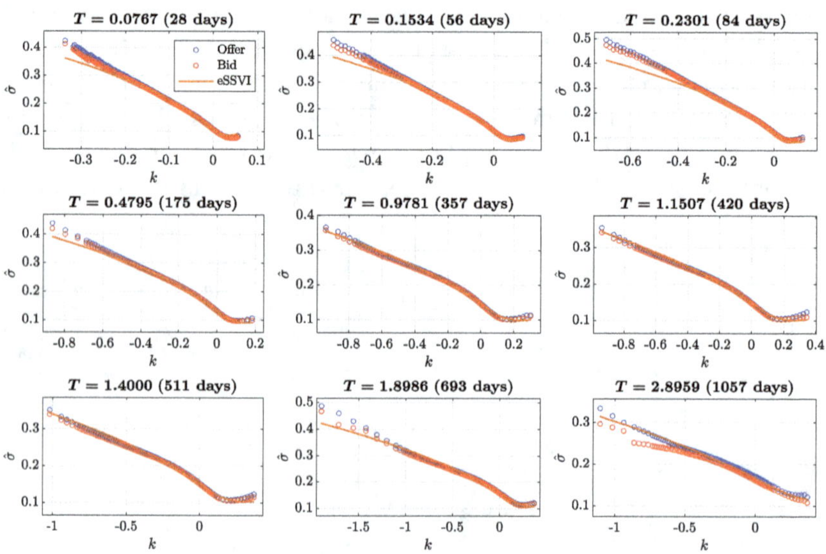

Figure 2. eSSVI smiles fit to regular S&P 500 index options as of January 23, 2020, in log-forward-moneyness k and implied volatility $\hat{\sigma}$ space. Red and blue circles are bid and offer implied volatilities, respectively, and the orange line presents the eSSVI fit.

[1]Note that non- and semi-parametric approaches have also been presented in the literature. An interpolation technique based on convex polynomials that requires the data to be arbitrage-free from the outset is presented in Ref. [33]. Natural cubic splines that smooth call prices and do not expect arbitrage-free input data are employed in Ref. [16] .

[2]SSVI has several attractive features. For example, the term structure of the ATMF-implied volatility may be seen as a (vector) parameter of the volatility surface [21]. As such, it does not need to be calibrated and can be observed

eSSVI, by making the parameter controlling the rotation of the smile maturity dependent. The formulation of the eSSVI parametrization is provided in Appendix A.3.

Figure 2 depicts the quality of the fit of eSSVI across nine listed regular SPX expiries as of January 23, 2020. Observe that the fit is generally good, except for the short-term deep out-of-the-money (OTM) put wing.

3. Local-Stochastic Volatility

Local-stochastic volatility was first introduced in Ref. [32] with the purpose of creating a model capable of recovering the vanilla smile while maintaining its realistic dynamics to correctly price exotic path-dependent derivatives. The hybrid LSV model aims to combine the advantages of LV and SV models while eliminating their drawbacks [31].

We consider a Heston-like LSV model that is, under the risk-neutral probability measure $\mathbb{Q}$, given by the following system of stochastic differential equations (SDEs):

$$dS(t) = (r(t) - q(t))S(t)dt + L(t, S(t))\sqrt{V(t)}S(t)dW^S(t), \quad (1)$$

$$dV(t) = \kappa(\theta - V(t))dt + \eta\sqrt{V(t)}dW^V(t), \quad (2)$$

$$dW^S(t)dW^V(t) = \rho dt, \quad (3)$$

where $r(t)$ and $q(t)$ are the deterministic, time-varying, continuously compounded risk-free interest rate and dividend yield inclusive of the borrow rate, respectively, $\kappa, \theta, \eta, V_0 \in \mathbb{R}_+$ denote the classic Heston parameters [30], $W^S(t)$ and $W^V(t)$ are $\mathbb{Q}$-Brownian motions, $\rho \in (-1, 1)$ is the instantaneous correlation between $W^S(t)$ and $W^V(t)$, and $L(t, S(t))$ is the state-dependent LV correction known as the leverage function [44]. The parameter κ controls the speed of mean reversion, θ is the long-term level of variance and η is the volatility of variance. The initial level of variance $V(0) = V_0$ is not observable and thus is treated as a model parameter. The process $V(t)$ remains positive and can reach 0 only if the so-called Feller condition, $2\kappa\theta > \eta^2$, is violated.

directly from traded options for a finite set of expiries. Moreover, another desirable property is the existence of tractable no-arbitrage conditions [28].

Equation (1) implies that the product $L(t, S(t))\sqrt{V(t)}$ gives the overall instantaneous volatility in the model [6]. The stochastic process $V(t)$ in Eq. (2) is responsible for matching the dynamics of the implied volatility smile, whereas the deterministic component $L(t, S(t))$ is introduced to recover the market-implied volatility surface [32].

In the local volatility model, the SDE governing the risk-neutral diffusive evolution of the current price of the underlying asset $S(t)$ is given by

$$dS(t) = (r(t) - q(t))S(t)dt + \sigma_{LV}(t, S(t))S(t)dW^S(t), \qquad (4)$$

where $\sigma_{LV}(t, S)$ is the state-dependent diffusion coefficient known as the local volatility function. The expression relating the function $\sigma_{LV}(t, S)$ to European option prices and their strike and maturity derivatives are given by [13, 15]. Assume that European call prices $C(K, T) = e^{-\int_0^T r(u)du}\, \mathbb{E}^{\mathbb{Q}}[(S(T)-K)^+]$ are known for a continuum of maturities T and strikes K. Then, by the so-called Dupire's formula, the local volatility function is given by

$$\sigma_{LV}^2(t, S) = 2\frac{\frac{\partial C}{\partial T} + (r(T) - q(T))K\frac{\partial C}{\partial K} + q(T)C}{K^2\frac{\partial^2 C}{\partial K^2}}\Bigg|_{T=t, K=S}. \qquad (5)$$

The proof of Eq. (5) is outlined, e.g., in Refs. [13, 19]. From a given spectrum of European option prices, with any strike $K \geq 0$ and expiry $T \geq 0$, one can employ the right-hand side of Eq. (5) to compute the unique local volatility surface that recovers the market prices of European options.

The LSV model should mimic the LV model so that the two processes have identical one-dimensional marginal distributions and the prices of European options match all strikes K and expiries T [37]. Using Gyöngy's theorem on mimicking processes, see [25] and Appendix A.1, we can match the diffusion terms of Eqs. (1) and (4) by

$$\sigma_{LV}(t, S) = \sqrt{\mathbb{E}^{\mathbb{Q}}\left[L(t, S(t))^2 V(t) | S(t) = S\right]}.$$

Rearranging the above equation, and because $L(t, S)$ is a deterministic function of t and S, we can obtain the expression for the leverage function:

$$L(t,S) = \frac{\sigma_{LV}(t,S)}{\sqrt{\mathbb{E}^{\mathbb{Q}}\left[V(t)|S(t)=S\right]}} = \sigma_{LV}(t,S)\sqrt{\frac{\int_{\mathbb{R}+} p(t,S,V)dV}{\int_{\mathbb{R}_+} Vp(t,S,V)dV}}, \tag{6}$$

where $p(t, S, V)$ denotes the transition probability density function of the LSV model [43]. Because the joint distribution of $S(t)$ and $V(t)$ is unknown, a closed-form representation of Eq. (6) for the Heston LSV model is not available [45]. The calibration procedure of $L(t, S)$ is presented in Appendix A.3. Note that Eq. (6) can intuitively be seen as a ratio between local volatility and the conditional expectation of stochastic volatility.[3]

By construction, the prices of European options under the LSV model always match the prices under the pure LV model. Therefore, even if the pure SV model fails to recover the market data, the LV correction compensates for this. Given this feature, we are allowed to study the sensitivity of any complex derivatives price with respect to the SV model parameters, such as the volatility of variance η or the spot-variance correlation ρ, while preserving an exact fit to the IVS.

Figure 3 shows that the Heston LSV model captures the correct dynamics of the IV smile and the typical market behavior, i.e., the fact that the skew moves in the same direction as the underlying level. In fact, in contrast to what we observed for the LV model, the IV smile shifts to the right for an increase in the index level and vice versa for a decrease [26].

Figure 4 allows us to observe that the forward-starting IV smiles generated by the Heston LSV model are approximately

[3]The model specifications directly imply two limiting cases. When $L(t, S) = 1$, for all S and t, the LSV model collapses to a pure SV model. Similarly, when $\eta = 0$, the process $V(t)$ becomes deterministic, we have $L(t, S) = \sigma_{LV}(t, S)/\sqrt{V(t)}$ and hence the LSV model boils down to a pure LV model [32].

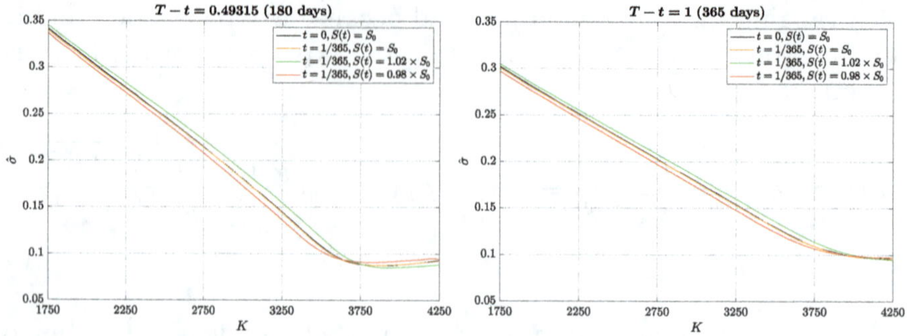

Figure 3. $T-t = 180$ and 365 days IV smile dynamics in the Heston LSV model calibrated to SPX options as of January 23, 2020. In black, the current IV smile. In orange, green and red, the forward IV smiles resulting from different levels at time $t = 1/365$.

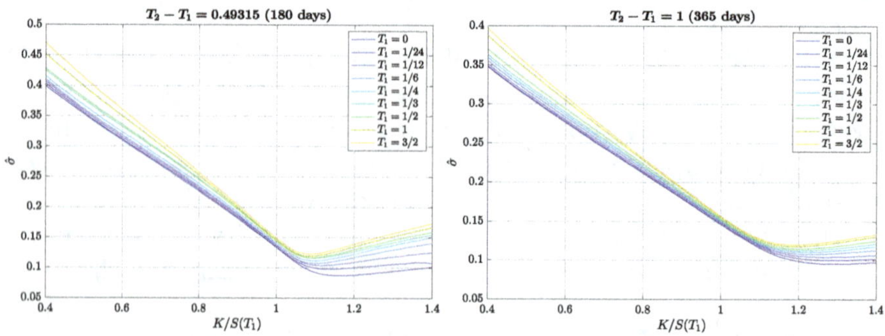

Figure 4. 180 and 365 days spot- and forward-starting implied volatility smiles generated by the Heston local-stochastic volatility model calibrated to SPX options as of January 23, 2020. T_1 denotes the forward start date and $T_2 - T_1$ the residual maturity.

time-homogeneous. Indeed, with increasing T_1, the skew is persisted; the forward IV smile is consistent with today's IV smile. This represents a great advantage of the LSV model in comparison to the commonly employed LV model [38].

The limitation of the LSV model is the non-trivial and computationally demanding calibration of the leverage function. Moreover, since the diffusion term in Eq. (1) depends not only on the current value of $S(t)$ but also on its probability distribution, the SDE is non linear and Ref. [24] argues that the existence of an LSV model for a given market IVS is not guaranteed, despite the opposite being a widespread belief in the quantitative finance community.

Yet, the Heston LSV model represents a suitable model for pricing the vol-of-vol and forward-smile risk. Autocallable structured notes are sensitive to these risks due to their high path and model dependency. In the following section, the focus is set on the comparison of the prices of such derivatives under the LV model and the Heston-like LSV model.

4. Autocallables Pricing

This section investigates the popular class of structured notes (SNs), known as autocallable barrier reverse convertibles (ABRCs). In particular, we compare the pricing of such exotic derivatives in the LV versus the Heston LSV model. SNs are generally issued at 100% of their face value, where a margin is included in the issue price. In this chapter, we focus on the theoretical values and thus exclude trading spreads, barrier shifts and sales margins. Moreover, payoffs are discounted with risk-free rates, thus ignoring issuers' credit risk.

4.1. *Payoff Definition and Risks*

The structure of an ABRC can assume different features and be defined with several distinct characteristics. A typical BRC can be decomposed into a zero-coupon bond (ZCB), a short D&I put option and a stream of coupons. The latter can be as follows: (i) contingent on the underlying asset prices observed at specific intermediate dates, i.e., be subject to down-and-out (D&O) barriers and thus be decomposed into a strip of digital call options, or (ii) guaranteed. Autocall denotes the enhancement with an early termination feature in the form of Bermudan U&O barriers, which, if hit, lead to the immediate repayment of the face value of the SN in addition to a coupon payment. We consider the features presented in Table 1.

Consider the set of observation dates $\mathcal{T} = \{T_1, \dots, T_N\}$, where $T_1 = T^O$ and $T_{i+1} - T_i = T^O$, for $i = 1, \dots, N-1$. Define $i^* := \inf\{i = 1, \dots, N-1 | S(T_i) \geq S(0) H_i^{AC}\} \wedge N$, and $L := \min_{T \in [0, T_N]}\{S(T)\}$

Table 1. Description of the main features determining the ABRC.

Feature	Notation	Description
Expiry tenor	T^E	Tenor corresponding to the final valuation date of the SN expressed in months, e.g., 12 months.
Observation tenor	T^O	Tenor corresponding to the length of the observation periods expressed in months, i.e., the time intervals between the dates at which the coupon barrier and autocall barrier are observed, e.g., 3 months.
Strike	K	Strike of the short put option expressed in % of the current spot $S(0)$, e.g., 90%. The gearing of the put option is given by $1/K$.
Knock-in barrier	H	D&I barrier level expressed in % of $S(0)$, e.g., 80%. If hit, it knocks in the short put option. It can be observed only at the final valuation date (European) or continuously (American).
Coupon	Y	Coupon level paid at the end of each observation period if the coupon barrier is not hit, e.g., 3% per annum (p.a.).
Coupon barrier	$\mathbf{H}^{\mathbf{Y}}$	D&O barrier levels expressed in % of $S(0)$, e.g., 80%. If hit, they invalidate or delay the coupon payment. They can be constant or variable and are observed at the end of each observation period.
Autocall coupon	$\mathbf{Y}^{\mathbf{AC}}$	Coupon levels paid upon early redemption expressed in percentage of the notional, e.g., 3%. They can be constant or "snowballing".
Autocall barrier	$\mathbf{H}^{\mathbf{AC}}$	U&O barrier levels expressed in % of $S(0)$, e.g., 100%. If hit, they trigger the early redemption of the SN. They can be constant or "step-down" and are observed at the end of each period (Bermudan).

Note: T^E, T^O, K, H and Y are scalars. $\mathbf{H}^{\mathbf{Y}}$, $\mathbf{Y}^{\mathbf{AC}}$ and $\mathbf{H}^{\mathbf{AC}}$ are $N \times 1$ vectors, where $N = T^E/T^O$ is the number of observation dates.

or $L := S(T_N)$ if the knock-in barrier H is observed continuously or only at the final valuation date T_N, respectively.

The final payoff of the ABRC for one unit of notional at time T_{i^*}, which is either the early redemption date or the final valuation date, is given by

$$h(T_{i^*}) = 1 + \begin{cases} \mathbb{1}_{\{S(T_N) \geq S(0)H_N^{AC}\}} \\ \quad Y_N^{AC} - \mathbb{1}_{\{L \leq S(0)H\}} \frac{1}{K}\left(K - \frac{S(T_N)}{S(0)}\right)^+, & T_{i^*} = T_N \cdot \\ Y_{i^*}^{AC}, & T_{i^*} < T_N \end{cases}$$

The final payoff consists of the face value of the ZCB, the autocall coupon (if any) and, in case $T_{i^*} = T_N$ (i.e., no early redemption occurs), the payout of the short D&I put option. Additionally, at the ith observation date T_i, for $i = 1, \ldots, i^*$, the holder of the ABRC receives the following coupon amount:

$$M(i)\mathbb{1}_{\{S(T_i) > S(0)H_i^Y\}} Y,$$

where, if the coupon barrier has the so-called "memory" feature, we have $M(1) = 1$ and $M(j) = j - \sup\{i = 1, \ldots, j-1 | S(T_i) > S(0)H_i^Y\} \vee 0$ for $j > 1$. Therefore, $M(i) - 1$ corresponds to the number of foregoing missed coupon payments at time T_i. If the coupon barrier has no memory, we have $M(j) = 1$ for all $j \geq 1$.

Thus, the fair value of the ABRC at time $t = 0$, denoted by $U(0)$, is given by the risk-neutral expectation of the discounted future coupon payments and the final payoff:

$$U(0) = \mathbb{E}^{\mathbb{Q}}\left[e^{-\int_0^{T_{i^*}} r(u)du} h(T_{i^*}) + \sum_{i=1}^{i^*} e^{-\int_0^{T_i} r(u)du} \right.$$
$$\left. M(i)\mathbb{1}_{\{S(T_i) > S(0)H_i^Y\}} Y \right]. \tag{7}$$

Note that U is path-dependent and T_{i^*} is a stopping time. Moreover, the BRC is a special case of ABRC with $\mathbf{H^{AC}} = \infty$ and hence $T_{i^*} = T_N$.

Consider the following ABRC on SPX priced as of January 23, 2020, and denominated in USD as our benchmark example: $T^E = 12$, $T^O = 3$, $K = 1.00$, $H = 0.80$ and European, $Y = 7.19\%$ p.a. as it leads to $U^{LV}(0) = 1$, $\mathbf{H^Y} = \mathbf{0}$ and thus the coupon is guaranteed, $\mathbf{Y^{AC}} = \mathbf{0}$, $\mathbf{H^{AC}} = \mathbf{1}$ and $N = 4$.

Figure 5 illustrates the scenarios for different paths of the underlying level. In Scenario 1, the underlying level at the observation

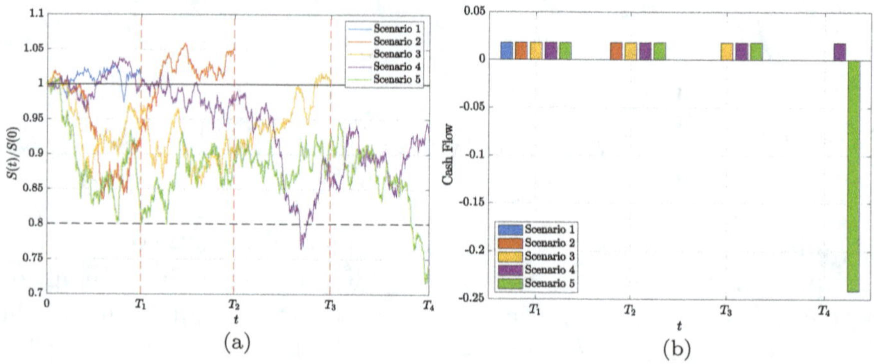

Figure 5. Different ABRC payoff scenarios for $T^E = 12$, $T^O = 3$, $K = 1.00$, $H = 0.80$ European, $Y = 7.19\%$ p.a., $\mathbf{H^Y} = \mathbf{0}$, $\mathbf{Y^{AC}} = \mathbf{0}$ and $\mathbf{H^{AC}} = \mathbf{1}$. (a) Underlying paths and scenario and (b) Cash flows excluding ZCB redemption.

date T_1 is above the autocall barrier, i.e., $S(T_1) \geq H_1^{AC} S(0)$. Therefore, the note is early redeemed at time T_1 with 100% payoff and a coupon payment of $\frac{1}{4} \times 7.19\%$ of the notional amount. Scenarios 2 and 3 are similar to the latter, however, the autocall barrier is breached at times T_2 and T_3, respectively. This implies that two and three coupon payments amounting each to $\frac{1}{4} \times 7.19\%$ are received by the note holder at times T_1, T_2 and T_1, T_2, T_3, respectively. In Scenarios 4 and 5, $S(T_i) < H_i^{AC} S(0)$, for $i = 1, 2, 3$, and thus the note holder receives all the coupon payments at times T_1, T_2, T_3 and T_4. In Scenario 4, $S(T_4) > HS(0)$, hence the note holder receives 100% of the face value. Whereas in Scenario 5, $S(T_4) \leq HS(0)$ and the note holder participates 1:1 to the negative performance of the underlying incurring a loss.

Figure 6(a) exhibits the LV and Heston LSV price of the ABRC for different levels of S at time $t = 0$. Due to the short D&I put option, the holder is short volatility and skew at the inception of the trade. Indeed, higher volatility and skew increase the probability of reaching the barrier H and the option to end ITM [8]. The exposure to the forward is long, which means that the holder is long the underlying asset level and short dividends, see Figure 6(b). In fact, a higher forward implies a lower probability of reaching the barrier H and the option to end ITM at expiry. Figure 6(b) also shows that the gamma $\frac{\partial^2 U}{\partial S^2}$ exposure is not single-signed. Remember that the issuer of the note takes the opposite risks on its books.

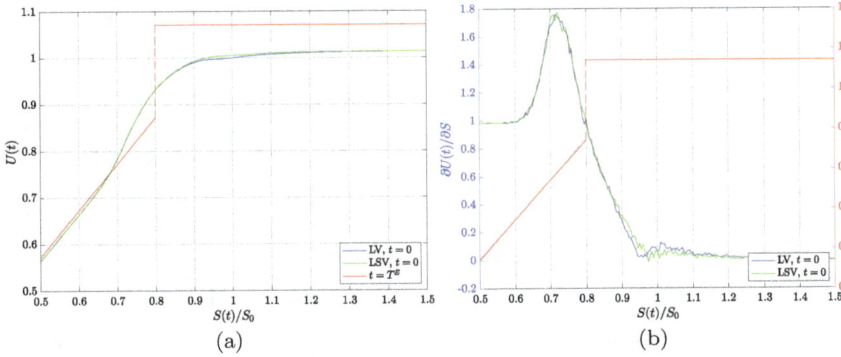

Figure 6. (a) Payoff diagram, price and (b) Sticky-moneyness delta at the inception of the benchmark ABRC for different S at $t = 0$.

Autocallables are known to have a strong model dependency due to the cancelable feature implied by the Bermudan U&O barriers. Consequently, static replication is not possible, and dynamic re-hedging with vanilla options is required as the underlying level moves [42].

As shown in Figure 7, the paths of the underlying level relative to the barrier levels are driving the vega dynamics of autocallables. In fact, as the underlying level falls, vega decreases initially and then increases to turn positive below the D&I barrier, see Figure 7(a). On the other hand, as the underlying level rises, vega tends toward zero because the early redemption of the note becomes more likely. Figure 7(b) suggests that the volatility exposure is also highly dynamic in the tenor dimension. This generates significant vega re-hedging costs for the issuers. As a matter of fact, a pricing model capable of capturing a realistic spot-volatility covariance, which is a known deficiency of the LV model, is essential [42].

We observe in Figure 6(a) that the price of the ABRC obtained using the Heston LSV model is strictly higher than the LV price, whereby the difference attains a maximum at around 97.50% of the current spot. In the subsequent sections, we analyze this closely.

Our price estimates are obtained by evaluating the expectation in Eq. (7) with QMC methods, whereby Sobol sequences of low-discrepancy quasi-random numbers are used. To ensure the comparability of the QMC estimates of the derivatives' prices between the two models, we employ the same quasi-random sequences, an

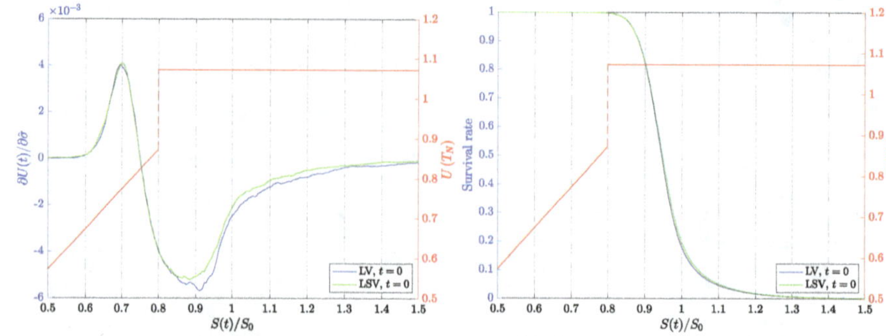

(a) Vega. (b) Survival rate, i.e., $\mathbb{P}[T_{i^*} = T_N]$.

Figure 7. (a) Vega computed with a parallel shift of the IVS and (b) survival rate of the benchmark ABRC for different S at $t = 0$.

Table 2. Y for different T^E computed as of January 23, 2020.

T^E	3	6	9	12	15	18	21	24	30	36	42
Y	3.99%	5.94%	6.85%	7.19%	7.18%	7.21%	7.12%	7.01%	6.80%	6.55%	6.31%
T^E	48	54	60	66	72	78	84	90	96	108	120
Y	6.08%	5.86%	5.73%	5.55%	5.40%	5.26%	5.13%	5.01%	4.87%	4.68%	4.53%

equidistant time grid with $m = 1000$ transition steps, and $n = 2^{15}$ paths as inputs for the simulations. For additional information, see Appendices A.2 and A.3. For variance reduction of the simulation estimates, we use the method of antithetic variates across the two models. The discussion of these methods goes beyond the scope of this chapter and is left to the interested reader, for example, see Ref. [22].

4.2. *Structure Sensitivity*

Here, we investigate which features from Table 1 lead to price differences between the LV and Heston LSV models and thus we determine which elements possess the highest model dependency and exposure to the vol-of-vol and the forward-smile risk. The assumed benchmark structure is that of Section 4.1 with extended T^E. The coupon level Y is computed for each T^E such that $U^{LV}(0) = 1$, leading to the results displayed in Table 2.

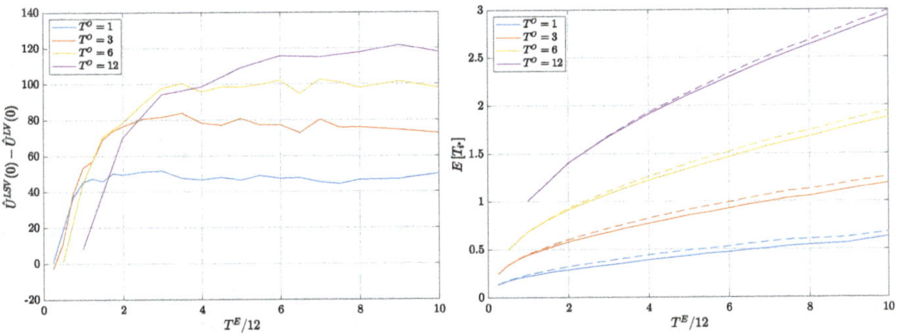

(a) Price differences in basis points (bps). (b) Expected expiries in years.

Figure 8. (a) $\hat{U}^{LSV}(0) - \hat{U}^{LV}(0)$ and (b) $\mathbb{E}^{\mathbb{Q}}[T_{i^*}]$ for different observation tenors T^O and across different expiry tenors T^E. In the right panel, the solid line is for LV and the dashed line for Heston LSV.

For the base payoff, the valuation difference, which we define as $\Delta^{LSV} := U^{LSV}(0) - U^{LV}(0)$, is driven uniquely by the autocall feature. In fact, leaving this aside, the payoff uniquely depends on the marginal distribution of $S(T_E)$, which is by construction the same under the two models.

Because of the path-dependent nature of ABRCs, we expect to find $\Delta^{LSV} > 0$. We proceed in the following with testing our claim by changing or adding some features while keeping the rest of the benchmark structure unchanged.

Figure 8(a) confirms our expectations as we observe $\hat{U}^{LSV}(0) > \hat{U}^{LV}(0)$ for all T^E and T^O. For the base case $T^O = 3$, the price difference is around 10 bps at $T^E = 6$ and increases rapidly to reach a constant level of approximately 80 bps at the 3-year expiry tenor. The same is for $T^O = 1, 6$, and 12, whereby the price differences settle around 50, 100, and 120 bps, respectively. In fact, the price differences demonstrate to be larger for longer T^O and tend to be positively related to the expected expiry $\mathbb{E}^{\mathbb{Q}}[T_{i^*}]$, see Fig. 8(b). This makes intuitive sense since the shorter the expected expiry, the smaller the impact of the decaying future ATMF skews in the LV model on the dynamical properties of $S(t)$.

Figure 9(a) shows that $\Delta^{LSV} > 0$, for all T^E and H. Moreover, for short tenors, Δ^{LSV} decreases with decreasing H. This trend then progressively reverses for longer T^E such that Δ^{LSV} decreases with

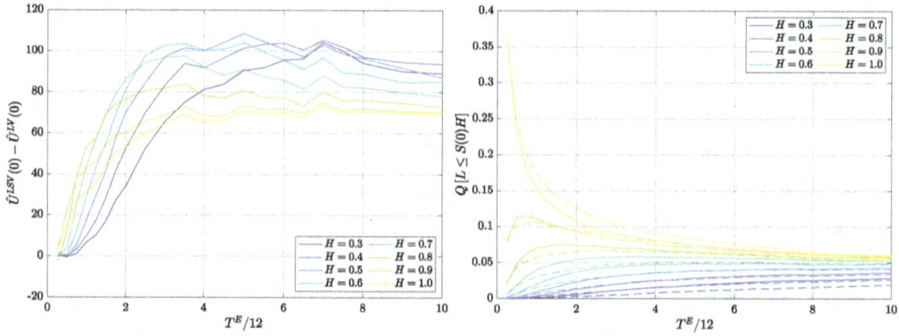

(a) Price differences in bps. (b) Knock-in probabilities.

Figure 9. (a) $\hat{U}^{LSV}(0) - \hat{U}^{LV}(0)$ and (b) $\mathbb{Q}[L \leq S(0)H]$ for different barriers H and across different expiry tenors T^E. In the right panel, the solid line is for LV and the dashed line for Heston LSV.

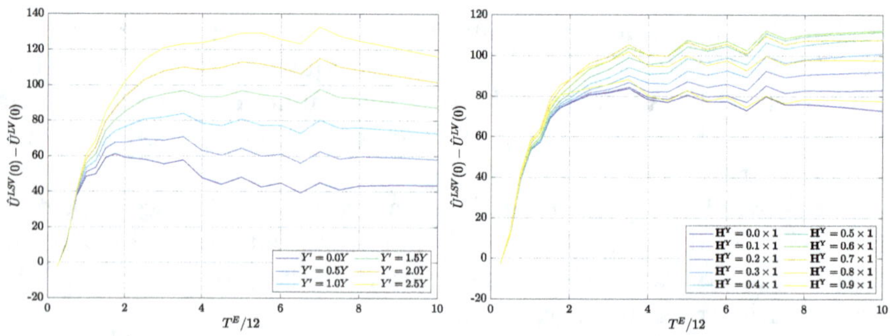

(a) Price differences in bps. (b) Price differences in bps.

Figure 10. $\hat{U}^{LSV}(0) - \hat{U}^{LV}(0)$ in bps for different coupon levels Y', left panel, and coupon barrier levels $\mathbf{H^Y}$ without memory, right panel, across various expiry tenors T^E.

higher H. The knock-in probabilities are, except for $H = 0.9, 1$, marginally higher under the LV model, see Figure 9(b).

Figure 10(a) exhibits that Δ^{LSV} scales linearly with the coupon level. From Figure 10(b), we observe that for a fixed T^E, Δ^{LSV} is a concave function of $\mathbf{H^Y}$. Indeed, a maximum is attained at $\mathbf{H^Y} = 0.6 \times \mathbf{1}$, while, for $\mathbf{H^Y} < 0.6 \times \mathbf{1}$ and $\mathbf{H^Y} > 0.6 \times \mathbf{1}$, Δ^{LSV} decreases. The guaranteed coupon case, i.e., $\mathbf{H^Y} = \mathbf{0}$, defines the lower boundary for Δ^{LSV}. As a result, the coupon barrier generally increases Δ^{LSV} and hence the structure's model dependency.

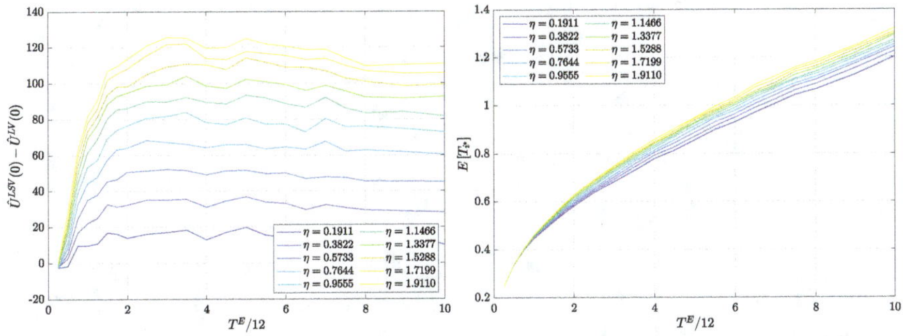

(a) Price differences in bps, $\mathbf{H^{AC}} = \mathbf{1}$. (b) Expected expiries in years, $\mathbf{H^{AC}} = \mathbf{1}$.

Figure 11. $\hat{U}^{LSV}(0) - \hat{U}^{LV}(0)$ for different volatilities of variance levels η across various expiry tenors T^E. In the right panel, the corresponding Heston LSV expected expiries $\mathbb{E}^{\mathbb{Q}}[T_{i^*}]$.

The impacts of the autocall coupon and the autocall barrier level are analyzed in Appendix B.1. All in all, the results presented in this section suggest that the features of the structure and their effect on the model dependency and exposure to the vol-of-vol as well as the forward-smile risk should be taken into consideration when pricing and risk-managing ABRCs.

4.3. *Parameter Sensitivity*

Here, we assess the sensitivity of the ABRC's LSV valuation with respect to the Heston parameters.[4] We consider the same benchmark structure on SPX as defined in Section 4.1.

Figure 11 portrays Δ^{LSV} for different levels of η, i.e., the volatility of variance parameter. As expected, larger values of η lead to higher price differences between the Heston LSV and LV models, in addition to longer $\mathbb{E}^{\mathbb{Q}}[T_{i^*}]$. This confirms the sensitivity of autocallable derivatives to the vol-of-vol and forward-smile risk, see also Figure 12(a). As $\eta \to 0$, we see that $\Delta^{LSV} \to 0$ since, by construction, the LSV model converges to the LV model. Moreover, we observe that the impact of higher η on Δ^{LSV} becomes progressively smaller.

[4]In principle, we could also alter the eSSVI surface parameters and explore the results. However, the fit to European call and put option market prices would be compromised.

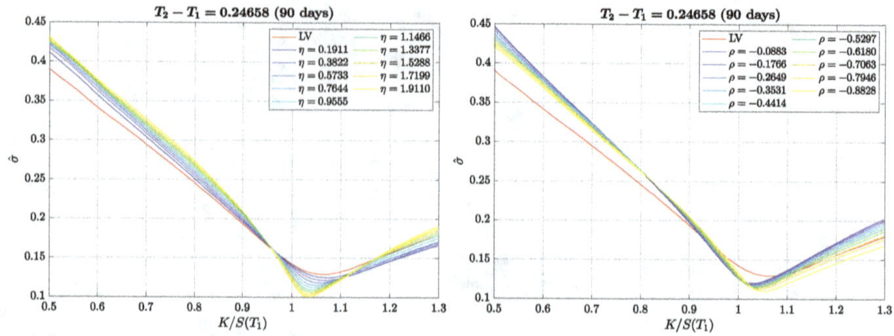

(a) 90-days Forward IV smile for different η. (b) 90-days Forward IV smile for different ρ.

Figure 12. $T_1 = 3$ months forward-starting IV smiles generated by the Heston-like LSV model calibrated to SPX option as of January 23, 2020, for different levels of Heston parameters (a) η and (b) ρ.

Next, we study the influence of η on the forward IV smiles. Figure 12(a) shows that the forward ATM skew steepens with increasing η. Therefore, the future volatility of implied volatilities rises with η. On the other hand, the forward ATM implied volatility levels decrease with higher η, thus implying higher prices in accordance with the ABRC's short volatility exposure for the note holder.

Figure 13 suggests that Δ^{LSV} decreases with higher spot-variance correlation levels, whereas the expected time to expiry lengthens. The price differences are nearly linear in ρ and constant across T^E. The influence of increasing ρ can be explained by a flatter forward ATM IV skew and the lower close to ATM forward IVs, see Figure 12(b). Intuitively, as the underlying level moves higher, the volatility decreases by a larger extent for lower correlations. This phenomenon is reflected by the lower forward-starting IVs in the call wing. Hence, with lower volatility, the early redemption and knock-in probabilities increase and decrease, respectively, while pushing the ABRC valuations higher.

The sensitivity of the ABRC's price with respect to the speed of mean reversion κ, the long-term variance level θ, and the initial level of variance V_0 is analyzed in Appendix B.2. The main takeaway of this section is that the Heston LSV model allows us to control for the spot-implied volatility dynamics through the SV parameters while recovering European call and put option prices and effectively impacting the prices of exotic derivatives.

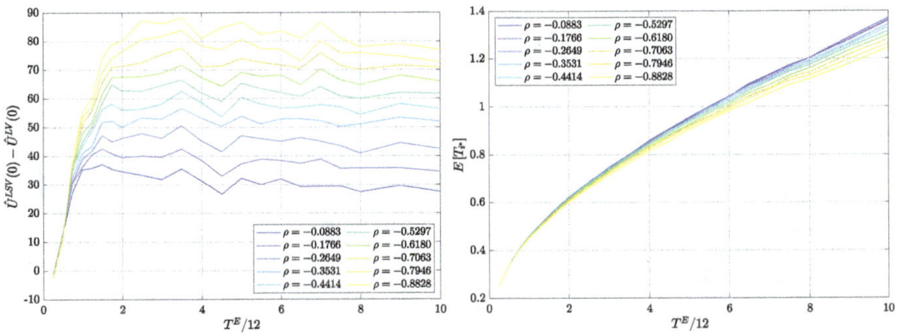

(a) Price differences in bps. (b) Expected expiries in years.

Figure 13. $\hat{U}^{LSV}(0) - \hat{U}^{LV}(0)$ for different correlation levels ρ across various expiry tenors T^E. In the right panel, the corresponding Heston LSV expected expiries $\mathbb{E}^{\mathbb{Q}}[T_{i^*}]$.

4.4. *Underlying Sensitivity*

Here, we assess underlying specific sensitivities of the valuation differences of ABRCs between the Heston LSV and the LV models. First, we test the impact of different forward levels on the benchmark structure referencing SPX. Second, we study the degree of model dependence across different underlyings. We consider the following indices: SPX, NDX, DJX and RUT. These indices represent popular choices for investors seeking exposure to the US market via ABRCs. The studied benchmark structure remains that of Section 4.1.

We compute the SPX ABRC prices assuming different constant and continuously compounded dividend yields $q \in \{0.00, 0.01, \ldots, 0.09\}$. The results are displayed in Figure 14(a) and suggest that, for short expiry tenors $T^E < 24$, Δ^{LSV} is positive and slightly increasing with q. Beyond $T^E \approx 24$, however, Δ^{LSV} decreases with lower forward prices. Moreover, for $q \geq 0.07$, Δ^{LSV} even becomes negative for sufficiently large T^E, indicating that Heston LSV prices fall below LV prices. Figure 14(b) exhibits the knock-in probabilities, namely $\mathbb{Q}\left[L \leq S(0)H\right]$. As the observation suggests and as discussed in Section 4.1, the probability of breaching the D&I barrier decreases with the forward level. Interestingly, the LV model generally implies higher knock-in probabilities than the Heston LSV model for $T^E < 24$, whereas the opposite holds true for $T^E \geq 24$. This explains the evolution of Δ^{LSV} along T^E.

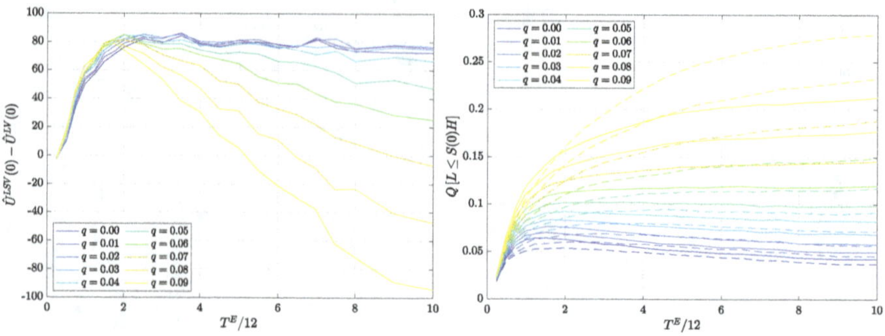

(a) Price differences in bps.

(b) Expected expiries in years.

Figure 14. (a) $\hat{U}^{LSV}(0) - \hat{U}^{LV}(0)$ and (b) $\mathbb{Q}[L \leq S(0)H]$ for different dividend yields q and across different T^E. In the right panel, the solid line is for LV and the dashed line for Heston LSV.

Table 3. Y for different underlyings and T^E computed as of January 23, 2020, for the benchmark ABRC.

	T^E	3	6	9	12	15	18	21	24	30	36	42
NDX	Y	5.15%	7.25%	8.02%	8.31%	8.27%	8.13%	7.93%	7.78%	7.39%	7.06%	6.81%
DJX	Y	3.56%	5.61%	6.70%	7.18%	7.32%	7.29%	7.20%	7.08%	6.85%	6.55%	6.31%
RUT	Y	4.65%	6.70%	7.56%	7.84%	7.83%	7.71%	7.55%	7.45%	7.15%	6.84%	6.55%
	T^E	48	54	60	66	72	78	84	90	96	108	120
NDX	Y	6.48%	6.27%	6.05%	5.82%	5.66%	5.50%	5.34%	5.23%	5.09%	4.86%	4.68%
DJX	Y	6.09%	5.92%	5.71%	5.56%	5.43%	5.28%	5.14%	5.03%	4.92%	4.71%	4.54%
RUT	Y	6.27%	6.07%	5.87%	5.69%	5.53%	5.36%	5.23%	5.10%	4.98%	4.77%	4.57%

Next, we study the sensitivity of ABRC valuation given different underlying indices. Appendix B.3 presents the eSSVI and Heston parameters calibrated to SPX, NDX, DJX and RUT options as of January 23, 2020.

The pricing of the base structure with the same coupon across all indices would lead to biased and uninterpretable results. Therefore, before computing Δ^{LSV}, we calculate the value of the coupon Y for each underlying such that $U^{LV}(0) = 1$, see Tables 2 and 3. Note that, for a fixed tenor T^E, the coupon is greater for underlyings exhibiting higher IVs, see Appendix B.3. Moreover, to isolate the effect of higher coupons, we also run the calculations for $Y = 0$.

Figure 15 shows Δ^{LSV} for the four indices and across different expiry tenors T^E. In the left panel, the coupon is set according to Table 3, whereas in the right panel, it is fixed to $Y = 0$. Despite

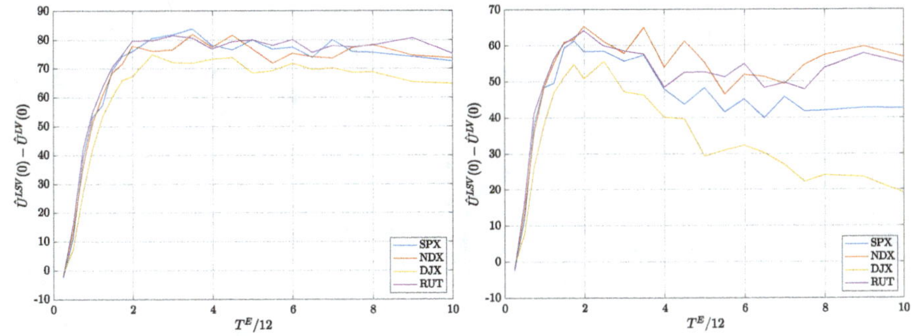

(a) Y as in Table 3. (b) $Y = 0$.

Figure 15. $\hat{U}^{LSV}(0) - \hat{U}^{LV}(0)$ for the indices SPX, NDX, DJX and RUT across expiry tenors T^E.

the differences in the Heston parameters, the eSSVI surface and the coupon amounts, the values of Δ^{LSV} are relatively close to each other for SPX, NDX and RUT, see Figure 15(a). Due to the lower forward, Δ^{LSV} is around 10 bps lower for DJX. However, Figure 15(b) suggests that, with $Y = 0$, an underlying specific pattern arises such that the indices with higher forward and higher implied volatilities tend to exhibit higher Δ^{LSV} and vice versa.

This analysis shows us that underlying-implicit characteristics such as forwards and IV levels do influence the additional cost of ABRCs implied by enhancing LV with an SV component. For instance, lower forward levels increase knock-in probabilities.

4.5. *Market Sensitivity*

Finally, we assess how the market environment affects Δ^{LSV} by repeating the above analysis on the previously studied benchmark structure. We define four volatility regimes proxied by the VIX level: (i) 9.14, i.e., low as of November 3, 2017, (ii) 31.37, i.e., medium-low as of June 23, 2020, (iii) 53.54, i.e., medium-high as of March 31, 2020, and (iv) 75.91, i.e., high as of March 17, 2020.

Observe the significant impact of the market volatility regime on Δ^{LSV} in Figure 16. The low-volatility regime is presented in Figures 16(a) and 16(b) and the high regime in Figures 16(c) and 16(d). Moreover, Figures 16(a) and 16(c) depict Δ^{LSV} for the benchmark structure with the coupon Y defined such that $U^{LV}(0) = 1$,

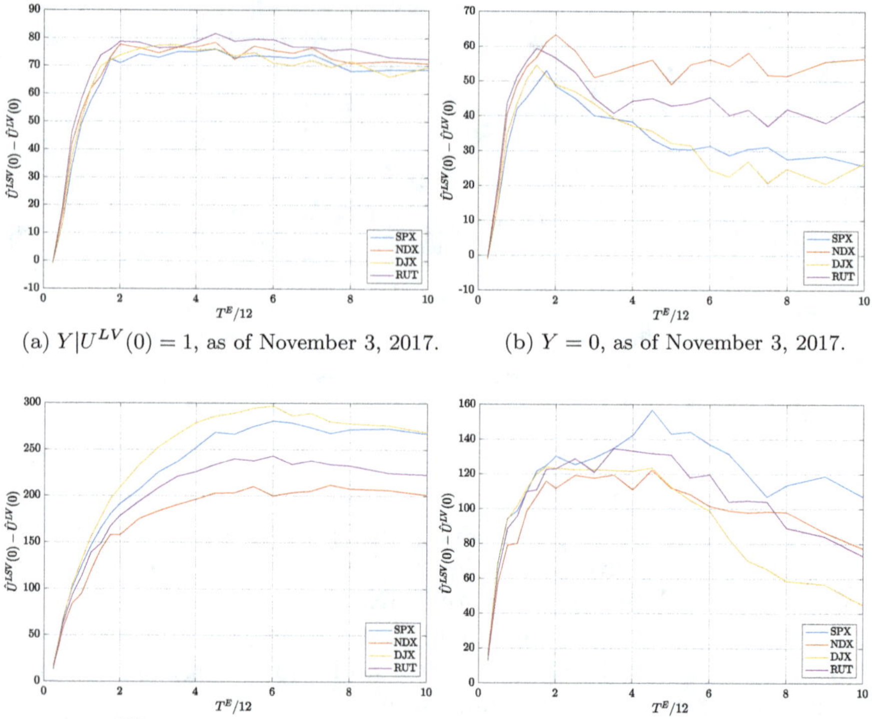

(a) $Y|U^{LV}(0) = 1$, as of November 3, 2017. (b) $Y = 0$, as of November 3, 2017.

(c) $Y|U^{LV}(0) = 1$, as of March 17, 2020. (d) $Y = 0$, as of March 17, 2020.

Figure 16. $\hat{U}^{LSV}(0) - \hat{U}^{LV}(0)$ for SPX, NDX, DJX and RUT across expiry tenors T^E, in low (subplots (a) and (b) and high (subplots (c) and (d)) volatility regimes and for different Y.

whereas Figure 16(b) and 16(d) show the results for $Y = 0$, hence isolating the impact of Y on Δ^{LSV}. Note that the medium-low and medium-high regimes, together with additional results, are presented in Appendix B.4.

For SPX, $Y = 0$, and $T^E = 48$, we obtain $\Delta^{LSV} \approx 50$, 80, 120 and 140 bps in low, medium-low, medium-high, and high volatility markets, respectively.

Accounting for the higher coupon levels, the price differences become even more important: $\Delta^{LSV} \approx 70$, 145, 190 and 250 bps, respectively. This applies directly to the other indices as well. Note also that Δ^{LSV} tends to be more spread out across the indices in highly volatile markets. This indicates that underlying specific characteristics assume more weight. Furthermore, high implied volatility

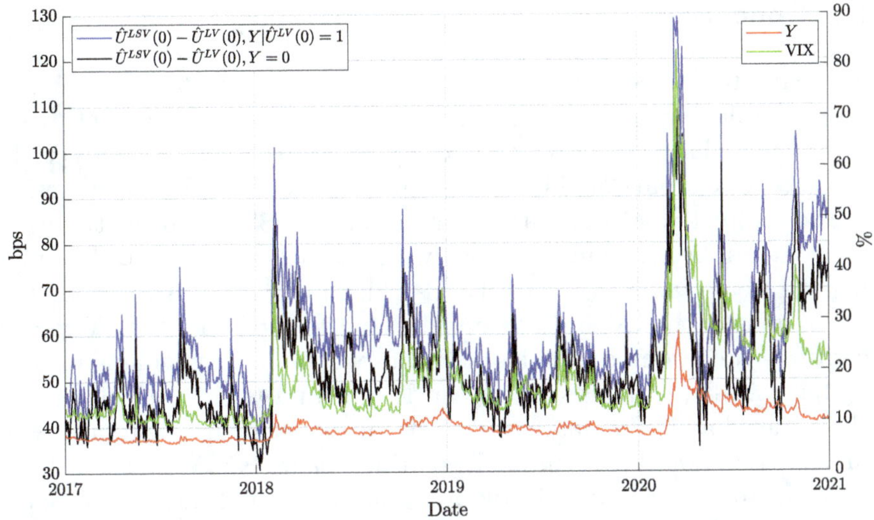

Figure 17. Evolution of $\hat{U}^{LSV}(0) - \hat{U}^{LV}(0)$ over the period January 3, 2017–December 31, 2020, for the benchmark ABRC. The green and red lines are the VIX and Y levels in percentage, respectively, see right y-axis. In blue is Δ^{LSV} for Y such that $U^{LV}(0) = 1$ and in black is Δ^{LSV} for $Y = 0$ in bps, see left y-axis.

and high forward imply larger model valuation differences in line with Section 4.4.

Figure 17 depicts the evolution of Δ^{LSV} for the $T^E = 12$ benchmark structure on SPX over the period spanning from January 3, 2017, to December 31, 2020. Observe a significant positive relationship between the VIX level, the coupon Y, and the model valuation differences Δ^{LSV}. The price differences amount on average to 60 bps for the ABRC under consideration. The minimum and maximum Δ^{LSV} are 37 and 130 bps, respectively, and the standard deviation is 14 bps.

This observation is only partially explained by higher coupons that can be obtained by selling a more expensive put option in periods of high implied volatilities; compare the black and blue lines in Figure 17. Indeed, the main drivers are the higher volatility-of-variance and lower spot-variance correlation (see Section 4.3) resulting from the calibration of the Heston model in stressed markets.

The results show that the model dependency implicit in autocallable derivatives and reflected in the valuation differences is tied to market's implied volatility level.

5. Conclusion

This chapter investigates the main drivers that affect the pricing of autocallable barrier reverse convertibles, structured products that represent a large share of the equity exotic derivatives market. In the theoretical part of this chapter, we first address the construction of the implied volatility surface based on the eSSVI parametrization of total implied variance. Then, we motivate our choice of applying the LSV model to price ABRCs. This motivation is given by the limitations of the LV and SV models. On the one hand, the LV model captures the wrong dynamics of the implied volatility smile and thus systematically misprices the forward-smile and vol-of-vol risk [6]. On the other hand, SV models do not produce enough curvature to match the short-term implied volatility skew. Consequently, both types of models are unsuitable for pricing and risk-managing path-dependent derivatives such as autocallables. Since the LSV models succeed in combining the advantages of the LV and SV models while eliminating their limitations, we employ the Heston-like LSV model in our analysis.

The main contribution of this chapter is an in-depth empirical analysis of the pricing of single-asset autocallable barrier reverse convertibles in the Heston local-stochastic volatility model. Employing quasi-Monte Carlo experiments, we investigate the sensitivity of the prices of autocallable derivatives referencing major US indices such as the S&P 500 in the Heston LSV model versus the LV model with respect to the derivative structure, model parameters, referenced underlying and volatility regime. Generally, we find autocallable barrier reverse convertibles to be valued higher in the Heston LSV model compared to the LV model and hence the price differences to be positive.

The empirical analysis consists of four parts. First, we show that the derivative structure has a profound impact on the valuation differences. For instance, longer U&O barrier observation tenors and higher coupon levels lead to larger price differences. Second, we demonstrate that the valuation differences increase with the volatility-of-variance η, whereas they decrease with the correlation ρ, the speed of mean reversion κ and the long-term level of variance θ (see Appendix B). Third, we analyze underlying specific characteristics such as the dividend yield and the implied volatility level.

We determine that lower forwards reduce the valuation differences, whereas underlyings exhibiting higher implied volatility levels tend to produce larger valuation differences. Finally, we find that the difference between Heston LSV and LV model valuations is positively related to the market's implied volatility level.

There are several directions for future research that this chapter leaves open. For instance, our work can be extended by considering underlyings from different asset classes, such as FX, see Ref. [10], or multi-underlying autocallables in the spirit of Ref. [11], whereby the payoff is written on the "worst-of". Moreover, we focus on the pricing of autocallables, i.e., the valuation differences at the inception of the trades, and not on the hedging. Hence, we do not study how the valuation differences evolve during the lifetime of the trade as, for example, the underlying level moves towards the barriers with the related risk management implications. Furthermore, more advanced models, such as the two-factor forward variance model from [6], can be considered for driving the stochastic component of LSV models.

Autocallables are the most traded equity-linked exotic derivatives with yearly volumes amounting to 100 billion euros [40]. Their growth has been exponential since their introduction in 2003 [12]. As a result, the market is well developed, the competition is high and the margins for autocallables issuers are tightening. In this context and especially for major US indices such as the ones considered in our analysis, price differences of 50–100 basis points caused by modeling assumptions that underestimate the costs of autocall vega re-hedging can translate into booking many unprofitable trades for the issuers. Therefore, the results of our work suggest that the correct pricing of autocallables is of utmost importance in consideration of the recent significant losses incurred by leading issuers.

Appendix A. Theoretical Results

A.1. *Gyöngy's Theorem*

Theorem A.1. *Let $Y(t)$ be an Itô process with $Y(0) = 0$ satisfying*

$$dY(t) = \beta(t,\omega)\,dt + \delta(t,\omega)\,dW(t),$$

where $\beta(t,\omega)$ and $\delta(t,\omega)$ are bounded adapted processes such that $\delta(t,\omega)\delta(t,\omega)^\top$ is uniformly positive definite and ω is a sample path of the Brownian motion $W(t)$. Then, there exists a Markov process $Z(t)$ satisfying

$$dZ(t) = b(t, Z(t))\, dt + d(t, Z(t))\, dW(t),$$

with non-random coefficients which admit a weak solution $Z(t)$ having the same (marginal) distribution as $Y(t)$ for every t. Moreover, $Z(t)$ can be constructed via

$$b(t,z) = \mathbb{E}\left[\beta(t,\omega)|Y(t)=z\right] \quad \textit{and}$$
$$d(t,z)d(t,z)^\top = \mathbb{E}\left[\delta(t,\omega)\delta(t,\omega)^\top|Y(t)=z\right].$$

A.2. *Heston LSV Model: Discretization*

For the discretization of the instantaneous variance process $V(t)$, we rely on the quadratic-exponential (QE) scheme of [3]. For the discretization of the underlying asset price process $S(t)$, we follow [44], whose approach is inspired by [3] and outlined in the following.

By recalling that $W^S(t)$ is almost surely equal to $\rho W^V(t) + \sqrt{1-\rho^2}W(t)^\perp$, where $W^V(t)$ and $W(t)^\perp$ are independent $\mathbb{Q}$-Brownian motions, we can rewrite the SDE from Eq. (1) as follows:

$$\begin{aligned} dS(t) &= (r(t)-q(t))S(t)dt + \rho L(t,S(t))\sqrt{V(t)}S(t)dW^V(t) \\ &\quad + \sqrt{1-\rho^2}L(t,S(t))\sqrt{V(t)}S(t)dW^\perp(t). \end{aligned} \tag{8}$$

Applying Itô's lemma to $\log S(t)$, where the dynamics of $S(t)$ and $V(t)$ are given by Eqs. (8) and (2), respectively, we obtain the following:

$$\begin{aligned} d\log S(t) &= \left(r(t)-q(t)-\frac{1}{2}L^2(t,S(t))V(t)\right)dt \\ &\quad + \rho L(t,S(t))\sqrt{V(t)}dW^V(t) \\ &\quad + \sqrt{1-\rho^2}L(t,S(t))\sqrt{V(t)}dW^\perp(t). \end{aligned}$$

In integral form, we have the following:

$$\begin{aligned}\log S(t_{j+1}) &= \log S(t_j) + \int_{t_j}^{t_{j+1}} (r(u) - q(u))\, du \\ &\quad - \frac{1}{2}\int_{t_j}^{t_{j+1}} L^2(u, S(u))V(u)du \\ &\quad + \rho \int_{t_j}^{t_{j+1}} L(u, S(u))\sqrt{V(u)}dW^V(u) \\ &\quad + \sqrt{1-\rho^2}\int_{t_j}^{t_{j+1}} L(u, S(u))\sqrt{V(u)}dW^{\perp}(u).\end{aligned}$$

As the effective variance process is also driven by a state-dependent LV component, we perform a local freezing of $L(u, S(u))$, i.e., we use the approximation

$$\begin{aligned}&\int_{t_j}^{t_{j+1}} L(u, S(u))\sqrt{V(u)}dW^V(u) \\ &\quad \approx L(t_j, S(t_j)) \int_{t_j}^{t_{j+1}} \sqrt{V(u)}dW^V(u),\end{aligned}$$

which leads to

$$\begin{aligned}\log S(t_{j+1}) &= \log S(t_j) + \log\frac{F(0, t_{j+1})}{F(0, t_j)} - \frac{1}{2}\int_{t_j}^{t_{j+1}} L^2(u, S(u))V(u)du \\ &\quad + \frac{\rho}{\eta}L(t_j, S(t_j))\Bigg(V(t_{j+1}) \\ &\quad - V(t_j) - \kappa\theta(t_{j+1} - t_j) + \kappa\int_{t_j}^{t_{j+1}} V(u)du\Bigg) \\ &\quad + \sqrt{1-\rho^2}\int_{t_j}^{t_{j+1}} L(u, S(u))\sqrt{V(u)}dW^{\perp}(u).\end{aligned}$$

In the Euler scheme, integrals with respect to time are approximated by

$$\int_{t_j}^{t_{j+1}} a(Y(u))du \approx a(Y(t_j))(t_{j+1} - t_j).$$

Moreover, as $W(t)^{\perp}$ is independent of $V(t)$, by Itô's isometry, and conditional on $\int_{t_j}^{t_{j+1}} L^2(u, S(u))V(u)du$ and $V(t_j)$, we have the following:

$$\int_{t_j}^{t_{j+1}} L(u, S(u))\sqrt{V(u)}dW^{\perp}(u)$$
$$\sim \mathcal{N}\left(0, \int_{t_j}^{t_{j+1}} L^2(u, S(u))V(u)d(u)\right).$$

The discretized process $\log \hat{S}(t)$ finally reads:

$$\begin{aligned}\log \hat{S}(t_{j+1}) = \log \hat{S}(t_j) + \log \frac{F(0, t_{j+1})}{F(0, t_j)} \\ - \frac{1}{2}\hat{L}^2(t_j, \hat{S}(t_j))\hat{V}(t_j)(t_{j+1} - t_j) \\ + \frac{\rho}{\eta}\hat{L}(t_j, \hat{S}(t_j))\Big(\hat{V}(t_{j+1}) - \hat{V}(t_j) \\ - \kappa\theta(t_{j+1} - t_j) + \kappa\hat{V}(t_j)(t_{j+1} - t_j)\Big) \\ + \sqrt{1-\rho^2}\sqrt{\hat{L}^2(t_j, \hat{S}(t_j))\hat{V}(t_j)}\sqrt{t_{j+1} - t_j}Z^S_{j+1},\end{aligned} \tag{9}$$

for $j = 0, \ldots, m-1$, where $Z^S_1, \ldots, Z^S_m$ are i.i.d. $\mathcal{N}(0, 1)$ variables independent of the discretized process $\hat{V}(t)$, which is obtained with the QE scheme, and

$$\hat{L}(t_j, \hat{S}(t_j)) = \frac{\sigma_{LV}(t_j, \hat{S}(t_j))}{\sqrt{\mathbb{E}^{\mathbb{Q}}\left[V(t_j) \mid S(t_j) = \hat{S}(t_j)\right]}}. \tag{10}$$

In the following section, we address the approximation of conditional expectation in Eq. (10) and the derivation of σ_{LV}. It is worth noting that the calibration and simulation of the model can occur simultaneously.

A.3. *Heston LSV Model: Calibration*

The LSV model is generally calibrated in two steps [43]. First, the pure stochastic volatility model, i.e., Heston [30] in our implementation, is calibrated to market data. In the second step, the calibration of the leverage function $L(t, S)$, which corrects the volatilities implied by the pure SV model toward the volatilities implied by the pure LV model, takes place.

Different approaches have been proposed for the calibration of the leverage function. Our implementation follows closely [44], which proposes a novel Monte Carlo technique for the evaluation of the conditional expectation $\mathbb{E}^{\mathbb{Q}}[V(t) \mid S(t) = S]$. Their idea is presented in the following and is similar to Ref. [24].

The approach consists in simulating the Heston LSV model with the discretization scheme in Eq. (9) for $S(t)$ combined with the QE scheme of [3] for $V(t)$. To update the value of $\hat{S}$ from t_j to t_{j+1}, we need to establish the two elements: $\sigma_{LV}(t_j, S)$ and $\mathbb{E}[V(t_j) \mid S(t_j) = S]$. For the first component, we rely on the formulation of Eq. (5) in terms of log-forward-moneyness $k := \log K/F(0,T)$ and total implied variance $w(k,T) := \hat{\sigma}^2\left(e^k F(0,T), T\right)$:

$$\sigma_{LV}^2\left(e^k F(0,T), T\right) = \frac{\frac{\partial w}{\partial T}}{1 - \frac{k}{w}\frac{\partial w}{\partial k} + \frac{1}{4}\left(-\frac{1}{4} - \frac{1}{w} + \frac{k^2}{w^2}\right)\left(\frac{\partial w}{\partial k}\right)^2 + \frac{1}{2}\frac{\partial^2 w}{\partial k^2}}.$$

The above equation stems from the fact that implied volatilities are widely used to quote market prices of options. Thus, we can rewrite the option price $C(K,T)$ as $C^{BS}(K,T,\hat{\sigma}(K,T))$ and express Eq. (5) in terms of $\hat{\sigma}(K,T)$ or in our case, but equivalently, in terms of $w(k,T)$. The reader is referred to Ref. [19] for the proof. We take the same approach to derive the local volatility function for the simulation of the pure LV model.

The expression for w is given by the eSSVI parametrization of Ref. [28]. For any option maturity $T \geq 0$, the eSSVI formula describes w as a function of k and the ATMF total implied variance $\theta_T := w(0,T)$:

$$w(k, \theta_T) = \frac{\theta_T}{2}\left(1 + \rho(\theta_T)\varphi(\theta_T)k + \sqrt{(\varphi(\theta_T)k + \rho(\theta_T))^2 + 1 - \rho(\theta_T)^2}\right), \quad (11)$$

where $\varphi : \mathbb{R}_+^* \mapsto \mathbb{R}_+^*$ is a smooth curvature function such that $\lim_{T\to 0}\theta_T\varphi(\theta_T)$ exists in $\mathbb{R}$ and $\rho(\theta_T) \in (-1,1)$ controls the rotation of the smile [21]. It is further assumed that θ is a function of T

at least of class $\mathcal{C}^1$ on $\mathbb{R}_+^*$ and that $\theta_0 := \lim_{T\to 0}\theta_T = 0$ because an ATM option with 0 time to maturity has no value [21].

Since eSSVI is an extension of SVI, the implied variance $\hat{\sigma}^2\left(e^k F(0,T), T\right)$ is linear in k for $|k| \to \infty$ and a fixed T [21]. Hence, it is consistent with the moment formula from [35].

For φ, we rely on the so-called "power-law" representation:

$$\varphi(\theta) = \eta\theta^{-\lambda}, \tag{12}$$

where $\lambda \in (0,1)$ and $\eta > 0$ to ensure positivity, while, for ρ, Ref. [27] finds the following to work well for equity indices:

$$\rho(\theta) = \rho_m + (\rho_0 - \rho_m)\exp\{-a\theta\}, \tag{13}$$

where $|\rho_0| < 1, |\rho_m| < 1$ and $a \geq 0$. The theorems that give the conditions on the parameters in Eqs. (11)–(13) for the eSSVI surface to be free of static arbitrage are presented in Refs. [21] and [28].

The second component, namely the evaluation of the conditional expectation, is more complex. The main challenge is the fact that, for each simulated realization of $S(t)$, exactly one single corresponding realization of $V(t)$ is available [44].

Following Ref. [44], we use a non-parametric approach enhanced with a continuous approximation. Assume that, for each t_j, $j = 1,\ldots,m$, we have a set of n Monte Carlo realizations $\{(\hat{S}_i(t_j), \hat{V}_i(t_j))\}_{i=1}^n$, simulated according to the scheme of Eq. (9) and the quadratic-exponential scheme, respectively, for which we need to evaluate the conditional expectation in Eq. (10).

To overcome the fact that for each $\hat{S}_i(t_j)$ we dispose of exactly one value of $\hat{V}_i(t_j)$, and hence the expectation conditional on $\hat{S}_i(t_j)$ is equal to $\hat{V}_i(t_j)$, we partition $\hat{S}(t_j)$ into ℓ mutually exclusive bins, whereby each bin is defined to contain nearly the same number of paths [44]. Define by $\{(\bar{S}_i(t_j), \bar{V}_i(t_j))\}_{i=1}^n$ the set of ordered realizations such that $\bar{S}_1(t_j) \leq \cdots \leq \bar{S}_n(t_j)$; the set of bins is then given by:

$$\mathcal{B} = \{(b_k, b_{k+1}]\}_{k=1}^{\ell},$$

where $b_1 = \bar{S}_1(t_j)$, $b_{\ell+1} = \bar{S}_n(t_j)$ and $b_k = \bar{S}_{(k-1)n/\ell}(t_j)$, for $k = 2,\ldots,\ell$. Note that the set of bins $\mathcal{B}$ is dependent on the time step t_j.

For a specific realization $S \in (b_k, b_k+1]$, [44] shows that the following approximation is justified and appropriate:

$$\begin{aligned}\mathbb{E}^{\mathbb{Q}}\left[V(t_j) \mid S(t_j)=S\right] &\approx \frac{\mathbb{E}^{\mathbb{Q}}\left[V(t_j)\mathbb{1}_{S(t_i)\in(b_k,b_{k+1}]}\right]}{\mathbb{Q}\left(S\left(t_i\right)\in(b_k,b_{k+1}]\right)}\\ &\approx \frac{\frac{1}{n}\sum_{j=1}^{n}\hat{V}_i(t_j)\mathbb{1}_{S\in(b_k,b_{k+1}]}}{\mathbb{Q}(\hat{S}\left(t_i\right)\in(b_k,b_{k+1}])}\\ &= \frac{\ell}{n}\sum_{i\in\mathcal{I}_k}\hat{V}_i(t_j), \end{aligned} \tag{14}$$

where $\mathcal{I}_k$ denotes the set of path numbers corresponding to the kth bin B_k, i.e., $\mathcal{I}_k = \{i \mid (\hat{S}_i(t_j), \hat{V}_i(t_j)) \in B_k\}$, and $\mathbb{1}$ is the indicator function.

With Eq. (14), the conditional expectation is approximated by means of a step-function. The continuous approximation (CA) consists of connecting the mid points of the approximations obtained with the non-parametric method described above [44]. In contrast to the simple method, the CA is continuous and provides a greater fit to the theoretical conditional expectation, see Figure 18. For an increasing number of simulations n and bins ℓ, the approximation recovered by the non-parametric method converges to the theoretical value [44].

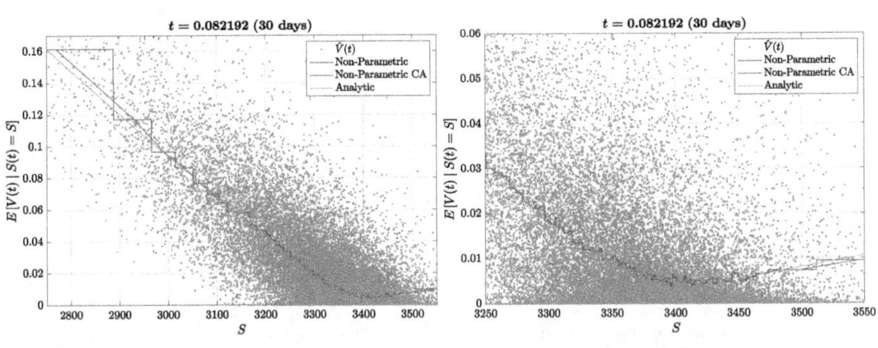

Figure 18. Approximation of the conditional expectation $\mathbb{E}^{\mathbb{Q}}\left[V(t) \mid S(t)=S\right]$, where the joint dynamics of $(S(t), V(t))_{t\geq 0}$ is given by the Heston model with $\kappa = 3.7764$, $\theta = 0.0365$, $\eta = 0.9555$, $\rho = -0.7946$ and $V_0 = 0.0141$. $T_{max} = 1057$ days, $\ell = 100$, $n = 2^{14}$ and $m = 1057$.

Figure 18 allows us to graphically visualize the functioning of the non-parametric method and the quality of the approximations for the Heston model. Figure 19 illustrates the non-parametric approximation of the conditional expectation for the Heston LSV model. For the latter, we cannot show a comparison with the theoretical value as this is not available analytically. Here, T_{max} corresponds to the longest listed SPX expiry as of January 23, 2020.

Figure 20 exhibits the approximate leverage function $\hat{L}(t, S)$ calibrated to SPX options as of January 23, 2020. We observe that the local volatility correction lies in the interval $[0.5, 1.5]$ and that its values close to ATMF are around 1. This is in accordance with Ref. [29], which claims that, in order to maintain the dynamic properties of the underlying SV model, the value of $L(t, S)$ around ATMF should be close to 1 and its skew not too remarkable.

The fact that the leverage function approximation is not smooth is due to the non-parametric approximation method and depends on the choice of the number of bins ℓ as well as the number of MC paths n. Yet, this does not have a significant impact on prices. Also, observe in Figure 20 that the non-parametric method does not allow recovering an approximation for the conditional expectation in low probability density areas, i.e., for $K \to 0$ or $K \to \infty$, and especially for $T \to 0$.

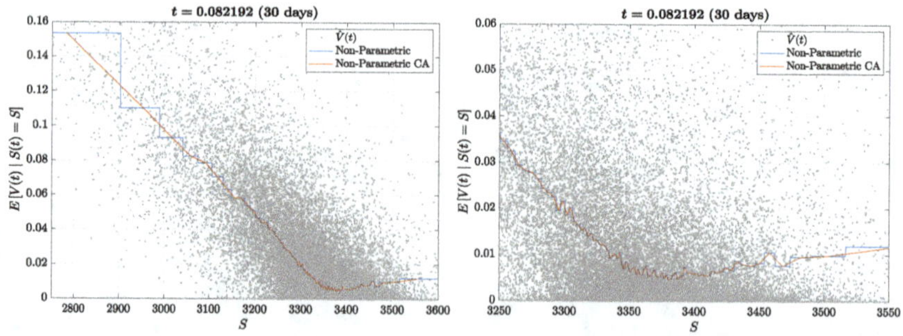

Figure 19. Approximation of the conditional expectation $\mathbb{E}^{\mathbb{Q}}[V(t) \mid S(t) = S]$, where the joint dynamics of $(S(t), V(t))_{t\geq 0}$ is given by the system of SDEs from Eqs. (1)–(3). The LV function is obtained as of January 23, 2020, $T_{max} = 1057$ days, $\ell = 100$, $n = 2^{14}$ and $m = 1057$. The Heston parameters are as in Figure 18.

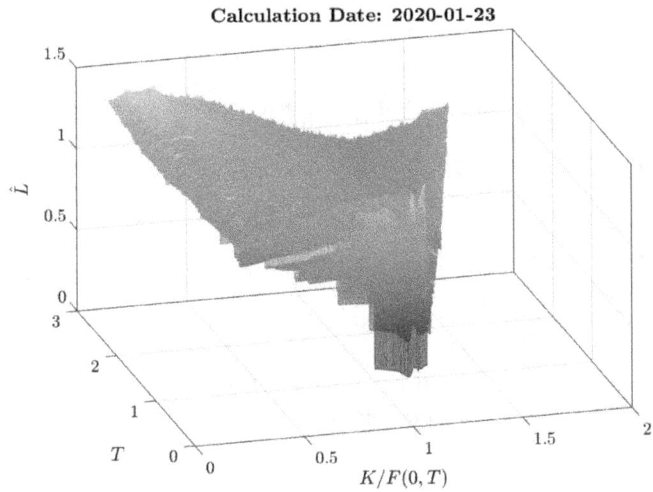

Figure 20. Leverage function approximation calibrated to SPX options as of January 23, 2020. The parameters for the approximation are $T_{max} = 1057$ days, $\ell = 200$, $n = 2^{18}$, and $m = 1057$.

Table 4. $\bar{Y}^{AC}$ for different T^E computed as of January 23, 2020.

T^E	3	6	9	12	15	18	21	24	30	36	42
$\bar{Y}^{AC}$	6.24%	9.03%	10.39%	10.96%	11.06%	11.24%	11.23%	11.13%	11.00%	10.8%	10.67%
T^E	48	54	60	66	72	78	84	90	96	108	120
$\bar{Y}^{AC}$	10.37%	10.15%	10.13%	9.92%	9.74%	9.69%	9.52%	9.37%	9.17%	8.99%	8.96%

Appendix B. Empirical Results

B.1. *Autocallables Pricing: Structure Sensitivity*

To investigate the impact of the autocall coupon, we set $Y = 0$ and solve for $\mathbf{Y^{AC}}$ such that $U^{LV}(0) = 1$ for each T^E. The results are presented in Table 4. For each period $i = 1, \ldots, N$, we define the autocall coupon $\mathbf{Y^{AC}}$ to be "snowballing", i.e., $Y_i^{AC} = i\frac{T^O}{12}\bar{Y}^{AC}$.

Similar to Figure 8(a), Figure 21(a) shows that the Heston LSV model leads to higher prices compared to LV, whereby the difference Δ^{LSV} is generally larger the longer the observation tenor T^O. However, for $T^O = 6$ and 12, we note that Δ^{LSV} increases almost

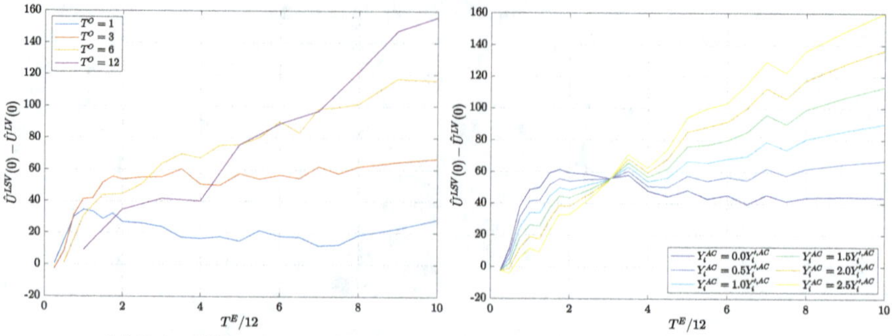

(a) Price differences in bps.

(b) Price differences in bps.

Figure 21. $\hat{U}^{LSV}(0) - \hat{U}^{LV}(0)$ for different observation tenors T^O and autocall coupon levels $\mathbf{Y^{AC}}$ across various expiry tenors T^E.

linearly with T^E. Moreover, in contrast to Figure 8(a), the price differences are smaller for short expiry tenors and vice versa for longer expiry tenors. For $T^O = 1$ and 3, Δ^{LSV} is smaller compared to the base case for all T^E. To summarize, our observation implies that, for long T^O and for $T^E > 72$, the autocall coupon implies a larger model dependency compared to the standard coupon case, while the reverse situation applies for $T^E \leq 72$.

Figure 21(b) exhibits that, for a fixed T^E, Δ^{LSV} scales linearly with $\mathbf{Y^{AC}}$. However, in the time dimension, we observe an inflection point at around the 3-year expiry tenor. For $T^E < 36$, Δ^{LSV} decreases with increasing $\mathbf{Y^{AC}}$, while, for $T^E > 36$, we observe that Δ^{LSV} increases with $\mathbf{Y^{AC}}$.

To analyze the impact of the autocall barrier level, we assume again the base case outlined in Section 4.1. Figure 22 displays the price differences between Heston LSV and LV for several constant autocall barrier levels.

We observe that, for low barrier levels, the high probability of early redemption translates into short expected expiries and minor Δ^{LSV}. Essentially, if $\mathbf{H^{AC}}$ is low, the autocallable derivative becomes a short fixed maturity structure.

We observe the same for high $\mathbf{H^{AC}}$. Thereby, low probabilities of breaching the autocall barriers essentially induce fixed maturity into the structure and reduce its path dependency. As a consequence, the Heston LSV and LV prices agree, up to a pricing error induced by different discretization schemes. This leads, for a fixed expiry tenor

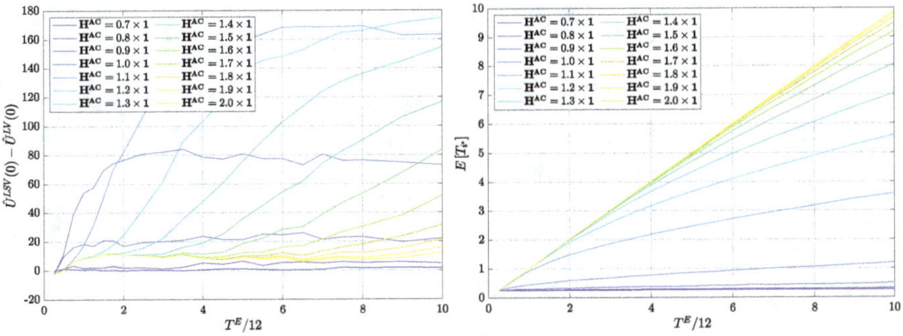

(a) Price differences in bps. (b) Expected expiries in years.

Figure 22. In the left panel, $\hat{U}^{LSV}(0) - \hat{U}^{LV}(0)$ for different constant autocall barrier levels $\mathbf{H^{AC}}$ and across different T^E. In the right panel, the LV implied $\mathbb{E}^{\mathbb{Q}}[T_{i^*}]$.

T^E, to a concave dependency between $\mathbf{H^{AC}}$ and Δ^{LSV}, where the structures whose autocall barrier levels imply $\mathbb{E}^{\mathbb{Q}}[T_{i^*}] \approx \frac{1}{2}T^E$ exhibit larger price differences. For a 6-year ABRC with $\mathbf{H^{AC}} = 1.1 \times \mathbf{1}$, the price difference implied by our models is as high as 1.70%.

A popular feature of ABRCs known as "step-down" generally refers to linearly decreasing autocall barrier levels. Consider, for instance, $T^E = 18$ and $T^O = 3$, then, if $H_1^{AC} = 1$ and $H_N^{AC} = 0.95$, we have $H_i^{AC} = H_1^{AC} + \frac{i-1}{N-1}(H_1^{AC} - H_N^{AC})$, for $i = 2, ..., N-1$, i.e., $\mathbf{H^{AC}} = (1.00, 0.99, 0.98, 0.97, 0.96, 0.95)$. The step-down feature reduces the impact of LSV by reducing significantly the expected expiry $\mathbb{E}^{\mathbb{Q}}[T_{i^*}]$, as shown in Figure 23. The lower the last barrier level H_N^{AC}, the smaller the model valuation differences Δ^{LSV}.

B.2. *Autocallables Pricing: Parameter Sensitivity*

Observing Figure 11, the magnitude of the effect of an increase in η is roughly constant across expiry tenors for $T^E \geq 36$. However, for autocall barrier levels that lead to a longer expected time to expiry, such as in Figure 22, we expect this to increase with T^E.

In fact, our claim is confirmed by Figure 24, which exhibits Δ^{LSV} across different expiry tenors T^E and volatility of variance levels η for the benchmark ABRC with higher autocall barriers, i.e., $\mathbf{H^{AC}} = 1.2 \times \mathbf{1}$.

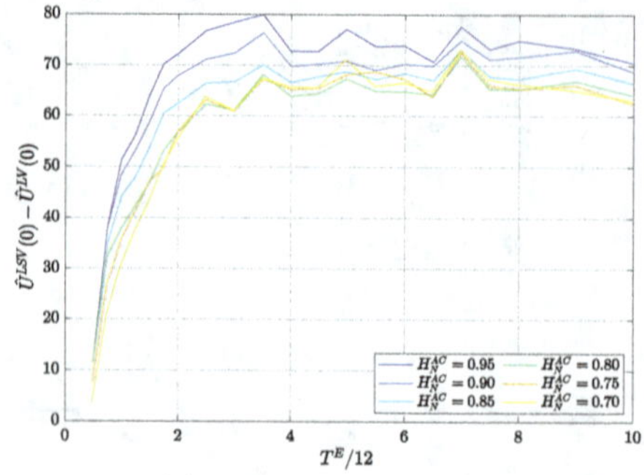

(a) Price differences in bps.

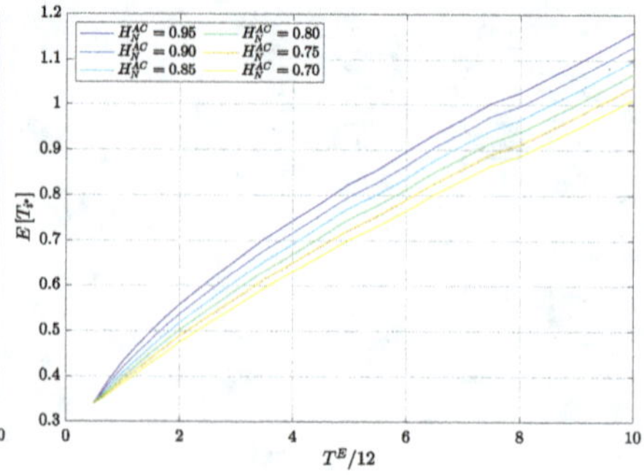

(b) Expected expiries in years.

Figure 23. In the left panel, $\hat{U}^{LSV}(0) - \hat{U}^{LV}(0)$ for different step-down autocall barrier levels $\mathbf{H}^{\mathbf{AC}}$ and across different T^E, $H_1^{AC} = 1$. In the right panel, the LV implied $\mathbb{E}^{\mathbb{Q}}[T_{i^*}]$.

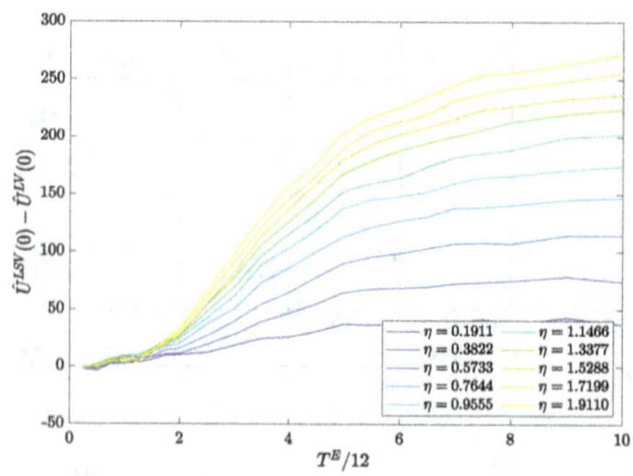

(a) Price differences in bps, $\mathbf{H}^{\mathbf{AC}} = 1.2 \times \mathbf{1}$.

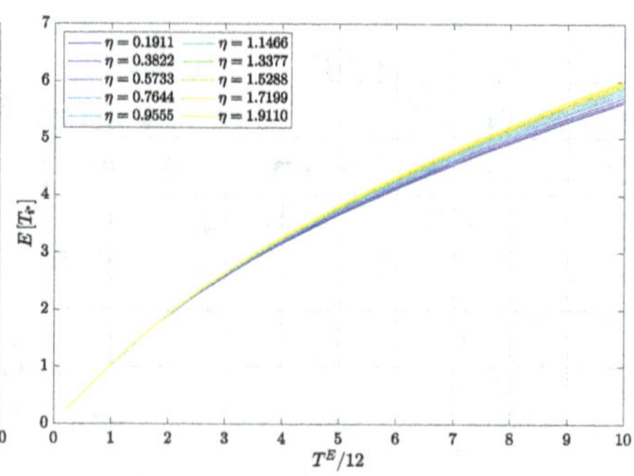

(b) Expected expiries in years, $\mathbf{H}^{\mathbf{AC}} = 1.2 \times \mathbf{1}$.

Figure 24. $\hat{U}^{LSV}(0) - \hat{U}^{LV}(0)$ for different volatility of variance levels η across various expiry tenors T^E. In the right panel, the corresponding Heston LSV expected expiries $\mathbb{E}^{\mathbb{Q}}[T_{i^*}]$.

We observe in Figure 25 the sensitivity of the ABRC's price with respect to the speed of mean reversion. Thereby, Δ^{LSV} is inversely related to κ. The effect is nearly constant across T^E for the basic ABRC.

Similar to η, although in opposite direction, the effect of κ on Δ^{LSV} becomes increasingly smaller for larger values of κ. Furthermore, the autocall probability increases with κ, leading to a shorter expected time to expiry. Inspection of the forward-starting IV smile provides insights for our observation.

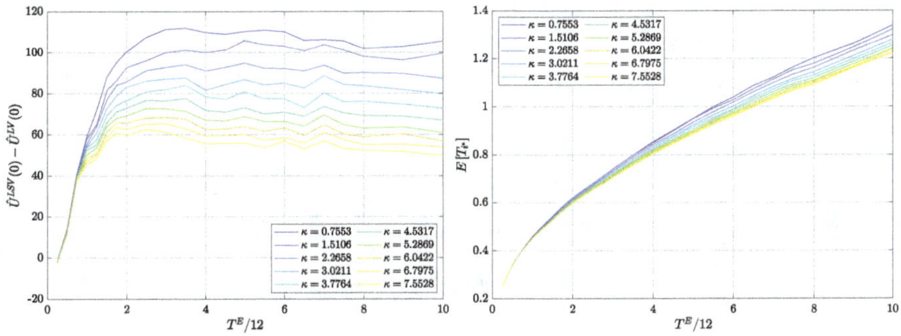

(a) Price differences in bps. (b) Expected expiries in years.

Figure 25. $\hat{U}^{LSV}(0) - \hat{U}^{LV}(0)$ for different speed of mean reversion levels κ across various expiry tenors T^E. In the right panel, the corresponding LSV expected expiries $\mathbb{E}^{\mathbb{Q}}[T_{i^*}]$.

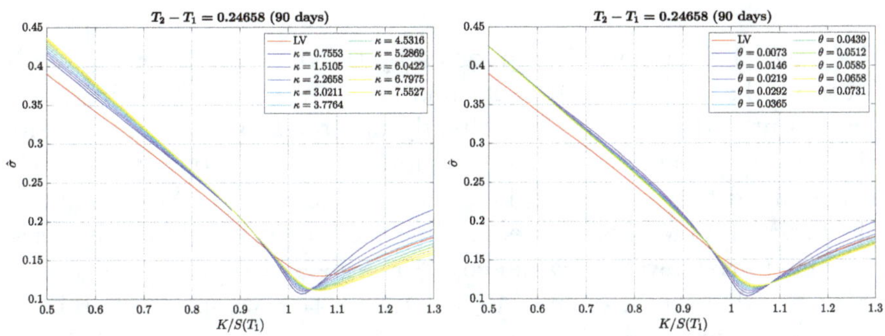

(a) 90-days Forward IV smile for different κ. (b) 90-days Forward IV smile for different θ.

Figure 26. $T_1 = 3$ months forward-starting IV smiles generated by the Heston-like LSV model calibrated to SPX option as of January 23, 2020, for different levels of κ and θ.

As shown in Figure 26(a), the forward ATM skew decreases with increasing κ. In turn, this leads to lower future vol-of-vol levels and higher forward ATM IVs. Hence, the ABRC's prices are driven lower, implying reduced differences between the Heston LSV and LV models. Intuitively, large values of κ imply that the volatility becomes "less stochastic" as any shock in the volatility process is rapidly tamed by the high speed of mean reversion.

For the long-term variance level, we expect the Heston LSV price of the ABRC to be decreasing with θ. Indeed, larger θ means higher long-term volatility levels, and the ABRC's vega is negative, see

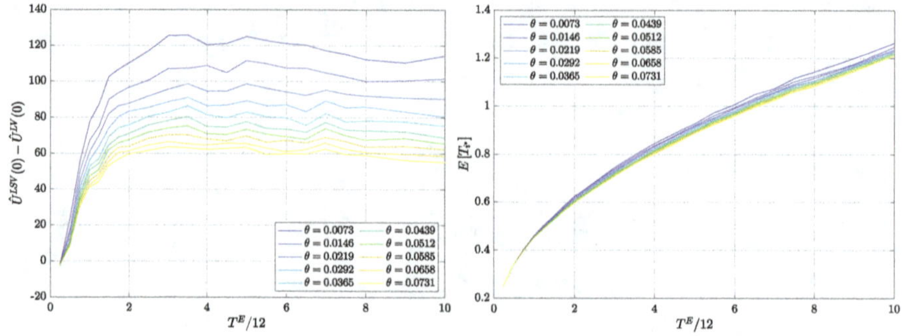

(a) Price differences in bps. (b) Expected expiries in years.

Figure 27. $\hat{U}^{LSV}(0) - \hat{U}^{LV}(0)$ for different long-term variance levels θ across various expiry tenors T^E. In the right panel, the corresponding LV expected expiries $\mathbb{E}^{\mathbb{Q}}[T_{i^*}]$.

Figure 7(a). Our claim is supported by the observation of Figure 27. Observe that Δ^{LSV} is inversely related to θ. The relationship is not linear but rather concave, as already observed for η and κ. In addition, $\mathbb{E}^{\mathbb{Q}}[T_{i^*}]$ decreases with θ. The influence of Heston's θ parameter is explained by the forward IV smile in Figure 26(b). With higher θ, the forward ATM skew flattens, while the forward ATM IVs increase.

The initial level of variance V_0 has negligible influence on the valuation differences of the ABRC between the two models and hence no result is presented.

B.3. *Autocallables Pricing: Underlying Sensitivity*

Tables 5 and 6 exhibit the eSSVI and Heston parameters calibrated to SPX, NDX, DJX and RUT options as of January 23, 2020, respectively. The eSSVI parameters are very close among the four indices. The main difference lies in the vector parameter θ, which denotes the AMTF term structure of total implied variance, displayed in the right panel of Figure 28.

The AMTF implied volatilities of SPX and DJX essentially agree, while RUT and NDX exhibit around 2% and 3% higher IV levels, respectively. On the other hand, Heston parameters are further apart, although the values of θ and V_0 reflect what is mentioned above about the ATMF implied volatility term structures.

Table 5. eSSVI parameters calibrated to SPX, NDX, DJX and RUT traditional, weekly, and end-of-month options as of January 23, 2020.

	η	λ	ρ_m	ρ_0	a
SPX	0.6066	0.5929	−0.7564	−0.4245	651.0968
NDX	0.5692	0.5741	−0.7593	−0.3328	724.3588
DJX	0.5752	0.5771	−0.7715	−0.4323	200.0267
RUT	0.5706	0.5971	−0.6823	−0.3437	387.2297

Table 6. Heston parameters calibrated to SPX, NDX, DJX and RUT traditional options as of January 23, 2020.

	κ	θ	η	ρ	V_0
SPX	3.7764	0.0365	0.9555	−0.7946	0.0141
NDX	3.5723	0.0463	0.8791	−0.7784	0.0242
DJX	2.0432	0.0388	0.5728	−0.7919	0.0159
RUT	4.6137	0.0409	1.0805	−0.7206	0.0205

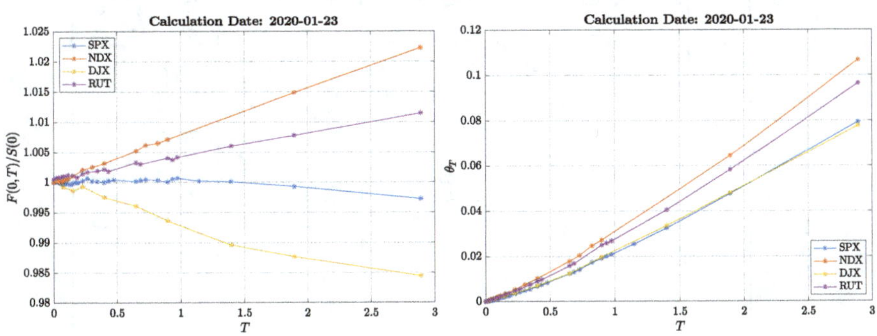

Figure 28. SPX, NDX, DJX and RUT ATMF total implied variance and forwards term structure as of January 23, 2020.

The left panel of Figure 28 displays the forwards in percentage of the spot, i.e., $F(0, T)/S(0)$, for different tenors T. The constituents of DJX and SPX are paying higher dividends compared to those of RUT and NDX as reflected by their forward curves. Implied dividend

Table 7. VIX levels, ATMF implied volatilities and forwards versus different tenors T as of November 3, 2017, June 23, 2020, March 31, 2020, and March 17, 2020, respectively.

				$\sigma(F(0,T),T)$					$F(0,T)/S(0)$				
		VIX	T	1/4	1/2	1	2	3	1/4	1/2	1	2	3
2017-11-03	SPX	9.14		0.0923	0.1098	0.1309	0.1525	0.1628	0.9995	0.9993	0.9990	1.0013	1.0052
	NDX			0.1350	0.1497	0.1647	0.1755	0.1905	1.0008	1.0028	1.0072	1.0188	1.0317
	DJX			0.1009	0.1167	0.1325	0.1436	0.1485	0.9971	0.9957	0.9955	0.9936	0.9933
	RUT			0.1397	0.1541	0.1708	0.1827	0.1911	1.0001	1.0006	1.0017	1.0057	1.0118
2020-06-23	SPX	31.37		0.2652	0.2717	0.2545	0.2381	0.2298	0.9969	0.9938	0.9876	0.9754	0.9640
	NDX			0.2809	0.2848	0.2666	0.2536	0.2485	0.9995	0.9984	0.9967	0.9924	0.9887
	DJX			0.2945	0.2914	0.2632	0.2434	0.2378	0.9955	0.9911	0.9839	0.9709	0.9564
	RUT			0.3575	0.3445	0.3009	0.2691	0.2543	0.9982	0.9966	0.9940	0.9878	0.9848
2020-03-31	SPX	53.54		0.3920	0.3469	0.2974	0.2554	0.2331	0.9942	0.9933	0.9945	0.9853	0.9784
	NDX			0.3948	0.3388	0.2921	0.2579	0.2415	0.9969	0.9969	0.9976	1.0003	1.0002
	DJX			0.4571	0.3874	0.3301	0.2938	0.2631	0.9919	0.9892	0.9805	0.9595	0.9464
	RUT			0.4430	0.3849	0.3273	0.2849	0.2650	0.9909	0.9890	0.9858	0.9837	0.9840
2020-03-17	SPX	75.91		0.5872	0.4779	0.3763	0.2944	0.2875	0.9861	0.9815	0.9771	0.9690	0.9600
	NDX			0.5776	0.4679	0.3682	0.3000	0.2696	0.9902	0.9886	0.9835	0.9774	0.9741
	DJX			0.6313	0.5026	0.3960	0.3357	0.3340	0.9832	0.9769	0.9659	0.9441	0.9278
	RUT			0.5941	0.4874	0.3834	0.3195	0.2931	0.9817	0.9786	0.9716	0.9591	0.9483

yields inclusive of borrow rates for the longest maturity are 2.08%, 1.64%, 1.15% and 0.78%, respectively.

B.4. *Autocallables Pricing: Market Sensitivity*

Table 7 outlines the underlying information that defines four volatility regimes as proxied by the VIX: low as of November 3, 2017, medium-low as of June 23, 2020, medium-high as of March 31, 2020, and high as of March 17, 2020.

Figures 29(a) and 29(c) depict Δ^{LSV} for the benchmark structure with the coupon Y defined such that $U^{LV}(0) = 1$, whereas Figure 29(b) and 29(d) show the results for $Y = 0$, hence isolating the impact of Y on Δ^{LSV}. Medium-low and medium-high volatility

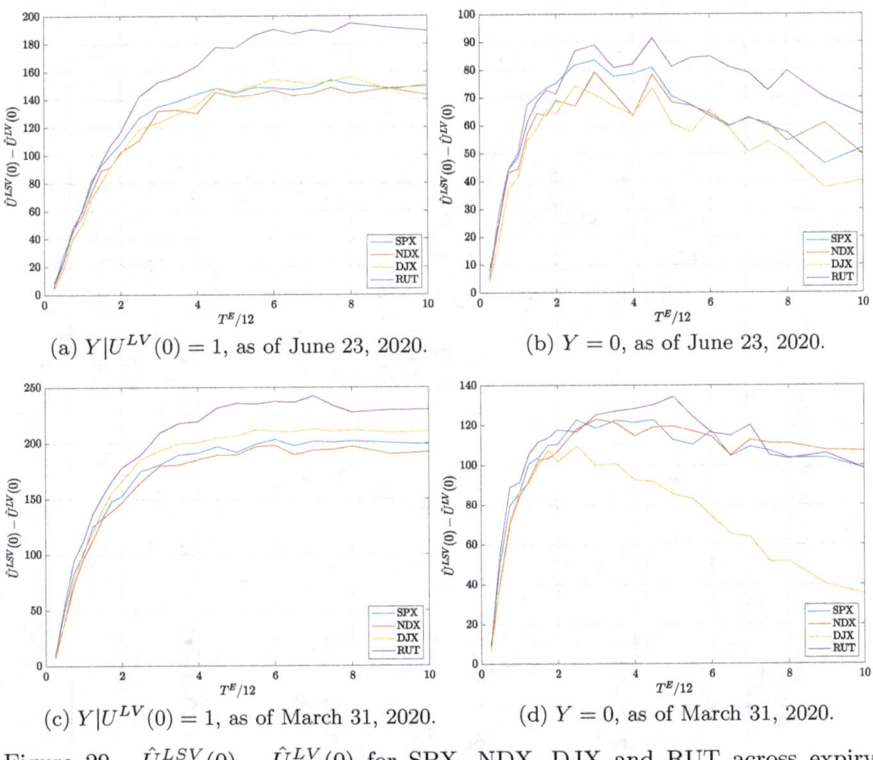

(a) $Y|U^{LV}(0) = 1$, as of June 23, 2020.

(b) $Y = 0$, as of June 23, 2020.

(c) $Y|U^{LV}(0) = 1$, as of March 31, 2020.

(d) $Y = 0$, as of March 31, 2020.

Figure 29. $\hat{U}^{LSV}(0) - \hat{U}^{LV}(0)$ for SPX, NDX, DJX and RUT across expiry tenors T^E, in medium-low and medium-high volatility regimes and for different coupon amounts Y.

Table 8. eSSVI and Heston parameters calibrated to options data in different volatility regimes for SPX, NDX, DJX and RUT.

		eSSVI					Heston				
		η	λ	ρ_m	ρ_0	a	κ	θ	η	ρ	V_0
2017-11-03	SPX	0.7303	0.5981	−0.7126	−0.3635	676.32	2.8555	0.0401	1.0806	−0.7473	0.0046
	NDX	0.6122	0.5816	−0.6759	−0.1902	513.85	4.4025	0.0428	1.0791	−0.6989	0.0135
	DJX	0.6499	0.6135	−0.6243	−0.0435	589.12	3.9711	0.0325	1.0894	−0.6900	0.0052
	RUT	0.6504	0.5918	−0.6141	−0.2397	364.16	4.3905	0.0464	1.2418	−0.6534	0.0173
2020-06-23	SPX	0.9664	0.4963	−0.7633	−0.2269	340.68	2.0230	0.0964	1.3275	−0.8176	0.1052
	NDX	0.9439	0.4900	−0.6838	−0.2543	306.51	1.7808	0.1040	1.2268	−0.7328	0.1126
	DJX	0.7798	0.5500	−0.7816	−0.3627	83.62	1.7819	0.0860	1.1351	−0.8111	0.1284
	RUT	1.1080	0.4078	−0.7628	−0.3608	120.76	1.7505	0.1032	1.3331	−0.7843	0.1911
2020-03-31	SPX	0.7710	0.5231	−0.8321	−0.4816	137.92	4.6048	0.0805	2.2566	−0.8245	0.3137
	NDX	0.7687	0.5227	−0.7706	−0.2908	212.56	4.2299	0.0766	2.0220	−0.7809	0.2971
	DJX	1.1234	0.4049	−0.6938	−0.5099	4854.88	3.8431	0.0882	2.1734	−0.7513	0.4058
	RUT	1.1092	0.4148	−0.7463	−0.4252	125.98	4.6056	0.1118	2.8350	−0.7620	0.4234
2020-03-17	SPX	1.1246	0.3460	−0.9227	−0.6585	120.92	6.0662	0.0940	3.4464	−0.8911	0.8440
	NDX	0.6885	0.4514	−0.9641	−0.9273	3841.28	6.4882	0.0780	2.4367	−0.8998	0.7813
	DJX	1.2104	0.2882	−0.8558	−0.8092	1449.55	5.8442	0.0938	3.7716	−0.8190	1.0221
	RUT	0.9665	0.3153	−0.9951	−0.9929	1449.54	5.5594	0.1057	2.6639	−0.9176	0.7730

regimes are presented here. An interested reader can compare the results to Figure 16.

Table 8 exhibits the eSSVI and Heston parameters calibrated to options data as of the four scenario dates from Section 4.5. Observe that, in stressed markets, the calibration of the Heston model tends to produce large values of η, κ, V_0 and θ as well as low spot-variance correlations ρ. Even though, as shown in Appendix B.2, high θ and κ tend to reduce Δ^{LSV}, the effect of high η and low ρ appears to be prevailing. Indeed, Δ^{LSV} increases with the volatility level of the underlying, as shown in Figures 16 and 29.

Acknowledgments

In memory of Peter Carr.

References

[1] Y. Aït-Sahalia and A. W. Lo. Nonparametric estimation of state-price densities implicit in financial asset prices. *The Journal of Finance*, 53(2):499–547, 1998.

[2] T. Alm, B. Harrach, D. Harrach, and M. Keller. A Monte Carlo pricing algorithm for autocallables that allows for stable differentiation. *Journal of Computational Finance*, 17(1):43–70, 2013.

[3] L. Andersen. Simple and efficient simulation of the Heston stochastic volatility model. *Journal of Computational Finance*, 11(3):1–42, 2008.

[4] H. Bartholomew. SocGen mulls sale of structured product books after big losses. Risk.net. Retrieved from https://www.risk.net/derivatives/7663541/socgen-mulls-sale-of-structured-product-books-after-big-losses, 2020.

[5] H. Bartholomew, N. Somasundaram, and L. Becker. Natixis's 260m hit blamed on big books and Kospi3 product. Risk.net. Retrieved from https://www.risk.net/derivatives/6229806/natixiss-eu260m-hit-linked-to-rapid-asia-expansion-and-kospi3-leverage, 2018.

[6] L. Bergomi. *Stochastic Volatility Modeling*, 1st Edition. CRC Press, Boca Raton, FL, 2016.

[7] F. Black and M. Scholes. *The Pricing of Options and Corporate Liabilities. The Journal of Political Economy*, 81(3):637–654, 1973.

[8] M. Bouzoubaa and A. Osseiran. *Exotic Options and Hybrids: A Guide to Structuring, Pricing and Trading*, 1st Edition. John Wiley & Sons, Hoboken, NJ, 2010.
[9] I. J. Clark. *Foreign Exchange Option Pricing: A Practitioner's Guide*, 1st Edition. John Wiley & Sons, Chichester, 2011.
[10] A. Cozma, M. Mariapragassam, and C. Reisinger. Convergence of an Euler scheme for a hybrid stochastic-local volatility model with stochastic rates in foreign exchange markets. *SIAM Journal on Financial Mathematics*, 9(1):127–170, 2018.
[11] A. De Col and P. Kuppinger. The interplay between stochastic volatility and correlations in equity autocallables. Available at SSRN, 2017.
[12] G. Deng, J. Mallett, and C. McCann. Modeling autocallable structured products. *Journal of Derivatives and Hedge Funds*, 17(4):326–340, 2016.
[13] E. Derman and I. Kani. Riding on a smile. *Risk*, 7:32–39, 1994.
[14] B. Dumas, J. Fleming, and R. E. Whaley. Implied volatility functions: Empirical tests. *The Journal of Finance*, 53(6):2059–2106, 1998.
[15] B. Dupire. Pricing with a smile. *Risk*, 7(1):18–20, 1994.
[16] M. R. Fengler. Arbitrage-free smoothing of the implied volatility surface. *Quantitative Finance*, 9(4):417–428, 2009.
[17] M. R. Fengler. Option data and modeling BSM implied volatility. In J.-C. Duan, W. K. Härdle, and James E. Gentle, editors, *Handbook of Computational Finance*, 1st Edition. Springer, Berlin, pp. 117–142, 2012.
[18] C. P. Fries and M.S. Joshi. Perturbation stable conditional analytic Monte-Carlo pricing scheme for autocallable products. *International Journal of Theoretical and Applied Finance*, 14(2):197–219, 2011.
[19] J. Gatheral. *The Volatility Surface: A Practitioner's Guide*, 1st Edition, John Wiley & Sons, Hoboken, 2006.
[20] J. Gatheral and A. Jacquier. Convergence of Heston to SVI. *Quantitative Finance*, 11(8):1129–1132, 2011.
[21] J. Gatheral and A. Jacquier. Arbitrage-free SVI volatility surfaces. *Quantitative Finance*, 14(1):59–71, 2014.
[22] P. Glasserman. *Monte Carlo Methods in Financial Engineering*. Springer, New York, 2004.
[23] T. Guillaume. Autocallable structured products. *The Journal of Derivatives*, 22(3):73–94, 2015.
[24] J. Guyon and P. Henry-Labordère. Being particular about calibration. *Risk*, 25(1):88–93, 2012.

[25] I. Gyöngy. Mimicking the one-dimensional marginal distributions of processes having an Ito differential. *Probability Theory and Related Fields*, 71(4):501–516, 1986.

[26] P. Hagan, D. Kumar, A. Lesniewski, and D. Woodward. Managing smile risk. *The Best of Wilmott*, 1:249–296, 2002.

[27] S. Hendricks. Extending the SSVI model with arbitrage-free conditions. Master's thesis, Delft University of Technology, 2016.

[28] S. Hendriks and C. Martini. The extended SSVI volatility surface. *Journal of Computational Finance*, 22(5):25–39, 2019.

[29] P. Henry-Labordère. Calibration of local stochastic volatility models to market smiles: A Monte-Carlo approach. *Risk Magazine*, September:112–117, 2009.

[30] S. L. Heston. A closed-form solution for options with stochastic volatility with applications to bond and currency options. *The Review of Financial Studies*, 6(2):327–343, 1993.

[31] C. Homescu. Local Stochastic Volatility Models: Calibration and Pricing. Available at SSRN, 2014.

[32] M. Jex, R. Henderson, and D. Wang. Pricing exotics under the smile. *Risk*, 12:72–75, 1999.

[33] N. Kahalé. An arbitrage-free interpolation of volatilities. *Risk*, 17(5):102–106, 2004.

[34] K. Kyoung-Kuk and L. Dong-Young. A recursive method for static replication of autocallable structured products. *Quantitative Finance*, 19(4):647–661, 2019.

[35] R. W. Lee. The moment formula for implied volatility at extreme strikes. *Mathematical Finance*, 14(3):469–480, 2004.

[36] OptionMetrics. *IvyDB US File and Data Reference Manual.* Retrieved from https://wrds-www.wharton.upenn.edu/documents/1504/IvyDB_US_Reference_Manual_rn2hAXz.pdf, 2021.

[37] V. Piterbarg. Markovian projection method for volatility calibration. Available at SSRN, 2006.

[38] R. Rebonato. *Volatility and Correlation: The Perfect Hedger and the Fox*, 2nd edn. John Wiley & Sons, Hoboken, NJ, 2004.

[39] Y. Ren, D. Madan, and M. Q. Qian. Calibrating and pricing with embedded local volatility models. *Risk*, 20(9):138–143, 2007.

[40] G. Salon. *Equity Autocalls and Vanna negative carries: Pricing and hedging with a simple add-on*. Available at SSRN, 2019.

[41] A. Sepp. Efficient numerical pde methods to solve calibration and pricing problems in local stochastic volatility models. *Global Derivatives Trading & Risk Management*, 2011.

[42] N. Sherif. Calling out autocallable pricing. Risk.net. Retrieved from https://www.risk.net/our-take/6348336/calling-out-autocallable-pricing, 2019.

[43] Y. Tian, Z. Zhu, G. Lee, F. Klebaner, and K. Hamza. Calibrating and pricing with a stochastic-local volatility model. *The Journal of Derivatives*, 22(3):21–39, 2015.

[44] A. W. Van der Stoep, L. A. Grzelak, and C. W. Oosterlee. The Heston stochastic-local volatility model: Efficient Monte Carlo simulation. *International Journal of Theoretical and Applied Finance*, 17(7):1450045, 30 pp, 2014.

[45] A. W. Van der Stoep, L. A. Grzelak, and C. W. Oosterlee. A novel monte carlo approach to hybrid local volatility models. *Quantitative Finance*, 17(9):1347–1366, 2017.

https://doi.org/10.1142/9789811280306_0011

Chapter 11

Not All Oil Storage Shocks Are Alike: The Case of WTI during Times of COVID-19

Helyette Geman* and Yuanye Ma†

Johns Hopkins University, Baltimore, USA

Birkbeck College, London, UK

**hgeman1@jhu.edu*

†*yma35@jhu.edu*

Abstract

In this chapter, we revisit and adjust the famous theory of storage, introduced by Kaldor 1939, to the WTI crude oil during the COVID-19 time in 2020. The theory of storage describes features regularly observed in commodity markets, among which are the relationships between the size of inventory held by producers and consumers of a given commodity and the volatility of spot and future prices on one hand and the shape of the forward curve on the other hand (Working, 1949). We show that storage capacity in Cushing was a much more explanatory factor than production or imports during the period when the pandemic news broke out in the Western world. This property can be explained by the remarkable lack of storage that existed in Cushing, the delivery point of the NYMEX Futures contracts at that time, and brought, for the first time in the history of oil markets, WTI prices to the value of minus 37 dollars.

Keywords: Oil markets, Storage scarcity, WTI price crash, Oil price forecasting

1. Introduction

Many extraordinary things took place in 2020 in the oil world: first, the large supply of US shale oil mentioned above was accompanied by a collapse in demand which occurred on a planet where millions of barrels were hitting the markets, at a time when planes were not flying and cars not driving, and the world consumption of 100 million barrels of oil prevailing at the end of 2019 was reduced by one third, creating in turn very large inventories. Oil refineries in the US were consuming at the beginning of the month of April 2020 half of the oil they were refining the year before. Along the same lines, the reference paper of Kilian [3] argues that the remarkable rise in oil prices between 2003 and 2008 was due to unexpected fluctuations in global real activity during that time period rather than a surprise diminution of oil supplies. They also mention the possible explanation of the peak oil hypothesis, namely the prediction that oil production would peak around 2006. Fifteen years later, peak oil is not discussed anymore and many oil experts estimate that 2019 may have been the year of peak oil demand, with the structural decline being due to the remarkable growth of renewable energy on one hand and natural gas replacing crude oil whenever feasible because it produces fewer emissions.

A key element in our period of analysis in this section was the extreme scarcity of storage capacity in the US during the first quarter of 2020; it had never prevailed before to that extent and led to the unprecedented picture of three dozens of very large crude carriers idle for a number of weeks off the coast of California. This lack of storage created the largely negative price of minus 37 dollars reached on April 20, 2020, by the first nearby WTI contract when long positions were hastily liquidated the day before expiry because of the non-availability of storage in Cushing, Oklahoma — the inconvenient delivery point far away from both coasts of the US and Gulf of Mexico as well. Moreover, several major oil companies owning tanks at the Cushing hub had leased them to smaller companies which in turn had subleased spaces to traders, further reducing availability. According to The Tank Tiger, a terminal storage clearing house in New Jersey and a major actor in brokering transactions, essentially all tanks were leased or subleased by mid-March 2020; this came as a shock to a number of hedge funds that had never really thought before of the crucial aspect of storage in physical delivery, sparking panic at the time of awareness. Interestingly, some of them are fully aware of the challenges of storage when it comes to much more esoteric assets, such as Bitcoins or electricity, but until April 2020, they had not extended the argument to barrels of oil.

The rest of this chapter is organized as follows: Section 1 examines the importance of supply versus storage capacity in explaining the WTI prices during the pre-COVID period and after. Section 2 analyzes the relationship between price volatility and storage capacity during the same periods. Section 3 revisits the results of Working [2] relative to the spread of the forward curves and inventories.

2. Oil Prices, Supply and Storage

The theory of storage, introduced by Kaldor in 1939 [1] and extended by Working in 1949, describes features regularly observed in commodity markets, among which are the relationships between the size of inventories held by commercial consumers of a given commodity and the volatility of spot and future prices on one hand and the shape of the forward curve on the other hand.

In detail, the theory of storage states the following:

- When available inventories of the commodity are high,
  - futures prices tend to be in contango,
  - the volatility of spot and futures prices tends to be low.
- When available inventories of the commodity are low,
  - futures prices tend to be in backwardation,
  - the volatility of spot and futures prices tends to increase.

Contango and backwardation are defined in terms of forward curves where we plot futures written on the same underlying against the maturity of the futures contracts. We call a forward curve in contango if the longer-dated futures are trading at a premium relative to the shorter-dated futures. Conversely, backwardation refers to the situation where the shorter-dated futures are more expensive. Examples of forward curves in contango and backwardation on different days are displayed in Figure 1. Forward curve is a key object in the commodity market, reflecting the market's view on the current expectation of the prices. It implies the benefit (or cost) of owning the

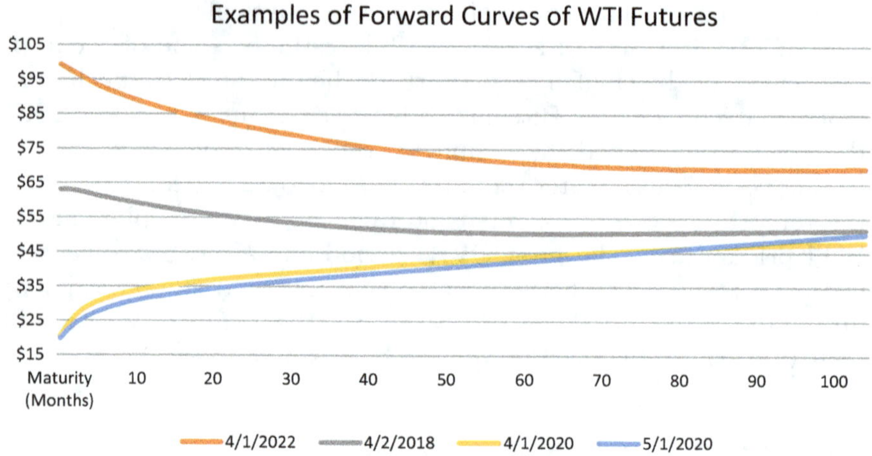

Figure 1. Examples of forward curves of WTI futures on four different days.

physical commodity, which is the so-called convenience yield, through the spot-forward relationship. Let r and g denote the continuously compounded risk-free rate and convenience yield. The spot-forward relationship can be written as

$$F(t,T) = S_t \cdot e^{(r-g)(T-t)},$$

where $F(tT)$ is the futures price observed on day t with maturity T.

Our goal in this chapter is to revisit the theory of storage and show that in the case of WTI crude oil prices during 2020, it was storage capacity which played the crucial role remarkably in agreement with the name of the theory. We propose accordingly to examine the importance of storage and supply in terms of their explanatory power of the price dynamics.

The prices of West Intermediate Texas (WTI) we employ are acquired from Bloomberg and represent the daily closing price of the first nearby future contract (Bloomberg ticker CL1) traded on the New York Mercantile Exchange (NYMEX) over the period 01/01/2018–12/31/2020. The storage and supply data are collected from the weekly release by the Energy Information Administration every Wednesday at 10:30 AM (holiday schedule exemptions apply). The supply data classically include a combination of crude oil production in the United States and crude oil imports into the United States. The storage data represent the (above-ground) inventory of crude oil

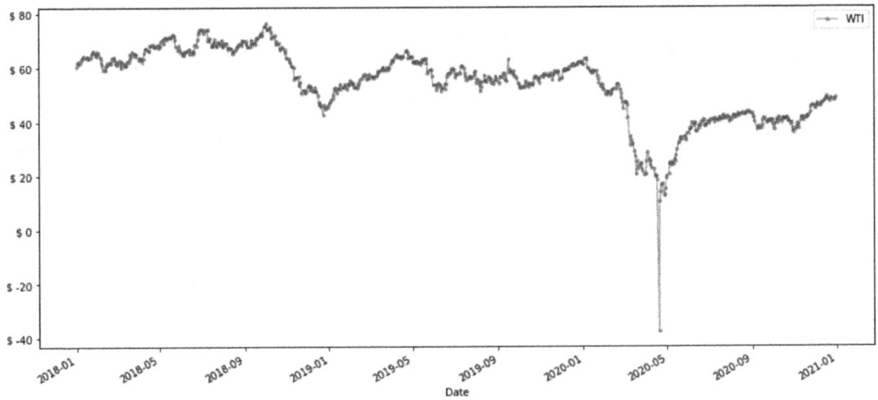

Figure 2. WTI front-month futures prices in 2018–2020.

in the United States excluding the State Petroleum Reserve and the remaining storage capacity is inferred accordingly. The Wednesday EIA weekly release reports the storage and supply data in the preceding week. All datetimes in this paper on the EIA data are moved by one week to reflect the accurate storage or supply level in that week.

We first display a trajectory of oil prices in Figure 2 represented by the first nearby future over the period of analysis, with prices mean reverting between the levels of 50 and 75 dollars during the months of January 2018–February 2020, before declining and collapsing to unprecedented negative values on April 20, 2020.

Note that the frequency of the WTI prices is daily, but only weekly data are available on the storage and supply. We use the weekly averaged prices for WTI instead in the rest of this chapter to match the frequency. Figure 3 displays the weekly averaged WTI prices, and Figure 4 depicts the oil remaining storage capacity specifically at Cushing, Oklahoma, the physical delivery point of WTI. We can observe the gigantic drop to the very low level of 10 million barrels in the week of April 20, 2020, in the same week when the first nearby WTI price went to the negative of 37 dollars. The production and import of crude oil in the US are shown in Figure 5. The production on one hand has been increasing until mid-2020, thanks to the exploitation of shale oil starting in 2014. On the other hand, import has been trending downwards in the same time period.

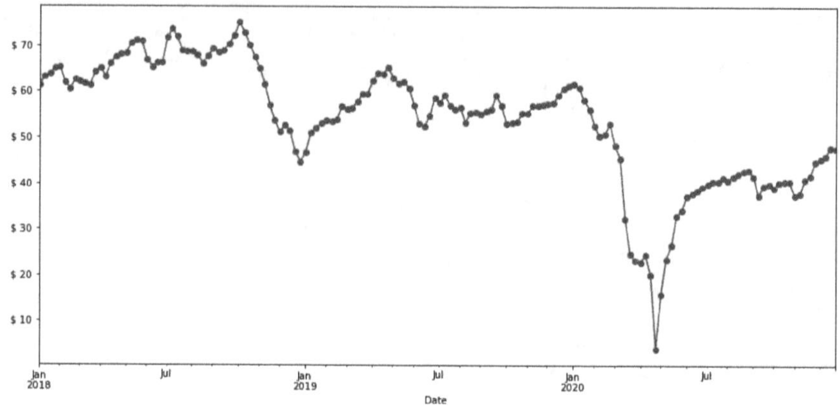

Figure 3. WTI front-month futures weekly averaged prices in 2018–2020.

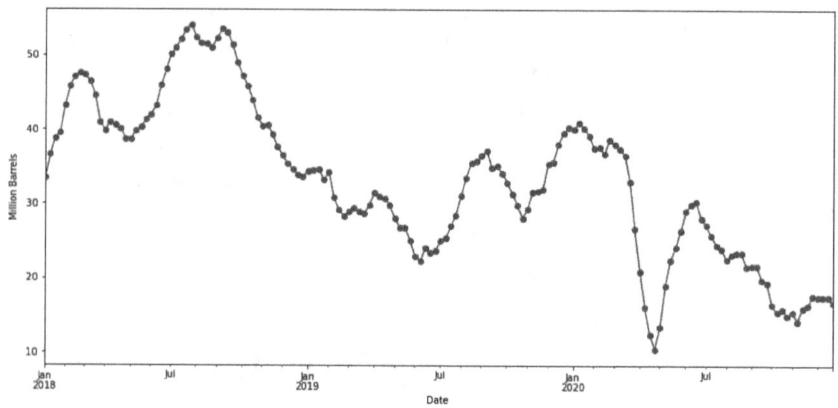

Figure 4. Storage capacity available at Cushing OK in 2018–2020.

After mid-2020, the drop in production and import is of magnitudes smaller than in WTI prices. This is in agreement with the findings of Herwartz and Plodt [4] who observe that 'an oil-specific demand shock triggers a large shift in the price of oil but only a small shift in crude oil production'.

2.1. *Chow Test of Structural Breaks*

Before we discuss the Chow test, ADF test is applied to the original and the first differenced series to check stationarity. *P*-values of the

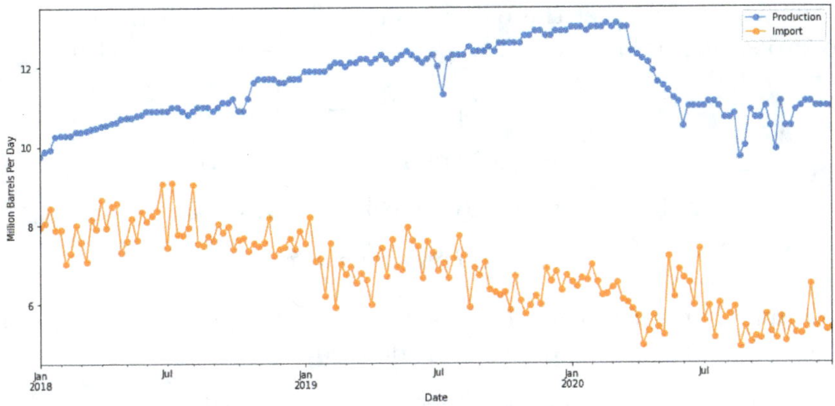

Figure 5. US production and import of crude oil in 2018–2020.

Table 1. *P*-values of ADF tests on the original and first differenced series.

	WTI weekly prices	Cushing storage	US production	US import
Original series	0.201	0.329	0.463	0.776
First differenced series	0.001	0.000	0.000	0.000

ADF test are displayed in Table 1. At 5% significance level, ADF tests reject the null for the four first differenced series, namely WTI weekly prices, Cushing storage, US production and US import, while fail to reject the null for the original series. Therefore, the following analysis in Section 1 will be conducted with the first differenced series.

We test for structural break point in the period of analysis by applying Chow test (Chow, 1960) for the pre-pandemic time (2018–2019) and the COVID-19 time (2020). Chow test is carried out by regressing the WTI weekly prices on the Cushing storage and US production and import (all four being first differenced). Formally, using the notation WTI_t, Sto_t, $Prod_t$ and Imp_t to denote the four, Chow test is performed by modeling WTI_t as a linear regression of Sto_t, $Prod_t$ and Imp_t on the entire time span from $t = 1$ to $t = T$:

$$\Delta WTI_t = \beta_0 + \beta_1 \Delta Sto_t + \beta_2 \Delta Prod_t + \beta_3 \Delta Imp_t \; for \, t = 1, \ldots, T. \tag{1}$$

Then we test whether there is enough evidence to split the time span to two subdomains $t = 1, \ldots, t_{bp}$ and $t = t_{bp} + 1, \ldots, T$, with

$$\Delta WTI_t = \beta_{1,0} + \beta_{1,1}\Delta Sto_t + \beta_{1,2}\Delta Prod_t + \beta_{1,3}\Delta Imp_t \text{ for } t = 1, \ldots, t_{bp}, \quad (2)$$

$$\Delta WTI_t = \beta_{2,0} + \beta_{2,1}\Delta Sto_t + \beta_{2,2}\Delta Prod_t + \beta_{2,3}\Delta Imp_t \text{ for } t = t_{bp} + 1, \ldots, T. \quad (3)$$

The null hypothesis of Chow test is $\beta_{1,0} = \beta_{2,0}$, $\beta_{1,2} = \beta_{2,2}$ and $\beta_{1,3} = \beta_{2,3}$. The test statistic F is defined as

$$F = \frac{(SSR - (SSR_1 + SSR_2))/k}{(SSR_1 + SSR_2)/(N_1 + N_2 - 2k)},$$

where SSR, SSR_1, SSR_2 are the sum of square residuals from regression Equation 1, Equation 2 and Equation 3, respectively, N_1, N_2 are the number of observations in each time fragment, and k is the number of regressors. The test statistic F follows an F-distribution with degrees of freedom k and $N_1 + N_2 - 2k$.

Chow test on whether there is enough evidence to break the entire 2018–2020 period of analysis into pre-pandemic time (2018–2019) and the COVID-19 time (2020), on the first differenced series, returns a test statistic $F = 2.867$ with degrees of free $k = 4$ and $N_1 + N_2 - 2k = 147$, resulting in a P-value of 0.025. At a 5% significant level, the null is rejected, and hence we identify the beginning of 2020 as a structural break point.

2.2. *Correlations Between Storage, Supply and WTI Prices*

We turn to the analysis during the COVID-19 time in 2020. The regression in Equation 4 returns

$$\Delta WTI_t = \underset{(0.820)}{0.1260} + \underset{(0.000)}{0.0010}\Delta Sto_t + \underset{(0.651)}{-0.0007}\Delta Prod_t + \underset{(0.354)}{-0.0008}\Delta Imp_t \quad (4)$$

with coefficients on the top and P-values associated with the coefficients in the bottom parentheses. Variance Inflation Factor (VIF) is checked for each regressor to preclude multicollinearity. Results of

Table 2. Variance inflation factor for each regressor.

	Cushing storage	US production	US import
VIF	1.025	1.073	1.079

VIFs are displayed in Table 2, all of which are less than 1.1, indicating little evidence for multicollinearity. The R^2 of the regression is 24.3%. Cushing storage is the only regressor significant at 5%, with a positive coefficient indicating a positive correlation between the two.

Given the relatively low R^2 observed in the regression, we examine the potential nonlinear correlation between WTI prices and the three factors by conducting the Spearman rank correlation test. For two samples X and Y of size n, the Spearman rank correlation can be calculated as

$$r = 1 - \frac{6 \sum_{i=1}^{n} d_i^2}{n\left(n^2 - 1\right)},$$

where $d_i = rank(X_i)\text{-}rank(Y_i)$ for each point in the samples.

The Spearman rank correlation ranges from -1 to 1 (like the Pearson correlation). But in the case where the Spearman rank correlation is equal to 1, it indicates that the two variables are related by a monotonically increasing function, rather than a linear function as indicated by a perfect Pearson correlation.

The statistic $t = r\sqrt{\frac{n-2}{1-r^2}}$ asymptotically follows a t-distribution with the degree of freedom $n-2$. We test the null hypothesis H0: the Spearman rank correlation between WTI prices and Cushing storage, US production and US import. The Spearman correlations and the P-values associated are shown in Table 3. At 5% significance level, the null is rejected for only the Cushing storage, implying a significant Spearman correlation between the change in WTI prices and the change in Cushing storage in 2020. The Spearman correlation is 0.507, strongly positive, which is in agreement with the intuition that the unprecedented fall of WTI is closed related to the extreme scarcity of storage capacity available at Cushing, Oklahoma. In comparison, the Spearman correlation is computed in the same manner for the pre-pandemic period as well. It is reduced to 0.119 between

Table 3. Results of Spearman rank correlation test between ΔWTI_t and each factor in 2020.

	Cushing storage	US production	US import
Spearman rank correlation	0.507	−0.045	−0.068
P-value	0.000	0.753	0.633

the changes in WTI prices and Cushing storage, with a P-value of 0.229 which is not significant at 5% level.

3. WTI Price Volatility and Storage Capacity

The negative correlation between commodity volatility and inventory, an important piece of the theory of storage, has been studied and tested in a vast body of literature (see for instance, Ref. [5]). In this section, we aim to exhibit the interesting and unusual property that, during the year 2020, it was in fact between storage capacity and WTI price volatility that a negative correlation existed and that the correlation was higher during the time of extreme storage scarcity.

3.1. *Annualized 30-day WTI Volatility vs Cushing Storage*

The WTI volatility is the annualized 30-day volatility of the WTI daily return acquired from Bloomberg (weekly averaged to match frequency as well). The storage data are the same as in Section 1. Figure 6 displays the trajectory of the WTI volatility in the period of analysis and shows that the pattern of the volatility significantly changed in the time of extreme storage scarcity. An immediate observation is that since the volatility is calculated over the past 30 days, there could exist lagged effect between the volatility and the Cushing storage. The Spearman cross-correlations are computed to check for the lagged effect with max lag equal to 4. Table 4 lists the Spearman cross-correlations. Unsurprisingly, the most significant Spearman correlation is observed at lag 1 with P-value less than 0.05, indicating that there exist a 1-week lag between the WTI volatility and the Cushing storage.

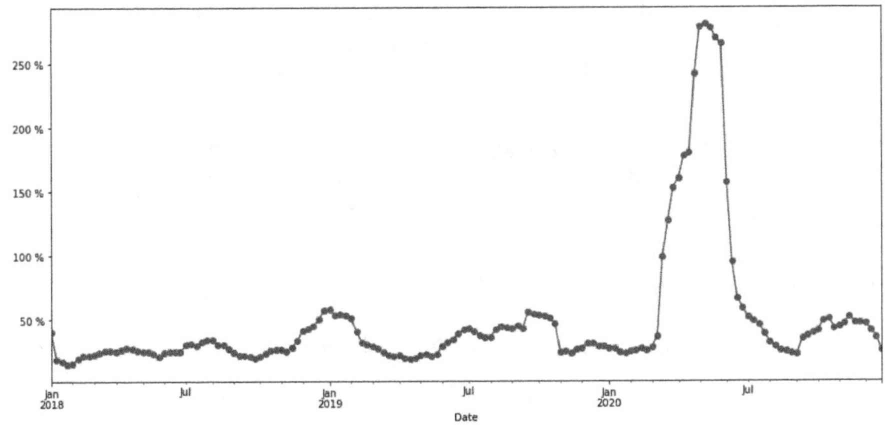

Figure 6. WTI front-month futures weekly averaged 30-day annualized volatility in 2018–2020.

Table 4. Results of Spearman cross correlation test between ΔVol_t and ΔSto_t.

	Lag = 0	Lag = 1	Lag = 2	Lag = 3	Lag = 4
Spearman cross-correlation	−0.108	−0.196	−0.190	−0.157	−0.141
P-value	0.181	0.015	0.019	0.054	0.084

Table 5. P-values of different test statistics for Granger causality test between ΔVol_t and ΔSto_{t-1}.

	F-test of SSR	χ^2 test of SSR	Likelihood ratio test
Test statistic	6.508	6.637	6.498
P-value	0.012	0.010	0.011

Granger causality test, which is established for testing whether the lagged values of one series can provide statistically significant information about future values of the other series, is conducted as well to double-check the lagged effect. Multiple test statistics are available for the Granger causality test, and the three test statistics computed are displayed in Table 5. The null is rejected for each choice from the three at 5% level, confirming that lag 1 is significant.

We move on to verifying the existence of the structural break at the beginning of 2020. A Chow test is established with lag 1 as

Table 6. Results of Lag-1 Spearman correlation test between ΔVol_t and ΔSto_{t-1}.

	2018–2019	2020
Spearman correlation	−0.001	−0.488
P-value	0.995	0.000

follows:

$$\begin{aligned}\Delta Vol_t &= \beta_{1,0} + \beta_{1,1}\Delta Sto_{t-1} + \beta_{1,2}\Delta Prod_{t-1}\\ &\quad + \beta_{1,3}\Delta Imp_{t-1}\ for\, t = 2, \ldots, t_{bp},\\ \Delta Vol_t &= \beta_{2,0} + \beta_{2,1}\Delta Sto_{t-1} + \beta_{2,2}\Delta Prod_{t-1},\\ &\quad + \beta_{2,3}\Delta Imp_{t-1}\ for\, t = t_{bp} + 1, \ldots, T,\end{aligned}$$

where Vol is the weekly 30-day volatility of WTI. The Chow test reports the F statistic of 5.532 with P-value of 0.000, confirming that the beginning of 2020 is a structural break point at 5% significance level.

The lag-1 Spearman correlation between the changes in the weekly 30-day WTI volatility and Cushing storage in 2018–2019 and in 2020 are computed and listed in Table 6. We observe significant negative correlation between Cushing storage capacity and WTI volatility, which is not exhibited in the years before. Interestingly, Geman and Ohana [6]), who analyzed the relation between WTI and price volatility in a period covering the years 2000, also showed that the correlation became much higher when the economic quantity explaining the volatility — in their case above ground inventory, like in the regular theory of storage where storage means the inventory that is stored — became extremely scarce.

4. WTI Forward Spread and Storage

We turn here to the last important piece of the theory of storage, namely the relationship between the spread of the forward curve and Inventory, as introduced in Working [2]. Again, and remarkably, the results are significant when inventory is replaced by remaining storage capacity at Cushing. Classically, to eliminate the potential seasonality in the prices of commodities, the forward spread is defined as

$$13 \text{ month} - \text{Future front month Future.}$$

We here follow the definition even though seasonality does not exist in the modern crude oil market.

Figure 7 plots together the price trajectories of the front-month WTI and the 13-month WTI, respectively. We can observe that before 2020, the forward curve is mostly in backwardation or small contango since the first nearby price is generally higher than the 13-month future price. However, during the pandemic time, the curve was in a heavy contango. This observation goes in line with Working's results, which state that in times of high inventory, the forward curve is in contango as the price of storage is higher than the benefit of owning the physical commodities, leading to a negative net convenience yield.

The WTI forward spread is weekly averaged as well to match the frequency of the Cushing storage. ADF test on the forward spread and the first differenced series yield P-values of 0.388 and 0.000, respectively. Chow test on the changes in the WTI forward spread and Cushing storage, US production and US import yields an F statistic of 5.407 with P-value of 0.000, confirming the beginning of 2020 is a structural break for WTI forward spread.

Figure 7. WTI front-month and 13-th month futures prices in 2018–2020.

Table 7. Results of Spearman correlation test between ΔFS_t and ΔSto_t.

	2018–2019	2020
Spearman correlation	−0.178	−0.522
P-value	0.07	0.000

Moving on to the Spearman correlation between the changes in WTI forward spread and Cushing storage, we list the results in Table 7. At 5% significance level, we discover that the negative correlation between the WTI forward spread and storage is significant only for the COVID-19 time. The strong negative Spearman correlation confirms that our 'adjusted' theory of storage is validated in 2020.

References

[1] N. Kaldor. Speculation and economic stability. *The Review of Economic Studies*, 7:1–27, 1936.

[2] H. Working. The theory of the price of storage. *American Economic Review*, 39:1254–1262, 1949.

[3] L. Kilian. Not all oil price shocks are alike: Disentangling demand and supply shocks in the crude oil market. *American Economic Review*, 99(3):1053–1069, 2009.

[4] H. Herwartz and M. Plodt. The macroeconomic effects of oil price shocks: Evidence from a statistical identification approach. *Journal of International Money and Finance*, 61:30–44, 2016.

[5] H. Geman and V. Nguyen. Soybean inventory and forward curve dynamics. *Management Science*, 51(7):1076–1091, 2005.

[6] H. Geman and S. Ohana. Spread of the forward curve and inventories in the US crude oil and natural gas markets. *Energy Economics*, 31(4):576–585, 2009.

https://doi.org/10.1142/9789811280306_0012

Chapter 12

Total Positivity and Relative Convexity of Option Prices

Paul Glasserman[*,‡] **and Dan Pirjol**[†,§]

[*]*Business School, Columbia University, USA*
[†]*Business School, Stevens Institute of Technology, USA*
[‡]*pg20@columbia.edu*
[§]*dpirjol@stevens.edu*

Abstract
This chapter studies total positivity and relative convexity properties in option pricing models. We introduce these properties in the Black–Scholes setting by showing the following: out-of-the-money calls are totally positive in strike and volatility, out-of-the-money puts have a reverse sign rule property, calls and puts are convex with respect to at-the-money prices and relative convexity of option prices implies a convexity-in-time property of the underlying. We then extend these properties to other models, including scalar diffusions, mixture models and certain Lévy processes. We show that relative convexity typically holds in time-homogeneous local volatility models through the Dupire equation. We develop implications of these ideas for empirical option prices, including constraints on the at-the-money skew. We illustrate connections with models studied by Peter Carr, including the variance-gamma, CGMY, Dagum and logistic density models.

Keywords: Total positivity, Relative convexity, Option prices, Levy processes, Implied volatility skew

1. Introduction: Three Properties of the Black–Scholes Model

We begin our discussion with three apparently little-known properties of the Black–Scholes model, which we formulate in this introduction. The rest of this chapter develops a general framework underlying these properties, extends the properties to other models and examines their empirical implications. We highlight several points of contact with models studied by Peter Carr.

Total positivity: For $k, v > 0$, define the call price function

$$c_{BS}(k,v) = \Phi\left(-\frac{\log k}{v} + \frac{v}{2}\right) - k\Phi\left(-\frac{\log k}{v} - \frac{v}{2}\right) \tag{1}$$

and set

$$c_{BS}(k,0) = (1-k)^+, \quad c_{BS}(0,v) = 1. \tag{2}$$

The usual Black–Scholes call option price for underlying price S_0, strike K, maturity T, discount factor e^{-rT} and volatility σ is then given by $S_0 c_{BS}(e^{-rT}K/S_0, \sigma\sqrt{T})$. We show in Section 3 that the function c_{BS} has the following total positivity property: for any $n = 1, 2, \ldots$, any $1 \le k_1 < \cdots < k_n$ and any $0 < v_1 < \cdots < v_n$,

$$\begin{vmatrix} c_{BS}(k_1, v_1) & \cdots & c_{BS}(k_1, v_n) \\ \vdots & & \vdots \\ c_{BS}(k_n, v_1) & \cdots & c_{BS}(k_n, v_n) \end{vmatrix} \ge 0, \tag{3}$$

where the expression on the left is the determinant of the indicated matrix. The restriction to $k_1 \ge 1$ is necessary; total positivity is a property of out-of-the money options.

Relative convexity: The function $v \mapsto c_{BS}(k,v)$ is neither convex nor concave for $k > 0$; "volga" can be positive or negative. However, call prices have a *relative* convexity property.

Suppose f and g are continuous and strictly increasing functions on an interval $[a,b]$. Then f is *convex with respect to* g if $f \circ g^{-1}$ is convex on $[g(a), g(b)]$. This says that a graph of f becomes convex when plotted against g. In [12], we showed the following: For any $k_1, k_2 > 0$, if $\log^2 k_2 > \log^2 k_1$, then $c_{BS}(k_2, \cdot)$ is convex with respect to $c_{BS}(k_1, \cdot)$ on every interval $[a, b]$, $0 < a < b < \infty$. In particular, every $c_{BS}(k, \cdot)$ is convex with respect to the at-the-money prices $c_{BS}(1, \cdot)$, so the at-the-money case is the "least" convex of the functions $c_{BS}(k, \cdot)$. Note that k_1 and k_2 may be on opposite sides of 1.

Convexity in time: Consider a driftless geometric Brownian motion

$$dS_t = \sigma S_t dW_t, \quad S_0 = 1, \tag{4}$$

with W a standard Brownian motion. The martingale property of S_t implies that for any convex function $\phi : (0, \infty) \to \mathbb{R}$,

$$0 \le t_1 \le t_2 \Rightarrow \mathbb{E}[\phi(S_{t_1})] \le \mathbb{E}[\phi(S_{t_2})], \tag{5}$$

provided the expectations exist. In other words, S_t, $t \ge 0$, is increasing in the convex order. In Section 3.3, we show that, for $0 \le t_1 \le t_2 \le t_3$,

$$\begin{aligned}\Phi(\sigma\sqrt{t_2}/2) - \Phi(\sigma\sqrt{t_1}/2) &\le \Phi(\sigma\sqrt{t_3}/2) - \Phi(\sigma\sqrt{t_2}/2)\\ &\Rightarrow \mathbb{E}[\phi(S_{t_2})] - \mathbb{E}[\phi(S_{t_1})] \le \mathbb{E}[\phi(S_{t_3})] - \mathbb{E}[\phi(S_{t_2})]\end{aligned} \tag{6}$$

for all convex ϕ for which the expectations are well defined and finite. The right side of (6) is a type of convexity in time, in the sense that the time increments of the expectation $\mathbb{E}[\phi(S_t)]$ are increasing. Whereas the monotonicity property (5) holds for all $t_1 \le t_2$, the convexity property in (6) holds only for appropriately spaced t_i; the left side of (6) specifies the appropriate spacing.

We will see that these properties are interrelated. Relative convexity across strikes implies total positivity (3) but only for $n = 2$. Relative convexity is in turn implied by a total positivity condition on a derivative of c_{BS}. The dynamic convexity property (6) is a consequence of relative convexity of option prices.

Section 2 presents background on total positivity and relative convexity, and it develops the basic connections between these properties and option prices. Section 3 proves the three properties discussed in this introduction. Section 4 establishes total positivity properties in other models, including non-negative scalar diffusions with non-negative drift, mixture models, the Dagum and logistic density models (Carr and Torricelli [7]) and certain Lévy processes, including the variance-gamma (Madan and Seneta [26], Madan, Carr, and Chang [24]) and CGMY (Carr *et al.* [4]) models. Section 5 develops a connection between relative convexity of option prices and the Dupire [9] equation. Section 6 derives consequences of total positivity, including a static replication property and constraints on the at-the-money skew.

2. Preliminaries

This section summarizes some background material on total positivity and relative convexity, and it lays out basic implications for option prices. The properties of total positivity we need can be found in Chapter 2 of Karlin [19] and Chapter 18 of Marshall, Olkin, and Arnold [27]. Background on relative convexity is available in Cargo [3] and Chapter 3 of Hardy, Littlewood, and Pólya [13].

2.1. *Total Positivity*

Let $K(\cdot,\cdot)$ be a function on the product of two intervals $I_x \times I_y$. The function K is *totally positive of order* r (TP_r) if, for all $n = 1,\ldots,r$, all $x_1 < \cdots < x_n \in I_x$ and all $y_1 < \cdots < y_n \in I_y$,

$$\det[K(x_i, y_j)]_{i,j=1,\ldots,n} \geq 0. \tag{7}$$

The function K is *totally positive* (TP_∞ or simply TP) if it is TP_r for all $r = 1, 2, \ldots$. (If $K(\cdot, y)$ integrates to one for all values of y, it is sometimes called a *Pólya type* density, but we will not use this terminology.)

In verifying total positivity conditions, we will frequently start from functions that are known to be TP or TP_r and then apply transformations that preserve these properties. We will use the following known properties. In each case, the variables x, y range over intervals, including possibly all of $\mathbb{R}$:

$$(x,y) \mapsto e^{xy} \text{ is TP,} \tag{8}$$

$$(x,y) \mapsto \mathbf{1}\{x > y\} \text{ and } (x,y) \mapsto \mathbf{1}\{x \geq y\} \text{ are TP,} \tag{9}$$

$$(x,y) \mapsto (x-y)^+ \text{ is TP.} \tag{10}$$

These properties also hold with x and y interchanged. Properties (11)–(13) hold for any $r \in \{2, 3, \ldots, \infty\}$.

$$\text{If} \quad K(\cdot,\cdot) \quad \text{is } \mathrm{TP}_r \quad \text{and} \quad a(\cdot), b(\cdot) \geq 0, \quad \text{then}$$
$$(x,y) \mapsto a(x)b(y)K(x,y) \text{ is } \mathrm{TP}_r. \tag{11}$$

If $g(\cdot)$, $h(\cdot)$ are monotone in the same direction, then

$$K(\cdot,\cdot)\ \mathrm{TP}_r \text{ implies } K(g(\cdot), h(\cdot)) \text{ is } \mathrm{TP}_r. \tag{12}$$

If K and L are TP_r, then

$$M(x,y) = \int K(x,z)L(z,y)\, dz \;\text{ is } \mathrm{TP}_r. \tag{13}$$

This property is called the *basic composition formula.* It holds with the integral replaced by a sum or, more generally, an integral with respect to a sigma-finite measure.

For strictly positive K, TP_2 is equivalent to monotonicity of ratios in the sense that

$$\frac{K(x_2,y)}{K(x_1,y)} \text{ is increasing in } y, \text{ for } x_1 < x_2.$$

(Here and throughout we use the term "increasing" in its weak sense, and we use "strictly increasing" where the strong sense is intended.) If K is strictly positive and differentiable in x, then it is TP_2 if and only if

$$\frac{\partial}{\partial x} \log K(x,y) \text{ is increasing in } y. \tag{14}$$

If K is strictly positive and twice differentiable, then it is TP_2 if and only if

$$\frac{\partial^2}{\partial x \partial y} \log K(x,y) \geq 0. \tag{15}$$

It is thus easy to see that TP_2 is preserved under multiplication but not ordinarily under addition.

If $x_1 < x_2$ and $y_1 < y_2$ imply

$$\det\begin{pmatrix} K(x_1, y_1) & K(x_1, y_2) \\ K(x_2, y_1) & K(x_2, y_2) \end{pmatrix} \leq 0,$$

then K is called RR_2, for *reverse rule of order 2*. More generally,

$$K \text{ is } \mathrm{RR}_r \text{ if (7) holds for all } n = 1, \ldots, r, \text{ all}$$
$$x_1 > \cdots > x_n \text{ and all } y_1 < \cdots < y_n. \tag{16}$$

Note that the x_i and y_j are monotone in opposite directions in this definition. Interchanging adjacent rows or columns of a matrix changes the sign of the determinant, so we could equivalently take the x_i to be in increasing order and the y_j in decreasing order.

Properties (11) and (12) hold with TP_r replaced by RR_r. In the basic composition formula (13), if K is RR_r and L is TP_r, then M is RR_r. These properties follow from the corresponding properties in the TP_r case by reversing the order of one argument.

We will see that whereas out-of-the money calls are often TP_r, out-of-the-money puts are often RR_r.

Other applications of total positivity properties have appeared in the mathematical finance literature. Kijima [17] used the TP_2 property of certain transition densities $g(t, x, y)$ in the spatial variables (x, y) to prove convexity of option prices in the spot asset price variable. In contrast, we use TP and RR properties in the variables (t, y). Zipkin [32] applied total positivity to derive properties of bond prices in stochastic interest rates models. Keller-Ressel [16] used total positivity to classify the possible yield curve shapes in the two-factor Vasicek model.

2.2. *Relative Convexity*

As in Section 1, if f and g are continuous, strictly increasing functions on $[a, b]$, then f is convex with respect to g (which we abbreviate "f cxw g") if $f \circ g^{-1}$ is convex. If f'/g' is defined throughout (a, b), then Theorem 1 of Cargo [3] gives

$$f \text{ cxw } g \iff f'/g' \text{ is increasing on } (a, b). \tag{17}$$

If f''/f' and g''/g' are defined throughout (a, b), then Theorem 2 of Cargo [3] gives

$$f \text{ cxw } g \iff g''/g' \leq f''/f' \text{ throughout } (a, b). \tag{18}$$

Theorem 3 of Cargo [3] gives

$$f \text{ cxw } g \iff \begin{vmatrix} 1 & g(t_1) & f(t_1) \\ 1 & g(t_2) & f(t_2) \\ 1 & g(t_3) & f(t_3) \end{vmatrix} \geq 0, \quad \text{for all } a \leq t_1 < t_2 < t_3 \leq b. \tag{19}$$

Taking $g(t) = t$ in (19) and expanding the determinant yield the definition of ordinary convexity of f.

2.3. *Interconnections*

To summarize implications of these properties for option prices, we consider an underlying asset $S_T \geq 0$, $S_0 \equiv 1$, with $\mathbb{E}[S_T] = 1$, for all $T > 0$. We assume that S_T has a strictly positive probability density $f(\cdot, T)$ on $(0, \infty)$, for each $T > 0$. Its cumulative distribution function $F(x, T)$ satisfies

$$1 - F(x, T) = \int_x^\infty f(u, T)\, du. \tag{20}$$

Define, for $K \geq 0$ and $T > 0$,

$$C(K, T) = \mathbb{E}[(S_T - K)^+] = \int_0^\infty (x - K)^+ f(x, T) dx, \tag{21}$$

with $C(K, 0) = (1 - K)^+$. To simplify the discussion, we will suppose that $C(K, T)$ is differentiable in T, with

$$\partial_T C(K, T) > 0, \quad \forall K, T > 0, \tag{22}$$

which holds in great generality.

Figure 1 summarizes some implications among properties of f, F and C. The implications from TP properties to TP_2 properties hold automatically; we include them because it is sometimes easier (or no harder) to work with the first column of implications than the second. The implications from f to F are standard; we include them for completeness. The properties in the figure are stated for $x, K \geq 1$.

Proposition 2.1. *The implications in Figure* 1 *hold with* $x, K \geq 1$, $T > 0$.

$$
\begin{array}{ccccl}
f(x,T)\ \mathrm{TP} & \Longrightarrow & f(x,T)\ \mathrm{TP}_2 & & \\
\Downarrow^{a} & & \Downarrow & & \\
1-F(x,T)\ \mathrm{TP} & \Longrightarrow & 1-F(x,T)\ \mathrm{TP}_2 & \Longleftrightarrow^{b'} & -C(\cdot,T_2)\ \mathrm{cxw}\ -C(\cdot,T_1), \forall 0<T_1<T_2 \\
\Downarrow & & \Downarrow & & \\
C(K,T)\ \mathrm{TP} & \Longrightarrow & C(K,T)\ \mathrm{TP}_2 & & \\
\Uparrow & & \Uparrow^{c} & & \\
\partial_T C(K,T)\ \mathrm{TP} & \Longrightarrow & \partial_T C(K,T)\ \mathrm{TP}_2 & \Longleftrightarrow^{b} & C(K_2,\cdot)\ \mathrm{cxw}\ C(K_1,\cdot), \forall 1\le K_1<K_2 \\
 & & & & \Uparrow^{d} \\
 & & & & f(x,T)\ \mathrm{TP}_3 \text{ and put-call symmetry holds}
\end{array}
$$

Figure 1. Implications among total positivity and relative convexity properties for out-of-the-money calls. The properties in the figure are stated for $x \geq 1$ and $K \geq 1$. An alternative to the implication (d) is discussed in Remark 2.2.

Proof. We prove the labeled implications in the figure; the others work the same way. We postpone the proof of implication (d) to Proposition 3.6.

(a) For $x \geq 1$, apply (9) and the basic composition formula (13) to conclude that

$$1 - F(x,T) = \int_1^\infty \mathbf{1}\{y > x\} f(y,T)\, dy$$

inherits total positivity from f. TP is similarly preserved by

$$C(K,T) = \int_1^\infty \mathbf{1}\{x > K\}[1 - F(x,T)]\, dx.$$

(b) From (17) we get that

$$C(K_2,\cdot)\ \mathrm{cxw}\ C(K_1,\cdot) \Longleftrightarrow \frac{\partial_T C(K_2,T)}{\partial_T C(K_1,T)} \text{ increasing in } T.$$

The condition that this holds for all $1 \leq K_1 < K_2$ is equivalent to the condition that $\partial_T C(K,T)$ is TP_2 in $K \geq 1$, $T > 0$.

(b') This implication is the same as (b) but with the roles of T and K interchanged:

$$-C(\cdot,T_2)\ \mathrm{cxw}\ -C(\cdot,T_1) \Longleftrightarrow \frac{-\partial_K C(K,T_2)}{-\partial_K C(K,T_1)} \uparrow K$$

$$\Longleftrightarrow \frac{1 - F(K,T_2)}{1 - F(K,T_1)} \uparrow K,$$

where we have used $\uparrow$ to abbreviate "increasing in." Requiring the last condition for all $K \geq 1$ and all $0 < T_1 \leq T_2$ is equivalent to requiring that $1 - F(K,T)$ be TP_2 for $K \geq 1$, $T > 0$.

(*c*) For $K \geq 1$, we have $C(K,0) = 0$. We can therefore write

$$C(K,T) = \int_0^\infty \mathbf{1}\{t \leq T\} \partial_T C(K,t)\, dt$$

and use the basic composition formula (13). □

Remark 2.2. Alternative to (d): The relation $C(K_2,\cdot)$ cxw $C(K_1,\cdot)$ also follows if $f(x,T)$ is TP_3 for $x \geq 0$, $T > 0$. This claim is similar to Lemma 3 of Molenaar and van Zwet [28], although no explicit proof is given there. By applying (10) and the basic composition formula (13) to (21), we conclude that if $f(x,T)$ is TP_3 for $x \geq 0$, $T > 0$, then $C(K,T)$ is TP_3 for $K \geq 0$, $T > 0$. This means that, for any $0 \leq K_0 < K_1 < K_2$,

$$\begin{vmatrix} C(K_0,T_0) & C(K_1,T_0) & C(K_2,T_0) \\ C(K_0,T_1) & C(K_1,T_1) & C(K_2,T_1) \\ C(K_0,T_2) & C(K_1,T_2) & C(K_2,T_2) \end{vmatrix} \geq 0, \quad \forall 0 \leq T_0 < T_1 < T_2. \tag{23}$$

If we take $K_0 = 0$, the values in the first column of (23) all become 1. The conclusion that $C(K_2,\cdot)$ is convex with respect to $C(K_1,\cdot)$ then follows from (19). However, we will see that the condition that $f(x,T)$ be TP_3 throughout $x \geq 0$, $T > 0$ is rarely satisfied; our examples typically restrict the range of x over which total positivity properties hold.

For out-of-the-money ($K \leq 1$) puts, we have

$$P(K,T) = \mathbb{E}[(K - S_T)^+] = \int_0^1 (K - x)^+ f(x,T) dx \tag{24}$$

$$= \int_0^1 \mathbf{1}\{x \leq K\} F(x,T) dx, \tag{25}$$

and, for $x \in [0,1]$,

$$F(x,T) = \int_0^1 \mathbf{1}\{u \leq x\} f(u,T) du. \tag{26}$$

$$
\begin{array}{ccccl}
f(x,T)\ \mathrm{RR} & \Longrightarrow & f(x,T)\ \mathrm{RR}_2 & & \\
\Downarrow^{a} & & \Downarrow & & \\
F(x,T)\ \mathrm{RR} & \Longrightarrow & F(x,T)\ \mathrm{RR}_2 & \Longleftrightarrow^{b'} & P(\cdot,T_1)\ \mathrm{cxw}\ P(\cdot,T_2), \forall 0<T_1<T_2 \\
\Downarrow & & \Downarrow & & \\
P(K,T)\ \mathrm{RR} & \Longrightarrow & P(K,T)\ \mathrm{RR}_2 & & \\
\Uparrow & & \Uparrow^{c} & & \\
\partial_T P(K,T)\ \mathrm{RR} & \Longrightarrow & \partial_T P(K,T)\ \mathrm{RR}_2 & \Longleftrightarrow^{b} & P(K_1,\cdot)\ \mathrm{cxw}\ P(K_2,\cdot), \forall K_1<K_2\le 1 \\
 & & & & \Uparrow^{d} \\
 & & & & f(x,T)\ \mathrm{TP}_3 \text{ and put-call symmetry holds}
\end{array}
$$

Figure 2. Implications among RR and relative convexity properties for out-of-the-money puts. The properties are stated for $x, K \in (0,1]$.

The TP conditions in Figure 1 have been replaced with RR conditions in Figure 2. The TP properties in Figure 1 have no direct relationship with the RR properties in Figure 2 because Figure 2 depends on the distribution of S_T in $(0,1)$, whereas Figure 1 depends on the distribution of S_T in $(1,\infty)$. However, the two sets of conditions are related under a symmetry condition discussed after the following proposition.

Proposition 2.3. *The implications in Figure 2 hold with $x, K \in (0,1]$, $T > 0$.*

Proof. We postpone the proof of implication (d) to Proposition 3.6. Implication (a) and the other downward implications in Figure 2 follow from applying the basic composition formula (13) to (26) and (25). For (b), we again apply (17) to get

$$P(K_1,\cdot)\ \mathrm{cxw}\ P(K_2,\cdot) \Longleftrightarrow \frac{\partial_T P(K_1,T)}{\partial_T P(K_2,T)} \uparrow T,$$

and this is equivalent to the condition that $\partial_T P(K,T)$ is RR_2. Implication (b') works the same way, noting that

$$P(\cdot,T_1)\ \mathrm{cxw}\ P(\cdot,T_2) \Longleftrightarrow \frac{\partial_K P(K,T_1)}{\partial_K P(K,T_2)} \uparrow K \Longleftrightarrow \frac{F(K,T_1)}{F(K,T_2)} \uparrow K.$$

The proof of (c) is analogous to that for calls. For $K \le 1$, we have $P(K,0) = 0$. We can therefore write

$$P(K,T) = \int_0^\infty \mathbf{1}\{t \le T\} \partial_T P(K,t)\, dt$$

and use the basic composition formula. □

To see why several TP properties in Figure 1 are accompanied by RR properties in Figure 2, it is helpful to consider settings in which *put-call symmetry* holds, meaning

$$C(K,T) = KP(1/K,T), \quad K,T > 0. \tag{27}$$

As the mapping $K \mapsto 1/K$ reverses the direction of monotonicity in K, it follows from (27) that $C(K,T)$ is TP_r on $(1,\infty)\times(0,\infty)$ if and only if $P(K,T)$ is RR_r on $(0,1)\times(0,\infty)$.

Related properties hold for distributions and densities. With the normalization $\mathbb{E}[S_T] = 1$ and the condition $\mathbb{P}(S_T > 0) = 1$ introduced earlier, we may define

$$\tilde{F}(x,T) = \mathbb{E}\left[S_T \mathbf{1}\{1/S_T \leq x\}\right]. \tag{28}$$

Then $\tilde{F}(\cdot,T)$ is the cumulative distribution of $1/S_T$ under the "share measure" defined by S_T. Theorem 2.2(b) of Carr and Lee [5] shows that put-call symmetry holds at T if and only if $\tilde{F}(\cdot,T) = F(\cdot,T)$. If $\tilde{F}(\cdot,T)$ and $F(\cdot,T)$ have densities $\tilde{f}(\cdot,T)$ and $f(\cdot,T)$, respectively, then we can write (28) as

$$\int_0^x \tilde{f}(y,T)dy = \int_{1/x}^{\infty} yf(y,T)dy.$$

Differentiating both sides with respect to x yields

$$\tilde{f}(x,T) = \frac{1}{x^3} f(1/x,T). \tag{29}$$

If put-call symmetry holds, then $\tilde{f} = f$, and reversing the steps leading to (29) proves the converse. If $\tilde{f} = f$, then any TP/RR property of either density is shared by the other, leading to the following result:

Proposition 2.4. *If put-call symmetry holds, then*

(i) *$f(x,T)$ is TP_r on $(1,\infty)\times(0,\infty)$ if and only if $f(x,T)$ is RR_r on $(0,1)\times(0,\infty)$,*
(ii) *$C(K,T)$ is TP_r on $(1,\infty)\times(0,\infty)$ if and only if $P(K,T)$ is RR_r on $(0,1)\times(0,\infty)$.*

Proof. Because the mapping $x \mapsto 1/x$ reverses the direction of monotonicity, (29) implies that $f(x,T)$ is TP_r on $(1,\infty)\times(0,\infty)$ if and only if $\tilde{f}(x,T)$ is RR_r on $(0,1)\times(0,\infty)$. If put-call symmetry holds, then $\tilde{f} = f$, and claim (i) follows. Claim (ii) follows similarly, as noted just after (27). □

3. The Black–Scholes Setting: Three Properties Revisited

3.1. *Total Positivity*

The Black–Scholes function c_{BS} in (1)–(2) is a special case of the call price in (21) in which the underlying has a lognormal distribution. For $v > 0$, define the lognormal random variable

$$X_v = e^{vZ - v^2/2}, \quad Z \sim N(0,1). \tag{30}$$

Then

$$c_{BS}(K,v) = \mathbb{E}[(X_v - K)^+] = \int_0^\infty (x-K)^+ f_{LN}(x,v)\,dx \tag{31}$$

$$= \int_{-\infty}^\infty (e^x - K)^+ \frac{1}{v}\varphi\left(\frac{x}{v} + \frac{v}{2}\right) dx \tag{32}$$

where f_{LN} is the density of X_v, and φ is the standard normal density.

Lemma 3.1. *The function*

$$(x,v) \mapsto \frac{1}{v}\varphi\left(\frac{x}{v} + \frac{v}{2}\right) \tag{33}$$

is TP in (x,v), for $x \geq 0$ and $v > 0$, and it is RR for $x \leq 0$ and $v > 0$.

Proof. Recall from (8) that the function $(x,y) \mapsto e^{xy}$ is TP. Now apply (12) with $h(x) = x^2, g(v) = -1/(2v^2)$, noting that h is increasing on $[0,\infty)$ but decreasing on $(-\infty,0]$. Thus,

$$(x,v) \mapsto e^{-\frac{x^2}{2v^2}} \tag{34}$$

is TP on $[0,\infty)\times(0,\infty)$ and RR on $(-\infty,0]\times(0,\infty)$. The function (33) can be written as the product of (34) and non-negative functions of x and v,

$$\frac{1}{v}\varphi\left(\frac{x}{v}+\frac{v}{2}\right)=\frac{e^{-\frac{1}{8}v^2}}{\sqrt{2\pi}v}\cdot e^{-\frac{x^2}{2v^2}}\cdot e^{-\frac{1}{2}x}. \tag{35}$$

By (11), (35) thus inherits the TP and RR properties of (34). □

Lemma 3.2. *The lognormal density of μX_v, $\mu, v>0$,*

$$f_{LN}(x,v;\mu)=\frac{1}{\sqrt{2\pi}vx}e^{-\frac{1}{2v^2}(\log(x/\mu)+\frac{1}{2}v^2)^2},\quad x>0,$$

is TP for $x\geq\mu$, $v>0$, and RR for $x\in(0,\mu]$, $v>0$.

Proof. The lognormal density can be expressed as

$$f_{LN}(x,v;\mu)=\frac{1}{x}\cdot\frac{1}{v}\varphi\left(\frac{\log(x/\mu)}{v}+\frac{v}{2}\right).$$

The function $x\mapsto\log(x/\mu)$ is increasing, and the function $x\mapsto 1/x$ is non-negative. It therefore follows from (11) and (12) that the density inherits the claimed TP and RR properties from (33). □

We omit the parameter μ from f_{LN} when $\mu=1$ and write

$$f_{LN}(x,v)=\frac{1}{\sqrt{2\pi}vx}e^{-\frac{1}{2v^2}(\log x+\frac{1}{2}v^2)^2}. \tag{36}$$

The TP_2/RR_2 case of Lemma 3.2 is illustrated in Figure 3. The figure plots the ratio $f_{LN}(x,\sigma_1)/f_{LN}(x,\sigma_2)$, with $\sigma_1<\sigma_2$; we put the smaller value of σ_i in the numerator to avoid dividing by numbers close to zero. The ratio is increasing for $x\in(0,1]$ and decreasing for $x\geq 1$. The ratio $f_{LN}(x,\sigma_1)/f_{LN}(x,\sigma_2)$ measures the likelihood of drawing the value x from the smaller-volatility distribution, relative to the likelihood of drawing it from the higher-volatility distribution. This likelihood ratio decreases as x moves away from 1 in either direction.

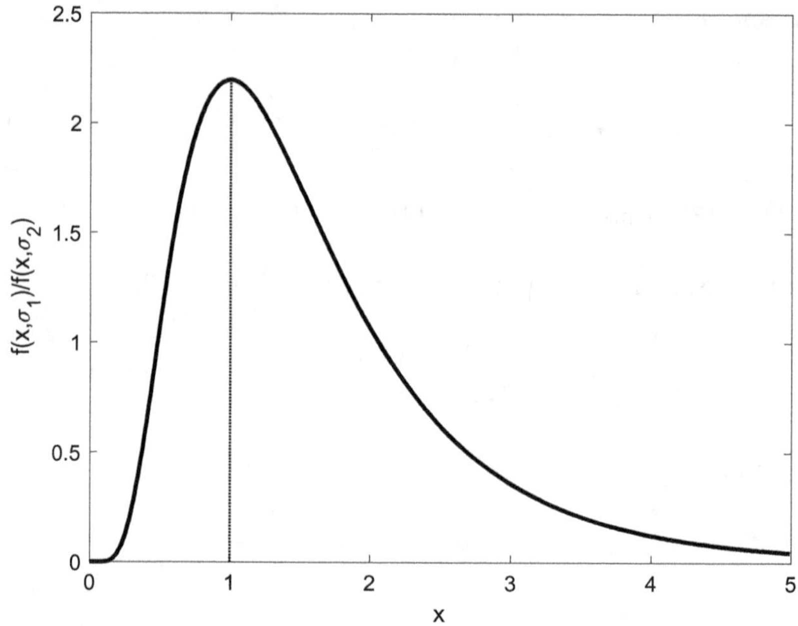

Figure 3. The ratio $f(x, \sigma_1)/f(x, \sigma_2)$, $\sigma_1 = 0.5 < \sigma_2 = 1$, is increasing for $x \in (0, 1]$ and decreasing for $x \geq 1$.

We can now prove the TP property in (3) for calls and the corresponding property for puts with

$$p_{BS}(K, v) = \mathbb{E}[(K - X_v)^+] = \int_0^\infty (K - x)^+ f_{LN}(x, v)dx$$
$$= \int_{-\infty}^\infty (K - e^x)^+ \frac{1}{v}\varphi\left(\frac{x}{v} + \frac{v}{2}\right) dx. \tag{37}$$

Theorem 3.3. *The Black–Scholes call function $c_{BS}(K, v)$ is TP on $[1, \infty) \times (0, \infty)$, and the put function $p_{BS}(K, v)$ is RR on $[0, 1] \times (0, \infty)$.*

Proof. For $K \geq 1$, the lower limit of integration in (31) can be set at 1. The claim for calls thus follows from applying Lemma 3.2 to Proposition 2.1. Similarly, for $K \in [0, 1]$, we may take the upper limit in the first integral of (37) to be 1 and apply Lemma 3.2 to Proposition 2.3. □

The functions $(e^x - K)^+$ and $(K - e^x)^+$ inherit total positivity from $(x - K)^+$ and $(K - x)^+$, so Theorem 3.3 can also be proved using the second integral in (32) and (37) and the properties of the density of the log-underlying in Lemma 3.1.

Theorem 3.3 is formulated in terms of the normalized functions c_{BS} and p_{BS}. We can make the dependence on other parameters explicit by writing (for $S_0, r, \sigma > 0$ and $K, T \geq 0$)

$$\begin{aligned} C_{BS}(S_0, K, r, \sigma, T) &= e^{-rT}\mathbb{E}[(S_0 e^{rT} X_{\sigma\sqrt{T}} - K)^+] \\ &= S_0 c_{BS}(e^{-rT}K/S_0, \sigma\sqrt{T}). \end{aligned} \tag{38}$$

We now see that, holding S_0, r and T fixed,

$$(K, \sigma) \mapsto C_{BS}(S_0, K, r, \sigma, T) \text{ is TP for } K \geq S_0 e^{rT},\ \sigma > 0.$$

Holding S_0, r and σ fixed,

$$(K, T) \mapsto C_{BS}(S_0, Ke^{rT}, r, \sigma, T) \text{ is TP for } K \geq S_0 e^{rT},\ T > 0. \tag{39}$$

This follows from (38). The first argument of c_{BS}, $e^{-rT}K/S_0$, is the strike expressed as forward moneyness. If we fix σ and vary T, the TP property holds with respect to forward moneyness rather than strike. If we fix T and vary σ, the TP property holds whether we vary the strike or the forward moneyness.

The properties in Theorem 3.3 extend to the option deltas

$$\Delta_{BS,c}(K, v) = \mathbb{E}[X_v \mathbf{1}\{X_v > K\}] = \Phi\left(-\frac{\log K}{v} + \frac{v}{2}\right) \tag{40}$$

and

$$\Delta_{BS,p}(K, v) = -\mathbb{E}[X_v \mathbf{1}\{X_v \leq K\}] = -\Phi\left(\frac{\log K}{v} - \frac{v}{2}\right). \tag{41}$$

The proof does not rely on the explicit expressions available in the Black–Scholes and follows from the TP/RR properties of the density of the underlying asset. We state the following for the negative put delta because the RR_1 property entails non-negativity.

Corollary 3.4. *The Black–Scholes call delta $\Delta_{BS,c}(K,v)$ is TP on $[1,\infty)\times(0,\infty)$, and the negative put delta $-\Delta_{BS,p}(K,v)$ is RR on $[0,1]\times(0,\infty)$.*

Proof. For $K\geq 1$,

$$\Delta_{BS,c}(K,v)=\int_1^\infty x\mathbf{1}\{x>K\}f_{LN}(x,v)\,dx.$$

The function $(x,K)\mapsto x\mathbf{1}\{x>K\}$ is TP, by (9) and (11), and the density is TP for $x\geq 1$, $v>0$, by Lemma 3.2, so the result follows by the basic composition formula. The put delta works the same way. □

The delta properties in this corollary could be inserted into Figures 1 and 2, in the sense that they hold whenever the density $f(x,T)$ is TP for $x\geq 1$, $T>0$, and RR for $x\in(0,1]$, $T>0$.

3.2. *Relative Convexity*

We now revisit the relative convexity property discussed in the introduction.

Theorem 3.5. *For any $\sigma>0$, the pricing functions $c_{BS}(K,\sigma\sqrt{T})$ and $p_{BS}(K,\sigma\sqrt{T})$ satisfy the cxw properties in Figures 1 and 2, respectively.*

Proof. We proved in Lemma 3.2 that $f_{LN}(x,v)$ is TP for $x\geq 1$, $v>0$, and it is RR for $x\in(0,1]$, $v>0$. Tracing the implications in Figures 1 and 2, we conclude that, for $0<v_1<v_2$, $-c_{BS}(\cdot,v_2)$ is cxw $-c_{BS}(\cdot,v_1)$ on $[1,\infty)$, and $p_{BS}(\cdot,v_1)$ is cxw $p_{BS}(\cdot,v_2)$ on $[0,1]$. By property (12), these properties are preserved if we replace the argument v with $\sigma\sqrt{T}$.

We established relative convexity and $c_{BS}(K_2,\cdot)$ and $c_{BS}(K_1,\cdot)$ in [12]. Direct calculation shows that

$$\frac{\partial_v c_{BS}(K_2,v)}{\partial_v c_{BS}(K_1,v)}=\sqrt{\frac{K_2}{K_1}}e^{-\frac{1}{2v^2}\left(\log^2 K_2-\log^2 K_1\right)}. \tag{42}$$

If $\log^2 K_2>\log^2 K_1$, this ratio is increasing in v, making $c_{BS}(K_2,\cdot)$ cxw $c_{BS}(K_1,\cdot)$, in light of the condition in (17). This relative convexity property then holds for $T\mapsto c_{BS}(K,\sigma\sqrt{T})$. As $\partial_v p_{BS}(K,v)=\partial_v c_{BS}(K,v)$, the same argument works for puts. □

Equation (42) implies $c_{BS}(K_2, \cdot)$ cxw $c_{BS}(K_1, \cdot)$ whenever $\log^2 K_2 > \log^2 K_1$. Unlike the TP properties we have discussed, this condition allows K_1 and K_2 to be on opposite sides of 1. This relative convexity property can be thought of as the combination of two more basic properties. First, we have $c_{BS}(K_2, \cdot)$ cxw $c_{BS}(K_1, \cdot)$ for $1 \le K_1 < K_2$, and then this property extends to strikes on opposite sides of 1 through symmetry. Using put-call symmetry and then put-call parity we get

$$c_{BS}(1/K, v) = p_{BS}(K, v)/K = c_{BS}(K, v)/K + 1/K - 1, \qquad (43)$$

so $\partial_v c_{BS}(1/K, v) = \partial_v c_{BS}(K, v)/K$, and therefore $\partial_v c_{BS}(1/K_2, v)/ \partial_v c_{BS}(K_1, v)$ is increasing in v if and only if $\partial_v c_{BS}(K_2, v)/ \partial_v c_{BS}(K_1, v)$ is increasing in v.

As in the discussion surrounding (38), for discounted option prices, relative convexity holds through forward moneyness. In other words,

$$T \mapsto C_{BS}(S_0, K_2 e^{rT}, r, \sigma, T) \;\text{ cxw }\; T \mapsto C_{BS}(S_0, K_1 e^{rT}, r, \sigma, T),$$

if $\log^2(K_2/S_0) > \log^2(K_1/S_0)$.

In [12], we used relative convexity to compare option prices under mixtures of lognormal densities. If an option price is convex in a parameter, then randomizing that parameter increases the price, by Jensen's inequality. As the Black–Scholes formula is not convex in volatility, the effect of randomizing volatility is ambiguous. The relative convexity property provides a test for which randomizations of volatility increase the price of an option and thus increase its implied volatility. We derive a related test for the "convexity in time" property in Section 3.3.

We conclude this section with a proof of the implication (d) in Figures 1 and 2.

Proposition 3.6. *Suppose S_T has a density $f(x, T)$ that is TP_3 for $x \ge 1$, $T > 0$, and RR_3 for $x \in (0, 1]$, $T > 0$. Suppose the put-call symmetry property (27) holds. Then $C(K_2, \cdot)$ cxw $C(K_1, \cdot)$, for $1 \le K_1 < K_2$, and $P(K_1, \cdot)$ cxw $P(K_2, \cdot)$, for $0 < K_1 < K_2 \le 1$.*

Proof. For any $0 < K_1 < K_2$ and any $0 < x_1 < x_2 < x_3$, we have

$$\begin{vmatrix} 1 & (x_1 - K_1)^+ & (x_1 - K_2)^+ \\ 1 & (x_2 - K_1)^+ & (x_2 - K_2)^+ \\ 1 & (x_3 - K_1)^+ & (x_3 - K_2)^+ \end{vmatrix} \geq 0. \tag{44}$$

This can be verified directly. It also follows from the fact that $(x - K_2)^+$ is an increasing convex function of the increasing function $(x - K_1)^+$. Now suppose $1 < K_1 < K_2$. We integrate the elements of (44) against $f(x_1, T_1)f(x_2, T_2)f(x_3, T_3)$ over $1 < x_1 < x_2 < x_3 < \infty$. Applying the basic composition formula (13) and the TP_3 property of $f(x, T)$, we find that

$$\begin{vmatrix} 1 - F(1, T_1) & C(K_1, T_1) & C(K_2, T_1) \\ 1 - F(1, T_2) & C(K_1, T_2) & C(K_2, T_2) \\ 1 - F(1, T_3) & C(K_1, T_3) & C(K_2, T_3) \end{vmatrix} \geq 0, \quad \forall 0 \leq T_1 < T_2 < T_3. \tag{45}$$

For puts, we start from the fact that for any $1 \leq K_1 < K_2$ and any $0 < y_1 < y_2 < y_3$, we have

$$\begin{vmatrix} 1 & (1/K_1 - y_1)^+ & (1/K_2 - y_1)^+ \\ 1 & (1/K_1 - y_2)^+ & (1/K_2 - y_2)^+ \\ 1 & (1/K_1 - y_3)^+ & (1/K_2 - y_3)^+ \end{vmatrix} \leq 0. \tag{46}$$

Integrating against $f(y_1, T_1)f(y_2, T_2)f(y_3, T_3)$ for $0 < y_1 < y_2 < y_3 < 1$, using the RR_3 property of f and the basic composition formula yields a positive determinant

$$\begin{vmatrix} F(1, T_1) & P(1/K_1, T_1) & P(1/K_2, T_1) \\ F(1, T_2) & P(1/K_1, T_2) & P(1/K_2, T_2) \\ F(1, T_3) & P(1/K_1, T_3) & P(1/K_2, T_3) \end{vmatrix} \geq 0, \quad \forall 0 \leq T_1 < T_2 < T_3 .$$

By the put-call symmetry relation $P(1/K, T) = C(K, T)/K$ and the linearity of the determinant in each column, this gives

$$\begin{vmatrix} F(1, T_1) & C(K_1, T_1) & C(K_2, T_1) \\ F(1, T_2) & C(K_1, T_2) & C(K_2, T_2) \\ F(1, T_3) & C(K_1, T_3) & C(K_2, T_3) \end{vmatrix} \geq 0, \quad \forall 0 \leq T_1 < T_2 < T_3.$$

This matrix and the one in (45) differ only in their first column. If we add their first columns, the determinant of the resulting matrix is the sum of the determinants of the original matrices. Thus,

$$\begin{vmatrix} 1 & C(K_1,T_1) & C(K_2,T_1) \\ 1 & C(K_1,T_2) & C(K_2,T_2) \\ 1 & C(K_1,T_3) & C(K_2,T_3) \end{vmatrix} \geq 0, \quad \forall 0 \leq T_1 < T_2 < T_3.$$

By (19), this proves the claim for call option prices. The corresponding statement for puts follows from put-call symmetry. □

The distinction between TP_3 and TP_2 is difficult to appreciate intuitively, but Karlin [19], p.23, shows that TP_3 densities have a distinctive convexity-preserving property. In a discrete-time Markov chain setting, Karlin [18], p.93, establishes a link between TP_3 and unimodality of certain transition probabilities.

The proof of Proposition 3.6 can be extended to show that $\mathrm{TP}_r/\mathrm{RR}_r$, $r > 3$, conditions on $f(x,t)$ imply higher-order notions of relative convexity for option prices; see the discussion and references in Section 6.1.

3.3. *Convexity in Time*

We now revisit the convexity-in-time property (6). Suppose

$$dS_t = \sigma S_t \, dW_t, \quad S_0 = 1,$$

with W_t a standard Brownian motion.

Theorem 3.7. *If* $0 \leq t_1 \leq t_2 \leq t_3$ *satisfy*

$$\Phi(\sigma\sqrt{t_2}/2) - \Phi(\sigma\sqrt{t_1}/2) \leq \Phi(\sigma\sqrt{t_3}/2) - \Phi(\sigma\sqrt{t_2}/2), \tag{47}$$

then

$$\mathbb{E}[\phi(S_{t_2})] - \mathbb{E}[\phi(S_{t_1})] \leq \mathbb{E}[\phi(S_{t_3})] - \mathbb{E}[\phi(S_{t_2})], \tag{48}$$

for all convex functions ϕ *for which the expectations are well defined and finite.*

Taking ϕ to be an option payoff, (48) becomes a constraint on the forward prices of calendar spreads. This constraint holds simultaneously for all puts and calls at all strikes, if the dates satisfy (47).

Proof. We know from Theorem 3.5 that $c_{BS}(K,\cdot)$ is cxw $c_{BS}(1,\cdot)$, for all $K \geq 0$. We have

$$c_{BS}(1,v) = 2\Phi\left(\frac{v}{2}\right) - 1, \quad v_u \equiv c_{BS}^{-1}(1,u) = 2\Phi^{-1}\left(\frac{u+1}{2}\right).$$

By the definition of relative convexity, $u \mapsto c_{BS}(K, v_u)$ is convex in $u > 0$, for all $K \geq 0$. In other words, $u \mapsto \mathbb{E}[(X_{v_u} - K)^+]$ is convex in $u > 0$ for all $K \geq 0$, with X_{v_u} as in (30).

Let U_1, U_2 be positive random variables, independent of the X_v random variables. Suppose that $U_1 \leq_{cx} U_2$, meaning that they are convexly ordered, and thus meaning that $\mathbb{E}[g(U_1)] \leq \mathbb{E}[g(U_2)]$, for all convex functions g for which the expectations are well defined and finite. Then

$$\begin{aligned}\mathbb{E}[(X_{v_{U_1}} - K)^+] &= \mathbb{E}[\mathbb{E}[(X_{v_{U_1}} - K)^+|U_1]] = \mathbb{E}[c_{BS}(K, v_{U_1})] \\ &\leq \mathbb{E}[c_{BS}(K, v_{U_2})] = \mathbb{E}[\mathbb{E}[(X_{v_{U_2}} - K)^+|U_2]] \\ &= \mathbb{E}[(X_{v_{U_2}} - K)^+],\end{aligned}$$

where the inequality follows from the convexity of $u \mapsto c_{BS}(K, v_u)$. Thus, call payoffs have larger expectations under $X_{v_{U_2}}$ than $X_{v_{U_1}}$. By Theorem 3.A.1(a) of Shaked and Shanthikumar [31], this implies that $X_{v_{U_1}} \leq_{cx} X_{v_{U_2}}$. In other words, we have shown that

$$U_1 \leq_{cx} U_2 \Rightarrow X_{v_{U_1}} \leq_{cx} X_{v_{U_2}}.$$

By Theorem 2.1 of Belzunce and Shaked [2], this implies that $u \mapsto \mathbb{E}[\phi(X_{v_u})]$ is convex for all convex ϕ. Thus, for $u_1 \leq u_2 \leq u_3$,

$$\begin{aligned}u_2 - u_1 \leq u_3 - u_2 \Rightarrow \mathbb{E}[\phi(X_{v_{u_2}})] &- \mathbb{E}[\phi(X_{v_{u_1}})] \\ &\leq \mathbb{E}[\phi(X_{v_{u_3}})] - \mathbb{E}[\phi(X_{v_{u_2}})].\end{aligned} \tag{49}$$

Now suppose (47) holds and set

$$u_i = 2\Phi\left(\frac{\sigma\sqrt{t_i}}{2}\right) - 1, \quad i = 1, 2, 3.$$

Then (47) implies $u_2 - u_1 \leq u_3 - u_2$, so the right side of (49) holds. But

$$v_{u_i} = 2\Phi^{-1}\left(\frac{u_i + 1}{2}\right) = \sigma\sqrt{t_i},$$

so $X_{v_{u_i}}$ has the distribution of S_{t_i}, and the right side (49) coincides with (48). □

The key to this result is the relative convexity of option prices with respect to at-the-money prices. One may ask, more generally, given a martingale S_t, what condition do dates t_i need to satisfy to yield the convexity-in-time property (48)? If options on S_t are cxw at-the-money prices, then if (48) holds for at-the-money calls (as in (47)), it holds for *all* convex payoffs. In other words, if the relative convexity property holds, then at-the-money prices determine the spacing of dates required for convexity in time. A class of models for which such a relative convexity result holds is described in Theorem 5.1.

As discussed, for example, in Hirsch *et al.* [14], an integrable process X_t, $t \geq 0$, is a *peacock* if it is increasing in the convex order, meaning that $t_1 \leq t_2 \Rightarrow \mathbb{E}[\phi(X_{t_1})] \leq \mathbb{E}[\phi(X_{t_2})]$, for all convex functions ϕ for which the expectations exist. Kellerer's theorem (Hirsch *et al.* [14], p.3) states that X_t, $t \geq 0$, is a peacock if and only if there exists a martingale M_t, $t \geq 0$, such that X_t and M_t have the same distribution for every $t \geq 0$. The condition in (48) replaces monotonicity in the convex order with a type of convexity in the convex order. It could be interesting to explore the consequences of combining the two properties.

4. Total Positivity in Other Models

4.1. *Scalar Diffusions*

Suppose $S_t, t \geq 0$, is a martingale diffusion and a non-negative strong Markov process with a transition density $g(t, x, y)$, meaning that, for any $u \geq 0$ and any $0 \leq a < b$,

$$\mathbb{P}(S_{u+t} \in (a, b)|S_u = x) = \int_a^b g(t, x, y)\, dy.$$

Karlin [18] established several total positivity properties of g. With $S_0 = 1$, the marginal density of S_T at time T becomes $f(x, T) = g(T, 1, x)$. Theorem 5.3(i) of Karlin [18] then states that

$$f(x, T) \text{ is TP for } x \geq 1,\ T > 0. \tag{50}$$

Karlin's result applies more generally with a non-negative drift, so it applies to $1/S_t$, if S_t is strictly positive. If we write $\tilde{f}(\cdot, t)$ for the density of $1/S_t$, then (50) applies to $\tilde{f}$. But $\tilde{f}(x,t) = f(1/x,t)/x^2$, $x > 0$ so $\tilde{f}(x,T)$ TP for $x \geq 1$, $T > 0$ implies

$$f(x,T) \text{ RR} \quad \text{for } x \in (0,1],\ T > 0. \tag{51}$$

In the case of geometric Brownian motion, properties (50)–(51) reduce to the properties we derived explicitly for the lognormal density in Lemma 3.2. These TP and RR properties of $f(x,T)$ are the conditions appearing in the upper-left corners of Figures 1 and 2, so their consequences in the figures hold as well. In particular, the TP and RR properties we proved for calls and puts in Theorem 3.3 hold for essentially all martingale scalar diffusions, indicating that these properties are fundamental and not peculiarities of the Black–Scholes setting.

4.2. *Bachelier Model*

We mainly consider non-negative underlying assets, but to show that this restriction can be relaxed, we briefly consider the Bachelier model. Let W_t be a standard Brownian motion, with $W_0 = 0$, and define

$$c_B(K,T) = \mathbb{E}[(W_T - K)^+] = \int_{-\infty}^{\infty} (x-K)^+ \varphi(x/\sqrt{T})/\sqrt{T}\, dx.$$

Arguing as we did in Lemma 3.1, we see that

$$\frac{1}{\sqrt{T}} \cdot \frac{e^{-x^2/2T}}{\sqrt{2\pi}}$$

is TP in $x \geq 0$, $T > 0$, and RR in $x \leq 0$, $T > 0$. For $K > 0$, we may take the lower limit of integration in $c_B(K,T)$ to be zero and conclude that $c_B(K,T)$ is TP in $K, T > 0$. A similar argument shows that out-of-the-money puts are RR in $K \leq 0$, $T > 0$.

4.3. *Asian Options*

For a standard Brownian motion W, define

$$A_T = \int_0^T e^{\sigma W_t + (r-\sigma^2/2)t}\, dt, \quad r \geq 0.$$

Donati-Martin, Ghomrasni and Yor [8] show that A_T has the same distribution as Y_T, where

$$dY_t = (rY_t + 1)\,dt + \sigma Y_t dW_t, \quad Y_0 = 0.$$

Theorem 5.3(i) of Karlin [18] implies that the density $f(\cdot, T)$ of Y_T (and therefore of A_T) is TP on $(0,\infty) \times (0,\infty)$. Thus,

$$(K,T) \mapsto e^{-rT}\mathbb{E}[(A_T - K)^+] \text{ is TP for } K,T > 0.$$

We can formulate this statement as a statement about Asian options (options on A_T/T) with strike K/T,

$$(K,T) \mapsto e^{-rT}\mathbb{E}[(A_T/T - K/T)^+] \text{ is TP for } K,T > 0.$$

4.4. *Continuous Volatility Mixtures*

For the driftless geometric Brownian motion in (4), S_T has the lognormal distribution of $X_{\sigma\sqrt{T}}$, with X_v as in (30). Consider a mixture of lognormals under which σ has a probability density $w(\cdot)$. The density of the mixture is given by

$$f_w(x,T) = \int_0^\infty f_{LN}(x, \sigma\sqrt{T})w(\sigma)\,d\sigma = \int_0^\infty f_{LN}(x,v)g(v,T)dv,$$
$$g(v,T) = w(v/\sqrt{T})/\sqrt{T}. \tag{52}$$

The following result provides a condition on w implying TP_2 and RR_2 properties for f_w, from which the implications in Figures 1 and 2 then follow.

Proposition 4.1. *Suppose $w(\sigma) > 0$ for all $\sigma > 0$, and suppose w is differentiable. If $\sigma \mapsto \sigma w'(\sigma)/w(\sigma)$ is decreasing, then $f_w(x,T)$ is TP_2 in $x \geq 1$, $T > 0$, and it is RR_2 in $x \in (0,1]$, $T > 0$.*

Proof. If we can show that $g(v,T)$ is TP_2 in $v, T > 0$, then the conclusion will follow by applying the basic composition formula (13) to (52), recalling the TP and RR properties of f_{LN} proved in Lemma 3.2.

To show that $g(v,T)$ is TP_2, we need to show that for any $v_1 < v_2$, the ratio $w(v_2/\sqrt{T})/w(v_1/\sqrt{T})$ is increasing in T. By differentiating with respect to T, we see that this ratio is increasing if

$$v_2 w'(v_2/\sqrt{T})w(v_1/\sqrt{T}) - v_1 w(v_2/\sqrt{T})w'(v_1/\sqrt{T}) \leq 0.$$

This holds if

$$\sigma_2 w'(\sigma_2)w(\sigma_1) \leq \sigma_1 w'(\sigma_1)w_2(\sigma_2),$$

whenever $\sigma_1 < \sigma_2$. In other words, it holds if $\sigma w'(\sigma)/w(\sigma)$ is decreasing in σ. □

The condition in Proposition 4.1 on the elasticity $\sigma w'(\sigma)/w(\sigma)$ is satisfied by, for example, the exponential density $w(\sigma) = \lambda e^{-\lambda\sigma}$, $\lambda > 0$, for which

$$\sigma \frac{w'(\sigma)}{w(\sigma)} = -\lambda\sigma$$

is strictly decreasing in σ.

4.5. *Discrete Volatility Mixtures*

By requiring $w(\sigma) > 0$ for all $\sigma > 0$ in Proposition 4.1, we ensure that all points $v/\sqrt{T}$, $v, T > 0$, are in the support of w and therefore that all (v, T) are in the support of g. Without this condition on w, the support of g will not in general be a product set, so the approach in Proposition 4.1 does not apply. In particular, we need a different approach for the case of a mixture over finitely many values of σ.

For positive weights w_i, $i = 1, \ldots, n$, summing to 1, and distinct volatilities $\sigma_i > 0$, $i = 1, \ldots, n$, define the finite mixture of lognormal densities,

$$f_w(x,T) = \sum_{i=1}^{n} w_i f_{LN}(x, \sigma_i\sqrt{T}), \tag{53}$$

with f_{LN} as in (36). For $i, j = 1, \ldots, n$, define

$$\Delta_{ij}(x,T) = \frac{1}{\sigma_i^2 T} + \frac{1}{\sigma_j^2 T} - \frac{(\sigma_i^2 - \sigma_j^2)^2}{\sigma_i^2\sigma_j^2}\left(\frac{1}{8} + \frac{\log^2 x}{2\sigma_i^2\sigma_j^2 T^2}\right). \tag{54}$$

Proposition 4.2. *Suppose that for all x in some interval (x_0, x_1) and all T in some interval (T_0, T_1) we have*

$$\sum_{i=1}^{n} \frac{w_i^2}{\sigma_i^2 T} f_{LN}^2(x, \sigma_i\sqrt{T}) + \sum_{i<j} w_i w_j \Delta_{ij}(x,T) f_{LN}(x, \sigma_i\sqrt{T})$$

$$f_{LN}(x, \sigma_j\sqrt{T}) \geq 0. \tag{55}$$

Then $f_w(x,T)$ is TP$_2$ on $(x_0, x_1) \times (T_0, T_1)$ if $x_0 \geq 1$, and it is RR$_2$ if $x_1 \leq 1$.

A sufficient condition for (55) is to have $\Delta_{ij}(x,T) \geq 0$ throughout $(x_0, x_1) \times (T_0, T_1)$, for all i, j. This would require $x_0, T_0 > 0$ and $x_1 < \infty$ because $\Delta_{ij}(x,T)$ becomes negative as x_0 or T_0 approaches zero and as $x_1 \to \infty$. Condition (55) is also satisfied if the matrix with diagonal entries $1/\sigma_i^2 T$ and off-diagonal entries $\Delta_{ij}(x,T)/2$ is positive semidefinite.

Proof. The proof consists in showing that the condition in (55) is equivalent to the condition $[\partial^2_{xT} \log f_w(x,T)]/\log x \geq 0$. For $x > 1$, this inequality makes f_w TP$_2$, in light of condition (15), and for $x \in (0,1)$, it makes f_w RR$_2$.

Differentiation yields

$$\partial^2_{xT} \log f_w = \frac{\partial^2_{xT} f_w \cdot f_w - \partial_T f_w \cdot \partial_w f_w}{f_w^2}.$$

The sign of this expression is determined by its numerator, which we can expand to get

$$\sum_{i,j=1}^{n} w_i w_j \Big(f_{LN}(x, \sigma_i\sqrt{T}) \partial^2_{xT} f_{LN}(x, \sigma_j\sqrt{T})$$

$$- \partial_T f_{LN}(x, \sigma_i\sqrt{T}) \partial_x f_{LN}(x, \sigma_j\sqrt{T}) \Big).$$

This expression can be written as

$$\sum_{i=1}^{n} w_i^2 \Big(f_{LN}(x, \sigma_i\sqrt{T}) \partial^2_{xT} f_{LN}(x, \sigma_i\sqrt{T})$$

$$- \partial_T f_{LN}(x, \sigma_i\sqrt{T}) \partial_x f_{LN}(x, \sigma_i\sqrt{T}) \Big) \tag{56}$$

$$
\begin{aligned}
&+\sum_{i<j} w_i w_j \Big(f_{LN}(x,\sigma_i\sqrt{T})\partial^2_{xT} f_{LN}(x,\sigma_j\sqrt{T}) \\
&+ f_{LN}(x,\sigma_j\sqrt{T})\partial^2_{xT} f_{LN}(x,\sigma_i\sqrt{T}) \qquad (57)\\
&- \partial_T f_{LN}(x,\sigma_i\sqrt{T})\partial_x f_{LN}(x,\sigma_j\sqrt{T}) \\
&- \partial_T f_{LN}(x,\sigma_j\sqrt{T})\partial_x f_{LN}(x,\sigma_i\sqrt{T})\Big). \qquad (58)
\end{aligned}
$$

Differentiating the lognormal density yields the following identities:

$$
\begin{aligned}
\partial_x f_{LN}(x,\sigma\sqrt{T}) &= D_x(x,\sigma,T) f_{LN}(x,\sigma\sqrt{T}),\\
D_x(x,\sigma,T) &= -\frac{3}{2x} - \frac{\log x}{\sigma^2 T x}, \qquad (59)\\
\partial_T f_{LN}(x,\sigma\sqrt{T}) &= D_T(x,\sigma,T) f_{LN}(x,\sigma\sqrt{T}),\\
D_T(x,\sigma,T) &= -\frac{1}{2T} + \frac{\log^2 x}{2\sigma^2 T^2} - \frac{\sigma^2}{8} \qquad (60)
\end{aligned}
$$

and

$$
\begin{aligned}
\partial^2_{xT} f_{LN}(x,\sigma\sqrt{T}) = &\left(\frac{\log x}{\sigma^2 T^2 x} + D_x(x,\sigma,T) D_T(x,\sigma,T)\right)\\
&\times f_{LN}(x,\sigma\sqrt{T}). \qquad (61)
\end{aligned}
$$

With these substitutions, the coefficient of w_i^2 in (56) thus becomes

$$
\frac{\log x}{\sigma_i^2 T^2 x} f^2_{LN}(x,\sigma_i\sqrt{T}).
$$

The coefficient of $w_i w_j$ in (57)–(58) becomes the product of $f_{LN}(x,\sigma_i\sqrt{T}) f_{LN}(x,\sigma_j\sqrt{T})$ and

$$
\begin{aligned}
&\frac{\log x}{\sigma_i^2 T x} + \frac{\log x}{\sigma^2 T x} + [D_T(x,\sigma_i,T) - D_T(x,\sigma_j,T)]\\
&\times [D_x(x,\sigma_i,T) - D_x(x,\sigma_j,T)]. \qquad (62)
\end{aligned}
$$

Substituting the expressions for D_x and D_T from (59)–(60) into (62) and simplifying shows that (56)–(58) equals $\log x$ times the expression on the left side of (55). □

The condition $\Delta_{ij} \geq 0$ holds on the boundary and interior of an ellipse in coordinates $(\log x, T)$ defined by

$$\log^2 x + \left(\frac{1}{2}\sigma_i\sigma_j T - r\right)^2 \leq r^2, \qquad r := 2\sigma_i\sigma_j \frac{\sigma_i^2 + \sigma_j^2}{(\sigma_i^2 - \sigma_j^2)^2}.$$

The ellipse is centered at $(x, T) = (1, \frac{2r}{\sigma_i\sigma_j})$ and spans the range $0 \leq T \leq \frac{4r}{\sigma_i\sigma_j}$ and $0 \leq |\log x| \leq r$. The TP_2 property holds in the half-ellipse with $x > 1$, and the RR_2 property holds in the half-ellipse with $x < 1$.

The argument in Proposition 4.2 leads to a condition for relative convexity of option prices. Option prices in the Gaussian mixture model with density (53) are linear combinations of Black–Scholes prices,

$$c_{mix}(K, T) = \sum_{i=1}^{n} w_i c_{BS}(K, \sigma_i\sqrt{T}).$$

Taking a derivative with respect to T gives

$$\partial_T c_{mix}(K, T) = \frac{1}{2}K^2 \sum_{i=1}^{N} w_i \sigma_i^2 f_{LN}(K, \sigma_i\sqrt{T}),$$

where we used the result

$$\partial_T c_{BS}(K, \sigma\sqrt{T}) = \frac{1}{2}\sigma^2 K^2 f_{LN}(K, \sigma\sqrt{T}).$$

Thus, $\partial_T c_{mix}$ is itself a linear combination of lognormal densities with positive coefficients. We can now apply the argument in Proposition 4.2, with w_i replaced by $K^2\sigma_i^2 w_i/2$, to conclude that if $\Delta_{ij} \geq 0$, for all i, j, then $\partial_T c_{mix}$ is TP_2. This in turn is equivalent (see Figure 1) to the relative convexity property $c_{mix}(K_2, \cdot)$ cxw $c_{mix}(K_1, \cdot)$, for $1 \leq K_1 < K_2$.

4.6. *The Dagum Density*

In one of his last publications (Carr and Torricelli [7]), Peter Carr studied option prices when the underlying has a Dagum density on

$(0, \infty)$,

$$f_D(x,T) = (a(T)-1)(1+x^{-a(T)})^{\frac{1}{a(T)}-2}x^{-a(T)-1},$$
$$a(T) = 1/\sqrt{1-e^{-\sigma^2 T}}. \tag{63}$$

For fixed a, this is a special case of the general three-parameter Dagum density. The density in (63) has been normalized to have a mean of 1. The parameterization in (63) makes $a(T) > 1$ and decreasing in T, and those are the only properties of $a(\cdot)$ we need.

Proposition 4.3. *The Dagum density $f_D(x,T)$ is TP_2 for $x \geq 1$, $T > 0$, and it is RR_2 for $x \in (0,1]$, $T > 0$.*

This result is somewhat surprising. The properties asserted for $x \geq 1$ and $x \in (0,1]$ are consistent with the properties in (50)–(51) for scalar diffusions, but (63) was not derived from a stochastic process. Carr and Torricelli [7] ended their paper with a comment that they were investigating diffusion processes that support the pricing formulas in their paper.

Proof. We temporarily suppress the dependence of a on T and write

$$\log f_D(x,a) = \log(a-1) - \left(\frac{2a-1}{a}\right)\log(1+x^{-a}) - (a+1)\log x. \tag{64}$$

Then

$$\frac{d}{dx}\log f_D(x,a) = \frac{2a-1}{x(x^a+1)} - \frac{a+1}{x}, \tag{65}$$

and

$$\frac{d^2}{dadx}\log f_D(x,a) = \frac{2x(x^a+1)-(2a-1)x^{a+1}\log x}{x^2(x^a+1)^2} - \frac{1}{x}. \tag{66}$$

This expression is non-negative if and only if

$$2(x^a+1) - (2a-1)x^a\log x \geq (x^a+1)^2. \tag{67}$$

If $x \leq 1$, then (recalling that $a > 1$)

$$(x^a+1)^2 \leq 2(x^a+1) \leq 2(x^a+1) - (2a-1)x^a\log x,$$

so (67) holds. Conversely, if $x \geq 1$, then

$$(x^a + 1)^2 \geq 2(x^a + 1) \geq 2(x^a + 1) - (2a - 1)x^a \log x.$$

Thus, the mixed second derivative in (66) is non-negative if and only if $x \leq 1$. As $a(T)$ is decreasing in T, we conclude that

$$\frac{d^2}{dTdx} \log f_D(x, T) \geq 0 \Longleftrightarrow x \geq 1.$$

This condition is equivalent to the TP_2 and RR_2 properties in the statement of the proposition. □

Remark 4.4. The Carr–Toricelli density (63) is invariant under the transformation (29) associated with the change to the share measure: explicit computation shows that (63) satisfies the relation $f_D(x, T) = f_D(1/x, T)/x^3$. This implies put-call symmetry, so, by Proposition 2.4, the RR_2 property of the density for $0 < x \leq 1$ is equivalent to the TP_2 property for $x \geq 1$.

4.7. *The Logistic Density*

Carr and Torricelli [7] also studied option prices in a model with risk-neutral density of logistic form

$$f_L(x, T) = \frac{1}{4s(T)} \cdot \frac{1}{\cosh^2(\frac{x - S_0}{2s(T)})}, \tag{68}$$

where $s(T) > 0$ is an increasing function of maturity. The support of $f_L(\cdot, T)$ is the entire real axis. Whereas the Dagum model is proposed as an alternative to the Black–Scholes model, the logistic model is an alternative to the Bachelier model, appropriate for assets that can take both positive and negative values. We prove a $\mathrm{TP}_2/\mathrm{RR}_2$ property for this model, similar to that obtained for the Dagum model.

Proposition 4.5. *Assume $S_0 = 0$. Then $f_L(x, T)$ is TP_2 for $x \geq 0$, $T > 0$ and RR_2 for $x \leq 0, T > 0$.*

Proof. The TP_2/RR_2 property is determined by the sign of the cross-derivative

$$\begin{aligned}\partial^2_{xT} \log f_L(x,T) &= -2\partial^2_{xT} \log\cosh\left(\frac{x}{2s(T)}\right)\\ &= -2\partial_T\left(\frac{1}{2s(T)}\tanh\frac{x}{2s(T)}\right).\end{aligned} \tag{69}$$

The partial T-derivative is evaluated as

$$\begin{aligned}\partial_T\left[\frac{1}{2s(T)}\tanh\frac{x}{2s(T)}\right] = -\frac{s'(T)}{2s^2(T)}\Bigg(&\tanh\frac{x}{2s(T)}\\ &+\frac{x}{2s(T)}\cosh^{-2}\left(\frac{x}{2s(T)}\right)\Bigg).\end{aligned} \tag{70}$$

The final result can be put into the form

$$\partial^2_{xT} \log f_L(x,T) = \frac{s'(T)}{s^2(T)}\frac{g_L(\frac{x}{2s(T)})}{\cosh^2(\frac{x}{2s(T)})}, \tag{71}$$

where $g_L(z) := \sinh z \cosh z + z$.

For all $x \geq 0$, we have $g_L(\frac{x}{2s(T)}) \geq 0$. Furthermore, since $s'(T) > 0$ the expression in (71) is non-negative for all $x \geq 0$. This proves the TP_2 claim. The RR_2 claim follows from $g_L(\frac{x}{2s(T)}) \leq 0$ for $x \leq 0$. □

These properties of the density extend to out-of-the-money calls and puts, as in the Bachelier model discussed in Section 4.2.

4.8. *Lévy Process Models*

We consider Lévy process models defined as time-changed Brownian motions. To this end, recall that a subordinator V_t is a Lévy process with increasing sample paths, that is, a Lévy process with no Brownian component, a non-negative drift and a Lévy measure that assigns measure zero to $(-\infty, 0)$. (See, e.g., Kyprianou [22] for basic properties Lévy processes and Lévy measures.) We assume $V_0 = 0$.

We consider underlying assets of the form

$$S_T = e^{\sigma W(V_T)+\theta V_T - mT}, \tag{72}$$

where W is a standard Brownian motion, and $\sigma > 0$, θ and m are scalar parameters. For $u \in \mathbb{R}$, define the cumulant generating function $\psi(u)$ of V_1,

$$\psi(u) = \log \mathbb{E}[e^{uV_1}], \tag{73}$$

which is finite for all $u \in (-\infty, u_0)$, for some $u_0 \geq 0$, because $V_1 \geq 0$. It follows from the infinite divisibility of V_t that, for all $t > 0$,

$$\mathbb{E}[e^{uV_t}] = e^{\psi(u)t}. \tag{74}$$

We then have

$$\mathbb{E}[e^{\sigma W(V_T)+\theta V_T}] = \mathbb{E}[e^{(\sigma^2/2+\theta)V_T}] = e^{\psi(\sigma^2/2+\theta)T}. \tag{75}$$

If $\psi(\sigma^2/2+\theta) < \infty$ and we set $m = \psi(\sigma^2/2+\theta)$, then the underlying asset in (72) satisfies $\mathbb{E}[S_T] = 1$, for all $T \geq 0$. In particular, if $\theta = -\sigma^2/2$, then the condition $\mathbb{E}[S_T] = 1$ holds with $m = 0$.

Our goal is to extend TP properties from the subordinator V_t to options on S_T. We consider some examples for motivation.

Gamma process: In the variance-gamma model (Madan and Seneta [26], Madan, Carr, and Chang [24]), the subordinator is a gamma process in which, for each $t > 0$, V_t has the gamma distribution $G(t/\nu, 1/\nu)$, $\nu > 0$, with density

$$g(x,t,\nu) = \frac{x^{t/\nu-1}}{\Gamma(t/\nu)\nu^{t/\nu}} e^{-x/\nu}, \quad x > 0. \tag{76}$$

We know from (8) that the function $x^t = e^{t \log x}$ is TP in $x > 0$ and $t > 0$. It follows that g in (76) is TP in $x > 0$ and $t > 0$. In addition, we have

$$e^{\psi(u)} = \left(\frac{1}{1-u\nu}\right)^{1/\nu}, \quad u < 1/\nu.$$

Inverse Gaussian process: In the normal inverse Gaussian model (Barndorff-Nielsen [1]), the subordinator is an inverse Gaussian process in which, for each $t > 0$, V_t has the inverse Gaussian density

$$g(x,t,\mu) = \frac{t}{\sqrt{2\pi x^3}} e^{\mu t} e^{-\frac{1}{2}(t^2x^{-1}+\mu^2 x)}, \quad x > 0, \mu > 0.$$

Much as in the proof of Lemma 3.1, the function $(x,t) \mapsto e^{-t^2x^{-1}/2}$ is TP in $x, t > 0$. Writing the density as

$$\frac{te^{\mu t}}{\sqrt{2\pi}} \cdot \frac{e^{-\frac{1}{2}\mu^2 x}}{x^{3/2}} \cdot e^{-\frac{1}{2}t^2x^{-1}},$$

we see that the density is the product of a non-negative function of t, a non-negative function of x, and a TP function and is therefore TP. In addition, we have (Kyprianou [22], p. 9)

$$e^{\psi(u)} = \sqrt{\mu^2 - 2u} - \mu, \quad u < \mu^2/2.$$

Stable subordinators: Karlin [18], Section 9, considers stable subordinators with support on $[0,\infty)$ with index $\alpha \in (0,1)$, for which V_t has the distribution of $t^{1/\alpha}V_1$ and, for $s > 0$,

$$\mathbb{E}[e^{-sV_t}] = e^{\psi(-s)t} = e^{-ts^\alpha}.$$

Karlin [18], p.90, shows that the density $g_\alpha(x,t)$ of V_t is TP in $x, t > 0$ for $\alpha = 1/k$, $k = 2, 3, \ldots$. Karlin [19], p.122, notes that the TP property does not hold for other α.

Compound Poisson process: A compound Poisson process with intensity $\lambda > 0$ and jump-size density h has density

$$g(x,t) = e^{-\lambda t} \sum_{n=0}^{\infty} \frac{\lambda^n t^n}{n!} h^{(n)}(x), \tag{77}$$

where $h^{(n)}$ denotes the n-fold convolution of h with itself. Suppose $h(x) = 0$ for $x \leq 0$, so all jumps are positive. Suppose h has the property that

$$(x,y) \mapsto h(x-y) \text{ is } \mathrm{TP}_r, \tag{78}$$

then $g(x,t)$ is TP_r. This is shown in Karlin [18], p.65, for the case $r = \infty$, but the result holds for all $r = 2, 3, \ldots$, as follows. By Theorem 3.7(i) of Karlin [18], (78) implies that $h^{(n)}(x)$ is TP_r in x and n; the Poisson mass function is TP in n and t because t^n is TP, so $g(x,t)$ in (77) is TP_r in x and t by the discrete version of the basic composition formula (13). A probability density h satisfying (78) is called a Pólya frequency function of order r. With $r = 2$, (78) is equivalent to requiring h to be log-concave, as can be seen by applying the second-derivative condition in (15).

We now return to the model in (72) of an underlying asset defined through a time-changed Brownian motion, and we consider TP properties of options on this underlying, based on TP properties of the density of the subordinator. Let

$$\begin{aligned} \tilde{C}(K,T) &= e^{-rT}\mathbb{E}[(S_T - K)^+] \text{ and} \\ \tilde{P}(K,T) &= e^{-rT}\mathbb{E}[(K - S_T)^+], \quad K \geq 0, \quad T > 0. \end{aligned}$$

We have included explicit discount factors in this setting to clarify the role of the factor e^{-mT} introduced in (72). The inclusion of the discount factor has no bearing on any TP or RR properties of $\tilde{C}(K,T)$ or $\tilde{P}(K,T)$.

The following result applies, in particular, to the variance gamma model and the normal inverse Gaussian model.

Proposition 4.6. *Suppose that V_t has a density $g(v,t)$ that is TP_n in $v > 0$ and $t > 0$. If $m \equiv \psi(\theta + \sigma^2/2) < \infty$, then $\tilde{C}(e^{-mT}K,T)$ is TP_n in $K \geq 1$, $T > 0$, and $\tilde{P}(e^{-mT}K,T)$ is RR_n in $K \in [0,1]$, $T > 0$. In particular, if $\theta = -\sigma^2/2$, then $m = 0$ and $\tilde{C}(K,T)$ is TP_n and $\tilde{P}(K,T)$ is RR_n.*

Proof. Let $f(\cdot,t)$ denote the density of $\sigma W(V_t) + \theta V_t$. Then

$$f(x,t) = \int_0^\infty \varphi\left(\frac{x-\theta v}{\sigma\sqrt{v}}\right)\frac{1}{\sigma\sqrt{v}}g(v,t)\,dv. \tag{79}$$

Write

$$\varphi\left(\frac{x-\theta v}{\sigma\sqrt{v}}\right)\frac{1}{\sigma\sqrt{v}} = e^{-x^2/2\sigma^2 v}\cdot\frac{e^{x\theta/\sigma^2}}{\sqrt{2\pi}}\cdot\frac{e^{-\theta^2 v/2\sigma^2}}{\sigma\sqrt{v}}. \tag{80}$$

The first factor is TP in $x \geq 0$, $v > 0$; the second and third factors are non-negative functions of x and v separately, so the product is TP. Applying the basic composition formula to (79), we conclude that $f(x,t)$ is TP_n in $x \geq 0$, $t > 0$. As the function $(x, K) \mapsto (e^x - K)^+$ is TP, another application of the basic composition formula shows that

$$C(K,T) \equiv \int_0^\infty (e^x - K)^+ f(x,T)\, dx$$

is TP_n in $K \geq 1$, $T > 0$. But then $e^{-rT-mT}C(K,T)$ is TP_n, and

$$\begin{aligned} e^{-rT-mT}C(K,T) &= e^{-rT}\int_0^\infty (e^{x-mT} - e^{-mT}K)^+ f(x,T)\, dx \\ &= \tilde{C}(e^{-mT}K, T). \end{aligned}$$

It remains to consider puts. For $x \leq 0$, the direction of monotonicity of $x \mapsto -x^2/2\sigma^2$ in (80) is reversed, so $e^{-x^2/2\sigma^2 v}$ becomes RR rather than TP. It then follows that the full product in (80) is RR, for $x \leq 0$, $v > 0$. Applying the basic composition formula to

$$P(K,T) = \int_{-\infty}^0 (K - e^x)^+ f(x,T)\, dx$$

shows that $P(K,T)$ is RR_n in $K \in [0,1]$, $T > 0$, if f is TP_n. Multiplying by e^{-rT-mT} shows that $\tilde{P}(e^{-mT}K, T)$ is RR_n in $K \in [0,1]$, $T > 0$. □

Compound Poisson processes are useful as approximations to infinite-intensity Lévy processes, and this property leads to another way to verify the TP_n condition for Proposition 4.6. Suppose the Lévy measure of the subordinator V_t has a density, and suppose that density is log-concave. Shaked and Shanthikumar [30], Lemma 4.1, show that the density $g(x,t)$ of V_t is then TP_2 in $x, t > 0$. Their argument is based on observing that if h is log-concave then (77) is TP_2, and then passing to the limit for the infinite-activity case. This argument holds for general TP_n: if the Lévy density is a Pólya frequency function of order n (in the sense of (78)), then the subordinator has a TP_n density $g(x,t)$.

The Lévy densities of the gamma process, the inverse Gaussian process and the stable subordinator are not log-concave. However, they are all decreasing, and this leads to the following result, which will also allow us to consider certain CGMY models.

Proposition 4.7. *Suppose the Lévy measure of the subordinator V_t has a decreasing density on $(0,\infty)$. Suppose $\theta = 0$ in (72). If $m \equiv \psi(\sigma^2/2) < \infty$, then $\tilde{C}(e^{-mT}K,T)$ is TP_2 in $K \geq 1$, $T > 0$, and $\tilde{P}(e^{-mT}K,T)$ is RR_2 in $K \in [0,1]$, $T > 0$.*

Proof. Let $G(\cdot,t)$ and $F(\cdot,t)$ denote the cumulative distribution functions of V_t and $\sigma W(V_t)$, respectively. Then

$$F(x,t) = \mathbb{P}(\sigma W(V_t) \leq x) = \int_0^\infty \Phi\Big(\frac{x}{\sigma\sqrt{v}}\Big) dG(v,t). \tag{81}$$

We can write the function inside the integral as

$$\Phi\left(\frac{x}{\sigma\sqrt{v}}\right) = \int_{-\infty}^\infty 1\{u \leq x\}\varphi\left(\frac{u}{\sigma\sqrt{v}}\right)\frac{1}{\sigma\sqrt{v}}\,du. \tag{82}$$

We know (see (80)) that for $u < 0$, $v > 0$, $\varphi(u/\sigma\sqrt{v})$ is RR, so it follows from the basic composition formula that (82) is RR in $x < 0$, $v > 0$. By Proposition 5.1(b) of Shaked and Shanthikumar [30], the fact that V_t has a decreasing Lévy density implies that $G(x,t)$ is TP_2. We can now apply Theorem 2.1(ii) of Lynch, Mimmack and Proschan [23] to (81) to conclude that F is RR_2 in $x < 0$, $t > 0$. The result of Lynch *et al.* [23] states that if G and the integrand in (81) are both TP_2, then F is TP_2. Our integrand is RR_2. The change of variables $u = 1/v$ and $s = 1/t$ makes the integrand TP_2 (because it reverses the direction of one argument) while keeping G TP_2 (because it reverses the directions of both arguments), thus showing that F is TP_2 in $x < 0$ and $1/t > 0$, which implies that F is RR_2 in $x < 0$, $t > 0$.

By the symmetry of the normal distribution,

$$1 - F(x,t) = \mathbb{P}(\sigma W(V_t) > x) = \mathbb{P}(\sigma W(V_t) \leq -x) = F(-x,t),$$

so $1 - F$ is TP_2 in $x, t > 0$.

We now have, by the basic composition formula, that, for $K \geq 1$, $T > 0$,

$$C(K,T) = \mathbb{E}[(e^{\sigma W(V_T)} - K)^+] = \int_1^\infty \mathbf{1}\{y > K\}[1 - F(\log y, t)]\, dy$$

is TP_2because $1 - F(\log y, t)$ is TP_2 in $y > 1$, $t > 0$. Similarly, for $K \in [0, 1]$,

$$P(K,T) = \mathbb{E}[(K - e^{\sigma W(V_T)})^+] = \int_0^1 \mathbf{1}\{y \leq K\} F(\log y, t)\, dy$$

is RR_2. Multiplying $C(K,T)$ and $P(K,T)$ by e^{-rT-mT} concludes the proof. □

CGMY process: Madan and Yor [25] show that the CGMY process of Carr *et al.* [4] can be written in the form (72). In their Proposition 5, they show that the Lévy measure for the corresponding subordinator has a density

$$C_Y \frac{1}{1 + v^{1+Y/2}} e^{(A^2-B^2)v/2} \mathbb{E}\left[e^{-B^2 vX/2}\right],$$

where C_Y is a constant that depends on the parameter Y, $A = (G-M)/2$, $B = (G+M)/2$, and X is a non-negative random variable. More precisely, Proposition 5 derives this expression in the symmetric case $A = 0$, and the general case follows from p.33 of Madan and Yor [25]. For any $G, M \geq 0$, we have $A^2 \leq B^2$, and the density is a decreasing function of v, as required for Proposition 4.7.

5. Relative Convexity and the Dupire Equation

As illustrated in Figure 1, relative convexity properties for call options imply TP_2 properties for call options. We now show that it is sometimes possible to derive relative convexity properties from TP_2-like conditions. To do this we will need to relate certain derivatives with respect to maturity to derivatives with respect to the underlying. The tool for this conversion is the Dupire [9] equation, which specializes the Fokker–Planck equation to option payoffs.

5.1. *The Driftless Case*

We first consider the driftless case, which is simpler. Suppose the underlying asset S_t, $t \geq 0$, is a positive Ito process satisfying, for some $\sigma : (0, \infty) \to (0, \infty)$,

$$dS_t = \sigma(S_t) S_t \, dW_t, \quad S_0 = 1. \tag{83}$$

Then S_t is a strong Markov process and, under modest conditions on σ (see Theorem 2.1 of Fournier and Printemps [10]),

$$S_t \text{ has a density } f(\cdot, t), \text{ for all } t > 0. \tag{84}$$

Suppose option prices $C(K, T) = \mathbb{E}[(S_T - K)^+]$ satisfy the Dupire equation

$$\partial_T C(K, T) = \frac{1}{2} \sigma^2(K) K^2 f(T, K), \quad T > 0, \quad K \geq 0. \tag{85}$$

The following result shows that through (85), we can convert TP properties of the density to relative convexity properties of option prices.

Theorem 5.1. *Suppose conditions (83)–(85) hold, and suppose $f(x, t) > 0$, for all $x, t > 0$. If $1 \leq K_1 < K_2$, then $C(K_2, \cdot)$ is cxw $C(K_1, \cdot)$ on $(0, \infty)$. If $0 < K_1 < K_2 \leq 1$, then $C(K_1, \cdot)$ is cxw $C(K_2, \cdot)$ on $(0, \infty)$.*

Proof. By Karlin's [19] Theorem 5.3, which we discussed in Section 4.1, $f(x, t)$ is TP in $x \geq 1$, $T > 0$. In particular, then, $f(K_2, T)/f(K_1, T)$ is increasing in T, for $1 \leq K_1 < K_2$. It then follows from (85) that, for $1 \leq K_1 < K_2$,

$$\frac{\partial_T C(K_2, T)}{\partial_T C(K_1, T)} = \frac{\sigma^2(K_2) K_2^2 \, f(K_2, T)}{\sigma^2(K_1) K_1^2 \, f(K_1, T)} \tag{86}$$

is increasing in T. By condition (17), this means that $C(K_2, \cdot)$ is cxw $C(K_1, \cdot)$. For the second claim, $f(x, t)$ is RR in $x \in (0, 1]$, $t > 0$, as noted in (51). It follows that for $0 < K_1 < K_2 \leq 1$, the ratio in (86) is decreasing in T, so its reciprocal is increasing in T, from which the claimed relative convexity follows. □

Taking $K_1 = 0$ in the second part of the theorem yields $C(K_1, \cdot) \equiv 1$. This makes the corresponding determinant in (19) equal to zero, so relative convexity holds trivially in this case.

If we take a time-dependent volatility $\sigma(S_t, t)$ in (83), then it is clear from (86) that the theorem continues to hold, provided $\sigma(K, T)$ is TP_2 in $K \geq 1$, $T > 0$, and RR_2 for $K \in (0, 1]$, $T > 0$.

5.2. *Constant Drift Rate*

Now suppose that, for some $r \geq 0$,

$$dS_t = rS_t\,dt + \sigma(S_t)S_t\,dW_t, \quad S_0 = 1. \tag{87}$$

Fix an expiration date $T > 0$. The forward price $F_t = e^{r(T-t)}S_t$ satisfies $F_T = S_T$ and

$$dF_t = \sigma_F(F_t, t)F_t\,dW_t, \quad \sigma_F(x, t) = \sigma(xe^{-r(T-t)}).$$

With $C(K, T) = \mathbb{E}[(F_T - K)^+]$, the Dupire equation takes the form

$$\partial_T C(K, T) = \frac{1}{2}\sigma_F^2(K, T)K^2 f(K, T), \quad T > 0, \quad K \geq 0, \tag{88}$$

where $f(\cdot, T)$ is the common density of F_T and S_T. Note that $\sigma_F(K, T) = \sigma(K)$. Thus, convexity of $C(K_2, \cdot)$ with respect to $C(K_1, \cdot)$ is again determined by the ratio (86). The density f has the TP property (50). The reciprocal process $1/S_t$ satisfies

$$d(1/S_t) = (\sigma^2(S_t) - r)/S_t\,dt - \sigma(S_t)/S_t\,dW_t,$$

If $\sigma^2(x) \geq r$, for all $x > 0$, then (51) holds as well. Thus, Theorem 5.1 extends to this setting.

To incorporate discounting at rate r and an arbitrary initial value S_0 for the underlying asset in (87), we proceed as we did for the Black–Scholes setting in Section 3.2. We have $\mathbb{E}[e^{-rT}S_T] = S_0$, so

$$\begin{aligned} C(K, T; S_0, r) &= e^{-rT}\mathbb{E}[(S_T - K)^+] \\ &= S_0\mathbb{E}[(S_T e^{-rT}/S_0 - e^{-rT}K/S_0)^+] \\ &= S_0 C(e^{-rT}K/S_0, T). \end{aligned}$$

The functions

$$T \mapsto C(K_i e^{rT}, T; S_0, r) = S_0 C(K_i/S_0, T)$$

inherit relative convexity from $C(K_i, T)$:

Corollary 5.2. *Suppose (84), (87) and (88) hold with $r \geq 0$. For $S_0 \leq K_1 < K_2$,*

$$T \mapsto C(K_2e^{rT}, T; S_0, r) \text{ cxw } T \mapsto C(K_1e^{rT}, T; S_0, r).$$

Suppose in addition that the process $1/S_t$ is well defined and $\sigma^2(x) \geq r$, for all $x \in (0, \infty)$. Then for $0 < K_1 < K_2 \leq S_0$, the cxw relation is reversed.

Thus, for discounted options prices, relative convexity should be formulated in terms of forward moneyness rather than fixed strikes. The condition $\sigma^2(x) \geq r$ ensures that $1/S_t$ has non-negative drift and thus implies that (51) holds.

6. Implications of Total Positivity

6.1. *Option Price Constraints*

Total positivity properties imply constraints on option prices. If $C(K, T)$ is TP_2 for $K \geq 1$, $T > 0$, then the price ratios

$$\frac{C(K_2, T)}{C(K_1, T)} \quad \text{and} \quad \frac{C(K, T_2)}{C(K, T_1)}$$

are increasing in $T > 0$ and $K \geq 1$, respectively, for $1 \leq K_1 < K_2$ and $0 < T_1 < T_2$. Assuming differentiability, these monotonicity properties can be formulated as non-negativity conditions on derivatives with respect to T and K.

Similar but increasingly complex properties can be derived from higher-order total positivity. For example, if OTM call prices are twice differentiable and TP_3, then

$$\frac{C(K_3, \cdot)}{C(K_1, \cdot)} \text{ cxw } \frac{C(K_2, \cdot)}{C(K_1, \cdot)} \text{ on } (0, \infty)$$

and

$$\frac{C(\cdot, T_3)}{C(\cdot, T_1)} \text{ cxw } \frac{C(\cdot, T_2)}{C(\cdot, T_1)} \text{ on } (1, \infty),$$

with $1 \leq K_1 < K_2 < K_3$ and $0 < T_1 < T_2 < T_3$. Corresponding statements hold for OTM puts if the ordering of the strikes is reversed.

These relationships and their generalization to higher orders to total positivity can be derived through the connection between total positivity and Tchebycheff systems, particularly Theorem 1.2 in Chapter XI of Karlin and Studden [20].

6.2. *Constraints on the ATM Implied Volatility Skew*

We now explore constraints on implied volatilities imposed by total positivity properties of option prices. As in previous sections, we write $C(K,T)$ for $\mathbb{E}[(S_T-K)^+]$, with S_T having density $f(\cdot,T)$ on $(0,\infty)$. We assume the normalization $S_0=1$. The implied volatility $\sigma_{BS}(K,T)$ solves $C(K,T)=c_{BS}(K,\sigma_{BS}(K,T)\sqrt{T})$. It will be convenient to work with the unannualized volatility (or total standard deviation)

$$v(K,T)=\sigma_{BS}(K,T)\sqrt{T}. \tag{89}$$

Familiar monotonicity properties of $C(K,T)$ impose constraints on $v(K,T)$:

- For any submartingale S_t, we have $C(K,T)$ increasing in T and therefore $v(K,T)$ increasing in T.
- The absence of butterfly arbitrage $\partial_K^2 C(K,T)\geq 0$ constrains a combination of volatility, its slope and its convexity with respect to strike K. At the ATM point, this constraint takes the form (see, for example, [21] p. 5)

  $$1+v(1,T)\partial_K v(1,T)-\frac{1}{4}v^2(1,T)(\partial_K v(1,T))^2+v(1,T)\partial_K^2 v(1,T)\geq 0.$$

  This constraint gives a lower bound on convexity $\partial_K^2 v(1,T)$ for given volatility and skew.
- Strike monotonicity

  $$\partial_K C(K,T)\leq 0, \quad \partial_K(P(K,T)/K)\geq 0. \tag{90}$$

  The second inequality is an improvement (Gatheral [11]) over the weaker monotonicity relation $\partial_K P(K,T)\geq 0$.

To similarly derive implications of total positivity properties, we record the following result:

Lemma 6.1. *Suppose that $C(K,T)$ and $P(K,T)$ are strictly positive. If the density $f(x,T)$ is TP_2 in $x \geq 1$, $T > 0$, then the ratio*

$$R_c(K,T) := \frac{\partial_K C(K,T)}{C(K,T)}, \quad K \geq 1,$$

is increasing in $T > 0$. If $f(x,T)$ is RR_2 in $x \in (0,1]$, $T > 0$, then the ratio

$$R_p(K,T) := -\frac{\partial_K P(K,T)}{P(K,T)}, \quad 0 < K \leq 1,$$

is increasing in $T > 0$.

Proof. We know from Figure 1 that the TP_2 condition on f implies that $C(K,T)$ is TP_2 for $K \geq 1$, $T > 0$. From (14) we know that this implies that $\partial_K \log C(K,T)$ is increasing in T, for $K \geq 1$, so $R_c(K,T)$ is increasing in T, for $K \geq 1$. The RR_2 condition on f implies that $P(K,T)$ is RR_2 for $K \in (0,1]$, $T > 0$. This in turn implies that $\partial_K \log P(K,T)$ is decreasing in T, for $K \in (0,1]$, so $R_p(K,T)$ is increasing in T. □

The partial derivatives appearing in the numerators of these ratios are related to the prices of digital options $D_c(K,T) = \mathbb{E}[\mathbf{1}\{S_T > K\}]$ and $D_p(K,T) = \mathbb{E}[\mathbf{1}\{S_T < K\}]$ as

$$D_c(K,T) = -\partial_K C(K,T), \quad D_p(K,T) = -\partial_K C(K,T).$$

The TP/RR conditions in the lemma thus imply the ratios of the digital options to the corresponding vanilla options are monotonic in maturity.

Assuming differentiability of the implied volatility, define the normalized ATM skew

$$s(T) := \frac{\partial_K \sigma_{BS}(1,T)}{\sigma_{BS}(1,T)} = \frac{\partial_K v(1,T)}{v(1,T)}. \tag{91}$$

For simplicity, we drop the K argument when referring to the ATM value and write $v(T)$ for $v(1,T)$.

The skew ratio $s(T)$ is bounded from below and above by the model-free Hodges [15] bounds, following from (90),

$$-\frac{\Phi(-v/2)}{v\varphi(v/2)} \leq s(T) \leq \frac{\Phi(-v/2)}{v\varphi(v/2)}\,.$$

The monotonicity properties in Lemma 6.1 lead to bounds on the time derivative of the skew ratio at the ATM point when option prices satisfy total positivity conditions.

Proposition 6.2. *Suppose the implied volatility is differentiable in $K, T > 0$. Suppose $C(K,T)$ is TP_2 for $K \geq 1$, $T > 0$, and suppose $P(K,T)$ is RR_2 for $K \in (0,1]$, $T > 0$ (for example, if the density $f(x,T)$ has these properties). Then the time-derivative of the ATM skew ratio $s(T)$ defined in (91) satisfies the bounds*

$$\begin{aligned}\frac{1}{2}\frac{v'(T)}{v(T)}&\left\{-\frac{1}{2\Phi(v(T)/2)-1} + s(T) f_S(v(T))\right\} \leq s'(T)\\ &\leq \frac{1}{2}\frac{v'(T)}{v(T)}\left\{\frac{1}{2\Phi(v(T)/2)-1} + s(T) f_S(v(T))\right\}, \qquad (92)\end{aligned}$$

where $v'(T) = \partial_T v(1,T)$, and

$$f_S(v) := \frac{2v\varphi(v/2)}{2\Phi(v/2)-1} - 2 + \frac{v^2}{2}$$

is a positive increasing function that vanishes at $v = 0$.

The first few terms in the expansion of $f_S(v)$ around $v = 0$ are

$$f_S(v) = \frac{1}{3}v^2 + \frac{1}{180}v^4 + O(v^6).$$

Proof. The bounds follow from the monotonicity conditions on R_c and R_p in Lemma 6.1. By the definition of implied volatility, $C(K,T) = c_{BS}(K, v(K,T))$, with $v(K,T)$ as in (89). As v is differentiable, the numerator of $R_c(K,T)$ is given by

$$\begin{aligned}\frac{d}{dK}C(K,T) &= \partial_K c_{BS}(K,v(K,T)) + \partial_v c_{BS}(K,v(K,T))\partial_K v(K,T)\\ &= -\Phi(d_2) + \varphi(d_1)\partial_K v(K,T),\end{aligned}$$

where we used

$$\partial_K c_{BS}(K,v) = -\Phi(d_2), \quad \partial_v c_{BS}(K,v) = \varphi(d_1)$$

with

$$d_1 = -\frac{\log K}{v} + \frac{v}{2}, \quad d_2 = -\frac{\log K}{v} - \frac{v}{2}.$$

Thus,

$$R_c(K,T) = \frac{-\Phi(d_2) + \varphi(d_1)\partial_K v(K,T)}{c_{BS}(K,v(K,T))}.$$

Similarly,

$$R_p(K,T) = \frac{-\Phi(-d_2) - \varphi(d_1)\partial_K v(K,T)}{p_{BS}(K,v(K,T))}.$$

From Lemma 6.1, we know that our $\mathrm{TP}_2/\mathrm{RR}_2$ conditions on out-of-the-money calls and puts imply that these ratios are increasing functions of T, for $K \geq 1$ and $K \leq 1$, respectively. At $K = 1$, we can use (91) to replace $\partial_K v(K,T)$ with $s(T)v(T)$ to get

$$R_c(1,T) = \frac{-\Phi(-\frac{1}{2}v(T)) + s(T)v(T)\varphi(\frac{1}{2}v(T))}{2\Phi(\frac{1}{2}v(T)) - 1}$$

Taking the T-derivative of this function and requiring its positivity gives the lower bound on $s'(T)$ in (92). Similarly,

$$R_p(1,T) = \frac{-\Phi(\frac{1}{2}v(T)) + s(T)v(T)\varphi(\frac{1}{2}v(T))}{2\Phi(\frac{1}{2}v(T)) - 1}.$$

Taking the T-derivative of this function and requiring its positivity gives the upper bound on $s'(T)$ in (92). □

6.3. *A Static Replication Property*

The determinant conditions defining total positivity properties can be interpreted as statements about static replication. To formulate this interpretation a bit more generally, suppose $h(T)$, $T \geq 0$, is the expected payoff of a contract with maturity T. Suppose that for some $1 \leq K_1 < \cdots < K_n$ and all $0 \leq T_1 < \cdots < T_{n+1}$ we have

$$\begin{vmatrix} C(K_1, T_1) & \cdots & C(K_1, T_{k+1}) \\ \vdots & & \vdots \\ C(K_k, T_1) & \cdots & C(K_k, T_{k+1}) \\ h(T_1) & \cdots & h(T_{k+1}) \end{vmatrix} \geq 0, \quad k = 2, 3, \ldots, n. \tag{93}$$

Condition (93) holds, for example, if the out-of-the-money calls $C(K,T)$ are TP_{n+1} and h is the expected payoff of a call with a strike price greater than K_n. In the terminology of Karlin and Studden [20], (93) states that h is an element of $\mathcal{C}(C(K_1, \cdot), \ldots, C(K_n, \cdot))$, a convex cone generated by the functions $C(K_i, \cdot)$.

We are asking if the value $h(T)$ can be replicated with a portfolio of European options $C(K_i, T)$ in such a way that the replication holds for a range of values T. This question is related to the Carr–Madan [6] formula, which replicates an arbitrary European payoff using European options of the same maturity. However, we are interested in whether a replication can be found for multiple maturities, and we do not necessarily require that h be derived from the same underlying asset, as long as (93) holds.

Consider an approximating portfolio of options

$$h_n(T) = \sum_{i=1}^{n} a_i C(K_i, T),$$

where the a_i could be positive or negative. Suppose we try to choose the coefficients so that the replication is perfect at certain predetermined maturities $0 < T_1 < \cdots < T_n$. This condition gives n equations for the n unknown coefficients a_i

$$\sum_{i=1}^{n} a_i C(K_i, T_j) = h(T_j), \quad j = 1, 2, \ldots, n. \tag{94}$$

If OTM calls are strictly TP_n, meaning that we have a strict inequality in the determinant condition (7), then the system of equations (94) has a unique solution. But the condition (93) further implies that either $h_n \equiv h$ or the equality $h_n(T) = h(T)$ has no solutions T other than the prescribed maturities $\{T_j\}_{j=1}^n$. This follows from Theorem 2.1 in Chapter 6 of Karlin [19], which states that the replication error

$$h(T) - \sum_{i=1}^{n} a_i C(K_i, T) \tag{95}$$

changes sign at most n times as T varies over $(0, \infty)$. Moreover, if the replication error changes sign n times, then the final sign is positive. (Karlin's [19] Theorem 2.1 makes the equivalent statement that the initial sign is $(-1)^n$.) It follows from point (iii) on page 34 in Karlin and Studden [20] that (95) has only simple zeros, and these coincide with the points at which (95) changes sign.

6.4. *Constraints from Relative Convexity*

Relative convexity constrains option prices and thus implicitly constrains implied volatilities. Consider a model in which call prices $C(K, T)$ are twice differentiable in T and strictly increasing in T. Suppose the call prices satisfy

$$1 \leq K_1 < K_2 \Longrightarrow C(K_2, \cdot) \text{ cxw } C(K_1, \cdot), \tag{96}$$

as in Figure 1. This property extends to baskets of options in the following sense. Suppose $1 \leq K_1, \ldots, K_n$ are all smaller than $K_{n+1}, \ldots, K_{n+m}$, and suppose $a_1, \ldots, a_n, b_1, \ldots, b_m > 0$. Then (96) implies

$$\sum_{j=1}^{m} b_j C(K_{n+j}, \cdot) \text{ cxw } \sum_{i=1}^{n} a_i C(K_i, \cdot). \tag{97}$$

To see why, recall from (17) that (96) implies that $\partial_T C(K_2, T)/\partial_T C(K_1, T)$ is increasing in T. For the strikes in the baskets, we therefore have $\partial_T[\partial_T C(K_{n+j}, T)/\partial_T C(K_i, T)] \geq 0$, $i = 1, \ldots, n$,

$j = 1, \ldots, m$, i.e.,

$$\partial_T^2 C(K_{n+j}, T)\partial_T C(K_i, T) - \partial_T C(K_{n+j}, T)\partial_T^2 C(K_i, T) \geq 0.$$

And then

$$\sum_{i=1}^{n}\sum_{j=1}^{m} a_i b_j \left(\partial_T^2 C(K_{n+j}, T)\partial_T C(K_i, T)\right. \\ \left. - \partial_T C(K_{n+j}, T)\partial_T^2 C(K_i, T)\right) \geq 0,$$

so

$$\sum_{j=1}^{m} b_j \partial_T^2 C(K_{n+j}, T) \sum_{i=1}^{n} a_i \partial_T C(K_i, T) \\ - \sum_{j=1}^{m} b_j \partial_T C(K_{n+j}, T) \sum_{i=1}^{n} a_i \partial_T^2 C(K_i, T) \geq 0,$$

which implies that

$$\partial_T \sum_{j=1}^{m} b_j C(K_{n+j}, T) \Big/ \partial_T \sum_{i=1}^{n} a_i C(K_i, T)$$

is increasing in T, as required for (97).

Applying Theorem 3 of Palmer [29], we find that if (96) holds and $1 \leq K_1 < K_2 < K_3$, then

$$\log\left(e^{C(K_2,\cdot)} + e^{C(K_3,\cdot)}\right) \text{ cxw } C(K_1, \cdot).$$

Is the log-sum-of-exponentials relevant to option pricing? Carr and Torricelli [7] suggested that it is, albeit in a different context.

6.5. *Empirical Tests for TP$_2$/RR$_2$ Properties*

We present empirical tests of the TP$_2$/RR$_2$ properties of option prices using market data. For this test we use European SPX index options from *OptionMetrics*.

Several practical issues have to be addressed when performing such a test:

Table 1. The first few expiries of the SPX index options, the forward price $F(T)$ and the number of strikes for which option pricing data are available. The pricing date is 4-Oct-2021, with closing price $S_0 = 4300.46$.

Expiry	$F(T)$	n_K
15-Oct-2021	4300.86	407
19-Nov-2021	4295.84	367
17-Dec-2021	4290.59	399

(i) Market option prices are available on a discrete grid of values of strikes K_i and maturities T_j. For any other values of (K, T), interpolation would be needed. In order to avoid additional errors introduced by interpolation, we used only options with listed strikes and maturities.
The first few option expiries are listed in Table 1. We used the first three expiries for this test.

(ii) For each expiry T, we compute the forward price $F(T)$ as the strike at which the difference between call and put mid-prices vanishes. For this computation, we use linear interpolation between consecutive strikes.

(iii) The tests are performed first using option mid-prices and then accounting for the bid-ask spread.

Define

$$\delta_{ij} := \begin{cases} C_{\text{mid}}(K_i, T_1)C_{\text{mid}}(K_j, T_2) & \\ \quad -C_{\text{mid}}(K_i, T_2)C_{\text{mid}}(K_j, T_1) & \text{for } F < K_i < K_j \\ P_{\text{mid}}(K_i, T_1)P_{\text{mid}}(K_j, T_2) & \\ \quad -P_{\text{mid}}(K_i, T_2)P_{\text{mid}}(K_j, T_1) & \text{for } K_j < K_i < F. \end{cases}$$

If TP_2/RR_2 holds for OTM calls/puts, one has $\delta_{ij} \geq 0$.

The plots in Figure 4 show the values of (K_i, K_j) with $\delta_{ij} < 0$, corresponding to exceptions from TP_2/RR_2, separately for OTM calls (left) and OTM puts (right). The blue dots use the mid-prices for both terms in the difference δ_{ij}.

In order to test the impact of the bid-ask spread, the yellow dots show violations using ask $\cdot$ ask $-$ bid $\cdot$ bid. This test is asking whether

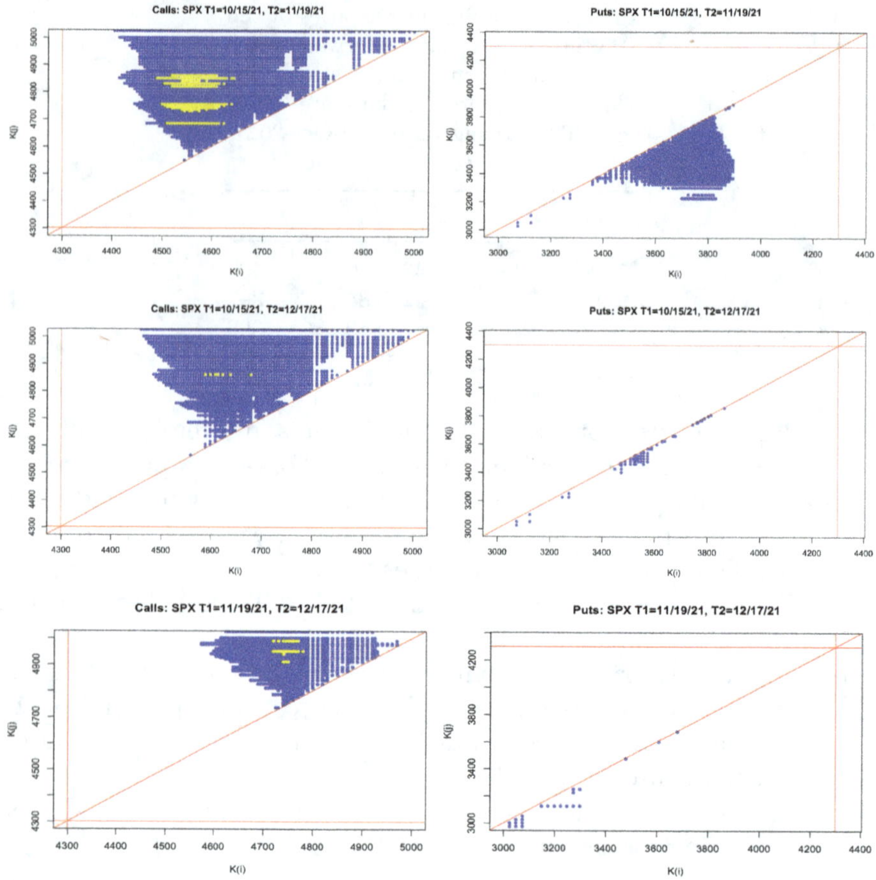

Figure 4. Points in the plane (K_i, K_j) with $\delta_{ij} < 0$. They correspond to exceptions from TP_2 property for OTM call options (left) and from RR_2 property for OTM put options (right). Upper: $T_1 = 10/15/21, T_2 = 11/19/21$, middle: $T_1 = 10/15/21, T_2 = 12/17/21$ and lower: $T_1 = 11/19/21, T_2 = 12/17/21$. The vertical/horizontal red lines are at $K = S_0$. Pricing date 10/4/21.

violations of the $\mathrm{TP}_2/\mathrm{RR}_2$ properties are large enough that they cannot be explained by the spread. There are no exceptions for puts using this test.

The results of the test suggest that the $\mathrm{TP}_2/\mathrm{RR}_2$ properties are well satisfied in a region of strikes around the ATM point and at short maturities. The RR_2 for puts appears to be better satisfied than the TP_2 property for calls.

Away from the ATM point there are more exceptions. In this region, the bid-ask spread increases so the accuracy of the test decreases. It is notable that when using the most favorable version of the difference in δ_{ij}, using bids and asks instead of mid-prices, the exceptions disappear for the puts and are considerably reduced for the calls.

Acknowledgment

We thank Umberto Cherubini for his comments and suggestions.

References

[1] O. Barndorff-Nielsen. Processes of normal inverse Gaussian type. *Finance and Stochastics*, 2: 41–68, 1998.

[2] F. Belzunce and M. Shaked. Stochastic comparisons of mixtures of convexly ordered distributions with applications in reliability theory. *Statistics and Probability Letters*, 53:363–372, 2001.

[3] G. T. Cargo. Comparable means and generalized convexity. *Journal of Mathematical Analysis and Application*, 12:387–392, 1965.

[4] P. Carr, H. Geman, D. Madan, and M. Yor. The fine structure of asset returns: An empirical investigation. *Journal of Business*, 75:305–332, 2002.

[5] P. Carr and R. Lee. Put-call symmetry: Extensions and applications. *Mathematical Finance*, 19(4):523–560, 2009.

[6] P. Carr and D. Madan. Towards a theory of volatility trading. In *Volatility: New Estimation Techniques for Pricing Derivatives*, edited by R.A. Jarrow, vol. 29, pp. 417–427, 1998. Risk Books, London.

[7] P. Carr and L. Torricelli. Additive logistic processes in option pricing. *Finance and Stochastics*, 25(4):689–724, 2021.

[8] C. Donati-Martin, R. Ghomrasni, and M. Yor. On certain Markov processes attached to exponential functionals of Brownian motion; application to Asian options. *Revista Matematica Iberoamericana*, 17(1):179–193, 2001.

[9] B. Dupire. Pricing with a smile. *Risk*, 7:18–20, 1994.

[10] N. Fournier and J. Printemps. Absolute continuity for some one-dimensional processes. *Bernoulli*, 16(2):343–360, 2010.

[11] J. Gatheral. *The Volatility Skew: Arbitrage Constraints and Asymptotic Behaviour*. Merrill Lynch, New York, 1999.

[12] P. Glasserman and D. Pirjol. W-shaped implied volatility curves and the Gaussian mixture model to appear Quantitative Finance. *Quantitative Finance*, 23(4):557–577, 2022.

[13] G.M. Hardy, J.E. Littlewood, and G. Pólya. *Inequalities*, Second Edition. Cambridge University Press, Cambridge, UK, 1952.

[14] F. Hirsch, C. Profeta, B. Roynette, and M. Yor. *Peacocks and Associated Martingales, with Explicit Constructions.* Springer-Verlag, Berlin, 2011.

[15] H. M. Hodges. Arbitrage bounds on the implied volatility strike and term structures of European-style options. *Journal of Derivatives*, 3:23–35, 1996.

[16] M. Keller-Ressel. Total positivity and the classification of term structure shapes in the two-factor Vasicek model. *International Journal of Theoretical and Applied Finance*, 24(5):2150027, 2021.

[17] M. Kijima. Monotonicity and convexity of option prices revisited. *Mathematical Finance*, 12(4):411–425, 2002.

[18] S. Karlin. Total positivity, absorption probabilities and applications. *Transactions of the American Mathematical Society*, 111:33–107, 1964.

[19] S. Karlin. *Total Positivity.* Stanford University Press, Stanford, CA, 1968.

[20] S. Karlin and W. Studden. *Tchebycheff Systems: With Applications in Analysis and Statistics.* Interscience Publishers, New York, 1966.

[21] T. Klassen. Necessary and sufficient no-arbitrage conditions for the SSVI/S3 volatility curve. January 31, 2016. Available at SSRN: https://ssrn.com/abstract=2725700 or http://dx.doi.org/10.2139/ssrn.2725700.

[22] A. Kyprianou. *Introductory Lectures on Lévy Process Fluctuations and Applications.* Springer-Verlag, Berlin, 2006.

[23] J. Lynch, G. Mimmack, and F. Proschan. Uniform stochastic orderings and total positivity. *Canadian Journal of Statistics*, 15(1):63–69, 1987.

[24] D. B. Madan, P. Carr, and E. C. Chang. The variance gamma process and option pricing. *European Finance Review*, 2:79–105, 1998.

[25] D. Madan and M. Yor. Representing the CGMY and Meixner Lévy procesess as time changed Brownian motions. *Journal of Computational Finance*, 12(1):27–47, 2008.

[26] D. B. Madan and E. Seneta. The variance gamma model for share market returns. *Journal of Business,* 63(4):511–524, 1990.

[27] A. W. Marshall, I. Olkin, and B. C. Arnold. *Inequalities: Theory of Majorization and Its Applications*, Second Edition. Springer, New York, 2009.

[28] W. Molenaar and W. R. van Zwet. On mixtures of distributions. *Annals of Mathematical Statistics*, 37(1):281–283, 1966.

[29] J. A. Palmer. Relative convexity. Electrical and Computer Engineering Department, University of California at San Diego, 2003.

[30] M. Shaked and J. G. Shanthikumar. On the first-passage times of pure jump processes. *Journal of Applied Probability*, 25(3):501–509, 1988.

[31] M. Shaked and J. G. Shanthikumar. *Stochastic Orders*, *Springer Series in Statistics*. Springer, New York, 2007.

[32] P. H. Zipkin. The relationship between risk and maturity in a stochastic setting. *Mathematical Finance*, 2:33–46, 1992.

https://doi.org/10.1142/9789811280306_0013

Chapter 13

Supervised Deep Neural Networks (DNNs) for Pricing/Calibration of Vanilla/Exotic Options Under Various Different Processes*

Tugce Karatas[†,¶], **Amir Oskoui**[‡,‖], **and Ali Hirsa**[§,**]

[†]*Tugce Karatas, Morgan Stanley, New York, USA*
[‡]*Amir Oskoui, Amazon, Rockville, Maryland, USA*
[§]*Ali Hirsa, Columbia University, New York, USA*
[¶]*tk2757@columbia.edu*
[‖]*amir.osko@gmail.com*
[**]*ali.hirsa@columbia.edu*

Abstract
We apply supervised deep neural networks (DNNs) for pricing and calibration of both vanilla and exotic options under both diffusion and pure-jump processes with and without stochastic volatility. We train our neural network models under different numbers of layers, neurons per layer and various different activation functions in order to find which combinations work better empirically. For training, we consider various different loss functions and optimization routines. We demonstrate that

*We would like to thank participants at Shanghai Advanced Institute of Finance, Shanghai, China, Orient Securities, Shanghai, China, and Cubist Systematic Strategies, New York, for their comments and suggestions on this study. Errors are our own responsibility.

deep neural networks exponentially expedite option pricing compared to commonly used option pricing methods which consequently make calibration and parameter estimation super fast.

Keywords: Machine learning, Derivatives, Deep neural networks

1. Introduction

A major component of model calibration and parameter estimation are derivatives pricing. Aside from few cases, there is no closed-form solution for derivatives pricing. In computational finance, it is critical to find a fast and accurate approximation for cases where there is no analytical solution. Some of these approaches could be very time-consuming and to possess a model that is accurate and fast in pricing is central. Movement in time can make the calculated values obsolete. Hence, the time it takes to re-compute these values is pivotal in derivatives business. Sometimes it is possible to exploit redundancies in the calculations, for example, pricing via fast Fourier techniques (FFT) [1], which results in a vector of prices on the same underlier for different strikes. To do so, it takes advantage of redundant matrix operations and cuts down on computational cost. In the setting of neural networks, once training is done, the mapping from input parameters $\mathbf{X}$ to an output price $\mathbf{y}$ has been optimized to give the smallest loss, through many iterations of updates on weights and biases in combination with permutations of nonlinear activation functions. In Figure 1, we illustrate the collection of deep learning activation functions. Hence, with its trained architecture, the calculation of prices using neural networks both with and without feedback connections which mimic the idea of context or memory in the brain (i.e., recurrent and feedforward neural networks, respectively) becomes elementary and at the same time super fast.

In this chapter, we revisit the original work of Das and Culkin (2017) that used deep neural networks for option pricing and explore various architectures and extend the work to more advanced models and different contracts. We show how feedforward neural networks can be used in the context of derivative pricing to achieve speed-ups of many orders of magnitude. As are the laws of conservation, the speed-up comes with a cost of accuracy. However, we show the loss in accuracy is well within a worst-case estimate of bid-ask spreads,

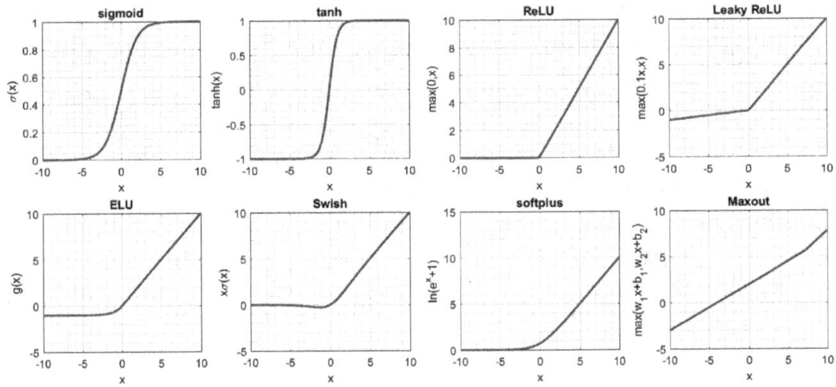

Figure 1. Collection of deep learning activation functions.

making the method practical. We demonstrate how to create labels to train the model for vanilla and exotic options (with weak and strong path dependence) under diffusion and pure-jump processes with and without stochastic volatility [2–4]. To optimize speed and accuracy of the neural network's learning, we use many perturbations of hyper-parameters (i.e., number of layers, neurons per layer and activation functions). In particular, we show how European, barrier and American option prices can be trained and priced out-of-sample swiftly and accurately under geometric Brownian motion (GBM) [5] and variance gamma (VG) [6], both with and without stochastic arrivals [2,3]. We show that this method trumps traditional techniques for option pricing which results in super-fast calibration and parameter estimation.

1.1. *Introduction to Models*

To model market behavior, we used four different processes: (a) geometric Brownian motion (GBM) [5], (b) geometric Brownian motion with stochastic arrival (GBMSA), a.k.a Heston stochastic volatility model [2], (c) variance-gamma (VG) model [6] and (4) variance gamma with stochastic arrival (VGSA) [3].

The first two are pure diffusion processes with constant and stochastic volatility, respectively. The last two are pure-jump processes, mirroring the diffusion cases, VG has constant volatility whereas VGSA has stochastic arrivals to allow for volatility clustering [3]. GBM as in the Black–Merton–Scholes model is the most well known for derivatives pricing [5]. However, its assumption of a constant volatility does not reflect market behavior, leading to an implied volatility surface that facilitates model inputs to match market prices. The variance-gamma process is a pure-jump process with time-changed Brownian motion to account for high activity [6]. It is shown that with addition of two extra parameters skewness and kurtosis, we can closely fit the smile across strikes for a fixed maturity [6]. Both GBMSA and VGSA are stochastic volatility models for diffusion and jump processes, respectively, with an effort to model non-constant volatility, as is observed in the market, enabling "us to calibrate to option price surfaces across both strike and maturity simultaneously" [7].

2. Brief Introduction to Neural Networks

2.1. *Feedforward Neural Networks*

Here, we will briefly introduce feedforward neural networks, but for a more detailed discussion of DNNs, we refer the reader to Chapter 6 of Deep Learning by Goodfellow, Bengio and Courville . Feedforward neural networks, also called deep feedforward networks, are considered "quintessential" to deep learning with the goal of approximating a function: f^* [8], where the network defines a mapping $\boldsymbol{y} = f(\boldsymbol{x}; \boldsymbol{\theta})$ and learns the appropriate parameter set $\boldsymbol{\theta}$ that leads to an optimal function approximation. The network is basically a composition of many different functions in a chain. The more of these functions that are applied to your input data $\mathbf{X}$, the more **layers** in your network. The length of functions compositely applied is in a sense the **depth** of the model. These networks must be trained in order to mimic a function or model.

Training data are provided accompanying the input x so that the learning algorithm can decide how to use its layers to produce values as close as possible to $\hat{y}$. During training, we have an optimizer that drives the output of the neural network $y = f(x)$ to match $\hat{y} = f^*(x)$. Hence, the neural network learns to use its layers to minimize an **objective function**, in our case a mean-squared-error function:

$$MSE = \frac{1}{N}\sum_{i=1}^{N}(y - \hat{y})^2.$$

The training data only indicate what values the output layer must approximate for each input x; however, they do not directly indicate

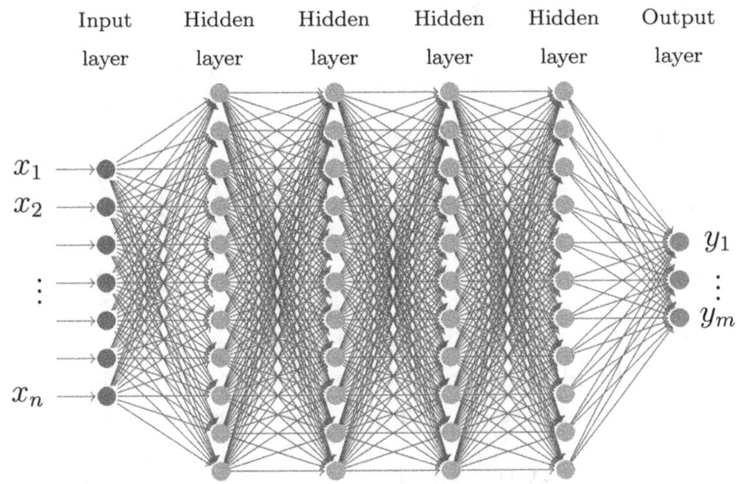

Figure 2. A graphical visualization of a deep neural network.

how to use the layers to optimally approximate f^*. When initially looking at training data, it is not clear what the appropriate output for each layer should be, which is why they are referred to as **hidden layers** in a "neural" network.

The term neural comes from a loose inspiration of neuroscience and the dimensionality of these hidden layers, as the width of each layer is based on the number of elements within it that are mapping a vector to a scalar via a nonlinear activation function. In that sense, each of these elements is analogous to a **neuron** because they are taking inputs from many different things and applying their own activation function [8]. A visualization of both depth and width in a feedforward neural network can be seen in Figure 2.

2.2. *Convolutional Neural Networks*

Another way of specializing neural networks to replicate complex functions in high dimensions is convolutional neural networks, also referred to as CNNs [9]. They often work well with data that "have a clear grid-structured topology" like time-series data or image data which are 1D and 2D grids, respectively [8]. Their huge success in practical applications for high-dimensional functions leads us to believe it could be tremendously useful and intuitive to use in the context of Asian options as they have a grid-like topology [10].

2.3. *"Wide" vs "Deep"*

In Figure 3, there is a visualization of the "effect of depth" showing how an increased number of layers in a neural network (i.e., deepness) results in higher accuracy of prediction shown by Goodfellow *et al.* (2014d). This seems like a compelling point that favors deepness of the neural network; however, Zogoruyko and Komadakis (2017) noted that by doubling the number of layers, accuracy was only improved by a fraction of a percent, leading to a "problem of diminishing feature reuse, which makes these networks very slow to train." They demonstrated how a "wide" neural network (meaning the number of hidden units is at least twice the input dimension) of only 16 layers could outperform "deep" neural networks including "thousand-layer-deep networks, achieving new state-of-the-art results on CIFAR, SVHN and COCO and significant improvements on ImageNet." In the context of derivative pricing, we have also explored these two compelling arguments and the results can be seen

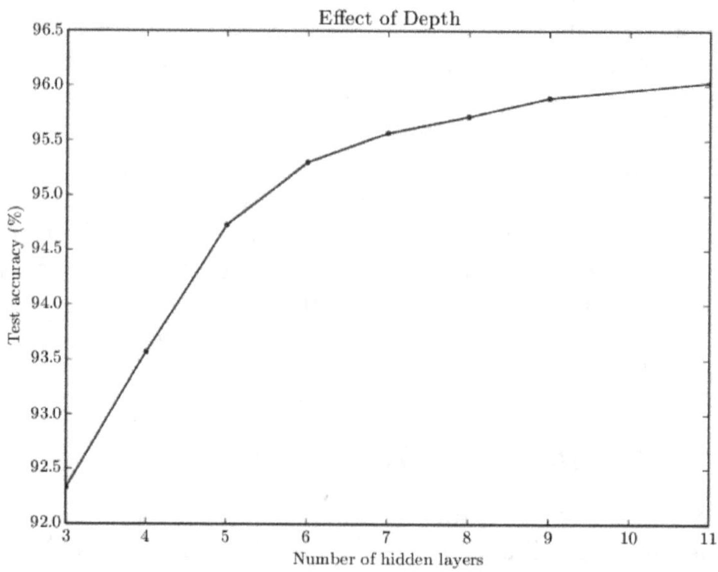

Figure 3. Empirical results showing that deeper networks generalize better when used to transcribe multi-digit numbers from photographs of addresses. Data from Goodfellow *et al.* (2014d). The test set accuracy consistently increases with increasing depth. [5]

in Figure 9. This result clearly highlighted the diminishing accuracy of the networks with an increase in depth, resulting in us to explore an optimal width for our hidden layers as shown in Figure 8 which will be discussed further.

2.4. *Dropout*

After exhausting the width and depth dimensions of our neural network, another idea worth exercising is dropout, which is introduced by Srivastava *et al.* (2014) [11]. To prevent overfitting of the model, we can force our neural network to learn the more robust features in conjunction with many different random subsets of the other neurons. This is called dropout because nodes of the network are dropped with a probability 1-p at each training stage.

2.5. *Choice of Optimizer and Global vs. Local Convergence*

Once this structure has been integrated into the neural network, optimization can be done using a choice of either gradient descent or more sophisticated routines like RMSProp, Adam or stochastic gradient descent (SGD) with momentum. Hence, as for deciding the choice of optimizer in this architecture, we introduce some insights, both local and global, studied by Soltanolkotabi *et al.* (2018) for reaching optima on wide and overparameterized neural networks [12]. For a 2-layered neural network with leaky ReLU activation function, Soudry and Carmon (2016) have shown that a global minimum can be obtained using gradient descent on a modified loss function; however, this doesn't evince that the global minimum of the original loss function is reached [13]. Li and Yuan (2017) have introduced identity mapping, by which SGD always converges to the global minimum for a 2-layered neural network with ReLU activation function under the standard weight initialization scheme [14]. Under similar realistic assumptions, Kawaguchi's studies showed that all local minima are global minima using nonlinear activation functions [15]. Additionally, under several assumptions, Choromanska *et al.* (2015) have simplified the loss function to a polynomial with i.i.d. Gaussian coefficients, showing that using stochastic gradient descent all critical points found “are local minima of high quality” meaning the test error value is comparable to that at the global minima [16]. They concluded that global minima are more difficult to reach with larger networks, but in practice, it’s “irrelevant as global minimum often leads to overfitting” [16].

To further generalize previous studies, Kawaguchi *et al.* (2018) show that without the overparameterization or any simplification assumption, local minima of the DNN are theoretically “no worse than the globally optimal values of corresponding classical machine learning models” [17]. This theoretical observation was supported empirically using stochastic gradient descent with momentum as their optimizer during training for ReLU, leaky ReLU and absolute value activation functions [17]. Around the same time, Allen-Zhu *et al.* (2018) noted that under the non-degenerate input and over-parameterization assumption, global optima can be reached using simple algorithms such as SGD during training of the DNN, but this result cannot be extended to testing [18]. Furthermore, Kingma and Ba (2014) have introduced Adam (adaptive moment estimation) optimization routine and they have shown that Adam converges faster compared to SGD and RMSProp when a neural network with ReLU activation function is trained [19]. These theoretical and empirical findings lead us to use more sophisticated optimization routines rather than gradient descent.

For our problem, we first used stochastic gradient descent (SGD) as the optimization routine which was painfully slow in training the model as expected. We then utilized RMSprop and Adam optimization routines since they are both commonly used by practitioners. Adam was of particular interest because it combines advantages from both AdaGrad and RMSProp, which are both extensions to stochastic gradient descent. Based on our empirical observations, both RMSprop and Adam converges much faster than SGD. Furthermore, Adam seems to work better than RMSprop, in parallel with what was expected from its bias-correction term and the insights mentioned above for an overparameterized DNN with ReLU, leaky ReLU and absolute value activation functions [19, 20]. Thus, for the remainder of this chapter, Adam is used as our optimization routine for training the network.

3. Labels and Parameter Selection

In order to implement supervised deep neural networks, many labels are needed for training. These labels are generated from existing[2] models. Table 1 shows some classical techniques for pricing options and it shows under a given model which types of options can be used for pricing. Monte Carlo simulation is commonly considered the slowest among these methods, and when it comes to trees, they have an order of complexity that is quadratic with each time step. Now, even though discretization may lead Monte Carlo simulation in terms of speeds and they both have a very wide domain of option types and models where they can be used, they are both still considered computationally expensive in practice. Leaving us with the transform techniques like the FFT method, which may be named "fast" but still takes a reasonable amount of time to run and these transforms are not applicable for path-dependent options. This results in the crux of our problem, in other words, the most expensive and computationally time-consuming step when using supervised deep neural networks is generating labels from these existing methodologies. Once labels are generated, training feedforward neural networks become almost trivial.

After deciding on which method and model to use for each option, the next step is to decide on market and model parameter ranges. Before going through model parameters for each option, we first start by deciding on the range of market parameters, which will be the same throughout all models and options. As we stated before, supervised deep neural networks necessitate creating a large number of labels from existing models. There are a general set of parameters that are common among all of these models: initial stock price (S_0), strike price (K), maturity (T), interest rate (r) and dividend yield (q). Using the fact that option prices are linear homogeneous in S_0 and K as seen in Black–Merton–Scholes option pricing formula, instead of considering both S_0 and K as two separate parameters, we will

[2]By existing models, we mean analytical or computational models used for derivatives pricing, e.g., transform techniques, numerical solutions of PDEs or PIDEs, Monte Carlo simulation and the like.

Table 1. Pricing schemes for various different models/processes.

Model	Pricing model/method: Transform techniques			PDEs/PIDEs			MC simulation			DNN		
	Vanilla	Weak	Exotic	Vanilla	Weak	Exotic	Vanilla	Weak	Exotic	Vanilla	Weak	Exotic
GBM	✓	✓	×	✓	✓	✓	✓	✓	✓	✓	✓	✓
VG	✓	✓	×	✓	✓	✓	✓	✓	✓	✓	✓	✓
GBMSA	✓	✓	×	✓	✓	✓	✓	✓	✓	✓	✓	?
VGSA	✓	✓	×	✓	✓	✓	✓	✓	✓	✓	✓	?

Table 2. Product and market parameters.

Parameter	Range
Moneyness (S_0/K)	$0.8 \rightarrow 1.2$
Maturity (T)	1 day $\rightarrow$ 3 years
Dividend rate (q)	$0\% \rightarrow 3\%$
Risk free rate (r)	$1\% \rightarrow 3\%$

only consider the ratio S_0/K that is the option moneyness. Table 2 shows the product and market parameters we have considered for each model. For training, we generated labels within 20% moneyness. The range for the maturity of the options is from 1 day to 3 years.

3.1. *European Options*

In the case of vanilla options, there are many available methods for pricing including Fast Fourier Transform (FFT), trees and Monte Carlo simulation. Leading us to build a Deep Neural Network (DNN) trained on closed-form generated call and put prices from the Black–Merton–Scholes formula for the GBM model. For the VG, VGSA and GBMSA models, the deep neural network is trained using labels obtained via FFT considering we have the characteristic function of the logarithm of the stock price process under these models.

The process begins with creating an input parameter matrix $\mathbf{X}$, which consists of different combinations of market and model parameters. Here, model parameters are volatility (σ) for the GBM model; volatility (σ), skewness (θ) and kurtosis (ν) for the VG model; rate of mean reversion (κ), correlation between stock and variance (ρ), long term variance (θ), volatility of variance (σ) and the initial variance (v_0) for the GBMSA model; and volatility (σ), skewness (θ), kurtosis (ν), rate of mean reversion (κ), the long-term rate of time change (η) and the volatility of the time change (λ) for the VGSA model. Table 3 shows the ranges of model parameters we have considered for European options.

After determining the ranges for the parameters, the parameter combinations are sampled via two different approaches. The first one is non-quasi approach, where parameter combinations are sampled at

Table 3. Model parameters.

GBM	Range	VG	Range	GBMSA	Range	VGSA	Range
σ	$0.05 \to 0.50$	σ	$0.05 \to 0.50$	σ	$0.05 \to 0.50$	σ	$0.05 \to 0.50$
		θ	$-0.90 \to -0.05$	κ	$0.20 \to 2.00$	θ	$-0.90 \to -0.05$
		ν	$0.05 \to 1.00$	ρ	$-0.90 \to -0.10$	ν	$0.05 \to 1.00$
				θ	$0.01 \to 0.20$	κ	$0.20 \to 3.00$
				v_0	$0.01 \to 0.20$	η	$0.01 \to 0.20$
						λ	$0.01 \to 0.20$

random, uniformly over the given ranges of market and model parameters. The second approach is the quasi approach. For this approach, we benefit from Halton sequences [21], which are deterministic and of low discrepancy. Here, we considered a 5D Halton sequence for the GBM model, 7D for the VG model, 9D for GBMSA model and 10D for the VGSA model. For this approach, Halton sequences are generated in the R platform as the first step. Then, the value of each parameter is obtained by multiplying the numbers, which are obtained from Halton sequences, with the range of the parameter and summing it with the lower bound of the corresponding parameter.

After the parameter ranges and sampling methods are chosen, the next step is to decide on the training size. Here, we considered four different training sizes, which are 40,000, 80,000, 160,000 and 240,000, in order to observe the effect of the training size on the performance. Each data set is generated separately. As expected, the discrepancy between data points decreases as training size increases. For this reason, it is expected that the performance of the model increases as training size increases.

Once the input parameter matrix $\mathbf{X} = [\mathbf{S_0}/\mathbf{K}, \mathbf{T}, \mathbf{r}, \mathbf{q}, \boldsymbol{\sigma}]$ is produced for the GBM model, the output vector $\boldsymbol{y} = \mathbf{EC}/\mathbf{K}$ is obtained by using the closed form Black–Merton–Scholes formula, where $\mathbf{EC}$ is the price of European call option. For VG, GBMSA and VGSA models, the output vector $\boldsymbol{y} = \mathbf{EC}/\mathbf{K}$ is obtained by using the FFT algorithm for corresponding input parameter matrices $\mathbf{X}$. Therefore, $(\mathbf{X}, \boldsymbol{y})$ will form the training set of the deep neural network.

3.2. *Barrier Options*

To introduce some path dependence, we transition implementation to barrier options, for which, closed-form solutions are available in the

GBM setting. However, prices are usually computed using Monte Carlo simulation for beyond GBM.[3] In this section, we will focus on pricing an Up-and-Out Put (UOP) options, where the variance-gamma and geometric Brownian motion models are used to describe the market both with and without stochastic arrivals. The ranges of all product and market parameters are the same as that of European options as in Table 2 except the range of $\mathbf{H}/\mathbf{K}$, where $\mathbf{H}$ is the barrier level. Since we used the normalized values for stock prices and option prices, we consider the normalized values of barrier levels as well. For $\mathbf{H}/\mathbf{K}$, we consider the range between $\mathbf{S_0}/\mathbf{K}$ and 1.2, where 1.2 is the upper bound for moneyness considered before. The reason behind the lower bound of this range is that the barrier level must be greater than the initial stock price for up-and-out barrier options. Furthermore, the ranges of the model parameters come from Table 3 as in European options. Again, the parameter combinations are sampled at random uniformly over the given ranges of market and model parameters.

Once the input parameter matrix $\mathbf{X} = [\mathbf{S_0}/\mathbf{K}, \mathbf{H}/\mathbf{K}, \mathbf{T}, \mathbf{r}, \mathbf{q}, \boldsymbol{\sigma}]$ is produced for the GBM model, the output vector $\boldsymbol{y} = \mathbf{UOP}/\mathbf{K}$ is obtained by using the closed form solution. Here, $\mathbf{UOP}$ is the price of up-and-out put options. For the GBMSA and VGSA models, the output vector $\boldsymbol{y} = \mathbf{UOP}/\mathbf{K}$ is obtained by using Monte Carlo procedure for their corresponding input parameter matrices $\mathbf{X}$. This procedure is based on 10,000 price paths of the underlying for the GBMSA model and 8000 price paths of the underlying for the VGSA model where each simulated path has 100 time steps. For details on how to simulate GBMSA or VGSA processes, see [7] page 239.

3.3. *American Options*

Now to really get to see where neural networks can transform the norm for pricing times, we introduce the strong path dependence of American options to this architecture. American options are usually priced using either Monte Carlo simulation or tree methods. Since both of these methods are relatively time-consuming, we

[3]Depends on the payoff, we can apply transform techniques like the Cosine-Fourier (COS) method [22] for pricing some barrier options, however for this study, we tried Monte Carlo methods for pricing.

construct a fully connected feedforward neural network trained on the prices of American options generated via the Ju–Zhong (JZ) approximation in the GBM model. With input parameter matrix $\mathbf{X} = [\mathbf{S_0}/\mathbf{K}, \mathbf{T}, \mathbf{r}, \mathbf{q}, \boldsymbol{\sigma}]$, the output vector $\boldsymbol{y} = \mathbf{AJZ}/\mathbf{K}$ is obtained by using the Ju–Zhong approximation. Here, $\mathbf{JZ}$ is the price of American put options under the Ju–Zhong approximation. Therefore, $(\mathbf{X}, \boldsymbol{y})$ will form the training set of the deep neural network. While generating input parameter matrices for American options, we used the non-quasi approach, which is described in Section 3.1. Therefore, market parameter combinations are generated at random uniformly over the ranges provided in Table 2, and the model parameter σ is generated from a uniform random distribution over the range between 0.05 and 0.50.

4. Training

Once training sets $(\mathbf{X}, \boldsymbol{y})$ are obtained for each model and option type, they are fed to the deep neural network algorithm. We train each model under a different number of layers, a different number of neurons per layer and various different activation function combinations in order to observe which combinations work better empirically under given training sets.

4.1. *Structure/Architecture*

Nonlinearity in the model is introduced through activation functions. We use different combinations of activation functions. In this experiment, we have considered exponential linear unit (elu), rectified linear unit (relu), leaky rectified linear unit (leaky relu) and sigmoid activation functions. For both sigmoid and tanh functions, if the input is either very large or small, the slope of the activation becomes very small resulting in a slow down for gradient descent making either of these functions not well suited for hidden layers [23]. However, to not rule anything out, we have still stress-tested permutations of these activation functions and visualized the results. There is a common preference toward rectified linear unit (relu) for hidden layers as its derivative is 1 for all positive inputs and 0 for negative ones, and to avoid a zero derivative in many cases, leaky relu can be substituted [24].

As we expected, Figures 4 and 5 illustrate that a sigmoid activation function is not suitable for our structure, and going forward, we will omit using it in our model and continue with the combinations of elu, relu and leaky relu activation functions. After testing all possible combinations of these three activation functions for 2, 3 and 4 number of layers, we realized that the trained models with initial activation function of leaky relu perform better compared to

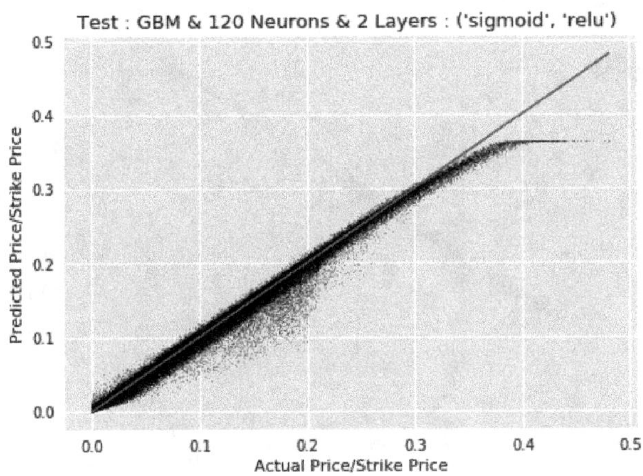

Figure 4. Sample 1.

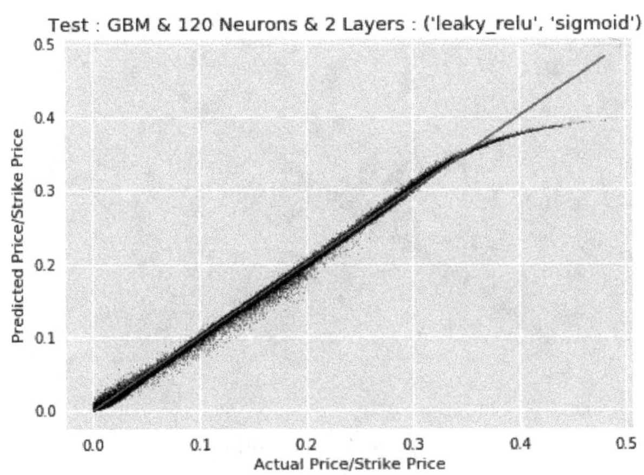

Figure 5. Sample 2.

other trained models. Figures 6 and 7 are good examples for this argument. This argument is not only valid for the GBM model but is also true for other processes as well. Based on these empirical observations, we will set the initial activation function as leaky relu and test different combinations of activation functions for other hidden layers. We will then select the trained model with the smallest MSE value or the largest R^2 value as our pricing neural net.

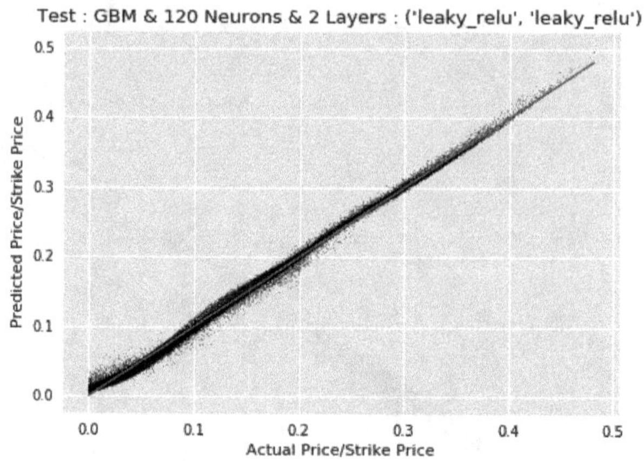

Figure 6. Sample 3.

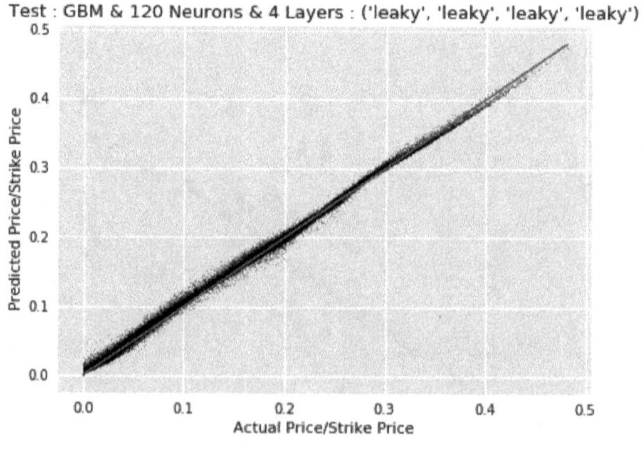

Figure 7. Sample 4.

4.2. *Diagnostics*

After testing different combinations of activation functions, the next step is to test the effect of a different number of layers as well as a different number of neurons per layer. In the first experiment, we keep the number of layers and the set of activation functions fixed and vary the number of neurons per layer. Figure 8 shows how the R^2 value changes as the number of neurons per layer increases. Here, we train deep neural network with European call option prices under the GBM model. There are four hidden layers, and the activation function is leaky relu for each hidden layer. We can see in Figure 8 that as the number of neurons per layer increases, the neural net model performs better, but there are diminishing returns. After 120 neurons per layer, there is a plateauing result, making it pointless to increase the number of neurons per layer further. Hence, we used 120 neurons per layer as default.

In Figure 9, we examine the model performance as the number of layers is increased. We show how root mean square error (RMSE) changes when we increase the number of layers for European call options under the GBM model. This finding is pretty consistent for other models. It can be seen in Figure 9 that as the number of layers increases, the model performance gets better. But this improvement is limited to four layers. After that, as soon as we use five layers or higher, RMSE value increases. It can be interpreted in a way that as we increase the number of layers, after some point, there will be an

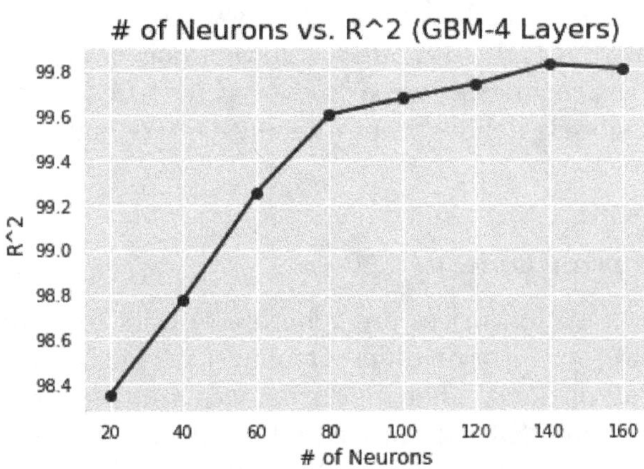

Figure 8. Number of neurons vs. R^2.

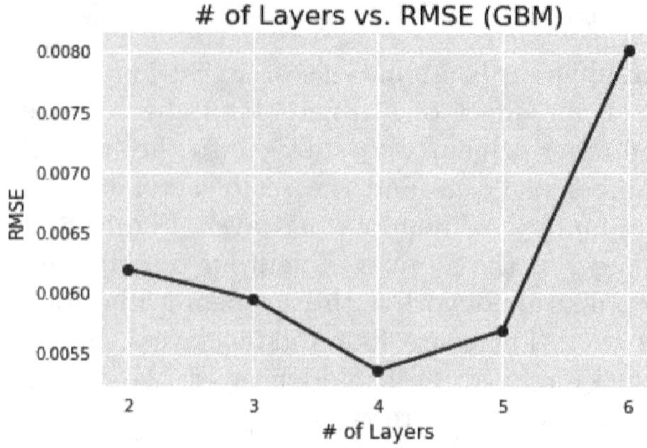

Figure 9. Number of layers vs. RMSE.

overparametrization problem. Based on this observation, we cap the number of layers in our neural network to four.

5. Validation

Once we obtain the optimal neural network architecture for each model and each option type, we need to check the architecture's validity. In order to do so, we check our trained model for three cases: (1) interpolation, (2) deep-out-of-the-money and (3) longer maturity. In the first case, we just validate it for interpolated points on our testing set. In the second case, we keep everything else fixed and test how the trained models behave when S_0/K is between 0.6 and 0.8. In the third case, we keep everything else fixed and test how the trained models behave when the maturity is between 3 years and 5 years.

5.1. *European Options*

European call option prices are generated under four different models; hence, we obtain four different neural network architectures for European call options. Their performances are measured in terms of mean square error (MSE) and R^2 values. Table 4 provides the summary of the empirical results for the trained models under GBM and VG, and Table 5 provides the summary of the empirical results for

Table 4. European option pricing under GBM and VG.

	GBM				VG			
Training set size	40,000	80,000	160,000	240,000	40,000	80,000	160,000	240,000
In-sample								
MSE	0.000060	0.000034	0.000029	0.000018	0.000678	0.000059	0.000046	0.000028
R^2	99.32%	99.62%	99.67%	99.79%	94.18%	99.50%	99.61%	99.76%
Deep-out-of-the-money								
MSE	0.000065	0.000054	0.000022	0.000014	0.000376	0.000071	0.000050	0.000042
R^2	95.37%	96.17%	98.47%	98.70%	83.78%	96.92%	97.83%	98.17%
Longer maturity								
MSE	0.000348	0.000184	0.000191	0.000129	0.004338	0.000643	0.000524	0.000378
R^2	97.34%	98.59%	98.54%	99.01%	69.03%	95.41%	96.26%	97.30%

Table 5. European option pricing under GBMSA and VGSA.

	GBMSA				VGSA			
Training set size	40,000	80,000	160,000	240,000	40,000	80,000	160,000	240,000
In-sample								
MSE	0.000122	0.000059	0.000032	0.000025	0.000240	0.000230	0.000244	0.000092
R^2	98.48%	99.22%	99.60%	99.69%	98.23%	98.31%	98.21%	99.32%
Deep-out-of-the-money								
MSE	0.000066	0.000032	0.000021	0.000016	0.000226	0.000324	0.000271	0.000150
R^2	93.48%	96.88%	97.97%	98.46%	94.00%	91.38%	92.79%	96.00%
Longer maturity								
MSE	0.000362	0.000237	0.000158	0.000103	0.000647	0.000724	0.000755	0.000377
R^2	96.36%	97.61%	98.41%	98.97%	95.92%	95.43%	95.23%	97.62%

the trained models under the GBMSA and VGSA models. For all these tables, the in-sample test size and the test sizes for deep-out-of-the-money and longer maturity cases are taken as 60,000.

According to the results in Tables 4 and 5, it can be observed that as the training size increases, the performance of the trained models increases but there are diminishing returns. The second result is that the performance of the trained neural net under the GBM model is better than all other processes. This is probably because as the number of parameters increases, the process becomes more complicated to learn and probably more labels are needed to train them.

As for one example, Figure 10 shows the performance of the architecture for the GBMSA model under in-sample test data, deep-out-of-the-money and longer maturity extrapolation data.

Furthermore, we have also studied the case where the training data set is generated with deep-out-of-the-money European call option prices under the GBM model. Therefore, by keeping all other parameter ranges the same, we generated the training data set with S_0/K between 0.6 and 0.8. Table 6 provides the summary of the empirical results for the corresponding trained model under the GBM model. As in the previous tables, we check our trained model for interpolation and longer maturity cases. We also check our model for the case where S_0/K is between 0.8 and 1.2, and it is under out-of-the-money label in Table 6. When the results are compared with the results in Table 4, it is seen that in-sample results are very similar. However, it is also seen that extrapolation results are better in Table 6. Therefore, it can be concluded that although we trained the model with deep-out-of-the-money option prices, the neural network provides good predictions when the option prices are out-of-the-money. It is important to note that by out-of-the-money, we mean the moneyness between 0.8 and 1.2.

Up until now, we have only obtained results using the non-quasi approach. In order to see how well the quasi approach works, we implemented it for generating data for European call options under the GBM model. Figure 11 shows the results obtained for both non-quasi and quasi approaches. It is shown that when the data are generated by using Halton sequences, the model fit is slightly better.

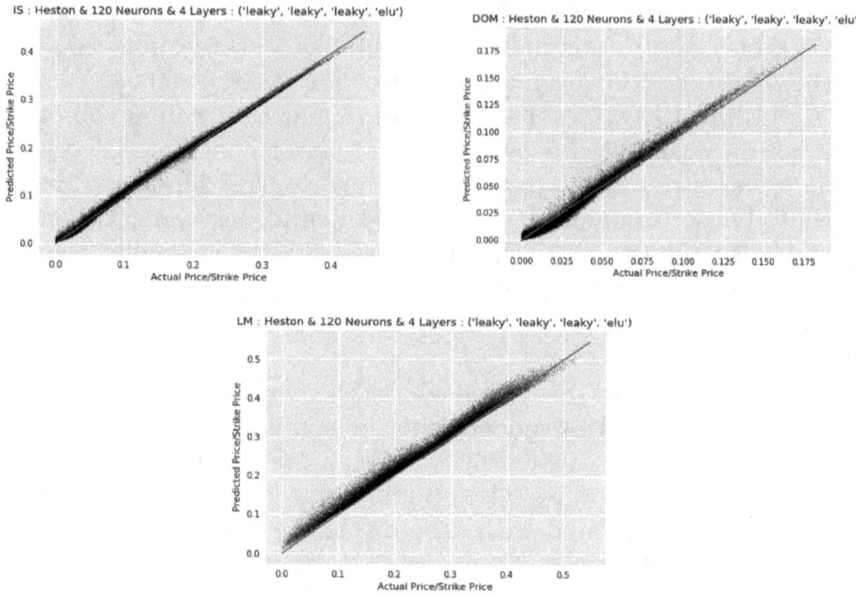

Figure 10. Performance of pricing machine under GBMSA model — EC.

Table 6. European option pricing under GBM-2.

Training set size	40,000	80,000	160,000	240,000
In-sample				
MSE	0.000138	0.000042	0.000029	0.000018
R^2	99.30%	99.79%	99.85%	99.91%
Out-of-the-money				
MSE	0.000166	0.000034	0.000020	0.000014
R^2	98.09%	99.61%	99.78%	99.84%
Longer maturity				
MSE	0.001845	0.000311	0.000285	0.000221
R^2	92.75%	98.78%	98.88%	99.13%

5.2. *Barrier Options*

Up-and-out barrier put option prices are generated under three different models; hence, we implemented three different neural networks for pricing UOPs. For the GBMSA and VGSA models, we take the

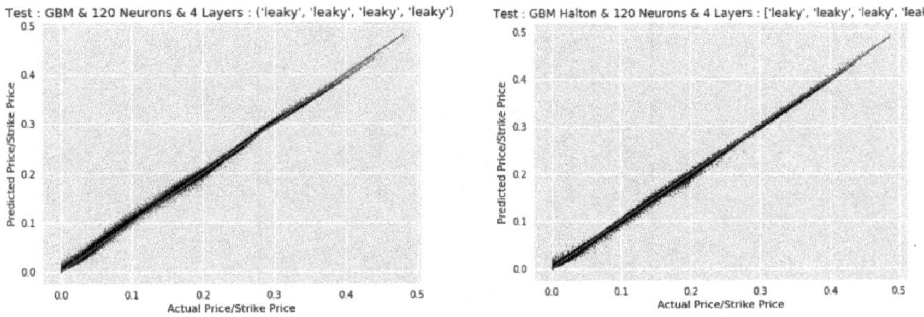

Figure 11. Non-quasi approach vs. quasi approach under GBM model — EC.

maximum training size as 160,000 because Monte Carlo procedure is computationally expensive, and from the last section, we know that the performances of the models trained with 160,000 data points and 240,000 data points are close enough. Table 7 provides the summary of the empirical results for the trained models under the GBM, GBMSA and VGSA models.

As it is seen in Table 7, as the number of parameters in the model decreases, the performance of the trained model increases. As an example, Figure 12 shows the performance of GBM model under in-sample test data and longer maturity extrapolation data.

As in the case of European options, we also applied the quasi approach for up-and-out barrier put options under the GBM model. Figure 13 shows the results obtained with both non-quasi and quasi approaches. We can conclude that when the data are generated under the quasi approach, the model fit is better.

5.3. *American Options*

American call option prices were generated under the GBM model using the Ju–Zhong approximation. The empirical results from the neural network trained using these data are summarized in Table 8. Additionally, Figure 14 shows the performance of this architecture, trained under the Ju–Zhong approximation of the GBM model, for in-sample test data and deep-out-of-the-money extrapolation data from left to right, respectively.

Table 7. Barrier option pricing under GBM, GBMSA and VGSA.

	GBM				GBMSA			VGSA		
Training set size	40,000	80,000	160,000	240,000	40,000	80,000	160,000	40,000	80,000	160,000
In-sample										
MSE	0.000159	0.000038	0.000017	0.000016	0.000114	0.000083	0.000026	0.000149	0.000089	0.000031
R^2	95.60%	98.94%	99.54%	99.57%	96.65%	97.55%	99.24%	95.13%	97.09%	99.00%
Deep-out-of-the-money										
MSE	0.000684	0.000617	0.000766	0.000562	0.001230	0.000965	0.000764	0.002254	0.001733	0.001275
R^2	83.64%	67.65%	91.29%	93.61%	85.43%	91.68%	90.04%	67.53%	75.86%	82.86%
Longer maturity										
MSE	0.000490	0.000107	0.000042	0.000048	0.000288	0.000167	0.000053	0.000163	0.000160	0.000067
R^2	86.92%	97.15%	98.87%	98.71%	91.48%	95.07%	98.43%	94.06%	94.16%	97.55%

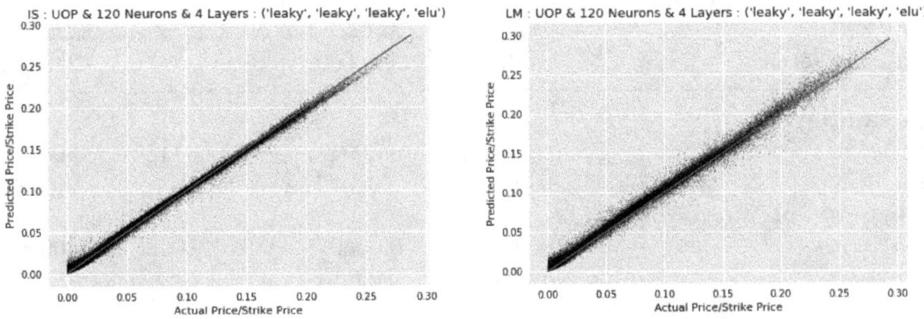

Figure 12. Performance of pricing machine under GBM model — UOBP.

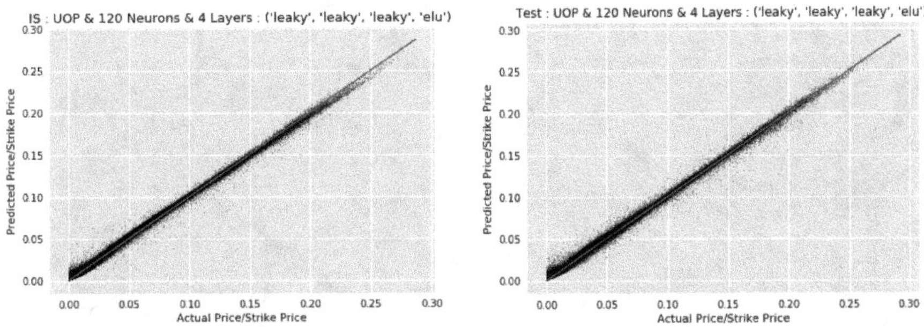

Figure 13. Non-quasi approach vs. quasi approach under GBM model — UOBP.

6. Deep Neural Network vs. Recurrent Neural Network

Although the trained feedforward neural network for pricing American call options performs well, as mentioned earlier, it is pretty expensive to generate labels for American options. Knowing American options are strongly path-dependent options, we might benefit from recurrent neural networks in pricing them. While generating data, input parameters (except maturity) are sampled at random uniformly over the ranges defined before. For maturity, we define discrete time steps from 1 to 12 months. Figure 15 provides a comparison between the performances of deep neural networks and recurrent neural networks. According to the numerical results, the MSE value of DNN model is slightly smaller than that of the RNN model. On the other hand, there is a big gap between training times of the two models. In our experiment training, DNNs took 50% more time than RNNs.

Table 8. American option pricing under GBM.

Training set size	40,000	80,000	160,000	240,000
In-sample				
MSE	0.000196	0.000187	0.000113	0.000025
R^2	99.04%	99.10%	99.45%	99.88%
Deep-out-of-the-money				
MSE	0.000221	0.000078	0.000098	0.000092
R^2	82.70%	93.88%	92.30%	92.79%
Longer maturity				
MSE	0.000788	0.000500	0.000364	0.000812
R^2	97.55%	98.44%	98.87%	97.48%

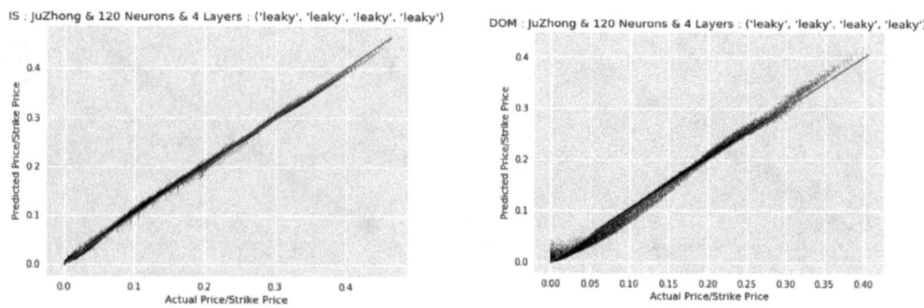

Figure 14. Performance of pricing machine trained on the Ju–Zhong approximation of GBM model — JZ.

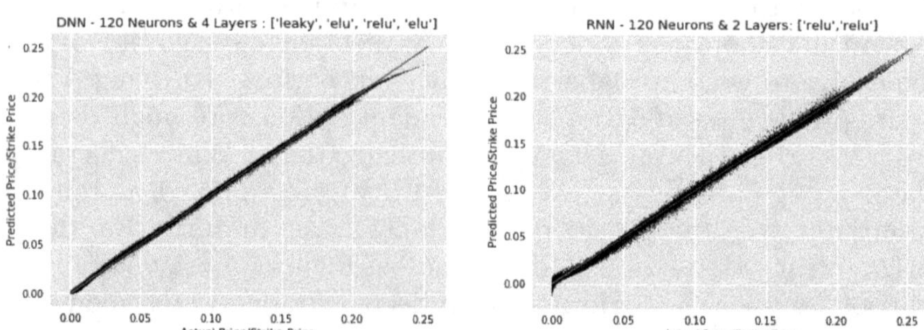

Figure 15. DNN vs. RNN.

Although neural networks are proficient at storing implicit knowledge, they struggle with memorization of facts (i.e., a working memory). Human beings' ability to be able to hold memory and affiliate it with some context is critical for problem solving. Hence, a recurrent neural network, or in other words a neural network equipped with feedback loops, can "not only rapidly and 'intentionally' store and retrieve facts but also sequentially reason with them" [8], enticing us to further explore the possibilities of an RNN's architecture in our future works.

7. Conclusion

In this chapter, we utilized a fully connected feedforward neural network to price vanilla, barrier and American options under the GBM, VG, GBMSA and VGSA regimes and explore the benefits of introducing recurrent neural networks to this task. The crux of the problem is creating labels and selecting hyper-parameters for training of the deep neural network. We used sample sizes of 300,000 points for training and 60,000 points for validation. We observed with an increase in depth in layers and neurons per layer the accuracy of the predictions increases but eventually diminishes. Once the training is done, the model can be used for derivative pricing for market parameters both within and reasonably outside the initial range of the training set with very low error. We also compared the performances of feedforward and recurrent neural networks for American put options. We observed that training time of RNNs is almost half of the training time of DNNs, which encourages us to explore RNNs further in our future work. All in all, once labels are created, training and predicting options prices are very inexpensive computationally. This architecture results in speed-ups of many orders of magnitude, making it practical and easy to implement and use.

References

[1] P. Carr and D. Madan. Option valuation using the fast Fourier transform. *Journal of Computational Finance*, 2(4):61–73, 1999.

[2] S. L. Heston. A closed-form solution for options with stochastic volatility with applications to bond and currency options. *The Review of Financial Studies*, 6(2):327–343, 1993.

[3] P. Carr, H. Geman, D. B. Madan, and M. Yor. Stochastic volatility for Lévy processes. *Mathematical Finance*, 13(3):345–382, 2003.

[4] A. Hirsa and D. B. Madan. Pricing american options under variance gamma. *Journal of Computational Finance*, 7(2):63–80, 2004.

[5] F. Black and M. Scholes, The pricing of options and corporate liabilities. *Journal of Political Economy*, 81(3):637–654, 1973.

[6] D. B. Madan, P. P. Carr, and E. C. Chang. The variance gamma process and option pricing. *Review of Finance*, 2(1):79–105, 1998.

[7] A. Hirsa. *Computational Methods in Finance.* CRC Press, Boca Raton, Florida, 2016.

[8] I. Goodfellow, Y. Bengio, A. Courville, and Y. Bengio. *Deep Learning*, Vol. 1. MIT Press, Cambridge, 2016.

[9] Y. LeCun, B. E. Boser, J. S. Denker, D. Henderson, R. E. Howard, W. E. Hubbard, and L. D. Jackel. Handwritten digit recognition with a back-propagation network. In editor D. Touretzky. *Advances in Neural Information Processing Systems.* Morgan-Kaufmann, Burlington, MA, 2:396–404, 1989.

[10] J. Vecer and M. Xu. Pricing Asian options in a semimartingale model. *Quantitative Finance*, 4(2):170–175, 2004.

[11] N. Srivastava, G. Hinton, A. Krizhevsky, I. Sutskever, and R. Salakhutdinov. Dropout: A simple way to prevent neural networks from overfitting. *The Journal of Machine Learning Research*, 15(1): 1929–1958, 2014.

[12] M. Soltanolkotabi, A. Javanmard, and J. D. Lee. Theoretical insights into the optimization landscape of over-parameterized shallow neural networks. *IEEE Transactions on Information Theory*, 65:742–769, 2017. arXiv preprint arXiv:1707.04926.

[13] D. Soudry and Y. Carmon. No bad local minima: Data independent training error guarantees for multilayer neural networks. *arXiv*, abs/1605.08361, 2016. arXiv preprint arXiv:1605.08361.

[14] Y. Li and Y. Yuan. Convergence analysis of two-layer neural networks with ReLU activation. In editor I. Guyon and U. Von Luxburg and S. Bengio and H. Wallach and R. Fergus and S. Vishwanathan and R. Garnett. *Advances in Neural Information Processing Systems.* Curran Associates, Inc, 30:597–607, 2017. https://proceedings.neurips.cc/paper_files/paper/2017/file/a96b65a721e561e1e3de768ac819ffbb-Paper.pdf.

[15] K. Kawaguchi. Advances in Neural Information Processing Systems. In editor D. Lee and M. Sugiyama and U. Luxburg and I.

Guyon and R. Garnett, *Deep Learning without Poor Local Minima*. Curran Associates, Inc., 29, 2016, arXiv:1605. 07110v3. https://proceedings.neurips.cc/paper_files/paper/2016/file/f2fc990265c712c49d51a18a32b39f0c-Paper.pdf

[16] A. Choromanska, M. Henaff, M. Mathieu, B. A. Gerard, 37 and Y. LeCun. The loss surfaces of multilayer networks. Proceedings of the 18th International Conference on Artificial Intelligence and Statistics (AISTATS), JMLR: W&CP volume 38, 2015, San Diego, CA, USA.

[17] Kawaguchi K, Huang J, Kaelbling LP. Effect of Depth and Width on Local Minima in Deep Learning. *Neural Comput*, 31(7):1462–1498, 2019. doi: 10.1162/neco_a_01195. Epub 2019 May 23. PMID: 31120383.

[18] Z. Allen-Zhu, Y. Li, and Z. Song. A convergence theory for deep learning via over-parameterization, In editor Chaudhuri, Kamalika and Salakhutdinov, Ruslan *Proceedings of the 36th International Conference on Machine Learning*, PMLR, 97:242–252, 2019. arXiv preprint arXiv:1811.03962. https://proceedings.mlr.press/v97/allen-zhu19a.html

[19] D. P. Kingma and J. Ba. Adam: A method for stochastic optimization. *CoRR*, abs/1412.6980, 2014, arXiv preprint arXiv:1412.6980.

[20] S. Ruder. An overview of gradient descent optimization algorithms. *arXiv*, abs/1609.04747, 2016, preprint arXiv:1609.04747.

[21] J. H. Halton. On the efficiency of certain quasi-random sequences of points in evaluating multi-dimensional integrals. *Numerische Mathematik*, 2(1):84–90, 1960.

[22] F. Fang and C. W. Oosterlee. Pricing early-exercise and discrete barrier options by Fourier-cosine series expansions. *Numerische Mathematik*, 114(1):27, 2009.

[23] X. Glorot and Y. Bengio. Understanding the difficulty of training deep feedforward neural networks. In *Proceedings of the Thirteenth International Conference on Artificial Intelligence and Statistics*, 2010, pp. 249–256.

[24] X. Glorot, A. Bordes, and Y. Bengio. Deep sparse rectifier neural networks. In *Proceedings of the Fourteenth International Conference on Artificial Intelligence and Statistics*, 2011, pp. 315–323.

[25] R. Culkin and S. R. Das. Machine learning in finance: The case of deep learning for option pricing. *Journal of Investment Management*, 15(4):92–100, 2017.

[26] S. Zagoruyko and N. Komodakis. Wide residual networks, In editor Richard C. Wilson and Edwin R. Hancock and William A. P. Smith, *Proceedings of the British Machine Vision Conference*, 2016, BMVA Press. arXiv preprint arXiv:1605.07146. https://dblp.org/rec/conf/bmvc/ZagoruykoK16.bib.

[27] J. De Spiegeleer, D. B. Madan, S. Reyners, and W. Schoutens. Machine learning for quantitative finance: Fast derivative pricing, hedging and fitting. *Quantitative Finance*, 18(10):1635–1643, 2018.

[28] J. M. Hutchinson, A. W. Lo, and T. Poggio. A nonparametric approach to pricing and hedging derivative securities via learning networks. *The Journal of Finance*, 49(3):851–889, 1994.

[29] P. Carr, H. Geman, D. B. Madan, and M. Yor. The fine structure of asset returns: An empirical investigation. *The Journal of Business*, 75(2):305–332, 2002.

[30] W. Fu and A. Hirsa. Ali, Fast Pricing of American Options Under Variance Gamma (June 7, 2019). *Journal of Computational Finance*, 25(1):29–49.

https://doi.org/10.1142/9789811280306_0014

Chapter 14

Asset Price Bubbles, Wealth Preserving, Dominating and Replicating Trading Strategies

Robert A. Jarrow[*,‡] **and Yuxuan Liu**[†,§]

[*] *Samuel Curtis Johnson Graduate School of Management, Cornell University, Ithaca, NY 14853, USA*

[†] *Operations Research and Industrial Engineering, Cornell University, Ithaca, NY 14853, USA*

[‡] *raj15@cornell.edu*

[§] *yl2999@cornell.edu*

Abstract

This chapter studies an arbitrage-free, competitive and frictionless market with trading in a single risky asset and money market account, where the risky asset exhibits a price bubble. We analyze two sets of self-financing and admissible trading strategies in this market. The first are simple trading strategies, and the second are trading strategies that replicate or super-replicate the risky asset's payoffs at the model's horizon. We show that, in both sets, there exist wealth preserving trading strategies, i.e., trading strategies whose initial value equals the present value of their future cash flows. And, in the second set, we show that there are wealth preserving replicating trading strategies that dominate buying and holding the risky asset. The practical applications of these insights are discussed.

Keywords: Asset price bubbles, Strict local martingales, Dominating trading strategies, Asset pricing, Continuous-time model

1. Introduction

In an arbitrage-free, competitive and frictionless market, asset price bubbles can theoretically exist (see Jarrow 2015 [10] for a discussion of the theoretical models). And, there is mounting empirical evidence that asset price bubbles exist in reality as well (see Jarrow, Kchia, Protter 2011 [13], Obayashi, Protter, Yang 2017 [25] and Jarrow and Kwok 2021 [14]). In light of these facts, we study how to trade an asset that exhibits a price bubble. Should you short the asset in hopes of covering the position after the bubble bursts? Or, should you buy the asset in hopes of selling it before the bubble bursts? Furthermore, suppose you want to buy the asset today in order to obtain the asset's payoff at some future time T. Is there a trading strategy that can be used to avoid the losses that occur if the bubble bursts on or before T?

Understanding the answers to these questions is the necessary first step to trading assets with price bubbles. And, they are essential to characterize an investor's optimal portfolio in the presence of asset price bubbles. To state our answers to these questions, we need some definitions.

Consider a market consisting of a single risky asset with no cash flows and a money market with time horizon $[0, T]$. A wealth preserving trading strategy is one where the present value of the trading strategy's cash flows is equal to its initial investment. A dominating trading strategy is one that satisfies three conditions: (i) the trading strategy's initial cost is less than or equal to the cost of buying the risky asset, (ii) its payoff at time T is never less than the payoff to the risky asset and (iii) with positive probability its payoff at time T is strictly greater. Such a trading strategy dominates a buy and hold position in the risky asset, hence the terminology.

Given these definitions, we prove the following results in an arbitrage-free market with bubbles. These results provide the answers to the three questions previously posed:

- Shorting the asset in hopes of covering the short before time T is infeasible because with strictly positive probability, it implies possible borrowing before time T that is greater than any fixed amount. Hence, this trading strategy is impossible given realistic borrowing constraints.

- Buying and holding the risky asset until time T are strictly wealth decreasing and therefore a suboptimal trading strategy.
- Simple buy and sell trading strategies over $[0, \tau]$, with $\tau < T$ a stopping time, exist that are wealth preserving, i.e., maintain one's initial wealth. An example of such a trading strategy is to sell the risky asset the first time the risky asset price hits a fixed and predetermined level $k > S_0$, where S_0 is the risky asset's time 0 price. Hence, buying an asset with a bubble and selling it at an optimally determined future date is a reasonable trading strategy.
- In a complete market, there exist self-financing trading strategies that exactly replicate the asset's time T payoff, which are both wealth preserving and dominating. These replicating trading strategies are dynamic and involve holding the risky asset in non-zero quantities over the entire time horizon $[0, T]$. For diffusion processes, it can be shown that these replicating strategies hold less than one unit of the risky asset at all times prior to T. Hence, there exist replicating trading strategies that obtain the asset's time T payoff and avoid the losses that occur if the bubble bursts on or before T.
- In an incomplete market, we provide a characterization of all wealth preserving and dominating self-financing trading strategies that super-replicate the asset's time T payoff. Analogous to a complete market, these dynamic trading strategies avoid the losses that occur if the bubble bursts on or before T and provide at least the asset's payoff at time T.

The importance of these insights are two-fold. First, in a complete or incomplete market with asset price bubbles, these results show that it is possible to replicate an index's payoff using a wealth preserving trading strategy at lower cost than via a buy and hold position in the asset. This implies that in a market with bubbles, financial institutions that provide indexed funds for clients (e.g., an S&P 500 index fund) can create an index at less cost than by using the traditional method of buying and holding the assets in the index. Second, these results can be used to facilitate the characterization of the solution to an investor's portfolio optimization problem in a market with bubbles.

This chapter lies within the literature studying the local martingale theory of bubbles, recently developed by Loewenstein and

Willard 2000 [21], Cox and Hobson 2005 [2], Heston, Loewenstein, Willard 2007 [8] and Jarrow, Protter, Shimbo 2007 [17] and 2010 [18]. For a review of the local martingale theory of bubble mathematics, see Protter 2013 [26]. The papers by Loewenstein and Willard 2000 [22], Jarrow 2017 [11] and Herdegen and Herrmann 2018 [6] include, as part of their content, a solution to an investor's optimal portfolio when asset prices exhibit bubbles. One can view our paper as studying the properties of an investor's feasible set in these portfolio optimization problems. In this regard, the insights of this chapter can be used to understand and characterize an investor's optimal trading strategy in the presence of price bubbles, see Jarrow and Liu 2022 [16].

An outline for this chapter is as follows: Section 2 presents the model, and Section 3 discusses optimal stopping times that characterize the asset's market price. Section 4 explores simple trading strategies and Section 5 analyzes replicating and super-replicating admissible self-financing trading strategies. Section 6 concludes this chapter.

2. The Model

This section briefly reviews the local martingale theory of bubbles.

2.1. *The Setup*

We consider a continuous time, continuous trading model on a finite horizon $[0, T]$. The randomness is represented by $(\Omega, \mathcal{F}, \mathbb{F}, \mathbb{P})$, which is a filtered complete probability space where the filtration $\mathbb{F} = (\mathcal{F}_t)_{t\geq 0}$ satisfies the usual hypothesis with $\mathcal{F}_T = \mathcal{F}$. The market is assumed to be competitive and frictionless. Competitive means that traders act as price takers, believing their trades have no quantity impact on the market price. Frictionless means that there are no transaction costs and no trading constraints.

Traded in the economy are a risky asset and a money market account (mma) that is locally riskless. The normalized market price of the risky asset is given by a non-negative semimartingale $(S_t)_{0\leq t\leq T}$ adapted to $\mathbb{F}$. Without loss of generality, we assume that no cash flows are paid to the risky asset.

Trading strategies are defined to be holdings in the risky asset that are predictable (i.e., depending on only current and past information) and holdings in the mma that are optional. To exclude doubling strategies from discussion, we only consider trading strategies that are admissible (the value of the trading strategy is bounded below). A trading strategy is self-financing if it requires no cash inflows or outflows except at times 0 and T. Specifically, denote by $\mathscr{O}$ the optional σ-algebra and $\mathscr{L}(S)$ the set of predictable processes for which the stochastic integral with respect to S exists.

An admissible self-financing trading strategy (s.f.t.s.) with initial wealth x and wealth process X is the tuple of stochastic processes $(\alpha_0, \alpha) \in (\mathscr{O}, \mathscr{L}(S))$ such that there exists some constant c where

$$X_t = \alpha_0 + \alpha_t \cdot S_t = x + \int_0^t \alpha_u dS_u \geq c, \quad \forall t \in [0, T].$$

The first equality represents the trading strategy's wealth at time t, which equals the number of units of the mma plus the number of shares of the risky asset times its market price. The second equality is the self-financing condition, which states that the trading strategy's time t wealth equals the initial wealth plus the accumulated capital gains from the trading strategy over $[0, T]$. The third inequality is the admissibility condition, which represents a uniform lower bound on the wealth process. This lower bound represents a borrowing constraint. We denote by $\mathcal{A}(x)$ the set of admissible s.f.t.s. $(\alpha_0, \alpha) \in (\mathscr{O}, \mathscr{L}(S))$ given an initial wealth x.

A simple arbitrage opportunity is an admissible s.f.t.s. $(\alpha_0, \alpha) \in \mathcal{A}(x)$ with initial wealth $x = 0$ and wealth process X such that

$$\mathbb{P}(X_T \geq 0) = 1 \quad \text{and}$$
$$\mathbb{P}(X_T > 0) > 0.$$

A *Free Lunch with Vanishing Risk* (FLVR) is an admissible s.f.t.s. that is an extension of a simple arbitrage opportunity that includes (the limits of) approximate simple arbitrage opportunities. We say the market satisfies *No Free Lunch with Vanishing Risk* (NFLVR) if there exists no FLVR.

We invoke the following assumption.

Assumption 2.1. The market satisfies NFLVR.

An equivalent local martingale measure $\mathbb{Q}$ is any probability measure on $(\Omega, \mathcal{F})$ such that for $A \in \mathcal{F}$, $\mathbb{Q}(A) = 0$ iff $\mathbb{P}(A) = 0$ (in symbols $\mathbb{Q} \sim \mathbb{P}$) and S is a $\mathbb{Q}$ local martingale. This implies that for all $t \in [0, T]$, there exists a sequence of stopping time $\tau_n \to T$ a.s. such that

$$\mathbb{E}^{\mathbb{Q}}[S_{T\wedge\tau_n}|\mathcal{F}_t] = S_t,$$

where $\mathbb{E}^{\mathbb{Q}}[\cdot]$ denotes expectation under $\mathbb{Q}$.

Define $\mathcal{M}$ to be the set of *equivalent local martingale measures* (ELMM). By the first fundamental theorem of asset pricing, the assumption of NFLVR implies that there exists an *ELMM*, i.e., $\mathcal{M} \neq \emptyset$.

A market is defined to be complete with respect to some $\mathbb{Q} \in \mathcal{M}$ if for any non-negative payoff $Z_T \in L^1(\mathbb{Q})$ at time T, there exists an $x \geq 0$ and $(\alpha_0, \alpha) \in \mathscr{A}(x)$ such that

$$x + \int_0^T \alpha_u dS_u = Z_T,$$

and the wealth process

$$X_t = \alpha_0 + \alpha_t \cdot S_t = x + \int_0^t \alpha_u dS_u$$

is a $\mathbb{Q}$ martingale.

By the second fundamental theorem of asset pricing, in a complete market satisfying NFLVR, the ELMM is unique. In a complete market, $\mathbb{E}^{\mathbb{Q}}[\cdot]$ gives the unique present value operator to determine the arbitrage-free price of any $Z \in L^1(\mathbb{Q})$ at time t, which is $\mathbb{E}^{\mathbb{Q}}[Z_T|\mathcal{F}_t]$.

In an incomplete market, $\mathbb{E}^{\mathbb{Q}}[\cdot]$ represents only one of the infinite number of present value operators consistent with NFLVR. We will study both complete and incomplete markets in the following. For more discussion on these topics, see Jarrow 2021 [12], Chapter 2.

2.2. *Wealth Preserving and Dominating Trading Strategies*

Under NFLVR, because the wealth process X of any admissible s.f.t.s. in $\mathcal{A}(x)$ is uniformly bounded below, it is a $\mathbb{Q}$ local martingale.

And, by Fatou's lemma, it is a $\mathbb{Q}$ supermartingale. We record this fact as a lemma.

Lemma 2.2 (Wealth processes). *Assume NFLVR. Then, the wealth process X of any admissible s.f.t.s. in $\mathcal{A}(x)$ is a $\mathbb{Q}$ supermartingale, i.e., for all $t \in [0,T]$,*

$$\mathbb{E}^{\mathbb{Q}}[X_T|\mathcal{F}_t] \leq X_t,$$

where $\mathbb{E}^{\mathbb{Q}}[\cdot]$ denotes expectation under $\mathbb{Q}$.

In particular, this implies

$$\mathbb{E}^{\mathbb{Q}}[X_T] \leq X_0 = x.$$

Because $\mathbb{E}^{\mathbb{Q}}[\cdot]$ represents a present value operator, this lemma states that all admissible s.f.t.s.'s are wealth non-increasing. This is consistent with the market not admitting any arbitrage opportunities, which would be wealth increasing. We say that an admissible s.f.t.s. with wealth process X is wealth preserving if X is a $\mathbb{Q}$ martingale, i.e., $\mathbb{E}^{\mathbb{Q}}[X_T] = X_0 = x$.

An admissible s.f.t.s. with wealth process X is said to be a dominating if there exists an admissible s.f.t.s. $(\alpha_0, \alpha) \in \mathscr{A}(x)$ such that $x < S_0$ and

$$x + \int_0^T \alpha_u dS_u = S_T \quad \text{a.s.}$$

The market is said to satisfy No Dominance (ND) if there exists no such dominating s.f.t.s.

Not all admissible s.f.t.s. are wealth preserving. Indeed, there exists a class of admissible s.f.t.s. called suicide strategies, which are wealth decreasing. A suicide strategy is any admissible s.f.t.s. $(\alpha_0, \alpha) \in \mathcal{A}(x)$ with initial wealth $x = 0$ and wealth process X such that

$$\begin{aligned} &\mathbb{P}(X_t \geq -k) = 1, \quad \text{for all t} \in [0,\mathrm{T}] \quad \text{and} \\ &\mathbb{P}(X_T = -k) = 1 \quad \text{for } k > 0. \end{aligned}$$

This trading strategy loses k units of the mma for sure over $[0,T]$ and is wealth decreasing, i.e., $\mathbb{E}^{\mathbb{Q}}[X_T] = -k < X_0 = 0$. For more details, see Jarrow 2021 [12], Chapter 2.

If our market is populated by investors $i \in \mathbb{I}$ with beliefs represented by a probability measure $\mathbb{P}_i \sim \mathbb{P}$ and preferences such that they prefer more wealth to less, then when selecting admissible s.f.t.s., they would restrict consideration to wealth preserving and dominating admissible s.f.t.s. This insight motivates our study of such trading strategies given in the following.

2.3. *The Local Martingale Theory of Bubbles*

Given the above setup, we can now introduce the notion of an asset price bubble. Given the market satisfies NFLVR, $\mathcal{M} \neq \emptyset$. To define the fundamental value, we need to choose an element of $\mathcal{M}$. If the market is complete, then $\mathcal{M}$ is the singleton set, and we choose that element. If the market is incomplete, then there exists an infinite number of ELMMs.

To identify a unique equivalent local martingale measure in an incomplete market, one assumes that the market studied is embedded in a larger market that includes the trading of derivatives on the risky asset (e.g., call and put options with different strikes and maturities). There are two possible cases in the extended market. First is that these traded derivatives complete the market and therefore the equivalent local martingale measure is again uniquely determined by the second fundamental theorem of asset pricing. The papers by Eisenberg and Jarrow 1994 [4], Dengler and Jarrow 1997 [3] and Schwartz 2017 [27] provide models with markets where this is the case. Second is that even with the traded derivatives, the extended market is incomplete. However, in this case, under certain conditions, the traded derivatives' price processes may provide enough information to identify a unique local martingale measure consistent with these prices. The papers by Jacod and Protter 2010 [9] and Schweizer and Wissel 2008 [28] study such extended but incomplete markets. For subsequent use, we assume that the unique ELMM chosen by the market is determined by either of these two alternatives.

Given the $\mathbb{Q} \in \mathcal{M}$ chosen by the market, we define the fundamental value of the risky asset under $\mathbb{Q}$ by

$$\tilde{S}_t = \mathbb{E}^{\mathbb{Q}}[S_T|\mathcal{F}_t].$$

This represents the time t of present value of buying and holding the asset until time T. As such, this definition is consistent with the standard definition of an asset's fundamental value used in the classic economics literature (see Jarrow 2015 [10]).

Next, we define the risky asset's bubble to be

$$\beta_t = S_t - \tilde{S}_t,$$

which represents the deviation of the risky asset's market price from its fundamental value.

Given these definitions, it is as follows:

1. $\beta_t \geq 0$ for all $t \in [0, T]$.
2. β is not constantly zero if and only if S is a strict local martingale under the chosen ELMM.
3. If $\beta_s = 0$ for some $s \in [0, T]$, then $\beta_t \equiv 0$ for $t \in [s, T]$.

Indeed, since S is a local martingale bounded from below, then by Fatou's lemma, it is a supermartingale. Hence, we have $S_t \geq \mathbb{E}^{\mathbb{Q}}[S_T|\mathcal{F}_t]$ and β is non-negative. S is a true martingale if and only if $\beta_t \equiv 0$.

The importance of these properties for the subsequent analysis is that they imply that an asset price bubble bursts on or before time T with probability one. And, if it burst before time T, it cannot be "reborn."

Moreover, we have the following characterization of asset price bubbles:

Theorem 2.3 (Bubble characterization). *For S which is a local martingale measure $\mathbb{Q}$,(1) $-$ (3) are equivalent. If S has bounded jumps, then they are all equivalent to* (4).

1. *S exhibits a bubble.*
2. *S is a strict supermartingale under $\mathbb{Q}$.*
3. $\mathbb{E}^{\mathbb{Q}}[S_T] < S_0$.
4. $\limsup_{x\to\infty} x\mathbb{Q}(\sup_{t\in[0,T]} S_t > x) > 0$.

Proof. By definition, S has a bubble if 2.3 holds. Furthermore, if S is a non-negative local martingale, then by Fatou's lemma, S is a supermartingale. 2.3 is a necessary and sufficient condition for S to be a strict supermartingale.

Define $\zeta_x := \inf\{t \in [0, T] : S_t \geq x\}$. For each $x > S_0$, given S has bounded jumps, S^{ζ_x} is a bounded local martingale and hence a true martingale so that by optional sampling theorem

$$S_0 = \mathbb{E}^{\mathbb{Q}} S_{\zeta_x \wedge T} = \mathbb{E}^{\mathbb{Q}}[S_T \mathbb{1}_{\zeta_x \geq T} + x \mathbb{1}_{\zeta_x < T}].$$

Letting $x \to +\infty$, we have by dominated convergence that

$$\lim_{x \to \infty} \mathbb{E}^{\mathbb{Q}}[S_T \mathbb{1}_{\zeta_x \geq T}] = \mathbb{E}^{\mathbb{Q}}[\lim_{x \to \infty} S_T \mathbb{1}_{\zeta_x \geq T}] = \mathbb{E}^{\mathbb{Q}}[S_T],$$

and, therefore,

$$S_0 - \mathbb{E}^{\mathbb{Q}}[S_T] = \limsup_{x \to \infty} x \mathbb{Q}(\zeta_x < T) = \limsup_{x \to \infty} x \mathbb{Q}(\sup_{t \in [0,T]} S_t > x).$$

Hence 2.3 is equivalent to 2.3. □

Condition (4) is very revealing. It states that an asset price bubble exists if and only if for any given future asset price x, the "expected value" of the price process exceeding x is non-zero as x approaches infinity. Here we provide several examples of asset price processes with bubbles.

Example 2.4 (Local volatility model). Suppose that under $\mathbb{Q}$, S is given by the following local volatility model

$$dS_t = \sigma(S_t) dW_t,$$

where W is a $\mathbb{Q}$ standard Brownian motion. Then S is a strict local martingale if and only if

$$\int_{\epsilon}^{\infty} \frac{1}{\sigma(x)^2} dx < \infty.$$

See Mijatovic and Urusov 2012 [23]. An example is the CEV process with $\sigma(x) = x^{\delta+1}$ for some $\delta > 0$.

Example 2.5 (A bubble construction). A risky asset price process with a bubble can be obtained by constructing the fundamental value and the bubble processes separately. Suppose that $\tilde{S}$ is a uniformly integrable martingale on $[0, T]$ and β is a non-negative local martingale such that $\beta_0 > 0$ and $\beta_T = 0 \quad a.s.$ Define $S_t = \tilde{S}_t + \beta_t$, which is a strict local martingale. One example of such a β is given by

$$d\beta_t = \frac{\beta_t}{\sqrt{T-t}} dW_t, \tag{1}$$

where W is a Brownian motion. Then, β is a time-changed Brownian motion such that $\lim_{t \to T} \beta_t = 0, \quad a.s.$

Alternatively, we could let β be given by the simple single jump process

$$\beta_t = \frac{1}{T-t}\mathbb{1}_{t<\tau},$$

where τ is the bubble's crash time, which is uniformly distributed. Then it can be verified that β is a martingale on $[0,T)$ but a strict local martingale on $[0,T]$ since β converges to 0 almost surely.

Moreover, one can construct single jump strict local martingales for any distribution of crash time τ with support $[0,T)$. For example, let h_t be a deterministic process such that $h_0 = 0$ but $\lim_{t\to T} h_t = +\infty$. And we define $\tau = \inf\{t : \tilde{S}_t \leq h_t\}$ for some continuous true martingale $\tilde{S}$. Then the corresponding process β is a bubble process, the crash time of which depends on the evolution of the fundamental value.

2.4. *Asset Return Explosion Times*

This section presents an alternative asset price bubble characterization theorem. For this section, assume that S is a continuous process and $\mathbb{F} = (\mathcal{F}_t)_{t\geq 0}$ is the filtration generated by S.

First we need the following lemma:

Lemma 2.6 (Exponential martingales). *For any positive continuous local martingale S, there exists a continuous local martingale M with $M_0 = 1$ such that $S = S_0\mathcal{E}(M)$, where $\mathcal{E}(\cdot)$ is the stochastic exponential.*

Given the stochastic exponential representation of the asset price as $S_t = S_0\mathcal{E}(M_t)$, M_t corresponds to the asset's cumulative return over $[0,T]$.

Now, define the sequence of stopping times $\zeta_n := \inf\{t \in [0,T] : [M]_t \geq n\}$ and the limit $\zeta := \mathop{lim}\limits_{n\to\infty} \zeta_n$, which exists since ζ_n is a non-decreasing sequence. Then, because $[M,M]_{t\wedge\zeta_n}$ is bounded by n, $S_{t\wedge\zeta_n}$ is a true martingale by Novikov's criterion.

Define the Radon–Nikodym density process $Z_{t\wedge\zeta_n} := \frac{S_{t\wedge\zeta_n}}{S_0}$. Note that $Z_0 = Z_{0\wedge\zeta_n} = 1$. Define the associated measure $\mathbb{R}_n$ by

$$\mathbb{R}_n(A) := \int_A Z_{T\wedge\zeta_n} d\mathbb{Q}$$

for $A \in \mathcal{F}_{\zeta_n}$. It is a probability measure because the optional sampling theorem and the martingale property imply that $\mathbb{E}^{\mathbb{R}_n}[\mathbb{1}_\Omega] = \mathbb{E}^{\mathbb{Q}}[Z_{\zeta_n}] = 1$.

This construction gives a consistent family of probability measures $\{\mathbb{R}_n\}_{n\geq 1}$, that is,

$$\mathbb{R}_{n+1}|_{\mathcal{F}_{\zeta_n}}(A) = \mathbb{R}_n(A)$$

for $A \in \mathcal{F}_{\zeta_n}$.

Proof. Note that

$$\begin{aligned}\mathbb{R}_{n+1}|_{\mathcal{F}_{\zeta_n}}(A) &= \mathbb{E}^{\mathbb{Q}}[Z_{\zeta_{n+1}}\mathbb{1}_A] = \mathbb{E}^{\mathbb{Q}}\left[\mathbb{E}^{\mathbb{Q}}\left[Z_{\zeta_{n+1}}\mathbb{1}_A|\mathcal{F}_{\zeta_n}\right]\right] \\ &= \mathbb{E}^{\mathbb{Q}}\left[\mathbb{1}_A\mathbb{E}^{\mathbb{Q}}\left[Z_{\zeta_{n+1}}|\mathcal{F}_{\zeta_n}\right]\right] = \mathbb{E}^{\mathbb{Q}}[Z_{\zeta_n}\mathbb{1}_A] = \mathbb{R}_n(A).\end{aligned}$$

The second to last equality holds because $\mathbb{E}^{\mathbb{Q}}[Z_{\zeta_{n+1}}|\mathcal{F}_{\zeta_n}] = Z_{\zeta_n}$. □

Hence, there exists extended probability measure $\mathbb{R}$ on $\mathcal{F}_{\zeta-} := \sigma\left(\bigcup_n \mathcal{F}_{\zeta_n}\right)$ such that for all n and $A \in \mathcal{F}_{\zeta_n}$ (see Cherny 2002 [1]),

$$\mathbb{R}|_{\mathcal{F}_{\zeta_n}}(A) = \mathbb{R}_n(A).$$

Note that this construction implies that if $\mathbb{Q}|_{\mathcal{F}_{\zeta-}}(A) = 0$, then $\mathbb{R}(A) = 0$ for $A \in \mathcal{F}_{\zeta-}$, that is, $\mathbb{R}$ is absolutely continuous with respect to $\mathbb{Q}$ on $\mathcal{F}_{\zeta-}$, in symbols $\mathbb{Q}|_{\mathcal{F}_{\zeta-}} \gg \mathbb{R}$.

Using this measure, we can prove the following theorem:

Proposition 2.7 (Bubble characterization for continuous price processes).

$$\mathbb{E}^{\mathbb{Q}}[S_t] = S_0\mathbb{R}(\zeta > t).$$

Hence, S is a strict local martingale and exhibits a bubble if and only if $\mathbb{R}(\zeta \leq T) > 0$.

Proof. When M is continuous, $Z_t := \mathcal{E}(M_t)$ satisfies

$$Z_t = 0 \quad \text{if} \quad \zeta \leq t \leq T.$$

Now,

$$Z_{t\wedge\zeta_n} = Z_{t\wedge\zeta_n} 1_{t<\zeta_n} + Z_{t\wedge\zeta_n} 1_{\zeta_n \leq t} = Z_t 1_{t<\zeta_n} + Z_{\zeta_n} 1_{\zeta_n \leq t}.$$

Taking expectations,

$$\begin{aligned} 1 = \mathbb{E}^{\mathbb{Q}}[Z_{t\wedge\zeta_n}] &= \mathbb{E}^{\mathbb{Q}}[Z_t 1_{t<\zeta_n}] + \mathbb{E}^{\mathbb{Q}}[Z_{\zeta_n} 1_{\zeta_n \leq t}] \\ &= \mathbb{E}^{\mathbb{Q}}[Z_t 1_{t<\zeta_n}] + \mathbb{E}^{\mathbb{Q}}\left[\frac{d\mathbb{R}_n}{d\mathbb{Q}} 1_{\zeta_n \leq t}\right] = \mathbb{E}^{\mathbb{Q}}[Z_t 1_{t<\zeta_n}] + \mathbb{R}_n(\zeta_n \leq t). \end{aligned}$$

Using the definition of $\mathbb{R}$ gives

$$1 = \mathbb{E}^{\mathbb{Q}}[Z_t 1_{t<\zeta_n}] + \mathbb{R}(\zeta_n \leq t).$$

Taking limits, we get

$$1 = \lim_{n\to\infty} \mathbb{E}^{\mathbb{Q}}[Z_t 1_{t<\zeta_n}] + \lim_{n\to\infty} \mathbb{R}(\zeta_n \leq t).$$

For the first term on the right side, note that $Z_t 1_{t<\zeta_n} \leq Z_t$ and $\mathbb{E}^{\mathbb{Q}}[Z_t] \leq 1$. By dominated convergence, we get $\lim_{n\to\infty} \mathbb{E}^{\mathbb{Q}}[Z_t 1_{t<\zeta_n}] = \mathbb{E}^{\mathbb{Q}}[Z_t 1_{t<\zeta}]$ because $\lim_{n\to\infty} 1_{t<\zeta_n} = 1_{t<\zeta}$ a.s. $\mathbb{Q}$. But, $Z_t 1_{\zeta\leq t} = 0$. Hence,

$$\mathbb{E}^{\mathbb{Q}}[Z_t 1_{t<\zeta}] = \mathbb{E}^{\mathbb{Q}}[Z_t 1_{t<\zeta}] + \mathbb{E}^{\mathbb{Q}}[Z_t 1_{\zeta\leq t}] = \mathbb{E}^{\mathbb{Q}}[Z_t].$$

For the second term,

$$\lim_{n\to\infty} \mathbb{R}(\zeta_n \leq t) = \mathbb{R}(\lim_{n\to\infty} \zeta_n \leq t) = \mathbb{R}(\zeta \leq t).$$

Substitution yields

$$1 = \mathbb{E}^{\mathbb{Q}}[Z_t] + \mathbb{R}(\zeta \leq t).$$

Using the definition of $\frac{S_t}{S_0} = Z_t$, we get

$$\mathbb{E}^{\mathbb{Q}}[S_t] = S_0 \mathbb{R}(t < \zeta).$$

□

This proposition states that a bubble exists if the quadratic variation of the cumulative return process $[M]$ explodes under $\mathbb{R}$ before or at time T with positive probability.

We can use this characterization to generate additional examples of asset price bubble processes.

Example 2.8 (Stochastic volatility). Suppose that we have the following dynamics of the risky asset:

$$dS_t = S_t\sigma(Y_t)dW_t,$$

where state variable Y is given by

$$dY_t = \mu^Y(t, Y_t)dt + \sigma^Y(t, Y_t)dW_t.$$

Then by Proposition 2.7, it follows that S is a strict local martingale if and only if

$$\mathbb{R}(\zeta > T) < 1,$$

where Y is given by, under $\mathbb{R}$,

$$dY_t = (\mu^Y(t, Y_t) + \sigma(t, Y_t)\sigma^Y(t, Y_t))dt + \sigma^Y(t, Y_t)d\tilde{W}.$$

Example 2.9 (Return process explosion time). Suppose h is a continuous $\mathbb{R}$ martingale such that $h_t = \frac{d\mathbb{Q}}{d\mathbb{R}}|_{\mathcal{F}_t}$ and f is a continuous non-negative $\mathbb{R}$ martingale. Define τ_0 the first hitting time of zero of process h. Then under $\mathbb{Q}$, the process $S_t = \frac{f_t}{h_t}\mathbb{1}_{\tau_0 > t}$ is a strict local martingale if $\mathbb{R}(\tau_0 \leq T) > 0$.

3. Optimal Stopping Times

This section studies a characterization of the risky asset's market price in a market with price bubbles. In this regard, we have the following proposition:

Proposition 3.1 (The risky asset market price).

$$S_t = ess \sup_{\tau \in \mathcal{T}(t,T)} \mathbb{E}^{\mathbb{Q}}[S_\tau|\mathcal{F}_t],$$

where $\mathcal{T}(t, T)$ is the collection of stopping times that are bounded between t and T.

Proof. Since S_t is a non-negative local martingale under $\mathbb{Q}$, it is a supermartingale. This implies that $S_t \geq E^{\mathbb{Q}}[S_\tau | \mathcal{F}_t]$ for any stopping time τ. Hence, $S_t \geq \underset{\tau \in [t,T]}{ess\,sup}\, E^{\mathbb{Q}}[S_\tau | \mathcal{F}_t]$.

Conversely, consider a localizing sequence of stopping times $\tau^n \to T$ with $\tau^n \leq T$ for all n. Under this sequence, $S_{\tau^n \wedge t}$ is a martingale under $\mathbb{Q}$ for all n, hence $S_{\tau^n \wedge s} = E^{\mathbb{Q}}[S_{\tau^n \wedge t} | \mathcal{F}_s]$ for $s \leq t \leq T$. Assume $s < \tau^n \wedge t$, then $S_s = E^{\mathbb{Q}}[S_{\tau^n \wedge t} | \mathcal{F}_s]$.

For $t = T$, we have $S_s = E^{\mathbb{Q}}[S_{\tau^n \wedge T} | \mathcal{F}_s] = E^{\mathbb{Q}}[S_{\tau^n} | \mathcal{F}_s]$. Hence, for the stopping time $\tau^n \in [t, T]$, we have $S_t = E^{\mathbb{Q}}[S_{\tau^n} | \mathcal{F}_t]$. This implies $\underset{\tau \in [t,T]}{ess\,sup}\, E^{\mathbb{Q}}[S_\tau | \mathcal{F}_t] \geq S_t$, which completes the proof. □

We call any stopping time that attains the essential supremum an optimal stopping time. If S is a true martingale under $\mathbb{Q}$, then for any stopping time τ, by the optional sampling theorem, we have $\mathbb{E}^{\mathbb{Q}}[S_\tau | \mathcal{F}_t] = S_t$. When there are no bubbles, every stopping time is optimal. However, if S is a strict local martingale, then there exist strictly suboptimal stopping times. Indeed, an example is the deterministic stopping time $\tau \equiv T$. In this case, $S_t > E^{\mathbb{Q}}[S_T | \mathcal{F}_t]$ because S is a strict local martingale.

The proof of the previous theorem generates the following corollary:

Corollary 3.2 (Localizing sequence). *If τ_n is a localizing sequence of stopping times, then τ_n is an optimal stopping time for all n.*

We can identify a useful localizing sequence. Define a sequence of stopping times on the time domain $[0, T]$ as

$$\pi_n := \inf\{t \in [0, T] : |S_t| \geq n\}.$$

This sequence is strictly increasing if S_t is continuous or S_t has bounded jumps.

Proof. If S_t is continuous, then S_t cannot jump to $n + 1$ before it hits n, so $\tau_{n+1} > \tau_n$.

If S_t has bounded jumps, then S_t can possibly jump to $n + 1$ before it hits n, so $\tau_{n+1} = \tau_n$ is possible.

But, because the size of a jump is bounded by K, then $S_{\pi_n} + \Delta S_{\pi_n} \leq s_{\pi_n} + K$, so $\pi_{n+K+1} = \inf\{t \in [0, T] : |s_t| \geq$

$n + K + 1\} > \pi_n$. Redefine the sequence on this subsequence to make it strictly increasing. This completes the proof. □

Hence, because it is a non-decreasing sequence,

$$\pi_\infty := \lim_{n\to\infty} \pi_n \quad a.s. \quad \mathbb{Q}.$$

We have $S_{\pi_\infty} = lim_n S_{\pi_n} = \infty$ a.s. $\mathbb{Q}$. The process S_t is said to explode if $\pi_\infty \leq T$. But, S_t is a $\mathbb{Q}$ supermartingale and any stopping time $\pi_\infty \leq T$, by the optional sampling theorem, satisfies

$$lim_n E[S_{\pi_n}] = E[S_{\pi_\infty}] \leq S_0.$$

Hence, S_t does not explode under $\mathbb{Q}$, and

$$\lim_{n\to\infty} \pi_n = \infty \quad a.s. \quad \mathbb{Q}.$$

This implies that π_n is a localizing sequence for the local martingale S_t. By the corollary, the τ_n are optimal stopping times.

If S is continuous, Proposition 2.7 provides a characterization of optimal stopping times.

Proposition 3.3 (Characterization optimal stopping times). *Let S be a continuous process and $\mathbb{F}$ the filtration generated by S.*

A stopping time $\tau \in \mathcal{T}(t,T)$ is optimal if and only if

$$\mathbb{R}(\zeta > \tau) = 1.$$

Recall the stopping time $\zeta_n := \inf\{t \in [0,T] : [M]_t \geq n\}$ with respect to the quadratic variation of the cumulative return process M. Under the hypothesis of this proposition, M is continuous with $M_0 = 1$. This implies that $\zeta_n < \zeta$ a.s. $\mathbb{Q}$ for all n, which also implies that $\zeta_n < \zeta$ a.s. $\mathbb{R}$ because $\{\zeta_n < \zeta\} \in \mathcal{F}_{\zeta-}$ and $\mathbb{Q}\,|_{\mathcal{F}_{\zeta-}} \gg \mathbb{R}$. Hence, the ζ_n are optimal stopping times.

4. Simple Trading Strategies

This section studies simple trading strategies, where a simple trading strategy is defined to be a buy and sell over $[0,\tau]$, where $\tau \leq T$ is a stopping time. More formally, a simple trading strategy is given by

$$\alpha_t := \mathbb{1}_{[0,\tau)}(t) \qquad \text{and}$$
$$\alpha_0(t) := S_{t\wedge\tau} - S_t\mathbb{1}_{[0,\tau)}(t)$$

with the wealth process $X_t = S_{t\wedge\tau}$ for $t \in [0,T]$, where the initial wealth invested is $x = S_0$. As defined, we see that this trading strategy is self-financing and admissible, and its lower bound is zero because $S_t \geq 0$.

We note that the subsequent analysis applies equally well to a finite number of buys and sells over the time period.

Remark 4.1 (Naked short selling). Simple trading strategies involving a short and cover are not admissible and excluded from the preceding definition. Indeed, if S is a strict local martingale, then it is unbounded above. Hence, $-S$ is unbounded below, and the s.f.t.s. $(\alpha_t := -\mathbb{1}_{[0,\tau)}(t),\ \alpha_0(t) := S_{t\wedge\tau} - S_t\mathbb{1}_{[0,\tau)}(t))$ with wealth process $X_t = -S_{t\wedge\tau}$ is not admissible.

An example of such a simple trading strategy is shorting the stock and covering the position at time T, after the bubble bursts. Because it violates admissibility, it is not a feasible trading strategy in practice since it implies unlimited borrowing with positive probability. The violation of admissibility explains why this short and cover trading strategy over $[0,T]$, in an arbitrage-free market, cannot remove asset price bubbles.

4.1. *No Bubbles*

If S has no bubbles and is a $\mathbb{Q}$ martingale, then all such admissible simple trading strategies, by the optional sampling theorem, are $\mathbb{Q}$ martingales, and hence wealth preserving. There can exist no dominating s.f.t.s. because the existence of an equivalent martingale measure implies that the market satisfies ND by the third fundamental theorem of asset pricing (see Jarrow and Larsson 2012 [15]).

4.2. *Bubbles*

This section explores admissible simple trading strategies when the risky asset exhibits a bubble. First, it is easy to see that buying and holding the risky asset over $[0,T]$ is wealth decreasing. Indeed, the initial cost is S_0, and the present value of the trading strategy is equal to $\mathbb{E}^{\mathbb{Q}}[S_T] < S_0$ because the asset is a $\mathbb{Q}$ strict supermartingale. As such, it is a suboptimal trading strategy.

However, we now show that there exist simple trading strategies that are wealth preserving, and in the process, this demonstration provides an economic interpretation of the optimal stopping times in Section 3 that generate a localizing sequence for the $\mathbb{Q}$ local martingale S.

With respect to the simple trading strategies just defined, when a "sell" occurs at an optimal stopping time that is an element of a localizing sequence, the trading strategy is wealth preserving. This follows because on the time interval $[0,\tau_n]$, the risky asset is a $\mathbb{Q}$ local martingale so that the wealth process X satisfies

$$\mathbb{E}^{\mathbb{Q}}[X_T] = \mathbb{E}^{\mathbb{Q}}[S_{\tau_n}] = S_0 = x.$$

Consequently, the wealth process of such a simple trading strategy is a $\mathbb{Q}$ martingale. Interestingly, however, it is not a dominating trading strategy because the time T payoff, $X_T = S_{\tau_n}$, may not be greater than or equal to S_T at time T with $\mathbb{Q}$ probability one.

For risky asset processes that are continuous or have bounded jumps, one such wealth preserving simple trading strategy is to buy the risky asset at time t and sell it the first time the risky asset price hits the level n, i.e., at the stopping time $\pi_n := \inf\{t \in [0,T] : |S_t| \geq n\}$.

Another wealth preserving simple trading strategy for continuous price processes is to buy the risky asset at time t and sell it the first time the quadratic variation of the cumulative return process hits the level n, i.e., at the stopping time $\zeta_n := \inf\{t \in [0,T] : [M]_t \geq n\}$. Note that for all of these simple trading strategies, the selling time must occur strictly before time T, and consequently, they are not dominating.

5. Replicating and Super-replicating Admissible s.f.t.s.

This section studies wealth preserving and dominating admissible s.f.t.s. that replicate or super-replicate the risky asset's time T payoffs. In a market with no bubbles, a buy and hold trading strategy over $[0, T]$ replicates the asset's time T payoffs and is wealth preserving. And, as is well known, in a market with no bubbles, there are no dominating admissible s.f.t.s.

In contrast, as shown in the previous section, this is not true in a market with bubbles. When the asset exhibits a bubble, the simple buy and hold trading strategy that generates the asset's time T payoff is wealth decreasing. This section shows that there exist dominating trading strategies that replicate or super-replicate the asset's time T payoffs.

For this section, we assume that S exhibits a price bubble and is a $\mathbb{Q}$ strict local martingale for some $\mathbb{Q} \in \mathcal{M}$. There are two cases to study: complete and incomplete markets.

5.1. *Complete Markets*

We assume that the market is complete with respect to some $\mathbb{Q} \in \mathcal{M}$, hence, by the second fundamental theorem of asset pricing, the ELMM is unique. In such a market, No Dominance (ND) is violated because by market completeness, there exists an admissible s.f.t.s. $(\alpha_0, \alpha) \in \mathscr{A}(x)$ with initial investment x where

$$x + \int_0^T \alpha_u dS_u = S_T \tag{2}$$

and the wealth process

$$X_t = \alpha_0(t) + \alpha_t S_t = x + \int_0^t \alpha_u dS_u \tag{3}$$

is a $\mathbb{Q}$ martingale, which implies that $x = \mathbb{E}^{\mathbb{Q}}[S_T] = \tilde{S}_0$. Hence, the trading strategy is wealth preserving. Since $\mathbb{Q}$ is a strict local martingale, we have that $x = \mathbb{E}^{\mathbb{Q}}[S_T] = \tilde{S}_0 < S_0$, which shows that it is also a dominating trading strategy.

The remainder of this section characterizes the standard buy and hold trading strategy. Because $\mathbb{Q} \in \mathcal{M}$ is unique, the fundamental value $\tilde{S}_t$ and the bubble β_t are uniquely defined, where $\tilde{S}_t = \mathbb{E}^{\mathbb{Q}}[S_T \mid \mathcal{F}_t]$ and $\beta_t = S_t - \tilde{S}_t \geq 0$. First, note that this implies $X_t = \tilde{S}_t$, hence we can rewrite expression (3) as

$$\tilde{S}_t = \tilde{S}_0 + \int_0^t \alpha_u dS_u = \alpha_0(t) + \alpha_t S_t. \tag{4}$$

Therefore, the bubble process can be written as

$$\begin{aligned}\beta_t = S_t - \tilde{S}_t &= \beta_0 + \int_0^t (1 - \alpha_u) dS_u \\ &= \beta_0 + \int_0^t \alpha_u^\beta dS_u = \alpha_0^\beta(t) + \alpha_t^\beta S_t,\end{aligned}$$

where $\alpha^\beta := 1 - \alpha$ and $\alpha_0^\beta := -\alpha_0$.[1]

This implies that the buy and hold trading strategy in the risky asset can be decomposed into two parts:

- the position that generates the fundamental value $(\alpha_0, \alpha) \in \mathscr{A}(\tilde{S}_0)$,
- the position that generates the bubble $(\alpha_0^\beta, \alpha^\beta) \in \mathscr{A}(\beta_0)$. Note that $\beta_T = 0$ a.s. but $\beta_0 > 0$, so α^β corresponds to a suicide strategy.

We can use this observation to generate bubble processes that depend on the fundamental value process.

Example 5.1 (Suicide strategies and bubbles). Bubble processes can be constructed that depend on the fundamental value in the following manner. Assume that $\tilde{S}$ follows a geometric Brownian motion, which is a true martingale. Additionally, assume that the bubble process is of the form

$$\beta_t = \int_0^t \tilde{\alpha}_u^\beta d\tilde{S}_u.$$

We can construct an admissible s.f.t.s. $\tilde{\alpha}^\beta$ that is a suicide strategy as follows. First, partition $(0, T) = \bigcup_{i=1}^\infty (T_{i-1}, T_i]$, where $T_i = \left(1 - \frac{1}{2^i}\right) T$. For each of these time intervals, choose $\tilde{\alpha}_i^\beta$ such that the probability of the wealth process β_t hitting zero is $p_i > 0$. Then, we have the following result:

[1]This follows from $\beta_t + \tilde{S}_t = S_t$ and $\alpha^\beta := 1 - \alpha$.

The process $\tilde{\alpha}_i^\beta$ is a suicide strategy if and only if

$$\prod_i (1 - p_i) = 0.$$

Hence,

$$S_t = \tilde{S}_t + \int_0^t \tilde{\alpha}_u^\beta d\tilde{S}_u$$

is a risky asset process with a bubble.

The following corollary characterizes this replicating trading strategy for continuous Markov processes. It is a direct consequence of expression (4), recognizing that $\tilde{S}_t = \mathbb{E}^{\mathbb{Q}}[S_T|\mathcal{F}_t]$.

Corollary 5.2 (Characterization of the replicating trading strategy). *If S is a continuous Markov process, and* $\mathbb{E}^{\mathbb{Q}}[S_T|S_t]$ is *a $C^{1,2}$ function of time t and risky asset price S_t, then*

$$\alpha_t = \frac{\partial \mathbb{E}^{\mathbb{Q}}[S_T|S_t]}{\partial S_t}.$$

Proof. If S is a Markov process, then $\tilde{S}_t = \mathbb{E}^{\mathbb{Q}}[S_T|\mathcal{F}_t] = \mathbb{E}^{\mathbb{Q}}[S_T|S_t]$. Ito's lemma gives

$$d\tilde{S}_t = \left(\frac{\partial \tilde{S}_t}{\partial t} + \frac{1}{2} \frac{\partial^2 \tilde{S}_t}{\partial S_t^2} \right) d \langle S, S \rangle_t + \frac{\partial \tilde{S}_t}{\partial S_t} dS_t.$$

Equating the integrand of dS_t in expression (4) completes the proof. □

As shown, for a continuous Markov process, the replicating trading strategy is the partial derivative of the asset's conditional expected value with respect to the asset's price at time t. The next question we study is whether the replicating trading strategy $(\alpha_0, \alpha) \in \mathscr{A}(\tilde{S}_0)$ in expression (2) has a non-zero position in the underlying asset for all times, i.e., it is not a simple wealth preserving trading strategy as discussed in Section 4. In this regard, we have the following result:

Theorem 5.3 (Non-zero holdings in the asset). *Assume $\tilde{S}$ is a $\mathcal{H}^1$ martingale. Then,*

$$\alpha_t \neq 0, \mathbb{Q} \times \lambda[0,T]$$

when $[\tilde{S}]_t$ increases, and the ratio $\frac{\alpha^\beta}{\alpha}$ is unbounded where λ is the Lebesgue measure.

Proof. By associativity of stochastic integration, one can verify that

$$dS_t = \frac{1}{\alpha_t} d\tilde{S}_t.$$

Because S_t is finite a.e., this implies $\alpha_t \neq 0, \mathbb{Q} \times \lambda[0,T]$ when $[\tilde{S}]_t$ increases.

Next, we have

$$\beta_t = \int_0^t \frac{\alpha_u^\beta}{\alpha_u} d\tilde{S}_u.$$

By definition, we have

$$\mathbb{E}^{\mathbb{Q}}[[\tilde{S}]_t^{1/2}] < \infty, \quad \forall t,$$

since $\tilde{S}$ is a $\mathcal{H}^1$ martingale. Suppose the integrand $\frac{\alpha^\beta}{\alpha}$ is bounded by $K > 0$, we have from Burkholder–Davis–Gundy inequalities that there exists $C_1 > 0$ such that

$$\begin{aligned}\mathbb{E}^{\mathbb{Q}}[\sup_{0\leq u\leq t} |\beta_u|] &\leq C_1 \mathbb{E}^{\mathbb{Q}}[[\beta_t]^{1/2}] \\ &= C_1 \mathbb{E}^{\mathbb{Q}}[[\int \frac{\alpha^\beta}{\alpha} d\tilde{S}]^{1/2}] \\ &\leq C_1 K \mathbb{E}[[\tilde{S}_t]^{1/2}] < \infty.\end{aligned}$$

Hence β is a local martingale of class (DL), so is a proper martingale contradiction. Therefore, process $\frac{\alpha^\beta}{\alpha}$ is unbounded. □

Hence, these replicating trading strategies do not include the simple wealth preserving trading strategies in Section 4, which have a zero holding in the risky asset after time τ and before T. The result that the ratio $\frac{\alpha^\beta}{\alpha}$ is unbounded implies, recalling that $S_t = S_t(\alpha_t^\beta + \alpha_t)$, that the proportion of the asset's price represented by the bubble is unbounded above.

From the construction of the suicide strategy, we see that α^β could be negative or positive. As a result, the replicating trading strategy's position in the risky asset may be greater than or smaller than 1 share, and sometimes it is a negative holding in the risky asset! The latter case happens if the bubble is larger than the fundamental value. However, for a class of diffusion models, we can show that this replicating trading strategy's holding in the risky asset is positive and less than one.

Theorem 5.4 (Time-homogeneous diffusion). *Suppose that the risky asset S with state-space $\mathbb{R}^+$ is governed by the following SDE:*

$$dS_t = \sigma(S_t)dW_t, \ S_0 \in [0, \infty),$$
$$S_t \equiv 0, \ t \geq \tau_0 := \inf\{t \in [0, \infty) : S_t = 0\},$$

where W_t is a Brownian motion and $\sigma : \mathbb{R}^+ \mapsto \mathbb{R}^+$ is a continuous function such that $\sigma(x) > 0, \forall x \in (0, \infty)$.

Assume further that

$$\tilde{S}_t = \mathbb{E}^{\mathbb{Q}}[S_T|\mathcal{F}_t] := f(t, S_t)$$

is a $C^{1,2}$ function of time t and risky asset price S_t. Then,

$$0 \leq \alpha_t \leq 1 \ a.s.$$

for all $t \in [0, T]$.

Proof. Since the process is continuous and Markov, by Corollary 5.2, it suffices to show that

$$0 \leq \frac{\partial}{\partial x} f(t, x) \leq 1.$$

To show $\frac{\partial}{\partial x} f(t, x) \geq 0$, note that by the comparison theorem (see Karatzas and Shreve 1988 [19], p. 293) we have $f(t, x)$ is increasing in x for any fixed t.

To show $\frac{\partial}{\partial x} f(t,x) \leq 1$, it suffices to show that $f(t,x)$ is concave in x for any fixed t. The time-homogenous diffusion possesses a non-exploding solution (see Karatzas and Shreve 1988 [19], p. 332). And, the Feynman–Kac theorem is valid in such case (see the Appendix). Note that

$$f(t,x) = \mathbb{E}^{\mathbb{Q}}[S_T|S_t = x],$$

where f is the minimal solution of the following partial differential equation (the solution to which is not unique if S is a strict local martingale)

$$\partial_t f(t,x) + \frac{\sigma^2(x)}{2}\partial_{xx} f(t,x) = 0.$$

Because stochastic differential equation is homogeneous, we have $f(t,x) = \mathbb{E}[S_T|S_t = x] = \mathbb{E}[S_{T-t}|S_0 = x]$. By supermartingale property of S, $f(t,x)$ is non-decreasing in t for all x. Thus, $\partial_t f(t,x) \geq 0$. The Feynman–Kac partial differential equation implies that $\partial_{xx} f(t,x) \leq 0$ and thus f is concave and

$$\partial_x f(t,x) \leq 1$$

since $0 \leq f(t,x) \leq x$. This completes the proof. □

Example 5.5 (CEV process). The CEV process evolution $dS_t = S_t^{\delta+1} dW_t$ with $\delta > 0$ is a strict local martingale. From Linetsky and Mendoza 2010 [20], we have that

$$f(t,x) = \mathbb{E}^{\mathbb{Q}}[S_T|S_t = x] = xG\left(\upsilon, \frac{x^{-2\delta}}{2\delta^2(T-t)}\right),$$

where $\upsilon = \frac{1}{2\delta}$ and

$$G(\upsilon, x) = \frac{\int_0^y u^{\upsilon-1} e^{-u} du}{\Gamma(\upsilon)}.$$

The trading strategy can be explicitly computed as

$$\alpha_t = \frac{\partial}{\partial x} f(t,x) = xG\left(\upsilon, \frac{x^{-2\delta}}{2\delta^2(T-t)}\right) - \frac{x^{\alpha} e^{-\frac{x^{-2\delta}}{2\delta^2(T-t)}}}{\Gamma(\upsilon)\delta(T-t)} < 1,$$

where $\alpha = \frac{2\delta-1}{2\delta^2(T-t)} - 2\delta$.

Note that as $t \uparrow T$, $\lim_{t \to T} \frac{\partial}{\partial x} f(t,x) = 1$ for all $x > 0$.

We can also obtain the following corollary:

Corollary 5.6 (Time-homogeneous diffusions). *There does not exist a time-homogeneous diffusion bubble process β.*

Proof. Suppose β is a non-negative, strict local martingale such that $\beta_T = 0$ *a.s.* and $\beta_0 > 0$, then we have for any $t \in (0,T)$,

$$\mathbb{E}[\beta_t|\beta_0] = \mathbb{E}[\beta_T|\beta_{T-t} = \beta_0] = 0.$$

Hence, $\beta_t = 0$ *a.s.* $\forall t > 0$, contradicting the continuity of diffusion process. □

This means that either the market price or the fundamental value process has to be a time-inhomogeneous diffusion. We can extend Theorem 5.4 to a time-inhomogeneous diffusion using the explosion time characterization of a strict local martingale.

Theorem 5.7 (Trading strategy within [0, 1]). *Let*

$$dS_t = S_t\sigma(t,S_t)dW_t,$$

where $\sigma(t,x)$ is a positive $C^{1,2}$ function such that for any given t, $\sigma(t,x)$ is an increasing function in x. Let $\mathbb{F}$ be the filtration generated by S. Define

$$R(t,x) := \mathbb{R}(\zeta > T|S_t = x),$$

where from Proposition 2.7

$$\tilde{S}_t = S_t R(t,S_t).$$

Assume $R(t,\cdot) \in C^1$ for all t. Then,

$$\alpha_t \in [0,1], \forall t \in [0,T].$$

Proof. By the same proof as in Theorem 5.4, we have $\alpha_t \geq 0$. To show $\alpha_t \leq 1$, since

$$\alpha_t = \frac{\partial(xR(t,x))}{\partial x}|_{x=S_t} = R(t,S_t)z + S_t\partial_x R(t,S_t),$$

it suffices to show that $R(t,\cdot)$ is a decreasing function. Abusing notation, we define the process $\sigma_t = \sigma(t,S_t)$. By Ito's formula and Girsanov's theorem, under the measure $\mathbb{R}$,

$$\begin{aligned} d\sigma_t = &\left(\partial_t\sigma(t,S_t) + \frac{1}{2}\left(\partial_{xx}\sigma(t,S_t)\right)\sigma^2(t,S_t)\right)dt \\ &+ \left(\partial_x\sigma(t,S_t)\right)\sigma(t,S_t)dW_t^{\mathbb{R}}, \end{aligned} \tag{5}$$

where $W^{\mathbb{R}}$ is an $\mathbb{R}$-Brownian motion. For any fixed t and $x_1 \leq x_2$, by a comparison theorem for stochastic differential equations (see p. 293 in [19]), we have

$$\sigma_u^{t,y_1} \geq \sigma_u^{t,y_2}, \ \forall u \geq t,$$

where $\{\sigma_u^{t,y_i}\}_{u\in[t,T]}$ is the solution to the stochastic differential equation 5 with initial value at time t, $y_i = \sigma(t,x_i)$. Because σ_t is a continuous process, $\zeta = \lim_n\{u : \sigma_u \geq n\}$. Hence, we have $R(t,x_1) \geq R(t,x_2)$ since by the comparison result, the process σ^{t,y_1} explodes before σ^{t,y_2}. □

Example 5.8 (Complete market with stochastic volatility). Consider the price evolution

$$\begin{aligned} dS_t &= S_t\sigma_t^3 dW_t, \\ d\sigma_t &= \sigma_t dW_t. \end{aligned}$$

By the Markov property,

$$\tilde{S}_t = \mathbb{E}[S_T|\mathcal{F}_t] = g(t,S_t,\sigma_t),$$

where $g(t,x,v) = \mathbb{E}[S_t|S_t = x, \sigma_t = v]$. Then, by Theorem 5.7, we have

$$g(t,x,v) = xR(T-t,v),$$

where $R(t,v) = \mathbb{R}(\zeta > t|\sigma_0 = v)$ and σ_t follows

$$d\sigma_t = \sigma_t^3 dt + \sigma_t dW_t^{\mathbb{R}}$$

with $W^{\mathbb{R}}$ an $\mathbb{R}$-Brownian motion.[2] It can be shown that

$$R(t, v) = 2N(1/v\sqrt{t}) - 1,$$

where $N(\cdot)$ is the cumulative distribution function of a standard normal distribution.

Finally, by Ito's formula and the fact that $\tilde{S}$ is a local martingale (so the dt term is zero), we have

$$d\tilde{S} = R(T-t, \sigma_t)dS_t + S_t \frac{\partial_v R(T-t, \sigma_t)}{\partial \sigma_t} d\sigma_t.$$

Substituting $d\sigma_t = \sigma_t dW_t = \sigma_t \left(\frac{dS_t}{S_t \sigma_t^3}\right)$ into the above expression, we have

$$d\tilde{S}_t = R(T-t, \sigma_t)dS_t + \frac{\partial_v R(T-t, \sigma_t)}{\sigma_t^2} dS_t,$$

so

$$\alpha_t = R(T-t, \sigma_t) + \frac{\partial_v R(T-t, \sigma_t)}{\sigma_t^2}.$$

The above results apply to only Markov processes, but for a large class of non-Markov models, we could also specify the wealth preserving strategy by use of Malliavin calculus.

Example 5.9 (The dominating trading strategy). Consider the following model in a complete financial market:

$$\begin{aligned} d\tilde{S}_t &= \tilde{S}_t \sigma(\tilde{S}_t)(\theta(\beta_t, \tilde{S}_t)dt + dW_t), \\ d\beta_t &= \sigma^\beta(t, \beta_t)(\theta(\beta_t, \tilde{S}_t) + dW_t), \end{aligned}$$

where β is the bubble process such that $\beta_T = 0$, *a.s.* and θ is the market price of risk. In this model, the market price of risk depends on both the fundamental value and the bubble.

---

[2]The conditional probability of explosion of the quadratic variation, $R(t, v)$, only depends on the volatility because the evolution of the volatility does not depend on the asset's price.

Then, we have using the Clark–Ocone formula that

$$S_T = \mathbb{E}^{\mathbb{Q}}[S_T] + \int_0^T \mathbb{E}^{\mathbb{Q}}[\mathcal{D}_t S_T - S_T \int_t^T \mathcal{D}_t \theta_s d\tilde{W}_s | \mathcal{F}_t] d\tilde{W}_t,$$

where for any t, $\mathcal{D}_t$ is the Malliavin derivative operator (see, for example, Nualart 2006 [24]). By the chain rule of Malliavin calculus, we have that

$$\mathcal{D}_t \theta_s = \theta'(\beta_s) \mathcal{D}_t \beta_s.$$

And, $\mathcal{D}_t \beta_s$ has the following SDE:

$$d(\mathcal{D}_t \beta_s) = \partial_x \sigma^{\beta}(t, \beta_t)(\mathcal{D}_t \beta_s) dW_s.$$

In this model, β is the state variable that drives the evolution of the market.

Finally, in this case, we have

$$\alpha_t = \frac{1}{\tilde{S}_t \sigma(\tilde{S}_t) + \sigma^{\beta}(t, \beta_t)} \left[\mathbb{E}^{\mathbb{Q}}[\mathcal{D}_t S_T - S_T \int_t^T \mathcal{D}_t \theta_s d\tilde{W}_s | \mathcal{F}_t] \right].$$

Example 5.10 (Counterexamples to $\alpha_t \in [0, 1]$).

1. ($\alpha_t < 0$) Suppose that the fundamental value and bubble are given by the following processes:

$$d\beta_t = \sigma_t^{\beta} dW_t^{\mathbb{Q}},$$
$$d\tilde{S}_t = \sigma_t^{\tilde{S}} dW_t^{\mathbb{Q}},$$

where

$$\sigma_t^{\beta} = -2\sqrt{T} \frac{(1 + \tilde{S}_t)\beta_t}{\sqrt{T - t}}$$

and

$$\sigma_t^{\tilde{S}} = \tilde{S}_t(\beta_t \wedge 1).$$

By Novikov's condition, $\tilde{S}$ is a proper positive martingale. And, β is a local martingale. Furthermore, $\beta_T = 0$ *a.s.*, so it is a strict local martingale, and hence a bubble process. Note that β is also a positive proper martingale on $[0, T)$, since $\tilde{S}$ does not explode on $[0, T]$.

Both σ^β and $\sigma^{\tilde{S}}$ are non-zero and have $\frac{\sigma^\beta}{\sigma^{\tilde{S}}} < -2, \forall t \in [0,T)$. This shows that

$$dS_t = \left(\frac{\sigma_t^\beta}{\sigma_t^{\tilde{S}}} + 1\right) d\tilde{S}_t,$$

which implies that

$$d\tilde{S}_t = \frac{1}{\frac{\sigma_t^\beta}{\sigma_t^{\tilde{S}}} + 1} dS_t.$$

Hence, $\alpha_t = \frac{1}{\frac{\sigma_t^\beta}{\sigma_t^{\tilde{S}}}+1}$, which is strictly negative throughout the whole period, i.e., the wealth preserving and dominating trading strategy has a negative position in the risky asset over $[0,T)$.

2. ($\alpha_t > 1$) Suppose that $\tilde{S}$ is a geometric Brownian motion with unit volatility and $S_0 = 1$. Define the bubble process β as follows:

$$d\beta_t = -\left(\beta_t \wedge \frac{1}{3}\right) dW_t^{\mathbb{Q}}, t \in [0, (T/2) \wedge \tau_{1/2}^{\tilde{S}}),$$

$$d\beta_t = \frac{\beta_t}{\sqrt{T-t}} dW_t^{\mathbb{Q}}, t \in [(T/2) \wedge \tau_{1/2}^{\tilde{S}}, T],$$

where $\tau_{1/2}^{\tilde{S}} = \inf\{t : \tilde{S}_t \leq 1/2\}$. The choice of $\tau_{1/2}^{\tilde{S}} = \inf\{t : \tilde{S}_t \leq 1/2\}$ guarantees that the volatility of S is never zero so the market is complete. By construction, the volatility of S is smaller than $\tilde{S}$, which implies using expression (4) that $\alpha > 1$ on $[0, (T/2) \wedge \tau_{1/2}^{\tilde{S}})$.

This completes the counterexamples.

Let S be a continuous Markov process with $\mathbb{F}$ the filtration generated by S, and define

$$R(t,x) := \mathbb{R}(\zeta > T | S_t = x).$$

Recall from Proposition 2.7 that

$$\tilde{S}_t = x\mathbb{R}(\tau > T | S_t = x) = \alpha_0(t) + \alpha_t x.$$

We can prove the following result:

Proposition 5.11 (Rate of change of percentage holdings in the risky asset). *Assume $R(t,x)$ is differential in x for all $t \in [0,T]$ a.s. $\mathbb{Q}$. Then,*

$$\frac{\alpha_t S_t}{\tilde{S}_t} = 1 - S_t \frac{d \log R(t, S_t)}{dS_t}.$$

Proof. Given $x\mathbb{R}(\tau > T | S_t = x) = \alpha_0(t) + \alpha_t x$, taking a derivative with respect to x yields

$$\alpha_t = R(t,x) - x\frac{dR(t,x)}{dx}.$$

But $\alpha_t S_t = \alpha_t x = xR(t,x) - x^2 \frac{dR(t,x)}{dx}$. Hence,

$$\frac{\alpha_t S_t}{\tilde{S}_t} = \frac{xR(t,x) - x^2 \frac{dR(t,x)}{dx}}{xR(t,x)} = 1 - x\frac{d \log R(t,x)}{dx}.$$ □

This proposition implies that as the market price $S_t = x$ increases, if $\frac{d \log R(t,x)}{dx}$ increases, then the holdings in the risky asset as a percent of the fundamental value, within the replicating trading strategy, decrease. But, $\frac{d \log R(t,x)}{dx}$ measures the percentage change in the size of the bubble, so as the bubble percentage increases, the holdings in the risky asset as a percent of the fundamental value decline.

5.2. *Incomplete Markets*

This section studies super-replicating admissible s.f.t.s. in an incomplete market. Because the market is incomplete, the set of ELMMs contains an infinite number of elements. We assume that the market selects a particular ELMM, $\tilde{\mathbb{Q}} \in \mathcal{M}$, for use in defining the asset's fundamental value. The asset's price bubble is defined with respect to $\tilde{\mathbb{Q}} \in \mathcal{M}$.

In this incomplete market, for any $\mathbb{Q} \in \mathcal{M}$, the risky asset price process S is a non-negative $\mathbb{Q}$ local martingale, hence a supermartingale. This implies $\mathbb{E}^{\mathbb{Q}}[S_T] \leq S_0$ for all $\mathbb{Q} \in \mathcal{M}$, hence, $\sup_{\mathbb{Q}\in\mathcal{M}} \mathbb{E}^{\mathbb{Q}}[S_T] \leq S_0$. Define the process

$$Y_t := \operatorname*{ess\,sup}_{\mathbb{Q}\in\mathcal{M}} \mathbb{E}^{\mathbb{Q}}[S_T|\mathcal{F}_t],$$

where $Y_0 = \sup_{\mathbb{Q}\in\mathcal{M}} \mathbb{E}^{\mathbb{Q}}[S_T] \leq S_0$ and $Y_T = S_T$. Y is a supermartingale for all $\mathbb{Q} \in \mathcal{M}$. By the optional decomposition theorem (see

Follmer and Kabanov 1998 [5]), there exists a non-decreasing cadlag adapted process C with $C_0 = 0$ and an $\alpha \in \mathscr{L}(S)$ such that

$$Y_t = Y_0 + \int_0^t \alpha dS_t - C_t, \tag{6}$$

where $\int_0^t \alpha dS_t$ is a $\mathbb{Q}$ local martingale for all $\mathbb{Q} \in \mathcal{M}$.

Consider the trading strategy represented by $(\alpha_0(t), \alpha_t)$ with α as given in expression (6), $\alpha_0(t) := \tilde{Y}_t - \alpha_t S_t$, and the wealth process

$$\tilde{Y}_t = \sup_{\mathbb{Q}\in\mathcal{M}} \mathbb{E}^{\mathbb{Q}}[S_T] + \int_0^t \alpha dS_t = \alpha_0(t) + \alpha_t S_t. \tag{7}$$

This trading strategy $(\alpha_0(t), \alpha_t) \in \mathcal{A}(\sup_{\mathbb{Q}\in\mathcal{M}_l} \mathbb{E}^{\mathbb{Q}}[S_T])$ because it is self-financing by construction, and it is admissible since $\tilde{Y}_t = Y_t + C_t \geq 0$ a.s. For this admissible s.f.t.s., we have

$$Y_t = \tilde{Y}_t - C_t$$

which implies that Y represents the wealth process of an admissible trading strategy with a cumulative cash outflow of C_t over $[0, t]$. The trading strategy $(\alpha_0(t), \alpha_t) \in \mathcal{A}(\sup_{\mathbb{Q}\in\mathcal{M}} \mathbb{E}^{\mathbb{Q}}[S_T])$ is said to super-replicate the risky asset's time T payoff because

$$\tilde{Y}_T = S_T + C_T \geq S_T \quad a.s.$$

(see Jarrow 2021 [12], Chapter 8 for more details on super-replication trading strategies).

Hence, the trading strategy $(\alpha_0(t), \alpha_t) \in \mathcal{A}(\sup_{\mathbb{Q}\in\mathcal{M}} \mathbb{E}^{\mathbb{Q}}[S_T])$ is a dominating trading strategy if $\tilde{\mathbb{Q}}(\tilde{Y}_T = Y_T + C_T > Y_T) > 0$ because its initial cost $\tilde{Y}_0 = \sup_{\mathbb{Q}\in\mathcal{M}} \mathbb{E}^{\mathbb{Q}}[S_T] \leq S_0$ and $\tilde{\mathbb{Q}}(\tilde{Y}_T = Y_T + C_T \geq Y_T) = 1$, where $\tilde{\mathbb{Q}} \in \mathcal{M}$ is the ELMM chosen by the market under which S is a strict local martingale. It is wealth preserving if $\tilde{Y}_t$ is a $\tilde{\mathbb{Q}}$ martingale. These insights are formalized in the following proposition:

Proposition 5.12 (Wealth preserving and dominating s.f.t.s.). *The super-replicating admissible s.f.t.s.* $(\alpha_0(t), \alpha_t) \in \mathcal{A}(\sup_{\mathbb{Q}\in\mathcal{M}} \mathbb{E}^{\mathbb{Q}}[S_T])$ *from expression (7) with wealth process*

$$\tilde{Y}_t = \sup_{\mathbb{Q}\in\mathcal{M}} \mathbb{E}^{\mathbb{Q}}[S_T] + \int_0^t \alpha dS_t = \alpha_0(t) + \alpha_t S_t$$

(1) *is dominating iff* $\tilde{\mathbb{Q}}(\tilde{Y}_T > S_T) > 0$,
(2) *is wealth preserving iff* $\tilde{Y}_t$ *is a* $\tilde{\mathbb{Q}}$ *martingale,*

where $\tilde{\mathbb{Q}} \in \mathcal{M}$ *is the ELMM chosen by the market under which* S *is a strict local martingale.*

The following corollary characterizes this super-replicating trading strategy for continuous Markov processes:

Corollary 5.13 (Characterization of the super-replicating trading strategy). *If* S *is a continuous Markov process, and* $\operatorname{ess\,sup}_{\mathbb{Q}\in\mathcal{M}} \mathbb{E}^{\mathbb{Q}}[S_T|S_t]$ is *a* $C^{1,2}$ *function of time* t *and risky asset price* S_t, *then*

$$\alpha_t = \frac{\partial \left(\operatorname{ess\,sup}_{\mathbb{Q}\in\mathcal{M}} \mathbb{E}^{\mathbb{Q}}[S_T|S_t] \right)}{\partial S_t}.$$

Proof. If S is a Markov process, then $\mathbb{E}^{\mathbb{Q}}[S_T|\mathcal{F}_t] = \mathbb{E}^{\mathbb{Q}}[S_T|S_t]$.
Ito's lemma on expression $Y_t := \operatorname{ess\,sup}_{\mathbb{Q}\in\mathcal{M}_l} \mathbb{E}^{\mathbb{Q}}[S_T|S_t]$ gives

$$dY_t = \left(\frac{\partial Y_t}{\partial t} + \frac{1}{2}\frac{\partial^2 Y_t}{\partial S_t^2} \right) d\langle S, S\rangle_t + \frac{\partial Y_t}{\partial S_t} dS_t.$$

Equating the integrand of dS_t in expression (6) completes the proof. □

As shown, for a continuous Markov process, the super-replicating trading strategy is just the partial derivative of the essential supremum of the conditional expected value with respect to the asset's price at time t.

Remark 5.14 (Essential Supremum Attained). In general, if the set of uniformly integrable martingale measures is non-empty, then it is always true that there exists a $\mathbb{Q} \in \mathcal{M}$ such that

$$Y_0 := \sup_{\mathbb{Q}\in\mathcal{M}} \mathbb{E}^{\mathbb{Q}}[S_T] = S_0.$$

Indeed, clearly, we have $Y_0 \leq S_0$ by the supermartingale property. If $\mathbb{Q}_{UI}$ is a uniformly integrable martingale measure, then we have $Y_0 = \sup_{\mathbb{Q}\in\mathcal{M}} \mathbb{E}^{\mathbb{Q}}[S_T] \geq \mathbb{E}^{\mathbb{Q}_{UI}}[S_T] = S_0$. Note that it is possible that $Y_0 = S_0$ and there is no true martingale measure (see Example 3.7 in Herdegen and Schweizer 2015 [7]).

We next give an example where there exists a uniformly integrable martingale measure, the essential supremum is obtained and the super-replicating trading strategy $\alpha \equiv 1$. Here, the trading strategy is neither a dominating strategy nor a wealth preserving strategy.[3]

Example 5.15 (Super-replicating trading strategy). Suppose that the market contains two independent $\mathbb{Q}$ — Brownian motions B^1 and B^2. Define $\sigma := \inf\{t : \mathcal{E}(B^2)_{A_t} = k\} \wedge T$ for some fixed $k > 0$, where $\mathcal{E}$ denotes the stochastic exponential and A_t is a strictly increasing process such that $\lim_{t \to T} A_t = \infty$. Define the risky asset price to be

$$S_t = \mathcal{E}(B^1)_{A_{t \wedge \sigma}}.$$

Define $Z = \mathcal{E}(B^2)_{A_{t \wedge \sigma}}$. Then, we have the following:

- S is a strict $\mathbb{Q}$ local martingale.
- Z is a positive martingale so that $\mathbb{Q}^* \sim \mathbb{Q}$, where $Z_T = \frac{d\mathbb{Q}^*}{d\mathbb{Q}}$.
- Under $\mathbb{Q}^*$, S is a true martingale so

$$\operatorname*{ess\ sup}_{\mathbb{Q} \in \mathcal{M}_l} \mathbb{E}^{\mathbb{Q}}[S_T | S_t] = \mathbb{E}^{\mathbb{Q}^*}[S_T | \mathcal{F}_t] = S_t.$$

This implies

$$\alpha_t = \frac{\partial (\mathbb{E}^{\mathbb{Q}^*}[S_T | \mathcal{F}_t])}{\partial S_t} = 1, \forall t \in [0, T].$$

6. Conclusion

This chapter studies an arbitrage-free, frictionless and competitive market with trading in a single risky asset and a money market account, where the risky asset exhibits a price bubble. We study various self-financing and admissible trading strategies that are wealth preserving and take a positive holding in the risky asset. Included in this class are dominating trading strategies that replicate or super-replicate the payoffs to the risky asset at the model's horizon.

[3]Note that when a martingale measure exists, this implies that the economy satisfies no dominance. Hence, the buy and hold trading strategy generating the asset's time T payoff cannot be otherwise attained.

The insights of this chapter can be used to understand and characterize an investor's optimal trading strategy in the presence of price bubbles, in this regard, see Jarrow and Liu 2022 [16].

Appendix

Lemma A.1. *Suppose that*

$$dS_t = \sigma(S_t)dW_t$$

where $\mathbb{P}(S_t \in (a,b)) > 0$ *for all* $a < b \in \mathbb{R}$, *and define* $f(t,x) = \mathbb{E}[S_T|S_t = x]$ *for* $x \in [0,\infty)$.

And, U *is any non-negative classical solution to PDE:*

$$\partial_t u + \frac{\sigma^2}{2}\partial_{xx}u = 0, (t,x) \in [0,T] \times \mathbb{R}^+,$$
$$u(T,x) = x, x \in \mathbb{R}^+.$$

First, the process $f(t,S_t)$ *is a true martingale since we have* $f(t,S_t) = \mathbb{E}[S_T|\mathcal{F}_t]$. *And,* $f(T,S_T) = S_T$. *Second, we have* $U(t,S_t)$ *is a local martingale since it is driftless by Ito's formula. Finally, it is a supermartingale since it is bounded from below. Then, we have*

$$\begin{aligned} U(t,S_t) &\geq \mathbb{E}[U(T,S_T)|\mathcal{F}_t] \\ &= \mathbb{E}[S_T|\mathcal{F}_t] \\ &= f(t,S_t). \end{aligned}$$

In particular, we have $f(t,x) \leq U(t,x), \forall(t,x) \in [0,T] \times \mathbb{R}^+$.

References

[1] A. Cherny. Families of consistent probability measures. *Theory of Probability and Its Applications*, 46(1): 118–121, 2002.

[2] A. Cox and D. Hobson. Local martingales, bubbles and option prices. *Finance Stoch.*, 9: 477–492, 2005.

[3] H. Dengler and R. Jarrow. Option pricing using a binomial model with random time steps (A Formal Model of Gamma Hedging). *Review of Derivatives Research*, 1:107–138, 1997.

[4] L. Eisenberg and R. Jarrow. Option pricing with random volatilities in complete markets. *Review of Quantitative Finance and Accounting*, 4:5–17, 1994.

[5] H. Follmer and Y. M. Kabanov. Optional decomposition and Lagrange multipliers. *Finance and Stochastics*, 2:69–81, 1998.

[6] M. Herdegen and S. Herrmann. Strict local martingales and optimal investment in a Black–Scholes model with a bubble. *Mathematical Finance*, 29(1):285–328, 2018.

[7] M. Herdegen, and M. Schweizer. Economics-based financial bubbles (and why they imply strict local martingales) (No. 15-05). Swiss Finance Institute, 2015.

[8] S. L. Heston, M. Loewenstein and G. A. Willard. Options and bubbles. *Rev. Financial Stud.*, 20:359–390, 2007.

[9] J. Jacod and P. Protter. Risk neutral compatibility with option prices. *Finance and Stochastics*, 14:285–315, 2010.

[10] R. Jarrow. Asset price bubbles. *Annual Review of Financial Economics*, 7:201–218, 2015.

[11] R. Jarrow. On the existence of competitive equilibrium in frictionless and incomplete stochastic asset markets. *Mathematics and Financial Economics*, 11(4):455–477, 2017.

[12] R. Jarrow. *Continuous-time Asset Pricing Theory*: A Martingale-*Based Approach*, 2nd Edition. Springer, Berlin, 2021.

[13] R. Jarrow, Y. Kchia, and P. Protter. How to detect an asset bubble. *SIAMJ. Financ. Math*, 2:839–865, 2011.

[14] R. Jarrow and S. Kwok. Inferring financial bubbles from option data. *Journal of Applied Econometrics*, 1–21, 2021.

[15] R. Jarrow and M. Larsson. The meaning of market efficiency. *Mathematical Finance*, 22(1):1–30, 2012.

[16] R. Jarrow and Y. Liu. Portfolio optimization in the presence of asset price bubbles. Working paper, Cornell University, 2022.

[17] R. Jarrow, P. Protter and K. Shimbo. Asset price bubbles in complete markets. In *Advances in Mathematical Finance*, Appl. Numer. Harmon. Anal., Birkhauser, Boston, MA, 2007, pp. 97–121.

[18] R. Jarrow, P. Protter, and K. Shimbo. Asset price bubbles in incomplete markets. *Math. Finance,* 20:145–185, 2010.

[19] I. Karatzas and S. Shreve. *Brownian Motion and Stochastic Calculus*, Springer, Berlin, 1988.

[20] V. Linetsky and R. Mendoza. Constant elasticity of variance (cev) diffusion model. *Encyclopedia of Quantitative Finance*, 2010.

[21] M. Loewenstein and G. A. Willard. Local martingales, arbitrage, and viability. Free snacks and cheap thrills. *Economic Theory*, 16:135–161, 2000.

[22] M. Loewenstein and G. A. Willard. Rational equilibrium asset-pricing bubbles in continuous trading models. *J. Economic Theory*, 91:17–58, 2000.

[23] A. Mijatovic and M. Urusov. On the martingale property of certain local martingales. *Probab. Theory Relat. Fields*, 152:1–30, 2012.

[24] D. Nualart. *The Malliavin Calculus and Related Topics.* Springer, Berlin, 2006, vol. 1995, pp. 317.

[25] Y. Obayashi, P. Protter, and S. Yang. The lifetime of a financial bubble. *Mathematics and Financial Economics*, 11:45–63, 2017.

[26] P. Protter. A mathematical theory of financial bubbles. In *Paris-Princeton Lectures on Mathematical Finance.* Lecture Notes in Mathematics, Springer, Berlin, 2013, vol. 2081, pp. 1–108.

[27] D. Schwarz. Market completion with derivative securities. *Finance and Stochastics*, 21:263–284, 2017.

[28] M. Schweizer and J. Wissel. Term structures of implied volatilities: Absence of arbitrage and existence results. *Mathematical Finance*, 18:77–114, 2008.

https://doi.org/10.1142/9789811280306_0015

Chapter 15

EMA-Type Trading Strategies Maximize Utility under Partial Information*

Xiaodong Chen[†] **and Roger Lee**[‡]

University of Chicago, Department of Mathematics,
Chicago, IL, USA
[†] *xdchen1994@gmail.com,*
[‡] *rogerlee@math.uchicago.edu*

Abstract

Consider a partially informed trader who does not observe the true drift of a financial asset. Under Gaussian price dynamics with stochastic unobserved drift, including cases of mean-reversion and momentum dynamics, we take a filtering approach to solve explicitly for trading strategies which maximize expected logarithmic, exponential and power utility. We prove that the optimal strategies depend on current price and an exponentially weighted moving average (EMA) price, and in some cases current wealth, not on any other stochastic variables. We establish optimality over *all* price-history-dependent strategies satisfying integrability criteria, not just EMA-type strategies. Thus the condition that the optimal trading strategy reduces to a function of EMA and current price is not an assumption but rather a consequence of our analysis. We solve explicitly for the optimal parameters of the EMA-type strategies and verify optimality rigorously.

*Dedicated to Peter Carr. We thank the refereeing/editorial team, and Dilip Madan, and conference participants at Maryland, NYU, IMPA, SIAM and the Bachelier Congress, for their valuable comments.

Keywords: EMA, EWMA, Exponentially weighted moving average, Kalman-Bucy filter, Partial information, Optimal trading, Expected utility maximization, Mean reversion, Momentum

1. Introduction

Consider a partially informed trader who does not observe the drift of a financial asset driven by a hidden stochastic state variable. This framework includes cases where the drift pulls the market price to revert toward a hidden stochastic state variable that represents the "fair value" of the financial asset, as well as cases where the drift is a hidden "momentum" variable. The trader who dynamically trades this asset faces the question of what strategy to follow, given the price history.

On one hand, various *technical analysis* approaches include buy/sell signals that depend on comparing the current price against a *moving average* or exponentially weighted moving average (EMA) of recent prices. It is common in practice to assess the empirical performance of such signals by backtesting on historical data, but this does not address the foundational questions of proving rigorously that trading strategies should use moving average signals in the first place and justifying exactly what explicit functional form should map the moving averages into optimal trades.

On the other hand, the *stochastic control* approach defines the objective of maximizing the expected utility of terminal wealth and solves the optimization problem under various assumptions, beginning with the Merton [17] problem which assumes a known constant drift and extending to cases of stochastic but observable drift [1, 10]. Further extensions [2–7, 9, 13, 14] incorporate a *filtering* approach to find strategies optimized for the *partial information* case of unobserved drift but without explicitly linking the solutions to the EMA of observable prices. Alternatively, assuming full information, other approaches exogenously impose moving-average dynamics on the price paths or constraints of moving-average type on the strategy space [12, 16].

Building on the partial information approach, this chapter's main contributions are three-fold.

First, we prove that the optimal position is a function of only: an EMA (which, in our terminology, always designates an explicit moving average of observable *price levels*, not of Brownian increments), the current price and in some cases, current wealth, and we solve for this optimal function explicitly, by expressing the Kalman–Bucy filter as an EMA. We do not constrain the optimization to maximize *within* some class of exogenously specified EMA-type strategies nor do we exogenously impose EMA-type dynamics for the price process. Rather, starting with SDEs (without lags/averaging) for the state variables, we optimize over *all* admissible functions of the entire price history and *conclude*, endogenously, that an EMA-type strategy wins.

Second, we obtain exact and *explicit* formulas for the optimal trading strategies given partial information in all cases: not only exponential and log utility but also power utility, and for dynamics which include both mean-reversion and momentum cases. The explicit nature of the solutions not only simplifies implementation but also provides intuition and insight into which factors drive which features of the optimal trades in which directions.

Third, in proving optimality relative to a specified universe of admissible strategies, we verify rigorously not only that the claimed optimal strategy is admissible but also moreover that it satisfies a stronger regularity condition, namely a natural sup-integrability condition purely on the induced value function, essentially establishing some control over the severity of the strategy's drawdowns.

2. Mean-Reverting and Momentum Dynamics

On a probability space $(\Omega, \mathcal{F}, \mathbb{P})$ with filtration $\{\mathcal{F}_t\}_{t\geq 0}$ supporting Brownian motions W and Z with correlation $\rho \in (-1, 1)$, let X and Θ be the unique strong solutions to the linear SDEs

$$\mathrm{d}X_t = (\tilde{\kappa}\Theta_t - \kappa_x X_t)\mathrm{d}t + \sigma_x \mathrm{d}W_t, \tag{1}$$

where $\tilde{\kappa} > 0$ and $\kappa_x \geq 0$ and $\sigma_x > 0$, and

$$\mathrm{d}\Theta_t = (\mu - \kappa_\theta \Theta_t)\mathrm{d}t + \sigma_\theta \mathrm{d}Z_t, \tag{2}$$

where $\kappa_\theta \geq 0$ and $\sigma_\theta > 0$.

Here X models the price of some underlying asset or combination of assets. For instance, X could be the spread between two futures contracts or X could be the price of a long-short combination of two stocks, at some fixed ratio. The drift of X contains the unobserved factor Θ. The case $\tilde{\kappa} = \kappa_x > 0$ produces mean-reversion dynamics where the level of X reverts toward Θ. The case $(\tilde{\kappa}, \kappa_x) = (1, 0)$ produces "momentum" dynamics where the drift of the non-stationary process X *is* Θ.

The hidden drift driver Θ itself varies stochastically. If $\kappa_\theta > 0$, then Θ reverts toward long-term level μ/κ_θ; on the other hand, if $\kappa_\theta = 0$, then Θ has constant drift μ.

Both X and Θ are adapted to $\mathcal{F}$, the *full-information* filtration. Let $\mathcal{F}^X$ denote the *partial-information* filtration generated by the observed price process X alone.

2.1. *The Kalman–Bucy Filter*

Section 2.1 applies the Kalman–Bucy filter [8, 15, 19] to express the model (1,2) in terms of processes adapted to the partial information filtration $\mathcal{F}^X$.

With respect to $\mathcal{F}^X$, the drift factor Θ is unobserved but does admit an estimate

$$\hat{\Theta}_t := \mathbb{E}(\Theta_t | \mathcal{F}_t^X) \tag{3}$$

with an uncertainty quantified by the conditional variance

$$\gamma_t := \mathrm{Var}(\Theta_t | \mathcal{F}_t^X) = \mathbb{E}\Theta_t^2 - \mathbb{E}\hat{\Theta}_t^2 \tag{4}$$

which is deterministic and satisfies the ODE

$$\frac{\mathrm{d}\gamma_t}{\mathrm{d}t} = -2\kappa_\theta \gamma_t + \sigma_\theta^2 - \left(\frac{\tilde{\kappa}\gamma_t}{\sigma_x} + \sigma_\theta \rho \right)^2. \tag{5}$$

Hence

$$\gamma_t = \frac{\sigma_x^2}{\tilde{\kappa}^2} \left(R \frac{e^{2Rt} + g}{e^{2Rt} - g} - \kappa_\theta - \rho \frac{\sigma_\theta \tilde{\kappa}}{\sigma_x} \right), \tag{6}$$

where

$$R := \sqrt{\kappa_\theta^2 + 2\rho\kappa_\theta \frac{\sigma_\theta \tilde{\kappa}}{\sigma_x} + \left(\frac{\sigma_\theta \tilde{\kappa}}{\sigma_x} \right)^2} \tag{7}$$

and

$$g := \frac{\gamma_0\tilde{\kappa}^2 + \sigma_\theta\sigma_x\tilde{\kappa}\rho + \sigma_x^2\kappa_\theta - \sigma_x^2 R}{\gamma_0\tilde{\kappa}^2 + \sigma_\theta\sigma_x\tilde{\kappa}\rho + \sigma_x^2\kappa_\theta + \sigma_x^2 R} < 1. \tag{8}$$

Thus, for all $\gamma_0 \geq 0$, we have $\gamma_t \to \bar{\gamma}$ as $t \to \infty$, where

$$\bar{\gamma} := \frac{\sigma_x^2}{\tilde{\kappa}^2}\left(R - \kappa_\theta - \rho\frac{\sigma_\theta\tilde{\kappa}}{\sigma_x}\right) \tag{9}$$

represents the long-term or steady-state level of uncertainty about Θ; moreover $\operatorname{sgn} g = \operatorname{sgn}(\gamma_0 - \bar{\gamma})$, and in particular $g = 0$ if and only if $\gamma_0 = \bar{\gamma}$.

Defining x by

$$\mathrm{d}x_t = \frac{1}{\sigma_x}\mathrm{d}X_t + \frac{\kappa_x}{\sigma_x}X_t\mathrm{d}t = \frac{\tilde{\kappa}}{\sigma_x}\Theta_t\mathrm{d}t + \mathrm{d}W_t, \tag{10}$$

we have

$$\mathrm{d}\hat{\Theta}_t = (\mu - \kappa_\theta\hat{\Theta}_t)\mathrm{d}t + \sigma_{\hat{\theta}}(t)\mathrm{d}\nu_t, \tag{11}$$

where

$$\sigma_{\hat{\theta}}(t) := \frac{\tilde{\kappa}\gamma_t}{\sigma_x} + \sigma_\theta\rho = \frac{\sigma_x}{\tilde{\kappa}}\left(R\frac{e^{2Rt} + g}{e^{2Rt} - g} - \kappa_\theta\right) \tag{12}$$

and the "innovation" process

$$\nu_t := x_t - \int_0^t \frac{\tilde{\kappa}}{\sigma_x}\hat{\Theta}_s\mathrm{d}s \tag{13}$$

is an $\mathcal{F}^X$-Brownian motion. Therefore,

$$\mathrm{d}X_t = \sigma_x\mathrm{d}x_t - \kappa_x X_t\mathrm{d}t = (\tilde{\kappa}\hat{\Theta}_t - \kappa_x X_t)\mathrm{d}t + \sigma_x\mathrm{d}\nu_t \tag{14}$$

which, together with (11), shows that $(X_t, \hat{\Theta}_t)$ is Markov with respect to the partial information filtration $\mathcal{F}^X$.

2.2. *The Filter is a Moving Average of Price Levels*

The estimate $\hat{\Theta}$ of the hidden drift factor given the entire price history reduces to a combination of an *EMA* of trailing *price levels* and the current price level. Proposition 2.1 makes this precise.

Proposition 2.1. *We have*

$$\hat{\Theta}_t = J(t)\frac{\mu}{\kappa_\theta} + \frac{1}{F(t)}\hat{\Theta}_0 - \frac{\sigma_{\hat{\theta}}(0)}{\sigma_x F(t)}X_0 + \frac{\sigma_{\hat{\theta}}(t)}{\sigma_x}X_t + \int_0^t K(s,t)X_s\mathrm{d}s, \tag{15}$$

where

$$\begin{aligned} F(t) &:= \exp\left(R\int_0^t \frac{e^{2Rs}+g}{e^{2Rs}-g}\mathrm{d}s\right) = \frac{e^{Rt}-ge^{-Rt}}{1-g}, \\ J(t) &:= \frac{\kappa_\theta(e^{Rt}-1)(e^{Rt}-g)}{R(e^{2Rt}-g)}, \\ K(s,t) &:= \frac{g(R+\kappa_x)(R+\kappa_\theta)e^{-R(t+s)} - (R-\kappa_x)(R-\kappa_\theta)e^{-R(t-s)}}{\tilde{\kappa}\,(1-ge^{-2Rt})}. \end{aligned} \tag{16}$$

Proof. We have

$$\begin{aligned} \mathrm{d}\hat{\Theta}_t &= (\mu - \kappa_\theta\hat{\Theta}_t)\mathrm{d}t + \sigma_{\hat{\theta}}(t)\left(\mathrm{d}x_t - \frac{\tilde{\kappa}}{\sigma_x}\hat{\Theta}_t\mathrm{d}t\right) \\ &= \left(\mu - (\kappa_\theta + \frac{\tilde{\kappa}}{\sigma_x}\sigma_{\hat{\theta}}(t))\hat{\Theta}_t\right)\mathrm{d}t + \sigma_{\hat{\theta}}(t)\mathrm{d}x_t \\ &= \left(\mu - R\frac{e^{2Rt}+g}{e^{2Rt}-g}\hat{\Theta}_t\right)\mathrm{d}t + \sigma_{\hat{\theta}}(t)\mathrm{d}x_t. \end{aligned} \tag{17}$$

To simplify the drift, the "integrating factor" $F(t)$ was chosen such that the dynamics of the product $F(t)\hat{\Theta}_t$ can be written in terms of (t, X) without reference to $\hat{\Theta}_t$. Explicitly,

$$\begin{aligned} \mathrm{d}(F(t)\hat{\Theta}_t) &= \hat{\Theta}_t F'(t)\mathrm{d}t + F(t)\mathrm{d}\hat{\Theta}_t = \mu F(t)\mathrm{d}t + F(t)\sigma_{\hat{\theta}}(t)\mathrm{d}x_t \\ &= \mu F(t)\mathrm{d}t + \frac{1}{\sigma_x}\Lambda(t)\mathrm{d}X_t + \frac{\kappa_x}{\sigma_x}\Lambda(t)X_t\mathrm{d}t, \end{aligned} \tag{18}$$

where $\Lambda(t) := F(t)\sigma_{\hat{\theta}}(t)$. Then

$$F(t)\hat{\Theta}_t - F(0)\hat{\Theta}_0 = \mu \int_0^t F(s)\mathrm{d}s + \frac{\kappa_x}{\sigma_x} \int_0^t \Lambda(s) X_s \mathrm{d}s \\ + \frac{1}{\sigma_x}\left(\Lambda(t)X_t - \Lambda(0)X_0 - \int_0^t X_s \mathrm{d}\Lambda(s)\right),$$

hence

$$\hat{\Theta}_t = \frac{1}{F(t)}\hat{\Theta}_0 + \frac{\mu}{F(t)}\int_0^t F(s)\mathrm{d}s + \frac{\sigma_{\hat{\theta}}(t)}{\sigma_x}X_t - \frac{\sigma_{\hat{\theta}}(0)}{\sigma_x F(t)}X_0 \\ + \frac{1}{\sigma_x F(t)}\int_0^t (\kappa_x \Lambda(s) - \Lambda'(s))X_s \mathrm{d}s. \tag{19}$$

Now J and K were defined to satisfy

$$J(t) = \frac{\kappa_\theta}{F(t)}\int_0^t F(s)\mathrm{d}s \qquad \text{and} \qquad K(s,t) = \frac{\kappa_x \Lambda(s) - \Lambda'(s)}{\sigma_x F(t)},$$

hence (15) follows from (19). □

For functions $f_{1,2} : [0,\infty) \to \mathbb{R}$, let the notation $f_1(t) \sim f_2(t)$ mean that $f_1/f_2 \to 1$ as $t \to \infty$.

Then the coefficients of μ/κ_θ, $\hat{\Theta}_0$, X_0 and X_t have, respectively, asymptotic behavior

$$\begin{aligned} J(t) &\sim \frac{\kappa_\theta}{R}(1 - e^{-Rt}), \\ \frac{1}{F(t)} &\sim e^{-Rt}, \\ -\frac{\sigma_{\hat{\theta}}(0)}{\sigma_x F(t)} &\sim \frac{R-\kappa_\theta}{\tilde{\kappa}}e^{-Rt} \qquad \text{if } R \neq \kappa_\theta, \text{ otherwise} \sim -\frac{2gR}{\tilde{\kappa}}e^{-Rt}, \\ \frac{\sigma_{\hat{\theta}}(t)}{\sigma_x} &\sim \frac{R-\kappa_\theta}{\tilde{\kappa}} \qquad \text{if } R \neq \kappa_\theta, \text{ otherwise} \sim \frac{2gR}{\tilde{\kappa}}e^{-2Rt}. \end{aligned} \tag{20}$$

In the case $g = 0$, these asymptotic equivalences hold with *equality* for *all* $t \geq 0$, and

$$K(s,t) = -\frac{(R-\kappa_x)(R-\kappa_\theta)}{\tilde{\kappa}}e^{-R(t-s)}.$$

Remark 2.2. Let $g = 0$, let $\kappa_\theta > 0$ and let t be large. Then the non-vanishing terms in (15) are

$$J(t)\frac{\mu}{\kappa_\theta} + \frac{\sigma_{\hat{\theta}}(t)}{\sigma_x}X_t + \frac{(\kappa_x - R)(R - \kappa_\theta)}{\tilde{\kappa}}\int_0^t e^{-R(t-s)}X_s\mathrm{d}s$$

$$\approx \frac{\kappa_\theta}{R}\cdot\frac{\mu}{\kappa_\theta} + \left(1 - \frac{\kappa_\theta}{R}\right)\cdot\frac{\kappa_x}{\tilde{\kappa}} \cdot\left(\frac{R}{\kappa_x}X_t + \left(1 - \frac{R}{\kappa_x}\right)\int_0^t Re^{-R(t-s)}X_s\mathrm{d}s\right) \tag{21}$$

which is a *weighted average* of

▷ the long-term Θ mean μ/κ_θ (with weight κ_θ/R),
▷ an observed average X-level (with weight $1 - \kappa_\theta/R$), scaled by $\kappa_x/\tilde{\kappa}$ to convert into a Θ level because $\frac{\kappa_x}{\tilde{\kappa}}X$ reverts toward Θ.

In turn, the average X-level is itself a weighted average (with weights R/κ_x and $1 - R/\kappa_x$) of

▷ the current X_t,
▷ an *exponentially weighted moving average* (EMA): $\int_0^t Re^{-R(t-s)}X_s\mathrm{d}s$.

The decay rate of the EMA is R from (7), where

$$R^2 = \frac{\kappa_\theta^2\sigma_x^2 + 2\rho\kappa_\theta\sigma_\theta\tilde{\kappa}\sigma_x + \sigma_\theta^2\tilde{\kappa}^2}{\sigma_x^2}. \tag{22}$$

Intuitively, this ratio balances the trade-off between two factors: On one hand, the greater the variation of the observed X levels — as measured by the σ_x^2 in the denominator — the longer the effective "window" over which the X averaging should be done, and therefore the smaller the decay rate R. On the other hand, the greater the variation of the X-undetermined part of the Θ dynamics, the less informative the older X data as an indicator of the current Θ level, and therefore the larger the R; this variation of the X-undetermined part of Θ can be expressed by rewriting (2):

$$\mathrm{d}\tilde{\kappa}\Theta_t = -(\tilde{\kappa}\mu - \kappa_x\kappa_\theta X_t)\mathrm{d}t - \kappa_\theta\mathrm{d}X_t + \kappa_\theta\sigma_x\mathrm{d}W_t + \tilde{\kappa}\sigma_\theta\mathrm{d}Z_t \tag{23}$$

which has eliminated Θ from the $\mathrm{d}t$ term, making both the $\mathrm{d}t$ and $\mathrm{d}X$ terms $\mathcal{F}^X$-observable; the remaining variation, taking into account the correlation between $\mathrm{d}W$ and $\mathrm{d}Z$, is given by the numerator of (22).

Because the EMA is an average of *observable prices*, the main practical challenge in calculating EMA is obtaining the volatility and mean reversion parameters, which determine the decay rate R. Those parameters may be estimated, in principle, from time-series data of X, given the explicit expressible transition densities in this model or alternatively inferred from a back-testing approach.

2.3. $\mathcal{F}^X$-dynamics of Price, Drift and Wealth

Denote the estimated instantaneous drift of X by

$$Y_t := \tilde{\kappa}\hat{\Theta}_t - \kappa_x X_t \tag{24}$$

which has dynamics

$$\begin{aligned} \mathrm{d}Y_t &= \tilde{\kappa}[(\mu - \kappa_\theta\hat{\Theta}_t)\mathrm{d}t + \sigma_{\hat{\theta}}(t)\mathrm{d}\nu_t] - \kappa_x(Y_t\mathrm{d}t + \sigma_x\mathrm{d}\nu_t) \\ &= (\tilde{\kappa}\mu - \kappa_\theta\tilde{\kappa}\hat{\Theta}_t - \kappa_x Y_t)\mathrm{d}t + (\tilde{\kappa}\sigma_{\hat{\theta}}(t) - \kappa_x\sigma_x)\mathrm{d}\nu_t \\ &= (\tilde{\kappa}\mu - \kappa_\theta(Y_t + \kappa_x X_t) - \kappa_x Y_t)\mathrm{d}t + (\tilde{\kappa}\sigma_{\hat{\theta}}(t) - \kappa_x\sigma_x)\mathrm{d}\nu_t. \end{aligned} \tag{25}$$

Suppose that some $\mathcal{F}^X$-adapted processes H and V satisfy

$$\mathrm{d}V_t = H_t\mathrm{d}X_t \tag{26}$$

(for which sufficient conditions are given in Section 4.1). Refer to H as the *control* process or the *trading strategy* and V as the *wealth* process. Implicit in the specification (26) are zero interest rates and frictionless markets.

Then (X, Y, V) have $\mathcal{F}^X$-dynamics

$$\begin{aligned} \mathrm{d}X_t &= Y_t\mathrm{d}t + \sigma_x\mathrm{d}\nu_t, \\ \mathrm{d}Y_t &= (\tilde{\kappa}\mu - (\kappa_\theta + \kappa_x)Y_t - \kappa_\theta\kappa_x X_t)\mathrm{d}t + \sigma_x\bar{\sigma}(t)\mathrm{d}\nu_t, \\ \mathrm{d}V_t &= Y_t H_t\mathrm{d}t + \sigma_x H_t\mathrm{d}\nu_t, \end{aligned} \tag{27}$$

where

$$\bar{\sigma}(t) := \frac{\tilde{\kappa}\sigma_{\hat{\theta}}(t)}{\sigma_x} - \kappa_x = R\frac{e^{2Rt} + g}{e^{2Rt} - g} - \kappa_\theta - \kappa_x \tag{28}$$

is the ratio of the signed $\mathcal{F}^X$-volatilities of Y and X.

3. Optimal Strategies

For fixed $T > 0$, we will solve for H to maximize expected utility of terminal wealth

$$\mathbb{E}U(V_T) \tag{29}$$

for a utility function $U \in \{U_{\text{exp}}, U_{\text{pow}}, U_{\log}\}$, where

$$\begin{aligned} U_{\log}(v) &:= \log v, \\ U_{\text{pow}}(v) &:= \frac{v^{1-q}}{1-q}, \qquad q > 1, \\ U_{\text{exp}}(v) &:= -\exp(-pv), \qquad p > 0, \end{aligned} \tag{30}$$

where q and p are risk-aversion parameters in the cases of power and exponential utility, respectively.

For any continuous function $G : [0,T] \times O \to \mathbb{R}$ that is $C^{1,2}$ on $(0,T) \times O$, where O is an open subset of $\mathbb{R}^3$, let $\mathcal{L}G$ denote the function $(0,T) \times O \times \mathbb{R} \to \mathbb{R}$ defined by

$$\begin{aligned} \mathcal{L}G(t,x,y,v,\mathsf{H}) := {} & G_t + yG_x + (\mu\tilde{\kappa} - \kappa_\theta\kappa_x x - (\kappa_\theta + \kappa_x)y)G_y \\ & + y\mathsf{H}G_v + \frac{\sigma_x^2}{2}G_{xx} + \frac{\sigma_x^2\bar{\sigma}(t)^2}{2}G_{yy} + \frac{\mathsf{H}^2\sigma_x^2}{2}G_{vv} \\ & + \sigma_x^2\bar{\sigma}(t)G_{xy} + \mathsf{H}\sigma_x^2\bar{\sigma}(t)G_{vy} + \mathsf{H}\sigma_x^2 G_{xv}. \end{aligned} \tag{31}$$

The partial derivatives of G are denoted by subscripts and evaluated at (t,x,y,v,H).

Proposition 3.1. *If $G_{vv} < 0$ on $(0,T) \times O$, then for each $(t,x,y,v,\mathsf{H}) \in (0,T) \times O \times \mathbb{R}$,*

$$\begin{aligned} \mathcal{L}\mathcal{G} \le {} & G_t + yG_x + (\mu\tilde{\kappa} - \kappa_\theta\kappa_x x - (\kappa_\theta + \kappa_x)y)G_y + \frac{\sigma_x^2}{2}G_{xx} + \sigma_x^2\bar{\sigma}(t)G_{xy} \\ & + \frac{\sigma_x^2\bar{\sigma}(t)^2}{2}G_{yy} - \frac{(yG_v + \sigma_x^2 G_{xv} + \sigma_x^2\bar{\sigma}(t)G_{yv})^2}{2\sigma_x^2 G_{vv}}. \end{aligned} \tag{32}$$

Equality holds if

$$\mathsf{H} = \frac{yG_v + \sigma_x^2 G_{xv} + \sigma_x^2\bar{\sigma}(t)G_{yv}}{-\sigma_x^2 G_{vv}}. \tag{33}$$

Proof. This follows from regarding $\mathcal{L}G$ as a quadratic in H with negative coefficient on H^2. □

Given processes (X, Y, V, H) as introduced in the previous section, define the process $\mathcal{L}^H G$ by

$$(\mathcal{L}^H G)_t := \mathcal{L}G(t, X_t, Y_t, V_t, H_t).$$

Remark 3.2. Intuitively, the operator $\mathcal{L}^H$ is the infinitesimal generator of the H-controlled process (t, X, Y, V). By finding G such that the right-hand side of (32) vanishes, with terminal condition given by the utility of terminal wealth, we will solve the Hamilton–Jacobi–Bellman equation

$$\sup_H \mathcal{L}^H G = 0, \qquad G(T, x, y, v) = U(v), \tag{34}$$

for G and H, which will be rigorously verified to be the value function and optimal trading strategy, respectively.

3.1. *Log Utility*

In the case of log utility ($U = U_{\log}$), let

$$G(t, x, y, v) = A(t)x^2 + B(t)xy + C(t)y^2 + \alpha(t)x + \beta(t)y + D(t) + U_{\log}(v), \tag{35}$$

where $A, B, C, D, \alpha, \beta$ are given in the following:

Proposition 3.3. *In the case $U = U_{\log}$, define*

$$\begin{aligned} A(t) &= -\kappa_x \kappa_\theta \bar{A}(t), & B(t) &= \kappa_x \kappa_\theta \bar{B}(t), \\ \alpha(t) &= 2\tilde{\kappa}\mu \bar{A}(t), & \beta(t) &= -\tilde{\kappa}\mu \bar{B}(t) \end{aligned} \tag{36}$$

and $D(t) = \int_t^T \mu\tilde{\kappa}\beta(s) + \sigma_x^2 A(s) + \sigma_x^2 \bar{\sigma}(s)^2 C(s) + \sigma_x^2 \bar{\sigma}(s) B(s) \mathrm{d}s$, *where, with* $\tau := T - t$,

$$\begin{aligned} \bar{A}(t) &= -\frac{(\kappa_x - \kappa_\theta)^2 + 4e^{-(\kappa_x+\kappa_\theta)\tau}\kappa_x\kappa_\theta - e^{2\kappa_\theta t}\kappa_x(\kappa_x + \kappa_\theta) - e^{2\kappa_x t}\kappa_\theta(\kappa_x + \kappa_\theta)}{4\sigma_x^2(\kappa_x - \kappa_\theta)^2(\kappa_x + \kappa_\theta)}, \\ \bar{B}(t) &= -\frac{(e^{-\kappa_\theta \tau} - e^{-\kappa_x \tau})^2}{2\sigma_x^2(\kappa_x - \kappa_\theta)^2}, \\ C(t) &= \frac{(\kappa_x - \kappa_\theta)^2 + 4e^{-(\kappa_x+\kappa_\theta)\tau}\kappa_x\kappa_\theta - e^{-2\kappa_x \tau}\kappa_x(\kappa_x + \kappa_\theta) - e^{-2\kappa_\theta \tau}\kappa_\theta(\kappa_x + \kappa_\theta)}{4\sigma_x^2(\kappa_x - \kappa_\theta)^2(\kappa_x + \kappa_\theta)} \end{aligned} \tag{37}$$

for $\kappa_x \neq \kappa_\theta$, *otherwise* $\bar{A}(t) = \frac{(1+2\kappa_x\tau+2\kappa_x^2\tau^2)e^{-2\kappa_x\tau}-1}{8\sigma_x^2\kappa_x}$, $\bar{B}(t) = -\frac{\tau^2 e^{-2\kappa_x\tau}}{2\sigma_x^2}$ *and* $\bar{C}(t) = \frac{\tau e^{-2\kappa_x\tau}}{2\sigma_x^2} - \bar{A}(t)$.

Then G *defined by* (35) *satisfies* $G(T,x,y,v) = U_{\log}(v)$ *and* $\mathcal{L}^H G \leq 0$ *for arbitrary* H. *The trading strategy defined by*

$$\begin{aligned} H_t^* &= h_t^* V_t, \\ h_t^* &= \frac{Y_t}{\sigma_x^2} \end{aligned} \tag{38}$$

attains equality $\mathcal{L}^{H^*} G = 0$.

Proof. Direct substitution shows that, for this (G, H^*), the right-hand side of (32) vanishes, the right-hand side of (33) evaluated at (t, X_t, Y_t, V_t) produces H_t^*, and $G(T,x,y,v) = U_{\log}(v)$. □

Our attention is mainly on trading strategies (to be further interpreted and discussed in Sections 3.2 and 3.3), but explicit formulas for value functions can also be useful, for instance, in calculating how much additional initial endowment is needed in the partial information case to attain the same optimized expected utility as in the full information case, thus measuring the value of information.

3.2. *Exponential Utility*

In the cases of exponential and power utility, define

$$G(t,x,y,v) = e^{A(t)x^2+B(t)xy+C(t)y^2+\alpha(t)x+\beta(t)y+D(t)}U(v), \tag{39}$$

where $A, B, C, D, \alpha, \beta$ will be defined in the following (and will depend on whether $U = U_{\exp}$ or $U = U_{\text{pow}}$).

In the case of exponential utility, the interdependencies of the ODEs for $A, B, C, D, \alpha, \beta$ may be resolved sequentially by solving a sequence of scalar ODEs. The result is as follows:

Proposition 3.4. *In the case* $U = U_{\exp}$, *define*

$$\begin{aligned} A(t) &= -\frac{\kappa_x^2\kappa_\theta^2}{2\sigma_x^2}\bar{A}(t), \qquad B(t) = \frac{\kappa_x\kappa_\theta}{\sigma_x^2}\bar{B}(t), \qquad C(t) = -\frac{1}{2\sigma_x^2}\bar{C}(t), \\ \alpha(t) &= \frac{\tilde{\kappa}\mu\kappa_x\kappa_\theta}{\sigma_x^2}\bar{A}(t), \qquad \beta(t) = -\frac{\tilde{\kappa}\mu}{\sigma_x^2}\bar{B}(t) \end{aligned} \tag{40}$$

and

$$\begin{aligned}
\bar{A}(t) &= \frac{2R\tau - 3 + 4e^{-R\tau} - e^{-2R\tau} - ge^{-2RT}(2R\tau - 4e^{R\tau} + e^{2R\tau} + 3)}{2R^3(1 - ge^{-2RT})}, \\
\bar{B}(t) &= \frac{(e^{R\tau} - 1)^2}{2R^2} \times \frac{e^{2Rt} - g}{e^{2RT} - g}, \\
\bar{C}(t) &= \frac{e^{2R\tau} - 1}{2R} \times \frac{e^{2Rt} - g}{e^{2RT} - g}, \\
D(t) &= \int_t^T \mu\tilde{\kappa}\beta(s) + \sigma_x^2 A(s) + \sigma_x^2 \bar{\sigma}(s)^2 C(s) + \sigma_x^2 \bar{\sigma}(s) B(s) \mathrm{d}s,
\end{aligned} \tag{41}$$

where $\tau := T - t$.

Then G *defined by* (39) *satisfies* $G(T, x, y, v) = U_{\exp}(v)$ *and* $\mathcal{L}^H G \leq 0$ *for arbitrary* H*. The trading strategy defined by*

$$\begin{aligned}
H_t^* := h_t^* := &\frac{\alpha(t) + \bar{\sigma}(t)\beta(t)}{p} + \frac{1 + \sigma_x^2 B(t) + 2\sigma_x^2 \bar{\sigma}(t) C(t)}{p\sigma_x^2} Y_t \\
&+ \frac{2A(t) + \bar{\sigma}(t)B(t)}{p} X_t
\end{aligned} \tag{42}$$

attains equality $\mathcal{L}^{H^*} G = 0$.

Proof. Direct substitution shows that, for this (G, H^*), the right-hand side of (32) vanishes, the right-hand side of (33) evaluated at (t, X_t, Y_t, V_t) produces H_t^*, and $G(T, x, y, v) = U_{\exp}(v)$. □

Remark 3.5. The prospective optimal trading strategy (42) or equivalently

$$H_t^* = \frac{1 + \kappa_\theta\kappa_x \bar{B}(t) - \bar{\sigma}(t)\bar{C}(t)}{p\sigma_x^2} Y_t + \frac{\kappa_\theta\kappa_x \bar{A}(t) - \bar{\sigma}(t)\bar{B}(t)}{p\sigma_x^2} (\mu\tilde{\kappa} - \kappa_\theta\kappa_x X_t) \tag{43}$$

is a linear combination of two "drifts" of X:

- First, $Y_t = \tilde{\kappa}\hat{\Theta}_t - \kappa_x X_t$ is the "instantaneous" drift of X. If $\kappa_x \neq 0$, then this is the drift of X toward its estimated "instantaneous" estimated reversion level $\hat{\Theta}_t\tilde{\kappa}/\kappa_x$.
- Second, $\mu\tilde{\kappa} - \kappa_x\kappa_\theta X_t$ is the "forward-looking" drift of X. If $\kappa_x\kappa_\theta \neq 0$, then this is the drift of X toward its long-term reversion level $\mu\tilde{\kappa}/(\kappa_\theta\kappa_x)$.

The coefficients on these two drifts have the effect of reducing the bet sizes when some notion of overall "risk" (or aversion to risk) is high:

- The denominator $p\sigma_x^2$ is higher (and therefore scales the position sizes toward 0) when risk aversion p is higher or when the X volatility σ_x is higher.
- The 1 in the first numerator multiplies $Y_t/(p\sigma_x^2)$, producing the purely *myopic* component that depends only on the instantaneous drift Y_t, instantaneous variance σ_x, and risk aversion p, in a ratio analogous to the Merton solution, but here with a filtered drift.
- As $t \to T$, the myopic direction dominates the long-term prospects: the coefficient on the instantaneous drift approaches the Merton weight $1/(p\sigma_x^2)$, while the coefficient on the long-term drift approaches 0.
- Both numerators have a positive contribution from the product $\kappa_\theta\kappa_x$ of the mean reversion rates of X and Θ. Intuitively, the stronger this is, the smaller the variability of the expected profits, and the bigger the bet sizes that the trader should make.
- Both numerators include $-\bar{\sigma}(t)$, the negative of the ratio of the signed $\mathcal{F}^X$-volatilities of Y and X. Intuitively, in the case that $\bar{\sigma} < 0$, the random fluctuations of Y and X have negative correlation, so when the price X moves against the trader, the drift Y moves in favor of the trader, mitigating the losses. Of course, prices X that move in favor of the trader are also mitigated by drifts Y that move against the trader; this two-sided mitigation of risk causes risk-averse utility maximizers to increase position sizing, hence the negative sign on $\bar{\sigma}$.
- The coefficient on the forward-looking drift can be negative. For instance, in the case that $g = \kappa_x = \kappa_\theta = 0$, we have $\bar{\sigma}(t) = R$ and $H_t^* = \frac{(1-R\bar{C}(t))}{p\sigma_x^2}Y_t - \frac{R\bar{B}(t)}{p\sigma_x^2}\mu\tilde{\kappa}$, which places a negative coefficient on the forward-looking drift $\mu\tilde{\kappa}$, in contrast to the positive coefficient on the instantaneous drift Y_t. The intuition is that increasing a positive forward-looking drift causes the optimal current position to become *less* positive because it becomes more advantageous to *delay* up-sizing that bet until a later date, when the drift is expected to be more favorable.

3.3. *Power Utility*

In the case $U = U_{\text{pow}}$, the G continues to be defined by (39), but the $A, B, C, D, \alpha, \beta$ differ from the coefficients in the $U = U_{\text{exp}}$ case; in particular, under power utility, the interdependencies of the ODEs for $A, B, C, D, \alpha, \beta$ cannot be resolved sequentially but rather require the solution of a matrix Riccati equation. In the case where the initial uncertainty is at the equilibrium level $\gamma_0 = \bar{\gamma}$, the $\bar{\sigma}(t)$ and thus the Riccati coefficients are constant, leading to an explicit solution, whose existence for all $t \in [0, T]$ is guaranteed by Lemma 3.6, based in part on [18] Lemma 4.1.

Lemma 3.6. *In the case $\gamma_0 = \bar{\gamma}$ and $\kappa_x \kappa_\theta \neq 0$, let $\mathbf{I} \in \mathbb{R}^{2\times 2}$ be the identity matrix and define*

$$S := \begin{pmatrix} \frac{2\sigma_x^2}{q} & \frac{2\sigma_x^2\bar{\sigma}}{q} \\ \frac{2\sigma_x^2\bar{\sigma}}{q} & \frac{2\sigma_x^2\bar{\sigma}^2}{q} \end{pmatrix}, \qquad P := \begin{pmatrix} 0 & \frac{1}{q} \\ -\kappa_x\kappa_\theta & \frac{(1-q)\bar{\sigma}}{q} - \kappa_\theta - \kappa_x \end{pmatrix},$$
$$Q := \begin{pmatrix} 0 & 0 \\ 0 & \frac{q-1}{2q\sigma_x^2} \end{pmatrix}. \tag{44}$$

For $\varepsilon \geq 0$ define $\Phi_\varepsilon, \Psi_\varepsilon : [0, T] \to \mathbb{R}^{2\times 2}$ by $\Phi_\varepsilon(T) = \mathbf{I}$, $\Psi_\varepsilon(T) = -\varepsilon\mathbf{I}$, and, for all $t < T$, by

$$\frac{\mathrm{d}}{\mathrm{d}t}\begin{pmatrix} \Phi_\varepsilon \\ \Psi_\varepsilon \end{pmatrix} = \begin{pmatrix} P & S \\ Q & -P^* \end{pmatrix}\begin{pmatrix} \Phi_\varepsilon \\ \Psi_\varepsilon \end{pmatrix}. \tag{45}$$

Then $M_\varepsilon(t) := \Phi_\varepsilon^{-1}(t)\Psi_\varepsilon(t)$ is well defined and negative semi-definite for all $t \in [0, T]$, all $\varepsilon \geq 0$. In particular, this conclusion holds for M_0, equivalently M.

Proof. The ODE (45) satisfies a Lipschitz condition, which implies the existence, uniqueness and continuous dependence on boundary conditions (and in particular, on ε) of $\Phi_\varepsilon(t)$ and $\Psi_\varepsilon(t)$.

To show that $\Phi_\varepsilon(t) =: (\phi_{ij}(t))_{1\leq i,j\leq 2}$ and $\Psi_\varepsilon(t) =: (\psi_{ij}(t))_{1\leq i,j\leq 2}$ are invertible on $[0, T)$, suppose to the contrary that there exists some $t_0 \in [0, T)$ and some non-zero $\pi \in \mathbb{R}^2$ such that $\Phi_\varepsilon(t_0)\pi = \mathbf{0}$ or

$\Psi_\varepsilon(t_0)\pi = \mathbf{0}$. Let $u(t) := \Phi_\varepsilon(t)\pi$ and $v(t) := \Psi_\varepsilon(t)\pi$. Then

$$\begin{aligned}\frac{\mathrm{d}}{\mathrm{d}t}(u^*(t)v(t)) &= (u^*(t)P^* + v^*(t)S)v(t) + u^*(t)(Qu(t) - P^*v(t)) \\ &= u^*(t)Qu(t) + v^*(t)Sv(t),\end{aligned} \tag{46}$$

hence

$$\int_{t_0}^{T} u^*(t)Qu(t) + v^*(t)Sv(t)\mathrm{d}t = u^*(T)v(T) - u^*(t_0)v(t_0) = -\varepsilon\pi^*\pi. \tag{47}$$

Because $q > 1$ implies Q and S are positive semi-definite, we have $\varepsilon = 0$. Because $t_0 < T$, we have

$$u^*(t)Qu(t) = v^*(t)Sv(t) = 0, \qquad t \in [t_0, T]. \tag{48}$$

In particular, $0 = u^*(T)Qu(T) = \pi^*Q\pi$, so $\pi = c\mathbf{e}_1$ for some scalar $c \neq 0$, where $\{\mathbf{e}_1, \mathbf{e}_2\}$ is the standard basis of $\mathbb{R}^2$. Hence, $u(t) = \Phi(t)\pi = c\phi_{11}(t)\mathbf{e}_1 + c\phi_{21}(t)\mathbf{e}_2$. Substituting into (48), we have $\phi_{21}(t) = 0$ for all $t \in [t_0, T]$. By (45), we have $\dot{\Phi} = P\Phi + S\Psi$. Comparing the $(2,1)$ entry of both sides, at all $t \in (t_0, T)$,

$$-\kappa_\theta\kappa_x\phi_{11}(t) + \frac{2\sigma_x^2\bar{\sigma}}{q}\psi_{11}(t) + \frac{2\sigma_x^2\bar{\sigma}^2}{q}\psi_{21}(t) = 0,$$

but taking $t \to T$ contradicts $\kappa_x\kappa_\theta \neq 0$.

So $\Phi_\varepsilon(t)$ and $\Psi_\varepsilon(t)$ are invertible for all $\varepsilon \geq 0$ and $t < T$, and $\Phi_0(T)$ is also invertible.

For all $\varepsilon \geq 0$, then $M_\varepsilon(t) := \Phi_\varepsilon^{-1}(t)\Psi_\varepsilon(t)$ exists for all $t \leq T$ and is invertible for all $t < T$.

For $\varepsilon > 0$, therefore, $M_\varepsilon(T)$ negative definite implies $M_\varepsilon(t)$ negative definite for all $t \in [0, T]$.

For each $t \in [0, T]$, by continuous dependence, $M_0(t) = \lim_{\varepsilon\to 0} M_\varepsilon(t)$ is negative semi-definite. □

Proposition 3.7. *In the case $\gamma_0 = \bar{\gamma}$, let*

$$\begin{aligned} \mathcal{H}_s^{\pm}(t) &:= \sinh\left(\frac{z_\pm}{\sqrt{q}}(t-T)\right), \\ \mathcal{H}_c^{\pm}(t) &:= \cosh\left(\frac{z_\pm}{\sqrt{q}}(t-T)\right), \end{aligned} \tag{49}$$

where

$$\begin{aligned} a &:= (q-1)(\bar{\sigma}+\kappa_x+\kappa_\theta)^2 + \kappa_x^2 + \kappa_\theta^2, \\ b &:= \sqrt{a^2 - 4q\kappa_x^2\kappa_\theta^2}, \\ z_\pm &:= \sqrt{\frac{a \pm b}{2}}. \end{aligned} \tag{50}$$

(I) *In the case $\kappa_x\kappa_\theta \neq 0$, define matrix-valued $\Phi, \Psi : [0,T] \to \mathbb{R}^{2\times 2}$ by $\Phi = (\phi_{ij})_{1\le i,j\le 2}$ and $\Psi = (\psi_{ij})_{1\le i,j\le 2}$, where*[1]

$$\begin{aligned} \psi_{11} &:= \sum_{+,-} \mp \frac{(q-1)\sqrt{q}\kappa_x^2\kappa_\theta^2}{2\sigma_x^2 b z_\pm}\mathcal{H}_s^{\pm}(t), & \psi_{12} &:= \sum_{+,-} \pm \frac{(q-1)\kappa_x\kappa_\theta}{2b\sigma_x^2}\mathcal{H}_c^{\pm}(t), \\ \psi_{21} &:= -\psi_{12}, & \psi_{22} &:= \sum_{+,-} \pm \frac{q-1}{2\sigma_x^2}\frac{z_\pm}{b\sqrt{q}}\mathcal{H}_s^{\pm}(t) \end{aligned} \tag{51}$$

and

$$\begin{aligned} \phi_{11} &:= \sum_{+,-}\left(\pm(\kappa_x+\kappa_\theta)\frac{z_\mp}{b}\mathcal{H}_s^{\pm}(t) \mp \frac{z_\mp^2+\kappa_x\kappa_\theta}{b}\mathcal{H}_c^{\pm}(t)\right), \\ \phi_{12} &:= \sum_{+,-}\left(\pm\left(\frac{z_\pm}{b\sqrt{q}} + \frac{\sqrt{q}}{bz_\pm}\kappa_x\kappa_\theta\right)\mathcal{H}_s^{\pm}(t) \mp \frac{\kappa_\theta+\kappa_x}{b}\mathcal{H}_c^{\pm}(t)\right), \\ \phi_{21} &:= \sum_{+,-}\left(\mp(z_\mp^2+q\kappa_x\kappa_\theta)\frac{z_\pm}{b\sqrt{q}}\mathcal{H}_s^{\pm}(t) \pm \kappa_x\kappa_\theta\frac{(q-1)\bar{\sigma}+q(\kappa_x+\kappa_\theta)}{b}\mathcal{H}_c^{\pm}(t)\right), \\ \phi_{22} &:= \sum_{+,-}\left(\mp((q-1)\bar{\sigma}+q(\kappa_x+\kappa_\theta))\frac{z_\pm}{b\sqrt{q}}\mathcal{H}_s^{\pm}(t) \pm \frac{z_\pm^2+\kappa_x\kappa_\theta}{b}\mathcal{H}_c^{\pm}(t)\right). \end{aligned} \tag{52}$$

[1] If $b \notin \mathbb{R}$, it does not matter which branch to choose for the complex square root because (51,52) are invariant under the transformation $(b, z_\pm, \mathcal{H}_s^{\pm}, \mathcal{H}_c^{\pm}) \mapsto (-b, z_\mp, \mathcal{H}_s^{\mp}, \mathcal{H}_c^{\mp})$, and likewise, the branch of z does not matter due to the symmetry $(z_\pm, \mathcal{H}_s^{\pm}, \mathcal{H}_c^{\pm}) \mapsto (-z_\pm, -\mathcal{H}_s^{\pm},, \mathcal{H}_c^{\pm})$.

Then Φ is invertible for all $t \in [0,T]$. Define A, B, C, α, β and M by

$$\begin{pmatrix} A(t) & \frac{B(t)}{2} \\ \frac{B(t)}{2} & C(t) \end{pmatrix} := M(t) := \Psi(t)\Phi^{-1}(t) \quad \text{and} \quad \begin{aligned} \alpha(t) &:= -\frac{2\mu\tilde{\kappa}}{\kappa_\theta\kappa_x}A(t) \\ \beta(t) &:= -\frac{\mu\tilde{\kappa}}{\kappa_\theta\kappa_x}B(t) \end{aligned} \tag{53}$$

and $D(t) := \int_t^T \frac{\begin{array}{c}2q\sigma_x^2 A(s) + 2q\sigma_x^2\bar{\sigma}(s)B(s) + 2q\sigma_x^2\bar{\sigma}(s)^2C(s) \\ +2q\mu\tilde{\kappa}\beta(s) + (1-q)\sigma_x^2(\alpha(s)+\bar{\sigma}(s)\beta(s))^2\end{array}}{2q} ds.$

(II) *In the case $\kappa_x\kappa_\theta = 0$, let $A = B = \alpha = 0$, and*

$$\begin{aligned} C(t) &:= \frac{q-1}{2\sigma_x^2} \times \frac{\mathcal{H}_s^+(t)}{(\bar{\sigma} - q(\kappa_x + \kappa_\theta + \bar{\sigma}))\mathcal{H}_s^+(t) + \sqrt{aq}\mathcal{H}_c^+(t)}, \\ \beta(t) &:= \frac{(1-q)\tilde{\kappa}\mu}{\sigma_x^2\sqrt{a/q}} \times \frac{\mathcal{H}_c^+(t) - 1}{(\bar{\sigma} - q(\kappa_x + \kappa_\theta + \bar{\sigma}))\mathcal{H}_s^+(t) + \sqrt{aq}\mathcal{H}_c^+(t)}, \end{aligned} \tag{54}$$

and D be as above.

Then, in both (I) and (II) *cases, G defined by* (39) *satisfies $G(T,x,y,v) = U_{\text{pow}}(v)$ and $\mathcal{L}^H G \leq 0$ for arbitrary H. The trading strategy defined by*

$$\begin{aligned} h_t^* = &\frac{\alpha(t) + \bar{\sigma}(t)\beta(t)}{q} + \frac{1 + \sigma_x^2 B(t) + 2\sigma_x^2\bar{\sigma}(t)C(t)}{q\sigma_x^2}Y_t \\ &+ \frac{2A(t) + \bar{\sigma}(t)B(t)}{q}X_t, \end{aligned} \tag{55}$$

$$H_t^* = h_t^* V_t \tag{56}$$

attains equality $\mathcal{L}^{H^*}G = 0$.

Proof. In the case $\kappa_x\kappa_\theta \neq 0$, the definitions (51,52) of Φ and Ψ satisfy the $\varepsilon = 0$ case of (45), hence $\Phi = \Phi_0$ and $\Psi = \Psi_0$. By Lemma 3.6, therefore, Φ is invertible and M exists. We have

$$\begin{aligned} M'(t) &= \frac{\mathrm{d}}{\mathrm{d}t}(\Psi(t)\Phi^{-1}(t)) = \Psi'(t)\Phi^{-1}(t) - \Psi(t)\Phi^{-1}(t)\Phi'(t)\Phi^{-1}(t) \\ &= (Q\Phi(t) - P^*\Psi(t))\Phi^{-1}(t) - \Psi(t)\Phi^{-1}(t)(P\Phi(t) + S\Psi(t))\Phi^{-1}(t) \\ &= -M(t)SM(t) - P^\top M(t) - M(t)P + Q. \end{aligned} \tag{57}$$

Calculating the derivatives of (39) and simplifying using the A', B' and C' formulas contained in the M' expression (57) shows that, for this (G, H^*), the right-hand side of (32) vanishes and the right-hand side of (33) evaluated at (t, X_t, Y_t, V_t) produces H_t^*; moreover, G satisfies the U_{pow} terminal condition. In the case $\kappa_x\kappa_\theta \neq 0$, the proof is by direct substitution. □

Remark 3.8. Thus the prospective optimal trading strategy in the power utility $\kappa_x\kappa_\theta \neq 0$ case is

$$\begin{aligned} H_t^* &= \frac{1+\kappa_x\kappa_\theta\bar{B}(t) - \bar{\sigma}(t)\bar{C}(t)}{q\sigma_x^2} Y_t V_t \\ &\quad + \frac{\kappa_x\kappa_\theta\bar{A}(t) - \bar{\sigma}(t)\bar{B}(t)}{q\sigma_x^2}(\mu\tilde{\kappa} - \kappa_x\kappa_\theta X_t)V_t, \end{aligned}$$

where $\bar{A}(t) := -\frac{2\sigma_x^2}{\kappa_x^2\kappa_\theta^2}A(t)$, $\bar{B}(t) := \frac{\sigma_x^2}{\kappa_x\kappa_\theta}B(t)$, and $\bar{C}(t) := -2\sigma_x^2 C(t)$.

As in the case of exponential utility, the optimal control is proportional to a linear combination of the "instantaneous" drift Y_t and the "forward-looking" drift $\tilde{\kappa}\mu - \kappa_x\kappa_\theta X_t$, and the coefficients on these drifts have similar interpretations to the exponential case.

Unlike the case of exponential utility, the power-utility maximizer takes position sizes that are proportional also to current wealth V_t.

The results (42) and (55) show that the only stochastic variables on which the optimal strategy depends are X_t, V_t and an exponentially weighted moving average (EMA) of X.

4. Verification

Let us rewrite the definitions (35) and (39):

$$G(t,x,y,v) := e^{f(t,x,y)}U(v), \qquad U \in \{U_{\text{exp}}, U_{\text{pow}}\}, \tag{58}$$

$$G(t,x,y,v) := f(t,x,y) + U(v), \qquad U = U_{\text{log}}, \tag{59}$$

where

$$f(t,x,y) := A(t)x^2 + B(t)xy + C(t)y^2 + \alpha(t)x + \beta(t)y + D(t).$$

Here $A, B, C, D, \alpha, \beta$ are defined by (40, 41) in case $U = U_{\text{exp}}$, by (53) in case $U = U_{\text{pow}}$ and by (36, 37) in case $U = U_{\text{log}}$. Any of

$G, f, A, B, C, D, \alpha, \beta$ may be written with a subscript U if we wish to emphasize their dependence on U.

Lemma 4.1. *In the cases $U = U_{\exp}$ and $U = U_{\text{pow}}$, we have*

$$\sup_{(t,\omega)\in[0,T]\times\Omega} f(t, X_t, Y_t) < \infty. \tag{60}$$

Proof. If $\kappa_x\kappa_\theta \neq 0$, then for all $t \in [0, T)$, we have

$$\begin{aligned} f(t, x, y) &= A(t)(x - x_0)^2 + B(t)(x - x_0)y + C(t)y^2 \\ &\quad + D(t) - x_0^2 A(t) \quad \text{where } x_0 := \frac{\mu\tilde{\kappa}}{\kappa_x\kappa_\theta} \\ &\leq D(t) - x_0^2 A(t) \end{aligned} \tag{61}$$

because $\begin{pmatrix} A(t) & B(t)/2 \\ B(t)/2 & C(t) \end{pmatrix}$ is negative semi-definite, which is verified in the case $U = U_{\exp}$ by

$$\begin{aligned} 4A(t)C(t) - B^2(t) &= \frac{\kappa_x^2\kappa_\theta^2\left(e^{R\tau} - 1\right)\left(e^{2Rt} - g\right)}{2\sigma_x^4 R^4\left(e^{2RT} - g\right)} \\ &\quad \times \left(R\tau + e^{R\tau}(R\tau - 2) + 2\right) > 0 \end{aligned} \tag{62}$$

and $A(t) < 0$, and is verified in the case $U = U_{\text{pow}}$ by Lemma 3.6.

If $\kappa_x\kappa_\theta = 0$, then in both cases $U = \{U_{\exp}, U_{\text{pow}}\}$, we have $C(t) < 0$, hence

$$f(t, x, y) = C(t)y^2 + \beta(t)y + D(t) \leq D(t) - \beta(t)^2/(4C(t)). \tag{63}$$

From either (61) or (63), the result follows because D, A and β^2/C are all bounded. □

4.1. *Admissible Controls*

Given (X_0, Y_0), let (X, Y) be the unique strong solution to the linear SDE (from (27))

$$\begin{aligned} \mathrm{d}X_t &= Y_t\mathrm{d}t + \sigma_x\mathrm{d}\nu_t, \\ \mathrm{d}Y_t &= (\tilde{\kappa}\mu - (\kappa_\theta + \kappa_x)Y_t - \kappa_\theta\kappa_x X_t)\mathrm{d}t + \sigma_x\bar{\sigma}(t)\mathrm{d}\nu_t. \end{aligned} \tag{64}$$

Let $\mathbb{H}$ denote the set of progressively measurable h such that

$$\mathbb{E}\int_0^T h_t^2 \mathrm{d}t < \infty. \tag{65}$$

Moreover, Y is Gaussian, hence $\int_0^T Y_s^2 \mathrm{d}s < \infty$ which allows us to define for $h \in \mathbb{H}$:

$$X_t^h := \int_0^t Y_s h_s \mathrm{d}s + \int_0^t \sigma_x h_s \mathrm{d}\nu_s. \tag{66}$$

Given initial wealth $V_0 > 0$ in case $U \in \{U_{\log}, U_{\text{pow}}\}$, or $V_0 \in \mathbb{R}$ in case $U = U_{\exp}$, define

$$\begin{aligned} V_t^H &:= V_0 + X_t^h, && \text{if } U = U_{\exp}, \\ V_t^H &:= V_0\, \mathcal{E}(X^h)_t, && \text{if } U \in \{U_{\log}, U_{\text{pow}}\}, \end{aligned} \tag{67}$$

where $\mathcal{E}$ denotes the stochastic (Doleans–Dade) exponential. Thus we have wealth dynamics

$$\mathrm{d}V_t^H = H_t \mathrm{d}X_t, \qquad \text{where } H_t := \begin{cases} h_t & \text{if } U = U_{\exp} \\ h_t V_t^H & \text{if } U \in \{U_{\text{pow}}, U_{\log}\}. \end{cases} \tag{68}$$

In cases $U = U_{\exp}$ or $U = U_{\text{pow}}$, let $r := p$ or $r := q - 1$, respectively, and let

$$\begin{aligned} \xi_t^h &:= f_x(t, X_t, Y_t)\sigma_x + f_y(t, X_t, Y_t)\sigma_x \bar{\sigma}(t) - r\sigma_x h_t, \\ \Xi_t^h &:= \exp\left(\int_0^T \xi_s^h \mathrm{d}\nu_s - \frac{1}{2}\int_0^T (\xi_s^h)^2 \mathrm{d}t\right). \end{aligned} \tag{69}$$

Definition 4.2 (Admissible trading strategies). Let $\mathcal{A}_U$ (abbreviated as $\mathcal{A}$) denote the set of admissible controls: all $h \in \mathbb{H}$ such that H satisfies (i) and (ii):

(i) In the cases $U \in \{U_{\text{pow}}, U_{\log}\}$, the wealth process is a.s. positive: $V_t^H > 0$.

(ii) In the cases $U \in \{U_{\exp}, U_{\text{pow}}\}$, the strategy h satisfies

$$\mathbb{E}(\Xi_T^h) = 1. \tag{70}$$

This condition is implied by a sufficient condition on the wealth process alone:

Proposition 4.3. *In the cases $U \in \{U_{\exp}, U_{\text{pow}}\}$, for $h \in \mathbb{H}$ satisfying (i), a sufficient condition for* (70) *is*

$$\mathbb{E} \sup_{t\in[0,T]} |G(t, X_t, Y_t, V_t^H)| < \infty. \tag{71}$$

In turn, a sufficient condition for (71) *is the following sup-integrability condition, involving no other stochastic variables aside from wealth:*

$$\mathbb{E} \sup_{t\in[0,T]} |U(V_t^H)| < \infty. \tag{72}$$

For instance, a sufficient condition for (72) *is that wealth be bounded below: $V_t^H > v^H$ for some non-random $v^H \in \mathbb{R}$ in the exponential case or non-random $v^H > 0$ in the power case.*

Proof. By Lemma 4.1, condition (72) implies (71).

To obtain (70), let $G_t := G(t, X_t, Y_t, V_t^h)$. Then,

$$\mathrm{d}G(t, X_t, Y_t, V_t^h) = (\mathcal{L}^H G)_t \mathrm{d}t + \xi_t^h G_t \mathrm{d}\nu_t \tag{73}$$

and

$$\begin{aligned} G_t &= G_0\, \mathcal{E}\left(\int_0^\cdot \frac{(\mathcal{L}^H G)_s}{G_s}\mathrm{d}s + \int_0^\cdot \xi^h \mathrm{d}\nu_s\right)_t \\ &= G_0 \exp\left(\int_0^t \frac{(\mathcal{L}^H G)_s}{G_s}\mathrm{d}s + \int_0^t \xi^h \mathrm{d}\nu_s - \frac{1}{2}\int_0^t (\xi_s^h)^2 \mathrm{d}s\right) \le G_0 \Xi_t^h \end{aligned} \tag{74}$$

because $G < 0$ and Propositions 3.4/3.7 imply $\mathcal{L}^H G \le 0$. So, if (71) holds, then

$$\mathbb{E} \sup_{t\in[0,T]} \Xi_t^h \le \mathbb{E} \sup_{t\in[0,T]} \frac{G_t}{G_0} < \infty,$$

hence Ξ^h is a true martingale and (70) follows. □

Next, we verify admissibility and optimality of the strategy h^* defined by (42) in case $U = U_{\exp}$, by (55) in case $U = U_{\text{pow}}$ and by (38) in case $U = U_{\log}$.

Proposition 4.4 (Admissibility). *We have $h^* \in \mathcal{A}$. Indeed it satisfies the stronger condition* (71).

Proof. We have h^* Gaussian, therefore in $\mathbb{H}$:

In the log and power cases, $V_0^{H^*} > 0$, and V^{H^*} is a stochastic exponential, hence $V_t^{H^*} > 0$.

In the power and exponential cases, to show H^* satisfies (71), let $G_t^* := G(t, X_t, Y_t, V_t^{H^*})$. Then

$$\mathrm{d}G_t^* = \big(\lambda_0(t) + \lambda_1(t)X_t + \lambda_2(t)Y_t\big)G_t^*\mathrm{d}\nu_t, \tag{75}$$

where the $\lambda_i(t)$ are deterministic and bounded on $[0, T]$ for $i = 0, 1, 2$. (Indeed, in the exponential case, they are constant: $\lambda_0 = \lambda_1 = 0$ and $\lambda_2 = -1/\sigma_x$.) In both power and exponential cases, then G^* is a stochastic exponential. Lemma 4.5 shows that G^* satisfies the Benes condition; therefore [11] Theorem 2.1 concludes that G^* is a martingale. Applying Doob's $L \log L$ maximal inequality to $-G^* = |G^*|$, we have

$$\mathbb{E} \sup_{t\in[0,T]} |G_t^*| \le \frac{e}{e-1}(1 + \mathbb{E}(|G_T^*| \log^+ |G_T^*|)),$$

so it suffices to show that $\mathbb{E}(|G_T^*| \log |G_T^*|) < \infty$.

The proof of [11] Theorem 2.1 defines a sequence of stopping times $\tau_n \uparrow \infty$ and establishes that $\sup_n \mathbb{E}(|G^*_{T\wedge\tau_n}| \log |G^*_{T\wedge\tau_n}|) < \infty$. Therefore,

$$\begin{aligned}\mathbb{E}(|G_T^*| \log |G_T^*|) &= \mathbb{E}(\liminf_{n\to\infty} |G^*_{T\wedge\tau_n}| \log |G^*_{T\wedge\tau_n}|)\\ &\le \liminf_{n\to\infty} \mathbb{E}(|G^*_{T\wedge\tau_n}| \log |G^*_{T\wedge\tau_n}|) < \infty \end{aligned} \tag{76}$$

as claimed. □

Lemma 4.5. *Given $T > 0$, there exists some constant C such that for all $t \in [0, T]$*

$$(1 + |X_t| + |Y_t|)^2 \le C\Big(1 + \sup_{s\le t} \nu_s^2\Big). \tag{77}$$

Proof. We have

$$\hat{\Theta}_t = e^{-\kappa_\theta t}\hat{\Theta}_0 + \sigma_{\hat{\theta}}(t)\nu_t + \int_0^t (\mu - (\kappa_\theta \sigma_{\hat{\theta}}(t) + \sigma'_{\hat{\theta}}(t))\nu_s)e^{\kappa_\theta(s-t)}\mathrm{d}s,$$

$$X_t = e^{-\kappa_x t}X_0 + \sigma_x \nu_t + \int_0^t (\kappa_\theta \hat{\Theta}_s - \kappa_x \sigma_x \nu_s)e^{\kappa_x(s-t)}\mathrm{d}s. \tag{78}$$

Therefore, there exists C such that

$$|\hat{\Theta}_t| + |X_t| \leq C\big(1 + \sup_{s\leq t}|\nu_s|\big), \tag{79}$$

which implies (77). □

4.2. *Verification Theorem*

To verify optimality of h^*, some key steps, that h^* satisfies (71) and hence the true martingale condition (70), were confirmed in Propositions 4.3 and 4.4. One step remains as follows:

Proposition 4.6 (Verification Theorem). *In all cases* $U \in \{U_{\text{exp}}, U_{\text{pow}}, U_{\text{log}}\}$, *we have*

$$\sup_{h\in\mathcal{A}} \mathbb{E}U(V_T^H) = \mathbb{E}U(V_T^{H^*}) = G(0, X_0, Y_0, V_0), \tag{80}$$

where H *is driven by* h *via* (68). *Thus* h^* *is optimal and attains expected utility* G.

Proof. For any $h \in \mathcal{A}$ we have $\mathcal{L}^H G \leq 0$ by Propositions 3.3/3.4/3.7. Let $G_t^H := G(t, X_t, Y_t, V_t^H)$.

For $0 \leq r \leq t \leq T$, by Ito's rule,

$$G_t^H = G_r^H + \int_r^t \mathcal{L}^H G(s, X_s, Y_s, V_s^H)\mathrm{d}s + M_t - M_r \leq G_r^H + M_t - M_r, \tag{81}$$

where in the U_{exp} and U_{pow} cases, $M_t = \Xi_t^h$ is a true martingale by (70) and in the U_{log} case,

$$M_t = \int_0^t \Big(\sigma_x(2A(t)X_s + B(s)Y_s + \alpha(s)) + \sigma_x\bar{\sigma}(t)(B(t)X_s + 2C(s)Y_s + \beta(s)) + \sigma_x h_t\Big)\mathrm{d}\nu_s \tag{82}$$

from (59,64,68), which is a true martingale because X and Y are Gaussian and h satisfies (65).

Thus G^H is a supermartingale in all cases of U, and

$$G(0, X_0, Y_0, V_0) \geq \mathbb{E}U(V_T^H). \tag{83}$$

In particular, if $h = h^*$, then by combining $h \in \mathcal{A}$ from Proposition 4.4 and $\mathcal{L}^{H^*}G = 0$ from Propositions 3.3/3.4/3.7, the inequalities (81, 83) hold with equality, proving (80). □

5. Conclusion

Maximizing expected utility from trading an asset following multi-dimensional Gaussian dynamics with stochastic unobserved drift of mean-reversion or momentum type, we conclude that the optimal trading strategy, given the entire history of the asset price, depends on only a few stochastic variables: an exponential moving average (EMA) of price, the current price and, in some cases, current wealth. The sufficiency of EMA-type strategies emerges endogenously as a conclusion, not an assumption, of our results, which rigorously verify optimality under exponential/power/log utility. The solutions are explicit, including formulas for the (not necessarily positive) weightings of EMA and current price, the decay rate in the EMA and the balance between forward-looking and myopic estimates of drift.

References

[1] M. Boguslavsky and E. Boguslavskaya. Arbitrage under power. *RISK magazine*, 2004, pp. 69–73.

[2] S. Brendle. Portfolio selection under incomplete information. *Stochastic Processes and their Applications*, 116:701–723, 2006.

[3] M. H. A. Davis and S. Lleo. *Risk-Sensitive Investment Management.* World Scientific, Singapore, 2014.

[4] J. Detemple. Asset pricing in a production economy with incomplete information. *Journal of Finance*, 41(2):383–391, 1986.

[5] J.-P. Fouque, A. Papanicolaou, and R. Sircar. Filtering and portfolio optimization with stochastic unobserved drift in asset returns. *Communications in Mathematical Sciences*, 13(4):935–953, 2015.

[6] R. Frey, A. Gabih, and R. Wunderlich. Portfolio optimization under partial information with expert opinions. *International Journal of Theoretical and Applied Finance*, 15(1):18, 2012.

[7] P. Guasoni. Asymmetric information in fads models. *Finance and Stochastics*, 10:159–177, 2006.

[8] G. Kallianpur. *Stochastic Filtering Theory*. Springer, Berlin, 1980.

[9] I. Karatzas and X. Zhao. Bayesian adaptive portfolio optimization. In *Handbooks in Mathematical Finance: Option Pricing, Interest Rates and Risk Management*, Chapter 17. Cambridge University Press, 2001, pp. 632–669.

[10] T. Suk Kim and E. Omberg. Dynamic nonmyopic portfolio behavior. *Review of Financial Studies*, 9(1):141–161, 1996.

[11] F. Klebaner and R. Liptser. When a stochastic exponential is a true martingale. extension of a method of benes. *Theory of Probability and Its Applications*, 58(1):38–62, 2014.

[12] R. S. J. Koijen, J. Carlos Rodríguez, and A. Sbuelz. Momentum and mean reversion in strategic asset allocation. *Management Science*, 55(7):1199–1213, 2009.

[13] P. Lakner. Optimal trading strategy for an investor: The case of partial information. *Stochastic Processes and their Applications*, 76: 77–97, 1998.

[14] S. Lee and A. Papanicolaou. Pairs trading of two assets with uncertainty in co-integration's level of mean reversion. *International Journal of Theoretical and Applied Finance*, 19(08):36, 2016.

[15] R. Liptser and A. Shiryaev. *Statistics of Random Processes II*, 2nd Edition. Springer, Berlin, 2001.

[16] M. Lorig, Z. Zhou, and B. Zou. A mathematical analysis of technical analysis. *Applied Mathematical Finance*, 26(1):38–68, 2019.

[17] R. C. Merton. Lifetime portfolio selection under uncertainty: The continuous-time case. *Review of Economics and Statistics*, 51(3): 247–257, 1969.

[18] W. Reid. *Riccati Differential Equations*. Academic Press, New York, 1972.

[19] J. Xiong. *An Introduction to Stochastic Filtering Theory*. Oxford University Press, Oxford, UK, 2008.

https://doi.org/10.1142/9789811280306_0016

Chapter 16

Option Returns*

Dilip B. Madan[†,¶], **Wim Schoutens**[‡,‖], **and King Wang**[§,**]

[†]*Robert H. Smith School of Business, University of Maryland, College Park, MD 20742, USA*

[‡]*Department of Mathematics, K. U. Leuven, CelestijnenLaan, 200B, B-300 Leuven, Belgium*

[§]*Derivative Product Stats, Morgan Stanley, 1585 Broadway 5th Floor, New York, NY 10036, USA*

[¶]*dbm@umd.edu*

[‖]*wim.schoutens@kuleuven.be*

[**]*king.wang@morganstanley.com*

Abstract

Nonlinear martingale theory is used to form lower and upper price processes straddling a martingale. The martingale return is then modeled in terms of risk charges associated with the returns on the straddling lower and upper processes. The move to physically expected returns is made via the usual covariation risk factors. There are however two covariation terms: one for the lower and the other for the upper return. The expected returns are then seen to incorporate in addition to covariation considerations that address the martingale, the risk charges that assess out of martingale issues. The theory is tested on prices of options for 10 underliers over 170 days covering 4 maturities and 21 strikes. It is observed that the risk charges have positive significant coefficients while the upper covariation has a positive price with the lower covariation receiving a negative price.

*This paper is the private opinion of the authors and does not necessarily reflect the policy and views of Morgan Stanley.

Keywords: Measure distortions, Backward stochastic partial integro-differential equations, Bilateral gamma process, Risk exposures, Risk charges

1. Introduction

Options as an asset class offer investors return opportunities that differ from those offered by the underlying assets themselves. They incorporate leverage effects and offer exposures to movements in volatility and changes in the structure of tail risks on both sides. Ref. [8] document the leverage effects across the range of strikes for call and put options with the former returns being positive while the latter are negative both sets increase with strikes under certain assumptions on the nature of the pricing kernel. The implications of non-monotonically decreasing kernels are taken up in Schlag and Sichert (2020). The formulation of volatility changes and jump risk exposures along with jumps in volatility and liquidity as risk factors for the option markets are investigated in Ref. [15] and Ref. [7]. Non-linearity of factor exposures is addressed in Ref. [16] while the effects of volatility are studied in Ref. [13], Ref. [4] and Ref. [14]. Divorcing variance issues from leverage using delta-hedged returns is focused on in Ref. [2]. Comparisons with model-simulated outcomes are made in Ref. [3]. It is anticipated that factor impacts vary with both maturity and moneyness with such variations explicitly incorporated in Ref. [16], for example. Many of the studies are on options written on the S&P 500 index representing a market wide factor. This chapter will include the sector Exchange Traded Funds (ETFs) as well.

The difficulty with options as an asset class is that, unlike stocks that represent the same asset on two successive dates, options change their moneyness and maturity character over time and can be seen to be different assets at two different time points. With a view toward avoiding such issues, the approach taken here is to study the structure of instantaneous returns. Specifically for any calibrated option pricing model, one may evaluate the return $r(x)$ to the option, given a jump in the logarithm of the underlying asset price of x. Recent time series data on daily returns are then employed to estimate the physical arrival rate $k(x)$ of jumps of size x by fitting the observed tail probabilities to a Lévy process pure jump model with arrival rates $k(x)$. The instantaneous expected return is then estimated by integrating $r(x)$ with respect to $k(x)$. For an underlying pure jump Lévy process and the stock itself as the asset we have $r(x) = (e^x - 1)$ and the continuously compounded expected rate of return μ per unit time is

$$\mu = \int_{-\infty}^{\infty} (e^x - 1)\, k(x) dx. \tag{1}$$

More generally, we perform the same calculation for an option price. Denote by $w(S)$ the price of an option when the underlying asset price is S. For a risk neutrally calibrated option pricing model delivering the function $w(S)$, we define

$$r(x) = \frac{w(Se^x) - w(S)}{w(S)}. \tag{2}$$

The mean return μ_w on the option is then evaluated as

$$\mu_w = \int_{-\infty}^{\infty} r(x) k(x) dx. \tag{3}$$

The integrals were truncated at an absolute return of 30%.

Most asset pricing studies focus attention on the martingale condition asserting that in the absence of arbitrage and under the law of one price, discounted prices are martingales. As a consequence, expected excess returns over an interest rate are seen as the negative of the covariation of returns with the returns on the measure change density. Modeling this density as adapted to various constructed factors delivers the asset pricing equations to be estimated and evaluated for their included risk premia. Such an approach with regard to options is taken in Ref. [7] with factors representing volatility, jump risks, jumps in volatility and liquidity.

Here we go beyond this context by recognizing that option markets provide a rich set of quotes on the bid and offer prices of options from which risk-neutral calibrations are often made to mid-quotes as candidate prices for a market under the law of one price. The basic data, however, are that on the bid and offer prices themselves. The literature on continuous-time two-price economies under no-arbitrage models the two prices as nonlinear martingales that lie below and above the martingale by the subtraction or addition of risk charges. The lower price is seen as an infimum of expectations over a variety of alternative measures while the upper price is a similar supremum. The gaps between the upper price and the martingale or the martingale and the lower price are the risk charges. Modeling the upper and lower prices directly themselves as nonlinear martingales leads to equations for the physical of statistically expected returns on the bid and offer prices themselves. Averaging these two price expected returns as a candidate expected return leads to asset pricing equations that include in addition to the classical covariation considerations, an additional role for the risk charges as risk factors.

Denoting by $w_b(S)$, $w_a(S)$ the lower or bid and upper or ask prices for an option when the underlying asset price is S one defines the lower and upper returns by

$$r_b(x) = \frac{w_b(Se^x) - w_b(S)}{w_b(S)}, \tag{4}$$

$$r_a(x) = \frac{w_a(Se^x) - w_a(S)}{w_a(S)}. \tag{5}$$

The corresponding mean returns μ_{w_b}, μ_{w_a} are

$$\mu_{w_b} = \int_{-\infty}^{\infty} r_b(x)k(x)dx, \tag{6}$$

$$\mu_{w_a} = \int_{-\infty}^{\infty} r_a(x)k(x)dx. \tag{7}$$

An average of the models for μ_{w_b}, μ_{w_a} may be taken to model μ_w. Additionally, one may test the models for μ_{w_b}, μ_{w_a} directly. However, a direct test of μ_{w_b}, μ_{w_a} requires a careful calibration of the sets of measures over which lower and upper prices are formulated. Here we work with a fixed and uncalibrated selection and employ averages of the resulting equations for μ_{w_b}, μ_{w_a} as alternative models for μ_w that incorporate risk charges as explanatory factors in addition to covariation considerations. Covariations deal with martingale considerations while risk charges address issues of distance to martingale or how far out of martingale matters may diverge.

The outline of the rest of this chapter is as follows: Section 2 introduces the nonlinear martingale equations for the lower and upper prices and their asset pricing implications. Section 3 goes on to develop the asset pricing equations for the lower and upper prices directly. The models for calibrating mid-quotes, bid and ask option prices and the time series of daily returns are presented in Section 4. The specific modeling of bid and ask prices using measure distortions is developed in Section 5. The measurement of two-sided risk premia for stochastic volatility and jumps is formulated in Section 6. The data employed in this chapter are described in Section 7. Relationship of the data to earlier results in the literature is detailed in Section 8. Asset pricing tests are formulated and conducted in Section 9. Time-series results on the structure of risk premia are reported in Section 10. Extensions to two-sided jump risk and stochastic volatility are reported in Section 11. Asset pricing tests for the lower and upper prices directly are formulated and reported in Section 12. Section 13 concludes.

2. Nonlinear Martingale Models for Two Price Economies

Nonlinear martingales differ from martingales as follows. For any martingale $M(t) = E\left[M(T)|\mathcal{F}_t\right]$, it is the case that

$$M(t) + \int_t^T dM(u) = M(T). \tag{8}$$

The martingale $(M(t),\ 0 < t < T)$ is a solution of the backward stochastic equation (8), for as an equation in t one is moving backwards in time, starting at T from $M(T)$. For a nonlinear martingale, there is a positive process, which is interpreted here as a process of risk charges $(RC_L(t),\ 0 < t < T)$ and the lower price satisfies a backward stochastic equation of the form

$$L(t) + \int_t^T RC_L(u)du + \int_t^T dM(u) = \chi \tag{9}$$

for some terminal random variable χ. Similarly, for the upper price, there is in general a different positive process of risk charges $(RC_U(t),\ 0 < t < T)$ with the upper price satisfying the equation

$$U(t) - \int_t^T RC_U(u)du + \int_t^T dM(u) = \chi. \tag{10}$$

The gap between the martingale and the lower price is the accumulated risk charge as is the case for the gap between the upper price and the martingale. The risk charge is a charge for the risk exposure embedded in the martingale and the exact form of the risk charge and the associated backward equations (9) and (10) to be solved for the lower and upper prices depend on the structure of the martingale. The risk charges are the drivers of the associated backward stochastic equations and the existence and uniqueness of solutions to these backward stochastic equations requires that drivers be uniformly Lipschitz.

Applications of nonlinear martingales for testing models for required returns for the upper and lower prices of equity assets were made in Ref. [11]. Candidate lower and upper equity prices were approximated by the minimum of five daily lows and the maximum of five daily highs. Unlike equity assets, the option markets provide a rich source of direct quotes on the lower and upper price daily by strike and maturity for each underlying asset.

In building models for risk charges, it is helpful to step back at this point and contemplate the local risk and its charge for a small time step. Over such a small time step of the martingale increment, let the possible values of the increment be x, $-\infty < x < \infty$, with the probability density $f(x)$. The expected value by construction is zero. The lower local-risk charge however is the gap between the expectation and an infimum of other candidate expectations taken under other densities. Let the other admissible densities be defined by a concave distribution function on the unit interval $\Psi(u)$, $0 \leq u \leq 1$, by the property that for every measurable set A and alternative probability density $h(x)$

$$H(A) \leq \Psi(F(A)), \tag{11}$$

$$H(A) = \int_A h(x)dx, \tag{12}$$

$$F(A) = \int_A f(x)dx. \tag{13}$$

The infimum of expectations over such densities is given by (Refs. ([5], [6])) the distorted expectation or expectation under a distorted probability distribution function or

$$b = \int_{-\infty}^{\infty} x d\Psi(F(x)) \tag{14}$$

$$= -\int_{-\infty}^{0} \Psi(F(x))dx + \int_{0}^{\infty} (1 - \Psi(F(x)))\, dx. \tag{15}$$

Note also that the expectation is given by

$$0 = -\int_{-\infty}^{0} F(x)dx + \int_{0}^{\infty} (1 - F(x))dx. \tag{16}$$

The gap is then given by the lower local-risk charge

$$rc_L = \int_{-\infty}^{\infty} (\Psi(F(x)) - F(x))dx. \tag{17}$$

For the upper local-risk charge, one first takes the supremum of expectations under the admissible densities. From the relations between suprema and infima and defining

$$\widehat{F}(x) = 1 - F(x), \tag{18}$$

$$\widehat{\Psi}(u) = 1 - \Psi(1 - u), \tag{19}$$

one observes that the supremum of expectations is given by

$$a = \int_{-\infty}^{\infty} x d\widehat{\Psi}(\widehat{F}(x)) \tag{20}$$

$$= -\int_{-\infty}^{0} \widehat{\Psi}(\widehat{F}(x))dx + \int_{0}^{\infty} \left(1 - \widehat{\Psi}(\widehat{F}(x))\right) dx \tag{21}$$

and the upper local-risk charge is

$$rc_U = \int_{-\infty}^{\infty} \left(\widehat{F}(x) - \widehat{\Psi}(\widehat{F}(x))\right) dx. \tag{22}$$

Observe that Ψ is concave and above the identity while $\widehat{\Psi}$ is convex and below the identity.

Refs. ([20], [21]) took limits of discrete-time models to formulate risk charges for continuous time pure-jump martingales by introducing measure distortions in place of probability distortions. The measure distortions were also used earlier in Eberlein, Madan, Pistorius and Yor (2013). Nonlinear martingales based on probability distortions were employed in Ref. [10]. For measure distortions, one introduces the functions G^+, G^- respectively concave/convex and above/below the identity defined on the positive half-line instead of the unit interval. Consider a pure-jump martingale with ν the possibly adapted jump-compensator.

The lower and upper local-risk charges are then given by

$$RC_L(u) = \int_0^\infty (G^+(K_u(x)) - K_u(x))dx + \int_0^\infty (L_u(x) - G^-(L_u(x))\, dx, \quad (23)$$

$$RC_U(u) = \int_0^\infty (K_u(x) - G^-(K_u(x)))dx + \int_0^\infty (G^+(L_u(x)) - L_u(x))\, dx, \quad (24)$$

$$K(x) = \nu\left((\Delta M_u)^- > x\right), \quad (25)$$

$$L(x) = \nu\left((\Delta M_u)^+ > x\right). \quad (26)$$

Equations (9) and (10) with risk charges defined by Equations (23) and (24) are referred to as backward stochastic partial integro-differential equations as the risk charges are given by integrals of distorted tail measures. By construction, the risk charges are positive processes.

Begin now with the equation for the discounted stock price being a risk-neutral martingale. We then have that

$$e^{-rt}S(t) = \widetilde{E}_t\left[e^{-rT}S(T)\right], \quad (27)$$

where $\widetilde{E}_t$ denotes a t conditional risk-neutral expectation. More generally, for any contingent claim with no intermediate cash flows and price process $w(t, S(t))$, we have that

$$e^{-rt}w(t, S(t)) + \int_t^T e^{-ru}\left[w(u, S(u_-)e^x) - w(u, S(u_-)\right](m(dx, du) - \widetilde{\nu}(dx, du)) = e^{-rT}w(T, S(T)) \quad (28)$$

for a risk-neutral compensating measure $\widetilde{\nu}(dx, du)$ for the integer-valued random measure for the jumps being $m(dx, du)$.

Define the upper and lower valuations by measure distortions as

$$\mathcal{L} = -\int_0^\infty G^+(K(a))da + \int_0^\infty G^-(L(a))da, \quad (29)$$

$$\mathcal{U} = -\int_0^\infty G^-(K(a))da + \int_0^\infty G^+(L(a))da. \quad (30)$$

The valuation itself is given by

$$\mathcal{V} = -\int_0^{\infty} K(a)da + \int_0^{\infty} L(a)da. \tag{31}$$

Proposition 2.1. *The risk-neutral drifts for the lower and upper valuations are given by*

$$\widetilde{E}_t\left[\frac{1}{\widetilde{L}_w(t)}\frac{d\widetilde{L}_w(t)}{dt}\right] = r + \widetilde{rc}_{Lg}, \tag{32}$$

$$\widetilde{E}_t\left[\frac{1}{\widetilde{U}_w(t)}\frac{d\widetilde{U}_w(t)}{dt}\right] = r - \widetilde{rc}_{Ug}, \tag{33}$$

where

$$\widetilde{rc}_{Lg} = \mathcal{V} - \mathcal{L}, \tag{34}$$

$$\widetilde{rc}_{Ug} = \mathcal{U} - \mathcal{V}. \tag{35}$$

Proof. The lower nonlinear risk-neutral martingale satisfies

$$\begin{aligned} & e^{-rt}\widetilde{L}_w(t) + \int_t^T \widetilde{RC}_{L_w}(u)du \\ & \quad + \int_t^T e^{-ru}\left[w(u, S(u_{-})e^{x}) - w(u, S(u_{-}))\right](m(dx, du) - \widetilde{\nu}(dx, du)) \\ & = e^{-rT}w(T, S(T)). \end{aligned}$$

Taking conditional expectations on both sides and differentiating on both sides yields

$$-re^{-rt}\widetilde{L}_w(t)dt - \widetilde{RC}_{L_w}(t)dt + e^{-rt}\widetilde{L}_w(t)\widetilde{E}_t\left[\frac{d\widetilde{L}_w(t)}{\widetilde{L}_w(t)}\right] = 0$$

or that

$$\widetilde{E}_t\left[\frac{1}{\widetilde{L}_w(t)}\frac{d\widetilde{L}_w(t)}{dt}\right] = r + \frac{\widetilde{RC}_{L_w}(t)}{e^{-rt}\widetilde{L}_w(t)}.$$

We may define the risk charge on a dollar by the charge on

$$z(x) = \frac{w(t, S(t_{-})e^{x}) - w(t, S(t_{-}))}{w(t, S(t_{-}))}$$

and then write

$$\widetilde{E}_t \left[\frac{1}{\widetilde{L}_w(t)} \frac{d\widetilde{L}_w(t)}{dt} \right] = r + \widetilde{rc}_{Lg}.$$

The equation for the upper price is using a similar argument

$$\widetilde{E}_t \left[\frac{1}{\widetilde{U}_w(t)} \frac{d\widetilde{U}_w(t)}{dt} \right] = r - \widetilde{rc}_{Ug}.$$

Note the upper and lower risk charges are respectively defined by deviations between upper valuations and valuations and valuations and lower valuations. □

We now make the transition from risk-neutral excess drifts that are positive for the lower price and negative for the upper price to physical drift rates. For this purpose, when working with probabilities, we have

$$\widetilde{E}_t \left[\frac{1}{\widetilde{L}_w(t)} \frac{d\widetilde{L}_w(t)}{dt} \right] = E_t \left[\frac{1}{\widetilde{L}_w(t)} \frac{d\widetilde{L}_w(t)}{dt} \right] + cov_P \left(\frac{dQ}{dP}, \frac{1}{\widetilde{L}_w(t)} \frac{d\widetilde{L}_w(t)}{dt} \right), \tag{36}$$

$$\widetilde{E}_t \left[\frac{1}{\widetilde{U}_w(t)} \frac{d\widetilde{U}_w(t)}{dt} \right] = E_t \left[\frac{1}{\widetilde{U}_w(t)} \frac{d\widetilde{U}_w(t)}{dt} \right] + cov_P \left(\frac{dQ}{dP}, \frac{1}{\widetilde{U}_w(t)} \frac{d\widetilde{U}_w(t)}{dt} \right). \tag{37}$$

For exposures $z(x)$ that are zero near zero, one may ignore a small neighborhood of zero and approximate the risk-neutral and physical integrations with respect to risk-neutral and physical Lévy measures as compound Poisson integrations with risk-neutral arrival rates as $\lambda\widetilde{p}(x)$ with physical counterpart $\theta p(x)$ for risk-neutral and physical jump size densities $\widetilde{p}, p$ and aggregate risk-neutral and physical arrival rates λ, θ.

We then write

$$\begin{aligned}\int z(x)\lambda\widetilde{p}(x)dx &= \int z(x)\lambda\frac{\widetilde{p}(x)}{p(x)}p(x)dx \\ &= \int z(x)\lambda p(x)dx + cov_P\left(z(x)\lambda, \frac{\widetilde{p}(x)}{p(x)}\right) \\ &= \frac{\lambda}{\theta}\int z(x)\theta p(x)dx + cov_P\left(z(x)\lambda, \frac{\widetilde{p}(x)}{p(x)}\right) \\ &\approx \frac{\lambda}{\theta}\int z(x)k(x)dx + cov_P\left(z(x)\lambda, \frac{\widetilde{p}(x)}{p(x)}\right). \end{aligned} \tag{38}$$

We thus write

$$\widetilde{E}_t\left[\frac{1}{\widetilde{L}_w(t)}\frac{d\widetilde{L}_w(t)}{dt}\right] \approx \frac{\lambda}{\theta}E_t\left[\frac{1}{\widetilde{L}_w(t)}\frac{d\widetilde{L}_w(t)}{dt}\right] + cov_P\left(\frac{\lambda}{\widetilde{L}_w(t)}\frac{d\widetilde{L}_w(t)}{dt}, \frac{\widetilde{p}(x)}{p(x)}\right), \tag{39}$$

$$\widetilde{E}_t\left[\frac{1}{\widetilde{U}_w(t)}\frac{d\widetilde{U}_w(t)}{dt}\right] \approx \frac{\lambda}{\theta}E_t\left[\frac{1}{\widetilde{U}_w(t)}\frac{d\widetilde{U}_w(t)}{dt}\right] + cov_P\left(\frac{\lambda}{\widetilde{U}_w(t)}\frac{d\widetilde{U}_w(t)}{dt}, \frac{\widetilde{p}(x)}{p(x)}\right). \tag{40}$$

It follows that the physical expected returns for the lower and upper prices may then be represented by the usual negated covariation considerations along with the effects of risk charges addressing out of martingale considerations.

$$E_t\left[\frac{1}{\widetilde{L}_w(t)}\frac{d\widetilde{L}_w(t)}{dt}\right] = -\theta cov_P\left(\frac{1}{\widetilde{L}_w(t)}\frac{d\widetilde{L}_w(t)}{dt}, \frac{\widetilde{p}(x)}{p(x)}\right) + \frac{\theta}{\lambda}\left(r + \mathcal{V} - \mathcal{L}\right), \tag{41}$$

$$E_t\left[\frac{1}{\widetilde{U}_w(t)}\frac{d\widetilde{U}_w(t)}{dt}\right] = -\theta cov_P\left(\frac{1}{\widetilde{U}_w(t)}\frac{d\widetilde{U}_w(t)}{dt}, \frac{\widetilde{p}(x)}{p(x)}\right) + \frac{\theta}{\lambda}(r + \mathcal{V} - \mathcal{U}). \tag{42}$$

Proposition 2.2. *Approximating the physically expected return by a weighted average of the physical lower and upper variations yields* *the resulting martingale and out of martingale asset pricing equation as*

$$E_t\left[\frac{1}{w(t)}\frac{dw(t)}{dt}\right] = \frac{\theta}{\lambda}r + Acov_P\left(\lambda\frac{d\widetilde{L}_w(t)}{\widetilde{L}_w(t)dt}, \frac{\widetilde{p}(x)}{p(x)}\right) + Bcov_P\left(\frac{d\widetilde{U}_w(t)}{\widetilde{U}_w(t)dt}, \frac{\widetilde{p}(x)}{p(x)}\right) + C\left(\mathcal{V} - \mathcal{L}\right) + D\left(\mathcal{U} - \mathcal{V}\right). \tag{43}$$

The two covariation terms may by Equation (38) be evaluated by integrating the lower and upper per dollar exposures with respect to the risk-neutral and physical Lévy densities and taking their difference. The risk charges come from direct computations of measure distorted valuations. The resulting asset pricing equation may be seen as incorporating both martingale plus out of martingale features. For measure distortions calibrated to data on bid and ask prices, the coefficients A and B should be unity while C, D should be equal and opposite in sign reflecting the ratio of aggregate arrival rates. For a fixed and arbitrary measure distortion, all four coefficients may be estimated to reflect different levels of marginal contributions from the four components.

3. Nonlinear Martingale Models for the Upper and Lower Prices Directly

For a direct modeling of expected returns on the bid or lower price and the ask or upper price, one may begin the analysis from different martingales. Here, following on from Ref. [22], we invoke comonotone additivity and postulate two martingale models for the bid or lower prices of calls coupled with the ask or upper prices of puts. This pairing recognizes that long calls and short puts are comonotone assets and the two martingale models are for claims increasing in the underlying stock price and claims decreasing in the underlying stock price. The forward price for both processes at each maturity is separately estimated by incorporating a continuous dividend yield as an additional parameter. Taking the cue from call prices, the prices $w_b(S)$ refer to the martingale model for claims increasing the underlying asset while the prices $w_a(S)$ refer to the martingale model for claims decreasing in the underlying asset price. We therefore have two martingales that we write as $M_b(t)$ and $M_a(t)$ with

$$M_b(t) + \int_t^T dM_b(u) = M_b(T), \tag{44}$$

$$M_a(t) + \int_t^T dM_a(u) = M_a(T). \tag{45}$$

Associated with these martingales are lower and upper price processes $L_b(t), U_b(t)$ and $L_a(t)$ and $U_a(t)$ that reflect risk charges subtracted and added to the martingale to deliver the lower and upper prices for claims respectively increasing or decreasing in the underlying asset price. These risk charges may be denoted $rc_{b,L}$, $rc_{b,U}$ and $rc_{a,L}$, $rc_{a,U}$. The risk-neutral compensating Lévy measures are $\widetilde{k}_b(x)$ and $\widetilde{k}_a(x)$. The physical Lévy compensators come from a time series analysis of daily returns and are as previously estimated to be $k(x)$.

The analysis of the previous section may then be repeated with respect to these martingales to write four asset pricing equations for the lower and upper returns on claims increasing and decreasing respectively in the underlying asset.

$$E_t\left[\frac{1}{\widetilde{L}_{w_b}(t)}\frac{d\widetilde{L}_{w_b}(t)}{dt}\right] = -\theta cov_P\left(\frac{1}{\widetilde{L}_{w_b}(t)}\frac{d\widetilde{L}_{w_b}(t)}{dt}, \frac{\widetilde{p}_b(x)}{p(x)}\right) + \frac{\theta}{\lambda}\left(r + \mathcal{V}_b - \mathcal{L}_b\right), \tag{46}$$

$$E_t\left[\frac{1}{\widetilde{U}_{w_b}(t)}\frac{d\widetilde{U}_{w_b}(t)}{dt}\right] = -\theta cov_P\left(\frac{1}{\widetilde{U}_{w_b}(t)}\frac{d\widetilde{U}_{w_b}(t)}{dt}, \frac{\widetilde{p}_b(x)}{p(x)}\right) + \frac{\theta}{\lambda}(r + \mathcal{V}_b - \mathcal{U}_b), \tag{47}$$

$$E_t\left[\frac{1}{\widetilde{L}_{w_a}(t)}\frac{d\widetilde{L}_{w_a}(t)}{dt}\right] = -\theta cov_P\left(\frac{1}{\widetilde{L}_{w_a}(t)}\frac{d\widetilde{L}_{w_a}(t)}{dt}, \frac{\widetilde{p}_a(x)}{p(x)}\right) + \frac{\theta}{\lambda}\left(r + \mathcal{V}_a - \mathcal{L}_a\right), \tag{48}$$

$$E_t\left[\frac{1}{\widetilde{L}_{w_a}(t)}\frac{d\widetilde{L}_{w_a}(t)}{dt}\right] = -\theta cov_P\left(\frac{1}{\widetilde{L}_{w_a}(t)}\frac{d\widetilde{L}_{w_a}(t)}{dt}, \frac{\widetilde{p}_a(x)}{p(x)}\right) + \frac{\theta}{\lambda}\left(r + \mathcal{V}_a - \mathcal{L}_a\right). \tag{49}$$

Proposition 3.1. *Approximating the physically expected return for increasing/decreasing claims by a weighted average of the corresponding physical lower and upper variations yields the resulting martingale and out of martingale lower and upper asset pricing equations for increasing/decreasing claims as*

$$E_t\left[\frac{1}{w_b(t)}\frac{dw_b(t)}{dt}\right] = \frac{\theta}{\lambda}r + Acov_P\left(\lambda\frac{d\widetilde{L}_{w_b}(t)}{\widetilde{L}_{w_b}(t)dt}, \frac{\widetilde{p}_b(x)}{p(x)}\right) + Bcov_P\left(\frac{d\widetilde{U}_{w_b}(t)}{\widetilde{U}_{w_b}(t)dt}, \frac{\widetilde{p}_b(x)}{p(x)}\right) + C\left(\mathcal{V}_b - \mathcal{L}_b\right) + D\left(\mathcal{U}_b - \mathcal{V}_b\right), \tag{50}$$

$$E_t\left[\frac{1}{w_a(t)}\frac{dw_a(t)}{dt}\right] = \frac{\theta}{\lambda}r + Acov_P\left(\lambda\frac{d\widetilde{L}_{w_a}(t)}{\widetilde{L}_{w_a}(t)dt}, \frac{\widetilde{p}_a(x)}{p(x)}\right) + Bcov_P\left(\frac{d\widetilde{U}_{w_a}(t)}{\widetilde{U}_{w_a}(t)dt}, \frac{\widetilde{p}_a(x)}{p(x)}\right) + C\left(\mathcal{V}_a - \mathcal{L}_a\right) + D\left(\mathcal{U}_a - \mathcal{V}_a\right). \tag{51}$$

The equations to be estimated and reported on in the paper are those of Propositions 2 and 3. They will be estimated on option data for ten underliers across four maturities every ten days over the period January 2015 through December 2021. Results will be reported over the whole data set and partitioned by maturity, by moneyness, by asset and by asset and maturity. The calculations require the computations of exposures and their integration with respect to specific Lévy densities that are both distorted and undistorted. The following two sections describe the Lévy models employed and the measure distortions associated with them.

4. Risk-Neutral and Physical Arrival Rate Models

The Gaussian distribution is well known to be a maximal entropy density on the real line that is also a limit law. These features have recommended its adoption as a model for returns that when consistently describing returns over arbitrary intervals of continuous time deliver the Brownian motion model for log returns or continuously compounded returns. However, continuous time may be viewed as an analytical fiction artificially lining up an uncountable infinity of time points into a line. The ordering into a line falls apart once infinitesimals are recognized as part of the field of numbers. Models of physical time recognize both (i) that time is increasing and (ii) when related to measures of activity time is also uncertain. All increasing processes with uncertainty or a martingale component are pure jump processes. A maximal entropy-increasing process on the positive half line that is also a limit law is the gamma process. Ref. [18] and Ref. [19] time changed Brownian motion by such a gamma process to arrive at the variance-gamma model. The variance-gamma model is also expressible as the difference between two independent gamma processes with different scale coefficients but the same speeds. Ref. [17] introduced the bilateral gamma model that allowed for different speeds on the two sides. Ref. [25] and Ref. [24] examined and confirmed the empirical adequacy of the bilateral gamma model with respect to daily return data and risk-neutral distributions embedded in option prices. They observed additionally that markets may be seen to take the escalator up and the elevator down with upmoves that are faster and smaller than the down-side counterparts. We therefore employ as a base model describing risk-neutral and or physical arrival rates those associated with bilateral gamma densities at unit time. The model has four parameters for speed and scale on the two sides that also calibrate effectively mean and variance rates for the upward and downward movements.

For two standard independent gamma processes $\gamma_p(t)$, $\gamma_n(t)$ with unit mean and variance rates and scale parameters b_p, b_n and speed parameters c_p, c_n, the associated bilateral gamma process $X(t)$ is defined as

$$X(t) = b_p\gamma_p(c_pt) - b_n\gamma_n(c_nt). \tag{52}$$

The characteristic function follows directly from that for the gamma process and is given by

$$\begin{aligned}\phi_{BG}(u,t) &= E\left[\exp\left(iuX(t)\right)\right] \\ &= \left(\frac{1}{1-iub_p}\right)^{c_pt}\left(\frac{1}{1+iub_n}\right)^{c_nt}.\end{aligned} \tag{53}$$

The convexity correction factor ω, for fixing the forward risk neutrally, is

$$\begin{aligned}\omega &= -\ln(E[\exp(X(1))]) \\ &= c_p\ln(1-b_p) + c_n\ln(1+b_n).\end{aligned} \tag{54}$$

The Lévy measure or arrival rate function is given by

$$k_{BG}(x) = c_p\frac{\exp(x/b_p)}{x}\mathbf{1}_{x>0} + c_n\frac{\exp\left(-|x|/b_n\right)}{|x|}\mathbf{1}_{x<0}. \tag{55}$$

The parameters calibrate the drift, δ, volatility, ν, skewness, ψ, and kurtosis, κ, of the distribution. Explicitly in terms of the parameters we have that

$$\delta = b_pc_p - b_nc_n, \tag{56}$$

$$\nu = \sqrt{b_p^2c_p + b_n^2c_n}, \tag{57}$$

$$\psi = 2\frac{b_p^3c_p - b_n^3c_n}{\nu^3}, \tag{58}$$

$$\kappa = 3 + 6\frac{b_p^4c_p + b_n^4c_n}{\nu^4}. \tag{59}$$

The density is also available in closed form using the Whittaker W function. Specifically, for $x > 0$, the density is given by

$$f_{BG}(x) = \left(\frac{1}{b_p}\right)^{c_p} \left(\frac{1}{b_n}\right)^{c_n} \left(\frac{1}{(1/b_p + 1/b_n)^{(c_p+c_n)/2}\Gamma(c_p)}\right)$$
$$\times x^{(c_p+c_n)/2-1} \exp\left(-x/2(1/b_p + 1/b_n)\right)$$
$$\times W\left(\frac{c_p - c_n}{2}, \frac{c_p + c_n - 1}{2}, \left(\frac{1}{b_p} + \frac{1}{b_n}\right)x\right). \tag{60}$$

For $x < 0$, the roles of b_p, c_p and b_n, c_n are reversed.

5. Measure Distortions

The measure distortions employed denoted $G^+(x), G^-(x)$ that are concave/convex and above/below the identity were introduced in Ref. [9]. They are defined as

$$G^+(x) = x + a(1 - e^{-cx})^{\frac{1}{1+\gamma}},$$
$$G^-(x) = x - \frac{b}{c}(1 - e^{-cx}).$$

They have been recently used in designing Markovian trading strategies in Ref. [12] with reasonable trading outcomes for the parameter setting $a = 100$, $b = 1$, $c = 0.01$ and $\gamma = 0.25$. Strategies for calibrating measure distortions are discussed in Ref. [23] and the references therein. Examples of sample calibrations are also presented in the references. Here we follow Ref. [12] and employ the parameter set 100, 1, 0.01 and 0.25 for a, b, c and γ. All the valuations with and without measure distortions are accomplished numerically.

6. Two-Sided Risk Premia for Jumps and Stochastic Volatility

The use of separate models for the motion of asset prices on the two sides as embodied in the bilateral gamma process allows for a separate assessment of volatility and jump risk premia on the two sides. The two scale parameters b_p, b_n by altering scale lift jump risk premia separately for the positive and negative moves while leaving premia for the small jumps relatively unchanged as is manifested by the arrival rate exponential decay functions on the two sides. The two speed parameters c_p and c_n lift all arrival rates uniformly and reflect movements in volatility again separately on the two sides.

For each option in the data set for all names, days, strikes and maturities, one may evaluate the price gradients with respect to the four parameters as a measure of the asset's responsiveness to movements in jump risk premia and volatility on the two sides. The sensitivity of mean returns on option assets to these gradients then permits an assessment of two-sided jump risk and volatility premia. The asset pricing equations will be expanded to accommodate a measurement of such risk premia.

7. Data and Their Bilateral Gamma Representation

The data on option prices employed covers daily market close information of European option bid, ask and mid-quote prices over the period January 2015 through and including December 2021 for 10 underlying assets. The underlying assets are SPY the exchange-traded fund (ETF) tracking the S&P 500 index and nine Sector ETFs with the tickers XLB, XLE, XLF, XLI, XLK, XLP, XLU, XLV and XLY. Information was extracted every 10 days for around 170 days for each of the 10 underliers. There may be some 20–30 maturities trading on each underlier each day and we selected data on four maturities closest to a month, quarter, half year and a year.

The first step toward and evaluation of instantaneous returns was a bilateral gamma summary of these data. This was done by fitting for each underlying asset i, for each day t and each maturity τ a risk-neutral bilateral gamma model yielding parameters $\widetilde{\theta}_{i,t,\tau} = (\widetilde{b}_p, \widetilde{c}_p, \widetilde{b}_n, \widetilde{c}_n)_{i,t,\tau}$. The variance-gamma special case of the bilateral gamma has been employed to mark option books on many underliers worldwide using such procedures. The bilateral gamma only improves upon this representation. The output of these estimations delivers access to Lévy densities $\widetilde{k}_{i,t,\tau}(x)$ and option price functions $w_{i,t,\tau}(K_j)$ evaluated at a unit forward under zero rates and dividend yields with 21 strikes ranging from 0.8 to 1.2 in steps of 0.02. The full data set then had 138,096 options ranging over all 10 underliers, 4 maturities, 21 strikes and around 170 days. The per dollar exposure $z_{i,t,\tau,j}(x)$ of each option to jumps of size x for x ranging between -0.3 and 0.3 in steps of 10 basis points excluding zero may then be evaluated using the bilateral gamma parameters by evaluating the ratio of the post-jump option price to the pre-jump price less unity. The expectations of these exposures measure distorted or not may then be determined to obtain the upper, lower and undistorted valuations on integrations with distorted or undistorted levels of $\widetilde{k}_{i,t,\tau}(x)$ using G^+ and G^- for the distortions. The results deliver 138,096 triples $(\widetilde{y}_{L,i,t,\tau,j}, \widetilde{y}_{V,i,t,\tau,j}, \widetilde{y}_{U,i,t,\tau,j})$ for the lower $\widetilde{y}_L$, upper $\widetilde{y}_U$ and undistorted valuations $\widetilde{y}_V$. These are all risk-neutral or distorted risk-neutral valuations.

In addition, for each underlier i and date t, we take 63 days of immediately prior daily returns and estimate a physical bilateral gamma model by matching observed tail probabilities with model probabilities using Ref. [1] weighting. The resulting parameters are $\theta_{it} = (b_p, c_p, b_n, c_n)_{it}$. They give us access to the physical Lévy density $k_{it}(x)$. The exposures $z_{i,t,\tau,j}(x)$ may then be integrated, distorted or undistorted with respect to $k_{it}(x)$ to produce the lower, upper and undistorted physical valuations $(y_{L,i,t,\tau,j}, y_{V,i,t,\tau,j}, y_{U,i,t,\tau,j})$. The candidates for the instantaneous expected option returns are the variables $y_{V,i,t,\tau,j}$.

8. Observations on Instantaneous Expected Option Returns

Ref. [8] argued that under certain conditions, expected option returns should be negative on puts, positive on calls and increasing with respect to strike levels. Additionally, Ref. [14] argue that call returns decline with volatility while put returns rise. While Ref. [13] argue for higher returns when realized volatilities dominate the implied volatilities. Here, we address these features in our collection of instantaneous expected option returns.

With respect to put call returns, the quartiles across the full sample for puts are -19.36, -6.83 and -1.21. The corresponding values for calls are 3.52, 19.24 and 52.52. By and large, the put returns are negative while the call returns are positive. With respect to the dependency on strikes, given the wide range of strikes involved across the many underliers, we regressed the instantaneous expected option return on log strikes and their squares to obtain that

$$\begin{aligned} y_V &= 0.0367 + 1.5742\log(K) + 3.6793\log(K)^2, \\ &\quad (35.14) \quad (263.41) \qquad\qquad (70.43) \\ R^2 &= 0.43\%. \end{aligned}$$

There is thus a clear positive and convex relationship between the option returns and strike levels. The results hold up and are comparable when partitioned by underlier and maturity, though the $R^{2\prime}s$ rise to between 20 and 40.

With regard to the Ref. [14] observation on differentiating call and put returns with respect to the effects of volatility, it is not clear which volatility is meant. There is the physical volatility of the stock that we have estimated each day for each asset using a bilateral gamma model for daily returns over the prior quarter. Additionally, there is the risk-neutral volatility associated with the variance of the risk-neutral distribution. To address this aspect, we regressed near money call and put option returns on the logarithm of the risk-neutral and statistical volatilities. The results are presented in Table 1. We observe a significant negative relationship with respect to calls on the risk-neutral volatility, but the relationship for puts is also negative but not significant. With respect to physical volatilities,

Table 1. Regressions on volatility.

	Constant	Coeff.	RSQ
Risk-neutral vols.			
Calls	0.0550	−0.0526	0.18
	(6.09)	−(7.61)	
Puts	−0.1162	−0.0077	0.03
	(−21.19)	(−1.85)	
Physical vols.			
Calls	0.2984	0.0403	0.23
	(14.12)	(8.29)	
Puts	−0.3929	−0.0650	3.51
	(−32.53)	(−23.40)	

both relationships are significant but positive for calls and negative for puts.

Regarding the Ref. [13] relationship between returns and the spread of the physical over the risk-neutral volatility, we regressed the returns over the full sample on the logarithm of the ratio of the physical to risk-neutral volatility. The result was

$$y_V = 0.1749 + 0.0577 \ln\left(\frac{volts}{volrn}\right) + 0.0052\left(\ln\left(\frac{volts}{volrn}\right)\right)^2.$$
$$(10.76) \qquad (6.23) \qquad\qquad\qquad (3.80)$$

The R^2 was zero and is not reported. The variables *volts* and *volrn* are the return volatilities as implied by the bilateral gamma parameter estimates obtained statistically and from the option surface at the appropriate maturity.

9. Martingale and Out of Martingale Asset Pricing Tests

The first test to be accomplished is that of Equation (43). The left-hand side variable is the vector y_V of length 138096 covering the ten names, for around 170 days for four maturities and 21 strikes. On the right-hand side, we have two covariations and two risk charges. The covariations can be evaluated are evaluates as follows:

$$cvL = -cov_P\left(\lambda\frac{d\widetilde{L}_w(t)}{\widetilde{L}_w(t)dt}, \frac{\widetilde{p}(x)}{p(x)}\right) = y_{L,i,t,\tau,j} - \widetilde{y}_{L,i,t,\tau,j}, \quad (61)$$

$$cvU = -cov_P\left(\lambda\frac{d\widetilde{U}_w(t)}{\widetilde{U}_w(t)dt}, \frac{\widetilde{p}(x)}{p(x)}\right) = y_{U,i,t,\tau,j} - \widetilde{y}_{U,i,t,\tau,j}. \quad (62)$$

The two risk charges are given by

$$rcL = \mathcal{V} - \mathcal{L} = \widetilde{y}_{e,i,t,\tau,j} - \widetilde{y}_{L,i,t,\tau,j}, \quad (63)$$
$$rvU = \mathcal{U} - \mathcal{V} = \widetilde{y}_{U,i,t,\tau,j} - \widetilde{y}_{e,i,t,\tau,j}. \quad (64)$$

The regressions that are run are for

$$y_V = \alpha + b_L * cvL + b_U * cvU + c_L * rcL + c_U * rcU + \varepsilon_V. \quad (65)$$

Table 2. Tests of Equation (43).

Constant	cvL	cvU	rcL	rcU	RSQ
Full sample					
−0.1313	−0.1264	0.1262	0.1251	0.1246	33.55
(−76.1)	(−101.1)	(100.8)	(102.7)	(100.6)	
Maturity 1 month					
−0.1342	−0.1256	0.1328	0.1341	0.1211	49.29
(−2.14)	(51.2)	(55.0)	(57.3)	(49.4)	
Maturity 3 months					
−0.1043	−0.0896	0.0886	0.1006	0.0599	48.36
(3.18)	(−32.1)	(31.8)	(32.2)	(21.5)	
Maturity 6 months					
0.0027	−0.1340	0.1334	0.1148	0.1413	59.73
(0.43)	(−70.0)	(69.5)	(47.5)	(70.3)	
Maturity 1 year					
−0.1419	−0.1483	0.1480	0.1381	0.1684	59.56
(−35.6)	(−74.2)	(74.0)	(49.0)	(65.7)	
		Moneyness <−10%			
−0.4077	−0.0899	0.1084	0.1133	0.0808	75.17
(−20.7)	(−54.8)	(72.6)	(80.1)	(46.6)	
−10%<Moneyness<10%					
−0.1098	−0.1393	0.1383	0.1418	0.1297	37.85
(−21.4)	(−76.9)	(76.1)	(79.6)	(73.3)	
Moneyness > 10%					
0.0146	−0.0602	0.0595	0.0633	0.0569	61.89
(0.31)	(−28.9)	(28.6)	(31.4)	(27.6)	

The regressions are reported on the full sample, by maturity and by moneyness in Table 2. They are reported by underlier in Table 3. We observe quite consistently that the two risk charges are positively significant as is the covariation with upper returns. The covariation with lower returns is negatively priced.

10. Time-Series Structure of Risk Premia

With a view toward exploring the time patterns of the two covariation and risk charge premia embedded in required returns, the asset pricing equation (43) was estimated separately for each date across

Table 3. Tests of Equation (43).

	Constant	cvL	cvU	rcL	rcU	RSQ
Separately by asset						
SPY	−0.0118	−0.0316	0.0305	0.0359	0.0268	25.14
	(−0.18)	(−8.78)	(8.47)	(10.81)	(7.46)	
XLB	−0.1650	−0.0356	0.0334	0.0419	0.0306	82.61
	(−10.3)	(−8.3)	(7.8)	(10.2)	(7.2)	
XLE	−0.1540	−0.1116	0.1126	0.1191	0.1010	96.62
	(−8.28)	(−44.1)	(45.8)	(51.7)	(39.4)	
XLF	−0.1940	−0.1602	0.1596	0.1614	0.1541	89.67
	(−14.6)	(−33.8)	(33.5)	(34.8)	(33.0)	
XLI	−0.0179	−0.0333	0.0328	0.0356	0.0308	56.12
	(−0.67)	(−9.2)	(9.0)	(9.9)	(8.6)	
XLK	−0.0651	−0.1017	0.1002	0.1024	0.0954	56.03
	(−2.65)	(−26.0)	(25.5)	(26.7)	(24.9)	
XLP	−0.0098	−0.0683	0.0687	0.0695	0.0661	39.86
	(−0.19)	(−11.8)	(11.9)	(12.2)	(11.5)	
XLU	−0.0655	−0.1363	0.1353	0.1279	0.1383	53.83
	(0.78)	(−38.9)	(38.9)	(37.7)	(39.8)	
XLV	0.1225	−0.0880	0.0866	0.0843	0.0814	37.76
	(3.7)	(−17.3)	(16.9)	(16.7)	(16.5)	
XLY	−0.0377	−0.0522	0.0507	0.0550	0.0453	87.69
	(−1.5)	(−16.0)	(15.5)	(17.1)	(14.3)	

all underliers, maturities and strikes. The total number of days with bilateral gamma parameter representations was 542 starting on January 2, 2015, and ending December 31, 2021. The number of assets across underliers, maturities and strikes for each day varied with a median of 252 and lower and upper quartiles of 231 and 252, respectively. The minimum was 63 and the maximum was 840. The 542 regressions produced times series of risk premia b_L, b_U for the lower and upper covariations and risk premia c_L, c_U for the lower and upper risk charges. Figures 1 and 2 present graphs for the four risk premia over time.

We observe that the upper covariation premium is positive while the lower covariation premium is negative and the former is above the latter. The risk charge premia are generally positive with the lower risk charge having a slightly higher premia. Table 4 presents selected percentiles for the four premia that were generally all significant with percentiles for the t-statistics presented in Table 5.

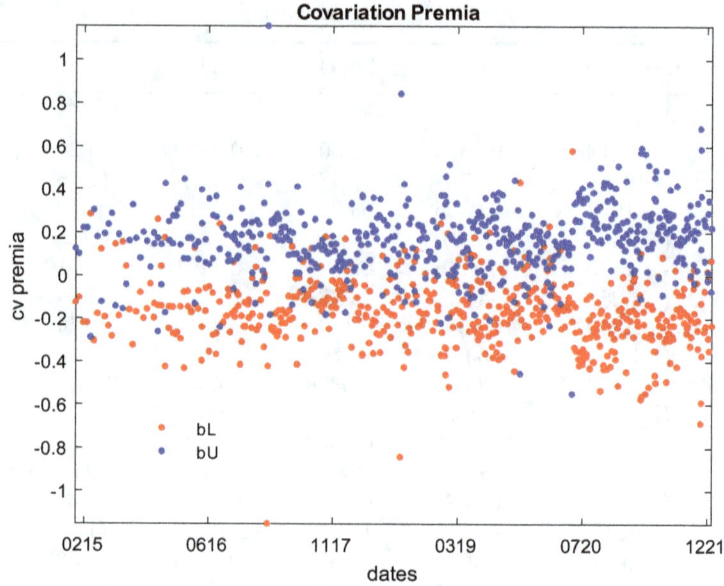

Figure 1. Covariation risk premia with respect to the lower and upper returns over the years 2015 through 2021.

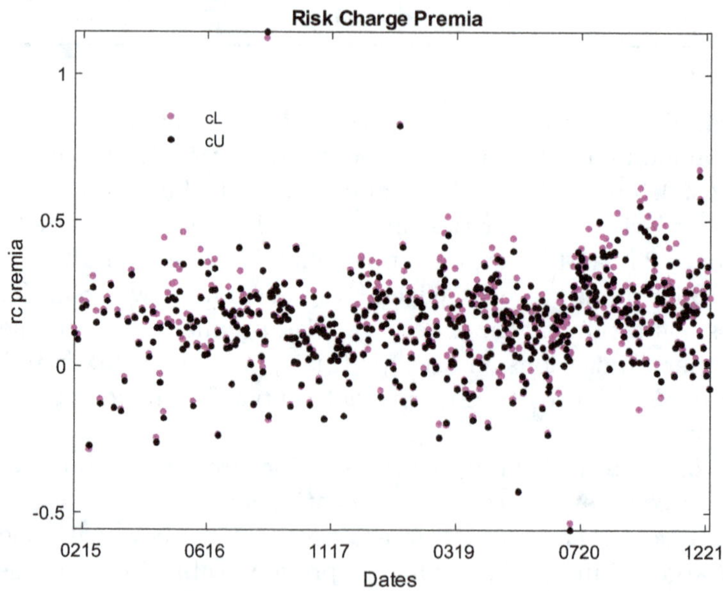

Figure 2. Risk charge risk premia for the lower and upper risk charges over the years 2015 through 2021.

Table 4. Risk premia percentiles.

Percentile	b_L	b_U	c_L	c_U
1	−0.5593	−0.2310	−0.2253	−0.2362
5	−0.4144	−0.1035	−0.0957	−0.1034
10	−0.3553	−0.0299	−0.0246	−0.0286
25	−0.2559	0.0779	0.0807	0.0742
50	−0.1723	0.1722	0.1741	0.1660
75	−0.0801	0.2551	0.2563	0.2416
90	0.0279	0.3555	0.3548	0.3212
95	0.1028	0.4125	0.4112	0.3790
99	0.2381	0.5746	0.5785	0.5023

Table 5. Risk premia t-statistics percentiles.

Percentile	b_L	b_U	c_L	c_U
1	−39.29	−12.17	−12.79	−11.85
5	−18.61	−4.56	−4.06	−4.81
10	−13.77	−0.99	−0.79	−0.93
25	−9.07	2.66	2.67	2.57
50	−6.17	6.28	6.25	6.03
75	−2.66	9.32	9.21	8.85
90	0.89	13.99	13.93	13.45
95	4.60	18.80	18.50	19.25
99	12.06	46.53	43.03	39.92

Additionally, we observe that when b_L is negative, then b_U, c_L and c_U are positive, and when b_L is negative, then b_U, c_L and c_U are all negative.

11. Two-Sided Jump Risk and Volatility Premia

The results of martingale and out of martingale asset pricing are extended to accommodate risk premia for up- and down-side jump risk premia and volatility. The covariation terms and risk charges are expanded to include the differential of returns with respect to the logarithms of b_p, c_p, b_n and c_n. The logarithmic derivatives measure sensitivities to percentage changes that reflect pure numbers devoid of scale considerations. Table 6 presents the results for the full sample, the four maturities and the three moneyness categories. Positive jump risk is positively priced while negative jump risk is negatively priced. Stochastic volatility on the two sides is not really priced, but for the longer maturities, it is negatively priced for the down-side volatility.

Table 7 reports the results for the 10 underliers. The R^2 is given below the name of the underlier. Risk premia for SPY have a different pattern to the other underliers pricing lower covariation positively and upper covariation and the two risk charges negatively. Stochastic volatility is not really priced, but positive and negative jump risks are positively and negatively priced, respectively.

The effects of the covariation and risk charge terms are comparable to those before the addition of jump and volatility risk terms. The positive jump risk has a consistently zero coefficient and it is not reported. For the positive and negative volatility terms, the premia are positive and slightly significant sometimes. Strongly and consistently negatively significant is the down-side jump risk premia. The signs are reversed for out of the money options.

12. Lower and Upper Returns Modeled Directly

This section reports on directly modeling the expected returns on the lower and upper prices. For this exercise, we begin with martingales for the lower prices of calls and upper prices of puts for prices w_b. A second martingale is fitted to the upper prices of calls and lower prices of puts for prices w_a. We then construct risk-neutral measure distorted valuations $\widetilde{y}^{(b)}_{L,i,t,\tau,j}$, $\widetilde{y}^{(b)}_{e,i,t,\tau,j}$, $\widetilde{y}^{(b)}_{U,i,t,\tau,j}$ around the martingale w_b. Similarly, we construct $\widetilde{y}^{(a)}_{L,i,t,\tau,j}$, $\widetilde{y}^{(a)}_{e,i,t,\tau,j}$, $\widetilde{y}^{(a)}_{U,i,t,\tau,j}$ around the martingale w_a. In addition, we integrate exposures for w_b, w_a against the physical bilateral gamma Lévy measures to form $y^{(b)}_{L,i,t,\tau,j}$, $y^{(b)}_{e,i,t,\tau,j}$, $y^{(b)}_{U,i,t,\tau,j}$ and $y^{(b)}_{L,i,t,\tau,j}$, $y^{(b)}_{e,i,t,\tau,j}$, $y^{(b)}_{U,i,t,\tau,j}$.

The covariations are defined by

$$cvL^{(b)} = y^{(b)}_{L,i,t,\tau,j} - \widetilde{y}^{(b)}_{L,i,t,\tau,j}, \tag{66}$$

$$cvU^{(b)} = y^{(b)}_{U,i,t,\tau,j} - \widetilde{y}^{(b)}_{U,i,t,\tau,j}, \tag{67}$$

Table 6. Tests of Equation (43) extended for two-sided jump and volatility risk.

Constant	cvL	cvU	rcL	rcU	dlogb$_p$	dlogc$_p$	dlogb$_n$	dlogc$_n$
Full sample (RSQ = 52.19)								
−0.0790	−0.0946	0.0943	0.0959	0.0908	0.6063	$-1.689e-4$	−2.3106	−0.0018
(−5.4)	(−85.6)	(85.2)	(89.4)	(82.6)	(37.7)	(−0.01)	(−109.2)	(−0.12)
Maturity 1 month (RSQ = 55.41)								
−0.1958	−0.1253	0.1258	0.1267	0.1211	0.2880	−0.0012	−2.0357	0.0160
(−3.7)	(54.4)	(55.3)	(57.5)	(52.7)	(1.64)	(−0.05)	(−34.1)	(0.23)
Maturity 3 months (RSQ = 64.90)								
−0.0392	0.0021	−0.0027	0.0287	−0.0353	0.9831	12.963	−1.0482	−1.7172
(−1.6)	(0.85)	(−1.09)	(10.9)	(−13.5)	(65.7)	(0.03)	(−1.21)	(−1.75)
Maturity 6 months (RSQ = 68.12)								
−0.0632	−0.1331	0.1325	0.1208	0.1350	0.4158	273.35	24.954	−0.2843
(−12.2)	(−87.8)	(87.2)	(62.9)	(80.1)	(52.0)	(0.42)	(24.1)	(−3.94)
Maturity 1 year (RSQ = 59.80)								
−0.1413	−0.1487	0.1484	0.1393	0.1681	0.0617	550.33	−4.7513	0.0018
(−34.6)	(−74.0)	(73.8)	(48.4)	(65.6)	(0.48)	(1.52)	(−2.21)	(1.37)
Moneyness <−10% (RSQ = 79.16)								
−0.4276	−0.0885	0.1116	0.1151	0.0807	−21.177	−0.1379	1.9315	−0.0089
(−23.2)	(−58.7)	(81.3)	(88.8)	(50.7)	(−6.7)	(−0.31)	(43.1)	(−0.79)
−10% <Moneyness <10% (RSQ = 47.59)								
−0.1392	−0.1493	0.1483	0.1490	0.1423	0.1570	$-8.918e-4$	5.3186	$-3.075e-4$
(−29.3)	(−88.7)	(87.8)	(90.2)	(86.1)	(8.9)	(−0.22)	(54.4)	(−0.05)
Moneyness > 10% (RSQ = 67.98)								
0.0560	−0.0396	0.0392	0.0424	0.0375	0.7365	$3.79e-4$	8.3181	−0.0235
(1.3)	(−20.0)	(19.7)	(22.0)	(19.1)	(31.5)	(0.01)	(23.6)	(−0.42)

Table 7. Tests of Equation (43) extended for two-sided jump and volatility risk.

	Constant	cvL	cvU	rcL	rcU	b_p	c_p	b_n	c_n
Separately by asset									
SPY	−0.0747	0.0268	−0.0274	−0.0147	−0.0325	1.0770	$4.8e-4$	−4.8636	2.9541
58.68	(−1.5)	(9.3)	(−9.5)	(−5.6)	(−11.2)	(47.9)	(0.03)	(−8.5)	(1.4)
XLB	−0.0715	−0.0224	0.0203	0.0332	0.0106	1.1586	85.38	−8.8884	0.1347
90.11	(−5.7)	(−6.9)	(6.3)	(10.7)	(3.3)	(7.0)	(0.3)	(−50.9)	(0.04)
XLE	−0.1459	−0.1066	0.1075	0.1146	0.0952	39.111	362.56	−0.9180	0.0397
96.75	(−7.74)	(−41.4)	(43.6)	(49.8)	(36.3)	(3.65)	(0.41)	(−10.2)	(0.95)
XLF	−0.1157	−0.1060	0.1045	0.1087	0.0999	−7.9385	777.29	−6.3734	−0.0094
94.76	(−12.0)	(−30.3)	(29.7)	(31.7)	(28.9)	(−10.4)	(0.73)	(−58.6)	(−2.1)
XLI	−0.0149	−0.0431	0.0423	0.0477	0.0365	−0.5585	968.05	−3.5544	−0.1598
61.99	(−0.56)	(−10.9)	(10.8)	(12.5)	(9.4)	(−4.2)	(0.07)	(−22.8)	(−0.14)
XLK	−0.0131	−0.1030	0.1013	0.1038	0.0964	−0.3143	43.5664	−1.8542	−17.196
56.55	(−0.45)	(−26.2)	(25.7)	(26.8)	(25.0)	(−1.6)	(0.10)	(−5.69)	(−2.99)
XLP	0.0519	−0.0021	0.0021	0.0054	$-5.9e-5$	1.6036	21.629	−2.6194	−0.0314
55.24	(1.19)	(−0.39)	(0.38)	(1.01)	(−0.01)	(1.87)	(0.008)	(−29.62)	(−0.14)
XLU	−0.0107	−0.1219	0.1288	0.1271	0.1184	64.488	457.03	−0.3435	0.7682
59.24	(−0.14)	(−36.3)	(39.2)	(39.9)	(34.8)	(19.9)	(0.45)	(−2.9)	(0.62)
XLV	0.0080	−0.0669	0.0648	0.0750	0.0522	−0.2412	127.43	−11.25	$4.5e-4$
67.68	(0.33)	(−18.1)	(17.5)	(20.5)	(14.6)	(−3.0)	(0.16)	(−57.7)	(−0.04)
XLY	0.0341	−0.0121	0.0109	0.0161	0.0063	0.3919	6060.2	0.5791	−2.8053
88.38	(1.3)	(−2.7)	(2.5)	(3.7)	(1.5)	(12.4)	(0.36)	(2.12)	−(2.07)

$$cvL^{(a)} = y^{(a)}_{L,i,t,\tau,j} - \widetilde{y}^{(a)}_{L,i,t,\tau,j}, \tag{68}$$

$$cvL^{(a)} = y^{(a)}_{L,i,t,\tau,j} - \widetilde{y}^{(a)}_{L,i,t,\tau,j}. \tag{69}$$

The risk charges are defined by

$$rcL^{(b)} = \widetilde{y}^{(b)}_{e,i,t,\tau,j} - \widetilde{y}^{(b)}_{L,i,t,\tau,j}, \tag{70}$$

$$rcU^{(b)} = \widetilde{y}^{(b)}_{U,i,t,\tau,j} - \widetilde{y}^{(b)}_{e,i,t,\tau,j}, \tag{71}$$

$$rcL^{(a)} = \widetilde{y}^{(a)}_{e,i,t,\tau,j} - \widetilde{y}^{(a)}_{L,i,t,\tau,j}, \tag{72}$$

$$rcU^{(a)} = \widetilde{y}^{(a)}_{U,i,t,\tau,j} - \widetilde{y}^{(a)}_{e,i,t,\tau,j}. \tag{73}$$

We then define

$$y^{(b)}_V = y^{(b)}_{e,i,t,\tau,j}, \tag{74}$$

$$y_V = y^{(a)}_{e,i,t,\tau,j}. \tag{75}$$

The regressions that are run are for

$$y^{(b)}_V = a + b^{(b)}_L cvL^{(b)} + b^{(b)}_U cvU^{(b)} + c^{(b)}_L rcL^{(b)} + c^{(b)}_U rcU^{(b)} + \varepsilon^{(b)}, \tag{76}$$

$$y^{(a)}_V = a + b^{(a)}_L cvL^{(a)} + b^{(a)}_U cvU^{(a)} + c^{(a)}_L rcL^{(a)} + c^{(a)}_U rcU^{(a)} + \varepsilon^{(a)}. \tag{77}$$

We report here just the results on the full sample:

$$\begin{aligned} y^{(b)}_V &= \underset{(-7.3)}{-0.2614} - \underset{(-245.1)}{0.1575} * cvL^{(b)} + \underset{(244.0)}{0.1558} * cvU^{(b)} + \underset{(249.8)}{0.1572} * rcL^{(b)} + \underset{(241.6)}{0.1528} * rcU^{(b)}, \\ R^{2(b)} &= 99.59, \\ y^{(a)}_V &= \underset{(-2.2)}{-0.0648} - \underset{(-39.7)}{0.0529} * cvL^{(a)} + \underset{(39.1)}{0.0522} * cvU^{(a)} + \underset{(41.8)}{0.0540} * rcL^{(a)} + \underset{(38.5)}{0.0510} * rcU^{(a)}, \\ R^{2(a)} &= 14.51. \end{aligned}$$

For both the lower and upper expected return rates, a significant role is played by both the lower and upper covariations with the former covariation being negatively priced while the latter one is positively priced. Both risk charges have positive effects on returns.

13. Conclusion

The theory of nonlinear martingales is employed to develop lower and upper price processes that straddle any martingale. The risk-neutral expectation is then modeled in terms of risk charges associated with the returns on the straddling lower and upper prices. The move to physically expected returns is then made via the usual covariation risk factors. There are however two covariation terms: one for the lower and the other for the upper valuation. The expected returns are then seen to incorporate in addition to covariation considerations that address the martingale, the risk charges that assess out of martingale issues. The theory is tested on prices of options for 10 underliers over 170 days covering 4 maturities and 21 strikes. It is observed that the risk charges have positive significant coefficients while the upper covariation has a positive price with the lower covariation receiving a negative price.

References

[1] T. W. Andersen and D. A. Darling. Asymptotic theory of certain "Goodness of Fit" criteria based on stochastic processes. *The Annals of Mathematical Statistics*, 23:193–212, 1952.

[2] G. Bakshi and N. Kapadia. Delta hedged gains and the negative market volatility risk premium. *Review of Financial Studies*, 16:527–566, 2003.

[3] M. Broadie, M. Chernov, and M. Johannes. Understanding option returns. *Review of Financial Studies*, 29:4493–4529, 2009.

[4] J. Cao and B. Han. Cross-section of option returns and idiosyncratic stock volatility. *Journal of Financial Economics*, 108:231–249, 2013.

[5] A. Cherny and D. B. Madan. New measures for performance evaluation. *Review of Financial Studies*, 22:2571–2606, 2009.

[6] A. Cherny and D. B. Madan. Markets as a counterparty: An introduction to conic finance. *International Journal of Theoretical and Applied Finance*, 13:1149–1177, 2010.

[7] G. M. Constantinides, J. C. Jackwerth, and A. Savov. The puzzle of index option returns. *Review of Asset Pricing Studies*, 3:229–257, 2013.

[8] J. D. Coval and T. Shumway. Expected option returns. *Journal of Finance*, 56:983–1009, 2001.

[9] E. Eberlein, D. B. Madan, M. Pistorius, and M. Yor. Bid and ask prices as non-linear continuous time G-expectations based on distortions. *Mathematics and Financial Economics*, 8:265–289, 2014.

[10] E. Eberlein, D. B. Madan, M. Pistorius, W. Schoutens, and M. Yor. Two price economies in continuous time. *Annals of Finance*, 10:71–100, 2014.

[11] R. J. Elliott, D. B. Madan, and T. K. Siu. Lower and upper pricing of financial assets. *Probability, Uncertainty, and Quantitative Risk*, 7:45–66, 2022.

[12] R. J. Elliott, D. B. Madan, and K. Wang. High dimensional Markovian trading of a single stock. SSRN paper no. 3980938, 2022.

[13] A. Goyal and A. Saretto. Cross-section of option returns and volatility. *Journal of Financial Economics*, 94:310–326, 2009.

[14] G. Hu and K. Jacobs. Volatility and expected option returns. *Journal of Financial and Quantitative Analysis*, 55:1025–1060, 2020.

[15] G. Hu and Y. Liu. The pricing of volatility and jump risks in the cross-section of index option returns. *Journal of Financial and Quantitative Analysis*, 57:2385–2411, 2021. https://doi.org/10.1017/S0022109022000333.

[16] C. S. Jones. A nonlinear factor analysis of S&P 500 index option returns. *Journal of Finance*, 59:2325–2363, 2006.

[17] U. Küchler and S. Tappe. Bilateral Gamma distributions and processes in financial mathematics. *Stochastic Processes and their Applications*, 118:261–283, 2008.

[18] D. B. Madan and E. Seneta. The variance gamma (VG) model for share market returns. *Journal of Business*, 63:511–524, 1990.

[19] D. Madan, P. Carr, and E. Chang. The variance gamma process and option pricing. *Review of Finance*, 2:79–105, 1998.

[20] D. B. Madan, M. Pistorius, and M. Stadje. Convergence of $BSD\Delta Es$ driven by random walks to BSDEs: The Case of (In)Finite Activity Jumps with General Driver. *Stochastic Processes and Their Applications*, 126:1553–1584, 2016.

[21] D. B. Madan, M. Pistorius, and M. Stadje. On dynamic spectral risk measures, a limit theorem and optimal portfolio allocation. *Finance and Stochastics*, 21:1073–1102, 2017.

[22] D. B. Madan and W. Schoutens. Two processes for two prices. *International Journal of Theoretical and Applied Finance*, 17:1–19, 2014.

[23] D. B. Madan and W. Schoutens. *Nonlinear Valuation and Non-Gaussian Risks in Finance.* Cambridge University Press, Cambridge, U.K, 2022.

[24] D. B. Madan, W. Schoutens, and K. Wang. Measuring and monitoring the efficiency of markets. *International Journal of Theoretical and Applied Finance*, 20(8):32, 2017.

[25] D. B. Madan and K. Wang. Asymmetries in financial returns. *International Journal of Financial Engineering*, 4:4, 2017.

[26] C. Schlag and T. Sichert. The shape of the pricing kernel and expected option returns, Working Paper, Stockholm School of Economics, 2021.

https://doi.org/10.1142/9789811280306_0017

Chapter 17

Supermartingale Brenier's Theorem with Full-Marginal Constraint*

Erhan Bayraktar[†,¶], **Shuoqing Deng**[‡,‖], and **Dominykas Norgilas**[§,**]

[†]*Department of Mathematics, University of Michigan, Ann Arbor, MI, USA*

[‡]*Department of Mathematics, The Hong Kong University of Science and Technology, Clear Water Bay, Hong Kong*

[§]*Department of Mathematics, University of Michigan, Ann Arbor, MI, USA*

[¶]*erhan@umich.edu*

[‖]*masdeng@ust.hk*

[**]*dnorgila@umich.edu*

Abstract

We explicitly construct the supermartingale version of the Fréchet–Hoeffding coupling in the setting with infinitely many marginal constraints. Our construction is based on the Markovian iteration of one-period optimal supermartingale couplings. We show that the constructed processes solve the continuous-time supermartingale optimal transport

*The authors are grateful to Xiaolu Tan for fruitful discussions.

[†]E.B. was partially supported by the National Science Foundation under grant DMS-2106556 and by the Susan M. Smith chair.

[‡]S.D. was partially supported by the Start-up Grant of HKUST.

problem for a particular family of (path-dependent) cost functions. The explicit computations are provided in the following three cases: the uniform case, the Bachelier model and the geometric Brownian motion case.

Keywords: Supermartingale optimal transport, Brenier's theorem, PCOCD

1. Introduction

The classical optimal transport (OT) problem, first introduced by Monge and then relaxed by Kantorovich, has the following formulation: given two probability measures μ_0, μ_1 on $\mathbb{R}$ and a cost (or payoff) function $c : \mathbb{R} \times \mathbb{R} \to \mathbb{R}$, the goal is to minimize (or maximize) the value $\mathbb{E}^{\mathbb{P}}[c(X_0, X_1)]$ among all probability measures $\mathbb{P}$ such that $\mathbb{P} \circ X_0^{-1} = \mu_0$ and $\mathbb{P} \circ X_1^{-1} = \mu_1$. Under the Spence–Mirrlees condition $c_{xy} > 0$, the maximizing transport plan is characterized by Brenier's theorem (see Brenier [18] and Rachev and Rüschendorf [61]) and corresponds to the Fréchet–Hoeffding (or quantile) coupling π^{FH}.

Motivated by the applications in financial mathematics, the Martingale Optimal Transport (MOT) problem was introduced by Beiglböck *et al.* [8] (in the discrete-time setting) and Galichon *et al.* [36] (in the continuous-time setting) and has been widely studied since then. Given two probability measures μ_0, μ_1 which are increasing in convex order, the problem consists in minimizing (or maximizing) $\mathbb{E}^{\mathbb{P}}[c(X_0, X_1)]$ among all martingale measures $\mathbb{P}$ such that $\mathbb{P} \circ X_0^{-1} = \mu_0$ and $\mathbb{P} \circ X_1^{-1} = \mu_1$. Under the so-called martingale Spence–Mirrlees condition $c_{xyy} > 0$, the maximizer corresponds to the so-called left-curtain martingale coupling π^{lc}, introduced by Beiglböck and Juillet [12]. π^{lc} was explicitly constructed by Henry-Labordère and Touzi [42] using ODE arguments (and under some technical assumptions). The general construction was later obtained by Hobson and Norgilas [48] using geometric arguments and properties of the potential functions of marginals.

The financial motivation of MOT comes from the robust sub/super-replication of financial derivatives in a market where the underlying asset and the corresponding vanilla options with certain maturities are available for trading. From the well-known Breenden–Litzenberger formula (see [17]), the marginal distributions of the underlying asset can be then obtained using the prices of vanilla options. Each sensible pricing model should be calibrated to the given market data and thus should produce the same marginal distributions at fixed times. The search for a model that produces the highest no-arbitrage price of an exotic claim, among all calibrated models, then naturally corresponds to the MOT problem. For more recent developments of MOT problems, see, for example, Acciaio *et al.* [1], Backhoff-Veraguas *et al.* [2,3], Beiglböck *et al.* [6,7,9–11,16], Beiglböck and Juillet [12,13], Brückerhoff *et al.* [20], Campi *et al.* [21], De Marco and Henry-Labordère [30], Dolinsky and Soner [31], Fahim nad Huang [34], Gaoyue *et al.* [39], Hobson and Neuberger [46], Hobson and Klimmek [45], Hobson and Norgilas [47], Nutz *et al.* [58] and Wiesel [63].

The problem of finding the models that give robust no-arbitrage bounds for the prices of exotic derivatives was initially studied in the seminal work of Hobson [49] by means of the Skorokhod Embedding Problem (SEP). SEP consists in finding a stopping time τ of a Brownian motion B such that B_τ has a prescribed law. This approach generated developments in many (probabilistic and financially motivated) directions, see, for example, Brown *et al.* [19], Madan and Yor [56], Cox *et al.* [23,27], Cox and Obłój [25,26] and Davis *et al.* [29]. See also the survey papers on SEP by Obłój [59] and Hobson [44].

More recently, the Supermartingale Optimal Transport (SOT) problem was introduced by Nutz and Stebegg [57]. Given two probability measures μ_0, μ_1 which are increasing in convex-decreasing order, the problem consists in minimizing (or maximizing) $\mathbb{E}^{\mathbb{P}}[c(X_0, X_1)]$ among all supermartingale measures $\mathbb{P}$ such that $\mathbb{P}\circ X_0^{-1} = \mu_0$ and $\mathbb{P}\circ X_1^{-1} = \mu_1$. In particular, the authors of [57] introduced two canonical supermartingale couplings, namely the increasing supermartingale coupling π^I and the decreasing supermartingale coupling π^D. These transport plans are canonical in the sense that they can be equivalently characterized by any, and then all, of the following properties: the optimality (in terms of minimization or maximization problem) for a large class of cost functions, the monotonicity of the support and the order-theoretic minimality. (The optimal couplings in the OT and MOT settings have similar characterizations.)

In this chapter, we shall focus on the continuous-time case, which corresponds to a suitable limit of the multimarginal SOT problem.

Given a continuous family of marginal distributions $(\mu_t)_{t\in[0,1]}$, which is non-decreasing in convex-decreasing order, we call a stochastic process that is calibrated to all marginals $(\mu_t)_{t\in[0,1]}$ a *PCOCD* ("Processus Croissant pour l'Ordre Convexe Décroissant" in French). Note that in the martingale case, such a process is baptized as a peacock (*PCOC* for short) and is extensively studied in the book of Hirch *et al.* [43].

We will closely follow Henri-Labordère *et al.* [41]: in the martingale setting, by considering a Markovian iteration of the one-period left-curtain martingale couplings π^{lc}, the authors obtained a pure-jump process in the spirit of the local Lévy models introduced by Carr *et al.* [22] and showed that it solves a particular continuous-time MOT problem. Our main goal is to extend the results of Henri-Labordère *et al.* [41] to the supermartingale setting.

In the supermartingale case, the construction is different in the following aspects. First, in the martingale case, the left-curtain and the right-curtain transport plans are symmetric, see Henry-Labordre *et al.* [41, Remark 3.12]. More precisely, the limiting process, associated with the left-curtain coupling, is driven by downward jumps and upward drift, while in the right-curtain case, it is the upward jumps and downward drift that drive the limiting process. On the other hand, in the supermartingale case, the increasing supermartingale transport plan and the decreasing supermartingale transport plan demonstrate different behavior, see Bayraktar *et al.* [4, 5]. In the increasing case, the limiting process is a martingale in the interior of the support of marginals and possesses strict supermartingale characteristics when it escapes to the upper boundary of the support (it jumps from the upper all the way down to the lower boundary). In the case of the decreasing supermartingale coupling, there are martingale and supermartingale regions in the interior of the support. Once the boundary curve (that separates these two regions) is hit, the process becomes deterministic and follows a decreasing (w.r.t. time) curve.

Second, in case of the decreasing supermartingale coupling, there might exist multiple *phase transition curves* for the limiting process that divide the martingale and strict supermartingale regions. To obtain explicit solutions, in this chapter, we will impose certain conditions that will guarantee the uniqueness of the phase transition curve. On the other hand, if the increasing supermartingale coupling is used for construction, then the regime-switching boundary is unique and is always given by the upper boundary of the support of the marginal distributions.

In financial terms, the dual SOT problem corresponds to the super-replication of an exotic payoff using semi-static strategies with no short-selling constraints. In order to prove the optimality of the limiting process, we will modify the arguments of Henry-Labordère *et al.* [42] and explicitly construct a candidate optimal dual strategy for a large (but very particular) class of cost functions. The choice of dual variables is closely related to the martingale and strict supermartingale regions of a candidate optimal transport plan. In the case of the decreasing supermartingale coupling, the dual methods are related to those of the dual MOT problem when the right-curtain martingale coupling is optimal, and also the classical OT duality when the quantile coupling is an optimizer. The strategies must be modified accordingly, if the construction of the limiting process is based on the increasing supermartingale coupling.

The rest of this chapter is organized as follows: In Section 2, we recall the formulation of the discrete-time supermartingale transport problem and introduce the continuous-time SOT problem. In Section 3, we provide the convergence theorem, which gives the characterization of the limiting process, and the optimality theorem, which shows that the limiting process solves a continuous-time SOT problem for a class of cost functions. In Section 4, we explicitly obtain the limiting process when the marginals correspond to uniform measures on bounded support, normal distributions with decreasing means (Brownian motion with drift) and log-normal distributions (geometric Brownian motion). In Appendix A and B, we collect some important results regarding one-period OT, MOT and SOT problems.

2. Supermartingale Optimal Transport Problem

2.1. *Discrete-Time Supermartingale Optimal Transport*

Let $\mathcal{M}$ (resp., $\mathcal{P}$) be the set of finite (resp., probability) Borel measures on $\mathbb{R}$ with finite first moments. The support of $\eta \in \mathcal{M}$, denoted by $\text{supp}(\eta)$, is the smallest closed set $I \subseteq \mathbb{R}$ with $\eta(I) =$

$\eta(\mathbb{R})$. We set $\ell_\eta := \inf\{k \in \text{supp}(\eta)\} \in [-\infty, \infty)$ and $r_\eta := \sup\{k \in \text{supp}(\eta)\} \in (-\infty, \infty]$. The mean of $\eta \in \mathcal{M}$ is denoted by $\overline{\eta}$ so that the barycenter of η is given by $\overline{\eta}/\eta(\mathbb{R})$.

Throughout this chapter, for any random variable ξ, the expectation of ξ is defined as $\mathbb{E}[\xi] := \mathbb{E}[\xi^+] - \mathbb{E}[\xi^-]$ with the convention $\infty - \infty = -\infty$.

The canonical process on $\mathbb{R}^2$ is denoted by (X_0, X_1) so that for $i = 0, 1$, $X_i(x_0, x_1) = x_i$ for all $(x_0, x_1) \in \mathbb{R}^2$. For $\mu_0, \mu_1 \in \mathcal{P}$, let $\mathcal{P}(\mu_0, \mu_1)$ be the set of (Borel) probability measures on $\mathbb{R}^2$ with first and second marginals μ_0 and μ_1, respectively. (Each $\mathbb{P} \in \mathcal{P}(\mu_0, \mu_1)$ is often called a transport plan or coupling of μ_0 and μ_1.) Then $X_0 \sim^{\mathbb{P}} \mu_0$, $X_1 \sim^{\mathbb{P}} \mu_1$ for all $\mathbb{P} \in \mathcal{P}(\mu_0, \mu_1)$. We also introduce the set of supermartingale couplings of μ_0 and μ_1:

$$\mathcal{S}_2(\mu_0, \mu_1) := \{\mathbb{P} \in \mathcal{P}(\mu_0, \mu_1) : \mathbb{E}^{\mathbb{P}}[X_1 | X_0] \le X_0 \ \mathbb{P}\text{-a.s.}\}.$$

By the classical result of Strassen [62], $\mathcal{S}_2(\mu_0, \mu_1)$ is non-empty if and only if $\mu_0 \le_{cd} \mu_1$, i.e., μ_0 is smaller than μ_1 in convex-decreasing order. Recall that $\mu_0 \le_{cd} \mu_1$ if $\mu_0(\phi) \le \mu_1(\phi)$ for all convex and non-increasing $\phi : \mathbb{R} \to \mathbb{R}$, where for a measurable $f : \mathbb{R} \to \mathbb{R}$ and $\eta \in \mathcal{M}$, we write $\eta(f) = \int_{\mathbb{R}} f d\eta$. Note that $\overline{\mu}_0 \le \overline{\mu}_1$ whenever $\mu_0 \le_{cd} \mu_1$. On the other hand, if $\mu_0 \le_{cd} \mu_1$ and $\overline{\mu}_0 = \overline{\mu}_1$, then $\mathcal{S}_2(\mu_0, \mu_1)$ reduces to the set of martingale couplings of μ_0 and μ_1. Indeed, every supermartingale with constant mean is a martingale.

For a (Borel) measurable reward (or cost) function $c : \mathbb{R}^2 \to \mathbb{R}$, a two-marginal supermartingale transport problem is defined by

$$\mathbf{P}_2(\mu_0, \mu_1) := \sup_{\mathbb{P} \in \mathcal{S}_2(\mu_0, \mu_1)} \mathbb{E}^{\mathbb{P}}\left[c(X_0, X_1)\right]. \tag{1}$$

Suppose that there exists $a_0, a_1 : \mathbb{R} \to \mathbb{R}$ that are μ_0- and μ_1-integrable, respectively, and such that $|c(x, y)| \le a_0(x) + a_1(y)$, $x, y \in \mathbb{R}$. Then in the case c satisfies the following *supermartingale Spence–Mirrlees* condition:

$$c(x', \cdot) - c(x, \cdot) \text{ is decreasing and convex for all } x < x',$$

Nutz and Stebegg [57] proved that the supremum in (1) is attained by the so-called *increasing* supermartingale coupling π^I. Note that, in the case c is smooth, supermartingale Spence–Mirrlees condition can be equivalently stated in terms of cross-derivatives: $c_{xy} \leq 0$ and $c_{xyy} \geq 0$. On the other hand, if $-c$ is supermartingale Spence–Mirrlees, then the optimizer is given by the *decreasing* supermartingale coupling π^D. The main focus of this chapter is on π^D (see Appendix B.1).

We now describe the dual problem that is associated with (1). We write $(\phi, \psi, h) \in \mathcal{D}_2(\mu_0, \mu_1)$ if $\phi, \psi, h : \mathbb{R} \to \mathbb{R}$ are (Borel) measurable functions such that $(\int_{\mathbb{R}}(\phi \vee 0)d\mu_0) \vee (\int_{\mathbb{R}}(\psi \vee 0)d\mu_1) < \infty$, $h \geq 0$ and

$$c(x, y) \leq \phi(x) + \psi(y) + h(x)(y - x), \quad x, y \in \mathbb{R}.$$

Then the weak duality holds

$$\mathbf{P}_2(\mu_0, \mu_1) \leq \mathbf{D}_2(\mu_0, \mu_1) := \inf_{(\varphi,\psi,h)\in\mathcal{D}_2(\mu_0,\mu_1)} \{\mu_0(\varphi) + \mu_1(\psi)\}. \quad (2)$$

Nutz and Stebegg [57] showed that the strong duality (i.e., equality in (2)) holds under some additional assumptions (for example, if $\mu_0 \leq_{cd} \mu_1$ are *irreducible*). In general (and without the irreducibility condition), the strong duality and the existence of dual optimizers can still be obtained, provided one agrees to switch from a point-wise to a quasi-sure formulation of the dual problem. An explicit construction of optimal dual variables is (under some further assumptions) provided in Appendix B.2.

Problem (1) can be easily extended to a T-period (or $(T+1)$-marginal) setting if we restrict to cost functions $c : \mathbb{R}^{T+1} \to \mathbb{R}$ of the form $c(x_0, \ldots, x_T) = \sum_{i=1}^{T} c_i(x_{i-1}, x_i)$, $(x_0, \ldots, x_T) \in \mathbb{R}^{T+1}$, for a collection of one-period (Borel) cost functions $c_i : \mathbb{R} \to \mathbb{R}$, $i = 1, \ldots, T$. More precisely, we are given a sequence of probability measures $\mu_0, \ldots, \mu_T \in \mathcal{P}$ satisfying $\mu_0 \leq_{cd} \cdots \leq_{cd} \mu_T$, and the goal is to maximize

$$\mathbb{E}^{\mathbb{P}}[c(X_0, \ldots, X_T)] = \sum_{i=1}^{T} \mathbb{E}^{\mathbb{P}}[c_i(X_{i-1}, X_i)] \quad (3)$$

over all (Borel) probability measures $\mathbb{P}$ on $\mathbb{R}^{T+1}$ such that $X_i \sim^{\mathbb{P}} \mu_i$, $i = 0, \ldots, T$, and satisfying $\mathbb{E}^{\mathbb{P}}[X_i | X_0, \ldots, X_{i-1}] \leq X_{i-1}$ $\mathbb{P}$-a.s., for all $i = 1, \ldots, T$. (For the martingale version with general cost functions $c : \mathbb{R}^{T+1} \to \mathbb{R}$, see Nutz *et al.* [58], while a corresponding continuous-time extension is given by Juillet *et al.* [20].) Then, if each c_i (or $-c_i$)

is supermartingale Spence–Mirrlees, the optimal supermartingale coupling (with fixed $T+1$ marginals) can be obtained by a Markovian iteration of the increasing (or decreasing) one-period supermartingale transport plans.

2.2. *Continuous-Time Supermartigale Optimal Transport*

In this section, we introduce a continuous-time supermartingale optimal transport problem under full-marginal constraint, as the limit of the multi-period supermartingale optimal transport introduced at the end of Section 2.1.

Let $\Omega := \mathbb{D}([0,1],\mathbb{R})$ be the canonical space of all càdlàg paths on $[0,1]$, X the canonical process and $\mathbb{F} = (\mathcal{F}_t)_{0\le t\le 1}$ the canonical filtration generated by X, i.e., $\mathcal{F}_t := \sigma(\{X_s, 0 \le s \le t\})$. We denote by $\mathcal{S}_\infty$ the collection of all supermartingale measures on Ω, i.e., under each $\mathbb{P} \in \mathcal{S}_\infty$, the canonical process X is a supermartingale. We equip $\mathcal{S}_\infty$ with the weak convergence topology throughout this chapter. By the classical results (see, for example, Karandikar [54]), there is a non-decreasing process $([X]_t)_{t\in[0,1]}$, defined on Ω, and which coincides with the $\mathbb{P}$-quadratic variation of X, $\mathbb{P}$-a.s. for every supermartingale measure $\mathbb{P} \in \mathcal{S}_\infty$. Denote by $[X]^c_\cdot$ the continuous part of $[X]_\cdot$.

Given a family of (integrable) probability measures $\mu = (\mu_t)_{0\le t\le 1}$, we denote by $\mathcal{S}_\infty(\mu) \subset \mathcal{S}_\infty$ the collection of all supermartingale measures on Ω such that $X_t \sim^{\mathbb{P}} \mu_t$ for all $t \in [0,1]$. In particular, from Ewald and Yor [33], we know that $\mathcal{S}_\infty(\mu)$ is non-empty if and only if the family $(\mu_t)_{0\le t\le 1}$ is non-decreasing in convex-decreasing order and $t \mapsto \mu_t$ is right-continuous.

For all $t \in [0,1]$, we denote by $-\infty \le \ell_t := \ell_{\mu_t} \le r_{\mu_t} =: r_t \le \infty$ the left and right extreme boundaries of $\mathrm{supp}(\mu_t)$. Suppose that $\mu_s \le_{cd} \mu_t$ for all $0 \le s \le t \le 1$. Then since $x \mapsto p_k(x) := (k-x)^+$ is convex and non-increasing for all $k \in \mathbb{R}$, we have that $\mu_s(p_k) \le \mu_t(p_k)$ for $k \in \mathbb{R}$. In particular, $\mu_s((-\infty,k)) > 0$ implies that $\mu_t((-\infty,k)) > 0$, from which it follows that $t \mapsto \ell_t$ is non-increasing. Note that, in general, $t \mapsto r_t$ may fail to be non-decreasing. In addition, if μ_t admits a density function for all $t \in [0,1]$ and $t \mapsto \mu_t$ is continuous w.r.t. the weak convergence topology, then $t \mapsto l_t$ and $t \mapsto r_t$ are continuous (see Henry-Labordère and Touzi [42, p. 2805]).

As in Henry-Labordère *et al.* [41] (see also Hobson and Klimmek [45]), our continuous-time SOT problem arises as a limit of the multi-period SOT problems, by considering the limit of the reward function $\sum_{i=1}^{T} c_i(x_{t_{i-1}}, x_{t_i})$ as in (3), where $(t_i)_{0\leq i\leq T}$ is a partition of $[0,1]$ with $\max_{1\leq i\leq T}|t_i - t_{i-1}| \to 0$ as $T \to \infty$. To obtain the convergence, we need the pathwise Itô calculus.

Definition 2.1 (Föllmer [35]). Let $\pi_n = (0 = t_0^n < \cdots < t_n^n = 1)$, $n \geq 1$, be partitions of $[0,1]$ with $|\pi_n| := \max_{1\leq k\leq n} |t_k^n - t_{k-1}^n| \to 0$ as $n \to \infty$. A càdlàg path $\mathbf{x} : [0,1] \to \mathbb{R}$ has a finite quadratic variation along $(\pi_n)_{n\geq 1}$ if the sequence of measures on $[0,1]$,

$$\sum_{1\leq k\leq n} (\mathbf{x}_{t_k^n} - \mathbf{x}_{t_{k-1}^n})^2 \delta_{\{t_{k-1}\}}(dt),$$

converges weakly to a measure $[\mathbf{x}]^F$ on $[0,1]$. For each $t \in [0,1]$, set $[\mathbf{x}]_t^F := [\mathbf{x}]^F([0,t])$, and let $[\mathbf{x}]_\cdot^{F,c}([0,t])$ be the continuous part of this non-decreasing path.

The following will be one of our standing assumptions:

Assumption 2.2. The cost function $c : \mathbb{R}^2 \to \mathbb{R}$ is in $C^3((l_1, \max_{0\leq t\leq 1} r_t) \times (l_1, \max_{0\leq t\leq 1} r_t))$ and satisfies

$$c(x,x) = c_y(x,x) = 0, \quad c_{xyy} < 0, \quad c_{xy} > 0,$$
$$(x,y) \in \left(l_1, \max_{0\leq t\leq 1} r_t\right) \times \left(l_1, \max_{0\leq t\leq 1} r_t\right).$$

Following Hobson and Klimmek [45], we then have (in fact, a weaker assumption on c would suffice, see Touzi *et al.* [42]) the following:

Lemma 2.3. *Let Assumption* 2.2 *hold true. Then for every path* $\mathbf{x} \in \Omega$ *with finite quadratic variation* $[\mathbf{x}]^F$ *along a sequence of partitions* $(\pi_n)_{n\geq 1}$*, we have*

$$\sum_{k=0}^{n-1} c(\mathbf{x}_{t_k^n}, \mathbf{x}_{t_{k-1}^n}) \to \frac{1}{2}\int_0^1 c_{yy}(\mathbf{x}_t, \mathbf{x}_t) d[\mathbf{x}]_t^{F,c} + \sum_{0\leq t\leq 1} c(\mathbf{x}_{t-}, \mathbf{x}_t).$$

The non-decreasing process $[X]_\cdot$, as in Karandikar [54], is defined for every càdlàg path $\mathbf{x}$ and coincides $\mathbb{P}$-a.s. with both the quadratic variation and $[\mathbf{x}]^F$, for every $\mathbb{P} \in \mathcal{S}_\infty$. This and Lemma 2.3 motivates us to define the following continuous-time reward function:

$$C(\mathbf{x}) := \frac{1}{2}\int_0^1 c_{yy}(\mathbf{x}_t, \mathbf{x}_t) d[\mathbf{x}]_t^c + \sum_{0\le t\le 1} c(\mathbf{x}_{t-}, \mathbf{x}_t), \quad \text{for all } \mathbf{x} \in \Omega,$$

where the integral and the sum are defined using positive and negative parts with a convention $\infty - \infty = -\infty$.

The continuous-time supermartingale optimal transport problem is now given by

$$\mathbf{P}_\infty(\mu) := \sup_{\mathbb{P}\in\mathcal{S}_\infty(\mu)} \mathbb{E}^{\mathbb{P}}\left[C(X)\right]. \tag{4}$$

Note that $\sum_{0\le t\le 1} c(X_{t-}, X_t) < \infty$ $\mathbb{P}$-a.s. for all $\mathbb{P} \in \mathcal{S}_\infty$, see Henry-Labordèrè *et al.* [41, Remark 2.5].

We now follow Henry–Labordèrè *et al.* [41] and introduce the dual formulation of the problem (4). First, we introduce the set of admissible semi-static trading strategies. Let $\mathbb{H}_0$ be the class of $\mathbb{F}$-predictable and locally bounded processes $H : [0,1] \times \Omega \to \mathbb{R}$, i.e., there exists an increasing family of $\mathbb{F}$-stopping times $(\tau_n)_{n\ge1}$ taking values in $[0,1] \cup \{\infty\}$ such that $H_{\cdot\wedge\tau_n}$ is bounded for all $n \ge 1$ and $\tau_n \to \infty$ as $n \to \infty$. Then, for all $H \in \mathbb{H}_0$ and under every supermartingale measure $\mathbb{P} \in \mathcal{S}_\infty$, one can define the integral, denoted by $H \cdot X$, see Jacod and Shiryaev [51, Chapter I.4]. Define

$$\mathcal{H} := \{H \in \mathbb{H}_0 : H \ge 0 \text{ and } H \cdot X \text{ is a } \mathbb{P}\text{-supermartingale for every } \mathbb{P} \in \mathcal{S}_\infty\}.$$

For the static strategy, we denote by $M([0,1])$ the space of all finite signed measures on $[0,1]$ which is a Polish space under the weak convergence topology and by Λ the class of all measurable maps $\lambda : \mathbb{R} \to M([0,1])$ which admit a representation $\lambda(x, dt) = \lambda_0(t, x)\gamma(dt)$ for some finite non-negative measure γ on $[0,1]$ and some measurable function $\lambda_0 : [0,1] \times \mathbb{R} \to \mathbb{R}$ which is bounded on $[0,1] \times K$ for all compact K of $\mathbb{R}$. We then denote

$$\Lambda(\mu) := \{\lambda \in \Lambda : \mu(|\lambda|) < \infty\}, \quad \text{where}$$
$$\mu(|\lambda|) := \int_0^1 \int_{\mathbb{R}} |\lambda_0(t,x)|\mu_t(dx)\gamma(dt).$$

We also introduce a family of random measures $\delta^X = (\delta_t^X)_{0\leq t\leq 1}$, associated with the canonical process X, by setting $\delta_t^X(dx) := \delta_{X_t}(dx)$. In particular, one has

$$\delta^X(\lambda) = \int_0^1 \lambda(X_t, dt) = \int_0^1 \lambda_0(t, X_t)\gamma(dt).$$

The set of admissible superhedging strategies with no short-selling constraint is defined by

$$\mathcal{D}_\infty := \{(H,\lambda) \in \mathcal{H} \times \Lambda(\mu) : \delta^X(\lambda) + (H \cdot X)_1$$
$$\geq C(X_\cdot), \mathbb{P}\text{-a.s.}, \forall \mathbb{P} \in \mathcal{S}_\infty\},$$

and then the dual problem is given by

$$\mathbf{D}_\infty(\mu) := \inf_{(H,\lambda)\in\mathcal{D}_\infty(\mu)} \mu(\lambda). \tag{5}$$

Furthermore, the weak duality holds: $\mathbf{P}_\infty(\mu) \leq \mathbf{D}_\infty(\mu)$.

3. Main Results

Our contribution splits into three parts: First, we construct a continuous-time supermartingale with given marginals $(\mu_t)_{t\in[0,1]}$. This is achieved as an accumulation point of a sequence $(\mathbb{P}^n)_n$ of solutions of n-period supermartingale transport problems. We then characterize the limiting law further and show that it corresponds to the distribution of a local Lévy process. Finally, we prove that this limit solves the continuous-time supermartingale optimal transport problem (4). The last point is achieved by proving the strong duality $\mathbf{P}_\infty(\mu) = \mathbf{D}_\infty(\mu)$ and explicitly constructing an optimal superhedging strategy.

3.1. *Convergence of the Sequence* $(\mathbb{P}^n)_{n\geq 1}$

For every $t \in [0,1]$, we denote by $\mathbb{R} \ni x \mapsto F(t,x)$ and $[0,1] \ni u \mapsto F^{-1}(t,u)$ the cumulative distribution function and the corresponding right-continuous inverse (w.r.t. the x-variable) of the probability measure μ_t. For $t \in [0,1)$, $\epsilon \in (0, 1-t]$ and $x, y \in \mathbb{R}$, let

$$\delta^\epsilon F(t,x) := F(t+\epsilon, x) - F(t,x)$$

and define

$$E := \{(t,x) : t \in [0,1], x \in (l_t, r_t)\}.$$

Assumption 3.1.

(i) The marginal distributions $\mu = (\mu_t)_{t\in[0,1]}$ belong to $\mathcal{P}$ and are non-decreasing in convex-decreasing and $t \mapsto \mu_t$ is continuous w.r.t. the weak convergence topology.
(ii) $F \in C_b^4(E)$. In particular, for all $t \in [0,1]$, the measure μ_t has a density function $f(t,\cdot)$ such that $f(t,\cdot) > 0$ on (ℓ_t, r_t).
(iii) There exists $\epsilon_1 \in (0,1]$ such that for all $t \in [0,1)$ and $0 < \epsilon \leq \epsilon_1 \wedge (1-t)$, μ_t and $\mu_{t+\epsilon}$ satisfy the dispersion assumption:

- There exists $m_\epsilon(t) < m^\epsilon(t)$ such that $\ell_{t+\epsilon} \leq \ell_t \leq m_\epsilon(t) < m^\epsilon(t) \leq r_t \leq r_{t+\epsilon}$, with $\ell_{t+\epsilon} < \ell_t \wedge m_\epsilon(t)$ and $m^\epsilon(t) \vee r_t < r_{t+\epsilon}$.
- Furthermore, $f(t+\epsilon,\cdot) < f(t,\cdot)$ on $(m_\epsilon(t), m^\epsilon(t))$, $f(t+\epsilon,x) = f(t,x)$ for $x \in \{m_\epsilon(t), m^\epsilon(t)\}$ and $f(t+\epsilon,\cdot) > f(t,\cdot)$ on $(\ell_{t+\epsilon}, m_\epsilon(t)) \cup (m^\epsilon(t), r_{t+\epsilon})$.

Note that Assumption B(iii) is precisely Assumption A.3, and thus all the results of Appendix B are valid.

Remark 3.2. Under Assumption 3.1, several further implications follow. First, since, for all $t \in [0,1]$, $f(t,\cdot) > 0$ on (ℓ_t, r_t), we have that $\inf_{x\in[-K,K]\cap(\ell_t,r_t)} f(t,x) > 0$ for all $K > 0$. Furthermore, due to the dispersion assumption (see Assumption 3.1(iii)), for every $t \in [0,1)$ and sufficiently small $\epsilon \in (0,1-t]$, the function $x \mapsto \delta^\epsilon F(t,x)$ attains the (unique) maximum and minimum at $m_\epsilon(t)$ and $m^\epsilon(t)$, respectively. It is also easy to see that, for all $x \in (\ell_t, r_t)$, $\int_x^\infty (y-x)\delta^\epsilon F(t,dy) > 0$. In particular, Assumption 3.1 implies Henry-Labordère *et al.* [41, Assumption 3.1].

In the rest of this chapter, we will always work with $(\mu_t)_{t\in[0,1]}$ satisfying Assumption 3.1.

Fix $t \in [0,1)$ and $\epsilon \in (0, 1-t]$ and consider a pair of marginals $(\mu_t, \mu_{t+\epsilon})$. Then the corresponding decreasing supermartingale coupling can be determined by a pair of functions $(T_d^\epsilon(t,\cdot) = \hat{T}_d^{\mu_t,\mu_{t+\epsilon}}(\cdot), T_u^\epsilon(t,\cdot) = \hat{T}_u^{\mu_t,\mu_{t+\epsilon}}(\cdot))$, where $(\hat{T}_d^{\mu_t,\mu_{t+\epsilon}}(\cdot), T_u^\epsilon(t,\cdot))$ are as in Appendix B.1. Furthermore, set $x_1^\epsilon(t) := x_1^{\mu_t,\mu_{t+\epsilon}}$ and $y_1^\epsilon(t) := y_1^{\mu_t,\mu_{t+\epsilon}}$, where $x_1^{\mu_t,\mu_{t+\epsilon}}$ is defined by (B.50), while $y_1^{\mu_t,\mu_{t+\epsilon}}$ is given by (B.51).

Recall that the canonical space of càdlàg paths $\Omega := \mathbb{D}([0,1]\mathbb{R})$ is a Polish space equipped with the Skorokhod topology, while X denotes the canonical process. Let $(\pi_n)_{n\geq 1}$ be a sequence of partitions of $[0,1]$ so that each $\pi_n = (t_k^n)_{0\leq k\leq n}$ is such that $0 = t_0^n < \cdots < t_n^n = 1$. Suppose in addition that $|\pi_n| := \max_{1\leq k\leq n}(t_k^n - t_{k-1}^n) \to 0$ as $n \to \infty$. Then, for every partition π_n, by considering the marginal distributions $(\mu_{t_k^n})_{0\leq k\leq n}$, one obtains an $(n+1)$-marginal (or n-period) SOT problem, where the goal is to maximize

$$\mathbb{E}\left[\sum_{0\leq k\leq n-1} c(\tilde{X}_k^n, \tilde{X}_{k+1}^n)\right]$$

among all discrete-time supermartingales $\tilde{X}^n = (\tilde{X}_k^n)_{0\leq k\leq n}$ satisfying marginal constraints. Under Assumptions 2.2 and 3.1, the iterated n-period decreasing supermartingale coupling is the solution to the above supermartingale transport problem. Let $\Omega^{*,n} := \mathbb{R}^{n+1}$ be the canonical space of discrete-time process, and $X^n = (X_k^n)_{0\leq k\leq n}$ be the canonical process on $\Omega^{*,n}$. Then, under the optimal supermartingale measure $\mathbb{P}^{*,n}$, X^n is a discrete-time supermartingale and at the same time a Markov chain, characterized by $T_u^{\Delta t_{k+1}^n}(t_k^n,\cdot)$, $T_d^{\Delta t_{k+1}^n}(t_k^n,\cdot)$ with $\Delta t_{k+1}^n := t_{k+1}^n - t_k^n$, induced by the two marginals $(\mu_{t_k^n}, \mu_{t_{k+1}^n})$, see Appendix B.1. We then extend the Markov chain X^n to a continuous-time càdlàg process $X^{*,n} = (X_t^{*,n})_{0\leq t\leq 1}$ defined by

$$X_t^{*,n} := \sum_{k=1}^{n} X_{k-1}^n \mathbf{1}_{[t_{k-1}^n, t_k^n)}(t), \quad t \in [0,1]$$

and define the probability measure $\mathbb{P}^n := \mathbb{P}^{*,n} \circ (X^{*,n})^{-1}$ on Ω.

We further denote by $\mathbf{m}(\delta^\epsilon F(t,\cdot))$ (resp. $\mathbf{m}(\partial_t F(t,\cdot)))$ the set of all local minimizers of functions $\delta^\epsilon F(t,\cdot))$ (resp., $\partial F(t,\cdot)))$. Let $\mathbf{M}(\partial_t F(t,\cdot))$ be the set of local maximizers of $\partial F(t,\cdot))$. Note that, by Assumption 3.1, $\mathbf{m}(\delta^\epsilon F(t,\cdot)) = \{m^\epsilon(t)\}$ and $\mathbf{M}(\delta^\epsilon F(t,\cdot)) = \{m_\epsilon(t)\}$ for all $0 < \epsilon \le \epsilon_1 \wedge (1-t)$.

Assumption 3.3.

(i) There is a constant $\epsilon_2 > 0$ such that, for all $t \in [0,1]$ and $0 < \epsilon \le \epsilon_2 \wedge (1-t)$, we have $\mathbf{m}(\partial_t F(t,\cdot)) = \{m_t\}$ and $\mathbf{M}(\partial_t F(t,\cdot)) = \{\tilde{m}_t\}$.
(ii) Let $m^0(t) = m_t$. Then the map $(t,\epsilon) \mapsto m^\epsilon(t)$ is continuous (and hence uniformly continuous with continuity modulus ρ_0) on $\{(t,\epsilon) : 0 \le \epsilon \le \epsilon_2, 0 \le t \le 1-\epsilon\}$.

Proposition 3.4. *Suppose that Assumptions* 3.1 *and* 3.3 *are valid. Then, the sequence* $(\mathbb{P}^n)_{n\ge1}$ *is tight w.r.t. the Skorokhod topology on* Ω. *Moreover, every limit point* $\mathbb{P}^0$ *satisfies* $\mathbb{P}^0 \in \mathcal{S}_\infty(\mu)$.

The proof of Proposition 3.4 requires two additional lemmas:

Lemma 3.5. *Let* $(\mu_t)_{t\in[0,1]}$ *be a family of probability measures in* $\mathcal{P}$ *which are increasing in convex-decreasing order. Then,* $(\mu_t)_{t\in[0,1]}$ *is uniformly integrable, i.e.,*

$$\lim_{K\to+\infty} \sup_{0\le t\le 1} \int |x| \mathbf{1}_{\{|x|\ge K\}} \mu_t(dx) = 0.$$

Proof. Using the inequality $|x|\mathbf{1}_{\{|x|\ge K\}} \le 2(|x| - \frac{K}{2})\mathbf{1}_{\{|x|\ge \frac{K}{2}\}}$, we have that

$$\begin{aligned}
&\sup_{0\le t\le 1} \int |x| \mathbf{1}_{\{|x|\ge K\}} \mu_t(dx) \\
&\quad = \sup_{0\le t\le 1} \int 2(|x| - \frac{K}{2}) \mathbf{1}_{\{|x|\ge \frac{K}{2}\}} \mu_t(dx)
\end{aligned}$$

$$\leq 2 \sup_{0\leq t\leq 1} \int \left(x - \frac{K}{2}\right) \mathbf{1}_{\{x\geq \frac{K}{2}\}}\mu_t(dx)$$

$$+ 2 \sup_{0\leq t\leq 1} \int \left(-x - \frac{K}{2}\right) \mathbf{1}_{\{x\leq -\frac{K}{2}\}}\mu_t(dx)$$

$$= 2 \sup_{0\leq t\leq 1} C_{\mu_t}(\frac{K}{2}) + 2 \sup_{0\leq t\leq 1} P_{\mu_t}\left(-\frac{K}{2}\right)$$

$$= 2C_{\tilde{\mu}}\left(\frac{K}{2}\right) + 2P_{\mu_1}\left(-\frac{K}{2}\right) \to 0, \quad \text{when } K \to \infty,$$

where $\tilde{\mu}$ is some probability measure on $\mathbb{R}$ with the same mass and mean with μ_0. We now explain the last equality. First, $x \mapsto (-x - \frac{K}{2})^+$ is convex and non-increasing, and thus using the convex-decreasing ordering of $(\mu_t)_{t\in[0,1]}$, we obtain that $\sup_{0\leq t\leq 1} P_{\mu_t}(-\frac{K}{2}) = P_{\mu_1}(-\frac{K}{2})$. On the other hand, $\sup_{0\leq t\leq 1} C_{\mu_t}(\frac{K}{2}) = C_{\tilde{\mu}}(\frac{K}{2})$ follows from the fact that the point-wise supremum of a family of convex functions is convex, and $\lim_{|x|\to\infty}\{\sup_{0\leq t\leq 1} C_{\mu_t}(x) - \{\overline{\mu_0} - \mu_0(\mathbb{R})x\}\} = 0$. Therefore, there exists some probability measure $\tilde{\mu}$ such that $\tilde{\mu}(\mathbb{R}) = \mu_0(\mathbb{R})$, $\overline{\mu_0} = \overline{\tilde{\mu}}$ and $C_{\tilde{\mu}} = \sup_{0\leq t\leq 1} C_{\mu_t}$. □

Recall that $(\mu_t)_{t\in[0,1]}$ satisfies Assumption 3.1. Now, for fixed $t \in [0,1)$, $\epsilon \in (0, 1-t]$ and $x \in (r_t, m^\epsilon(t))$ denote by $q^\epsilon(t,x)$ the conditional probability of the (martingale) upward jump under the decreasing supermartingale coupling so that $q^\epsilon(t,x) = \frac{x - T_d^\epsilon(t,x)}{T_u^\epsilon(t,x) - T_d^\epsilon(t,x)}$. Note that, for $x \leq x_1^\epsilon(t)$, $T_u^\epsilon(t,x) = \infty$ and therefore $q^\epsilon(t,x) = 0$.

Furthermore, define $J_d^\epsilon(t,\cdot)$, $J_u^\epsilon(t,\cdot)$ by

$$J_d^\epsilon(t,x) = x - T_d^\epsilon(t,x), \quad J_u^\epsilon(t,x) = T_u^\epsilon(t,x) - x, \quad x \in (\ell_t, r_t),$$

so that $J_d^\epsilon(t,\cdot)$, $J_u^\epsilon(t,\cdot)$ correspond to the downward and upward distance each particle travels (between times t and $t+\epsilon$) under the decreasing supermartingale coupling, conditioned it started at x. (Note that $J_u^\epsilon(t,x) = \infty$ for $x \leq x_1^\epsilon(t)$, but this happens with zero probability.)

Lemma 3.6. *Suppose Assumptions* 3.1 *and* 3.3 *hold. Then, we have the following*:

(i) *For every $K > 0$, there is a constant C_1, independent of (t, x, ϵ) such that*

$$J_d^\epsilon(t,x) + q^\epsilon(t,x) \le C_1\epsilon, \quad \forall x \in [-K,K] \cap (l_t, r_t) \cap (x_1^\epsilon(t), m_t^\epsilon).$$

(ii) *For every $K > 0$, there is a constant C_2, independent of (t, x, ϵ) such that*

$$J_d^\epsilon(t,x) \le C_2\epsilon, \quad \forall x \in [-K,K] \cap (l_t, x_1^\epsilon(t)].$$

Proof. (i) Since $\mu_t|_{[x_1^\epsilon(t),r_t)} \le_c \mu_{t+\epsilon}|_{[y_1^\epsilon(t),r_{t+\epsilon})}$ and the decreasing supermartingale coupling $\hat{\mathbb{P}}^{\mu_t,\mu_{t+\epsilon}}$ coincides with the right-curtain coupling of $\mu_t|_{[x_1^\epsilon(t),r_t)} \le_c \mu_{t+\epsilon}|_{[y_1^\epsilon(t),r_{t+\epsilon})}$ (see Appendix B.1), the result follows immediately from Henry-Labordère and Touzi [42, Lemma 6.4] applied to the right-curtain coupling.

(ii) For $x \le x_1^\epsilon(t)$, $T_d^\epsilon(t,x) = F^{-1}(t+\epsilon, F(t,x))$ and therefore

$$\begin{aligned} J_d^\epsilon(t,x) &= F^{-1}(t+\epsilon, F(t+\epsilon,x)) - F^{-1}(t+\epsilon, F(t,x)) \\ &= \frac{1}{f(t+\epsilon, F^{-1}(t+\epsilon,\xi))}\delta^\epsilon F(t,x), \end{aligned}$$

for some ξ between $F(t+\epsilon,x)$ and $F(t,x)$ by the mean value theorem. Now, one draws the desired conclusion from the fact that $|\delta^\epsilon F| \le C\epsilon$, for some constant $C > 0$. □

We are now ready to prove Proposition 3.4.

Proof of Proposition 3.4. Recall that $\mathbb{P}^n$ is a supermartingale measure on the canonical space Ω induced by the continuous-time supermartingale $X^{*,n}$ under the probability $\mathbb{P}^{*,n}$. The supermartingale $X^{*,n}$ jumps only at discrete time points relative to the partition $\pi_n = (t_k^n)_{0\le k\le n}$. Moreover, at time t_{k+1}^n, on $\{x_1^\epsilon(t_k^n) \le X_{t_n^k}\}$, the upward jump size is $J_u^\epsilon(t_n^k, X_{t_n^k})$ and downward jump size is $J_u^\epsilon(t_n^k, X_{t_n^k})$, where $\epsilon := t_{k+1}^n - t_k^n$. In addition, at time t_{k+1}^n and on $\{x_1^\epsilon(t_k^n) \ge X_{t_n^k}\}$, the downward jump size is $J_d^\epsilon(t_n^k, X_{t_n^k})$ with probability 1.

For given positive constants C, θ, we introduce

$$\begin{aligned} \mathcal{E}_n(C,\theta) := \inf\{\Pi_{i=j}^{k-1}(1 - C(t_{i+1}^n - t_i^n)) :\ &\text{for some } s \in [0,1) \text{ and} \\ &0 \le j \le k \le n \text{ such that } s \le t_j^n \le t_{k+1}^n \le s+\theta\}. \end{aligned}$$

(i) First, using Jacod and Shiryaev [51, Theorem VI.4.5], we show that $(\mathbb{P}^n)_{n\geq 1}$ is tight. Let $\tau := 1 \wedge \inf\{s : |X_s| \geq K\}$, and τ is a stopping time w.r.t. the canonical filtration generated by $(X_s)_{0\leq s\leq 1}$. In addition,

$$\begin{aligned}
&K\mathbb{P}^n\left[\sup_{0\leq t\leq 1}|X_t|\geq K\right]\\
&\leq \mathbb{E}^{\mathbb{P}^n}\left[|X_\tau|\right]\\
&= \mathbb{E}^{\mathbb{P}^n}\left[X_\tau + 2X_\tau^-\right] \leq \mathbb{E}^{\mathbb{P}^n}\left[X_0 + 2X_\tau^-\right]\\
&\leq \mathbb{E}^{\mathbb{P}^n}\left[X_0 + 2X_1^-\right] \leq \mathbb{E}^{\mathbb{P}^n}\left[|X_0|\right] + 2\mathbb{E}^{\mathbb{P}^n}\left[|X_1|\right] < +\infty,
\end{aligned}$$

where in the above, the first inequality comes from Markov inequality, $\mathbb{P}^{*,n}\circ(X^{*,n})^{-1} = \mathbb{P}^n\circ X^{-1}$, and the fact that $X_t^{*,n}$ is piecewise constant. The third inequality comes from optional stopping theorem and the fact that X^- is a submartingale. Let $\eta > 0$ be an arbitrary small real number, then there is some $K > 0$ such that

$$\mathbb{P}^n\left[\sup_{0\leq t\leq 1}|X_t|\geq K\right] \leq \eta, \quad \text{for all } n\geq 1.$$

We can assume w.l.o.g. that K satisfies $-K < m_t < K$ for all $t\in[0,1]$; recall Assumption 3.3.

The remaining proof is almost identical to the proof of [41, Proposition 3.2]. However, in few places, the supermartingale transitions appear (which are not present in [41]) and thus we sketch the arguments.

Denote in addition that $r^K(t) := r_t \wedge K$ and $\ell^K(t) := \ell_t \vee (-K)$. Let $\delta > 0$, then it follows from Lemma 3.6 that $J_d^\epsilon(t_n^k, X_{t_n^k})$ is uniformly bounded by $C\epsilon$ for some constant C on $D_\delta^K := \{(t,x) : l^K(t) + \delta/2 \leq x \leq m_t\}$. Let $\theta > 0$ satisfy $\theta \leq \frac{\delta}{2C}$ and $|l^K(t+\theta) - l^K(t)| + |r^K(t+\theta) - r^K(t)| \leq \delta/2$. Let S, T be two stopping times w.r.t. the filtration generated by $X^{*,n}$ such that $0\leq S\leq T\leq S+\theta\leq 1$. Since, by Lemma 3.6, the big jumps of $X^{*,n}$ correspond to $J_u^\epsilon(t_n^k, X_{t_n^k})$ and not to $J_d^\epsilon(t_n^k, X_{t_n^k})$, using the same arguments as in the proof of [41, Proposition 3.2], we have that

$$\mathbb{P}^{*,n}[\sup_{0\le t\le 1}|X_t^{*,n}|\le K, |X_T^{*,n}-X_S^{*,n}|\ge\delta]\le 1-\mathcal{E}_n(C,\theta).$$

It follows that

$$\begin{aligned}
&\limsup_{\theta\to 0}\limsup_{n\to\infty}\mathbb{P}^{*,n}[|X_T^{*,n}-X_S^{*,n}|\ge\delta]\\
&\le \limsup_{\theta\to 0}\limsup_{n\to\infty}\mathbb{P}^{*,n}\left[\sup_{0\le t\le 1}|X_t^{*,n}|\le K, |X_T^{*,n}-X_S^{*,n}|\ge\delta\right]\\
&\quad+\mathbb{P}^{*,n}\left[\sup_{0\le t\le 1}|X_t^{*,n}|\ge K\right]\\
&\le \limsup_{\theta\to 0}\limsup_{n\to\infty}(1-\mathcal{E}_n(C,\theta))+\eta=\eta.
\end{aligned}$$

Since $\eta>0$ can be arbitrarily small, we conclude that

$$\limsup_{\theta\to 0}\limsup_{n\to\infty}\mathbb{P}^{*,n}[|X_T^{*,n}-X_S^{*,n}|\ge\delta]=0.$$

Finally, Jacod and Shiryaev [51, Theorem VI.4.5] show that $(\mathbb{P}^n)_{n\ge 1}$ is tight.

(ii) Let $\mathbb{P}^0$ be a limit of $(\mathbb{P}^n)_{n\ge 1}$. Then repeating the arguments of the second part of the proof of [41, Proposition 3.2] (which relies on the continuity of $F(t,x)$), we obtain that $\mathbb{P}^0\circ X_t^{-1}=\mu_t$.

(iii) In the last step, we show that X is still a supermartingale under $\mathbb{P}^0$. For every $K>0$, we first define the auxiliary process $X_t^K:=(-K)\vee X_t\wedge K$. Given $s<t$ and $\varphi(s,X.)$ a bounded continuous, $\mathcal{F}_s$-measurable function, it follows from weak convergence that

$$\lim_{n\to+\infty}\mathbb{E}^{\mathbb{P}^n}[\varphi(s,X.)(X_t^K-X_s^K))]=\mathbb{E}^{\mathbb{P}^0}[\varphi(s,X.)(X_t^K-X_s^K))].$$

As X is a $\mathbb{P}^n$-supermartingale, we have that

$$\begin{aligned}
&\mathbb{E}^{\mathbb{P}^n}[\varphi(s,X.)(X_t^K-X_s^K))]\\
&\le -\mathbb{E}^{\mathbb{P}^n}[\varphi(s,X.)(X_t\mathbf{1}_{\{|X_t|\ge K\}}-X_s\mathbf{1}_{\{|X_s|\ge K\}})]\\
&\le |\mathbb{E}^{\mathbb{P}^n}[\varphi(s,X.)(X_t\mathbf{1}_{\{|X_t|\ge K\}}-X_s\mathbf{1}_{\{|X_s|\ge K\}})]|\\
&\le 2|\varphi|_\infty\sup_{0\le t\le 1}\int|x|\mathbf{1}_{\{|x|\ge K\}}\mu_t(dx)\\
&\to 0,\quad \text{as } K\to\infty,
\end{aligned}$$

where the last inequality follows from Lemma 3.5 and the above convergence is uniformly in n. Finally, by the dominated convergence theorem, we have that

$$\begin{aligned}
&\mathbb{E}^{\mathbb{P}^0}[\varphi(s, X_\cdot)(X_t - X_s))] \\
&= \lim_{K\to\infty} \mathbb{E}^{\mathbb{P}^0}[\varphi(s, X_\cdot)(X_t^K - X_s^K))] \\
&= \lim_{K\to\infty} \lim_{n\to+\infty} \mathbb{E}^{\mathbb{P}^n}[\varphi(s, X_\cdot)(X_t^K - X_s^K))] \\
&\le 0.
\end{aligned}$$

As φ is arbitrary, we conclude that X is a $\mathbb{P}^0$-supermartingale.

3.2. *Characterization of the Limiting Process*

To further analyze the limiting process of the previous section, we consider the decreasing supermartingale coupling (see Appendix B) of two marginals μ_t and $\mu_{t+\epsilon}$. Recall that $x_1^\epsilon(t)$ denotes the unique phase transition point which divides the martingale region (to the right of $x_1^\epsilon(t)$) and the supermartingale region (to the left of $x_1^\epsilon(t)$). In the supermartingale region, the mass at $x \le x_1^\epsilon(t)$ is transported (through the quantile coupling) to the destination $T_d^\epsilon(t, x) = F^{-1}(t+\epsilon, F(t, x))$. In the martingale region, the two supporting maps T_u^ϵ and T_d^ϵ are characterized in Proposition B.4.

Set $\epsilon_0 := \epsilon_1 \wedge \epsilon_2$, where ϵ_1, ϵ_2 are as in Assumptions 3.1 and 3.3, respectively.

Assumption 3.7.

(i) The map $(t, \epsilon) \mapsto x_1^\epsilon(t)$ is uniformly continuous (with continuity modulus ρ_1) and also uniformly bounded on $\{(t, \epsilon) : 0 < \epsilon \le \epsilon_0, 0 \le t \le 1 - \epsilon\}$:

(ii) For every $t \in [0, 1]$, $r_t = r \in (-\infty, \infty]$.

(iii) For every $t \in [0, 1]$, we have $\partial_{tx} f(t, m_t) > 0$.

Lemma 3.8. *Suppose that Assumptions 3.1, 3.3, 3.7(i) and (ii) hold. Then the limit* $\lim_{\epsilon\to 0} x_1^\epsilon(t)$ *exists. Moreover, if we denote the limit by* $x_1(t)$*, then* $t \mapsto x_1(t)$ *is continuous and uniquely determined* *by the equation*

$$\int_{x_1(t)}^{+\infty} (x_1(t) - \xi)\partial_t f(t, \xi) d\xi = 0, \quad t \in [0, 1].$$

Proof. It follows from Lemma B.3 that $x_1^\epsilon(t)$ is unique for all $t \in [0, 1)$, $\epsilon \in (0, \epsilon_0]$. From Assumption 3.7 (i), using the Arzelà–Ascoli theorem, we have that $x_1^\epsilon(t)$ converges when $\epsilon \to 0$, and the limit remains a continuous function.

Using the properties of the decreasing supermartingale coupling (see Appendix B), we have that $x_1^\epsilon(t)$ and $y_1^\epsilon(t)$ satisfy the mean and mass preservation conditions:

$$\int_{x_1^\epsilon(t)}^{r_t} f(t, x) dx = \int_{y_1^\epsilon(t)}^{r_{t+\epsilon}} f(t + \epsilon, x) dx,$$

$$\int_{x_1^\epsilon(t)}^{r_t} x f(t, x) dx = \int_{y_1^\epsilon(t)}^{r_{t+\epsilon}} x f(t + \epsilon, x) dx.$$

Rearranging and using that $r_t = r_{t+\epsilon}$ gives

$$\int_{x_1^\epsilon(t)}^{r_t} (f(t, x) - f(t + \epsilon, x)) dx = \int_{y_1^\epsilon(t)}^{x_1^\epsilon(t)} f(t + \epsilon, x) dx,$$

$$\int_{x_1^\epsilon(t)}^{+\infty} x(f(t, x) - f(t + \epsilon, x)) dx = \int_{y_1^\epsilon(t)}^{x_1^\epsilon(t)} x f(t + \epsilon, x) dx.$$

Using Taylor's expansion $f(t + \epsilon, x) - f(t, x) = \partial_t f(t, x)\epsilon + \frac{1}{2}\partial_{tt} f(\xi_1, x)\epsilon^2$ (with $\xi_1 \in (t, t + \epsilon)$) in the first equation above and applying the mean value theorem for definite integrals, we get that

$$-\epsilon \int_{x_1^\epsilon(t)}^{+\infty} \partial_t f(t, x) dx - \frac{1}{2}\epsilon^2 \int_{x_1^\epsilon(t)}^{+\infty} \partial_{tt} f(\xi_1, x) dx = (x_1^\epsilon(t) - y_1^\epsilon(t)) f(t, \xi_2),$$

where ξ_2 lies in $[y_1^\epsilon(t), x_1^\epsilon(t)]$. Letting ϵ tend to 0 on both sides, the l.h.s. tends to 0, and consequently, the r.h.s. also tends to 0. It follows that $\lim_{\epsilon\to 0} x_1^\epsilon(t) = \lim_{\epsilon\to 0} y_1^\epsilon(t)$. Dividing both sides by ϵ, we get

$$-\int_{x_1^\epsilon(t)}^{+\infty} \partial_t f(t,x)dx = \frac{x_1^\epsilon(t) - y_1^\epsilon(t)}{\epsilon} f(t,\xi_2) + O(\epsilon). \tag{6}$$

Similarly,

$$-\int_{x_1^\epsilon(t)}^{+\infty} x\partial_t f(t,x)dx = \frac{x_1^\epsilon(t) - y_1^\epsilon(t)}{\epsilon} \xi_2 f(t,\xi_2) + O(\epsilon). \tag{7}$$

Note that Assumption 3.7(ii) ensures that $x \mapsto \partial_t f(t,x)$ is not a constant.

Combining (6) and (7) and letting ϵ tend to 0, we get that

$$\int_{x_1(t)}^{+\infty} (x - x_1(t))\partial_t f(t,x)dx = 0.$$

□

Remark 3.9. Assumption 3.7(ii) can be relaxed. For example, if $t \mapsto r_t$ is differentiable, then the equation that characterizes $x_1(t)$, as in Lemma 3.8, can be shown to be of the following form:

$$\int_{x_1(t)}^{r_t} (x_1(t) - \xi)\partial_t f(t,\xi)d\xi = -f(t,r_t)(x_1(t) - r_t)\frac{dr_t}{dt}, \quad t \in [0,1].$$

Consequently, the subsequent arguments would have to be adjusted. Since our main motivation is the examples that satisfy Assumption 3.7(ii), we do not include the details.

We also introduce T_u through the following integral equation:

$$\int_x^{T_u(t,x)} (x - \xi)\partial_t f(t,\xi)d\xi = 0. \tag{8}$$

Proposition 3.10. *Suppose that Assumptions* 3.1, 3.3, 3.7(*i*) *and* (*ii*) *hold. For $x \in (x_1(t), m_t)$,* (8) *has the unique solution $T_u(t,x)$ on* (m_t, r_t).

Proof. Define $G(t,x,y) := \int_x^y (x-\xi)\partial_t f(t,\xi)d\xi$, as $y \mapsto G(t,x,y)$ is continuous, it is enough to show that, for $x \in [x_1(t), m_t)$, $y \mapsto G(t,x,y)$ is decreasing on $y \in [m_t, \infty)$, $G(t,x,m_t) > 0$ and $G(t,x,+\infty) < 0$.

We first show that for $x \in [x_1(t), m_t]$, $y \mapsto G(t,x,y)$ is decreasing on $y \in [m_t, \infty)$. Indeed, for $m_t \le y_1 < y_2$, we have

$$G(t,x,y_2) - G(t,x,y_1) = \int_{y_1}^{y_2} (x-\xi)\partial_t f(t,\xi)d\xi < 0,$$

where the last inequality follows from the fact that $\xi > y_1 \ge m_t \ge x$ and $\partial_t f(t,\xi) > 0$ on $[y_1, y_2]$ (as $x \mapsto \partial_t F(t,x)$ is increasing on (m_t, ∞)).

Note that the equation $\partial_t F(t,x) = 0$ has a unique solution under Assumption 3.3, and we denote it by $\bar{x}(t)$. Now let us show that $x \mapsto G(t,x,+\infty)$ is decreasing on $(x_1(t), \bar{x}(t))$ and increasing on $(\bar{x}(t), m_t)$. Indeed,

$$\begin{aligned}\partial_x G(t,x,+\infty) &= \int_x^{+\infty} \partial_t f(t,\xi)d\xi = \partial_t F(t,+\infty) - \partial_t F(t,x)\\ &= -\partial_t F(t,x),\end{aligned}$$

which is negative on $(x_1(t), \bar{x}(t))$ and positive on $(\bar{x}(t), m_t)$. To show $G(t,x,+\infty) < 0$ for all $x_1(t) < x < m_t$, it is enough to show that $G(t,x_1(t),+\infty) \le 0$ and $G(t,m_t,+\infty) \le 0$. Note that from Lemma 3.8, $x_1(t)$ satisfies that

$$\int_{x_1(t)}^{+\infty} (x_1(t)-\xi)\partial_t f(t,\xi)d\xi = 0,$$

i.e., $G(t,x_1(t),+\infty) = 0$. Moreover, as $G(t,m_t,m_t) = 0$ and $y \mapsto G(t,m_t,y)$ is strictly decreasing on $y \in [m_t,\infty]$ which is shown above, it follows that $G(t,m_t,+\infty) < 0$.

In addition, $x \mapsto G(t,x,m_t)$ is decreasing on the interval $(x_1(t), m_t)$:

$$\partial_x G(t,x,m_t) = \int_x^{m_t} \partial_t f(t,\xi)d\xi = \partial_t F(t,m_t) - \partial_t F(t,x) < 0.$$

It follows that $G(t,x,m_t) > G(t,m_t,m_t) = 0$. □

We further define j_u and j_d for $t \in [0,1], x \in (x_1(t), m_t)$ by $j_u(t,x) := T_u(t,x) - x$ and $j_d(t,x) := \frac{\partial_t F(t,x) - \partial_t F(t,T_u(t,x))}{f(t,x)}$. The following lemma analyzes the asymptotic behavior of T_d^ϵ, T_u^ϵ and $q^\epsilon(t,x)$

in the martingale region and when ϵ is small. The proof is analogous to the proof of Henry-Labordère *et al.* [41, Lemma 6.6] when applied to the right-curtain coupling, and thus omitted.

Lemma 3.11. *Suppose that Assumptions* 3.1, 3.3, 3.7(i) *and* (ii) *hold.*

For $0 < \delta < K < \infty$, *let* $E_{\delta,K} := \{(t,x) : t \in [0,1], (m_t - K) \vee x_1(t) < x \leq m_t - \delta\}$. *Define* $j_d^\epsilon(t,x) := \frac{\partial_t F(t,x) - \partial_t F(t, T_u^\epsilon(t,x))}{f(t+\epsilon,x)}$. *Then* $T_u^\epsilon(t,x)$ *and* $T_d^\epsilon(t,x)$ *admit the following expansions*:

$$T_u^\epsilon(t,x) - x := J_u^\epsilon(t,x) = j_u(t,x) + (\epsilon \vee \rho_0(\epsilon)) e_u^\epsilon(t,x)$$

and

$$x - T_d^\epsilon(t,x) := J_d^\epsilon(t,x) = \epsilon j_d^\epsilon(t,x) + \epsilon^2 e_d^\epsilon(t,x),$$

with $e_d^\epsilon(t,x)$ *and* $e_u^\epsilon(t,x)$ *bounded on* $E_{\delta,K}$. *Consequently, there exists a constant* $C_{\delta,K}$ *such that the probability of the upward jump* q^ϵ *admits the asymptotic expansion*:

$$\begin{aligned} q^\epsilon(t,x) = \frac{J_d^\epsilon(t,x)}{J_u^\epsilon(t,x) + J_d^\epsilon(t,x)} &= \epsilon \frac{j_d(t,x)}{j_u(t,x)} + C_{\delta,K}\epsilon\,(\epsilon \vee \rho_0(\epsilon))\,, \\ \textit{for } (t,x) \in E_{\delta,K}. \end{aligned} \tag{9}$$

The following lemma considers the asymptotic expansion of J_d^ϵ in the supermartingale region.

Lemma 3.12. *Suppose that Assumptions* 3.1, 3.3, 3.7(i) *and* (ii) *hold.*

For $0 < K < \infty$, *let* $E_K := \{(t,x) : t \in [0,1], (x_1(t) - K) \vee l_t \leq x \leq x_1(t)\}$. *Then,* $x - T_d^\epsilon(t,x) = J_d^\epsilon(t,x) = \epsilon j_d^\epsilon(t,x) + \epsilon^2 e_d^\epsilon(t,x)$, *with* $j_d^\epsilon(t,x) := \frac{1}{f(t+\epsilon,x)} \partial_t F(t,x)$, *and* $e_d^\epsilon(t,x)$ *bounded on* E_K.

Proof. For $J_d^\epsilon(t,x)$, applying Taylor's expansion to the first order, we have that

$$\begin{aligned}
J_d^\epsilon(t,x) &= x - T_d^\epsilon(t,x) = F^{-1}(t+\epsilon, F(t+\epsilon,x)) - F^{-1}(t+\epsilon, F(t,x)) \\
&= \frac{\partial F^{-1}}{\partial x}(t+\epsilon, F(t+\epsilon,x))\,[F(t+\epsilon,x) - F(t,x)] \\
&\quad + \frac{1}{2}\frac{\partial^2 F^{-1}}{\partial x^2}(t+\epsilon, c)\,[F(t+\epsilon,x) - F(t,x)]^2 \\
&= \frac{1}{f(t+\epsilon,x)}\,[F(t+\epsilon,x) - F(t,x)] \\
&\quad + \frac{1}{2}(-1)\frac{f'(t+\epsilon,\xi)}{f^3(t+\epsilon,\xi)}\,[F(t+\epsilon,x) - F(t,x)]^2,
\end{aligned}$$

where in the above, c is between $F(t,x)$ and $F(t+\epsilon,x)$, and $\xi = F^{-1}(t+\epsilon,c)$. Applying further second-order Taylor's expansion to the first $F(t+\epsilon,x) - F(t,x)$ and first-order Taylor's expansion to the second $F(t+\epsilon,x) - F(t,x)$, we have

$$\begin{aligned}
J_d^\epsilon(t,x) &= \frac{1}{f(t+\epsilon,x)}\left[\partial_t F(t,x)\epsilon + \frac{1}{2}\partial_{tt}F(\xi_1,x)\epsilon^2\right] \\
&\quad - \frac{1}{2}\frac{f'(t+\epsilon,\xi)}{f^3(t+\epsilon,\xi)}\,[\partial_t F(\xi_2,x)\epsilon]^2 \\
&= \frac{\partial_t F(t,x)}{f(t+\epsilon,x)}\epsilon + \left[\frac{\partial_{tt}F(\xi_1,x)}{2f(t+\epsilon,x)}\right. \\
&\quad \left. - \frac{f'(t+\epsilon,\xi)}{2f^3(t+\epsilon,\xi)}\,(\partial_t F(\xi_2,x))^2\right]\epsilon^2,
\end{aligned}$$

with ξ_1, ξ_2 between t and $t+\epsilon$. Hence the expansion of J_d^ϵ is valid, with

$$\begin{aligned}
|e_T^\epsilon(t,x)| \le \sup_{t\le s\le t+\epsilon, F^{-1}(t+\epsilon,F(t,x))\le\xi\le x} &\left|\frac{\partial_{tt}F(s,\xi)}{2f(s,\xi)}\right. \\
&\left. - \frac{f'(s,\xi)}{2f^3(s,\xi)}\,(\partial_t F(s,\xi))^2\right|.
\end{aligned}$$

□

For $t \in [0, 1]$, extend the definition of j_d to $(\ell_t, x_1(t)]$ by setting $j_d(t, x) := \frac{1}{f(t,x)} \partial_t F(t, x)$. For the main result of this section, we need one additional result.

Lemma 3.13. *Suppose that Assumptions* 3.1, 3.3 *and* 3.7 *hold.*

(i) T_u *is strictly decreasing in* x *on* $(x_1(t), m_t)$.
(ii) $j_d(t, x)\mathbf{1}_{\{x_1(t)<x<m_t\}}, j_u(t, x)\mathbf{1}_{\{x_1(t)<x<m_t\}}, \frac{j_d}{j_u}(t, x)\mathbf{1}_{\{x_1(t)<x<m_t\}}$ *and* $j_d(t, x)\mathbf{1}_{\{x\le x_1(t)\}}$ *are all locally Lipschitz in* $(t, x) \in \{0 \le t \le 1, (-K \vee l_t) \le x \le (K \wedge r_t)\}$.

Proof.

(i) Differentiating both sides of (8) with respect to $x \in (x_1(t), m_t)$, we get that

$$\partial_x T_u(t, x)\,(x - T_u(t, x))\,\partial_t f(t, T_u(t, x)) + \int_x^{T_u(t,x)} \partial_t f(t, \xi) d\xi = 0.$$

Hence

$$\partial_x T_u(t, x) = \frac{\partial_t F(t, T_u(t, x)) - \partial_t F(t, x)}{(x - T_u(t, x))\,\partial_t f(t, T_u(t, x))} < 0, \tag{10}$$

where the last inequality follows from $\partial_t F(t, T_u(t, x)) > \partial_t F(t, x)$.

(ii) Using Assumption 3.3 and repeating the arguments of the proof of [41, Lemma 3.6] (applied to the right-curtain coupling case), we get that all $j_d(t, x)\mathbf{1}_{\{x_1(t)<x<m_t\}}, j_u(t, x)\mathbf{1}_{\{x_1(t)<x<m_t\}}, \frac{j_d}{j_u}(t, x)\mathbf{1}_{\{x_1(t)<x<m_t\}}$ are locally Lipschitz. It is left to verify the regularity of the function $j_d(t, x)\mathbf{1}_{\{x\le x_1(t)\}}$. But Assumption 3.1 and the definition $j_d(t, x) = \frac{1}{f(t,x)} \partial_t F(t, x)$ immediately imply the local Lipschitz property. □

In the following, we provide a characterization of the limit of the sequence $(\mathbb{P}^n)_{n\ge1}$. The limiting process is a pure-jump process that is similar in spirit to the local Lévy models introduced by Carr, Geman, Madan and Yor [22]. (See also [41] for the related martingale case.)

Theorem 3.14. *Suppose that Assumptions* 3.1, 3.3 *and* 3.7 *hold. Then* $\mathbb{P}^n \to \mathbb{P}^0$, *where* $\mathbb{P}^0$ *is the unique weak solution to the SDE*:

$$X_t = X_0 + \int_0^t j_u(t, X_{s-})(dN_s - \nu_s ds)\mathbf{1}_{\{x_1(s)<X_{s-}<m_s\}} - \int_0^t \mathbf{1}_{\{X_{s-}\le x_1(s)\}} j_d(t, X_{s-})ds, \tag{11}$$

and $(N_s)_{0\le s\le 1}$ *is a unit size jump process with predictable compensated process* $(\nu_s)_{0\le s\le 1}$ *given by*

$$\nu_s := \frac{j_d}{j_u}(s, X_{s-})\mathbf{1}_{\{x_1(s)<X_{s-}<m_s\}},$$

where $x_1(t)$ *is given by Lemma* 3.8, $j_u(t,x) := T_u(t,x) - x$ *and* $j_d(t,x) := \frac{\partial_t F(t,x) - \partial_t F(t, T_u(t,x))}{f(t,x)}$ *for* $x \in (x_1(t), m_t)$, $j_d(t,x) := \frac{1}{f(t,x)}\partial_t F(t,x)$ *for* $x \in (\ell_t, x_1(t)]$ *and* T_u *is characterized by* (8) *on* $x \in (x_1(t), m_t)$.

Proof. By Proposition 3.4, the sequence of supermartingale measures $(\mathbb{P}^n)_{n\ge 1}$ induced by the decreasing supermartingale transport plan is tight. We shall prove that any limit of $(\mathbb{P}^n)_{n\ge 1}$ provides a weak solution to (11). Our strategy is identical to that of Henry-Labordère and Touzi [42, Theorem 3.7], and thus we only present the steps that are affected by the supermartingale feature of our construction.

For all $\mathbf{x} \in \Omega := \mathbb{D}([0,1], \mathbb{R})$ and $\varphi \in C_b^1(\mathbb{R})$, we define

$$\begin{aligned} M_t(\varphi, \mathbf{x}) &:= \varphi(\mathbf{x}_t) - \int_0^t j_d(s, \mathbf{x}_{s-})D\varphi(\mathbf{x}_{s-})\mathbf{1}_{\{x_1(s)<\mathbf{x}_{s-}<m_s\}}ds \\ &\quad - \int_0^t \left[[\varphi(\mathbf{x}_{s-} + j_u(s, \mathbf{x}_{s-})) - \varphi(\mathbf{x}_{s-})]\frac{j_d}{j_u}(s, \mathbf{x}_{s-})\right] \\ &\quad \times \mathbf{1}_{\{x_1(s)<\mathbf{x}_{s-}<m_s\}}ds - \int_0^t j_d(s, \mathbf{x}_{s-})D\varphi(\mathbf{x}_{s-})\mathbf{1}_{\{\mathbf{x}_{s-}\le x_1(s)\}}ds. \end{aligned}$$

The process $M(\varphi, X)$ is progressively measurable w.r.t. the canonical filtration $\mathbb{F}$. For every constant $p > 0$, we introduce an $\mathbb{F}$-stopping time and the corresponding stopped canonical process

$$\tau_p := \inf\{t \geq 0 : |X_t| \geq p \text{ or } |X_{t-}| \geq p\}, \ X_t^p := X_{t\wedge\tau_p}.$$

Denote further $J(\mathbf{x}) := \{t > 0 : \Delta\mathbf{x}(t) \neq 0\}$, $V(\mathbf{x}) := \{a > 0 : \tau_a(\mathbf{x}) < \tau_{a+}(\mathbf{x})\}$ and

$$V'(\mathbf{x}) := \{a > 0 : \tau_a(\mathbf{x}) \in J(\mathbf{x}) \text{ and } |\mathbf{x}(\tau_a(\mathbf{x}))| = a\}.$$

By extracting a subsequence, we can suppose w.l.o.g. that $\mathbb{P}^n \to \mathbb{P}^0$ weakly. To prove that $\mathbb{P}^0$ is a weak solution to SDE (11), it is enough to show that $(M_t(\varphi, X))_{t\in[0,1]}$ is a local martingale under $\mathbb{P}^0$ for every $\varphi \in C_b^1(\mathbb{R})$. Since the functions j_d and j_u are locally Lipchitz but not necessarily uniformly bounded, as in the proof of Henry-Labordère and Touzi [42, Theorem 3.7], we need to adapt the localization technique in Jacod and Shiryaev [51].

First, since $\mathbb{P}^n$ is induced by the Markov chain $(X^n, \mathbb{P}^{*,n})$ for all $n \geq 1$, we have

$$\mathbb{E}_{t_k^n}^{\mathbb{P}^n}[\varphi(X_{t_{k+1}^n}) - \varphi(X_{t_k^n})] = \alpha_u + \alpha_d + \alpha_{\tilde{d}},$$

where

$$\begin{aligned}
\alpha_u &:= \mathbb{E}_{t_k^n}^{\mathbb{P}^n}\Big[\{\varphi(X_{t_k^n} + J_u^{\epsilon_k^n}(t_k^n, X_{t_k^n})) - \varphi(X_{t_k^n})\} \\
&\quad \times \frac{J_d^{\epsilon_k^n}}{J_d^{\epsilon_k^n} + J_u^{\epsilon_k^n}}\mathbf{1}_{\{x_1^{\epsilon_k^n}(t_k^n) < X_{t_k^n} < m^{\epsilon_k^n}(t_k^n)\}}\Big], \\
\alpha_d &:= \mathbb{E}_{t_k^n}^{\mathbb{P}^n}\Big[\{\varphi(X_{t_k^n} - J_d^{\epsilon_k^n}(t_k^n, X_{t_k^n})) - \varphi(X_{t_k^n})\} \\
&\quad \times \frac{J_u^{\epsilon_k^n}}{J_d^{\epsilon_k^n} + J_u^{\epsilon_k^n}}\mathbf{1}_{\{x_1^{\epsilon_k^n}(t_k^n) < X_{t_k^n} < m^{\epsilon_k^n}(t_k^n)\}}\Big], \\
\alpha_{\tilde{d}} &:= \mathbb{E}_{t_k^n}^{\mathbb{P}^n}\Big[\{\varphi(X_{t_k^n} - J_d^{\epsilon_k^n}(t_k^n, X_{t_k^n})) - \varphi(X_{t_k^n})\}\mathbf{1}_{\{X_{t_k^n} \leq x_1^{\epsilon_k^n}(t_k^n)\}}\Big],
\end{aligned}$$

with $\epsilon_k^n := t_{k+1}^n - t_k^n$ (also recall that, under the present assumptions (dispersion assumption in particular), $x_1^{\epsilon_k^n}(t_k^n)$ is the unique regime-switching boundary).

By the continuity of $(\epsilon, t) \mapsto (m^\epsilon(t), x_1^\epsilon(t))$ and noting that the density $f(t,x) \in C_b^3(E)$, we have that for ϵ_k^n small and for all $s \in [t_k^n, t_{k+1}^n]$,

$$
\begin{aligned}
&|\mathbb{E}_{t_k^n}^{\mathbb{P}^n}[\mathbf{1}_{\{x_1^{\epsilon_k^n}(t_k^n)<X_{t_k^n}<m^{\epsilon_k^n}(t_k^n)\}} - \mathbf{1}_{\{x_1(s)<X_s<m_s\}}]| \\
&\quad \leq |\int_{x_1^{\epsilon_k^n}(t_k^n)}^{x_1(s)} f(t,x)dx| + |\int_{m^{\epsilon_k^n}(t_k^n)}^{m_s} f(t,x)dx| = O(\rho_0(\epsilon_k^n) \vee \rho_1(\epsilon_k^n)).
\end{aligned}
$$

Then, using Lemma 3.11 and the arguments of [41, Theorem 3.7], we have that

$$
\begin{aligned}
\alpha_u = \mathbb{E}_{t_k^n}^{\mathbb{P}^n}\Bigg[\int_{t_k^n}^{t_{k+1}^n} &[\varphi(X_s + j_u(s, X_s)) - \varphi(X_s)] \\
&\times \frac{j_d}{j_u}(s, X_s)\mathbf{1}_{\{x_1(s)<X_s<m_s)\}}ds\Bigg], \\
\alpha_d = -\mathbb{E}_{t_k^n}^{\mathbb{P}^n}&\left[\int_{t_k^n}^{t_{k+1}^n} j_d(s, X_s)D\varphi(X_s)\mathbf{1}_{\{x_1(s)<X_s<m_s\}}ds\right] \\
&+ O(\epsilon_k^n(\epsilon_k^n \vee \rho_0(\epsilon_k^n) \vee \rho_1(\epsilon_k^n))).
\end{aligned}
$$

Similarly, using Lemma 3.12, we have that

$$
\begin{aligned}
\alpha_{\tilde{d}} = -\mathbb{E}_{t_k^n}^{\mathbb{P}^n}&\left[\int_{t_k^n}^{t_{k+1}^n} j_d(s, X_s)D\varphi(X_s)\mathbf{1}_{\{X_s\leq x_1(s))\}}ds\right] \\
&+ O(\epsilon_k^n(\epsilon_k^n \vee \rho_0(\epsilon_k^n) \vee \rho_1(\epsilon_k^n))).
\end{aligned}
$$

Now let $0 \leq s < t \leq 1$, $p \in \mathbb{N}$, $\phi_s(X.)$ be an $\mathcal{F}_s$-measurable bounded random variable on Ω such that $\phi : \Omega \to \mathbb{R}$ is continuous under the Skorokhod topology. Then,

$$
\begin{aligned}
&\mathbb{E}^{\mathbb{P}^n}[\phi_s(X.)(M_{t\wedge\tau_p}(\varphi, X) - M_{s\wedge\tau_p}(\varphi, X))] \\
&\quad \leq C_p(|\pi_n| \vee \rho_0(|\pi_n|) \vee \rho_1(|\pi_n|))
\end{aligned}
$$

for some constant $C_p > 0$. The remaining arguments are those of [41, Theorem 3.7] and are thus omitted. □

3.3. *Optimality of the Local Lévy Process*

In this section, we establish the optimality of the previously obtained limiting process to the continuous-time primal problem $\mathbf{P}_\infty$.

We will need the optimal dual strategy (in discrete time one-period case) which is given in Lemma B.5; in the following, we denote $h^\epsilon := \hat{h}^{\mu_t,\mu_{t+\epsilon}}, \varphi^\epsilon := \hat{\varphi}^{\mu_t,\mu_{t+\epsilon}}, \psi^\epsilon := \hat{\psi}^{\mu_t,\mu_{t+\epsilon}}$.

Now let us introduce the optimal dual strategies for the continuous-time transport problem. First, we define the dynamic strategy h^* by

$$
\begin{aligned}
&h^*(t,x) = 0, \quad \text{when } x \le x_1(t),\\
&\partial_x h^*(t,x) = \frac{c_x(x,T_u(t,x)) - c_x(x,x)}{j_u(t,x)}, \quad x_1(t) < x < m_t,\\
&\lim_{x\downarrow x_1(t)} h^*(t,x) = 0,\\
&h^*(t,x) = h^*(t,T_u^{-1}(t,x)) - c_y(T_u^{-1}(t,x),x), \quad \text{when } x \ge m_t.
\end{aligned}
$$

We remark that from the above definition, for all $t \in [0,1]$, $x \mapsto h^*(t,x)$ is continuous both at $x_1(t)$ and m_t. In addition, ψ^* is defined, up to a constant, by

$$
\partial_x \psi^*(t,x) := -h^*(t,x), \quad (t,x) \in E = \{(t,x) : t \in [0,1], x \in (l_t, r_t)\}.
$$

Now, using the same arguments as [41, Corollary 3.10] together with the fact that $h^*(t,x) = 0$ for $t \in [0,1]$ and $x \le x_1(t)$, we have that $\psi^* \in C^{1,1}(E)$.

For the (static part of the) dual limiting strategy, let $\gamma^*(dt) := \delta_{\{0\}}(dt) + \delta_{\{1\}}(dt) + Leb(dt)$ be a finite measure on $[0,1]$, where Leb denotes the Lebesgue measure on $[0,1]$.

One further defines λ_0^* and $\bar{\lambda}_0^*$ by $\lambda_0^*(0,x) := \psi^*(0,x)$, $\lambda_0^*(1,x) := \psi^*(1,x)$, $\bar{\lambda}_0^*(0,x) := |\psi^*(0,x)|$ and $\bar{\lambda}_0^*(1,x) := \sup_{t\in[0,1]} |\psi^*(t,x)|$, and for all $(t,x) \in (0,1) \times \mathbb{R}$,

$$
\begin{aligned}
\lambda_0^*(t,x) &:= \partial_t \psi^*(t,x) + \mathbf{1}_{\{x_1(t)<x\le m_t\}} \big(\partial_x \psi^* j_d\\
&\qquad + \nu[\psi^* - \psi^*(\cdot,T_u) + c(\cdot,T_u)]\big) + \mathbf{1}_{\{x\le x_1(t)\}} \partial_x \psi^* j_d,\\
\bar{\lambda}_0^* &:= \partial_t \psi^*(t,x) + \mathbf{1}_{\{x_1(t)<x<m_t\}} \big(\partial_x \psi^* j_d + \nu[\psi^* - \psi^*(\cdot,T_u)]\big) \,|\\
&\qquad + \mathbf{1}_{\{x_1(t)<x<m_t\}} \nu[|c(\cdot,T_u)|] + \mathbf{1}_{x\le x_1(t)} |\partial_x \psi^* j_d|.
\end{aligned}
$$

Finally, we define $\lambda^*(x,dt) := \lambda_0^*(t,x)\gamma^*(dt)$ and $\bar{\lambda}^*(x,dt) := \bar{\lambda}_0^*(t,x)\gamma^*(dt)$.

The following result shows that the limiting process of the previous sections solves the continuous-time supermartingale optimal transport problem. Let H^* be the $\mathbb{F}$-predictable process on Ω defined by

$$H_t^* := h^*(t, X_{t-}), \quad t \in [0,1].$$

Theorem 3.15. *Suppose that Assumptions* 2.2, 3.1, 3.3 *and* 3.7 *hold and that*

$$\mu(\bar{\lambda}^*) = \int_0^1 \int_{\mathbb{R}} \bar{\lambda}_0^*(t,x)\mu_t(dx)\gamma^*(dt) < \infty. \tag{12}$$

Then the supermartingale transport problem (4) *is solved by the local Lévy process* (11). *Moreover, we have that* $(H^*, \lambda^*) \in \mathcal{D}_\infty(\mu)$ *and the following duality is valid:*

$$\mathbb{E}^{\mathbb{P}^0}[C(X_\cdot)] = \mathbf{P}_\infty(\mu) = \mathbf{D}_\infty(\mu) = \mu(\lambda^*),$$

and the optimal value is given by

$$\mu(\lambda^*) = \int_0^1 \int_{x_1(t)}^{m_t} \frac{j_d(t,x)}{j_u(t,x)} c(x, x + j_u(t,x)) f(t,x)\, dx\, dt.$$

In order to prove Theorem 3.15, we consider the following partition of $[0,1]$: $\pi_n = (t_k^n)_{0 \le k \le n}$, where $t_k^n := k\epsilon$ with $\epsilon = \frac{1}{n}$. In the following, we shall simplify the notation t_k^n to t_k. Remind that under every $\mathbb{P}^n$, we have the following super-replication inequality:

$$\sum_{k=0}^{n-1} (\varphi^\epsilon(t_k, X_{t_k}) + \psi^\epsilon(t_k, X_{t_{k+1}})) + \sum_{k=0}^{n-1} h^\epsilon(t_k, X_{t_k})(X_{t_{k+1}} - X_{t_k})$$
$$\ge \sum_{k=0}^{n-1} c(X_{t_k}, X_{t_{k+1}}). \tag{13}$$

We further define $\Psi^* : \Omega \to \mathbb{R}$ by

$$\Psi^*(\mathbf{x}) := \psi^*(1, \mathbf{x}_1) - \psi^*(0, \mathbf{x}_0) - \int_0^1 (\partial_t \psi^*(t, \mathbf{x}_t)$$
$$+ j_d(t, \mathbf{x}_t) \mathbf{1}_{\{\mathbf{x}_t < m_t\}} \partial_x \psi^*(t, \mathbf{x}_t))dt$$

$$+ \int_0^1 \frac{j_d(t, \mathbf{x}_t)}{j_u(t, \mathbf{x}_t)} \mathbf{1}_{\{x_1(t) < \mathbf{x}_t < m_t\}} \left(\psi^*(t, \mathbf{x}_t)\right.$$
$$\left. - \psi^*(t, \mathbf{x}_t + j_u(t, \mathbf{x}_t)) + c(\mathbf{x}_t, \mathbf{x}_t + j_u(t, \mathbf{x}_t))\right) dt.$$

To prove Theorem 3.15, we need several auxiliary results. The proof of the following lemma relies on Lemmas 3.11 and 3.12 but otherwise is the same as the proof of [41, Lemma 6.7], and thus we omit the details.

Lemma 3.16. *Under Assumptions* 2.2, 3.1 *and* 3.3, *we have that*

$$T_u^\epsilon \mathbf{1}_{\{x_1^\epsilon(t) < x < m_t^\epsilon\}} \to T_u \mathbf{1}_{\{x_1(t) < x < m_t\}}, \; h^\epsilon \to h^*,$$
$$\partial_t \psi^\epsilon \to \partial_t \psi^*, \; \psi^\epsilon \to \psi^*$$

locally uniformly on $E = \{(t, x) : t \in [0, 1], x \in (l_t, r_t)\}$.

Lemma 3.17. *Suppose Assumptions* 2.2, 3.1 *and* 3.3 *hold. Then for every càdlàg path* $\mathbf{x} \in \mathbb{D}([0, 1], \mathbb{R})$ *taking value in* (l_1, r_1), *we have*

$$\lim_{n \to \infty} \sum_{k=0}^{n-1} \left(\varphi^\epsilon(t_k, \mathbf{x}_{t_k}) + \psi^\epsilon(t_k, \mathbf{x}_{t_{k+1}})\right) \to \Psi^*(\mathbf{x}), \quad \text{as } \epsilon \to 0.$$

Proof. The arguments are almost identical to those of [41, Lemma 6.9], and thus we only briefly sketch them. First note that

$$\sum_{k=0}^{n-1} \left(\varphi^\epsilon(t_k, \mathbf{x}_{t_k}) + \psi^\epsilon(t_k, \mathbf{x}_{t_{k+1}})\right)$$
$$= \sum_{k=0}^{n-1} \left(\varphi^\epsilon(t_k, \mathbf{x}_{t_k}) + \psi^\epsilon(t_k, \mathbf{x}_{t_k})\right) + \psi^\epsilon(t_{n-1}, \mathbf{x}_1)$$
$$+ \sum_{k=1}^{n-1} \left(\psi^\epsilon(t_{k-1}, \mathbf{x}_{t_k}) - \psi^\epsilon(t_k, \mathbf{x}_{t_k})\right) - \psi^\epsilon(0, \mathbf{x}_0).$$

Then by Lemma 3.16 and the arguments of [41, Lemma 6.9], as $\epsilon \to 0$, we have that $\psi^\epsilon(t_{n-1}, \mathbf{x}_1) \to \psi^*(1, \mathbf{x}_1)$,

$$\sum_{k=1}^{n-1} \left(\psi^\epsilon(t_{k-1}, \mathbf{x}_{t_k}) - \psi^\epsilon(t_k, \mathbf{x}_{t_k})\right) \to - \int_0^1 \partial_t \psi^*(t, \mathbf{x}_t) dt,$$

and $\sum_{k=0}^{n-1}\left(\varphi^\epsilon(t_k,\mathbf{x}_{t_k})+\psi^\epsilon(t_k,\mathbf{x}_{t_k})\right)\mathbf{1}_{\{x_1^\epsilon(t_k)<\mathbf{x}_{t_k}<m^\epsilon(t_k)\}}$ converges to

$$\begin{aligned}&\int_0^1 -\partial_x\psi^*(t,\mathbf{x}_t)j_d(t,\mathbf{x}_t)dt\\ &\quad+\int_0^1 \frac{j_d(t,\mathbf{x}_t)}{j_u(t,\mathbf{x}_t)}\mathbf{1}_{\{x_1(t)<\mathbf{x}_t<m_t\}}\left(\psi^*(t,\mathbf{x}_t)\right.\\ &\quad\left.-\psi^*(t,\mathbf{x}_t+j_u(t,\mathbf{x}_t))+c(\mathbf{x}_t,\mathbf{x}_t+j_u(t,\mathbf{x}_t))\right)dt.\end{aligned}$$

Finally, using similar arguments, and noting that $c(x,x)=0$ for all $x\in\mathbb{R}$, we have that

$$\begin{aligned}&\sum_{k=0}^{n-1}\left(\varphi^\epsilon(t_k,\mathbf{x}_{t_k})+\psi^\epsilon(t_k,\mathbf{x}_{t_k})\right)\mathbf{1}_{\{\mathbf{x}_{t_k}\le x_1^\epsilon(t_k)\}}\\ &\qquad\to-\int_0^1 j_d(t,\mathbf{x}_t)\mathbf{1}_{\{\mathbf{x}_t\le x_1(t)\}}\partial_x\psi^*(t,\mathbf{x}_t)dt,\end{aligned}$$

which concludes the proof. □

Lemma 3.18. *Suppose that Assumptions* 2.2, 3.1, 3.3 *and* 3.7 *hold and* $\mu(\bar{\lambda}^*)<\infty$. *Then for the probability measure* $\mathbb{P}^0$ *given in Theorem* 3.14, *we have that*

$$\begin{aligned}\mathbb{E}^{\mathbb{P}^0}[C(X.)]&=\mathbb{E}^{\mathbb{P}^0}[\Psi^*(X.)]=\mu(\lambda^*)\\ &=\int_0^1\int_{x_1(t)}^{m_t}\frac{j_d(t,x)}{j_u(t,x)}c(x,x+j_u(t,x))f(t,x)\,dx\,dt.\end{aligned}$$

Proof. The arguments are almost identical to those of [41, Lemma 6.10] (adapted to the right-curtain coupling situation). We only need to adapt various definitions to include the supermartingale regions governed by $t\mapsto x_1(t)$.

By Itô's formula, the following process is a local martingale:

$$\begin{aligned}&\psi^*(t,X_t)-\psi^*(0,X_0)-\int_0^1\left(\partial_t\psi^*(t,X_t)\right.\\ &\quad+\left(j_d(t,X_t)\mathbf{1}_{\{x_1(t)<X_t<m_t\}}+j_d(t,X_t)\mathbf{1}_{\{X_t\le x_1(t)\}}\right)\\ &\quad\left.\partial_x\psi^*(t,X_t)\right)dt+\int_0^1\frac{j_d(t,x_t)}{j_u(t,x_t)}\mathbf{1}_{\{x_1(t)<X_t<m_t\}}\left(\psi^*(t,X_t)\right.\\ &\quad\left.-\psi^*(t,X_t+j_u(t,X_t))\right)dt.\end{aligned}$$

Moreover, using the fact that $\mu(\bar{\lambda}^*) < \infty$ together with the dominated convergence theorem, we have that

$$\mathbb{E}^{\mathbb{P}^0}[\Psi^*(X_\cdot)] = \int_0^1 \int_{x_1(t)}^{m_t} \frac{j_d(t,x)}{j_u(t,x)} c(x, x + j_u(t,x)) f(t,x)\, dx\, dt.$$

To compute $\mathbb{E}^{\mathbb{P}^0}[C(X_\cdot)]$, noting that $[X]_t^c = 0$, $\mathbb{P}^0$-a.s., and the process

$$Y_t := \sum_{s \le t} |c(X_{s-}, X_s)| - \int_0^t |c(X_{s-}, X_{s-} + j_u(t, X_{s-})| \\ \times \frac{j_d(t, X_{s-})}{j_u(t, X_{s-})} \mathbf{1}_{\{x_1(t) < X_t < m_t\}}\, dt$$

is a local martingale. The remainder of the proof follows the arguments of [42, Lemma 6.10]. □

In the following lemma, we establish the continuous limit of the dynamic part. The proof relies on Lemma 3.16 but otherwise is identical to the proof of [41, Lemma 6.11] and is thus omitted.

Lemma 3.19. *Suppose Assumptions* 3.1, 3.3 *and* 3.7 *hold. Then the following convergence in probability* (*as* $\epsilon \to 0$) *holds under every supermartingale measure* $\mathbb{P} \in \mathcal{S}_\infty$:

$$\sum_{k=1}^{n-1} h^\epsilon(t_k, X)(X_{t_{k+1}} - X_{t_k}) \to \int_0^1 h^*(t, X_{t-}) dX_t.$$

Finally, we provide the proof of Theorem 3.15.

Proof of Theorem 3.15. Using the discrete superhedging duality (13), together with the convergence results of Lemmas 2.3, 3.17 and 3.19, we have that under every $\mathbb{P} \in \mathcal{S}_\infty$, (Ψ^*, h^*) superhedges the continuous-time cost $C(X_\cdot)$:

$$\Psi^*(X_\cdot) + \int_0^1 h^*(t, X_{t-}) dX_t \\ \ge \int_0^1 \frac{1}{2} c_{yy}(X_t, X_t) d[X]_t^c + \sum_{0 \le t \le 1} c(X_{t-}, X_t), \quad \mathbb{P}\text{-a.s.}$$

By the weak duality,

$$\mathbb{E}^{\mathbb{P}^0}[C(X.)] \leq \mathbf{P}_\infty(\mu) \leq \mathbf{D}_\infty(\mu) \leq \mu(\lambda^*).$$

Then Lemma 3.18 concludes the proof.

4. Examples

In this section, we will consider three examples of supermartingales matching a given PCOCD. Contrary to the martingale case of [41,52] (that covers left-curtain and right-curtain couplings), in the supermartingale context, the increasing and decreasing couplings provide significantly different dynamics in continuous time.

4.1. *Uniform Distribution with Bounded Support*

In this section, the family of marginal distributions $(\mu_t)_{t\in[0,1]}$ satisfies

$$\mu_t = \frac{1}{e^t + e^{2t}} \lambda_{[-e^{2t}, e^t]}, \quad t \in [0,1]. \tag{14}$$

(This example was also considered in the martingale case by Juillet [52].) Our goal is to explicitly determine the quantities that define the SDE given in Theorem 3.14.

Note that $\ell_t = -e^{2t}$ and $r_t = e^t$ for all $t \in [0,1]$. Furthermore, $(\mu_t)_{t\in[0,1]}$ satisfies Assumption 3.1 with $m_\epsilon(t) = \ell_t$ and $m^\epsilon(t) = r_t$, for each $t \in [0,1)$ and $\epsilon \in (0, 1-t]$. Recall that m_ϵ, m^ϵ maximizes and minimizes, respectively, the function $x \mapsto F(t+\epsilon, x) - F(t,x)$. Observe that m_ϵ, m^ϵ are independent of $\epsilon > 0$. By direct computation, we have that, for all $t \in (0,1)$, $\partial_t F(t,\cdot)$ is minimized and maximized at $m_t = e^t$ and $\tilde{m}_t = -e^{2t}$. Then $m^0(t) := m_t = \lim_{\epsilon\downarrow 0} m^\epsilon(t) = e^t$ for all $t \in [0,1]$. It is now easy to see that $(\mu_t)_{t\in[0,1]}$ satisfies Assumption 3.3. However, since $t \mapsto r_t$ is not constant and $m_t = r_t$, Assumption 3.7 does not hold. For this reason, most of the results of Section 3.2 (that lead to Theorem 3.14) cannot be applied, and thus we will prove the relevant statements by direct calculations.

Now, fix $t \in [0,1)$ and $\epsilon \in (0, 1-t]$ and consider the decreasing supermartingale coupling $\hat{\mathbb{P}}^{\mu_t, \mu_{t+\epsilon}}$ of μ_t and $\mu_{t+\epsilon}$ (see Appendix B.1). Since, Assumption 3.1 is satisfied, the phase transition point that separates the martingale and supermartingale regions is unique, see Lemma B.3. The transition threshold is denoted by

$$x_1^\epsilon(t) := x_1^{\mu_t,\mu_{t+\epsilon}},$$

see (B.50).

Lemma 4.1. *If* $(\mu_t)_{t\in[0,1]}$ *is given by* (14), *then the phase transition* $x_1^\epsilon(t)$ *is given by*

$$x_1^\epsilon(t) = \frac{e^t(e^{2(t+\epsilon)} - e^{t+\epsilon} + e^t) + e^{2t}(e^t - 2e^{t+\epsilon})}{e^{t+\epsilon} + e^{2(t+\epsilon)} - e^t - e^{2t}}. \tag{15}$$

Furthermore, the limit $x_1(t) := \lim_{\epsilon\downarrow 0} x_1^\epsilon(t)$ *exists and is given by*

$$x_1(t) = \frac{-e^t}{1+2e^t} \in (-e^{2t}, e^t), \quad t \in [0,1]. \tag{16}$$

Proof. To determine $x_1^\epsilon(t) \in (\ell_t, r_t)$, we use the fact that under the decreasing supermartingale coupling $\hat{\mathbb{P}}^{\mu_t,\mu_{t+\epsilon}}$, $\mu|_{[x_1^\epsilon(t),r_t)}$ is mapped to $\nu|_{[y_1^\epsilon(t),r_{t+\epsilon})}$ in a martingale way, where $y_1^\epsilon(t) = y_1^{\mu_t,\mu_{t+\epsilon}}$ (see (B.51)). In particular, the pair $(x_1^\epsilon(t), y_1^\epsilon(t))$ is uniquely determined by the mass and mean preservation condition

$$\int_{x_1^\epsilon(t)}^{r_t} z^i \mu_t(dz) = \int_{y_1^\epsilon(t)}^{r_{t+\epsilon}} z^i \mu_{t+\epsilon}(dz), \quad i = 0,1. \tag{17}$$

Direct computation leads to

$$\frac{e^t - x_1^\epsilon(t)}{e^t + e^{2t}} = \frac{e^{t+\epsilon} - y_1^\epsilon(t)}{e^{t+\epsilon} + e^{2(t+\epsilon)}}, \quad \frac{e^{2t} - (x_1^\epsilon(t))^2}{e^t + e^{2t}} = \frac{e^{2(t+\epsilon)} - (y_1^\epsilon(t))^2}{e^{t+\epsilon} + e^{2(t+\epsilon)}}.$$

Solving the above equations gives

$$x_1^\epsilon(t) = \frac{e^t(e^{2(t+\epsilon)} - e^{t+\epsilon} + e^t) + e^{2t}(e^t - 2e^{t+\epsilon})}{e^{t+\epsilon} + e^{2(t+\epsilon)} - e^t - e^{2t}},$$

$$y_1^\epsilon(t) = x_1^\epsilon(t) - e^{t+\epsilon} + e^t.$$

By letting $\epsilon \downarrow 0$, direct calculation (using L'Hôpital's rule) gives that $x_1(t) = \frac{-e^t}{1+2e^t}$ (note that $\lim_{\epsilon\downarrow 0} y_1^\epsilon(t) = x_1(t)$), which concludes the proof. □

Even though not all Assumptions 3.1, 3.3 and 3.7 are satisfied in the case of (14), the following result shows that the statement of Theorem 3.14 remains true.

Proposition 4.2. *If $(\mu_t)_{t\in[0,1]}$ is given by* (14), *then the statement of Theorem* 3.14 *holds, and the corresponding SDE is explicitly given by*

$$X_t = X_0 + \int_0^t \mathbf{1}_{\{X_{s-}>x_1(s)\}} j_u(s, X_{s-})(dN_s - \nu_s ds)$$
$$- \int_0^t \mathbf{1}_{\{X_{s-}\le x_1(s)\}} \tilde{\nu}_s ds,$$

where $(N_s)_{0\le s\le 1}$ is a unit size jump process with predictable compensated process $(\nu_s)_{0\le s\le 1}$ given by $\nu_s := \frac{j_d}{j_u}(s, X_{s-})$, with $j_d(s,x) = \frac{1}{2}\frac{e^s - x}{1+e^s}(1+2e^s)$, $j_u(s,x) = e^s - x$ and $\tilde{\nu}_s := \frac{e^{2s} - x(1+2e^s)}{1+e^s}$.

In addition, if Assumption 2.2 *and the integrability condition* (12) *are satisfied, then the above process is the optimal solution for the primal problem* (4) *and the conclusion of Theorem* 3.15 *holds.*

Proof. Since, for $t \in [0,1]$, we have that $m_t = r_t$, it follows that $\mathbf{1}_{\{x_1(t)<X_{t-}<m_t\}} = \mathbf{1}_{\{X_{t-}>x_1(t)\}}$ a.s. We now determine (j_d, j_u).

For $t \in [0,1)$ and $\epsilon \in (0, 1-t]$, we consider the one-period decreasing supermartingale coupling $\hat{\mathbb{P}}^{\mu_t,\mu_{t+\epsilon}}$, which is supported on the graphs of two functions $T_u^\epsilon(t,\cdot) = T_u^{\mu_t,\mu_{t+\epsilon}}(\cdot)$, $T_d^\epsilon(t,\cdot) = T_d^{\mu_t,\mu_{t+\epsilon}}(\cdot)$, see Appendix B.1. On $(x_1^\epsilon(t), m^\epsilon(t) = r_t)$, $(T_d^\epsilon(t,\cdot), T_u^\epsilon(t,\cdot))$ can be determined from the mass and mean preservation condition

$$\int_x^{T_u^\epsilon(t,x)} z^i \mu_t(dz) = \int_{T_d^\epsilon(t,x)}^{T_u^\epsilon(t,x)} z^i \mu_{t+\epsilon}(dz), \quad i = 0, 1.$$

Note that since $T_u^\epsilon(t,x) \ge m^\epsilon(t) = r_t$ for $x \le r_t$, we have that $\int_x^{T_u^\epsilon(t,x)} z^i \mu_t(dz) = \int_x^{r_t} z^i \mu_t(dz)$ for $i = 0, 1$. Then direct calculation gives that

$$\frac{e^t - x}{e^t + e^{2t}} = \frac{T_u^\epsilon(t,x) - T_d^\epsilon(t,x)}{e^{t+\epsilon} + e^{2(t+\epsilon)}},$$
$$T_u^\epsilon(t,x) = x + e^t - T_d^\epsilon(t,x), \quad x \in (x_1^\epsilon(t), e^t).$$

It follows that

$$x - T_d^\epsilon(t,x) = \frac{1}{2}\frac{e^t - x}{e^t + e^{2t}}\left[e^{t+\epsilon} - e^t + e^{2(t+\epsilon)} - e^{2t}\right], \quad x \in (x_1^\epsilon(t), e^t).$$

This further leads to

$$\begin{aligned} j_d(t,x) &:= \lim_{\epsilon\downarrow 0} j_d^\epsilon(t,x) := \lim_{\epsilon\downarrow 0}\frac{x - T_d^\epsilon(t,x)}{\epsilon} \\ &= \frac{1}{2}\frac{e^t - x}{1+e^t}(1+2e^t), \quad x \in (x_1(t), e^t), \\ j_u(t,x) &:= \lim_{\epsilon\downarrow 0}(T_u^\epsilon(t,x) - x) = e^t - x, \quad x \in (x_1(t), e^t). \end{aligned}$$

Then also

$$\frac{j_d}{j_u}(t,x) = \frac{1}{2}\frac{1+2e^t}{1+e^t}, \quad x \in (x_1(t), e^t).$$

If we define T_u by $T_u(t,x) := \lim_{\epsilon\downarrow 0} T_u^\epsilon(t,x)$, then $T_u(t,x) = e^t$ for $x \in (x_1(t), e^t)$, which is clearly non-decreasing and continuous.

The definition of j_d on $[0,1) \times (\ell_t, x_1(t)]$ remains the same:

$$j_d(t,x) := \lim_{\epsilon\downarrow 0} j_d^\epsilon(t,x) = \lim_{\epsilon\downarrow 0}\frac{x - T_d^\epsilon(t,x)}{\epsilon}, \quad x \in (-e^{2t}, x_1(t)].$$

The explicit form is recovered by using the fact that $T_d^\epsilon(t,x) = F^{-1}(t+\epsilon, F(t,x))$ for $x \le x_1^\epsilon(t)$. Direct computation gives that

$$j_d(t,x) = \frac{e^{2t} - x(1+2e^t)}{1+e^t}, \quad x \in (-e^{2t}, x_1(t)].$$

It follows that the statements of Lemmas 3.11, 3.12 and 3.13(ii) (and consequently Theorem 3.14) hold, which proves the first part of the present proposition.

The second claim is established by following the arguments of the proof of Theorem 3.15. In particular, we need continuity of T_u, Lemmas 3.13(ii) and 3.16. However, these results (by direct computation) also hold in the present setting, □

Increasing supermartingale coupling: Let $(\mu_t)_{t\in[0,1]}$ be as in (14). Fix $t \in [0,1)$ and $\epsilon \in (0, 1-t]$, and denote by $\bar{\mathbb{P}}^{\mu_t,\mu_{t+\epsilon}}$ the increasing supermartingale coupling of μ_t and $\mu_{t+\epsilon}$ (see Nutz and Stebegg [57] and Bayraktar *et al.* [4]).

The main difference between $\bar{\mathbb{P}}^{\mu_t,\mu_{t+\epsilon}}$ and the decreasing supermartingale coupling $\hat{\mathbb{P}}^{\mu_t,\mu_{t+\epsilon}}$ is that $\bar{\mathbb{P}}^{\mu_t,\mu_{t+\epsilon}}$ is constructed by working from left to right and mapping $\mu_t|_{(-\infty,x]}$ to the shadow measure $S^{\mu_{t+\epsilon}}(\mu_t|_{(-\infty,x]})$, for each $x\in\mathbb{R}$. The construction of $\hat{\mathbb{P}}^{\mu_t,\mu_{t+\epsilon}}$ is similar but works from right to left and thus considers the measures $(\mu_t|_{[x,\infty)})_{x\in\mathbb{R}}$ and their corresponding 'shadows' in $\mu_{t+\epsilon}$.

The main feature of $\bar{\mathbb{P}}^{\mu_t,\mu_{t+\epsilon}}$ is that there exists the unique point $x_1^\epsilon(t)\in(\ell_t,r_t)$ such that $\bar{\mathbb{P}}^{\mu_t,\mu_{t+\epsilon}}$ is a martingale on $(-\infty,x_1^\epsilon(t)]\times\mathbb{R}$ and strict supermartingale elsewhere. In particular,

- On $(-\infty,x_1^\epsilon(t)]\times\mathbb{R}$, $\bar{\mathbb{P}}^{\mu_t,\mu_{t+\epsilon}}$ coincides with the left-curtain martingale coupling of $\mu_t|_{(-\infty,x_1^\epsilon(t)]}$ and $S^{\mu_{t+\epsilon}}(\mu_t|_{(-\infty,x_1^\epsilon(t)]})$.
- The support of $(\mu_t-\mu_t|_{(-\infty,x_1^\epsilon(t)]})$ is strictly to the right of the support of $(\mu_{t+\epsilon}-S^{\mu_{t+\epsilon}}(\mu_t|_{(-\infty,x_1^\epsilon(t)]}))$.
- On $(x_1^\epsilon(t),\infty)\times\mathbb{R}$, $\bar{\mathbb{P}}^{\mu_t,\mu_{t+\epsilon}}$ coincides with the *antitone* coupling of $(\mu_t-\mu_t|_{(-\infty,x_1^\epsilon(t)]})$ and $(\mu_{t+\epsilon}-S^{\mu_{t+\epsilon}}(\mu_t|_{(-\infty,x_1^\epsilon(t)]}))$.

See Bayraktar *et al.* [4] for details. (In fact, these properties hold for any measures $\mu\le_{cd}\nu$ and not necessarily $\mu_t\le_{cd}\mu_{t+\epsilon}$ as in (14).) The left-curtain martingale coupling was introduced by Beiglböck and Juillet [12] (it is the symmetric counterpart of the right-curtain martingale coupling, see Appendix A.2). The aforementioned antitone coupling of two measures η,χ (with $\eta(\mathbb{R})=\chi(\mathbb{R})$ and atom-less η) is denoted by $\pi^{a,\eta,\chi}$ and given by

$$\pi^{a,\eta,\chi}(dx,dy)=\eta(dx)\delta_{F_\chi^{-1}(\chi(\mathbb{R})-F_\eta(x))}(dy).$$

Note that $\pi^{a,\eta,\chi}$ is supported on a graph of a decreasing function $x\mapsto F_\chi^{-1}(\chi(\mathbb{R})-F_\eta(x))$.

Lemma 4.3. *If $(\mu_t)_{t\in[0,1]}$ is defined by (14), then the phase transition $x_1^\epsilon(t)$ is given by*

$$x_1^\epsilon(t)=\frac{e^{3t}(1-e^{2\epsilon})+e^t(2e^\epsilon+e^t(1+e^\epsilon))}{1+e^\epsilon+e^t(1+e^{2\epsilon})},\qquad t\in[0,1),\quad \epsilon\in(0,1-t]. \tag{18}$$

In particular, under $\bar{\mathbb{P}}^{\mu_t,\mu_{t+\epsilon}}$, $\mu_t|_{(\ell_t,x_1^\epsilon(t)]}$ *is mapped to* $\mu_{t+\epsilon}|_{[y_1^\epsilon(t),r_t)}$ *in a martingale way, where*

$$y_1^\epsilon(t) = x_1^\epsilon(t) - e^{t+\epsilon} - e^{2t},$$

while $\mu_t|_{(x_1^\epsilon(t),\infty)})$ *is mapped to* $\mu_{t+\epsilon}|_{(-\infty,y_1^\epsilon(t))}$ *in a strict supermartingale way.*

Furthermore, the limit $x_1(t) := \lim_{\epsilon\downarrow 0} x_1^\epsilon(t)$ *exists and is given by*

$$x_1(t) = e^t = r_t, \quad t \in [0,1]. \tag{19}$$

Proof. To determine $x_1^\epsilon(t) \in (\ell_t, r_t)$, we use the fact that $x_1^\epsilon(t)$ is the largest $x \in (\ell_t, r_t)$ for which $\mu_t|_{(\ell_t,x]} \leq_c S^{\mu_{t+\epsilon}}(\mu_t|_{(\ell_t,x]})$ and that $r_{S^{\mu_{t+\epsilon}}(\mu_t|_{(\ell_t,x_1^\epsilon(t)]})} = \sup\{k \in supp(S^{\mu_{t+\epsilon}}(\mu_t|_{(\ell_t,x_1^\epsilon(t)]}))\} = r_t$. Using that $(\mu_t)_{t\in[0,1]}$ are given by (14) and the properties of the shadow measures, it follows that $\mu_t|_{(\ell_t,x_1^\epsilon(t)]} \leq_c S^{\mu_{t+\epsilon}}(\mu_t|_{(\ell_t,x_1^\epsilon(t)]}) = \mu_{t+\epsilon}|_{[y_1^\epsilon(t),r_{t+\epsilon})}$ for some (unique) $y_1^\epsilon(t) \in (\ell_{t+\epsilon}, \ell_t)$. In particular, the pair $(x_1^\epsilon(t), y_1^\epsilon(t))$ is uniquely characterized by the mass and mean preservation condition

$$\int_{\ell_t}^{x_1^\epsilon(t)} z^i \mu_t(dz) = \int_{y_1^\epsilon(t)}^{r_{t+\epsilon}} z^i \mu_{t+\epsilon}(dz), \quad i = 0, 1. \tag{20}$$

Direct computation leads to

$$\frac{x_1^\epsilon(t) + e^{2t}}{e^t + e^{2t}} = \frac{e^{t+\epsilon} - y_1^\epsilon(t)}{e^{t+\epsilon} + e^{2(t+\epsilon)}}, \quad \frac{(x_1^\epsilon(t))^2 - e^{4t}}{e^t + e^{2t}} = \frac{e^{2(t+\epsilon)} - (y_1^\epsilon(t))^2}{e^{t+\epsilon} + e^{2(t+\epsilon)}}.$$

Solving the above equations gives

$$x_1^\epsilon(t) = \frac{e^{3t}(1 - e^{2\epsilon}) + e^t(2e^\epsilon + e^t(1 + e^\epsilon))}{1 + e^\epsilon + e^t(1 + e^{2\epsilon})}, \quad y_1^\epsilon(t) = x_1^\epsilon(t) - e^{t+\epsilon} - e^{2t}.$$

Letting $\epsilon \downarrow 0$ gives that $x_1(t) = e^t$ and $y_1^\epsilon(t) = -e^{2t}$, which concludes the proof. □

It is well known (see Henry-Labordre̊ and Touzi [42]) that the left-curtain martingale coupling (of two measures in convex order) is supported on the graphs of two functions that can be computed explicitly. The following gives an explicit representation of $\bar{\mathbb{P}}^{\mu_t,\mu_{t+\epsilon}}$ in terms of the supporting functions:

Lemma 4.4. *Let* $(\mu_t)_{t\in[0,1]}$ *be given by* (14). *Fix* $t \in [0,1)$ *and* $\epsilon(0, 1-t]$. *Let* $x_1^\epsilon(t)$ *be as in Lemma* 4.3.

Then $\bar{\mathbb{P}}^{\mu_t,\mu_{t+\epsilon}}$ is given by

$$\bar{\mathbb{P}}^{\mu_t,\mu_{t+\epsilon}}(dx,dy) = \mu(dx)\mathbf{1}_{[x_1^\epsilon(t),e^t)}(x)\delta_{\bar{T}_d^\epsilon(t,x)}(dy) + \mu(dx)\mathbf{1}_{(-e^{2t},x_1^\epsilon(t))}\left\{\frac{\bar{T}_u^\epsilon(t,x)-x}{\bar{T}_u^\epsilon(t,x)-\bar{T}_d^\epsilon(t,x)}\delta_{\bar{T}_d^\epsilon(t,x)}(dy) + \frac{x-\bar{T}_d^\epsilon(t,x)}{\bar{T}_u^\epsilon(t,x)-\bar{T}_d^\epsilon(t,x)}\delta_{\bar{T}_u(x)}(dy)\right\},$$

where

$$T_u^\epsilon(t,x) = \frac{1}{2}\left\{\frac{e^\epsilon(1+e^{t+\epsilon})(x+e^{2t})}{1+e^t} + x - e^{2t}\right\}, \quad x \in (-e^{2t}, x_1^\epsilon(t)),$$

$$T_d^\epsilon(t,x) = x - e^{2t} - T_u^\epsilon(t,x), \quad x \in (-e^{2t}, x_1^\epsilon(t)),$$

$$T_d^\epsilon(t,x) = \left(e^{t+\epsilon} + e^{2(t+\epsilon)}\right)\left(1 - \frac{x+e^{2t}}{e^t+e^{2t}}\right) - e^{2t} \quad x \in [x_1^\epsilon(t), e^t).$$

Proof. Since, on $(\ell_t, x_1^\epsilon(t)) \times (y_1^\epsilon(t), r_{t+\epsilon})$, $\bar{\mathbb{P}}^{\mu_t,\mu_{t+\epsilon}}$ coincides with the left-curtain martingale coupling of $\mu_t|_{(\ell_t,x_1^\epsilon(t))}$ and $\mu_{t+\epsilon}|_{(y_1^\epsilon(t),r_{t+\epsilon})}$, the supporting functions $(T_d^\epsilon(t,\cdot), T_u^\epsilon(t,\cdot))$ can be determined from the mass and mean preservation condition

$$\int_{-e^{2t}}^{x} z^i \mu_t(dz) = \int_{T_d^\epsilon(t,x)}^{T_u^\epsilon(t,x)} z^i \mu_{t+\epsilon}(dz), \quad i = 0, 1.$$

The direct computation gives that

$$\frac{x+e^{2t}}{e^t+e^{2t}} = \frac{T_u^\epsilon(t,x) - T_d^\epsilon(t,x)}{e^{t+\epsilon}+e^{2(t+\epsilon)}},$$

$$T_d^\epsilon(t,x) = x - e^{2t} - T_u^\epsilon(t,x), \quad x \in (-e^{2t}, x_1^\epsilon(t)).$$

Solving for $T_u^\epsilon(t,x)$ (which is easy) gives the required representations of the supporting functions on $(-e^{2t}, x_1^\epsilon(t))$.

To obtain $T_d^\epsilon(t,\cdot)$ on $[x_1^\epsilon(t), r_t)$, we use that $\bar{\mathbb{P}}^{\mu_t,\mu_{t+\epsilon}}$ coincides with the antitone coupling $\pi^{a,\mu_t|_{[x_1^\epsilon(t),r_t)},\mu_{t+\epsilon}|_{(\ell_{t+\epsilon},y_1^\epsilon(t)]}}$ of $\mu_t|_{[x_1^\epsilon(t),r_t)}$ and $\mu_{t+\epsilon}|_{(\ell_{t+\epsilon},y_1^\epsilon(t),r_{t+\epsilon}]}$. It follows that

$$T_d^\epsilon(t,x) = F^{-1}(t+\epsilon, 1 - F(t,x)), \quad x \in [x_1^\epsilon(t), r_t),$$

with $F(t,x) = (x+e^{2t})/(e^t+e^{2t})$, which proves the claim. □

Now define $J_d^\epsilon(t,x) = x - T_d^\epsilon(t,x)$ for $x \in (\ell_t, r_t)$ and $J_u^\epsilon(t,x) = T_u^\epsilon(t,x) - x$ for $x \in (\ell_t, x_1^\epsilon(t))$. Then direct computation gives that

$$j_d(t,x) := \lim_{\epsilon \downarrow 0} J_d^\epsilon(t,x) = e^{2t} + \lim_{\epsilon \downarrow 0} T_u^\epsilon(t,x) = e^{2t} + x,$$
$$x \in (\ell_t = -e^{2t}, x_1(t) = r_t = e^t) \tag{21}$$

and

$$j_u(t,x) := \lim_{\epsilon \downarrow 0} \frac{J_u^\epsilon(t,x)}{\epsilon} = \frac{1+2e^{2t}}{2} \frac{x+e^{2t}}{1+e^t}, \quad x \in (-e^{2t}, e^t). \tag{22}$$

Proposition 4.5. *Let* $(\mu_t)_{t\in[0,1]}$ *be as in* (14). *For each* $n \geq 1$, *let* $\mathbb{P}^n := \mathbb{P}^{*,n} \circ (X^{*,n})^{-1}$, *where* $\mathbb{P}^{*,n}$ *is the* n*-period supermartingale coupling (w.r.t. partition* π_n*) obtained through the Markovian iteration of one-period increasing supermartingale couplings* $\overline{\mathbb{P}}^{\mu_{t_k^n}, \mu_{t_{k+1}^n}}$. *(Here* $X^{*,n}$ *is the piece-wise constant canonical process, see Section* 3.)

Then the sequence $(\mathbb{P}^n)_{n\geq 1}$ *is tight w.r.t. the Skorokhod topology on* Ω.

Moreover, any accumulation point of $(\mathbb{P}^n)_{n\geq 1}$, *denoted by* $\mathbb{P}^0$, *is the law of the following SDE*:

$$X_t = X_0 - \int_0^t j_d(t, X_{s-})(dN_s - \nu_s ds) - \sum_{s\leq t} \mathbf{1}_{\{X_{s-}=e^s\}}(e^s + e^{2s}),$$

where $(N_s)_{0\leq s\leq 1}$ *is a unit size jump process, with predictable compensator* $\nu_s := \frac{j_u}{j_d}(s, X_{s-})$ *with* j_d, j_u *as in* (21), (22).

Finally, if Assumption 2.2 *holds with* $c_{xyy} > 0$ *and* $c_{xy} < 0$, *then* $\mathbb{P}^0$ *solves* $\mathbf{P}_\infty(\mu)$ *and the strong duality* $\mathbf{P}_\infty(\mu) = \mathbf{D}_\infty(\mu)$ *holds.*

Proof. The tightness of $(\mathbb{P}^n)_{n\geq 1}$ is guaranteed by Proposition 3.4.

The proof of the SDE characterization of $\mathbb{P}^0$ and its optimality use similar arguments as in Theorems 3.14 and 3.15. Some notable difference arises due to the fact that the construction is based on the one-period increasing supermartingale coupling (and not on he decreasing one). For example, the drift part of X is determined by j_u (and thus by the upward transitions of the increasing supermartingale coupling), while the jumps of X are governed by j_d (and thus arise from the downward transitions of the increasing coupling). In particular, the terms α_u, α_d (which are defined as in the proof of Theorem 3.14) will determine the integral part of the SDE. This does not introduce new arguments and thus we omit the details.

In order to explain the summation term that appears in the SDE, we turn to the term $\alpha_{\tilde{d}}$ (see the proof of Theorem 3.14):

$$\alpha_{\tilde{d}} = \mathbb{E}^{\mathbb{P}^n}_{t^n_k}[\{\varphi(X_{t^n_k} - J^{\epsilon^n_k}_d(t^n_k, X_{t^n_k})) - \varphi(X_{t^n_k})\}\mathbf{1}_{\{x^{\epsilon^n_k}_1(t^n_k)\le X_{t^n_k}<e^{t^n_k}\}}],$$

where $\epsilon^n_k = t^n_{k+1} - t^n_k$. Note that in the present setting, $x^\epsilon_1(t) \to e^t$, and thus in the limit, the supermartingale region $[x^\epsilon_1(t), r_t)$ becomes a single point. Using this together with the fact that $J^\epsilon_d(t,x) \to e^{2t}+x$, we obtain that

$$\alpha_{\tilde{d}} = \mathbb{E}^{\mathbb{P}^n}_{t^n_k}\left[\sum_{t^n_k\le s\le t^n_{k+1}} [\varphi(-e^{2s}) - \varphi(e^s)]\,\mathbf{1}_{\{X_s=e^s\}}\right] + O(\epsilon^n_k(\epsilon^n_k \vee \rho_1(\epsilon^n_k))),$$

which, in the limit, determines the summation term $\sum_{s\le t}\mathbf{1}_{\{X_{s-}=e^s\}}$ $(e^s + e^{2s})$ of the SDE.

For the optimality, the arguments are similar to those of Theorem 3.15. The candidate optimal dual strategies should be redefined to reflect the fact that we are working with the increasing supermartingale coupling (or the left-curtain martingale coupling in the martingale region). In the limit, we have that X is a martingale on (ℓ_t, r_t), $t \in [0,1]$, and has a strict supermartingale transition (a jump down to the lower boundary ℓ_t) only if it escapes to the upper boundary r_t at time t. Hence the dual strategies (see Section 3.3) in fact can be defined as in Henry-Labordère *et al.* [41, Eq. (3.9), (3.10), (3.11)]:

$$\partial_x h^*(t,x) = \tfrac{c_x(x,x)-c_x(x,T_d(t,x))}{j_d(t,x)}, \quad x \in (\ell_t, r_t),$$
$$\lim_{x\uparrow x_1(t)=e^t} h^*(t,x) = 0 = h^*(t,e^t).$$

We remark that from the above definition, for all $t \in [0,1]$, $x \mapsto h^*(t,x)$ is continuous. In addition, ψ^* is defined, up to a constant, by

$$\partial_x\psi^*(t,x) := -h^*(t,x), \quad (t,x) \in E = \{(t,x) : t \in [0,1], x \in (l_t, r_t)\}.$$

The limiting arguments that prove optimality of (h^*, ψ^*) are as in the decreasing case, and thus we omit the details. □

4.2. *Bachelier Dynamics with Negative Drift*

In this section, we consider the marginals $(\mu_t)_{t\in(0,1]}$ such that each μ_t has the density

$$f(t,x) = \frac{1}{\sqrt{2\pi t}} e^{-\frac{(x+t)^2}{2t}}, \quad t \in (0,1]. \tag{23}$$

Note that Assumption 3.1 is almost satisfied; indeed μ_0 is left undefined. We could overcome this by introducing $\delta > 0$ and then working with $t \in [\delta, 1]$. Alternatively, we could specify $\tilde{\mu}_t$ to have density $f(t+\delta, \cdot)$ for each $t \in [0,1]$. For the convenience of notation, we choose to work on $(0,1]$.

Fix $t \in (0,1)$ and $\epsilon \in (0, 1-t]$. Since $m_\epsilon(t)$ and $m^\epsilon(t)$, as in Assumption 3.1, correspond to two unique crossing points of the densities $f(t,\cdot), f(t+\epsilon,\cdot)$, by direct computation, one easily obtains that

$$m^2 = \frac{t(t+\epsilon)}{\epsilon} \ln \frac{t+\epsilon}{t} + (t+\epsilon)t, \quad m \in \{m_\epsilon(t), m^\epsilon(t)\}.$$

On the other hand, straightforward calculations show that m_t (resp., $\tilde{m}_t$), the minimizer (resp., maximizer) of $\partial_t F(t,\cdot)$, is given by $m_t = -\tilde{m}_t = \sqrt{t(t+1)}$. Note that $m_t = \lim_{\epsilon\downarrow 0} m^\epsilon(t), \tilde{m}_t = \lim_{\epsilon\downarrow 0} m_\epsilon(t)$, for each $t \in (0,1)$. It follows that Assumption 3.3 holds.

Our next goal is to show that $(\mu_t)_{t\in(0,1]}$ also satisfies Assumption 3.7. Since, $r_t = \infty$ for all $t \in (0,1]$, Assumption 3.7(ii) is immediate. For Assumption 3.7 (iii), simple calculations lead to

$$\partial_{tx} f(t,x) = t^{-\frac{5}{2}} \Phi'\left(\frac{x+t}{\sqrt{t}}\right) \left[x + t + \frac{1}{2}(t-x)\left(\frac{(x+t)^2}{t} - 1\right)\right],$$

where $\Phi(x) := \int_{-\infty}^{x} \frac{1}{\sqrt{2\pi}} e^{-\frac{t^2}{2}} dt$ is the c.d.f. of the standard normal random variable. Now using that $m_t = \sqrt{t(t+1)}$, we consequently have that $\partial_{tx} f(t, m_t) = t^{-2}\sqrt{t+1}\Phi'(\sqrt{t} + \sqrt{t+1}) > 0$.

It is left to verify Assumption 3.7(i). Let $x_1^\epsilon(t)$ be the unique phase transition point of the decreasing supermartingale coupling of μ_t and $\mu_{t+\epsilon}$, see Section B.1.

Lemma 4.6. *Let $(\mu_t)_{t\in(0,1]}$ be specified by* (23). *Then, $x_1^\epsilon(t)$ is uniquely determined by the equation*

$$1-\Phi\left(\frac{x_1^\epsilon(t)+t}{\sqrt{t}}\right)=\frac{1}{\epsilon}(\sqrt{t+\epsilon}-\sqrt{t})\Phi'\left(\frac{x_1^\epsilon(t)+t}{\sqrt{t}}\right),$$

$$t\in(0,1),\ \epsilon\in(0,t-1].$$

Furthermore, the limit $x_1(t) := \lim_{\epsilon\downarrow 0} x_1^\epsilon(t)$ exists and is uniquely determined by the equation

$$2\sqrt{t}\left(1-\Phi\left(\frac{x_1(t)+t}{\sqrt{t}}\right)\right)=\Phi'\left(\frac{x_1(t)+t}{\sqrt{t}}\right). \tag{24}$$

The proof of Lemma 4.6 requires the following auxiliary result:

Lemma 4.7. *For each $t\in(0,1]$, the equation $2\sqrt{t}(1-\Phi(x))=\Phi'(x)$ admits a unique (real-valued) solution $x_t^*\in(-\infty,2\sqrt{t})$.*

Proof. The proof is an application of the intermediate value theorem. Let us consider the function $F(x) := 2\sqrt{t}(1-\Phi(x))-\Phi'(x)$. First, as $F'(x)=\Phi'(x)(x-2\sqrt{t})$, it is clear that $x\mapsto F(x)$ is continuous on $\mathbb{R}$, decreasing on $(-\infty,2\sqrt{t}]$, increasing on $[2\sqrt{t},\infty)$. Furthermore, $\lim_{x\to-\infty}F(x)=2\sqrt{t}>0$ and $\lim_{x\to\infty}F(x)=0$. It follows that the equation $F(x)=0$ admits a unique solution in the interval $(-\infty,2\sqrt{t})$. □

Proof of Lemma 4.6. To determine $x_1^\epsilon(t)\in(\ell_t,r_t)$, we use the fact that under the decreasing supermartingale coupling $\hat{\mathbb{P}}^{\mu_t,\mu_{t+\epsilon}}$, $\mu|_{[x_1^\epsilon(t),r_t)}$ is mapped to $\nu|_{[y_1^\epsilon(t),r_{t+\epsilon})}$ in a martingale way, where $y_1^\epsilon(t)=y_1^{\mu_t,\mu_{t+\epsilon}}$ (see (B.51)). In particular, the pair $(x_1^\epsilon(t),y_1^\epsilon(t))$ is uniquely determined by the mass and mean preservation condition

$$\int_{x_1^\epsilon(t)}^{r_t=\infty} z^i\mu_t(dz)=\int_{y_1^\epsilon(t)}^{r_{t+\epsilon}=\infty} z^i\mu_{t+\epsilon}(dz),\quad i=0,1. \tag{25}$$

Note that due to the dispersion assumption (see Assumption 3.1), we must have that $y_1^\epsilon(t)\le x_1^\epsilon(t)<m^\epsilon(t)$.

Now apply the change of variables: $\hat{x}_1^\epsilon(t) = \frac{x_1^\epsilon(t)+t}{\sqrt{t}}$, $\hat{y}_1^\epsilon(t) = \frac{y_1^\epsilon(t)+t+\epsilon}{\sqrt{t+\epsilon}}$. Then (25) with $i=0$ reads

$$\Phi(\hat{x}_1^\epsilon(t)) = \Phi(\hat{y}_1^\epsilon(t)). \tag{26}$$

For (25) with $i=1$, we first rewrite it as

$$\int_{x_1^\epsilon(t)}^\infty (x+t) f(t,x)dx + \epsilon \int_{x_1^\epsilon(t)}^\infty f(t,x)dx = \int_{y_1^\epsilon(t)}^\infty (x+t+\epsilon) f(t+\epsilon, x)dx,$$

by adding $(t+\epsilon)$ times Equation (25) with $i=0$ on both sides. Then direct calculation leads to

$$\sqrt{t}\Phi'(\hat{x}_1^\epsilon(t)) + \epsilon(1-\Phi(\hat{x}_1^\epsilon(t))) = \sqrt{t+\epsilon}\Phi'(\hat{y}_1^\epsilon(t)). \tag{27}$$

From (26), we get $\hat{x}_1^\epsilon(t) = \hat{y}_1^\epsilon(t)$ or equivalently $\frac{x_1^\epsilon(t)+t}{\sqrt{t}} = \frac{y_1^\epsilon(t)+t+\epsilon}{\sqrt{t+\epsilon}}$. By plugging this relation $\hat{x}_1^\epsilon(t) = \hat{x}_2^\epsilon(t)$ into (27), we obtain that

$$1-\Phi(\hat{x}_1^\epsilon(t)) = \frac{1}{\epsilon}(\sqrt{t+\epsilon}-\sqrt{t})\Phi'(\hat{x}_1^\epsilon(t)), \tag{28}$$

which is precisely the required algebraic equation that characterizes $x_1^\epsilon(t)$.

We now deal with the limit $x_1(t) := \lim_{\epsilon\downarrow 0} x_1^\epsilon(t)$.

Recall that $\epsilon_0 := \epsilon_1 \wedge \epsilon_2$, where ϵ_1, ϵ_2 are as in Assumptions 3.1 and 3.3, respectively.

For each (small) $\delta > 0$, define $F = F^\delta : \mathbb{R}^3 \to \mathbb{R}$ on $\{(t,\epsilon) : 0 \le \epsilon \le \epsilon_0,\ \delta \le t \le 1-\epsilon\} \times \mathbb{R}$ by

$$F(t,\epsilon,x) := (1-\Phi(x)) - \frac{\sqrt{t+\epsilon}-\sqrt{t}}{\epsilon}\frac{1}{\sqrt{2\pi}}e^{-\frac{x^2}{2}},$$
$$(t,\epsilon,x) \in [\delta, 1-\epsilon] \times (0,\epsilon_0] \times \mathbb{R} \tag{29}$$

and

$$F(t,0,x) := (1-\Phi(x)) - \frac{1}{2\sqrt{t}}\frac{1}{\sqrt{2\pi}}e^{-\frac{x^2}{2}}, \quad (t,x) \in [\delta,1] \times \mathbb{R}. \tag{30}$$

Note that, by (28), $F(t,\epsilon,\hat{x}_1^\epsilon(t)) = 0$ for all $\epsilon \in (0,\epsilon_0]$ and $t \in [\delta, 1-\epsilon]$.

Using Lemma 4.7, we define $\hat{x}_1^0(t)$, for all $t \in (0,1]$, to be the unique solution to $F(t,0,x) = 0$. Then $x_1^0(t)$ is defined as $x_1^0(t) := \sqrt{t}\hat{x}_1^0(t) - t$, for each $t \in (0,1]$. Note that $x_1^0(\cdot)$ is continuous if and only if $\hat{x}_1^0(\cdot)$ is. Now since $\hat{x}_1^0(t)$ uniquely satisfies $F(t,0,x) = 0$, we immediately have that $\lim_{\epsilon\downarrow 0}\hat{x}_1^\epsilon(t)$ exists, for all $t\in(0,1]$, and uniquely satisfies (24).

Lemma 4.8. *For $\epsilon\in[0,\epsilon_0]$ and $t\in(0,1]$, let $x_1^\epsilon(t)$ be given by Lemma 4.6 with $x_1^0(t):=x_1(t)=\lim_{\epsilon\downarrow 0}x_1^\epsilon(t)$.*

Then, for each (small) $\delta>0$, the map $(t,\epsilon)\mapsto x_1^\epsilon(t)$ is continuous on $\{(t,\epsilon):0\le\epsilon\le\epsilon_0,\ \delta\le t\le 1-\epsilon\}\times\mathbb{R}$.

Proof. Let F be defined as in (29) and (30). To prove the continuity of $(t,\epsilon)\mapsto x_1^\epsilon(t):=\sqrt{t}\hat{x}_1^\epsilon(t)-t$, we will use the implicit function theorem and show that $(t,\epsilon)\mapsto\hat{x}_1^\epsilon(t)$ is continuous, where $F(t,\epsilon,\hat{x}_1^\epsilon(t))=0$.

We claim that $(t,\epsilon,x)\mapsto F(t,\epsilon,x)$ is continuously differentiable.

First, for $0<\epsilon\le\epsilon_0$, we have that

$$\frac{\partial F}{\partial\epsilon}(t,\epsilon,x)=-\frac{1}{\sqrt{2\pi}}e^{-\frac{x^2}{2}}\frac{\frac{1}{2}(t+\epsilon)^{-\frac{1}{2}}\epsilon-(\sqrt{t+\epsilon}-\sqrt{t})}{\epsilon^2},$$

and it follows that $\lim_{\epsilon\to 0}\frac{\partial F}{\partial\epsilon}(t,\epsilon,x)=-\Phi'(x)\frac{1}{4}t^{-\frac{3}{2}}$. On the other hand,

$$\begin{aligned}\frac{\partial F}{\partial\epsilon}(t,0,x)&=\lim_{\epsilon\to 0}\frac{F(t,\epsilon,x)-F(t,0,x)}{\epsilon}\\&=\lim_{\epsilon\to 0}-\frac{1}{\sqrt{2\pi}}e^{-\frac{x^2}{2}}\frac{\frac{1}{2}t^{-\frac{1}{2}}\epsilon-(\sqrt{t+\epsilon}-\sqrt{t})}{\epsilon^2}=-\Phi'(x)\frac{1}{4}t^{-\frac{3}{2}},\end{aligned}$$

and hence $\frac{\partial F}{\partial\epsilon}$ is continuous. The continuities of $\frac{\partial F}{\partial t}$ and $\frac{\partial F}{\partial x}$ follow similarly by the direct computations.

Now we check that $\frac{\partial F}{\partial x}(t,\epsilon,x)|_{F(t,\epsilon,x)=0}\neq 0$. For $\epsilon\in[0,\epsilon_0]$, direct calculations show that

$$\frac{\partial F}{\partial x}(t,\epsilon,x)|_{F(t,\epsilon,x)=0}=\Phi'(x)\left[x\frac{1-\Phi(x)}{\Phi'(x)}-1\right]<0,$$

where for the inequality we use the fact that $\frac{1-\Phi(x)}{\Phi'(x)}<\frac{1}{x}$ when $x>0$ (for $x\le 0$ the inequality is trivially satisfied).

By the implicit function theorem, we get that $(t,\epsilon)\mapsto\hat{x}_1^\epsilon(t)$ is continuously differentiable on a compact set $\{(t,\epsilon):0\le\epsilon\le\epsilon_0,\ \delta\le t\le 1-\epsilon\}$ and consequently uniformly bounded and continuous. The regularity of $(t,\epsilon)\mapsto x_1^\epsilon(t)$ follows from the regularity of $(t,x)\mapsto\hat{x}_1^\epsilon(t)$. □

Since all the assumption required for Theorems 3.14 and 3.15 hold, we have the following:

Proposition 4.9. *Let $(\mu_t)_{t\in(0,1]}$ be specified by (23) and consider $t \mapsto x_1(t)$ as in Lemma 4.6. Then the SDE as in Theorem 3.14 is explicitly given by*

$$X_t = X_0 + \int_0^t j_u(s, X_{s-})(dN_s - \nu_s ds)\mathbf{1}_{\{x_1(s)<X_{s-}<m_s\}}$$
$$- \int_0^t \mathbf{1}_{\{X_{s-}\le x_1(s)\}} j_d(s, X_{s-})ds,$$

where $m_s = \sqrt{s(s+1)}$, $\nu_s(s, X_{s-}) := \frac{j_d}{j_u}(s, X_{s-})$ with $j_u(t,x) = T_u(t,x) - x$, and $j_d(t,x) = \frac{1}{2\sqrt{t}}(\tilde{T}_u(t,x) - 2\sqrt{t})e^{\frac{\hat{x}^2}{2}-\frac{\tilde{T}_u(t,x)^2}{2}} - \frac{\hat{x}}{2\sqrt{t}} + 1$, for $x \in (x_1(s), m_s)$, and $j_d(s, X_{s-}) := \frac{s-x}{2s}$ for $x \in (\ell_s, x_1(s)]$; here $\hat{x} := \frac{x+t}{\sqrt{t}}$ and $\tilde{T}_u(t,x) := \sqrt{t}T_u(t,x) - t$ is uniquely determined by the equation

$$(\tilde{T}_u(t,x) - \hat{x})(\tilde{T}_u(t,x) - 2\sqrt{t})\Phi'(\tilde{T}_u(t,x)) + 2\sqrt{t}\left(\Phi(\tilde{T}_u(t,x)) - \Phi(\hat{x})\right)$$
$$= \Phi'(\hat{x}) - \Phi'(\tilde{T}_u(t,x)).$$

In addition, if Assumption 2.2(ii) and the integrability condition (12) are satisfied, then the law $\mathbb{P}^0$ of the above process is the optimal solution for the primal problem (4), and the strong duality

$$\mathbb{E}^{\mathbb{P}^0}[C(X_\cdot)] = \mathbf{P}_\infty(\mu) = \mathbf{D}_\infty(\mu)$$

holds.

Proof. As it has been verified that Assumptions 3.1, 3.3 and 3.7 are valid (up to $t = 0$), using Theorems 3.14 and 3.15, we obtain the validity of the SDE and the optimality of $\mathbb{P}^0$. It is left to derive the explicit expressions of the terms T_u, j_u, j_d that define the SDE.

In the supermartingale region, i.e., for $x \in (\ell_t, x_1(t)]$, we have that

$$j_d(t,x) = \frac{1}{f(t,x)}\partial_t F(t,x) = \frac{\sqrt{t}}{\Phi'(\frac{x+t}{\sqrt{t}})}\partial_t \Phi(\frac{x+t}{\sqrt{t}}) = \frac{t-x}{2t}.$$

In the martingale region, i.e., for $x \in (x_1(t), m_t)$, using (8), we have that $T_u(t,x)$ is uniquely determined by

$$\int_x^{T_u(t,x)} (x-\xi)\frac{\partial}{\partial t}\left(\frac{1}{\sqrt{2\pi t}}e^{-\frac{(\xi+t)^2}{2t}}\right) d\xi = 0.$$

By a change of variables $\tilde{T}_u(t,x) := \sqrt{t}T_u(t,x) - t$, we obtain that $\tilde{T}_u(t,x)$ satisfies

$$\begin{aligned}(\tilde{T}_u(t,x) - \hat{x})(\tilde{T}_u(t,x) - 2\sqrt{t})\Phi'(\tilde{T}_u(t,x))\\ + 2\sqrt{t}\left(\Phi(\tilde{T}_u(t,x)) - \Phi(\hat{x})\right) = \Phi'(\hat{x}) - \Phi'(\tilde{T}_u(t,x)).\end{aligned}$$

Finally, for $x \in (x_1(t), m_t)$,

$$\begin{aligned} j_d(t,x) &= \frac{\partial_t F(t,x) - \partial_t F(t, T_u(t,x))}{f(t,x)} \\ &= \frac{1}{2\sqrt{t}}(\tilde{T}_u(t,x) - 2\sqrt{t})e^{\frac{\hat{x}^2}{2} - \frac{\tilde{T}_u(t,x)^2}{2}} - \frac{\hat{x}}{2\sqrt{t}} + 1,\end{aligned}$$

as required. □

Remark 4.10. Let $(\mu_t)_{t\in(0,1]}$ be specified by (23), and for $t \in (0,1)$ and $\epsilon \in (0, 1-t]$, consider the increasing supermartingale coupling of μ_t and $\mu_{t+\epsilon}$. Then there exists the unique threshold $x_1^\epsilon(t)$ such that $(\ell_t, x_1^\epsilon(t)]$ is a martingale region, while $(x_1^\epsilon(t), r_t)$ corresponds to the supermartingale region.

By changing variables $\hat{x}_1^\epsilon(t) = \frac{x_1^\epsilon(t)+t}{\sqrt{t}}$ and using similar arguments as in Lemma 4.6, we have that $x_1^\epsilon(t)$ uniquely solves

$$\epsilon\Phi(\hat{x}_1^\epsilon(t)) = \sqrt{t}\Phi'(\hat{x}_1^\epsilon(t)) + \sqrt{t+\epsilon}\Phi'(-\hat{x}_1^\epsilon(t)).$$

Then letting $\epsilon \downarrow 0$, we have that $\hat{x}_1^\epsilon(t) \to +\infty$ (provided the limit exists). It follows that $x_1^\epsilon(t) \to +\infty$, and therefore one could expect that the supermartingale transitions of the limiting SDE correspond to jumps from ∞ to $-\infty$.

This is in-line with our observations in Proposition 4.5 obtained in the uniform case. In particular, when the increasing supermartingale coupling is used in construction, and in the case of unbounded support of marginals, the convergence results may fail in general. We will consider these issues in our future research.

4.3. *Geometric Brownian Motion with Decreasing Average*

In this section, we consider the marginals $(\mu_t)_{t\in(0,1]}$ such that each μ_t has the density

$$f(t,x) = \frac{1}{x\sqrt{2\pi t}}e^{-\frac{(\ln x+t)^2}{2t}}, \quad t \in (0,1]. \tag{31}$$

Similar to the previous Bachelier case (see Section 4.2), we can introduce $\delta > 0$ and then work with $t \in [\delta, 1]$ (or $t \in [\delta, 1+\delta]$). For the convenience of notation, we shall work on $(0, 1]$.

Assumption 3.1 is clearly satisfied. Fix $t \in (0,1)$ and $\epsilon \in (0, 1-t]$. For $m_\epsilon(t)$ and $m^\epsilon(t)$ (as in Assumption 3.1), direct computation leads to

$$(\ln m)^2 = \frac{t(t+\epsilon)}{\epsilon}\ln\frac{t+\epsilon}{t} + (t+\epsilon)t, \quad m \in \{m_\epsilon(t), m^\epsilon(t)\}.$$

On the other hand, straightforward calculations show that m_t (resp., $\tilde{m}_t$), the minimizer (resp., maximizer) of $\partial_t F(t,\cdot)$, is given by $\ln m_t = -\ln\tilde{m}_t = \sqrt{t(t+1)}$. It follows that Assumption 3.3 is also valid.

We now show that $(\mu_t)_{t\in(0,1]}$ also satisfies Assumption 3.7. First, Assumption 3.7(ii) is immediate, as $r_t = \infty$ for all $t \in (0,1]$. For Assumption 3.7 (iii), simple calculations lead to

$$\partial_{tx} f(t, m_t) = t^{-\frac{3}{2}}\sqrt{t+1}\Phi'(\sqrt{t}+\sqrt{t+1})e^{-2\sqrt{t(t+1)}} > 0.$$

It is left to verify Assumption 3.7(i). Let $x_1^\epsilon(t)$ be the unique phase transition point of the decreasing supermartingale coupling of μ_t and $\mu_{t+\epsilon}$, see Section B.1.

Lemma 4.11. *Let $(\mu_t)_{t\in(0,1]}$ be specified by (31). Then, $x_1^\epsilon(t)$ is uniquely determined by the equation*

$$1 - \Phi\left(\frac{\ln x_1^\epsilon(t)}{\sqrt{t}}\right) = e^{-\frac{1}{2}\epsilon}\left[1 - \Phi\left(\frac{\ln x_1^\epsilon(t) + t}{\sqrt{t}} - \sqrt{t+\epsilon}\right)\right],$$
$$t \in (0,1),\ \epsilon \in (0, t-1].$$

Furthermore, the limit $x_1(t) := \lim_{\epsilon\downarrow 0} x_1^\epsilon(t)$ exists and is uniquely determined by the equation

$$\frac{1}{\sqrt{t}}\Phi'(\frac{\ln x_1(t)}{\sqrt{t}}) = 1 - \Phi(\frac{\ln x_1(t)}{\sqrt{t}}). \tag{32}$$

The proof of Lemma 4.11 requires the following auxiliary result:

Lemma 4.12. *For each* $t \in (0,1]$, *the equation* $\sqrt{t}(1-\Phi(x)) = \Phi'(x)$ *admits the unique (real-valued) solution* $x_t^* \in (-\infty, \sqrt{t})$.

Proof. The proof is similar to Lemma 4.7 and is an application of the intermediate value theorem. Hence we omit the details here. □

Proof of Lemma 4.11. To determine $x_1^\epsilon(t) \in (\ell_t, r_t)$, we use the fact that under the decreasing supermartingale coupling $\hat{\mathbb{P}}^{\mu_t,\mu_{t+\epsilon}}$, $\mu|_{[x_1^\epsilon(t), r_t)}$ is mapped to $\nu|_{[y_1^\epsilon(t), r_{t+\epsilon})}$ in a martingale way, where $y_1^\epsilon(t) = y_1^{\mu_t,\mu_{t+\epsilon}}$ (see (B.51)). In particular, the pair $(x_1^\epsilon(t), y_1^\epsilon(t))$ is uniquely determined by the mass and mean preservation condition

$$\int_{x_1^\epsilon(t)}^{r_t=\infty} z^i \mu_t(dz) = \int_{y_1^\epsilon(t)}^{r_{t+\epsilon}=\infty} z^i \mu_{t+\epsilon}(dz), \quad i = 0, 1. \tag{33}$$

Note that due to the dispersion assumption (see Assumption 3.1), we must have that $y_1^\epsilon(t) \le x_1^\epsilon(t) < m^\epsilon(t)$.

Now apply the change of variables: $\hat{x}_1^\epsilon(t) = \frac{\ln x_1^\epsilon(t)+t}{\sqrt{t}}$, $\hat{y}_1^\epsilon(t) = \frac{\ln y_1^\epsilon(t)+t+\epsilon}{\sqrt{t+\epsilon}}$. Then (33) with $i = 0$ reads

$$\Phi(\hat{x}_1^\epsilon(t)) = \Phi(\hat{y}_1^\epsilon(t)). \tag{34}$$

For (33) with $i = 1$, it is equivalent to

$$\int_{\hat{x}_1^\epsilon(t)}^{+\infty} \frac{1}{\sqrt{2\pi}} e^{-\frac{1}{2}(y-\sqrt{t})^2} dy = e^{-\frac{1}{2}\epsilon} \int_{\hat{y}_1^\epsilon(t)}^{+\infty} \frac{1}{\sqrt{2\pi}} e^{-\frac{1}{2}(y-\sqrt{t+\epsilon})^2} dy,$$

which leads to

$$1 - \Phi(\hat{x}_1^\epsilon(t) - \sqrt{t}) = e^{-\frac{1}{2}\epsilon}[1 - \Phi(\hat{y}_1^\epsilon(t) - \sqrt{t+\epsilon})]. \tag{35}$$

From (26), we get $\hat{x}_1^\epsilon(t) = \hat{y}_1^\epsilon(t)$ or equivalently $\frac{\ln x_1^\epsilon(t)+t}{\sqrt{t}} = \frac{\ln y_1^\epsilon(t)+t+\epsilon}{\sqrt{t+\epsilon}}$. By plugging $\hat{x}_1^\epsilon(t) = \hat{y}_1^\epsilon(t)$ into (35), we obtain that

$$1 - \Phi(\frac{\ln x_1^\epsilon(t)}{\sqrt{t}}) = e^{-\frac{1}{2}\epsilon}[1 - \Phi(\frac{\ln x_1^\epsilon(t) + t}{\sqrt{t}} - \sqrt{t+\epsilon})], \tag{36}$$

which characterizes $x_1^\epsilon(t)$.

We now deal with the limit $x_1(t) := \lim_{\epsilon \downarrow 0} x_1^\epsilon(t)$.

Recall that $\epsilon_0 := \epsilon_1 \wedge \epsilon_2$, where ϵ_1, ϵ_2 are as in Assumptions 3.1 and 3.3, respectively.

For each (small) $\delta > 0$, define $G = G^\delta : \mathbb{R}^3 \to \mathbb{R}$ on $\{(t,\epsilon) : 0 \le \epsilon \le \epsilon_0,\ \delta \le t \le 1-\epsilon\} \times \mathbb{R}$ by

$$G(t,\epsilon,x) := \frac{1}{\epsilon}\left\{(1-\Phi(x)) - e^{-\frac{1}{2}\epsilon}[1-\Phi(x+\sqrt{t}-\sqrt{t+\epsilon})]\right\},$$
$$(t,\epsilon,x) \in [\delta, 1-\epsilon] \times (0,\epsilon_0] \times \mathbb{R} \tag{37}$$

and

$$G(t,0,x) := (1-\Phi(x)) - \frac{1}{\sqrt{t}}\frac{1}{\sqrt{2\pi}}e^{-\frac{x^2}{2}}. \tag{38}$$

Note that, by (36), $G(t,\epsilon,\hat{x}_1^\epsilon(t)) = 0$ for all $\epsilon \in (0,\epsilon_0]$ and $t \in [\delta, 1-\epsilon]$.

Using Lemma 4.12, we define $\hat{x}_1^0(t)$, for all $t \in (0,1]$, to be the unique solution to $F(t,0,x) = 0$. Then $x_1^0(t)$ is defined as $x_1^0(t) := \exp\left(\sqrt{t}\hat{x}_1^0(t) - t\right)$, for each $t \in (0,1]$. Note that $x_1^0(\cdot)$ is continuous if and only if $\hat{x}_1^0(\cdot)$ is. Now since $\hat{x}_1^0(t)$ uniquely satisfies $F(t,0,x) = 0$, we immediately have that $\lim_{\epsilon\downarrow 0}\hat{x}_1^\epsilon(t)$ exists, for all $t \in (0,1]$, and uniquely satisfies (24).

Lemma 4.13. *For $\epsilon \in [0,\epsilon_0]$ and $t \in (0,1]$, let $x_1^\epsilon(t)$ be given by Lemma 4.11 with $x_1^0(t) := x_1(t) = \lim_{\epsilon\downarrow 0} x_1^\epsilon(t)$.*

Then, for each (small) $\delta > 0$, the map $(t,\epsilon) \mapsto x_1^\epsilon(t)$ is continuous on $\{(t,\epsilon) : 0 \le \epsilon \le \epsilon_0,\ \delta \le t \le 1-\epsilon\} \times \mathbb{R}$.

Proof. Let G be defined as in (37) and (38). To prove the continuity of $(t,\epsilon) \mapsto x_1^\epsilon(t) := \exp\left(\sqrt{t}\hat{x}_1^\epsilon(t) - t\right)$, we will use the implicit function theorem and show that $(t,\epsilon) \mapsto \hat{x}_1^\epsilon(t)$ is continuous, where $G(t,\epsilon,\hat{x}_1^\epsilon(t)) = 0$.

We claim that $(t,\epsilon,x) \mapsto G(t,\epsilon,x)$ is continuously differentiable. Indeed,

$$\lim_{\epsilon\to 0}\frac{\partial G}{\partial \epsilon}(t,\epsilon,x) = -\frac{1}{8}(1-\Phi(x)) + \frac{1}{8}\Phi'(x)t^{-\frac{3}{2}}(2t+1) + \frac{1}{8}\Phi''(x)t^{-1}$$
$$= \lim_{\epsilon\to 0}\frac{G(t,\epsilon,x) - G(t,0,x)}{\epsilon},$$

and hence $\frac{\partial G}{\partial \epsilon}$ is continuous. The continuities of $\frac{\partial G}{\partial t}$ and $\frac{\partial G}{\partial x}$ follow similarly by the direct computations.

Now we check that $\frac{\partial G}{\partial x}(t,\epsilon,x)|_{G(t,\epsilon,x)=0} \neq 0$. For $\epsilon \in [0,\epsilon_0]$, direct calculations show that

$$\begin{aligned}\frac{\partial G}{\partial x}(t,\epsilon,x)|_{G(t,\epsilon,x)=0} &= -\Phi'(x) + e^{-\frac{1}{2}\epsilon}\Phi'(x+\sqrt{t}-\sqrt{t+\epsilon})\\ &= -\frac{\Phi'(x)}{1-\Phi(x)} + \frac{\Phi'(x+\sqrt{t}-\sqrt{t+\epsilon})}{1-\Phi(x+\sqrt{t}-\sqrt{t+\epsilon})},\end{aligned}$$

and the desired conclusion follows.

We now study the monotonicity of the map $x \mapsto \frac{\Phi'(x)}{1-\Phi(x)}$:

$$\begin{aligned}\left(\frac{\Phi'(x)}{1-\Phi(x)}\right)' &= \frac{\Phi''(x)(1-\Phi(x)) + (\Phi'(x))^2}{(1-\Phi(x))^2}\\ &= \Phi'(x)\frac{\Phi'(x) - x(1-\Phi(x))}{(1-\Phi(x))^2} > 0,\end{aligned}$$

where in the last step, in the case $x > 0$, we use the inequality $\frac{1-\Phi(x)}{\Phi'(x)} < \frac{1}{x}$ (the case $x \geq 0$ is trivially satisfied). Hence $x \mapsto \frac{\Phi'(x)}{1-\Phi(x)}$ is strictly increasing. It follows that $\frac{\partial G}{\partial x}|_{G(t,\epsilon,x)=0} < 0$ for $\epsilon \in (0,\epsilon_0]$. Similarly, for $\epsilon = 0$, we have that

$$\frac{\partial G}{\partial x}(t,0,x)|_{G(t,0,x)=0} = -\Phi'(x) + \frac{1}{\sqrt{t}}\Phi'(x)x = -\Phi'(x) + x(1-\Phi(x)) < 0.$$

Finally, from the implicit function theorem, we have that $(t,\epsilon) \mapsto \ln x_1^\epsilon(t)$ is continuously differentiable on a compact set $\{(t,\epsilon) : 0 \leq \epsilon \leq \epsilon_0,\ \delta \leq t \leq 1-\epsilon\}$ and consequently uniformly bounded and continuous. □

Finally, we have the following characterization and the optimality of the limiting process:

Proposition 4.14. *Let $(\mu_t)_{t\in(0,1]}$ be specified by* (31) *and consider $t \mapsto x_1(t)$ as in Lemma* 4.11. *Then the SDE as in Theorem* 3.14 *is explicitly given by*

$$\begin{aligned}X_t = X_0 &+ \int_0^t j_u(s,X_{s-})(dN_s - \nu_s ds)\mathbf{1}_{\{x_1(s) < X_{s-} < m_s\}}\\ &- \int_0^t \mathbf{1}_{\{X_{s-} \leq x_1(s)\}} j_d(s,X_{s-})ds,\end{aligned}$$

where $m_s = e^{\sqrt{s(s+1)}}$, $\nu_s(s, X_{s-}) := \frac{j_d}{j_u}(s, X_{s-})$ *with* $j_u(t,x) = T_u(t,x) - x$ *and*

$$j_d(t,x) = \frac{x}{2}\left[e^{\frac{(\ln x+t)^2}{2t} - \frac{(\ln(T_S(t,x))+t)^2}{2t}}\left(\frac{\ln(T_u(t,x))}{\sqrt{t}} - \sqrt{t}\right) - \left(\frac{\ln x}{\sqrt{t}} - \sqrt{t}\right)\right],$$

for $x \in (x_1(s), m_s)$, *and* $j_d(s, X_{s-}) := x^{\frac{s-\ln x}{2s}}$ *for* $x \in (\ell_s, x_1(s)]$; *here* $T_u(t,x)$ *is uniquely determined by the following equation:*

$$\left(1 - \frac{x}{T_u(t,x)}\right)e^{-\frac{(\ln(T_u(t,x)))^2}{2t}}\ln(T_u(t,x))$$
$$= t\left(1 - \frac{x}{T_u(t,x)}\right)e^{-\frac{(\ln x)^2}{2t}} - t^{\frac{3}{2}}\left[\Phi\left(\frac{\ln(T_u(t,x))}{\sqrt{t}}\right) - \Phi\left(\frac{\ln x}{\sqrt{t}}\right)\right].$$

In addition, if Assumption 2.2(*ii*) *and the integrability condition* (12) *are satisfied, then the law* $\mathbb{P}^0$ *of the above process is the optimal solution for the primal problem* (4), *and the strong duality*

$$\mathbb{E}^{\mathbb{P}^0}[C(X_\cdot)] = \mathbf{P}_\infty(\mu) = \mathbf{D}_\infty(\mu)$$

holds.

Proof. As it has been verified that Assumptions 3.1, 3.3 and 3.7 are valid (up to $t = 0$), using Theorems 3.14 and 3.15, we obtain the validity of the SDE and the optimality of $\mathbb{P}^0$. It is left to derive the explicit expressions of the terms T_u, j_u, j_d that define the SDE.

The calculations are similar to those of Proposition 4.9, and we omit the details. □

Appendix

A. Brenier's Theorem

A.1. *Brenier's Theorem in Optimal Transport (OT)*

Let (X, Y) be a random vector in $\mathbb{R}^2$ and let $\mathcal{P}_2$ be the set of all (Borel) probability measures on $\mathbb{R}^2$. We denote respectively μ and ν the (integrable) marginal distributions of X and Y.

Let $c : \mathbb{R}^2 \to \mathbb{R}$ be a (measurable) cost, or payoff, function. The primal optimal transport problem corresponds to

$$P_{OT}(\mu,\nu) := \sup_{\mathbb{P}\in\mathcal{P}_2(\mu,\nu)} \mathbb{E}^{\mathbb{P}}[c(X,Y)], \quad \text{where}$$

$$\mathcal{P}_2(\mu,\nu) := \{\mathbb{P}\in\mathcal{P}_2 : X \sim_{\mathbb{P}} \mu, Y \sim_{\mathbb{P}} \nu\}.$$

The above optimization problem has a dual problem, which is defined by

$$D_{OT}(\mu,\nu) := \inf_{(\varphi,\psi)\in\mathcal{D}_s} \{\mu(\varphi)+\nu(\psi)\}, \quad \text{where}$$

$$\mathcal{D}_s := \{(\varphi,\psi) : \mu(\varphi\vee 0)+\nu(\psi\vee 0) < \infty, \varphi\oplus\psi \geq c\}.$$

In the above, $\varphi\oplus\psi(x,y) := \varphi(x)+\psi(y)$ and $\chi(f) := \int f d\chi$, for a (Borel) measure χ on $\mathbb{R}$ and a (Borel) measurable $f : \mathbb{R}\to\mathbb{R}$. Under mild conditions, it can be proved that the duality $P_{OT}(\mu,\nu) = D_{OT}(\mu,\nu)$ holds. (The notation $\mathcal{D}_s$ is motivated by the fact that, in financial terms, $(\varphi,\psi)\in\mathcal{D}_s$ corresponds to a *static* hedging strategy.)

Brenier's theorem gives the explicit expressions of the optimizers of both the primal and dual problems. In the case μ is atomless, a candidate primal optimizer is given by the Fréchet–Hoeffding (or quantile) coupling $\mathbb{P}_*$ defined by

$$\mathbb{P}_*(dx,dy) := \mu(dx)\delta_{T_*(x)}(dy), \tag{A.39}$$

push-forward map from μ to ν is where $T_* := F_\nu^{-1}\circ F_\mu$. Here F_ν^{-1} is the right-continuous inverse of (the c.d.f. of ν) F_ν: $F_\nu^{-1}(t) := \inf\{y : F_\nu > t\}$.

We further introduce candidate dual optimizers φ_* and ψ_* (up to a constant) by setting

$$\begin{aligned} \varphi_*(x) &:= c(x,T_*(x)) - \psi_*\circ T_*(x), \\ \psi_*'(y) &:= c_y(T_*^{-1}(y),y), \quad \forall x,y\in\mathbb{R}. \end{aligned} \tag{A.40}$$

Theorem A.1 (Brenier [18], Rachev and Rüschendorf [61]). *Suppose μ has no atoms. Let c be an upper semi-continuous function with (at most) linear growth. Assume that the partial derivative c_{xy} exists and satisfies the Spence–Mirrlees condition $c_{xy} > 0$.*

Let $\mathbb{P}_*$ be as in (A.39) and (φ_*,ψ_*) as in (A.40), and assume that $(\mu(\varphi_*\vee 0)+\nu(\psi_*\vee 0)) < \infty$.

Then $\mathbb{P}_* \in \mathcal{P}_2(\mu,\nu)$, $(\varphi_*,\psi_*) \in \mathcal{D}_s$ *and*

$$\int c(x, T_*(x))\mu(dx) = P_{OT}(\mu,\nu) = D_{OT}(\mu,\nu) = \mu(\varphi_*) + \nu(\psi_*).$$

Remark A.2. In the case $c_{xy} < 0$, then $P_{OT} = D_{OT}$ and the optimal coupling is the antitone coupling which is supported on $x \mapsto T^*(x) := F_\nu^{-1} \circ (1 - F_\mu(x))$. The dual optimizers are still defined through (A.40) but with T^* in place of T_*.

A.2. *Brenier's Theorem in Martingale Optimal Transport (MOT)*

Two (integrable) probability measures μ, ν on $\mathbb{R}$ are increasing in convex order, denoted by $\mu \leq_c \nu$, if for all convex functions $f : \mathbb{R} \to \mathbb{R}$, we have that $\mu(f) \leq \nu(f)$. By Strassen's classical result [62], $\mu \leq_c \nu$ is equivalent to non-emptiness of the set $\mathcal{M}_2(\mu,\nu) := \{\mathbb{P} \in \mathcal{P}_2(\mu,\nu) : \mathbb{E}^{\mathbb{P}}[Y|X] = X\}$.

In this section, we suppose that μ and ν have finite first moments, $\mu \leq_c \nu$, and the following dispersion assumption holds:

Assumption A.3 (Dispersion). μ, ν admit densities f_μ, f_ν that satisfy the following:

1. $f_\mu > 0$ on (ℓ_μ, r_μ), $f_\nu > 0$ on (ℓ_ν, r_ν), and $\ell_\nu \leq \ell_\mu < r_\mu \leq r_\nu$.
2. There exists $\ell_\mu < \underline{m} := \underline{m}^{\mu,\nu} < \overline{m} := \overline{m}^{\mu,\nu} < r_\mu$ such that

$$f_\mu > f_\nu, \quad \text{on } (\underline{m}, \overline{m}), \quad f_\nu > f_\mu \quad \text{on } (\ell_\nu, \underline{m}) \cup (\overline{m}, r_\nu),$$
$$f_\mu = f_\nu, \text{ on } \{\underline{m}, \overline{m}\}.$$

Remark A.4. Note that if $\overline{\mu} = \overline{\nu}$ and Assumption A.3 holds, then $\mu \leq_c \nu$. Furthermore, the difference of distribution functions $y \mapsto F_\nu(y) - F_\mu(y)$ attains the (unique) maximum and minimum at $\underline{m}^{\mu,\nu}$ and $\overline{m}^{\mu,\nu}$, respectively.

Given a (measurable) payoff function $c : \mathbb{R}^2 \to \mathbb{R}$, the primal problem of MOT is defined by

$$P_{MOT}(\mu,\nu) := \sup_{\mathbb{P} \in \mathcal{M}_2(\mu,\nu)} \mathbb{E}^{\mathbb{P}}[c(X,Y)].$$

The MOT problem also has a dual problem:

$$D_{MOT}(\mu,\nu) := \inf_{(\varphi,\psi,h)\in\mathcal{D}_{ss}} \{\mu(\varphi)+\nu(\psi)\},$$

where the set of dual variables is defined as follows:

$$\mathcal{D}_{ss} := \{(\varphi,\psi,h) : \mu(\varphi\vee 0)+\nu(\psi\vee 0) < \infty, h:\mathbb{R}\to\mathbb{R}, \varphi\oplus\psi+h^{\otimes} \geq c\}$$

with $\varphi\oplus\psi(x,y) := \varphi(x)+\psi(y)$ and $h^{\otimes}(x,y) := h(x)(y-x)$. (The notation $\mathcal{D}_{ss}$ is motivated by the fact that, in financial terms, $(\varphi,\psi,h)\in\mathcal{D}_{ss}$ corresponds to a *semi-static* hedging strategy, where the static part is (φ,ψ) and the dynamic part corresponds to h.)

We now introduce candidate optimal quantities. We start with a pair of functions $(T_d^{\mu,\nu}, T_u^{\mu,\nu})$ that will support the optimal coupling in the case $\mu\leq_c\nu$ satisfy Assumption A.3.

Set

$$g^{\mu,\nu}(x,y) := F_\nu^{-1}(F_\mu(x)+F_\nu(y)-F_\mu(y)), \quad x\in(\ell_\mu,r_\mu), y\in(\ell_\nu,r_\nu). \tag{A.41}$$

Define

$$T_d^{\mu,\nu}(x) = T_u^{\mu,\nu}(x) = x, \quad x\in[\overline{m}^{\mu,\nu}, r_\mu). \tag{A.42}$$

For $x\in(\ell_\mu,\overline{m}^{\mu,\nu})$, let $T_d^{\mu,\nu}(x)$ be the (unique) scalar such that

$$\int_{-\infty}^{x} [F_\nu^{-1}(F_\mu(\xi))-\xi] f_\mu(\xi)d\xi + \int_{-\infty}^{T_d(x)} \mathbf{1}_{(-\infty,\overline{m}^{\mu,\nu}]}(\xi)[g^{\mu,\nu}(x,\xi)-\xi](f_\nu(\xi)-f_\mu(\xi))d\xi = 0 \tag{A.43}$$

and set

$$T_u^{\mu,\nu}(x) = g^{\mu,\nu}(x, T_d^{\mu,\nu}(x)), \quad x\in(\ell_\mu,\overline{m}^{\mu,\nu}). \tag{A.44}$$

Remark A.5. The existence and uniqueness of (A.43) are given by Henry-Labordère and Touzi [42]. Furthermore, $T_d(x)\leq x\leq T_u(x)$ for all $x\in(\ell_\mu,r_\mu)$, and, under Assumption A.3, T_d, T_u are both continuous, T_d (resp., T_u) is strictly increasing (resp., decreasing) on $(\ell_\mu,\overline{m}^{\mu,\nu}]$. See Henry-Labordère and Touzi [42, Section 4] (note, however, that [42] constructed the left-curtain martingale coupling, while in this chapter, we are working with the right-curtain coupling.)

Using the pair $(T_d^{\mu,\nu}, T_u^{\mu,\nu})$, we now define a candidate martingale coupling through its disintegration w.r.t. the first marginal μ. Define a measure $\mathbb{P}^{\mu,\nu}$ on $\mathbb{R}^2$ by

$$\begin{aligned}\mathbb{P}^{\mu,\nu}(dx,dy) &= \mu(dx)\mathbf{1}_{[\overline{m}^{\mu,\nu},r_\mu)}(x)\delta_x(dy) + \mu(dx)\mathbf{1}_{(\ell_\mu,\overline{m}^{\mu,\nu})}(x)\\ &\quad\times\left[q^{\mu,\nu}(x)\delta_{T_u^{\mu,\nu}(x)}(dy) + (1-q^{\mu,\nu}(x))\delta_{T_d^{\mu,\nu}(x)}(dy)\right],\end{aligned} \tag{A.45}$$

where

$$q^{\mu,\nu}(x) := \frac{x - T_d^{\mu,\nu}(x)}{T_u^{\mu,\nu}(x) - T_d^{\mu,\nu}(x)}, \quad x \in (\ell_\mu, \overline{m}^{\mu,\nu}), \tag{A.46}$$

corresponds to the (conditional) martingale probability of jumping to $T_u^{\mu,\nu}(x)$ from x.

We now introduce a candidate triple $(\varphi_*, \psi_*, h_*) = (\varphi_*^{\mu,\nu}, \psi_*^{\mu,\nu}, h_*^{\mu,\nu})$ for the dual problem. To ease the notation, we will write $(T_d, T_u) = (T_d^{\mu,\nu}, T_u^{\mu,\nu})$.

Define h_*, up to a constant, by

$$\begin{aligned} h_* &= h_* \circ T_d^{-1} + c_y(\cdot,\cdot) - c_y(T_d^{-1},\cdot) \quad \text{on } [\overline{m}^{\mu,\nu}, r_\mu),\\ h_*' &= \frac{c_x(\cdot,T_u) - c_x(\cdot,T_d)}{T_u - T_d} \quad \text{on } (\ell_\mu, \overline{m}^{\mu,\nu}).\end{aligned} \tag{A.47}$$

(Note that the constant can be chosen such that h_* is continuous.) The (continuous) function ψ_* is then given (also up to a constant) by

$$\begin{aligned} \psi_*' &= c_y(T_d^{-1},\cdot) - h_* \circ T_d^{-1} \quad \text{on } [\overline{m}^{\mu,\nu}, r_\mu),\\ \psi_*' &= c_y(T_u^{-1},\cdot) - h_* \circ T_u^{-1} \quad \text{on } (\ell_\mu, \overline{m}^{\mu,\nu}).\end{aligned} \tag{A.48}$$

Finally, the function φ_* is defined by

$$\varphi_*(x) = \mathbb{E}^{\mathbb{P}^{\mu,\nu}}[c(X,Y) - \psi_*(Y)|X = x], \quad x \in (\ell_\mu, r_\mu). \tag{A.49}$$

Theorem A.6 (Henry-Labordère and Touzi [42, Theorems 4.5, 5.1]). *Suppose $\mu \leq_c \nu$ satisfies Assumption* A.3. *Assume further that $\int \varphi_* \vee 0 d\mu + \int \psi_* \vee 0 d\nu < \infty$ and that the partial derivative c_{xyy} exists and $c_{xyy} < 0$ on $\mathbb{R}^2$. Let $\mathbb{P}_* = \mathbb{P}^{\mu,\nu}$ be as in* (A.45) *and (φ_*, ψ_*, h_*) as in* (A.49), (A.48) *and* (A.47).

Then $\mathbb{P}_* \in \mathcal{M}_2(\mu,\nu)$, $(\varphi_*, \psi_*, h_*) \in \mathcal{D}_{ss}$ and the strong duality holds:

$$\mathbb{E}^{\mathbb{P}_*}[c(X,Y)] = P_{MOT}(\mu,\nu) = D_{MOT}(\mu,\nu) = \mu(\varphi_*) + \nu(\psi_*).$$

B. One-Period Supermartingale Optimal Transport

B.1. *Solution to the Primal SMOT Problem and Related Properties*

Let $\mu, \nu \in \mathcal{P}$ be in convex-decreasing order, i.e., $\mu \leq_{cd} \nu$ (for two measures η, χ on $\mathbb{R}$, we also write $\eta \leq \chi$ if $\eta(A) \leq \chi(A)$ for all Borel $A \subseteq \mathbb{R}$). Let $\mathcal{S}_2(\mu,\nu) := \{\mathbb{P} \in \mathcal{P}_2(\mu,\nu) : \mathbb{E}^{\mathbb{P}}[Y|X] \leq X\}$ be the set of supermartingale couplings with given marginals μ and ν. The following theorem defines the decreasing supermartingale coupling $\hat{\mathbb{P}} = \hat{\mathbb{P}}^{\mu,\nu} \in \mathcal{S}_2(\mu,\nu)$.

Theorem B.1 (Nutz and Stebegg [57]). *Suppose $\mu \leq_{cd} \nu$ and let $\hat{\mathbb{P}} \in \mathcal{S}_2(\mu,\nu)$ be the decreasing supermartingale coupling. It satisfies any, and then all, of the following properties*:

1. *$\hat{\mathbb{P}}$ solves* (1) *whenever c satisfies $c_{xyy} < 0$ and $c_{xy} > 0$.*
2. *For each $x \in \mathbb{R}$, $\hat{\mathbb{P}}|_{[x,\infty)\times\mathbb{R}}$ is the smallest element* (*w.r.t.* $\leq_{cd}$) *of $\{\theta : \mu|_{[x,\infty)} \leq_{cd} \theta \leq \nu\}$.*
3. *There exists $\Gamma \subseteq \mathbb{R}^2$ and $M \subset \mathbb{R}$ such that $\hat{\mathbb{P}}_*$ is second-order right-monotone and first-order left-monotone w.r.t.* (Γ, M) *in the sense of Definition* B.2.

Definition B.2. Let $(\Gamma, M) \in B(\mathbb{R}^2) \times B(\mathbb{R})$. We say

1. Γ is second-order right-monotone if for all $(x,y_1),(x,y_2),(x',y') \in \Gamma$ with $x' < x$ we have that $y' \notin (y_1,y_2)$.
2. (Γ, M) is first-order left-monotone if for all $(x_1,y_1),(x_2,y_2) \in \Gamma$ with $x_1 < x_2$ and $x_2 \notin M$ we have that $y_1 \leq y_2$.

The second property of $\hat{\mathbb{P}}$ in Theorem B.1 implies that, for each $x \in \mathbb{R}$, $\hat{\mathbb{P}}|_{[x,\infty)\times\mathbb{R}}$ is the shadow of $\mu|_{[x,\infty)}$ in ν: given $\mu_0 \leq \mu \leq_{cd} \nu$, the *shadow measure*, denoted by $S^{\nu}(\mu_0)$, is the smallest element (w.r.t. $\leq_{cd}$) of $\{\theta : \mu_0 \leq_{cd} \theta \leq \nu\}$.

Furthermore, the set M, that appears in the third property of $\hat{\mathbb{P}}$ in Theorem B.1, corresponds to the martingale points of $\hat{\mathbb{P}}$ in the sense that $\hat{\mathbb{P}}|_{M\times\mathbb{R}}$ is a martingale. The explicit constructions of $\hat{\mathbb{P}}$ and M were provided by Bayraktar *et al.* [5, Theorem 6.1, Proposition 5.1]. In particular, there exists $(x_n)_{n\geq 1}$ in $\mathbb{R}$ such that $M = \bigcup_{n\geq 1}[x_{n+1}, x_n)$ so that $\hat{\mathbb{P}}$ alternates between being a martingale and supermartingale at most countably many times. For each

$n \geq 1$, the transitions of $\hat{\mathbb{P}}$ on $[x_{n+1}, x_n)$ are of the right-curtain type (see (A.45)), while on $\mathbb{R} \setminus M$, $\hat{\mathbb{P}}$ mimics the transitions of the quantile coupling (see (A.39)).

For a measure η on $\mathbb{R}$, let $C_\eta : \mathbb{R} \to \mathbb{R}$ be given by $C_\eta(k) := \int_{\mathbb{R}} (x-k)^+ \eta(dx)$, $k \in \mathbb{R}$. Define $c^{\mu,\nu} : \mathbb{R} \to \mathbb{R}$ by

$$c^{\mu,\nu}(x) = \sup_{k \in \mathbb{R}} \{C_{\mu|_{[x,\infty)}}(k) - C_\nu(k)\}, \quad x \in \mathbb{R}.$$

Then, provided μ is atom-less, c is non-negative, non-decreasing and continuous and

$$c(x) = \overline{\mu|_{[x,\infty)}} - \overline{S^\nu(\mu|_{[x,\infty)})}.$$

See Bayraktar *et al.* [5, Lemmas 3.1, 5.1]. Then the first point (starting from the right, i.e., r_μ, and moving to the left toward ℓ_μ) where $\hat{\mathbb{P}}$ transitions from being a martingale to supermartingale is given by

$$x_1^{\mu,\nu} = \inf\{x \in \mathbb{R} : c^{\mu,\nu}(x) = 0\} \quad \text{with} \quad \inf \emptyset = r_\mu. \tag{B.50}$$

Furthermore, define

$$y_1^{\mu,\nu} = \ell_{S^\nu(\mu|_{[x_1^{\mu,\nu},\infty)})}. \tag{B.51}$$

Note that, since $\mu|_{[x_1^{\mu,\nu},\infty)} \leq_{cd} S^\nu(\mu|_{[x_1^{\mu,\nu},\infty)})$, we have that $y_1^{\mu,\nu} \leq x_1^{\mu,\nu}$.

Lemma B.3. *Suppose that* $\mu \leq_{cd} \nu$ *satisfy Assumption* A.3. *Let* $\hat{\mathbb{P}}$ *be the decreasing supermartingale coupling of Theorem* B.1.

Then the (μ*-a.s. unique) set of martingale points of* $\hat{\mathbb{P}}$ *is given by* $M = [x_1^{\mu,\nu}, r_\mu)$. *Furthermore, the second marginal of* $\hat{\mathbb{P}}|_{M \times \mathbb{R}}$ *is* $\nu|_{[y_1^{\mu,\nu}, r_\nu)}$.

Proof of Lemma B.3. We assume that $\overline{\mu} > \overline{\nu}$, since otherwise $\mu \leq_c \nu$, and there is nothing to prove. Indeed, if $\overline{\mu} = \overline{\nu}$, then $x_1^{\mu,\nu} = \ell_\mu$ and $\hat{\mathbb{P}} = \mathbb{P}^{\mu,\nu}$ is the right-curtain martingale coupling, see (A.45).

Suppose that $x_1^{\mu,\nu} \in (\ell_\mu, r_\mu]$. Let $\overline{m} := \overline{m}^{\mu,\nu}$. Note that $\mu|_{[\overline{m}, r_\mu)} \leq \nu$ and thus $\mu|_{[\overline{m}, r_\mu)} = S^\nu(\mu|_{[\overline{m}, r_\mu)})$. It follows that $x_1^{\mu,\nu} \leq \overline{m}$. In fact, since μ and $\nu - \mu|_{[\overline{m}, r_\mu)}$ both have strictly positive densities in the neighbourhood of $\overline{m}$ and $f_\mu > f_\nu$ to the left of $\overline{m}$, we must have that $x_1^{\mu,\nu} < \overline{m}$.

We now argue that $S^\nu(\mu|_{[x_1^{\mu,\nu},r_\mu)}) = \nu|_{[y_1(\mu,\nu),r_\nu)}$. First, using the associativity of the shadow measure (see Bayraktar *et al.* [4]), we have that

$$S^\nu(\mu|_{[x_1^{\mu,\nu},r_\mu)}) = \mu|_{[\overline{m},r_\mu)} + S^{\nu-\mu|_{[\overline{m},r_\mu)}}(\mu|_{[x_1^{\mu,\nu},\overline{m})}).$$

Thanks to the properties of the shadow measure ($S^{\nu-\mu|_{[\overline{m},r_\mu)}}(\mu|_{[x_1^{\mu,\nu},\overline{m})})$ has the smallest variance among all possible target laws of $\mu|_{[x_1^{\mu,\nu},\overline{m})}$ within $\nu - \mu|_{[\overline{m},r_\mu)}$), we have that

$$S^{\nu-\mu|_{[\overline{m},r_\mu)}}(\mu|_{[x_1^{\mu,\nu},\overline{m})}) = \nu|_{[y_1(\mu,\nu),\overline{m})} + (\nu - \mu|_{[\overline{m},r_\mu)})|_{(\overline{m},r_0)}$$

for some $r_0 \in (\overline{m}, r_\nu]$. But if $r_0 < r_\nu$, then $\nu - S^\nu(\mu|_{[x_1^{\mu,\nu},r_\mu)})$ charges $[r_0, r_\nu)$. Then, since $x_1^{\mu,\nu} < \overline{m} < r_0 < r_\nu$, we can find a small enough $x < x_1^{\mu,\nu}$ such that $\mu|_{[x,x_1^{\mu,\nu})} \leq_c S^{\nu - S^\nu(\mu|_{[x_1^{\mu,\nu},r_\mu)})}(\mu|_{[x,x_1^{\mu,\nu})})$, contradicting the minimality of $x_1^{\mu,\nu}$. It follows that $r_0 = r_\nu$.

It is left to show that $x_1^{\mu,\nu}$ is the (μ-a.s.) unique regime-switching point. For this we use the following observations. The transitions of the decreasing supermartingale coupling $\hat{\mathbb{P}}$ are either those of the right-curtain (see (A.45)) or the quantile coupling (see (A.39)), see Nutz and Stebegg [57] or Bayraktar *et al.* [5]. In particular, by the definition of $x_1^{\mu,\nu}$, we must have that (locally) to the left of $x_1^{\mu,\nu}$, $\hat{\mathbb{P}}$ corresponds to the quantile coupling of $\mu|_{(-\infty,x_1^{\mu,\nu})}$ and $\nu|_{(-\infty,y_1^{\mu,\nu})}$, denoted by π^q (which is just a restriction of the quantile coupling of μ and ν to $(-\infty, x_1^{\mu,\nu}) \times (-\infty, y_1^{\mu,\nu})$).

Under π^q, each $x \in (\ell_\mu, x_1^{\mu,\nu})$ is mapped to $F_\nu^{-1}(F_\mu(x))$. Note that $x \mapsto F_\nu^{-1}(F_\mu(x))$ is non-decreasing and continuous, and by construction (and the supermartingale requirement), we have that $F_\nu^{-1}(F_\mu(x_1^{\mu,\nu})) = y_1^{\mu,\nu} \leq x_1^{\mu,\nu}$. Let $\bar{x}$ be defined by $F_\mu(\bar{x}) = F_\nu(\bar{x})$. Due to Assumption A.3, $\bar{x}$ is unique and satisfies $\bar{x} \in (\underline{m}, \overline{m})$. In particular, $F_\nu > F_\mu$ on $(-\infty, \bar{x})$, while $F_\nu < F_\mu$ on $(\bar{x}, \infty)$.

If $x_1^{\mu,\nu} \leq \bar{x}$, then $F_\nu^{-1}(F_\mu(x)) < x$ for all $x < x_1^{\mu,\nu}$, and the quantile coupling provides strict supermartingale transitions on $(-\infty, x_1^{\mu,\nu})$. Then using characterization of $\hat{P}_*$ in terms of the shadow measure, it follows that $\hat{\mathbb{P}} = \pi^q$ on $(-\infty, x_1^{\mu,\nu})$, which proves our claim. On the other hand, $x_1^{\mu,\nu} > \bar{x}$ cannot happen, since then $y_1^{\mu,\nu} = F_\nu^{-1}(F_\mu(x_1^{\mu,\nu})) > x_1^{\mu,\nu}$, a contradiction.

Finally, provided that μ is atomless and using the construction of Bayraktar *et al.* [5], we have that the decreasing supermartingale coupling is supported on the graph of two functions $\hat{T}_d = \hat{T}^{\mu,\nu}_d, \hat{T}_u = \hat{T}^{\mu,\nu}_u : (\ell_\mu, r_\mu) \to (\ell_\nu, r_\nu)$. If, in addition, the dispersion assumption holds, then using Lemma B.3 and utilizing the construction and properties of the right-curtain martingale coupling $P^{\mu,\nu}$ (as in (A.45)), we have that $(\hat{T}_d, \hat{T}_u)$ satisfies some useful properties.

First,

$$\hat{T}_d(x) \le x \le \hat{T}_u(x) \text{ for all } x \in (\ell_\mu, r_\mu) \quad \text{and} \quad \hat{T}_d = \hat{T}_u \text{ on } [\overline{m}, r_\mu). \tag{B.52}$$

Furthermore,

$$\begin{aligned} &\hat{T}_d \text{ is continuous and strictly increasing on } (\ell_\mu, r_\mu), \\ &\hat{T}_d(x) = F_\nu^{-1} \circ F_\mu \text{ on } (\ell_\mu, x_1^{\mu,\nu}) \end{aligned} \tag{B.53}$$

and

$$\begin{aligned} &\hat{T}_u \text{ is continuous on } (x_1^{\mu,\nu}, r_\mu), \text{ strictly decreasing on } (x_1^{\mu,\nu}, \overline{m}), \\ &\hat{T}_u \equiv \infty \text{ on } (\ell_\mu, x_1^{\mu,\nu}]. \end{aligned} \tag{B.54}$$

In particular, in terms of $(\hat{T}_d, \hat{T}_u)$, the decreasing supermartingale coupling $\mathbb{P}^{\mu,\nu}$ is given by

$$\begin{aligned} \hat{\mathbb{P}}(dx, dy) = {} & \mu(dx)\mathbf{1}_{(\ell_\mu, x_1^{\mu,\nu}] \cup [\overline{m}, r_\mu)}(x)\delta_{\hat{T}_d(x)}(dy) \\ & + \mu(dx)\mathbf{1}_{(x_1^{\mu,\nu}, \overline{m})}\left\{ \frac{\hat{T}_u(x) - x}{\hat{T}_u(x) - \hat{T}_d(x)}\delta_{\hat{T}_d(x)}(dy) \right. \\ & \left. + \frac{x - \hat{T}_d(x)}{\hat{T}_u(x) - \hat{T}_d(x)}\delta_{\hat{T}_u(x)}(dy) \right\}. \end{aligned} \tag{B.55}$$

Equivalently, we can express $\hat{\mathbb{P}}$ in terms of the right-curtain coupling $\mathbb{P}^{\mu|_{[x_1^{\mu,\nu}, r_\mu)}, \nu|_{[y_1^{\mu,\nu} r_\nu)}}$ of $\mu|_{[x_1^{\mu,\nu}, r_\mu)}$ and $\nu|_{[y_1^{\mu,\nu} r_\nu)}$ (see (A.45)):

$$\begin{aligned} \hat{\mathbb{P}}(dx, dy) = {} & \mu(dx)\mathbf{1}_{(\ell_\mu, x_1^{\mu,\nu}]}(x)\delta_{F_\nu^{-1}(F_\mu(x))}(dy) \\ & + \mathbf{1}_{(x_1^{\mu,\nu}, r_\mu)}\mathbb{P}^{\mu|_{[x_1^{\mu,\nu}, r_\mu)}, \nu|_{[y_1^{\mu,\nu} r_\nu)}}(dx, dy). \end{aligned} \tag{B.56}$$

While the pair $(\hat{T}_d, \hat{T}_u)$ can be explicitly constructed using potential functions of the underlying measures (see Bayraktar *et al.* [5]), the following representation is more useful in the present context.

Recall the definition of $g = g_{\mu,\nu}$ (see (A.41)).

Proposition B.4. *For each $x \in [x_1^{\mu,\nu}, \overline{m}^{\mu,\nu})$, $\hat{T}_u(x)$ is uniquely characterized by the integral equation:*

$$\int_x^\infty [F_\nu^{-1}(F_\mu(\xi)) - \xi] f_\mu(\xi) d\xi + \int_{\hat{T}_u(x)}^\infty \mathbf{1}_{(x_1^{\mu,\nu},\infty)}(\xi)[g(x,\xi) - \xi](f_\nu(\xi) - f_\mu(\xi)) d\xi = 0$$

and $\hat{T}_d(x) = g(x, \hat{T}_u(x))$.

Proof. Since $\mu|_{[x_1^{\mu,\nu}, r_\mu)} \leq_c \nu|_{[y_1(\mu,\nu), r_\nu)}$ and the decreasing supermartingale coupling $\hat{\mathbb{P}}^{\mu,\nu}$ of $\mu \leq_{cd} \nu$ coincides with the right-curtain coupling of $\mu|_{[x_1^{\mu,\nu}, r_\mu)} \leq_c \nu|_{[y_1(\mu,\nu), r_\nu)}$ on $[x_1^{\mu,\nu}, r_\mu)$, the result follows immediately from the construction of the latter, which is given in Section A.2 (see (A.43) and (A.44)). $\square$

B.2. *Optimal Dual Strategy for Decreasing SMOT*

We introduce now the optimal dual strategies to the dual problem (5) in the case of the decreasing supermartingale coupling $\hat{\mathbb{P}} = \hat{\mathbb{P}}^{\mu,\nu}$ (see Theorem B.1) is optimal. Recall that the pair $(\hat{T}_d, \hat{T}_u)$ represents the supporting functions of $\hat{\mathbb{P}}$, while $x_1 = x_1^{\mu,\nu}$ is the unique threshold that separates martingale and supermartingale regions.

In the following, we suppose that $\mu \leq_{cd} \nu$ satisfies Assumption A.3.

We introduce the following triple $(\hat{\varphi}, \hat{\psi}, \hat{h}) = (\hat{\varphi}(\mu,\nu), \hat{\psi}(\mu,\nu), \hat{h}(\mu,\nu))$, as the candidate optimal dual strategies for $\mathbf{D}_2(\mu,\nu)$ (with $\mathbf{D}_2$ defined in (2)):

$$\begin{aligned}
&\hat{h}'(x) := \tfrac{c_x(x,\hat{T}_u(x)) - c_x(x,\hat{T}_d(x))}{\hat{T}_u(x) - \hat{T}_d(x)}, \quad x_1 < x < \overline{m},\\
&\lim_{x\downarrow x_1} \hat{h}(x) = 0,\\
&\hat{h}(x) := \hat{h}((\hat{T}_u)^{-1}(x)) - c_y((\hat{T}_u^{-1}(x), x), \quad x \geq \overline{m},\\
&\hat{h}(x) := 0, \quad x \leq x_1.
\end{aligned} \tag{B.57}$$

Note that, when $x = x_1$, $\hat{T}_u(x) = \infty$ and therefore $\hat{h}'(x) = 0$. Furthermore, $\hat{h}$ is continuous at $x \in \{x_1, \overline{m}\}$ (note that $c_y(x,x) = 0$ and $\lim_{x\to\overline{m}}(\hat{T}_u)^{-1}(x) = \overline{m}$).

Denoting $L^{-1}(x) := (\hat{T}_u)^{-1}(x)\mathbf{1}_{\{x\geq\overline{m}\}} + (\hat{T}_d)^{-1}(x)\mathbf{1}_{\{x<\overline{m}\}}$, we introduce $\hat{\psi}$, up to a constant, by

$$\hat{\psi}'(x) := c_y(L^{-1}(x), x) - \hat{h}(L^{-1}(x)).$$

Note that $\hat{\psi}$ can be chosen to be continuous, which then also makes

$$c(\cdot, \hat{T}_u(\cdot)) - \hat{\psi}(\hat{T}_u(\cdot)) - c(\cdot, \hat{T}_d(\cdot)) + \hat{\psi}(\hat{T}_d(\cdot)) - (\hat{T}_u(\cdot) - \hat{T}_d(\cdot))\hat{h}(\cdot)$$

continuous.

Finally, we define

$$\hat{\varphi}(x) := \mathbb{E}^{\hat{\mathbb{P}}}[c(X,Y) - \psi(Y)|X = x], \quad x \in \mathbb{R}.$$

Note that, for $x_1 \leq x \leq \overline{m}$,

$$\begin{aligned}\hat{\varphi}(x) &= \frac{x - \hat{T}_d(x)}{\hat{T}_u(x) - \hat{T}_d(x)}\left(c(x, \hat{T}_u(x)) - \hat{\psi}(\hat{T}_u(x))\right)\\ &\quad + \frac{\hat{T}_u(x) - x}{\hat{T}_u(x) - \hat{T}_d(x)}\left(c(x, \hat{T}_d(x)) - \hat{\psi}(\hat{T}_d(x))\right),\\ \hat{\varphi}(x) &:= c(x,x) - \hat{\psi}(x) = -\hat{\psi}(x), \quad x > \overline{m}\end{aligned}$$

and

$$\hat{\varphi}(x) := c(x, \hat{T}_d(x)) - \hat{\psi}(\hat{T}_d(x)), \quad x < x_1.$$

From our definitions, we immediately have that $\mathbb{E}^{\hat{\mathbb{P}}}[c(X,Y)] = \mu(\hat{\varphi}(X)) + \nu(\hat{\psi}(Y))$. It is left to show that the triple $(\hat{\varphi}, \hat{\psi}, \hat{h})$ defines a superhedge.

Lemma B.5. *Let $\mu \leq_{cd} \nu$ be such that Assumption* A.3 *holds. Suppose that the reward function $c : \mathbb{R}^2 \to \mathbb{R}$ satisfies Assumption* 2.2. *Assume further that $\int \hat{\varphi} \vee 0 d\mu + \int \psi \vee 0 d\nu < \infty$.*

We have that $(\hat{\varphi}, \hat{\psi}, \hat{h}) \in \mathcal{D}_2(\mu, \nu)$.

Proof. To obtain the proof, we need to show that $\hat{h} \geq 0$ and that $c(x,y) \leq \hat{\varphi}(x) + \hat{\psi}(y) + \hat{h}(x)(y - x)$ for all $x, y \in \mathbb{R}$. The second point, however, follows immediately from the arguments of the classical and martingale versions of Brenier's theorem (see Theorems A.1 and A.6).

We now verify that $h \geq 0$; we will use that $c(\cdot,\cdot) = c_y(\cdot,\cdot) = 0$ and $c_{xy} > 0$.

First, as $c_{xy} > 0$, we have that when $x_1 \leq x < \overline{m}$,

$$\hat{h}'(x) := \frac{c_x(x, \hat{T}_u(x)) - c_x(x, \hat{T}_d(x))}{\hat{T}_u(x) - \hat{T}_d(x)} > 0.$$

Hence, since $\hat{h}(x_1) = 0$, we have that $\hat{h}(x) \geq 0$ for all $x_1 \leq x < \overline{m}$.

For $x \geq \overline{m}$, as $x_1 \leq (\hat{T}_u)^{-1}(x) \leq \overline{m}$, we have that $\hat{h}((\hat{T}_u)^{-1}(x)) \geq 0$. In addition, as $c_y(x,x) = 0$ and $c_{xy} > 0$, we have that $c_y((\hat{T}_u)^{-1}(x), x) \leq 0$. It follows that

$$\hat{h}(x) = \hat{h}((\hat{T}_u)^{-1}(x)) - c_y((\hat{T}_u)^{-1}(x), x) \geq 0.$$

Since $\hat{h} \equiv 0$ on $(-\infty, x_1)$, the no short-selling constraint is satisfied. □

References

[1] B. Acciaio, M. Beiglböck, and G. Pammer. Weak transport for non-convex costs and model-independence in a fixed-income market. *Mathematical Finance*, 31(4):1423–1453, 2021.

[2] J. Backhoff-Veraguas, M. Beiglböck, M. Huesmann, and S. Källblad. Martingale Benamou–Brenier: A probabilistic perspective. *The Annals of Probability*, 48(5):2258–2289, 2020.

[3] J. Backhoff-Veraguas and G. Pammer. Stability of martingale optimal transport and weak optimal transport. *The Annals of Applied Probability*, 32(1):721–752, 2022.

[4] E. Bayraktar, S. Deng, and D. Norgilas. A potential-based construction of the increasing supermartingale coupling. arXiv preprint arXiv:2108.03450, 2021.

[5] E. Bayraktar, S. Deng, and D. Norgilas. Supermartingale shadow couplings: The decreasing case. arXiv preprint arXiv:2207.11732, 2022.

[6] M. Beiglböck, A. M. G. Cox, and M. Huesmann. Optimal transport and skorokhod embedding. *Inventiones Mathematicae*, 208(2):327–400, 2017.

[7] M. Beiglböck, A. M. G. Cox, and M. Huesmann. The geometry of multi-marginal skorokhod embedding. *Probability Theory and Related Fields*, 176(3):1045–1096, 2020.

[8] M. Beiglböck, P. Henry-Labordere, and F. Penkner. Model-independent bounds for option prices—a mass transport approach. *Finance and Stochastics*, 17(3):477–501, 2013.

[9] M. Beiglböck, P. Henry-Labordère, and N. Touzi. Monotone martingale transport plans and skorokhod embedding. *Stochastic Processes and their Applications*, 127(9):3005–3013, 2017.

[10] M. Beiglböck, D. Hobson, and D. Norgilas. The potential of the shadow measure. *Electronic Communications in Probability*, 27:1–12, 2022.

[11] M. Beiglböck, B. Jourdain, W. Margheriti, and G. Pammer. Approximation of martingale couplings on the line in the weak adapted topology. *Probability Theory and Related Fields*, 183:359–413. arXiv preprint arXiv:2101.02517, 2021.

[12] M. Beiglböck and N. Juillet. On a problem of optimal transport under marginal martingale constraints. *The Annals of Probability*, 44(1):42–106, 2016.

[13] M. Beiglböck and N. Juillet. Shadow couplings. *Transactions of the American Mathematical Society*, 374(7):4973–5002, 2021.

[14] M. Beiglböck and M. Nutz. Martingale inequalities and deterministic counterparts. *Electronic Journal of Probability*, 19:1–15, 2014.

[15] M. Beiglböck, M. Nutz, and F. Stebegg. Fine properties of the optimal Skorokhod embedding problem. *Journal of the European Mathematical Society*, 24(4):1389–1429, 2021.

[16] M. Beiglböck, M. Nutz, and N. Touzi. Complete duality for martingale optimal transport on the line. *The Annals of Probability*, 45(5):3038–3074, 2017.

[17] D. T. Breeden and R. H. Litzenberger. Prices of state-contingent claims implicit in option prices. *Journal of Business*, 4:621–651, 1978.

[18] Y. Brenier. Polar factorization and monotone rearrangement of vector-valued functions. *Communications on Pure and Applied Mathematics*, 44(4):375–417, 1991.

[19] H. Brown, D. Hobson, and L. C. G. Rogers. Robust hedging of barrier options. *Mathematical Finance*, 11(3):285–314, 2001.

[20] M. Brückerhoff, M. Huesmann, and N. Juillet. Shadow martingales–a stochastic mass transport approach to the peacock problem. *Electronic Journal of Probability*, 27:1–62, 2022.

[21] L. Campi, I. Laachir, and C. Martini. Change of numeraire in the two-marginals martingale transport problem. *Finance and Stochastics*, 21(2):471–486, 2017.

[22] P. Carr, H. Geman, D. B. Madan, and M. Yor. From local volatility to local Lévy models. *Quantitative Finance*, 4(5):581–588, 2004.

[23] A. M. G. Cox, D. Hobson, and J. Obłój. Pathwise inequalities for local time: Applications to skorokhod embeddings and optimal stopping. *The Annals of Applied Probability*, 18(5):1870–1896, 2008.
[24] A. M. G. Cox and D. G. Hobson. Skorokhod embeddings, minimality and non-centred target distributions. *Probability Theory and Related Fields*, 135(3):395–414, 2006.
[25] A. M. G. Cox and J. Obłój. Robust pricing and hedging of double no-touch options. *Finance and Stochastics*, 15(3):573–605, 2011.
[26] A. M. G. Cox and J. Obłój. On joint distributions of the maximum, minimum and terminal value of a continuous uniformly integrable martingale. *Stochastic Processes and their Applications*, 125(8):3280–3300, 2015.
[27] A. M. G. Cox, J. Obłój, and N. Touzi. The root solution to the multi-marginal embedding problem: An optimal stopping and time-reversal approach. *Probability Theory and Related Fields*, 173(1):211–259, 2019.
[28] A. M. G. Cox and J. Wang. Root's barrier: Construction, optimality and applications to variance options. *The Annals of Applied Probability*, 23(3):859–894, 2013.
[29] M. Davis, J. Obłój, and V. Raval. Arbitrage bounds for prices of weighted variance swaps. *Mathematical Finance*, 24(4):821–854, 2014.
[30] S. De Marco and P. Henry-Labordere. Linking vanillas and vix options: A constrained martingale optimal transport problem. *SIAM Journal on Financial Mathematics*, 6(1):1171–1194, 2015.
[31] Y. Dolinsky and H. Mete Soner. Martingale optimal transport and robust hedging in continuous time. *Probability Theory and Related Fields*, 160(1):391–427, 2014.
[32] Y. Dolinsky and H. Mete Soner. Martingale optimal transport in the skorokhod space. *Stochastic Processes and their Applications*, 125(10):3893–3931, 2015.
[33] C.-O. Ewald and M. Yor. On peacocks and lyrebirds: Australian options, Brownian bridges, and the average of submartingales. *Mathematical Finance*, 28(2):536–549, 2018.
[34] A. Fahim and Y.-J. Huang. Model-independent superhedging under portfolio constraints. *Finance and Stochastics*, 20(1):51–81, 2016.
[35] H. Föllmer. Calcul d'itô sans probabilités. In *Séminaire de Probabilités XV 1979/80*, Springer, 1981, pp. 143–150.
[36] A. Galichon, P. Henry-Labordere, and N. Touzi. A stochastic control approach to no-arbitrage bounds given marginals, with an application to lookback options. *The Annals of Applied Probability*, 24(1):312–336, 2014.

[37] P. Gassiat, H. Oberhauser, and G. Dos Reis. Root's barrier, viscosity solutions of obstacle problems and reflected fbsdes. *Stochastic Processes and their Applications*, 125(12):4601–4631, 2015.

[38] G. Guo, X. Tan, and N. Touzi. On the monotonicity principle of optimal skorokhod embedding problem. *SIAM Journal on Control and Optimization*, 54(5):2478–2489, 2016.

[39] G. Guo, X. Tan, and N. Touzi. Optimal skorokhod embedding under finitely many marginal constraints. *SIAM Journal on Control and Optimization*, 54(4):2174–2201, 2016.

[40] G. Guo, X. Tan, and N. Touzi. Tightness and duality of martingale transport on the skorokhod space. *Stochastic Processes and their Applications*, 127(3):927–956, 2017.

[41] P. Henry-Labordère, X. Tan, and N. Touzi. An explicit martingale version of the one-dimensional Brenier's theorem with full marginals constraint. *Stochastic Processes and their Applications*, 126(9):2800–2834, 2016.

[42] P. Henry-Labordère and N. Touzi. An explicit martingale version of the one-dimensional Brenier theorem. *Finance and Stochastics*, 20(3):635–668, 2016.

[43] F. Hirsch, C. Profeta, B. Roynette, and M. Yor. *Peacocks and Associated Martingales, with Explicit Constructions.* Springer Science & Business Media, Bocconi & Springer Series, Milan, 2011.

[44] D. Hobson. The skorokhod embedding problem and model-independent bounds for option prices. In *Paris-Princeton Lectures on Mathematical Finance 2010.* Springer, Berlin, 2011, pp. 267–318.

[45] D. Hobson and M. Klimmek. Model-independent hedging strategies for variance swaps. *Finance and Stochastics*, 16(4):611–649, 2012.

[46] D. Hobson and A. Neuberger. Robust bounds for forward start options. *Mathematical Finance: An International Journal of Mathematics, Statistics and Financial Economics*, 22(1):31–56, 2012.

[47] D. Hobson and D. Norgilas. Robust bounds for the american put. *Finance and Stochastics*, 23(2):359–395, 2019.

[48] D. Hobson and D. Norgilas. A construction of the left-curtain coupling. *Electronic Journal of Probability*, 27:1–46, 2022.

[49] D. G. Hobson. Robust hedging of the lookback option. *Finance and Stochastics*, 2(4):329–347, 1998.

[50] D. G. Hobson and D. Norgilas. The left-curtain martingale coupling in the presence of atoms. *The Annals of Applied Probability*, 29(3):1904–1928, 2019.

[51] J. Jacod and A. Shiryaev. *Limit Theorems for Stochastic Processes*, vol. 288. Springer Science & Business Media, Berlin, 2013.

[52] N. Juillet. Martingales associated to peacocks using the curtain coupling. *Electronic Journal of Probability*, 23:1–29, 2018.
[53] S. Källblad, X. Tan, and N. Touzi. Optimal skorokhod embedding given full marginals and azéma–yor peacocks. *The Annals of Applied Probability*, 27(2):686–719, 2017.
[54] R. L. Karandikar. On pathwise stochastic integration. *Stochastic Processes and their applications*, 57(1):11–18, 1995.
[55] H. G. Kellerer. Markov-komposition und eine anwendung auf martingale. *Mathematische Annalen*, 198(3):99–122, 1972.
[56] D. B. Madan and M. Yor. Making Markov martingales meet marginals: With explicit constructions. *Bernoulli*, 8:509–536, 2002.
[57] M. Nutz and F. Stebegg. Canonical supermartingale couplings. *The Annals of Probability*, 46(6):3351–3398, 2018.
[58] M. Nutz, F. Stebegg, and X. Tan. Multiperiod martingale transport. *Stochastic Processes and their Applications*, 130(3):1568–1615, 2020.
[59] J. Obłój. The skorokhod embedding problem and its offspring. *Probability Surveys*, 1:321–392, 2004.
[60] J. Obłój and P. Spoida. An iterated azéma-yor type embedding for finitely many marginals. *Ann. Probab.* 45:2210–2247. arXiv preprint arXiv:1304.0368, 2013.
[61] S. T. Rachev and L. Rüschendorf. *Mass Transportation Problems: Volume I: Theory*, vol. 1. Springer Science & Business Media, 1998.
[62] V. Strassen. The existence of probability measures with given marginals. *The Annals of Mathematical Statistics*, 36(2):423–439, 1965.
[63] J. Wiesel. Continuity of the martingale optimal transport problem on the real line. arXiv preprint arXiv:1905.04574, 2019.

https://doi.org/10.1142/9789811280306_0018

Chapter 18

Forward–Backward Stochastic Neural Networks: Deep Learning of High-Dimensional Partial Differential Equations

Maziar Raissi

Department of Applied Mathematics, University of Colorado Boulder, Boulder, Colorado 80309, USA

maziar.raissi@colorado.edu

Abstract

Classical numerical methods for solving partial differential equations suffer from the curse of dimensionality mainly due to their reliance on meticulously generated spatio-temporal grids. Inspired by modern deep learning-based techniques for solving forward and inverse problems associated with partial differential equations, we circumvent the tyranny of numerical discretization by devising an algorithm that is scalable to high dimensions. In particular, we approximate the unknown solution by a deep neural network which essentially enables us to benefit from the merits of automatic differentiation. To train the aforementioned neural network, we leverage the well-known connection between high-dimensional partial differential equations and forward–backward stochastic differential equations. In fact, independent realizations of a standard Brownian motion will act as training data. We test the effectiveness of our approach for a couple of benchmark problems spanning a number of scientific domains, including Black–Scholes–Barenblatt and Hamilton–Jacobi–Bellman equations, both in 100 dimensions.

Keywords: Forward–backward stochastic differential equations, Black–Scholes equations, Hamilton–Jacobi–Bellman equations, Stochastic control, Deep learning, Automatic differentiation

1. Introduction

Since their introduction [5, 13], backward stochastic differential equations have found many applications in areas like stochastic control, theoretical economics and mathematical finance. They have received considerable attention in the literature and interesting connections to partial differential equations have been obtained (see, e.g., Ref. [6] and the references therein). The key feature of backward stochastic differential equations is the random terminal condition that the solution is required to satisfy. These equations are referred to as forward–backward stochastic differential equations, if the randomness in the terminal condition is coming from the state of a forward stochastic differential equation. The solution to a forward–backward stochastic differential equation can be written as a deterministic function of time and the state process. Under suitable regularity assumptions, this function can be shown to be the solution of a parabolic partial differential equation [6]. A forward–backward stochastic differential equation is called uncoupled if the solution of the backward equation does not enter the dynamics of the forward equation and coupled if it does. The corresponding parabolic partial differential equation is semi-linear in case the forward–backward stochastic differential equation is uncoupled and quasi-linear if it is coupled.

In this work, we approximate the aforementioned deterministic function of time and space by a deep neural network. This choice is inspired by modern techniques for solving forward and inverse problems associated with partial differential equations, where the unknown solution is approximated either by a neural network [17, 22, 23] or a Gaussian process [19–21, 25]. Moreover, putting a prior on the solution is fully justified by the similar approach pursued in the past century by classical methods of solving partial differential equations, such as finite elements, finite differences or spectral methods, where one would expand the unknown solution in terms of an appropriate set of basis functions. However, the classical methods suffer from the curse of dimensionality mainly due to their reliance on spatio-temporal grids. In contrast, modern techniques avoid the tyranny of mesh generation, and consequently, the curse of dimensionality, by approximating the unknown solution with a neural network or a Gaussian process. Moreover, unlike the state-of-the-art deep learning-based algorithms for solving high-dimensional partial differential equations [4, 8, 26], our algorithm (upon a single round of training) results in a solution function that can be evaluated anywhere in the space-time domain, not just at the initial point.

2. Problem Setup and Solution Methodology

We consider coupled forward–backward stochastic differential equations of the general form:

$$\begin{aligned} dX_t &= \mu(t, X_t, Y_t, Z_t)dt + \sigma(t, X_t, Y_t)dW_t, \quad t \in [0, T], \\ X_0 &= \xi, \\ dY_t &= \varphi(t, X_t, Y_t, Z_t)dt + Z_t'\sigma(t, X_t, Y_t)dW_t, \quad t \in [0, T), \\ Y_T &= g(X_T), \end{aligned} \tag{1}$$

where W_t is a vector-valued Brownian motion. A solution to these equations consists of the stochastic processes X_t, Y_t and Z_t. It is shown in Refs. [2, 12] (see also Refs. [6, 7, 14]) that coupled forward–backward stochastic differential equations (1) are related to quasi-linear partial differential equations of the form

$$u_t = f(t, x, u, Du, D^2u) \tag{2}$$

with terminal condition $u(T, x) = g(x)$, where $u(t, x)$ is the unknown solution and

$$\begin{aligned} f(t, x, y, z, \gamma) = \varphi(t, x, y, z) - \mu(t, x, y, z)'z \\ - \frac{1}{2}\mathrm{Tr}[\sigma(t, x, y)\sigma(t, x, y)'\gamma]. \end{aligned} \tag{3}$$

Here, Du and D^2u denote the gradient vector and the Hessian matrix of u, respectively. In particular, it follows directly from Ito's formula (see, e.g., Ref. [6]) that solutions of equations (1) and (2) are related according to

$$Y_t = u(t, X_t), \quad \text{and} \quad Z_t = Du(t, X_t). \tag{4}$$

Inspired by recent developments in *physics-informed deep learning* [22, 23] and *deep hidden physics models* [17], we proceed by approximating the unknown solution $u(t, x)$ by a deep neural network. We obtain the required gradient vector $Du(t, x)$ by applying the chain rule for differentiating compositions of functions using automatic differentiation [3]. It is worth emphasizing that automatic differentiation is different from, and in several respects superior to, numerical or symbolic differentiation, two commonly encountered techniques of computing derivatives. In its most basic description [3], automatic differentiation relies on the fact that all numerical computations are ultimately compositions of a finite set of elementary operations for which derivatives are known. Combining the derivatives of the constituent operations through the chain rule gives the derivative of the overall composition. This allows accurate evaluation of derivatives at machine precision with ideal asymptotic efficiency and only a small constant factor of overhead. In particular, to compute the derivatives involved in equation (4), we rely on TensorFlow [1] which is a popular and relatively well-documented open-source software library for automatic differentiation and deep learning computations.

Parameters of the neural network representing $u(t, x)$ can be learned by minimizing the following loss function given explicitly in equation (6) obtained from discretizing the forward–backward stochastic differential equation (1) using the standard Euler–Maruyama scheme. To be more specific, let us apply the Euler–Maruyama scheme to the set of equations (1) and obtain

$$\begin{aligned} X^{n+1} &\approx X^n + \mu(t^n, X^n, Y^n, Z^n)\Delta t^n + \sigma(t^n, X^n, Y^n)\Delta W^n, \\ Y^{n+1} &\approx Y^n + \varphi(t^n, X^n, Y^n, Z^n)\Delta t^n + (Z^n)'\sigma(t^n, X^n, Y^n)\Delta W^n, \end{aligned} \tag{5}$$

for $n = 0, 1, \ldots, N-1$, where $\Delta t^n := t^{n+1} - t^n = T/N$ and $\Delta W^n \sim \mathcal{N}(0, \Delta t^n)$ is a random variable with mean 0 and standard deviation $\sqrt{\Delta t^n}$. The loss function is then given by

$$\sum_{m=1}^{M}\sum_{n=0}^{N-1} |Y_m^{n+1} - Y_m^n - \Phi_m^n \Delta t^n - (Z_m^n)' \Sigma_m^n \Delta W_m^n|^2 + \sum_{m=1}^{M} |Y_m^N - g(X_m^N)|^2, \tag{6}$$

which corresponds to M different realizations of the underlying Brownian motion. Here, $\Phi_m^n := \varphi(t^n, X_m^n, Y_m^n, Z_m^n)$ and $\Sigma_m^n := \sigma(t^n, X_m^n, Y_m^n)$. The subscript m corresponds to the mth realization of the underlying Brownian motion while the superscript n corresponds to time t^n. It is worth recalling from equations (4) that $Y_m^n = u(t^n, X_m^n)$ and $Z_m^n = Du(t^n, X_m^n)$, and consequently, the loss (6) is a function of the parameters of the neural network $u(t, x)$. Furthermore, from equation (5), we have

$$X_m^{n+1} = X_m^n + \mu(t^n, X_m^n, Y_m^n, Z_m^n)\Delta t^n + \sigma(t_m^n, X_m^n, Y_m^n)\Delta W_m^n,$$

and $X_m^0 = \xi$ for every m.

3. Related Work[1]

In Refs. [8, 26], the authors consider uncoupled forward–backward stochastic differential equations of the form

$$\begin{aligned} dX_t &= \mu(t, X_t)dt + \sigma(t, X_t)dW_t, \quad t \in [0, T], \\ X_0 &= \xi, \\ dY_t &= \varphi(t, X_t, Y_t, Z_t)dt + Z_t'\sigma(t, X_t)dW_t, \quad t \in [0, T), \\ Y_T &= g(X_T), \end{aligned} \tag{7}$$

which are subcases of the coupled equations (1) studied in this work. The above equations are related to the semi-linear and parabolic

[1]This section can be skipped in the first read.

class of partial differential equations:

$$u_t = \varphi(t, x, Du, D^2u) - \mu(t, x)'Du - \frac{1}{2}\text{Tr}[\sigma(t, x)\sigma(t, x)'D^2u]. \quad (8)$$

The authors of Refs. [8, 26] then devise an algorithm to compute $Y_0 = u(0, X_0) = u(0, \xi)$ by treating Y_0 and $Z_0 = Du(0, \xi)$ as parameters in their model. Then, they employ the Euler–Maruyama scheme to discretize equations (7). Their next step is to approximate the functions $Du(t^n, x)$ for $n = 1, \ldots, N-1$ at time steps t^n by $N-1$ different neural networks. This enables them to approximate $Z^n = Du(t^n, X^n)$ by evaluating the corresponding neural network at time t^n at the spatial point X^n. Moreover, no neural networks are employed in Refs. [8, 26] to approximate the functions $u(t^n, x)$. In fact, $Y^n = u(t^n, X^n)$ is computed by time marching using the Euler–Maruyama scheme used to discretize equations (7). Their loss function is then given by

$$\sum_{m=1}^{M} |Y_m^N - g(X_m^N)|^2, \quad (9)$$

which tries to match the terminal condition. The total set of parameters are consequently given by Y_0, Z_0 and the parameters of the $N-1$ neural networks used to approximate the gradients. There are a couple of major drawbacks associated with the method advocated in Refs. [8, 26].

The first and the most obvious drawback is that the number of parameters involved in their model grows with the number of points N used to discretize time. This is prohibitive especially in cases where one would need to perform long-time integration (i.e., when the final time T is large) or in cases where it is a requirement to employ smaller time step size Δt in order to increase the accuracy of the Euler–Maruyama scheme. The second major drawback is that the method as outlined in Refs. [8, 26] is designed in such a way that it is only capable of approximating $Y_0 = u(0, X_0) = u(0, \xi)$. This means that in order to obtain an approximation to $Y_t = u(t, X_t)$ at a later time $t > 0$, they will have to retrain their algorithm. The third drawback is that assuming Y_0 and Z_0 to act as parameters of the models in addition to approximating the gradients by $N-1$ distinct (not sharing any parameters) neural networks seems a little bit *ad hoc*.

In contrast, the method proposed in this work circumvents all of the drawbacks mentioned above by placing a neural network directly on the object of interest, the unknown solution $u(t, x)$. This choice is justified by the similar well-established approach taken by the classical methods of solving partial differential equations, such as finite elements, finite differences or spectral methods, where one would expand the unknown solution $u(t, x)$ in terms of an appropriate set of basis functions. In addition, modern methods for solving forward and inverse problems associated with partial differential equations approximate the unknown solution $u(t, x)$ by either a neural network [9, 11, 17, 22–24] or a Gaussian process [15, 16, 18–21, 25]. The classical methods suffer from the curse of dimensionality mainly due to their reliance on spatio-temporal grids. Here, inspired by the aforementioned modern techniques, we avoid the curse of dimensionality by approximating $u(t, x)$ with a neural network. It should be highlighted that the number of parameters of the neural network we use to approximate $u(t, x)$ is independent of the number of points N needed to discretize time (see equation (5)). Moreover, upon a single round of training, the neural network representing $u(t, x)$ can be evaluated anywhere in the space–time domain, not just at the initial point $u(0, X_0)$. Furthermore, we compute the required gradients $Du(t, x)$ by differentiating the neural network representing $u(t, x)$ using automatic differentiation. Consequently, the networks $Du(t, x)$ and $u(t, x)$ share the same set of parameters. This is fully justified by the theoretical connection (see equation (4)) between solutions of forward–backward stochastic differential equations and their associated partial differential equations. A major advantage of the approach pursued in this work is the reduction in the number of parameters employed by our model, which helps the algorithm generalize better during test time and consequently mitigate the well-known over-fitting problem.

In Ref. [4], a follow-up work on Refs. [8, 26], the authors extend their framework to fully nonlinear second-order partial differential equations of the general form

$$u_t = f(t, x, u, Du, D^2u), \tag{10}$$

with terminal condition $u(T, x) = g(x)$. Here, let X_t denote a high-dimensional stochastic process satisfying the forward stochastic differential equation

$$\begin{aligned} dX_t &= \mu(X_t)dt + \sigma(X_t)dW_t, \\ X_0 &= \xi, \end{aligned} \tag{11}$$

where $\mu(X_t)$ is the drift vector and $\sigma(X_t)$ is the diffusion matrix. It then follows directly from Ito's formula [6] that the processes

$$\begin{aligned} Y_t &:= u(t, X_t), \\ Z_t &:= Du(t, X_t), \\ \Gamma_t &:= D^2u(t, X_t), \\ A_t &:= \mathcal{L}Du(t, X_t) := Du_t(t, X_t) + \frac{1}{2}D\mathrm{Tr}[D^2u(t, X_t)\sigma(X_t)\sigma(X_t)^T] \end{aligned} \tag{12}$$

solve the second-order backward stochastic differential equation

$$\begin{aligned} dY_t &= f(t, X_t, Y_t, Z_t, \Gamma_t)dt + \frac{1}{2}\mathrm{Tr}[\Gamma_t\sigma(X_t)\sigma(X_t)^T]dt + Z_t^T dX_t, \\ dZ_t &= A_t dt + \Gamma_t dX_t, \\ Y_T &= g(X_T). \end{aligned} \tag{13}$$

Similar to their prior works [8, 26], the authors then devise an algorithm to compute $Y_0 = u(0, X_0) = u(0, \xi)$ by treating Y_0, $Z_0 = Du(0, \xi)$, $\Gamma_0 = D^2u(0, \xi)$ and $A_0 = \mathcal{L}Du(0, \xi)$ as parameters of their model. Then, they proceed by discretizing equations (13) by the Euler–Maruyama scheme. Their next step is to approximate the functions $D^2u(t^n, x)$ and $\mathcal{L}Du(t^n, x)$ for $n = 1, \ldots, N-1$, corresponding to each time step t^n, by $2(N-1)$ distinct neural networks. This enables them to approximate $\Gamma^n = D^2u(t^n, X^n)$ and $A^n = D^2u(t^n, X^n)$ by evaluating the corresponding neural networks at X^n. Moreover, no neural networks are employed in Ref. [4] to approximate the functions $u(t^n, x)$ and $Du(t^n, x)$. In fact, $Y^n = u(t^n, X^n)$ and $Z^n = Du(t^n, X^n)$ are computed by time marching using the Euler–Maruyama scheme applied to equations (13). Their loss function is then given by (9) which tries to match the terminal condition. The total set of parameters are consequently given by Y_0, Z_0, Γ_0, A_0 and the parameters of the $2(N-1)$ neural networks used to approximate the functions $D^2u(t^n, x)$ and $\mathcal{L}Du(t^n, x)$. This framework, being a descendant of Refs. [8, 26], also suffers from the drawbacks listed above. It should be emphasized that, although not pursued here, the framework proposed in this work can be straightforwardly extended to solve the second-order backward stochastic differential equations (13). The key (see, e.g., Ref. [6]) is to leverage the fundamental relationships (12).

4. Results

The proposed framework provides a universal treatment of coupled forward–backward stochastic differential equations of fundamentally different nature and their corresponding high-dimensional partial differential equations. This generality will be demonstrated by applying the algorithm to a wide range of canonical problems spanning a number of scientific domains including a 100-dimensional Black–Scholes–Barenblatt equation and a 100-dimensional Hamilton–Jacobi–Bellman equation. These examples are motivated by the pioneering works [4, 8, 26]. All data and codes used in this manuscript will be publicly available on GitHub at https://github.com/maziarraissi/FBSNNs.

4.1. *Black–Scholes–Barenblatt Equation in 100D*

Let us start with the following forward–backward stochastic differential equations:

$$\begin{aligned} dX_t &= \sigma \text{diag}(X_t) dW_t, \quad t \in [0, T], \\ X_0 &= \xi, \\ dY_t &= r(Y_t - Z_t' X_t)dt + \sigma Z_t' \text{diag}(X_t) dW_t, \quad t \in [0, T), \\ Y_T &= g(X_T), \end{aligned} \tag{14}$$

where $T = 1$, $\sigma = 0.4$, $r = 0.05$, $\xi = (1, 0.5, 1, 0.5, \ldots, 1, 0.5) \in \mathbb{R}^{100}$ and $g(x) = \|x\|^2$. The above equations are related to the Black–Scholes–Barenblatt equation

$$u_t = -\frac{1}{2}\text{Tr}[\sigma^2 \text{diag}(X_t^2) D^2 u] + r(u - (Du)'x), \tag{15}$$

with terminal condition $u(T, x) = g(x)$. This equation admits the explicit solution

$$u(t, x) = \exp\left((r + \sigma^2)(T - t)\right) g(x), \tag{16}$$

which can be used to test the accuracy of the proposed algorithm. We approximate the unknown solution $u(t, x)$ by a five-layer deep neural network with 256 neurons per hidden layer. Furthermore, we partition the time domain $[0, T]$ into $N = 50$ equally spaced intervals (see equations (5)). Upon minimizing the loss function (6), using the Adam optimizer [10] with mini-batches of size 100 (i.e., 100 realizations of the underlying Brownian motion), we obtain the results reported in Figure 1. In this figure, we are evaluating the learned solution $Y_t = u(t, X_t)$ at representative realizations (not seen during training) of the underlying high-dimensional process X_t. Unlike the state-of-the-art algorithms [4, 8, 26], which can only approximate $Y_0 = u(0, X_0)$ at time 0 and at the initial spatial point $X_0 = \xi$, our algorithm is capable of approximating the entire solution function

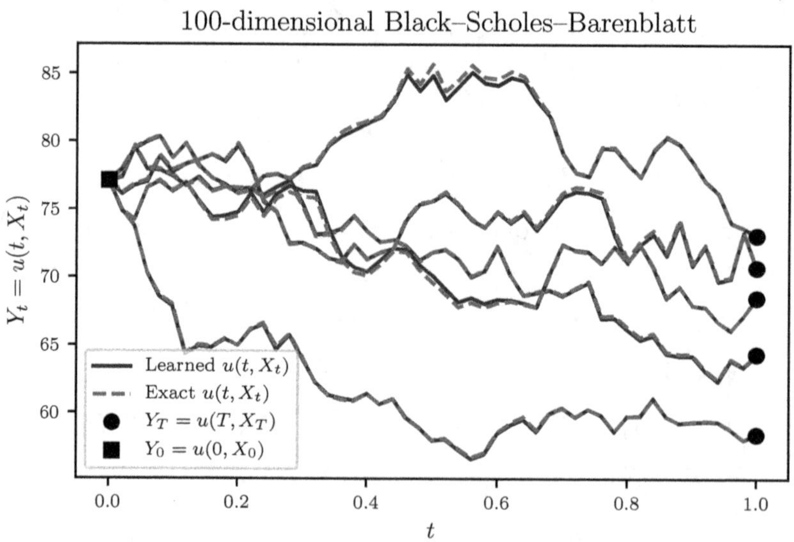

Figure 1. Black–Scholes–Barenblatt equation in 100D: Evaluations of the learned solution $Y_t = u(t, X_t)$ at representative realizations of the underlying high-dimensional process X_t. It should be highlighted that the state-of-the-art algorithms [4, 8, 26] can only approximate $Y_0 = u(0, X_0)$ at time 0 and at the initial spatial point $X_0 = \xi$.

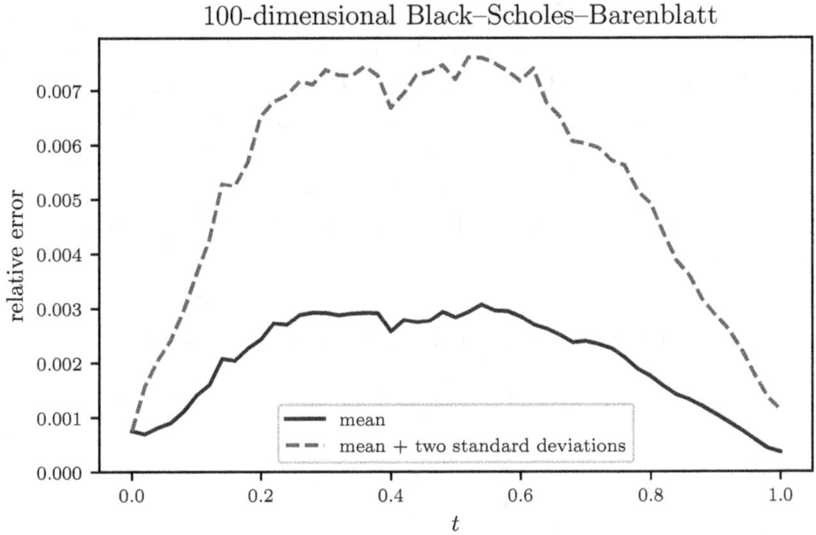

Figure 2. Black–Scholes–Barenblatt Equation in 100D: Mean and mean plus two standard deviations of the relative errors between model predictions and the exact solution computed based on 100 realizations of the underlying Brownian motion.

$u(t, x)$ in a single round of training as demonstrated in Figure 1. Figures such as this one are absent in Refs. [4, 8, 26], by design.

To further scrutinize the performance of our algorithm, in Figure 2, we report the mean and mean plus two standard deviations of the relative errors between model predictions and the exact solution computed based on 100 independent realizations of the underlying Brownian motion. It is worth noting that in Figure 1, we were plotting five representative examples of the 100 realizations used to generate Figure 2. The results reported in Figures 1 and 2 are obtained after 2×10^4, 3×10^4, 3×10^4, and 2×10^4 consecutive iterations of the Adam optimizer with learning rates of 10^{-3}, 10^{-4}, 10^{-5}, and 10^{-6}, respectively. The total number of iterations is therefore given by 10^5. Every 10 iterations of the optimizer takes about 0.88 s on a single NVIDIA Titan X GPU card. In each iteration of the Adam optimizer, we are using 100 different realizations of the underlying Brownian motion. Consequently, the total number of Brownian motion trajectories observed by the algorithm is given by 10^7. It is worth highlighting that the algorithm converges to the exact value

$Y_0 = u(0, X_0)$ in the first few hundred iterations of the Adam optimizer. For instance, after only 500 steps of training, the algorithms achieve an accuracy of around 2.3×10^{-3} in terms of relative error. This is comparable to the results reported in Refs. [4, 8, 26], both in terms of accuracy and the speed of the algorithm. However, to obtain more accurate estimates for $Y_t = u(t, X_t)$ at later times $t > 0$, we need to train the algorithm using more iterations of the Adam optimizer.

4.2. *Hamilton–Jacobi–Bellman Equation in 100D*

Let us now consider the following forward–backward stochastic differential equations:

$$\begin{aligned} dX_t &= \sigma dW_t, \quad t \in [0, T], \\ X_0 &= \xi, \\ dY_t &= \|Z_t\|^2 dt + \sigma Z_t' dW_t, \quad t \in [0, T), \\ Y_T &= g(X_T), \end{aligned} \tag{17}$$

where $T = 1$, $\sigma = \sqrt{2}$, $\xi = (0, 0, \ldots, 0) \in \mathbb{R}^{100}$ and $g(x) = \ln\left(0.5\left(1 + \|x\|^2\right)\right)$. The above equations are related to the Hamilton–Jacobi–Bellman equation

$$u_t = -\mathrm{Tr}[D^2 u] + \|Du\|^2, \tag{18}$$

with terminal condition $u(T, x) = g(x)$. This equation admits the explicit solution

$$u(t, x) = -\ln\left(\mathbb{E}\left[\exp\left(-g(x + \sqrt{2}W_{T-t})\right)\right]\right), \tag{19}$$

which can be used to test the accuracy of the proposed algorithm. In fact, due to the presence of the expectation operator $\mathbb{E}$ in equation (19), we can only approximately compute the exact solution. To be precise, we use 10^5 Monte Carlo samples to approximate the exact solution (19) and use the result as ground truth. We represent the unknown solution $u(t, x)$ by a five-layer deep neural network with 256 neurons per hidden layer. Furthermore, we partition the time domain $[0, T]$ into $N = 50$ equally spaced intervals (see equations (5)). Upon minimizing the loss function (6), using the Adam optimizer [10] with mini-batches of size 100 (i.e., 100 realizations of the underlying Brownian motion), we obtain the results reported in Figure 3. In this figure, we are evaluating the learned solution $Y_t = u(t, X_t)$ at a representative realization (not seen during training) of the underlying high-dimensional process X_t. It is worth noting that computing the exact solution (19) to this problem is prohibitively costly due to the need for the aforementioned Monte Carlo sampling strategy. That is why we are depicting only a single realization of the solution trajectories in Figure 3. Unlike the state-of-the-art algorithms [4, 8, 26], which can only approximate $Y_0 = u(0, X_0)$ at time 0 and at the initial spatial point $X_0 = \xi$, our algorithm is capable of approximating the entire solution function $u(t, x)$ in a single round of training as demonstrated in Figure 3.

To further investigate the performance of our algorithm, in Figure 4, we report the relative error between model prediction and the exact solution computed for the same realization of the underlying Brownian motion as the one used in Figure 3. The results reported

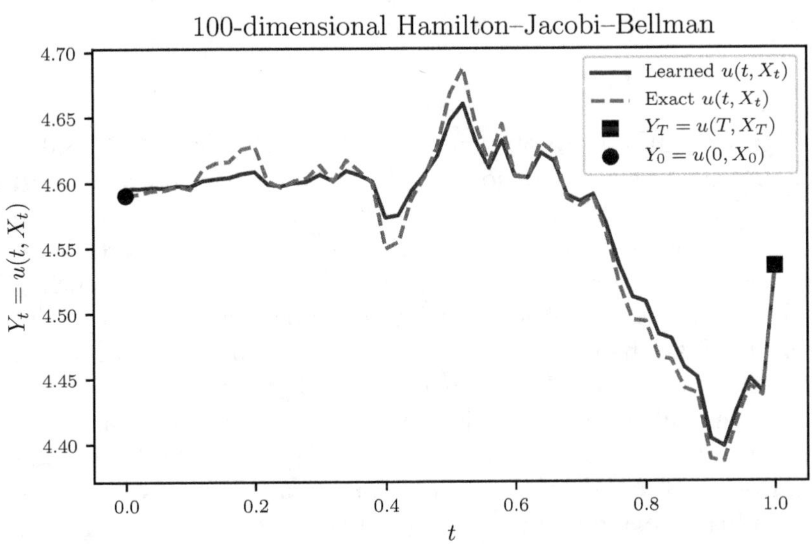

Figure 3. Hamilton–Jacobi–Bellman Equation in 100D: Evaluation of the learned solution $Y_t = u(t, X_t)$ at a representative realization of the underlying high-dimensional process X_t. It should be highlighted that the state-of-the-art algorithms [4, 8, 26] can only approximate $Y_0 = u(0, X_0)$ at time 0 and at the initial spatial point $X_0 = \xi$.

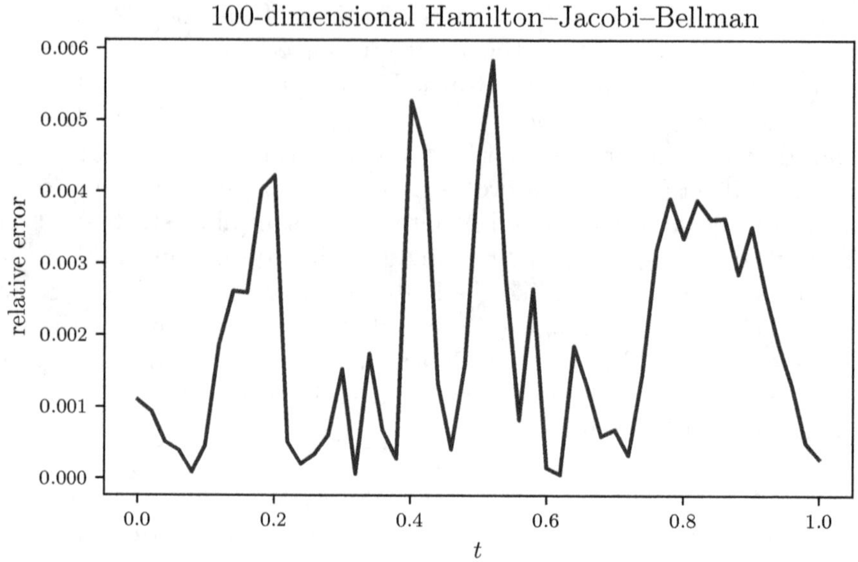

Figure 4. Hamilton–Jacobi–Bellman Equation in 100D: The relative error between model prediction and the exact solution computed based on a single realization of the underlying Brownian motion.

in Figures 3 and 4 are obtained after 2×10^4, 3×10^4, 3×10^4, and 2×10^4 consecutive iterations of the Adam optimizer with learning rates of 10^{-3}, 10^{-4}, 10^{-5}, and 10^{-6}, respectively. The total number of iterations is therefore given by 10^5. Every 10 iterations of the optimizer take about 0.79 second on a single NVIDIA Titan X GPU card. In each iteration of the Adam optimizer, we are using 100 different realizations of the underlying Brownian motion. Consequently, the total number of Brownian motion trajectories observed by the algorithm is given by 10^7. It is worth highlighting that the algorithm converges to the exact value $Y_0 = u(0, X_0)$ in the first few hundred iterations of the Adam optimizer. For instance, after only 100 steps of training, the algorithms achieve an accuracy of around 7.3×10^{-3} in terms of relative error. This is comparable to the results reported in Refs. [4,8,26], both in terms of accuracy and the speed of the algorithm. However, to obtain more accurate estimates for $Y_t = u(t, X_t)$ at later times $t > 0$, we need to train the algorithm using more iterations of the Adam optimizer.

4.3. *Allen–Cahn Equation in 20D*

Let us consider the following forward–backward stochastic differential equations:

$$\begin{aligned} dX_t &= dW_t, \quad t \in [0,T], \\ X_0 &= \xi, \\ dY_t &= (-Y_t + Y_t^3)dt + Z_t' dW_t, \quad t \in [0,T), \\ Y_T &= g(X_T), \end{aligned} \tag{20}$$

where $T = 0.3$, $\xi = (0,0,\ldots,0) \in \mathbb{R}^{20}$ and $g(x) = \left(2 + 0.4\|x\|^2\right)^{-1}$. The above equations are related to the Allen–Cahn equation

$$u_t = -0.5\mathrm{Tr}[D^2 u] - u + u^3, \tag{21}$$

with terminal condition $u(T,x) = g(x)$. We represent the unknown solution $u(t,x)$ by a five-layer deep neural network with 256 neurons per hidden layer. Furthermore, we partition the time domain $[0,T]$ into $N = 15$ equally spaced intervals (see equations (5)). Upon minimizing the loss function (6), using the Adam optimizer [10] with mini-batches of size 100 (i.e., 100 realizations of the underlying Brownian motion), we obtain the results reported in Figure 5. In this

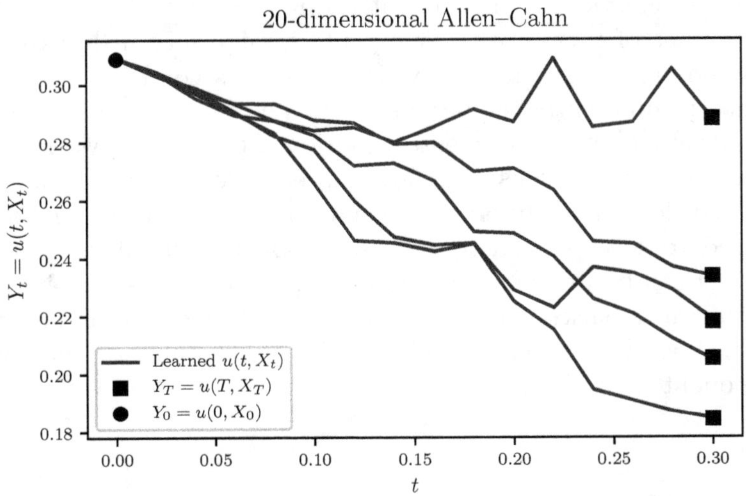

Figure 5. Allen–Cahn Equation in 20D: Evaluation of the learned solution $Y_t = u(t, X_t)$ at representative realizations of the underlying high-dimensional process X_t. It should be highlighted that the state-of-the-art algorithms [4,8,26] can only approximate $Y_0 = u(0, X_0)$ at time 0 and at the initial spatial point $X_0 = \xi$.

figure, we are evaluating the learned solution $Y_t = u(t, X_t)$ at five representative realizations (not seen during training) of the underlying high-dimensional process X_t. Unlike the state-of-the-art algorithms [4,8,26], which can only approximate $Y_0 = u(0, X_0) = 0.30879$ at time 0 and at the initial spatial point $X_0 = \xi$, our algorithm is capable of approximating the entire solution function $u(t, x)$ in a single round of training as demonstrated in Figure 5.

5. Summary and Discussion

In this work, we put forth a deep learning approach for solving coupled forward–backward stochastic differential equations and their corresponding high-dimensional partial differential equations. The resulting methodology showcases a series of promising results for a diverse collection of benchmark problems. As deep learning technology is continuing to grow rapidly in terms of methodological, algorithmic and infrastructural developments, we believe that this is a timely contribution that can benefit practitioners across a wide range of scientific domains. Specific applications that can readily enjoy these benefits include, but are not limited to, stochastic control, theoretical economics and mathematical finance.

In terms of future work, one could straightforwardly extend the proposed framework in this work to solve second-order backward stochastic differential equations (13). The key (see, e.g., Ref. [6]) is to leverage the fundamental relationships (12) between second-order backward stochastic differential equations and fully nonlinear second-order partial differential equations. Moreover, our method can be used to solve stochastic control problems, where in general, to obtain a candidate for an optimal control, one needs to solve a coupled forward–backward stochastic differential equation (1), where the backward components influence the dynamics of the forward component.

References

[1] M. Abadi, A. Agarwal, P. Barham, E. Brevdo, Z. Chen, C. Citro, G. S Corrado, A. Davis, J. Dean, M. Devin *et al.* Tensorflow: Large-scale

machine learning on heterogeneous distributed systems. https://www.usenix.org/system/files/conference/osdi16/osdi16-abadi.pdf.

[2] F. Antonelli. Backward-forward stochastic differential equations. *The Annals of Applied Probability*, 777–793, 1993. https://www.projecteuclid.org/journals/annals-of-applied-probability/volume-3/issue-3/Backward-Forward-Stochastic-Differential-Equations/10.1214/aoap/1177005363.full.

[3] A. G. Baydin, B. A. Pearlmutter, A. A. Radul, and J. M. Siskind. Automatic differentiation in machine learning: A survey. arXiv preprint, arXiv:1502.05767, 2015. https://www.jmlr.org/papers/volume18/17-468/17-468.pdf.

[4] C. Beck, A. Jentzen *et al.* Machine learning approximation algorithms for high-dimensional fully nonlinear partial differential equations and second-order backward stochastic differential equations. arXiv preprint, arXiv:1709.05963, 2017. https://link.springer.com/article/10.1007/s00332-018-9525-3.

[5] J.-M. Bismut. Conjugate convex functions in optimal stochastic control. *Journal of Mathematical Analysis and Applications*, 44(2):384–404, 1973.

[6] P. Cheridito, H. M. Soner, N. Touzi, and N. Victoir. Second-order backward stochastic differential equations and fully nonlinear parabolic PDEs. *Communications on Pure and Applied Mathematics*, 60(7):1081–1110, 2007.

[7] F. Delarue and S. Menozzi. A forward-backward stochastic algorithm for quasi-linear PDEs. *The Annals of Applied Probability*, 140–184, 2006. https://projecteuclid.org/journals/annals-of-applied-probability/volume-16/issue-1/A-forwardbackward-stochastic-algorithm-for-quasi-linear-PDEs/10.1214/105051605000000674.full.

[8] J. Han, A. Jentzen *et al.* Overcoming the curse of dimensionality: Solving high-dimensional partial differential equations using deep learning. https://www.pnas.org/doi/pdf/10.1073/pnas.1718942115.

[9] G. E. Karniadakis, I. G. Kevrekidis, L. Lu, P. Perdikaris, S. Wang, and L. Yang. Physics-informed machine learning. *Nature Reviews Physics*, 3(6):422–440, 2021.

[10] D. P. Kingma and J. B. Adam: A method for stochastic optimization. In editor Yoshua Bengio and Yann LeCun, *3rd International Conference on Learning Representations*, ICLR, San Diego, CA, USA, 2015, arXiv preprint, arXiv:1412.6980, 2014.

[11] L. Lu, X. Meng, Z. Mao, and G. E. Karniadakis. Deepxde: A deep learning library for solving differential equations. *SIAM Review*, 63(1):208–228, 2021.

[12] J. Ma, P. Protter, and J. Yong. Solving forward-backward stochastic differential equations explicitly- a four step scheme. *Probability Theory and Related Fields*, 98(3):339–359, 1994.

[13] E. Pardoux and S. Peng. Adapted solution of a backward stochastic differential equation. *Systems & Control Letters*, 14(1):55–61, 1990.

[14] E. Pardoux and S. Tang. Forward-backward stochastic differential equations and quasilinear parabolic PDEs. *Probability Theory and Related Fields*, 114(2):123–150, 1999.

[15] P. Perdikaris, M. Raissi, A. Damianou, N. D. Lawrence, and G. E. Karniadakis. Nonlinear information fusion algorithms for data-efficient multi-fidelity modelling. *Proceedings of the Royal Society A*, 473(2198):20160751, 2017.

[16] M. Raissi. Parametric Gaussian process regression for big data. *Computational Mechanics*, 64(2019):409–416. arXiv preprint, arXiv:1704.03144, 2017.

[17] M. Raissi. Deep hidden physics models: Deep learning of nonlinear partial differential equations. *The Journal of Machine Learning Research*, 19(1):932–955. arXiv preprint, arXiv:1801.06637, 2018.

[18] M. Raissi and G. Karniadakis. Deep multi-fidelity Gaussian processes. arXiv preprint, arXiv:1604.07484, 2016.

[19] M. Raissi and G. E. Karniadakis. Hidden physics models: Machine learning of nonlinear partial differential equations. *Journal of Computational Physics*, 357:125–141, 2018.

[20] M. Raissi, P. Perdikaris, and G. E. Karniadakis. Inferring solutions of differential equations using noisy multi-fidelity data. *Journal of Computational Physics*, 335:736–746, 2017a.

[21] M. Raissi, P. Perdikaris, and G. E. Karniadakis. Machine learning of linear differential equations using gaussian processes. *Journal of Computational Physics*, 348:683–693, 2017b.

[22] M. Raissi, P. Perdikaris, and G. E. Karniadakis. Physics informed deep learning (part ii): Data-driven discovery of nonlinear partial differential equations. *Journal of Computational physics* 378(2019):686–707. arXiv preprint, arXiv:1711.10566, 2017c.

[23] M. Raissi, P. Perdikaris, and G. E. Karniadakis. Physics informed deep learning (part i): Data-driven solutions of nonlinear partial differential equations.*Journal of Computational physics* 378(2019):686–707. arXiv preprint, arXiv:1711.10561, 2017d.

[24] M. Raissi, P. Perdikaris, and G. E. Karniadakis. Multistep neural networks for data-driven discovery of nonlinear dynamical systems. arXiv preprint, arXiv:1801.01236, 2018a.

[25] M. Raissi, P. Perdikaris, and G. E. Karniadakis. Numerical Gaussian processes for time-dependent and nonlinear partial differential

equations. *SIAM Journal on Scientific Computing*, 40(1):A172–A198, 2018b.

[26] E. Weinan, J. Han, and A. Jentzen. Deep learning-based numerical methods for high-dimensional parabolic partial differential equations and backward stochastic differential equations. *Communications in Mathematics and Statistics*, 5(4):349–380, 2017.

https://doi.org/10.1142/9789811280306_0019

Chapter 19

How to Design a Derivatives Market?

Bastien Baldacci*, Paul Jusselin†, and Mathieu Rosenbaum‡

École Polytechnique, Institut Polytechnique de Paris,
Route de Saclay, 91128 Palaiseau, France
*bastien.baldacci@polytechnique.edu
†paul.jusselin@polytechnique.edu
‡mathieu.rosenbaum@polytechnique.edu

Abstract
We consider the problem of designing a derivatives exchange aiming at addressing clients' needs in terms of listed options and providing suitable liquidity. We proceed into two steps: First, we use a quantization method to select the options that should be displayed by the exchange. Then, using a principal–agent approach, we design a make-take fees contract between the exchange and the market maker. The role of this contract is to provide incentives to the market maker so that he offers small spreads for the whole range of listed options, hence attracting transactions and meeting the commercial requirements of the exchange.

Keywords: Make-take fees, Market making, Derivatives, Market design, Quantization, Lloyd's algorithm, Financial regulation, High-frequency trading, Principal–agent problem, Stochastic control

1. Introduction

Nowadays, a typical role of an exchange is to give the possibility to investors to buy or sell financial products on electronic platforms in sufficiently large quantities and at reasonable prices. Therefore, exchanges have to set up their markets in a relevant way in order to achieve this goal. The issues related to market design cover a wide range of topics from the microstructure of electronic trading platforms to the basic question of selecting the products that will be traded on the exchange.

Recently, many papers have focused on the microstructural aspects of market design. For example, the way of choosing an optimal tick size is addressed in Ref. [4], where the authors study the relations between tick size, volatility and bid-ask bounce frequency. In Refs. [3, 7], the relevance of continuous trading and its comparison with a frequent batch auction system is discussed, while market fragmentation is analyzed in Ref. [9]. Macroscopic features have also been investigated, see, for example, Ref. [8], where different market structures are classified with respect to several criteria, such as matching mechanism, information feedback and bid structure.

Most of the research on market design focuses on stock markets. However, even if exchanges concentrate a large part of their activities on simple products, such as stocks or futures, many also offer their clients the possibility to trade more complex financial instruments, such as derivatives. Actually, there is very few academic literature on derivatives market design, mostly addressing the relationship between stock and option markets. For example, in Ref. [11], the authors investigate the factors influencing the selection of stocks for option listing. However, they neither question the optimality of those factors nor search for more relevant ones. The papers dealing with market design can in fact be separated into two groups: the ones that review and try to understand market practice and those proposing a theoretical framework in order to help exchanges improve their market design. Surprisingly, to our knowledge, there is no paper of the last kind dealing with derivatives market. In this chapter, we propose the first contribution in that direction.

We take the realistic point of view of an exchange that wants to organize, or reorganize, its derivatives market. We consider that the market is made of vanilla European options only that we view as independent of the underlying. By this, we mean that we deal with options that are used as hedging instruments and whose prices are essentially fixed by supply and demand. Finally, we suppose that the exchange has access to data allowing for the estimation of the distribution of options market demand. For example, if the exchange already has a derivatives market, it can use its own data, otherwise that of other exchanges. We focus on two issues: selecting the options that are going to be traded and attracting liquidity on those options.

The first issue faced by the exchange is the choice of the derivatives offered to the clients. Obviously, it is impossible for the exchange to propose all maturities and strikes on its platform. This would be very hard to manage from a technical point of view, and it would be impossible to guarantee liquidity on each option. As the maturities are quite standardized, the main challenge relies on strikes' selection satisfying clients' needs. Therefore, we consider that the exchange's problem is to select n call options (or equivalently n strikes), with fixed maturity, with the aim of maximizing the clients' satisfaction. We define a measurement of this satisfaction and write the exchange objective under the form of quantization problems. We refer to Refs. [6, 12] for an introduction to quantization. Such approach allows the exchange to select automatically a set of options based only on the data at its disposal.

The next goal of the exchange is to attract liquidity on its platform in order to increase the amount of executed orders. To do so, one way is to use a make-take fees system: the exchange typically associates a fee rebate to executed limit orders, while charging a transaction fee for market orders. This enables it to subsidize liquidity provision and tax liquidity consumption. In Ref. [5], the authors design the optimal make-take fees policy for a market with one market maker and a single underlying asset. This work has been extended in Ref. [2] to the case of multiple market makers. The general principle of the approach in Refs. [2, 5] is to consider that the exchange offers a contract to the market maker whose pay-off depends on the market order flow he generates. The problem of the exchange then boils down to designing the optimal contract in order to optimize the number of transactions.

However, in our setting, the problem faced by the exchange is more complex to several extents. The main difference with the framework of Refs. [2, 5] is that the exchange has to manage several assets simultaneously, namely the different options quoted on the platform. In order to focus on this issue, we assume that there is only one market maker setting bid and ask quotes for all available options. Another challenge for a derivatives exchange is the possible absence of quotations for far from the money options (or quotations with a too wide spread). Such issue arises essentially for commercial reasons. Indeed, an exchange does not wish to display to its clients a product with scarce liquidity. It wants to make sure that there is sufficient available volume on the market for the whole range of listed options. Therefore, the design of an optimal make-take fees policy for options market must aim at providing incentives to the market maker to lower the spreads, notably for far from the money options.

To do so, we are inspired by Refs. [2, 5], using a principal–agent framework. The exchange (the principal) has to design a contract toward the market maker (the agent) that maximizes a certain utility that depends on the behavior of the market maker. The main point is that the market maker's behavior, here the quoted spread on every available option, cannot be dictated by the exchange and depends on the contract. For example, if the contract offers high incentives for every executed ask market order, then it is likely that the ask price quoted by the market maker will be close to the mid-price. Formally, for a given contract, the market maker determines its behavior by solving a stochastic control problem. Then, in order to find the optimal contract, the exchange maximizes its expected utility over the set of admissible contracts, knowing the market maker's response to each contract.

This chapter is organized as follows: In Section 2, we explain how an exchange can select the options that will be traded on its platform using only market data. Then, in Section 3, we design the optimal contract that the exchange should offer to the market maker in order to maximize liquidity. Proofs and technical results are relegated to the Appendix.

2. Market-Driven Selection of the Listed Options

In this section, we build a method for the exchange to select the strikes that are going to be traded on its platform. This approach uses only data from trades volume reports and is based on a quantization algorithm. We illustrate this method by numerical experiments using data provided by Euronext.

2.1. *How to Choose the Strikes in Order to Match Market Demand?*

We consider European call options with strikes expressed in percentage of the spot price (in moneyness) and that the exchange wishes to select n strikes.[1] Choosing relevant strikes, the exchange's objective is to maximize the satisfaction of the investors. So, we focus in this section on the market-taking side of the trading flow. Section 3 will be rather devoted to market makers.

We measure the regret of a market taker associated with the execution of a market order as a function of the difference between the strike he would have ideally bought (or sold) and the strike he actually bought (or sold). More precisely, for a given maturity, consider strikes $K_1 < \cdots < K_n$ that represent the options listed by the exchange. When a market taker wants to buy an option with strike K, he sends a market order on the option whose strike is the nearest from K. Hence, he buys (or sells) the option with strike K_i, where i is such that

$$i = \arg\min_{1 \leq j \leq n} |K - K_j|.$$

We consider that the regret associated with this market order is $\rho(|K - K_i|)$, where ρ is an increasing function. Note that the regret of the market order can be written as follows:

$$\min_{1 \leq j \leq n} \rho(|K - K_j|).$$

We finally assume that the strike K is randomly chosen according to the distribution $\mathbb{P}^{mkt}$. This probability measure represents the law of market demand. Thus, the higher the demand for a given strike, the higher the probability that K is close to this strike. The exchange can easily estimate the distribution $\mathbb{P}^{mkt}$ using data from its own options

[1] We do not address here the problem of choosing the number of strikes to propose. This point is left for further research.

market or from other exchanges. The average regret of a market order is therefore written as follows:

$$\mathbb{E}^{mkt}[\min_{1\leq j\leq n} \rho(|K - K_j|)], \tag{1}$$

where $\mathbb{E}^{mkt}$ denotes the expectation when $K \sim \mathbb{P}^{mkt}$. The problem of the exchange is then to find the n-uplet $(K_i)_{1\leq i\leq n}$ that minimizes (1). Formally, this corresponds to the following minimization problem:

$$\underset{K_1\leq\cdots\leq K_n}{\arg\min}\ \mathbb{E}^{mkt}[\min_{1\leq j\leq n} \rho(|K - K_j|)]. \tag{2}$$

Here the expectation is computed for given $(K_i)_{1\leq i\leq n}$ and thus the goal is to find a minimizing sequence $(K_i)_{1\leq i\leq n}$. This type of optimization is classical in the field of signal or image processing and is called *quantization* problem. The main idea of quantization is to summarize the information contained in a complex probability measure into a uniform probability with finite support. As an example, it allows to compress a signal (or an image) by selecting among its spectrum a given number of frequencies that summarizes the signal with the smallest possible loss of information. For an introduction to quantization problem, see Refs. [6, 12].

In this chapter, we consider the quantization problem (2) when ρ is a power-law function of the form $\rho(x) = |x|^p$ with $p \geq 2$. The power-law function has the advantage to be symmetric and convex. Therefore, greater errors are increasingly penalized. As a consequence, we expect the solution of (2) to capture the features of the tails of $\mathbb{P}^{mkt}$. Moreover, the greater the p, the more large errors are penalized. Hence, for a large p, the $(K_i)_{1\leq i\leq n}$ solutions of (2) are likely to be more spread toward large strikes and contain more extreme values of the distribution $\mathbb{P}^{mkt}$.

2.2. *Solving the Quantization Problem*

In this section, we give some sufficient conditions that ensure that (2) has a unique solution. We also explain how (2) can be solved.

To get the existence of a solution to problem (2), we need to make the following assumption:

Assumption 2.1. The probability $\mathbb{P}^{mkt}$ is absolutely continuous with respect to the Lebesgue measure with density that is log-concave and compactly supported in $[0, \overline{K}], \overline{K} > 0$.

The assumption on the support of the probability is very reasonable since strikes between 0 and 200% of the spot price basically cover all the possible strikes of traded options. The log-concavity assumption is not really restrictive since it allows us to consider a wide class of probability distributions, such as exponential type and Gaussian laws. It is shown in [6, Theorem I-5.1] that under Assumption 2.1, Problem (2) admits a unique non-degenerate solution. The term non-degenerate simply means that the optimal set of strikes satisfies $K_1 < \cdots < K_n$.

We now present a way to approximate numerically the solution of (2). The idea behind the algorithm is that the solution $(K_i)_{1\leq i\leq n}$ can be seen as the fixed point of a function. This provides us a numerical method to approximate the $(K_i)_{1\leq i\leq n}$ that consists in iterating this function. This is known as Lloyd's algorithm, which is a very intuitive approach that searches step by step the solution of (2). A very convenient aspect of this algorithm is that it is automatic and easy to implement.

Lloyd's algorithm starts with an initial set of strikes $(K_i)_{1\leq i\leq n}$ and is made of three steps:

1. For any i, identify A_i the set of "wished" strikes that corresponds to market orders sent to the strike K_i. Equivalently, A_i contains all the strikes K which are closer to K_i than from any other K_j,
$$A_i = \{K, \text{ s.t } i = \underset{1\leq j\leq n}{\arg\min}|K - K_j|\}.$$
2. Set K_i' as the unique strike in A_i that minimizes the average regret of market orders sent with ideal strike in A_i. More precisely, K_i' is given by
$$K_i' = \underset{k\in A_i}{\arg\min}\ \mathbb{E}^{mkt}[|K - k|^p \mathbf{1}_{K\in A_i}].$$
3. Go back to Step 1 with $(K_i)_{1\leq i\leq n} = (K_i')_{1\leq i\leq n}$ (or stop if a certain stopping criterion is reached and consider $(K_i')_{1\leq i\leq n}$ as the approximate solution of (2)).

Lloyd's algorithm has a very clear interpretation in terms of selecting the optimal set of strikes: first, it identifies the area "controlled" by the $i - th$ strike and then improves the choice of the strikes. It is then intuitive that the solution of (2) is a fixed point of Lloyd's algorithm. The sets $(A_i)_{1\leq i\leq n}$ form a covering of $\mathbb{R}_+$ that is often called the Voronoï tessellation associated with the $(K_i)_{1\leq i\leq n}$. It is easy to show that, for Step 1,

$$A_1 = [0, K_1],\ A_n = [K_n, \overline{K}] \text{ and for } i \in \{2, \ldots, n-1\} :$$
$$A_i = \left[\frac{K_i + K_{i-1}}{2}, \frac{K_{i+1} + K_i}{2}\right].$$

A usual stopping criterion for Step 3 is when $(K_i')_{1\leq i\leq n}$ is too close from $(K_i)_{1\leq i\leq n}$. More precisely, the algorithm stops if

$$\sum_{i=1}^{n} |K_i' - K_i| < \varepsilon,$$

for a certain $\varepsilon > 0$. Note that, starting from a discrete-valued $\mathbb{P}^{mkt}$ (as will be the case here), when $p = 2$, Step 2 of Lloyd's algorithm boils down to compute the average realization of $\mathbb{P}^{mkt}$ conditional on being in A_i. This can be obtained instantaneously. However, when $p > 2$, Step 2 is not straightforward to compute in general. Yet the objective function being convex and taking the derivative with respect to k, a necessary and sufficient condition for k to be the solution of Step 2 is

$$\mathbb{E}[|K - k|^{p-2}(K - k)\mathbf{1}_{K\in A_i}] = 0$$

or equivalently

$$k = \frac{\mathbb{E}^{mkt}[K|K - k|^{p-2}\mathbf{1}_{K\in A_i}]}{\mathbb{E}^{mkt}[|K - k|^{p-2}\mathbf{1}_{K\in A_i}]}.$$

This characterizes the solution of Step 2 as a fixed point. Thus, one usually replaces Step 2 by its iterative version:

$$K_i' = \frac{\mathbb{E}^{mkt}[K|K - K_i|^{p-2}\mathbf{1}_{K\in A_i}]}{\mathbb{E}^{mkt}[|K - K_i|^{p-2}\mathbf{1}_{K\in A_i}]}.$$

From now on, we call Lloyd's algorithm the initial algorithm where we replace Step 2 with its approximate version. We prove in

Appendix A.1 that $(K_i)_{1\leq i\leq n}$ is the solution of (2) if and only if it is a fixed point of Lloyd's algorithm. The great strength of this method is that it is easy to implement, transparent and completely automatic. Note also that if $\mathbb{P}^{mkt}$ has a discrete support, say 10 strikes, then Lloyd's algorithm will not necessarily select those strikes as the solution of (2).

We now turn to numerical experiments illustrating the efficiency of our method.

2.3. *Application*

In this section, we apply our methodology to market data. First, we describe the data and then present our numerical results.

2.3.1. *Description of the Data*

We use data from Euronext, one of the main stock and option exchanges in Europe. The data set contains every trading day from the 3rd of December 2018 to the 24th of May 2019 and for every available options the total number of trades (buy and sell) during the day. Our data set is only made of transactions that occurred on the Euronext platform. In particular, we neither use OTC data nor data from another exchange. We choose for our example the most standard call options in terms of underlying on Euronext, namely options on the CAC 40 index. We report in Table 1 the number of call options traded each month for different ranges of maturity and in Table 2 the number of call options traded each month for each strike.

In Figure 1, we display the empirical distribution of traded option strikes (for all maturities) and the quantile plot of the maturity distribution in log-scale. The distribution of the strikes is unimodal, concentrated near the money and skewed toward the money strikes. In Figure 2, we provide the empirical distribution of traded options strikes for different ranges of maturity. We see that the distribution of the strikes depends on the maturity. In particular, the variance of the distribution is increasing with the maturity. The skewness toward the money strikes is present for any maturity.

Table 1. Number of options traded by maturity and month.

Maturity	December	January	February	March	April	May
$T \leq 1M$	135,951	99,202	96,323	191,357	161,937	108,491
$1M < T \leq 3M$	79,016	61,651	30,371	117,400	58,914	121,267
$3M < T \leq 6M$	10,990	13,279	15,979	33,901	11,227	11,779
$6M < T$	71,977	30,278	14,197	17,158	25,354	21,330

Table 2. Number of options traded by strike and month.

Strike (%)	December	January	February	March	April	May
20	0	0	0	0	55	10
30	1	1,692	2	381	0	0
40	0	77	0	80	3	41
50	58	417	0	328	2,031	1,948
60	1,933	152	31	323	691	2,092
70	1,402	1,928	653	3,837	2,412	2,956
80	12,814	12,952	3,400	10,118	14,689	12,147
90	113,210	114,463	10,465	247,877	184,835	147,362
100	159,075	68,747	130,002	94,714	50,621	90,528
110	5,811	3,586	12,253	1,766	83	2,205
120	869	94	64	11	0	16
130	1	11	0	0	0	0
140	0	0	0	0	2,012	1,960
150	0	0	0	381	0	1,602
160	1,720	271	0	0	0	0
170	1,040	20	0	0	0	0

2.3.2. *Numerical Results*

We now present our numerical results. Since the distribution of the strikes depends on the maturity and because short maturities are over-represented in our data, we split our data set into four subsets depending on the maturity:

- maturity less than 1 month,
- maturity between 1 and 3 months,
- maturity between 3 and 6 months,
- maturity larger than 6 months.

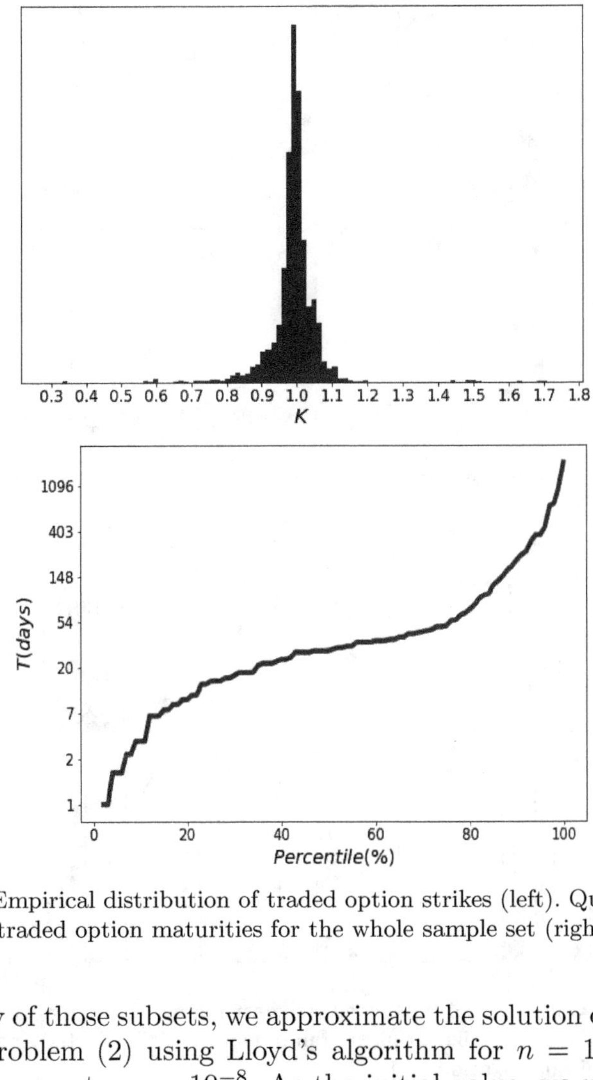

Figure 1. Empirical distribution of traded option strikes (left). Quantile plot in log-scale of traded option maturities for the whole sample set (right).

For any of those subsets, we approximate the solution of the quantization problem (2) using Lloyd's algorithm for $n = 10$ and with stopping parameter $\varepsilon = 10^{-8}$. As the initial value, we use n points $(K_i)_{1 \leq i \leq n}$ generated with uniform law between the 10th and 90th percentiles of the data set. In Figures 3 and 4, we plot a visualization of the quantization of the different sets obtained for $p = 2$ and $p = 8$.

The strikes selected by Lloyd's algorithm manage to reproduce some of the statistical properties of the demand distribution $\mathbb{P}^{mkt}$. In particular, for any range of maturity, the distribution of the

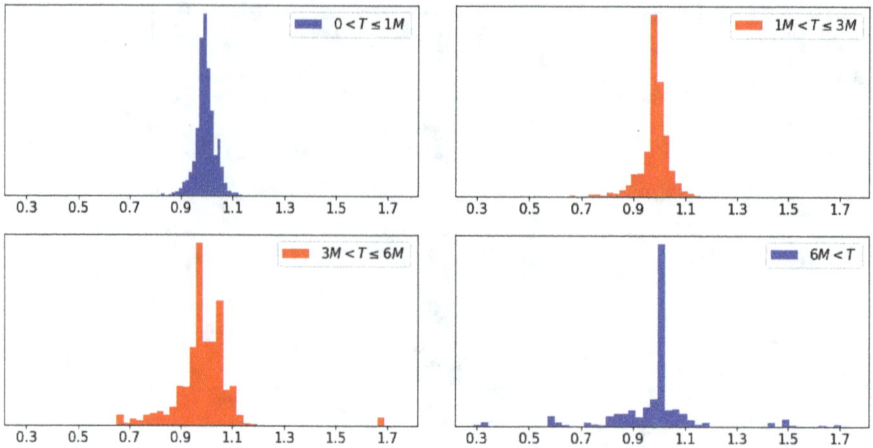

Figure 2. Empirical distribution of the strikes for different maturities.

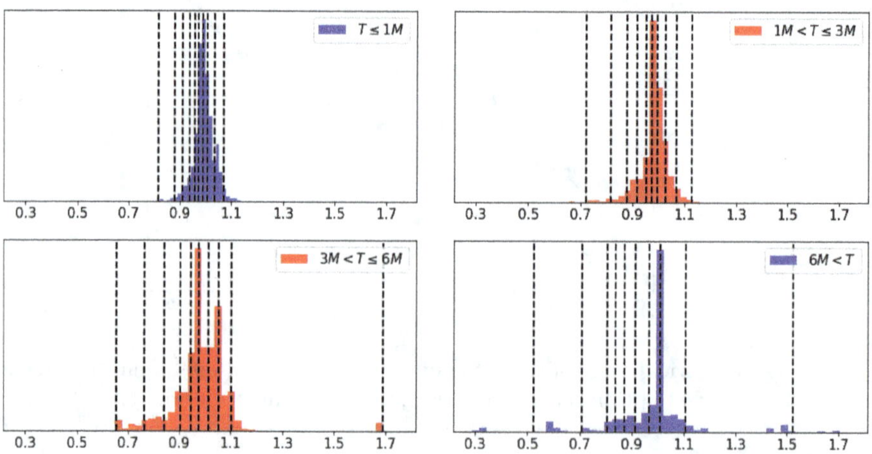

Figure 3. Quantization of the option strikes using $p = 2$ and $\varepsilon = 10^{-8}$. Empirical distribution of traded strikes is plotted in blue or red. The dotted lines correspond to the optimal quantization of $\mathbb{P}^{mkt}$.

$(K_i)_{1\le i\le n}$ is skewed toward in the money strikes. Also, the variance of the selected strikes is increasing with the maturity of market data.

We observe that for $p = 8$, the strikes selected by the quantization method are more spread toward large strikes than for $p = 2$. This is not surprising since the penalization of large errors is increasing with p for the regret function $|\cdot|^p$. Therefore, as expected, the larger

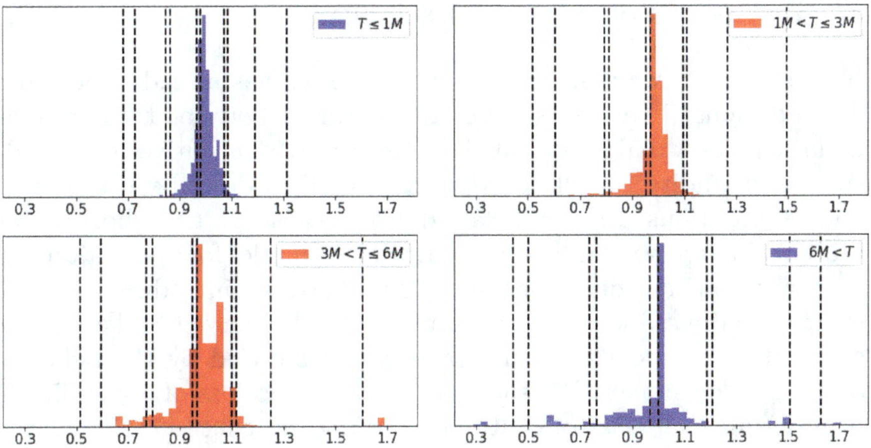

Figure 4. Quantization of the option strikes using $p = 8$ and $\varepsilon = 10^{-8}$. Empirical distribution of traded strikes is plotted in blue or red. The dotted lines correspond to the optimal quantization of $\mathbb{P}^{mkt}$.

the p, the more the solution of the quantization problem (2) contains extreme values of the distribution $\mathbb{P}^{mkt}$. We also note that the selected strikes for $p = 8$ exhibit some kind of redundancy: some of them are very close to each other. In practice, one would of course discard one of the two strikes being very close (it may then be interesting to take a smaller n). For practical applications, the easiest approach is probably to use $p = 2$. With this choice, Lloyd's algorithm is very fast and easy to implement. It also corresponds to the most documented case.

Finally, we insist on the fact that when an exchange uses our methodology for strikes selection, it is interesting, if possible, to include transactions from other exchanges and from the OTC market in the data set. This is because using only its own trade data may induce a bias in the strikes selection. For example, if for some reason clients of an exchange go to other venues to buy (or sell) out of the money options, then, in the exchange data set, there will be very few transactions reported on out of the money options. This will lead to inaccuracies since the demand for out of the money options will be underestimated.

We now turn to the problem of providing incentives to the market maker to quote attractive spreads in order to attract liquidity toward the selected options.

3. Incentive Policy of the Exchange

In this section, we assume that the exchange has already selected a list of options. The goal is to design a contract between the exchange and the market maker so that the latter receives incentives to provide suitable liquidity on all the options. We first describe the market and assumptions. In particular, due to the short time horizon we are working on, we can assume a Bachelier model for the underlying asset and constant delta for the options. Then, we introduce a class of tractable admissible contracts proposed to the market maker. These contracts are indexed on the transactions induced by the behavior of the market maker. We show that there is no loss of generality in considering such class of contracts. For a given contract, the market maker solves an optimization problem to deduce its optimal quotes for each option. Then, the exchange maximizes its expected utility over the set of admissible contracts, knowing the response of the market maker to a given contract.

The utility of the exchange is made of two parts: one component related to the actual Profit and Loss (PnL for short) due to transactions and one aiming at ensuring that enough liquidity is constantly posted on every option. As explained in the introduction, this second component addresses commercial constraints in order to make the exchange competitive. In particular, our model is flexible and can be designed so that the exchange has more interest in reducing the spreads for far from the money options, although not very traded, than for near the money options. We derive explicitly the optimal incentives that should be offered up to the resolution of a two-dimensional linear PDE.

We conclude this section with numerical results showing the impact of the incentive policy on the spread of the listed options. We emphasize that we adopt a financial engineering viewpoint in this section. Our goal is to provide a quantitative and operational answer to the lack of liquidity on certain options listed by the exchange.

3.1. *The Market*

This section is devoted to the description of the market model.

We consider a finite trading horizon time $T > 0$ and a probability space $(\Omega, \mathcal{F}, \mathbb{P}^0)$ under which all stochastic processes are defined.

Following Section 2, we work on a market where European call options with strike $k \in \mathcal{K} := \{K_1, \ldots, K_n\}$ and maturity $\tau \in \mathcal{T} := \{T_1, \ldots, T_m\}$ can be traded. We focus on call options but our results can be extended to put options in a straightforward manner.

Remark 3.1. Here, the set of strike and maturities is unspecified. However, the problem would naturally be studied over the set derived using the quantization method in the previous section. This means that the principal will design the contract proposed to the market-maker based on an exogeneous demand $\mathbb{P}^{mkt}$, measured empirically by aggregating demands over different venues.

The price of the underlying, observable by all market participants, has a dynamic given by

$$\mathrm{d}S_t = \sigma \mathrm{d}W_t, \tag{3}$$

where $\sigma > 0$ is the volatility of the asset and W is a one-dimensional Brownian motion. The choice of an arithmetic Brownian motion is motivated by the fact that we have in mind a time horizon T of one trading day or less. This is a reasonable assumption as the trading horizon of a market maker is usually one day, with the objective to end the trading day with a flat inventory. Therefore, the volatility σ must be interpreted as the daily volatility of the underlying asset. At this scale, Bachelier and Black–Scholes-type dynamics are quite indistinguishable. Moreover, the use of stochastic volatility would probably not be relevant here as the volatility process does not really diffuse over a single day.

Assuming zero interest rate, we write the price at time t of the call option with maturity τ and strike k as $C_t^{k,\tau}$. Its dynamic is given by

$$\mathrm{d}C_t^{k,\tau} = \sigma \Delta_t^{k,\tau} \mathrm{d}W_t, \tag{4}$$

where $\Delta_t^{k,\tau} := \mathcal{N}(d_t)$ is the Bachelier delta of the call option $C^{k,\tau}$ at time t, $\mathcal{N}(\cdot)$ is the cumulative distribution function of the standard Gaussian law and $d_t := \frac{S_t - k}{\sigma\sqrt{\tau}}$.

Remark 3.2. In this model, option prices are linear with respect to the underlying price, meaning that the value of the option comes from its delta. We could consider the full Bachelier dynamics of a call option, which include the gamma exposure. However, as we will make use of the constant delta assumption to obtain semi-explicit formulas, it is irrelevant to add such exposure (which moves way faster than the delta) in the option dynamics if it is assumed to be constant.

As we work over a short time horizon, the delta of the quoted options does not vary significantly. Hence, throughout this chapter, we assume it to be constant.

Assumption 3.3. We consider that

$$\Delta_t^{k,\tau} = \Delta^{k,\tau}.$$

This assumption, which can be relaxed, leads to technical simplifications. Note that in our problem setting, as the considered time horizon is one trading day, from a practical trading viewpoint, it is very reasonable to assume a constant delta (by taking the one at the opening of the market) and recalibrate it at the end of the day, although the "true" delta is of course time-varying as imposed by no-arbitrage constraints. This will lead to a different pay-off of the contract for the market maker in case of a significant price move from one day to another.

The market maker displays bid and ask quotes on the listed options. The market maker best bid price and best ask price at time t on the option with maturity τ and strike k are

$$P_t^{k,\tau,b} := C_t^{k,\tau} - \delta_t^{k,\tau,b}, \quad P_t^{k,\tau,a} = C_t^{k,\tau} + \delta_t^{k,\tau,a}, \quad t \in [0,T],$$

where the superscript b (resp., a) stands for bid (resp., ask). So, we consider that the market maker controls the spreads $\delta^{k,\tau} := (\delta^{k,\tau,a}, \delta^{k,\tau,b})$ on each option. The set of admissible controls for the market maker is therefore defined as

$$\begin{aligned} \mathcal{A} := \big\{ (\delta_t)_{t\in[0,T]} = (\delta_t^{k,\tau,i})_{t\in[0,T]}, k \in \mathcal{K}, \tau \in \mathcal{T}, i \in \{a,b\}, \\ \text{predictable and s.t } |\delta_t^{k,\tau,i}| \le \delta_\infty \big\}, \end{aligned} \tag{5}$$

where $\delta_\infty > 0$ is a constant, assumed to be large enough to satisfy technical conditions (see Appendix A.7). In practice, it is of course not restrictive to assume that the spreads are bounded.

We now describe the dynamics of the market order flow. For every listed option, the arrival of ask (resp., bid) market orders is modeled by a point process $N^{k,\tau,a}$ (resp., $N^{k,\tau,b}$). We expect the intensity of buy (resp., sell) market order arrivals to be a decreasing function of both the spread quoted by the market maker $\delta^{k,\tau}$ and the transaction cost $f^{k,\tau}$ collected by the exchange. This has quite natural interpretation as a wider spread or higher fee decreases the number of transactions on the considered option. Moreover, we know from the literature (see [4], [10] and [14]) that the average number of trades per unit of time for single assets is a decreasing function of the ratio between spread and volatility. Assuming the same kind of behavior for the options, this leads to the following form of the intensity function:

$$\lambda^{k,\tau}(\delta_t^{k,\tau,i}) := A\exp\left(-\frac{C}{\sigma}(\delta_t^{k,\tau,i} + f^{k,\tau})\right),$$

where A and C are positive constants that can be calibrated using market data and $f^{k,\tau}$ represents the fee fixed by the exchange for each market order. Furthermore, we assume that all market orders are of unit size.

Remark 3.4. In Equation (3), the efficient price is independent of the order flow. However, it is a direct extension to assume the dynamics

$$\mathrm{d}S_t = \sigma \mathrm{d}W_t + \sum_{(k,\tau)\in\mathcal{K}\times\mathcal{T}} \xi^{k,\tau}\left(\mathrm{d}N_t^{k,\tau,a} - \mathrm{d}N_t^{k,\tau,b}\right),$$

where $\xi^{k,\tau}$ represents the instantaneous impact of a trade on option $C^{k,\tau}$.

Remark 3.5. Without further constraint on the parameters of the principal–agent model, there could be a mismatch between the empirical distribution of trading over the different strikes and the one resulting from the optimal contract. In order to match those distributions, it is enough to choose the "neutral intensities" $(\lambda^{k,\tau})_{(k,\tau)} = Ae^{-\frac{C}{\sigma}f^{k,\tau}}$ proportional to the trading distribution.

The parameter A represents the average number of orders sent on the options market, whereas C is the sensitivity of the intensities with respect to the spread. A direct generalization is set in different order flow parameters $A^{k,\tau,i}$ for each side of each option. This helps us to model the fact that there is on average more trading on at-the-money and in-the-money options and that there is usually more option buyers than sellers. Note however that there are option sellers who want to benefit from the time premium when they sell derivatives. The main difficulty in our framework is that the market maker is dealing with multiple derivatives. If the market maker strategy depends on its inventory on each option, then the problem lies in dimension n, which becomes intricate for large n. However, we will see that we can circumvent this issue since, in our case, we can aggregate the risk factors related to the inventories through the delta-weighted cumulated inventory:

$$\mathcal{Q}_t := \sum_{(k,\tau)\in\mathcal{K}\times\mathcal{T}} \Delta^{k,\tau} Q_t^{k,\tau}, \tag{6}$$

where $Q_t^{k,\tau} := N_t^{k,\tau,b} - N_t^{k,\tau,a}$ is the number of options $C^{k,\tau}$ held by the market maker at time t. Each inventory is weighted by the corresponding Δ (see Section 3.2 for details). Thus, the quantity $\mathcal{Q}$ represents the marked-to-market value of the market maker's portfolio. It therefore contains the market risk carried by the market maker. For example, an out of the money option will account for a small part of the total risk and conversely for in the money options. Finally, we consider that the market maker has a critical absolute inventory $\overline{q} \in \mathbb{N}$. The intensity of the orders arrival is then

$$\lambda^{k,\tau,i} := \lambda^{k,\tau}(\delta_t^{k,\tau,i})\mathbb{1}_{\{\phi(i)\mathcal{Q}_{t-} > -\overline{q}\}} \text{ with } \phi(i) := \begin{cases} 1 \text{ if } i = a \\ -1 \text{ if } i = b. \end{cases}$$

Remark 3.6. Note that there is a direct link between the spread quoted by the market maker and his inventory process. Indeed, a lower spread $\delta^{k,\tau,b}$ (resp., $\delta^{k,\tau,a}$) on the bid (resp., ask) side of the listed option $C^{k,\tau}$ increases the intensity of orders arrival $\lambda^{k,\tau,b}$ (resp., $\lambda^{k,\tau,a}$). This leads to an increase (resp., decrease) of the inventory process $Q^{k,\tau}$. In other words, the market maker skews his quotes depending on the level of its aggregated inventory.

3.2. *Market Maker's Problem and Contract Representation*

In this section, we exhibit the class of contracts used by the exchange. We also explain and solve the market maker's problem for any admissible contract.

The PnL of the market maker is defined as the sum of the cash earned from his executed orders and of the value of his inventory on each traded option. Thus, using that $\sum_{(k,\tau)\in\mathcal{K}\times\mathcal{T}} Q_t^{k,\tau}\Delta^{k,\tau}S_t = \mathcal{Q}_t S_t$, it writes

$$PL_t^\delta := \mathcal{W}_t^\delta + \mathcal{Q}_t S_t, \tag{7}$$

where

$$\mathcal{W}_t^\delta := \sum_{(k,\tau)\in\mathcal{K}\times\mathcal{T}} \int_0^t P_u^{k,\tau,a}\mathrm{d}N_u^{k,\tau,a} - \int_0^t P_u^{k,\tau,b}\mathrm{d}N_u^{k,\tau,b}$$

stands for his cash process at time $t \in [0,T]$. This expression shows the relevance of the variable $\mathcal{Q}$ for the market maker. It represents the volatility of the market maker's PnL with respect to the underlying price movements. Using (4), a direct integration by parts leads to the following form of the PnL process:

$$PL_t^\delta := \sum_{i\in\{a,b\}} \sum_{(k,\tau)\in\mathcal{K}\times\mathcal{T}} \int_0^t \delta_u^{k,\tau,i}\mathrm{d}N_u^{k,\tau,i} + \mathcal{Q}_u\mathrm{d}S_u.$$

Remark 3.7. In this framework, we consider that there is no hedging of the market maker when he buys or sells an option. This can be added straightforwardly to the model in the spirit of [1]. The obtained results are not modified significantly.

Moreover, the exchange offers to the market maker a contract ξ, namely an $\mathcal{F}_T$-measurable random variable, which is added to his PnL at the end of the trading period. This contract aims at incentivizing the market maker to reduce the spread quoted for each option. More details are given in Section 3.3. The contract depends on all the transactions occurring between time 0 and time T, as well as on the efficient price moves.

Thus, taking an exponential utility function, the market maker maximizes the following functional of his wealth:

$$V_{\mathrm{MM}}(\xi) := \sup_{\delta \in \mathcal{A}} \mathbb{E}^{\delta}\left[-\exp\left(-\gamma\left(\xi + PL_T^{\delta}\right)\right)\right], \tag{8}$$

where $\gamma > 0$ denotes the market maker's risk aversion parameter and $\mathbb{E}^{\delta}$ the probability measure associated with a given control process $\delta \in \mathcal{A}$, see Appendix A.2.2 for details. For the well-posedness of Equation (8), we need integrability conditions on the contract ξ, see Appendix A.3 for details.

Finally, we consider that the market maker accepts a contract ξ only if its associated optimal expected utility $V_{\mathrm{MM}}(\xi)$ is above some fixed threshold $R < 0$. This threshold, called reservation utility of the agent, is the critical utility value under which the market maker has no interest in the contract. This quantity has to be taken into account carefully by the exchange before proposing a contract to the market makers.

We now introduce the class of contracts proposed to the market maker. Given $Y_0 > 0$, and predictable processes $Z := (Z^{C^{k,\tau}}, Z^{k,\tau,i})_{k\in\mathcal{K}\ \tau\in\mathcal{T}\ i\in\{a,b\}} \in \mathcal{Z}$ (see Appendix A.4 for a definition of $\mathcal{Z}$), we introduce a special class of remuneration $\xi = Y_T^{Y_0,Z}$ of the form

$$\begin{aligned} Y_T^{Y_0,Z} :=& Y_0 + \int_0^T \left(\sum_{i=a,b}\sum_{(k,\tau)\in\mathcal{K}\times\mathcal{T}} Z_r^{k,\tau,i}\mathrm{d}N_r^{k,\tau,i} + Z_r^{C^{k,\tau}}\mathrm{d}C_r^{k,\tau}\right) \\ &+ \left(\frac{1}{2}\gamma\sigma^2\left(\sum_{(k,\tau)\in\mathcal{K}\times\mathcal{T}} \Delta^{k,\tau}(Z_r^{C^{k,\tau}} + Q_r^{k,\tau})\right)^2 - H(Z_r, Q_r)\right)\mathrm{d}r, \end{aligned} \tag{9}$$

where for $(z,q) \in \mathbb{R}^{2\times\#\mathcal{K}\times\#\mathcal{T}} \times \mathbb{R}$ with $z := (z^{k,\tau})_{(k,\tau)\in\mathcal{K}\times\mathcal{T}}$, the function H, called Hamiltonian of the market maker, is defined by[2]

$$H(z,q) := \sup_{\delta\in\mathbb{R}^{2\times\#\mathcal{K}\times\#\mathcal{T}}} h(\delta, z, q)$$

[2]This Hamiltonian term appears naturally when applying the dynamic programming principle for the market maker's problem.

with

$$h(\delta, z, q) := \sum_{i=a,b} \sum_{(k,\tau)\in\mathcal{K}\times\mathcal{T}} \gamma^{-1}\left(1 - \exp\left(-\gamma\left(z^{k,\tau,i} + \delta^{k,\tau,i}\right)\right)\right)$$
$$\lambda^{k,\tau}(\delta^{k,\tau,i})\mathbb{1}_{\{\phi(i)\mathcal{Q}>-\bar{q}\}}.$$

Actually, it turns out that it is enough to consider contracts of the form (9). More precisely, we show that any admissible contract (in the sense of the integrability conditions specified in Appendix A.4) is of this form. We have the following lemma proved in Appendix A.5:

Lemma 3.8. *Any contract ξ satisfying* (20) *has a unique representation $\xi = Y_T^{Y_0,Z}$ for some $(Y_0, Z) \in \mathbb{R} \times \mathcal{Z}$.*

Furthermore, the terms defining (9) have natural interpretation:

- The compensation Y_0 is calibrated by the exchange to ensure the reservation utility constraint with level R of the market maker.[3]
- The term $Z^{C^{k,\tau}}$ is the compensation given to the market maker with respect to the volatility risk induced by the option $C^{k,\tau}$.
- Each time a trade is executed on the ask (resp., bid) side for the option $C^{k,\tau}$, the market maker is compensated by the term $Z^{k,\tau,a}$ (resp., $Z^{k,\tau,b}$).
- The term $\frac{1}{2}\gamma\sigma^2\left(\sum_{k=1}^{\mathcal{K}}\sum_{\tau=1}^{\mathcal{T}}\Delta(Z^{C^{k,\tau}} + Q^{k,\tau})\right)^2 - H(Z,Q)$ is a continuous coupon given to the market maker.

When the market maker remuneration is $Y^{Y_0,Z}$, its optimal response can be computed explicitly as a functional of Z.

Theorem 3.9. *For $\xi = Y^{Y_0,Z}$, the market maker utility is*

$$V_{\mathrm{MM}}(Y_T^{Y_0,Z}) = -\exp(-\gamma Y_0),$$

associated with the optimal bid-ask policy $\hat{\delta}_t^{k,\tau,i}(\xi) := \Delta^i(Z_t^{k,\tau,i})$, where

$$\Delta^i(Z_t^{k,\tau,i}) := (-\delta_\infty) \vee \left(-Z_t^{k,\tau,i} + \frac{1}{\gamma}\log\left(1 + \frac{\sigma\gamma}{C}\right)\right)$$
$$\wedge\, \delta_\infty \text{ for } (k,\tau,i) \in \mathcal{K}\times\mathcal{T}\times\{a,b\}. \tag{10}$$

[3]From Theorem 3.9, we see that taking $Y_0 = -\log(-R)$ ensures the reservation utility of the market maker.

Theorem 3.9 provides the optimal response of the market maker to any contract of the form (9), see Appendix A.6 for the proof. Moreover, from Equation (10), we get that the exchange can anticipate the optimal behavior of the market maker. It is therefore easy for the platform to compute its own utility for a given contract.

3.3. *Solving the Exchange's Problem*

In this section, we formalize the goal of the exchange and solve the problem of designing the optimal contract.

3.3.1. *Description of the Exchange's Problem*

We recall that the exchange has two objectives. The first one is to receive a high number of trades to collect the associated fees. The second is to have small spreads on its platform, in particular for far from the money options for which spreads are typically large. This is because the clients want to have sufficient liquidity on the whole list of options.

In order to quantify the first objective, we introduce a weighted version of the total number of trades:

$$\mathcal{N}_t = \sum_{i=a,b} \sum_{(k,\tau)\in\mathcal{K}\times\mathcal{T}} c^{k,\tau} N_t^{k,\tau,i},$$

where for any $(k,\tau) \in \mathcal{K}\times\mathcal{T}$, $c^{k,\tau} \geq 0$ represents the value attributed to a trade on the option $C^{k,\tau}$ by the exchange.[4] Hence, the more the exchange wants to attract liquidity on the option $C^{k,\tau}$, the higher the $c^{k,\tau}$ has to be. If the considered option is very liquid (at the money options, for example), the exchange may choose a rather small $c^{k,\tau}$.

To take into account the second objective, we consider the following quantity:

$$\mathcal{L}_T^{\delta} := \sum_{i=a,b} \sum_{(k,\tau)\in\mathcal{K}\times\mathcal{T}} \int_0^T \omega\left(\delta_t^{k,\tau,i} - \delta_\infty^{k,\tau}\right) \mathrm{d}N_t^{k,\tau,i}, \qquad (11)$$

[4]One can, for example, take $c^{k,\tau} = f^{k,\tau}$. In this case, $\mathcal{N}_T$ represents the total amount of fees collected by the exchange.

where $\omega \in [0,1)$,[5] and $\delta_\infty^{k,\tau}$ can be seen as a spread threshold the exchange would like to impose to the market maker. The more important the second objective for the exchange, the closer to one ω has to be chosen.

We thus consider that the exchange is looking for the contract ξ that maximizes the following quantity:

$$\mathbb{E}^{\hat{\delta}(\xi)}\left[-\exp\left(-\eta\left(\mathcal{N}_T - \mathcal{L}_T^{\delta(\xi)} - \xi\right)\right)\right], \tag{12}$$

where $\eta > 0$ is the risk aversion of the exchange and $\hat{\delta}(\xi)$ denotes the optimal response of the market maker given the contract ξ.

Remark 3.10. We consider that the exchange does not have a reservation utility. For example, we can assume that R is so that $\xi = 0$ is an admissible contract, which would lead to positive PnL for the exchange.

According to Lemma 3.8, we know that it is enough for the exchange to consider contracts of the form $Y_T^{Y_0,Z}$ with $(Y_0, Z) \in \mathbb{R} \times \mathcal{Z}$. So, (12) becomes

$$\mathbb{E}^{\hat{\delta}(Y^{Y_0,Z})}\left[-\exp\left(-\eta\left(\mathcal{N}_T - \mathcal{L}_T^{\delta(Y^{Y_0,Z})} - Y_T^{Y_0,Z}\right)\right)\right]. \tag{13}$$

Moreover, for a contract of the form $Y^{Y_0,Z}$, from Theorem 3.9, the exchange knows the best response $\hat{\delta}(Y^{Y_0,Z})$ of the market maker. Indeed, we recall that the optimal controls are given by

$$\hat{\delta}^{k,\tau,i}(Y^{Y_0,Z}) = \Delta^i(Z_t^{k,\tau,i}).$$

It implies that

$$\mathcal{L}_T^{\hat{\delta}(Y^{Y_0,Z})} = \mathcal{L}_T^Z := \sum_{i=a,b} \sum_{(k,\tau)\in\mathcal{K}\times\mathcal{T}} \int_0^T \omega\left(\Delta^i(Z_t^{k,\tau,i}) - \delta_\infty^{k,\tau}\right) \mathrm{d}N_t^{k,\tau,i}.$$

As in [5], we note that for a given contract $Y^{Y_0,Z}$, the market maker's optimal response does not depend on Y_0. The exchange objective function (13) being decreasing in Y_0, the maximization with respect

[5]The choice of $\omega \in [0,1)$ is for technical reasons only.

to Y_0 is achieved at the level $\hat{Y}_0 = -\log(-R)$.[6] Finally, the exchange problem becomes

$$V_0^E := \sup_{Z\in\mathcal{Z}} \mathbb{E}^{\Delta(Z)}\left[-\exp\left(-\eta\left(\mathcal{N}_T^Z - \mathcal{L}_T^Z - Y_T^{\hat{Y}_0,Z}\right)\right)\right]. \tag{14}$$

3.3.2. *Stochastic Control Approach for the Reduced Exchange Problem*

In this section, we solve the reduced exchange problem (14). We characterize the optimal contract components $Z^\star$ and explain how to compute them in practice.

To solve this stochastic control problem, we study the associated Hamilton–Jacobi–Bellman (HJB for short) equation. This approach characterizes an optimal $Z^\star$ solving (14) under the form of a feedback function. The following result is proved in Appendix A.7:

Theorem 3.11. *The maximization problem* (14) *admits a solution* $Z^\star$ *given by*

$$Z^{\star k,\tau,i}(t,\mathcal{Q}_{t^-}) := \frac{1}{a-b}\log\left(\frac{bx_2 U\left(t,\mathcal{Q}_{t^-}\right)}{ax_1^{k,\tau}U\left(t,\mathcal{Q}_{t^-}-\Delta^{k,\tau}\phi(i)\right)}\right)$$
$$\text{and } Z^{\star C^{k,\tau}}(t,Q_t^{k,\tau}) := -\frac{\gamma}{\gamma+\eta}Q_t^{k,\tau}, \tag{15}$$

for $(k,\tau,i)\in\mathcal{K}\times\mathcal{T}\times\{a,b\}$, *where* a, b, $(x_1^{k,\tau})_{k\in\mathcal{K},\tau\in\mathcal{T}}$ *and* x_2 *are constants defined in Appendix A.8 and where* $\tilde{U} := (-U)^{-\frac{C}{\sigma\eta(1-\omega)}}$ *is the unique solution of the following linear PDE on* $[0,T]\times\mathbb{R}$:

$$\begin{cases} 0 = \partial_t\tilde{U}(t,\mathcal{Q}) - \tilde{U}(t,\mathcal{Q})\frac{C\gamma\eta}{\gamma+\eta}\frac{\sigma}{2(1-\omega)}\mathcal{Q}^2 \\ \qquad + \sum\limits_{i=a,b}\sum\limits_{(k,\tau)\in\mathcal{K}\times\mathcal{T}}\hat{C}^{k,\tau}\tilde{U}\left(t,\mathcal{Q}-\Delta^{k,\tau}\phi(i)\right)\mathbf{1}_{\phi(i)\mathcal{Q}>-\bar{q}}, \\ \tilde{U}(T,\mathcal{Q}) = 1, \end{cases} \tag{16}$$

where $\hat{C}^{k,\tau}$ *are defined in Appendix A.8.*

[6]Note that $-\exp(-\hat{Y}_0) = R$.

Theorem 3.11 provides the incentives $Z^\star$ that maximize the exchange expected utility function, see Appendix A.7 for the proof. The optimal contract is therefore given by

$$\xi^\star = Y^{\hat{Y}_0, Z^*} = \hat{Y}_0 + \int_0^T \sum_{(k,\tau)\in\mathcal{K}\times\mathcal{T}} \left(\sum_{i=a,b} Z_r^{\star k,\tau,i} \mathrm{d}N_r^{k,\tau,i} + Z_r^{\star C^{k,\tau}} \mathrm{d}C_r^{k,\tau} \right)$$
$$+ \int_0^T \left(\frac{1}{2}\gamma\sigma^2 \left(\sum_{(k,\tau)\in\mathcal{K}\times\mathcal{T}} \Delta^{k,\tau} (Z_r^{\star C^{k,\tau}} + Q_r^{k,\tau}) \right)^2 - H(Z_r^\star, Q_r) \right) \mathrm{d}r. \tag{17}$$

We now provide some comments on the interpretation of the optimal incentives.

- The term $\int_0^T Z_u^{\star C^{k,\tau}} \mathrm{d}C_u^{k,\tau}$ in the optimal contract corresponds to part of the inventory risk process of the market maker $(Q_t^{k,\tau} C_t^{k,\tau})_{t\in[0,T]}$ that is supported by the exchange. As in [5], the proportion of risk handled by the platform on each option is $\frac{\gamma}{\gamma+\eta}$. Hence, the more risk-averse the exchange, the smallest this proportion.
- An application of Ito's formula gives the following approximation:

$$\log \left(\frac{\tilde{U}(t, \mathcal{Q})}{\tilde{U}\left(t, \mathcal{Q} - \Delta^{k,\tau}\phi(i)\right)} \right) \approx \phi(i) 2 \frac{\sigma}{C} (T-t) \tilde{C} \Delta^{k,\tau} \mathcal{Q}, \tag{18}$$

where $\tilde{C} := \frac{C\gamma\eta}{\gamma+\eta} \frac{\sigma}{2(1-\omega)}$. Thus, when the aggregated inventory is highly positive, the exchange provides incentives to the market maker so that it attracts buy market orders and tries to dissuade him to accept more sell market orders and conversely for a negative inventory.
- Numerically, we show that the incentive $Z^{\star k,\tau,a}$ and $Z^{\star k,\tau,b}$ given by (15) are increasing functions of the value $c^{k,\tau}$ that the principal associates with the option $C^{k,\tau}$. Hence, he logically provides higher incentives to an option he is more interested in.
- Although the principal manages a large number of listed options, we circumvent the curse of dimensionality by working with the aggregated inventory process. Note that the pay-off of the optimal

contract depends only on t and $\mathcal{Q}$. Thus, it is very easy to compute the exchange at the end of the trading day.

In practice, to implement the above methodology, one needs to compute the function $\tilde{U}$ in order to design the optimal contract. The first way to do this is to use a classical finite difference scheme on the PDE (16). In Section 3.4, we use this technique for some numerical experiments on our method.

Moreover, as PDE (16) is linear, we can also resort to a probabilistic representation to compute $\tilde{U}$ using a Monte Carlo method. More precisely, we have the following result which is a direct consequence of the Feynman–Kac formula.

Lemma 3.12. *We have the following representation:*

$$\tilde{U}(t,q) := \mathbb{E}\left[\exp\left(\int_t^T -\tilde{C}\left(\mathcal{Q}_s^{t,q}\right)^2 + \sum_{i=a,b}\sum_{(k,\tau)\in\mathcal{K}\times\mathcal{T}} \overline{\lambda}_s^{k,\tau,i}\mathrm{d}s\right)\right], \tag{19}$$

where

$$\mathcal{Q}_s^{t,q} = q + \int_t^s \sum_{(k,\tau)\in\mathcal{K}\times\mathcal{T}} \Delta^{k,\tau}\mathrm{d}\left(\overline{N}_u^{k,\tau,b} - \overline{N}_u^{k,\tau,a}\right),$$

where for any $(k,\tau) \in \mathcal{K}\times\mathcal{T}$ and $i = a$ or b, $\overline{N}^{k,\tau,i}$ is a point process with intensity $\overline{\lambda}_s^{k,\tau,i} := \hat{C}^{k,\tau}\mathbf{1}_{\{\phi(i)\mathcal{Q}_{s^-}^{t,q} > -\overline{q}\}}$, with $\hat{C}^{k,\tau}$ defined in Appendix A.8.

The proof is in the same vein as [5, Proposition 4.1]. We now turn to numerical illustrations of our make-take fees policy.

3.4. *Numerical Results*

For numerical experiments, we consider three options which are characterized by their delta. We fix the following parameters: $A = 1.5s^{-1}, \sigma = C = 0.3s^{-1/2}$, $f^{k,\tau} = [0.5, 0.8, 0.8]$ the vector of fees and $\delta_\infty^{k,\tau} = [2, 3, 3]$ the set of quotation thresholds. The first option is at the money, the second one is in the money and the third is out of

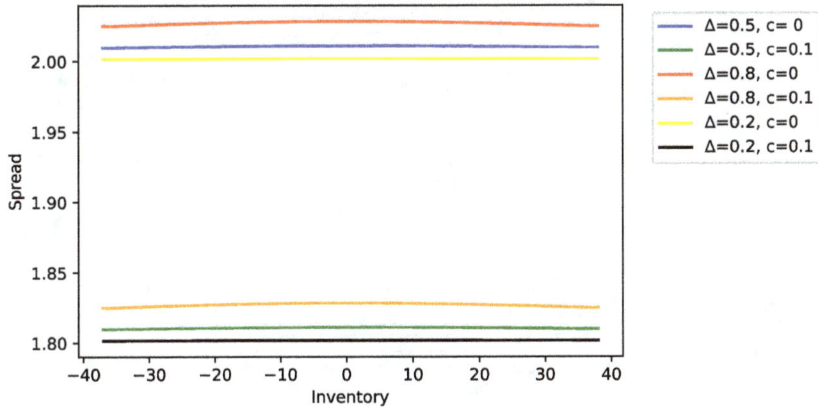

Figure 5. Spread at initial time with respect to the market maker inventory, $\omega = 0$.

the money, hence the following set of deltas $[0.5, 0.8, 0.2]$. Moreover, we take $\eta = 1, \gamma = 0.01, T = 100s, \overline{q} = 40$.

We analyze the impact of the penalty ω and the weight associated with each options $c^{k,\tau}$ in the value function of the exchange.

In Figure 5, we display the average bid-ask spread at initial time on each option for $\omega = 0$, and $c^{k,\tau}$ being equal to either 0 or 0.1. We see that a higher $c^{k,\tau}$ leads to a decrease in the spread for the option $C^{k,\tau}$. This result is in line with the form of the incentives in Theorem 3.11. Indeed, $Z^{\star k,\tau,i}$ is an increasing function of $c^{k,\tau}$ and $\hat{\delta}^{k,\tau,i}$ is a decreasing function of $Z^{\star k,\tau,i}$. Thus, increasing the interest of the principal for the option $C^{k,\tau}$ leads to a decrease in the spread proposed by the market maker on this option. This shows that the exchange has a direct control on each option he is interested in.

In Figure 6, we focus on the role of ω, equal to 0.1 on the spreads proposed by the market maker. As expected, a non-vanishing value of ω leads to a decrease in the spread for all the quoted options. This agrees with Theorem 3.11, where we see that the incentives are an increasing function of $\omega \in [0, 1)$. Thus, the exchange can influence the whole set of spreads proposed on the quoted options.

We conclude by showing in Figure 7 the behavior of the average spread with a higher ω equal to 0.2. We obtain similar effects as in Figure 6, namely a decrease in the spread on all quoted options for a higher ω.

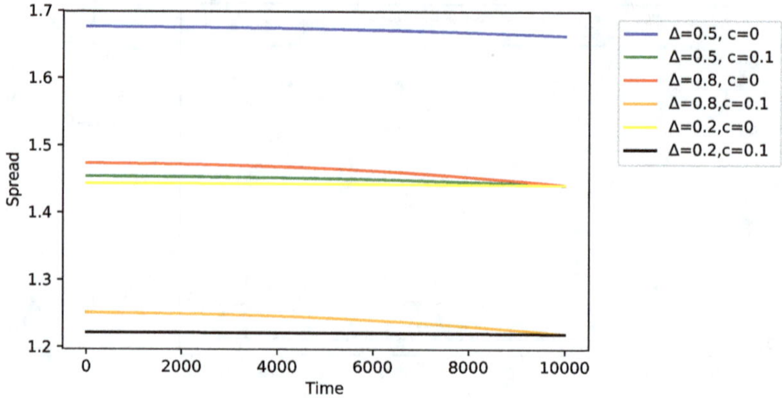

Figure 6. Optimal ask spread for a null inventory with respect to the remaining trading time (in seconds), $\omega = 0.1$.

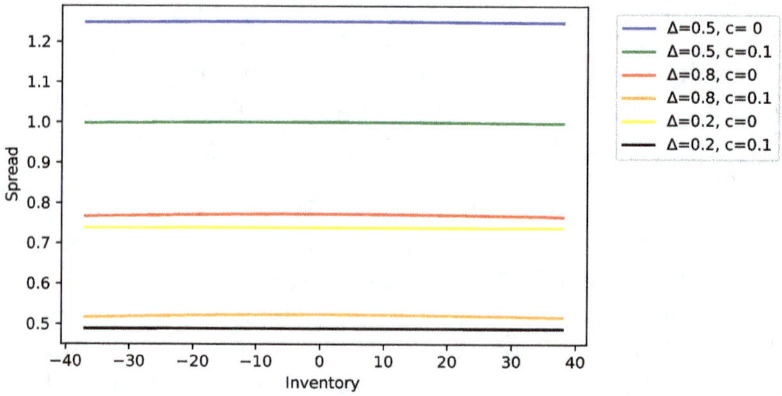

Figure 7. Spread at initial time with respect to the market maker inventory, $\omega = 0.2$.

3.5. *Conclusion*

This work is, to our knowledge, the first to address the problem of designing a derivatives exchange based solely on market data. In the first part, a simple market-driven methodology enables us to choose which options the exchange should select to attract market takers. In the second part, we provide a make-take fees policy between the exchange and the market maker which ensures a high quality of liquidity for the listed options.

Appendix

A.1. *Proof of the convergence of Lloyd's algorithm*

According to Paragraph 5.2 in [6], the set $(K_i)_{1\leq i\leq n}$ is a solution of (2) if and only if for any i, A_i has positive Lebesgue measure and.

$$\int_{A_i} |K_i - x|^{p-1}\text{sgin}(x - K_i)\mathbb{P}^{mkt}(\mathrm{d}x) = 0,$$

where sgin is the sign function. This is equivalent to

$$K_i = \frac{\int_{A_i} |K_i - x|^{p-2} x\mathbb{P}^{mkt}(\mathrm{d}x)}{\int_{A_i} |K_i - x|^{p-2}\mathbb{P}^{mkt}(\mathrm{d}x)} = \frac{\mathbb{E}^{mkt}[|K_i - K|^{p-2}K\mathbf{1}_{K\in A_i}]}{\mathbb{E}^{mkt}[|K_i - K|^{p-2}\mathbf{1}_{K\in A_i}]}.$$

Thus, $(K_i)_{1\leq i\leq N}$ is the solution of (2) if and only if it is a fixed point of Lloyd's algorithm.

We now give proofs and technical results for Section 3. They are mostly inspired by [5]. However, for sake of completeness, we provide rigorous derivations.

A.2. *Stochastic basis*

A.2.1. *Canonical Process*

In this section, we give an accurate definition of the probability space defined in Section 3.1. We consider a final horizon time $T > 0$ and the space $\Omega =: \Omega_c \times \Omega_d^{2\times\#\mathcal{T}\times\#\mathcal{K}}$ with Ω_c the set of continuous functions from $[0, T]$ into $\mathbb{R}$ and Ω_d the set of piecewise constant càdlàg functions from $[0, T]$ into $\mathbb{N}$. We consider Ω as a subspace of the Skorokhod space $\mathcal{D}([0, T], \mathbb{R}^{2\times\#\mathcal{T}\times\#\mathcal{K}+1})$ of càdlàg functions from $[0, T]$ into $\mathbb{R}^{2\times\#\mathcal{T}\times\#\mathcal{K}+1}$ and $\mathcal{F}$ the trace Borel σ-algebra on Ω, where the topology is the one associated with the usual Skorokhod distance on $\mathcal{D}([0, T], \mathbb{R}^{2\times\#\mathcal{T}\times\#\mathcal{K}+1})$.

We define $(\mathcal{X}_t)_{t\in[0,T]} := \left(W_t, (N_t^{k,\tau,i})_{i=a,b;k\in\mathcal{K};\tau\in\mathcal{T}}\right)$ as the canonical process on Ω, that is, for any $\omega = (w, n^{k,\tau,i}) \in \Omega$,

$$W_t(\omega) = w(t),\ N_t^{k,\tau,i}(\omega) = n^{k,\tau,i}(t).$$

A.2.2. *Probability Measure*

We now properly define $\mathbb{P}^0$ and the associated change of measure. We set the probability $\mathbb{P}^0$ on $(\Omega, \mathcal{F})$ such that under $\mathbb{P}^0$, W, $N^{k,\tau,i}$ are independent, W is a one-dimensional Brownian motion and the $N^{k,\tau,i}, k \in \mathcal{K}, \tau \in \mathcal{T}, i = a, b$ are Poisson processes with intensity $\lambda^{k,\tau,i}(0)$.[7] Finally, we endow the space $(\Omega, \mathcal{F})$ with the ($\mathbb{P}^0-$completed) canonical filtration $\mathbb{F} := (\mathcal{F}_t)_{t\in[0,T]}$ generated by $(\mathcal{X}_t)_{t\in[0,T]}$.

By (5), the control process must be predictable and uniformly bounded. The last assumption is required to define the associated probability measure. So, for $\delta \in \mathcal{A}$, we introduce the corresponding probability measure $\mathbb{P}^\delta$ under which $S_t = S_0 + \sigma W_t$ follows (3) and for $k \in \mathcal{K}, \tau \in \mathcal{T}, i \in \{a, b\}$, the

$$N_t^{\delta,k,\tau,i} := N_t^{k,\tau,i} - \int_0^t \lambda^{k,\tau}(\delta_r^{k,\tau,i})\mathbb{1}_{\{\phi(i)Q_{r-} > -\bar{q}\}} \mathrm{d}r$$

are martingales. This probability measure is defined by the corresponding Doléans–Dade exponential:

$$L_t^\delta := \exp\left(\sum_{i=a,b}\sum_{(k,\tau)\in\mathcal{K}\times\mathcal{T}} \int_0^t \mathbb{1}_{\{\phi(i)Q_{r-} > -\bar{q}\}}\left(\log\left(\frac{\lambda^{k,\tau}(\delta_r^{k,\tau,i})}{A}\right) \mathrm{d}N_r^{k,\tau,i}\right.\right.$$
$$\left.\left. - \left(\lambda^{k,\tau}(\delta_r^{k,\tau,i}) - A\right) \mathrm{d}r\right)\right),$$

which is a true martingale by the uniform boundedness of $\delta_t^{k,\tau,i}$.[8] We can therefore define the Girsanov change of measure $\frac{\mathrm{d}\mathbb{P}^\delta}{\mathrm{d}\mathbb{P}^0}|_{\mathcal{F}_t} = L_t^\delta$, for all $t \in [0, T]$. In particular, all the probability measures $\mathbb{P}^\delta$ indexed by $\delta \in \mathcal{A}$ are equivalent. We shall write $\mathbb{E}_t^\delta$ for the conditional expectation with respect to $\mathcal{F}_t$ under the probability measure $\mathbb{P}^\delta$.

---

[7]In other words, $\mathbb{P}^0$ is simply the product measure of the Wiener measure on Ω_c and the unique measure on $\Omega_d^{2\times\#\mathcal{T}\times\#\mathcal{K}}$ that makes the canonical process a homogeneous Poisson process with the prescribed intensity.

[8]The associated Novikov criterion is given in Ref. [13].

A.3. *Well-posedness of the optimization problems*

We give in this section the necessary integrability conditions ensuring that both exchange and market maker's problems are well defined. We consider the following assumptions:

$$\sup_{\delta\in\mathcal{A}} \mathbb{E}^{\delta}\left[\exp\left(-\gamma'\xi\right)\right] < +\infty, \text{ for some } \gamma' > \gamma,$$

$$\sup_{\delta\in\mathcal{A}} \mathbb{E}^{\delta}\left[\exp\left(\eta'\xi\right)\right] < +\infty, \text{ for some } \eta' > \eta. \tag{20}$$

Moreover, the following technical assumption is required in order to derive the best response of the market maker in Theorem 3.9:

$$\sup_{\delta\in\mathcal{A}} \sup_{t\in[0,T]} \mathbb{E}^{\delta}\left[\exp\left(-\gamma' Y_t^{0,Z}\right)\right] < +\infty, \text{ for some } \gamma' > \gamma. \tag{21}$$

Finally, we define $\mathcal{Z}$ as the set of predictable processes $(Z_t)_{t\in[0,T]}$ such that Conditions (20) and (21) are satisfied. This is the set of admissible contract components of the exchange.

A.4. *Dynamic programming principle*

In the spirit of Ref. [5], we provide a proof of a dynamic programming principle for the market maker's problem. Note that the same type of dynamic programming principle exists for the exchange's problem.

For any $\mathbb{F}$ stopping time $\tau \in [t,T]$ and $\mu \in \mathcal{A}_\tau$, we define

$$J_T(\tau,\mu) = \mathbb{E}_\tau^{\mu}\left[-\exp\left(-\gamma\left(\xi + \sum_{i=a,b}\sum_{(k,\tau)\in\mathcal{K}\times\mathcal{T}} \int_\tau^T \mu_u^{k,\tau,i} \mathrm{d}N_u^{k,\tau,i} + Q_u^{k,\tau}\mathrm{d}C_u^{k,\tau}\right)\right)\right],$$

where $\mathcal{A}_\tau$ denotes the restriction of $\mathcal{A}$ to controls on $[\tau,T]$. We also define the set $\mathcal{J}_{\tau,T} = (J_T(\tau,\mu))_{\mu\in\mathcal{A}_\tau}$. The continuation utility of the market maker is defined for any $\mathcal{F}$-stopping time τ by

$$V_\tau = \operatorname*{ess\,sup}_{\mu\in\mathcal{A}_\tau} J_T(\tau,\mu).$$

We first prove the following technical lemma:

Lemma A.1. *Let τ be a stopping time with values in $[t,T]$. Then there exists an increasing sequence $(\mu^n)_{n\in\mathbb{N}}$ in $\mathcal{A}_\tau$ such that $V_\tau = \lim_{n\to+\infty} J_T(\tau,\mu^n)$.*

Proof. For $\mu, \mu' \in \mathcal{A}_\tau$, we define

$$\hat{\mu} := \mu \mathbb{1}_{\{J_T(\tau,\mu) \geq J_T(\tau,\mu')\}} + \mu' \mathbb{1}_{\{J_T(\tau,\mu) \leq J_T(\tau,\mu')\}}.$$

We have $\hat{\mu} \in \mathcal{A}_\tau$ and by definition of $\hat{\mu}$, $J_T(\tau, \hat{\mu}) \geq \max(J_T(\tau,\mu), J_T(\tau,\mu'))$. Thus $\mathcal{J}_{\tau,T}$ is increasing, and we obtain the same result as in [5]. The conclusion follows. □

We set

$$\mathcal{D}_{t,T}(\delta) := \exp\left(-\gamma\left(\sum_{i=a,b}\sum_{(k,\tau)\in\mathcal{K}\times\mathcal{T}}\int_t^T \delta_u^{k,\tau,i} \mathrm{d}N_u^{k,\tau,i} + Q_u^{k,\tau}\mathrm{d}C_u^{k,\tau}\right)\right).$$

Given Lemma A.1, we can now prove the dynamic programming principle associated with (8).

Lemma A.2. *Let $t \in [0,T]$ and τ be an $\mathbb{F}$ stopping time with values in $[t,T]$. Then*

$$V_t = \operatorname*{ess\,sup}_{\delta\in\mathcal{A}} \mathbb{E}_t^\delta\left[-\mathcal{D}_{t,\tau}(\delta)V_\tau\right].$$

Proof. Let $t \in [0,T]$ and τ be a stopping time with values in $[t,T]$. First, by tower property, we have

$$\begin{aligned} V_t &= \operatorname*{ess\,sup}_{\delta\in\mathcal{A}} \mathbb{E}_t^\delta\left[-\mathcal{D}_{t,T}(\delta)\exp(-\gamma\xi)\right] \\ &= \operatorname*{ess\,sup}_{\delta\in\mathcal{A}} \mathbb{E}_t^\delta\left[\mathcal{D}_{t,\tau}(\delta)\mathbb{E}_\tau^\delta\left[-\mathcal{D}_{\tau,T}(\delta)\exp(-\gamma\xi)\right]\right]. \end{aligned}$$

Then, Bayes' rule yields

$$\begin{aligned} &\mathbb{E}_\tau^\delta\left[-\mathcal{D}_{\tau,T}(\delta)\exp(-\gamma\xi)\right] = \mathbb{E}_\tau^0\left[-\frac{L_T^\delta}{L_\tau^\delta}\mathcal{D}_{\tau,T}(\delta)\exp(-\gamma\xi)\right] \\ &\leq \operatorname*{ess\,sup}_{\delta\in\mathcal{A}} \mathbb{E}_\tau^\delta\left[\mathcal{D}_{\tau,T}(\delta)\exp(-\gamma\xi)\right] \\ &= V_\tau. \end{aligned}$$

Finally, we obtain

$$V_t \leq \operatorname*{ess\,sup}_{\mu\in\mathcal{A}} \mathbb{E}_t^\mu\left[V_\tau\mathcal{D}_{t,\tau}(\delta)\right].$$

We next prove the reverse inequality. Let $\delta \in \mathcal{A}$ and $\mu \in \mathcal{A}_\tau$. We define $(\delta \otimes_\tau \mu)_u = \delta_u 1_{\{0\leq u\leq\tau\}} + \mu_u 1_{\{\tau\leq u\leq T\}}$. Then, $\delta \otimes_\tau \mu \in \mathcal{A}$, and by tower property,

$$\begin{aligned}V_t &\geq \mathbb{E}_t^{\delta\otimes_\tau\mu}\left[-\mathcal{D}_{\tau,T}(\mu)\mathcal{D}_{t,\tau}(\delta)\exp\left(-\gamma\xi\right)\right]\\ &= \mathbb{E}_t^{\delta\otimes_\tau\mu}\left[\mathbb{E}_\tau^{\delta\otimes_\tau\mu}\left[-\mathcal{D}_{\tau,T}(\mu)\exp(-\gamma\xi)\right]\mathcal{D}_{t,\tau}(\delta)\right].\end{aligned}$$

Using Bayes' formula and noting that $\frac{L_T^{\delta\otimes_\tau\mu}}{L_\tau^{\delta\otimes_\tau\mu}} = \frac{L_T^\mu}{L_\tau^\mu}$, we have

$$\begin{aligned}\mathbb{E}_\tau^{\delta\otimes_\tau\mu}\left[-\mathcal{D}_{\tau,T}(\mu)\exp(-\gamma\xi)\right] &= \mathbb{E}_\tau^0\left[-\frac{L_T^\mu}{L_\tau^\mu}\mathcal{D}_{\tau,T}(\mu)\exp(-\gamma\xi)\right]\\ &= J_T(\tau,\mu).\end{aligned}$$

This implies

$$V_t \geq \mathbb{E}_t^{\delta\otimes_\tau\mu}\left[\mathcal{D}_{t,\tau}(\delta)J_T(\tau,\mu)\right].$$

We can therefore use again Bayes' rule and the fact that $\frac{L_\tau^{\delta\otimes_\tau\mu}}{L_t^{\delta\otimes_\tau\mu}} = \frac{L_\tau^\delta}{L_t^\delta}$ to obtain

$$\begin{aligned}V_t \geq \mathbb{E}_t^0\left[\frac{L_T^{\delta\otimes_\tau\mu}}{L_t^{\delta\otimes_\tau\mu}}\mathcal{D}_{t,\tau}(\delta)J_T(\tau,\mu)\right] &= \mathbb{E}_t^0\left[\mathbb{E}_\tau^0\left[\frac{L_T^{\delta\otimes_\tau\mu}}{L_\tau^{\delta\otimes_\tau\mu}}\frac{L_\tau^{\delta\otimes_\tau\mu}}{L_t^{\delta\otimes_\tau\mu}}\mathcal{D}_{t,\tau}(\delta)J_T(\tau,\mu)\right]\right]\\ &= \mathbb{E}_t^0\left[\mathbb{E}_\tau^0\left[\frac{L_T^{\delta\otimes_\tau\mu}}{L_\tau^{\delta\otimes_\tau\mu}}\right]\frac{L_\tau^{\delta\otimes_\tau\mu}}{L_t^{\delta\otimes_\tau\mu}}\mathcal{D}_{t,\tau}(\delta)J_T(\tau,\mu)\right]\\ &= \mathbb{E}_t^0\left[\frac{L_\tau^{\delta\otimes_\tau\mu}}{L_t^{\delta\otimes_\tau\mu}}\mathcal{D}_{t,\tau}(\delta)J_T(\tau,\mu)\right]\\ &= \mathbb{E}_t^\delta\left[\mathcal{D}_{t,\tau}(\delta)J_T(\tau,\mu)\right].\end{aligned}$$

Since the previous inequality holds for any $\mu \in \mathcal{A}_\tau$, we deduce from monotone convergence theorem together with Lemma A.1 that there exists a sequence $(\mu^n)_{n\in\mathbb{N}}$ of controls in $\mathcal{A}_\tau$ such that

$$\begin{aligned}V_t \geq \lim_{n\to+\infty}\mathbb{E}_t^\delta\left[\mathcal{D}_{t,\tau}(\delta)J_T(\tau,\mu^n)\right] &= \mathbb{E}_t^\delta\left[\mathcal{D}_{t,\tau}(\delta)\lim_{n\to+\infty}J_T(\tau,\mu^n)\right]\\ &= \mathbb{E}_t^\delta\left[\mathcal{D}_{t,\tau}(\delta)V_\tau\right].\end{aligned}$$

This concludes the proof. □

A.5. *Proof of Lemma 3.8*

We divide the proof into six steps.

Step 1: Derivation of the martingale representation. For $\delta \in \mathcal{A}$, it follows from the dynamic programming principle of Lemma A.2 that the process

$$U_t^\delta = V_t \mathcal{D}_{0,t}(\delta)$$

defines a $\mathbb{P}^\delta$-supermartingale for any $\delta \in \mathcal{A}$. By standard analysis, we may then consider it in its càdlàg version (by taking right limits along rationals). By the Doob–Meyer decomposition, we can write $U_t^\delta = M_t^\delta - A_t^\delta$, where M^δ is a $\mathbb{P}^\delta$-martingale and $A_t^\delta = A_t^{\delta,c} + A_t^{\delta,d}$ is an integrable non-decreasing predictable process such that $A_0^{\delta,c} = A_0^{\delta,d} = 0$ with pathwise continuous component $A^{\delta,c}$ and with $A^{\delta,d}$ a piecewise constant predictable process.

From the martingale representation theorem under $\mathbb{P}^\delta$, see Appendix A.1 in [5], there exists $\tilde{Z}^\delta = (\tilde{Z}^{\delta,S}, \tilde{Z}^{\delta,k,\tau,i})_{k\in\mathcal{K},\tau\in\mathcal{T},i=a,b}$ predictable such that

$$M_t^\delta = V_0 + \int_0^t \tilde{Z}_r^{\delta,S} \mathrm{d}S_r + \sum_{i=a,b} \sum_{(k,\tau)\in\mathcal{K}\times\mathcal{T}} \int_0^t \tilde{Z}_r^{\delta,k,\tau,i} \mathrm{d}N_r^{\delta,k,\tau,i}.$$

Step 2: Boundedness of the value function. We show that V is a negative process. In fact, thanks to the uniform boundedness of $\delta \in \mathcal{A}$, we have that

$$\frac{L_T^\delta}{L_t^\delta} \geq \alpha_{t,T} = \exp\left(-\sum_{i=a,b} \sum_{(k,\tau)\in\mathcal{K}\times\mathcal{T}} \frac{k}{\sigma} N_T^{k,\tau,i} - 2 \times \#\mathcal{T} \times \#\mathcal{K} A \mathrm{e}^{-\frac{kc_\infty}{\sigma}} (\mathrm{e}^{\frac{k}{\sigma}} + 1)(T-t)\right),$$

where $c_\infty := \max_{k,\tau} c^{k,\tau}$. Therefore,

$$V_t \leq \mathbb{E}_t^0 \left[-\alpha_{t,T} \exp\left(-\gamma(\delta_\infty \sum_{i=a,b} \sum_{(k,\tau)\in\mathcal{K}\times\mathcal{T}} N_T^{k,\tau,i} + \int_t^T Q_u^{k,\tau} \mathrm{d}C_u^{k,\tau}) \right) \mathrm{e}^{-\gamma\xi} \right] < 0.$$

Step 3: Identification of the coefficients (1/2). Let Y be the process defined for any $t \in [0,T]$ by $V_t = -\mathrm{e}^{-\gamma Y_t}$. As $A^{\delta,d}$ is a predictable point process and the jumps of $N^{k,\tau,i}, i = a,b$, are totally inaccessible stopping times under $\mathbb{P}^0$, we have $\langle N^{k,\tau,i}, A^{\delta,d}\rangle_t = 0$ a.s. Using Ito's formula, we obtain that

$$Y_T = \xi, \text{ and } \mathrm{d}Y_t = \sum_{i=a,b}\sum_{(k,\tau)\in\mathcal{K}\times\mathcal{T}} Z_t^{k,\tau,i}\mathrm{d}N_t^{k,\tau,i} + Z_t^S\mathrm{d}S_t - \mathrm{d}I_t - \mathrm{d}\tilde{A}_t^d,$$

with

$$\begin{aligned}
Z_t^{k,\tau,a} &= -\frac{1}{\gamma}\log\left(1+\frac{\tilde{Z}_t^{\delta,k,\tau,a}}{U_{t-}^{\delta}}\right) - \delta_t^{k,\tau,a},\\
Z_t^{k,\tau,b} &= -\frac{1}{\gamma}\log\left(1+\frac{\tilde{Z}_t^{\delta,k,\tau,b}}{U_{t-}^{\delta}}\right) - \delta_t^{k,\tau,b},\\
Z_t^S &= -\frac{\tilde{Z}_t^{\delta,S}}{\gamma U_{t-}^{\delta}} - \sum_{(k,\tau)\in\mathcal{K}\times\mathcal{T}} Q_{t-}^{k,\tau}\Delta^{k,\tau},\\
I_t &= \int_0^t \left(\overline{h}(\delta_r, Z_r, Q_r)\mathrm{d}r - \frac{1}{\gamma U_r^{\delta}}\mathrm{d}A_r^{\delta,c}\right),\\
\overline{h}(\delta, Z_t, Q_t) &= h(\delta, Z_t, Q_t) - \frac{1}{2}\gamma\sigma^2(Z_t^S + Q_t)^2,\\
\tilde{A}_t^d &= \frac{1}{\gamma}\sum_{s\le t}\log\left(1-\frac{\Delta A_t^{\delta,d}}{U_{t-}^{\delta}}\right).
\end{aligned}$$

In particular, the last relation between $\tilde{A}^d$ and $A^{\delta,d}$ shows that $\Delta a_t \geq 0$ is independent of $\delta \in \mathcal{A}$, with $a_t = -\frac{A_t^{\delta,d}}{U_{t-}^{\delta}}$ and abusing notations slightly, $\Delta a_t = -\frac{\Delta A_t^{\delta,d}}{U_{t-}^{\delta}}$.

In order to complete the proof, we argue in the subsequent steps that $Z \in \mathcal{Z}$ and that, for $t \in [0,T]$, $A_t^{\delta,d} = -\sum_{s\le t} U_{s-}^{\delta}\Delta a_s = 0$ so that $\tilde{A}_t^d = 0$ and $I_t = \int_0^t \overline{H}(Z_r, Q_r)\mathrm{d}r$, where

$$\overline{H}(Z_t, Q_t) = H(Z_t, Q_t) - \frac{1}{2}\gamma\sigma^2(Z_t^S)^2.$$

Step 4: Identification of the coefficients (2/2). Since $V_T = -1$, we get that

$$\begin{aligned}0 &= \sup_{\delta\in\mathcal{A}} \mathbb{E}^\delta[U_T^\delta] - V_0\\ &= \sup_{\delta\in\mathcal{A}} \mathbb{E}^\delta[U_T^\delta - M_T^\delta]\\ &= \gamma\sup_{\delta\in\mathcal{A}} \mathbb{E}^0\left[L_T^\delta \int_0^T U_{r^-}^\delta(\mathrm{d}I_r - \overline{h}(\delta, Z_r, Q_r)\mathrm{d}r + \frac{\mathrm{d}a_r}{\gamma})\right].\end{aligned}$$

Moreover, the controls being uniformly bounded, we have

$$U_t^\delta \leq -\beta_t = V_t\exp\left(-\gamma\left(\delta_\infty \sum_{i=a,b}\sum_{(k,\tau)\in\mathcal{K}\times\mathcal{T}} N_T^{k,\tau,i} + \int_0^t Q_u^{k,\tau}\mathrm{d}C_u^{k,\tau}\right)\right) < 0.$$

Then, using $A^{\delta,d} \geq 0, U^\delta \leq 0$ and $\mathrm{d}I_t - \overline{h}(\delta, Z_t, Q_t)\mathrm{d}t \geq 0$, we obtain

$$\begin{aligned}0 &\leq \sup_{\delta\in\mathcal{A}} \mathbb{E}^0\left[\alpha_{0,T}\int_0^T -\beta_{r^-}\left(\mathrm{d}I_r - \overline{h}(\delta, Z_r, Q_r)\mathrm{d}r + \frac{\mathrm{d}a_r}{\gamma}\right)\right]\\ &= -\mathbb{E}^0\left[\alpha_{0,T}\int_0^T \beta_{r^-}\left(\mathrm{d}I_r - \overline{H}(Z_r, Q_r)\mathrm{d}r + \frac{\mathrm{d}a_r}{\gamma}\right)\right].\end{aligned}$$

The quantities $\alpha_{0,T}\int_0^T \beta_{r^-}(\mathrm{d}I_r - \overline{H}(Z_r, Q_r))\mathrm{d}r$ and $\alpha_{0,T}$ $\int_0^T \beta_{r^-}\frac{\mathrm{d}a_r}{\gamma}$ being non-negative random variables, the result follows.

Step 5: Admissibility of the process Z. As ξ satisfies the conditions in (20), to prove that $Z \in \mathcal{Z}$, it is enough to show that for some $p > 0$,

$$\sup_{\delta\in\mathcal{A}}\sup_{t\in[0,T]} \mathbb{E}^\delta[\exp(-\gamma(p+1)Y_t)] < +\infty.$$

Using Hölder inequality together with the boundedness of the intensities of the $N^{k,\tau,i}$, we have that $\sup_{\delta\in\mathcal{A}} \mathbb{E}^\delta[|U_T^\delta|^{p'+1}] < +\infty$ for some $p' > 0$. We deduce

$$\sup_{\delta\in\mathcal{A}} \sup_{t\in[0,T]} \mathbb{E}^\delta[|U_t^\delta|^{p'+1}] = \sup_{\delta\in\mathcal{A}} \mathbb{E}^\delta[|U_T^\delta|^{p'+1}] < +\infty$$

because U^δ is a $\mathbb{P}^\delta$-negative supermartingale. The conclusion follows using again Hölder inequality, the uniform boundedness of the intensities of the $N^{k,\tau,i}$ and the fact that

$$\exp(-\gamma Y_t) = U_t^\delta \exp\left(\gamma\left(\sum_{i=a,b}\sum_{(k,\tau)\in\mathcal{K}\times\mathcal{T}}\int_0^t \delta_u^{k,\tau,i}\mathrm{d}N_u^{k,\tau,i} + Q_u^{k,\tau}\mathrm{d}C_u^{k,\tau}\right)\right).$$

Step 6: Uniqueness of the representation. Let $(Y_0, Z), (Y_0^{'}, Z^{'}) \in \mathbb{R}\times\mathcal{Z}$ be such that $\xi = Y_T^{Y_0,Z} = Y_T^{Y_0^{'},Z^{'}}$. By following the lines of the verification argument in the proof of Theorem 3.9, we obtain the equality $Y_t^{Y_0,Z} = Y_t^{Y_0^{'},Z^{'}}$ using the fact that the value of the continuation utility of the market maker satisfies

$$-\mathrm{e}^{-\gamma Y_t^{Y_0,Z}} = -\mathrm{e}^{-\gamma Y_t^{Y_0^{'},Z^{'}}} = \operatorname*{ess\,sup}_{\delta\in\mathcal{A}} \mathbb{E}_t^\delta\left[-\mathrm{e}^{-\gamma(PL_T^\delta - PL_t^\delta + \xi)}\right].$$

This in turn implies that for $t \in [0,T]$ $Z_t^{k,\tau,i}\mathrm{d}N_t^{k,\tau,i} = Z_t^{'k,\tau,i}\mathrm{d}N_t^{k,\tau,i}$ and $Z_t^S\sigma^2\mathrm{d}t = Z_t^{'S}\sigma^2\mathrm{d}t = \mathrm{d}\langle Y, S\rangle_t$. Consequently, $(Y_0, Z) = (Y_0^{'}, Z^{'})$.

A.6. *Proof of Theorem 3.9*

Let $\xi = Y_T^{Y_0,Z}$ with $(Y_0, Z) \in \mathbb{R}\times\mathcal{Z}$. We first prove that for an arbitrary set of controls $\delta \in \mathcal{A}$, we have $J_{\mathrm{MM}}(\delta,\xi) \le -\mathrm{e}^{-\gamma Y_0}$, where $J_{\mathrm{MM}}(\delta,\xi)$ is such that $V_{\mathrm{MM}}(\xi) = \sup_{\delta\in\mathcal{A}} J_{\mathrm{MM}}(\delta,\xi)$. Then, we will see that this inequality is in fact an equality when the corresponding Hamiltonian $h(\delta, z, q)$ is maximized. Denote

$$\overline{Y}_t := Y_t^{Y_0,Z} + \sum_{i=a,b}\sum_{(k,\tau)\in\mathcal{K}\times\mathcal{T}}\int_0^t \delta_u^{k,\tau,i}\mathrm{d}N_u^{k,\tau,i} + Q_u^{k,\tau}\mathrm{d}C_u^{k,\tau}$$

with $t \in [0, T]$. A direct application of Itô"s formula leads to

$$\mathrm{d}e^{-\gamma \overline{Y}_t} = \gamma e^{-\gamma \overline{Y}_{t-}} \Bigg(- \Bigg(\sum_{(k,\tau)\in\mathcal{K}\times\mathcal{T}} Q_t^{k,\tau} \Delta^{k,\tau} + Z_t^S \Bigg) \mathrm{d}S_t + (H(Z_t, Q_t) - h(\delta, Z_t, Q_t))\mathrm{d}t - \sum_{i=a,b} \sum_{(k,\tau)\in\mathcal{K}\times\mathcal{T}} \gamma^{-1} \left(1 - \exp\left(-\gamma \left(Z_t^{k,\tau,i} + \delta_t^{k,\tau,i}\right)\right)\right) \mathrm{d}N_t^{\delta,k,\tau,i} \Bigg).$$

Thus, $e^{-\gamma \overline{Y}_\cdot}$ is a $\mathbb{P}^\delta$-local submartingale. Thanks to Condition (21), the uniform boundedness of the intensities of the $N^{k,\tau,i}$ and Hölder inequality $\left(e^{-\gamma \overline{Y}_t}\right)_{t\in[0,T]}$ is uniformly integrable and hence is a true submartingale. Doob–Meyer decomposition theorem gives us that

$$\int_0^\cdot \gamma e^{-\gamma \overline{Y}_{t-}} \Bigg(- \Bigg(\sum_{(k,\tau)\in\mathcal{K}\times\mathcal{T}} Q_t^{k,\tau} \Delta^{k,\tau} + Z_t^S \Bigg) \mathrm{d}S_t - \sum_{i=a,b} \sum_{(k,\tau)\in\mathcal{K}\times\mathcal{T}} \gamma^{-1} \left(1 - \exp\left(-\gamma \left(Z_t^{k,\tau,i} + \delta_t^{k,\tau,i}\right)\right)\right) \mathrm{d}N_t^{\delta,k,\tau,i} \Bigg)$$

is a true martingale. This implies that

$$\begin{aligned} J_{\mathrm{MM}}(\delta, \xi) &= \mathbb{E}^\delta \left[-e^{-\gamma \overline{Y}_T} \right] \\ &= -e^{-\gamma Y_0} - \mathbb{E}^\delta \left[\int_0^T \gamma e^{-\gamma \overline{Y}_{t-}} \left(H(Z_t, Q_t) - h(\delta, Z_t, Q_t) \right) \mathrm{d}t \right] \\ &\leq -e^{-\gamma Y_0}. \end{aligned}$$

In addition to this, the previous inequality becomes an equality if and only if δ is chosen as the maximizer of the Hamiltonian h thus leading to the optimal quotes provided in Theorem 3.9. So, we deduce $J_{\mathrm{MM}}(\delta, \xi) = -e^{-\gamma Y_0}$. Finally, we have $V_{\mathrm{MM}}(\xi) = -e^{-\gamma Y_0}$ with optimal response $(\hat{\delta}_t)_{t\in[0,T]}$.

A.7. *Proof of Theorem 3.11*

We define for any map $v : [0,T] \times \mathbb{Z}^{\#\mathcal{K}\times\#\mathcal{T}} \longrightarrow (-\infty,0)$, $x \in \mathbb{R}$, $(k,\tau) \in \mathcal{K}\times\mathcal{T}$ and $(t,q) \in [0,T] \times \mathbb{Z}^{\#\mathcal{K}\times\#\mathcal{T}}$

$$v(t, q \ominus_{K_i,T_j} x) := v(t, q^{K_1,T_1}, q^{K_1,T_2}, \dots, q^{K_i,T_{j+1}}, q^{K_i,T_j} - x, q^{K_i,T_{j+2}}, \dots, q^{K_n,T_m}).$$

The Hamilton–Jacobi–Bellman equation of the stochastic control problem (14) is given by

$$0 = \partial_t v(t,q) + \mathcal{H}_E\left(t,q,v(t,\cdot)\right),\ v(T,q) = -1, \tag{22}$$

with

$$\mathcal{H}_E\left(t,q,v(t,\cdot)\right) = \sup_{z\in\mathcal{Z}} h_E\left(t,q,s,z,v(t,\cdot)\right),$$

$$\begin{aligned} h_E(t,q,s,z,v(t,\cdot)) = v(t,q) &\left(\frac{\eta}{2}\gamma\sigma^2\left(\sum_{(k,\tau)\in\mathcal{K}\times\mathcal{T}} \Delta^{k,\tau}(z^{C^{k,\tau}} + q^{k,\tau})\right)^2\right. \\ &\left.+\frac{\eta^2}{2}\sigma^2\left(\sum_{(k,\tau)\in\mathcal{K}\times\mathcal{T}} \Delta^{k,\tau} z^{C^{k,\tau}}\right)^2\right) \\ &+\sum_{i=a,b}\ \sum_{(k,\tau)\in\mathcal{K}\times\mathcal{T}} h^i_{k,\tau}\left(t, z^{k,\tau,i}, v(t,q),\right. \\ &\left. v\left(t, q\ominus_{k,\tau}\phi(i)\right)\right)\mathbf{1}_{\phi(i)\mathcal{Q}>-\bar{q}} \end{aligned}$$

and

$$h^i_{k,\tau}(t,z,y,y') = \left(y' x_1^{k,\tau} e^{az} - y x_2 e^{bz}\right) O_{k,\tau},$$

where

$$x_1^{k,\tau} = e^{-\eta(c^{k,\tau}+\omega(\delta_\infty^{k,\tau} - \gamma^{-1}\log(1+\frac{\sigma\gamma}{C}))},\ x_2 = \left(1+\eta\frac{1-(1+\frac{\sigma\gamma}{C})^{-1}}{\gamma}\right),$$

$$O_{k,\tau} = (1+\frac{\sigma\gamma}{C})^{-\frac{C}{\gamma\sigma}} e^{-\frac{C}{\sigma}f^{k,\tau}}$$

and

$$a = \eta(1-\omega) + \frac{C}{\sigma},\ b = \frac{C}{\sigma}.$$

Tedious but straightforward computations lead to the following optimizers:

$$z^{\star k,\tau,i} := \frac{1}{a-b}\log\left(\frac{bx_2 v\,(t,q)}{ax_1^{k,\tau} v\,(t, q \ominus_{k,\tau} \phi(i))}\right),$$

$$z^{\star C^{k,\tau}} := -\frac{\gamma}{\gamma+\eta} q^{k,\tau}.$$

Note that from these computations, we get that this above optimization makes sense only if we assume that there exists δ_∞ large enough so that for $i = a$ or b, $k \in \mathcal{K}, \tau \in \mathcal{T}$ and any t, q:

$$\left| - z_t^{\star k,\tau,i}(t,q) + \frac{1}{\gamma}\log\left(1 + \frac{\sigma\gamma}{C}\right)\right| < \delta_\infty. \tag{23}$$

We will check that we can make such choice at the end of the verification argument. Equation (22) is rewritten as follows:

$$\begin{aligned} 0 = {} & \partial_t v(t,q) + v(t,q)\frac{\gamma\eta^2}{\gamma+\eta}\frac{\sigma^2}{2}\left(\sum_{(k,\tau)\in\mathcal{K}\times\mathcal{T}} \Delta^{k,\tau} q^{k,\tau}\right)^2 \\ & - v(t,q)\sum_{i=a,b}\sum_{(k,\tau)\in\mathcal{K}\times\mathcal{T}} \tilde{C}^{k,\tau}\left(\frac{v(t,q)}{v(t, q\ominus_{k,\tau}\phi(i))}\right)^{\frac{C}{\sigma\eta(1-\omega)}} \mathbf{1}_{\phi(i)\mathcal{Q}>-\bar{q}}, \end{aligned} \tag{24}$$

where

$$\tilde{C}^{k,\tau} = x_2\left(\frac{x_2}{x_1^{k,\tau}}\right)^{\frac{a}{a-b}} O_{k,\tau}\left(\left(\frac{b}{a}\right)^{\frac{b}{a-b}} - \left(\frac{b}{a}\right)^{\frac{a}{a-b}}\right) > 0.$$

We now make the ansatz $v(t,q) = u(t,\mathcal{Q})$. We derive the following PDE

$$\begin{aligned} 0 = {} & \partial_t u(t,\mathcal{Q}) + u(t,\mathcal{Q})\frac{\gamma\eta^2}{\gamma+\eta}\frac{\sigma^2}{2}\mathcal{Q}^2 - u(t,\mathcal{Q})\sum_{i=a,b}\sum_{(k,\tau)\in\mathcal{K}\times\mathcal{T}} \tilde{C}^{k,\tau} \\ & \left(\frac{u(t,\mathcal{Q})}{u(t,\mathcal{Q}-\Delta^{k,\tau}\phi(i))}\right)^{\frac{C}{\sigma\eta(1-\omega)}} \mathbf{1}_{\phi(i)\mathcal{Q}>-\bar{q}}, \end{aligned} \tag{25}$$

with terminal condition $u(T,\mathcal{Q}) = -1$.

Using the classical change of variable $\tilde{u} := (-u)^{-\frac{C}{\sigma\eta(1-\omega)}}$, PDE (25) becomes

$$0 = \partial_t \tilde{u}(t,\mathcal{Q}) - \tilde{u}(t,\mathcal{Q})\frac{C\gamma\eta}{\gamma+\eta}\frac{\sigma}{2(1-\omega)}\mathcal{Q}^2 + \sum_{i=a,b}\sum_{(k,\tau)\in\mathcal{K}\times\mathcal{T}} \hat{C}^{k,\tau}\tilde{u}(t,\mathcal{Q}-\Delta^{k,\tau}\phi(i))\mathbf{1}_{\phi(i)\mathcal{Q}>-\bar{q}}, \tag{26}$$

where $\hat{C}^{k,\tau} := \tilde{C}^{k,\tau}\frac{C}{\sigma\eta(1-\omega)}$. Eventually, Cauchy–Lipschitz theorem provides the existence and uniqueness of a bounded solution to (26) and so to (24).

For the verification argument, we first introduce a technical lemma.

Lemma A.3. *Let $Z \in \mathcal{Z}, \xi = Y_T^{\hat{Y}_0,Z}$. We define*

$$K_t^Z := \exp\left(-\eta\left(\sum_{i=a,b}\sum_{(k,\tau)\in\mathcal{K}\times\mathcal{T}} c^{k,\tau}N_t^{k,\tau,i} - \int_0^t \omega\left(\Delta^i(Z_s^{k,\tau,i}) - \delta_\infty^{k,\tau}\right)\mathrm{d}N_s^{k,\tau,i} - Y_t^{Y_0,Z}\right)\right), \quad t\in[0,T].$$

There exists $\epsilon > 0$ such that

$$\sup_{t\in[0,T]} \mathbb{E}^{\hat{\delta}(Z)}\left[|K_t^Z|^{1+\epsilon}\right] < +\infty,$$

where $\hat{\delta}(Z)$ is defined in Theorem 3.9.

The proof is borrowed from [5]. We now verify that the unique solution v of Equation (22) coincides at any point $(0, Q_0)$ with the value v_0^E of the reduced problem (14). We also prove that in (14), the maximum is achieved for feedback controls issued from (15).

Using Itô's formula, we get

$$\begin{aligned}\mathrm{d}[v(t,Q_t)K_t^Z] = K_{t-}^Z\Big[&(h_E(t,Q_{t-},S_t,Z_t,v(t,\cdot)) - \mathcal{H}_E(t,Q_{t-},v(t,\cdot)))\,\mathrm{d}t \\ &+ v(t,Q_{t-})\eta\sum_{k=1}^{\mathcal{K}}\sum_{\tau=1}^{\mathcal{T}} Z_t^{C^{k,\tau}}\mathrm{d}C_t^{k,\tau} + \sum_{i=a,b}\sum_{k=1}^{\mathcal{K}}\sum_{\tau=1}^{\mathcal{T}} \\ &\left(e^{-\eta(c^{k,\tau}-Z_t^{k,\tau,i})}v(t,Q_{t-}^{k,\tau}-\phi(i)) - v(t,Q_{t-})\right)\mathrm{d}N_t^{\hat{\delta}(Z),k,\tau,i}\Big].\end{aligned}$$

The process K^Z is uniformly integrable on $[0,T]$ according to (21), Hölder inequality and the boundedness of the intensity of the processes $N^{k,\tau,i}$.

Moreover, v being uniformly bounded as a consequence of the Cauchy–Lipschitz theorem, the process $\left(v(t,Q_t)K_t^Z\right)_{t\in[0,T]}$ is a $\mathbb{P}^{\hat{\delta}(Z)}$ supermartingale and the local martingale term in the above equation is a true martingale. Hence,

$$v(0,Q_0) \geq \mathbb{E}^{\hat{\delta}(Z)}[v(T,Q_T)K_T^Z] = -\mathbb{E}^{\hat{\delta}(Z)}[K_T^Z]. \tag{27}$$

Since $Z \in \mathcal{Z}$ is arbitrary, we get

$$v(0,Q_0) \geq \sup_{Z\in\mathcal{Z}} -\mathbb{E}^{\hat{\delta}(Z)}[K_T^Z] = v_0^E.$$

The feedback form of Z, issued from (15), being bounded according to Equation (23), is admissible. Considering the process $Z^\star$, we get an equality instead of an inequality in the above equation.

For consistency, we now check that there does exist some constant δ_∞ such that (23) is satisfied. In the same vein as in Step 2 of the proof of Theorem 3.9, we can show that for any t and q, $v(t,q)$ is negative. Because of the compactness of the domain of v, the function is uniformly negative: we can find ε such that $v < -\varepsilon$ on $[0,T]\times\mathcal{D}$. Consequently, $\log\left(\frac{v(t,q)}{v(t,q^{k,\tau}\ominus_{k,\tau}\phi(i))}\right)$ is uniformly bounded in i, k, τ, t and q. Thus, we can always choose a δ_∞ satisfying (23).

References

[1] B. Baldacci, P. Bergault, and O. Guéant. Algorithmic market making for options. *Quantitative Finance*, 21(1):85–97, 2021.

[2] B. Baldacci, D. Possamaï, and M. Rosenbaum. Optimal make-take fees in a multi market-maker environment. *SIAM Journal on Financial Mathematics*, 12(1):446–486, 2021.

[3] E. Budish, P. Cramton, and J. Shim. The high-frequency trading arms race: Frequent batch auctions as a market design response. *The Quarterly Journal of Economics*, 130(4):1547–1621, 2015.

[4] K. Dayri and M. Rosenbaum. Large tick assets: implicit spread and optimal tick size. *Market Microstructure and Liquidity*, 7(4), 2016.

[5] O. El Euch, T. Mastrolia, M. Rosenbaum, and N. Touzi. Optimal make–take fees for market making regulation. *Mathematical Finance*, 31, 109–148. arXiv preprint arXiv:1805.02741, 2018.

[6] S. Graf and H. Luschgy. *Foundations of Quantization for Probability Distributions*. Springer, Berlin, 2007.

[7] P. Jusselin, T. Mastrolia, and M. Rosenbaum. Optimal auction duration: A price formation viewpoint. *Operations Research*, 69(6):1734–1745, 2021.

[8] J. Kalagnanam and D. C. Parkes. Auctions, bidding and exchange design. In *Handbook of Quantitative Supply Chain Analysis*, Springer, Berlin, 2004, pp. 143–212.

[9] S. Laruelle and C. A. Lehalle. *Market Microstructure in Practice.* World Scientific, Singapore, 2018.

[10] A. Madhavan, M. Richardson, and M. Roomans. Why do security prices change? a transaction-level analysis of nyse stocks. *The Review of Financial Studies*, 10(4):1035–1064, 1997.

[11] S. Mayhew and V. Mihov. How do exchanges select stocks for option listing? *The Journal of Finance*, 59(1):447–471, 2004.

[12] G. Pagès, H. Pham, and J. Printems. Optimal quantization methods and applications to numerical problems in finance. In *Handbook of Computational and Numerical Methods in Finance*, Springer, Berlin, 2004, pp. 253–297.

[13] A. Sokol. Optimal Novikov-type criteria for local martingales with jumps. *Electronic Communications in Probability*, 18:1–8, 2013.

[14] M. Wyart, J.-P. Bouchaud, J. Kockelkoren, M. Potters, and M. Vettorazzo. Relation between bid–ask spread, impact and volatility in order-driven markets. *Quantitative Finance*, 8(1):41–57, 2008.

https://doi.org/10.1142/9789811280306_0020

Chapter 20

A Moment Matching Calibration under the Bilateral Gamma Model and Its Application

Jingyan Zhang* and Wim Schoutens†

Department of Mathematics, KU Leuven, Celestijnenlaan 200B, 3001 Leuven, Belgium

**jingyan.zhang@kuleuven.be*

†wim.schoutens@kuleuven.be

Abstract

This chapter provides a closed-form solution for a moment matching calibration under the Bilateral Gamma (BG) model. The BG model is an exponential Lévy model with as underlying distribution a bilateral gamma distribution. The famous Variance-Gamma (VG) model is a special case of this BG model. Compared with the variance-gamma distributions, bilateral gamma distributions allow more flexible tail behaviors. Model calibration is a vital and classical problem of option pricing. The standard calibration process applies a search algorithm to find an optimal parameter set by minimizing an objective function representing the error between the model and market quotes. However, numerical optimization often suffers from local minima, an ill-posed problem, and the optimal result is sensitive to the initial value of the search algorithm. Moment matching calibration follows an alternative approach. It estimates the model parameters by matching a series of moments of the model with the corresponding market-implied moments. Hence, instead of applying a search algorithm, it obtains the optimal parameters by solving the moments matching equations, and thus it avoids the mentioned issues. Previous studies have developed the moment matching calibration for the mentioned VG model. This chapter provides an analytical solution of the moments matching equations for the BG model. Next, we evaluate its performance in a numerical study and compare a few variations of the methodology. As theoretically expected, the moment matching calibration under the BG model outperforms the moment matching calibration under the VG model. In terms of minimizing root-mean-squared errors, also as expected, it is suboptimal by construction compared with the search algorithm under the BG model. We quantify the gap and note that the straightforward moment matching calibration is obtained almost instantaneously in contrast to the search algorithm, which is rather time-consuming. Accordingly, we combine the moment matching calibration and standard calibration by using the moment matching solution as a plausible initial value for the search algorithm and improve model performance as such.

Keywords: Model calibration, Implied moments, Lévy model

1. Introduction

Given an option pricing model, the procedure to obtain model parameters from options market data is called model calibration. It is one of the classical and essential problems of option pricing models. It is used for exotic option pricing, hedging and risk management purposes.

Since Black and Scholes published their model in 1973, market participants have appreciated their model in option pricing and applied it to various market problems. However, due to its restrictive assumptions, the model has a series of drawbacks. Hence, over time many alternative models have been proposed, and one has developed a vast and diverse series of other pricing models to counter the shortcomings of the Black and Scholes model. With this, model calibration problems have come to the fore. The main idea is to construct an objective function representing the error between the model and the market. Minimizing this objective function would give a plausible parameter estimate, one that at least is the "closest" in some sense to the actual market setting.

Hence, given a certain underlier and a certain model with parameter set θ, a standard calibration approach is to minimize the sum of the errors between market prices, P, and model prices, $\hat{P}$ over all traded options on the given name, to find the optimized model parameters set θ^*:

$$\theta^* = \underset{\theta}{\operatorname{argmin}} \sum_i \omega_i h(P_i, \hat{P}_i(\theta)), \tag{1}$$

where P_i is the market price for the contract i and $\hat{P}_i$ is corresponding estimated model price, ω_i is a weight attached to this ith quote and $h(\cdot)$ is the error function employed.

In our study, we will minimize the Mean Squared Error (MSE):

$$\sum_{i=1}^{n} \frac{1}{n}(P_i - \hat{P}_i(\theta))^2 \tag{2}$$

and report typically its square root, the RMSE.

Standard model calibration aims to minimize the objective function, and although such calibration performs reasonably well in general, it suffers from a few problems. The results suffer from local minima. In addition, the different choices of objective functions will lead to significant differences in parameter sets but also in the exotic option pricing process [4,5]. Last but not least, the optimal result of the search algorithm is susceptible to the initial starting value of the search algorithm. Furthermore, it is quite time-consuming when the model parameter set is large.

To improve the performance of the calibration method, researchers developed various approaches. For example, by adding a convexifying penalty term to the objective function; another approach is improving the quality of feed option data by considering historical market prices. To improve the robustness of the calibration method, one has applied Bayesian estimations to obtain a comparable stable parameter set. Guillaume and Schoutens [6] proposed a moment matching market-implied calibration method which ameliorates the standard calibration method, mainly when applied to the Variance-Gamma (VG) model and sharply reduces the computation speed. Considering the excellent reported performance of the moment matching calibration method, in this paper, we apply it to the Bilateral Gamma (BG) model with the VG model as a special case.

The VG model is a pure jump process introduced by Carr *et al.* [3]. Küchler and Tappe [7] generalized the VG model and developed the BG model to describe different tail behavior on two sides of the return distribution. In essence, it allowed for two different shape parameters of the underlying gamma processes. In this study, we derive an analytical solution to the moment matching calibration equations under the BG model. Then, we evaluate its performance in the numerical study. Specifically, we compare the moment matching calibration under the BG and VG models. In particular, we calibrate the model to a time series of option data over various strikes and with different maturities.

The remaining parts of this chapter are organized as follows. In Section 2, we introduce the implied moments and the moments of the BG model and solve the moment matching calibration equations under the BG Model. In Section 3, we evaluate the calibration performance under the BG model and present the results of the numerical study. In Section 4, we discuss the model performance and numerical results and conclude.

2. Moment Matching Calibration under the Bilateral Gamma Model

2.1. *Market Implied Moments*

We will use the term "implied moments" for moments of the risk-neutral distribution obtained from option market data. In this subsection, we introduce these implied moments briefly and show how to calculate implied moments from given option market prices. In essence, it uses the same methodology as the methodology underlying the famous VIX index.

Volatility is the standard deviation, the square of the second central moment, of our return distribution and is the only model parameter for the Black and Scholes option pricing model. One could estimate it by matching the Black and Scholes option price with the market price. This market implied value is then called implied volatility and typically depends on the option's strike and maturity. Another approach is to estimate the volatility by inferring the risk-neutral distribution from the given option dataset at a particular maturity and then calculate the standard deviation directly. The advantage is that the estimation is no longer dependent on a particular choice of strike level. In addition, one could also infer higher moments from this risk-neutral distribution. In our study, we apply this model-free method to obtain the implied volatility and higher implied standardized moments.

Bakshi *et al.* [2] introduced a model-free estimation method which is also the reference of the CBOE to calculate the VIX index and SKEW index. Here, we introduce this method briefly. Bakshi and Madan [1] explained the theory behind this method. They also proved that any twice-differentiable payoff could be spanned by a portfolio of bonds, the underlying asset and out-of-the-money vanilla (put and call) options (see also Ref. [10]):

$$\begin{aligned} f(S_T) &= f(\kappa) + f^{'}(\kappa)((S_T-\kappa)^+ - (\kappa - S_T)^+) \\ &\quad + \int_0^{\kappa} f^{''}(K)(K-S_T)^+ dK + \int_{\kappa}^{\infty} f^{''}(K)(S_T-K)^+ dK, \end{aligned} \tag{3}$$

where κ is a certain strike value. Applying the put-call parity to the right side of Eq. (3), we get the expectation of a general claim payoff:

$$\begin{aligned} E_Q[f(S_T)] &= f(\kappa) + f^{'}(\kappa)(\exp((r-q)T)S_0 - \kappa) \\ &\quad + \exp(rT)\left(\int_0^{\kappa} f^{''}(K)EP(K,T)dK \right. \\ &\quad \left. + \int_{\kappa}^{\infty} f^{''}(K)EC(K,T)dK\right). \end{aligned} \tag{4}$$

Accordingly, we can deduce the Nth moment of the log asset return $X_T = \log\left(\frac{S_T}{S_0}\right)$ by considering the function $f(S_T) = \left(\log\left(\frac{S_T}{S_0}\right)\right)^N$:

$$\begin{aligned} &E_Q\left[\left(\log\left(\frac{S_T}{S_0}\right)\right)^N\right] \\ &\quad = \left(\log\left(\frac{\kappa}{S_0}\right)\right)^N + N\left(\log\left(\frac{\kappa}{S_0}\right)\right)^{N-1}\left(\frac{F_0}{\kappa} - 1\right) \end{aligned}$$

$$+ \exp(rT)\int_0^{\kappa} \frac{N}{K^2}\left((N-1)\left(\log\left(\frac{K}{S_0}\right)\right)^{N-2}\right.$$

$$\left. - \left(\log\left(\frac{K}{S_0}\right)\right)^{N-1}\right) EP(K,T)dK$$

$$+ \exp(rT)\int_{\kappa}^{\infty} \frac{N}{K^2}\left((N-1)\left(\log\left(\frac{K}{S_0}\right)\right)^{N-2}\right.$$

$$\left. - \left(\log\left(\frac{K}{S_0}\right)\right)^{N-1}\right) EC(K,T)dK, \tag{5}$$

where $F_0 = S_0 \exp((r-q)T)$.

However, the challenge of estimating the model-free implied moments is that we can not observe the option data for a continuum of strikes. One can (see, e.g., Madan and Schoutens [8]) use the trapezoidal rule to solve this computation problem. More precisely, Eq. (6) [8] is the truncated form of the Nth order moment of the risk-neutral log return $X_T = \log\left(\frac{S_T}{S_0}\right)$.

$$E_Q\left[\left(\log\left(\frac{S_T}{S_0}\right)\right)^N\right] = \left(\log\left(\frac{K_0}{S_0}\right)\right)^N + N\left(\log\left(\frac{K_0}{S_0}\right)\right)^{N-1}\left(\frac{F_0}{K_0}-1\right)$$

$$+ \exp(rT)N\sum_{i=1}^{M}\frac{\Delta K_i}{K_i^2}\left((N-1)\left(\log\left(\frac{K_i}{S_0}\right)\right)^{N-2}\right.$$

$$\left. - \left(\log\left(\frac{K_i}{S_0}\right)\right)^{N-1}\right) \mathrm{Price}(K_i,T), \tag{6}$$

where S_0 is the current underlying stock price, F_0 is the current forward price at maturity, T is the option maturity in years, r is the risk-free interest rate corresponding to the maturity T, K_i is the strike price of the ith out-of-the-money option ($K_i > F_0$ for call option, $K_i < F_0$ for put option), ΔK_i is the interval between strike prices as Eq. (7) shows:

$$\begin{cases} \Delta K_1 = K_2 - K_1, \\ \Delta K_i = \dfrac{K_{i+1} - K_{i-1}}{2}, \quad \forall i \neq 1 \textit{ or } N, \\ \Delta K_N = K_N - K_{N-1} \end{cases} \tag{7}$$

K_0 is the first strike price below the forward price F_0,
$Price(K_i, T)$ is the price for the option contract with strike price K_i and maturity T given by Eq. (8), where EC and EP are the midpoints of the corresponding bid and ask price of the European Call (EC) and the European Put (EP).

$$\begin{cases} \text{Price}(K_i, T) = EP(K_i, T), \\ \text{Price}(K_i, T) = \dfrac{EC(K_0, T) + EP(K_0, T)}{2}, \quad \forall i \neq 1 \text{ or } N. \\ \text{Price}(K_i, T) = EC(K_i, T) \end{cases} \tag{8}$$

After getting the Nth raw moment of the log return, $X_T = \log(\frac{S_T}{S_0})$, from Eq. (6), one could obtain the implied central moment and implied standardized moments from Eq. (9).

$$\begin{cases} \text{Var}(X_T) = E_Q[X_T^2] - (E_Q[X_T])^2, \\ \text{Skewness}(X_T) = \dfrac{E_Q[X_T^3] - 3E_Q[X_T]E_Q[X_T^2] + 2(E_Q[X_T])^3}{(\text{Var}(X_T))^{3/2}}, \\ \text{Kurtosis}(X_T) = \dfrac{\begin{matrix} E_Q[X_T^4] - 4E_Q[X_T]E_Q[X_T^3] \\ +6(E_Q[X_T])^2 E_Q[X_T^2] - 3(E_Q[X_T])^4 \end{matrix}}{(\text{Var}(X_T))^2}, \\ \text{Hyperskewness}(X_T) = \\ \quad \dfrac{\begin{matrix} E_Q[X_T^5] - 5E_Q[X_T]E_Q[X_T^4] + 10(E_Q[X_T])^2 E_Q[X_T^3] \\ -10(E_Q[X_T])^3 E_Q[X_T^2] + 4(E_Q[X_T])^5 \end{matrix}}{(\text{Var}(X_T))^{5/2}}, \end{cases} \tag{9}$$

where $E_Q[X_T^N]$ is the Nth raw moment of the risk-neutral distribution of X_T. In the following study, implied volatility is the square root of the variance in Eq. (9), implied skewness is Skewness, implied kurtosis is Kurtosis and implied hyperskewness is Hyperskewness in Eq. (9), respectively.

2.2. *Moments of Bilateral Gamma Distributions*

Küchler and Tappe [7] introduced the BG distribution for modeling financial market fluctuation. Compared with the VG distribution, the BG distribution allows for different shape parameters of two underlying gamma processes, thus allowing different tail behaviors on both sides of the distribution. It hence can be seen as an extension of the VG distribution allowing for more flexibility.

We say that X follows a BG distribution with parameters $c_p, b_p, c_n, b_n > 0$ if the characteristic function of $X \sim BG(u; c_p, b_p, c_n, b_n)$ is

$$\phi_{BG}(u; c_p, b_p, c_n, b_n) = \mathbb{E}[\exp(iuX)] = (1 - ib_pu)^{-c_p}(1 + ib_nu)^{-c_n}, \tag{10}$$

where i is the imaginary number. The corresponding cumulant generating function is

$$\psi_{BG}(u; c_p, b_p, c_n, b_n) = \ln \mathbb{E}[\exp(uX)] = -c_p \ln(1-b_pu) - c_n \ln(1+b_nu). \tag{11}$$

Taking partial derivatives of the above cumulant generating function, we get the nth order cumulant $\kappa_n = \frac{\partial^n}{\partial u^n}\psi(u)|_{u=0}$ which is given by

$$\kappa_n = (n-1)!(c_pb_p^n + (-1)^n c_nb_n^n). \tag{12}$$

From this, a straightforward calculation then gives for our BG distribution:

$$\begin{cases} \mathrm{Var}^{\mathrm{Model}}(X) = \kappa_2 = b_p^2c_p + b_n^2c_n, \\ \mathrm{Skewness}^{\mathrm{Model}}(X) = \dfrac{\kappa_3}{\kappa_2^{3/2}} = \dfrac{2(b_p^3c_p - b_n^3c_n)}{(b_p^2c_p + b_n^2c_n)^{3/2}}, \\ \mathrm{Kurtosis}^{\mathrm{Model}}(X) = 3 + \dfrac{\kappa_4}{\kappa_2^2} = 3 + \dfrac{6(b_p^4c_p + b_n^4c_n)}{(b_p^2c_p + b_n^2c_n)^2}, \\ \mathrm{Hyperskewness}^{\mathrm{Model}}(X) = \dfrac{\kappa_5 + 10\kappa_3\kappa_2}{\kappa_2^{5/2}} = \dfrac{24(b_p^5c_p - b_n^5c_n)}{(b_p^2c_p + b_n^2c_n)^{5/2}} \\ \quad + \dfrac{20(b_p^3c_p - b_n^3c_n)}{(b_p^2c_p + b_n^2c_n)^{3/2}}. \end{cases} \tag{13}$$

Note that for the associated Lévy process, $X = X_t, t > 0$, the increments follow $X_t \sim BG(tc_p, b_p, tc_n, b_n)$. Denoting the kth raw moment as $m_k = E[X_T^k]$, we have

$$\begin{cases} \mathrm{Var}^{\mathrm{Model}}(X_T) = E[(X_T - E(X_T))^2] = m_2 - m_1^2 = T(b_p^2 c_p + b_n^2 c_n), \\ \mathrm{Skewness}^{\mathrm{Model}}(X_T) = \dfrac{E[(X_T - E(X_T))^3]}{(\mathrm{Var}^{\mathrm{Model}}(X_T))^{3/2}} \\ = \dfrac{m_3 - 3m_1 m_2 + 2m_1^3}{(m_2 - m_1^2)^{3/2}} = \dfrac{2(b_p^3 c_p - b_n^3 c_n)}{\sqrt{T}(b_p^2 c_p + b_n^2 c_n)^{3/2}}, \\ \mathrm{Kurtosis}^{\mathrm{Model}}(X_T) = \dfrac{E[(X_T - E(X_T))^4]}{(\mathrm{Var}^{\mathrm{Model}}(X_T))^2} \\ = \dfrac{m_4 - 4m_1 m_3 + 6m_1^2 m_2 - 3m_1^4}{(m_2 - m_1^2)^2} = 3 + \dfrac{6(b_p^4 c_p + b_n^4 c_n)}{T(b_p^2 c_p + b_n^2 c_n)^2}, \\ \mathrm{Hyperskewness}^{\mathrm{Model}}(X_T) = \dfrac{E[(X_T - E(X_T))^5]}{(\mathrm{Var}^{\mathrm{Model}}(X_T))^{5/2}} \\ = \dfrac{m_5 - 5m_1 m_4 + 10m_1^2 m_3 - 10m_1^3 m_2 + 4m_1^5}{(m_2 - m_1^2)^{5/2}} \\ = \dfrac{24(b_p^5 c_p - b_n^5 c_n)}{T^{3/2}(b_p^2 c_p + b_n^2 c_n)^{5/2}} + \dfrac{20(b_p^3 c_p - b_n^3 c_n)}{\sqrt{T}(b_p^2 c_p + b_n^2 c_n)^{3/2}}. \end{cases} \tag{14}$$

We observe that the variance scales with T, skewness with $1/\sqrt{T}$ and excess kurtosis with a factor $1/T$.

2.3. *Moment Matching Calibration Procedure*

In this section, we introduce the moment matching calibration method under the BG model. Guillaume and Schoutens [6] introduced a moment matching calibration method under the VG model. They matched three parameters of the VG model with the corresponding implied moments and gave an analytical solution to the moment matching equations. In this study, we match the four model parameters of the BG model in a similar manner via an analytical solution of the corresponding moment matching equations.

A pure-jump exponential Lévy process is defined as Eq. (15):

$$S_t = \frac{S_0 \exp((r-q)t + X_t)}{E_Q[\exp(X_t)]} = S_0 \exp((r-q+\omega)t + X_t) \qquad (15)$$

where $X = \{X_t, t \geq 0\}$ is a Lévy model and $\omega = -\log(\phi_X(-i))$ is a convexity correction parameter to make the model risk-neutral. Assume $X = \{X_t, t \geq 0\}$ is a bilateral gamma process and hence where X_t follows the $BG(tc_p, b_p, tc_n, b_n)$ distribution.

The general moment matching calibration matches the implied moments with model moments and solves this equation system. The specific matching equations are shown as Eq. (16). Implied market moments are estimated (model-free) as described in Section 2.1 and the moments of the BG model as in Section 2.2.

$$\begin{cases} \mathrm{Var}^{\mathrm{Market}}(X_T) = \mathrm{Var}^{\mathrm{Model}}(X_T), \\ \mathrm{Skewness}^{\mathrm{Market}}(X_T) = \mathrm{Skewness}^{\mathrm{Model}}(X_T), \\ \mathrm{Kurtosis}^{\mathrm{Market}}(X_T) = \mathrm{Kurtosis}^{\mathrm{Model}}(X_T), \\ \mathrm{Hyperskewness}^{\mathrm{Market}}(X_T) = \mathrm{Hyperskewness}^{\mathrm{Model}}(X_T). \end{cases} \qquad (16)$$

Denoting the implied variance, skewness, kurtosis and hyperskewness (at a fixed maturity T) as v, s, k and f, respectively. Applying Eq. (14) to Eq. (16), we obtain the following system of moment matching equations:

$$\begin{cases} c_p b_p^2 + c_n b_n^2 = \dfrac{v}{T}, \\ c_p b_p^3 - c_n b_n^3 = \dfrac{s v^{3/2}}{2T}, \\ c_p b_p^4 + c_n b_n^4 = \dfrac{(k-3)v^2}{6T}, \\ c_p b_p^5 - c_n b_n^5 = \dfrac{(f-10s)v^{5/2}}{24T}. \end{cases} \qquad (17)$$

This moment matching equations admits a solution under the restriction $c_p, b_p, c_n, b_n > 0$ if and only if $6 + 3s^2 - 2k < 0$ (Condition 1) and $(2k-6)^2 + 30s^2 - 3sf > 0$ (Condition 2). The solution is given by

$$\begin{cases} c_p = (E + F/D)/(-2B^2), \\ b_p = (D + A)/(2C), \\ c_n = (E - F/D)/(-2B^2), \\ b_n = (D - A)/(2C), \end{cases} \tag{18}$$

where

$$\begin{cases} a = v/T, \quad b = \dfrac{sv^{3/2}}{2T}, \quad c = \dfrac{(k-3)v^2}{6T}, \quad d = \dfrac{(f-10s)v^{5/2}}{24T}, \\ A = ad - bc, \quad B = c^2 - bd, \quad C = ac - b^2, \quad D = \sqrt{A^2 + 4BC}, \\ E = b^4c - ab^2(c^2 + 2bd) + a^2(4bcd - c^3 - ad^2), \\ F = -bc^2(b^4 - 5ab^2c + 5a^2c^2) + (2b^2 - 3ac)(b^4 - 3ab^2c - a^2c^2)d + \\ a^2b(4b^2 - 7ac)d^2 + a^4d^3. \end{cases} \tag{19}$$

In case Condition 1 or Condition 2 is violated, the moment matching equations (16) admit no solution. Unfortunately, as we will see in our numerical study of the following section, such situations sometimes do occur in financial markets. A practical *ad hoc* way of dealing with such situations is to adjust the implied skewness, implied kurtosis and implied hyper-skewness. More precisely, in such situations, we will follow the adjusted method 1 of Guillaume and Schoutens [6], where one replaces implied skewness and implied kurtosis, (s, k), with the closest couple, $(s_a, k_a+\epsilon)$, which belonged to the existing domain. Then, we fixed the adjusted implied skewness and implied kurtosis and further checked whether it satisfied Condition 2. If not, we adjust implied hyper-skewness using the same method. We set ϵ equal to 0.1 to guarantee that a couple of values are in the interior of the existence domain.

Finally, we often make use of a different parametrization of the BG models, the so-called mean(μ)-variance(σ) parameterization of the BG model. These parameters provide a different intuitive understanding of the upside and downside returns. The connection between two parameterizations is given in Eq. (20), and details are described in Madan *et al.* [9].

$$\begin{cases} \mu_p = b_p c_p, \\ \sigma_p = b_p \sqrt{c_p}, \\ \mu_n = b_n c_n, \\ \sigma_n = b_n \sqrt{c_n}. \end{cases} \tag{20}$$

3. Numerical Studies

After inferring the analytical solution of moment matching equations, we apply it to real option market data. First, we present the statistics of option datasets in Section 3.1. Second, we calibrate the BG model on a particular day (2018-09-24) and show its calibrating performance as an illustration. Then, to illustrate this calibrating method under the BG model over time, we calibrate the BG model on contracts whose days to maturity (DTM) is nearest to 30 days for every trading day in 2018. Furthermore, we report on similar calibrations on contracts whose DTM is the nearest to 60 days, 90 days and 180 days. The evaluation method in this study is the RMSE given by

$$RMSE(\theta_t) = \sqrt{\frac{1}{N}\sum_{i=1}^{N}(P_i - \hat{P}_i(\theta_t))^2}, \tag{21}$$

where the market option price is P and the model option price is $\hat{P}$, θ_t is the parameter space at time t and N is the number of available market options at time t.

3.1. *Data*

There are 251 trading days in our dataset covering the year 2018 from 2018-01-02 to 2018-12-31. We only used out-of-money contracts and deleted market quotes that violated no-arbitrage constraints.

First, we illustrated the methodology on a particular date, namely 2018-09-24, and reported on the fitting for a series of available time to maturities (TTMs). Table 1 presents time to maturity (TTM), the

Table 1. Summary statistics of option quotes on 2018-09-24.

TTM	N quotes	N calls	N puts	Min X/S	Max X/S
1.2384	103	25	78	0.2912	1.4387
0.9890	93	25	68	0.3768	1.4387
0.7397	97	25	72	0.3425	1.4044
0.4712	93	25	68	0.3768	1.4044
0.3178	250	61	189	0.3425	1.2331
0.2411	269	62	207	0.3083	1.2331
0.1452	254	59	195	0.4110	1.1475
0.0685	248	57	191	0.5738	1.1133

number of quotes, call options and put options, and the minimum and maximum of the ratio of strike price and underlying price (X/S), also sometimes referred to as moneyness, of options with different TTM. The number of quotes sharply decreases for options with a TTM longer than 0.4712. Moreover, the minimum X/S decreases, and the maximum X/S increases as TTM increases.

Then, we select option quotes whose DTM is the nearest to 30 days into the 30 DTM option dataset. Moreover, we follow the same screening rules for the 60 DTM, 90 DTM and 180 DTM option datasets. Table 2 presents the statistics of time to maturity (TTM), the number of quotes, call options and put options, the minimum and maximum of the ratio of strike price and underlying price of approximately 30 DTM, 60 DTM, 90 DTM and 180 DTM option datasets. For almost all panels, the number of call options is lower than the number of put options. Furthermore, we observed that the average value of the minimum X/S is larger for the 30 DTM dataset than for the 180 DTM dataset and the average value of the maximum X/S is smaller for the 30 DTM dataset than for the 180 DTM dataset.

3.2. *Results*

In this numeric study, we evaluate the performance of the matching calibration under the BG model. First, we calibrated the BG model on 2018-09-24 for different maturities. In Figure 1(a), we show the implied moments corresponding to the different maturities. As expected, the implied variance shows an increasing trend; the implied skewness shows a decreasing trend except for the second

Table 2. Summary statistics of option quotes.

	Statistic	N	Mean	St. dev.	Min	Pctl (25)	Pctl (75)	Max
30 DTM	TTM	251	0.0836	0.0244	0.0384	0.0630	0.1041	0.1260
	N quotes	251	240.4980	21.5975	148	233.5	253.5	281
	N calls	251	64.9203	17.2082	13	53	77	110
	N puts	251	175.5777	15.5439	124	166	188	202
	Min X/S	251	0.5109	0.0927	0.3190	0.4505	0.5642	0.7832
	Max X/S	251	1.1318	0.0372	1.0287	1.1090	1.1549	1.3405
60 DTM	TTM	251	0.1666	0.0244	0.1178	0.1452	0.1836	0.2110
	N quotes	251	250.5219	19.8596	124	245	259	293
	N calls	251	71.2191	18.5855	28	58	85	127
	N puts	251	179.3028	14.6406	96	172	190	203
	Min X/S	251	0.4116	0.0558	0.2932	0.3653	0.4411	0.6204
	Max X/S	251	1.1759	0.0397	1.0856	1.1519	1.1961	1.3962
90 DTM	TTM	251	0.2465	0.0243	0.2000	0.2260	0.2685	0.2932
	N quotes	251	237.6813	35.6879	93	241	255	293
	N calls	251	67.0080	19.7628	21	57.5	75	144
	N puts	251	170.6733	25.4534	71	166	185	209
	Min X/S	251	0.3872	0.0530	0.2519	0.3475	0.4120	0.5514
	Max X/S	251	1.2123	0.0445	1.1128	1.1798	1.2408	1.3962
180 DTM	TTM	251	0.4939	0.0700	0.3644	0.4411	0.5466	0.6247
	N quotes	251	91.1554	8.7970	71	87	94	110
	N calls	251	24.2351	5.2027	9	22	26	39
	N puts	251	66.9203	8.1762	48	62	68	87
	Min X/S	251	0.3196	0.0907	0.1079	0.2617	0.3829	0.4882
	Max X/S	251	1.3214	0.0733	1.1631	1.2793	1.3607	1.5095

maturity; the implied kurtosis and the implied hyper-skewness also show a decreasing trend. Then we further check whether all of these implied standardized moments are not violating Condition 1 and 2, and hence we are in the existence domain of the matching equations. In Figure 1(b), the blue points are implied standardized moments; the red line is the border of the existence domain for Condition 1; the grey surface is the border of the existence domain for Condition 2. We observed that the implied standardized moments with the second maturity are out of the red line boundary; the first Condition 1 is, in that case, violated. So we make an adjustment as described above and then use the adjusted moments to calibrate the VG and BG models.

Table 3 presents the optimal parameter sets calibrated on 2018-09-24 using S&P500 option dataset with different expiration dates. The first column, TTM_i, is the time to maturity; the 2nd to 4th columns

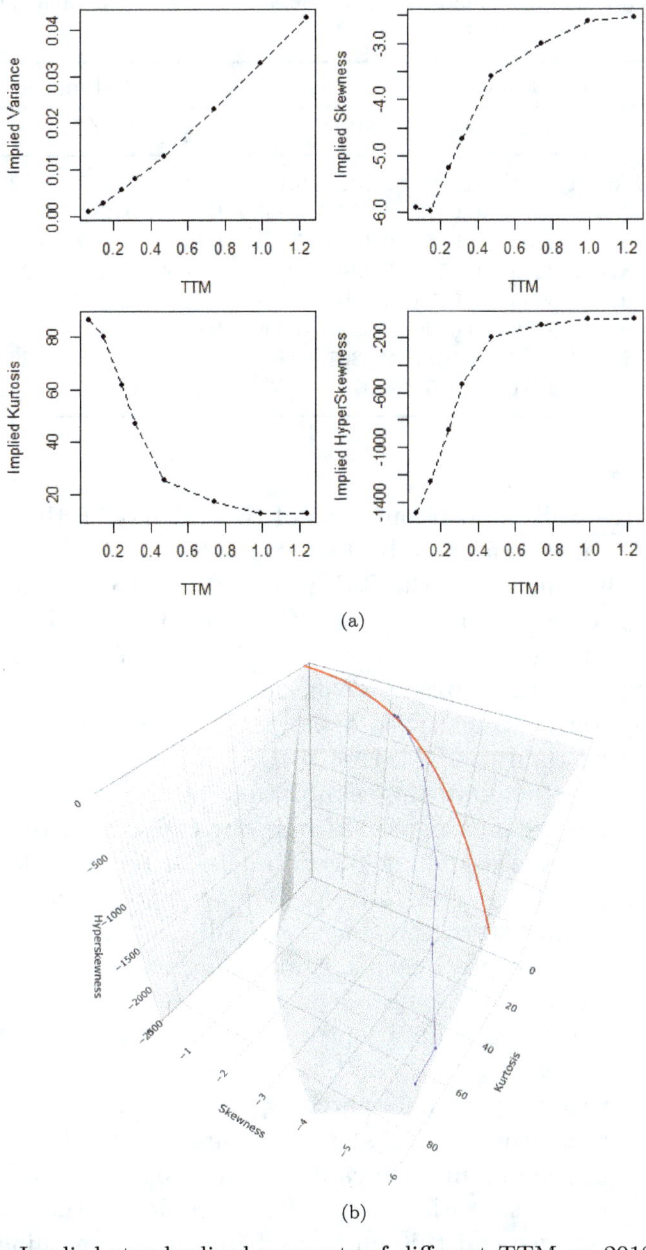

Figure 1. Implied standardized moments of different TTM on 2018-09-24. (a) Implied moments and (b) Existence domain.

Table 3. Optimum parameter sets calibrated on 2018-09-24 (moment matching calibration).

	The VG model				The BG model				
TTM_i	σ	ν	θ	RMSE	c_p	b_p	c_n	b_n	RMSE
0.0685	0.1068	1.3541	−0.0502	2.3319	6.1779	0.0254	0.5677	0.1382	1.7173
0.1452	0.1203	2.5215	−0.0471	4.3970	1.2500	0.0557	0.3544	0.2137	3.8644
0.2411	0.1317	3.2051	−0.0453	6.4726	2.8072	0.0442	0.2536	0.2696	4.7729
0.3178	0.1316	3.0246	−0.0525	7.2993	0.4545	0.0890	0.3225	0.2616	7.0029
0.4712	0.1226	2.0695	−0.0778	4.2300	0.0188	0.2244	0.5488	0.2202	5.5822
0.7397	0.1095	1.9202	−0.0996	4.6907	0.0002	0.6862	0.5767	0.2315	6.2681
0.9890	0.1137	1.9407	−0.1017	3.7307	1E-8	6.1104	0.6097	0.2327	5.3015
1.2384	0.1162	2.2851	−0.0955	4.9285	2E-9	8.7340	0.5035	0.2612	6.2660

are the three calibrated parameters of the VG model; the 6th to the 9th columns are the four calibrated parameters of the BG model; the 5th and 10th columns are the RMSE of calibrated VG model and BG model, respectively. The TTM in bold type corresponds to the case where we adjusted the implied standardized moments to satisfy the domain of matching calibration equations. From this table, it is clear that for option contracts with a short TTM, the RMSE of the BG model is lower than the RMSE of the VG model.

To improve the matching calibration performance, we further integrate the searching algorithm into our calibration process. The performance of the searching algorithm is better than the matching calibration, but it suffers from some shortfalls, for example, it is sensitive to the starting value and easily suffers from the local minima. Hence, we propose using matching calibrated parameters as starting values for the search algorithm. On the one hand, we expect this integrated calibration to perform better than the matching calibration; on the other hand, we expect the matching calibrated results to provide a plausible searching range for the searching algorithm. Moreover, the moments of this calibrated model are near to the sample moments, and the calibrated model would be more stable when the market prices show considerable fluctuation. In the following study, we call this integrated improved matching calibration. We perform the searching algorithm by minimizing the RMSE

Table 4. Optimum parameter sets calibrated on 2018-09-24 (improved moment matching calibration).

TTM_i	c_p	b_p	c_n	b_n	RMSE
0.0685	9.8013	0.0195	1.0843	0.0991	1.1311
0.1452	2.4035	0.0412	0.5753	0.1676	2.6112
0.2411	3.7267	0.0355	0.4155	0.2199	3.1379
0.3178	0.8702	0.0733	0.4982	0.2091	4.4210
0.4712	0.0332	0.2843	0.7608	0.1793	3.4568
0.7397	0.0004	1.2647	0.7259	0.2003	5.1083
0.9890	$1E-8$	5.7931	0.6746	0.2151	4.5608
1.2384	$4E-9$	7.9974	0.6453	0.2217	4.5736

between the market price option of options P and the model price of options $\hat{P}$. Table 4 shows the calibrated optimum parameter sets. As expected, the RMSE decreased a lot. Besides, we observed that the shape parameters present a decreasing trend while the scale parameters present an increasing trend. In other words, the speed for both upside and downside stock motion decreases while the scale for the upside and downside stock motion increases.

We further compare the moment matching calibration performance based on the BG and the VG models over a more extended period. Specifically, for every trading day in 2018, we select the option contracts with DTM nearest to 30 days into the 30 DTM dataset. Next, we apply the moment matching calibration under the BG and VG models to this dataset. We repeat this procedure for 60, 90 and 180 DTM datasets.

Figure 2 depicts the time series of the implied variance, skewness, kurtosis and hyper-skewness for the datasets with different DTM. We observe that implied variance increases with a longer DTM consistently over time. Next, we check whether the implied standardized moments satisfy the existence domain of the moment matching equations. There were 251 trading days in 2018 in total. For the 30 DTM dataset, there is only one day, 2018-02-05, when the implied standardized moments do not satisfy Condition 1, while the days that the implied standardized moments do not satisfy Condition 2 is 7.97%. For the 60 DTM dataset, again, only on one day, 2018-02-05, the implied standardized moments do not satisfy Condition 1,

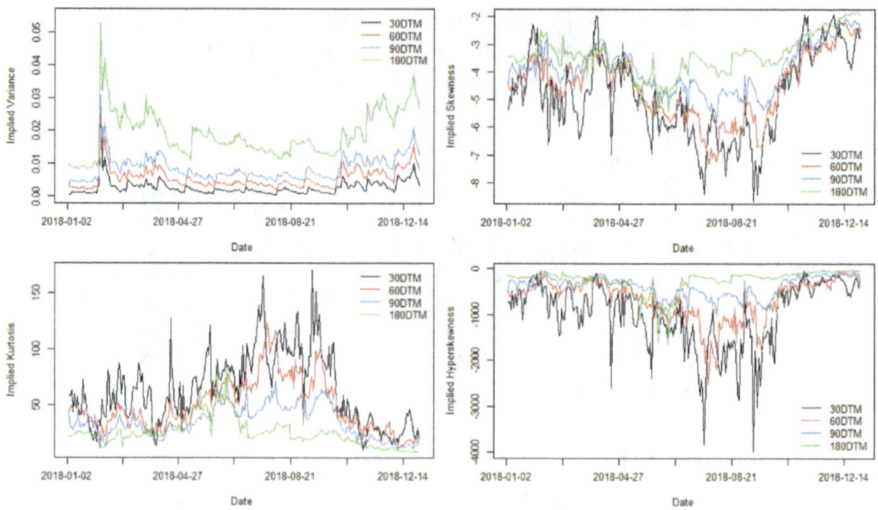

Figure 2. Implied moments of different DTMs.

while the days that the implied standardized moments do not satisfy Condition 2 is 6.37%. For the 90 DTM dataset, the days that the implied standardized moments do not satisfy Condition 1 is 1.99%, while the days that the implied standardized moments do not satisfy Condition 2 is 5.18%. For the 180 DTM dataset, the days that the implied standardized moments do not satisfy Condition 1 is 1.99%, while the days that the implied standardized moments do not satisfy Condition 2 is 10.36%.

Figure 3 gives a more intuitive view of the domain conditions for implied standardized moments of 30 DTM dataset. The blue points are implied standardized moments which are satisfying both conditions. The purple points are those which do not satisfy Condition 1. The yellow points in the green circle do not satisfy Condition 2. We also observe that there is no trading day when implied standardized moments are not satisfying both conditions. Figure 4 presents the domain conditions for implied standardized moments of 60 DTM, 90 DTM and 180 DTM datasets, respectively.

Figure 5 indicates that the RMSE of the BG model is lower than the VG model. It is not surprising to find this result because the

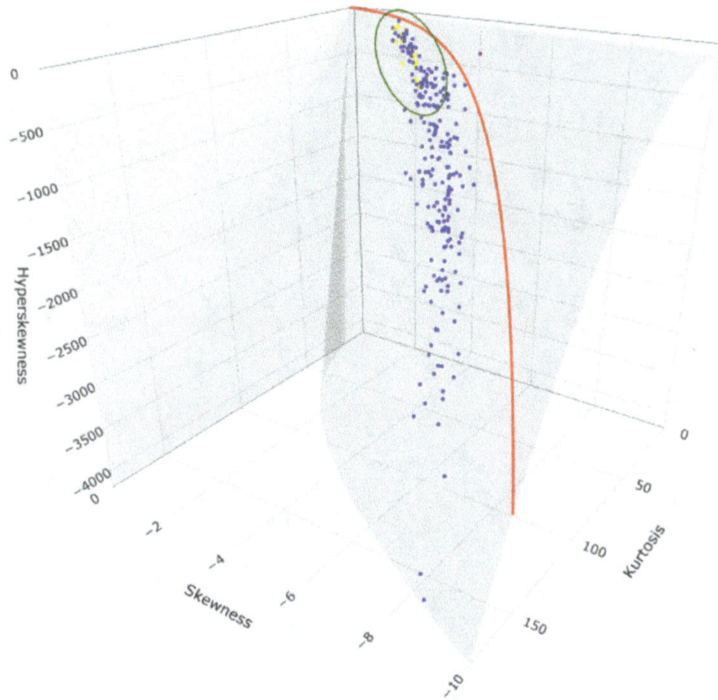

Figure 3. Domain condition for implied standardized moments of 30 DTM dataset.

BG model is more flexible in describing the tail behavior of financial return density than the variance gamma model. The VG model being a specific case of the BG model from a theoretical point would actually always enforce such an improvement. We further calculate the average improvement in 2018, which is 0.9735.

Figures 6, 7, and 8 show the performance of the moment matching calibration and the improved moment matching calibration under the BG model for option contracts for the various DTMs. Figure 6 is the line plot of RMSE of two calibrations for option contracts with 30 DTM during 2018-01-02 and 2018-12-31. It indicates that the improved moment matching calibration performance is better than the moment matching calibration. The RMSE of improved moment matching calibration is lower than the RMSE of moment matching calibration again by construction from a theoretical side.

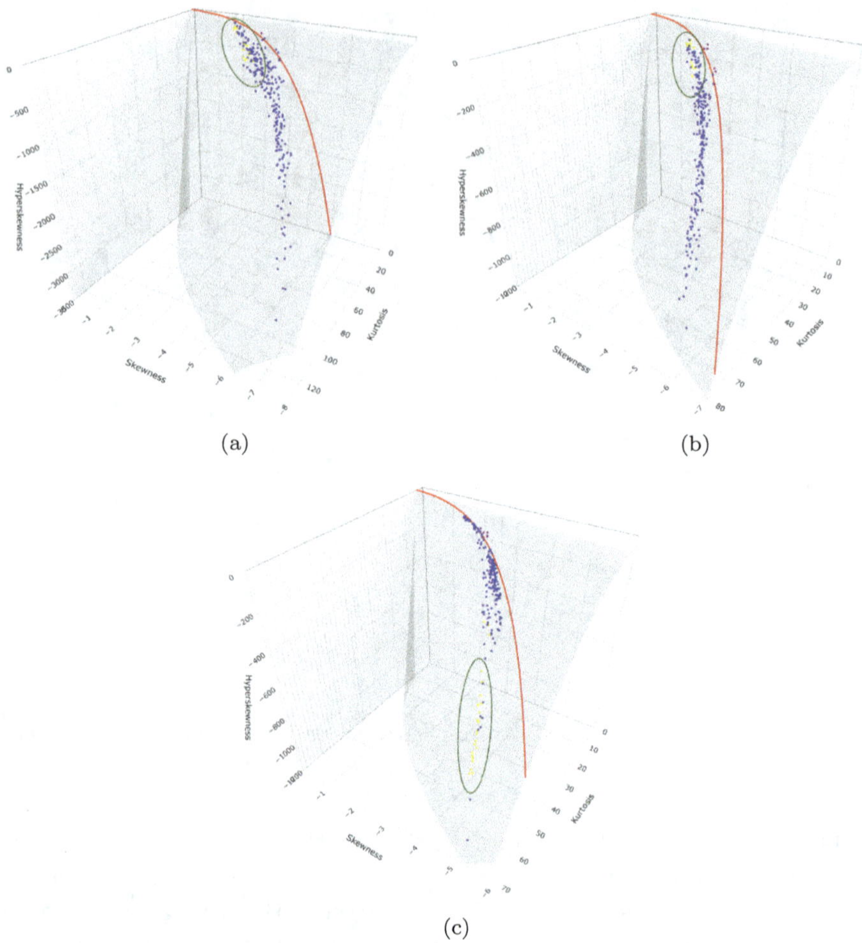

Figure 4. Domain condition for implied standardized moments of different DTMs. (a) 60 DTM, (b) 90 DTM, and (c) 180 DTM.

Moreover, the average RMSE improvement is 0.8213. Figures 7, 8, and 9 show the RMSE of calibration for options contracts with 60 DTM, 90 DTM, and 180 DTM. In the 60 DTM option dataset, we observed that the average difference in RMSE between the moment matching calibrating method and the improved moment matching is 1.1296, which is more significant than the difference between these two methods in 30 DTM option datasets. Furthermore, this phenomenon becomes more evident in 90 DTM and 180 DTM option

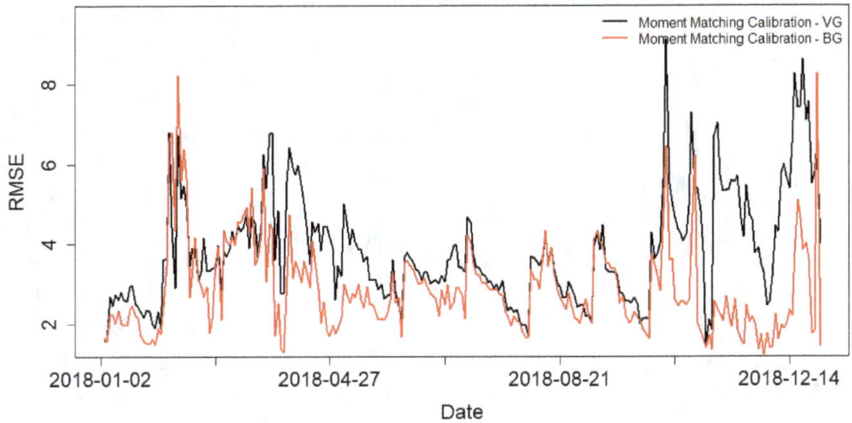

Figure 5. The RMSE of moment matching calibration under the VG and BG models on S&P500 options with 30 DTM from 2018-01-02 to 2018-12-31.

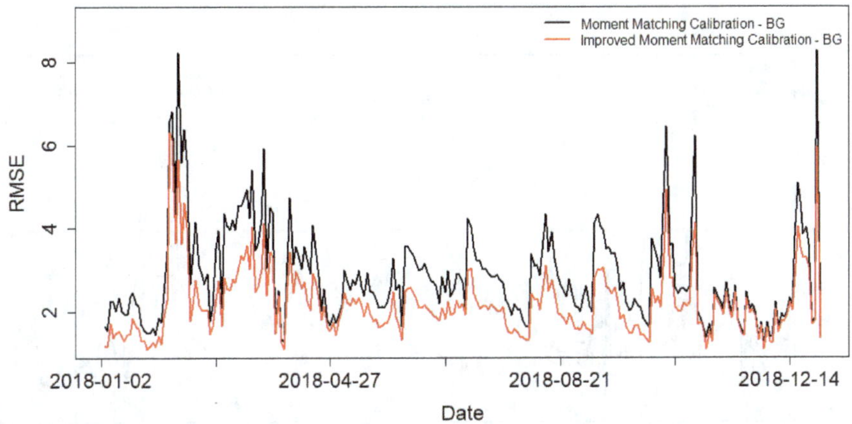

Figure 6. The RMSE of moment matching calibration and improved moment matching calibration based on BG model on S&P500 options with 30 DTM from 2018-01-02 to 2018-12-31.

datasets, where the average RMSE improvements are 1.4540 and 2.2787, respectively.

4. Conclusion

This chapter provides an analytical solution to the moment matching calibration problem under the BG model. Furthermore, it evaluates

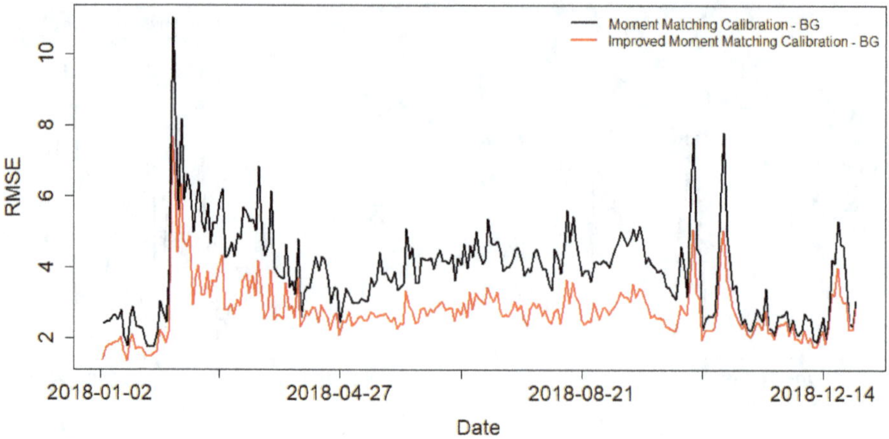

Figure 7. The RMSE of moment matching calibration and improved moment matching calibration based on BG model on S&P500 options with 60 DTM from 2018-01-02 to 2018-12-31.

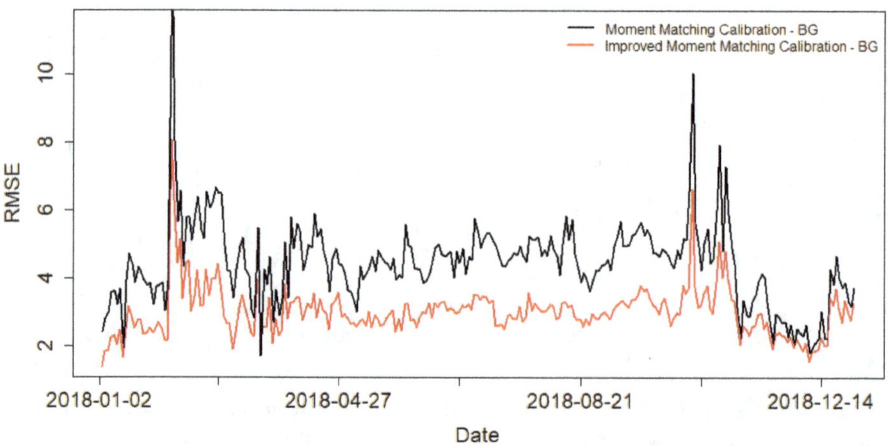

Figure 8. The RMSE of numerical optimizing, moments matching calibration, and combined calibration based on BG model on S&P500 options with 90 DTM from 2018-01-02 to 2018-12-31.

the moment matching calibration performance under the BG and VG models in the numerical study. It is not surprising to find that the calibrated results of the BG model are better than the VG model. In addition, using moment matching calibrated parameters as the initial

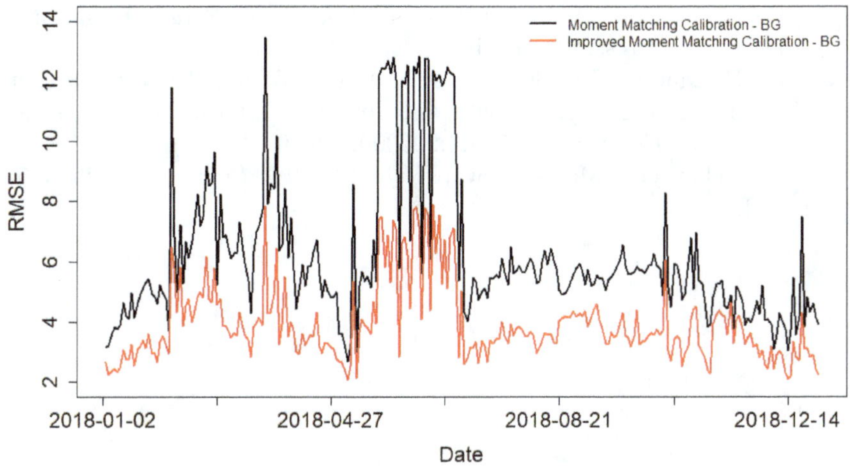

Figure 9. The RMSE of numerical optimizing, moments matching calibration, and combined calibration based on BG model on S&P500 options with 180 DTM from 2018-01-02 to 2018-12-31.

starting value of the numerical optimizing algorithm is a reasonable choice.

References

[1] G. Bakshi and D. Madan. Spanning and derivative-security valuation. *Journal of Financial Economics*, 55(2):205–238, 2000.

[2] G. Bakshi, N. Kapadia, and D. Madan. Stock return characteristics, skew laws, and the differential pricing of individual equity options. *The Review of Financial Studies*, 16(1):101–143, 2003.

[3] P. Carr, H. Geman, and D. B. Madan. Pricing and hedging in incomplete markets. *Journal of Financial Economics*, 62(1):131–167, 2001.

[4] K. Detlefsen and W. K Härdle. Calibration risk for exotic options. *The Journal of Derivatives*, 14(4):47–63, 2007.

[5] F. Guillaume and W. Schoutens. Calibration risk: Illustrating the impact of calibration risk under the Heston model. *Review of Derivatives Research*, 15(1):57–79, 2012.

[6] F. Guillaume and W. Schoutens. A moment matching market implied calibration. *Quantitative Finance*, 13(9):1359–1373, 2013.

[7] U. Küchler and S. Tappe. Bilateral gamma distributions and processes in financial mathematics. *Stochastic Processes and their Applications*, 118(2):261–283, 2008.

[8] D. Madan and W. Schoutens. *Applied Conic Finance*. Cambridge University Press, Cambridge, UK, 2016.

[9] D. B. Madan, W. Schoutens, and King Wang. Bilateral multiple gamma returns: Their risks and rewards. *International Journal of Financial Engineering*, 7(01):2050008, 2020.

[10] W. Schoutens. Moment swaps. *Quantitative Finance*, 5(6):525–530, 2005.

https://doi.org/10.1142/9789811280306_0021

Chapter 21

Exploiting Arbitrage Requires Short Selling

Eckhard Platen[*,‡] **and Stefan Tappe**[†,§]

[*] *Finance Discipline Group, School of Mathematical and Physical Sciences, University of Technology Sydney, PO Box 123, Broadway, NSW 2007, Australia*

[†] *Department of Mathematical Stochastics, Albert Ludwig University of Freiburg, Ernst-Zermelo-Strasse 1, D-79104 Freiburg, Germany*

[‡] *eckhard.platen@uts.edu.au*

[§] *stefan.tappe@math.uni-freiburg.de*

Abstract

We show that in a financial market given by semimartingales, an arbitrage opportunity, provided it exists, can only be exploited through short selling. This finding provides a theoretical basis for differences in regulation for financial services providers that are allowed to go short and those without short sales. The privilege to be allowed to short sell gives access to potential arbitrage opportunities, which creates by design a bankruptcy risk.

Keywords: Arbitrage opportunity, Short selling, Supermartingale deflator, Self-financing portfolio

1. Introduction

It seems to be a common belief that the exploitation of various forms of arbitrage requires short selling. Indeed, a number of well-known examples exist. However, providing a mathematically rigorous proof for such a statement turns out to be not trivial, as will be shown in this chapter.

There has been always a need for design and regulation of the activities of financial market participants. In particular, the granting of the privilege of short selling to some financial services providers raises the question of whether there is a theoretical link between the potential exploitation of arbitrage opportunities and short selling. Hedge funds and investment banks are typical examples of such privileged financial services providers. Short selling occurs when an investor or financial services provider borrows a security and sells it on the open market, planning to buy it back later for less money. The risk of loss on a short sale is theoretically unlimited since the price of the underlying asset can climb to any level. Exploiting arbitrage opportunities can be interpreted as a service to the market because it can remove inconsistencies between asset prices. Market participants with large quantities of assets under management, such as pension funds and mutual funds, should not engage in short selling because their risk of bankruptcy could destabilize the market and cause major economic damage. There are also a variety of other reasons for such market participants not to engage in short selling, including higher risk aversion of members, taxation and regulatory constraints aimed at protecting investors.

So far, the literature seems not to have clarified precisely the crucial link between short selling and exploiting arbitrage. Although there are papers dealing with financial markets under short sale constraints (see, for example, Refs. [1, 2, 12, 14, 16, 23, 28]), to the best of our knowledge, the literature has not emphasized so far in a mathematically precise manner the important fact that only through short selling one can exploit arbitrage opportunities. The goal of this chapter is to fill this gap and show that in a financial market consisting of non-negative semimartingales an arbitrage opportunity, provided it exists, can only be exploited through short selling.

Before we provide the mathematical formulation of our results (see Theorems 1.2–1.8), we outline the stochastic framework that we consider in this chapter; more details and the precise definitions can be found in Section 2. Let $\mathbb{S} = \{S^i : i \in I\}$ be a financial market with an arbitrary, possibly infinite index set I, consisting of at least two primary security accounts. These accounts could be cum-dividend stocks, savings accounts and combinations of derivatives and other securities offering collateral. We assume that the primary security accounts are non-negative semimartingales which cannot revive from bankruptcy and that at least one of these semimartingales is strictly positive. Summing up, for what follows, we make the following standing assumption:

Assumption 1.1. *Let $\mathbb{S} = \{S^i : i \in I\}$ be a financial market consisting of non-negative semimartingales which cannot revive from bankruptcy such that $S^i, S^i_- > 0$ for some $i \in I$.*

Let $\mathbb{P}_{\text{sf}}(\mathbb{S})$ be the space of all self-financing portfolios investing in finitely many assets, and let $\mathbb{P}_{\text{sf}}^{\delta \geq 0}(\mathbb{S})$ be the convex cone of all such portfolios without short selling. We fix a deterministic finite time horizon $T \in (0, \infty)$. Then a portfolio S^δ is an *arbitrage portfolio* if $S_0^\delta = 0$ and $S_T^\delta \in L_+^0 \setminus \{0\}$, where L_+^0 is the convex cone of all equivalence classes of non-negative random variables. This definition essentially says that an arbitrage portfolio generates under limited liability from zero initial capital some strictly positive wealth. If such an arbitrage portfolio does not exist, then the market satisfies *No-Arbitrage* (NA), which means that $\mathscr{K}_0 \cap L_+^0 = \{0\}$, where $\mathscr{K}_0$ denotes the convex cone of all outcomes of self-financing portfolios starting at zero. Often, one assumes that an arbitrage portfolio is non-negative (see, for example, Ref. [24]) or admissible (see, for example, Ref. [4] or [6]). For the sake of generality, in our upcoming first result, we do not assume that an arbitrage portfolio has to be non-negative or admissible.

Theorem 1.2. *For every arbitrage portfolio $S^\delta \in \mathbb{P}_{\text{sf}}(\mathbb{S})$, we have $S^\delta \notin \mathbb{P}_{\text{sf}}^{\delta \geq 0}(\mathbb{S})$.*

The above theorem states the fact that exploiting arbitrage requires short selling. Although this result seems intuitively plausible, the mathematical proof (provided in Section 2, also for the upcoming Theorems 1.3–1.8) is not obvious in the present semimartingale market framework. The proof is straightforward if the arbitrage portfolio goes negative in between (see Lemma 2.4) or if we consider financial market models in discrete time with strictly positive primary security accounts (see Proposition 3.1). However, in the present continuous time framework, where we also consider non-negative arbitrage portfolios, deeper results from martingale theory are required for the proof.

Similar results also hold true for weaker forms of arbitrage opportunities than the arbitrage portfolios considered above, such as so-called, arbitrages of the first kind or various types of free lunches, as defined later on. In the following results (Theorem 1.3–1.7), we will consider a sequence $(S^{\delta_n})_{n\in\mathbb{N}} \subset \mathbb{P}_{\rm sf}(\mathbb{S})$ of self-financing portfolios and assume that $\bigcup_{n\in\mathbb{N}} \operatorname{supp}(\delta_n)$ is finite. Here, for every $n \in \mathbb{N}$, the support of δ_n, denoted by $\operatorname{supp}(\delta_n)$, consists of all indices of those primary security accounts in which the trading strategy δ_n invests. We emphasize that the aforementioned condition that $\bigcup_{n\in\mathbb{N}} \operatorname{supp}(\delta_n)$ is finite is *always* satisfied if the index set I is finite, that is, the market $\mathbb{S}$ consists of finitely many assets.

A sequence $(S^{\delta_n})_{n\in\mathbb{N}} \subset \mathbb{P}_{\rm sf}(\mathbb{S})$ of self-financing portfolios is called an *arbitrage of the first kind* if $S_0^{\delta_n} \downarrow 0$ and there exists a random variable $\xi \in L^0_+ \setminus \{0\}$ such that $S_T^{\delta_n} \geq \xi$ for all $n \in \mathbb{N}$. Typically, the sequence $(S^{\delta_n})_{n\in\mathbb{N}}$ is assumed to be non-negative; see, for example [17]. If a non-negative arbitrage of the first kind does not exist, then we have $p(\xi) > 0$ for each $\xi \in L^0_+ \setminus \{0\}$, where

$$p(\xi) := \inf\{S_0^\delta : S^\delta \in \mathbb{P}_{\rm sf}(\mathbb{S}) \text{ such that } S^\delta \geq 0 \text{ and } S_T^\delta \geq \xi\}$$

denotes the superreplication price of ξ. This just means that the market satisfies *No-Arbitrage of the First Kind* (NA_1). For the sake of generality, in our upcoming result, we do not assume that an arbitrage of the first kind has to remain always non-negative.

Theorem 1.3. *Let $(S^{\delta_n})_{n\in\mathbb{N}} \subset \mathbb{P}_{\rm sf}(\mathbb{S})$ be an arbitrage of the first kind such that $\bigcup_{n\in\mathbb{N}} \operatorname{supp}(\delta_n)$ is finite. Then there exists an index $n_0 \in \mathbb{N}$ such that $S^{\delta_n} \notin \mathbb{P}_{\rm sf}^{\delta\geq 0}(\mathbb{S})$ for all $n \geq n_0$.*

A sequence $(S^{\delta_n})_{n\in\mathbb{N}}$ of self-financing portfolios is called an *asymptotic arbitrage of the first kind* if $S_0^{\delta_n} \downarrow 0$ and there exists a sequence of random variables $(\xi_n)_{n\in\mathbb{N}} \subset L^0_+$ such that $S_T^{\delta_n} \geq \xi_n$ for all $n \in \mathbb{N}$ and $\limsup_{n\to\infty} \mathbb{P}(\xi_n \geq 1) > 0$. If we even have

$\limsup_{n\to\infty} \mathbb{P}(\xi_n \geq 1) = 1$, then one also calls it a *strong asymptotic arbitrage of the first kind*, cf., e.g., Ref. [18] or [19]. Typically, the sequence $(S^{\delta_n})_{n\in\mathbb{N}}$ is assumed to be non-negative, see, for example, Ref. [17]. If a non-negative arbitrage of the first kind does not exist, then for every sequence $(S^{\delta_n})_{n\in\mathbb{N}}$ of non-negative self-financing portfolios and every sequence of random variables $(\xi_n)_{n\in\mathbb{N}} \subset L^0_+$ such that $S^{\delta_n}_T \geq \xi_n$ for all $n \in \mathbb{N}$ we have $\lim_{n\to\infty} \mathbb{P}(\xi_n \geq 1) = 0$, or equivalently $\xi_n \xrightarrow{\mathbb{P}} 0$; cf. Ref. [25, Lemma 5.10]. This just means that the market satisfies *No-Asymptotic Arbitrage of the First Kind* (NAA_1). It is well known that NAA_1 is equivalent to *No Unbounded Profit with Bounded Risk* (NUPBR), see, for example, Ref. [17]. For the sake of generality, in our upcoming result we do not assume that an asymptotic arbitrage of the first kind has to be non-negative.

Theorem 1.4. *Let $(S^{\delta_n})_{n\in\mathbb{N}} \subset \mathbb{P}_{\text{sf}}(\mathbb{S})$ be an asymptotic arbitrage of the first kind such that $\bigcup_{n\in\mathbb{N}} \text{supp}(\delta_n)$ is finite. Then we have $S^{\delta_n} \notin \mathbb{P}^{\delta\geq 0}_{\text{sf}}(\mathbb{S})$ for infinitely many $n \in \mathbb{N}$.*

Note that for a given asymptotic arbitrage of the first kind, the sequence $(\mathbb{P}(\xi_n \geq 1))_{n\in\mathbb{N}}$ does not need to be convergent. In this chapter, we suggest calling it a *limit arbitrage of the first kind* if the above condition $\limsup_{n\to\infty} \mathbb{P}(\xi_n \geq 1) > 0$ is replaced by the stronger condition $\lim_{n\to\infty} \mathbb{P}(\xi_n \geq 1) > 0$, implicitly meaning that the limit exists. In the case of a limit arbitrage of the first kind, the previous result can be improved as follows.

Theorem 1.5. *Let $(S^{\delta_n})_{n\in\mathbb{N}} \subset \mathbb{P}_{\text{sf}}(\mathbb{S})$ be a limit arbitrage of the first kind such that $\bigcup_{n\in\mathbb{N}} \text{supp}(\delta_n)$ is finite. Then there exists an index $n_0 \in \mathbb{N}$ such that $S^{\delta_n} \notin \mathbb{P}^{\delta\geq 0}_{\text{sf}}(\mathbb{S})$ for all $n \geq n_0$.*

We call a sequence $(S^{\delta_n})_{n\in\mathbb{N}}$ of self-financing portfolios with $S^{\delta_n}_0 = 0$ for all $n \in \mathbb{N}$ a *free lunch with vanishing risk* if there exist a random variable $\xi \in L^\infty_+ \setminus \{0\}$ and a sequence $(\xi_n)_{n\in\mathbb{N}} \subset L^\infty$ such that $\|\xi_n - \xi\|_{L^\infty} \to 0$ and $S^{\delta_n}_T \geq \xi_n$ for each $n \in \mathbb{N}$, where L^∞ denotes the Banach space of all equivalence classes of bounded random variables, and where L^∞_+ is the convex cone of all equivalence classes of non-negative bounded random variables. Typically, the sequence $(S^{\delta_n})_{n\in\mathbb{N}}$ is assumed to consist of admissible portfolios, which can become negative but remain above a critical level; see, for example,

Ref. [4] or [6]. If an admissible free lunch with vanishing risk does not exist, then we have $\overline{\mathscr{C}} \cap L^0_+ = \{0\}$, where $\mathscr{C} := (\mathscr{K}_0 - L^0_+) \cap L^\infty$ with $\mathscr{K}_0$ denoting the convex cone of all outcomes of admissible self-financing portfolios starting at zero, and where $\overline{\mathscr{C}}$ denotes the closure of $\mathscr{C}$ with respect to the norm topology on L^∞. This just means that the market satisfies the *No Free Lunch with Vanishing Risk* (NFLVR) condition. In our following result we do not assume that a free lunch with vanishing risk has to be admissible.

Theorem 1.6. *Let $(S^{\delta_n})_{n \in \mathbb{N}} \subset \mathbb{P}_{\text{sf}}(\mathbb{S})$ be a free lunch with vanishing risk such that $\bigcup_{n \in \mathbb{N}} \text{supp}(\delta_n)$ is finite. Then there exists an index $n_0 \in \mathbb{N}$ such that $S^{\delta_n} \notin \mathbb{P}^{\delta \geq 0}_{\text{sf}}(\mathbb{S})$ for all $n \geq n_0$.*

A sequence $(S^{\delta_n})_{n \in \mathbb{N}}$ of self-financing portfolios with $S^{\delta_n}_0 = 0$ for all $n \in \mathbb{N}$ is called a *free lunch with bounded risk* if there exist a random variable $\xi \in L^\infty_+ \setminus \{0\}$ and a sequence $(\xi_n)_{n \in \mathbb{N}} \subset L^\infty$ such that $\xi_n \xrightarrow{w^*} \xi$ and $S^{\delta_n}_T \geq \xi_n$ for each $n \in \mathbb{N}$, where $\xi_n \xrightarrow{w^*} \xi$ denotes weak-star convergence in L^∞, that is,

$$\mathbb{E}[\xi_n \eta] \to \mathbb{E}[\xi \eta] \quad \text{for all } \eta \in L^1.$$

Typically, the sequence $(S^{\delta_n})_{n \in \mathbb{N}}$ is assumed to consist of admissible portfolios; see, for example, Ref. [4] or [6]. If an admissible free lunch with bounded risk does not exist, then the market satisfies *No Free Lunch with Bounded Risk* (NFLBR), which means that $\widetilde{\mathscr{C}} \cap L^0_+ = \{0\}$, where $\widetilde{\mathscr{C}}$ denotes the closure of $\mathscr{C}$ with respect to the sequential weak-star topology on L^∞. In our following result, we do not assume that a free lunch with bounded risk has to be admissible.

Theorem 1.7. *Suppose that $(S^i_T)^{-1} \in L^\infty$, where the index $i \in I$ stems from Assumption 1.1. Furthermore, let $(S^{\delta_n})_{n \in \mathbb{N}} \subset \mathbb{P}_{\text{sf}}(\mathbb{S})$ be a free lunch with bounded risk such that $\bigcup_{n \in \mathbb{N}} \text{supp}(\delta_n)$ is finite. Then there exists an index $n_0 \in \mathbb{N}$ such that $S^{\delta_n} \notin \mathbb{P}^{\delta \geq 0}_{\text{sf}}(\mathbb{S})$ for all $n \geq n_0$.*

This result can be generalized as follows. Given an arbitrary directed set $(J, \leq)$, a net $(S^{\delta_j})_{j \in J}$ of self-financing portfolios with $S^{\delta_j}_0 = 0$ for all $j \in J$ is called a *free lunch* if there exist a random variable $\xi \in L^\infty_+ \setminus \{0\}$ and a net $(\xi_j)_{j \in J} \subset L^\infty$ such that $\xi_j \xrightarrow{w^*} \xi$ and

$S_T^{\delta_j} \geq \xi_j$ for each $j \in J$, where $\xi_j \overset{w^*}{\to} \xi$ denotes weak-star convergence in L^∞, that is,

$$\mathbb{E}[\xi_j \eta] \to \mathbb{E}[\xi \eta] \quad \text{for all } \eta \in L^1.$$

Typically, the net $(S^{\delta_j})_{j \in J}$ is assumed to consist of admissible portfolios; see, for example, Ref. [6]. If an admissible free lunch does not exist, then the market satisfies *No Free Lunch* (NFL), which means that $\overline{\mathscr{C}}^* \cap L^0_+ = \{0\}$, where $\overline{\mathscr{C}}^*$ denotes the closure of $\mathscr{C}$ with respect to the weak-star topology on L^∞. In our following result, we do not assume that a free lunch has to be admissible. Similarly as for the previous results, the following condition that $\bigcup_{j \in J} \operatorname{supp}(\delta_j)$ is finite is *always* satisfied if the index set I is finite, that is, the market $\mathbb{S}$ consists of finitely many assets.

Theorem 1.8. *Suppose that $(S_T^i)^{-1} \in L^\infty$, where the index $i \in I$ stems from Assumption 1.1. Furthermore, let $(S^{\delta_j})_{j \in J} \subset \mathbb{P}_{\mathrm{sf}}(\mathbb{S})$ be a free lunch such that $\bigcup_{j \in J} \operatorname{supp}(\delta_j)$ is finite. Then there exists an index $j_0 \in J$ such that $S^{\delta_j} \notin \mathbb{P}_{\mathrm{sf}}^{\delta \geq 0}(\mathbb{S})$ for all $j \geq j_0$.*

Let us briefly outline the essential steps for the proofs of Theorems 1.2–1.8. A crucial concept for the proofs is that of an *equivalent supermartingale deflator* (ESMD). First, we show that the existence of an ESMD implies the statements of Theorems 1.2–1.8 (see Propositions 2.6–2.11). In a second step, we show that in the present setting an ESMD always exists; see Proposition 2.14. This result seems to be of independent interest. The main ideas for the proof include a change of numéraire, a result about ESMDs from [23], and a σ-localization technique from Ref. [20].

We mention that supermartingale deflators and the related concept of a supermartingale measure have been used in various contexts in the mathematical finance literature; in particular in connection with short sale constraints, including Refs. [12, 16, 23, 28] and [2]. The papers [23] and [28] present versions of the fundamental theorem of asset pricing with short sale prohibitions. Further references, where supermartingales and supermartingale deflators are studied with a focus on applications in finance, include [22,34] and the recent paper [9].

The remainder of this chapter is organized as follows. In Section 2, we provide the proofs of our results, in Section 3, we briefly comment on discrete-time models, and in Section 4 we present several examples and illustrate how our examples with arbitrage portfolios which go negative link to asset and money market bubbles.

2. Proofs of the Results

In this section we provide the proofs of Theorems 1.2–1.8. First, we introduce the precise mathematical framework. Let $T \in (0, \infty)$ be a fixed finite time horizon, and let $(\Omega, \mathscr{F}, (\mathscr{F}_t)_{t \in [0,T]}, \mathbb{P})$ be a stochastic basis satisfying the usual conditions; see Ref. [11, Def. I.1.3]. Furthermore, we assume that $\mathscr{F}_0$ is $\mathbb{P}$-trivial. Then every $\mathscr{F}_0$-measurable random variable is $\mathbb{P}$-almost surely constant. As mentioned in Section 1, we consider a financial market $\mathbb{S} = \{S^i : i \in I\}$ consisting of non-negative semimartingales for an index set I with $|I| \geq 2$. Apart from the latter condition of having at least two elements, the index set I is arbitrary; in particular, it may be infinite, and thus possibly even uncountable. We assume that for each $i \in I$ the semimartingale S^i cannot revive from bankruptcy, which means that $S^i_t = 0$ for all $t \geq \tau^i$, where τ^i denotes the bankruptcy time of S^i given by

$$\tau^i := \inf\{t \in \mathbb{R}_+ : S^i_{t-} = 0 \text{ or } S^i_t = 0\}.$$

Furthermore, we assume that $S^i, S^i_- > 0$ for some $i \in I$.

For an $\mathbb{R}^d$-valued semimartingale X we denote by $L(X)$ the set of all X-integrable processes in the sense of vector integration; see Ref. [31] or [11, Sec. III.6]. For $\delta \in L(X)$ we denote by $\delta \cdot X$ the stochastic integral according to Ref. [31].

For a finite set $F \subset I$, we define the multi-dimensional semimartingale $S^F := (S^i)_{i \in F}$. We call a process $\delta = (\delta^i)_{i \in I}$ a *strategy* for $\mathbb{S}$ if its *support*

$$F := \operatorname{supp}(\delta) := \{i \in I : \delta^i \neq 0\} \tag{1}$$

is finite and we have $\delta^F \in L(S^F)$, where $\delta^F := (\delta^i)_{i \in F}$. We will also use the notation $\Delta(\mathbb{S})$ for the space of all strategies for $\mathbb{S}$. For a strategy $\delta \in \Delta(\mathbb{S})$ we define the *portfolio* $S^\delta := \delta \cdot S$, where we use the short-hand notation $\delta \cdot S := \sum_{i \in F} \delta^i S^i$ with $F := \operatorname{supp}(\delta)$. A strategy $\delta \in \Delta(\mathbb{S})$ and the corresponding portfolio S^δ are called *self-financing* for $\mathbb{S}$ if $S^\delta = S^\delta_0 + \delta \cdot S$, where $\delta \cdot S := \delta^F \cdot S^F$ is the stochastic integral according to Ref. [31] with $F := \mathrm{supp}(\delta)$. We denote by $\Delta_{\mathrm{sf}}(\mathbb{S})$ the space of all self-financing strategies.

Let $\mathbb{P}_{\mathrm{sf}}(\mathbb{S})$ be the space of all self-financing portfolios S^δ. We denote by $\mathbb{P}_{\mathrm{sf}}^{+}(\mathbb{S})$ the convex cone of all non-negative self-financing portfolios $S^\delta \geq 0$, and we denote by $\mathbb{P}_{\mathrm{sf}}^{\mathrm{adm}}(\mathbb{S})$ the convex cone of all admissible self-financing portfolios $S^\delta \geq -a$ for some $a \in \mathbb{R}_+$. Moreover, we denote by $\mathbb{P}_{\mathrm{sf}}^{\delta\geq 0}(\mathbb{S})$ the convex cone of all self-financing portfolios $S^\delta \in \mathbb{P}_{\mathrm{sf}}(\mathbb{S})$ such that $\delta \geq 0$, which means that $\delta^i \geq 0$ for all $i \in I$. A self-financing portfolio S^δ is called an *arbitrage portfolio* if $S_0^\delta = 0$ and $S_T^\delta \in L_+^0 \setminus \{0\}$.

Recall that we assume that $S^i, S_-^i > 0$ for some $i \in I$. The proofs of the following two auxiliary results are straightforward, and therefore omitted.

Lemma 2.1. *For each $\delta \in \Delta_{\mathrm{sf}}(\mathbb{S})$ we have $\delta^F \in \Delta_{\mathrm{sf}}(\mathbb{S}^F)$, where $F := \mathrm{supp}(\delta)$, and $\mathbb{S}^F$ denotes the finite market*

$$\mathbb{S}^F := \{S^j : j \in F \cup \{i\}\}.$$

Lemma 2.2. *Let $(\delta_n)_{n\in\mathbb{N}} \subset \Delta_{\mathrm{sf}}(\mathbb{S})$ be a sequence of self-financing strategies such that $F := \bigcup_{n\in\mathbb{N}} \mathrm{supp}(\delta_n)$ is finite. Then we also have $\delta_n^F \in \Delta_{\mathrm{sf}}(\mathbb{S}^F)$ for each $n \in \mathbb{N}$, where $\mathbb{S}^F$ denotes the finite market*

$$\mathbb{S}^F := \{S^j : j \in F \cup \{i\}\}.$$

Remark 2.3. In view of Lemmas 2.1 and 2.2, from now on we may assume that we have a finite market $\mathbb{S} = \{S^1, \ldots, S^d\}$ consisting of non-negative semimartingales for some $d \in \mathbb{N}$ with $d \geq 2$, such that the semimartingales $S^1, \ldots, S^{d-1} \geq 0$ cannot revive from bankruptcy, and we have $S^d, S_-^d > 0$.

Lemma 2.4. *For every self-financing portfolio $S^\delta \in \mathbb{P}_{\mathrm{sf}}(\mathbb{S})$ the property $S^\delta \in \mathbb{P}_{\mathrm{sf}}^{\delta\geq 0}(\mathbb{S})$ implies $S^\delta \in \mathbb{P}_{\mathrm{sf}}^{+}(\mathbb{S})$.*

Proof. Since $S^i \geq 0$ for all $i = 1, \ldots, d$, the property $\delta^i \geq 0$ for all $i = 1, \ldots, d$ implies $S^\delta = \delta \cdot S = \sum_{i=1}^d \delta^i S^i \geq 0$. □

Definition 2.5. Let $\mathbb{X}$ be a family of semimartingales, and let Z be a semimartingale such that $Z, Z_- > 0$. We call Z an *equivalent supermartingale deflator (ESMD)* for $\mathbb{X}$ if XZ is a supermartingale for all $X \in \mathbb{X}$.

The following Propositions 2.6–2.11 show the statements of Theorems 1.2–1.8, provided that an ESMD Z for $\mathbb{P}_{\rm sf}^{\delta \geq 0}(\mathbb{S}) \cap \mathbb{P}_{\rm sf}^{+}(\mathbb{S})$ exists.

Proposition 2.6. *Suppose that an ESMD Z for $\mathbb{P}_{\rm sf}^{\delta \geq 0}(\mathbb{S}) \cap \mathbb{P}_{\rm sf}^{+}(\mathbb{S})$ exists. Then for every arbitrage portfolio $S^\delta \in \mathbb{P}_{\rm sf}(\mathbb{S})$ we have $S^\delta \notin \mathbb{P}_{\rm sf}^{\delta \geq 0}(\mathbb{S})$.*

Proof. Let $S^\delta \in \mathbb{P}_{\rm sf}^{\delta \geq 0}(\mathbb{S}) \cap \mathbb{P}_{\rm sf}^{+}(\mathbb{S})$ be a self-financing portfolio such that $S_0^\delta = 0$ and $\xi := S_T^\delta \in L_+^0$. Since Z is an ESMD for $\mathbb{P}_{\rm sf}^{\delta \geq 0}(\mathbb{S}) \cap \mathbb{P}_{\rm sf}^{+}(\mathbb{S})$, the process $S^\delta Z$ is a non-negative supermartingale. By Doob's optional stopping theorem we obtain

$$\mathbb{E}[\xi Z_T] = \mathbb{E}[S_T^\delta Z_T] \leq \mathbb{E}[S_0^\delta Z_0] = 0,$$

and hence, we deduce that $\mathbb{E}[\xi Z_T] = 0$. Since $\xi \geq 0$ and $\mathbb{P}(Z_T > 0) = 1$, this shows $\xi = 0$. Consequently, the portfolio S^δ cannot be an arbitrage portfolio. Together with Lemma 2.4, this completes the proof. □

Proposition 2.7. *Suppose that an ESMD Z for $\mathbb{P}_{\rm sf}^{\delta \geq 0}(\mathbb{S}) \cap \mathbb{P}_{\rm sf}^{+}(\mathbb{S})$ exists. Let*

$$(S^{\delta_n})_{n \in \mathbb{N}} \subset \mathbb{P}_{\rm sf}(\mathbb{S})$$

be an arbitrage of the first kind. Then there exists an index $n_0 \in \mathbb{N}$ such that $S^{\delta_n} \notin \mathbb{P}_{\rm sf}^{\delta \geq 0}(\mathbb{S})$ for all $n \geq n_0$.

Proof. We have $S_0^{\delta_n} \downarrow 0$ and there exists a random variable $\xi \in L_+^0 \setminus \{0\}$ such that $S_T^{\delta_n} \geq \xi$ for all $n \in \mathbb{N}$. Suppose, contrary to the assertion above, there is a subsequence $(S^{\delta_{n_k}})_{k \in \mathbb{N}}$ such that $S^{\delta_{n_k}} \in \mathbb{P}_{\rm sf}^{\delta \geq 0}(\mathbb{S})$ for all $k \in \mathbb{N}$. Let $k \in \mathbb{N}$ be arbitrary. By Lemma 2.4 we have $S^{\delta_{n_k}} \in \mathbb{P}_{\rm sf}^{+}(\mathbb{S})$. Since Z is an ESMD for $\mathbb{P}_{\rm sf}^{\delta \geq 0}(\mathbb{S}) \cap \mathbb{P}_{\rm sf}^{+}(\mathbb{S})$, the process $S^{\delta_{n_k}} Z$ is a non-negative supermartingale, and hence by Doob's optional stopping theorem we obtain

$$\mathbb{E}[\xi Z_T] \leq \mathbb{E}\big[S_T^{\delta_{n_k}} Z_T\big] \leq \mathbb{E}\big[S_0^{\delta_{n_k}} Z_0\big] = S_0^{\delta_{n_k}} Z_0.$$

Since $S_0^{\delta_{n_k}} \downarrow 0$, we deduce that $\mathbb{E}[\xi Z_T] = 0$. Therefore, and since $\xi \geq 0$ and $\mathbb{P}(Z_T > 0) = 1$, we obtain the contradiction $\xi = 0$. □

Proposition 2.8. *Suppose that an ESMD Z for $\mathbb{P}_{\mathrm{sf}}^{\delta\geq 0}(\mathbb{S}) \cap \mathbb{P}_{\mathrm{sf}}^{+}(\mathbb{S})$ exists. Let*

$$(S^{\delta_n})_{n\in\mathbb{N}} \subset \mathbb{P}_{\mathrm{sf}}(\mathbb{S})$$

be an asymptotic arbitrage of the first kind. Then there is a subsequence $(S^{\delta_{n_k}})_{k\in\mathbb{N}}$ such that $S^{\delta_{n_k}} \notin \mathbb{P}_{\mathrm{sf}}^{\delta\geq 0}(\mathbb{S})$ for all $k \in \mathbb{N}$.

Proof. We have $S_0^{\delta_n} \downarrow 0$ and there exists a sequence of random variables $(\xi_n)_{n\in\mathbb{N}} \subset L_+^0$ such that $S_T^{\delta_n} \geq \xi_n$ for all $n \in \mathbb{N}$ and

$$\limsup_{n\to\infty} \mathbb{P}(\xi_n \geq 1) > 0. \tag{2}$$

Suppose, contrary to the assertion above, there is an index $n_0 \in \mathbb{N}$ such that $S^{\delta_n} \in \mathbb{P}_{\mathrm{sf}}^{\delta\geq 0}(\mathbb{S})$ for all $n \geq n_0$. According to Lemma 2.4, we have $S^{\delta_n} \in \mathbb{P}_{\mathrm{sf}}^{+}(\mathbb{S})$ for all $n \geq n_0$. By (2), there are $\epsilon \in (0,1]$ and a subsequence $(n_k)_{k\in\mathbb{N}}$ with $n_1 \geq n_0$ such that

$$\mathbb{P}(\xi_{n_k} \geq 1) \geq \epsilon \quad \text{for all } k \in \mathbb{N}. \tag{3}$$

By the von Weizsäcker theorem (see Ref. [33]), there exist another subsequence $(\xi_{n_{k_l}})_{l\in\mathbb{N}}$ and a non-negative random variable $\xi : \Omega \to [0,\infty]$ such that $(\xi_{n_{k_l}})_{l\in\mathbb{N}}$ is $\mathbb{P}$-almost surely Cesàro convergent to ξ. In other words, we have $\bar{\xi}_{n_{k_l}} \overset{\text{a.s.}}{\to} \xi$, where

$$\bar{\xi}_{n_{k_l}} := \frac{1}{l}\sum_{p=1}^{l} \xi_{n_{k_p}} \quad \text{for each } l \in \mathbb{N}.$$

Noting (3), according to Ref. [6, Lemma 9.8.6] (applied with $\eta = 1/2$,) we have

$$\mathbb{P}\left(\sum_{p=1}^{l} \xi_{n_{k_p}} \geq \frac{\epsilon l}{2}\right) \geq \frac{\epsilon/2}{1-\epsilon/2} = \frac{\epsilon}{2-\epsilon} \quad \text{for each } l \in \mathbb{N},$$

which implies

$$\mathbb{P}\left(\bar{\xi}_{n_{k_l}} \geq \frac{\epsilon}{2}\right) \geq \frac{\epsilon}{2-\epsilon} \quad \text{for each } l \in \mathbb{N}.$$

Therefore, and since $\bar{\xi}_{n_{k_l}} \xrightarrow{\mathbb{P}} \xi$, we have $\xi \neq 0$. Now, let $l \in \mathbb{N}$ be arbitrary. Since Z is an ESMD for $\mathbb{P}_{\rm sf}^{\delta \geq 0}(\mathbb{S}) \cap \mathbb{P}_{\rm sf}^{+}(\mathbb{S})$, the processes $S^{\delta_{n_{k_p}}} Z$, $p = 1, \ldots, l$ are non-negative supermartingales, and hence by Doob's optional stopping theorem, we obtain

$$\mathbb{E}\big[\bar{\xi}_{n_{k_l}} Z_T\big] = \frac{1}{l} \sum_{p=1}^{l} \mathbb{E}\big[\xi_{n_{k_p}} Z_T\big] \leq \frac{1}{l} \sum_{p=1}^{l} \mathbb{E}\Big[S_T^{\delta_{n_{k_p}}} Z_T\Big]$$

$$\leq \frac{1}{l} \sum_{k=1}^{l} \mathbb{E}\Big[S_0^{\delta_{n_{k_p}}} Z_0\Big] = Z_0 \sigma_l,$$

where $(\sigma_l)_{l \in \mathbb{N}} \subset (0, \infty)$ denotes the sequence

$$\sigma_l := \frac{1}{l} \sum_{p=1}^{l} S_0^{\delta_{n_{k_p}}}, \quad l \in \mathbb{N}.$$

Since $S_0^{\delta_{n_{k_l}}} \to 0$, we have $\sigma_l \to 0$. Therefore, by Fatou's lemma, we deduce that

$$\mathbb{E}[\xi Z_T] = \mathbb{E}\Big[\lim_{l \to \infty} \bar{\xi}_{n_{k_l}} Z_T\Big] \leq \liminf_{l \to \infty} \mathbb{E}\big[\bar{\xi}_{n_{k_l}} Z_T\big] \leq 0,$$

and hence $\mathbb{E}[\xi Z_T] = 0$. Since $\xi \geq 0$ and $\mathbb{P}(Z_T > 0) = 1$, we obtain the contradiction $\xi = 0$. □

Proposition 2.9. *Suppose that an ESMD Z for $\mathbb{P}_{\rm sf}^{\delta \geq 0}(\mathbb{S}) \cap \mathbb{P}_{\rm sf}^{+}(\mathbb{S})$ exists. Let*

$$(S^{\delta_n})_{n \in \mathbb{N}} \subset \mathbb{P}_{\rm sf}(\mathbb{S})$$

be a limit arbitrage of the first kind. Then there is an index $n_0 \in \mathbb{N}$ such that $S^{\delta_n} \notin \mathbb{P}_{\rm sf}^{\delta \geq 0}(\mathbb{S})$ for all $n \geq n_0$.

Proof. We have $S_0^{\delta_n} \downarrow 0$ and there exists a sequence of random variables $(\xi_n)_{n \in \mathbb{N}} \subset L_+^0$ such that $S_T^{\delta_n} \geq \xi_n$ for all $n \in \mathbb{N}$ and

$$\lim_{n \to \infty} \mathbb{P}(\xi_n \geq 1) > 0. \tag{4}$$

Suppose, contrary to the assertion above, there is a subsequence $(S^{\delta_{n_k}})_{k \in \mathbb{N}}$ such that $S^{\delta_{n_k}} \in \mathbb{P}_{\text{sf}}^{\delta \geq 0}(\mathbb{S})$ for all $k \in \mathbb{N}$. According to Lemma 2.4, we have $S^{\delta_{n_k}} \in \mathbb{P}_{\text{sf}}^{+}(\mathbb{S})$ for all $k \in \mathbb{N}$. By (4), there are $\epsilon \in (0,1]$ and an index $n_0 \in \mathbb{N}$ such that

$$\mathbb{P}(\xi_n \geq 1) \geq \epsilon \quad \text{for all } n \geq n_0. \tag{5}$$

Without loss of generality, we may assume that $n_0 \leq n_1$. By the von Weizsäcker theorem (see [33]), there exist another subsequence $(\xi_{n_{k_l}})_{l \in \mathbb{N}}$ and a non-negative random variable $\xi : \Omega \to [0,\infty]$ such that $(\xi_{n_{k_l}})_{l \in \mathbb{N}}$ is $\mathbb{P}$-almost surely Cesàro convergent to ξ. Now, as in the proof of Proposition 2.8, we derive the contradiction that simultaneously $\xi \neq 0$ and $\xi = 0$. □

Proposition 2.10. *Suppose that an ESMD Z for $\mathbb{P}_{\text{sf}}^{\delta \geq 0}(\mathbb{S}) \cap \mathbb{P}_{\text{sf}}^{+}(\mathbb{S})$ exists. Let*

$$(S^{\delta_n})_{n \in \mathbb{N}} \subset \mathbb{P}_{\text{sf}}(\mathbb{S})$$

be a free lunch with vanishing risk. Then there exists an index $n_0 \in \mathbb{N}$ such that $S^{\delta_n} \notin \mathbb{P}_{\text{sf}}^{\delta \geq 0}(\mathbb{S})$ for all $n \geq n_0$.

Proof. There exist a random variable $\xi \in L_+^{\infty} \setminus \{0\}$ and a sequence $(\xi_n)_{n \in \mathbb{N}} \subset L^{\infty}$ such that $\|\xi_n - \xi\|_{L^\infty} \to 0$ and $S_T^{\delta_n} \geq \xi_n$ for each $n \in \mathbb{N}$. Since $\xi \geq 0$ and the mapping $x \mapsto x^+$ is Lipschitz continuous, we also have $\|\xi_n^+ - \xi\|_{L^\infty} \to 0$, and hence $\|\xi_n^+\|_{L^\infty} \to \|\xi\|_{L^\infty}$. Moreover, since $\|\xi\|_{L^\infty} > 0$, there exists an index $n_0 \in \mathbb{N}$ such that $\|\xi_n^+\|_{L^\infty} > 0$ for each $n \geq n_0$. Now, let $n \geq n_0$ be arbitrary. We claim that $S^{\delta_n} \notin \mathbb{P}_{\text{sf}}^{\delta \geq 0}(\mathbb{S})$. Indeed, by Lemma 2.4, we may assume that $S^{\delta_n} \in \mathbb{P}_{\text{sf}}^{+}(\mathbb{S})$. Thus, since $S_T^{\delta_n} \geq 0$, we have $S_T^{\delta_n} \geq \xi_n^+$. Furthermore, since $S_0^{\delta_n} = 0$ and $\xi_n^+ \in L_+^{\infty} \setminus \{0\}$, the portfolio S^{δ_n} is an arbitrage portfolio. Therefore, by Proposition 2.6, we obtain $S^{\delta_n} \notin \mathbb{P}_{\text{sf}}^{\delta \geq 0}(\mathbb{S})$. □

Proposition 2.11. *Suppose that an ESMD Z for $\mathbb{P}_{\text{sf}}^{\delta \geq 0}(\mathbb{S}) \cap \mathbb{P}_{\text{sf}}^{+}(\mathbb{S})$ with $Z_T \in L^1$ exists. Let*

$$(S^{\delta_j})_{j \in J} \subset \mathbb{P}_{\text{sf}}(\mathbb{S})$$

be a free lunch. Then there exists an index $j_0 \in J$ such that $S^{\delta_j} \notin \mathbb{P}_{\text{sf}}^{\delta \geq 0}(\mathbb{S})$ for all $j \geq j_0$.

Proof. There exist a random variable $\xi \in L^\infty_+ \setminus \{0\}$ and a net $(\xi_j)_{j \in J} \subset L^\infty$ such that $\xi_j \overset{w^*}{\to} \xi$ and $S_T^{\delta_j} \geq \xi_j$ for each $j \in J$. Therefore, we have $\mathbb{E}[\xi_j \eta] \to \mathbb{E}[\xi \eta]$ for all $\eta \in L^1$. In particular, since $Z_T \in L^1$, we obtain

$$\mathbb{E}[\xi_j Z_T] \to \mathbb{E}[\xi Z_T]. \tag{6}$$

Suppose, contrary to the assertion above, that for every $j_0 \in J$ there exists $j \geq j_0$ such that $S^{\delta_j} \in \mathbb{P}_{\mathrm{sf}}^{\delta \geq 0}(\mathbb{S})$. According to Lemma 2.4, we have $S^{\delta_j} \in \mathbb{P}_{\mathrm{sf}}^+(\mathbb{S})$. Moreover, we have

$$\mathbb{E}[\xi_j Z_T] = 0. \tag{7}$$

Indeed, since Z is an ESMD for $\mathbb{P}_{\mathrm{sf}}^{\delta \geq 0}(\mathbb{S}) \cap \mathbb{P}_{\mathrm{sf}}^+(\mathbb{S})$, the process $S^{\delta_j} Z$ is a non-negative supermartingale, and hence, recalling that $S_0^{\delta_j} = 0$, by Doob's optional stopping theorem, we obtain

$$\mathbb{E}[\xi_j Z_T] \leq \mathbb{E}[S_T^{\delta_j} Z_T] \leq \mathbb{E}[S_0^{\delta_j} Z_0] = S_0^{\delta_j} Z_0 = 0.$$

Now, we will show that $\mathbb{E}[\xi Z_T] = 0$. Indeed, let $\epsilon > 0$ be arbitrary. Due to (6), there exists $j_0 \in J$ such that

$$|\mathbb{E}[\xi_j Z_T] - \mathbb{E}[\xi Z_T]| \leq \epsilon \quad \text{for all } j \geq j_0.$$

Thus, using (7), it follows that

$$\mathbb{E}[\xi Z_T] \leq \epsilon.$$

Since $\epsilon > 0$ was arbitrary, we deduce that $\mathbb{E}[\xi Z_T] = 0$. Now, noting that $\xi \geq 0$ and $\mathbb{P}(Z_T > 0) = 1$, we obtain the contradiction $\xi = 0$. □

Now, our goal is to prove that an ESMD Z for $\mathbb{P}_{\mathrm{sf}}^{\delta \geq 0}(\mathbb{S}) \cap \mathbb{P}_{\mathrm{sf}}^+(\mathbb{S})$ exists. Recall that due to Lemmas 2.1 and 2.2, we may assume that we are in the situation of Remark 2.3. We define $X^i := S^i / S^d$ for $i = 1, \ldots, d-1$ and the $\mathbb{R}^d$-valued semimartingale $\bar{X} := (X, 1)$, where $X := (X^1, \ldots, X^{d-1})$. Furthermore, we define $\mathbb{X} := \{X^1, \ldots, X^{d-1}\}$ and the discounted market $\bar{\mathbb{X}} := \{\bar{X}^1, \ldots, \bar{X}^d\}$. The following are two well-known results about the change of numéraire technique.

Lemma 2.12. [32, Prop. 5.2] *For an $\mathbb{R}^d$-valued predictable process δ the following statements are equivalent:*

(i) *We have* $\delta \in \Delta_{\mathrm{sf}}(\mathbb{S})$.
(ii) *We have* $\delta \in \Delta_{\mathrm{sf}}(\bar{\mathbb{X}})$.

If the previous conditions are fulfilled, then we have

$$S^\delta = S^d \bar{X}^\delta.$$

For a pair $(x, \theta) \in \mathbb{R} \times \Delta(\mathbb{X})$ the corresponding wealth process is defined as

$$X^{x,\theta} := x + \theta \cdot X.$$

Lemma 2.13. [32, Lemma 5.1] *There is a bijection between* $\mathbb{R} \times \Delta(\mathbb{X})$ *and* $\Delta_{\mathrm{sf}}(\bar{\mathbb{X}})$, *which is defined as follows*:

(1) *For* $\delta \in \Delta_{\mathrm{sf}}(\bar{\mathbb{X}})$, *we assign*

$$\delta \mapsto (x, \theta) := (X_0^\delta, \delta^1, \ldots, \delta^{d-1}) \in \mathbb{R} \times \Delta(\mathbb{X}).$$

(2) *For* $(x, \theta) \in \mathbb{R} \times \Delta(\mathbb{X})$, *we assign*

$$(x, \theta) \mapsto \delta = (\theta, X_-^{x,\theta} - \theta \cdot X_-) \in \Delta_{\mathrm{sf}}(\bar{\mathbb{X}}).$$

Furthermore, for all $(x, \theta) \in \mathbb{R} \times \Delta(\mathbb{X})$ *and the corresponding self-financing strategy* $\delta \in \Delta_{\mathrm{sf}}(\bar{\mathbb{X}})$, *we have*

$$\bar{X}^\delta = X^{x,\theta}.$$

Proposition 2.14. *Let* $\mathbb{S} = \{S^1, \ldots, S^d\}$ *be a financial market consisting of nonnegative semimartingales for some* $d \in \mathbb{N}$ *with* $d \geq 2$, *such that the semimartingales* $S^1, \ldots, S^{d-1} \geq 0$ *cannot revive from bankruptcy, and we have* $S^d, S^d_- > 0$. *Then the following statements are true*:

(1) *There exists an ESMD* Z *for* $\mathbb{P}_{\mathrm{sf}}^{\delta \geq 0}(\mathbb{S}) \cap \mathbb{P}_{\mathrm{sf}}^{+}(\mathbb{S})$.
(2) *If* $(S_T^d)^{-1} \in L^\infty$, *then the ESMD* Z *can be chosen such that* $Z_T \in L^1$.

Proof. According to Ref. [23, Thm. 1.3], there exists an ESMD Y for $\bar{\mathbb{X}}$ such that $Y_0 = 1$. We set

$$Z := Y / S^d. \tag{8}$$

Since $1 \in \bar{\mathbb{X}}$, the process Y is a supermartingale. Thus, if $(S_T^d)^{-1} \in L^\infty$, then we have $Z_T \in L^1$. Now, let $S^\delta \in \mathbb{P}_{\mathrm{sf}}^{\delta \geq 0}(\mathbb{S}) \cap \mathbb{P}_{\mathrm{sf}}^{+}(\mathbb{S})$ be arbitrary. By Lemma 2.12, we have $\bar{X}^\delta \in \mathbb{P}_{\rm sf}^{\delta \geq 0}(\bar{\mathbb{X}}) \cap \mathbb{P}_{\rm sf}^+(\bar{\mathbb{X}})$ and the identity

$$S^\delta = S^d \bar{X}^\delta. \tag{9}$$

We define the increasing sequence $(D_n)_{n \in \mathbb{N}}$ of predictable sets by $D_n := \{\|\delta\| \leq n\}$ for all $n \in \mathbb{N}$, and the sequence of predictable, bounded, non-negative processes $(\delta_n)_{n \in \mathbb{N}}$ as $\delta_n := \delta \mathbb{1}_{D_n}$ for all $n \in \mathbb{N}$. Let $n \in \mathbb{N}$ be arbitrary. By Lemma 2.13, we have

$$\bar{X}^{\delta_n} = X^{x_n, \theta_n}.$$

where $(x_n, \theta_n) \in \mathbb{R} \times \Delta(\mathbb{X})$ is given by

$$(x_n, \theta_n) := (X_0^{\delta_n}, \delta_n^1, \dots, \delta_n^{d-1}),$$

and we have

$$\delta_n = (\theta_n, X_-^{x_n, \theta_n} - \theta_n \cdot X_-).$$

Using integration by parts, we obtain

$$\begin{aligned} Y\bar{X}^{\delta_n} = YX^{x_n, \theta_n} &= x_n + \theta_n \boldsymbol{\cdot} (YX) + (X_-^{x_n, \theta_n} - \theta_n \cdot X_-) \boldsymbol{\cdot} Y \\ &= x_n + \delta_n \boldsymbol{\cdot} (Y\bar{X}), \end{aligned}$$

where $Y\bar{X}$ denotes the $\mathbb{R}^d$-valued supermartingale with components $Y\bar{X}^i$, $i = 1, \dots, d$, cf. Ref. [23, p. 2685]. By [32, Prop. 5.2] we have $\delta \in \Delta_{\rm sf}(Y\bar{\mathbb{X}})$, where $Y\bar{\mathbb{X}} := \{Y\bar{X}^1, \dots, Y\bar{X}^d\}$. Hence, using Ref. [11, Thm. III.6.19.a], letting $n \to \infty$ we obtain

$$Y\bar{X}^\delta = x + \delta \boldsymbol{\cdot} (Y\bar{X}).$$

Now, for each $n \in \mathbb{N}$, we obtain

$$\mathbb{1}_{D_n} \boldsymbol{\cdot} (Y\bar{X}^\delta) = \mathbb{1}_{D_n} \boldsymbol{\cdot} \big(\delta \boldsymbol{\cdot} (Y\bar{X})\big) = (\delta \mathbb{1}_{D_n}) \boldsymbol{\cdot} (Y\bar{X}) = \delta_n \boldsymbol{\cdot} (Y\bar{X}),$$

where we have used the associativity of the stochastic integral, see Ref. [31, Thm. 4.6]. It follows that $\mathbb{1}_{D_n} \boldsymbol{\cdot} (Y\bar{X}^\delta)$ is a supermartingale for each $n \in \mathbb{N}$. Hence, we deduce that $Y\bar{X}^\delta$ is a non-negative σ-supermartingale in the sense of Ref. [20], and by Ref. [20, Prop. 3.1], it follows that $Y\bar{X}^\delta$ is a supermartingale. Taking into account (8) and (9), this shows that ZS^δ is a supermartingale. Consequently, the process Z is an ESMD for $\mathbb{P}_{\rm sf}^{\delta \geq 0}(\mathbb{S}) \cap \mathbb{P}_{\rm sf}^+(\mathbb{S})$. □

Now, we are ready to provide the proofs of the results stated in Section 1. Recall that due to Lemmas 2.1 and 2.2, we may assume that we are in the situation of Remark 2.3. The proofs of Theorems 1.2–1.6 and 1.8 are a consequence of combining Propositions 2.6–2.11 with Proposition 2.14, and the proof of Theorem 1.7 is an immediate consequence of the more general Theorem 1.8.

3. Financial Market Models in Discrete Time

In this section, we briefly demonstrate how the proof of our main result can be simplified for discrete-time models with strictly positive primary security accounts. We assume that a discrete filtration $(\mathscr{F}_t)_{t=0,\dots,T}$ for some $T \in \mathbb{N}$ with $\mathscr{F}_0 = \{\Omega, \emptyset\}$ is given, and we consider a market $\mathbb{S} = \{S^i : i \in I\}$ consisting of non-negative, adapted processes $S^i \geq 0$ for all $i \in I$. As shown in Ref. [11, p. 14], this can be regarded as a particular case of the continuous time setting, which we have considered so far. In this particular setting, the space $\Delta_{\mathrm{sf}}(\mathbb{S})$ of all self-financing strategies consists of all predictable processes $\delta = (\delta_t)_{t=1,\dots,T}$ with finite support (1) such that

$$\delta_t \cdot S_t = \delta_{t+1} \cdot S_t \quad \text{for all } t = 1, \dots, T-1, \tag{10}$$

and the corresponding self-financing portfolio S^δ is given by

$$S_0^\delta = \delta_1 \cdot S_0, \tag{11}$$

$$S_t^\delta = \delta_t \cdot S_t, \quad t = 1, \dots, T. \tag{12}$$

If the primary security accounts are strictly positive, then we can provide an elementary proof of Theorem 1.2 for such discrete-time models by using the following result.

Proposition 3.1. *If $S^i > 0$ for all $i \in I$, then for every self-financing portfolio $S^\delta \in \mathbb{P}_{\mathrm{sf}}^{\delta \geq 0}(\mathbb{S})$ with $S_0^\delta = 0$ we have $\delta = 0$, and hence $S^\delta = 0$.*

Proof. Inductively we will show that $\delta_t = 0$ for all $t = 1, \dots, T$. For $t = 1$ note that by (11) we have $\delta_1 \cdot S_0 = 0$. Since $\delta_1^i \geq 0$ and $S_0^i > 0$ for all $i \in I$, we obtain $\delta_1 = 0$. We proceed with the induction step $t \to t+1$ and suppose that $\delta_t = 0$. Then by (10) we have $\delta_{t+1} \cdot S_t = 0$. Since $\delta_{t+1}^i \geq 0$ and $S_t^i > 0$ for all $i \in I$, we obtain $\delta_{t+1} = 0$, completing the proof. □

4. Examples

In this section, we present examples, where arbitrage portfolios can be explicitly computed, and verify that, in accordance with Theorem 1.2, these portfolios indeed require short selling.

Example 4.1. Consider the market $\mathbb{S} = \{S^1, S^2\}$ consisting of two primary security accounts such that $S_0^1 = S_0^2$ and $S_t^1 > S_t^2$ for all $t > 0$. For example, the assets could be $S_t^1 = e^t$ for $t \in \mathbb{R}_+$ and $S^2 = 1$. Then $\delta = (1, -1)$ is a self-financing strategy, and we obtain the non-negative arbitrage portfolio $S^\delta = S^1 - S^2$. In accordance with Theorem 1.2, we see that this arbitrage portfolio requires short selling.

In the following example, we consider a simple one-period model in discrete time, which is a particular case of the setting from Section 3.

Example 4.2. This example can be found in Ref. [7, Exercise 1.1.1]. The probability space $(\Omega, \mathscr{F}, \mathbb{P})$ is defined as follows. Let $\Omega := \{\omega_1, \omega_2, \omega_3\}$ with pairwise different elements $\omega_1, \omega_2, \omega_3$, the σ-algebra is given by the power set $\mathscr{F} := \mathfrak{P}(\Omega)$, and concerning the probability measure $\mathbb{P}$ we assume that $\mathbb{P}(\{\omega_i\}) > 0$ for all $i = 1, 2, 3$. The filtration $(\mathscr{F}_t)_{t=0,1}$ is given by $\mathscr{F}_0 := \{\Omega, \emptyset\}$ and $\mathscr{F}_1 := \mathscr{F}$. In this example, we have three primary security accounts. The values at time $t = 0$ are given by the vector $\pi \in \mathbb{R}^3$ defined as

$$\pi := \begin{pmatrix} 1 \\ 2 \\ 7 \end{pmatrix},$$

and the values at the terminal time $T = 1$ are given by the random vector $S : \Omega \to \mathbb{R}^3$ defined as

$$S(\omega_1) := \begin{pmatrix} 1 \\ 3 \\ 9 \end{pmatrix}, \quad S(\omega_2) := \begin{pmatrix} 1 \\ 1 \\ 5 \end{pmatrix} \quad \text{and} \quad S(\omega_3) := \begin{pmatrix} 1 \\ 5 \\ 10 \end{pmatrix}.$$

Hence, the market $\mathbb{S} = \{S^1, S^2, S^3\}$ consists of one savings account and two risky security accounts. Note that in this example every arbitrage portfolio $S^\delta \in \mathbb{P}_{\text{sf}}(\mathbb{S})$ is non-negative, that is, we have $S^\delta \in$

$\mathbb{P}^+_{\text{sf}}(\mathbb{S})$. It is easily verified that the market $\mathbb{S}$ admits arbitrage and that all arbitrage portfolios are specified by the set

$$\left\{ \begin{pmatrix} 3\xi \\ 2\xi \\ -\xi \end{pmatrix} : \xi > 0 \right\}.$$

Hence, in accordance with Theorem 1.2, each such arbitrage portfolio requires short selling. More precisely, in order to exploit arbitrage, we have to go short in the second risky primary security account, whereas for the first risky primary security account and for the savings account, we have long positions.

In the above two examples we have considered financial markets, where NA is not satisfied, that is, at least one non-negative arbitrage portfolio exists. Now, we are interested in markets satisfying NA and still admitting arbitrage portfolios which can go negative, e.g., admissible arbitrage portfolios, and to confirm the validity of Theorem 1.2 also for such arbitrage portfolios.

For what follows, we consider a finite market $\mathbb{S} = \{S^1, \ldots, S^d\}$ consisting of non-negative semimartingales. Suppose the model satisfies NA, that is, a non-negative arbitrage portfolio does not exist. We are interested in a criterion which ensures the existence of an arbitrage portfolio. As we will see in the following, such a criterion is the existence of a money market bubble. Important references about bubbles include, for example, Refs. [3,8,10,13,15] and the article [27] with an overview of the respective literature.

Before we proceed, let us clarify the relation between our upcoming results and existing results in the bubble literature. Usually, when introducing bubbles, one assumes that an equivalent risk-neutral probability measures $\mathbb{Q} \approx \mathbb{P}$ exists, which is equivalent to no-arbitrage in the sense of NFLVR. Then a price process S^i has a bubble if it is a strict supermartingale under the risk-neutral probability measure $\mathbb{Q}$. For what follows, we will drop the typical assumption that an equivalent risk-neutral probability measure exists, which means NFLVR, and only assume that NUPBR holds true.

Definition 4.3. The market $\mathbb{S}$ has a bubble if there are an index $i \in \{1, \ldots, d\}$ and a self-financing portfolio $S^\vartheta \in \mathbb{P}^+_{\text{sf}}(\mathbb{S})$ such that $S^\vartheta_0 < S^i_0$ and $S^\vartheta_T \geq S^i_T$. In this case, the bubble is S^i.

Remark 4.4. Since we assume NUPBR rather than NFLVR, our definition of a bubble only relates to non-negative, rather than admissible portfolios.

Lemma 4.5. *Suppose $S^i, S^i_- > 0$ for all $i = 1, \dots, d$, and that the market $\mathbb{S}$ has a bubble. Then there exists an arbitrage portfolio S^δ.*

Proof. There are an index $i \in \{1, \dots, d\}$ and a self-financing portfolio $S^\vartheta \in \mathbb{P}^+_{\text{sf}}(\mathbb{S})$ such that $S^\vartheta_0 < S^i_0$ and $S^\vartheta_T \geq S^i_T$. If $S^\vartheta_0 = 0$, then S^δ with $\delta := \vartheta$ is already an arbitrage portfolio. Now, we assume that $S^\vartheta_0 > 0$. Setting

$$\alpha := \frac{S^i_0}{S^\vartheta_0} > 1,$$

by Ref. [25, Lemma 7.21] the process $\delta := \alpha\vartheta - e_i$ is also a self-financing strategy for the market $\mathbb{S}$, and we have

$$S^\delta = \alpha S^\vartheta - S^i. \tag{13}$$

It follows that $S^\delta_0 = 0$ and $S^\delta_T > 0$, showing that S^δ is an arbitrage portfolio. □

Remark 4.6. As we can see from (13), the arbitrage portfolio S^δ is generally not admissible, in particular, it can happen that it goes negative.

For what follows, we recall that $\mathscr{M}$ denotes the space of all uniformly integrable martingales and that $\mathscr{M}_{\text{loc}}$ denotes the space of all local martingales. A semimartingale Z with $Z, Z_- > 0$ is called an *equivalent local martingale deflator* (ELMD) for $\mathbb{S}$ if $S^i Z \in \mathscr{M}_{\text{loc}}$ for each $i = 1, \dots, d$.

Lemma 4.7. *Suppose there exists an ELMD Z for $\mathbb{S}$ such that $S^i Z \in \mathscr{M}$ for each $i = 1, \dots, d$. Then the market $\mathbb{S}$ does not have a bubble.*

Proof. According to Ref. [26, Prop. C.3], the process Z is also an ELMD for $\mathbb{P}^+_{\text{sf}}(\mathbb{S})$. Let $i \in \{1, \dots, d\}$ and $S^\vartheta \in \mathbb{P}^+_{\text{sf}}(\mathbb{S})$ be such that $S^\vartheta_T \geq S^i_T$. By Ref. [11, Lemma I.1.44] and Doob's optional stopping theorem for non-negative supermartingales we obtain

$$\begin{aligned}(S^\vartheta_0 - S^i_0)Z_0 &= \mathbb{E}[S^\vartheta_0 Z_0] - \mathbb{E}[S^i_0 Z_0] \\ &\geq \mathbb{E}[S^\vartheta_T Z_T] - \mathbb{E}[S^i_T Z_T] = \mathbb{E}[(S^\vartheta_T - S^i_T)Z_T] \geq 0,\end{aligned}$$

and hence $S^\vartheta_0 \geq S^i_0$. □

The following result contains sufficient conditions for the converse statement of the previous result.

Lemma 4.8. *Suppose there exists an ELMD Z for $\mathbb{S}$ such that for some $i \in \{1, \ldots, d\}$, we have $S^i Z \notin \mathscr{M}$. Furthermore, we assume that $S_T^i Z_T \in L^1$ and that there exists a self-financing portfolio $S^\vartheta \in \mathbb{P}_{\mathrm{sf}}^+(\mathbb{S})$ such that*

$$S_t^\vartheta = \frac{\mathbb{E}[S_T^i Z_T | \mathscr{F}_t]}{Z_t}, \quad t \in [0, T]. \tag{14}$$

Then the market $\mathbb{S}$ has the bubble S^i.

Proof. By (14) we have $S^\vartheta Z \in \mathscr{M}$ and $S_T^\vartheta = S_T^i$. Furthermore, since $S^i Z \notin \mathscr{M}$, we have $\mathbb{E}[S_0^i Z_0] > \mathbb{E}[S_T^i Z_T]$. Therefore, we obtain

$$S_0^\vartheta Z_0 = \mathbb{E}[S_T^\vartheta Z_T] = \mathbb{E}[S_T^i Z_T] < S_0^i Z_0,$$

and hence $S_0^\vartheta < S_0^i$. □

We call every predictable, càdlàg, finite variation process B with $B_0 = 1$ and $B, B_- > 0$ a *savings account.*

Proposition 4.9. *Suppose that $S^d = B$ for some savings account B such that B and B^{-1} are bounded. Furthermore, we assume there exists a local martingale $D > 0$ with $D_0 = 1$ such that the multiplicative special semimartingale $Z = DB^{-1}$ is an ELMD for $\mathbb{S}$. Then the following statements are true:*

(1) *Non-negative arbitrage portfolios, non-negative (asymptotic) arbitrages of the first kind and non-negative free lunches (with vanishing/bounded risk) do not exist.*
(2) *If $D \in \mathscr{M}$, then an admissible free lunch with vanishing risk does not exist. In particular, an admissible arbitrage portfolio does not exist.*
(3) *If D is the unique local martingale with $D_0 = 1$ such that DB^{-1} is an ELMD for $\mathbb{S}$, then the existence of an admissible arbitrage portfolio (or, more generally, of an admissible free lunch with vanishing risk) implies that $D \notin \mathscr{M}$.*

Proof. These statements follow from Ref. [26, Thm. 4.2 and Thm. 4.4]. □

Recall that we are interested in market models satisfying NA for its non-negative self-financing portfolios but still admitting an arbitrage portfolio. The following remark summarizes our previous results:

Remark 4.10. Suppose we are in the situation of Proposition 4.9. Then the market $\mathbb{S}$ satisfies NUPBR, and hence, a non-negative arbitrage portfolio does not exist. Furthermore, the local martingale D is a supermartingale and a candidate for the density process of an equivalent risk-neutral probability measure $\mathbb{Q} \approx \mathbb{P}$ for the discounted market $\{S^1/B, \dots, S^{d-1}/B\}$, which exists if and only if D is a true martingale. Consider the following statements:

(a) There exists an admissible arbitrage portfolio.
(b) There exists an arbitrage portfolio.
(c) The market has a bubble.
(d) D is a strict local martingale.

Then the following statements are true:

(1) We have the implications (a) $\Rightarrow$ (b) and (d).
(2) If $S^i, S^i_- > 0$ for all $i = 1, \dots, d-1$, then we have the implication (c) $\Rightarrow$ (b).
(3) If D is the unique local martingale with $D_0 = 1$ such that DB^{-1} is an ELMD for $\mathbb{S}$, then we have the implication (d) $\Rightarrow$ (a).
(4) If $S^1 Z, \dots, S^{d-1} Z \in \mathscr{M}$, then we have the implication (c) $\Rightarrow$ (d).
(5) If there exists a self-financing portfolio $S^\vartheta \in \mathbb{P}^+_{\text{sf}}(\mathbb{S})$ such that

$$S_t^\vartheta = \frac{\mathbb{E}[D_T | \mathscr{F}_t]}{Z_t}, \quad t \in [0, T],$$

then we have the implication (d) $\Rightarrow$ (c).

In the upcoming result, we have situations where non-negative arbitrage portfolios do not exist and all the statements (a)–(d) hold.

Proposition 4.11. *Let W be an $\mathbb{R}$-valued Wiener process, and assume that the filtration $(\mathscr{F}_t)_{t \in [0,T]}$ is the right-continuous, completed filtration generated by W. Suppose that the market is of the form $\mathbb{S} = \{S, 1\}$, containing a continuous semimartingale $S > 0$ such that $S^{-1} \in \mathscr{M}_{\text{loc}}$ with $S^{-1} \notin \mathscr{M}$ and the quadratic variation $\langle S^{-1} \rangle$ are strictly increasing. Then the following statements are true:*

(1) *A non-negative arbitrage portfolio does not exist.*
(2) *There exists an admissible arbitrage portfolio.*
(3) *The market has a bubble.*

Proof. Without loss of generality, we may assume that $S_0 = 1$. Setting $Z := D := S^{-1}$, we have $Z \in \mathscr{M}_{\text{loc}}$. Thus Z is an ELMD for $\mathbb{S}$, and hence, a non-negative arbitrage portfolio does not exist.

Now, let Y be any ELMD for $\mathbb{S}$ with $Y_0 = 1$. By the martingale representation theorem (see Ref. [11, Thm. III.4.33]), there exist $\theta, \sigma \in L^2_{\text{loc}}(W)$ and $A \in \mathscr{V}$ such that $Y = \mathscr{E}(-\theta \cdot W)$ and $S = \mathscr{E}(A + \sigma \cdot W)$. Furthermore, by Yor's formula (see [11, II.8.19]), we obtain

$$YS = \mathscr{E}\big((\sigma - \theta) \cdot W + A - \sigma\theta \cdot \lambda\big),$$

where λ denotes the Lebesgue measure. Since $YS \in \mathscr{M}_{\text{loc}}$, there exists $a \in L^1_{\text{loc}}(A)$ such that $A = a \cdot \lambda$ up to an evanescent set, and it follows that $\theta = a/\sigma$ λ-a.e. $\mathbb{P}$-a.e. Therefore, we have $Y = \mathscr{E}(-(a/\sigma) \cdot W)$ up to an evanescent set. Since Y was an arbitrary ELMD for $\mathbb{S}$ with $Y_0 = 1$, this proves the uniqueness of the ELMD Z. Hence, by Remark 4.10, there exists an admissible arbitrage portfolio.

Since Z is non-negative, it is also a supermartingale, and hence we have $Z_T \in L^1$. We define the martingale $M \in \mathscr{M}$ as

$$M_t := \mathbb{E}[Z_T | \mathscr{F}_t], \quad t \in [0, T].$$

By the martingale representation theorem (see Ref. [11, Thm. III.4.33]), there exist $H, K \in L^2_{\text{loc}}(W)$ such that $Z = Z_0 + H \cdot W$ and $M = M_0 + K \cdot W$. Since the quadratic variation $\langle Z \rangle = H^2 \cdot \lambda$ is strictly increasing, we have $H \neq 0$ up to an evanescent set. We define the predictable process $\theta := \frac{K}{H}$. Since the Wiener process W is continuous, we have $H, \theta H \in L^1_{\text{loc}}(W)$. Therefore, by the first associativity theorem for vector stochastic integrals with respect to local martingales (proven as Ref. [31, Thm. 4.6] by using Ref. [31, Lemma 4.4]), we have $\theta \in L^1_{\text{loc}}(Z)$ and

$$K \cdot W = (\theta H) \cdot W = \theta \cdot (H \cdot W) = \theta \cdot Z.$$

Therefore, we have

$$M = M_0 + \theta \cdot Z.$$

We define the $\mathbb{R}^2$-valued predictable process $\xi = (\eta, \theta)$ as

$$\eta := \theta \cdot Z - \theta Z.$$

Introducing the discounted market $\bar{\mathbb{S}} = \{1, Z\}$, we have $\xi \in \Delta_{\mathrm{sf}}(\bar{\mathbb{S}})$ and

$$M = M_0 + (1, Z)^{\xi} = M_0 + \eta + \theta Z.$$

By Ref. [32, Prop. 5.2], we have $\xi \in \Delta_{\mathrm{sf}}(\mathbb{S})$. Furthermore, we obtain

$$MS = M_0 S + (M - M_0)S = M_0 S + (S, 1)^{\xi} = M_0 S + \eta S + \theta.$$

Now, we define the $\mathbb{R}^2$-valued predictable process ϑ as

$$\vartheta := \xi + M_0 e_1.$$

By [25, Lemma 7.21], we have $\vartheta \in \Delta_{\mathrm{sf}}(\mathbb{S})$ and

$$(S, 1)^{\vartheta} = (S, 1)^{\xi} + M_0 S.$$

Therefore, we have

$$(S, 1)^{\vartheta} = MS,$$

which means that

$$(S, 1)^{\vartheta}_t = \frac{\mathbb{E}[Z_T | \mathscr{F}_t]}{Z_t}, \quad t \in [0, T].$$

Consequently, by Remark 4.10, the market has a bubble. □

Let us mention well-known examples of a market $\mathbb{S} = \{S, 1\}$, where S is given as the power of a Bessel process.

Example 4.12. For a Bessel process $S > 0$ of dimension $\delta > 2$, its power $Z := S^{2-\delta}$, which is a solution to the SDE

$$dZ_t = (2 - \delta) Z_t^{\frac{1-\delta}{2-\delta}} dW_t,$$

is a strict local martingale, see Ref. [29]. Therefore, Proposition 4.11 applies to the market $\mathbb{S} = \{S^{\delta - 2}, 1\}$.

Now, we provide an example of a financial market satisfying NA, and admitting an admissible arbitrage portfolio which can be computed explicitly.

Example 4.13. Consider the market $\mathbb{S} = \{S, 1\}$, where S is a Bessel process of dimension 3. By Proposition 4.11, the following statements are true:

(1) A non-negative arbitrage portfolio does not exist.
(2) There exists an admissible arbitrage portfolio.
(3) The market has a bubble.

The existence of arbitrage in this market model has been pointed out in Ref. [5], and explicit constructions of arbitrage portfolios are provided in Refs. [21] and [30]. Assume that $S_0 = 1$ and $T = 1$. Denoting by $\Phi : \mathbb{R} \to [0, 1]$ the distribution function of the standard normal distribution $\mathrm{N}(0, 1)$, we define the function $F : [0, 1] \times \mathbb{R} \to [0, \frac{1}{\Phi(1)}]$ as

$$F(t, x) := \frac{\Phi(x/\sqrt{1-t})}{\Phi(1)},$$

where for $t = 1$ and x positive this expression is understood to be $\frac{1}{\Phi(1)}$. Then, according to [21, Example 4.6], an arbitrage portfolio S^δ is given by the self-financing strategy $\delta = (\theta, \eta)$ defined by the continuous processes

$$\theta_t := \frac{\partial}{\partial x} F(t, S_t), \quad t \in [0, 1], \tag{15}$$

$$\eta := \theta \cdot S - \theta S, \tag{16}$$

and we have

$$S_t^\delta = F(t, S_t) - 1, \quad t \in [0, 1].$$

In particular, we see that this arbitrage portfolio is indeed admissible, that is, we have $S^\delta \in \mathbb{P}_{\mathrm{sf}}^{\mathrm{adm}}(\mathbb{S})$. However, this arbitrage portfolio cannot be non-negative, that is, we have $S^\delta \notin \mathbb{P}_{\mathrm{sf}}^{+}(\mathbb{S})$. Moreover, in accordance with Theorem 1.2, the arbitrage portfolio S^δ requires short selling, that is, we have $S^\delta \notin \mathbb{P}_{\mathrm{sf}}^{\delta \geq 0}(\mathbb{S})$. More precisely, as (15) shows, we have a long position $\theta > 0$ in the risky primary security account S. However, by (16) we have $\eta_0 = -\theta_0 < 0$, and hence, by the continuity of η, the stopping time $\tau := \inf\{t \in [0,1] : \eta_t = 0\}$ is strictly positive, which shows that we have the short position $\eta < 0$ on the stochastic interval $[\![0, \tau[\![$.

Funding Statement

Stefan Tappe gratefully acknowledges financial support from the Deutsche Forschungsgemeinschaft (DFG, German Research Foundation), project number 444121509.

Acknowledgments

The authors would like to thank Michael Schmutz and Andreas Haier from the Swiss Financial Market Supervisory Authority FINMA for fruitful discussions. The authors are also grateful to Claudio Fontana and Constantinos Kardaras for invaluable comments and remarks and to the referee for the careful study of this chapter and the valuable comments and suggestions.

References

[1] D. Coculescu and A. Dandapani. Insiders and their free lunches: The role of short positions. *SIAM J. Finan. Math.*, 13(3):877–902. https://doi.org/10.1137/20M1375826, 2022.

[2] D. Coculescu and M. Jeanblanc. Some no-arbitrage rules under short-sales constraints, and applications to converging asset prices. *Finance Stoch.*, 23(2):397–421, 2019.

[3] A. M. Cox and D. G. Hobson. Local martingales, bubbles and option prices. *Finance Stoch.*, 9(4):477–492, 2005.

[4] F. Delbaen and W. Schachermayer. A general version of the fundamental theorem of asset pricing. *Math. Ann.*, 300(3):463–520, 1994.

[5] F. Delbaen and W. Schachermayer. Arbitrage possibilities in Bessel processes and their relations to local martingales. *Probab. Theory Related Fields*, 102(3):357–366, 1995.

[6] F. Delbaen and W. Schachermayer. *The Mathematics of Arbitrage*. Springer Finance. Springer, Berlin, 2008.

[7] H. Föllmer and A. Schied. *Stochastic Finance*, 4th Edition. De Gruyter, Berlin, 2016.

[8] P. Guasoni and M. Rásonyi. Fragility of arbitrage and bubbles in local martingale diffusion models. *Finance Stoch.*, 19(2):215–231, 2015.

[9] P. Harms, C. Liu, and A. Neufeld. Supermartingale deflators in the absence of a numéraire. *Math. Financ. Econ.*, 15(4):885–915, 2021.

[10] S. L. Heston, M. Loewenstein, and G. A. Willard. Options and bubbles. *Rev. Financial Studies*, 20(2):359–390, 2007.

[11] J. Jacod and A. N. Shiryaev. *Limit Theorems for Stochastic Processes.* Number 288 in Grundlagen der mathematischen Wissenschaften, 2nd Edition. Springer, Berlin, 2003.

[12] R. A. Jarrow and M. Larsson. Informational efficiency under short sale constraints. *SIAM J. Finan. Math.*, 6(1):804–824, 2015.

[13] R. A. Jarrow and D. B. Madan. Arbitrage, martingales, and private monetary value. *Journal of Risk*, 3(1):73–90, 2000.

[14] R. A. Jarrow, P. Protter, and S. Pulido. The effect of trading futures on short sale constraints. *Math. Finance*, 25(2):311–338, 2015.

[15] R. A. Jarrow, P. Protter, and K. Shimbo. Asset price bubbles in incomplete markets. *Math. Finance*, 20(2):145–185, 2010.

[16] E. Jouini and H. Kallal. Arbitrage in securities markets with short-sales constraints. *Math. Finance*, 5(3):197–232, 1995.

[17] Y. M. Kabanov, C. Kardaras, and S. Song. No arbitrage of the first kind and local martingale numéraires. *Finance Stoch.*, 20(4):1097–1108, 2016.

[18] Y. M. Kabanov and D. O. Kramkov. Large financial markets: Asymptotic arbitrage and contiguity. *Probab. Theory Appl.*, 39(1):222–229, 1994.

[19] Y. M. Kabanov and D. O. Kramkov. Asymptotic arbitrage in large financial markets. *Finance Stoch.*, 2(2):143–172, 1998.

[20] J. Kallsen. σ-localization and σ-martingales. *Theory Probab. Appl.*, 48(1):152–163, 2004.

[21] I. Karatzas and C. Kardaras. The numéraire portfolio in semimartingale financial models. *Finance Stoch.*, 11(4):447–493, 2007.

[22] C. Kardaras. Generalized supermartingale deflators under limited information. *Math. Finance*, 23(1):186–197, 2013.

[23] C. Kardaras and E. Platen. On the semimartingale property of discounted asset-price processes. *Stoch. Proc. Appl.*, 121(11):2678–2691, 2011.

[24] E. Platen and D. Heath. *A Benchmark Approach to Quantitative Finance.* Springer Finance. Springer, Berlin, 2010.

[25] E. Platen and S. Tappe. No-arbitrage concepts in topological vector lattices. *Positivity*, 25(5):1853–1898, 2021.

[26] E. Platen and S. Tappe. No arbitrage and multiplicative special semimartingales. *Adv. in Appl. Probab.*, 55(3), 1033–1074, 2023. https://doi.org/10.1017/apr2022.62.

[27] P. Protter. A mathematical theory of financial bubbles. In V. Henderson and R. Sircar (eds.), *Paris-Princeton Lectures on Mathematical Finance*, vol. 2081. Springer, Cham, 2013, pp. 1–108.

[28] S. Pulido. The fundamental theorem of asset pricing, the hedging problem and maximal claims in financial markets with short sales prohibitions. *Ann. Appl. Probab.*, 24(1):54–75, 2014.

[29] D. Revuz and M. Yor. *Continuous Martingales and Brownian Motion.* Springer, Berlin, 1990.

[30] J. Ruf. Hedging under arbitrage. *Math. Finance*, 23(2):297–317, 2013.

[31] A. N. Shiryaev and A. S. Cherny. Vector stochastic integrals and the fundamental theorem of asset pricing. *Proc. Steklov Inst. Math.*, 237:12–56, 2002.

[32] K. Takaoka and M. Schweizer. A note on the condition of no unbounded profit with bounded risk. *Finance Stoch.*, 18(2):393–405, 2014.

[33] H. von Weizsäcker. Can one drop L^1-boundedness in Komlós subsequence theorem? *Amer. Math. Monthly*, 111(10):900–903, 2004.

[34] G. Žitković. A filtered version of the bipolar theorem of Brannath and Schachermayer. *J. Theor. Probab.*, 15(1):41–61, 2002.

https://doi.org/10.1142/9789811280306_0022

Chapter 22

Power Laws in Market Microstructure

Umut Çetin[*,‡] **and Henri Waelbroeck**[†,§]

[*] *Department of Statistics, London School of Economics and Political Science, 10 Houghton St., London, WC2A 2AE, UK*

[†] *Baruch College, CUNY, NY, USA and AlgoCortex LLC*

[‡] *u.cetin@lse.ac.uk*

[§] *h.waelbroeck@algocortex.com*

Abstract

We develop an equilibrium model for market impact of trades when investors with private signals execute via a trading desk. Fat tails in the signal distribution lead to a power law for price impact, while the impact is logarithmic for lighter tails. Moreover, the tail distribution of the equilibrium trade volume obeys a power law. The spread decreases with the degree of noise trading and increases with the number of insiders. In case of a monopolistic insider, the last slice traded against the limit order book is priced at the fundamental value of the asset reminiscent of the Kyle models in continuous time. However, competition among insiders leads to aggressive trading, hence vanishing profit in the limit. The model also predicts that the order book flattens as the amount of noise trading increases converging to a model with proportional transactions costs with non-vanishing spread.

Keywords: Limit order book, Price impact, Power laws, Equilibrium, Market microstructure, h-transform

1. Introduction

Kyle [17] studies in a simple but remarkably powerful framework a single risk neutral informed trader and a number of non-strategic uninformed liquidity traders submitting orders to a market maker, who aggregates all the orders and clear the market at a single price. Consequently, Kyle's uniform auction model does not produce a bid-ask spread and predicts a linear price impact of trades. However, his model allows for an explicit characterization of equilibrium parameters, including the optimal strategy of the informed trader as well as the equilibrium pricing rule. This in turn allows one to analyze how the private information is disseminated to the market and gets incorporated into the prices over time. In particular, *Kyle's lambda* yields an explicit measurement of market's liquidity and the extent of linear price impact.

On the other hand, empirical data provide some clues as to the shape and scale of market impact. There is a strong consensus among the practitioners that the impact is a concave function of trade size (see [28]). But biases in the data, a low signal-to-noise ratio and other issues hinder a precise determination of the functional form of market impact, particularly for large trades where data are sparse. Impact functions used in practice range from square root to logarithm (e.g., [1, 3, 11, 23, 28] and [30]). We contribute to this debate using a rational expectations approach.

Understanding the exact shape of the price impact is of utmost importance for optimal trade execution (see Bouchaud *et al.* [7]). Portfolio managers endeavor to find mispriced assets in order to beat their benchmarks. When they decide to change their holdings to take advantage of a mispricing, they create orders in an order management system and the trading desk routes these orders to broker dealers for execution. However, this new order causes prices to move to a different level due to the price impact of the trade. The value lost by not being able to execute at the decision price is called *implementation shortfall* (see Ref. [21]) and understanding how this shortfall scales with trade size is essential to optimize the investment management process. A market impact model is needed in order to maximize net trading profits, optimize position sizes, limit liquidity risk and estimate a portfolio's capacity.

Various models yield similar results for small trade sizes but they yield very different predictions for the impact of large trades. This is unfortunate since the large trades typically dominate the aggregate implementation shortfall for most portfolios. Indeed, [8] finds that large trades (above 10,000 shares) from institutional traders account for approximately 48% of the aggregate volume and the moderate trades (500–9,999 shares) by institutions make up 38% of the trading volume. Yet, large trades are fewer in number, their implementation shortfall most exposed to market noise and their size most subject to selection bias: a manager may execute a large trade because she can. This makes empirical testing difficult. The absence of a consensus on the shape of market impact for large trades motivates the search for a theoretical framework that would capture the essential features of trading and yet be sufficiently parsimonious to be testable.

To address these issues, we propose a market microstructure model for the price impact that shares features from Kyle [17] and Glosten [13]. Our results provide the micro-foundations for a large number of empirical findings including those on price impact and volume. To the best of our knowledge, this is the first model to establish the rules governing the power laws for the price impact function in an equilibrium setting.[1] The liquidity suppliers in our model face adverse selection due to the existence of informed traders (henceforth called *insiders*). Different from Ref. [17], but consistent with the modern practice, they move first by posting limit orders as in Ref. [13]. We assume following [13] that the resulting offer curve is competitive so that the limit prices are given by 'tail expectations.' That the marginal cost of a trade depends on the trade size leads to *discriminatory pricing*.

We show that whether the market impact follows a power law or a logarithmic law depends on the distribution of the fundamental value, which is the private signal of the insiders. The price impact, and equivalently the implementation shortfall, has a power law if the market believes that the fundamental value has fat tails while lighter tails are responsible for a logarithmic behavior.

Our model makes sharp predictions on the shape of market impact based on the asset's return distribution. Ignoring for a moment the difference between the risk-neutral returns distribution and the

[1]See also Nadtochiy [19] for an explanation of concave price impact in a continuous-time setting. However, price is not determined in a rational expectations equilibrium setting in Ref. [19].

physical distribution,[2] the asset's conditional return distribution is predicted by options market participants who encode their views in the options data. The shape of this distribution is sensitive to the event calendar, for example, the shape and scale of the impact function for large trade in a biopharmaceutical company ahead of a major drug approval release would be quite different from the shape and scale of market impact for the same stock when no news is expected. An investment manager with an active trading strategy in this kind of company would be able to label trades as "pre-announcement" and "other" and, over time, calibrate an impact model for each of these two cases. The goodness of fit measures for the predicted shapes from this chapter would provide a test of our theory.[3]

Our framework also allows us to compute the tails of the probability distribution associated with the aggregate volume. For a large class of distributions that can be used to model the liquidation value, we demonstrate that the tail of the trade size obeys a power law.

The power-law behavior of order sizes has been documented previously in various contexts: Reference [15] showed that the market volume in a time interval Δt has a power-law tail with exponent 1.7, Ref. [18] considered off-book trades and found an exponent ranging from 1.59 to 1.74, Ref. [12] estimated the exponent to be in the neighborhood of 1.5 and Ref. [29] reconstructed metaorders in Spanish stock exchange using data with brokerage codes and found that the metaorder transaction size distribution has a power-law tail with exponent 1.7. And in a study performed directly on institutional trade data from Alliance Bernstein, Ref. [3] found a tail exponent of 1.56 for metaorder sizes. Our model gives an equilibrium-based explanation for the magnitude of these exponents.

One of the most striking features of our model is its tractability while allowing general distributions for the fundamental value. We characterize the equilibrium strategy of insiders and the

[2]This is in fact consistent with the assumption that the market makers are risk-neutral. The more realistic case with risk-averse market makers that leads to the risk-neutral measure being different than the physical one is left to future research.

[3]To formulate a test based on the options montage is more involved, in no small part because wide spreads in option markets make pricing in the tails quite challenging. Such a project lies outside the scope of this chapter.

corresponding market impact of trades as a solution of an integral equation. While an analytic solution to this equation can be found only in few examples, its numerical implementation is straightforward and fast.

The solution of this integral equation is given by the fixed point of a highly nonlinear operator, the existence of which is shown using Schauder's fixed point theorem in Sections 3 and 4. Although this integral equation arises from a one-period consideration, we obtain *a priori* estimates on its solution using a space-time h-transform of a standard Brownian motion on $[0, 1]$ and via comparison arguments on the solutions of the resulting h-path process. These estimates also allowed us to bound the fixed point(s) of the original integral equation by the extremal fixed points of two *better-behaved* and, most importantly, *monotone* integral operators. Such a comparison was essential in establishing the power laws considered in this chapter.

Although the exact form of the market impact can only be solved numerically, we are nevertheless able to obtain the exact analytic asymptotics when the order size is large using the theory of regular variation. Moreover, due to the scaling property of the noise demand, these asymptotics still provide a good approximation for small orders if the variance of the noise demand is relatively small. The error in such an approximation appears to be still low even in the case of higher variance as confirmed visually by our numerical studies and should provide a good benchmark for empirical works.

Due to the discriminatory pricing by the liquidity suppliers, our model produces a non-zero bid-ask spread in equilibrium. We find that the minimal bid-ask spread for an *infinitesimal trade* is the same regardless of the variance of the noise trades. The shape of the order book, however, is not invariant to the changes in this variance; on the contrary, the order book flattens as it increases. In particular, the spread associated with a non-infinitesimal trade size decreases with the amount of noise trading consistent with the experimental findings of Bloomfield *et al.* [6]. In the limit, the equilibrium converges to a model with proportional transaction costs.

Our proof of the existence of equilibrium assumes that the fundamental value of the asset is bounded. However, our numerical experiments suggest that equilibrium exists for a large class of unbounded distributions commonly found in the literature and used in practice. Moreover, the asymptotics for these solutions agree with the analytical forms that our theory predicts. Yet, unlike the bounded case, an equilibrium may not exist for all unbounded distributions. Given the premise of numerical results and our formal calculations, we conjecture that the existence of equilibrium requires a sufficient amount of competition among insiders if the signal distribution exhibit fat tails. This is intuitive given the fact that the liquidity suppliers post limit prices using tail expectations in equilibrium. Since the noise demand is Gaussian, the large orders are more likely to be informed and the tail risk in the total demand is completely determined by the signal distribution as the insiders' aggregate demand is a monotone function of the fundamental value. Therefore, fat tails in the signal distribution increase the liquidity suppliers' need for compensation. Moreover, sizable fat tails are typically associated with excessive variance. Our model predicts that such risks arising from the signal distribution cause the market to break down unless the risk is reduced to a manageable level by strong enough competition among informed traders.

Even though we model the interactions in a single period model, our framework also has the flavor of a continuous-time Kyle model considered by Ref. [2]. Indeed, in case of a monopolistic insider, we show that conditional on the asset value $V = v$ the last infinitesimal slice of the aggregate order traded by the desk against the order book is priced at v on average, reminiscing the convergence of the equilibrium price to the liquidation value by the end of the trading horizon in the continuous-time Kyle model. Thus, all private information gets incorporated into market prices once the last slice has been traded.

The above 'convergence' result motivates the analysis of the case of multiple insiders. In the same vein as Ref. [16], we also model and solve the imperfect competition among $N \geq 2$ insiders who observe the liquidation value V perfectly. As in Ref. [16], this competition leads to more aggressive trading. When the signal distribution is continuous, we find that (conditional on $V = v$) the average price for the last slice traded by the desk exceeds v if the insiders are buying in equilibrium, which can be attributed to more aggressive buying due to competition. An analogous observation holds when the optimal strategy in equilibrium is to sell. We obtain an explicit formula for the aggregate profit of the insiders that shows that it converges to 0 in the limit as the number of insiders increases.

This chapter is related to the 'econophysics' literature that uses the concepts of physics to study economic issues. Gabaix *et al.* [12] argue that "[econophysics] is similar in spirit to behavioral economics in that it postulates simple plausible rules of agent behavior,..." and develop a theory of large institutional trades by assuming that the liquidity providers' preferences exhibit first-order risk aversion justified by prospect theory and institutional practices. While we share the same motivation of explaining the power laws observed in the data for price impact and trade size as Ref. [12], we instead follow a rational expectations approach to establish these laws. Thus, our model can be interpreted as a merger between econophysics and the market microstructure theory.

This chapter also relates to the literature on limit order markets. The case of liquidity suppliers moving first and submitting limit orders to be later hit by potentially informed market order was first studied by Refs. [13] and [24]. Glosten [13] is more concerned on the equilibrium among the liquidity suppliers for a given market order and there is no general existence result for an equilibrium that incorporates the optimal strategies of both the limit order traders as well as the strategic trader submitting the market order with the exception of a special case given in an example. Moreover, studies of Refs. [4] and [26] on the limit order book and the order flow in Paris Bourse and Stockholm Stock Exchange found evidence that contradicts the predictions of Ref. [13] and support a concave price impact function. [26] also stressed the need for a richer theoretical model to replicate the empirical observations. More recent works on limit order markets are mainly set in continuous time and a short list would include Refs. [10,14,20] and [25]. However, the sheer complexity of equilibrium in continuous time required these works to impose very restrictive assumptions to have a tractable model such as traders being able to trade only once (essentially making it a collection of one period models) or only for one unit of the asset. We, on the other hand, establish the existence of equilibrium for general distributions and without any restriction on the trading strategy of the strategic traders and characterize it via an integral equation that possesses an easy numerical solution.

Structure of this chapter is as follows: We present the trading model and the first implications of equilibrium in the following section. In Sections 3 and 4, we demonstrate the existence of an equilibrium under mild assumptions. Section 5 considers the asymptotic behavior of market impact and the distribution of trade volume in equilibrium. Further properties of equilibrium along with some comparative statics are given in Section 6. Numerical solutions are provided in Section 7. Moreover, Section 8 explores an alternative same-price allocation model numerically and compares the results with those of the trading desk model. Section 9 contains the concluding remarks and directions for future study. The Appendix contains some auxiliary results and the proofs not presented in the main text.

2. The Market Structure and Equilibrium

Our model is built upon Glosten [13] and the trading takes place in one period. All random variables in this section are assumed to be defined on a complete probability space $(\Omega, \mathcal{F}, P)$ and E is the expectation operator associated with P. There are four types of agents interacting in this market:

(1) Competitive (infinitely many) *liquidity suppliers* move first and place limit orders that give rise to an order book. The resulting *limit order book* is identified by some non-decreasing function $h : \mathbb{R} \to \mathbb{R}$ and, therefore, a market order of size x traded against the order book incurs the cost of

$$\int_0^x h(y)dy.$$

In other words, $h(y)$ corresponds to marginal price of the yth share.

(2) A *trading desk*, which acts as a broker for its clients, does not trade for its own account but only gathers and executes orders for its clients. At the beginning of the day, the desk does not have any orders. Any arriving order of size y is priced at

$$\int_0^y h(Y + x)dx, \tag{1}$$

where Y is the accumulated number of shares from prior orders. The desk does not publish Y and, thus, its clients do not observe Y prior to submitting their orders. However, they are aware of the form of the pricing rule given by (1).

(3) *Noise traders* whose cumulative demand for the traded asset is given by a random variable $Z \sim N(0, \sigma^2)$ are non-strategic. Z is independent of V, which is the random variable representing the liquidation value of the asset. V is assumed to be non-constant.
(4) $N \geq 1$ risk neutral *insider(s)*, who know(s) V and choose(s) a trade size to maximize their expected profit conditional on their private information. The cumulative demand of the insiders will be denoted by X. N is assumed to be deterministic and, therefore, known to the market participants.

We assume that noise traders as well as insiders are the clients of the desk. The desk aggregates all orders and trades $Z + X$ with the liquidity suppliers. Moreover, noise trades are assumed to arrive to the desk prior to the informed order(s).

Let us first consider the case $N = 1$. Since the accumulated number of shares from prior orders equals Z when the insider's order arrives at the desk, the insider is charged

$$\int_0^X h(Z + y)dy \tag{2}$$

for an order of X units. Observe that the insider will always prefer buying via the desk to buying from the order book since she will get a better price from the desk in case the noise traders are selling. Noise traders, on the other hand, are indifferent between two trading venues under our assumption that they arrive slightly earlier to the market than the informed trader.

The cost given by (1) can be justified by Bertrand competition for orders from a strategic trader (informed or uninformed) among brokerage firms each of which has already received noise orders of size Y_i. We assume the strategic trader does not split her trades among different brokers consistent with the market practice. Note that one does not have to assume that Y_is are the same, but the pairs (Y_i, V) have the same distribution over the firms.

Another, and more common, approach in the industry is to charge all orders the same average price. That is, the insider's cost of trading X units via the trading desk equals $\frac{X}{X+Z} \int_0^{X+Z} h(y)dy$, while the noise trades are priced at $\frac{Z}{X+Z} \int_0^{X+Z} h(y)dy$. However, such a cost structure makes the model analytically intractable. Nevertheless, we analyze this model numerically in Section 8 and find that it shares the same qualitative features and same asymptotic price impacts with the equilibrium arising from the cost structure of (2).

2.1. *Optimal Strategies for the Informed*

Let us next consider the optimization problem for the insider facing (2) as her trading cost. Note that the expected profit of the insider from a market order of size x is, therefore, given by

$$E^v \left[Vx - \int_0^x h(Z+y)dy \right],$$

where E^v is the expectation operator for the insider with the private information $V = v$. Since h is assumed to be non-decreasing, the first-order condition characterizes the unique X^* achieving the maximum expected profit via $V = F(X^*)$, where

$$F(x) := \int_{-\infty}^{\infty} h(x+z)q(\sigma, z)dz \tag{3}$$

and $q(\sigma, \cdot)$ is the probability density function of a mean-zero Gaussian random variable with variance σ^2. Note that since h^* is non-decreasing and not constant, F is strictly increasing and one-to-one. Thus, $X^* = F^{-1}(V)$.

We shall also consider the case of multiple insiders trading via the same desk and knowing the value of V. We assume that informed orders arrive simultaneously and the desk charges each insider an amount proportional to their order size. Therefore, the expected profit of an individual insider placing an order of size x is given by

$$E^v \left[Vx - \frac{x}{U+x} \int_0^{U+x} h(Z+y)dy \right],$$

where U denotes the aggregate demand of the other insiders.

The first-order condition associated with the above optimization problem of an individual insider is again given by

$$v = E^v\left[\frac{x}{U+x}h(Z+U+x) + \frac{U}{(U+x)^2}\int_0^{U+x} h(Z+u)du\right].$$

As every insider has symmetric information and is risk-neutral, the equilibrium demand x^* for each insider must be the same and satisfy

$$v = E^v\left[\frac{h(Z+Nx^*)}{N} + \frac{N-1}{N^2x^*}\int_0^{Nx^*} h(Z+u)du\right].$$

Denoting the total informed demand by X^*, the above can be rewritten as $V = F(X^*)$, where

$$F(x) := E^v\left[\frac{h(Z+x)}{N} + \frac{N-1}{Nx}\int_0^{x} h(Z+u)du\right], \tag{4}$$

and $F(0)$ is interpreted by continuity to be $E^v[h(Z)]$.

Note that the marginal cost function F always satisfies $F(x) \leq E^v[h(Z+x)]$ for $x > 0$ since the marginal price h is increasing. Recall that $E^v[h(Z+x)]$ is the marginal cost of buying x units for a monopolist insider. Thus, the expression of the marginal cost via (4) can be viewed as a weighted combination of the marginal cost for the monopolist and the average cost of buying x units. The weight placed on the average cost vanishes in case of monopolist and is increasing to 1 as the number of insiders increases.

Moreover, it follows from the monotonicity of h that F defined via (4) is strictly increasing. Also note that (4) reduces to (3) when $N = 1$. Thus, we shall always refer to (4) when discussing the optimal strategies of the insiders regardless of the value of N.

2.2. *Equilibrium and First Properties*

In what follows, the total informed demand will be denoted by X and we assume following Ref. [13] that limit prices are given by 'tail expectations.' That is, denoting the total demand $X + Z$ by Y,

$$h(y) = \begin{cases} E[V|Y \geq y], & \text{if} \quad y > 0, \\ E[V|Y \leq y], & \text{if} \quad y < 0. \end{cases} \tag{5}$$

The value $h(0)$ is not relevant for the subsequent computations and can be freely chosen to be any value between the best ask $h(0+) := \lim_{y \downarrow 0} h(y)$ and the best bid $h(0-) := \lim_{y \uparrow 0} h(y)$.

The definition (5) entails that liquidity suppliers earn zero aggregate profit on average. Indeed, the expected profit is given by

$$E\left[\int_0^Y (h(y) - V)dy\right] = \int_0^\infty E[(h(y) - V)\mathbf{1}_{[Y \geq y]}]dy \\ + \int_{-\infty}^0 E[(V - h(y))\mathbf{1}_{[Y \leq y]}]dy = 0,$$

where the last equality is due to the definition of the conditional expectation.

Definition 2.1. The pair (h^*, X^*) is an equilibrium if h^* is non-decreasing and non-constant, $X^* \in \mathbb{R}$ and

i) h^* satisfies (5) with $Y = X^* + Z$,
ii) X^* is the profit maximising order size for the insider(s) given h^*. That is, $V = F(X^*)$, where F is given by (4).

The strict monotonicity of F leads to the following result that in particular yields an explicit formula for the aggregate profit of the insiders.

Proposition 2.1. *Let (X^*, h) be an equilibrium and F defined by (4).*

(1) *For any $x \in \mathbb{R}$, we have*

$$E^v[h(x + Z)] = F(x) + \frac{N(N-1)}{x^N} \int_0^x (F(x) - F(y))y^{N-1}dy \\ = F(x) + N(N-1) \int_0^1 (F(x) - F(xy))y^{N-1}dy. \tag{6}$$

(2) $E^v[h(X^*+Z)] = v$ *when* $N=1$ *and, in general,*

$$E^v[h(X^*+Z)] = v + (N-1)\int_0^1 (v - F(y^{\frac{1}{N}}F^{-1}(v)))dy. \quad (7)$$

Thus, $E^v[h(X^*+Z)] > v$ *(resp.,* $E^v[h(X^*+Z)] < v$*) if* $F^{-1}(v) \in (0,\infty)$ *(resp.,* $F^{-1}(v) \in (-\infty, 0)$*).*

(3) *The aggregate expected profit of the insiders conditional on* $V = v$ *is given by*

$$\begin{aligned}\pi^*(v) &:= E^v\left[\int_0^{X^*}(v - h(y+Z))dy\right] \\ &= N\int_0^{F^{-1}(v)}(v - F(y))\left(\frac{y}{F^{-1}(v)}\right)^{N-1}dy \\ &= F^{-1}(v)\int_0^1 (v - F(y^{\frac{1}{N}}F^{-1}(v)))dy \quad (8)\end{aligned}$$

with the second and third equalities being valid if $F^{-1}(v)$ *is finite.*

(4) *The expected loss of noise traders is given by*

$$\int_0^\infty \frac{h(y) - h(-y)}{2}P(|Z| \geq y)dy. \quad (9)$$

Moreover, if the aggregate mid-spread *function* S *defined as* $S(x) := \int_0^x \frac{h(y)-h(-y)}{2}dy$ *satisfies* $\lim_{x\to\infty} S(x)P(Z \geq x) = 0$, *then the above loss equals*

$$\int_0^\infty S(y)P(|Z| \in dy) = E[S(|Z|)]. \quad (10)$$

Since the liquidity suppliers earn zero profit on average, (10) implies that the *ex ante* profit of insiders is given by $E[S(|Z|)]$. Thus, the larger the spread, the bigger the insiders' profit. Moreover, since S is concave and increasing, this profit (or the loss of the noise traders) is bounded by $S(E[|Z|]) = S(\sigma\sqrt{\frac{2}{\pi}}) \leq S(\sigma)$. This upper bound corresponds to the aggregate spread at the expected noise volume.

The expression (7) reveals an interesting feature of our model akin to Kyle's model in continuous time. Observe that $h(X^*+Z)$ can be viewed as the last slice that is traded with the limit order traders.

Thus, when there is a monopolistic insider, (7) shows that the final slice is priced at the actual value of V similar to the convergence of the equilibrium price to the liquidation value of the asset in the continuous time version of the Kyle model studied in Ref. [2] for general payoffs.

This 'convergence' may disappear when the liquidation value of the asset is observed by more than one insider as in Ref. [16]. If the distribution of the fundamental value does not possess any atoms, the optimal strategy of the insiders will be finite for any realization v of V. In this case, $E^v[h(X^* + Z)] > v$ when the optimal strategy is to buy. The intuition, as observed earlier by Ref. [16], behind this overvaluation is that competition leads to more aggressive trading and results in higher market valuation.

In practice, an important trading benchmark for traders is *the implementation shortfall.* Reference [21] defines it as the difference between a 'paper trading' benchmark and the actual trading costs. Assuming that the benchmark is given by the *ex ante* valuation $E[V]$, the associated shortfall in our context can be defined as follows:

Definition 2.2. The implementation shortfall associated with trading x units is given by

$$IS(x) := \frac{1}{x}\int_0^x E[h(Z+y)]dy.$$

Observe that $IS(x)$ is simply the expected average cost of trading x units. As the following result shows, it is smaller than the marginal cost $F(x)$, which is given by the first-order condition (4).

Proposition 2.2. *Let h be a function that defines the order book and $F(x)$ be given by the first-order condition (4). Then,*

$$IS(x) = N\int_0^1 F(xy)y^{N-1}dy.$$

In particular, $IS(x) < F(x)$ for $x > 0$ and $IS(x) > F(x)$ for $x < 0$.

3. Characterization of Equilibrium

The aim of this section is to identify the integral equations whose solutions determine an equilibrium (X^*, h^*). Writing h instead of h^*

to ease the exposition and using the definition of h when $y > 0$, we get

$$\begin{aligned} h(y) &= E[V|X^* + Z \geq y] = E[V|F^{-1}(V) \geq y - Z] \\ &= E[V|V \geq F(y - Z)]. \end{aligned}$$

Similarly, $h(y) = E[V|V \leq F(y - Z)]$ for $y < 0$.

Next introduce the right-continuous functions $\Phi^\pm$ and $\Pi^\pm$ via

$$\begin{aligned} &\Phi^+(y) := E[V\mathbf{1}_{[V>y]}],\ \Pi^+(y) := P(V > y), \\ &\Phi^-(y) := E[V\mathbf{1}_{[V\leq y]}],\ \Pi^-(y) := P(V \leq y) = 1 - \Pi^+(y). \end{aligned}$$

Note that $\Phi^+(y-) = E[V\mathbf{1}_{[V\geq y]}]$ and $\Pi^+(y-) = P(V \geq y)$ are the *unnormalized* upper tail expectation and the upper tail probability, respectively.

Now let us compute $h(y)$ for $y > 0$ using the fact that $\Phi^+(x) = \Phi^+(x-)$ for almost all x:

$$h(y) = \frac{E[V\mathbf{1}_{[V\geq F(y-Z)]}]}{P(V \geq F(y - Z))} = \frac{\int_{-\infty}^{\infty} \Phi^+(F(y - z))q(\sigma, z)dz}{\int_{-\infty}^{\infty} \Pi^+(F(y - z))q(\sigma, z)dz}. \tag{11}$$

Similarly, for $y < 0$,

$$h(y) = \frac{\int_{-\infty}^{\infty} \Phi^-(F(y - z))q(\sigma, z)dz}{\int_{-\infty}^{\infty} \Pi^-(F(y - z))q(\sigma, z)dz}. \tag{12}$$

In order to obtain an equation for F it will be convenient to define, for any continuous g, the mappings

$$\begin{aligned} \phi_g^+(x) &:= \frac{\int_{-\infty}^{\infty} \Phi^+(g(z))q(\sigma, x - z)dz}{\int_{-\infty}^{\infty} \Pi^+(g(z))q(\sigma, x - z)dz} \quad \text{and} \\ \phi_g^-(x) &:= \frac{\int_{-\infty}^{\infty} \Phi^-(g(z)q(\sigma, x - z)dz}{\int_{-\infty}^{\infty} \Pi^-(g(z))q(\sigma, x - z)dz}. \end{aligned}$$

Let us also set

$$\phi_g(x) := \phi_g^+(x)\mathbf{1}_{x\geq 0} + \phi_g^-(x)\mathbf{1}_{x<0}. \tag{13}$$

Now, combining (4), (11) and (12) yields an equation for F:

$$F(x) = \frac{1}{N}\int_{-\infty}^{\infty} q(\sigma, x-z)\phi_F(z)dz + \frac{N-1}{Nx}\int_0^x dy \int_{-\infty}^{\infty} \times q(\sigma, y-z)\phi_F(z)dz. \tag{14}$$

Assuming one can change the order of integration above,[4] then (14) can be rewritten as

$$F(x) = \int_{-\infty}^{\infty} \left\{ \frac{1}{N} q(\sigma, x-z) + \frac{N-1}{N}\bar{q}(\sigma, x, z) \right\} \phi_F(z)dz, \tag{15}$$

with

$$\bar{q}(\sigma, x, z) := \mathbf{1}_{x\neq 0}\frac{1}{x}\int_0^x q(\sigma, y-z)dy + \mathbf{1}_{x=0}q(\sigma, z). \tag{16}$$

The preceding calculations show that the existence of a solution for the above integral equation is a necessary condition for equilibrium. Validity of the converse is obvious and we, thus, have the following:

Theorem 3.1. *Equilibrium exists if and only if there exists a function $F : \mathbb{R} \to \mathbb{R}$ that satisfies (14). Given such a solution F, (X^*, h^*) constitutes an equilibrium, where $X^* = F^{-1}(V)$ and h^* is defined via (11) and (12).*

In view of the above theorem, finding an equilibrium boils down to finding a solution of (14). Moreover, equilibrium will be uniquely defined if there exists a unique solution of (14). As usual, solutions of (14) will be identified as fixed points of a mapping.

Before analyzing in depth this fixed-point problem, we shall first consider some settings in which equilibrium is explicitly solvable. Note that since h is increasing, its right and left limits exist. In particular, $h(0+)$ is the lowest ask price and $h(0-)$ is the highest ask price. Thus, *the bid-ask spread* is given by $h(0+) - h(0-)$ in equilibrium.

[4]We shall see later that this is justified when V is bounded from below.

Definition 3.1. V is said to be symmetric if V and $-V$ have the same distribution. That is, $\Pi^+(y-) = \Pi^-(-y)$ for all y.

Proposition 3.1. *Suppose that V is symmetric and there exists a unique solution F to (14). Then F is symmetric, i.e., $F(x) = -F(-x)$ for all x. Moreover, any symmetric solution of (14) is also a solution of*

$$F(x) = \frac{1}{N}\int_0^\infty q_0(\sigma, x-z)\phi_F^+(z)dz + \frac{N-1}{Nx}\int_0^x dy \times \int_0^\infty q_0(\sigma, y-z)\phi_F^+(z)dz, \tag{17}$$

where $q_0(\sigma, x, z) := q(\sigma, x-z) - q(\sigma, x+z)$.

Proof. Observe that $-\Phi^+(y-) = E[-V\mathbf{1}_{[V\geq y]}] = E[-V\mathbf{1}_{[-V\leq -y]}] = E[V\mathbf{1}_{[V\leq -y]}] = \Phi^-(-y)$. Thus, utilizing the fact that Φ^+ and Π^+ differ from their left limits at most at countably many points and q is symmetric around zero, we obtain

$$\begin{aligned}
&\int_{-\infty}^\infty q(\sigma, -x-z)\phi_F(z)dz \\
&= \int_{-\infty}^0 dz\, q(\sigma, x-z)\frac{\int_{-\infty}^\infty \Phi^+(F(-u))q(\sigma, z-u)du}{\int_{-\infty}^\infty \Pi^+(F(-u))q(\sigma, z-u)du} \\
&\quad + \int_0^\infty dz\, q(\sigma, x-z)\frac{\int_{-\infty}^\infty \Phi^-(F(-u))q(\sigma, z-u)du}{\int_{-\infty}^\infty \Pi^-(F(-u))q(\sigma, z-u)du} \\
&= -\int_{-\infty}^0 dz\, q(\sigma, x-z)\frac{\int_{-\infty}^\infty \Phi^-(-F(-u))q(\sigma, z-u)du}{\int_{-\infty}^\infty \Pi^-(-F(-u))q(\sigma, z-u)du} \\
&\quad - \int_0^\infty dz\, q(\sigma, x-z)\frac{\int_{-\infty}^\infty \Phi^+(-F(-u))q(\sigma, z-u)du}{\int_{-\infty}^\infty \Pi^+(-F(-u))q(\sigma, z-u)du} \\
&= -\int_{-\infty}^\infty q(\sigma, -x-z)\phi_G(z)dz,
\end{aligned}$$

where $G(x) := -F(-x)$. Moreover,

$$
\begin{aligned}
-\frac{1}{x}\int_0^{-x} dy \int_{-\infty}^{\infty} q(\sigma, y-z)\phi_F(z)dz
&= \frac{1}{x}\int_0^{x} dy \int_{-\infty}^{\infty} q(\sigma, -y-z)\phi_F(z)dz \\
&= -\frac{1}{x}\int_0^{x} dy \int_{-\infty}^{\infty} q(\sigma, y-z)\phi_G(z)dz.
\end{aligned}
$$

Thus, $-G$ is also a solution of (14), which establishes the first assertion. The second assertion follows from a change of variable in (14) as above and using the assumed symmetry of F. □

Example 3.1. Suppose that $P(V=1) = P(V=-1) = \frac{1}{2}$. Then, the unique symmetric solution of (14) is defined by

$$
\begin{aligned}
F(x) = \frac{1}{N}\int_0^{\infty} q_0(\sigma, x, z)dz + \frac{N-1}{Nx}\int_0^x dy \\
\times \int_0^{\infty} dz q_0(\sigma, y, z), \quad x \geq 0.
\end{aligned}
$$

In this case, it is easily seen that in equilibrium $X^* = \infty$ (resp., $X^* = -\infty$) if $V = 1$ (resp., $V = -1$). Moreover, $h^*(y) = \mathbf{1}_{[y>0]} - \mathbf{1}_{[y<0]}$.

Although the insiders' optimal market order is to buy or sell an infinite amount cumulatively, their profit remains finite. Indeed, when $V = 1$, the aggregate expected profit is given by

$$
\int_0^{\infty} E^1(1 - h(Z+y))dy = 2E^1\left(\int_0^{\infty} \mathbf{1}_{[Z<-y]}dy\right) = \sigma\sqrt{\frac{2}{\pi}}.
$$

Note that the total profit is independent of N.

Example 3.2. Consider the case $P(V=-1) = P(V=0) = P(V=1) = \frac{1}{3}$. Then, similar considerations as above should yield $F(\infty) = 1$ and $F(-\infty) = -1$. Moreover, symmetry considerations lead to $F(0) = 0$, which suggests that the insider does not trade when $V = 0$.

Indeed, the unique solution of (14) is given by

$$F(x) = \frac{1}{N}\int_0^\infty q_0(\sigma, x, z)\frac{1}{1+P(Z\geq z)}dz + \frac{N-1}{Nx}\int_0^x dy\int_0^\infty dz q_0(\sigma, y, z)\frac{1}{1+P(Z\geq z)}.$$

Differently from Example 3.1, the order book will not be flat since the insider does not trade when $V = 0$. One can obtain h^* via (12) and (11). Alternatively, for $y > 0$

$$h(y) = \frac{E[V\mathbf{1}_{[X^*(V)+Z\geq y]}]}{P(X^*(V)+Z\geq y)} = \frac{P(V=1)}{P(V=1)+P(V=0, Z\geq y)} = \frac{P(V=1)}{P(V=1)+P(V=0)P(Z\geq y)} = \frac{1}{1+P(Z\geq y)},$$

where the first equality follows from the fact that $X^*(V)$ is infinite when $V = -1$ or 1. Similarly, for $y < 0$, $h(y) = -\frac{1}{1+P(Z\leq y)}$. In particular, the bid-ask spread is given by $h(0+) - h(0-) = \frac{4}{3}$ and is again independent of the noise volume and of N.

3.1. *Existence of Equilibrium*

We shall denote by m (resp., M) lower (resp., upper) endpoint of the support of the random variable V. Note that, since V is assumed non-degenerate, we have $-\infty \leq m < M \leq \infty$.

Define on the support of V

$$\Psi^{\pm}(y) := \frac{\Phi^{\pm}(y)}{\Pi^{\pm}(y)} \tag{18}$$

so that $\Psi^+(y) = E[V|V > y]$ and $\Psi^-(y) = E[V|V \leq y]$.

We impose the following condition on the function F to ensure that the integral equation (14) is well defined and changing the order of integration in (15) is justified.

Assumption 3.1. $\int_{-\infty}^0 \phi_F^-(z)q(\sigma, z)dz > -\infty$.

Observe that the above is automatically satisfied if V is bounded from below in view of (22) in the following section. Moreover, if F is a continuous function satisfying (14) and V is symmetric, it satisfies the above assumption, too.

One of the useful consequences of the above assumption is that the marginal tradings costs are strictly increasing.

Lemma 3.1. *Let F be a continuous non-decreasing solution of (14) or (30) satisfying Assumption 3.1. Then,* $\lim_{x\to\infty} F(x) = M$ *and* $\lim_{x\to-\infty} F(x) = m$*. Moreover, F is strictly increasing.*

This gives rise to the following sufficient condition for equilibrium. Note that since V is bounded under the hypothesis of the theorem, Assumption 3.1 is satisfied.

Theorem 3.2. *Suppose $-\infty < m < M < \infty$. Then, there exists an equilibrium.*

4. Existence of a Solution for the Fixed Point Equation

This section is devoted to the proof of Theorem 3.2 using Schauder's fixed-point theorem. The following lemma provides the key foundations for the estimates that are used to prove the existence of a fixed point.

Lemma 4.1. *Let $g : \mathbb{R} \to \mathbb{R}$ be a continuous function and u^+ (resp., u^-) be the unique solution of*

$$u_t + \sigma^2 u_{xx} = 0, \qquad u(1,x) = \Pi^+(g(x)) \ (\text{resp. } u(1,x) = \Pi^-(g(x))). \tag{19}$$

Then, the following hold:

(1) *There exists a solution B on a filtered probability space $(\Omega, \mathcal{F}, (\mathcal{F}_t), \mathbb{Q})$ to the following SDE:*

$$dB_t = \sigma dW_t + \sigma^2 \frac{u_x(t, B_t)}{u(t, B_t)} dt, \quad B_0 = x, \tag{20}$$

where u is either u^+ or u^- and W is a Brownian motion with $W_0 = 0$.

(2) $\phi_g^+(x) = \mathbb{E}^{\mathbb{Q}^+}[\Psi^+(g(B_1))]$ *and* $\phi_g^-(x) = \mathbb{E}^{\mathbb{Q}^-}[\Psi^-(g(B_1))]$, *where $(B, \mathbb{Q}^+)$ (resp., $(B, \mathbb{Q}^-)$) corresponds to the solution of (20) if*

$u = u^+$ (resp., $u = u^-$) and $\mathbb{E}^{\mathbb{Q}}$ stands for the expectation under $\mathbb{Q}$.

(3) $\phi_g^+(0) > \phi_g^-(0)$.

(4) *Suppose further that g is non-decreasing. Then, $\phi_g^{\pm}$ are non-decreasing, too. Consequently, ϕ_g is non-decreasing. Moreover,*

$$\phi_g^+(x) \leq \mathbb{E}^{\mathbb{Q}^+}[\Psi^+(g(\sigma W_1 + x))], \tag{21}$$

$$\phi_g^-(x) \geq \mathbb{E}^{\mathbb{Q}^-}[\Psi^-(g(\sigma W_1 + x))]. \tag{22}$$

Proof. We shall prove the claims for u^+ only, the corresponding proof for u^- being analogous.

(1) Note that

$$u^+(t,x) = \int_{-\infty}^{\infty} \Pi^+(g(z)) \frac{1}{\sqrt{2\pi\sigma^2(1-t)}} \exp\left(-\frac{(x-z)^2}{2\sigma^2(1-t)}\right) dz.$$

Then, if β is a Brownian motion on a filtered probability space $(\Omega, \mathcal{F}, (\mathcal{F}_t), \mathbb{P})$ with $\beta_0 = 0$, $u^+(t, B_t)$ is a bounded martingale with $u^+(1, B_1) = \Pi^+(g(B_1)$, where $B = \sigma\beta + x$. Thus, we can define a new measure $\mathbb{Q}$ on $(\Omega, \mathcal{F})$ by

$$\frac{d\mathbb{Q}}{d\mathbb{P}} = \frac{u(1, B_1)}{u(0, B_0)}.$$

By means of Girsanov's theorem, under $\mathbb{Q}$, B solves (20).

(2) Observe that

$$\begin{aligned}\phi_g^+(x) &= \frac{\mathbb{E}\left[\Psi^+(g(B_1))\Pi^+(g(B_1))\right]}{\mathbb{E}\left[\Pi^+(g(B_1))\right]} \\ &= \frac{\mathbb{E}\left[\Psi^+(g(B_1))u^+(1,B_1)\right]}{\mathbb{E}\left[u(1,B_1)\right]} = \mathbb{E}^{\mathbb{Q}}\left[\Psi^+(g(B_1))\right].\end{aligned}$$

(3) The claim is equivalent to

$$\begin{aligned}&\int_{-\infty}^{\infty} \Phi^+(g(z))q(\sigma,z)dz \int_{-\infty}^{\infty} \Pi^-(g(z))q(\sigma,z)dz \\ &\quad - \int_{-\infty}^{\infty} \Phi^-(g(z))q(\sigma,z)dz \int_{-\infty}^{\infty} \Pi^+(g(z))q(\sigma,z)dz > 0.\end{aligned}$$

Using $\Phi^+ = E[V] - \Phi^-$ and $\Pi^+ + \Pi^- = 1$, the above is valid if and only if

$$0 < \int_{-\infty}^{\infty} \Phi^+(g(z))q(\sigma, z)dz - E[V] \int_{-\infty}^{\infty} \Pi^+(g(z))q(\sigma, z)dz$$
$$= \int_{-\infty}^{\infty} \left(\Psi^+(g(z)) - E[V]\right) q(\sigma, z)\Pi^+(g(z))dz,$$

which holds since for any x we have $\Psi^+(x) \geq \Psi^+(m) = E[V]$ in view of Lemma A.1 and Ψ^+ is not constant.

(4) Now, suppose g is non-decreasing, which in turn implies $u_x^+ \leq 0$ since Π^+ is non-increasing. Therefore, as $\frac{u_x(t,x)}{u(t,x)}$ is Lipschitz on $[0, t]$ for any $t < T$, the standard comparison results for SDEs applied to (20) in conjunction with Lemma A.1 imply

$$\mathbb{E}^{\mathbb{Q}}\left[\Psi^+(g(B_1))\middle|B_0 = y\right] \geq \mathbb{E}^{\mathbb{Q}}\left[\Psi^+(g(B_1))\middle|B_0 = x\right] \quad \text{if } y \geq x$$

since we can construct all these solutions indexed by their starting point on the same probability space due to the local Lipschitz property of u_x^+/u^+. This shows the desired monotonicity ϕ_g^+. Similarly, the same comparison principle yields that the solution of (20) is bounded from above by $\sigma W_t + x$ in case of $u = u^+$ since $u_x^+ \leq 0$. Combined with the monotonicity property of $\Psi^+(g)$, we deduce $\phi_g^+(x) \leq \mathbb{E}^{\mathbb{Q}}\left[\Psi^+(g(\sigma W_1 + x))\right]$.

□

Proof of Theorem 3.2 The proof will be an application of Schauder's fixed-point theorem. Note that since V takes values in $[m, M]$, so does $\Psi^{\pm}$. This justifies the representation (15) for F. Since in equilibrium h must also be taking values in $[m, M]$, we must expect F to take values in $[m, M]$, too. Thus, we can concentrate on functions on $\mathbb{R}$ that take values in $[m, M]$. Moreover, F will possess a derivative that is bounded by

$$K_0 := (|m| + M) \int_{-\infty}^{\infty} |z| \frac{e^{-\frac{z^2}{2\sigma^2}}}{\sigma^3\sqrt{2\pi}} dz \left(\frac{1}{N} + \frac{N-1}{2N}\right) < \infty.$$

To see this, first observe that

$$\begin{aligned}\frac{\partial \bar{q}(\sigma, x, z)}{\partial x} &= \frac{q(\sigma, x-z) - \bar{q}(\sigma, x, z)}{x}\\ &= \frac{1}{x^2}\int_0^x \{q(\sigma, x-z) - q(\sigma, y-z)dy\}\\ &= \frac{1}{x^2}\int_0^x uq_x(\sigma, u-z)du.\end{aligned}$$

Therefore,

$$\begin{aligned}\left|\frac{d}{dx}F(x)\right| &\leq \int_{-\infty}^{\infty} |\phi_F(z)| \left\{\frac{|q_x(\sigma, x-z)|}{N}\right.\\ &\quad \left. + \frac{N-1}{Nx^2}\int_0^{|x|} u|q_x(\sigma, u-z)|du\right\} dz\\ &\leq (|m| + M)\left\{\frac{1}{N}\int_{-\infty}^{\infty} |z-x|\frac{e^{-\frac{(z-x)^2}{2\sigma^2}}}{\sigma^3\sqrt{2\pi}}dz\right.\\ &\quad \left. + \frac{N-1}{Nx^2}\int_0^{|x|} duu \int_{-\infty}^{\infty} |z-u|\frac{e^{-\frac{(z-u)^2}{2\sigma^2}}}{\sigma^3\sqrt{2\pi}}dz\right\}\\ &= (|m| + M)\int_{-\infty}^{\infty} |z|\frac{e^{-\frac{z^2}{2\sigma^2}}}{\sigma^3\sqrt{2\pi}}dz\left(\frac{1}{N} + \frac{N-1}{2N}\right).\end{aligned}$$

We shall show the existence of a fixed point in the normed space $\mathcal{X} := L^2(\mathbb{R}, \mu_0)$, i.e., the space of Borel measurable functions that are square integrable with respect to μ_0, where

$$\mu_0(dx) = \frac{1}{\sqrt{2\pi}}e^{-\frac{x^2}{2}}dx.$$

Note that μ_0 is equivalent to the Lebesgue measure on $\mathbb{R}$. Next define

$$\begin{aligned}D_0 : \{g | g : \mathbb{R} \mapsto [m, M] \text{ is such that } |g(x) - g(y)|\\ \leq K_0|x-y|, \forall x, y \in \mathbb{R}\}\end{aligned}$$

and let

$$D := \{g \in \mathcal{X} | g = g_0,\ \mu_0\text{-a.e. for some } g_0 \in D_0\}.$$

It is easy to see that D is a convex subset of $\mathcal{X}$.

Next define the operator T on $\mathcal{X}$ via

$$Tg(x) := \int_{-\infty}^{\infty} \left\{ \frac{1}{N} q(\sigma, x-z) + \frac{N-1}{N} \bar{q}(\sigma, x, z) \right\} \phi_{\bar{g}}(z) dz,$$

where $\bar{g} := (g \vee m) \wedge M$ and ϕ_g and $\bar{q}$ are as defined in (13) and (16), respectively. Note that for each x,

$$\left\{ \frac{1}{N} q(\sigma, x-z) + \frac{N-1}{N} \bar{q}(\sigma, x, z) \right\} dz$$

is a probability measure on $\mathbb{R}$.

Step 1 *(T maps D into itself):* It is easy to verify that Tg is continuous and takes values in $[m, M]$ in view of Lemma 4.1 and that

$$\int_{-\infty}^{\infty} \left\{ \frac{1}{N} q(\sigma, x-z) + \frac{N-1}{N} \bar{q}(\sigma, x, z) \right\} dz = 1.$$

Moreover, Tg is differentiable with a derivative bounded by K_0 by using the above computations that led to the estimate K_0. Thus, $Tg \in D_0 \subset D$.

Step 2 *(D is compact):* Let $(g_n) \subset D$. Then there exists $(g_n^0) \subset D_0$ such that μ_0-a.e. we have $g_n = g_n^0$ for each $n \geq 1$. Then by Arzela–Ascoli theorem, there exists a subsequence that converges uniformly on compacts to a continuous function g^0. Without loss of generality, let us assume that g_n^0 converges to g^0. Note that necessarily $|g^0(x) - g^0(y)| \leq K_0|x-y|$ for all $x, y \in \mathbb{R}$, i.e., $g^0 \in D_0$. Finally, as g_ns are uniformly bounded and μ_0 is a probability measure, the dominated convergence theorem yields $g_n \to g^0$ in $L^2(\mathbb{R}, \mu_0)$.

Step 3 *($T : D \to D$ is continuous):* Suppose $g_n \to g$ in D as $n \to \infty$. In view of the definition of D, we may assume without loss of generality that g_ns are continuous since changing g_n on a Lebesgue null set does not alter the value of Tg_n. By another application of Arzela–Ascoli theorem, there exists a subsequence that converges pointwise to some continuous function, which we may identify with g due to the uniqueness of L^2-limits up to a null set. Thus, we may assume g is continuous, too.

Moreover, the same argument shows that every subsequence of g_n has a further subsequence that converges to g pointwise since continuous functions that agree on Lebesgue null sets should agree at every point. Thus, $g_n \to g$ pointwise as $n \to \infty$.

Next, since ϕ_{g_n} is uniformly bounded, the dominated convergence theorem yields

$$\lim_{n\to\infty} Tg_n(x) = \int_{-\infty}^{\infty} dz \left\{ \frac{1}{N} q(\sigma, x - z) + \frac{N-1}{N} \bar{q}(\sigma, x, z) \right\} \times \lim_{n\to\infty} \phi_{g_n}(z).$$

On the other hand, Lemma 4.1 and Girsanov theorem imply for $z > 0$

$$\phi_{g_n}(z) = \frac{\mathbb{E}\left[\Psi^+(g_n(\sigma\beta_1 + z))\Pi^+(g_n(\sigma\beta_1 + z))\right]}{u^n(0, z)},$$

where $\mathbb{E}$ is the expectation operator for $\mathbb{P}$ under which β is a standard Brownian motion, and u^n is the function u^+ in Lemma 4.1 defined by the terminal condition $\Pi^+(g_n)$. Since Ψ^+ and Π^+ are continuous except on a Lebesgue null set, the dominated convergence theorem yields

$$\begin{aligned}&\lim_{n\to\infty} \mathbb{E}[\Psi^+(g_n(\sigma\beta_1 + z))\Pi^+(g_n(\sigma\beta_1 + z))] \\ &\quad = \mathbb{E}[\Psi^+(g(\sigma\beta_1 + z))\Pi^+(g(\sigma\beta_1 + z))].\end{aligned}$$

Similarly,

$$\begin{aligned}\lim_{n\to\infty} u^n(0, z) &= \lim_{n\to\infty} \mathbb{E}[\Pi^+(g_n(\sigma\beta_1 + z))] \\ &= \mathbb{E}[\Pi^+(g(\sigma\beta_1 + z))].\end{aligned}$$

Thus, we have shown $\lim_{n\to\infty} \phi_{g_n}(z) = \phi_g(z)$ for $z > 0$. Analogous arguments yield the convergence for $z \le 0$, which in turn establishes the pointwise convergence of Tg_n to T_g, i.e.,

$$\lim_{n\to\infty} Tg_n(x) = Tg(x), \qquad x \in \mathbb{R}.$$

This yields the claim by an application of the dominated convergence theorem since Tg_ns are uniformly bounded.

Therefore, there exists a $g \in D$ such that $g = Tg$ by Schauder's fixed point theorem. The claim now follows from Theorem 3.1. □

Under the hypotheses of Theorem 3.2, it is clear that $m < F(x) < M$ for $x \in \mathbb{R}$. However, in view of the bounds given by (21) and (22), it is possible to obtain sharper bounds on any solution of (14).

Theorem 4.1. *Suppose $-\infty < m < M < \infty$ and let $\Psi^{\pm}$ be as in (18). Then the following statements are valid.*

(1) *There exists a maximal non-decreasing solution*[5] *to*

$$\begin{aligned} R(x) = & \int_0^{\infty} dz \left\{ \frac{1}{N} q(\sigma, x - z) + \frac{N-1}{N} \bar{q}(\sigma, x, z) \right\} \\ & \times \int_{-\infty}^{\infty} \Psi^{+}(R(y)) q(\sigma, z - y) dy \\ & + E[V] \int_{-\infty}^{0} dz \left\{ \frac{1}{N} q(\sigma, x - z) + \frac{N-1}{N} \bar{q}(\sigma, x, z) \right\}. \end{aligned} \tag{23}$$

Moreover, this maximal solution is not constant and any solution of (14) is bounded from above by this maximal solution.

(2) *There exists a minimal nondecreasing solution*[6] *to*

$$\begin{aligned} l(x) = & E[V] \int_0^{\infty} dz \left\{ \frac{1}{N} q(\sigma, x - z) + \frac{N-1}{N} \bar{q}(\sigma, x, z) \right\} \\ & + \int_{-\infty}^{0} dz \left\{ \frac{1}{N} q(\sigma, x - z) + \frac{N-1}{N} \bar{q}(\sigma, x, z) \right. \\ & \left. \times \int_{-\infty}^{\infty} \Psi^{-}(l(y)) q(\sigma, z - y) dy \right\}. \end{aligned} \tag{24}$$

Moreover, this minimal solution is not constant and any solution of (14) is bounded from below by this minimal solution.

[5] R is a maximal non-decreasing solution if $R(x) \geq r(x)$ for all $x \in \mathbb{R}$, where r is any other non-decreasing solution.

[6] l is a minimal non-decreasing solution if $l(x) \leq L(x)$ for all $x \in \mathbb{R}$, where L is any other non-decreasing solution.

Proof.

(1) Let $\mathcal{D}$ be the space of nondecreasing functions on $\mathbb{R}$ that take values in $[m, M]$ and define an operator T on $\mathcal{D}$ via

$$\begin{aligned} Tr(x) = & \int_0^\infty dz \left\{ \frac{1}{N} q(\sigma, x-z) + \frac{N-1}{N} \bar{q}(\sigma, x, z) \right\} \\ & \times \int_{-\infty}^{\infty} \Psi^+(r(y)) q(\sigma, z-y) dy \\ & + E[V] \int_{-\infty}^{0} dz \left\{ \frac{1}{N} q(\sigma, x-z) + \frac{N-1}{N} \bar{q}(\sigma, x, z) \right\}. \end{aligned}$$

First, observe that $Tr_1 \geq Tr_2$ if $r_1 \leq r_2$ since Ψ^+ is non-decreasing. Thus, setting $r_0 \equiv m$ and $r_n = Tr_{n-1}$ for $n \geq 1$, we observe that r_n is an increasing sequence of non-decreasing continuous functions taking values in $[m, M]$. Thus, the limit, r_∞ exists, is non-decreasing and continuous by Dini's theorem. It also follows from the dominated convergence theorem and that Ψ^+ has only countably many discontinuities that r_∞ is a solution of (23).

Now let $\mathcal{E}$ denote the set of all solutions of (23) in $\mathcal{D}$ and define

$$R^*(x) := \sup_{r \in \mathcal{E}} r(x).$$

Clearly, R^* takes values in $[m, M]$. Due to the aforementioned monotonicity, $TR^* \geq Tr = r$ for all $r \in \mathcal{E}$. Consequently, $TR^* \geq R^*$. Setting $g_0 = R^*$ and $g_n = Tg_{n-1}$ for $n \geq 1$, we again obtain an increasing sequence which converges to some element r of $\mathcal{E}$. Moreover, $r \geq R^*$, which in turn implies $r = R^*$ by the construction of R^*.

Note that if R^* is constant, it has to equal M since $R^*(\infty) = M$. However, under this assumption, the right side of (23) equals

$$\begin{aligned} & \int_0^\infty dz \left\{ \frac{1}{N} q(\sigma, x-z) + \frac{N-1}{N} \bar{q}(\sigma, x, z) \right\} \\ & \quad \times (M \mathbf{1}_{z>0} + E[V] \mathbf{1}_{z<0}) < M \end{aligned}$$

as $E[V] < M$. Thus, R^* cannot be constant.

To show the final assertion, let F be a solution of (14). Since $\Psi^- \leq E[V]$ and that $\phi_F^+(z) \leq \int_{-\infty}^{\infty} \Psi^+(F(y))q(\sigma, z-y)dy$ by (21), we deduce that

$$F(x) \leq TF(x).$$

As above, setting $g_0 = F$ and $g_n = Tg_{n-1}$ for $n \geq 1$, we again obtain an increasing sequence which converges to a member of $\mathcal{E}$, which proves the claim.

(2) Since $\Psi^- \leq E[V]$, the proof follows the similar lines as above and, hence, omitted. □

5. Market Impact Asymptotics

The shape of market impact as a function of trade size is important to practitioners to address capacity and position sizing. Various functional forms have been explored in the literature (see, e.g., Refs. [3], [12], [23], and [28]), including $\sqrt{X}$ and $\log(1+aX)$. Rejecting either of these forms empirically is challenging due to three practical difficulties: (1) the spread and market impact terms are collinear for small orders, (2) signal-to-noise ratios are weak for executions that take a small percentage of market volume and (3) for very large trades, order sizes are often increased if liquidity is available or reduced if liquidity is hard to find, leading to bias in the data. In the absence of clear empirical evidence, theoretical predictions for the shape of market impact provide valuable insight into how trading costs scale with trade size.

Motivated by this need, we draw our attention in this section to the *market impact* associated with large orders. More precisely, we will be computing the asymptotics of the marginal cost of trades, which is given by the function F. As we shall see later, the asymptotic form of F will coincide (up to a scaling factor) with that of the implementation shortfall IS. We will also be able to compute the tail asymptotics of the distribution of the total demand in equilibrium using *the theory of regular variation.*

Definition 5.1. A function $g : (0, \infty) \to (0, \infty)$ is said to be *regularly varying of index* ρ at ∞ if

$$\lim_{\lambda \to \infty} \frac{g(\lambda x)}{g(\lambda)} = x^\rho, \quad \forall x > 0.$$

Analogously, a function $g : (-\infty, 0) \to (0, \infty)$ is said to be regularly varying of index ρ at $-\infty$ if $g(-x)$ is regularly varying of index ρ at ∞.

Roughly speaking, a function of regular variation behaves like a power function asymptotically. We shall obtain our asymptotic results under a mild condition on the distribution of V.

Assumption 5.1. Π^+ has a continuous derivative on (m, M). Moreover, $\Psi_x^+(M) := \lim_{x\to M} \frac{d}{dx}\Psi^+(x)$ and $\Psi_x^-(m) := \lim_{x\to m} \frac{d}{dx}\Psi^-(x)$ exist and equal the left and right derivatives, respectively, at finite end points. Moreover, $\Psi_x^+(M)\Psi_x^-(m) \neq 0$[7].

Observe that when M is finite and the left derivative of Ψ^+ at M exists,

$$\Psi_x^+(M) = \lim_{x\to M} \frac{M - \Psi^+(x)}{M - x} \leq \lim_{x\to M} \frac{M - x}{M - x} = 1.$$

Similarly, $\Psi_x^-(m) \leq 1$ if m is finite under an analogous condition.

In this section, we will mainly focus on the asymptotics of F and IS. However, it is easy to see from (4) that F and h behave similarly for large values. For a more rigorous demonstration, suppose $M - F$ is regularly varying at ∞ with exponent ρ^+. Recalling the measure ν defined in (B.50), we formally obtain

$$\begin{aligned}\lim_{x\to\infty} \frac{M - h(x)}{M - F(x)} &= \lim_{x\to\infty} \int_{-\infty}^{\infty} \nu(x, 1, dy) \frac{M - \Psi^+(F(xy))}{M - F(x)} \\ &= \Psi_x^+(M) 1^{\rho^+} = \Psi_x^+(M),\end{aligned} \tag{25}$$

using the mean value theorem and the continuity of the derivative of Ψ^+ together with the fact that the F is regularly varying with index ρ^+ since the measure $\nu(x, 1, dy)$ converges to the point mass at 1 as $x \to \infty$. This shows that marginal price is also regularly varying with the same index ρ^+.

The next result is the first description of the asymptotics of solutions of (14).

---

[7] This last condition is automatically satisfied if $M = \infty$ and $m = -\infty$ since $\Psi^+(\infty) = -\Psi^-(-\infty) = \infty$.

Theorem 5.1. *Assume Assumption 5.1, $N > 1$ and $-\infty < m < M < \infty$. Let F be any solution of (14). Then, the following statements are valid:*

(1) *$M - F$ is regularly varying of index ρ^+ at ∞, with $\rho^+ = \frac{\Psi_x^+(M)-1}{1-\frac{\Psi_x^+(M)}{N}}$. Moreover, if $\Psi_x^+(M) = 1$ and there exist an integer $n \geq 1$ and a real constant $k \in (0, \infty)$ such that*[8]

$$\lim_{x \to M} \frac{\Psi^+(x) - x}{(M - x)^{n+1}} = \frac{1}{k},$$

the following asymptotics hold:

$$M - F(x) \sim \left(\frac{N}{N-1}\frac{n}{k}\right)^{-\frac{1}{n}} (\log x)^{-\frac{1}{n}}, \quad x \to \infty. \tag{26}$$

(2) *$F - m$ is regularly varying of index ρ^- at $-\infty$, with $\rho^- = \frac{\Psi_x^-(m)-1}{1-\frac{\Psi_x^-(m)}{N}}$. Moreover, if $\Psi_x^-(m) = 1$, and there exist an integer $n \geq 1$ and a real constant $k \in (0, \infty)$ such that*

$$\lim_{x \to m} \frac{x - \Psi^-(x)}{(x - m)^{n+1}} = \frac{1}{k},$$

then

$$F(x) - m \sim \left(\frac{N}{N-1}\frac{n}{k}\right)^{-\frac{1}{n}} (\log |x|)^{-\frac{1}{n}}, \quad x \to -\infty. \tag{27}$$

---

[8] In case $\Psi_x^+(M) \neq 1$, this limit condition is valid with $n = 0$ and $k = (1 - \Psi_x^+(M))^{-1}$. Thus, this additional regularity assumption can be viewed as an extension of the existing regularity that holds when $\rho^+ \neq 0$. In particular, if V has a probability density p with

$$p(x) \propto (M - x)^\beta \exp\left(-\frac{\Sigma}{(M - x)^n}\right),$$

for some $\beta \in \mathbb{R}$, $\Sigma > 0$, and $n \geq 1$, the limit condition holds with $k = n\Sigma$. Analogous considerations apply in the second part.

The lengthy and technical proof of the above result is given in the Appendix. However, we can give a quick motivation of why the regular variation exponent is as given. To this end, define $\gamma(x) := \lim_{\alpha\to\infty} \frac{M-F(\alpha x)}{M-F(\alpha)}$ for $x \geq 1$. Then, using the integral equation (14) and taking the appropriate ratios, one can formally 'show' that

$$\gamma(x) = \frac{\Psi_x^+(M)}{N}\gamma(x) + \Psi_x^+(M)\frac{N-1}{Nx}\int_0^x \gamma(y)dy.$$

The initial condition $\gamma(1) = 1$ next reveals that $\gamma(x) = x^{\rho^+}$.

Observe that the asymptotic shape of marginal costs (or, equivalently, marginal prices) is independent of the noise variance. This stems from the tail expectation condition that defines the order book. Recall that, for $y > 0$, the marginal price of the yth share purchased is given by $h(y) = E[V|F(y+Z)]$. Since the noise demand Z is mostly concentrated around two standard deviations in the neighborhood of 0, i.e., the large trades are most likely coming from the informed traders, the impact of the noise distribution on the asymptotic behavior of the marginal price is negligible in equilibrium. This is also responsible for the price impact depending on return distribution only by its tail.

Indeed, the power law of the price impact only depends on the number of insiders, i.e., the intensity of the competition among the informed, and the particular tail mass index $\Psi_x^+(M)$. To see why $\Psi_x^+(M) < 1$ is an indication of fat tails, consider the situation where the distribution Π^+ exhibit fat tails, i.e., power-like behavior, in the sense that for large x,

$$\frac{\Pi_x^+(x)}{\Pi^+(x)} \sim -\alpha(M-x)^{-1}, \quad \alpha > 0.$$

Since $\frac{M-\Psi^+(x)}{M-x} = \frac{\int_x^M \Pi^+(y)dy}{(M-x)\Pi^+(x)} - 1$, a direct application of the L'Hôpital rule implies $\Psi_x^+(M) = \frac{\alpha}{1+\alpha} < 1$. This shows in view of Theorem 5.1 that the price impact obeys a power law when the arithmetic return of the risky asset has a fat-tailed distribution.

In the preceding example, the magnitude of ρ^+ equals $\frac{1}{1+\alpha\frac{N-1}{N}}$. That is, the impact gets bigger as the returns distribution has fatter tails (smaller α) and increased competition among insiders results in smaller impact. We shall see analogous features when we discuss unbounded return distributions in Section 7.

We have seen in Proposition 2.2 that the implementation shortfall is smaller than F. In view of Theorem 5.1, we have a more precise relationship for large x.

Corollary 5.1. *Assume Assumption 5.1, $N > 1$ and $-\infty < m < M < \infty$, and let (h^*, X^*) be an equilibrium. Suppose that F^* is given by (4), with h being replaced by h^*. Then,*

$$M - IS^*(x) \sim \frac{N}{N+\rho^+}(M - F^*(x)), \qquad x \to \infty,$$
$$IS^*(x) - m \sim \frac{N}{N+\rho^-}(F^*(x) - m), \qquad x \to -\infty,$$

where ρ^+ and ρ^- are as in Theorem 5.1.

Corollary 5.1 shows that for large N implementation shortfall and the marginal cost of trading are almost indistinguishable. This is even more pronounced when $M - F$ (resp., $F - m$) is slowly varying, i.e., $\rho^+ = 0$ (resp., $\rho^- = 0$). Combined with (25), the above yields

$$M - IS^*(x) \sim \frac{N - \Psi_x^+(M)}{\Psi_x^+(M)(N-1)+}(M - h^*(x)), \qquad x \to \infty.$$

Observe that IS can be estimated from market data using the open limit order book governed by h. Moreover, the returns distribution, hence $\Psi_x^+(M)$, can be estimated from the option data. Thus, the above relationship gives a statistic to estimate the number of informed traders in the market.

5.1. *Equilibrium Distribution of the Traded Volume*

The above results will also allow us to compute the distribution of the traded volume in equilibrium. Although this will be achieved under an additional regularity assumption on the distribution of the asset value V, it will be satisfied for practically all distributions typically appearing in applications.

Corollary 5.2. *Assume Assumption 5.1, $N > 1$ and $-\infty < m < M < \infty$. Let F be any solution of (14). Then, the following statements are valid:*

(1) *Suppose that there exist an integer* $n \geq 0$ *and a real constant* $k \in (0, \infty)$ *such that*

$$\lim_{x \to M} \frac{\Psi^+(x) - x}{(M - x)^{n+1}} = \frac{1}{k}.$$

Then, $\Pi^+(F)$ *is regularly varying at* ∞ *of index* $-\frac{\Psi_x^+(M)}{1 - \frac{\Psi_x^+(M)}{N}}$.

(2) *Suppose that there exist an integer* $n \geq 0$ *and a real constant* $k \in (0, \infty)$ *such that*

$$\lim_{x \to M} \frac{x - \Psi^-(x)}{(x - m)^{n+1}} = \frac{1}{k}.$$

Then, $\Pi^-(F)$ *is regularly varying at* $-\infty$ *of index* $-\frac{\Psi_x^-(m)}{1 - \frac{\Psi_x^-(m)}{N}}$.

This seemingly technical result uncovers the distribution of the total volume traded in equilibrium. Indeed, for $x > 0$,

$$P(X^* > x) = P(F^{-1}(V) > x) = P(V > F(x)) = \Pi^+(F(x)).$$

Thus, under the hypothesis of Corollary 5.2, the tail distribution of equilibrium X^* is regularly varying at infinity. That is,

$$P(X^* > x) = x^{-\zeta^+} s(x),$$

where s is a slowly varying function and $\zeta^+ := \frac{\Psi_x^+(M)}{1 - \frac{\Psi_x^+(M)}{N}}$.

Moreover, since the aggregate order is given by $Y^* = X^* + Z$ and Z and V are independent, we have for $y > 0$

$$\begin{aligned} P(Y^* > y) &= \int_{-\infty}^{\infty} dz P(X^* > y - z) q(\sigma, z) \\ &= \int_{-\infty}^{\infty} dz P(X^* > z) q(\sigma, y - z), \end{aligned}$$

which can easily be shown to be regularly varying at infinity with the same index. Thus,

$$P(Y^* > y) = y^{-\zeta^+} s(y), \quad y > 0, \tag{28}$$

for some regularly varying s. In particular, if V has lighter tails, i.e., $\Psi_x^+(M) = 1$, $P(Y^* > y)$ is regularly varying of index $-\frac{N}{N-1}$.

Analogous computations yield for the sell side

$$P(Y^* < -y) = y^{-\zeta^-} s(y), \quad y > 0, \tag{29}$$

where $\zeta^- := \frac{\Psi_x^-(m)}{1-\frac{\Psi_x^-(m)}{N}}$.

6. Further Properties of Equilibrium and Comparative Statics

The following scaling property of F is inherited from the analogous property of the Gaussian distribution:

Proposition 6.1. *Let $F(1;\cdot)$ be a solution of (14) with $\sigma = 1$. Then the function $x \mapsto F(1;\frac{x}{\sigma})$ solves (14).*

Proof.

$$\begin{aligned}
F\Big(1;\frac{x}{\sigma}\Big) &= \frac{1}{N}\int_{-\infty}^{\infty} q\Big(1,\frac{x}{\sigma}-z\Big)\phi_F(z)dz \\
&\quad + \sigma\frac{N-1}{Nx}\int_0^{\frac{x}{\sigma}} dy\int_{-\infty}^{\infty} q(1,y-z)\phi_F(z)dz \\
&= \frac{1}{N}\int_{-\infty}^{\infty} q\Big(\sigma,x-z\Big)\phi_F\Big(\frac{z}{\sigma}\Big)dz \\
&\quad + \frac{N-1}{Nx}\int_0^{x} dy\int_{-\infty}^{\infty} q\Big(1,\frac{y}{\sigma}-z\Big)\phi_F(z)dz \\
&= \frac{1}{N}\int_{-\infty}^{\infty} q\Big(\sigma,x-z\Big)\phi_F\Big(\frac{z}{\sigma}\Big)dz \\
&\quad + \frac{N-1}{Nx}\int_0^{x} dy\int_{-\infty}^{\infty} q(\sigma,y-z)\phi_F\Big(\frac{z}{y}\Big)dz.
\end{aligned}$$

Similar manipulations yield

$$\phi_F^{\pm}\Big(\frac{z}{y}\Big) = \frac{\int_{-\infty}^{\infty}\Phi^{\pm}\Big(F\Big(1;\frac{u}{y}\Big)\Big)q\Big(\sigma,u-z\Big)du}{\int_{-\infty}^{\infty}\Pi^{\pm}\Big(F\Big(1;\frac{u}{y}\Big)\Big)q(\sigma,u-z)du},$$

which establishes the claim. □

The above simplifies the numerical analysis of the model considerably. A straightforward corollary to this result is the following, whose proof is left to the reader.

Corollary 6.1. *Consider the solutions of (14) for any σ.*

(1) *If (14) has a unique solution for some σ, it has a unique solution for all σs.*
(2) *If (14) has a unique solution for some σ, $F(0)$ does not depend on σ.*
(3) *Let $h(\sigma; \cdot)$ be the function defined via (11) and (12), where F is the unique solution of (14) for the given σ. Then, $h(\sigma; x) = h(1; \frac{x}{\sigma})$ for all $x \neq 0$.*
(4) *Suppose (14) has a unique solution for some σ and let $X^*(\sigma)$ be the optimal order size for the given σ. Then, $X^*(\sigma) = \sigma X^*(1)$.*

In particular, h inherits the same scaling property of F. A simple but striking consequence of this property concerns the equilibrium bid-ask spread. The following result is immediate, hence its proof is omitted.

Corollary 6.2. *Suppose that uniqueness holds for the solutions of (14). Then, $h(0+) - h(0-)$ does not depend on σ. Moreover, for fixed x, $h(x)$ is decreasing in σ for $x > 0$ and increasing in σ for $x < 0$. Consequently, the aggregate mid-spread S is decreasing in σ.*

The liquidity suppliers charge a minimal bid-ask spread that does not vanish even if the amount of 'noise' trading is excessively large. On the other hand, the spread associated with any trade size $y > 0$, i.e., $h(y) - h(-y)$, and, therefore, the aggregate mid-spread S is decreasing with the amount of noise trading, consistent with the experimental findings of Ref. [6]. Moreover, in the limit as $\sigma \to \infty$, the order book, i.e., gets flatten and converges to the one that yields transaction costs that are proportional to the order size.

Uniqueness of solutions also allows us to discuss the dependency of aggregate insider profit and the expected loss of noise traders on the noise variance. In particular, the aggregate profit of insiders is increasing in noise variance as expected. The following is a direct consequence of Proposition 2.1.

Corollary 6.3. *Suppose that uniqueness holds for the solutions of (14) and denote by $\pi(\sigma)$ the aggregate wealth of the insiders in equilibrium. Then, $\pi(\sigma) = \sigma\pi(1)$.*

Similarly, the expected loss of noise traders is given by $\sigma E[S(1, \sigma^{-1}|Z|)]$ where $S(1, \cdot)$ is the aggregate mid-spread function in equilibrium for $\sigma = 1$.

Another consequence of the uniqueness of solutions of (3.11) is that the aggregate expected profit of the insiders vanishes as $N \to \infty$.

Proposition 6.2. *Suppose that $-\infty < m < M < \infty$, there exists a unique solution F_N of (14) for each $N \geq 1$, and uniqueness holds for the solutions of*

$$F(x) = \frac{1}{x} \int_0^x dy \int_{-\infty}^{\infty} q(\sigma, y - z)\phi_F(z)dz. \tag{30}$$

Assume further that Π^+ is continuous. Then $F_\infty = \lim_{N\to\infty} F_N$ exists and solves (30). Moreover, $\lim_{N\to\infty} \pi^*(v) = 0$, where π^* is the aggregate expected profit as defined in (8).

Proof. First, observe that ϕ_F is bounded since V is. Thus the dominated convergence theorem in conjunction with the continuity of Π^+ and consequently that of Φ^+ and Φ^- show that both $\liminf F_N$ and $\limsup F_N$ solve (30). As (30) can have at most one solution, $F_\infty := \lim F_N$ exists.

Also note that F_∞ is strictly increasing and continuous by Lemma 3.1. Thus, $\lim_{N\to\infty} F_N^{-1}(v) = F_\infty^{-1}(v) \in \mathbb{R}$, and

$$\begin{aligned}
\lim_{N\to\infty} \pi^*(v) &= \lim_{N\to\infty} F_N^{-1}(v)N \int_0^1 (v - F_N(F_N^{-1}(v)y)y^{N-1}dy \\
&= F_\infty^{-1}(v) \lim_{N\to\infty} N \int_0^1 (v - F_N(F_N^{-1}(v)y)y^{N-1}dy.
\end{aligned}$$

Since each F_N takes values in (m, M), $\lim_{N\to\infty} F_N(F_N^{-1}(v)y) = F_\infty(F_\infty^{-1}(v)y)$ and the measure $Ny^{N-1}dy$ on $[0, 1]$ converges weakly to the point mass at 1, we have

$$\lim_{N\to\infty} N \int_0^1 (v - F_N(F_N^{-1}(v)y)y^{N-1}dy = v - F_\infty(F_\infty^{-1}(v)) = 0.$$

□

We believe the aggregate profit of the insiders decreases and the spread increases in the number of insiders. Although we are not able to prove these intuitive properties, it is observed in all numerical studies that we perform in the following section.

7. Numerical Studies

This section is devoted to the description of results obtained in the previous version via a naive numerical search for a fixed point: Starting with an F_0, we compute $F_{n+1} = TF_n$ until the distance between successive iterations becomes negligibly small, where TF corresponds to the right side of (14). Although the proofs of the statements concerning the existence of equilibrium and its asymptotics relied on a boundedness assumption, we shall also present the solutions to the fixed point problems associated with equilibria with unbounded signals.

Since σ can be absorbed into the units for measuring equity in view of Proposition 6.1, we will set $\sigma = 1$ in all numerical tests with no loss of generality in this section.

We consider first the case of bounded signals that was the focus of the previous section.

7.1. *Bounded Signals*

7.1.1. *Truncated Gaussian Distribution:*

If signals are drawn from the truncated Gaussian distribution with density $p(v) = \frac{1}{erf(\frac{M}{\sqrt{2\Sigma}})\sqrt{2\pi\Sigma}}e^{-\frac{v^2}{2\Sigma}}$ for $v \in [-M, M]$, the numerical solution for equilibrium F converges to the upper bound as $M - F(x) \sim 1/x^{\frac{N-1}{2N}}$ in accordance with the predictions of Theorem 5.1. We show F and the theoretical prediction for its asymptotic behavior in Figure 1.

7.1.2. *Logit-normal distribution:*

If price is a probability-weighted average over two possible outcomes $v_{\pm} = p_0 \pm 1$, where the probability is a sigmoidal function of a Gaussian generator potential g as $p = \frac{1}{1+e^{-g}}$, the signals distribution

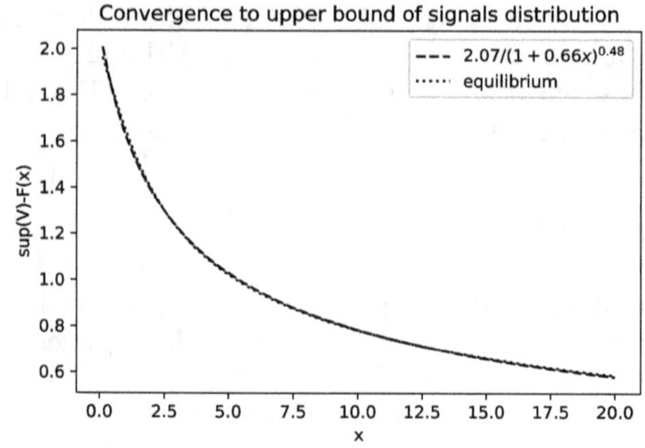

Figure 1. The asymptotic behavior of F is shown for the case where signals are drawn from a truncated Gaussian distribution.

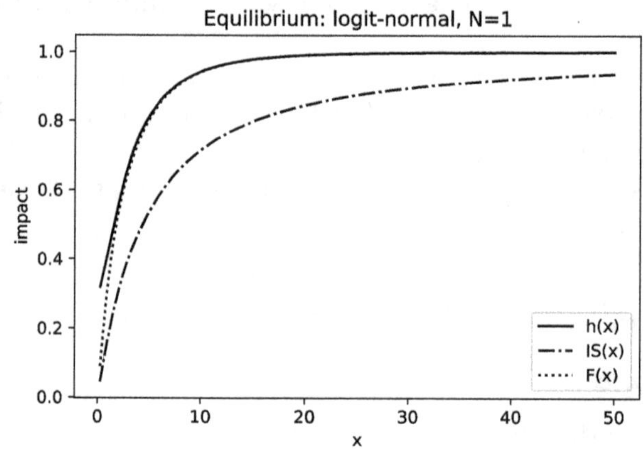

Figure 2. Equilibrium impact and shortfall for logit-normal signals for the case of an insider ($N = 1$).

is the logit-normal distribution with density $p(v) = \sqrt{\frac{2}{\pi\Sigma}} \frac{e^{-\frac{ln^2(\frac{1-v}{1+v})}{2\Sigma}}}{1-v^2}$. This distribution has support in $[-1, 1]$.

We show the equilibrium solution for F, the order book h and the implementation shortfall for logit-normal signals, in Figure 2.

Note that the logit normal distribution does not satisfy the hypothesis of Theorem 5.1. Thus, our theory cannot predict the asymptotics of F for this distribution. However, the following formal

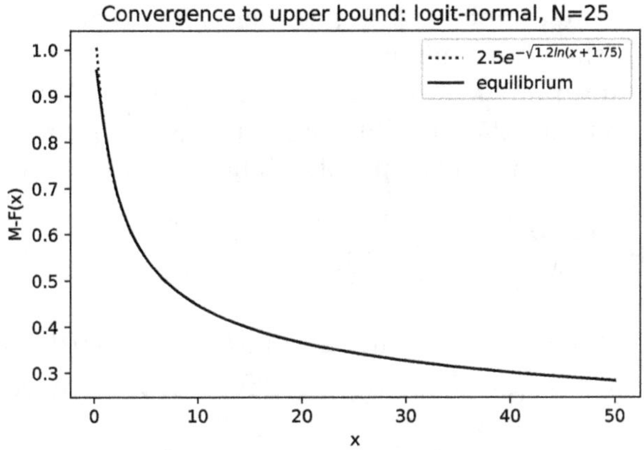

Figure 3. Convergence to the upper bound for $M = 1$ when signals are drawn from a logit-normal distribution and shared with $N = 25$ traders.

arguments yield the asymptotics that seem to be verified by the numerical experiments. Observe that for $x >> \sigma$, (4) becomes

$$F(x) \approx \frac{1}{N}h(x) + \frac{N-1}{Nx}\int_0^x h(u)du. \tag{31}$$

It follows that $F(x) + xF'(x) \approx h(x) + \frac{1}{N}xh'(x)$. Moreover, for large values of x, we roughly have $h(x) \approx \Psi^+(F(x))$. Let us consider the large N limit and drop the $1/N$ term. Using the approximation $erfc(x) \approx \frac{e^{-x^2}}{x\sqrt{\pi}}(1 - \frac{1}{2x^2})$ and expanding to first-order in $1/\log(x)$, we find that asymptotically

$$xF' = \frac{\Sigma(1-F)}{log(1-F)},$$

which yields $F \to 1 - e^{-k\sqrt{\log(x)}}$.

The numerical solution shown in Figure 3 for $N = 25$ is consistent with this asymptotic form.

7.2. *Unbounded Signals*

In the rest of this section, we place emphasis on unbounded signals, that is, when the support of V is unbounded. Although we do not have a theoretical justification for the existence of a solution for (14) in the case of unbounded signals, we were able to arrive at numerical solutions via the above numerical search.

The asymptotic behavior of $F(x)$ for large signals will depend on the tail behavior of the distribution of V. Assuming the interchange of limits and integrals in the proof of Theorem 5.1, we can show that

$$\gamma(x) = \frac{\Psi_x^+(\infty)}{N}\gamma(x) + \frac{N-1}{Nx}\Psi_x^+(\infty)\int_0^x \gamma(y)dy, \quad x > 0,$$

where $\gamma(x) := \lim_{\alpha\to\infty} \frac{F(\alpha x)}{F(\alpha)}$ in case of $M = \infty$. Solution of the above equation immediately yields that, for $N > 1$, F is regularly varying at ∞ of order ρ^+, where

$$\rho^+ = \frac{\Psi_x^+(\infty) - 1}{1 - \frac{\Psi_x^+(\infty)}{N}}. \tag{32}$$

Observe that when $M = \infty$, $\Psi_x^+(\infty) \geq 1$ in contrast to the bounded case, where $\Psi_x^+(M) \leq 1$. Since ρ^+ must be non-negative, this places the restriction on N:

$$N > \Psi_x^+(\infty) \tag{33}$$

unless $\Psi_x^+(\infty) = 1$. Thus, we conjecture that (33) is a necessary condition for the existence of equilibrium when $M = \infty$. Observe that for a fat-tailed unbounded distribution, $\Psi_x^+(\infty) > 1$. Thus, a sufficient competition among insiders is necessary for the equilibrium to exist. Such a condition is always satisfied in the bounded case since $\Psi_x^+(M) \leq 1$ for $M < \infty$.

As in the bounded case F will be slowly varying at infinity when $\Psi_x^+(\infty) = 1$. In this case, if we assume

$$\lim_{x\to\infty} (\Psi^+(x) - x)x^{n-1} = \frac{1}{k} \tag{34}$$

for some $k > 0$ and $n \geq 1$, formal calculations yield

$$F(x) \sim \left(\frac{N}{N-1}\frac{n}{k}\right)^{\frac{1}{n}} (\log x)^{\frac{1}{n}}, \quad x \to \infty. \tag{35}$$

Tables 1 and 2 summarize the predicted asymptotics for a class of distributions commonly used in the literature and practice. As can be

Table 1. Distributions with power-law impact.

Distribution	Density	ρ^+
Beta prime	$x^{\lambda-1}(1+x)^{-(\lambda+\alpha)}$	$\left(\frac{N-1}{N}\alpha-1\right)^{-1}$
Fréchet	$(x-\beta)^{-(1+\alpha)}\exp\left\{-\left(\frac{x-\beta}{s}\right)^{-\alpha}\right\}$	$\left(\frac{N-1}{N}\alpha-1\right)^{-1}$
Lomax	$\left(1+\frac{x}{\lambda}\right)^{-(\alpha+1)}$	$\left(\frac{N-1}{N}\alpha-1\right)^{-1}$
Pareto	$x^{-(\alpha+1)}$	$\left(\frac{N-1}{N}\alpha-1\right)^{-1}$
Student	$\left(1+\frac{x^2}{\alpha}\right)^{-(\alpha+1)/2}$	$\left(\frac{N-1}{N}\alpha-1\right)^{-1}$

Notes: In the above, probability densities are given up to a scaling factor and implicit constraints are enforced to ensure they are well defined with finite mean. Moreover, $N > \frac{\alpha}{\alpha-1}$ in all of the above.

Table 2. Distributions with logarithmic impact.

Distribution	Density	Asymptotics
Exponential	$\exp(-\lambda x)$	$\frac{N}{\lambda(N-1)}\log x$
Gaussian	$\exp(-(x-\mu)^2/\Sigma)$	$\sqrt{\frac{2\Sigma N}{N-1}}\sqrt{\log x}$
Inverse Gaussian	$x^{-3/2}\exp\left(-\frac{\lambda(x-\mu)^2}{2\mu^2 x}\right)$	$\frac{2N\mu^2}{\lambda(N-1)}\log x$
Normal Inverse Gaussian	$\frac{K_1(\lambda\zeta(x))}{\pi\zeta(x)}\exp(\delta\gamma+\beta(x-\mu))$	$\frac{N}{(N-1)(\lambda+\beta-1)}\log x$
Weibull	$x^{d-1}\exp(-\lambda^p x^p)$	$\left(\frac{N}{\lambda^p(N-1)}\right)^{1/p}(\log x)^{1/p}$

Notes: In the above, probability densities are given up to a scaling factor and implicit constraints are enforced to ensure they are well defined with finite mean. Moreover, $\zeta(x) := \delta^2 + (x-\mu)^2$ for the normal inverse Gaussian distribution.

observed by Table 1, the impact gets bigger as the return distribution has fatter tails (smaller α). At the same time, the market also needs more competition among the informed traders in order to function. Note that as $\alpha \to 1$, the mean and the variance of the distributions listed therein diverge to ∞. Thus, the liquidity suppliers are only willing to make the market if this excessive risk is shared with a large amount of informed trading.

7.2.1. *Gaussian signals*

We assume that the mean of V equals 0. The numerical solution is shown in Figure 4 together with the $\sqrt{\log x}$ asymptotic behavior.

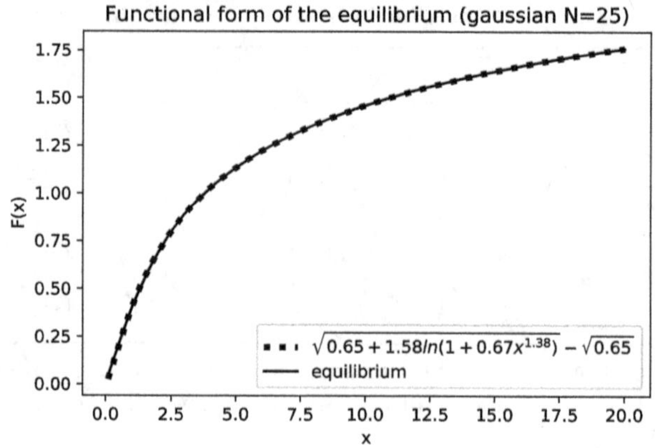

Figure 4. Functional form of the equilibrium for Gaussian signals, for $N = 25$.

7.2.2. *Lognormal signals*

For a lognormal distribution, the mean is an arbitrary scale factor which we set to 1 and, thus, the density is $p(v) = \frac{1}{\sqrt{2\pi\Sigma v}} e^{-\frac{(ln(v)+\Sigma/2)^2}{2\Sigma}}$. We choose a large signal variance $\sqrt{\Sigma} = 10\%$ in our numerical experiments below, illustrative of an earnings announcement for a high-volatility name. Moreover, we translate the distribution by 1 so that the mean is 0. The equilibrium solutions for h, F and IS are shown for various values of N in Figure 5.

The lognormal distribution does not satisfy the conditions of Theorem 5.1. Thus, we do not have a theoretical prediction for the asymptotic market impact. However, we find numerically that the asymptotic form is $\sqrt{\log(x)}$ in Figure 6. Evidence for more concave impact function than the square root was reported in Ref. [3]. In addition, one of us (HW) has had the opportunity to consider the shape of the impact function for asset managers with different order generation processes. We cite two relevant (unpublished) examples here. The impact function for a quantitative fund with no discernible intraday alpha is closest to a logarithmic one consistent with the findings of Bershova and Rakhlin. However, for a manager with non-discretionary executions rich in small-cap biopharmaceutical trades and other hard-to-execute orders, we found the log function to be too concave to explain the impact of large trades whereas a square root function fit the data well.

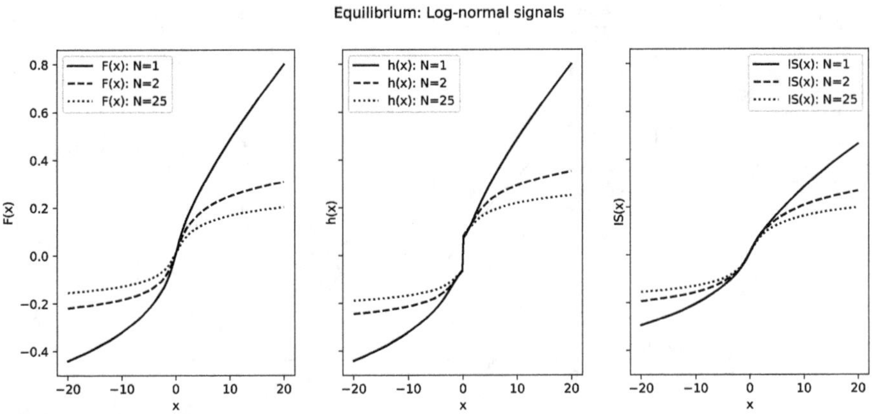

Figure 5. Equilibrium solutions for lognormal signals for the cases of an insider ($N = 1$) and shared signals with $N = 2$, $N = 25$. The discontinuity of $h(x)$ at the origin is the bid-ask spread.

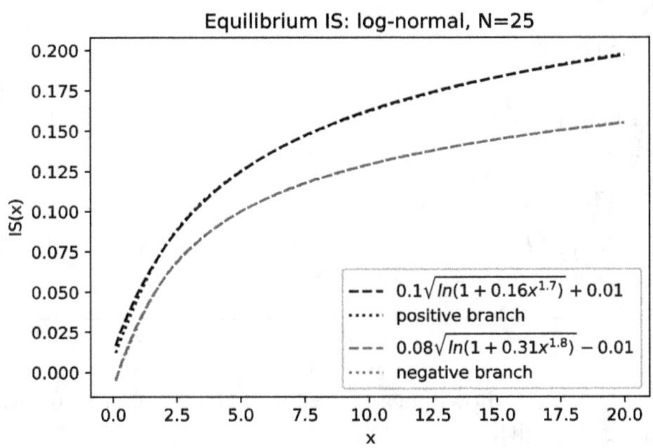

Figure 6. Functional form of the equilibrium for lognormal signals, for $N = 25$. The lognormal distribution is not symmetric and this results in a notable difference between the positive and negative branches for cost as a function of trade size.

The aggregate profit is a decreasing function of the number of informed investors and we show the profit as a function of trade size below for various values of N in Figure 7. Moreover, Figure 8 shows how the spread depends on the number of informed investors.

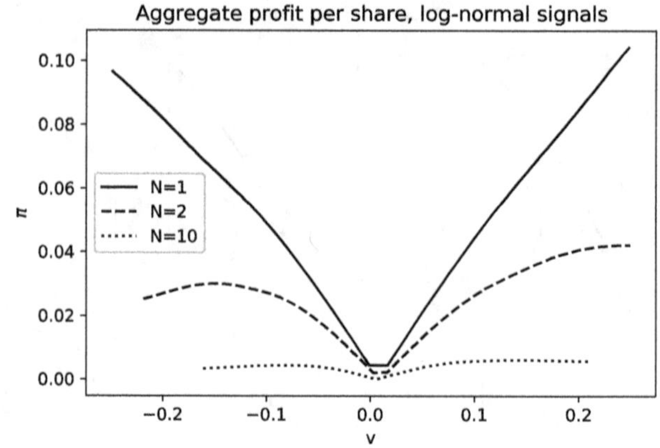

Figure 7. Aggregate investor profit per share for lognormal signals.

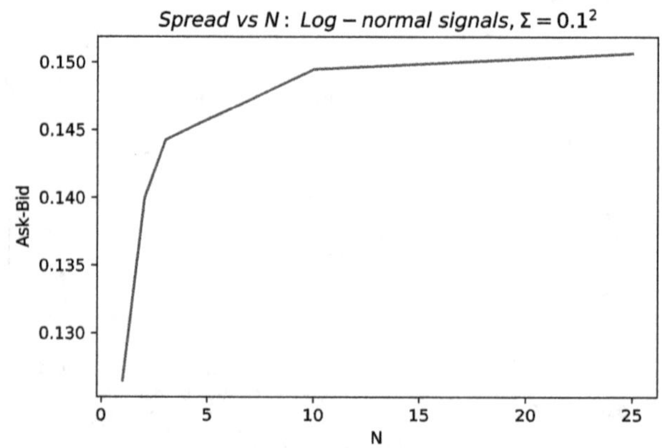

Figure 8. The spread is shown as a function of the number of informed investors, for lognormal signals with $\sqrt{\Sigma} = 10\%$.

7.2.3. *Student signals*

We explore the effect of fat tails in the signal distribution next. We consider the case where signals are drawn from a Student t-distribution with $\alpha = 3$, $p(v) \sim \frac{1}{(1+\frac{v^2}{\Sigma})^2}$. This is reminiscent of some empirical studies such as Ref. [22]. However, we note that we are assuming a Student distribution of *arithmetic* returns. The power-law tail of geometric returns in Plerou's study implies an infinite expected price.

In view of Table 1, the expected asymptotics is $F(x) \sim x^{1/(\alpha-1-\frac{\alpha}{N})}$. Moreover, our conjecture predicts no equilibrium when $N \le \frac{\alpha}{\alpha-1} = \frac{3}{2}$. Indeed, no numerical solution for F can be found when $N = 1$. The equilibrium is asymptotically parabolic for $N = 2$ (theoretical $\rho^+ = 2$), linear for $N = 3$ (theoretical $\rho^+ = 1$) and concave for $N \ge 4$. The numerical solutions are shown in Figure 9. For $N = 25$, the asymptotic exponent is $F(x) \sim x^{25/47}$ according to our theory. The numerical solution is compared to this prediction in Figure 10.

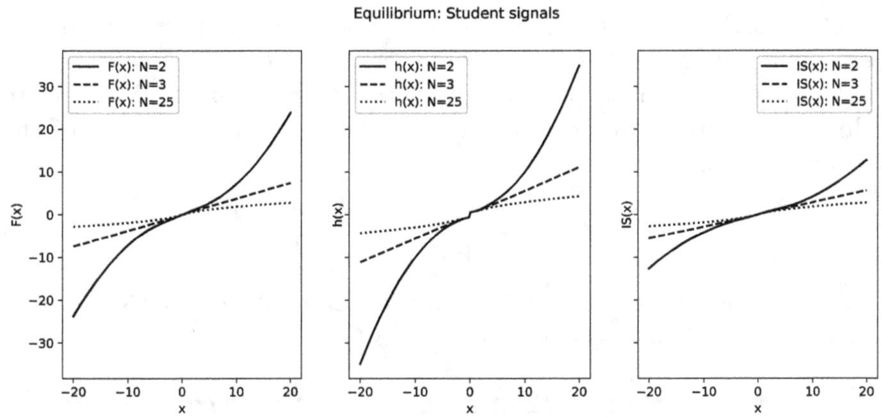

Figure 9. Equilibrium solutions for Student signals for the cases $N = 2$, $N = 3$ and $N = 25$.

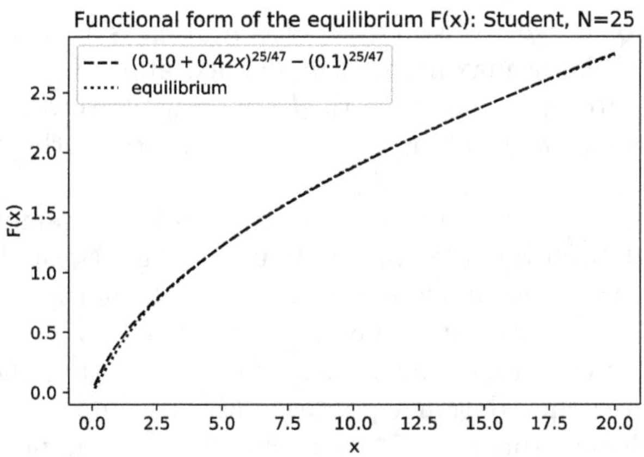

Figure 10. Functional form of the equilibrium for Student signals for $\alpha = 3$, $N = 25$.

The case of power-law tailed signal distributions was considered previously by Farmer *et al.* in the case of perfect competition between insiders [9]. One can view their model as the limiting case of the one considered herein as $N \to \infty$ in case of a Pareto-tailed distribution with exponent 3.

8. Same-Price Allocation

An alternative framework also of interest to practitioners is one where portfolio managers and noise traders submit their orders to an aggregator, which merges the orders into a block ("metaorder", in the literature), liquidates $X+Z$ for some average price and allocates shares with the same average price to noise traders and insiders. We refer to this framework as *same-price allocation.* The expected profit of the insiders in this case is

$$E^v\left[VX - \frac{X}{X+Z}\int_0^{X+Z} h(y)dy\right]. \tag{36}$$

In this case, the corresponding first-order condition for the maximization problem is given by $V = F(X^*)$, where

$$F(x) = E^v\left[\frac{x}{Z+x}\frac{h(Z+x)-\bar{h}(Z+x)}{N} + \bar{h}(Z+x)\right],$$

where $\bar{h}(x) = \frac{1}{x}\int_0^x h(y)dy$ and h is given by the tail expectation as above.

The problem with this first-order condition is that it is not clear whether it yields a maximum as F defined above is not necessarily increasing. However, our numerical experiments always suggest an increasing solution yielding a 'numerical' proof of the existence of equilibrium.

The solutions are similar in form and share the same asymptotic behavior for both bounded and unbounded signal distributions. We show in Figure 11 as an example the case of lognormal signals.

Figure 12 compares the same-price allocation model to the trading desk model in the case of Gaussian signals. The dotted lines represent the same-price liquidation equilibria. Market impact is somewhat greater with same-price liquidation than for the trading desk model, for $N > 1$. For the insider case, the two are essentially identical.

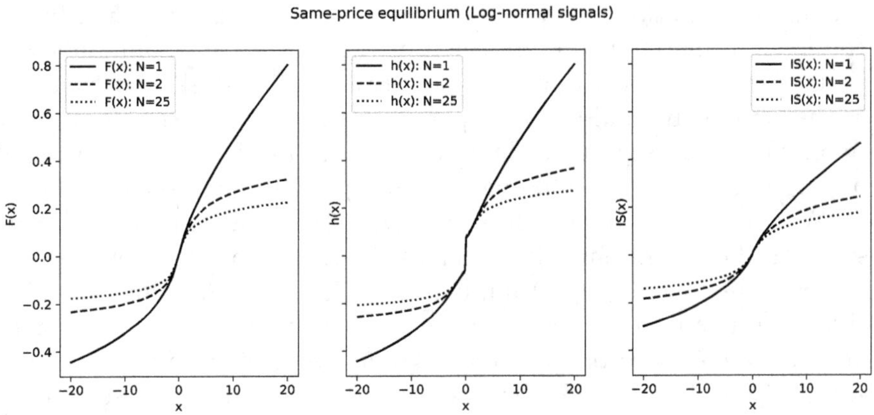

Figure 11. Equilibrium solutions for same-price liquidation with lognormal signals for the cases of an insider ($N = 1$), and shared signals with $N = 2$, $N = 25$.

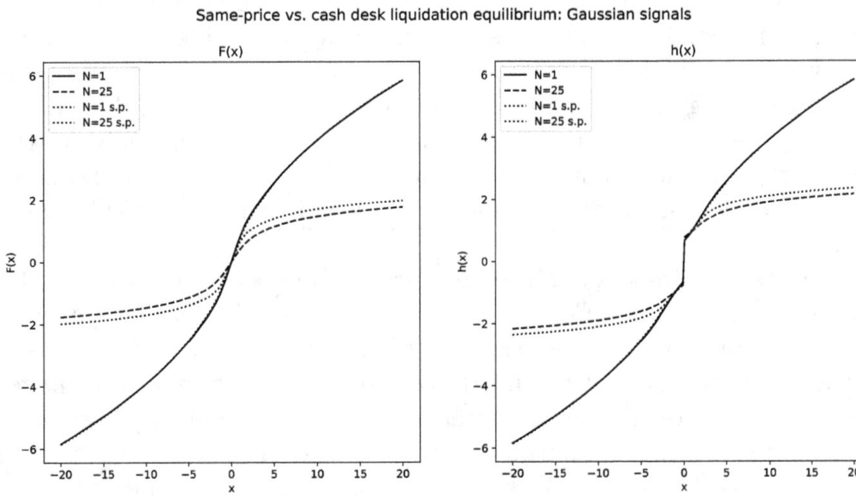

Figure 12. Equilibrium for Gaussian signals, comparing the same-price and trading desk liquidation models ($N = 1, 2, 25$). Dotted lines represent the same-price liquidation equilibrium.

9. Conclusion

Since empirical data on very large trades is sparse and often biased, it is important to develop a theoretical understanding of the process in order to discriminate between various proposals for the shape of the impact function. We proposed an asymmetric information-based equilibrium model where informed investors draw a signal and send their orders along with noise traders to a trading desk that executes at the net cost to liquidate the aggregate amount against a limit order book. Our results provide the micro-foundations for a large number of empirical findings including those on price impact and volume.

We found that market impact is asymptotically a power of trade size if the signal has fat tails, whereas the impact becomes of the form $(\log x)^{1/p}$ for some $p > 0$ for lighter tails. Moreover, for fat-tailed signal distributions, an equilibrium only exists if there is a sufficient amount of competition. The trade volume also obeys a power law in equilibrium. The spread decreases with the amount of noise trading and, although we do not have an analytic proof, the bid-ask spread seems to be an increasing and bounded function of the number of informed investors.

A relevant and arguably more realistic extension of our framework while still remaining in a static setting is to consider the scenario in which the insiders receive different but possibly correlated signals regarding the liquidation value. On the other hand, due to our assumption that the insiders' orders arrive simultaneously at the desk, the optimization problem of each insider requires the solution of a nonlinear filtering problem even in the case of Gaussian signals.

In reality, limit order markets are dynamic and thus the order books change over time reflecting the changes in market parameters. The analytic characterization of the equilibrium in the current framework in terms of the fixed point of an integral operator makes us optimistic regarding an extension of the current framework to a dynamic setting in continuous time. However, continuous trading brings extra flexibilities to portfolio choice, including the option to place a market or limit order at each trade, resulting in a more complicated model. This extension, though extremely interesting, will thus be left for future research.

Appendix A. Auxiliary Results and Proofs

Lemma A.1. *Ψ^+ and Ψ^- are non-decreasing on the support of V.*

Proof. Suppose $x < y$. Note that Ψ^+ is non-decreasing if $E[V\mathbf{1}_{[V>y]}]P(V > x) - E[V\mathbf{1}_{[V>x]}]P(V > y) \geq 0$. Indeed, the left side of the above equals

$$\begin{aligned}
&E[(V-y)\mathbf{1}_{[V>y]}]P(V > x) - E[(V-y)\mathbf{1}_{[V>x]}]P(V > y)\\
&\quad = E[(V-y)\mathbf{1}_{[V>y]}](P(V > x) - P(V > y))\\
&\qquad -E[(V-y)\mathbf{1}_{[x<V\leq y]}]P(V > y),
\end{aligned}$$

which is non-negative since $V - y \leq 0$ on the set $[x < V \leq y]$.

The second assertion is proved analogously. □

Proof of Proposition 2.1

(1) Let $g(x) := E^v[h(x+Z)]$. By direct differentiation, the expression (4) implies

$$xF(x) = x\frac{g(x)}{N} + \frac{N-1}{N}\int_0^x g(y)dy, \tag{A.37}$$

which is equivalent to the ODE $x\frac{g'(x)}{N} + g = F(x) + xF'(x)$. Recall that $g(0) = E^v[h(Z)] = F(0)$ by construction. Thus, the unique solution of the above ODE with this initial condition is given by

$$\begin{aligned}
g(x) &= NF(x) - \frac{N(N-1)}{x^N}\int_0^x F(y)y^{N-1}dy\\
&= F(x) + \frac{N(N-1)}{x^N}\int_0^x (F(x) - F(y))y^{N-1}dy.
\end{aligned}$$

This yields (6) after a change of variable.

(2) The above also yields (7) due to the first-order condition $F(X^*) = V$. The remaining assertions are direct consequences of the strict monotonicity of F.

(3) Note that the total expected profit is given by

$$\int_0^{X^*}(v - E^v[h(y+Z)])dy = \int_0^{X^*}(v - g(y))dy$$
$$= vX^* - \frac{N}{N-1}\left(X^*F(X^*) - X^*\frac{g(X^*)}{N}\right)$$
$$= -\frac{vX^*}{N-1} + \frac{X^*g(X^*)}{N-1} = \frac{X^*}{N-1}(g(X^*) - v)$$
$$= N\int_0^{X^*}(v - F(y))\left(\frac{y}{X^*}\right)^{N-1}dy,$$

where the second equality follows from (A.37) and the third is due to $F(X^*) = V$.

(4) Observe that

$$\int_0^Z h(y)dy = \int_0^\infty h(y)\mathbf{1}_{[Z\geq y]}dy - \int_{-\infty}^0 h(y)\mathbf{1}_{[Z\leq y]}dy.$$

Taking expectations and using the symmetry of Z, we obtain

$$E[\int_0^Z h(y)dy] = \int_0^\infty (h(y) - h(-y))P(Z \geq y)dy$$
$$= \int_0^\infty \frac{h(y) - h(-y)}{2}P(|Z| \geq y)dy$$

and prove the first claim. The second claim follows directly from integration by parts. □

Proof of Proposition 2.2. Note that $E[h(y+Z)] = E^v[h(y+Z)]$ for all y. We shall show the result for $N > 1$, the remaining case is similar and easier. Using the first representation in (6), we obtain

$$\int_0^x E[h(y+Z)]dy = N\int_0^x F(y)dy - N(N-1)\int_0^x dyy^{-N}$$
$$\times \int_0^y dzF(z)z^{N-1} = N\int_0^x F(y)dy$$
$$-N(N-1)\int_0^x dzF(z)z^{N-1}\int_z^x dyy^{-N}$$

$$= N\int_0^x F(y)dy + N\int_0^x dzF(z)z^{N-1}$$
$$\times (x^{-N+1} - z^{-N+1})$$
$$= N\int_0^x dzF(z)\left(\frac{z}{x}\right)^{N-1} = xN\int_0^1 dzF(xz)z^{N-1},$$

which yields the first assertion once divided by x. The remaining claims follow from $F(xy) < F(x)$ (resp., $F(xy) > F(x)$) for $x > 0$ (resp., $x < 0$) and for all $y \in (0,1)$ since F is strictly increasing. □

Proof of Lemma 3.1 We give the proof for the solutions of (14), the analogous property of the solutions of (30) can be proven similarly.

Monotone convergence theorem in conjunction with Assumption 3.1 implies

$$\lim_{x\to\infty}\int_{-\infty}^{\infty} q(\sigma,z)\phi_F(x+z)dz = \int_{-\infty}^{\infty} q(\sigma,z)\lim_{x\to\infty}\phi_F(x+z)dz.$$

Moreover, $\lim_{x\to\infty}\phi_F(x+z) = \Psi^+(F(\infty)-)$. To see this, first note that

$$\phi_F^+(z+x) = \frac{\int_{-\infty}^{\infty}\Psi^+(F(u))\Pi^+(F(u))\frac{1}{\sqrt{2\pi\sigma^2}}\exp\left(-\frac{(x+z-u)^2}{2\sigma^2}\right)du}{\int_{-\infty}^{\infty}\Pi^+(F(u))\frac{1}{\sqrt{2\pi\sigma^2}}\exp\left(-\frac{(x+z-u)^2}{2\sigma^2}\right)du}.$$

Next, the measure

$$\frac{\Pi^+(F(u)q(\sigma,z+x-u)du}{\int_{-\infty}^{\infty}\Pi^+(F(u)q(\sigma,z+x-u)du}$$

converges to the point mass at ∞. Indeed, for any $0 < a < \infty$, we have

$$\frac{\int_{-\infty}^{a}\Pi^+(F(u)q(\sigma,z+x-u)du}{\int_{-\infty}^{\infty}\Pi^+(F(u)q(\sigma,z+x-u)du}$$
$$= \frac{\int_{-\infty}^{a}\Pi^+(F(u)\exp\left(-\frac{u^2}{2\sigma^2}+\frac{u(z+x)}{\sigma^2}\right)du}{\int_{-\infty}^{\infty}\Pi^+(F(u)\exp\left(-\frac{u^2}{2\sigma^2}+\frac{u(z+x)}{\sigma^2}\right)du}$$

$$\leq \frac{\exp\left(\frac{a(z+x)}{\sigma^2}\right)\int_{-\infty}^{a}\Pi^+(F(u)\exp\left(-\frac{u^2}{2\sigma^2}\right)du}{\int_{2a}^{\infty}\Pi^+(F(u)\exp\left(-\frac{u^2}{2\sigma^2}+\frac{u(z+x)}{\sigma^2}\right)du}$$

$$\leq \frac{\exp\left(\frac{-a(z+x)}{\sigma^2}\right)\int_{-\infty}^{a}\Pi^+(F(u)\exp\left(-\frac{u^2}{2\sigma^2}\right)du}{\int_{2a}^{\infty}\Pi^+(F(u)\exp\left(-\frac{u^2}{2\sigma^2}\right)du},$$

which converges to 0 as $x \to \infty$.

Thus, using the representation of F via (15), we deduce $F(\infty) = \Psi^+(F(\infty)-)$. Note that changing the order of integration is justified thanks to Assumption 3.1. On the other hand, $\Psi^+(x-) > x$ for any $x < M$ since $P(V > x) > 0$ whenever $x < M$. This in turn implies $F(\infty) = M$. Similarly, $\lim_{x\to-\infty} F(x) = m$. Thus, F is strictly increasing in view of (15) and Lemma 4.1 since $m \neq M$ and, therefore, ϕ_F is not constant. □

Appendix B. Proof of Impact Asymptotics

We shall first start with the asymptotics of solutions of (23) and (24) which will later allow us to compute the asymptotics of interest.

Theorem B.1. *Suppose that $N > 1$, $-\infty < m < M < \infty$, and Assumption 5.1 holds. Then, the following statements are valid:*

(1) *Set $G := M - R$, where R is any non-decreasing solution of (23). Then, G is regularly varying of index $\rho^+ = \frac{\Psi_x^+(M)-1}{1-\frac{\Psi_x^+(M)}{N}}$.*
(2) *Set $G := l - m$, where l is any non-decreasing solution of (24). Then, G is regularly varying of index $\rho^- = \frac{\Psi_x^-(m)-1}{1-\frac{\Psi_x^-(m)}{N}}$.*

Proof. Only the proof of the first statement will be given, proof of the second being similar. We can assume without loss of generality that $E[V] = 0$ since, otherwise, we can replace V by $V - E[V]$ and redefine Ψ^+ and R accordingly.

By means of a straightforward change of variable, we obtain for $x > 0$

$$\begin{aligned}\frac{G(\alpha x)}{G(\alpha)} &= \frac{1}{N}\int_0^\infty dz q\Big(\frac{\sigma}{\alpha}, x - z\Big) \int_{-\infty}^\infty dy q\Big(\frac{\sigma}{\alpha}, z - y\Big) \\ &\quad \times \frac{M - \Psi^+(R(\alpha y))}{M - R(\alpha)} + \frac{N-1}{N}\int_0^\infty dz \bar{q}\Big(\frac{\sigma}{\alpha}, x, z\Big) \\ &\quad \times \int_{-\infty}^\infty dy q\Big(\frac{\sigma}{\alpha}, y - z\Big)\frac{M - \Psi^+(R(\alpha y))}{M - R(\alpha)} + \frac{M}{M - R(\alpha)} \\ &\quad \times \int_{-\infty}^0 dz \left\{\frac{1}{N} q\Big(\frac{\sigma}{\alpha}, x - z\Big) + \frac{N-1}{N}\bar{q}\Big(\frac{\sigma}{\alpha}, x, z\Big)\right\} \end{aligned} \tag{B.38}$$

Observe that the measure $q(\frac{\sigma}{\alpha}, x - z)dz$ converges to the Dirac measure at point x as $\alpha \to \infty$.

Step 1: For $y > 0$,

$$\frac{(M - \Psi^+(R(\alpha y))}{M - R(\alpha)} = \frac{(M - R(\alpha y))\Psi^+_x(y^*)}{M - R(\alpha)}$$

for some $y^* \geq R(\alpha y)$ by the mean value theorem, where Ψ^+_x stands for the derivative of Ψ^+, since $\Psi^+(M) = M$. Thus,

$$\begin{aligned}\lim_{\alpha\to\infty}\frac{(M - \Psi^+(R(\alpha y))}{M - R(\alpha)} &= \frac{(M - R(\alpha y))\Psi^+_x(y^*)}{M - R(\alpha)} \\ &= \Psi^+_x(M)\lim_{\alpha\to\infty}\frac{G(\alpha y)}{G(\alpha)}\end{aligned} \tag{B.39}$$

as $R(\infty) = M$.

Step 2: Let $\gamma_*(x) := \liminf_{\alpha\to\infty}\frac{G(\alpha x)}{G(\alpha)}$. Then, in view of the first step, Fatou's lemma yields

$$\gamma_*(x) \geq \frac{\Psi^+_x(M)}{N}\gamma_*(x) + \frac{N-1}{Nx}\Psi^+_x(M)\int_0^x \gamma_*(y)dy.$$

Thus, if $\gamma^*(x) = 0$ for some $x > 0$, it must be 0 for almost all $x > 0$. However, $\gamma_*(x) \geq 1$ for all $x \in (0, 1)$ since G is decreasing. Thus, $\gamma_* > 0$ for all $x > 0$. In particular, γ_* is bounded away from 0 on $[0, n]$ for any $n \geq 1$.

Step 3: It follows from Step 2 and Corollary 2.0.5 in Ref. [5] that

$$\frac{x^d}{C} \leq \frac{G(\alpha x)}{G(\alpha)} \leq Cx^c \text{ for } x \geq 1 \quad \text{and} \quad \alpha \geq \alpha_0$$

for some constants c, d, C and α_0. Moreover, since for $x < 1$, we have

$$\frac{G(\alpha x)}{G(\alpha)} = \left(\frac{G(\alpha x x^{-1})}{G(\alpha x))}\right)^{-1},$$

and $\alpha x > \alpha_0$ for large enough α, we deduce that the mapping $(\alpha, x) \mapsto \frac{G(\alpha x)}{G(\alpha)}$ is bounded when x belongs to bounded intervals in $(0, \infty)$.

Step 4: Moreover,

$$(M - R(\alpha))\alpha \geq \frac{N-1}{N} \int_0^\alpha du \int_0^\infty dzq(\sigma, u - z)$$
$$\int_{-\infty}^\infty dy(M - \Psi^+(R(y)))q(\sigma, z - y),$$

which in turn implies

$$\frac{1}{M - R(\alpha)} \leq K\alpha, \qquad \alpha > 1 \text{ for some } K < \infty. \tag{B.40}$$

Since $\frac{G(\alpha x)}{G(\alpha)}$ is bounded when x belongs to bounded intervals in $(0, \infty)$ by Step 3, we obtain, for any $\varepsilon > 0$,

$$\lim_{\alpha \to \infty} \int_{-\infty}^\infty dzq\Big(\frac{\sigma}{\alpha}, x - z\Big) \int_{z-\varepsilon}^{z+\varepsilon} dyq\Big(\frac{\sigma}{\alpha}, z - y\Big)$$
$$\times \frac{M - \Psi^+(R(\alpha y))}{M - R(\alpha)} = \Psi_x^+(M)\gamma(x), \tag{B.41}$$

where $\gamma(x) := \lim_{\alpha \to \infty} \frac{G(\alpha x)}{G(\alpha)}$ in view of (B.39) provided that the limit exists.

Furthermore, in view of (B.40), we also have

$$\int_{-\infty}^{\infty} dzq\Big(\frac{\sigma}{\alpha}, x-z\Big) \int_{\mathbb{R}\setminus(z-\varepsilon,z+\varepsilon)} dyq\Big(\frac{\sigma}{\alpha}, z-y\Big) \\ \times \frac{M-\Psi^{+}(R(\alpha y))}{M-R(\alpha)} \le KM \int_{-\infty}^{\infty} dzq\Big(\frac{\sigma}{\alpha}, x-z\Big) \\ \times \int_{\mathbb{R}\setminus(z-\varepsilon,z+\varepsilon)} dy\alpha q\Big(\frac{\sigma}{\alpha}, z-y\Big) \to 0 \text{ as } \alpha\to\infty. \tag{B.42}$$

Step 5: Applying the arguments of Step 4 to the second and the third integrals in (B.38) now shows that for $x > 0$

$$\gamma(x) = \frac{\Psi_x^{+}(M)}{N}\gamma(x) + \frac{N-1}{Nx}\Psi_x^{+}(M)\int_0^x \gamma(y)dy. \tag{B.43}$$

In particular, $\lim_{\alpha\to\infty}\frac{G(\alpha x)}{G(\alpha)}$ exists. Using the initial condition that $\gamma(1) = 1$, direct manipulations show that

$$\gamma(x) = x^{\rho^{+}}.$$

□

Theorem B.2. *Assume that $N > 1$, $-\infty < m < M < \infty$, Π^{+} has a continuous derivative and Assumption 5.1 holds. Then, the following statements are valid:*

(1) *Suppose that $\Psi_x^{+}(M) = 1$ and there exist an integer $n \ge 1$ and a real constant $k \in (0,\infty)$ such that*

$$\lim_{x\to M}\frac{\Psi^{+}(x)-x}{(M-x)^{n+1}} = \frac{1}{k}.$$

Then, the following asymptotics[9] hold:

$$M - R(x) \sim \left(\frac{N}{N-1}\frac{n}{k}\right)^{-\frac{1}{n}} (\log x)^{-\frac{1}{n}}, \quad x\to\infty, \tag{B.44}$$

where R is any solution of (23).

[9]We write $f(x) \sim g(x)$, $x \to \pm\infty$ if $\lim_{x\to\pm\infty}\frac{f(x)}{g(x)} = 1$.

(2) *Suppose that* $\Psi^-_x(m) = 1$ *and there exist an integer* $n \geq 1$ *and a real constant* $k \in (0, \infty)$ *such that*

$$\lim_{x \to m} \frac{x - \Psi^-(x)}{(x-m)^{n+1}} = \frac{1}{k}.$$

Then

$$l(x) - m \sim \left(\frac{N}{N-1}\frac{n}{k}\right)^{-\frac{1}{n}} (\log|x|)^{-\frac{1}{n}}, \quad x \to -\infty, \qquad \text{(B.45)}$$

where l *is any solution of (24).*

Proof. We shall again only give the proof the first statement and assume without loss of generality that $E[V] = 0$. For any $\alpha > 0$, define

$$r(\alpha, x) := \frac{R(\alpha x) - R(\alpha)}{(M - R(\alpha))^{n+1}}.$$

Straightforward manipulations similar to the ones employed in the proof of Theorem B.1 leads to

$$\begin{aligned}
r(\alpha, x) &= -\frac{R(\alpha)}{(M - R(\alpha))^{n+1}} \int_{-\infty}^{0} dz \left\{\frac{1}{N} q\left(\frac{\sigma}{\alpha}, x - z\right)\right. \\
&\quad \left. + \frac{N-1}{N}\bar{q}\left(\frac{\sigma}{\alpha}, x, z\right)\right\} + \int_0^\infty dz \left\{\frac{1}{N} q\left(\frac{\sigma}{\alpha}, x - z\right)\right. \\
&\quad \left. + \frac{N-1}{N}\bar{q}\left(\frac{\sigma}{\alpha}, x, z\right)\right\} \int_1^\infty dy q\left(\frac{\sigma}{\alpha}, z - y\right) \\
&\quad \times \frac{\Psi^+(R(\alpha y)) - R(\alpha)}{(M - R(\alpha))^{n+1}} + \int_0^\infty dz \left\{\frac{1}{N} q\left(\frac{\sigma}{\alpha}, x - z\right)\right. \\
&\quad \left. + \frac{N-1}{N}\bar{q}\left(\frac{\sigma}{\alpha}, x, z\right)\right\} \int_{-\infty}^{1} dy q\left(\frac{\sigma}{\alpha}, z - y\right) \\
&\quad \times \frac{\Psi^+(R(\alpha y)) - R(\alpha)}{(M - R(\alpha))^{n+1}} \leq \int_0^\infty dz \left\{\frac{1}{N} q\left(\frac{\sigma}{\alpha}, x - z\right)\right.
\end{aligned}$$

$$
\begin{aligned}
&+\frac{N-1}{N}\bar{q}\Big(\frac{\sigma}{\alpha},x,z\Big)\Big\}\int_1^\infty dyq\Big(\frac{\sigma}{\alpha},z-y\Big)\\
&\times\frac{\Psi^+(R(\alpha y))-R(\alpha)}{(M-R(\alpha))^{n+1}}+\int_0^\infty dz\left\{\frac{1}{N}q\Big(\frac{\sigma}{\alpha},x-z\Big)\right.\\
&+\frac{N-1}{N}\bar{q}\Big(\frac{\sigma}{\alpha},x,z\Big)\Big\}\int_{-\infty}^1 dyq\Big(\frac{\sigma}{\alpha},z-y\Big)\\
&\times\frac{\Psi^+(R(\alpha))-R(\alpha)}{(M-R(\alpha))^{n+1}}\leq K+\int_0^\infty dz\left\{\frac{1}{N}q\Big(\frac{\sigma}{\alpha},x-z\Big)\right.\\
&+\frac{N-1}{N}\bar{q}\Big(\frac{\sigma}{\alpha},x,z\Big)\Big\}\int_1^\infty dyq\Big(\frac{\sigma}{\alpha},z-y\Big)\\
&\times\frac{\Psi^+(R(\alpha y))-R(\alpha)}{(M-R(\alpha))^{n+1}}
\end{aligned}
$$

for some $K>0$ independent of α, where the first inequality follows from that $R\geq E[V]=0$ and $R(\alpha y)\leq R(\alpha)$ for $y\leq 1$ and the second is due to the boundedness of $\frac{\Psi^+(R(\alpha y))-R(\alpha)}{(M-R(\alpha))^{n+1}}$.

Moreover, for $y>1$,

$$
\begin{aligned}
\frac{\Psi^+(R(\alpha y))-R(\alpha)}{(M-R(\alpha))^{n+1}}&=\frac{\Psi^+(R(\alpha y))-R(\alpha y)}{(M-R(\alpha))^{n+1}}+r(\alpha,y)\\
&\leq\frac{\Psi^+(R(\alpha y))-R(\alpha y)}{(M-R(\alpha y))^{n+1}}+r(\alpha,y)
\end{aligned}
$$

due to the monotonicity of R. Thus, utilizing the boundedness of $\frac{\Psi^+(R(\alpha y))-R(\alpha)}{(M-R(\alpha))^{n+1}}$ once more, we arrive at

$$
\begin{aligned}
r(\alpha,x)\leq\kappa+\int_0^\infty dz\left\{\frac{1}{N}q\Big(\frac{\sigma}{\alpha},x-z\Big)+\frac{N-1}{N}\bar{q}\Big(\frac{\sigma}{\alpha},x,z\Big)\right\}\\
\times\int_1^\infty dyq\Big(\frac{\sigma}{\alpha},z-y\Big)r(\alpha,y),
\end{aligned}
\tag{B.46}
$$

for some $\kappa\in(0,\infty)$ that is independent of α.

Step 1: Let κ be as above and consider the operator $T : C([1,\infty),[0,\infty)) \to C([1,\infty),[0,\infty))$ defined by

$$Tf(x) = \kappa + \int_0^\infty dz \left\{ \frac{1}{N} q\Big(\frac{\sigma}{\alpha}, x - z\Big) + \frac{N-1}{N} \bar{q}\Big(\frac{\sigma}{\alpha}, x, z\Big) \right\} \times \int_1^\infty dy q\Big(\frac{\sigma}{\alpha}, z - y\Big) f(y).$$

Clearly, T is increasing, i.e., $Tf \geq Tg$ if $f \geq g$.

Step 2: For $z \geq 0$ and $c \in \mathbb{R}$,

$$\int_c^\infty dy q\Big(\frac{\sigma}{\alpha}, z - y\Big) y = \frac{\sigma^2}{\alpha^2} q\Big(\frac{\sigma}{\alpha}, z - c\Big) + z \int_{c-z}^\infty dy q\Big(\frac{\sigma}{\alpha}, y\Big) \leq z + \frac{\sigma}{\alpha\sqrt{2\pi}}. \tag{B.47}$$

Thus, if $f(x) = \beta x + \delta$ for some $\beta > 0$ and $\delta \geq 0$, we have

$$\begin{aligned} Tf(x) &\leq \delta + \kappa + \frac{\sqrt{2}\sigma\beta}{\alpha\sqrt{\pi}} + \frac{\beta x}{N} + \beta \frac{N-1}{xN} \int_0^x y dy \\ &= \delta + \kappa + \frac{\sqrt{2}\sigma\beta}{\alpha\sqrt{\pi}} + \frac{\beta x(N+1)}{2N} \leq \delta + \kappa \\ &\quad + \beta \left(\frac{\sqrt{2}\sigma}{\alpha\sqrt{\pi}} + \frac{3x}{4} \right), \end{aligned}$$

where the last inequality is due to the hypothesis that $N \geq 2$. In particular, given $\beta = \gamma\kappa$ for some $\gamma > 4$, $Tf \leq f$ whenever $\alpha \geq \frac{4\sqrt{2}\sigma\gamma}{\sqrt{\pi}(\gamma-4)}$.

Step 3: Define

$$\mathcal{D}(\alpha) := \{ f : [1,\infty) \to [0,\infty) : f \text{ is continuous and } f(x) \leq 5\kappa x + \frac{1}{(M - R(\alpha))^n} \forall x \geq 1 \}$$

and observe that the restriction of $r(\alpha,\cdot)$ to $[1,\infty)$ belongs to $\mathcal{D}(\alpha)$ for all $\alpha > 0$.

In view of Step 2, we have that $T\mathcal{D}(\alpha) \subset \mathcal{D}(\alpha)$ for large enough α. Thus, it admits a fixed point in $\mathcal{D}(\alpha)$ for large enough α by Tarski's theorem (Theorem 1 in Ref. [27]). In fact, it admits a unique fixed point. Indeed, if f and g are two fixed points of T in $\mathcal{D}(\alpha)$,

$$(f-g)(x) = \int_0^\infty dz \left\{ \frac{1}{N} q\left(\frac{\sigma}{\alpha}, x-z\right) + \frac{N-1}{N} \bar{q}\left(\frac{\sigma}{\alpha}, x, z\right) \right\} \times \int_1^\infty dy q\left(\frac{\sigma}{\alpha}, z-y\right)(f-g)(y).$$

Thus,

$$\inf_{x\geq 1}(f-g)(x) \geq \inf_{x\geq 1}(f-g)(x) \inf_{x\geq 1} \int_0^\infty dz \left\{ \frac{1}{N} q\left(\frac{\sigma}{\alpha}, x-z\right) + \frac{N-1}{N} \bar{q}\left(\frac{\sigma}{\alpha}, x, z\right) \right\} \int_1^\infty dy q\left(\frac{\sigma}{\alpha}, z-y\right) = c \inf_{x\geq 1}(f-g)(x)$$

for some $c \in (0,1)$. Since $\inf_{x\geq 1}(f-g)(x) < \infty$, the above implies $\inf_{x\geq 1}(f-g)(x) \leq 0$. Applying the same argument to $g-f$, we deduce $f = g$.
Moreover, taking $f^*(x) = 5\kappa x$ and utilizing the previous step we deduce that the unique fixed point is bounded from above by f^*. Theorem 1 in Ref. [27] now yields that $r(\alpha, \cdot) \leq f^*$ for large enough α in view of (B.46).

Step 4: In view of Step 3, we have that $r(\alpha, x) \leq 10\kappa$ for all $x \in [1,2]$ for large enough α. Thus, Theorem 3.1.5 in Ref. [5] yields $r(\alpha, \cdot)$ is bounded in bounded subintervals of $(0,\infty)$ uniformly in α.

Step 5: In view of Step 4 and using arguments similar to the ones used in Steps 4 and 5 of the proof of Theorem B.1, we arrive at

$$\gamma(x) = \frac{1}{k} + \frac{\gamma(x)}{N} + \frac{N-1}{xN} \int_0^x \gamma(y)dy,$$

where $\gamma(x) := \lim_{\alpha\to\infty} r(\alpha, x)$ for $x > 0$. The unique solution of the above equation with $\gamma(1) = 0$ is given by

$$\gamma(x) = \frac{N}{k(N-1)} \log x.$$

Step 6: Let $g(x) := \exp\left((M - R(x))^{-n}\right)$ and observe that

$$\begin{aligned}
\frac{g(\alpha x)}{g(\alpha)} &= \exp\left(\frac{(M-R(\alpha))^n - (M-R(\alpha x))^n}{(M-R(\alpha))^n (M-R(\alpha x))^n}\right) \\
&= \exp\left(\frac{\begin{array}{c}(R(\alpha x) - R(\alpha))\sum_{i=0}^{n-1}(M-R(\alpha)^{n-1-i} \\ (M-R(\alpha x)^i\end{array}}{(M-R(\alpha))^n (M-R(\alpha x))^n}\right) \\
&= \exp\left(\frac{R(\alpha x) - R(\alpha)}{(M-R(\alpha))^{n+1}} \frac{M-R(\alpha)}{M-R(\alpha x)} \sum_{i=0}^{n-1}\right. \\
&\quad \left. \times \left(\frac{M-R(\alpha)}{M-R(\alpha x)}\right)^{n-1-i}\right),
\end{aligned}$$

which converges to $\exp(n\gamma(x))$ as $\alpha \to \infty$ since $M - R$ is slowly varying at ∞. Thus,

$$g(x) = x^{\frac{N}{N-1}\frac{n}{k}} s(x), \quad x > 0.$$

where s is a slowly varying function at ∞. That is,

$$(M - R(x))^{-n} = \frac{N}{N-1}\frac{n}{k}\log x + \log s(x).$$

Since $\lim_{x\to\infty} \frac{\log s(x)}{\log x} = 0$ (cf. Proposition 1.3.6 (i) and (iii) in Ref. [5]), we have

$$M - R(x) \sim \left(\frac{N}{N-1}\frac{n}{k}\right)^{-\frac{1}{n}} (\log x)^{-\frac{1}{n}}, \quad x \to \infty.$$

□

Corollary B.1. *Assume that $N > 1$, $-\infty < m < M < \infty$, and Assumption 5.1 holds. Then, the following statements are valid:*

(1) *Suppose that there exist an integer $n \geq 0$ and a real constant $k \in (0, \infty)$ such that*

$$\lim_{x\to M} \frac{\Psi^+(x) - x}{(M-x)^{n+1}} = \frac{1}{k}.$$

Then, $\Pi^+(R)$ is regularly varying at ∞ of index $-\frac{\Psi_x^+(M)}{1-\frac{\Psi_x^+(M)}{N}}$, where R is any solution of (23).

(2) *Suppose that there exist an integer $n \geq 0$ and a real constant $k \in (0, \infty)$ such that*

$$\lim_{x \to M} \frac{x - \Psi^-(x)}{(x - m)^{n+1}} = \frac{1}{k}.$$

Then, $\Pi^-(l)$ is regularly varying at $-\infty$ of index $-\frac{\Psi_x^-(m)}{1 - \frac{\Psi_x^-(m)}{N}}$, where l is any solution of (24).

Proof. Again we only prove the first statement. The hypothesis implies $\Psi^+(x) - x$ is regularly varying with index $n+1$ at M. Thus, $\Psi^+(R) - R$ is regularly varying of index $(n+1)\rho^+$ at ∞, which in particular implies

$$\lim_{x \to \infty} \frac{\Psi^+(R(x)) - R(x)}{\int_x^\infty \frac{\Psi^+(R(y)) - R(y)}{y} dy} = - \lim_{x \to \infty} \frac{x(\Psi_x^+(R(x)R'(x) - R'(x))}{\Psi^+(R(x)) - R(x)}$$
$$= -(n+1)\rho^+, \tag{B.48}$$

in view of Theorem 1.5.11(ii) in Ref. [5].

Moreover, direct manipulations yield $\Pi^+(x) = \frac{\int_x^M \Pi^+(y)dy}{\Psi^+(x) - x}$, which in turn implies $-\frac{\Pi_x^+(x)}{\Pi^+(x)} = \frac{\Psi_x^+(x)}{\Psi^+(x) - x}$. Therefore,

$$\begin{aligned}\lim_{x \to \infty} \frac{x\Pi_x^+(R(x))R'(x)}{\Pi^+(R(x))} &= - \lim_{x \to \infty} \frac{xR'(x)\Psi_x^+(R(x))}{\Psi^+(R(x)) - R(x)} \\ &= -(n+1)\rho^+ - \lim_{x \to \infty} \frac{xR'(x)}{\Psi^+(R(x)) - R(x)} \\ &= -(n+1)\rho^+ - k \lim_{x \to \infty} \frac{xR'(x)}{(M - R(x))^{n+1}},\end{aligned}$$

where the second equality follows from (B.48).

Note that if $\Psi_x^+(M) < 1$, $n = 0$ and $k = \frac{1}{1 - \Psi^+(M)}$. In this case,

$$\lim_{x \to \infty} \frac{xR'(x)}{M - R(x)} = -\rho^+$$

by Theorem 1.5.11(ii) in Ref. [5]. Thus,

$$\lim_{x\to\infty}\frac{x\Pi_x^+(R(x))R'(x)}{\Pi^+(R(x))}=\rho^+(k-1)=-\frac{\Psi_x^+(M)}{1-\frac{\Psi_x^+(M)}{N}}.$$

An application of Exercise 1.11.13 in Ref. [5] to $1/\Pi^+(R)$ establishes the claim.

Now, suppose $\Psi_x^+(M)=1$ and observe that n is necessarily bigger than 0 and $\rho^+=0$ in this case. Recall the function g in Step 6 of the proof of Theorem B.2 and note that

$$\lim_{x\to\infty}\frac{xg'(x)}{g(x)}=\frac{Nn}{(N-1)k}$$

by another application of Theorem 1.5.11(i) in Ref. [5]. Since

$$\frac{xg'(x)}{g(x)}=\frac{xnR'(x)}{(M-R(x))^{n+1}},$$

we arrive at

$$\lim_{x\to\infty}\frac{xR'(x)}{(M-R(x))^{n+1}}=\frac{N}{k(N-1)}.$$

Therefore,

$$\lim_{x\to\infty}\frac{x\Pi_x^+(R(x))R'(x)}{\Pi^+(R(x))}=-\frac{N}{N-1}=-\frac{\Psi_x^+(M)}{1-\frac{\Psi_x^+(M)}{N}},$$

and we again conclude by means of Exercise 1.11.13 in Ref. [5]. □

We are now ready to prove the asymptotics that are of our main interest.

Proof of Theorem 5.1 We shall give a proof of the first statement as the second one can be proven along similar lines.

By means of a change of variable employed in earlier proofs we obtain for $x>0$

$$\frac{G(\alpha x)}{G(\alpha)}=\frac{1}{N}\int_0^\infty dzq\Big(\frac{\sigma}{\alpha},x-z\Big)\int_{-\infty}^\infty \nu(\alpha,z,dy)dy\frac{M-\Psi^+(F(\alpha y))}{M-F(\alpha)}$$
$$+\frac{N-1}{N}\int_0^\infty dz\bar{q}\Big(\frac{\sigma}{\alpha},x,z\Big)\int_{-\infty}^\infty \nu(\alpha,z,dy) \qquad \text{(B.49)}$$

$$\times\, dy \frac{M-\Psi^{+}(F(\alpha y))}{M-F(\alpha)} + \frac{1}{M-F(\alpha)} \int_{-\infty}^{0}$$

$$\times\, dz \left\{ \frac{1}{N} q\Big(\frac{\sigma}{\alpha}, x-z\Big) + \frac{N-1}{N} \bar{q}\Big(\frac{\sigma}{\alpha}, x, z\Big) \right\} \phi_F(\alpha z),$$

where

$$\nu(\alpha, z, dy) := \frac{\Pi^{+}(F(\alpha y) q\Big(\frac{\sigma}{\alpha}, y-z\Big))}{\int_{-\infty}^{\infty} du \Pi^{+}(F(\alpha u) q\Big(\frac{\sigma}{\alpha}, u-z\Big))} dy. \tag{B.50}$$

We shall first demonstrate that for $z > 0$ the measure $\nu(\alpha, z, dy)$ converges to the Dirac measure at point z as $\alpha \to \infty$. Indeed, let R^* be the maximal solution of (23) and observe that for any $\varepsilon > 0$ and $z > 0$

$$\begin{aligned} \nu(\alpha, z, (\mathbb{R}\backslash(z-\varepsilon, z+\varepsilon))) &= \frac{\int_{\mathbb{R}\backslash(z-\varepsilon,z+\varepsilon)} dy \Pi^{+}(F(\alpha y) q\Big(\frac{\sigma}{\alpha}, y-z\Big)}{\int_{-\infty}^{\infty} du \Pi^{+}(F(\alpha u) q\Big(\frac{\sigma}{\alpha}, u-z\Big)} \\ &\le \frac{\int_{\mathbb{R}\backslash(z-\varepsilon,z+\varepsilon)} dy q\Big(\frac{\sigma}{\alpha}, y-z\Big)}{\int_{0}^{\infty} du \Pi^{+}(R(\alpha u) q\Big(\frac{\sigma}{\alpha}, u-z\Big)}, \end{aligned}$$

where the last inequality is due to the fact that $F \le R^*$ by Theorem 4.1.

Moreover, since $\Pi^{+}(R)$ is regularly varying at ∞ with some index $r \le 0$ by Corollary B.1, we have $\Pi^{+}(R(\alpha u) \ge c(1+u)^{r-\delta}\alpha^{r-\delta}$ for some $c > 0$ for all $u \ge 0$ by Proposition 1.3.6(v) in Ref. [5]. Therefore,

$$\nu(\alpha, z, (\mathbb{R}\backslash(z-\varepsilon, z+\varepsilon))) \le \frac{\alpha^{\delta-r} \int_{\mathbb{R}\backslash(z-\varepsilon,z+\varepsilon)} dy q\Big(\frac{\sigma}{\alpha}, y-z\Big)}{c \int_{0}^{\infty} du (1+u)^{r-\delta} q\Big(\frac{\sigma}{\alpha}, u-z\Big)}, \tag{B.51}$$

the right side of which converges to 0 as $\alpha \to \infty$. Similarly, we can show

$$\lim_{\alpha \to \infty} \nu(\alpha, z, (-\infty, z-\varepsilon)) = 0.$$

Step 1: Let $\gamma_*(x) := \liminf_{\alpha\to\infty} \frac{G(\alpha x)}{G(\alpha)}$. It follows from the same argument in Step 2 of the proof of Theorem B.1 that γ_* is bounded away from 0 on $[0, n]$ for any $n \geq 1$. This in turn implies the mapping $(\alpha, x) \mapsto \frac{G(\alpha x)}{G(\alpha)}$ is bounded when x belongs to bounded intervals in $(0, \infty)$ as in Step 3 of the same proof.

Step 2: Moreover, since $F \leq R^*$, (B.40) yields

$$\frac{1}{M - R(\alpha)} \leq K\alpha, \qquad \alpha > 1 \text{ for some } K < \infty.$$

Thus, the arguments of Steps 4 and 5 of the proof of Theorem B.1 are still applicable due to (B.51) and that $\Psi_F^- \leq E[V]$. Consequently, γ still satisfies (B.43), where $\gamma(x) = \lim_{x\to\infty} \frac{G(\alpha x)}{G(\alpha)}$. In particular, $\gamma(x) = x^{\rho^+}$.

Step 3: If $\Psi_x^+(M)$, the proof of Theorem B.2 can be applied verbatim once we show that $f(\alpha, \cdot)$ is bounded in $[1, 2]$ uniformly in α, where

$$f(\alpha, x) := \frac{F(\alpha x) - F(\alpha)}{(M - F(\alpha))^{n+1}}.$$

Since $F(\alpha)$ is eventually larger than $E[V]$ and $\phi_F(z) \leq E[V]$ for $z < 0$, we have for large enough α

$$\begin{aligned} f(\alpha, x) &= \int_{-\infty}^{0} dz \left\{ \frac{1}{N} q\Big(\frac{\sigma}{\alpha}, x - z\Big) + \frac{N-1}{N} \bar{q}\Big(\frac{\sigma}{\alpha}, x, z\Big) \right\} \\ &\quad \times \frac{\phi_F(\alpha z) - F(\alpha)}{(M - F(\alpha))^{n+1}} + \int_{0}^{\infty} dz \left\{ \frac{1}{N} q\Big(\frac{\sigma}{\alpha}, x - z\Big) \right. \\ &\quad \left. + \frac{N-1}{N} \bar{q}\Big(\frac{\sigma}{\alpha}, x, z\Big) \right\} \int_{-\infty}^{\infty} \nu(\alpha, z, dy) \\ &\quad \times \frac{\Psi^+(F(\alpha y)) - F(\alpha)}{(M - F(\alpha))^{n+1}} \leq \int_{0}^{\infty} dz \left\{ \frac{1}{N} q\Big(\frac{\sigma}{\alpha}, x - z\Big) \right. \\ &\quad \left. + \frac{N-1}{N} \bar{q}\Big(\frac{\sigma}{\alpha}, x, z\Big) \right\} \int_{-\infty}^{\infty} q\Big(\frac{\sigma}{\alpha}, z - y\Big) \\ &\quad \times \frac{\Psi^+(F(\alpha y)) - F(\alpha)}{(M - F(\alpha))^{n+1}}, \end{aligned}$$

where the last inequality follows from Part (4) of Lemma 4.1 since $\Psi^+(F(\alpha y))$ is increasing in y for positive α. Thus, $f(\alpha,\cdot)$ can be shown to be bounded by the same function that bounds $r(\alpha,\cdot)$ introduces in the proof of Theorem B.2. Repeating the remaining arguments therein yields the claim.

□

Proof of Corollary 5.1. It follows from Theorem 3.1 that F^* must solve (14). In particular, F^* is regularly varying at ∞ of order ρ^+.

In view of Proposition 2.2, we have

$$\begin{aligned}\frac{M - IS^*(x)}{M - F^*(x)} &= N\int_0^1 \frac{M - F^*(xy)}{M - F^*(x)} y^{N-1} dy \\ &= \frac{N\int_0^x (M - F^*(y)) y^{N-1} dy}{x^N (M - F^*(x))}.\end{aligned}$$

Observe that $\lim_{y\to\infty}(M - F^*(y))y^{-\rho^+\varepsilon} = \infty$ by Proposition 1.3.6 (v) in Ref. [5]. Thus, $\int_0^\infty (M - F^*(y))y^{N-1}dy = \infty$. This justifies the application of the L'Hôpital rule to arrive at

$$\begin{aligned}\lim_{x\to\infty}\frac{M - IS^*(x)}{M - F^*(x)} &= \lim_{x\to\infty}\frac{N(M - F^*(x))x^{N-1}}{Nx^{N-1}(M - F^*(x)) - x^N F^*_x(x)} \\ &= \frac{1}{1 - \lim_{x\to\infty}\frac{xF^*_x(x)}{N(M - F^*(x))}} = \frac{1}{1 + \frac{\rho^+}{N}} = \frac{N}{N + \rho^+},\end{aligned}$$

where the third equality follows from Exercise 1.11.13 applied to $1/(M - F)$.

Asymptotic relationship near $-\infty$ is proved the same way. □

References

[1] R. Almgren, C. Thum, E. Hauptmann, and H. Li. Direct estimation of equity market impact. *Risk*, 18:58–62, 2005.
[2] K. Back. Insider trading in continuous time. *The Review of Financial Studies*, 5:387–409, 1992.
[3] N. Bershova and D. Rakhlin. The non-linear market impact of large trades: Evidence from buy-side order flow. *Quantitative Finance*, 13:1759–1778, 2013.

[4] B. Biais, P. Hillion, and C. Spatt. An empirical analysis of the limit order book and the order flow in the Paris bourse. *The Journal of Finance*, 50:1655–1689, 1995.
[5] N. H. Bingham, C. M. Goldie, and J. L. Teugels. *Regular Variation*, vol. 27. Cambridge University Press, Cambridge, 1989.
[6] R. Bloomfield, M. O'hara, and G. Saar. How noise trading affects markets: An experimental analysis. *The Review of Financial Studies*, 22:2275–2302, 2009.
[7] J.-P. Bouchaud, J. Bonart, J. Donier, and M. Gould. *Trades, Quotes and Prices: Financial Markets under the Microscope*, Cambridge University Press, Cambridge, 2018.
[8] S. Chakravarty. Stealth-trading: Which traders' trades move stock prices? *Journal of Financial Economics*, 61:289–307, 2001.
[9] J. D. Farmer, A. Gerig, F. Lillo, and H. Waelbroeck. How efficiency shapes market impact. *Quantitative Finance*, 13:1743–1758, 2013.
[10] T. Foucault, O. Kadan, and E. Kandel. Limit order book as a market for liquidity. *The Review of Financial Studies*, 18:1171–1217, 2005.
[11] X. Gabaix, P. Gopikrishnan, V. Plerou, and H. E. Stanley. A theory of power-law distributions in financial market fluctuations. *Nature*, 423:267–270, 2003.
[12] X. Gabaix, P. Gopikrishnan, V. Plerou, and H. E. Stanley. Institutional investors and stock market volatility. *The Quarterly Journal of Economics*, 121:461–504, 2006.
[13] L. R. Glosten. Is the electronic open limit order book inevitable? *The Journal of Finance*, 49:1127–1161, 1994.
[14] R. L. Goettler, C. A. Parlour, and U. Rajan. Equilibrium in a dynamic limit order market. *The Journal of Finance*, 60:2149–2192, 2005.
[15] P. Gopikrishnan, V. Plerou, X. Gabaix, and H. E. Stanley. Statistical properties of share volume traded in financial markets. *Physical Review E*, 62:R4493, 2000.
[16] C. W. Holden and A. Subrahmanyam. Long-lived private information and imperfect competition. *The Journal of Finance*, 47:247–270, 1992.
[17] A. S. Kyle. Continuous auctions and insider trading. *Econometrica*, 53:1315–1335, 1985.
[18] F. Lillo, M. Szabolcs, and J. D. Farmer. Theory for long memory in supply and demand. *Physical Review E*, 71:066122, 2005.
[19] S. Nadtochiy. A simple microstructural explanation of concave pice impact. Available at SSRN 3515008, 2020.
[20] C. A. Parlour. Price dynamics in limit order markets. *The Review of Financial Studies*, 11:789–816, 1998.

[21] A. F. Perold. The implementation shortfall: Paper versus reality. *Journal of Portfolio Management*, 14:4, 1988.

[22] V. Plerou, P. Gopikrishnan, L. A. Nunez Amaral, and E. H. Stanley. Scaling of the distribution of price fluctuations of individual companies. *Physical Review E*, 60:6519, 1999.

[23] M. Potters and J.-P. Bouchaud. More statistical properties of order books and price impact. *Physica A: Statistical Mechanics and its Applications*, 324:133–140, 2003.

[24] K. Rock. *The Specialist's Order Book and Price Anomalies*, tech. rep., Harvard University, 1989.

[25] I. Roşu. A dynamic model of the limit order book. *The Review of Financial Studies*, 22:4601–4641, 2009.

[26] P. Sandås. Adverse selection and competitive market making: Empirical evidence from a limit order market. *The Review of Financial Studies*, 14:705–734, 2001.

[27] A. Tarski. A lattice-theoretical fixpoint theorem and its applications. *Pacific Journal of Mathematics*, 5:285–309, 1955.

[28] N. Torre. *Market Impact Model Handbook*, BARRA, Berkeley, 1997.

[29] G. Vaglica, F. Lillo, E. Moro, and R. N. Mantegna. Scaling laws of strategic behavior and size heterogeneity in agent dynamics. *Physical Review E*, 77:036110, 2008.

[30] E. Zarinelli, M. Treccani, J. D. Farmer, and F. Lillo. Beyond the square root: Evidence for logarithmic dependence of market impact on size and participation rate. *Market Microstructure and Liquidity*, 1, 2015.

https://doi.org/10.1142/9789811280306_0023

Chapter 23

An Extension with Illustrations of the Azéma–Yor Algorithm for Solving Skorokhod Embedding Problem

Yuri Imamura[*,‡] **and Ju-Yi Yen**[†,§]

[*] *The School of Mathematics and Physics, Kanazawa University, Kakuma, Kanazawa 920-1192, JAPAN*
[†] *Department of Mathematical Sciences, University of Cincinnati, Cincinnati, Ohio 45221-0025, USA*
[‡] *imamuray@se.kanazawa-u.ac.jp*
[§] *ju-yi.yen@uc.edu*

Abstract
We recall and illustrate four methods: Azéma–Yor algorithm, Vallois algorithm, excursion method and Azéma exponential result, each one allowing to solve the Skorokhod embedding problem. In doing so, we consider more general stopping times than in the original Azéma–Yor algorithm.

Keywords: Azéma–Yor algorithm, Vallois algorithm, Excursion theory, Skorokhod embedding

1. Introduction and Motivation

1.1. *Background*

The celebrated Skorokhod embedding problem can be stated as the following:

Given a probability measure $\mu(dx)$ in $\mathbb{R}$, find a stopping time T of $(X_t)_{t\geq 0}$ such that X_T has law μ.

We shall focus on the case where the process $X = (X_t)_{t\geq 0}$ is taken to be Brownian motion $(B_t)_{t\geq 0}$. In this case, it has been demonstrated that the problem has many (non-interesting) solutions, for example, if $\mu = \delta_a$, then $T = \inf\{t : B_t = a\}$ is a solution to the problem. Another trivial solution is that for any probability measure μ, let $F_\mu(x)$ be the distribution function for μ, and let Φ denote the distribution function for a standard normal variable, then $T = \inf\{t \geq 1 : B_t = F_\mu^{-1}(\Phi(B_1))\}$, and that $\mathbb{E}[T] = \infty$ in this case. However, from a gambler's perspective, it is desirable that T be as small as possible. Hence, one usually considers the following additional condition:

$$(B_{t\wedge T})_{t\geq 0} \text{ is uniformly integrable.} \tag{1}$$

As a consequence of condition (1), it is necessary that $\mu(dx)$ satisfies the following:

$$\int |x| d\mu(x) < \infty \quad \text{and} \quad \int x d\mu(x) = 0. \tag{2}$$

It has been shown that for any probability $\mu(dx)$ on $\mathbb{R}$ satisfying (2), there exist solutions to Skorokhod embedding with target measure μ. The survey article written by Obłój [12] includes at least 21 solutions scattered in the literature.

Skorokhod embedding is often used to construct or embed martingales in Brownian motion. Since the 1970s, the field of quantitative finance makes extensive use of stochastic processes and probability theory, in particular, Brownian motion and martingale theory. Naturally, the feature of the Skorokhod embedding problem inspires researchers to investigate its applications in mathematical finance (see, e.g., Refs. [6, 7]). Let us briefly explain the context. The role of martingales in option pricing involves modeling the time evolution of a random price process $(X_t)_{t\geq 0}$ defined on $(\Omega, \mathcal{F}, \mathcal{F}_t, \mathbb{P})$.

The common assumption for deriving option pricing formulae is the principle of no-arbitrage. The mathematical interpretation of the absence of arbitrage possibilities is that there exists a risk-neutral probability measure $\mathbb{Q}$ equivalent to $\mathbb{P}$ under which the discounted prices of financial securities are martingales. Option prices with fixed maturity t can be used to identify the marginal distribution of the underlying asset under the measure $\mathbb{Q}$. Now, let μ_t denote the law of the one-dimension marginal of $(X_t)_{t\geq 0}$. We are concerned here with an arbitrage-free market, in other words, μ_t is the one-dimension marginal of a martingale, though the corresponding martingale might not be unique. On the other hand, any continuous martingale X can be written as a time-changed Brownian motion (possibly under an enlargement of the probability space). More precisely, there is a Brownian motion B with respect to a filtration $(\mathcal{F}_t)_{t\geq 0}$ such that for each $t \geq 0$, the bracket of X, $\langle X\rangle_t$, is an $\mathcal{F}$-stopping time and that $X_t = B_{\langle X\rangle_t}$. Therefore, there exists a one-to-one correspondence between the price model process and the solution of the Skorokhod embedding problem under certain conditions. Indeed, it was recognized by Carr–Geman–Madan–Yor that the price process can be written as a time-changed Brownian motion under the arbitrage free market [3].

The plan for the remainder of this chapter is the following: in Section 2, we give a brief survey on Azéma–Yor algorithm and Vallois algorithm for the Skorokhod embedding problem and their applications in finance. In Section 3, we study the excursion theory argument for the Skorokhod embedding problem. We also show how Azéma universal exponential result [1] allows us to bypass the method used by Azéma–Yor in Ref. [2] and the excursion method introduced in the same section. In Section 4, we illustrate examples stimulated by Azéma–Yor algorithm. We show how our examples and in fact a vast generalization of them may be included in the framework of excursion method, and we make explicit the corresponding law μ.

2. Some Existing Algorithms for Skorokhod Embedding and Their Applications in Finance

As mentioned earlier, there exist many solutions to the Skorokhod embedding problem with target measure μ. For this chapter, we are particularly interested in two solutions: one is derived by Azéma and Yor [2] and the other by Vallois [16,17]. We shall introduce these two algorithms and their applications in finance in this section.

In the sequel, $S_t = \sup_{s \leq t} B_s$ denotes the one-sided supremum of a Brownian motion, L_t is the local time of a Brownian motion at level 0 and $|B_t|$ is the reflected Brownian motion.

2.1. *Azéma–Yor Algorithm*

The Azéma–Yor algorithm [2] may be expressed in the following explicit form: given μ satisfying (2), and associate to μ in the following Hardy–Littlewood barycenter function:

$$\psi_\mu(x) = \frac{1}{\mu([x,\infty))} \int_{[x,\infty)} y\mu(dy), \tag{3}$$

then the Azéma–Yor algorithm is given by

$$T_{\text{AY}} := \inf\{t : S_t \geq \psi_\mu(B_t)\}, \tag{4}$$

see Figure 1 for illustration. Moreover,

Theorem 2.1 (Azéma–Yor [2]).

(i) $(B_{t\wedge T_{AY}}, t \geq 0)$ *is a uniformly integrable martingale.*
(ii) $B_{T_{AY}}$ *has the given law* $\mu(dx)$.

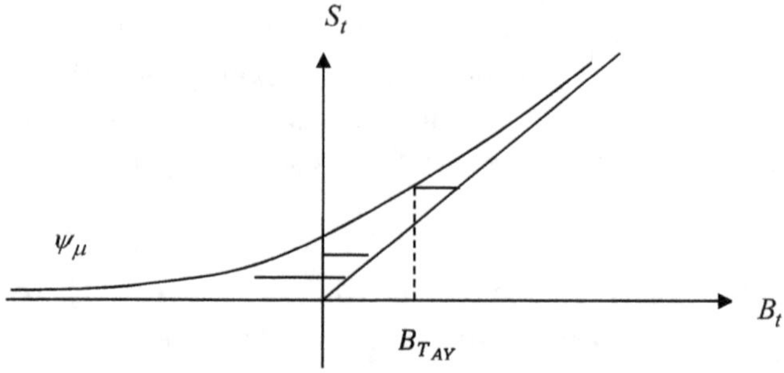

Figure 1. $B_{T_{AY}}$ is distributed as μ.

2.2. *Vallois Algorithm*

Vallois' construction is based on the local time L_t of the Brownian motion B_t at level 0 [16, 17]. Specifically, given μ satisfying (2), for certain functions h_- and h_+, Vallois algorithm is defined by

$$T_{\text{v}} = \inf\{t \geq 0 : B_t \notin (h_-(L_t), h_+(L_t))\}. \tag{5}$$

Indeed, there exist increasing functions h_- and h_+ such that $B_{T_{\text{v}}}$ has the given law μ and

$$\mathbb{E}[\Psi(L_T)] \leq \mathbb{E}[\Psi(L_{T_{\text{v}}})], \tag{6}$$

for all T, where B_T has the given law μ and Ψ is a convex function. Furthermore, Vallois shows that $(B_{t\wedge T_{\text{v}}}; t \geq 0)$ is a uniformly integrable martingale.

We remark that thanks to Lévy's well-known identity in law:

$$\big((S_t, S_t - B_t); t \geq 0\big) \overset{(\text{law})}{=} \big((L_t, |B_t|); t \geq 0\big), \tag{7}$$

it is not difficult to see the connection between Azéma–Yor algorithm (4) and Vallois algorithm (5). In fact, Vallois algorithm was done originally to counter the asymmetry in the Azéma–Yor construction.

2.3. *Applications in Finance — Optimal Stopping for Exotic Options*

Though a European option can be exercised only at maturity, an American-style option can be exercised at any time prior to maturity. A third type of option, called a hyper option, can be exercised many times prior to maturity. Thus, choosing optimal time(s) to exercise an option becomes interesting to study. We came across the idea of hyper option by reading Carr and Lee's work [5] in which they introduce hyper options with payoff contingent on the local time.

The optimal stopping problem in mathematical finance is concerned with choosing a time (or a family of times) which is prior to the maturity to exercise an exotic option such that the reward is maximized (or the cost is minimized). Formally, suppose we have a pricing/hedging function $F = F(X_t)$ defined on $(\Omega, \mathcal{F}, \mathcal{F}_t, \mathbb{P})$, and X_t

has the same one-dimensional marginal as the martingale B_T, where T is a family of stopping times, then the optimal stopping problem is to find T which optimizes $\mathbb{E}[F(X_t; t \geq 0)]$. We explain further the two algorithms introduced in this section.

2.3.1. *On Azéma–Yor Algorithm*

Let T be a stopping time where the given law of B_T is μ. Azéma–Yor [2] observed that for any $b > 0$, we may write

$$\begin{aligned}\mathbb{P}(S_T \geq b) \leq \mathbb{P}(S_{T_{\mathrm{AZ}}} \geq b) &= \mathbb{P}(B_{T_{\mathrm{AZ}}} \geq \phi(b)) \\ &= \mu([\phi(b), \infty)) := \bar{\mu}(\phi(b)),\end{aligned} \tag{8}$$

where ϕ is an inverse of ψ_μ and $\bar{\mu}$ is the tail distribution function. Therefore, the right-hand side of (8) is the least upper bound among all stopping times, and the optimal stopping time is T_{AZ}. Hence, Azéma–Yor algorithm is applied in [6–8] to find the bound of the price of exotic options and which gives robust hedging.

In this chapter, we show that the stopping time T is constructed by a function of S_t and B_t, and it is connected to the barycenter function ψ_μ.

2.3.2. *On Vallois Algorithm*

For an increasing function h, we consider the following stopping times:

$$\theta_h^{(a)} = \inf\{t : h(L_t, |B_t|) \geq a\}.$$

Now, together with (5) and (6), we can apply the algorithm to a financial derivative, precisely: suppose that a payoff function of American-style lookback option is given by Ψ, then the price of the option can be described as $\mathbb{E}[\Psi(L_{\theta_h^{(a)}})]$ which is bounded by $\mathbb{E}[\Psi(L_{T_{\mathrm{v}}})]$.

We remark that in Ref. [6], Cox, Hobson and Obłój apply Vallois' Skorokhod embedding to discuss robust pricing and hedging of options written on the local time.

We further remark that for the lookback barrier option, Hobson derives model-free lower and upper bounds in Ref. [8]; Carr and Chou show exact replication strategies for a lognormal model with constant but otherwise arbitrary risk-neutral drift in Ref. [4].

3. Connections between the Two Algorithms Introduced in Section 2

In view of remarkable features of both Azéma–Yor algorithm and Vallios algorithm which allow researchers to address pertinent application-level problems in finance, we are motivated to further investigate a broader class of stopping times related to them.

3.1. *The Excursion Theory*

We shall use here the Brownian excursion theory in the manner of Rogers [15] (see also Jeulin–Yor [10]) to relate the two algorithms discussed in Section 2. Our goal is to identify the laws of (S_T, B_T) or $(L_\theta, |B_\theta|)$ for the stopping times:

$$T_h^{(a)} = \inf\{t : h(S_t, S_t - B_t) \geq a\}$$

or

$$\theta_h^{(a)} = \inf\{t : h(L_t, |B_t|) \geq a\},$$

where $a \in \mathbb{R}$ and the non-negative function h defined on a domain $D \subset [0,\infty)^2$ is continuous with the following properties: $\lim_{(\lambda,x)\to(0,0)} h(\lambda, x) = 0$, and denoting indifferently $h(\lambda, x) \equiv h_\lambda(x)$, we assume that $h_\lambda(a)$ is strictly increasing and we denote by $h_\lambda^{-1}(\cdot)$ the inverse of h_λ:

$$h_\lambda^{(-1)}(a) = \inf\{x \geq 0 : h(\lambda, x) \geq a\}.$$

For simplicity, we suppose that $D = \{(\lambda, x) \in [0,\infty)^2 : h(\lambda, x) < a\}$ is connected. The study with respect to either of these stopping times, T or θ, yields that for the other one thanks to Lévy's well-known identity in law (7) recalled in Section 2. Thus we obtain that

$$S_{T_h^{(a)}} \overset{\text{(law)}}{=} L_{\theta_h^{(a)}}.$$

Our presentation involves a function of two variables h, from which we are able to deduce the target measure μ, that is, the law of $B_{T_h^{(a)}}$.

The excursion theory argument runs in the following equalities between random sets:

$$
\begin{aligned}
(L_{\theta_h^{(a)}} \geq l) &= (\theta_h^{(a)} \geq \tau_l) \\
&= (\forall \lambda \leq l, \ \text{for } t \in (\tau_{\lambda-}, \tau_\lambda), \ \text{one has: } h(\lambda, |B_t|) < a) \\
&= \Bigg(\sum_{\lambda \leq l} \mathbb{1}_{\{\sup_{\tau_{\lambda-} \leq t \leq \tau_\lambda} h(\lambda, |B_t|) \geq a\}} = 0 \Bigg),
\end{aligned} \tag{9}
$$

where $\tau_l = \inf\{s > 0 : L_s > l\}$. In our proof of Theorem 3.1, we shall deduce the formula for the tail distribution of $L_{\theta_h^{(a)}}$ from the last equality (9) above.

Now, we set $\lambda_+ = \sup_{(\lambda,x)\in D} \lambda$. We shall introduce the context of Theorem 3.1 by proposing a general formulation which encompasses both algorithms. The generalization in question concerns stopping times, such as $T_h^{(a)}$ or $\theta_h^{(a)}$.

Theorem 3.1. *For h and $a \geq 0$, there is the following formula:*

$$
\mathbb{P}(S_{T_h^{(a)}} \geq x) = \mathbb{P}(L_{\theta_h^{(a)}} \geq x) = \exp(-G(x)), \tag{10}
$$

where

$$
G(x) = \begin{cases} 0 & x \leq 0, \\ \int_0^x \frac{d\lambda}{h_\lambda^{-1}(a)} & 0 < x \leq \lambda_+, \\ \infty & x > \lambda_+. \end{cases}
$$

Proof. The process $N_l^h = \sum_{\lambda \leq l} \mathbb{1}_{\{\sup_{\tau_{\lambda-} \leq t \leq \tau_\lambda} h(\lambda, |B_t|) \geq a\}}$ is, by excursion theory, an inhomogeneous Poisson process, whose measure may be expressed simply in terms of the Itô excursion measure $\mathbf{n}$; precisely, we have

$$
(L_{\theta_h^{(a)}} \geq l) = (N_l^h = 0),
$$

hence

$$
\begin{aligned}
\mathbb{P}(L_{\theta_h^{(a)}} \geq l) &= \exp\left(- \int_0^l d\lambda \, \mathbf{n}\Big(\sup_{t \leq V(\varepsilon)} h(\lambda, |\varepsilon_t|) \geq a \Big) \right) \\
&= \exp\left(- \int_0^l \frac{d\lambda}{h_\lambda^{-1}(a)} \right),
\end{aligned} \tag{11}
$$

where we have denoted by ε the generic excursion, and by $V(\varepsilon)$ it's lifetime. The result needed for (11) is that the height of the generic excursion $\sup_{t\leq V(\varepsilon)} |\varepsilon_t|$ is distributed under $\mathbf{n}$ as $\left(\frac{dx}{x^2}\right)$. □

See Ref. [18], Chapter 5, for detailed description for the Itô measure $\mathbf{n}$.

3.2. *Azéma's Exponential Result*

In this section, we show that formula (10) may be seen as a consequence of Azéma's exponential result. We first state Azéma's result in Ref. [1]:

Proposition 3.2 (Azéma [1]). *Let $(A_t^{\mathcal{L}}, t \geq 0)$ be the predictable compensator of $1_{(\mathcal{L}\leq t)}$, where $\mathcal{L}$ stands for the end of a predictable set on $(\Omega, \mathcal{F}, (\mathcal{F}_t), P)$, i.e,*

$$\mathcal{L} = \sup\{t : (t, \omega) \in \Gamma\},$$

for Γ a predictable set. Then, under the hypothesis (C) and (A), for

(C) *all martingales are continuous,*
(A) *$\mathcal{L}$ avoids all $(\mathcal{F}_t)$ stopping times T, i.e., $\mathbb{P}(\mathcal{L} = T) = 0$,*

the variable $A_\infty^{\mathcal{L}}$ is a standard exponential variable with mean 1.

We now recover formula (11) by remarking that

$$\theta_h^{(a)} = \inf\{t : |B_t| \geq h_{L_t}^{-1}(a)\}.$$

Consequently, if we denote

$$\mathcal{L} = \sup\{t \leq \theta_h^{(a)} : B_t = 0\},$$

then a simple application of the Balayage formula (see Refs. [9], p. 216; [14], p. 260; [18], Chapter 2.4) yields

$$A_t^{\mathcal{L}} = \int_0^{(L_{\theta_h^{(a)}\wedge t})} \frac{d\lambda}{h_\lambda^{-1}(a)} = G(L_{\theta_h^{(a)}\wedge t}).$$

Consequently, applying Azéma's result, we obtain

$$\mathbb{P}(L_{\theta_h^{(a)}} \geq l) = \mathbb{P}(G(L_{\theta_h^{(a)}}) \geq G(l)) = \exp(-G(l)),$$

which is precisely formula (10).

4. Examples Stimulated by the Aźema–Yor Algorithm

In Section 2.1, we see that the Azéma–Yor algorithm is given by

$$T_{\mathrm{AY}} := \inf\{t : S_t \geq \psi_\mu(B_t)\},$$

where ψ_μ is the Hardy–Littlewood barycenter function of μ defined by (3). The stopping times $T_h^{(a)}$s in Theorem 3.1 are recognized as particular T_{AY}s. More precisely, from the assumption of h, we have

$$\begin{aligned}
T_h^{(a)} &= \inf\{t : h(S_t, S_t - B_t) \geq a)\} \\
&= \inf\{t : S_t - B_t \geq h_{S_t}^{-1}(a)\} \\
&= \inf\{t : S_t - h_{S_t}^{-1}(a) \geq B_t\} \\
&= \inf\{t : S_t \geq \psi_h^{(a)}(B_t)\},
\end{aligned}$$

where

$$\psi_h^{(a)}(x) = \begin{cases} 0, & \text{if } x \leq b_-, \\ \inf\{s : s - h_s^{-1}(a) \geq x\}, & \text{if } b_- < x < \lambda_+, \\ x, & \text{if } x \geq \lambda_+, \end{cases}$$

for $b_- = \inf_{(s,s-x)\in D} x$. Note the function $\psi_h^{(a)}$ is right continuous and non-decreasing, and $\psi_h^{(a)}(x) < \infty$ for all $x < b_+$.

Moreover, by the study of Skorokhod embedding problem in p. 276, Chapter 6, Revuz–Yor [14], We have that

$$\begin{aligned}\mu([x,\infty)) &= \mathbb{P}(B_{T_h^{(a)}} \geq x) \\ &= \mathbb{P}(S_{T_h^{(a)}} \geq \psi_h^{(a)}(x)) \\ &= \exp\left(-\int_0^{\psi_h^{(a)}(x)} \frac{ds}{h_s^{-1}(a)}\right) \\ &= \exp(-G(\psi_h^{(a)}(x))). \end{aligned} \tag{12}$$

We note that (12) leads to the result of Theorem 3.1. Therefore, the distributions of $B_{T_h^{(a)}}$ and $S_{T_h^{(a)}}$ are identified by the function G.

We give some explicit examples with various functions h in the following:

4.1. *The Azéma–Yor Fan*

We consider $h(\lambda, x) = \beta\lambda + (1-\beta)x$ for $\beta > 0$ and $\alpha > 0$. Then the stopping time of Azéma–Yor algorithm is written by

$$\begin{aligned} T_{(\beta,\alpha)} &:= T_h^{(\beta\alpha)} \\ &= \inf\{t : (1-\beta)S_t + \beta(S_t - B_t) \geq \beta\alpha\} \\ &= \inf\{t : S_t \geq \beta(B_t + \alpha)\}. \end{aligned} \tag{13}$$

The stopping time $T_{(\beta,\alpha)}$ was proposed by Lim, Yen and Yor in Ref. [11], which is called the Azéma–Yor fan since the barycenter function is the straight line. When $\beta = 0$, it is obvious that $T_{(\beta,\alpha)} = 0$, a.s. since Brownian motion oscillates at the initial point.

We shall show that the Azéma–Yor fan describes some remarkable examples discussed in the following sections. The cases $\beta = 1, 1.5$, and .5 are shown in Figure 2.

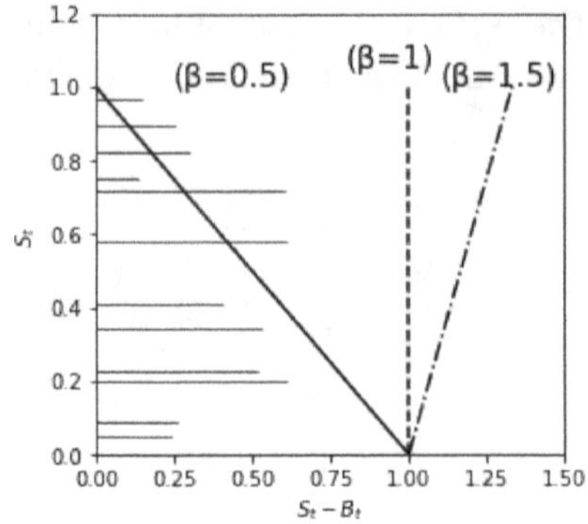

Figure 2. Azéma–Yor fan for $\beta = 0.5, 1, 1.5$.

4.1.1. *The Reflected Brownian Motion* ($\beta = 1$)

We first recall Lévy's identity (7) that $(S_t - B_t, t \geq 0)$ is a reflected Brownian motion. We consider

$$T_{(1,\alpha)} = \inf\{t : S_t - B_t = \alpha\}.$$

Then, $S_{T_{(1,\alpha)}}$ is an exponential variable. Therefore, $B_{T_{(1,\alpha)}}$ is a shifted exponential variable, that is, $B_{T^a_{(1)}}$ is distributed as $a(\mathbf{e} - 1)$, where $\mathbf{e}$ denotes a standard exponential variable.

4.1.2. *The BES(3)-Pitman Example* ($\beta = 1/2$)

Next, we recall Pitman's theorem that $(2S_t - B_t, t \geq 0)$ is a three-dimensional Bessel process (denoted by BES(3)) [13]. We consider here

$$T_{(\frac{1}{2},\frac{1}{2}\alpha)} = \inf\{t : 2S_t - B_t = \alpha\}.$$

It is well known, thanks to Pitman's theorem that $S_{T_{(\frac{1}{2},\frac{1}{2}\alpha)}}$ and $S_{T_{(\frac{1}{2},\frac{1}{2}\alpha)}} - B_{T_{(\frac{1}{2},\frac{1}{2}\alpha)}}$ are uniform on $[0, \alpha]$. Consequently, $B_{T_{(\frac{1}{2},\frac{1}{2}\alpha)}}$ is uniform on $[-\alpha, \alpha]$, and it is also independent from $T_{(\frac{1}{2},\frac{1}{2}\alpha)}$. The two classical examples above were further developed in Ref. [11] where a number of properties of distributions of the Azéma–Yor fan are discussed.

4.1.3. *The Case* $(0 < \beta < 1)$

In the case $0 < \beta < 1$, for $\lambda_+ = \frac{\alpha\beta}{1-\beta}(< \infty)$, $\{S_{T_h^{(a)}} = \lambda_+\}$ occurs with positive probability. Since we obtain that $h_\lambda^{-1}(a) = (1-\frac{1}{\beta})\lambda+\alpha$ and $\psi_h^{(a)}(x) = \beta(x+\alpha)$, the density function of $S_{T_{(\beta,\alpha)}}$ is equal to

$$\mathbb{P}\left(S_{T_{(\beta,\alpha)}} \in dx\right) = \frac{1}{\alpha}\left(\frac{(\beta-1)x}{\alpha\beta}+1\right)^{\frac{2\beta-1}{1-\beta}} \mathbb{1}_{[0,\frac{\alpha\beta}{1-\beta}]}(x)dx, \tag{14}$$

and the one of $B_{T_{(\beta,\alpha)}}$ is

$$\mathbb{P}\left(B_{T_{(\beta,\alpha)}} \in dx\right) = \frac{\beta}{\alpha}\left(\frac{(\beta-1)x}{\alpha}+\beta\right)^{\frac{2\beta-1}{1-\beta}} \mathbb{1}_{[-a,\frac{\alpha\beta}{1-\beta}]}(x)dx. \tag{15}$$

4.1.4. *The Case* $(1 < \beta)$

If $1 < \beta$, then $\lambda_+ = \infty$, and the values of $S_{T_{(\beta,\alpha)}}$ and $B_{T_{(\beta,\alpha)}}$ are unbounded above. Therefore, by the same calculations as (14) and (15), we obtain that

$$\mathbb{P}\left(S_{T_{(\beta,\alpha)}} \in dx\right) = \frac{1}{\alpha}\left(\frac{(\beta-1)x}{\alpha\beta}+1\right)^{\frac{2\beta-1}{1-\beta}} \mathbb{1}_{[0,\infty)}(x)dx \tag{16}$$

and

$$\mathbb{P}\left(B_{T_{(\beta,\alpha)}} \in dx\right) = \frac{\beta}{\alpha}\left(\frac{(\beta-1)x}{\alpha}+\beta\right)^{\frac{2\beta-1}{1-\beta}} \mathbb{1}_{[-a,\infty)}(x)dx. \tag{17}$$

4.2. *The Arc-Sin Law*

We consider the stopping time

$$T_h^{(1)} = \inf\{t \geq 0 : S_t^2(\cos^{-1}(B_t))^2 + B_t^2 \geq 1\},$$

where $h(\lambda, x) = \lambda^2(\cos^{-1}(\lambda - x))^2 + (\lambda - x)^2$ and its domain is $D = \{(\lambda, x) : h(\lambda, x) < 1,\ 0 \leq \lambda, x \leq 1\}$. We obtain that $h_\lambda^{-1}(a) =$

$\lambda - (\psi_h^{(1)})^{-1}(\lambda)$, where

$$\psi_h^{(1)}(x) = \begin{cases} 0, & \text{if } x < -1, \\ \frac{\sqrt{1-x^2}}{\cos^{-1}(x)}, & \text{if } |x| < 1, \\ x, & \text{if } x > 1. \end{cases}$$

Therefore, by (12), it holds that for $|x| < 1$,

$$\begin{aligned} \mathbb{P}(B_{T_h^{(a)}} \geq x) &= \exp\left(- \int_0^{\psi_h^{(a)}(x)} \frac{d\lambda}{\lambda - (\psi_h^{(1)})^{-1}(\lambda)} \right) \\ &= \exp\left(- \int_{-1}^{x} \frac{\sqrt{1-v^2} - v\cos^{-1}(v)}{(\psi_h^{(-1)}(v) - v)(\sqrt{1-v^2}(\cos^{-1}(v))^2)} dv \right) \\ &= \frac{\cos^{-1}(v)}{\pi}. \end{aligned}$$

Hence its density function is given by

$$\mathbb{P}(B_{T_h^{(1)}} \in dx) = \frac{1}{\pi\sqrt{1-x^2}} \mathbb{1}_{\{|x|<1\}} dx,$$

which is called the arc-sine law. Figure 3 illustrates this case.

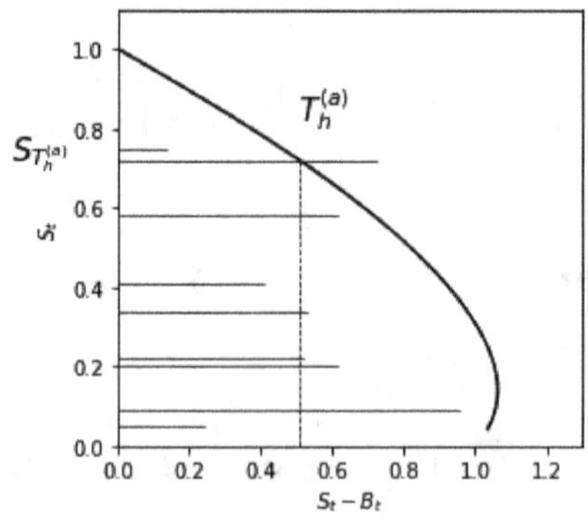

Figure 3. The arc-sin law.

4.3. *Linear Combinations of Power Functions*

We fix $a > 0$. We study the case

$$h(\lambda, x) = \lambda^p + x^q, \tag{18}$$

with parameter $p, q > 0$. Note that when $p = q = 1$, the corresponding stopping time coincides with $T_{(\frac{1}{2},2a)}$ of the Azèma–Yor fan defined by (13). Therefore, by results shown in Section 4.1.2, it is the first hitting time of BES(3), and μ is uniformly distributed on $[-4a, 4a]$.

We show the tail distribution function of $S_{T_h^{(a)}}$ in the following proposition:

Proposition 4.1. *If either $q \neq 1$ or $p \neq 1$ holds, then*

$$\mathbb{P}(S_{T_h^{(a)}} \in dx) = \frac{1}{(a-\lambda^p)^{\frac{1}{q}}} \exp\left(-\frac{a^{\frac{1}{p}-\frac{1}{q}}}{p} B\left(\frac{x^p}{a}; \frac{1}{p}, 1-\frac{1}{q}\right)\right)$$
$$\times \mathbb{1}_{(0,a^{\frac{1}{p}})}(x)dx,$$

where $B(c; \alpha, \beta) = \int_0^c x^\alpha (1-x)^{1-\beta} dx$ is the incomplete Beta function at $c \in (0,1)$ with parameter $\alpha > 0$ and $\beta \in \mathbb{R}$.

Proof. By Theorem 3.1, the tail distribution function is the exponential of $-G$. The upper bound of h for the first variable is $\lambda_+ = a^{1/p}$. The inverse function of h is $h_\lambda^{-1}(a) = (a - \lambda^p)^{1/q}$. By Theorem 3.1, G is obtained by

$$G(x) = \frac{a^{\frac{1}{p}-\frac{1}{q}}}{p} \mathbf{B}\left(\frac{x^p}{a}; \frac{1}{p}, 1-\frac{1}{q}\right). \qquad \square$$

Remark 4.2. Note that the function G is well defined on $[0, a^{1/p})$ and the left-limit at $a^{1/p}$ is characterized by q. When $0 < q \leq 1$, $G(x)$ diverges to infinity as x goes to $a^{1/p}$, hence $S_{T_h^{(a)}}$ and $B_{T_h^{(a)}}$ both have a continuous distribution at $a^{1/p}$. Therefore, we see that $S_{T_h^{(a)}} \neq B_{T_h^{(a)}}$, a.s. On the other hand, in the case $q > 1$, since G is discontinuous at $a^{1/p}$, $S_{T_h^{(a)}}$ and $B_{T_h^{(a)}}$ have atom at $a^{1/p}$.

Corollary 4.3. *For $p = 1/n$ with some natural number n and $q \neq 1$, the density function of $S_{T_h^{(a)}}$ is given by*

$$\mathbb{P}(S_{T_h^{(a)}} \in dx) = \frac{1}{(a - \lambda^{\frac{1}{n}})^{\frac{1}{q}}} e^{\frac{n!}{\left(1-\frac{1}{q}\right)_n} a^{n-\frac{1}{q}}} \prod_{k=0}^{n-1} e^{\frac{(k+1)_{n-k}}{\left(1-\frac{1}{q}+k\right)_{n-k}} x^{\frac{1}{n}+k} a^{n-\frac{1}{q}-k}} \\ \times \mathbb{1}_{(0,a^{\frac{1}{p}})}(x)dx,$$

where $m! = \prod_{i=1}^{m} i$ and $(x)_m = \prod_{i=0}^{m-1}(x+i)$.

Proof. Integrate both sides of the following equation:

$$\frac{\partial}{\partial x} x^\alpha (1-x)^\beta = \alpha x^{\alpha-1}(1-x)^{\beta-1} - (\alpha+\beta)x^\alpha(1-x)^{\beta-1},$$

we have the induction formula of the incomplete Beta function

$$\mathbf{B}(c; \alpha+1, \beta) = \frac{1}{\alpha+\beta}\left(\alpha \mathbf{B}(c; \alpha, \beta) - c^\alpha(1-c)^\beta\right),$$

for $c \in (0,1)$, $\alpha > 0$ and $\beta \neq 0$. For a natural number n, by using $\mathbf{B}(c; 1, \beta) = \frac{1}{\beta}(1 - (1-c)^\beta)$, we obtain that

$$\mathbf{B}(c; n, \beta) = \frac{(n-1)!}{(\beta)_n} - (1-c)^\beta \sum_{k=0}^{n-1} \frac{(k+1)_{n-k-1}}{(\beta+k)_{n-k}} c^k. \qquad \square$$

4.3.1. *The Circle Case ($p = q = 2$) (see Figure 4(a)).*

Letting $p = q = 2$ in (18), then the stopping time is given by

$$T_h^{(a)} = \inf\{t : S_t^2 + (S_t - B_t)^2 \geq a\}.$$

The upper bound of S_t is $\lambda_+ = \sqrt{a}$, and the inverse function of h is $h_\lambda^{-1}(a) = \sqrt{a - \lambda^2}$. Thus, we obtain that $G(x) = \sin^{-1}(\frac{x}{\sqrt{a}})$.

The Hardy–Littlewood barycenter function is

$$\psi_h^{(a)}(x) = \frac{1}{2}(x + \sqrt{2a - x^2}), \qquad (x \in [-\sqrt{a}, \sqrt{a}]).$$

Hence the density functions of $S_{T_h^{(a)}}$ and $B_{T_h^{(a)}}$ are as follows:

$$\mathbb{P}(S_{T_h^{(a)}} \in dx) = \frac{1}{\sqrt{a - x^2}} \exp\left(-\sin^{-1}\left(\frac{x}{\sqrt{a}}\right)\right) \mathbb{1}_{(0,\sqrt{a})}(x)dx \quad (19)$$

and

$$\mathbb{P}(B_{T_h^{(a)}} \in dx) = \frac{\sqrt{2}}{a - x\sqrt{2a - x^2}} \exp\left(-\sin^{-1}\left(\frac{x + \sqrt{2a - x^2}}{2\sqrt{a}}\right)\right) \times \mathbb{1}_{\{|x| < \sqrt{a}\}}dx.$$

From $\mathbb{P}(S_{T_h^{(a)}} > \sqrt{a}) = 0$ and (19), we note that

$$\begin{aligned}\mathbb{P}(S_{T_h^{(a)}} = \sqrt{a}) &= \lim_{x \to \sqrt{a}-} \mathbb{P}(S_{T_h^{(a)}} \geq x) \\ &= e^{-\frac{\pi}{4}} \\ &\neq 0.\end{aligned}$$

Therefore, $S_{T_h^{(a)}}$ has atom at $\sqrt{a}$. Similarly, $B_{T_h^{(a)}}$ also has atom at $\sqrt{a}$ with probability $e^{-\frac{\pi}{4}}$.

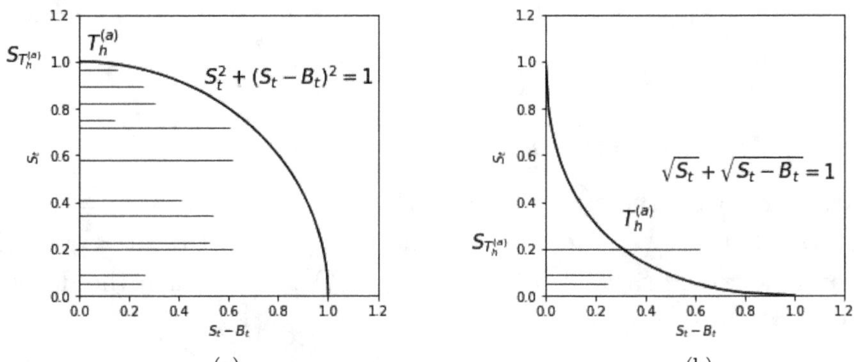

Figure 4. Linear combinations of power functions. (a) The circle case ($p = q = 2$) and (b) The convex boundary case ($p = q = \frac{1}{2}$).

4.3.2. *The Convex Boundary Case* ($p = q = \frac{1}{2}$) *(see Figure 4(b)).*

We consider the stopping time

$$T_h^{(a)} = \inf\{t : \sqrt{S_t} + \sqrt{S_t - B_t} \geq a\}.$$

Then the upper bound of S_t is $\lambda_+ = a^2$, $h_\lambda^{-1}(a) = \sqrt{a - \sqrt{\lambda}}$ and the Hardy–Littlewood barycenter function is

$$\psi_h^{(a)}(x) = \frac{(x + a^2)^2}{4a^2}, \qquad (|x| \leq a^2).$$

Hence, the density functions of $S_{T_h^{(a)}}$ and $B_{T_h^{(a)}}$ are given by

$$\mathbb{P}(S_{T_h^{(a)}} \in dx) = \frac{1}{\sqrt{a - \sqrt{x}}} e^{\frac{4}{3}\left(\sqrt{a-\sqrt{x}}(\sqrt{x}+2a) - 2a\sqrt{a}\right)} \mathbb{1}_{(0,a^2)}(x)dx$$

and

$$\mathbb{P}(B_{T_h^{(a)}} \in dx) = \sqrt{\frac{2a}{a^2 - x}} \exp\left(\frac{\sqrt{2}}{3a^{\frac{3}{2}}}(\sqrt{a^2 - x}(x + 5a^2) - 4\sqrt{2}a^3)\right) \times \mathbb{1}_{\{|x|<a^2\}} dx.$$

Since $\mathbb{P}(S_{T_h^{(a)}} \geq a^2) = \mathbb{P}(S_{T_h^{(a)}} = a^2) = 0$, $S_{T_h^{(a)}}$ never hits a^2 with probability 1.

4.4. *The Multiplication Case*

We begin with the study at time $T_h^{(a)}$ for the case $h(\lambda, x) = g(\lambda)x$, (or $h_\lambda^{-1}(a) = \frac{a}{g(\lambda)}$). Here we assume that $g : \mathbb{R}_+ \backslash \{0\} \to \mathbb{R}_+ \backslash \{0\}$ is continuous and satisfying $\lim_{(\lambda,x)\to(0,0)} g(\lambda)x = 0$. Then the density function of $S_{T_h^{(a)}}$ is given by

$$\mathbb{P}(S_{T_h^{(a)}} \in dx) = \frac{g(x)}{a} \exp\left(-\frac{1}{a}\int_0^x g(\lambda)d\lambda\right) \mathbb{1}_{\{x\geq 0\}} dx.$$

4.4.1. *The Case* $(g(\lambda) = \lambda^p)$

For $p > 0$, we set $g(\lambda) = \lambda^p$. Then the stopping time is $T_h^{(a)} = \inf\{t : S_t^p(S_t - B_t) = a\}$. Thus, $S_{T_h^{(a)}}$ has Weibull distribution with parameters $(p+1, \alpha(p+1))$ and its density function is given by

$$\mathbb{P}(S_{T_h^{(a)}} \in dx) = \frac{x^p}{a} e^{-\frac{x^{p+1}}{a(p+1)}} \mathbb{1}_{\{x\geq 0\}} dx.$$

In particular, when $p = 1$, $B_{T_h^{(a)}}$ has the following density function:

$$\mathbb{P}(B_{T_h^{(a)}} \in dx) = \frac{x + \sqrt{x^2 + a}}{2a} e^{-\frac{\left(x+\sqrt{x^2+a}\right)^2}{8a}} dx.$$

4.4.2. *The Case* $(g(\lambda) = 1/(\lambda + 1))$

Fix $0 < a < 1$, and set $h(\lambda, x) = \frac{x}{\lambda+1}$. Then the stopping time $T_h^{(a)}$ is reduced to the Azéma–Yor fan since

$$\begin{aligned} T_h^{(a)} &= \inf\{t : \frac{1}{S_t + 1}(S_t - B_t) \geq a\} \\ &= T_{(\frac{1}{1-a}, a)}, \end{aligned}$$

where $T_{(\frac{1}{1-a}, a)}$ is defined in (13). Since $1 < \frac{1}{1-a}$, the density functions of $S_{T_h^{(a)}}$ and $B_{T_h^{(a)}}$ are given in (16) and (17), respectively.

4.4.3. *The Case* $(g(\lambda) = 1/\sqrt{\lambda^2 + 1})$

We consider the case $g(\lambda) = 1/\sqrt{\lambda^2 + 1}$. Since $\psi_h^{(a)}(x) = \frac{x^2-1}{2x}$, the density functions are given by

$$\mathbb{P}(S_{T_h^{(a)}} \in dx) = \frac{1}{a\sqrt{x^2+1}} \left(x + \sqrt{x^2+1}\right)^{\frac{1}{a}} \mathbb{1}_{\{x\geq 0\}} dx$$

and

$$\mathbb{P}(B_{T_h^{(a)}} \in dx) = \frac{2x^{1+\frac{1}{a}}}{a(x^2+1)} dx.$$

The cases for $a = 0.1, 0.2, 0.3$ are demonstrated in Figure 5.

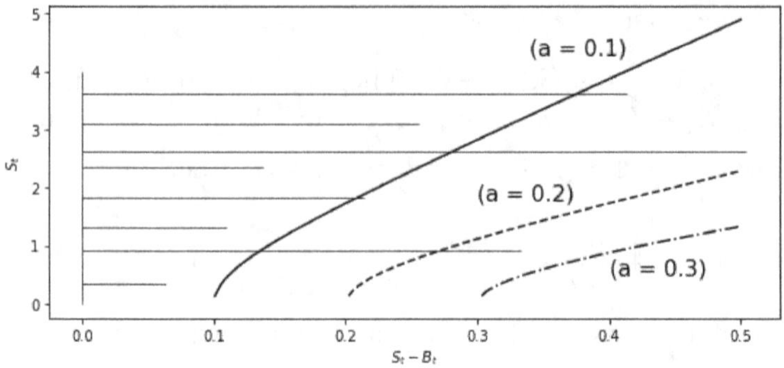

Figure 5. The case with $g(\lambda) = 1/\sqrt{\lambda^2+1}$ for $a = 0.1, 0.2, 0.3$.

Acknowledgment

This work was supported by JSPS KAKENHI Grant Number 20K03731. Ju-Yi Yen is grateful to the Mathematics Division of the National Center for Theoretical Sciences (Taiwan) for their hospitality and support during some extended visit.

References

[1] J. Azéma. Quelques applications de la théorie générale des processus. I. *Inventiones Mathematicae*, 18:293–336, 1972.

[2] J. Azéma and M. Yor. Une solution simple au problème de Skorokhod. In *Séminaire de Probabilités, XIII (Univ. Strasbourg, Strasbourg, 1977/78)*, volume 721 of *Lecture Notes in Math.*, Springer, Berlin, 1979, pp. 90–115.

[3] P. Carr, H. Geman, D. B. Madan, and M. Yor. The fine structure of asset returns: An empirical investigation. *The Journal of Business*, 75(2):305–332, 2002.

[4] P. Carr and A. Chou. Hedging complex barrier options. Working paper, NYU's Courant Institute and Enuvis Inc., 2002.

[5] P. Carr and R. Lee. From hyper options to options on local time. Unpublished Manuscript, 29 pages, 2005.

[6] A. M. G. Cox, D. Hobson, and J. Obłój. Pathwise inequalities for local time: Applications to Skorokhod embeddings and optimal stopping. *Annals of Applied Probability*, 18(5):1870–1896, 2008.

[7] D. Hobson. The Skorokhod embedding problem and model-independent bounds for option prices. In *Paris-Princeton Lectures on*

Mathematical Finance 2010, volume 2003 of *Lecture Notes in Math.*, Springer, Berlin, 2011, pp. 267–318.

[8] D. G. Hobson. Robust hedging of the lookback option. *Finance and Stochastics*, 2(4):329–347, 1998.

[9] M. Jeanblanc, M. Yor, and M. Chesney. *Mathematical Methods for Financial Markets*. Springer Finance. Springer-Verlag London Ltd., London, 2009.

[10] T. Jeulin and M. Yor. Sur les distributions de certaines fonctionnelles du mouvement brownien. In *Seminar on Probability, XV (Univ. Strasbourg, Strasbourg, 1979/1980) (French)*, volume 850 of *Lecture Notes in Math.*, Springer, Berlin, 1981, pp. 210–226.

[11] A. P. C. Lim, J.-Y. Yen, and M. Yor. Some examples of Skorokhod embeddings obtained from the Azéma-Yor algorithm. *Stochastic Processes and their Applications*, 123(2):329–346, 2013.

[12] J. Obłój. The Skorokhod embedding problem and its offspring. *Probability Survey*, 1:321–390 (electronic), 2004.

[13] J. W. Pitman. One-dimensional Brownian motion and the three-dimensional Bessel process. *Advances in Applied Probability*, 7(3):511–526, 1975.

[14] D. Revuz and M. Yor. *Continuous Martingales and Brownian Motion*, volume 293 of *Grundlehren der Mathematischen Wissenschaften [Fundamental Principles of Mathematical Sciences]*, 3rd Edition. Springer-Verlag, Berlin, 1999.

[15] L. C. G. Rogers. Williams' characterisation of the Brownian excursion law: Proof and applications. In *Seminar on Probability, XV (Univ. Strasbourg, Strasbourg, 1979/1980) (French)*, volume 850 of *Lecture Notes in Math.*, Springer, Berlin, 1981, pp. 227–250.

[16] P. Vallois. Quelques inégalités avec le temps local en zero du mouvement brownien. *Stochastic Processes and their Applications*, 41(1):117–155, 1992.

[17] P. Vallois. Le problème de Skorokhod sur **R**: une approche avec le temps local. In *Seminar on Probability, XVII*, volume 986 of *Lecture Notes in Math.*, Springer, Berlin, 1983, pp. 227–239.

[18] J.-Y. Yen and M. Yor. *Local Times and Excursion Theory for Brownian Motion*, volume 2088 of *Lecture Notes in Mathematics*. Springer, Cham, 2013. A tale of Wiener and Itô measures.

www.ingramcontent.com/pod-product-compliance
Lightning Source LLC
LaVergne TN
LVHW010537300926
849162LV00002B/163